THE NEGRO CARAVAN

Selected from
THE AMERICAN NEGRO: HIS HISTORY AND LITERATURE
William Loren Katz
GENERAL EDITOR

THE NEGRO CARAVAN

WRITINGS BY AMERICAN NEGROES

SELECTED AND EDITED BY STERLING

A. BROWN, HOWARD UNIVERSITY;

ARTHUR P. DAVIS, VIRGINIA UNION

UNIVERSITY; AND ULYSSES LEE,

LINCOLN UNIVERSITY

New Introduction by Julius Lester

ARNO PRESS AND THE NEW YORK TIMES
NEW YORK 1970

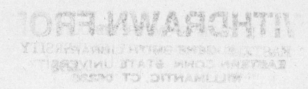

This book is respectfully dedicated to Ulysses Lee, who died January 7, 1969.

THE PUBLISHERS

INTRODUCTION TO THIS EDITION

Few BOOKS ACQUIRE THE STATUS OF LEGENDS, BUT THIS IS ONE. It was first published in 1941, and the outbreak of the war caused it to be even more ignored than it would have been normally. However, it acquired a place in the lives of black intellectuals, and those able to acquire a copy congratulated themselves for being the recipient of one of the Lord's few modern miracles. At long last, it is once more available.

The book is aptly named. It is a "caravan," a journey through black literature. Every literary form is represented, from the short story and novel to drama to historical, cultural, social and personal essays. Within each section, the selections are arranged chronologically, beginning with the earliest example of black writing in the particular genre to the most recent at the time of original publication. Thus, the reader is afforded the opportunity to study the evolution of black writing in style, subject matter and theme in each genre, not to mention having the sheer pleasure of reading works of which one had only heard or had never known existed.

The book opens with a selection from "The Heroic Slave," a long story by Frederick Douglass. In the next section there are excerpts from the two earliest known novels by blacks—William Wells Brown's "Clotel" and Martin Delaney's "Blake." Until the recent republication of long out-of-print works by blacks, "The Negro Caravan" was the only place one could read a part of another legend, Jean Toomer's "Cane" or Margaret Walker's great poem, "For My People," or anything by Zora Neale Hurston and Rudolph Fisher, to mention a few whose works are once again in print.

But "The Negro Caravan" still remains the best source for sampling the fiction of Walter White, Jessie Fauset, Wallace Thurman, or the poetry of Sterling Brown, Waring Cuney,

Countee Cullen, Frank Marshall Davis, Richard Wright and Owen Dodson. There is also a large selection of "folk literature": songs; aphorisms; religious, secular and protest songs; tales excerpted from Zora Hurston's classic, "Mules and Men." In the large nonfiction section, there are speeches, autobiographical and biographical writings, as well as essays. Each section of the book is preceded by an essay of the editor, which presents a history of black writing in the specific genre. These essays are as valuable as anything else in the book.

"The Negro Caravan" is important not only for the works presented, but for the point of view it exemplifies. The editors are aware that blacks had been represented in literature by whites, who honestly believed that they knew blacks better than did blacks themselves. Thus, one of the purposes of the anthology was to present blacks writing about blacks. "Negro authors . . . must be allowed the privilege and must assume the responsibility of being the ultimate portrayers of their own," the editors say in the introduction to the book. This assertion needs to be heeded as much today as when it was originally written.

The editors, however, do not use their anthology to falsify black literature. They are committed to black literature, but their commitment is not to one particular kind. This attitude is invaluable, particularly now, because it recognizes that black writers are black *and* American; each black writer decides for himself whenever he sits down to write which aspect of his inescapable duality he will emphasize. It is the tendency of too many black writers and critics to want to deny that the duality exists and to demand that all black writing fit one definition—black nationalism.

The editors of "The Negro Caravan" recognize, without apology, that a black poet, like Paul Laurence Dunbar, wrote "dialect" poetry and also poetry in Western metric traditions. Rather than praise the former and denigrate the latter, they present both for the value implicit in each. They eschew the term "Negro literature" as having no meaning, because "Negro writers [are] American writers." They go so far as to claim that Countee Cullen, who did not want to be considered a "Negro poet," was correct, because he was "an American poet who happen[ed] to be a Negro." While most black writers today quite rightly reject any such definition of themselves, it is of more than casual importance that Cullen's best poetry concerns itself with the condition of being a black American and not simply with being an American.

The same can be said of this anthology. The desire of black writers of the past to be accepted as American writers and not as black writers was a reaction against seeing their work treated by white publishers as "exotic," as something never to be considered as worthy of the same serious consideration given to white writers, particularly when those white writers were writing about blacks.

Because of the change in the social climate, the black writer today does not have this particular problem, but the present emphasis on blackness and the corresponding denial of Americanness is as false as Cullen's denial of blackness. The black American writer must realize that his blackness has been acted upon and has reacted to forces that are peculiarly American. Thus, his black experience is different from that of the Jamaican, Brazilian or Guinean. Indeed, there is something very American about the present romanticization of blackness. The present attitude is not one which will most easily free the black American writer spiritually to do that which only he can do—illuminate the consciousness of Man through the specifics of his own particular black experience.

"The Negro Caravan" lives with and exemplifies the duality of being black and American. It shows the richness and variety in black writing and, by doing so, represents the totality of black writing. It comes as close today as it did in 1941 to being the most important single volume of black writing ever published.

Julius Lester

THE NEGRO CARAVAN

PREFACE TO FIRST EDITION

THIS ANTHOLOGY of the writings of American Negroes has three purposes: (1) to present a body of artistically valid writings by American Negro authors, (2) to present a truthful mosaic of Negro character and experience in America, and (3) to collect in one volume certain key literary works that have greatly influenced the thinking of American Negroes, and to a lesser degree, that of Americans as a whole.

Several anthologies of prose and poetry by American Negro writers have preceded this one. All are useful to the student, but they generally represent either single types, such as James Weldon Johnson's pioneering *The Book of American Negro Poetry* (1922; revised and enlarged 1931), Newman I. White and Walter Clinton Jackson's *An Anthology of American Negro Verse* (1924), and Carter G. Woodson's *Negro Orators and Their Orations* (1925); or single periods, such as Benjamin Brawley's *Early Negro American Writers*; or a single form in a single period, such as Carter G. Woodson's *The Mind of the Negro as Reflected in Letters Written During the Crisis, 1800-1860*. Johnson's Anthology, Robert J. Kerlin's *Negro Poets and Their Poems* (1923, revised and enlarged 1935), and Countee Cullen's *Caroling Dusk* (1927) pay only slight attention to poets before Dunbar. Two anthologies attempting to cover the entire range of types and of periods are V. F. Calverton's *Anthology of American Negro Literature* (1929) and *Readings From Negro Authors*, edited by Otelia Cromwell, Lorenzo D. Turner, and Eva B. Dykes (1931). Both were prepared over a decade ago, and in that decade a large amount of publishing has been done by James Weldon Johnson, Charles Johnson, Langston Hughes, Zora Neale Hurston, Arna Bontemps, and Richard Wright, to name only a few of the better known writers. Even for the period before their publication dates, however, these books are far less comprehensive in scope than *The Negro Caravan*. There is very little in both books, for instance, representing the numerous and influential writers of the nineteenth century.

Comprehensiveness for its own sake was, of course, not an editorial aim. But comprehensiveness seemed a necessity for one of the aims of the book, namely, a more accurate and revealing story of the Negro writer than has ever been told before. Thus writers such as David Ruggles, Samuel Ringgold Ward, Charlotte Forten, Mrs. Keckley,

Charles Langston, to mention only a few who have never appeared in any similar anthology, are included, not as finds, but because their writings are interesting and pertinent.

A section of folk literature, ampler than in any similar anthology; the neglected antislavery pamphleteering and journalism; the little-known fugitive slave narratives; the earliest novels (never before anthologized); all of these inclusions do more than enlarge the scope of *The Negro Caravan*. They serve the editorial purposes, which are different from those of any preceding anthology.

The Negro Caravan should be useful, not only to students of American literature, but also to students of American social history. It presents the literary record of America's largest minority group, and in doing so it sheds light upon American culture and minority problems. It pieces out a mosaic more representative than is to be found in any other single volume. Many classes of Negroes, from many sections, undergoing many sorts of experiences, are shown in this mosaic. A cursory glance at the table of contents will reveal the highly composite make-up of the book.

The Negro Caravan covers the entire period of Negro expression—from the writings of Phillis Wheatley and Jupiter Hammon to the current fiction of Richard Wright. All literary types are represented. The selections are divided according to types into eight sections: Short Stories; Novels (selections); Poetry; Folk Literature; Drama; Speeches, Pamphlets, and Letters; Biography (Biography and Autobiography); and Essays (Historical, Social, Cultural, and Personal). Within each section the arrangement is chronological, except as noted in the historical essays, where the subject matter supersedes the chronology for reader interest. Each section begins with a historical and critical introduction explaining the history of the type as used by Negro authors. Each author's work is prefaced by a biographical and bibliographical note. There is a chronology of events in American history and literature that have significant pertinence to the writings of American Negroes, as well as a chronology of the history and literature of Negroes.

Passages have been omitted from several of the selections for reasons of space and interest. These omissions have been indicated by dots for short passages and by asterisks for longer passages. There have been no other editorial alterations in the selections except the correction of obvious errors and misprints. The typographical peculiarities of the nineteenth-century selections have been retained. The few summarized sections that were felt necessary for long short stories, are enclosed in brackets. The editors have supplied many titles of selections where the authors give no titles, or where the selections, standing

as units, seem to require more descriptive titles than the titles of the
larger works. Though the editors favor a simplified dialect, they have
kept the dialect as the authors wrote it, except in rare instances for
the sake of clarity.

Vernon Loggins' *The Negro Author* (1931) and Carter G. Woodson's *The Mind of the Negro As Reflected in Letters Written During
the Crisis, 1800-1860,* have been of great value in the preparation of this
anthology. The earlier anthologies have been useful, especially James
Weldon Johnson's *Book of American Negro Poetry* and Brawley's
Early Negro American Writers. Cooperation of authors and copyright
holders has been generous. Helpful advice came in from many sources;
especially to be singled out are the aids afforded by Arthur Spingarn
of New York and Henry P. Slaughter of Washington, bibliophiles
with great knowledge of the subject. Mr. Slaughter put his huge collection at our disposal for items difficult to find. Mrs. Dorothy Porter's
cooperativeness, patience, and resourcefulness were invaluable to us.
Her sure knowledge of the extensive collection of The Moorland
Room of the Howard University Founders' Library was a great help,
and but for her, many biographical facts would be missing. Walter
G. Daniel, Librarian of the Howard University Founders' Library,
kindly placed the facilities of the library at our disposal; members of
the library staffs at Howard, Hampton Institute, Lincoln University,
and Virginia Union University were generously cooperative. Invaluable
assistance in the last stages of preparing the manuscript was given
by Dean Charles H. Wesley, Dean Charles H. Thompson, and Professor Charles E. Burch of Howard University, and by Mrs. Virginia
Macbeth Jones of Richmond. Many of our colleagues have given us a
helping hand and words of good cheer. The numerous friends who
worked so strenuously in Richmond, Hampton, and Washington in the
last months of preparing manuscript must already know our gratitude.
The editors' families have watched the work from its inception with
interest and sympathy. To Daisy T. Brown and Clarice Davis, who
saw the work through with such unfailing and good-humored understanding, all three editors extend their heartfelt thanks.

Sterling A. Brown
Arthur P. Davis
Ulysses Lee

TABLE OF CONTENTS

III. POETRY

IV. FOLK LITERATURE

V. DRAMA

VI. SPEECHES, PAMPHLETS, AND LETTERS

VII. BIOGRAPHY

AUTOBIOGRAPHY

BIOGRAPHY

VIII. ESSAYS

HISTORICAL ESSAYS

SOCIAL ESSAYS

CULTURAL ESSAYS

PERSONAL ESSAYS

APPENDIX

THE NEGRO CARAVAN

INTRODUCTION

THE Negro has been a favored subject for American authors from the earliest years of the nation. Cooper, Melville, Poe, William Gilmore Simms, Bryant, Longfellow, Whittier, and many others tried their hands at picturing Negro life and character in portraits that turned out quite dissimilar. America's most popular novel and play, Harriet Beecher Stowe's *Uncle Tom's Cabin,* caused a flood of proslavery and antislavery arguments in fiction. Blackface minstrelsy, considered to be one of America's few original contributions to dramatic history, was for a long time the most popular theatrical entertainment in the United States, and its burlesque of what was considered to be Negro behavior is still influential in the moving pictures and in radio. During the period of local color, such white authors as Irwin Russell, Joel Chandler Harris, and Thomas Nelson Page made their literary reputations by exploiting Negro folkways.

In the twentieth century the literary popularity of Negro life and character has not abated. It is likely that Thomas Dixon, aided by David Wark Griffith in *The Birth of a Nation,* and supported by their latest disciple, Margaret Mitchell, in *Gone With the Wind,* has done more than historians and social scientists to implant in the American mind certain inflexible concepts of Reconstruction. Pulitzer Prize winners like Julia Peterkin and Paul Green, popular best sellers like Octavus Roy Cohen and Roark Bradford, and regionalists like DuBose Heyward and Erskine Caldwell, have reported and interpreted the Negro with great interest though with varying skill, honesty, and sympathy. On the twentieth-century stage, plays by white authors about the Negro have ranged from Edward Sheldon's *The Nigger* to such fantasies as Marc Connelly's *The Green Pastures* and John LaTouche's and Vernon Duke's *Cabin in the Sky,* and such militant plays as *Never No More* by James Knox Millen and *Stevedore* by Paul Peters and George Sklar.

White authors, basing their interpretations on necessarily limited knowledge derived from an outside view, run the risk of stereotyping Negro character. This is true even when they have the best intentions in the world toward their subject, and many, of course, did not have the best intentions.

> I swear their nature is beyond my comprehension. A strange
> people!—merry 'mid their misery—laughing through their tears,

like the sun shining through the rain. Yet what simple philosophers they! They tread life's path as if 'twere strewn with roses devoid of thorns, and make the most of life with natures of sunshine and song.

Any American reader could be forgiven for taking the above to refer to the Negro. It is actually a passage about the Irish, spoken by an English officer in a play that deals with one of the most tragic periods in the history of Ireland. It is one of the oddities of American culture that the three most popular figures in the comic gallery are the Negro, the Irishman, and the Jew, figures whose histories have more than their share of persecution and abuse. Other immigrant people have often been humorous butts.

It appears to be a literary truism that racial and minority groups are most often stereotyped by the majority. Today in Europe, conquered or threatened minorities receive substantially the same literary treatment that the Negro has received here for so many years. With certain honorable exceptions, more numerous in our own time, the white authors dealing with the American Negro have interpreted him in a way to justify his exploitation. Creative literature has often been a handmaiden to social policy.

Thus, in antebellum days, the Negro was shown to be, by his peculiar endowment, the perfect, natural slave. Southern preachers in their *Bible Defenses of Slavery;* physiologists with their "scientific" discoveries made at long range; political economists with their insistence that there should be "servile, laborious beings to perform servile, laborious offices" so that a small master class could sustain chivalry were warrants for J. P. Kennedy to write:

> No tribe of people have ever passed from barbarism to civilization whose progress has been more secure from harm, more genial to their character or better supplied with mild and beneficent guardianship adapted to the actual state of their intellectual feebleness, than the negroes of Swallow Barn.

Complementary to this contented slave was the comic Negro, the clown, the dearly beloved buffoon, seen at his best in the minstrel shows. His corollary was the wretched freedman, the Negro so unhappy among the cold, unsympathetic Yankees and so unequipped for freedom that he frequently stole back to the South on a sort of Underground Railroad in reverse. After emancipation these stereotypes were handled by persuasive authors like Thomas Nelson Page, who gave us the classic examples of slaves yearning for the good old days "befo' de War," speaking often, we fear, like ventriloquists' dummies. In

Reconstruction the wretched freedman became the brute, swaggering about, insulting, and assaulting, and it must be added, wanting to vote.

Abolitionist authors yielded also to the habit of stereotyping. Besides their idealized victims, they also created the "white slave," the tragic mulatto, who to most of the abolitionists seemed to be more tragically doomed than darker fellow bondsmen. Later writers have also emphasized, to an even greater degree, the woes of Negroes of mixed blood.

In the twentieth century the contented slave may be gone but his lineaments remain in his offspring who, though exchanging the cabin for the cabaret, is a creature of mirth and rhythm and song, free from worldly cares. The exotic primitive, unmoral and flamboyant, has been a popular stock figure in our time. Some writers, like Vachel Lindsay, Paul Morand, and Carl Van Vechten, have seen Africa resurgent in the contemporary Negro, the irresistible Congo cutting through the black. Revolting from a drab America standardized by the Babbitts, many authors turned to the Negro as a symbol of escape, and rather strangely, of unshackled freedom.

It is inaccurate to infer that all white authors have taken the easy way of stereotyping. Herman Melville refused to see peculiar endowments in the Negroes aboard the *Pequod,* or in the mutinying slaves of the *Benito Cereno.* From Cable, Twain, and Tourgée down to such authors as Paul Green, E. C. L. Adams, T. S. Stribling, DuBose Heyward, Evelyn Scott, Erskine Caldwell, William March, and Hamilton Basso—many white authors have honestly and courageously insisted upon proffering testimony that differed from that of countless more popular witnesses. But in the main, Negro life and character in American literature have been narrowly grooved, in a way to reinforce, whether consciously or not, American social policy toward the Negro.

The validity of much of the work of white authors cannot be denied, but the belief as expressed, for instance, in many publishers' announcements, that white authors know the Negro best is untenable to the editors of this anthology. They believe that the "inside view" is more likely to make possible the essential truth than "the outside." We go to French authors, Russian authors, German authors, for deeper understanding of those nations; to a Polish Jew, for instance, for deeper understanding of that minority; to working-class authors for deeper understanding of that class.

White authors offer such unimpeachable qualifications for understanding Negroes as playing with Negro children, attending Negro picnics and churches, and bossing Negro gangs. One states that her slaveholding ancestry enables her to interpret Negro character better than any Negro author could interpret it. The editors believe, however, that Negro authors, as they mature, must be allowed the privilege and must assume the responsibility of being the ultimate portrayers of their own.

When the Negro artist has expressed his own people, he has almost always refuted, or differed from, or at least complicated the simpler patterns of white interpretation. Thus, at the very time when J. P. Kennedy was complaisantly writing of the "intellectual feebleness" of the Negro of Swallow Barn, free Negroes in New York were editing and publishing their own newspapers, organs of outspoken propaganda for the antislavery cause; others were contributing money and articles to Garrison's *Liberator*. David Walker's celebrated and inflammatory *Appeal* was being circulated in the South in spite of sharp censorship. And Negroes had been publishing poetry and prose for over half a century. During the argumentative period of the eighteen forties and fifties, many narratives of fugitive slaves were written, powerful ammunition for the antislavery arsenal. Sometimes fictionalized or ghostwritten, sometimes dictated to abolitionists, and often, as in the instances of William Wells Brown and Frederick Douglass, written by the fugitives themselves, these autobiographies formed a popular American literary type, serving as useful sources for *Uncle Tom's Cabin*.

The record of the Negro author extends well over a century and a half. But Negro expression was not confined to the printed page, written under abolitionist sponsorship in the North. In the South, on cotton and tobacco plantations, in field and factory, along "slave row" and in the dank rooms adjoining the slave marts, in camp meetings and in secret brush arbors, the slaves were creating a fine body of folksong—such spirituals as "Swing Low, Sweet Chariot" and "Deep River," and such satires as "My ole mosser promise me." From these folk expressions of slavery to contemporary blues and worksongs, the folk Negro has revealed himself to be much more than contented slave, comic buffoon, and wretched freedman.

In the literature of American Negroes, these favorite stereotypes do not often appear. The self-effacing black mammy, the obsequious major-domo, the naïve folk, and the exotic primitive, to name instances, are seen from a different point of view and are presented with a different stress. This is not the same as denial of the existence of Negroes who resemble and serve as bases for the stereotyping. But Negro writers feel justly that these stereotypes have received far more attention than their importance in the total picture warrants, and that, being stereotypes, they are superficial, resulting from memory more than from observation and understanding. Negro authors write of their kinsfolk, their friends, the people with whom they rub shoulders daily. They find it hard to believe that these characters are as simplified as much literature has made them. And they know so many types of Negroes who have never found places in the books. Much Negro writing, of course, consciously revolting from the offending stereotypes, produces counter-stereotypes of its own. But whether a blues patched together in some dimly lit honky-tonk, or a novel perfected in the few hours after work, or an essay attacking the bias of history, Negro writings generally agree in giving a portrait of Negro life and character different from that which has been handed down for over a century.

A second unifying bond, related to this one, is the theme of struggle that is present in so much Negro expression. Before Emancipation, by far the greatest amount of writing was in the antislavery tradition. Speeches, often letters, pamphlets, poems, the first tentative groping novels, were all conceived as strokes for freedom. The folk expression of the slaves, especially in its more memorable form, the spirituals, shares this deep concern. Out of the storehouse of Christian ideas and idioms, the slave took those that spoke most of his condition, and transmuted them into poetry telling of tribulation and faith, symbolic, naturally indirect, in the way of good poetry, but none the less convincing. After Emancipation, Negro writers turned to the struggle for the rights and responsibilities of citizenship in a democracy. In the twentieth century, Negro writers continue to use both creative and informational literature to attack abuses and injustices and to demand that democracy live up to its name.

In spite of such unifying bonds as a common rejection of the popular stereotypes and a common "racial" cause, writings by Negroes do not seem to the editors to fall into a unique cultural pattern. Negro writers have adopted the literary traditions that seemed useful for their purposes. They have therefore been influenced by Puritan didacticism, sentimental humanitarianism, local color, regionalism, realism, naturalism, and experimentalism. Phillis Wheatley wrote the same high moralizing verse in the same poetic pattern as her contemporary poets in New England. While Frederick Douglass brought more personal knowledge and bitterness into his antislavery agitation than William Lloyd Garrison and Theodore Parker, he is much closer to them in spirit and in form than to Phillis Wheatley, his predecessor, and Booker T. Washington, his successor. Francis E. W. Harper wrote antislavery poetry in the spirit and pattern of Longfellow and Felicia Hemans; her contemporary, Whitfield, wrote of freedom in the pattern of Byron. And so it goes. Without too great imitativeness, many contemporary Negro writers are closer to O. Henry, Carl Sandburg, Edgar Lee Masters, Edna St. Vincent Millay, Waldo Frank, Ernest Hemingway, and

John Steinbeck than to each other. The bonds of literary tradition seem to be stronger than race.

The editors therefore do not believe that the expression "Negro literature" is an accurate one, and in spite of its convenient brevity, they have avoided using it. "Negro literature" has no application if it means structural peculiarity, or a Negro school of writing. The Negro writes in the forms evolved in English and American literature. "A Negro novel," "a Negro play" are ambiguous terms. If they mean a novel or a play by Negroes, then such works as *Porgy* and *The Green Pastures* are left out. If they mean works about Negro life, they include more works by white authors than by Negro, and these works have been most influential upon the American mind. The editors consider Negro writers to be American writers, and literature by American Negroes to be a segment of American literature. They believe that it would be just as misleading to classify Clifford Odets' plays about Jewish life as "Jewish literature" or James T. Farrell's novels of the Chicago Irish as "Irish literature" or some of William Saroyan's tales as "Armenian literature."

The chief cause for objection to the term is that "Negro literature" is too easily placed by certain critics, white and Negro, in an alcove apart. The next step is a double standard of judgment, which is dangerous for the future of Negro writers. "A Negro novel," thought of as a separate form, is too often condoned as "good enough for a Negro." That Negroes in America have had a hard time, and that inside stories of Negro life often present unusual and attractive reading matter are incontrovertible facts; but when they enter literary criticism these facts do damage to both the critics and the artists.

Negro writers are not numerous; their audience, with few exceptions, is small; the subject matter they know best is often controversial; and almost all of them make their livings from jobs other than writing. Yet they must ask that their books be judged as books, without sentimental allowances. In their own defense they must demand a single standard of criticism.

The editors do not hold that this anthology maintains an even level of literary excellence. A number of the selections have been included as essential to a balanced picture. Literature by Negro authors about Negro experience is a literature in process and like all such literature (including American literature) must be considered as significant, not only because of a body of established masterpieces, but also because of the illumination it sheds upon a social reality.

I
SHORT STORIES

THE SHORT STORY

EXCEPT for a few stories by Poe, William Gilmore Simms, and Melville's stirring *Benito Cereno,* short stories about Negro life were seldom attempted before the Civil War. For antislavery purposes, Lydia Maria Child and Isaac T. Hopper wrote short narratives of fugitive slaves, but these were as close to biography as they were to fiction. Similarly, two nineteenth-century Negro writers used the form, Frederick Douglass in his fictionalized account of Madison Washington and the uprising on the *Creole,* and William Wells Brown in numerous anecdotes throughout his volumes. It was not until the eighties, however, that a Negro writer of "short stories" emerged, when Charles W. Chesnutt began to contribute to magazines. By this time George Washington Cable, Thomas Nelson Page, and Joel Chandler Harris were already so widely accepted that the Negro in a short story was likely to be either a mulatto, tragically facing the quandary of mixed blood, or a mellowed raconteur entertaining the young white folks with tales of the plantation past or of the animal world. The Negro short-story writer entered upon the literary scene at a time when the short story had already taken definite form; by the mid-nineties the local-color mold had hardened, and James Lane Allen, Kate Chopin, Grace King, and a company of lesser contributors to the magazines had standardized the earlier fictional conception of the Negro character. In popular magazines for the next three decades the reliable purveyors of short fiction, such as Harry Stilwell Edwards, Ruth McEnery Stuart, O. Henry, Arthur Akers, E. K. Means, and Octavus Roy Cohen, continued to dominate the short story field.

The short story as a literary form in America has always been intended primarily for popular magazine publication; few collections of previously unpublished stories reach the literary market. In this medium, more than in others, the Negro author faces the dilemma of the divided audience. With the exception of the journals of two Negro organizations, the National Association for the Advancement of Colored People's *The Crisis* and the National Urban League's *Opportunity: Journal of Negro Life,* and a few fugitive publications, there have been no magazines with a primarily Negro audience in which Negro writers could place their short stories. *The Atlantic Monthly, Lippincott's The Saturday Evening Post, The American Mercury,* and *Esquire* have been the main outlets in the general magazine field. The necessity for magazine publication has affected the Negro short story profoundly. When Charles W. Chesnutt's stories began to appear in the better magazines (like other Negro writers, he had written pseudonymously for the pulp magazines), the racial identity of the author was an important consideration. The *Atlantic Monthly* had never before published the work of a Negro writer of fiction. For a dozen years after the appearance, in 1887, of the first story, "The Goophered Grapevine," the secret was kept until, with the appearance of "The Wife of His Youth," James McArthur, of the *Critic,* discovered that Chesnutt was a Negro. When he asked Walter Hines Page, then editor of the *Atlantic,* if he might mention that fact in his magazine, Page objected on the grounds that such an announcement might be injurious to the author's reputation. He finally consented, however, and the *Critic* unobtrusively mentioned Chesnutt as one who "faces the problems of the race to which he in part belongs." Thirty years later the problem cropped up again with the appearance of Langston Hughes' "A Good Job Gone" in *Esquire,* for though the matter here was handled with a shrewd eye upon circulation-building publicity, the concern of many of the magazine's readers was genuine. Hughes has written, in *Fighting Words:*

> Here are our problems: In the first place, Negro books are considered by editors and publishers as exotic. Negro material is placed, like Chinese material or Bali material or East Indian material, into a certain classification. Magazine editors will tell you, "We can use but so many Negro stories a year." (That "so many" meaning very few.) Publishers will say, "We already have one Negro novel on our list this fall."

> The market for Negro writers, then, is definitely limited as long as we write about ourselves. And the more truthfully we write about ourselves, the more limited our market becomes. Those novels about Negroes that sell best, by Negroes or whites, those novels that make the best-seller lists and receive the leading prizes, are almost always books that touch very lightly upon the facts of Negro life, books that make our black ghettos in the big cities seem very happy places indeed, and our plantations in the deep South idyllic in their pastoral loveliness . . . When we cease to be exotic, we do not sell well.

The importance of such a situation should not be underestimated. An author's audience inevitably makes its demands upon him, and even the most conscientious artist will make concessions to these demands. The Negro short-story writer, then, it might be objected, could easily solve his audience problem by producing the type of story that it demands. But the Negro author faces two audiences, the white American reader conditioned by the Pages and the Allens, and, later, by the Cohens, the Akerses, the Julia Peterkins, and the Roark Bradfords; and the Negro audience, equally conditioned by and liking the pópular magazine characters and at the same time demanding that Negro writers produce a more complimentary picture of Negro life. Making the quandary more complicated is, of course, the artist's own integrity. To satisfy both audiences is difficult; as a result, short stories by Negroes are limited in range, inventiveness, and appeal.

Yet Negro writers have produced a quantity of short stories. They fall roughly into two classes: those intended for magazines of general circulation, and those intended for Negro magazines. Each has its characteristic style and subject matter. The author finds himself restricted in his choice of themes in each case, for the Negro magazine is no more disposed to accept satirical, humorous, and closely critical stories than the general magazine is to publish polemical narratives. Chesnutt, as a pioneer, avoided certain of the restrictions by writing from a detached point of view. Paul Laurence Dunbar, his contemporary, undoubtedly felt so circumscribed that he accommodated his stories to the plantation tradition of his dialect poems. Alice Moore (later Alice Dunbar-Nelson) wrote stories of New Orleans that had no relation to Negro life. The short stories appearing at present in general magazines, with certain exceptions, follow literary patterns more than reality. Those appearing in the Negro magazines usually follow a pattern best described as the lynching—passing—race-praising tradition. In every case the Negro writer of short stories has had to consider an ethical responsibility in the selection of subject matter and in the delineation of character. Few short stories by Negro writers exist for the sake of the story alone. It is significant that one of the best constructed stories by a Negro, Chesnutt's "Baxter's Procrustes," deals with white characters. Almost always in the portrayal of Negro character the weight of social responsibility bears down upon and sometimes stunts artistic stature.

Thus, the *Opportunity-Crisis* story, as a type, follows the lynching—passing—race-praising pattern. The lynching story as the term is used here need not involve a destruction of life by mob violence; it may be concerned as well with the inevitable struggle of a character against odds arising out of racial prejudice, as effective a lyncher as a mob. The passing stories are legion. Usually a fair girl, who for economic reasons has crossed the color line, yearns to return to her people, if only for a week-end. Upon returning she enjoys a happiness so full that she either remains Negro, or, returning to the white world, does so with an aching heart. The stories of race praise may be simple chronicles of the beauty of a brown girl or extravagant stories of African heroism. Many stories of American Negroes show their heroines proud of their royal African lineage and of the superiority of the African heritage to the polyglot heritage of the rest of America. In few of these stories is there humor or deft characterization or psychological understanding; these elements are sacrificed to the burning message.

Chesnutt and Dunbar published more stories in general magazines than did even the most prominent of the writers of the New Negro Movement. The Dunbar stories are genial folksy tales of life on the plantation and in small towns, where the problems are those of the minister and his congregation, of a cook and her madame, of young love in brownskin. Occasionally, as in "The Tragedy at Three Forks," and "The Lynching of Jube Benson," both of which are concerned with the problem of mob violence, "At Shaft 11," dealing with a mining strike, and "The Ordeal of Mt. Hope," portraying the misadventures of a young minister trying to reform a small town, he touches the more serious problems of the Negro. But most of his stories, like "The Walls of Jericho," "The Trial Sermons on Bull-Skin," or "The Case of Ca'line," are gentle studies of the pleasanter aspects of Negro life. Chesnutt's stories, however, have deeper implications. His stories of the color line within the race, unique in their day, are still the best treatment of this theme; the tragedy of the mulatto and of lynching are combined in "The Sheriff's Children"; the sardonic contradictions arising from color prejudice among Negroes themselves are in "A Matter of Principle." His observation of social phenomena, sharpened perhaps by his work as court reporter; his realization of the effect of small slights upon character, seen at its best in "The Bouquet" and in "Uncle Wellington's Wives"; his sense of the effect of injustices short of lynching, as in "The Web of Circumstance," makes him one of the most important of Negro short-story writers. No writer since Chesnutt has combined the appreciation of the folk Negro, of the transplanted urban Negro, and of the foibles of the "upper tenth" in the way that Chesnutt did.

In company with Dunbar and Chesnutt, later Negro writers have divided their attention between stories that on the surface have no serious import beyond the selling of a story at once acceptable to editors and inoffensive to Negroes and those whose force grows directly out of the structure of the society in which their characters must live. Often, the Negro writer has shied away from the genuinely humorous aspects of Negro life made obnoxious by their continued exploitation at the hands of white writers; just so much of the reality of Negro life has been lost to the Negro short story. Though Rudolph Fisher, in such a story as "Blues of Steel," handled phases of life in the world of barbershops and poolrooms, Negro writers have generally left the province of the lodge parade or the burial-society picnic to those who see their burlesque qualities alone. The rhetoric-laden allegories and fantasies of W. E. B. DuBois' *Darkwater: The Twentieth-Century Completion of "Uncle Tom's Cabin"* (1919), wander far from the actualities of Negro life with its black Christ child born in Georgia and its Manhattan destroyed by a comet, are symptomatic of the lengths to which preoccupation with racial injustice can carry an author.

Rudolph Fisher made use of the rich materials of urban life in stories that not only reflect the surface qualities of the Harlem sector of Bagdad-on-the-Hudson, but also probe beneath the traditionally comic exteriors of his characters, disclosing even in his lighter tales something of the inner workings of his characters' minds. The wonder at the city, the milling life of Harlem's newcomers, the clash between conventionally fundamentalist morality and the newer, freer life of the metropolis are woven into the narrative of such stories as "The City of Refuge," "Vestiges," and "Miss Cynthie." One of Fisher's first stories, "High Yaller," won first prize in a *Crisis* story contest (1925).

From these contests and those held by *Opportunity* in the twenties, came a number of competent stories and a group of new writers. Arthur Huff Fauset won the first *Opportunity* prize (1926) with "Symphonesque," a story of religious and emotional ecstasy. John Matheus, whose "Fog" and "Swamp Moccasin" won·first prizes, has since written several other stories with backgrounds in Florida, the West Indies, and Africa. Eugene Gordon, Anita Scott Coleman, Edwin Sheen, Mary Louise French, and Marita Bonner were also on the prize lists. Unlike Fisher, however, most of the prize winners, once the contests were over, wrote little. Marita Bonner, with such a story as "The Makin's," has continued to write.

Among newer writers, John Henrik Clarke, with his stories of disinherited Negro youth; Chester Himes, with his tough-minded approach; and Ted Poston, with his sketches of untreated phases of Negro life, promise valuable additions to the short story. These writers, unlike the racial idealists, do not shrink from the harsher aspects of Negro life, but present the picture as they have observed it.

With the increased attention paid to psychological techniques by the literary world of the twenties and thirties, Negro short-story writers should have found their horizons greatly widened. The stories of William Faulkner and Erskine Caldwell, with their penetration behind the curtain which normally cloaks black-white relationships, cultivated an audience that, after the Harlem stories and novels of the twenties, should have been ready to accept even more valid interpretations of Negro life from Negro authors. No segment of American life offers more opportunities for the author inclined to probe into the workings of minds beset by many fears and conflicts arising out of a complex social orientation. Of the collections of short stories published in the past twenty years, Jean Toomer's *Cane* (1923), Eric Walrond's *Tropic Death* (1926), Langston Hughes' *The Ways of White Folks* (1934), and Richard Wright's *Uncle Tom's Children* (1939) come closest to penetrating the interior regions of Negro life politely overlooked by the racial idealists and inaccessible to white writers. Claude McKay's *Gingertown* (1932), while supplied with luxuriant tropical settings in its Jamaica stories and sketches, produces in its Harlem stories, such as "Near-White," "Mattie and Her Sweetman," or "Brownskin Blues," short-story variations on the themes developed in *Home to Harlem*. McKay's characters are approached broadside; their problems are simple, elemental, and so, for the most part, are they.

Zora Neale Hurston's *Mules and Men* (1935) contains folk tales and sketches from Florida, which, although they cannot be called short stories, are the only volumes since Chesnutt in which a Negro writer has made use of folklore. Miss Hurston's "Drenched in Light" and "The Gilded Six Bits," however, are among the few short stories dealing with the folk Negro in terms indicative of a full and sympathetic understanding of their lives.

Toomer, Walrond, Hughes, and Wright have written stories that indicate the latent possibilities in Negro life admirably suited to this literary type. Significantly, the first two authors, since the publication of their first volumes of short stories, have not explored Negro experience further. Significantly again, both were published by Boni and Liveright, a firm noted in the twenties for its liberal publishing policies. *Cane* is a collection of stories which, half prose, half poetry, touch the edges of areas in Negro life that have seldom found their way into literature. Most of the stories are portraits of essentially sensitive characters who, like Fern, the beautiful cream-colored girl, or Kabnis, a poet at heart who finds life as a Georgia schoolteacher dessicating, face problems peculiar to their race and class. Brooding behind Toomer's poetic prose are ugly, brutal facts of life as it is faced by Negroes which obtrude into what otherwise would be pastoral beauty. The stories are symbolic reproductions in miniature of a world in which even the finest soul is destroyed before it can begin to unfold; what laughter and joy there is in Toomer is hollow, mocking laughter and crazed, drugged, manufactured joy. In contrast to many another story of the period, Toomer's stories lift the lid from what appears to be the placid bourgeois life of Washington or the pleasant, rustic life of Georgia, and reveal a festering of the soul never indicated by the writers in the race-praise tradition. Similarly, the stories in *Tropic Death,* with their settings in the polychrome lands of the Caribbean, reveal the brittle, often maddeningly violent life of the Negroes of the hot countries. Complex racial and familial relations, superstition, sudden, harsh death with obeah as an aider and abettor, run through the volume. Walrond's ability to handle the West Indian psychology is as marked as is his ability to handle the dialect; in American magazines, his stories and sketches of West Indians in Harlem illuminate a seldom recognized facet of Negro life.

The Ways of White Folks leans heavily on satire and irony. But from Hughes's somewhat irreverent stories of kitchen slaveys, cultists, musicians, Negrophiles, and Negrophobes, the realities of Negro life swim into the consciousness of the reader, making him realize that there is a greater depth in Negro-white relationships of the most casual sort than other writers have suggested. Without truculence, Hughes counterpoises realized Negro characters and white types, disclosing to view several gradations of white attitudes. The result is a revelation of the breadth of unexplored areas available to Negro writers. Even when dealing with the tradition-bound problems of "passing" and miscegenation, Hughes is able to emphasize a phase of the subject that has generally escaped notice. This is because he accepts the fact of the situation as one which, readily understandable in itself, needs no explanation. It is the effect of the fact that interests him. The five long stories in Richard Wright's *Uncle Tom's Children* take an area for exploration that is even farther from that approved by the racial idealists. Wright's stories have been objected to on the grounds that they deal too heavily in violence and in brutality, but, dealing as they do with persons inured to violence through a lifetime of brutalizing influences that teach them to kill or be killed, or better, "kill for you will be killed in any event," their course could hardly be otherwise. Wright's Negroes are all of the heroic stock of Denmark Vesey and Nat Turner; their development may have been stunted by their environment, but the stuff of heroism is there. Silas in "Long Black Song," Sue in "Bright and Morning Star," can act in no other fashion if they are to retain any self-respect at all. Every one of the stories in *Uncle Tom's Children* is worthy of study as a clinical case illustrating the extremes to which the unhealthy race relations of the plantation South can lead men, black and white alike. No better introduction to the many-sided shapes that these relations can take on can be found than in the essay, "The Ethics of Living Jim-Crow."

The importance of these four writers lies in their realization that the world of the Negro is a complex one and that any short story setting out to picture even the smallest segment of that world must deal with characters who reflect all the complexities of their world. There are no simple, single-line Negroes; the facts of their existence in a world that at present remains split into mutually exclusive and yet constantly overlapping compartments prevents the development of such a character. In the short story, where a single incident's impact can be explored in all of its variegated coloring and shading, the Negro author has an opportunity to attempt a fuller delineation of such characters than is possible in other literary forms. Their full portrayal, however, has only begun.

FREDERICK DOUGLASS (1817-1895)

This little-known work of fiction by Frederick Douglass (see also p. 606) was published in *Autographs For Freedom* (1853), a gift book edited by Julia Griffiths to raise money for the antislavery cause. "The Heroic Slave" is a short story about Madison Washington, who led the famous uprising in 1841 on the "Creole," a ship engaged in the domestic slave trade. Douglass regrets that there are only "a few transient incidents," "a few glimpses of this great character"; he offers his story as one that speaks "of marks, traces, possibles, and probabilities." The selections below come from Parts Three and Four of the long story; the first two parts tell of Madison Washington's escape from Virginia to Canada and the aid given him by the Listwells, a white family of Ohio.

From The Heroic Slave

. . . JUST UPON THE EDGE of the great road from Petersburg, Virginia, to Richmond, and only about fifteen miles from the latter place, there stands a somewhat ancient and famous public tavern, quite notorious in its better days, as being the grand resort for most of the leading gamblers, horse-racers, cock-fighters, and slave-traders from all the country round about.[1] This old rookery, the nucleus of all sorts of birds, mostly those of ill omen, has, like everything else peculiar to Virginia, lost much of its ancient consequence and splendour; yet it keeps up some appearance of gaiety and high life, and is

[1] This building—The Halfway House—still stands.   (Editors' Note.)

still frequented, even by respectable travellers, who are unacquainted with its past history and present condition. Its fine old portico looks well at a distance, and gives the building an air of grandeur. A nearer view, however, does little to sustain this pretension. . . . The gloomy mantle of ruin is already outspread to envelop it, and its remains even but now remind one of a human skull, after the flesh has mingled with the earth. Old hats and rags fill the places in the upper windows once occupied by large panes of glass, and the moulding boards along the roofing have dropped off from their places, leaving holes and crevices in the rented wall for bats and swallows to build their nests in. The platform of the portico which fronts the highway is a rickety affair, its planks are loose, and in some places entirely gone, leaving effective man-traps in their stead for nocturnal ramblers. The wooden pillars, which once supported it, but which now hang as encumbrances, are all rotten, and tremble with the touch. A part of the stable, a fine old structure in its day, which has given comfortable shelter to hundreds of the noblest steeds of "the Old Dominion" at once, was blown down many years ago, and never has been, and probably never will be, rebuilt. The doors of the barn are in wretched condition; they will shut with a little human strength to help their worn-out hinges, but not otherwise. The side of the great building seen from the road is much discoloured in sundry places by slops poured from the upper windows, rendering it unsightly and offensive in other respects. Three or four great dogs, looking as dull and gloomy as the mansion itself, lie stretched out along the door-sills under the portico; and double the number of loafers, some of them completely rum-ripe, and others ripening, dispose themselves like so many sentinels about the front of the house. These latter understand the science of scraping acquaintance to perfection. They know everybody, and almost everybody knows them. Of course, as their title implies, they have no regular employment. They are (to use an expressive phrase) *hangers on,* or still better, they are what sailors would denominate *holders-on to the slack, in everybody's mess and in nobody's watch.* They are, however, as good as the newspaper for the events of the day, and they sell their knowledge almost as cheap. Money they seldom have; yet they always have capital the most reliable. They make their way with a succeeding traveller by intelligence gained from a preceding one. All the great names of Virginia they know by heart, and have seen their owners often. The history of the house is folded in their lips, and they rattle off stories in connection with it, equal to the guides at Dryburgh Abbey. He must be a shrewd man, and well skilled in the art of evasion, who gets out of the hands of these fellows without being at the expense of a treat. . . .

[A Mr. Listwell stops at the tavern to spend a night. After shaking off Wilkes, one of the tavern loungers, he goes to his room.]

Disgusted, and little alarmed withal, Mr. Listwell, who was not accustomed to such entertainment, at length retired, but not to sleep. He was *too* much wrought upon by what he had heard to rest quietly, and what snatches of sleep he got, were interrupted by dreams which were anything than pleasant. At eleven o'clock, there seemed to be several hundreds of persons crowding into the house. A loud and confused clamour, cursing and cracking of whips, and the noise of chains startled him from his bed; for a moment he would have given the half of his farm in Ohio to have been at home. This uproar was kept up with undulating course, till near morning. There was loud laughing,—loud singing,—loud cursing,—yet there seemed to be weeping and mourning in the midst of all. Mr. Listwell said he had heard enough during the forepart of the night to convince him that a buyer of men and women stood the best chance of being respected. And he, therefore, thought it best to say nothing which might undo the favourable opinion that had been formed of him in the bar-room by at least one of the fraternity that swarmed about it. While he would not avow himself a purchaser of slaves, he deemed it not prudent to disavow it. . . .

In this spirit he rose early in the morning, manifesting no surprise at what he had heard during the night. His quondam friend was soon at his elbow, boring him with all sorts of questions. All, however, directed to find out his character, business, residence, purposes, and destination. With the most perfect appearance of good nature and carelessness, Mr. Listwell evaded these meddlesome inquiries, and turned conversation to general topics, leaving himself and all that specially pertained to him out of discussion. Disengaging himself from their troublesome companionship, he made his way to an old bowling-alley, which was connected with the house, and which, like all the rest, was in very bad repair.

On reaching the alley Mr. Listwell saw, for the first time in his life, a slave-gang on their way to market. A sad sight truly. Here were one hundred and thirty human beings,—children of a common Creator—guilty of no crime—men and women, with hearts, minds, and deathless spirits, chained and fettered, and bound for the market, in a Christian country,—in a country boasting of its liberty, independence, and high civilization! Humanity converted into merchandise, and linked in iron bands, with no regard to decency or humanity!

All sizes, ages, and sexes, mothers, fathers, daughters, brothers, sisters, —all huddled together, on their way to market to be sold and separated from home, and from each other *forever*. And all to fill the pockets of men too lazy to work for an honest living, and who gain their fortune by plundering the helpless, and trafficking in the souls and sinews of men. As he gazed upon this revolting and heart-rending scene, our informant said he almost doubted the existence of a God of justice! And he stood wondering that the earth did not open and swallow up such wickedness.

In the midst of these reflections, and while running his eye up and down the fettered ranks, he met the glance of one whose face he thought he had seen before. To be resolved, he moved towards the spot. It was MADISON WASHINGTON! Here was a scene for the pencil! Had Mr. Listwell been confronted by one risen from the dead, he could not have been more appalled. He was completely stunned. A thunderbolt could not have struck him more dumb. He stood, for a few moments, as motionless as one petrified; collecting himself, he at length exclaimed, "Madison! is that you?"

The noble fugitive, but less astonished than himself, answered cheerily. "O yes, sir, they've got me again."

Thoughtless of consequences for the moment, Mr. Listwell ran up to his old friend, placing his hands upon his shoulders, and looked him in the face. Speechless they stood gazing at each other as if to be doubly resolved that there was no mistake about the matter, till Madison motioned his friend away, intimating a fear lest the keepers should find him there, and suspect him of tampering with the slaves.

"They will soon be out to look after us. You can come when they go to breakfast, and I will tell you all." . . .

[Listwell and Madison Washington manage a meeting. Since Listwell had helped Madison to escape to the North, he is curious about Madison's reenslavement. Madison explains that he had returned to Virginia to save his wife from slavery. He had been discovered by his master and his two sons, overpowered, and sold to a trader. Though wishing to buy Madison, Listwell is unable to do so, since the slave-traders had sworn to take him South. Listwell follows the coffle to Richmond.]

We pass over the hurry and bustle, the brutal vociferations of the slave-drivers in getting their unhappy gang in motion for Richmond; and we need not narrate every application of the lash to those who faltered in the journey. Mr. Listwell followed the train at a long distance, with a sad heart; and on reaching Richmond, left his horse at an hotel, and made his way to the wharf, in the direction of which he saw the slave-coffle driven. He was just in time to see the whole company embark for New Orleans. The thought struck him that, while mixing with the multitude, he might do his friend Madison one last service, and he stepped into a hardware store and purchased three strong *files*. These he took with him, and standing near the small boat, which lay in waiting to bear the company by parcels to the side of the brig that lay in the stream, he managed, as Madison passed him, to slip the files into his pocket, and at once darted back among the crowd.

All the company now on board, the imperious voice of the captain sounded, and instantly a dozen hardy seamen were in the rigging, hurrying aloft to unfurl the broad canvas of our Baltimore built American Slaver. The sailors hung about the ropes, like so many black cats, now in the round-tops, now in the cross-trees, now on the yard-arms; all was bluster and activity. Soon the broad topsail, the royal and top gallant sail were spread to the breeze. Round went the heavy windlass, clank, clank went the fall-bit,—the anchors weighed,—jibs, mainsails, and topsails hauled to the wind, and the long, low, black slaver, with her cargo of human flesh, careened, and moved forward to the sea.

Mr. Listwell stood on the shore, and watched the slaver till the last speck of her upper sails faded from sight, and announced the limit of human vision. "Farewell! farewell! brave and true man! God grant that brighter skies may smile upon your future than have yet looked down upon your thorny pathway."

* * * *

Just two months after the sailing of the Virginia slave brig, which the reader has seen move off to sea so proudly with her human cargo for the New Orleans market, there chanced to meet, in the Marine Coffee-house at Richmond, a company of *ocean birds,* when the following conversation, which throws some light on the subsequent history, not only of Madison Washington, but of the hundred and thirty human beings with whom we last saw him chained.

"I say, shipmate, you had rather rough weather on your late passage to Orleans?" said Jack Williams, a regular old salt, tauntingly, to a trim, compact, manly-looking person, who proved to be the first mate of the slave brig in question.

"Foul play, as well as foul weather," replied the firmly knit personage, evidently but little inclined to enter upon a subject which terminated so ingloriously to the captain and officers of the American slaver.

"Well, betwixt you and me," said Williams, "that whole affair on board of the *Creole* was miserably and disgracefully managed. Those black rascals got the upper hand of ye altogether: and in my opinion, the whole disaster was the result of ignorance of the real character of *darkies* in general. With half a dozen *resolute* white men, (I say it not boastingly,) I could have had the rascals in irons in ten minutes, not because I'm so strong, but I know how to manage 'em. With my back against the *caboose,* I could, myself, have flogged a dozen of them; and had I been on board, by every monster of the deep, every black devil of 'em all would have had his neck stretched from the yard-arm. Ye made a mistake in yer manner of fighting 'em. All that is needed in dealing with a set of *darkies,* is to show that yer not afraid of 'em. For my own part, I would not honour a dozen niggers by pointing a gun at one of 'em,—a good stout whip, or a stiff rope's end, is better than all the guns at Old Point to quell a *nigger* insurrection. Why, sir, to take a gun to a *nigger* is the best way you can select to tell him you are afraid of him, and the best way of inviting his attack."

This speech made quite a sensation among the company, and a part of them intimated solicitude for the answer which might be made to it. Our first mate replied, "Mr. Williams, all that you've now said sounds very well *here* on shore, where, perhaps, you have studied negro character. I do not profess to understand the subject as well as yourself; but it strikes me, you apply the same rule in dissimilar cases. It is quite easy to talk of flogging niggers here on land, where you have the sympathy of the community, and the whole physical force of the government, state and national, at your command; and where, if a negro shall lift his hand against a white man, the whole community, with one accord, are ready to unite in shooting him down. I say, in such circumstances, it's easy to talk of flogging negroes and of negro cowardice: but, sir, I deny that the negro is, naturally, a coward, or that your theory of managing slaves will stand the test of *salt* water. It may do very well for an overseer, a contemptible hireling, to take advantage of fears already in existence, and which his presence has no power to inspire; to swagger about, whip in hand, and discourse on the timidity and cowardice of negroes; for they have a smooth sea and a fair wind. It is one thing to manage a company of slaves on a Virginia plantation, and quite another thing to quell an insurrection on the lonely billows of the Atlantic, where every breeze speaks of courage and liberty. For the negro to act cowardly on shore, may be to act wisely; and I've some doubts whether *you,* Mr. Williams, would find it very convenient, were you a slave in Algiers, to raise your hand against the bayonets of a whole government." . . .

[As the argument waxes, the mate finally states his resolution never again to set his foot on the deck of a slave ship.]

"Indeed! indeed!" exclaimed Williams, derisively.

"Yes, *indeed*," echoed the mate; "but don't misunderstand me. It is not the high value that I set upon my life that makes me say what I have said; yet I am resolved never to endanger my life again in a cause which my conscience does not approve. I dare say *here* what many men *feel*, but *dare not speak*, that this whole slave-trading business is a disgrace and scandal to Old Virginia."

"Hold! hold on! shipmate," said Williams, "I hardly thought you'd have shown your colours so soon,—I'll be hanged if you're not as good an abolitionist as Garrison himself."

The mate now rose from his chair, manifesting some excitement. "What do you mean, sir," said he, in a commanding tone. *"That man does not live who shall offer me an insult with impunity."*

The effect of these words was marked; and the company clustered around. Williams, in an apologetic tone said, "Shipmate! keep your temper. I meant no insult. We all know that Tom Grant is no coward, and what I said about your being an abolitionist was simply this: you *might* have put down them black mutineers and murderers, but your conscience held you back."

"In that, too," said Grant, "you were mistaken. I did all that any man with equal strength and presence of mind could have done. The fact is, Mr. Williams, you underrate the courage as well as the skill of these negroes, and, further, you do not seem to have been correctly informed about the case in hand at all."

"All I know about it is," said Williams, "that on the ninth day after you left Richmond, a dozen or two of the niggers ye had on board, came on deck and took the ship from you;—had her steered into a British port, where, by-the-bye, every wooly head of them went ashore and was free. Now I take this to be a discreditable piece of business, and one demanding explanation." . . .

"I see," said Grant, "how you regard this case, and how difficult it will be for me to render our ship's company blameless in your eyes. Nevertheless, I will state the fact precisely as they came under my own observation. Mr. Williams speaks of 'ignorant negroes,' and, as a general rule, they are ignorant; but had he been on board the *Creole,* as I was, he would have seen cause to admit that there are exceptions to this general rule. The leader of the mutiny in question was just as shrewd a fellow as ever I met in my life, and was as well fitted to lead in a dangerous enterprise as any one white man in ten thousand. The name of this man, strange to say, (ominous of greatness,) was MADISON WASHINGTON. In the short time he had been on board, he had secured the confidence of every officer. The negroes fairly worshipped him. His manner and bearing were such, that no one could suspect him of a murderous purpose. The only feeling with which we regarded him was, that he was a powerful, good-disposed negro. He seldom spoke to any one, and when he did speak, it was with the utmost propriety. His words were well chosen, and his pronunciation equal to any schoolmaster. It was a mystery to us *where* he got his knowledge of language; but as little was said to him, none of us knew the extent of his intelligence and ability till it was too late. It seems he brought three files with him on board, and must have gone to work upon his fetters the first night out; and he must have worked well at that; for on the day of the rising, he got the irons *off eighteen* besides himself.

"The attack began just about twilight in the evening. Apprehending a squall, I had commanded the second mate to order all hands on deck, to take in sail. A few minutes before this I had seen Madison's head above the hatchway, looking out upon the white-capped waves at the leeward. I think I never saw him look more good-natured. I stood just about midship, on the larboard side. The captain was pacing the quarter-deck on the starboard side, in company with Mr. Jameson, the owner of most of the slaves on board. Both were armed. I had just told the men to lay aloft, and was looking to see my orders obeyed, when I heard the discharge of a pistol on the starboard side; and turning suddenly around, the very deck seemed covered with fiends from the pit. The nineteen negroes were all on deck, with their broken fetters in their hands, rushing in all directions. I put my hand quickly in my pocket to draw out my jack-knife; but before I could draw it, I was knocked senseless to the deck. When I came to myself, (which I did in a few minutes, I suppose, for it was yet quite light,) there was not a white man on deck. The sailors were all aloft in the rigging, and dared not come down. Captain Clarke and Mr. Jameson lay stretched on the quarter-deck,— both dying,—while Madison himself stood at the helm unhurt.

"I was completely weakened by the loss of blood, and had not recovered from the stunning blow which felled me to the deck; but it was a little too much for me, even in my prostrate condition, to see our good brig commanded by a *black murderer*. So I called out to the men to come down and take the ship, or die in the attempt. Suiting the action to the word, I started aft. 'You murderous villain,' said I, to the imp at the helm, and rushed upon him to deal him a blow, when he pushed me back with his strong, black arm, as though I had been a boy of twelve. I looked around for the men. They were still in the rigging. Not one had come down. I started towards Madison again. The rascal now told me to stand back. 'Sir,' said he, 'your life is in my hands. I could have killed you a dozen times over during this last half hour, and could kill you now. You call me a *black murderer.* I am not a murderer. God is my witness that LIBERTY, not *malice,* is the motive for this night's work. I have done no more to those dead men yonder, than they would have done to me in like circumstances. We have struck for our freedom, and if a true man's heart be in you, you will honour us for the deed. We have done that which you applaud your fathers for doing, and if we are murders, *so were they.'*

"I felt little disposition to reply to this impudent speech. By heaven, it disarmed me. The fellow loomed up before me. I forgot his blackness in the dignity of his manner, and the eloquence of his speech. It seemed as if the souls of both the great dead (whose names he bore) had entered him. To the sailors in the rigging he said: 'Men! the battle is over,—your captain is dead. I have complete command of this vessel. All resistance to my authority will be in vain. My men have won their liberty, with no other weapons but their own BROKEN FETTERS. We are nineteen in number. We do not thirst for your blood, we demand only our rightful freedom. Do not flatter yourselves that I am ignorant of chart or compass. I know both. We are now only about sixty miles from Nassau. Come down, and do your duty. Land us in Nassau, and not a hair of your heads shall be hurt.'

"I shouted, *Stay where you are, men,*—when a sturdy black fellow ran at me with a handspike, and would have split my head open, but for the interference of Madison, who darted between me and the blow. 'I know what you are up to,' said the latter to me. 'You want to navigate this brig into a slave port, where you would have us all hanged; but you'll miss it; before this brig shall touch a slave-cursed shore while I am on board, I will myself put a match to the magazine, and blow her, and be blown with her, into a thousand fragments. Now I have saved your life twice within these last twenty minutes,—for, when you lay helpless on the deck, my men were about to kill you. I held them in check. And if you now (seeing I am your friend and not your enemy) persist in your resistance to my authority, I give you fair warning, YOU SHALL DIE.'

"Saying this to me, he cast a glance into the rigging, where the terror-stricken sailors were clinging, like so many frightened monkeys, and commanded them to come down, in a tone from which there was no appeal for four men stood by with muskets in hand, ready at the word of command to shoot them down.

"I now became satisfied that resistance was out of the question; that my best policy was to put the brig into Nassau, and secure the assistance of the American consul at that port. I felt sure that the authorities would enable us to secure the murderers, and bring them to trial.

"By this time the apprehended squall had burst upon us. The wind howled furiously,—the ocean was white with foam, which, on account of the darkness, we could see only by the quick flashes of lightning that darted occasionally from the angry sky. All was alarm and confusion. Hideous cries came up from the slave women. Above the roaring billows a succession of heavy thunder rolled along, swelling the teriffic din. Owing to the great darkness, and a sudden shift of the wind, we found ourselves in the trough of the sea. When shipping a heavy sea over the starboard bow, the bodies of the captain and Mr. Jameson were washed overboard. For awhile we had dearer interests to look after than slave property. A more savage thundergust never swept the ocean. Our brig rolled and creaked as if every bolt would be started, and every thread of oakum would be pressed out of the seams. 'To the pumps! to the pumps!' I cried, but not a sailor would quit his grasp. Fortunately this squall soon passed over, or we must have been food for sharks.

"During all the storm Madison stood firmly at the helm, his keen eye fixed upon the binnacle. He was not indifferent to the dreadful hurricane; yet he met it with the equanimity of an old sailor. He was silent, but not agitated. The first words he uttered after the storm had slightly subsided, were characteristic of the man. 'Mr. Mate, you cannot write the bloody laws of slavery on those restless billows. The ocean, if not the land, is free.' I confess, gentlemen, I felt myself in the presence of a superior man; one who, had he been a white man, I would have followed willingly and gladly in any honourable enterprise. Our difference of colour was the only ground for difference of action. It was not that his principles were wrong in the abstract; for they are the principles of 1776. But I could not bring myself to recognize their application to one whom I deemed my inferior.

"But to my story. What happened now is soon told. Two hours after the frightful tempest had spent itself, we were plump at the wharf in Nassau. I sent two of our men immediately to our consul with a statement of facts, requesting his interference on our behalf. What he did, or whether he did anything, I don't know; but, by order of the authorities, a company of *black* soldiers came on board, for the purpose, as they said, of protecting the property. These impudent rascals, when I called on them to assist me in keeping the slaves on board, sheltered themselves adroitly under their instructions only to protect property,—and said they did not recognize *persons* as *property*. I told them that, by the laws of Virginia and the laws of the United States, the slaves on board were as much property as the barrels of flour in the hold. At this the stupid blockheads showed their *ivory*, rolled up their white eyes in horror, as if the idea of putting men on a footing with merchandise were revolting to their humanity. When these instructions were understood among the negroes, it was impossible for us to keep them on board. They deliberately gathered up their baggage before our eyes, and, against our remonstrances, poured through the gangway—formed themselves into a procession on the wharf,—bid farewell to all on board, and uttering the wildest shouts of exultation, they marched, amidst the deafening cheers of a multitude of sympathising spectators, under the triumphant leadership of their heroic chief and deliverer, MADISON WASHINGTON."

CHARLES W. CHESNUTT (1858-1932)

When Thomas Bailey Aldrich accepted Charles Waddell Chesnutt's "The Goophered Grapevine" for the *Atlantic Monthly* in 1887, the career of the first Negro writer to use the short story as a serious medium for literary expression began. Chesnutt (see also p. 161), though born in Cleveland, had been a teacher in North Carolina, the scene of the stories in his *The Conjure Woman* (1899, reissued in 1929); and, in the year that his first story was accepted, he was admitted to the Ohio bar. From that year until his death he was a resident of Cleveland. Though Uncle Julius, the narrator, is a Negro, *The Conjure Woman* is apparently written from the point of view of a white man; Chesnutt was so successful in taking this point of view that most reviewers did not suspect that the author was a Negro. His second volume, *The Wife of His Youth* (1899), collected his stories of the color line, in which the "Blue Vein Society" of the city of Groveland (Cleveland) plays an important part. "As a matter of fact," · Chesnutt wrote, "substantially all of my writings, with the exception of *The Conjure Woman,* have dealt with the problems of mixed blood, which, while in the main the same as those of the true Negro, are in some instances and in some respects much more complex and difficult of treatment." Chesnutt was here writing from the most personal of experiences, for he himself was what

anthropologists have called a "voluntary" Negro. His stories are
especially valuable for their fusion of a keen understanding of the
less obvious problems of living as a Negro in America and their
appreciation of the dramatic qualities in Negro life. In 1928 Chesnutt, "for his pioneer work as a literary artist depicting the life and
struggle of Americans of Negro descent," received the Spingarn
Achievement Award, a gold medal given annually to Americans of
African descent who have made distinguished contributions to their
chosen fields. The following is reprinted by permission
of Helen M. Chesnutt.

The Sheriff's Children

[The first pages of this story describe the village of Troy, county
seat of Branson County, North Carolina.]

A MURDER WAS A RARE EVENT in Branson County. Every well-
informed citizen could tell the number of homicides committed in
the county for fifty years back, and whether the slayer, in any given
instance, had escaped, either by flight or acquittal, or had suffered
the penalty of the law. So, when it became known in Troy early one
Friday morning in summer, about ten years after the war, that old
Captain Walker, who had served in Mexico under Scott, had left
an arm on the field of Gettysburg, had been foully murdered during
the night, there was intense excitement in the village. Business was
practically suspended, and the citizens gathered in little groups to
discuss the murder, and speculate upon the identity of the murderer.
It transpired from testimony at the coroner's inquest, held during
the morning, that a strange mulatto had been met going away from
Troy early Friday morning, by a farmer on his way to town. Other
circumstances seemed to connect the stranger with the crime. The
sheriff organized a posse to search for him, and early in the evening,
when most of the citizens of Troy were at supper, the suspected man
was brought in and lodged in the county jail.

By the following morning the news of the capture had spread
to the farthest limits of the county. A much larger number of people
than usual came to town that Saturday,—bearded men in straw hats
and blue homespun shirts, and butternut trousers of great amplitude
of material and vagueness of outline; women in homespun frocks and
slat-bonnets, with faces as expressionless as the dreary sandhills which
gave them a meagre sustenance.

The murder was almost the sole topic of conversation. A steady
stream of curious observers visited the house of mourning, and gazed

upon the rugged face of the old veteran, now stiff and cold in death; and more than one eye dropped a tear at the remembrance of the cheery smile, and the joke—sometimes superannuated, generally feeble, but always good-natured—with which the captain had been wont to greet his acquaintances. There was a growing sentiment of anger among these stern men, toward the murderer who had thus cut down their friend, and a strong feeling that ordinary justice was too slight a punishment for such a crime.

Toward noon there was an informal gathering of citizens in Dan Ayson's store.

"I hear it 'lowed that Square Kyahtah's too sick ter hol' co'te this evenin'," said one, "an' that the purlim'nary hearin' 'll haf ter go over 'tel nex' week." A look of disappointment went round the 'crowd.

"Hit's the durndes', meanes' murder ever committed in this caounty," said another, with moody emphasis.

"I s'pose the nigger 'lowed the Cap'n had some greenbacks," observed a third speaker.

"The Cap'n," said another, with an air of superior information, "has left two bairls of Confedrit money, which he 'spected 'd be good some day er nuther."

This statement gave rise to a discussion of the speculative value of Confederate money; but in a little while the conversation returned to the murder.

"Hangin' air too good fer the murderer," said one; "he oughter be burnt, stider bein' hung."

There was an impressive pause at this point, during which a jug of moonlight whiskey went the round of the crowd.

"Well," said a round-shouldered farmer, who, in spite of his peaceable expression and faded gray eye, was known to have been one of the most daring followers of a rebel guerrilla chieftain, "what air ye gwine ter do about it? Ef you fellers air gwine ter set down an' let a wuthless nigger kill the bes' white man in Branson, an' not say nuthin' ner do nuthin', I'll move outen the caounty."

This speech gave tone and direction to the rest of the conversation. Whether the fear of losing the round-shouldered farmer operated to bring about the result or not is immaterial to this narrative; but, at all events, the crowd decided to lynch the negro. They agreed that this was the least that could be done to avenge the death of their murdered friend, and that it was a becoming way in which to honor his memory. They had some vague notions of the majesty of the law and the rights of the citizen, but in the passion of the moment these sunk into oblivion; a white man had been killed by a negro.

"The Cap'n was an ole sodger," said one of his friends solemnly. "He'll sleep better when he knows that a co'te-martial has be'n hilt an' jestice done."

By agreement the lynchers were to meet at Tyson's store at five o'clock in the afternoon, and proceed thence to the jail, which was situated down the Lumberton Dirt Road (as the old turnpike ante-dating the plank-road was called), about half a mile south of the court-house. When the preliminaries of the lynching had been arranged, and a committee appointed to manage the affair, the crowd dispersed, some to go to their dinners, and some to secure recruits for the lynching party.

It was twenty minutes to five o'clock, when an excited negro, panting and perspiring, rushed up to the back door of Sheriff Camp-bell's dwelling, which stood at a little distance from the jail and some-what farther than the latter building from the court-house. A tur-baned colored woman came to the door in response to the negro's knock.

"Hoddy, Sis' Nance."

"Hoddy, Brer Sam."

"Is de shurff in?" inquired the negro.

"Yas, Brer Sam, he's eatin' his dinner," was the answer.

"Will yer ax 'im ter step ter de do' a minute, Sis' Nance?"

The woman went into the dining-room, and a moment later the sheriff came to the door. He was a tall, muscular man, of a ruddier complexion that is usual among Southerners. A pair of keen, deep-set gray eyes looked out from under bushy eyebrows, and about his mouth was a masterful expression, which a full beard, once sandy in color, but now profusely sprinkled with gray, could not entirely conceal. The day was hot; the sheriff had discarded his coat and vest, and had his white shirt open at the throat.

"What do you want, Sam?" he inquired of the negro, who stood hat in hand, wiping the moisture from his face with a ragged shirt-sleeve.

"Shurff, dey gwine ter hang de pris'ner w'at lock' up in de jail. Dey're comin' dis a-way now. I wuz layin' down on a sack er corn down at de sto', behine a pile er flour-bairls, w'en I hearn Doc' Cain en Kunnel Wright talkin' erbout it. I slip' outen de back do', en run here as fas' as I could. I hearn you say down ter de sto' once't dat you wouldn't let nobody take a pris'ner 'way fum you widout walkin' over yo' dead body, en I thought I'd let you know 'fo' dey come, so yer could pertec' de pris'ner."

The sheriff listened calmly, but his face grew firmer, and a determined gleam lit up his gray eyes. His frame grew more erect, and he unconsciously assumed the attitude of a soldier who momentarily expects to meet the enemy face to face.

"Much obliged, Sam," he answered. "I'll protect the prisoner. Who's coming?"

"I dunno who-all *is* comin'," replied the negro. "Dere's Mistah McSwayne, en Doc' Cain, en Maje' McDonal', and Kunnel Wright, en a heap er yuthers. I wuz so skeered I done furgot mo' d'n half un em. I spec' dey mus' be mos' here by dis time, so I'll git outen de way, fer I don't want nobody fer ter think I wuz mix' up in dis business." The negro glanced nervously down the road toward the town, and made a movement as if to go away.

"Won't you have some dinner first?" asked the sheriff.

The negro looked longingly in at the open door, and sniffed the appetizing odor of boiled pork and collards.

"I ain't got no time fer ter tarry, Shurff," he said, "but Sis' Nance mought gin me sump'n I could kyar in my han' en eat on de way."

A moment later Nancy brought him a huge sandwich of split cornpone, with a thick slice of fat bacon inserted between the halves, and a couple of baked yams. The negro hastily replaced his ragged hat on his head, dropped the yams in the pocket of his capacious trousers, and, taking the sandwich in his hand, hurried across the road and disappeared in the woods beyond.

The sheriff reentered the house, and put on his coat and hat. He then took down a double-barreled shotgun and loaded it with buckshot. Filling the chambers of a revolver with fresh cartridges, he slipped it into the pocket of the sack-coat which he wore.

A comely young women in a calico dress watched these proceedings with anxious surprise.

"Where are you going, father?" she asked. She had not heard the conversation with the negro.

"I am goin' over to the jail," responded the sheriff. "There's a mob comin' this way to lynch the nigger we've got locked up. But they won't do it," he added, with emphasis.

"Oh, father! don't go!" pleaded the girl, clinging to his arm; "they'll shoot you if you don't give him up."

"You never mind me, Polly," said her father reassuringly, as he gently unclasped her hands from his arm. "I'll take care of myself and the prisoner, too. There ain't a man in Branson County that would shoot me. Besides, I have faced fire too often to be scared away from my duty. You keep close in the house," he continued, "and if any one disturbs you just use the old horse-pistol in the top bureau drawer. It's a little old-fashioned, but it did good work a few years ago."

The young girl shuddered at this sanguinary allusion, but made no further objection to her father's departure.

The sheriff of Branson was a man far above the average of the community in wealth, education, and social position. His had been one of the few families in the county that before the war had owned large estates and numerous slaves. He had graduated at the State University at Chapel Hill, and had kept up some acquaintance with current literature and advanced thought. He had traveled some in his youth, and was looked up to in the county as an authority on all subjects connected with the outer world. At first an ardent supporter of the Union, he had opposed the secession movement in his native State as long as opposition availed to stem the tide of public opinion. Yielding at last to the force of circumstances, he had entered the Confederate service rather late in the war, and served with distinction through several campaigns rising in time to the rank of colonel. After the war he had taken the oath of allegiance, and had been chosen by the people as the most available candidate for the office of sheriff, to which he had been elected without opposition. He had filled the office for several terms, and was universally popular with his constituents.

Colonel or Sheriff Campbell, as he was indifferently called, as the military or civil title happened to be most important in the opinion of the person addressing him, had a high sense of the responsibility attaching to his office. He had sworn to do his duty faithfully, and he knew what his duty was, as sheriff, perhaps more clearly than he had apprehended it in other passages of his life. It was, therefore, with no uncertainty in regard to his course that he prepared his weapons and went over to the jail. He had no fears for Polly's safety.

The sheriff had just locked the heavy front door of the jail behind him when a half dozen horsemen, followed by a crowd of men on foot, came round a bend in the road and drew near the jail. They halted in front of the picket fence that surrounded the building, while several of the committee of arrangements rode on a few rods farther to the sheriff's house. One of them dismounted and rapped on the door with his riding-whip.

"Is the sheriff at home?" he inquired.

"No, he has just gone out," replied Polly, who had come to the door.

"We want the jail keys," he continued.

"They are not here," said Polly. "The sheriff has them himself." Then she added, with assumed indifference, "He is at the jail now."

The man turned away, and Polly went into the front room, from which she peered anxiously between the slats of the green blinds of a window that looked toward the jail. Meanwhile the messenger returned to his companions and announced his discovery. It looked as though the sheriff had learned of their design and was preparing to resist it.

One of them stepped forward and rapped on the jail door.

"Well, what is it?" said the sheriff, from within.

"We want to talk to you, Sheriff," replied the spokesman.

There was a little wicket in the door; this the sheriff opened, and answered through it.

"All right, boys, talk away. You are all strangers to me, and I don't know what business you can have." The sheriff did not think it necessary to recognize anybody in particular on such an occasion; the question of identity sometimes comes up in the investigation of these extra-judicial executions.

"We're a committee of citizens and we want to get into the jail."

"What for? It ain't much trouble to get into jail. Most people want to keep out."

The mob was in no humor to appreciate a joke, and the sheriff's witticism fell dead upon an unresponsive audience.

"We want to have a talk with the nigger that killed Cap'n Walker."

"You can talk to that nigger in the court-house, when he's brought out for trial. Court will be in session here next week. I know what you fellows want, but you can't get my prisoner to-day. Do you want to take the bread out of a poor man's mouth? I get seventy-five cents a day for keeping this prisoner, and he's the only one in jail. I can't have my family suffer just to please you fellows."

One or two young men in the crowd laughed at the idea of Sheriff Campbell's suffering for want of seventy-five cents a day; but they were frowned into silence by those who stood near them.

"Ef yer don't let us in," cried a voice, "we'll bus's' the do' open."

"Bust away," answered the sheriff, raising his voice so that all could hear. "But I give you fair warning. The first man that tries it will be filled with buckshot. I'm sheriff of this county; I know my duty, and I mean to do it."

"What's the use of kicking, Sheriff?" argued one of the leaders of the mob. "The nigger is sure to hang anyhow; he richly deserves it; and we've got to do something to teach the niggers their places, or white people won't be able to live in the county."

"There's no use talking, boys," responded the sheriff. "I'm a white man outside, but in this jail I'm sheriff; and if this nigger's to be hung in this county, I propose to do the hanging. So you fellows might as well right-about-face, and march back to Troy. You've had a pleasant trip, and the exercise will be good for you. You know *me*. I've got powder and ball, and I've faced fire before now, with nothing between me and the enemy, and I don't mean to surrender this jail while I'm able to shoot." Having thus announced his determination, the sheriff closed and fastened the wicket, and looked around for the best position from which to defend the building.

The crowd drew off a little, and the leaders conversed together in low tones.

The Branson County jail was a small, two-story brick building, strongly constructed, with no attempt at architectural ornamentation. Each story was divided into two large cells by a passage running from front to rear. A grated iron door gave entrance from the passage to each of the four cells. The jail seldom had many prisoners in it, and the lower windows had been boarded up. When the sheriff had closed the wicket, he ascended the steep wooden stairs to the upper floor. There was no window at the front of the upper passage, and the most available position from which to watch the movements of the crowd below was the front window of the cell occupied by the solitary prisoner.

The sheriff unlocked the door and entered the cell. The prisoner was crouched in a corner, his yellow face, blanched with terror, looking ghastly in the semi-darkness of the room. A cold perspiration had gathered on his forehead, and his teeth were chattering with affright.

"For God's sake, Sheriff," he murmured hoarsely, "don't let 'em lynch me; I didn't kill the old man."

The sheriff glanced at the cowering wretch with a look of mingled contempt and loathing.

"Get up," he said sharply. "You will probably be hung sooner or later, but it shall not be to-day, if I can help it. I'll unlock your fetters, and if I can't hold the jail, you'll have to make the best fight you can. If I'm shot, I'll consider my responsibility at an end."

There were iron fetters on the prisoner's ankles, and handcuffs on his wrists. These the sheriff unlocked, and they fell clanking to the floor.

"Keep back from the window," said the sheriff. "They might shoot if they saw you."

The sheriff drew toward the window a pine bench which formed a part of the scanty furniture of the cell, and laid his revolver upon it. Then he took his gun in hand, and took his stand at the side of the window where he could with least exposure of himself watch the movements of the crowd below.

The lynchers had not anticipated any determined resistance. Of course they had looked for a formal protest, and perhaps a sufficient show of opposition to excuse the sheriff in the eye of any stickler for legal formalities. They had not however come prepared to fight a battle, and no one of them seemed willing to lead an attack upon the jail. The leaders of the party conferred together with a good deal of animated gesticulation, which was visible to the sheriff from his outlook, though the distance was too great for him to hear what was said. At length one of them broke away from the group, and rode back to the main body of the lynchers, who were restlessly awaiting orders.

"Well, boys," said the messenger, "we'll have to let it go for the present. The sheriff says he'll shoot, and he's got the drop on us this time. There ain't any of us that want to follow Cap'n Walker jest yet. Besides, the sheriff is a good fellow, and we don't want to hurt 'im. But," he added, as if to reassure the crowd, which began to show signs of disappointment, "the nigger might as well say his prayers, for he ain't got long to live."

There was a murmur of dissent from the mob, and several voices insisted that an attack be made on the jail. But pacific counsels finally prevailed, and the mob sullenly withdrew.

The sheriff stood at the window until they had disappeared around the bend in the road. He did not relax his watchfulness when the last one was out of sight. Their withdrawal might be a mere feint, to be followed by a further attempt. So closely, indeed, was his attention drawn to the outside, that he neither saw nor heard the prisoner creep stealthily across the floor, reach out his hand and secure the revolver which lay on the bench behind the sheriff, and creep as noiselessly back to his place in the corner of the room.

A moment after the last of the lynching party had disappeared there was a shot fired from the woods across the road; a bullet whistled by the window and buried itself in the wooden casing a few inches from where the sheriff was standing. Quick as thought, with the instinct born of a semi-guerrilla army experience, he raised his gun and fired twice at the point from which a faint puff of smoke showed the hostile to have been sent. He stood a moment watching, and then rested his gun against the window, and reached behind him mechanically for the other weapon. It was not on the bench. As the sheriff realized this fact, he turned his head and looked into the muzzle of the revolver.

"Stay where you are, Sheriff," said the prisoner, his eyes glistening, his face almost ruddy with excitement.

The sheriff mentally cursed his own carelessness for allowing him to be caught in such a predicament. He had not expected anything of the kind. He had relied on the negro's cowardice and subordination in the presence of an armed white man as a matter of course. The sheriff was a brave man, but realized that the prisoner had him at an immense disadvantage. The two men stood thus for a moment, fighting a harmless duel with their eyes.

"Well, what do you mean to do?" asked the sheriff with apparent calmness.

"To get away, of course," said the prisoner, in a tone which caused the sheriff to look at him more closely, and with an involuntary feeling of apprehension; if the man was not mad, he was in a state of mind akin to madness, and quite as dangerous. The sheriff felt that he must speak the prisoner fair, and watch for a chance to turn the tables on him. The keen-eyed, desperate man before him was a different being altogether from the groveling wretch who had begged so piteously for life a few minutes before.

At length the sheriff spoke:—

"Is this your gratitude to me for saving your life at the risk of my own? If I had not done so, you would now be swinging from the limb of some neighboring tree."

"True," said the prisoner, "you saved my life, but for how long? When you came in, you said Court would sit next week. When the crowd went away they said I had not long to live. It is merely a choice of two ropes."

"While there's life there's hope," replied the sheriff. He uttered this commonplace mechanically, while his brain was busy in trying to think out some way of escape. "If you are innocent you can prove it."

The mulatto kept his eye upon the sheriff. "I didn't kill the old man," he replied; "but I shall never be able to clear myself. I was at his house at nine o'clock. I stole from it the coat that was on my back when I was taken. I would be convicted, even with a fair trial unless the real murderer were discovered beforehand."

The sheriff knew this only too well. While he was thinking what argument next to use, the prisoner continued:—

"Throw me the keys—no, unlock the door."

The sheriff stood a moment irresolute. The mulatto's eye glittered ominously. The sheriff crossed the room and unlocked the door leading into the passage.

"Now go down and unlock the outside door."

The heart of the sheriff leaped within him. Perhaps he might make a dash for liberty, and gain the outside. He descended the narrow stairs, the prisoner keeping close behind him.

The sheriff inserted the huge iron key into the lock. The rusty bolt yielded slowly. It still remained for him to pull the door open.

"Stop!" thundered the mulatto, who seemed to divine the sheriff's purpose. "Move a muscle, and I'll blow your brain out."

The sheriff obeyed; he realized that his chance had not yet come.

"Now keep on that side of the passage, and go back upstairs."

Keeping the sheriff under cover of the revolver, the mulatto followed him up the stairs. The sheriff expected the prisoner to lock him into the cell and make his own escape. He had about come to the conclusion that the best thing he could do under the circumstances was to submit quietly, and take his chances of recapturing the prisoner after the alarm had been given. The sheriff had faced death more than once upon the battlefield. A few minutes before, well armed, and with a brick wall between him and them he had dared a hundred men to fight; but he felt instinctively that the desperate man confronting him was not to be trifled with, and he was too prudent a man to risk his life against such heavy odds. He had Polly to look after, and there was a limit beyond which devotion to duty would be quixotic and even foolish.

"I want to get away," said the prisoner, "and I don't want to be captured; for if I am I know I will be hung on the spot. I am afraid," he added somewhat reflectively, "that in order to save myself I shall have to kill you."

"Good God!" exclaimed the sheriff in involuntary terror; "you would not kill the man to whom you owe your own life."

"You speak more truly than you know," replied the mulatto. "I indeed owe my life to you."

The sheriff started. He was capable of surprise, even in that moment of extreme peril. "Who are you?" he asked in amazement.

"Tom, Cicely's son," returned the other. He had closed the door and stood talking to the sheriff through the gated opening. "Don't you remember Cicely—Cicely whom you sold, with her child, to the speculator on his way to Alabama?"

The sheriff did remember. He had been sorry for it many a time since. It had been the old story of debts, mortgages, and bad crops. He had quarreled with the mother. The price offered for her and

her child had been unusually large, and he had yielded to the combination of anger and pecuniary stress.

"Good God!" he gasped, "you would not murder your own
father?"

"My father?" replied the mulatto. "It were well enough for me
to claim the relationship, but it comes with poor grace from you to
ask anything by reason of it. What father's duty have you ever performed for me? Did you give me your name, or even your protection? Other white men gave their colored sons freedom and
money, and sent them to the free States. *You* sold *me* to the rice
swamps."

"I at least gave you the life you cling to," murmured the sheriff.

"Life?" said the prisoner, with a sarcastic laugh. "What kind of a
life? You gave me your own blood, your own features,—no man
need look at us together twice to see that,—and you gave me a black
mother. Poor wretch! She died under the lash, because she had enough
womanhood to call her soul her own. You gave me a white man's
spirit, and you made me a slave, and crushed it out."

"But you are free now." said the sheriff. He had not doubted,
could not doubt, the mulatto's word. He knew whose passions coursed
beneath that swarthy skin and burned in the black eyes opposite his
own. He saw in this mulatto what he himself might have become had
not the safeguards of parental restraint and public opinion been thrown
around him.

"Free to do what?" replied the mulatto. "Free in name, but despised and scorned and set aside by the people to whose race I belong
far more than to my mother's."

"There are schools," said the sheriff. "You have been to school."
He had noticed that the mulatto spoke more eloquently and used
better language than most Branson County people.

"I have been to school, and dreamed when I went that it would
work some marvelous change in my condition. But what did I learn?
I learned to feel that no degree of learning or wisdom will change the
color of my skin and that I shall always wear what in my own country is a badge of degradation. When I think about it seriously I do
not care particularly for such a life. It is the animal in me, not the
man, that flees the gallows. I owe you nothing," he went on, "and expect nothing of you; and it would be no more than justice if I should
avenge upon you my mother's wrongs and my own. But still I hate
to shoot you; I have never yet taken human life—for I did *not* kill the
old captain. Will you promise to give no alarm and make no attempt
to capture me until morning, if I do not shoot?"

So absorbed were the two men in their colloquy and their own tumultuous thoughts that neither of them had heard the door below move upon its hinges. Neither of them had heard a light step come stealthily up the stairs, nor seen a slender form creep along the darkening passage toward the mulatto.

The sheriff hesitated. The struggle between his love of life and his sense of duty was a terrific one. It may seem strange that a man who could sell his own child into slavery should hesitate at such a moment, when his life was trembling in the balance. But the baleful influence of human slavery poisoned the very fountains of life, and created new standards of right. The sheriff was conscientious; his conscience had merely been warped by his environment. Let no one ask what his answer would have been; he was spared the necessity of a decision.

"Stop," said the mulatto," you need not promise. I could not trust you if you did. It is your life for mine; there is but one safe way for me; you must die."

He raised his arm to fire, when there was a flash—a report from the passage behind him. His arm fell heavily at his side, and the pistol dropped at his feet.

The sheriff recovered first from his surprise, and throwing open the door secured the fallen weapon. Then seizing the prisoner he thrust him into the cell and locked the door upon him; after which he turned to Polly, who leaned half-fainting against the wall, her hands clasped over her heart.

"Oh, father, I was just in time!" she cried hysterically, and wildly sobbing, threw herself into her father's arms.

"I watched until they all went away," she said. "I heard the shot from the woods and I saw you shoot. Then when you did not come out I feared something had happened, that perhaps you had been wounded. I got out the other pistol and ran over here. When I found the door open, I knew something was wrong, and when I heard voices I crept upstairs, and reached the top just in time to hear him say he would kill you. Oh, it was a narrow escape!"

When she had grown somewhat calmer, the sheriff left her standing there and went back into the cell. The prisoner's arm was bleeding from a flesh wound. His bravado had given place to a stony apathy. There was no sign in his face of fear or disappointment or feeling of any kind. The sheriff sent Polly to the house for cloth, and bound up the prisoner's wound with a rude skill acquired during his army life.

"I'll have a doctor come and dress the wound in the morning," he said to the prisoner. "It will do very well until then, if you will keep quiet. If the doctor asks you how the wound was caused, you can say that you were struck by the bullet fired from the woods. It would do you no good to have it known that you were shot while attempting to escape."

The prisoner uttered no word of thanks or apology, but sat in sullen silence. When the wounded arm had been bandaged, Polly and her father returned to the house.

The sheriff was in an unusually thoughtful mood that evening. He put salt in his coffee at supper, and poured vinegar over his pancakes. To many of Polly's questions he returned random answers. When he had gone to bed he lay awake for several hours.

In the silent watches of the night, when he was alone with God, there came into his mind a flood of unaccustomed thoughts. An hour or two before, standing face to face with death, he had experienced a sensation similar to that which drowning men are said to feel—a kind of clarifying of the moral faculty, in which the veil of the flesh, with its obscuring passions and prejudices, is pushed aside for a moment, and all the acts of one's life stand out, in the clear light of truth, in their correct proportions and relations,—a state of mind in which one sees himself as God may be supposed to see him. In the reaction following his rescue, this feeling had given place for a time to far different emotions. But now, in the silence of midnight, something of this clearness of spirit returned to the sheriff. He saw that he had owed some duty to this son of his,—that neither law nor custom could destroy a responsibility inherent in the nature of mankind. He could not thus, in the eyes of God at least, shake off the consequences of his sin. Had he never sinned this wayward spirit would never have come back from the vanished past to haunt him. As these thoughts came, his anger against the mulatto died away, and in its place there sprang up a great pity. The hand of parental authority might have restrained the passions he had seen burning in the prisoner's eyes when the desperate man spoke the words which had seemed to doom his father to death. The sheriff felt that he might have saved this fiery spirit from the slough of slavery; that he might have sent him to the free North, and given him there, or in some other land, an opportunity to turn to usefulness and honorable pursuits the talents that had run to crime, perhaps to madness; he might, still less, have given this son of his the poor simulacrum of liberty which men of his caste could possess in a slave-holding community; or least of all, but still something, he might have kept the boy on the plantation, where the burdens of slavery would have fallen lightly upon him.

The sheriff recalled his own youth. He had inherited an honored name to keep untarnished; he had had a future to make; the picture of a fair young bride had beckoned him on to happiness. The poor wretch now stretched upon a pallet of straw between the brick walls of the jail had had none of these things,—no name, no father, no mother—in the true meaning of motherhood,—and until the past few years no possible future, and that one vague and shadowy in its outline, and dependent for form and substance upon the slow solution of a problem in which there were many unknown quantities.

From what he might have done to what he might yet do was an easy transition for the awakened conscience of the sheriff. It occurred to him, purely as a hypothesis, that he might permit his prisoner to escape; but his oath of office, his duty as sheriff, stood in the way of such a course, and the sheriff dismissed the idea from his mind. He could, however, investigate the circumstances of the murder, and move Heaven and earth to discover the real criminal, for he no longer doubted the prisoner's innocence; he could employ counsel for the accused, and perhaps influence public opinion in his favor. An acquittal once secured, some plan could be devised by which the sheriff might in some degree atone for his crime against this son of his—against society—against God.

When the sheriff had reached this conclusion he fell into an unquiet slumber, from which he awoke late the next morning.

He went over to the jail before breakfast and found the prisoner lying on his pallet, his face turned to the wall; he did not move when the sheriff rattled the door:

"Good-morning," said the latter, in a tone intended to waken the prisoner.

There was no response. The sheriff looked more keenly at the recumbent figure; there was an unnatural rigidity about its attitude.

He hastily unlocked the door and, entering the cell, bent over the prostrate form. There was no sound of breathing; he turned the body over—it was cold and stiff. The prisoner had torn the bandage from his wound and bled to death during the night. He had evidently been dead several hours.

JEAN TOOMER (1894-)

Jean Toomer (see also p. 355) was born in Washington, D. C. Educated there and at the University of Wisconsin and the College of the City of New York, he decided in 1918 to pursue a literary career. His sketches, poems, and reviews have appeared in various national magazines. His first book, *Cane* (1923), a collection of sketches, short stories, and poems, startled literary America with its unusual

subject matter and its unique approach. In a foreword to *Cane* Waldo
Frank writes of Toomer: "A poet has arisen in that land who writes,
not as a Southerner, not as a rebel against Southerners, not as a
Negro, not as apologist or priest or critic: who writes as a poet."
"Blood Burning Moon" is from the first section of *Cane*, which deals
with Georgia; "Avey" is from the second section, which deals with
Washington. Both are reprinted by permission of the author and the
Horace Liveright Publishing Corporation.

Blood-Burning Moon

Up from the skeleton stone walls, up from the rotting floor boards
and the solid hand-hewn beams of oak of the pre-war cotton factory,
dusk came. Up from the dusk the full moon came. Glowing like a
fired pine-knot, it illumined the great door and soft showered the
Negro shanties aligned along the single street of factory town. The full
moon in the great door was an omen. Negro women improvised songs
against its spell.

Louisa sang as she came over the crest of the hill from the white
folks' kitchen. Her skin was the color of oak leaves on young trees
in fall. Her breasts, firm and up-pointed like ripe acorns. And her
singing had the low murmur of winds in fig trees. Bob Stone, younger
son of the people she worked for, loved her. By the way the world
reckons things, he had won her. By measure of that warm glow which
came into her mind at thought of him, he had won her. Tom Burwell,
whom the whole town called Big Boy, also loved her. But working in
the fields all day, and far away from her, gave him no chance to show
it. Though often enough of evenings he had tried to. Somehow, he
never got along. Strong as he was with hands upon the ax or plow,
he found it difficult to hold her. Or so he thought. But the fact was
that he held her to factory town more firmly than he thought for. His
black balanced, and pulled against, the white of Stone, when she
thought of them. And her mind was vaguely upon them as she came
over the crest of the hill, coming from the white folks' kitchen. As
she sang softly at the evil face of the full moon.

A strange stir was in her. Indolently, she tried to fix upon Bob or
Tom as the cause of it. To meet Bob in the canebrake, as she was going
to do an hour or so later, was nothing new. And Tom's proposal which
she felt on its way to her could be indefinitely put off. Separately, there
was no unusual significance to either one. But for some reason, they
jumbled when her eyes gazed vacantly at the rising moon. And from
the jumble came the stir that was strangely within her. Her lips

trembled. The slow rhythm of her song grew agitant and restless. Rusty black and tan spotted hounds, lying in the dark corners of porches or prowling around back yards, put their noses in the air and caught its tremor. They began plaintively to yelp and howl. Chickens woke up and cackled. Intermittently, all over the countryside dogs barked and roosters crowed as if heralding a weird dawn or some ungodly awakening. The women sang lustily. Their songs were cotton-wads to stop their ears. Louisa came down into factory town and sank wearily upon the step before her home. The moon was rising towards a thick cloud-bank which soon would hide it.

> Red nigger moon. Sinner!
> Blood-burning moon. Sinner!
> Come out that fact'ry door.

2

Up from the deep dusk of a cleared spot on the edge of the forest a mellow glow arose and spread fan-wise into the low-hanging heavens. And all around the air was heavy with the scent of boiling cane. A large pile of cane-stalks lay like ribboned shadows upon the ground. A mule, harnessed to a pole, trudged lazily round and round the pivot of the grinder. Beneath a swaying oil lamp, a Negro alternately whipped out at the mule, and fed cane-stalks to the grinder. A fat boy waddled pails of fresh-ground juice between the grinder and the boiling stove. Steam came from the copper boiling pan. The scent of cane came from the copper pan and drenched the forest and the hill that sloped to factory town, beneath its fragrance. It drenched the men in the circle seated around the stove. Some of them chewed at the white pulp of stalks, but there was no need for them to, if all they wanted was to taste the cane. One tasted it in factory town. And from factory town one could see the soft haze thrown by the glowing stove upon the low-hanging heavens.

Old David Georgia stirred the thickening syrup with a long ladle, and ever so often drew it off. Old David Georgia tended his stove and told tales about the white folks, about moonshining and cotton picking, and about sweet nigger gals, to the men who sat there about his stove to listen to him. Tom Burwell chewed cane-stalk and laughed with the others till someone mentioned Louisa. Till some one said something about Louisa and Bob Stone, about the silk stockings she must have gotten from him. Blood ran up Tom's neck hotter than the glow that flooded from the stove. He sprang up. Glared at the men and said, "She's my gal." Will Manning laughed. Tom strode over to him.

Yanked him up and knocked him to the ground. Several of Manning's friends got up to fight for him. Tom whipped out a long knife and would have cut them to shreds if they hadnt ducked into the woods. Tom had had enough. He nodded to Old David Georgia and swung down the path to factory town. Just then, the dogs started barking and the roosters began to crow. Tom felt funny. Away from the fight, away from the stove, chill got to him. He shivered. He shuddered when he saw the full moon rising towards the cloud-bank. He who didnt give a godam for the fears of old women. He forced his mind to fasten on Louisa. Bob Stone. Better not be. He turned into the street and saw Louisa sitting before her home. He went towards her, ambling, touched the brim of a marvelously shaped, spotted, felt hat, said he wanted to say something to her, and then found that he didnt know what he had to say, or if he did, that he couldnt say it. He shoved his big fists in his overalls, grinned, and started to move off.

"Youall want me, Tom?"

"Thats what us wants, sho, Louisa."

"Well, here I am—"

"An here I is, but that aint ahelpin none, all th same."

"You wanted to say something?"

"I did that, sho. But words is like th spots on dice: no matter how y fumbles em, there's times when they jes wont come. I dunno why. Seems like th love I feels fo yo done stole m tongue. I got it now. Whee! Louisa, honey, I oughtnt tell y, I feel I oughtnt cause yo is young an goes t church an I has had other gals, but Louisa I sho do love y. Lil gal, Ise watched y from them first days when youall sat right here befo yo door befo th well an sang sometimes in a way that like t broke m heart. Ise carried y with me into th fields, day after day, and after that, an I sho can plow when yo is there, an I can pick cotton. Yassur! Come near beatin Barlo yesterday. I sho did. Yassur! An next year if ole Stone'll trust me, I'll have a farm. My own. My bales will buy yo what y gets from white folks now. Silk stockings an purple dresses—course I dont believe what some folks been whisperin as t how y gets them things now. White folks always did do for niggers what they likes. An they jes cant help alikin yo, Louisa. Bob Stone likes y. Course he does. But not th way folks is awhisperin. Does he, hon?"

"I dont know what you mean, Tom."

"Course y dont. Ise already cut two niggers. Had t hon, t tell em so. Niggers always tryin t make somethin outa nothin. An then besides, white folks aint up t them tricks so much nowadays. Godam better not be. Leastawise not with you. Cause I wouldnt stand f it. Nassur."

"What would you do, Tom?"

"Cut him jes like I cut a nigger."

"No, Tom—"

"I said I would an there ain't no mo to it. But that aint th talk f now. Sing, honey Louisa, an while I'm listenin t y I'll be makin love."

Tom took her hand in his. Against the tough thickness of his own, hers felt soft and small. His huge body slipped down to the step beside her. The full moon sank upward into the deep purple of the cloud-bank. An old woman brought a lighted lamp and hung it on the common well whose bulky shadow squatted in the middle of the road, opposite Tom and Louisa. The old woman lifted the well-lid, took hold the chain, and began drawing up the heavy bucket. As she did so, she sang. Figures shifted, restless-like, between lamp and window in the front rooms of the shanties. Shadows of the figures fought each other on the gray dust of the road. Figures raised the windows and joined the old woman in song. Louisa and Tom, the whole street, singing:

> Red nigger moon. Sinner!
> Blood-burning moon. Sinner!
> Come out that fact'ry door.

3

Bob Stone sauntered from his veranda out into the gloom of fir trees and magnolias. The clear white of his skin paled, and the flush of his cheeks turned purple. As if to balance this outer change, his mind became consciously a white man's. He passed the house with its huge open hearth which, in the days of slavery, was the plantation cookery. He saw Louisa bent over that hearth. He went in as a master should and took her. Direct, honest, bold. None of this sneaking that he had to go through now. The contrast was repulsive to him. His family had lost ground. Hell no, his family still owned the niggers, practically. Damned if they did, or he wouldnt have to duck around so. What would they think if they knew? His mother? His sister? He shouldnt mention them, shouldnt think of them in this connection. There in the dark he blushed at doing so. Fellows about town were all right, but how about his friends up North? He could see them, incredible, repulsed. They didnt know. The thought first made him laugh. Then, with their eyes still upon him, he began to feel embarrassed. He felt the need of explaining things to them. Explain hell. They wouldnt understand, and moreover, who ever heard of a Southerner getting on his knees to any Yankee, or anyone. No sir. He was going to see Louisa to-night, and love her. She was lovely—in her way. Nigger way. What way was that? Damned if he knew. Must know. He'd known her long enough to know. Was there something about niggers that you couldnt know? Listening to them at church didnt tell you anything. Looking at them didnt tell you anything. Talking to them didnt tell you anything—unless it was gossip, unless they wanted to talk. Of course, about farming, and licker, and craps—but those werent nigger. Nigger was something more. How much more? Something to be afraid of, more? Hell no. Who ever heard of being afraid of a nigger? Tom Burwell. Cartwell had told him that Tom went with Louisa after she reached home. No sir. No nigger had ever been with his girl. He'd like to see one try. Some position for him to be in. Him, Bob Stone, of the Stone family, in a scrap with a nigger over a nigger girl. In the good old days . . . Ha! Those were the days. His family had lost ground. Not so much, though. Enough for him to have to cut through old Lemon's canefield by way of the woods, that he might meet her. She was worth it. Beautiful nigger gal. Why nigger? Why not, just gal? No, it was because she was nigger that he went to her. Sweet . . . The scent of boiling cane came to him. Then he saw the rich glow of the stove. He heard the voices of the men circled around it. He was about to skirt the clearing when he heard his own name mentioned. He stopped. Quivering. Leaning against a tree, he listened.

"Bad nigger. Yassur, he sho is one bad nigger when he gets started."

"Tom Burwell's been on th gang three times fo cuttin men."

"What y think he's a gwine t do t Bob Stone?"

"Dunno yet. He aint found out. When he does— Baby!"

"Young Stone aint no quitter an I ken tell y that. Blood of th old uns in his veins."

"Thats right. He'll scrap, sho."

"Be gettin too hot f niggers round this away."

"Shut up, nigger. Y dont know what y talkin bout."

Bob Stone's ears burned as though he had been holding them over the stove. Sizzling heat welled up within him. His feet felt as if they rested on red-hot coals. They stung him to quick movement. He circled the fringe of the glowing. Not a twig cracked beneath his feet. He reached the path that led to factory town. Plunged furiously down it. Halfway along, a blindness within him veered him aside. He crashed into the bordering canebrake. Cane leaves cut his face and lips. He tasted blood. He threw himself down and dug his fingers in the ground. The earth was cool. Cane-roots took the fever from his hands. After a long while, or so it seemed to him, the thought came to him that it must be time to see Louisa. He got to his feet and walked calmly to their meeting place. No Louisa. Tom Burwell had her. Veins in his forehead bulged and distended. Saliva moistened the dried blood on his lips. He bit down on his lips. He tasted blood. Not his own blood; Tom Burwell's blood. Bob drove through the cane and out again upon the road. A hound swung down the path before him towards factory town. Bob couldn't see it. The dog loped aside to let him pass. Bob's blind rushing made him stumble over it. He fell with a thud that dazed him. The hound yelped. Answering yelps came from all over the countryside. Chickens cackled. Roosters crowed, heralding the bloodshot eyes of southern awakening. Singers in the town were silenced. They shut their windows down. Palpitant between the rooster crows, a chill hush settled upon the huddled forms of Tom and Louisa. A figure rushed from the shadow and stood before them. Tom popped to his feet.

"Whats y want?"

"I'm Bob Stone."

"Yassur—an I'm Tom Burwell. Whats y want?"

Bob lunged at him. Tom side-stepped, caught him by the shoulder, and flung him to the ground. Straddled him.

"Let me up."

"Yassur—but watch yo doins, Bob Stone."

A few dark figures, drawn by the sound of scuffle, stood about them. Bob sprang to his feet.

"Fight like a man, Tom Burwell, an I'll lick y."

Again he lunged. Tom side-stepped and flung him to the ground. Straddled him.

"Get off me, you godam nigger you."

"Yo sho has started somethin now. Get up."

Tom yanked him up and began hammering at him. Each blow sounded as if it smashed into a precious, irreplaceable soft something. Beneath them, Bob staggered back. He reached in his pocket and whipped out a knife. "That's my game, sho."

Blue flash, a steel blade slashed across Bob Stone's throat. He had a sweetish sick feeling. Blood began to flow. Then he felt a sharp twitch of pain. He let his knife drop. He slapped one hand against his neck. He pressed the other on top of his head as if to hold it down. He groaned. He turned, and staggered towards the crest of the hill in the direction of white town. Negroes who had seen the fight slunk into their homes and blew the lamps out. Louisa, dazed, hysterical, refused to go indoors. She slipped, crumbled, her body loosely propped against the woodwork of the well. Tom Burwell leaned against it. He seemed rooted there.

Bob reached Broad Street. White men rushed up to him. He collapsed in their arms.

"Tom Burwell. . . ."

White men like ants upon a forage rushed about. Except for the taut hum of their moving, all was silent. Shotguns, revolvers, rope, kerosene, torches. Two high-powered cars with glaring search-lights. They came together. The taut hum rose to a low roar. Then nothing could be heard but the flop of their feet in the thick dust of the road. The moving body of their silence preceded them over the crest of the hill into factory town. It flattened the Negroes beneath it. It rolled to the wall of the factory, where it stopped. Tom knew that they were coming. He couldnt move. And then he saw the search-lights of the two cars glaring down on him. A quick shock went through him. He stiffened. He started to run. A yell went up from the mob. Tom wheeled about and faced them. They poured down on him. They swarmed. A large man with dead-white face and flabby cheeks came to him and almost jabbed a gun-barrel through his guts.

"Hands behind y, nigger."

Tom's wrists were bound. The big man shoved him to the well. Burn him over it, and when the woodwork caved in, his body would drop to the bottom. Two deaths for a godam nigger.

Louisa was driven back. The mob pushed in. Its pressure, its momentum was too great. Drag him to the factory. Wood and stakes already there. Tom moved in the direction indicated. But they had to drag him. They reached the great door. Too many to get in there. The mob divided and flowed around the walls to either side. The big man shoved him through the door. The mob pressed in from the sides. Taut humming. No words. A stake was sunk into the ground. Rotting floor boards piled around it. Kerosene poured on the rotting floor boards. Tom bound to the stake. His breast was bare. Nails scratches let little lines of blood trickle down and mat into the hair. His face, his eyes were set and stony. Except for irregular breathing, one would have thought him already dead. Torches were flung onto the pile. A great flare muffled in black smoke shot upward. The mob yelled. The mob was silent. Now Tom could be seen within the flames. Only his head, erect, lean, like a blackened stone. Stench of burning flesh soaked the air. Tom's eyes popped. His head settled downward. The mob yelled. Its yell echoed against the skeleton stone walls and sounded like a hundred yells. Like a hundred mobs yelling. Its yell thudded against the thick front wall and fell back. Ghost of a yell slipped through the flames and out the great door of the factory. It fluttered like a dying thing down the single street of factory town.

Louisa, upon the step before her home, did not hear it, but her eyes opened slowly. They saw the full moon glowing in the great door. The full moon, an evil thing, an omen, soft showering the homes of folks she knew. Where were they, these people? She'd sing, and perhaps they'd come out and join her. Perhaps Tom Burwell would come. At any rate, the full moon in the great door was an omen which she must sing to:

> Red nigger moon. Sinner!
> Blood-burning moon. Sinner!
> Come out that fact'ry door.

Avey

FOR A LONG WHILE she was nothing more to me than one of those skirted beings whom boys at a certain age disdain to play with. Just how I came to love her, timidly, and with a secret blush, I do not know. But that I did was brought home to me one night, the first night that Ned wore his long pants. Us fellers were seated on the curb before an apartment house where she had gone in. The young trees had not outgrown their boxes then. V Street was lined with them. When our legs grew cramped and stiff from the cold of the stone, we'd stand around a box and whittle it. I like to think now that there was a hidden purpose in the way we hacked them with our knives. I like to feel that something deep in me responded to the trees, the young trees that whinnied like colts impatient to be let free. . . . On the particular night I have in mind, we were waiting for the top-floor light to go out. We wanted to see Avey leave the flat. This night she stayed longer than usual and gave us a chance to complete the plans of how we were going to stone and beat that feller on the top floor out of town. Ned especially had it in for him. He was about to throw a brick up at the window when at last the room went dark. Some minutes passed. Then Avey, as unconcerned as if she had been paying an old-maid aunt a visit, came out. I don't know what she had on, and that sort of thing. But I do know that I turned hot as bare pavements in the summer-time when Ned boasted: "Hell, bet I could get her too if you little niggers weren't always spying and crabbing everything." I didn't say a word to him. It wasn't my way then. I just stood there like the others, and something like a fuse burned up inside of me. She never noticed us and swung along lazy and easy as anything. We sauntered to the corner and watched her till her door banged to. Ned repeated what he'd said. I didn't seem to care. Sitting around old Mush-Head's bread box, the discussion began. "Hang if I can see how she gets away with it," Doc started. Ned knew, of course. There was nothing he didn't know when it came to women. He dilated on the emotional needs of girls. Said they weren't much different from men in that respect. And concluded with the solemn avowal: "It does em good." None of us liked Ned much. We all talked dirt; but it was the way he said it. And then too, a couple of the fellers had sisters and caught Ned playing with them. But there was no disputing the superiority of his smutty wisdom. Bubs Sanborn, whose mother was friendly with Avey's, had overheard the old ladies talking. "Avey's mother's onto her," he said. We thought that only natural and began to guess at what would happen. Some one said she'd marry that fellow on the top floor. Ned called that a lie because Avey was going to marry nobody but him. We had our doubts about that, but we did agree that she'd leave school soon and marry some one. The gang broke up, and I went home, picturing myself as married.

Nothing I did seemed able to change Avey's indifference to me. I played basket-ball, and when I'd make a clean shot she'd clap with the others, louder than they, I thought. I'd meet her on the street, and there'd be no difference in the way she said hello. She never took the trouble to call me by my name. On the days for drill, I'd let my voice down a tone and call for a complicated maneuver when I saw her coming. She'd smile appreciation but it was an impersonal smile, never for me. It was on a summer excursion down to Riverview that she first seemed to take me into account. The day had been spent riding merry-go-rounds, scenic railways, and shoot-the-chutes. We had been in swimming and we had danced. I was a crack swimmer then. She didn't know how. I held her up and showed her how to kick her legs and draw her arms. Of course she didn't learn in one day, but she thanked me for bothering with her. I was also somewhat of a dancer. And I had already noticed that love can start on a dance floor. We danced. But though I held her tightly in my arms, she was way away. That college feller who lived on the top floor was somewhere making money for the next year. I imagined that she was thinking, wishing for him. Ned was along. He treated her until his money gave out. She went with another feller. Ned got sore. One by one the boys' money gave out. She left them. And they got sore. Everyone of them but me got sore. This is the reason I guess, why I had her to myself on the top deck of the Jane Mosely that night as we puffed up the Potomac, coming home. The moon was brilliant. The air was sweet like clover. And every now and then, a salt tang, a stale drift of sea-weed. It was not my fault if my mind went romancing. I should have

taken her in my arms the minute we were stowed in that old life-
boat. I dallied, dreaming. She took me in hers. And I could feel by
the touch of it that it wasn't a man-to-woman love. It made me restless. I felt chagrined. I didn't know what it was, but I did know
that I couldn't handle it. She ran her fingers through my hair and
kissed my forehead. I itched to break through her tenderness to
passion. I wanted her to take me in her arms as I knew she had
that college feller. I wanted her to love me passionately as she did
him. I gave her one burning kiss. Then she laid me in her lap as if
I were a child. Helpless. I got sore when she started to hum a lullaby.
She wouldn't let me go. I talked. I knew damned well that I could
beat her at that. Her eyes were soft and misty, the curves of her lips
were wistful, and her smile seemed indulgent of the irrelevance of
my remarks. I gave up at last and let her love me, silently, in her
own way. The moon was brilliant. The air was sweet like clover,
and every now and then, a salt tang, a stale drift of sea-weed . . .

The next time that I came close to her was the following summer
at Harper's Ferry. We were sitting on a flat projecting rock they
give the name of Lover's Leap. Some one is supposed to have jumped
off it. The river is about six hundred feet beneath. A railroad track
runs up the valley and curves out of sight where part of the mountain rock had to be blasted away to make room for it. The engines
of this valley have a whistle, and the echoes of which sound like
iterated gasps and sobs. I always think of them as crude music from
the soul of Avey. We sat there holding hands. Our palms were soft
and warm against each other. Our fingers were not tight. She would
not let them be. She would not let me twist them. I wanted to talk.
To explain what I meant to her. Avey was as silent as those great
trees whose tops we looked down upon. She has always been like
that. At least, to me. I had the notion that if I really wanted to, I
could do with her just what I pleased. Like one can strip a tree. I
did kiss her. I even let my hands cup her breasts. When I was
through, she'd seek my hand and hold it till my pulse cooled down.
Evening after evening we sat there. I tried to get her to talk about
that college feller. She never would. There was no set time to go
home. None of my family had come down. And as for hers, she
didn't give a hang about them. The general gossips could hardly
say more than they had. The boarding house porch was always
deserted when we returned. No one saw us enter, so the time was
set conveniently for scandal. This worried me a little, for I thought
it might keep Avey from getting an appointment in the schools.
She didn't care. She had finished normal school. They could give

her a job if they wanted to. As time went on, her indifference to things began to pique me: I was ambitious. I left the Ferry earlier than she did. I was going off to college. The more I thought of it, the more I resented, yes, hell, that's what it was, her downright laziness. Sloppy indolence. There was no excuse for a healthy girl to take life so easy. Hell! she was no better than a cow. I was certain that she was a cow when I felt an udder in a Wisconsin stock-judging class. Among those energetic Swedes, or whatever they are, I decided to forget her. For two years I thought I did. When I'd come home for the summer she'd be gone. We never wrote; she was too damned lazy for that. But what a bluff I put up about forgetting her. The girls up that way, at least the ones I knew, haven't got the stuff: they don't know how to love. Giving themselves completely was tame beside just the holding of Avey's hand. One day I received a note from her. The writing I decided, was slovenly. She wrote on a torn bit of note-book paper. The envelope had a faint perfume that I remembered. A single line told me she had lost her school and was going away. I comforted myself with the reflection that shame held no pain for one so indolent as she. Nevertheless, I left Wisconsin that year for good. Washington had seemingly forgotten her. I hunted Ned. Between curses, I caught his opinion of her. She was no better than a whore. I saw her mother on the street. The same old pinchbeck, jerky-gaited creature that I'd always known.

Perhaps five years passed. The business of hunting a job or something or other had bruised my vanity so that I could recognize it. I felt old. Avey and my real relation to her. I thought I came to know. I wanted to see her. I had been told that she was in New York. As I had no money, I hiked and bummed my way there. I got work in a ship-yard and walked the streets at night, hoping to meet her. Failing in this, I got to work to save enough to pay my fare back home. One evening in early June, just at the time when dusk is most lovely on the eastern horizon, I saw Avey, indolent as ever, leaning on the arm of a man, strolling under the recently lit arc-lights of U Street. She had almost passed before she recognized me. She showed no surprise. The puff over her eyes had grown heavier. The eyes themselves were still sleepy-large, and beautiful. I had almost concluded-indifferent. "You look older," was what she said. I wanted to convince her that I was, so I asked her to walk with me. The man whom she was with, and whom she never took the trouble to introduce, at a nod from her, hailed a taxi, and drove away. That gave me a notion that was what she had been used to. Her dress was of some fine, costly stuff. I suggested the park, and then added that the grass might stain her skirt. Let it stain, she said, for where it came from there are others.

I have a spot in Soldier's Home to which I always go when I want the simple beauty of another's soul. Robins spring about the lawn all day. They leave their footprints in the grass. I imagine that the grass at night smells sweet and fresh because of them. The ground is high, Washington lies below. Its light spreads like a blush against the darkened sky. Against the soft dusk sky of Washington. And when the wind is from the South, soil of my homeland falls like a fertile shower upon the lean streets of the city. Upon my hill is Soldier's Home. I know the policeman who watches the place of nights. When I go there alone, I talk to him. I tell him I come there to find truth that people bury in their hearts. I tell him that I do not come there with a girl to do the thing he's paid to watch out for. I look deep in his eyes when I say these things, and he believes me. He comes over to see who it is on the grass. I say hello to him. He greets me in the same manner and goes off searching for other black splotches upon the lawn. Avey and I went there. A band in one of the buildings a fair distance off was playing a march. I wished they would stop. Their playing was like a tin spoon in one's mouth. I wanted the Howard Glee Club to sing "Deep River" from the road. . . . Other than the first comments, Avey had been silent. I started to hum a folk-tune. She slipped her hand in mine. Pillowed her head as best she could upon my arm. Kissed the hand that she was holding and listened, or so I thought, to what I had to say. I traced my development from the early days up to the present time, the phase in which I could understand her. I described her own nature and temperament. Told how they needed a larger life for their expression. How incapable Washington was of understanding that need. How it could not meet it. I pointed out that in lieu of proper channels her emotions had overflowed into paths that dissipated them. I talked, beautifully I thought, about an art that would be born, an art that would open the way for women the likes of her. I asked her to hope, and build up an inner life against the coming of that day. I recited some of my own things to her. I sang, with a strange quiver in my voice, a promise-song. And then I began to wonder why her hand had not once returned a single pressure. My old-time feeling about her laziness came back. I spoke sharply. My policeman friend passed by. I said hello to him. As he went away, I began to visualize certain possibilities. An immediate and urgent passion swept over me. Then I looked at Avey. Her heavy eyes were closed. Her breathing was as faint and regular as a child's in slumber.

My passion died. I was afraid to move lest I disturb her. Hours and hours, I guess it was, she lay there. My body grew numb. I shivered. I coughed. I wanted to get up and whittle at the boxes of young trees. I withdrew my hand. I raised her head to waken her. She did not stir. I got up and walked around. I found my policeman friend and talked to him. We both came up, and bent over her. He said that it would be all right for her to stay there just so long as she got away before the workmen came at dawn. A blanket was borrowed from a neighbor's house. I sat beside her through the night. I saw the dawn steal over Washington. The Capitol dome looked like a gray ghost ship drifting in from sea. Avey's face was pale, and her eyes were heavy. She did not have the gray crimson-splashed beauty of the dawn. I hated to wake her. Orphan-woman . . .

RUDOLPH FISHER (1897-1934)

Rudolph Fisher (see also p. 203) was born in Washington, D. C. He was educated in the Providence, R. I., public schools, Brown University, and the Howard University Medical School. He practiced roentgenology in New York City. His story output includes "High Yaller," "Guardian of the Law," "Ringtail," "Blades of Steel," and "Vestiges"; "The City of Refuge" (which appeared in *The Atlantic Monthly* in 1925) and "Miss Cynthie" (which appeared in *Story* in 1933) have been reprinted by Edward O'Brien in his anthologies of the best short stories of the year. "Miss Cynthie" is here reprinted by permission of the editors of *Story* Magazine.

Miss Cynthie

FOR THE FIRST TIME IN HER LIFE somebody had called her "madam." She had been standing, bewildered but unafraid, while innumerable Red Caps appropriated piece after piece of the baggage arrayed on the platform. Neither her brief seventy years' journey through life nor her long two days' travel northward had dimmed the live brightness of her eyes, which, for all their bewilderment, had accurately selected her own treasures out of the row of luggage and guarded them vigilantly. "These yours, madam?"

The biggest Red Cap of all was smiling at her. He looked for all the world like Doc Crinshaw's oldest son back home. Her little brown face relaxed; she smiled back at him.

"They got to be. You all done took all the others."

He laughed aloud. Then—"Carry 'em in for you?"

She contemplated his bulk. "Reckon you can manage it—puny little feller like you?"

Thereupon they were friends. Still grinning broadly, he surrounded himself with her impedimenta, the enormous brown extension-case on one shoulder, the big straw suitcase in the opposite hand, the carpet-bag under one arm. She herself held fast to the umbrella. "Always like to have sump'm in my hand when I walk. Can't never tell when you'll run across a snake."

"There aren't any snakes in the city."

"There's snakes everywhere, chile."

They began the tedious hike up the interminable platform. She was small and quick. Her carriage was surprisingly erect, her gait astonishingly spry. She said:

"You liked to took my breath back yonder, boy, callin' me 'madam.' Back home everybody call me 'Miss Cynthie.' Even their chillun. Black folks, white folks too. 'Miss Cynthie.' Well, when you come up with that 'madam' o' yourn, I say to myself, 'Now, I wonder who that chile's a-grinnin' at? 'Madam' stands for mist'ess o' the house, and I sho' ain' mist'ess o' nothin' in this hyeh New York.'"

"Well, you see, we call everybody 'madam.'"

"Everybody?—Hm." The bright eyes twinkled. "Seem like that's worry me some—if I was a man."

He acknowledged his slip and observed, "I see this isn't your first trip to New York."

"First trip any place, son. First time I been over fifty mile from Waxhaw. Only travelin' I've done is in my head. Ain' seen many places, but I's seen a passel o' people. Reckon places is pretty much alike after people been in 'em awhile."

"Yes, ma'am. I guess that's right."

"You ain' no reg'lar bag-toter, is you?"

"Ma'am?"

"You talk too good."

"Well, I only do this in vacation-time. I'm still in school."

"You is. What you aimin' to be?"

"I'm studying medicine."

"You is?" She beamed. "Aimin' to be a doctor, huh? Thank the Lord for that. That's what I always wanted my David to be. My grandchile hyeh in New York. He's to meet me hyeh now."

"I bet you'll have a great time."

"Mussn't bet, chile. That's sinful. I tole him 'for' he left home, I say, 'Son, you the only one o' the chillun what's got a chance to amount to sump'm. Don't th'ow it away. Be a preacher or a doctor.

Work yo' way up and don' stop short. If the Lord don' see fit for
you to doctor the soul, then doctor the body. If you don' get to be
a reg'lar doctor, be a tooth-doctor. If you jes' can't make that, be a
foot-doctor. And if you don' get that fur, be a undertaker. That's
the least you must be. That ain' so bad. Keep you acquainted with
the house of the Lord. Always mind the house o' the Lord—whatever
you do, do like a church-steeple: aim high and go straight.' "

"Did he get to be a doctor?"

"Don'· b'lieve he did. Too late startin', I reckon. But he's done
succeeded at sump'm. Mus' be at least a undertaker, 'cause he started
sendin' the homefolks money, and he come home las' year dressed
like Judge Pettiford's boy what went off to school in Virginia.
Wouldn't tell none of us 'zackly what he was doin', but he said he
wouldn' never be happy till I come and see for myself. So hyeh I is."
Something softened her voice. "His mammy died befo' he knowed
her. But he was always sech a good chile—" The something was
apprehension. "Hope he *is* a undertaker."

They were mounting a flight of steep stairs leading to an exit-
gate, about which clustered a few people still hoping to catch sight
of arriving friends. Among these a tall young brown-skinned man
in a light grey suit suddenly waved his panama and yelled, "Hey,
Miss Cynthie!"

Miss Cynthie stopped, looked up, and waved back with a delighted
umbrella. The Red Cap's eyes lifted too. His lower jaw sagged.

"Is that your grandson?"

"It sho' is," she said and distanced him for the rest of the climb.
The grandson, with an abandonment that superbly ignored onlookers,
folded the little woman in an exultant, smothering embrace. As soon
as she could, she pushed him off with breathless mock impatience.

"Go 'way, you fool, you. Aimin' to squeeze my soul out my body
befo' I can get a look at this place?" She shook herself into the sem-
blance of composure. "Well. You don't look hungry, anyhow."

"Ho-ho! Miss Cynthie in New York! Can y' imagine this? Come
on. I'm parked on Eighth Avenue."

The Red Cap delivered the outlandish luggage into a robin's egg
blue open Packard with scarlet wheels, accepted the grandson's dollar
and smile, and stood watching the car roar away up Eighth Avenue.

Another Red Cap came up. "Got a break, hey, boy?"

"Dave Tappen himself—can you beat that?"

"The old lady hasn't seen the station yet—starin' at him."

"That's not the half of it, bozo. That's Dave Tappen's grandmother. And what do you s'pose she hopes?"

"What?"

"She hopes that Dave has turned out to be a successful undertaker!"

"Undertaker? Undertaker!"

They stared at each other a gaping moment, then doubled up with laughter.

"Look—through there—that's the Chrysler Building. Oh, hellelujah! I meant to bring you up Broadway—"

"David—"

"Ma'am?"

"This hyeh wagon yourn?"

"Nobody else's. Sweet buggy, ain't it?"

"David—you ain't turned out to be one of them moonshiners, is you?"

"Moonshiners—? Moon—Ho! No indeed, Miss Cynthie. I got a better racket 'n that."

"Better which?"

"Game. Business. Pick-up."

"Tell me, David. What is yo' racket?"

"Can't spill it yet, Miss Cynthie. Rather show you. Tomorrow night you'll know the worst. Can you make out till tomorrow night?"

"David, you know I always wanted you to be a doctor, even if 'twasn' nothin' but a foot-doctor. The very leas' I wanted you to be was a undertaker."

"Undertaker! Oh, Miss Cynthie!—with my sunny disposition?"

"Then you ain' even a undertaker?"

"Listen, Miss Cynthie. Just forget 'bout what I am for awhile. Must till tomorrow night. I want you to see for yourself. Tellin' you will spoil it. Now stop askin', you hear?—because I'm not answerin'— I'm surprisin' you. And don't expect anybody you meet to tell you. It'll mess up the whole works. Understand? Now give the big city a break. There's the elevated train going up Columbus Avenue. Ain't that hot stuff?"

Miss Cynthie looked. "Humph!" she said. "'Tain' half high as that trestle two mile from Waxhaw."

She thoroughly enjoyed the ride up Central Park West. The stagger lights, the extent of the park, the high, close, kingly buildings, remarkable because their stoves cooled them in summer as well as heated them in winter, all drew nods of mild interest. But what gave her special delight was not these: it was that David's car so effortlessly sped past the headlong drove of vehicles racing northward.

They stopped for a red light; when they started again their

machine leaped forward with a triumphant eagerness that drew from her an unsuppressed "Hot you, David! That's it!"

He grinned appreciatively. "Why, you're a regular New Yorker already."

"New York nothin'! I done the same thing fifty years ago—befo' I knowed they was a New York."

"What!"

"'Deed so. Didn' I use to tell you 'bout my young mare, Betty? Chile, I'd hitch Betty up to yo' grandpa's buggy and pass anything on the road. Betty never knowed what another horse's dust smelt like. No 'ndeedy. Shuh, boy, this ain' nothin' new to me. Why that broke-down Fo'd yo uncle Jake's got ain' nothin'—nothin' but a sorry mess. Done got so slow I jes' won' ride in it—I declare I'd rather walk. But this hyeh thing, now, this is right nice." She settled back in complete, complacent comfort, and they sped on, swift and silent.

Suddenly she sat erect with abrupt discovery.

"David—well—bless my soul!"

"What's the matter, Miss Cynthie?"

Then he saw what had caught her attention. They were travelling up Seventh Avenue now, and something was miraculously different. Not the road; that was as broad as ever, wide, white gleaming in the sun. Not the houses; they were lofty still, lordly, disdainful, supercilious. Not the cars; they continued to race impatiently onward, innumerable, precipitate, tumultuous. Something else, something at once obvious and subtle, insistent, pervasive, compelling.

"David—this mus' be Harlem!"

"Good Lord, Miss Cynthie—!"

"Don' use the name of the Lord in vain, David."

"But I mean—gee!—you're no fun at all. You get everything before a guy can tell you."

"You got plenty to tell me, David. But don' nobody need to tell me this. Look a yonder."

Not just a change of complexion. A completely dissimilar atmosphere. Sidewalks teeming with leisurely strollers, at once strangely dark and bright. Boys in white trousers, berets, and green shirts, with slickened black heads and proud swagger. Bareheaded girls in crisp organdie dresses, purple, canary, gay scarlet. And laughter, abandoned strong Negro laughter, some falling full on the ear, some not heard at all, yet sensed—the warm life-breath of the tireless carnival to which Harlem's heart quickens in summer.

"This is it," admitted David. "Get a good eyeful. Here's One Hundred and Twenty-fifth Street—regular little Broadway. And here's the Alhambra, and up ahead we'll pass the Lafayette."

"What's them?"

"Theatres."

"Theatres? Theatres. Humph! Look, David—is that a colored folks church?" They were passing a fine gray-stone edifice.

"That? Oh. Sure it is. So's this one on this side."

"No! Well, ain' that fine? Splendid big church like that for colored folks."

Taking his cue from this, her first tribute to the city he said, "You ain't seen nothing yet. Wait a minute."

They swung left through a side-street and turned right on a boulevard. "What do you think o' that?" And he pointed to the quarter-million-dollar St. Mark's.

"That a colored church, too?"

" 'Tain' no white one. And they built it themselves, you know. Nobody's hand-me-down gift."

She heaved a great happy sigh. "Oh, yes, it was a gift, David. It was a gift from on high." Then, "Look a hyeh—which a one you belong to?"

"Me? Why, I don't belong to any—that is, none o' these. Mine's over in another section. Y'see, mine's Baptist. These are all Methodist. See?"

"M-m. Uh-huh. I see."

They circled a square and slipped into a quiet narrow street overlooking a park, stopping before the tallest of the apartment-houses in the single commanding row.

Alighting, Miss Cynthie gave this imposing structure one sidewise, upward glance, and said, "Y'all live like bees in a hive, don't y'? —I boun' the women does all the work, too." A moment later, "So this is a elevator? Feel like I'm glory-bound sho' nuff."

Along a tiled corridor and into David's apartment. Rooms leading into rooms. Luxurious couches, easy-chairs, a brown-walnut grand piano, gay-shaded floor lamps, panelled walls, deep rugs, treacherous glass-wood floors—and a smiling golden-skinned girl in a gingham housedress, approaching with outstretched hands.

"This is Ruth, Miss Cynthie."

"Miss Cynthie!" said Ruth.

They clasped hands. "Been wantin' to see David's girl ever since he first wrote us 'bout her."

"Come—here's your room this way. Here's the bath. Get out of your things and get comfy. You must be worn out with the trip."

"Worn out? Worn out? Shuh. How you gon' get worn out on a train? Now if 'twas a horse, maybe, or Jake's no-count Fo'd—but a train—didn' but one thing bother me on that train."

"What?"

"When the man made them beds down, I jes' couldn' manage to undress same as at home. Why, s'posin' sump'm bus' the train open— where'd you be? Naked as a jay-bird in dew-berry time."

David took in her things and left her to get comfortable. He returned, and Ruth, despite his reassuring embrace, whispered:

"Dave, you can't fool old folks—why don't you go ahead and tell her about yourself? Think of the shock she's going to get—at her age."

David shook his head. "She'll get over the shock if she's there looking on. If we just told her, she'd never understand. We've got to railroad her into it. Then she'll be happy."

"She's nice. But she's got the same ideas as all old folks—"

"Yea—but with her you can change 'em. Specially if everything is really all right. I know her. She's for church and all, but she believes in good times too, if they're right. Why, when I was a kid—" He broke off. "Listen!"

Miss Cynthie's voice came quite distinctly to them, singing a jaunty little rhyme:

> *"Oh I danced with the gal with the hole in her stockin',*
> *And her toe kep' a-kickin' and her heel kep' a-knockin'—*
>
> *'Come up, Jesse, and get a drink o' gin,*
> *'Cause you near to the heaven as you'll ever get ag'in'."*

"She taught me that when I wasn't knee-high to a cricket," David said.

Miss Cynthie still sang softly and merrily:

> *"Then I danced with the gal with the dimple in her cheek,*
> *And if she'd 'a' kep' a-smilin', I'd 'a' danced for a week—"*

"God forgive me," prayed Miss Cynthie as she discovered David's purpose the following night. She let him and Ruth lead her, like an early Christian martyr, into the Lafayette Theatre. The blinding glare of the lobby produced a merciful self-anaesthesia, and she entered the sudden dimness of the interior as involuntarily as in a dream . . . .

Attendants outdid each other for Mr. Dave Tappen. She heard him tell them, "Fix us up till we go on," and found herself sitting between Ruth and David in the front row of a lower box. A miraculous device of the devil, a motion-picture that talked, was just ending. At her feet the orchestra was assembling. The motion-picture faded out amid a scattered round of applause. Lights blazed and the orchestra burst into an ungodly rumpus.

She looked out over the seated multitude, scanning row upon row of illumined faces, black faces, white faces, yellow, tan, brown; bald heads, bobbed heads, kinky and straight heads; and upon every countenance, expectancy—scowling expectancy in this case, smiling in that, complacent here, amused there, commentative elsewhere, but everywhere suspense, abeyance, anticipation.

Half a dozen people were ushered down the nearer aisle to reserved seats in the second row. Some of them caught sight of David and Ruth and waved to them. The chairs immediately behind them in the box were being shifted. "Hello, Tap!" Miss Cynthie saw David turn, rise, and shake hands with two men. One of them was large, bald and pink, emanating good cheer; the other short, thin, sallow with thick black hair and a sour mien. Ruth also acknowledged their greeting. "This is my grandmother," David said proudly. "Miss Cynthie, meet my managers, Lou and Lee Goldman." "Pleased to meet you," managed Miss Cynthie. "Great lad, this boy of yours," said Lou Goldman. "Great little partner he's got, too," added Lee. They also settled back expectantly.

"Here we go!"

The curtain rose to reveal a cotton-field at dawn. Pickers in blue denim overalls, bandanas, and wide-brimmed straws, or in gingham aprons and sun-bonnets, were singing as they worked. Their voices, from clearest soprano to richest bass, blended in low concordances, first simply humming a series of harmonies, until, gradually, came words, like figures forming in mist. As the sound grew, the mist cleared, the words came round and full, and the sun rose bringing light as if in answer to the song. The chorus swelled, the radiance grew, the two, as if emanating from a single source, fused their crescendos, till at last they achieved a joint transcendence of tonal and visual brightness.

"Swell opener," said Lee Goldman.

"Ripe," agreed Lou.

David and Ruth arose. "Stay here and enjoy the show, Miss Cynthie. You'll see us again in a minute."

"Go to it, kids," said Lou Goldman.

"Yea—burn 'em up," said Lee.

Miss Cynthie hardly noted that she had been left, so absorbed was she in the spectacle. To her, the theatre had always been the antithesis of the church. As the one was the refuge of righteousness, so the other was the stronghold of transgression. But this first scene awakened memories, captured and held her attention by offering a blend of truth and novelty. Having thus baited her interest, the show now pro-

ceeded to play it like the trout through swift-flowing waters of wickedness. Resist as it might, her mind was caught and drawn into the
impious subsequences.

The very music that had just rounded out so majestically now
distorted itself into ragtime. The singers came forward and turned to
dancers; boys, a crazy, swaying background, threw up their arms and
kicked out their legs in a rhythmic jamboree; girls, an agile, brazen
foreground, caught their skirts up to their hips and displayed their
copper calves, knees, thighs, in shameless, incredible steps. Miss
Cynthie turned dismayed eyes upon the audience, to discover that
mob of sinners devouring it all with fond satisfaction. Then the dancers
separated and with final abandon flung themselves off the stage in
both directions.

Lee Goldman commented through the applause, "They work easy,
them babies."

"Yea," said Lou. "Savin' the hot stuff for later."

Two black-faced cotton-pickers appropriated the scene, indulging
in dialogue that their hearers found uproarious.

"Ah'm tired."

"Ah'm hongry."

"Dis job jes' wears me out."

"Starves me to death."

"Ah'm so tired—you know what Ah'd like to do?"

"What?"

"Ah'd like to go to sleep and dream I was sleepin'.'"

"What good dat do?"

"Den I could wake up and still be 'sleep."

"Well y'know what Ah'd like to do?"

"No. What?"

"Ah'd like to swaller me a hog and a hen."

"What good dat do?"

"Den Ah'd always be full o' ham and eggs."

"Ham? Shuh. Don't you know a hog has to be smoked 'fo' he's
a ham?"

"Well, if I swaller him, he'll have a smoke all around him, won'
he?"

Presently Miss Cynthie was smiling like everyone else, but her smile
soon fled. For the comics departed, and the dancing girls returned,
this time in scant travesties on their earlier voluminous costumes—tiny
sun-bonnets perched jauntily on one side of their glistening bobs,
bandanas reduced to scarlet neck-ribbons, waists mere brassieres, skirts
mere gingham sashes.

And now Miss Cynthie's whole body stiffened with a new and surpassing shock; her bright eyes first widened with unbelief, then slowly grew dull with misery. In the midst of a sudden great volley of applause her grandson had broken through that bevy of agile wantons and begun to sing.

He too was dressed as a cotton-picker, but a Beau Brummel among cotton pickers; his hat bore a pleated green band, his bandana was silk, his overalls blue satin, his shoes black patent leather. His eyes flashed, his teeth gleamed, his body swayed, his arms waved, his words came fast and clear. As he sang, his companions danced a concerted tap, uniformly wild, ecstatic. When he stopped singing, he himself began to dance, and without sacrificing crispness of execution, seemed to absorb into himself every measure of the energy which the girls, now merely standing off and swaying, had relinquished.

"Look at that boy go," said Lee Goldman.

"He ain't started yet," said Lou.

But surrounding comment, Dave's virtuosity, the eager enthusiasm of the audience were all alike lost on Miss Cynthie. She sat with stricken eyes watching this boy whom she'd raised from a babe, taught right from wrong, brought up in the church, and endowed with her prayers, this child whom she had dreamed of seeing a preacher, a regular doctor, a tooth-doctor, a foot-doctor, at the very least an under-taker—sat watching him disport himself for the benefit of a sinsick, flesh-hungry mob of lost souls, not one of whom knew or cared to know the loving kindness of God; sat watching a David she'd never foreseen, turned tool of the devil, disciple of lust, unholy prince among sinners.

For a long time she sat there watching with wretched eyes, saw portrayed on the stage David's arrival in Harlem, his escape from 'old friends' who tried to dupe him; saw him working as a trap-drummer in a night-club, where he fell in love with Ruth, a dancer; not the gentle Ruth Miss Cynthie knew, but a wild and shameless young savage who danced like seven devils—in only a girdle and breast-plates; saw the two of them join in a song-and-dance act that eventually made them Broadway headliners, an act presented *in toto* as the pre-finale of this show. And not any of the melodies, not any of the sketches, not all the comic philosophy of the tired-and-hungry duo, gave her figure a moment's relaxation or brightened the dull defeat in her staring eyes. She sat apart, alone in the box, the symbol, the epitome of supreme failure. Let the rest of the theatre be riotous, clamoring for more and more of Dave Tappen, "Tap," the greatest tapster of all time, idol of

uptown and downtown New York. For her, they were lauding simply
an exhibition of sin which centered about her David.

"This'll run a year on Broadway," said Lee Goldman.

"Then we'll take it to Paris."

Encores and curtains with Ruth, and at last David came out on the
stage alone. The clamor dwindled. And now he did something quite
unfamiliar to even the most consistent of his followers. Softly, delicate-
ly, he began to tap a routine designed to fit a particular song. When
he had established the rhythm, he began to sing the song:

> *"Oh I danced with the gal with the hole in her stockin','*
> *And her toe kep' a-kickin' and her heel kep' a-knockin'—*
>
> *'Come up, Jesse, and get a drink o' gin,*
> *'Cause you near to the heaven as you'll ever get ag'in'—"*

As he danced and sang this song, frequently smiling across at Miss
Cynthie, a visible change transformed her. She leaned forward in-
credulously, listened intently, then settled back in limp wonder. Her
bewildered eyes turned on the crowd, on those serried rows of shrift-
less sinners. And she found in their faces now an overwhelmingly
curious thing: a grin, a universal grin, a gleeful and sinless grin such
as not the nakedest chorus in the performance had produced. In a
few seconds, with her own song, David had dwarfed into unim-
portance, wiped off their faces, swept out of their minds every trace
of what had seemed to be sin; had reduced it all to mere trivial detail
and revealed these revelers as a crowd of children, enjoying the guile-
less antics of another child. And Miss Cynthie whispered

"Bless my soul! They didn' mean nothin' . . . They jes' didn' see
no harm in it—"

> *"Then I danced with the gal with the dimple in her cheek,*
> *And if she'd 'a' kep' a-smilin', I'd 'a' danced for a week—*
> *'Come up, Jesse—'"*

The crowd laughed, clapped their hands, whistled. Someone threw
David a bright yellow flower. "From Broadway!"

He caught the flower. A hush fell. He said:

"I'm really happy tonight, folks. Y'see this flower? Means success,
don't it? Well, listen. The one who is really responsible for my success
is here tonight with me. Now what do you think o' that?"

The hush deepened.

"Y'know folks, I'm sump'm like Adam—I never had no mother.

But I've got a grandmother. Down home everybody calls her Miss Cynthie. And everybody loves her. Take that song I just did for you. Miss Cynthie taught me that when I wasn't knee-high to a cricket. But that wasn't all she taught me. Far back as I can remember, she used to always say one thing: Son, do like a church steeple—aim high and go straight. And for doin' it—" he grinned, contemplating the flower—"I get this."

He strode across to the edge of the stage that touched Miss Cynthie's box. He held up the flower.

"So y'see, folks, this isn't mine. It's really Miss Cynthie's." He leaned over to hand it to her. Miss Cynthie's last trace of doubt was swept away. She drew a deep breath of revelation; her bewilderment vanished, her redoubtable composure returned, her eyes lighted up; and no one but David, still holding the flower toward her, heard her sharply whispered reprimand:

"Keep it, you fool. Where's yo' manners—givin' 'way what somebody give you?"

David grinned:

"Take it, tyro. What you tryin' to do—crab my act?"

Thereupon, Miss Cynthie, smiling at him with bright, meaningful eyes, leaned over without rising from her chair, jerked a tiny twig off the stem of the flower, then sat decisively back, resolutely folding her arms, with only a leaf in her hand.

"This'll do me," she said.

The finale didn't matter. People filed out of the theatre. Miss Cynthie sat awaiting her children, her foot absently patting time to the orchestra's jazz recessional. Perhaps she was thinking, "God moves in a mysterious way," but her lips were unquestionably forming the words:

> "—danced with the gal—hole in her stockin'—
> —toe kep' a-kickin'—heel kep' a-knockin'."

JOHN F. MATHEUS (1887-   )

John F. Matheus, born in Kyser, West Virginia, in 1887, was educated in the public schools of Steubenville, Ohio, and at Western Reserve, Columbia (A. M., 1921), Chicago, and the Sorbonne. He has done research work in Haiti, Cuba, and Liberia, countries that have provided settings for several of his plays and short stories. In 1925 he won the *Opportunity* short-story contest with "Fog," and in 1926 he won first prize for the personal-experience section, second prize in the drama section, and honorable mention in both the short-

story and poetry sections. Since 1922 he has been professor of Romance
languages at West Virginia State College. The following is reprinted
by permission of the author and *Opportunity: Journal of Negro Life.*

Fog

THE STIR OF LIFE echoed. On the bridge between Ohio and West
Virginia was the rumble of heavy trucks, the purr of high power
engines in Cadillacs and Paiges, the rattle of Fords. A string of loaded
freight cars pounded along on the C. & P. tracks, making a thunderous,
if tedious way to Mingo. A steamboat's hoarse whistle boomed forth
between the swish, swish, chug, chug of a mammoth stern paddle
wheel with the asthmatic poppings of the pistons. The raucous shouts
of smutty-speaking street boys, the noises of a steam laundry, the
clank and clatter of a pottery, the godless voices of women from
Water Street houses of ill fame, all these blended in a sort of modern
babel, common to all the towers of destruction erected by modern
civilization.

These sounds were stirring when the clock sounded six on top of
the Court House, that citadel of Law and Order, with the statue of
Justice looming out of an alcove above the imposing stone entrance,
blindfolded and in her right hand the scales of Judgment. Even so
early in the evening the centers from which issued these inharmonious
notes were scarcely visible. This sinister cloak of a late November
twilight Ohio Valley fog had stealthily spread from somewhere
beneath the sombre river bed, down from somewhere in the lowering
West Virginia hills. This fog extended its tentacles over city and river,
gradually obliterating traces of familiar landscapes. At five-thirty the
old Panhandle bridge, supported by massive sandstone pillars, stalwart,
as when erected fifty years before to serve a generation now passed
behind the portals of life, this *old* bridge had become a spectral outline against the sky as the toll keepers of the *new* bridge looked northward up the Ohio River.

Now at six o'clock the fog no longer distorted; it blotted out,
annihilated. One by one the street lights came on, giving an uncertain
glare in spots, enabling peeved citizens to tread their way homeward
without recognizing their neighbor ten feet ahead, whether he might
be Jew or Gentile, Negro or Pole, Slav, Croatian, Italian or one
hundred per cent American.

An impatient crowd of tired workers peered vainly through the
gloom to see if the headlights of the interurban car were visible through
the thickening haze. The car was due at Sixth and Market at six-ten

and was scheduled to leave at six-fifteen for many little towns on the West Virginia side.

At the same time as these uneasy toilers were waiting, on the opposite side of the river the car had stopped to permit some passengers to descend and disappear in the fog. The motorman, flagged and jaded by the monotony of many stoppings and startings, waited mechanically for the conductor's bell to signal, "Go ahead."

The fog was thicker, more impenetrable. It smothered the headlight. Inside the car in the smoker, that part of the seats nearest the motorman's box, partitioned from the rest, the lights were struggling bravely against a fog of tobacco smoke, almost as opaque as the dull grey blanket of mist outside.

A group of red, rough men, sprawled along the two opposite bench-formed seats, paralled to the sides of the car, were talking to one another in the thin, flat colorless English of their mountain state, embellished with the homely idioms of the coal mine, the oil field, the gas well.

"When does this here meetin' start, Bill?"

"That air notice read half after seven."

"What's time now?"

"Damned 'f I know. Hey, Lee, what time's that pocket clock of yourn's got?"

"Two past six."

There was the sound of a match scratching against the sole of a rough shoe.

"'Gimme a light, Lafe."

In attempting to reach for the burning match before its flame was extinguished, the man stepped forward and stumbled over a cheap suitcase of imitation leather. A vile looking stogie fell in the aisle.

"God! Your feet're bigger'n Bill's."

The crowd laughed uproariously. The butt of this joke grinned and showed a set of dirty nicotine stained teeth. He recovered his balance in time to save the flaring match. He was a tremendous man, slightly stooped, with taffy colored, straggling hair and little pig eyes.

Between initial puffs he drawled: "Now you're barkin' up the wrong tree. I only wear elevens."

"Git off'n me, Lee Cromarty," growled Bill. "You hadn't ought to be rumlin' of *my* feathers the wrong way—and you a-plannin' to ride the goat."

Lafe, a consumptive appearing, undersized, bovine eyed individual, spat out the remark: "Naow, there! You had better be kereful. Men have been nailed to the cross for less than that."

"Ha! ha!—ho! ho! ho!"

There was a joke to arouse the temper of the crowd.

A baby began to cry lustily in the rear and more commodious end of the car reserved for nonsmokers. His infantine wailing smote in sharp contrast upon the ears of the hilarious joshers, filling the silence that followed the subsidence of the laughter.

"Taci, bimba. Non aver paura!"

Nobody understood the musical words of the patient, Madonna-eyed Italian mother, not even the baby, for it continued its yelling. She opened her gay colored shirt waist and pressed the child to her bosom. He was quieted.

"She can't speak United States, but I bet her Tony Spaghetti votes the same as you an' me. The young 'un 'll have more to say about the future of these Nunited States than your children an' mine unless we carry forward the word such as we are going to accomplish tonight."

"Yeh, you're damned right," answered the scowling companion of the lynx-eyed citizen in khaki clothes, who had thus commented upon the foreign woman's offspring.

"They breed like cats. They'll outnumber us, unless—"

A smell of garlic stifled his speech. Nick and Mike Axaminter, late for the night shift at the La Belle, bent over the irate American deluging him with the odor of garlic and voluble, guttural explosions of a Slovak tongue.

"What t' hell! Git them buckets out o' my face, you hunkies, you!"

Confused and apologetic the two men moved forward.

"Isn't this an awful fog, Barney," piped a gay, girlish voice.

"I'll tell the world it is," replied her red-haired companion, flinging a half smoked cigarette away in the darkness as he assisted the girl to the platform.

They made their way to a vacant seat in the end of the car opposite the smoker, pausing for a moment respectfully to make the sign of the cross before two Sisters of Charity, whose flowing black robes and ebon headdress contrasted strikingly with the pale whiteness of their faces. The nuns raised their eyes, slightly smiled and continued their orisons on dark decades of rosaries with pendant crosses of ivory.

"Let's sit here," whispered the girl. "I don't want to be by those niggers."

In a few seconds they were settled. There were cooings of sweet words, limpid-eyed soul glances. They forgot all others. The car was theirs alone.

"Say, boy, ain't this some fog. Yuh can't see the old berg."

" 'Sthat so. I hadn't noticed."

Two Negro youths thus exchanged words. They were well dressed and sporty.

"Well, it don't matter, as long as it don't interfere with the dance."

"I hope Daisy will be there. She's some stunnin' high brown an' I don't mean maybe."

"O boy!"

Thereupon one began to hum "Daddy, O Daddy" and the other whistled softly the popular air from "Shuffle Along" entitled "Old-Fashioned Love."

"Oi, oi! Ven I say vill dis car shtart. Ve must mek dot train fur Pittsburgh."

"Ach, Ish ka bibble. They can't do a thing without us, Laban."

They settled down in their seats to finish the discussions in Yiddish, emphasizing the conversation with shrugs of the shoulder and throaty interjections.

In a set apart to themselves, for two seats in front and behind were unoccupied, sat an old Negro man and a Negro woman, evidently his wife. Crowded between them was a girl of fourteen or fifteen.

"This heah is suah cu'us weather," complained the old man.

"We all nevah had no sich fog in Oklahoma."

The girl's hair was bobbed and had been straightened by "Poro" treatment, giving her an Egyptian cast of features.

"Gran' pappy," said the girl, "yo' cain't see ovah yander."

"Ain't it de troot, chile."

"Ne' min', sugah," assured the old woman. "Ah done paid dat 'ployment man an' he sayed yo' bound tuh lak de place. Dis here lady what's hirin yo' is no po' trash an' she wants a likely gal lak yo' tuh ten' huh baby."

Now these series of conversations did not transpire in chronological order. They were uttered more or less simultaneously during the interval that the little conductor stood on tiptoe in an effort to keep one hand on the signal rope, craning his neck in a vain and dissatisfied endeavor to pierce the miasma of the fog. The motorman chafed in his box, thinking of the drudging lot of the laboring man. . . .

The garrulous group in the smoker were smouldering cauldrons of discontent. In truth their dissatisfaction ran the gamut of hate. It was stretching out to join hands with an unknown and clandestine host to plot, preserve, defend their dwarfed and twisted ideals.

The two foreign intruders in the smoker squirmed under the merciless, half articulate antipathy. They asked nothing but a job to make some money. In exchange for that magic English word job, they endured the terror that walked by day, the boss. They grinned stupidly at profanity, dirt, disease, disaster. Yet they were helping to make America.

Three groups in the car on this foggy evening were united under the sacred mantle of a common religion. Within its folds they sensed vaguely a something of happiness. The Italian mother radiated the joy of her child. Perhaps in honor of her and in reverence the two nuns with downcast eyes, trying so hard to forget the world, were counting off the rosary of the blessed Virgin—"Ave, Maria," "Hail, Mary, full of grace, the Lord is with thee; blessed art thou among women."

The youth and his girl in their tiny circle of mutual attraction and affection could not as in Edwin Markham's poem widen the circle to include all or even to embrace that small circumscribed area of humanity within the car.

And the Negroes? Surely there was no hate in their minds. The gay youths were rather indifferent. The trio from the South, journeying far for a greater freedom of self expression philosophically accepted the inevitable "slings and arrows of outrageous fortune."

The Jews were certainly enveloped in a racial consciousness, unerringly fixed on control and domination of money, America's most potent factor in respectability.

The purplish haze of fog contracted. Its damp presence slipped into the car and every passenger shivered and peered forth to see. Their eyes were as the eyes of the blind!

At last the signal bell rang out staccato. The car suddenly lurched forward, shaking from side to side the passengers in their seats. The wheels scraped and began to turn. Almost at once a more chilling wetness filtered in from the river. In the invisibility of the fog it seemed that one was traveling through space, in an aeroplane perhaps, going nobody knew where.

The murmur of voices buzzed in the smoker, interrupted by the boisterous outbursts of laughter. A red glare tinted the fog for a second and disappeared. La Belle was "shooting" the furnaces. Then a denser darkness and the fog.

The car lurched, scintillating sparks flashed from the trolley wire, a terrific crash—silence. The lights went out. Before anybody could think or scream, there came a falling sensation, such as one experiences when dropped unexpectedly in an elevator or when diving through the scenic railways of the city amusement parks, or more exactly when one has a nightmare and dreams of falling, falling, falling.

"The bridge has given way. God! The muddy water! The fog! Darkness. Death."

These thoughts flashed spontaneously in the consciousness of the rough ignorant fellows, choking in the fumes of their strong tobacco, came to the garlic-scented "hunkies," to the Italian Madonna, to the Sisters of Charity, to the lover boy and his lover girl, to the Negro youths, to the Jews thinking in Yiddish idioms, to the old Negro man and his wife and the Egyptian-faced girl, with the straightened African hair, even to the bored motorman and the weary conductor.

To drown, to strangle, to suffocate, to die! In the dread silence the words screamed like exploding shells within the beating temples of terror-stricken passengers and crew.

Then protest, wild, mad, tumultuous, frantic protest. Life at bay and bellowing furiously against its ancient arch-enemy and antithesis —Death. An oath, screams,—dull, paralyzing, vomit-stirring nausea. Holy, unexpressed intimacies, deeply rooted prejudices were roughly shaken from their smug moorings. The Known to be changed for an Unknown, the ever expected, yet unexpected, Death. No! No! Not that.

Lee Cromarty saw things in that darkness. A plain, one-story frame house, a slattern woman on the porch, an overgrown, large hipped girl with his face. Then the woman's whining, scolding voice and the girl's bashful confidences. What was dimming that picture? What cataract was blurring his vision? Was it fog?

To Lafe, leader of the crowd, crouched in his seat, his fingers clawing the air for a grasping place, came a vision of a hill-side grave, —his wife's—and he saw again how she looked in her coffin—then the fog.

"I'll not report at the mine," thought Bill. "Wonder what old Bunner will say to that." The mine foreman's grizzled face dangled for a second before him and was swallowed in the fog.

Hoarse, gasping exhalations. Men, old men, young men, sobbing. "Pièta! Madre mia!—Mercy, Virgin Mary! My child!"

No thoughts of fear or pain on the threshold of death, that shadow from whence all children flow, but all the Mother Love focused to save the child.

"*Memorare,* remember, O most gracious Virgin Mary, that never was it known that any one who fled to thy protection, implored thy help and sought thy intercession was left unaided."

The fingers sped over the beads of the rosary. But looming up, unerasable, shuttled the kaleidoscope of youth, love, betrayal, renunciation, the vows. *Miserere, Jesu!*

> "Life is ever lord of Death
> And Love can never lose its own."

The girl was hysterical, weeping, screaming, laughing. Did the poet dream an idle dream, a false mirage? Death is master. Death is stealing Love away. How could a silly girl believe or know the calm of poesie?

The boy crumbled. His swagger and bravado melted. The passionate call of sex became a blur. He was not himself, yet he was looking at himself, a confusion in space, in night, in Fog. And who was she hanging limp upon his arm?

That dance? The jazz dance? Ah, the dance! The dance of Life was ending. The orchestra was playing a dirge and Death was leading the Grand March. Fog! Impenetrable fog!

All the unheeded, forgotten warnings of ranting preachers, all the prayers of simple black mothers, the Mercy-Seat, the Revival, too late. Terror could give no articulate expression to these muffled feelings. They came to the surface of a blunted consciousness, incoherent.

Was there a God in Israel? Laban remembered Russia and the pogrom. The old Negro couple remembered another horror. They had been through the riots in Tulsa. There they had lost their son and his wife, the Egyptian-faced girl's father and mother. They had heard the whine of bullets, the hiss of flame, the howling of human wolves, killing in the most excruciating manner. The water was silent. The water was merciful.

The old woman began to sing in a high quavering minor key:

> "Lawdy, won't yo' ketch mah groan,
> Oh Lawdy, Lawdy, won't yo' ketch my groan."

The old man cried out: "Judgment! Judgment!"

The Egyptian-faced girl wept. She was sore afraid, sore afraid. And the fog was round about them.

Time is a relative term. . . . What happened inside the heads of these men and women seemed to them to have consumed hours instead of seconds. The conductor mechanically grabbed the trolley rope, the motorman threw on the brakes.

The reaction came. Fear may become inarticulate and paralyzed. Then again it may become belligerent and self-protective, striking blindly in the maze. Darkness did not destroy completely the sense of direction.

"The door! the exit!"

A mad rush to get out, not to be trapped without a chance, like rats in a trap.

"Out of my way! Damn you—out of my way!"

Somebody yelled: "Sit still!"

Somebody hissed: "Brutes! Beasts!"

Another concussion, accompanied by the grinding of steel. The car stopped, lurched backward, swayed, and again stood still. Excited shouts reechoed from the ends of the bridge. Automobile horns tooted. An age seemed to pass, but the great smash did not come. There was still time—maybe. The car was emptied.

"Run for the Ohio end!" someone screamed.

The fog shut off every man from his neighbor. The sound of scurrying feet reverberated, of the Italian woman and her baby, of the boy carrying his girl, of the Negro youths, of the old man and his wife, half dragging the Egyptian-faced girl, of the Sisters of Charity, of the miners. Flitting like wraiths in Homer's Hades, seeking life.

In five minutes all were safe on Ohio soil. The bridge still stood. A street light gave a ghastly glare through the fog. The whore houses on Water Street brooded evily in the shadows. Dogs barked, the Egyptian-faced girl had fainted. The old Negro woman panted, "Mah Jesus! Mah Jesus!"

The occupants of the deserted car looked at one another. The icy touch of the Grave began to thaw. There was a generous intermingling. Everybody talked at once, inquiring, congratulating.

"Look after the girl," shouted Lee Cromarty. "Help the old woman, boys."

Bells began to ring. People came running. The ambulance arrived The colored girl had recovered. Then everybody shouted again. Profane miners, used to catastrophe, were strangely moved. The white boy and girl held hands.

"Sing us a song, old woman," drawled Lafe.

"He's heard mah groan. He done heard it," burst forth the old woman in a song flood of triumph.

> "Yes, he conquered Death and Hell,
> An' He never said a mumblin' word,
> Not a word, not a word."

"How you feelin', Mike," said Bill to the garlic eater.

"Me fine. Me fine."

The news of the event spread like wildfire. The street was now crowded. The police arrived. A bridge official appeared, announcing the probable cause of the accident, a slipping of certain supports. The girders fortunately had held. A terrible tragedy had been prevented.

"I'm a wash-foot Baptist an' I don't believe in Popery," said Lafe, "but, fellers, let's ask them ladies in them air mournin' robes to say a prayer of thanksgiving for the bunch."

The Sisters of Charity did say a prayer, not an audible petition for the ears of men, but a whispered prayer for the ears of God, the Benediction of Thanksgiving, uttered by the Catholic Church through many years, in many tongues and places.

"De profundis," added the silently moving lips of the white-faced nuns. "Out of the depths have we cried unto Thee, O Lord. And Thou hast heard our cries."

The motorman was no longer dissatisfied. The conductor's strength had been renewed like the eagle's.

"Boys," drawled Lafe, "I'll be damned if I'm goin' to that meetin' tonight."

"Nor me," affirmed Lee Cromarty.

"Nor me," repeated all the others.

The fog still crept from under the bed of the river and down from the lowering hills of West Virginia—dense, tenacious, stealthy, chilling, but from about the hearts and minds of some rough, unlettered men another fog had begun to lift.

CECIL BLUE (1903-   )

Cecil A. Blue, now professor of English at Lincoln University (Missouri), was born in British Columbia and received his education at Harvard (A. M., 1926) and at the University of Michigan. His story, "The Flyer," won the *Opportunity* short-story contest in 1927. It is reprinted by permission of the author and *Opportunity*.

The "Flyer"

When "Number 13" ran into the Charlotte station at 4:30 P. M., Timothy Hawkins, colored passenger, got his first opportunity to make a confession. Not that there weren't other passengers in the Jim Crow car—there were at least a dozen. But not a single one of them gave the slightest suggestion of possessing that magnetism of personality which Mr. Hawkins vaguely conceived to be the prerequisite of a confidant. On the contrary, they sat munching or giggling with stupid expressions on their faces. So Timothy had given up the idea of striking up an acquaintanceship when the train was only ten minutes out of Salisbury; and, with his black velour hat pulled down over his face, and his jaw comfortably propped upon his huge palm, had kept his mouth shut for ninety minutes.

But now the occasion presented itself.

For the want of something more interesting to do, Tim had pulled up the train window and stuck his head out. And when he spied "Sonny" Langford leaning against a post and balancing a wheelbarrow by the handle as if it were no more than a walking cane, he gave such a start that a spot on the back of his head collided rather sharply with the edge of the window frame. He uttered a mild epithet, and in the same breath shouted at Sonny.

"Hi dah. . . . Yeh, you." And he grinned.

The person addressed, a lanky, dark-brown Negro in blue overalls and wilted tan colored cap, turned and stared vacuously. But on being reassured, he rested the barrow against the post, and careened with a slightly halting gait in the direction of the train window.

"Well ah'll be . . .," he exclaimed on recognizing the passenger, and stopped dead for an instant. Then, with a leap, he attained the train window. Two huge palms clasped with a dull reverberation.

"Wat you doin' on dis yah train, buoy?"

"How be yuh, Sonny? Buoy, I'se sho glad to see yuh."

But if Tim had interpreted the interrogation as only a form of greeting, Sonny had intended a literal translation. An explanation of the anomalous position of Tim Hawkins was certainly the prerogative of an old "buddy." Hadn't they worked together for years, and gone around together before Sonny had gotten married and been dragged up to Charlotte by his wife? . . . Tim, a free man, travelling!

"Wheh you comin from Tim? Still livin in King's Mountain, ain't you?" he asked, more to the point.

And here was the opportunity for the confession—an old friend, a regular fellow. But, strangely, the desire for expression had disappeared. An hour ago, Tim would have laid bare his soul, craving sympathy. Now, with the desire gone, he was thinking with calm irony of something his wife had once said: "Don trust them niggahs." Of course he felt a momentary shame at recalling the sentiment in connection with Sonny Langford. But, after all, the apothegm was universal, and Sonny would be the last one to come under it—unless he had changed considerably in three or four years. Nevertheless, there was no confession to be made.

In a composed, semi-formal tone, Tim began to recite the details of the trip to Salisbury . . . how glad he was to see his sister after five years; her hospitality; the nice people that he had met, etc. But the enthusiasm which Sonny expected was nowhere in view. In its stead was a restrained, deliberate manner, and insipid, sentimental details. Was this Tim Hawkins? Surely Tim would have let loose in such a place as Salisbury. Sonny was tempted to ask outright, "How 'bout the gals? Any liquor?" But no. Perhaps four years had made a great deal of change.

"So das how come you on heah, huh? Lawd, who would a thought it? Seem lak you nevah wanted to leave dat hole . . . an dat woman. Ah sho would lak to see uh." And to show that neither of them had lost their sense of humor, they both laughed profusely.

"Yeh, I ain't rid on a train fuh fo yeahs," added Tim. "Man, ah sho was a sca'd baby . . . when dat train stahted to rum'lin . . . an grat'in . . . an commenced to m-o—o-ve. Ha ha-a-h-h-."

"Ha ha-h-h-h," echoed Sonny.

"All aboard," sounded the cavernous voices of the train-men. Suddenly Tim remembered where he was: his conversation with Sonny could be interrupted whenever the train saw fit to move. Yes, he was on a train, going from Salisbury to King's Mountain. Salisbury! Lilian! But he was going in an opposite direction, away. The holiday was over. Before he could summon any inhibitory strength, something in him had given way, and he felt as if some heavy liquid were rushing into his heart, causing it to swell. Salisbury! The locomotive bell started its clanging; the train jerked and shivered, and began to creep away.

"Bye, bye buddy," the porter was saying, walking beside the train, "Ah sho was glad to see you, buoy."

"Bye Sonny," replied Tim, waving his hand. And he was waving not only to Sonny Langford, but to the city, and more especially, to that other city, where she lived. He was feeling her soft hand in his. Then, as the hands parted, the heart over-flowed, drowning all restraints:

"Buoy, dah sho's some prutty wimmen in Sals'bry."

Coming so suddenly, and uttered with such enthusiasm, the remark elicited a series of titters from the other passengers. Sonny too laughed, saying to himself, "Same ol Tim, . . . Same ol Tim." But to Timothy Hawkins the words were cathartic—they had taken the place of tears. He drew in his head and settled back in the seat, oblivious of the conglomerate noise of the train, the increasing speed.

To the other passengers, Tim was certainly enjoying a good sleep. Neither the screaming of the baby up front, nor the guffawing of some young beaus who had taken over the entire rear portion of the car, disturbed him.

But although grown callous to his immediate surroundings, Tim's

mind was far from unconscious. He was rehearsing with that peculiarly delightful pleasure which accompanies certain recollections, the
events of his three days in Salisbury. And the presiding goddess over
all his thoughts, whose image diffused a roseate glow, was a certain
cinnamon-colored girl, with large black eyes, round faced and full-
bosomed. He remembered the party at which he had first seen her,
and how gracefully she swayed by him, her body sensitive to every
motion of the dance. Later, there had been gin, cigars . . . and more
music. And to think that he had held her in his arms . . . had kissed
her. He, Timothy Hawkins. Oh, the memory was flattering.

He pictured himself at another time seated on a cushiony sofa in
her house, gazing into soft black eyes, eyes innocent and ingenuous.

"Do you love me?" he had asked.

"Do you think I do?"

What an answer. It left Tim's unsophisticated mind confused and
groping for a reply. "Yes" or "No" would have been entirely inap-
propriate. The situation demanded more urbanity than was his.
Luckily, she had come to his rescue: "But you got a wife."

The remark, uttered with such candor, had suddenly illuminated
his mind. Convinced of her affection for him, he suddenly saw in this
girl the dormant passion of womanhood hungering for the love of
a strong man. No, she wasn't one of those butterflies; she was the
apotheosis of the finest qualities of the woman. She was a goddess,
not to be desecrated. And she loved him. She had allowed him to
kiss her—had yielded fully to his kisses. If he hadn't been married
he would have gone for a parson that very night. A thrill of exhilaration diffused itself through the reclining body of Timothy Hawkins,
causing him to shift in his seat.

That had been the climax of Tim's sojourn in Salisbury. He had
promised Bessie to be back by Saturday night, and he didn't want to
disappoint her. Bessie was a good woman, quiet and industrious. But
she was so peculiar in some things. Indeed, she was often perplexing,
mysterious. For instance, she had said to him one day: "You don't
need to worry, daddy; when you're taw'd, ah'm taw'd too." Jim did
not try to analyze the cryptic remark then. But days later the full
meaning dawned on him spontaneously. That was Bessie, she never
said much, but she always meant what she said. As long as he carried
out his part of the bargain, he could depend on her. . . . Yes, she
too had something admirable about her, even though he could not
see below the surface of her nature. She was not the Madonna of the
soft black eyes, but of resolute suffering and blistered hands. He had
found himself two goddesses.

II

He had not ridden on a train for four years—not since he had married Bessie. Many times when they were working out on the country roads, he used to see the famous "Flyer" go shooting by on the other side of a valley. Gee, she looked pretty. The motion!

And then this Spring had come bringing with it an unusual spirit of restlessness. Tim felt as if some genius of the fresh earth, and the green swaying pine-trees, and the singing birds were beckoning to him—as if the earth was trying to make him feel his kinship to it. And there was that particular afternoon barely a week ago—an afternoon of dazzling, thin sunshine, of bracing air, of whistling birds. There were the men in khaki and blue, singing and sweating, as they swung the pickaxes with wide curves. A familiar sustained whistle in the distance, and Tim relaxed his muscles even before the pick had fallen. When it fell, he left it sticking in the red earth, and straightened up. The whistle shrieked again, nearer. A heavy rumbling sound, and the "Flyer" came galloping from behind the curve of a pine forest.

"Da she go," said several of the men with momentary glances of admiration between the strokes of their picks. Black and powerful, with the power of twenty sleek horses, it galloped along the tracks. Tim stood gazing at the passing monster with a blank expression. But in his body the blood was racing along with the locomotive. It was almost dragging him off his feet. . . . Then the phenomenon disappeared; and with his eyes riveted on the glistening cliff behind which the last coach had slipped out of sight, he felt for the smooth handle of the pick.

Then the thing had happened.

"Wha you lookin so sad fuh, Tim? Is you sick?" said Bessie to him when he came home from work that afternoon.

Strange, he had never thought of that. . . . The picture of the "Flyer," which had impressed itself so vividly upon his mind that day, now flashed before him, phantom-like. And the birds were singing, and the trees were blowing in the wind, and "dah she go," the workmen were saying, as they had said many a time before. The desire of weeks became suddenly tangible, articulate.

"Ahm jes kind'a tah'd, Bess. Reck'n ah needs a rest. Yuh know, evah since ah had dat in'gestion, ah kin feel mahsef gettin' dizzy lak, sometimes. Dis aftahnoon, foh instance, we was diggin on de Shelby road. An all of a sudden ah got to feelin so dizzy, ah had to stop fuh a lil whal."

"Think you bettah see doc Hooper?"

"Guess ah bettah."

That night when Tim came in, he said to Bessie, "Ah done seen doc. Dropped in on de way to meet'n. T'aint nothin de mattah wif me—cept'n dat ah needs a lil res. Just a day or two. He say dat'll do me moh good dan all de med'cn in de world."

From behind the table lamp he stole a glance at Bessie's face. No the suggestion did not draw forth any visible displeasure. She sat sewing just as calmly as ever. . . . But why shouldn't he go? She wouldn't miss him for just two or three days.

He ventured putting the suggestion in concrete form:

"Ah could run up to Sals'bry foh a day or two to see Sis Jane. Get back Sat'day night. How bout dat?"

"Reck'n it'll be a'right!" That was all Bessie said, in a voice that was absolutely even and unemotional. Nor, again, was there any sign on her face—neither in the lines of her thin salmon-pink lips nor in her brittle black eyes.

"Ah reck'n de boss will let me off."

Nothing else was said on the subject until the following Wednesday morning. As he was rising from the breakfast table in the kitchen, he said to her: "Reck'n ah'll leave on de Fliah, Bess. Das de bes one. Fix coupla shirts an sox fuh me, will yuh?"

When Tim returned at noon, he found everything ready. He had had no qualms about that; Bessie was always to be depended on. What a lucky fellow he was! The train left at 3:15. He would have time to eat a good dinner and dress leisurely. The street car would take him to the station in ten minutes.

The dinner was important, of course. Apropos of that point, he made a complimentary remark to the effect that a fellow couldn't be certain of a decent meal while he was away from home. Unfortunately, Bessie did not hear it. . . . Yes, the dinner was important. But today the toilet was by no means a subordinate affair. To Tim it was a big holiday. Within a short while he would be a passenger behind the powerful black engine, shooting by houses and fields. Too bad they had finished the job out on the Shelby road; otherwise, he could wave to the boys.

"Yuh ought to dress fuss, Tim," Bessie suggested. That's right, he should dress first. Eating in one's best clothes alters the process considerably. Then, too, taking a bath on a full stomach might give one the cramps.

When he came out of the bedroom, after a full forty-five minutes, he showed the effects of a laborious preparation. Tiny beads of vaseline glistened on his crinkly hair; his brown face betrayed the lavish use of some emolument; his steel-blue suit, with trousers bulging at the waist, was pressed into stiff edges; and his red shoes glistened faintly in the crepuscular light of the kitchen floor.

"Mah, you looks real sma't," commented Bessie, in a tone that was neither affectionate nor derisive. And knowing that she was sincere, Tim smiled sheepishly.

At her suggestion, he ate leisurely and heartily. The food was nice and hot. . . . Of course she didn't eat with him; she very seldom did. As a matter of fact, you could hardly say that she ate—a bit here and a bit there. Cooking takes away one's appetite, she said. Nevertheless, she took a great deal of pride in preparing those things that Tim liked.

While he ate, she busied herself in preparing a box of lunch for him,—ham sandwiches, egg sandwiches, cake, bananas. "Dat's some woman," said Tim to himself as he gulped down the coffee.

When the time came for leaving, Bessie helped him on with his overcoat, and pulled down the jacket. Then she gave him the two packages—the lunch and the shirts.

In the parlor, he turned around to bid her good-bye. "Bye, Bess," he said. She presented her lips. They were a little stiff, and the kiss was somewhat perfunctory. But what did it matter? She was true steel.

III

And now he was returning home, more restless than when he had left, and tired out in body. Try as he would, he could not keep out of his mind a foolish bit of music that he had heard on the victrola: "Gwine home, wone be long." He found himself repeating the bar over and over, as if there were some salutary cynicism in it.

But cynical self-delusion could not long sustain him. It seemed that the nearer he approached King's Mountain, the more disagreeably obtruding became his thoughts. He tried to live in the past—to lose himself again in pleasant recollection of the incidents of his holiday. . . . the girl Lilian . . . lights . . . music . . . happy-go-lucky fellows with gin bottles. But, instead, he found himself juxtaposing the immediate past and the immediate future. . . . Perhaps he shouldn't have told Bessie that lie about the doctor . . . but he just had to get away. And to have asked her to go with him would have been just the same as not going at all. Oh, well, she didn't care about those things anyway. Funny woman!

When the candy man came around, bawling his wares in an unintelligible gibberish, Tim straightened up, and beckoned him. The most attractive things in the basket were some large glass pistols, filled with gaily colored hard candy. He thought of the two kids next door, and bought one of the pistols.

"Now, got any choc'lat candy?"

"Naw, but ah kin git yuh some.

"A'right."

The vender returned with three boxes. Tim selected the largest and most attractive looking one. The transaction completed and the presents stowed away, he sank back to his former comfortable posture.

The interruption seemed to have driven still farther away all salutary images. Even single scenes were momentary and elusive. A baby was screaming up front; somebody was continually opening and closing the door; the young bucks in the rear were cackling incessantly. Luckily, there was only a minute or two more of riding.

By the time the conductor bawled out his "King's Mount'n . . . King's Mount'n," night had fallen on the countryside. The lamps had been lighted half an hour before; and now there was a lugubrious contrast in the lighted train and the thick blackness without. Tim got up and stretched. Then he took up his packages—the newspaper package with the dirty shirts, the box of candy—and shuffled toward the door behind the group of dandies.

Yes, he was a little tired. That was the only way he could account for the eagerness with which he stepped off the train. Of course, he reasoned with himself, riding in a coach—a Jim Crow—isn't anything like riding up in the locomotive. That *must* be very different.

In the street he stopped to decide between the street-car and a taxi-cab. But before he could come to a decision an industrious colored driver had settled the question by fairly pulling him into a near-by automobile. "Might as well," thought Tim, as the car swung sharply around in a semi-circle. Then he began to examine his surroundings.

"New boat, ain't it?" he inquired of the chauffeur, after a minute of observation.

"Month old."

"Ah thought," replied the passenger, and settled back in the cushiony seat. How different from the rattling, jolting ride on the train. There was an elegant restraint in the dark paint, glistening in the yellow rays from the tiny lamp overhead. The motor hummed steadily, to the easy roll of the car, as it rode the bumps of Carmel Street.

"Lil mo. . . . Das right. . . ."

The car began to slow up, almost as if of its own accord.

"My, heah in no time," he added (with inward regret) as the car came to a dead stop. Then, as he was paying the driver, he ventured half-apologetically: "Ah don want to be personal, but what do dis yah baby set yuh back? "Whew" he exclaimed upon hearing the figure, "dis yah ain lak a Foad, is it?" The car jerked off, and Tim turned toward the house.

As he was opening the gate, he noticed that the house was in complete darkness. Instantly, a thought flashed across his mind. Ten chances to one Bessie had understood him to say that he would get back Sunday rather than Saturday. And, after all, he was foolish to say Saturday. What could he have been thinking about? . . . More than likely, she was out shopping. Well, there would be plenty to eat. He was hungry.

But as he opened the door he felt as if a gust of cold wind had been suddenly blown at him. Bessie wasn't in the habit of letting the fire go out. She must have been out a long time. And he didn't have a match.

Confronted with the problem of finding his way to the kitchen, Tim did not follow out the process of reasoning to account for his wife's absence. He began to feel his way cautiously, through the small front parlor, cluttered with chairs and small tables, into the middle room, which, on rare occasions, was used as a dining room. This too was chilly. "What the . . ." He checked himself. In the kitchen he stumbled against a chair, striking his shin. The collision peeved him. He ran his hand violently along the wall over the kitchen table, and upset the match-safe. The matches fell, pit . . . pit . . . pit . . . all over the table and on the floor. "Hell," he muttered. Picking up one, he scratched it on his heels. The sharp spurt and glow was an encouraging relief to the deserted stillness of the house. The oil lamp was in its accustomed place on the shelf, the reflected rays of light streaming from its bright chimney as if it were some miniature light-house. Then, at last, light.

The kitchen appeared unusually tidy and ordered. The stove was sedate in a new coat of polish; the floor seemed recently scrubbed; the bottles and glasses on the shelves were all neatly arranged. But more significant than all this was the fact that the windows were locked. For the first time, a definite misgiving loomed afar off in the mind of Timothy Hawkins. Not that there was any anomaly in the appearance of the kitchen; Bessie always took a pride in her house. But there were the other circumstances: the cold and musty-smelling house, the locked windows. What could all this mean? For a moment he remained standing in the middle of the room, his hands stuck in his overcoat pocket, his mind confused and groping. Then the ideas began to rearrange themselves, to fall in their proper places. The grim truth which had been hovering in the distance like some malignant fiend drew nearer and nearer, and finally became a part of his consciousness. And as it struck the brains, his heart winced under its rapier thrusts. Bessie was gone.

For the want of definite resolution, he walked into the bedroom and lighted the lamp there. The signs were the same: everything neatly arranged, the windows locked. He took off his hat, threw it on the bed, and sat down in a chair. What was to be done? Curiously enough, he did not feel any anger. The desertion of his wife seemed more like retributive justice. Without any inner struggle, he accepted the responsibility; it was he who had broken the pledge—at least, the pledge as she had understood it. She was no truant. She had said, "When you're taw'd, ah'm taw'd too, daddy" . . . and he had not understood. Hard, exacting justice.

But having unconsciously absorbed some of the tenets of this stolid doctrine of life, Tim felt that to give himself over to pangs of conscience would be useless and unmanly. Whatever softness would creep into his heart he would throw out. He was not even sure that he was capable of remorse. . . . On the other hand, he could not realize the inconsistency of trying to make clear to himself just how the woman had come to definite knowledge of his hypocrisy. To rehearse in his mind with solid cynicism the possible events leading up to the desertion was to purge his conscience in a way conformable to her code. That which had been responsible for his misfortune would be at the same time his succor. And *he* was the man.

He got up and walked back to the kitchen. It seemed to have grown chillier, even though he had not yet taken off his overcoat. Perhaps he had better make a fire. Lifting the lid off the stove, he saw that newspaper and wood had been carefully arranged. On the floor was a bucket of coal. All he needed to do was apply the match. Funny woman! . . . Yes she must have seen the doctor. But whether the interview was accidental or the consequence of a suspicion, he could not decide. . . . He applied the match and saw the hot flames shoot up and envelop the wood. . . . No, he shouldn't have lied to her; that was the only thing he regretted. What could she have thought of him? He could see that familiar sneering smile on her face.

Undecided as to his next step, Tim suddenly remembered that he was hungry. He hadn't eaten anything but a ham sandwich since leaving Salisbury. In the ice-box he found eggs, cold macaroni, and ham. The coffee-can was nearly full. With superfluous vigor he set himself to the task. The meat was soon sizzling in the pan; the coffee pot spouted steam. Gradually the kitchen became filled with the heavy vapor of greases. But there was something suggestive of the amateur in this. The rich, complex odor of the expert cook that Bessie was had given place to this insipid mixture of hot grease and coffee. Tim could not but feel that he was out of place—that he was a man playing a woman's role. Though but an amateur smoker (curiously, he had never became addicted to the habit of tobacco-chewing so common among his acquaintances) he went into the bedroom after his pipe. A few draws, perhaps, would relieve his nerves.

He ate scantily of the meal, the coffee being the only thing for which he had any appetite. Then he thought of something else to do. Oh yes, the candy. He would take the glass pistol to the kids next door. Should he take the chocolates too? No use giving away a dollar and a half, he decided.

Before going out of the house he resolved upon a plan of forestalling any inquiry on the part of his neighbor. "Dat mouthy woman," he said to himself. If he wasn't careful, she would get everything out of him. He could picture her spreading the news at church next morning, and the sisters and brothers listening with wide-open eyes. Everybody would be talking about how Tim Hawkins's wife ran away from him. The disagreeableness of the prospect loomed so formidable to Tim that he was almost tempted to shut himself in. But, after all, they would find out sooner or later, unless—

A few moments later he was knocking at Mrs. Johnson's door. Fortunately, the door was opened by little Sammy.

"Lo, Sam. How's yoh mammy? . . . Ah brung dis fuh you an Sistah. Now, don eat it all yohsef—yoh lil rascal you."

The boy grinned with delight as he clasped the prize and jumped away from an affectionate poke. But before he could close the door, the shrill voice of his mother, with its customary ingratiating overtones, came from the rear:

"Hi, Tim, wat yuh stan'n out dah fuh, col as tis. Come on in and shut dat doh." But the fly was prepared to elude the spider this once, at any rate.

"In a hurry, Miss Johnson—got to run down to de drug stoh." And before Mrs. Johnson could marshal her wits, Tim was gone—towards the drug store.

At the corner he stopped to get himself together. Where was he going? Perhaps he had better walk a little farther out of sight, because it would be just like that woman to come out of her house and watch his movements. . . . At First and Carmel he stopped again. To go farther would mean running into some good brother or sister returning home from the Saturday night's shopping. There was somebody familiar coming up Carmel street now. Turning to the left, he walked briskly down First Street, past the Friendship Baptist Church. As it was darker in this section, the lights being more widely separated, he could go more slowly. A few blocks to the left, and two to the left again, would bring him home. Had he been out long enough to have gone to the drug store and back? An any rate, by walking slowly up Prospect, he would have succeeded in wasting enough time.

It had turned even colder. But the brisk walk had set the blood racing through his body, driving out all chillness. And although he had all reason to be tired, he felt, instead, fresh and energetic. His mind became suddenly clear and alert. He took advantage of this mental clarity to question himself, to analyze his position. Here he was walking the streets at eleven o'clock of a Saturday night, dodging here and there as if he were some criminal. Why? His wife had left him. But that was not the first time such a thing happened in the world. Then what? The question was for *him* to decide. Did he want her, or didn't he? If he did not, then he would simply have to hold his feet to the fire—the snickerings and whisperings and all. (How detestable to see a *man* gossiping!) . . . If he did want her back, then he would have to go in search of her. Which was it to be? And with the question, his thoughts became enmeshed again in all sorts of conflicting opinions.

When he turned into Carmel Street, the problem was still unsolved. After all, *he* was the man. Why should he go chasing after any woman? Let her come back herself—if she wanted to. But would she want to? She was such an enigma, and Tim had no precedent to guide him. The best thing would be to wait a little while. On the other hand, there was the scandal.

As he was passing Mrs. Johnson's house he noticed that the light in the front parlor was out—and, if he wasn't mistaken, a dark shadow had just slipped away from the window. "The cat!" thought Tim, and turned resolutely into his gate.

But the effect of the observation was more disturbing than his assumed cynicism was willing to admit. It made more tangible to him what was at first only a shadowy fear. "None o huh damn business, anyhow." Nevertheless, as he was going up the steps he saw visions of the parson taking some such text as, "Husbands, love your wives." Hadn't this happened about a year ago, when Annie Morris and her husband broke up? And how everybody looked at everybody else so innocently that Sunday morning, as if to say, "Well who would a thought it?" when all the time they were chuckling inwardly, and overflowing with malicious pleasure. The blood went racing through his brains. A solution to the perplexing situation required calm thought.

He drew out his door key violently, only to find, on turning the knob, that he had gone out and left the door unlocked. "Yoh sho mus be worried, son," he said to himself in an ineffective attempt at humorous cynicism. "Calm yohself." And as he opened the door, a gleam of light from the kitchen struck his eyes. Lawd, he had even forgotten to put the light out. Well. . . .

"Who dat," came a nervous voice from the rear, and Tim stopped short. Could it be. . . . ?

"Tim?"

"Bessie?"

He hesitated a few moments to collect himself. Then, removing his coat and hat, he walked with calm steps back to the kitchen. A crisp odoriferous smell, and a gush of warm air greeted his entry. At the stove Bessie, in her usual house dress, was making coffee.

"Wat you waste all dat meat fuh, Tim? Ef ah had known you was comin' back so soon ah sho wouldn't a gone from dis house. . . . Wast'n all dat meat."

"Thought ah was hungrier'n ah was." . . . Should he ask her where she had been for such a long time? No, let her tell him herself.

"You know, sistah Saunders done passed away dis ev'n. Ah been ovah dah help'n sence yestiddy. Funr'l tomorrow."

"Poor ole soul! . . . Say, leh me try a cup o dat coffee, will yuh?"

GEORGE SCHUYLER (1895-)

George S. Schuyler (see also p. 213) was born in Providence, Rhode Island in 1895. He was educated in the public schools of Syracuse, New York. From 1912 to 1920 he was in the United States Army, serving as a first lieutenant in the World War. He has been on the editorial staffs of *The Messenger* and of *The Pittsburgh Courier* and *The Crisis*, and has written numerous stories, articles, and reviews in *The American Mercury*, *The World Tomorrow*, *New Masses*, *Modern Quarterly*, *Opportunity*, *The Crisis*, and *The Nation*. His novel *Black No More*, was published in 1931; *Slaves, Today: A Story of Liberia* was published the same year. "Black Warriors" are more character sketches than short stories; "Woof," a similar sketch of a hard-bitten Army man, was published in *Harlem Magazine*. Good character drawing appears in "Memoirs of a Pearl-Diver," Schuyler's reporting of his experiences as dishwasher, and "Black Magic." The following is reprinted by permission of *The American Mercury*.

From Black Warriors

Once, after an unusually large pay day winning, Rain-in-the-Face, our company gambling king, took a bunch of us to town to help him celebrate. We piled off the street car at the Totem Pole and our host led us into a well-appointed saloon. It was not a place frequented by the Seattle Aframericans. We bellied to the long bar, the five of us, and ordered whiskey.

The bartender surveyed us coldly and calmly waited on a white customer who had come in behind us. Finally he turned to us and asked sharply, "Are you lookin' for Sam?"

"Who's Sam?" asked Rain-in-the-Face. He was a smooth, black fellow of solemn mien and what apprehensive Nordics call a smart nigger. He hailed originally from Savannah and spoke fluently the geechie gibberish of Yamacraw. He boasted of a high-school education and interpreted current events at our Sunday morning barber-shop forums.

"Sam's the porter," replied the gentleman in the white jacket, winking at the customer he had just served, "an' he's just gone home fer th' day."

"Well, he might come back," said Rain-in-the-Face, winking at us, "so we'll have five whiskies while we're waiting."

The bartender grimly set the drinks in front of us. We drank. Then he took the five empty glasses and one by one smashed them to pieces on the floor. "That's what we do with our glasses when you kind o' people drink outta 'm," he explained.

"A'right," said Rain-in-the-Face, indulging in one of his infrequent grins, "we'll have another round. We don't care what you do with your glasses."

Five more glasses were filled, emptied quickly and returned to the bar. One by one they were picked up and deliberately smashed on the floor. The bartender glared and placed his hands on his hips.

"Make it five beers next time," Rain-in-the-Face ordered. "Th' big glasses cost more!"

The beer was served and the glasses promptly broken, but the bartender was plainly tiring of the play.

"Why don't you fellas go where yer wanted?" he asked.

"If we on'y went where we was wanted, we wouldn't go nowheres," remarked our host.

"Well, I don't care," the bartender replied. "We don' serve colored. That's the boss's orders."

"But we're soldiers in uniform," argued Rain-in-the-Face.

"Don't make no diffrence, yer colored."

"A'right," quoth our host, suddenly inspired with an idea, "we'll go, but we'll be back."

We filed out, much to the relief of the bartender, and assembling on the corner, Rain-in-the-Face informed us that he was going to fix that guy. Four blocks down the street he led us into a Negro saloon. It was full of soldiers from the First Battalion, most of them broke but eager for liquor. Rain-in-the-Face gathered about forty of them around him and with our gang in the van, retraced his steps to the exclusive barroom.

The forty-five of us crowded into the place and lined up with our feet on the long brass rail. The bartender was thunderstruck.

"What do you people want?" he asked weakly.

"Beer all around," ordered Rain-in-the-Face, tossing a five-dollar gold piece on the mahogany.

The bartender scratched his head, grinned a little sheepishly, and drew the foaming lager. We tossed it off, set down the glasses, and waited.

"You win," said the bartender. "Have another on the house."

[CAPTAIN JACKSON]

[Captain Jackson had just received his commission in the 1917 Des Moines Training Camp.]

During the Christmas holidays he went on leave of absence to see his father and mother, who had returned to Mississippi to live. The Jim Crow laws did not yield to the war sentimentalism, so Jackson rode into his home town in the colored coach. As he stepped from it, he noticed a number of white soldiers in the station.

"Look at that nigger in captain's uniform," somebody yelled. Jackson hurried through the colored waiting-room with his suitcase. At the street door a crowd of soldiers and civilians met him.

"Don't think we're gonna salute you, nigger," they warned. Jackson tried to push his way through but they pushed him back.

"Where'd you get that uniform, darkey?" they asked. "Why don't you make us salute you?"

They had completely surrounded him by now and he glanced helplessly to the right and left. There was not a kind look on any of the faces circling him.

"Let me through, please?" he requested, with as much dignity as he could muster.

"Oh, so yah wanna git away, eh?" jeered the ringleader. "Well, wait'll we git some souvenirs."

He reached out and took the insignia off one of Jackson's shoulder straps. Another hand took the other. Somebody snatched his hat off. Deft fingers unfastened his Expert Rifleman badge. Willing hands pinioned his arms while equally willing fists pummeled him. They were all laughing.

Jackson suddenly broke loose with a wrench and fought his way through the mob. Down the street he ran with the pack after him. Mr. Sanders, a friend of his father, saved him by pulling him in his automobile and driving rapidly off. Later on by a circuitous route he took him home. "Better stay in th' house, Wilbur," the white man said as he drove off.

Jackson was a sight. His well-tailored uniform was dirty and torn. He was bruised and scratched and one leather leggin was missing. His mother had hardly finished, attending his hurts when the telephone rang. Old Mr. Jackson answered it.

"Dave," came a kindly voice over the wire, "bettah tell youah boy tuh git outta town 'fore it gits too late. They're comin' after 'im."

In a suit of his father's clothes, with a slouch hat pulled over his ears, Jackson caught the next train out of town. Christmas Day and the day after he rode in a dirty, cramped coach, getting to safer soil.

The day after New Year's Day, when the officers on holiday leave had returned to duty, the comedian of the mess, a jovial second lieutenant, was reading aloud one of the patriotic blurbs from the Creel Press Bureau in Washington and a few of the cynics were smiling. Jackson came in and sat down. He ate in silence. Then suddenly, to everyone's surprise, he blurted out, "For Christ's sake will you stop reading that bunk!"

LANGSTON HUGHES (1902-   )

The Ways of White Folks (1934) by Langston Hughes (see also p. 366) is unusual in that it is one of the few instances in which a Negro author uses satire to reveal the attitudes of whites towards Negroes. In other short stories, such as "The Professor," Hughes's satire is directed at Negroes themselves. "Slave on the Block" is reprinted by permission of the author and of Alfred A. Knopf, Inc., publishers of *The Ways of White Folks*.

Slave on the Block

THEY WERE PEOPLE who went in for Negroes—Michael and Anne—the Carraways. But not in the social-service, philanthropic sort of way, no. They saw no use in helping a race that was already too charming and naive and lovely for words. Leave them unspoiled and just enjoy them, Michael and Anne felt. So they went in for the Art of Negroes—the dancing that had such jungle life about it, the songs that were so simple and fervent, the poetry that was so direct, so real. They never tried to influence that art, they only bought it and raved over it, and copied it. For they were artists, too.

In their collection they owned some Covarrubias originals. Of course Covarrubias wasn't a Negro, but how he caught the darky spirit! They owned all the Robeson records and all the Bessie Smith. And they had a manuscript of Countee Cullen's. They saw all the plays with or about Negroes, read all the books, and adored the Hall Johnson Singers. They had met Doctor DuBois, and longed to meet Carl Van Vechten. Of course they knew Harlem like their own backyard, that is, all the speakeasies and night clubs and dance halls, from the Cotton Club and the ritzy joints where Negroes couldn't go themselves, down to places like the Hot Dime, where white folks couldn't get in—unless they knew the man. (And tipped heavily.)

They were acquainted with lots of Negroes, too—but somehow the Negroes didn't seem to like them very much. Maybe the Carraways gushed over them too soon. Or maybe they looked a little like poor white folks, although they were really quite well off. Or maybe they tried too hard to make friends, dark friends, and the dark friends suspected something. Or perhaps their house in the Village was too far from Harlem, or too hard to find, being back in one of those queer and expensive little side streets that had once been ⟨a⟩lleys before the art invasion came. Anyway, occasionally, a furtive Negro might accept their invitation for tea, or cocktails; and sometimes a lesser Harlem celebrity or two would decorate their rather slow parties; but one seldom came back for more. As much as they loved Negroes, Negroes didn't seem to love Michael and Anne.

But they were blessed with a wonderful colored cook and maid—until she took sick and died in her room in their basement. And then the most marvellous ebony boy walked into their life, a boy as black as all the Negroes they'd ever known put together.

"He is the jungle," said Anne when she saw him.

"He's 'I Couldn't Hear Nobody Pray,'" said Michael.

For Anne thought in terms of pictures: she was a painter. And

Michael thought in terms of music: he was a composer for the piano. And they had a most wonderful idea of painting pictures and composing music that went together, and then having a joint "concert-exhibition" as they would call it. Her pictures and his music. The Carraways, a sonata and a picture, a fugue and a picture. It would be lovely, and such a novelty, people would have to like it. And many of their things would be Negro. Anne had painted their maid six times. And Michael had composed several themes based on the spirituals, and on Louis Armstrong's jazz. Now here was this ebony boy. The essence in the flesh.

They had nearly missed the boy. He had come, when they were out, to gather up the things the cook had left, and take them to her sister in Jersey. It seems that he was the late cook's nephew. The new colored maid had let him in and given him the two suitcases of poor dear Emma's belongings, and he was on his way to the Subway. That is, he was in the hall, going out just as the Carraways, Michael and Anne, stepped in. They could hardly see the boy, it being dark in the hall, and he being dark, too.

"Hello," they said. "Is this Emma's nephew?"

"Yes'm," said the maid. "Yes'm."

"Well, come in," said Anne, "and let us see you. We loved your aunt so much. She was the best cook we ever had."

"You don't know where *I* could get a job, do you?" said the boy. This took Michael and Anne back a bit, but they rallied at once. So charming and naive to ask right away for what he wanted.

Anne burst out, "You know, I think I'd like to paint you."

Michael said, "Oh, I say now, that would be lovely! He's so utterly Negro."

The boy grinned.

Anne said, "Could you come back tomorrow?"

And the boy said, "Yes, indeed, I sure could."

The upshot of it was that they hired him. They hired him to look after the garden, which was just about as big as Michael's grand piano —only a little square behind the house. You know those Village gardens. Anne sometimes painted it. And occasionally they set the table there for four on a spring evening. Nothing grew in the garden really, practically nothing. But the boy said he could plant things. And they had to have some excuse to hire him.

The boy's name was Luther. He had come from the South to his relatives in Jersey, and had had only one job since he got there, shining shoes for a Greek in Elizabeth. But the Greek fired him because the boy wouldn't give half his tips over to the proprietor.

"I never heard of a job where I had to pay the boss, instead of the boss paying me," said Luther. "Not till I got here."

"And then what did you do?" said Anne.

"Nothing. Been looking for a job for the last four months."

"Poor boy," said Michael; "poor, dear boy."

"Yes," said Anne. "You must be hungry." And they called the cook to give him something to eat.

Luther dug around in the garden a little bit that first day, went out and bought some seeds, came back and ate some more. They made a place for him to sleep in the basement by the furnace. And the next day Anne started to paint him, after she'd bought the right colors.

"He'll be good company for Mattie," they said. "She claims she's afraid to stay alone at night when we're out, so she leaves." They suspected, though, that Mattie just liked to get up to Harlem. And they thought right. Mattie was not as settled as she looked. Once out, with the Savoy open until three in the morning, why come home? That was the way Mattie felt.

In fact, what happened was that Mattie showed Luther where the best and cheapest hot spots in Harlem were located. Luther hadn't even set foot in Harlem before, living twenty-eight miles away, as he did, in Jersey, and being a kind of quiet boy. But the second night he was there Mattie said, "Come on, let's go. Working for white folks all day, I'm tired. They needn't think I was made to answer telephones all night." So out they went.

Anne noticed that most mornings Luther would doze almost as soon as she sat him down to pose, so she eventually decided to paint Luther asleep. "The Sleeping Negro," she would call it. Dear, natural childlike people, they would sleep anywhere they wanted to. Anyway, asleep, he kept still and held the pose.

And he *was* an adorable Negro. Not tall, but with a splendid body. And a slow and lively smile that lighted up his black, black face, for his teeth were very white, and his eyes, too. Most effective in oil and canvas. Better even than Emma had been. Anne could stare at him at leisure when he was asleep. One day she decided to paint him nude, or at least half nude. A slave picture, that's what she would do. The market at New Orleans for a background. And call it "The Boy on the Block."

So one morning when Luther settled down in his sleeping pose, Anne said, "No," she had finished that picture. She wanted to paint him now representing to the full the soul and sorrow of his people. She wanted to paint him as a slave about to be sold. And since slaves in warm climates had no clothes, would he please take off his shirt.

Luther smiled a sort of embarrassed smile and took off his shirt. "Your undershirt, too," said Anne. But it turned out that he had on a union suit, so he had to go out and change altogether. He came back and mounted the box that Anne said would serve just then for a slave block, and she began to sketch. Before luncheon Michael came in, and went into rhapsodies over Luther on the box without a shirt, about to be sold into slavery. He said he must put him into music right now. And he went to the piano and began to play something that sounded like Deep River in the jaws of a dog, but Michael said it was a modern slave plaint, 1850 in terms of 1933. Vieux Carré remembered on 135th Street. Slavery in the Cotton Club.

Anne said, "It's too marvellous!" And they painted and played till dark, with rest periods in between for Luther. Then they all knocked off for dinner. Anne and Michael went out later to one of Lew Leslie's new shows. And Luther and Mattie said, "Thank God!" and got dressed up for Harlem.

Funny, they didn't like the Carraways. They treated them nice and paid them well. "But they're too strange," said Mattie, "they make me nervous."

"They is mighty funny," Luther agreed.

They didn't understand the vagaries of white folks, neither Luther nor Mattie, and they didn't want to be bothered trying.

"I does my work," said Mattie. "After that I don't want to be painted, or asked to sing songs, nor nothing like that."

The Carraways often asked Luther to sing, and he sang. He knew a lot of southern work-songs and reels, and spirituals and ballads.

> *"Dear Ma, I'm in hard luck:*
> *Three days since I et,*
> *And the stamp on this letter's*
> *Gwine to put me in debt."*

The Carraways allowed him to neglect the garden altogether. About all Luther did was pose and sing. And he got tired of that.

Indeed, both Luther and Mattie became a bit difficult to handle as time went on. The Carraways blamed it on Mattie. She had got hold of Luther. She was just simply spoiling a nice simple young boy. She was old enough to know better. Mattie was in love with Luther.

At least, he slept with her. The Carraways discovered this one night about one o'clock when they went to wake Luther up (the first time they'd ever done such a thing) and ask him if he wouldn't sing his own marvellous version of John Henry for a man who had just came from Saint Louis and was sailing for Paris tomorrow. But Luther

wasn't in his own bed by the furnace. There was a light in Mattie's
room, so Michael knocked softly. Mattie said, "Who's that?" And
Michael poked his head in, and here were Luther and Mattie in bed
together!

Of course, Anne condoned them. "it's so simple and natural for
Negroes to make love." But Mattie, after all, was forty if she was a day.
And Luther was only a kid. Besides Anne thought that Luther had
been ever so much nicer when he first came than he was now. But
from so many nights at the Savoy, he had became a marvellous dancer,
and he was teaching Anne the Lindy Hop to Cab Calloway's records.
Besides, her picture of "The Boy on the Block" wasn't anywhere near
done. So they kept him. At least, Anne kept him, although Michael
said he was getting a little bit bored with the same Negro always in
the way.

For Luther had grown a bit familiar lately. He smoked up all
their cigarettes, drank their wine, told jokes on them to their friends,
and sometimes even came upstairs singing and walking about the
house when the Carraways had guests in who didn't share their
enthusiasm for Negroes, natural or otherwise.

Luther and Mattie together were a pair. They quite frankly lived
with one another now. Well, let that go. Anne and Michael prided
themselves on being different; artists. you know, and liberal-minded
people—maybe a little scatter-brained, but then (secretly, they felt)
that came from genius. They were not ordinary people, bothering
about the liberties of others. Certainly, the last thing they would do
would be to interfere with the delightful simplicity of Negroes.

But Mattie must be giving Luther money and buying him clothes.
He was dressing awfully well. And on her Thursday afternoons off
she would come back loaded with packages. As far as the Carraways
could tell, they were all for Luther.

And sometimes there were quarrels drifting up from the basement.
And often, all too often, Mattie had moods. And it was pretty awful
having two hard and glowering people around the house. Anne
couldn't paint and Michael couldn't play.

One day, when she hadn't seen Luther for three days, Anne called
downstairs and asked him if he wouldn't please come up and take off
his shirt and get on the box. The picture was almost done. Luther
came dragging his feet upstairs and humming:

> "Before I'd be a slave
> I'd be buried in ma grave
> And go home to my Jesus
> And be free."

And that afternoon he let the furnace go almost out.

That was the state of things when Michael's mother (whom Anne had never liked) arrived from Kansas City to pay them a visit. At once neither Mattie nor Luther liked her either. She was a mannish old lady, big and tall, and inclined to be bossy. Mattie, however, did spruce up her service, cooked delicious things, and treated Mrs. Carraway with a great deal more respect than she did Anne.

"I never play with servants," Mrs. Carraway had said to Michael, and Mattie must have heard her.

But Luther, he was worse then ever. Not that he did anything wrong, Anne thought, but the way he did things! For instance, he didn't need to sing now all the time, especially since Mrs. Carraway had said she didn't like singing. And certainly not songs like "You Rascal, You."

But all things end! With the Carraways and Luther it happened like this: One forenoon, quite without a shirt (for he expected to pose) Luther came sauntering through the library to change the flowers in the vase. He carried red roses. Mrs. Carraway was reading her morning scripture from the Health and Life.

"Oh, good morning," said Luther. "How long are you gonna stay in this house?"

"I never liked familiar Negroes," said Mrs. Carraway, over her nose glasses.

"Huh!" said Luther. "That's too bad! I never liked poor white folks."

Mrs. Carraway screamed, a short loud, dignified scream. Michael came running in bathrobe and pajamas. Mrs. Caraway grew tall. There was a scene. Luther talked. Michael talked, Anne appeared.

"Never, never, never," said Mrs. Carraway, "have I suffered such impudence from servants—and a nigger servant—in my own son's house."

"Mother, Mother, Mother," said Michael. "Be calm. I'll discharge him." He turned on the nonchalant Luther. "Go!" he said, pointing toward the door. "Go, go!"

"Michael," Anne cried, "I haven't finished 'The Slave on the Block.'" Her husband looked nonplussed. For a moment he breathed deeply.

"Either he goes or I go," said Mrs. Carraway, firm as a rock.

"He goes," said Michael with strength from his mother.

"Oh!" cried Anne. She looked at Luther. His black arms were full of roses he had brought to put in the vases. He had on no shirt. "Oh!" His body was ebony.

"Don't worry 'bout me!" said Luther. "I'll go."

"Yes, we'll go," boomed Mattie from the doorway, who had come up from below, fat and belligerent. "We've stood enough foolery from you white folks! Yes, we'll go. Come on, Luther.

What could she mean, "stood enough?" What had they done to them, Anne and Michael wondered. They had tried to be kind. "Oh!"

"Sneaking around knocking on our door at night," Mattie went on. "Yes, we'll go. Pay us! Pay us! Pay us!" So she remembered the time they had come for Luther at night. That was it.

"I'll pay you," said Michael. He followed Mattie out.

Anne looked at her black boy.

"Good-bye," Luther said. "You fix the vases."

He handed her his armful of roses, glanced impudently at old Mrs. Carraway and grinned—grinned that wide, beautiful, white-toothed grin that made Anne say when she first saw him, "He looks like the jungle." Grinned, and disappeared in the dark hall, with no shirt on his back.

"Oh," Anne moaned distressfully, "my 'Boy on the Block'!"

"Huh!" snorted Mrs. Carraway.

TED POSTON (1906-   )

Ted Poston, born in Hopkinsville, Kentucky, was educated in the local public schools, at Tennessee Agricultural and Industrial State College and at New York University. He worked as tobacco stemmer, porter, shoeshine boy, dining-car waiter, Pullman porter, and seaman before he went into newspaper work in 1928. Since then he has worked for the *Pittsburgh Courier,* the *New York Contender,* the *Amsterdam News,* and the New York *Post.* In 1932-1933 he was one of a group of Negroes who went to Russia to make motion pictures, a project that did not materialize. After some time in Germany, he returned to America. From his experiences as a reporter he has gathered material for several stories and sketches of Negro workers, among them "Law and Order in Norfolk" and "A Matter of Record." "The Making of Mamma Harris" is here reprinted by permission of the author and of *The New Republic.*

The Making of Mamma Harris

SHE WAS A SCRAWNY hardbitten little woman and she greeted me with that politely blank stare which Negroes often reserve for hostile whites or prying members of their own race.

I had been directed to her tenement in Richmond's ramshackle Negro section by another woman, a grayhaired old grandmother whose gnarled hands had been stemming tobacco for five decades.

"The white folks down at union headquarters is all right," she had said, "and we love 'em—especially Mr. Marks. But if you want to know about us stemmers and the rumpus we raised, you better go see Mamma Harris. She's Missus CIO in Richmond."

The blank look softened on the thin dark face when I mentioned this.

"Must've been Sister Jones," she said, still standing near the door. "They all call me Mamma though. Even if I ain't but forty-nine and most of 'em old enough to be my grandmammy."

I edged toward a rocking chair on the other side of the bed.

"I'm a CIO man myself," I remarked. "Newspaper Guild. Our local boys just fixed up the Times-Dispatch this morning."

She yelled so suddenly that I almost missed the rocker.

"Bennie!" she called toward the kitchen, "you hear that, Bennie? CIO's done organized The Dispatch. Moved right in this morning. What I tell you? We gonna make this a union town yet!"

A hulking overalled Negro appeared in the kitchen doorway. His booming bass voice heightened his startling resemblance to Paul Robeson.

"Dispatch?" he thundered. "God Amighty, we do come on."

Mrs. Harris nodded in my direction.

"He's a CIO man from up New York. Wants to know about our rumpus out at Export. He's a Guilder too, just like the white 'uns."

Benny limped toward the other chair.

"They give us hell," he said, "but we give it right back to 'em. And it was we'uns who come out on top. The cops was salty. Wouldn't even let us set down and rest. But I told the women, I told 'em 'Sit down' and they did. Right in front of the cops too. Didn't I, Louise?"

Mrs. Harris nodded energetically from her perch on the bed.

"You dead did. And they didn't do nothing neither. They 'fraid of the women. You can outtalk the men. But us women don't take no tea for the fever."

Bennie boomed agreement. "There was five hundred of the women on the picket line and only twenty of us mens. But we sure give 'em hell. I talked right up to them cops, didn't I, Louise? Didn't I?"

Finally Mrs. Harris got around to the beginning.

"I wasn't no regular stemmer at first," she said, "but I been bringing a shift somewhere or other since I was eight. I was took out of school then and give a job minding chillun. By the time I was ten I was cooking for a family of six. And I been scuffling ever since.

"But I don't work in no factory till eight years ago. Then I went out to Export. Well, it took me just one day to find out that preachers don't know nothing about hell. They ain't worked in no tobacco factory."

Bennie was smiling to himself and gazing at the ceiling.

"Them cops beat up them strikers something awful out at Vaughn's," he said. "They even kicked the women around. But they didn't do it to us, huh, Louise? We stood right up to 'em."

Mrs. Harris waved aside the interruption.

"Then there was this scab," she went on, "only he ain't no scab then, cause we don't have no union. We ain't even heerd of no union nowhere then, but I knew something was bound to happen. Even a dog couldn't keep on like we was. You know what I make then? Two dollars and eighty cents a week. Five dollars was a too bad week."

"I put in eighty-two and a half hours one week," Bennie said, "and they only give me $18.25. I think about this one day when one of them cops . . ."

Mrs. Harris shushed him.

"Now this scab—only he ain't no scab then—he rides me from the minute I get to Export. He's in solid with the man and he always brags he's the ringtail monkey in this circus. He's a stemmer like the rest of us but he stools for the white folks.

"There's two hundred of us on our floor alone and they only give us four and half and five cents a pound. You only get paid for the stems. And some of them stems is so puny they look like horse hair."

Bennie was chuckling softly to himself but a glance from Mrs. Harris held the cops at bay for the moment.

"And as if everything else wasn't bad enough, there was this scab. We's cramped up on them benches from kin to can't, and he's always snooping around to see nobody don't pull the stem out the center instead of pulling the leaf down both sides separate. This dust just eats your lungs right out of you. You start dying the day you go in."

She coughed automatically and continued.

"Well, I keep this up for six long years. And this scab is riding me ever' single day. He's always riding everybody and snitching on them what don't take it. He jump me one day about singing and I ain't got no voice nohow. But I like a song and I gotta do something to ease my mind or else I go crazy.

"But he jump me this morning and tell me to shut up. Well, that's my cup. Six years, but this once is too often. So I'm all over him like gravy over rice. I give him a tongue-lashing what curled every nap on his head."

For a moment she had the same beaming look which Bennie displayed when he spoke of the cops.

"I sass him deaf, dumb and blind, and he takes it. But all the time he's looking at me kinder queer. And all at once he says 'You mighty salty all of a sudden; you must be joining up with this union foolishness going on around here.'

"You coulda knocked me over with a Export stem. I ain't even heard nothing about no union. But as soon as he cuts out, I start asking around. And bless my soul if they ain't been organizing for a whole full week. And I ain't heerd a peep."

"I ain't heerd nothing neither then," Benny put in, "and I been there fifteen years."

Mrs. Harris caught another breath.

"Well, I don't only go to the next meeting downtown, but I carries sixty of the girls from our floor. They remember how I sass this scab and they're all with me. We plopped right down in the first row of the gallery. And when they asked for volunteers to organize Export, I can't get to my feet quick enough."

"I come in right after," Bennie remarked.

"And it ain't no time," Mrs. Harris continued, "before we got seven hundred out of the thousand what works in Export. The man is going crazy mad and the scab is snooping overtime. But they can't fire us. The boom time is on and the warehouse is loaded to the gills."

She paused dramatically.

"And then on the first of August, 1938, we let 'em have it. We called our strike and closed up Export tight as a bass drum."

Bennie couldn't be shushed this time.

"The cops swooped down like ducks on a June bug," he said, "but we was ready for 'em. I was picket captain and there was five hundred on the line. And all five hundred was black and evil."

Mrs. Harris was beaming again.

"Then this scab came up with a couple hundred others and tried to break our line," she recalled, "but we wasn't giving a crip a crutch or a dog a bone. I made for that head personal—but the cops wouldn't let me at 'im."

"I stayed on the line for twenty-four hours running," Bennie chuckled, "and I didn't take a inch from none of them cops."

"And we wasn't by ourselves neither," Mrs. Harris went on. "The preachers, Dr. Jackson, the Southern Aid Society and all the other union people help us. GWU and them garment ladies give us a hundred dollars right off the bat. Malgamate sent fifty. The ship folks down in Norfolk come through, and your white Guild boys here give ten dollars too."

"It was them white garment ladies what sent the cops," Bennie cut in. "They come out five hundred strong and parade around the factory. They got signs saying 'GWU Supports Export Tobacco Workers.'

"Them cops jump salty as hell. '*White* women,' they say, 'white women out here parading for niggers.' But they don't do nothing. Because we ain't taking no stuff from nobody.

"We was out eighteen days," Mrs. Harris said, "and the boss was losing money hand over fist. But you know how much we spend in them eighteen days? Over seven hundred dollars."

Her awed tones made it sound like seven thousand.

"But it was worth it. We win out and go back getting ten, eleven and twelve cents a pound. And better still we can wear our union buttons right out open. We might even got them scabs fired if we wanted, but we didn't want to keep nobody out of work."

Bennie stopped smiling for the first time.

"We might be better off if we did," he said soberly. "I bet we do next time."

Mrs. Harris explained.

"They been sniping away at us ever since we win. They give the scabs all the breaks and lay off us union people first whenever they can. They give all the overtime to the scabs and even let 'em get away with stripping the stem down the center. But we ain't licked yet. We still got two hundred members left and we still got union conditions."

Her face brightened again.

"And we fixed that old scab—even if he is been there nineteen years. We moved him off our floor completely, and he ain't allowed to ride nobody.

"We got a good set of people downtown now and we're reorganizing right along. By the time our new contract comes up in June, we'll probably have the whole thousand."

"And if we strike again, and them cops jump salty"—Bennie began.

And this time Mamma Harris let him pursue the subject to his heart's content.

CHESTER HIMES (1907-)

Like O. Henry, Chester Himes began to publish short stories while serving a prison term. While in the Ohio State Penitentiary he wrote for *Abbott's Monthly* and for *Esquire,* contributing to the latter magazine "To Red Hell," based on the penitentiary fire of 1930. He has also contributed to *Opportunity* and to *Coronet.* "The Night's for Cryin' " is here reprinted by permission of the author and of *Esquire.*

"The Night's For Cryin' "

BLACK BOY SLAMMED his Tom Collins down on the bar with an irritated bang, turned a slack scowl toward Gigilo.

Gigilo, yellow and fat like a well-fed hog, was saying in a fat, whiskey-thickened voice: "Then she pulled out a knife and cut me 'cross the back. I just looked at 'er. Then she threw 'way the knife and hit me in the mouth with her pocketbook. I still looked at her. Then she raised her foot and stomped my corns. I pushed her down then."

Black Boy said: "Niggah, ef'n yo is talkin' tuh me, Ah ain' liss'nin'." Black Boy didn't like yellow niggers, he didn't want no yellow nigger talking to him now, for he was waiting for Marie, his high yellow heart, to take her to her good-doing job.

Gigilo took another sip of rye, but he didn't say anymore.

Sound bubbled about them, a bubble bursting here in a strident laugh, there in accented profanity. A woman's coarse, heavy voice said: "Cal, Ah wish you'd stop Fo'-Fo' frum drinkin' so much" . . . A man's flat, unmusical drone said: "Ah had uh ruff on 632 and 642 come out." He had repeated the same words a hundred solid times. . . . "Aw, she ain' gibin' dat chump nuttin'," a young, loud voice clamored for attention . . . A nickel victrola in the rear blared a husky, negroid bellow: "*Anybody heah wanna buy . . .*"

The mirror behind the bar reflected the lingering scowl on Black Boy's face, the blackest blot in the ragged jam of black and yellow faces lining the bar.

Wall lights behind him spilled soft stain on the elite at the tables. Cigarette smoke cut thin blue streamers ceilingward through the muted light, mingled with whiskey fumes and perfume scents and Negro smell. Bodies squirmed, inching riotous-colored dresses up from yellow, shapely legs. Red-lacquered nails gleamed like bright blood drops on the stems of whiskey glasses, and the women's yellow faces looked like powdered masks beneath sleek hair, bruised with red mouths.

Four white people pushed through the front door, split a hurried, half apologetic path through the turn of displeased faces toward the cabaret entrance at the rear. Black Boy's muddy, negroid eyes followed them, slightly resentful.

A stoop-shouldered, consumptive-looking Negro leaned over Black Boy's shoulder and whispered something in his ear.

Black Boy's sudden strangle blew a spray of Tom Collins over the bar. He put the tall glass quickly down, sloshing the remaining liquid over his hand. His red tongue slid twice across his thick, red lips, and his slack, plate-shaped face took on a popeyed expression, as startlingly unreal beneath the white of his precariously perched Panama as an eight ball with suddenly sprouted features. The puffed, bluish scar on his left cheek, memento of a pick-axe duel on a chain gang, seemed to swell into an embossed reproduction as a shell explosion, ridges pronging off from it in spokes.

He slid back from his stool, his elbow digging into a powdered, brownskin back to his right, caught on his feet with a flatfooted clump. Standing, his body was big, his six foot height losing impressiveness in slanting shoulders and long arms like an ape's.

He paused for a moment, undecided, a unique specimen of sartorial splendor—white Panama stuck on the back of his shiny shaved skull, yellow silk polo shirt dirtied slightly by the black of his bulging muscles, draped trousers of a brilliant pea green, tight waisted and slack hanging above size eleven shoes of freshly shined tan.

The woman with the back turned a ruffled countenance, spat a stream of lurid profanity at him through twisted red lips. But he wedged through the jam toward the door, away from her, smashed out of the Log Cabin bar into a crowd of idling avenue pimps.

The traffic lights at the corner turned from green to red. Four shiny, new automobiles full of laughing black folks, purred casually through the red. A passing brownskin answered to the call of "Babe," paused before her "nigger" in saddle-backed stance, arms akimbo, tight dress tightened on the curve of her hips.

Black Boy's popped eyes filled with yellow specks, slithered across the front of the weather-stained Majestic Hotel across the street, lingering a searching instant on every woman whose face was light. Around the corner, down on Central Avenue, he caught a fleeting glimpse of a yellow gal climbing into a green sedan, then a streetcar clanged across his vision.

He pulled in his red lips, wet them with his tongue. Then he broke into a shuffling, flat-footed run—through the squawk of a horn, across suddenly squealing brakes, never looked around. A taxidriver's curse lashed him across the street. His teeth bared slightly, but the bloated unreality of his face never changed.

He turned right in front of the Majestic, roughed over a brown dandy with two painted crones, drew up at the corner, panting. The green sedan burnt rubber, pulled right through the red light in a whining, driving first.

But too late to keep Black Boy from catching a flash of the pretty, frightened face of Marie and the nervous profile of the driver bent low over the wheel. A yellow nigger. He turned and watched the red tail-light sink into the distant darkness, his body twisting on flatly planted feet. His bulging eyes turned a vein-laced red. Sweat popped out on his face, putting a sheen on its lumpy blackness, grew in beads on his shiny head, trickled in streams down his body.

He turned and ran for a cab, but his actions were dogged now instead of apprehensive. He'd already seen Marie with that yellow hotel nigger. He caught a cab pointing the right way, said: "Goose it, Speed," before he swung through the open door.

Speed goosed it. The cab took sudden life, jumped ahead from the shove of eight protesting cylinders. Black Boy leaned tensely forward, let the speedometer needle hit fifty before he spoke. "Dar's uh green sedan up front, uh fo'do' job. Latch on it'n earn dis dime, big dime."

The lank, loose-bodied brown boy driving threw him a careless, toothy grin, coiled around the wheel. He headed into the red light at Cedar Avenue doing a crisp seventy, didn't slacken. He pulled inside the line of waiting cars, smashed into the green while the red still lingered in his eyes. The green turned to red at Carnegie, and the car in front stopped, but he burst the red wide open doing a sheer eighty-five, leaning on the horn.

"Ri' at Euclid," Black Boy directed through lips that hung so slack they seemed to be turned wrong side out. He was gambling on those yellow folk seeking the protection of their white folk where they worked, for they had lost the green sedan.

The driver braked for the turn, eyes roving for traffic cops. He didn't see any and he turned at a slow fifty, not knowing whether the light was red, white or blue. The needle walked right up the street numbers, fifty-seven at 57th Street, seventy-one at 71st. It was hovering on eighty again when Black Boy said: "Turn 'round."

That lanky darky wouldn't have turned nobody's car in the world like that but another darky's.

Marie was just getting out of the green sedan in front of the Regis where she worked as a maid. When she heard that shrill cry of rubber on asphalt she broke into a craven run.

Black Boy hit the pavement in a flat-footed lope, caught her just as she was about to climb the lobby stairs. He never said a word, he just reached around from behind and smacked her in the face with the open palm of his right hand. She drew up short against the blow. Then he hit her under her right breast with a short left jab and chopped three rights into her face when she turned around with the edge of his fist like he was driving nails.

She wilted to her knees and he bumped her in the mouth with his knee, knocking her sprawling on her side. He kicked her in the body three rapid, vicious times, slobber drooling from his slack, red lips. His bloated face was a tar ball in the spill of sign light, his eyes too dull to notice. Somehow his Panama still clung on his eight ball head, whiter than ever, and his red lips were a split, bleeding incision in his black face.

Marie screamed for help. Then she whimpered. Then she begged. "Doan kill me, Black Boy, daddy deah, honey darlin', daddy-daddy deah. Marie luvs yuh, daddy darlin'. Doan kill yo' lil' honeybunch, Marie . . ."

The yellow boy, slowly following from the car, paused a moment in indecision as if he would get back in and drive away. But he couldn't bear seeing Black Boy kick Marie. The growth of emotion was visible in his face before it pushed him forward.

After an instant he realized that that was where he worked as a bellhop, that those white folk would back him up against a strange nigger. He stepped quickly over to Black Boy, spoke in a cultural peremptory voice: "Stop kicking that woman, you dirty black nigger."

Black Boy turned his bloated face toward him. His dull eyes explored him, dogged. His voice was flatly telling him: "You keep outta dis, yellow niggah. Dis heah is mah woman an' Ah doan lak you no way."

The yellow boy was emboldened by the appearance of two white men in the hotel doorway. He stepped over and slung a weighted blow to Black Boy's mouth. Black Boy shifted in quick rage, drew a spring-blade barlow chiv and slashed the yellow boy to death before the two white men could run down the stairs. He broke away from their restraining hands, made his way to the alley beside the theater in his shambling, flat-footed run before the police cruiser got there.

He heard Marie's loud, fear-shrill voice crying: "He pulled a gun on Black Boy, He pulled a gun on Black Boy. Ah saw 'im do it—"

He broke into a laugh, satisfied. She was still his . . .

Three rapid shots behind him stopped his laugh, shattered his face into black fragments. The cops had begun shooting without calling halt. He knew that they knew he was a "dinge," and he knew they wanted to kill him, so he stepped into the light behind Clark's Restaurant, stopped dead still with upraised hands, not turning around.

The cops took him down to the station and beat his head into an open, bloody wound from his bulging eyes clear around to the base of his skull—"You'd bring your nigger cuttings down on Euclid Avenue, would you, you black—"

They gave him the electric chair for that.

But if it is worrying him, he doesn't show it during the slow drag of days in death row's grilled enclosure. He knows that that high yellow gal with the ball-bearing hips is still his, heart, soul and body. All day long, you can hear his loud, crowing voice, kidding the other condemned men, jibing the guards, telling lies. He can tell some tall lies, too—"You know, me'n Marie wuz in Noo Yawk dat wintah. Ah won leben grands in uh dice game'n bought her uh sealskin—"

All day long, you can hear his noisy laugh.

Marie comes to see him as often as they let her, brings him fried chicken and hot, red lips; brings him a wide smile and tiny yellow specks in her big, brown, ever-loving eyes. You can hear his assured love-making all over the range, his casual "honeybunch," his chuckling, contented laugh.

All day long . . .

It's at night, when she's gone and the cells are dark and death row is silent, that you'll find Black Boy huddled in the corner of his cell, thinking of her, perhaps in some other nigger's loving arms. Crying softly. Salty tears making glistening streaks down the blending blackness of his face.

RICHARD WRIGHT (1909-   )

Richard Wright (see also pp. 401, 1050) was born near Natchez, Mississippi. Because his family was constantly on the move, his education was erratic. By fifteen when he ran away from home, he had lived in Natchez, Jackson, Greenwood, and Carters, in Mississippi; Elaine, Helena, and West Helena, in Arkansas; and Memphis, in Tennessee. He has worked at many jobs, "from ditch-digging to clerking in a post office"; during the depression, while working on the Chicago Federal Writers' Project, he won a *Story Magazine* contest with *Uncle Tom's Children* (1938), the first story of which, "Big Boy Leaves Home," had already appeared in *The New Caravan* (1936). Since then he has written the much-discussed novel, *Native*

Son, a Book-of-the-Month Club choice. The dramatization of his novel, written in collaboration with Paul Green and produced by Orson Welles, was one of the best plays of the 1940-1941 New York season. In 1939 he was awarded a Guggenheim Fellowship and in 1941, the Spingarn Medal. His "Bright and Morning Star," originally published in the *New Masses,* has now been reprinted in the revised edition of *Uncle Tom's Children.* It is here reprinted by permission of the author and of Harper and Brothers.

Bright and Morning Star

SHE STOOD WITH HER BLACK FACE some six inches from the moist window-pane and wondered when on earth would it ever stop raining. It might keep up like this all week, she thought. She heard rain droning upon the roof and high up in the wet sky her eyes followed the silent rush of a bright shaft of yellow that swung from the airplane beacon in far off Memphis. Momently she could see it cutting through the rainy dark; it would hover a second like a gleaming sword above her head, then vanish. She sighed, troubling, Johnny-Boys been trampin in this slop all day wid no decent shoes on his feet. . . . Through the window she could see the rich black earth sprawling outside in the night. There was more rain than the clay could soak up; pools stood everywhere. She yawned and mumbled: "Rains good n bad. It kin make seeds bus up thu the groun er it kin bog things down lika watah-soaked coffin." Her hands were folded loosely over her stomach and the hot air of the kitchen traced a filmy veil of sweat on her forehead. From the cook stove came the soft singing of burning wood and now and then a throaty bubble rose from a pot of simmering greens.

"Shucks, Johnny-Boy coulda let somebody else do all tha runnin in the rain. Theres others bettah fixed fer it than he is. But, naw! Johnny-Boy ain the one t trust nobody t do nothin. Hes gotta do it *all* hisself. . . ."

She glanced at a pile of damp clothes in a zinc tub. Waal, Ah bettah git t work. She turned, lifted a smoothing iron with a thick pad of cloth, touched a spit-wet finger to it with a quick, jerking motion: *smiiitz!* Yeah; its hot! Stooping, she took a blue work-shirt from the tub and shook it out. With a deft twist of her shoulders she caught the iron in her right hand; the fingers of her left hand took a piece of wax from a tin box and a frying sizzle came as she smeared the bottom. She was thinking of nothing now; her hands followed a life-long ritual of toil. Spreading a sleeve, she ran the hot iron to and fro until the wet cloth became stiff. She was deep in the midst of her work when a song rose up out of the far off days of her childhood and broke through half-parted lips:

> *Hes the Lily of the Valley, the Bright n Mawnin Star*
> *Hes the Fairest of Ten Thousan t mah soul . . .*

A gust of wind dashed rain against the window. Johnny-Boy oughta c mon home n eat his suppah. Aw, Lawd! Itd be fine ef Sug could eat wid us tonight! Itd be like ol times! Mabbe aftah all it wont be long fo he comes back. Tha lettah Ah got from im las week said *Don give up hope.* . . . Yeah; we gotta live in hope. Then both of her sons, Sug and Johnny-Boy, would be back with her.

With an involuntary nervous gesture, she stopped and stood still, listening. But the only sound was the lulling fall of rain. Shucks, ain no usa me ackin this way, she thought. Ever time they gits ready to hol them meetings Ah gits jumpity. Ah been a lil scared ever since Sug went t jail. She heard the clock ticking and looked. Johnny-Boys a *hour* late! He sho mus be havin a time doin all tha trampin, trampin thu the mud. . . . But her fear was a quiet one; it was more like an intense brooding than a fear; it was a sort of hugging of hated facts so closely that she could feel their grain, like letting cold water run over her hand from a faucet on a winter morning.

She ironed again, faster now, as if she felt the more she engaged her body in work the less she would think. But how could she forget Johnny-Boy out there on those wet fields rounding up white and black Communists for a meeting tomorrow? And that was just what Sug had been doing when the sheriff had caught him, beat him, and tried to make him tell who and where his comrades were. Po Sug! They sho musta beat the boy somethin awful! But, thank Gawd, he didnt talk! He ain no weaklin, Sug ain! Hes been lion-hearted all his life long.

That had happened a year ago. And now each time those meetings came around the old terror surged back. While shoving the iron a cluster of toiling days returned; days of washing and ironing to feed Johnny-Boy and Sug so they could do party work; days of carrying a hundred pounds of white folks' clothes upon her head across fields sometimes wet and sometimes dry. But in those days a hundred pounds was nothing to carry carefully balanced upon her head while stepping by instinct over the corn and cotton rows. The only time it had seemed heavy was when she had heard of Sug's arrest. She had been coming home one morning with a bundle upon her head, her hands swinging idly by her sides, walking slowly with her eyes in front of her, when Bob, Johnny-Boy's pal, had called from across the fields and had come and told her that the sheriff had got Sug. That morning the bundle had become heavier than she could ever remember.

And with each passing week now, though she spoke of it to no one, things were becoming heavier. The tubs of water and the smoothing iron and the bundle of clothes were becoming harder to lift, with her back aching so; and her work was taking longer, all because Sug was gone and she didn't know just when Johnny-Boy would be taken too. To ease the ache of anxiety that was swelling her heart, she hummed, then sang softly:

> *He walks wid me, He talks wid me*
> *He tells me Ahm His Own. . . .*

Guiltily, she stopped and smiled. Looks like Ah jus cant seem t fergit them ol songs, no mattah how hard Ah tries. . . . She had learned them when she was a little girl living and working on a farm. Every Monday morning from the corn and cotton fields the slow strains had floated from her mother's lips, lonely and haunting; and later, as the years had filled with gall, she had learned their deep meaning. Long hours of scrubbing floors for a few cents a day had taught her who Jesus was, what a great boon it was to cling to Him, to be like Him and suffer without a mumbling word. She had poured the yearning of her life into the songs, feeling buoyed with a faith beyond this world. The figure of the Man nailed in agony to the Cross, His burial in a cold grave, His transfigured Resurrection, His being breath and clay, God and Man—all had focused her feelings upon an imagery which had swept her life into a wondrous vision.

But as she had grown older, a cold white mountain, the white folks and their laws, had swum into her vision and shattered her songs and their spell of peace. To her that white mountain was temptation, something to lure her from her Lord, a part of the world God had made in order that she might endure it and come through all the stronger, just as Christ had risen with greater glory from the tomb. The days crowded with trouble had enhanced her faith and she had grown to love hardship with a bitter pride; she had obeyed the laws of the white folks with a soft smile of secret knowing.

After her mother had been snatched up to heaven in a chariot of fire, the years had brought her a rough workingman and two black babies, Sug and Johnny-Boy, all three of whom she had wrapped in the charm and magic of her vision. Then she was tested by no less than

God; her man died, a trial which she bore with the strength shed by the grace of her vision; finally even the memory of her man faded into the vision itself, leaving her with two black boys growing tall, slowly into manhood.

Then one day grief had come to her heart when Johnny-Boy and Sug had walked forth demanding their lives. She had sought to fill their eyes with her vision, but they would have none of it. And she had wept when they began to boast of the strength shed by a new and terrible vision.

But she had loved them, even as she loved them now; bleeding, her heart had followed them. She could have done no less, being an old woman in a strange world. And day by day her sons had ripped from her startled eyes her old vision, and image by image had given her a new one, different, but great and strong enough to fling her into the light of another grace. The wrongs and sufferings of black men had taken the place of Him nailed to the Cross; the meager beginnings of the party had become another Resurrection; and the hate of those who would destroy her new faith had quickened in her a hunger to feel how deeply her new strength went.

"Lawd, Johnny-Boy," she would sometimes say, "Ah just wan them white folks t try t make me tell *who* is *in* the party n who *ain!* Ah just wan em t try, n Ahll show em somethin they never thought a black woman could have!"

But sometimes like tonight, while lost in the forgetfulness of work, the past and the present would become mixed in her; while toiling under a strange star for a new freedom the old songs would slip from her lips with their beguiling sweetness.

The iron was getting cold. She put more wood into the fire, stood again at the window and watched the yellow blade of light cut through the wet darkness. Johnny-Boy ain here yit. . . . Then, before she was aware of it, she was still, listening for sounds. Under the drone of rain she heard the slosh of feet in mud. Tha ain Johnny-Boy. She knew his long, heavy footsteps in a million. She heard feet come on the porch. Some woman. . . . She heard bare knuckles knock three times, then once. Thas some of them comrads! She unbarred the door, cracked it a few inches, and flinched from the cold rush of damp wind.

"Whos tha?"

"Its me!"

"Who?"

"Me, Reva!"

She flung the door open.

"Lawd, chile c mon in!"

She stepped to one side and a thin, blond-haired white girl ran through the door; as she slid the bolt she heard the girl gasping and shaking her wet clothes. Somethings wrong! Reva wauldna walked a mile t mah house in all this slop fer nothin! Tha gals stuck onto Johnny-Boy. Ah wondah ef anything happened t im?

"Git on inter the kitchen, Reva, where its warm."

"Lawd, Ah sho is wet!"

"How yuh reckon yuhd be, in all tha rain?"

"Johnny-Boy ain here *yit*?" asked Reva.

"Naw! N ain no usa yuh worryin bout im. Jus yuh git them shoes off! Yuh wanna ketch yo deatha col?" She stood looking absently. Yeah; its somethin about the party er Johnny-Boy thas gone wrong. Lawd, Ah wondah ef her pa knows how she feels bout Johnny-Boy? "Honey, yuh hadnt oughta come out in sloppy weather like this."

"Ah had t come, An Sue."

She led Reva to the kitchen.

"Git them shoes off n git close t the stove so yuhll git dry!"

"An Sue, Ah got somethin t tell yuh . . ."

The words made her hold her breath. Ah bet its somethin bout Johnny-Boy!

"Whut, honey?"

"The sheriff wuz by our house tonight. He come to see pa."

"Yeah?"

"He done got word from somewheres bout tha meetin tomorrow."

"Is it Johnny-Boy, Reva?"

"Aw, naw, An Sue! Ah ain hearda word bout im. Ain yuh seen im tonight?"

"He ain come home t eat yit."

"Where kin he be?"

"Lawd knows, chile."

"Somebodys gotta tell them comrades tha meetings off," said Reva. "The sheriffs got men watchin our house. Ah had t slip out t git here widout em followin me."

"Reva?"

"Hunh?"

"Ahma ol woman n Ah wans yuh t tell me the truth."

"Whut, An Sue?"

"Yuh ain tryin t fool me, is yuh?"

"*Fool* yuh?"

"Bout Johnny-Boy?"

"Lawd, naw, An Sue!"

"Ef theres anythin wrong jus tell me, chile. Ah kin stan it."

She stood by the ironing board, her hands as usual folded loosely over her stomach, watching Reva pull off her water-clogged shoe. She was feeling that Johnny-Boy was already lost to her; she was feeling the pain that would come when she knew it for certain; and she was feeling that she would have to be brave and bear it. She was like a person caught in a swift current of water and knew where the water was sweeping her and did not want to go on but had to go on to the end.

"It ain nothin bout Johnny-Boy, An Sue," said Reva. "But we gotta do somethin er we'll all git inter trouble."

"How the sheriff know about tha meetin?"

"Thas whut pa wans t know."

"Somebody done turned Judas."

"Sho looks like it."

"Ah bet it wuz some of them new ones," she said.

"Its hard t tell," said Reva.

"Lissen, Reva, yuh oughta stay her n git dry, but yuh bettah git back n tell yo pa Johnny-Boy ain here n Ah don know when hes gonna show up. *Some*bodys gotta tell them comrades t stay erway from yo pas house."

She stood with her back to the window, looking at Reva's wide, blue eyes. Po critter! Gotta go back thu all tha slop! Though she felt sorry for Reva, not once did she think that it would not have to be done. Being a woman, Reva was not suspect; she would *have* to go. It was just as natural for Reva to go back through the cold rain as it was for her to iron night and day, or for Sug to be in jail. Right now, Johnny-Boy was out there on those dark fields trying to get home. Lawd, don let em git im tonight! In spite of herself her feelings became torn. She loved her son and, loving him, she loved what he was trying to do. Johnny-Boy was happiest when he was working for the party, and her love for him was for his happiness. She frowned, trying hard to fit something together in her feelings: for her to try to stop Johnny-Boy was to admit that all the toil of years meant nothing; and to let him go meant that sometime or other he would be caught, like Sug. In facing it this way she felt a little stunned, as though she had come suddenly upon a blank wall in the dark. But outside in the rain were people, white and black, whom she had known all her life. Those people depended upon Johnny-Boy, loved him and looked to him as a man and leader. Yeah; hes gotta keep on; he cant stop now. . . . She looked at Reva; she was crying and pulling her shoes back on with reluctant fingers.

"Whut yuh carryin on tha way fer, chile?"

"Yuh done los Sug, now yuh sendin Johnny-Boy . . ."

"Ah got t, honey."

She was glad she could say that. Reva believed in black folks and not for anything in the world would she falter before her. In Reva's trust and acceptance of her she had found her first feelings of humanity; Reva's love was her refuge from shame and degradation. If in the early days of her life the white mountain had driven her back from the earth, then in her last days Reva's love was drawing her toward it, like the beacon that swung through the night outside. She heard Reva sobbing.

"Hush, honey!"

"Mah brothers in jail too! Ma cries ever day . . ."

"Ah knows, honey."

She helped Reva with her coat; her fingers felt the scant flesh of the girl's shoulders. She don git ernuff t eat, she thought. She slipped her arms around Reva's waist and held her close for a moment.

"Now, yuh stop that cryin."

"A-a-ah c—c—cant hep it. . . ."

"Everythingll be awright; Johnny-Boyll be back."

"Yuh think so?"

"Sho, chile. Cos he will."

Neither of them spoke again until they stood in the doorway. Outside they could hear water washing through the ruts of the street.

"Be sho n send Johnny-Boy t tell the folks t stay erway from pas house," said Reva.

"Ahll tell im. Don yuh worry."

"Good-bye!"

"Good-bye!"

Leaning against the door jamb, she shook her head slowly and watched Reva vanish through the falling rain.

II

She was back at her board, ironing, when she heard feet sucking in the mud of the back yard; feet she knew from long years of listening were Johnny-Boy's. But tonight, with all the rain and fear, his coming was like a leaving, was almost more than she could bear. Tears welled to her eyes and she blinked them away. She felt that he was coming so that she could give him up; to see him now was to say good-bye. But it was a good-bye she knew she could never say; they were not that way toward each other. All day long they could sit in the same room and not speak; she was his mother and he was her son. Most of the time a nod or a grunt would carry all the meaning that she wanted to convey to him, or he to her. She did not even turn her head when he heard him come stomping into the kitchen. She heard him pull up a chair, sit, sigh, and draw off his muddy shoes; they fell to the floor with heavy thuds. Soon the kitchen was full of the scent of his drying socks and his burning pipe. Tha boys hongry! She paused and looked at him over her shoulder; he was puffing at his pipe with his head tilted back and his feet propped up on the edge of the stove; his eyelids drooped and his wet clothes steamed from the heat of the fire. Lawd, that boy gits mo like his pa every day he lives, she mused, her lips breaking in a slow faint smile. Hols tha pipe in his mouth just like his pa usta hol his. Wondah how they woulda got erlong ef his pa hada lived? They oughta liked each other, they so mucha like. She wished there could have been other children besides Sug, so Johnny-Boy would not have to be so much alone. A man needs a woman by his side. . . . She thought of Reva; she liked Reva; the brightest glow her heart had ever known was when she had learned that Reva loved Johnny-Boy. But beyond Reva were cold white faces. Ef theys caught it means *death*. . . . She jerked around when she heard Johnny-Boy's pipe clatter to the floor. She saw him pick it up, smile sheepishly at her, and wag his head.

"Gawd, Ahm sleepy," he mumbled.

She got a pillow from her room and gave it to him.

"Here," she said.

"Hunh," he said, putting the pillow between his head and the back of the chair.

They were silent again. Yes, she would have to tell him to go back out into the cold rain and slop; maybe to get caught; maybe for the last time; she didn't know. But she would let him eat and get dry before telling him that the sheriff knew of the meeting to be held at Lem's tomorrow. And she would make him take a big dose of soda before he went out; soda always helped to stave off a cold. She looked at the clock. It was eleven. Theres time yit. Spreading a newspaper on the apron of the stove, she placed a heaping plate of greens upon it, a knife, a fork, a cup of coffee, a slab of cornbread, and a dish of peach cobbler.

"Yo suppahs ready," she said.

"Yeah," he said:

He did not move. She ironed again. Presently, she heard him eating. When she could no longer hear his knife tinkling against the edge of the plate, she knew he was through. It was almost twelve now. She would let him rest a little while longer before she told him. Till one er'clock, mabbe. Hes so tired. . . . She finished her ironing, put away

the board, and stacked the clothes in her dresser drawer. She poured
herself a cup of black coffee, drew up a chair, sat down and drank.

"Yuh almos dry," she said, not looking around.

"Yeah," he said, turning sharply to her.

The tone of voice in which she had spoken had let him know
that more was coming. She drained her cup and waited a moment
longer.

"Reva wuz here."

"Yeah?"

"She lef bout an hour ergo."

"Whut she say?"

"She said ol man Lem hada visit from the sheriff today."

"Bout the meetin?"

"Yeah."

She saw him stare at the coals glowing red through the crevices of
the stove and run his fingers nervously through his hair. She knew he
was wondering how the sheriff had found out. In the silence he would
ask a wordless question and in the silence she would answer wordlessly.
Johnny-Boys too trustin, she thought. Hes trying t make the party
big n hes takin in folks fastern he kin git t know em. You cant trust
ever white man yuh meet. . . .

"Yuh know, Johnny-Boy, yuh been takin in a lotta them white
folks lately . . ."

"Aw, ma!"

"But, Johnny-Boy . . ."

"Please, don talk t me bout tha now, ma."

Yuh ain t ol t lissen n learn, son," she said.

"Ah know whut yuh gonna say, ma. N yuh wrong. Yuh cant
judge folks jus by how yuh feel bount em n by how long yuh done
knowed em. Ef we start tha we wouldnt have *no*body in the party.
When folks pledge they word t be with us, then we gotta take em
in. Wes too weak t be choosy."

He rose abruptly, rammed his hands into his pockets, and stood
facing the window; she looked at his back in a long silence. She knew
his faith; it was deep. He had always said that black men could not
fight the rich bosses alone; a man could not fight with every hand
against him. But he believes so hard hes blind, she thought. At odd
times they had had these arguments before; always she would be
pitting her feeling against the hard necessity of his thinking, and
always she would lose. She shook her head. Po Johnny-Boy he don
know . . .

"But ain nona our folks tol, Johnny-Boy," she said.

"How yuh know?" he asked. His voice came low and with a tinge of anger. He still faced the window and now and then the yellow blade of light flicked across the sharp outine of his black face.

"Cause Ah know em," she said.

"*Any*body mighta tol," he said.

"It wuznt nona *our* folks," she said again.

She saw his hand sweep in a swift arc of disgust.

"*Our* folks! Ma, who in Gawd's name is *our* folks?"

"The folks we wuz born n raised wid, son. The folks we *know*!"

"We can't make the party grow tha way, ma."

"It mighta been Booker," she said.

"Yuh don know."

". . . er Blattberg . . ."

"Fer Chrissakes!"

". . . er any of the fo-five others whut joined las week."

"Ma, yuh jus don wan me t go out tonight," he said.

"Yo ol ma wans yuh t be careful, son."

"Ma, when yuh start doubtin folks in the party, then there ain no end."

"Son, Ah knows ever black man n woman in this parta the county," she said, standing too. "Ah watched em grow up; Ah even helped birth n nurse some of em; Ah knows em *all* from way back. There ain none of em that *coulda* tol! The folks Ah know jus don open they dos n ast death t walk in! Son, it wuz some of them *white* folks! Yuh jus mark mah word n wait n see!"

"Why is it gotta be *white* folks?" he asked. "Ef they tol, then theys jus Judases, thas all."

"Son, look at whuts befo yuh."

He shook his head and sighed.

"Ma, Ah done tol yuh a hundred times. Ah can't see white n Ah cant see black," he said. "Ah sees rich men n Ah sees po men."

She picked up his dirty dishes and piled them in a pan. Out of the corners of her eyes she saw-him sit and pull on his wet shoes. Hes goin! When she put the last dish away he was standing fully dressed, warming his hands over the stove. Jus a few mo minutes now n he'll be gone, like Sug, mabbe. Her throat tightened. This black man's fight takes *ever*thin! Looks like Gawd put us in this worl jus t beat us down!

"Keep this, ma," he said.

She saw a crumpled wad of money in his outstretched fingers.

"Naw; yuh keep it. Yuh might need it."

"It ain mine, ma. It berlongs t the party."

"But, Johnny-Boy, yuh might hafta go erway!"

"Ah kin make out."

"Don fergit yosef too much son."

"Ef Ah don come back theyll need it."

He was looking at her face and she was looking at the money.

"Yuh keep tha," she said slowly. "Ahll give em the money."

"From where?"

"Ah got some."

"Where yuh git it from?"

She sighed.

"Ah been savin a dollah a week fer Sug ever since hes been in jail."

"Lawd, ma!"

She saw the look of puzzled love and wonder in his eyes. Clumsily, he put the money back into his pocket.

"Ahm gone," he said.

"Here; drink this glass of soda watah."

She watched him drink, then put the glass away.

"Waal," he said. "Take the stuff outta yo pockets!"

She lifted the lid of the stove and he dumped all the papers from his pocket into the fire. She followed him to the door and made him turn round.

Lawd, yuh tryin to maka revolution n yuh cant even keep yo coat buttoned." Her nimble fingers fastened his collar high around his throat. "There!"

He pulled the brim of his hat low over his eyes. She opened the door and with the suddenness of the cold gust of wind that struck her face, he was gone. She watched the black fields and the rain take him, her eyes burning. When the last faint footstep could no longer be heard, she closed the door, went to her bed, lay down, and pulled the cover over her while fully dressed. Her feelings coursed with the rhythm of the rain: Hes gone! Lawd, Ah *know* hes gone! Her blood felt cold.

III

She was floating in a grey void somewhere between sleeping and dreaming and then suddenly she was wide awake, hearing and feeling in the same instant the thunder of the door crashing in and a cold wind filling the room. It was pitch black and she stared, resting on her elbows, her mouth open, not breathing, her ears full of the sound of tramping feet and booming voices. She knew at once: They lookin fer im! Then, filled with her will, she was on her feet, rigid, waiting, listening.

"The lamps burnin!"

"Yuh see her?"

"Naw!"

"Look in the kitchen!"

"Gee, this place smells like niggers!"

"Say, somebody's here er been here!"

"Yeah; theres fire in the stove!"

"Mabbe hes been here n gone?"

"Boy, look at these jars of jam!"

"Niggers make good jam!"

"Git some bread!"

"Heres some cornbread!"

"Say, lemme git some!"

"Take it easy! Theres plenty here!"

"Ahma take some of this stuff home!"

"Look, heres a pota greens!"

"N some hot cawffee!"

"Say, yuh guys! C mon! Cut it out! We didn't come here for a feas!"

She walked slowly down the hall. They lookin fer im, but they ain got im yit! She stopped in the doorway, her gnarled, black hands as always folded over her stomach, but tight now, so tightly the veins bulged. The kitchen was crowded with white men in glistening raincoats. Though the lamp burned, their flashlights still glowed in red fists. Across her floor she saw the muddy tracks of their boots.

"Yuh white folks git outta mah house!"

There was quick silence; every face turned toward her. She saw a sudden movement, but did not know what it meant until something hot and wet slammed her squarely in the face. She gasped, but did not move. Calmly, she wiped the warm greasy liquor of greens from her eyes with her left hand. One of the white men had thrown a handful of greens out of the pot at her.

"How they taste, ol bitch?"

"Ah ast yuh t git outta mah house!"

She saw the sheriff detach himself from the crowd and walk toward her.

"Now, Anty . . ."

"White man, don yuh *Anty* me!"

"Yuh ain got the right sperit!"

"Sperit hell! Yuh git these men outta mah house!"

"Yuh ack like yuh don like it!"

"Naw, Ah don like it, n yuh knows dam wall Ah don!"

"Whut yuh gonna do bout it?"

"Ahm tellin yuh t git outta mah house!"

"Gittin sassy?"

"Ef telling yuh t git outta mah house is sass, then Ahm sassy!"

Her words came in a tense whisper; but beyond, back of them, she was watching, thinking, judging the men.

"Listen, Anty," the sheriff's voice came soft and low. "Ahm here t hep yuh. How come yuh wanna ack this way?"

"Yuh ain never heped yo *own* sef since yuh been born," she flared. "How kin the likes of yuh hep me?"

One of the white men came forward and stood directly in front of her.

"Lissen, nigger woman, yuh talkin t *white* men!"

"Ah don care who Ahm talkin t!"

"Yuhll wish some day yuh did!"

"Not t the likes of yuh!"

"Yuh need somebody t teach yuh how t be a good nigger!"

"*Yuh* cant teach it t me!"

"Yuh gonna change yo tune."

"Not longs mah bloods warm!"

"Don git smart now!"

"Yuh git outta mah house!"

"Spose we don go?" the sheriff asked.

They were crowded around her. She had not moved since she had taken her place in the doorway. She was thinking only of Johnny-Boy as she stood there giving and taking words; and she knew that they, too, were thinking of Johnny-Boy. She knew they wanted him, and her heart was daring them to take him from her.

"Spose we don go?" the sheriff asked again.

"Twenty of yuh runnin over one ol woman! Now, ain yuh white men glad yuh so brave?"

The sheriff grabbed her arm.

"C mon, now! Yuh done did ernuff sass for one night. Wheres tha nigger son of yos?"

"Don yuh wished yuh knowed?"

"Yuh wanna git slapped?"

"Ah ain never seen one of yo kind tha wuznt too low fer . . ."

The sheriff slapped her straight across her face with his open palm. She fell back against a wall and sank to her knees.

"Is tha whut white men do t nigger women?"

She rose slowly and stood again, not even touching the place that ached from his blow, her hands folded over her stomach.

"Ah ain never seen one of yo kind tha wuznt too low fer . . ."

He slapped her again; she reeled backward several feet and fell on her side.

"Is tha whut we too low t do?"

She stood before him again, dry-eyed, as though she had not been struck. Her lips were numb and her chin was wet with blood.

"Aw, let her go! Its the nigger we wan!" said one.

"Wheres that nigger son of yos?" the sheriff asked.

"Find im," she said.

"By Gawd, ef we hafta find im we'll kill im!"

"He wont be the only nigger yuh ever killed," she said.

She was consumed with a bitter pride. There was nothing on this earth, she felt then, that they could not do to her but that she could take. She stood on a narrow plot of ground from which she would die before she was pushed. And then it was, while standing there feeling warm blood seeping down her throat, that she gave up Johnny-Boy, gave him up to the white folks. She gave him up because they had come tramping into her heart demanding him, thinking they could get him by beating her, thinking they could scare her into making her tell where he was. She gave him up because she wanted them to know that they could not get what they wanted by bluffing and killing.

"Wheres this meetin gonna be?" the sheriff asked.

"Don yuh wish yuh knowed?"

"Ain there gonna be a meetin?"

"How come yuh astin me?"

"There *is* gonna be a meeting," said the sheriff.

"Is it?"

"Ah gotta great mind t choke it outta yuh!"

"Yuh so smart," she said.

"We ain playin wid yuh!"

"Did Ah say yuh wuz?"

"Tha nigger son of yos is erroun here somewheres n we aim t find him," said the sheriff. "Ef yuh tell us where he is n ef he talks, mabbe he'll git off easy. But ef we hafta find im, we'll kill im! Ef we hafta find im, then yuh git a sheet t put over im in the mawnin, see? Gut yuh a sheet, cause hes gonna be dead!"

"He won't be the only nigger yuh ever killed," she said again.

The sheriff walked past her. The others followed. Yuh didn't git whut yuh wanted! she thought exultingly. N yuh ain gonna *never* git it! Hotly, something ached in her to make them feel the intensity of her pride and freedom; her heart groped to turn the

bitter hours of her life into words of a kind that would make them
feel that she had taken all they had done to her in her stride and
could still take more. Her faith surged so strongly in her she was
all but blinded. She walked behind them to the door, knotting and
twisting her fingers. She saw them step to the muddy ground.
Each whirl of the yellow beacon revealed glimpses of slanting rain.
Her lips moved, then she shouted:

"Yuh didnt git whut yuh wanted! N yuh ain gonna nevah git it!"

The sheriff stopped and turned; his voice came low and hard.

"Now, by Gawd, thas ernuff outta yuh!"

"Ah know when Ah done said ernuff!"

"Aw, naw, yuh don!" he said. "Yuh don know when yuh
done said ernuff, but Ahma teach yuh ternight!"

He was up the steps and across the porch with one bound. She
backed into the hall, her eyes full on his face.

"Tell me when yuh gonna stop talkin!" he said, swinging his fist.

The blow caught her high on the cheek; her eyes went blank;
she fell flat on her face. She felt the hard heel of his wet shoes coming
into her temple and stomach.

"Lemme hear yuh talk some mo!"

She wanted to, but could not; pain numbed and choked her.
She lay still and somewhere out of the grey void of unconsciousness
she heard someone say: *aw fer chrissakes leave her erlone its the*
nigger we wan. . . .

IV

She never knew how long she had lain huddled in the dark hallway. Her first returning feeling was of a nameless fear crowding the
inside of her, then a deep pain spreading from her temple downward over her body. Her ears were filled with the drone of rain and
she shuddered from the cold wind blowing through the door. She
opened her eyes and at first saw nothing. As if she were imagining
it, she knew she was half-lying and half-sitting in a corner against
a wall. With difficulty she twisted her neck and what she saw made
her hold her breath—a vast white blur was suspended directly above
her. For a moment she could not tell if her fear was from the blur
or if the blur was from her fear. Gradually the blur resolved itself
into a huge white face that slowly filled her vision. She was stone
still, conscious really of the effort to breathe, feeling somehow that
she existed only by the mercy of that white face. She had seen it
before; its fear had gripped her many times; it had for her the fear
of all the white faces she had ever seen in her life. *Sue* . . . As from

a great distance, she heard her name being called. She was regaining consciousness now, but the fear was coming with her. She looked into the face of a white man, wanting to scream out for him to go; yet accepting his presence because she felt she had to. Though some remote part of her mind was active, her limbs were powerless. It was as if an invisible knife had split her in two, leaving one half of her lying there helpless, while the other half shrank in dread from a forgotten but familiar enemy. *Sue its me Sue its me* . . . Then all at once the voice came clearly.

"Sue, its me! Its Booker!"

And she heard an answering voice speaking inside of her, Yeah, its Booker . . . The one whut jus joined . . . She roused herself, struggling for full consciousness; and as she did so she transferred to the person of Booker the nameless fear she felt. It seemed that Booker towered above her as a challenge to her right to exist upon the earth.

"Yuh awright?"

She did not answer; she started violently to her feet and fell.

"Sue, yuh hurt!"

"Yah," she breathed.

"Where they hit yuh?"

"Its mah head," she whispered.

She was speaking even though she did not want to; the fear that had hold of her compelled her.

"They beat yuh?"

"Yeah."

"Them bastards! Them Gawddam bastards!"

She heard him saying it over and over; then she felt herself being lifted.

"Naw!" she gasped.

"Ahma take yuh t the kitchen!"

"Put me down!"

"But yuh cant stay here like this!"

She shrank in his arms and pushed her hands against his body; when she was in the kitchen she freed herself, sank into a chair, and held tightly to its back. She looked wonderingly at Booker. There was nothing about him that should frighten her so, but even that did not ease her tension. She saw him go to the water bucket, wet his handkerchief, wring it, and offer it to her. Distrustfully, she stared at the damp cloth.

"Here; put this on yo forehead . . ."

"Naw!"

"C mon; itll make yuh feel bettah!"

She hesitated in confusion. What right had she to be afraid when someone was acting kindly as this toward her? Reluctantly, she leaned forward and pressed the damp cloth to her head. It helped. With each passing minute she was catching hold of herself, yet wondering why she felt as she did.

"What happened?"

"Ah don know."

"Yuh feel bettah?"

"Yeah."

"Who all wuz here?"

"Ah don know," she said again.

"Yo head still hurt?"

"Yeah."

"Gee, Ahm sorry."

"Ahm awright," she sighed and buried her face in her hands.

She felt him touch her shoulder.

"Sue, Ah got some bad news fer yuh . . ."

She knew; she stiffened and grew cold. It had happened; she stared dry-eyed, with compressed lips.

"Its mah Johnny-Boy," she said.

"Yeah; Ahm awful sorry t halfta tell yuh this way. But Ah thought yuh oughta know . . ."

Her tension eased and a vacant place opened up inside of her. A voice whispered, Jesus, hep me!

"W-w-where is he?"

"They got im out to Foleys Woods tryin t make im tell who the others is."

He ain gonna tell," she said. "They just as wall kill im, cause he ain gonna nevah tell."

"Ah hope he don," said Booker. "But he didnt hava chance t tell the others. They grabbed im jus as he got t the woods."

Then all the horror of it flashed upon her; she saw flung out over the rainy countryside an array of shacks where white and black comrades were sleeping; in the morning they would be rising and going to Lem's; then they would be caught. And that meant terror, prison, and death. The comrades would have to be told; she would have to tell them; she could not entrust Johnny-Boy's work to another, and especially not to Booker as long as she felt toward him as she did. Gripping the bottom of the chair with both hands, she tried to rise; the room blurred and she swayed. She found herself resting in Booker's arms.

"Lemme go!"

"Sue, yuh too weak t walk!"

"Ah gotta tell em!" she said

"Set down, Sue! Yuh hurt! Yuh sick!"

When seated, she looked at him helplessly.

"Sue, lissen! Johnny-Boys caught. Ahm here. Yuh tell me who they is n Ahll tell em."

She stared at the floor and did not answer. Yes; she was too weak to go. There was no way for her to tramp all those miles through the rain tonight. But should she tell Booker? If only she had somebody like Reva to talk to! She did not want to decide alone; she must make no mistake about this. She felt Booker's fingers pressing on her arm and it was as though the white mountain was pushing her to the edge of a sheer height; she again exclaimed inwardly, Jesus, hep me! Booker's white face was at her side, waiting. Would she be doing right to tell him? Suppose she did not tell and then the comrades were caught? She could not ever forgive herself for doing a thing like that. But maybe she was wrong; maybe her fear was what Johnny-Boy had always called "jus foolishness." She remembered his saying, Ma we can't make the party grow ef we start doubtin everbody. . . .

"Tell me who they is, Sue, n Ahll tell em. Ah jus joined n Ah don know who they is."

"Ah don know who they is," she said.

"Yuh *gotta* tell me who they is, Sue!"

"Ah told yuh Ah don know."

"Yuh *do* know! C mon! Set up n talk!"

"Naw!"

"Yuh wan em all t git *killed*?"

She shook her head and swallowed. Lawd, Ah don blieve in this man!

"Lissen, Ahll call the names n yuh tell me which ones is in the party n which ones ain, see?"

"Naw!"

"Please, Sue!"

"Ah don know," she said.

"Sue, yuh ain doin right by em. Johnny-Boy wouldn't wan yuh t be this way. Hes out there holdin up his end. Les hol up ours . . ."

"Lawd, Ah don know . . ."

"Is yuh scareda me cause Ahm *white*? Johnny-Boy ain like tha. Don let all the work we done go fer nothin."

She gave up and bowed her head in her hands.

"Is it Johnson? Tell me, Sue?"

"Yeah," she whispered in horror; a mounting horror of feeling herself being undone.

"Is it Green?"

"Yeah."

"Murphy?"

"Lawd, Ah don know!"

"Yuh gotta tell me, Sue!"

"Mistah Booker, please leave me erlone . . ."

"Is it Murphy?"

She answered yes to the names of Johnny-Boy's comrades; she answered until he asked her no more. Then she thought, How he know the sheriffs men is watchin Lems house? She stood up and held onto her chair, feeling something sure and firm within her.

"How yuh know about Lem?"

"Why . . . How Ah know?"

"Whut yuh doin here this tima night? How yuh know the sheriff got Johnny-Boy?"

"Sue, don yuh blieve in me?"

She did not, but she could not answer. She stared at him until her lips hung open; she was searching deep within herself for certainty.

"You meet Reva?" she asked.

"Reva?"

"Yeah; Lems gal?"

"Oh, yeah. Sho, Ah met Reva."

"She tell yuh?"

She asked the question more of herself than of him; she longed to believe.

"Yeah," he said softly. "Ah reckon Ah oughta be goin t tell em now."

"Who?" she asked. "Tell *who*?"

The muscles of her body were stiff as she waited for his answer; she felt as though life depended upon it.

"The comrades," he said.

"Yeah," she sighed.

She did not know when he left; she was not looking or listening. She just suddenly saw the room empty and from her the thing that had made her fearful was gone.

V

For a space of time that seemed to her as long as she had been upon the earth, she sat huddled over the cold stove. One minute she would say to herself, They both gone now; Johnny-Boy n Sug . . . Mabbe Ahll never see em ergin. Then a surge of guilt would blot out her longing. "Lawd, Ah shouldna tol!" she mumbled. "But no man kin be so lowdown as t do a thing like tha . . ." Several times she had an impulse to try to tell the comrades herself; she was feeling a little better now. But what good would that do? She had told Booker the names. He jus couldnt be a Judas t po folks like us . . . He *couldnt!*

"An Sue!"

Thas Reva! Her heart leaped with an anxious gladness. She rose without answering and limped down the dark hallway. Through the open door, against the background of rain, she saw Reva's face lit now and then to whiteness by the whirling beams of the beacon. She was about to call, but a thought checked her. Jesus, hep me! Ah gotta tell her bout Johnny-Boy . . . Lawd, Ah can't!

"An Sue, yuh there?"

"C mon in, chile!"

She caught Reva and held her close for a moment without speaking.

"Lawd, Ahm sho glad yuh here," she said at last.

"Ah thought somethin had happened t yuh," said Reva, pulling away. "Ah saw the do open . . . Pa told me to come back n stay wid yuh tonight . . ." Reva paused and started. "W-w-whuts the mattah?"

She was so full of having Reva with her that she did not understand what the question meant.

"Hunh?"

"Yo neck . . ."

"Aw, it ain nothin, chile. C mon in the kitchen."

"But theres blood on yo neck!"

"The sheriff wuz here . . ."

"Them fools! Whut they wanna bother yuh fer? Ah could kill em! So hep me Gawd, Ah could!"

"It ain nothin," she said.

She was wondering how to tell Reva about Johnny-Boy and Booker. Ahll wait a lil while longer, she thought. Now that Reva was here, her fear did not seem as awful as before.

"C mon, lemme fix yo head. An Sue. Yoh hurt."

They went to the kitchen. She sat silent while Reva dressed her scalp. She was feeling better now; in just a little while she would tell Reva. She felt the girl's finger pressing gently upon her head.

"Tha hurt?"

"A lil, chile."

"Yuh po thing!"

"It ain nothin."

"Did Johnny-Boy come?"

She hesitated.

"Yeah."

"He done gone t tell the others?"

Reva's voice sounded so clear and confident that it mocked her. Lawd, Ah cant tell this chile . . .

"Yuh told im, didn't yuh, An Sue?"

"Y-y-yeah . . ."

"Gee! Thas good! Ah told pa he didnt hafta worry ef Johnny-Boy got the news. Mabbe thingsll come out awright."

"Ah hope . . ."

She could not go on; she had gone as far as she could. For the first time that night she began to cry.

"Hush, An Sue! Yuh awways been brave. Itll be awwright!"

"Ain nothin awwright, chile. The worls jus too much fer us. Ah reckon."

"Ef you cry that way itll make me cry."

She forced herself to stop. Naw; Ah cant carry on tha way in fronta Reva . . . Right now she had a deep need for Reva to believe in her. She watched the girl get pine-knots from behind the stove, rekindle the fire, and put on the coffee pot.

"Yuh wan some cawffee?" Reva asked.

"Naw, honey."

"Aw, c mon, An Sue."

"Jusa lil, honey."

"Thas the way to be. Oh, say, Ah fergot," said Reva, measuring out spoonsful of coffee. "Pa told me t tell yuh t watch out fer tha Booker man. Hes a stool."

She showed not one sign of outward movement or expression, but as the words fell from Reva's lips she went limp inside.

"Pa tol me soon as Ah got back home. He got word from town . . ."

She stopped listening. She felt as though she had been slapped to the extreme outer edge of life, into a cold darkness. She knew now what she had felt when she had looked up out of her fog of pain and had seen Booker. It was the image of all the white folks, and the fear that went with them, that she had seen and felt during her lifetime. And again, for the second time that night, something she had felt had come true. All she could say to herself was, Ah didnt like im! Gawd knows, Ah didn't! Ah told Johnny-Boy it wuz some of them white folks . . .

"Here; drink yo cawffee . . ."

She took the cup; her fingers trembled, and the steaming liquid spilt onto her dress and leg.

"Ahm sorry, An Sue!"

Her leg was scalded, but the pain did not bother her.

"Its awright," she said.

"Wait; lemme put some lard on tha burn!"

"It don hurt."

"Yuh worried bout somethin."

"Naw, honey."

"Lemme fix yuh so mo cawffee."

"Ah don wan nothin now, Reva."

"Waal, buck up. Don be tha way . . .

They were silent. She heard Reva drinking. No; she would not tell Reva; Reva was all she had left. But she had to do something, some way, somehow. She was undone too much as it was; and to tell Reva about Booker or Johnny-Boy was more than she was equal to; it would be too coldly shameful. She wanted to be alone and fight this thing out with herself.

"Go t bed, honey. Yuh tired."

"Naw; Ahm awright, An Sue."

She heard the bottom of Reva's empty cup clank against the top of the stove. Ah *got* t make her go t bed! Yes; Booker would tell the names of the comrades to the sheriff. If she could only stop him some way! That was the answer, the point, the star that grew bright in the morning of new hope. Soon, maybe half an hour from now, Booker would reach Foleys Woods. Hes boun t go the long way, cause he don know no short cut, she thought. Ah could wade the creek n beat im there. : . . But what would she do after that?

"Reva, honey, go t bed. Ahm awright. Yuh need res."

"Ah ain sleepy, An Sue!"

"Ah knows whuts bes fer yuh, chile. Yuh tired n wet."

"A wanna stay up wid yuh."

She forced a smile and said:

"Ah don think they gonna hurt Johnny-Boy . . ."

"Fer *real*, An Sue?"

"Sho, honey."

"But Ah wanna wait up wid yuh."

"Thas mah job, honey. Thas whut a mas fer, t wait up fer her chullun."

"Good night, An Sue."

"Good night, honey."

She watched Reva pull up and leave the kitchen; presently she heard the shucks in the mattress whispering, and she knew that Reva had gone to bed. She was alone. Through the cracks of the stove she saw the fire dying to grey ashes; the room was growing cold again. The yellow beacon continued to flit past the window and the rain still drummed. Yes; she was alone; she had done this awful thing alone; she must find some way out, alone. Like touching a festering sore, she put her finger upon that moment when she had shouted her defiance to the sheriff, when she had shouted to feel her strength. She had lost Sug to save others; she had let Johnny-Boy go to save others; and then in a moment of weakness that came from too much strength she had lost all. If she had not shouted to the sheriff, she would have been strong enough to have resisted Booker; she would have been able to tell the comrades herself. Something tightened in her as she remembered and understood the fit of fear she had felt on coming to herself in the dark hallway. A part of her life she thought she had done away with forever had had hold of her then. She had thought the soft, warm past was over; she had thought that it did not mean much when now she sang: *"Hes the Lily of the Valley, the Bright n Mawnin Star . . ."* The days when she had sung that song were the days when she had not hoped for anything on this earth, the days when the cold mountain had driven her into the arms of Jesus. She had thought that Sug and Johnny-Boy had taught her to forget Him, to fix her hope upon the fight of black men for freedom. Through the gradual years she had believed and worked with them, had felt strength shed from the grace of their terrible vision. That grace had been upon her when she had let the sheriff slap her down; it had been upon her when she had risen time and again from the floor and faced him. But she had trapped herself with her own hunger; to water the long dry thirst of her faith her pride had made a bargain which her flesh could not keep. Her having told the names of Johnny-Boy's comrades was but an incident in a deeper horror. She stood up and looked at the floor while call and counter-call, loyalty and counter-loyalty struggled in her soul. Mired she was between two abandoned worlds, living, but dying without the strength of the grace that either gave.

The clearer she felt it the fuller did something well up from the depths of her for release; the more urgent did she feel the need to fling into her black sky another star, another hope, one more terrible vision to give her the strength to live and act. Softly and restlessly she walked about the kitchen, feeling herself naked against the night, the rain, the world; and shamed whenever the thought of Reva's love crossed her mind. She lifted her empty hands and looked at her writhing fingers. Lawd, whut kin Ah do now? She could still wade the creek and get to Foley's Woods before Booker. And then what? How could she manage to see Johnny-Boy or Booker? Again she heard the sheriff's threatening voice: Git yuh a sheet, cause hes gonna be dead! The sheet! Thas it, the *sheet!* Her whole being leaped with will; the long years of her life bent toward a moment of focus, a point. Ah kin go wid mah sheet! Ahll be doin whut he said! Lawd Gawd in Heaven, Ahma go lika nigger woman wid mah windin sheet t git mah dead son! But then what? She stood straight and smiled grimly; she had in her heart the whole meaning of her life; her entire personality was poised on the brink of a total act. Ah know! Ah *know!* She thought of Johnny-Boy's gun in the dresser drawer. Ahll hide the gun in the sheet n go aftah Johnny-Boy's body. . . . She tiptoed to her room, eased out the dresser drawer, and got a sheet. Reva was sleeping; the darkness was filled with her quiet breathing. She groped in the drawer and found the gun. She wound the gun in the sheet and held them both under her apron. Then she stole to the bedside and watched Reva. Lawd, hep her! But mabbe shes bettah off. This had t happen sometimes . . . She n Johnny-Boy couldna been together in this here South . . . N Ah couldn't tell her bout Booker. Itll come out awright n she wont nevah know. Reva's trust would never be shaken. She caught her breath as the shucks in the mattress rustled dryly; then all was quiet and she breathed easily again. She tiptoed to the door, down the hall, and stood on the porch. Above her the yellow beacon whirled through the rain. She went over muddy ground, mounted a slope, stopped and looked back at her house. The lamp glowed in her window, and the yellow beacon that swung every few seconds seemed to feed it with light. She turned and started across the fields, holding the gun and sheet tightly, thinking, Po Reva . . . Po critter . . . Shes fas ersleep . . .

VI

For the most part she walked with her eyes half shut, her lips tightly compressed, leaning her body against the wind and the driving rain, feeling the pistol in the sheet sagging cold and heavy in her fingers. Already she was getting wet; it seemed that her feet found every puddle of water that stood between the corn rows.

She came to the edge of the creek and paused, wondering at what point was it low. Taking the sheet from under her apron, she wrapped the gun in it so that her finger could be upon the trigger. Ahll cross here, she thought. At first she did not feel the water; her feet were already wet. But the water grew cold as it came up to her knees; she gasped when it reached her waist. Lawd, this creeks high! When she had passed the middle, she knew that she was out of danger. She came out of the water, climbed a grassy hill, walked on, turned a bend and saw the lights of autos gleaming ahead. Yeah; theys still there! She hurried with her head down. Wonda did Ah beat im here? Lawd, Ah *hope* so! A vivid image of Booker's white face hovered a moment before her eyes and a surging will rose up in her so hard and strong that it vanished. She was among the autos now. From nearby came the hoarse voices of the men.

"Hey, yuh!"

She stopped, nervously clutching the sheet. Two white men with shotguns came toward her.

"Whut in hell yuh doin out here?"

She did not answer.

"Didn't yuh hear somebody speak t yuh?"

"Ahm comin aftah mah son," she said humbly.

"Yo *son*?"

"Yessuh."

"Whut yo son doin out here?"

"The sheriff's got im."

"Holy Scott! Jim, its the niggers ma!"

"What yuh got there?" asked one.

"A sheet."

"A *sheet*?"

"Yessuh."

"Fer whut?"

"The sheriff tol me t bring a sheet t git his body."

"Waal, waal . . ."

"Now, ain tha somethin?"

The white men looked at each other.

"These niggers sho love one ernother," said one.

"N tha ain no lie," said the other.

"Take me t the sheriff," she begged.

"Yuh ain givin us *orders*, is yuh?"

"Nawsuh."

"We'll take yuh when wes good n ready."

"Yessuh."

"So yuh wan his body?"

"Yessuh."

"Waal, he ain dead yit."

"They gonna kill im," she said.

"Ef he talks they wont."

"He ain gonna talk," she said.

"How yuh know?"

"Cause he ain."

"We got ways of makin niggers talk."

"Yuh ain got no way fer im."

"You thinka lot of that black Red, don yuh?"

"Hes mah son."

"Why don yuh teach im some sense?"

"Hes mah son," she said again.

"Lissen, ol nigger woman, yuh stand there wid yo hair white. Yuh got bettah sense than t blieve tha niggers kin make a revolution . . ."

"A black republic," said the other one, laughing.

"Take me t the sheriff," she begged.

"Yuh his ma," said one. "Yuh kin make im talk n tell whos in this thing wid im."

"He ain gonna talk," she said.

"Don yuh wan im t live?"

She did not answer.

"C mon, les take her t Bradley."

They grabbed her arms and she clutched hard at the sheet and gun; they led her toward the crowd in the woods. Her feelings were simple; Booker would not tell; she was there with the gun to see to that. The louder became the voices of the men the deeper became her feeling of wanting to right the mistake she had made; of wanting to fight her way back to solid ground. She would stall for time until Booker showed up. Oh, ef theyll only lemme git close t Johnny-Boy! As they led her near the crowd she saw white faces turning and looking at her and heard a rising clamor of voices.

"Whos tha?"

"A nigger woman!"

"Whut she doin out here?"

"This is his ma!" called one of the men.

"Whut she want?"

"She brought a sheet t cover his body!"

"He ain dead yit!"

"They tryin t make im talk!"

"But he will be dead soon ef he don open up!"

"Say, look! The niggers ma brought a sheet t cover up his body!"

"Now, ain tha sweet?"

"Mabbe she wans t hol a prayer meetin!"

"Did she git a preacher?"

"Say, go git Bradley!"

"O.K.!"

The crowd grew quiet. They looked at her curiously; she felt their cold eyes trying to detect some weakness in her. Humbly, she stood with the sheet covering the gun. She had already accepted all that they could do to her.

The sheriff came.

"So yuh brought yo sheet, hunh?"

"Yessuh," she whispered.

"Looks like them slaps we gave yuh learned yuh some sense, didnt they?"

She did not answer.

"Yuh don need tha sheet. Yo son ain dead yit," he said, reaching toward her.

She backed away, her eyes wide.

"Naw!"

"Now, lissen, Anty!" he said. "There ain no use in yuh ackin a fool! Go in there n tell tha nigger son of yos t tell us whos in this wid im, see? Ah promise we wont kill im ef he talks. We'll let him git outta town."

"There ain nothin Ah kin tell im," she said.

"Yuh wan us t kill im?"

She did not answer. She saw someone lean toward the sheriff and whisper.

"Bring her erlong," the sheriff said.

They led her to a muddy clearing. The rain streamed down through the ghostly glare of the flashlights. As the men formed a semi-circle she saw Johnny-Boy lying in a trough of mud. He was tied with rope; he lay hunched and one side of his face rested in a pool of black water. His eyes were staring questioningly at her.

"Speak t im," said the sheriff.

If she could only tell him why she was here! But that was impossible; she was close to what she wanted and she stared straight before her with compressed lips.

"Say, nigger!" called the sheriff, kicking Johnny-Boy. "Here's yo ma!"

Johnny-Boy did not move or speak. The sheriff faced her again.

"Lissen, Anty," he said. "Yuh got mo say wid im than anybody. Tell im t talk n hava chance. Whut he wanna pertect the other niggers n white folks fer?"

She slid her finger about the trigger of the gun and looked stonily at the mud.

"Go t him," said the sheriff.

She did not move. Her heart was crying out to answer the amazed question in Johnny-Boy's eyes. But there was no way now.

"Wall, yuhre astin fer it. By Gawd, we gotta way to *make* yuh talk t im," he said, turning away. "Say, Tim, git one of them logs n turn that nigger upside-down n put his legs on it!"

A murmur of assent ran through the crowd. She bit her lips; she knew what that meant.

"Yuh wan yo nigger son crippled?" she heard the sheriff ask.

She did not answer. She saw them roll the log up; they lifted Johnny-Boy and laid him on his face and stomach, then they pulled his legs over the log. His knee-caps rested on the sheer top of the log's back and the toes of his shoes pointed groundward. So absorbed was she in watching that she felt that it was she who was being lifted and made ready for torture.

"Git a crowbar!" said the sheriff.

A tall, lank man got a crowbar from a nearby auto and stood over the log. His jaws worked slowly on a wad of tobacco.

"Now, its up t yuh Anty," the sheriff said. "Tell the man what t do!"

She looked into the rain. The sheriff turned.

"Mabbe she think wes playin. Ef she don say nothin, then break em at the knee-caps!"

"O.K., Sheriff!"

She stood waiting for Booker. Her legs felt weak; she wondered if she would be able to wait much longer. Over and over she said to herself, Ef he come now Ahd kill em both!

"She ain saying nothin, Sheriff!"

"Waal, Gawddammit, let im have it!"

The crowbar came down and Johnny-Boy's body lunged in the mud and water. There was a scream. She swayed, holding tight to the gun and sheet.

"Hol im! Git the other leg!"

The crowbar fell again. There was another scream.

"Yuh break em?" asked the sheriff.

The tall man lifted Johnny-Boy's legs and let them drop limply again, dropping rearward from the kneecaps. Johnny-Boy's body lay still. His head had rolled to one side and she could not see his face.

"Jus lika broke sparrow wing," said the man, laughing softly.

Then Johnny-Boy's face turned to her; he screamed.

"Go way, ma! Go way!"

It was the first time she had heard his voice since she had come out to the woods; she all but lost control of herself. She started violently forward, but the sheriff's arm checked her.

"Aw naw! Yuh had yo chance!" He turned to Johnny-Boy. "She kin go ef yuh talk."

"Mistah, he ain gonna talk," she said.

"Go way, ma!" said Johnny-Boy.

"Shoot im! Don make im suffah so," she begged.

"He'll either talk or he'll never hear yuh ergin," the sheriff said. "Theres other things we kin do t im."

She said nothing.

"What yuh come here fer, ma?" Johnny-Boy sobbed.

"Ahm gonna split his eardrums," the sheriff said. "Ef yuh got anythin t say t im yuh bettah say it *now!*"

She closed her eyes. She heard the sheriff's feet sucking in mud. Ah could save im! She opened her eyes; there were shouts of eagerness from the crowd as it pushed in closer.

"Bus em, Sheriff!"

"Fix im so he can't hear!"

"He knows how t do it, too!"

"He busted a Jew boy tha way once!"

She saw the sheriff stoop over Johnny-Boy, place his flat palm over one ear and strike his fist against it with all his might. He placed his palm over the other ear and struck again. Johnny-Boy moaned, his head rolling from side to side, his eyes showing white amazement in a world without sound.

"Yuh wouldn't talk t im when yuh had the chance," said the sheriff. "Try n talk now."

She felt warm tears on her cheeks. She longed to shoot Johnny-Boy and let him go. But if she did that they would take the gun from her, and Booker would tell who the others were. Lawd, hep me! The men were talking loudly now, as though the main business was over. It seemed ages that she stood there watching Johnny-Boy roll and whimper in his world of silence.

"Say, Sheriff, heres somebody lookin fer yuh!"

"Who is it?"

"Ah don know!"

"Bring em in!"

She stiffened and looked around wildly, holding the gun tight. Is tha Booker? Then she held still, feeling that her excitement might betray her. Mabbe Ah kin shoot em both; Mabbe Ah kin shoot *twice!* The sheriff stood in front of her, waiting. The crowd parted and she saw Booker hurrying forward.

"Ah know em all, Sheriff!" he called.

He came full into the muddy clearing where Johnny-Boy lay.

"Yuh mean yuh got the names?"

"Sho! The ol nigger . . ."

She saw his lips hang open and silent when he saw her. She stepped forward and raised the sheet.

"Whut . . ."

She fired, once; then, without pausing, she turned, hearing them yell. She aimed at Johnny-Boy, but they had their arms around her, bearing her to the ground, clawing at the sheet in her hand. She glimpsed Booker lying sprawled in the mud, on his face, his hands stretched out before him; then a cluster of yelling men blotted him out. She lay without struggling, looking upward through the rain at the white faces above her. And she was suddenly at peace; they were not a white mountain now; they were not pushing her any longer to the edge of life. Its awright . . .

"She shot Booker!"

"She hada gun in the sheet!"

"She shot im right thu the head!"

"Whut she shoot im fer?"

"Kill the bitch!"

"Ah *thought* somethin wuz wrong bout her!"

"Ah wuz fer givin it t her from the firs!"

"Thas whut yuh git fer treatin a nigger nice!"

"Say, Bookers dead!"

She stopped looking into the white faces, stopped listening. She waited, giving up her life before they took it from her; she had done what she wanted. Ef only Johnny-Boy . . . She looked at him, he lay looking at her with tired eyes. Ef she could only tell im! But he lay already buried in a grave of silence.

"Whut yuh kill im fer, hunh?"

It was the sheriff's voice; she did not answer.

"Mabbe she wuz shootin at yuh, Sheriff?"

"Whut yuh kill im fer?"

She felt the sheriff's foot come into her side; she closed her eyes.

"Yuh black bitch!"

"Let her have it!"

"Yuh reckon she foun out bout Booker?"

"She mighta."

"Jesus Chris, whut yuh dummies *waitin* on!"

"Yeah; kill her!"

"Kill em *both*!"

"Let her know her nigger sons dead firs!"

She turned her head toward Johnny-Boy; he lay looking puzzled in a world beyond the reach of voices. At leas he can't hear, she thought.

"C mon, let im have it!"

She listened to hear what Johnny-Boy could not. They came, two of them, one right behind the other; so close together that they sounded like one shot. She did not look at Johnny-Boy now; she looked at the white faces of the men, hard and wet in the glare of the flashlights.

"Yuh hear tha, nigger woman?"

"Did tha surprise im? Hes in hell now wonderin whut hit im!"

"C mon! Give it t her, Sheriff!"

"Lemme shoot her, Sheriff! It wuz mah pal she shot!"

"Awright, Pete! Thas fair ernuff!"

She gave up as much of her life as she could before they took it from her. But the sound of the shot and the streak of fire that tore its way through her chest forced her to live again, intensely. She had not moved, save for the slight jarring impact of the bullet. She felt the heat of her own blood warming her cold, wet back. She yearned suddenly to talk. "Yuh didn't git whut yuh wanted! N yuh ain gonna nevah git it! Yuh didn't kill me; Ah come here by mahsef . . ." She felt rain falling into her wide-open, dimming eyes and heard faint voices. Her lips moved soundlessly. *Yuh didnt git yuh didnt yuh didnt* . . . Focused and pointed she was, buried in the depths of her star, swallowed in its peace and strength; and not feeling her flesh growing cold, cold as the rain that fell from the invisible sky upon the doomed living and the dead that never dies.

II
NOVELS (SELECTIONS)

THE NOVEL

THE earliest Negro novelists, wrote to plead a cause, and their successors have almost always followed their example. When the antislavery agents, William Wells Brown and Martin Delany, tried their hands at the novel, they found a technique ready-made—that of the propaganda novel of Dickens, Mrs. Gaskell, and Mrs. Stowe. The phenomenal success of *Uncle Tom's Cabin,* pleading their own burning cause, must have prompted their fiction.

But unlike the nineteenth-century reform novelists who were professionals, practising their craft over many years in many books, Brown and Delany squeezed novel writing into careers crowded with antislavery work, remote from the literary world. It is not surprising that their only two ventures, are immature, structurally imperfect, and sentimental. Both had good tales to tell, but they just did not learn, and probably could not find time to learn how to write novels. Their weakness was not that they wrote propaganda, but that they wrote propaganda badly.

Brown's *Clotel, or The President's Daughter,* the first novel by an American Negro, was published in London in 1853. *Clotel* was franker than *Uncle Tom's Cabin* in showing the widespread miscegenation in the old South (a subject of considerable interest to Brown). Even before the antislavery controversy, Thomas Jefferson had been attacked by his enemies as the father of children by slave women, and similar charges against other presidents featured antislavery polemics. In its American edition, however, renamed *Clotel: A Tale of the Southern States* (1864), President Jefferson was replaced by an American Senator. The first title of the novel led one to expect more scandal than really appears; it is Clotel's grandmother who was the "president's daughter," Clotel's father being a Virginia congressman. Woes are heaped upon the luckless heroines, who are in the worst "blood and tears" tradition, but Clotel survives to be an Angel of Mercy in the Civil War hospitals. Brown tried to tumble all sorts of incidents derived from his old knowledge of slavery and his new acquaintance with books into a small volume, with the results that many scenes are tantalizingly undeveloped. Though bits of racy realism show good observation and a knack for rendering scenes, *Clotel* is important only historically.

Martin Delany's *Blake, or the Huts of America* (1859), the second novel by a Negro, is dismissed by Vernon Loggins as puerile. The charge seems excessive. The fragments that have come down to us are weak in structure and unconvincing in situation and dialect. The central character, a stereotyped "noble savage," is too articulate, farseeing, and lucky in his unhampered extensive wanderings through the South organizing the slaves for a future uprising. Nevertheless the novel has its value. It is inaccurate to term it an analogue of *Uncle Tom's Cabin,* for it varies greatly, being much more concerned with the slaves than with white characters, and stressing the spirit of discontent and revolt in even the ordinary fieldhand. The novel quickly leaves the conventional story of the separation of a slave husband and wife and goes on to a sort of picaresque plot so that interesting and significant characters and activities can be presented. In spite of the lumbering style and strained dialect, *Blake* contains some pictures of slavery more convincing than anything in *Uncle Tom's Cabin* or *Clotel.* The final installment in the truncated form of the novel that we possess tells how the rashness of a drunken Negro windbag leads to the discovery of a plot for an uprising in New Orleans. This episode is more than the work of a propagandist; it is the work of a novelist who knows how to bring off a dramatic scene.

It was a long time before the third novel by an American Negro was published in America. This was Frances Harper's *Iola Leroy, or Shadows Uplifted* (1892). In his introduction, William Still characterized the book better than he knew:

> Doubtless the thousands of colored Sunday schools in the South, in casting about for an interesting, moral storybook, full of practical lessons, will not be content to be without *Iola Leroy.*

Mrs. Harper stated that her story's "mission would not be in vain if it awaken in the hearts of our countrymen a stronger sense of justice and a more Christlike humanity . . ." *Iola Leroy* is full of "ennobling sentiments"; it is as dull as it is pious. There are repetitions of situations from Brown's *Clotel,* something of a forecast of a sort of literary inbreeding which causes Negro writers to be influenced by other Negroes more than should ordinarily be expected. Iola is young, modest, refined, beautiful. The daughter of a white father and a quadroon mother, she was kept ignorant of her colored blood and educated as white. When the father dies suddenly, some of his relatives sell her into slavery. The Civil War breaks out providentially, and Iola serves as a nurse to the troops. After the war she is honorably wooed by white men, but she finally marries a young Negro doctor thus described: "The blood of a proud aristocratic ancestry was flowing through his veins, and generations of blood admixture had effaced all trace of his negro lineage."

Dunbar's four novels are not so inept as *Iola Leroy*, but they are still conventional and weak. *The Uncalled* (1898), the story of the conflict in a young white man's mind over whether he should enter the ministry or not; *The Love of Landry* (1900), a sentimental story of life in Colorado; *The Fanatics* (1901), a romance of the Civil War as it affected the whites in a small Ohio town, are all curiously unrelated to Negro life. Dunbar took too seriously his own ill-considered statement: "We must write like the white man. I do not mean imitate them; but our life is now the same." What resulted was a curious "racelessness" of his characters. *The Sport of the Gods* (1904) shows Dunbar turning to the problems of an uprooted Southern family in New York. In spite of a plot overridden with coincidences, this last novel gives a cross section of life that bears witness to more social awareness and more bitterness than any other of his works. The promise of this novel was checked by Dunbar's early death.

Charles W. Chesnutt, according to Joel E. Spingarn,

> is a true pioneer, but we should be underestimating his achievement if we thought of it merely in terms of its subject matter or material . . . What is important is not that Mr. Chesnutt was the first to discover or deal with the material, but that he was the first to give it life.

The House Behind the Cedars (1900) is concerned with the border line of color, which Chesnutt handled more fully than any other Negro writer. The situation is predictable: an idealized octoroon is loved by a white aristocrat who is ignorant of her racial identity. After the discovery she dies a pathetic death. Her only loyal lover is a Negro. Brown's octoroon, Clotel, after dishonorable proposals from whites, had married a white Frenchman, upon whose death she married a heroic black man; Mrs. Harper's octoroon, Iola, turned down dishonorable and honorable proposals from whites to marry in her own race. *The House Behind the Cedars* is a better novel than its predecessors, however, containing sidelights on social conditions that reveal an informed, close observer. *The Marrow of Tradition* (1901), Chesnutt's best novel, goes much deeper in social analysis. The Wilmington, North Carolina, race riot is the climax of the book, but the train of events leading up to it is laid with the realism that was entering the problem novel. *The Colonel's Dream* (1906) dramatizes the conflict in the South between deep-grooved prejudice and idealistic reform. There was little in Chesnutt's time to make him optimistic, and the conflict is resolved with tragic irony. Chesnutt used melodramatic devices and occasionally stilted language, in the manner of the fiction of his time. But there is no gainsaying his insight into the social realities of the South, nor his ability to tell a gripping story.

Chesnutt wrote no novels in the last decades of his life. Only a few novels were published by Negroes in the first years of the century. Sutton Grigg's *Unfettered* (1902) and *The Hindered Hand* (1905) are answers to books like Thomas Dixon's vilifying *The Leopard's Spots* (see p. 884). Beautiful heroines, "the very essence of loveliness," and noble heroes, "ebonylike Apollos," are models of decorum. Long dissertations on the race problem, and unconvincing, melodramatic treatments of violence to the Negro make the books more tracts than novels. J. W. Grant's *Out of the Darkness* (1909) and Robert L. Waring's *As We See It* (1910) are slightly better.

Because of his undeniable grasp of social problems and his militancy, W. E. B. DuBois was far closer to Chesnutt than these others, but he was inferior to Chesnutt as a novelist. *The Quest of the Silver Fleece* (1911) is part keen analysis of the politics, economics, and education of the postwar South, and part allegory. This fusion, not always successfully achieved, is in DuBois's second novel, *The Dark Princess* (1928), which is part fantasy, urging a union of the darker races of the world, and part mordant criticism of both America's treatment of the Negro and the Negro's own weaknesses.

Even James Weldon Johnson's *Autobiography of an Ex-Colored Man* (1912) is a purpose novel. The propaganda is more insinuated than direct, however, and the start that Dunbar's *The Sport of the Gods* made toward the showing of various strata in Negro life away from plantation log cabins is continued here with notable additions. This novel is definitely a forerunner: Southern rural life seen in its own terms, the Bohemian life of Negroes in New York, and the problem of "passing" are done with quiet realism. But the style is more that of the essay than of fiction, and the "problem" comes in for long discussion. A very popular novel among Negroes, first published in 1917 but brought up to date only this year (1941), is J. A. Roger's *From "Superman" to Man,* which is a compendium of anthropological and sociological information strung on a mere thread of narrative.

The early Negro novelists seemed to look upon lynchings as necessities for their novels, but they often succeeded only in getting an effect of stagey villainy and not ghastly terror. Far more cogent was Walter White's *Fire in the Flint* (1925), a swiftly paced novel by a man who probably knows more actual details of the rope and faggot mobs than any other American (see p. 1005). *Fire in the Flint* is more than a lynching novel, however; it is the first novel after Chesnutt's to show the lives of ambitious, moderately successful Negroes in the South. White's *Flight* (1928) is also something of a pioneering book, giving inside views of "passing." There have been numerous novels about this romantic subject, but *Flight* probably remains the best.

The years between 1924 and the present have been the most productive of novels by Negroes. A few novelists and many readers agreed with James Weldon Johnson's hero in *The Autobiography of an Ex-Colored Man* that American literature had too little about "colored people who live in respectable homes and amidst a fair degree of culture." Jessie Fauset, writing about what she knew best, turned to this type of character in *There Is Confusion* (1924). Wearying of caricature and underestimation, Miss Fauset performed pioneering service in attempting to describe the Negro middle class. But realism yielded to idealizing, with a heavy dash of argumentation. In her last three novels, Miss Fauset has made the phenomenon of "passing" more important and spectacular than it really is in middle-class Negro life. *Comedy, American Style* (1933), however, has power in its revelation of the tragedy that can be caused by color prejudice within the race itself. Nella Larsen's *Quicksand* (1928) and *Passing* (1930) are concerned with upper-class Negro life, and again "passing" has an undue importance, though it is rendered with some technical dexterity.

During the New Negro movement, many young artists stepped free from the "problem," or rendered it implicitly rather than explicitly. That is, they tried to be novelists rather than lecturers. Claude McKay in his unabashedly naturalistic *Home to Harlem* (1928) has a sort of ribald poetry, rooted in the setting of Harlem speak-easies and buffet flats, and railroad dining cars. This picaresque strain is continued in *Banjo* (1929), a tale of beachcombers in Marseilles, which nevertheless shows McKay yielding to the lecturer's impulse. *Banana Bottom* (1931), a pastoral though realistic picture of McKay's native Jamaica, has memorable characters and scenes. McKay insists rightly that he created his characters "without sandpaper or varnish." Many of them are definitely alive and vigorous.

Rudolph Fisher is the first Negro to write social comedy. *The Walls of Jericho* (1928) is bright with the wisecracking "jiving" of Harlem, and with satire that is highly intelligent, though at times it edges into caricature. It gives more of the reality of Harlem, however, than many more pretentious books. *The Conjure Man Dies* (1932) is the first Negro venture into the detective story. Countee Cullen's *One Way to Heaven* (1932) reveals a comic and satiric gift that readers of the author's lyrics could hardly have expected.

The Menckenite influence of the period found George Schuyler the most apt disciple. *Black No More* (1931) joined pungent satire and farce in its story of a scientific discovery that turned Negroes white. Schuyler is merciless with professional race-men of both races who gain money and prestige from race agitation. Schuyler "spoofed" the demagoguery but not real efforts at race advance, which he has himself energetically seconded. *Black No More* was a refreshing start at satiric racial self-criticism, but the author has confined his later work mainly to journalism. Wallace Thurman was a caustic satirist, lampooning intraracial color snobbishness in *The Blacker the Berry* (1929), and debunking some of the exaggerations of the New Negro movement in *Infants of the Spring* (1932). This novel, in the tradition of Carl Van Vechten's *Nigger Heaven,* deals with an uprooted intelligentsia who desperately wanted to be the Negro counterpart of Hemingway's "Lost Generation." Thurman was a clear-eyed observer, but a careless novelist.

Negro life in the South did not attract many of the novelists of the twenties, who preferred the Mecca of Harlem. A poetic novel, dealing with boyhood in what was close to a folk setting, was Langston Hughes's *Not Without Laughter* (1930). Life in a small Kansas town, a transplanted bit out of the South, is sympathetically presented. *Ollie Miss* (1935) by George Wylie Henderson, somewhat in the tradition of Julia Peterkin's *Scarlet Sister Mary,* nevertheless has faithful realism in its portrait of life close to the soil. George Lee's *River George* (1936) is one of the first novels to deal with the inequities of sharecropping. The educated hero, returning to his people to help them out of their ruts, runs into concerted opposition, and takes to outlawry. Not always convincing, *River George* still has passages of power and insight into the psychology of the cotton belt.

Zora Neale Hurston has written more fully than any other Negro of Southern rural life. She has made good use of her knowledge of Negro folkways and speech in *Jonah's Gourd Vine* (1934) and *Their Eyes Were Watching God* (1937), both novels laid in her native Florida, generally in self-contained all-Negro communities. Sympathy and authenticity mark her work.

Sporting life at the turn of the century is revealed in Arna Bontemps' *God Sends Sunday* (1931), a winning story about the ups-and-downs of Little Augie the jockey. A more serious re-creation of history is Bontemps' *Black Thunder* (1936), which tells of Gabriel's abortive insurrection in the Virginia of 1800. The novel is a poetic rendering of a dramatic episode in American history, a type of novel attempted so far only in the less successful *Princess Malah* (1933) by John Hill and *Fugitives of the Pearl* by John E. Paynter, a fictionalized version of his historical essay on the runaways. The only novel that deals with the Negro soldier in the first World War is Victor Daly's *Not Only War* (1932), a novel of protest against prejudice more than a portrait of army life in the trenches or behind the lines.

Recent fiction by Negroes is in the tradition of social realism. Waters E. Turpin's *These Low Grounds* (1937) carries a family's history from slavery to the present, with revealing documentation of Negro life on the Eastern Shore of Maryland. *O Canaan!* (1939) traces the rise and fall of a Negro family and its fellow migrants from Mississippi to Chicago during the World War. It deals with the rackets that developed during prohibition, only to be broken up by criminal syndicates. Details of the South Side social scene are in a measure complementary to Farrell's *Studs Lonigan* trilogy.

Richard Wright's highly successful *Native Son* (1940), the most widely read and discussed novel by a Negro, is the best example of the new social realism. Written with great craftsmanship, courage, and insight, *Native Son* pleads a burning cause. More powerful than any other protest literature, this novel shows the vicious influences on personality of a frustrating ghettolike environment. It has the narrative drive of a sensational murder thriller, but Wright's analysis of the social forces that make Bigger Thomas is far more important.

William Attaway's *Let Me Breathe Thunder* (1939) is a capable novel in the Steinbeck tradition, dealing with white vagabonds; his *Blood on the Forge,* published this year (1941), is a ground-breaking novel in its dealing with the Negro worker in the steel mills. Attaway is an addition to the school of American social realists, and his future will bear watching.

With the work of these later writers, as various as their purposes and techniques may be, fiction by Negroes may be said to have come of age. The literary inbreeding that caused too many Negro novelists to repeat the stock characters and situations is disappearing. The awareness of and apprenticeship to the masters of the craft of fiction, American, English, or Continental European; the increasing contact with white writers of good will toward Negro fellow-craftsmen; the recognition that dramatic presentation can convey ideas and protest better than lecturing; the frank recognition of weaknesses among Negroes, and the refusal to show only Negro victims and white villains; an audience losing its hypersensitivity and growing in its respect for the artist; all of these may mean a genuine advance in the fiction by Negro authors. Great areas of Negro life remain unexplored, many of them even untouched. The Negro working class, the various strata of the Negro middle class; urban life in both the South and North (outside Harlem) are some of these areas. Even the fields covered—the rural South and Harlem—still call for interpreters. There are many Harlems, for instance, a long way from Van Vechten's "Nigger Heaven," that could furnish backgrounds for good novels. There is little fiction dealing with college life, with the Negro professional class, with the Negro church, business, white-collar employment, or with Negroes in entertainment and athletics. When one considers the many shelves of fiction dealing with the Negro, he must be struck by the way white novelists, from Cooper down to the very present, outnumber Negro novelists. The story of the Negro in America has been handled largely by outsiders. This by itself should constitute a challenge to Negro authors.

The selections given below are designed as a mosaic of Negro experience, more than as any adequate presentation of the novelists' powers. Admittedly this type of selection is bound to do some injustice to the novels, but it is necessary in an anthology of this sort, and the novelists have been cooperative in permitting it. As far as possible, the selections were made as narrative units, capable of standing separately. It is hoped, however, that many will stir a desire to read the entire works.

WILLIAM WELLS BROWN (1816-1884)

The following excerpts are taken from the third edition of William Wells Brown's historic novel (see also p. 625); this edition is called *Clotelle, or the Colored Heroine* (1867). Brown advises his readers that the two leading characters are real personages and that the author witnessed many of the incidents. The first part of the book is the better because there seems to be more of Brown's remembered observation there, and less of his remembered reading.

[Speculating in Slaves]

DICK JENNINGS THE SLAVE-SPECULATOR, was one of the few Northern men, who go to the South and throw aside their honest mode of obtaining a living and resort to trading in human beings. A more repulsive-looking person could scarcely be found in any community of bad looking men. Tall, lean and lank, with high cheek-bones, face much pitted with the small-pox, gray eyes with red eyebrows, and sandy whiskers, he indeed stood alone without mate or fellow in looks. Jennings prided himself upon what he called his goodness of heart, and was always speaking of his humanity. As many of the slaves whom he intended taking to the New Orleans market had been raised in Richmond, and had relations there, he determined to leave the city early in the morning, so as not to witness any of the scenes so common on the departure of a slave-gang to the far South. In this, he was most successful; for not even Isabella, who had called at the prison several times to see her mother and sister, was aware of the time that they were to leave.

The slave-trader started at early dawn, and was beyond the confines of the city long before the citizens were out of their beds. As a slave regards a life on the sugar, cotton, or rice plantation as even worse than death, they are ever on the watch for an opportunity to escape. The trader, aware of this, secures his victims in chains before he sets out on his journey. On this occasion, Jennings had the men chained in pairs, while the women were allowed to go unfastened, but were closely watched.

After a march of eight days, the company arrived on the banks of the Ohio River, where they took a steamer for the place of their destination. Jennings had already advertised in the New Orleans papers, that he would be there with a prime lot of ablebodied slaves, men and women, fit for field-service, with a few extra ones calculated for house-servants,—all between the ages of fifteen and twenty-five years; but like most men who make a business of speculating in human beings, he often bought many who were far advanced in years, and would try to pass them off for five or six years younger than they were. Few persons can arrive at anything approaching the real age of the negro, by mere observation, unless they are well acquainted with the race. Therefore, the slave-trader frequently carried out the deception with perfect impunity.

After the steamer had left the wharf and was fairly out on the bosom of the broad Mississippi, the speculator called his servant Pompey to him; and instructed him as to getting the negroes ready for market. Among the forty slaves that the trader had on this occasion, were some whose appearance indicated that they had seen some years and had gone through considerable service. Their gray hair and whiskers at once pronounced them to be above the ages set down in the trader's advertisement. Pompey had long been with Jennings, and understood his business well, and if he did not take delight in the discharge of his duty, he did it at least with a degree of alacrity, so that he might receive the approbation of his master.

Pomp, as he was usually called by the trader, was of real negro blood, and would often say, when alluding to himself, "Dis nigger am no counterfeit, he is de 'ginuine artikle. Dis chile is none of your haf-and-haf, dere is no bogus about him."

Pompey was of low stature, round face, and, like most of his race, had a set of teeth, which, for whiteness and beauty, could not be surpassed; his eyes were large, lips thick, and hair short and woolly. Pompey had been with Jennings so long, and had seen so much of buying and selling of his fellow-creatures, that he appeared perfectly indifferent to the heart-rending scenes which daily occurred in his presence. Such is the force of habit:—

> "Vice is a monster of such frightful mien,
> That to be hated, needs but to be seen;
> But seen too oft, familiar with its face,
> We first endure, then pity, then embrace."

It was on the second day of the steamer's voyage, that Pompey selected five of the oldest slaves, took them into a room by themselves, and commenced preparing them for market.

"Now," said he, addressing himself to the company, "I is de chap dat is to get you ready for de Orlèans market, so dat you will bring marser a good price. How old is you?" addressing himself to a man not less than forty.

"If I live to see next sweet-potato-digging time, I shall be either forty or forty-five, I don't know which."

"Dat may be," replied Pompey; "but now you is only thirty years old,—dat's what marser says you is to be."

"I know I is more den dat," responded the man.

"I can't help nuffin' about dat," returned Pompey; "but when you get into de market and any one ax you how old you is, and you tell um you is forty or forty-five, marser will tie you up and cut you all to pieces. But if you tell um dat you is only thirty, den he won't. Now remember dat you is thirty years old and no more."

"Well den, I guess I will only be thirty when they ax me."

"What's your name?" said Pompey, addressing himself to another. "Jeems."

"Oh! Uncle Jim, is it?"

"Yes."

"Den you must have all them gray whiskers shaved off, and all dem gray hairs plucked out of your head." This was all said by Pompey in a manner which showed that he knew what he was about.

"How old is you?" asked Pompey of a tall, strong-looking man. "What's your name?"

"I am twenty-nine years old, and my name is Tobias, but they calls me Toby."

"Well, Toby, or Mr. Tobias, if dat will suit you better, you are now twenty-three years old; dat's all,—do you understand dat?"

"Yes," replied Toby.

Pompey now gave them all to understand how old they were to be when asked by persons who were likely to purchase, and then went and reported to his master that the old boys were all right.

"Be sure," said Jennings, "that the niggers don't forget what you have taught them, for our luck this time in the market depends upon their appearance. If any of them have so many gray hairs that you cannot pluck them out, take the blacking and brush, and go at them."

*   *   *   *   *

It was half-past twelve, and the passengers, instead of retiring to their berths once more assembled at the gambling-tables. The practice of gambling on the western waters has long been a source of annoyance to the more moral persons who travel on our great rivers. Thousands of dollars often change owners during a passage from St. Louis or Louisville to New Orleans, on a Mississippi steamer. Many men are completely ruined on such occasions, and duels are often the consequence.

"Go call my boy, steward," said Mr. Jones, as he took his cards one by one from the table.

In a few minutes a fine-looking, bright-eyed mulatto boy, apparently about sixteen years of age, was standing by his master's side.

"I am broke, all but my boy," said Jones, as he ran his fingers through his cards; "but he is worth a thousand dollars, and I will bet the half of him."

"I will call you," said Thompson, as he laid five hundred dollars at the feet of the boy, who was standing on the table, and at the same time throwing down his cards before his adversary.

"You have beaten me," said Jones; and a roar of laughter followed from the other gentleman as poor Joe stepped down from the table.

"Well, I suppose I owe you half the nigger," said Thompson, as he took hold of Joe and began examining his limbs.

"Yes," replied Jones, "he is half yours. Let me have five hundred dollars, and I will give you a bill of sale of the boy."

"Go back to your bed," said Thompson to his chattel, "and remember that you now belong to me."

The poor slave wiped the tears from his eyes, as, in obedience, he turned to leave the table.

"My father gave me that boy," said Jones, as he took the money, "and I hope, Mr. Thompson, that you will allow me to redeem him."

"Most certainly, sir," replied Thompson. "Whenever you hand over the cool thousand the negro is yours."

Next morning, as the passengers were assembling in the cabin and on deck, and while the slaves were running about waiting on or looking for their masters, poor Joe was seen entering his new master's stateroom, boots in hand.

"Who do you belong to?" inquired a gentleman of an old negro, who passed along leading a fine Newfoundland dog which he had been feeding.

"When I went to sleep las' night," replied the slave, "I 'longed to Massa Carr; but he bin gamblin' all night, an' I don't know who I 'longs to dis mornin'."

Such is the uncertainty of a slave's life. He goes to bed at night the pampered servant of his young master, with whom he has played in childhood, and who would not see his slave abused under any consideration, and gets up in the morning the property of a man whom he has never before seen.

[Quadroon; Octoroon]

A FEW MILES OUT OF RICHMOND is a pleasant place, with here and there a beautiful cottage surrounded by trees so as scarcely to be seen. Among these was one far retired from the public roads, and almost hidden among the trees. This was the spot that Henry Linwood had selected for Isabella, the eldest daughter of Agnes. The young man hired the house, furnished it, and placed his mistress there, and for many months no one in his father's family knew where he spent his leisure hours.

When Henry was not with her, Isabella employed herself in looking after her little garden and the flowers that grew in front of her cottage. The passion-flower, peony, dahlia, laburnum, and other plants, so abundant in warm climates, under the tasteful hand of Isabella, lavished their beauty upon this retired spot, and miniature paradise.

Although Isabella had been assured by Henry that she should be free and that he would always consider her as his wife, she nevertheless felt that she ought to be married and acknowledged by him. But this was an impossibility under the State laws, even had the young man been disposed to do what was right in the matter. Related as he was, however, to one of the first families in Virginia, he would not have dared to marry a woman of so low an origin, even had the laws been favorable.

Here, in this secluded grove, unvisited by any other except her lover, Isabella lived for years. She had become the mother of a lovely daughter, which its father named Clotelle. The complexion of the child was still fairer than that of its mother. Indeed, she was not darker than other white children, and as she grew older she more and more resembled her father.

As time passed away, Henry became negligent of Isabella and his child, so much so, that days and even weeks passed without their seeing him, or knowing where he was. Becoming more acquainted with the world, and moving continually in the society of young women of his own station, the young man felt that Isabella was a burden to him, and having as some would say, "outgrown his love," he longed to free himself of the responsibility; yet every time he saw the child, he felt that he owed it his fatherly care.

Henry had now entered into political life, and been elected to a seat in the legislature of his native State; and in his intercourse with his friends had become acquainted with Gertrude Miller, the daughter of a wealthy gentleman living near Richmond. Both Henry and Gertrude were very good-looking, and a mutual attachment sprang up between them.

Instead of finding fault with the unfrequent visits of Henry, Isabella always met him with a smile, and tried to make both him and herself believe that business was the cause of his negligence. When he was with her, she devoted every moment of her time to him, and never failed to speak of the growth and increasing intelligence of Clotelle.

The child had grown so large as to be able to follow its father on his departure out to the road. But the impression made on Henry's feelings by the devoted woman and her child was momentary. His heart had grown hard, and his acts were guided by no fixed principle. Henry and Gertrude had been married nearly two years before Isabella knew anything of the event, and it was merely by accident that she became acquainted with the facts.

One beautiful afternoon, when Isabella and Clotelle were picking wild strawberries some two miles from their home, and near the roadside, they observed a one-horse chaise driving past. The mother turned her face from the carriage not wishing to be seen by strangers, little dreaming that the chaise contained Henry and his wife. The child, however, watched the chaise, and startled her mother by screaming out at the top of her voice, "Papa! papa!" and clapped her little hands for joy. The mother turned in haste to look at the strangers, and her eyes encountered those of Henry's pale and dejected countenance. Gertrude's eyes were on the child. The swiftness with which Henry drove by could not hide from his wife the striking resemblance of the child to himself. The young wife had heard the child exclaim "Papa! papa!" and she immediately saw by the quivering of his lips and the agitation depicted in his countenance, that all was not right.

MARTIN R. DELANY (1812-1885)

In 1839 Martin R. Delany (see also p. 634) went down the Mississippi to New Orleans, and continued a tour of several months of Texas, Mississippi, Louisiana, and Arkansas. According to his biographer, Frank Rollin, "the experienced gained among the slaves of the Southwest was carefully garnered up for future usefulness." The biographer makes no mention, however, of Delany's novel, *Blake; or The Huts of America* (1859). This novel was announced in the first issue of the *Anglo-African Magazine* (January 1859) as "A Tale of the Mississippi Valley, The Southern United States and Cuba," giving ". . . in the most familiar manner the formidable understanding among the slaves throughout the United States and Canada . . . The hero [is] an educated West Indian black, who deprived of his liberty by fraud when young and brought to the United States, in maturer age, at the instance of his wife being sold from him, sought revenge through the medium of a deep laid secret organization." Though the plot sounds implausible, facts that should be borne in mind are Delany's own tour through the sections of which he wrote, his planning with John Brown to alter the Underground Railroad so that Kansas instead of Canada was the terminus, and his fearless spirit. Delany had been threatened with tarring and feathering in northern Ohio, but armed with a butcher's knife and hatchet, he stood the proslavery mob at bay. When the fugitive slave bill passed, Delany spoke to the mayor of Pittsburgh in a public address: "If any man approaches that house in search of a slave—I care not who he may be, whether constable or sheriff, magistrate or even judge of the Supreme Court—nay, let it be he who sanctioned this act to become a law, surrounded by his cabinet as his bodyguard . . . if he crosses the threshold of my door, and I do not lay him a lifeless corpse at my feet, I hope the grave may refuse my body a resting place, and righteous Heaven my spirit a home." The editorial note stated that *Blake* contained some eighty chapters and about 600 pages, and hoped that Delany would place the work into the hands of a publisher before he went to Africa. What happened to it is a mystery. Only seven installments, from January to August, 1859, ran in the *Anglo-African Magazine*.

[Conspiracy]

ON LEAVING THE PLANTATION carrying them hanging upon his arm, thrown across his shoulders, and in his hands Henry had a bridle, halter, blanket, girt, and horsewhip, the emblems of a faithful servant in discharge of his master's business.

By shrewdness and discretion such was his management as he passed along, that he could tell the name of each place and proprietor, long before he reached them. Being a scholar, he carefully kept a record of the plantations he had passed, that when accosted by a white, as an overseer or patrol, he invariably pretended to belong to a back estate, in search of his master's race horse. If crossing a field, he was taking a near cut; but if met in a wood, the animal was in the forest, as being a great leaper no fence could debar him, though the forest was fenced and posted. The blanket a substitute for a saddle, was in reality carried for a bed.

With speed unfaltering and spirits unflinching, his first great strive was to reach the Red River, to escape from his own state as quickly as possible. Proceeding on in the direction of the Red River country, he met with no obstruction, except in one instance, when he left his assailant quietly upon the earth. A few days after the inquest was held upon the body of the deceased overseer—verdict of the Jury, "By hands unknown."

On approaching the river, after crossing a number of streams, as the Yazoo, Ouchita, and such, he was brought to sad reflections. A dread came over him, difficulties lay before him, dangers stood staring him in the face at every step he took. Here for the first time since his maturity of manhood responsibilities rose up in a shape of which he had no conception. A mighty undertaking, such as had never before been ventured upon, and the duty revolving upon him, was too much for a slave with no other aid than the aspirations of his soul panting for liberty. Reflecting upon the peaceful hours he once enjoyed as a professing Christian, and the distance which slavery had driven him from its peaceful portals, here in the wilderness, determining to renew his faith and dependence upon Divine aid, when falling upon his knees, he opened his heart to God, as a tenement of the Holy Spirit.

"Arm of the Lord awake! renew my faith, confirm my hope, perfect me in love. Give strength, give courage, guide and protect my pathway, and direct me in my course!" Springing to his feet as if a weight had fallen from him, he stood up a new man.

The river is narrow, the water red as if colored by iron rust, the channel winding. Beyond this river lies his hopes, the broad plains of Louisiana with a hundred thousand bondsmen, seeming anxiously to await him. . . .

While gazing upon the stream in solemn reflection for Divine aid to direct him, logs came floating down, which suggested a proximity to the raft with which sections of that stream is filled, when going but a short distance up, he crossed in safety to the Louisiana side. His faith was now fully established, and thenceforth, Henry was full of hope and confident of success.

Reaching Alexandria with no obstruction, his first secret meeting was held in the hut of Aunt Dilly. Here he found them all ready for an issue.

"Am dis you chile" said the old woman, stooping with age, sitting on a low stool in the chimney corner; "dis many day, I heahn on yeh!" though Henry had just entered on his mission. From Alexandria he passed rapidly on to Latuer's making no immediate stops, preferring to organize at the more prominent places.

This is a mulatto planter, said to have come from the isle of Guadaloupe. Riding down the road upon a pony at a quick gallop, was a mulatto youth, a son of the planter, an old black man on foot keeping close to the horse's heels.

"Whose boy are you?" enquired the young mulatto, who had just dismounted, the old servant holding his pony.

"I'm in search of master's race horse."

"What is your name?" farther enquired the young mulatto.

"Gilbert, sir."

"What do you want?"

"I am hungry, sir."

"Dolly," said he to an old black woman at the woodpile; "show this man into the negro quarter, and give him something to eat; give him a cup of milk. Do you like milk, my man?"

"Yes sir, I have no choice when hungry; anything will do."

"Da is none heah but claubah; maus Eugene," replied the old cook.

"Give him that," said the young master. "You people like that kind of stuff I believe; our negroes like it."

"Yes sir," replied Henry, when the lad left.

"God knows'e needn' talk 'bout wat we po' black folks eat, case da don' ghin us nothin' else but dat an' caun bread," muttered the old woman.

"Don't they treat you well, aunty?" enquired Henry.

"God on'y knows my chile, wat we suffeh."

"Who was that old man who ran behind your master's horse?"

"Dat Nathan, my husban'."

"Do they treat him well, aunty?"

"No chile, wus an' any dog, da beat 'im foh little an nothin'."

"Is Uncle Nathan religious?"

"Yes, chile, ole man an' I's been sahvin' God dis many day, for yeh baun! Wen any on 'em in de house git sick, den da sen foh 'Uncle Nathan' come pray foh dem; 'Uncle Nathan' mighty good den!"

"Do you know that the Latuers are colored people?"

"Yes, chile; God bless yeh soul yes! Case huh mammy ony dead two-three yehs, an' she black as me."

"How did they treat her?"

"Not berry well; she nus da childen; an eat in a house arter all done."

"What did Latuer's children call her?"

"Da call huh 'mammy,' same like wite folks childen call de nus."

"Can you tell me, aunty, why they treat you people so badly, knowing themselves to be colored, and some of the slaves related to them?"

"God bless yeh hunny, de wite folks, dese plantehs make 'em so; da run heah, an' tell 'em da mus'n treat deh niggehs well, case da spile 'em."

"Do the white planters frequently visit here?"

"Yes, huny, yes, da heah some on 'em all de time eatin' an' drinkin' long wid de old men; da on'y tryin' git wat little 'e got, dat alll Da te'nd to be great frien' de ole man; but laws a massy hunny, I doh mine dese wite folks no how!"

"Does your master ever go to their houses and eat with them?"

"Yes, chile, some time'e go, but den half on 'em got nothin' fit to eat; da hab fat poke an' bean, caun cake an' sich like, dat all da got, some on 'em."

"Does Mr. Latuer give them better at his table?"

"Laws hunny, yes; yes'n deed chile! 'E got mutton—some time whole sheep mos'—fowl, pig, an' ebery tum ting a nuddeh, 'e got so much ting dah, I haudly know wat cook fus."

"Do the white planters associate with the family of Latuer?"

"One of 'em, ten 'e coatin de dahta; I don't recon 'e gwine hab heh. Da cah [can't] fool long wid 'Toyeh's gals dat way."

"Whose girls, Metoyers?"

"Yes chile."

"Do you mean the wealthy planters of that name?"

"Dat same, chile."

"Well, I want to understand you: You don't mean to say that they are colored people?"

"Yes, hunny, yes; da good culled folks as any body. Some five-six boys an five-six gals on 'em; da all rich."

"How do they treat their slaves?"

"Da boys all mighty haud mastas, da gals all mighty good; sahvants all like 'em."

"You seem to understand the people very well, aunty. Now please tell me what kind of masters there are generally in the Red river country."

"Haud 'nough chile, haud 'nough, God on'y knows!"

"Do the colored masters treat theirs generally worse than the whites?"

"No hunny, 'bout da same."

"That's just what I want to know. What are the usual allowances for slaves?"

"Da 'low de fiel' han' two suit a yeah foh umin [women] one long linen coat,[1] make suit, an' foh man, pantaloon an' jacket."

"How about eating?"

"Half peck meal ah day foh family uh fo!"

"What about weekly privileges? Do you have Saturday to yourselves?"

"Land hunny, no! no chile, no! Da do'n 'low us no time, 'tall. Da 'low us ebery uddeh Sunday wash ouh close; dat all de time we git."

"Then you don't get to sell anything for yourselves?"

"No, hunny, no! Da don' 'low pig, chicken, tucky, goose, bean, pea, tateh, nothin' else."

"Well aunty, I'm glad to meet you, and as evening's drawing nigh, I must see your husband a little, then go."

"God bless yeh chile whar ebeh yeh go! Yeh ain' arteh no race-hos, dat yeh ain't."

"You got something to eat my man, did you?" enquired the lad, Eugene, at the conclusion of his interview with Uncle Nathan.

"I did sir, and feasted well!" replied Henry in conclusion; "Goodbye!" and he left for the next plantation suited to his objects.

"God bless de baby!" said old Aunt Dolly as Uncle Nathan entered the hut, referring to Henry.

"Ah, chile!" replied the old man with tears in his eyes; "my yeahs has heahn dis day!"

* * * * *

[1] Coat,—a term used by slaves for frock.

Approaching Crane's on Little River, the slaves were returning from the field to the gin. Many being females some of whom were very handsome, had just emptied their baskets. So little clothing had they, and so loosely hung the tattered fragments about them, that they covered themselves behind the large empty baskets tilted over on the side, to shield their person from exposure.

The overseer engaged in another direction, the master absent, and the family at the great house, a good opportunity presented for an inspection of affairs.

"How do you do, young woman?" saluted Henry.

"How de do, sir!" replied a sprightly, comely young mulatto girl, who stood behind her basket with not three yards of cloth in the tattered relic of the only garment she had on.

"Who owns this place?"

"Mr. Crane sir," she politely replied with a smile.

"How many slaves has he?"

"I don'o; some say five a' six hunded."

"Do they all work on this place?"

"No sir, he got two-three places."

"How many on this place?"

"Oveh a hundred an 'fifty."

"What allowances have you?"

"None sir."

"What! no Saturday to yourselves?"

"No sir."

"They allow you Sundays, I suppose."

"No, sir, we work all day ev'ry Sunday."

"How late do you work?"

"Till we can' see to pick no mo' cotton; but w'en its moon light, we pick till ten o'clock at night."

"What time do you get to wash your clothes?"

"None sir; da on'y 'low us one suit ev'ry New Yehs day,[2] an' us gals take it off every Satady night aftah de men all gone to bed and wash it fah Sunday."

"Why do you want clean clothes on Sunday, if you have to work on that day?"

"It's de Laud's day, an' we wa to be clean, and we feel betteh."

"How do the men do for clean clothes?"

"We wash de men's clothes afteh da go to bed."

"And you say you are only allowed one suit a year? Now young woman; I don't know your name but—"

---

[2] Some Red River planters do not allow their slaves but one suit a year.

"Nancy, sir."

"Well Nancy, speak plainly, and don't be backward; what does your one suit consist of?"

"A frock sir, made out er coarse tow linen."

"Only one piece, and no under clothes at all?' '

"Dat's all sir!" replied she modestly looking down and drawing the basket which sufficiently screened her, still closer to her person.

"Is that which you have on a sample of the goods your clothes are made of?"

"Yes, sir, dis is da kine."

"I would like to see some other of your girls."

"Stop sir, I go call Susan!" when gathering up, and drawing around and before her, a surplus of the back section, the only remaining sound remnant of the narrow tattered garment that she wore, off she ran behind the gin, where lay in the sun, a number of girls to rest themselves during their hour of "spell."

"Susan!" she exclaimed rather loudly; "I do'n want you gals!" she pleasantly admonished, as the whole twelve or fifteen rose from their resting place, and came hurriedly around the building, Nancy and Susan in the lead. They instinctively as did Nancy, drew thair garments around and about them, on coming in sight of the stranger. Standing on the outside of the fence, Henry politely bowed as they approached.

"Dis is Susan, sir!" said Nancy, introducing her friend with blind simplicity.

"How de do, sir!" saluted she, a modest and intelligent, very pretty young black girl, of good address.

"Well Susan!" replied Henry; "I don't want anything but to see you girls; but I will ask you this question: how many suits of clothes do they give you a year?"

"One sir."

"How many pieces make a suit?"

"Jus' one frock"; and they simultaneously commenced drawing still closer before, the remnant of coarse garment, which hung in tatters about them.

"Don't you have shoes and stockings in winter?"

"We no call foh shoes, case 'taint cole much; on'y some time little fros'."

"How late in the evening do you work?"

"Da fiel' han's dah;" pointing to those returning to the field; "da work till bed time, but we gals heah, we work in de gin, and spell each other ev'ry twelve ouahs."

"You're at leisure now; who fills your places?"

"Nutha set a' han's go to work, fo' you come."

"How much cotton do they pick for a task?"

"Each one mus' pick big basket full, an' fetch it in f'om da fiel' to de gin, else da git thirty lashes."

"How much must the women pick as a task?"

"De same as de men."

"That can't be possible!" said Henry, looking over the fence down upon their baskets; "how much do they hold?"

"I dis membeh sir, but good 'eal."

"I see on each basket marked 225 lbs.; is that the quantity they hold?"

"Yes sir, dat's it."

"All mus' be in ghin certain or else da git whipped; sometime de men help 'em."

"How can they do this when they have their own to carry?"

"Da put deres on de head, an' ketch holt one side de women basket. Sometimes they leave part in de fiel', an' go back afteh it."

"Do you get plenty to eat?"

"No sir, da feeds us po'ly; sometime, we do'n have mo'n half nough!"

"Did you girls ever work in the field?"

"O yes sir! all uv us, on'y we wan't strong nough to fetch in ouh cotton, den da put us in de gin."

"Where would you rather work; in the gin or in the field?"

"If 'twant foh carryin' cotton, we'd rather work in de fiel'."

"Why so girls?"

"Case den da would'n be so many ole wite plantehs come an' look at us, like we was show!"

"Who sees that the tasks are all done in the field?"

"Da Drivah."

"Is he a white man?"

"No sir, black."

"Is he a free man?"

"No sir, slave."

"Have you no white overseer?"

"Yes sir, Mr. Dorman."

"Where is Dorman when you are at work?"

"He out at de fiel' too."

"What is he doing there?"

"He watch Jesse, da drivah."

"Is Jesse a pretty good fellow?"

"No sir, he treat black folks like dog, he all de time beat 'em, when da no call to do it."

"How did he treat you girls when you worked in the field?"

"He beat us if we jist git little behind de rest in pickin'! Da wite folks made 'im bad."

"Point him out to me and after tonight, he'll never whip another. Now girls, I see that you are smart intelligent young women, and I want you to tell me why it is, that your master keeps you all here at work in the gin, when he could get high prices for you, and supply your places with common cheap hands at half the money?"

"Case we gals won' go! Da been mo'n a dozen plantehs heah lookin' at us, an' want to buy us foh house keepehs, an' we won't go; we die fus!" said Susan with a shudder.

"Yes," repeated Nancy, with equal emotion; "we die fus!"

"How can you prevent it girls; won't your master sell you against your will?"

"Yes sir, he would, but da plantehs da don't want us widout we willin' to go."

* * * * *

From Texas Henry went into the Indian Nation near Fort Towson, Arkansas.

"Make yourself at home sir!" invited Mr. Culver, the intelligent old Chief of the United Nation; "and Josephus will attend to you," referring to his nephew Josephus Braser, an educated young chief and counsellor among his people.

"You are slaveholders I see, Mr. Culver!" said Henry.

"We are sir, but not like the white men," he replied.

"How many do you hold?"

"About two hundred on my two plantations."

"I can't well understand how a man like you can reconcile your principles with the holding of slaves and——"

"We have had enough of that!" exclaimed Dr. Donald, with a tone of threatening authority.

"Hold your breath sir, else I'll stop it!" in a rage replied the young chief.

"Sir," responded the Doctor; "I was not speaking to you, but only speaking to that Negro!"

"You're a fool!" roared Braser springing to his feet.

"Come, come, gentlemen!" admonished the old Chief; "I think you are both going mad! I hope you'll behave something better."

"Well, uncle, I can't endure him! He assumes so much authority!"

replied he. "He'll make the Indians slaves just now, then Negroes will have no friends."

Donald was a white man, who had married among the Indians a sister of the old Chief and aunt to the young, for the sake of her wealth and a home. A physician without talents, he was unable to make a business and unwilling to work.

"Mr. Bras——"

"I want nothing more of you," interrupted Braser, "and don't——"

"Josephus, Josephus!" interrupted the old Chief; "you will surely let the Doctor speak!"

Donald stood pale and trembling before the young Choctaw born to command, when receiving no favor he left the company muttering "nigger!"

"Now you see," said Mr. Culver as the Doctor left the room; "the difference between a white man and Indian holding slaves. Indian work side by side with black man, eat with him, drink with him, rest with him and both lay down in shade together; white man even won't let you talk! In our Nation Indian and black all marry together. Indian like black man very much, only he don't fight 'nough. Black man in Florida fight much, and Indian like 'im heap!"

"You make, sir, a slight mistake about my people. They would fight if in their own country they were united as the Indians here, and not scattered thousands of miles apart, as they are. You should also remember, that the Africans have never permitted a subjugation of their country by foreigners as the Indians have theirs, and Africa today is still peopled by Africans, whilst America, the home of the Indian who is fast passing away, is now possessed and ruled by foreigners."

"True, true!" said the old Chief looking down reflectingly; "too true! I had not thought that way before. Do you think the white man couldn't take Africa if he wanted?"

"He might by a combination, and I still am doubtful whether then he could if the Africans were determined as formerly to keep him out. You will also remember, that the whites came in small numbers to America, and then drove the Indians from their own soil, whilst the blacks got in Africa as slaves, are taken by their own native conquerors, and sold to white men as prisoners of war."

"That is true sir, true!" sighed the old Chief; "the Indian like game before the bow, is passing away before the gun of the white man!"

"What I now most wish to learn is, whether in case that the blacks should rise, they may have hope or fear from the Indian?"

"I'm an old mouthpiece, been puffing out smoke and talk many seasons for the entertainment of the young and benefit of all who come among us. The squaws of the great men among the Indians in Florida were black women, and the squaws of the black men were Indian women. You see the vine that winds around and holds us together. Don't cut it, but let grow till bimeby, it git so stout and strong, with many, very many little branches attached, that you can't separate them. I now reach to you the pipe of peace and hold out the olive-branch of hope! Go on young man, go on. If you want white man to love you, you must fight 'im!" concluded the intelligent old Choctaw.

"Then sir, I shall rest contented, and impart to you the object of my mission," replied Henry.

"Ah hah!" exclaimed the old Chief after an hour's seclusion with him, "ah hah! Indian have something like that long-go. I wonder your people ain't got it before! That what make Indian strong; that what make Indian and black man in Florida hold together. Go on young man, go on! May the Great Spirit make you brave!" exhorted Mr. Culver, when the parties retired for the evening, Henry rooming with the young warrior Braser.

By the aid of the young Chief and kindness of his uncle, the venerable old brave, Henry was conducted quite through the nation on a pony placed at his service, affording to him an ample opportunity of examining into the condition of things. He left the settlement with the regrets of the people, being the only instance in which his seclusions were held with the master instead of the slave.

CHARLES W. CHESNUTT (1858-1932)

Charles Waddell Chesnutt (see also p. 27), after his success with the short story, turned to the novel form. *The House Behind the Cedars,* a novel of the color line, appeared in 1900; *The Marrow of Tradition,* from which the following selection is taken, in 1901; and *The Colonel's Dream,* a story of a Southern colonel whose dream of reform is smashed by the bigotry of a small North Carolina town, in 1905. *The Marrow of Tradition* has its scene laid in Wellington (Wilmington, North Carolina) at the time of the 1898 race riots. *The Marrow of Tradition,* exploring the tenuous connections of the white and Negro lines of the same family, is a close study of race relations in the South at the end of the century. The chapter, "The Storm Breaks," is one of the earliest examples of racial conflict in fiction. It is reprinted by permission of Helen M. Chesnutt.

[The Storm Breaks]

THE WELLINGTON RIOT began at three o'clock in the afternoon of a day as fair as was ever selected for a deed of darkness. The sky was clear, except for a few light clouds that floated, white and feathery, high in air, like distant islands in a sapphire sea. A salt-laden breeze from the ocean a few miles away lent a crisp sparkle to the air.

At three o'clock sharp the streets were filled, as if by magic, with armed white men. The negroes, going about, had noted, with uneasy curiosity, that the stores and places of business, many of which closed at noon, were unduly late in opening for the afternoon, though no one suspected the reason for the delay; but at three o'clock every passing colored man was ordered, by the first white man he met, to throw up his hands. If he complied, he was searched, more or less roughly, for fire-arms, and then warned to get off the street. When he met another group of white men the scene was repeated. The man thus summarily held up seldom encountered more than two groups before disappearing across lots to his own home or some convenient hiding-place. If he resisted any demand of those who halted him—But the records of the day are historical; they may be found in the newspapers of the following date, but they are more firmly engraved upon the hearts and memories of the people of Wellington. For many months there were negro families in the town whose children screamed with fear and ran to their mothers for protection at the mere sight of a white man.

Dr. Miller had received a call, about one o'clock, to attend a case at the house of a well-to-do colored farmer, who lived some three or four miles from the town, upon the very road, by the way, along which Miller had driven so furiously a few weeks before, in the few hours that intervened before Sandy Campbell would probably have been burned at the stake. The drive to his patient's home, the necessary inquiries, the filling of the prescription from his own medicine-case, which he carried along with him, the little friendly conversation about the weather and the crops, and, the farmer being an intelligent and thinking man, the inevitable subject of the future of their race,—these, added to the return journey, occupied at least two hours of Miller's time.

As he neared the town on his way back, he saw ahead of him half a dozen men and women approaching, with fear written in their faces, in every degree from apprehension to terror. Women were weeping and children crying, and all were going as fast as seemingly lay in their power, looking behind now and then as if pursued by some deadly enemy. At sight of Miller's buggy they made a dash for cover, disappearing, like a covey of frightened partridges, in the underbrush along the road.

Miller pulled up his horse and looked after them in startled wonder. "What on earth can be the matter?" he muttered, struck with a vague feeling of alarm. A psychologist, seeking to trace the effects of slavery upon the human mind, might find in the South many a curious illustration of this curse, abiding long after the actual physical bondage had terminated. In the olden time the white South labored under the constant fear of negro insurrections. Knowing that they themselves, if in the negroes' place, would have risen in the effort to throw off the yoke, all their reiterated theories of negro subordination and inferiority could not remove that lurking fear, founded upon the obscure consciousness that the slaves ought to have risen. Conscience, it has been said, makes cowards of us all. There was never, on the continent of America, a successful slave revolt, nor one which lasted more than a few hours, or resulted in the loss of more than a few white lives; yet never was the planter free from the fear that there might be one.

On the other hand, the slave had before his eyes always the fear of the master. There were good men, according to their lights,—according to their training and environment,—among the Southern slaveholders, who treated their slaves kindly, as slaves, from principle, because they recognized the claims of humanity, even under the dark skin of a human chattel. There was many a one who protected or pampered his negroes, as the case might be, just as a man fondles his dog,— because they were his; they were part of his estate, an integral part of the entity of property and person which made up the aristocrat; but with all this kindness, there was always present, in the consciousness of the lowest slave, the knowledge that he was in his master's power, and that he could make no effectual protest against the abuse of that authority. There was also the knowledge, among those who could think at all, that the best of masters was himself a slave to a system, which hampered his movements but scarcely less than those of his bondmen.

When, therefore, Miller saw these men and women scampering into the bushes, he divined, with this slumbering race consciousness which years of culture had not obliterated, that there was some race trouble on foot. His intuition did not long remain unsupported. A black head was cautiously protruded from the shrubbery, and a black voice—if such a description be allowable—addressed him:—

"Is dat you, Doctuh Miller?"

"Yes. Who are you, and what's the trouble?"

"What's de trouble, suh? Why, all hell's broke loose in town yonduh. De w'ite folks is riz 'gins' de niggers, an say dey 're gwine ter kill eve'y nigger dey kin lay han's on."

Miller's heart leaped to his throat, as he thought of his wife and child. This story was preposterous; it could not be true, and yet there must be something in it. He tried to question his informant, but the man was so overcome with excitement and fear that Miller saw clearly that he must go farther for information. He had read in the Morning Chronicle, a few days before, the obnoxious editorial quoted from the Afro-American Banner, and had noted the comment upon it by the white editor. He had felt, as at the time of its first publica- cation, that the editorial was ill-advised. It could do no good, and was calculated to arouse the animosity of those whose friendship, whose tolerance, at least, was necessary and almost indispensable to the col- ored people. They were living, at the best, in a sort of armed neutrality with the whites; such a publication, however serviceable elsewhere, could have no other effect in Wellington than to endanger this truce and defeat the hope of a possible future friendship. The right of free speech entitled Barber to publish it; a larger measure of common-sense would have made him withhold it. Whether it was the republication of this article that had stirred up anew the sleeping dogs of race prejudice and whetted their thirst for blood, he could not yet tell; but at any rate, there was mischief on foot.

"Fer Gods sake, doctuh, don't go no closeter ter dat town," pleaded his informant, "er you'll be killt sho'. Come on wid us, suh, an' tek keer er yo'se'f. We're gwine ter hide in de swamps till dis thing is over!"

"God, man!" exclaimed Miller, urging his horse forward, "my wife and child are in the town!"

Fortunately, he reflected, there were no patients confined in the hospital,—if there should be anything in this preposterous story. To one unfamiliar with Southern life, it might have seemed impossible that these good Christian people, who thronged the churches on Sun- day, and wept over the sufferings of the lowly Nazarene, and sent missionaries to the heathen, could be hungering and thirsting for the blood of their fellow men; but Miller cherished no such delusion. He knew the history of his country; he had the threatened lynching of Sandy Campbell vividly in mind; and he was fully persuaded that to race prejudice, once roused, any horror was possible. That women or children would be molested of set purpose he did not believe, but that they might suffer by accident was more than likely.

As he neared the town, dashing forward at the top of his horse's speed, he heard his voice called in a loud and agitated tone, and glancing around him, saw a familiar form standing by the roadside, gesticulating vehemently.

He drew up the horse with a suddenness that threw the faithful and obedient animal back upon its haunches. The colored lawyer, Watson, came up to the buggy. That he was laboring under great and unusual excitement was quite apparent from his pale face and frightened air.

"What's the matter, Watson?" demanded Miller, hoping now to obtain some reliable information.

"Matter!" exclaimed the other. "Everything's the matter! The white people are up in arms. They have disarmed the colored people, killing half a dozen in the process, and wounding as many more. They have forced the mayor and aldermen to resign, have formed a provisional city government *á la française,* and have ordered me and a half a dozen other fellows to leave town in forty-eight hours, under pain of sudden death. As they seem to mean it, I shall not stay so long. Fortunately, my wife and children are away. I knew you were out here, however, and I thought I'd come out and wait for you, so that we might talk the matter over. I don't imagine they mean you any harm, personally, because you tread on nobody's toes; but you're too valuable a man for the race to lose, so I thought I'd give you warning. I shall want to sell you my property, too, at a bargain. For I'm worth too much to my family to dream of ever attempting to live here again."

"Have you seen anything of my wife and child?" asked Miller, intent upon the danger to which they might be exposed.

"No; I didn't go to the house. I inquired at the drugstore and found out where you had gone. You needn't fear for them,—it is not a war on women and children."

"War of any kind is always hardest on the women and children," returned Miller; "I must hurry on and see that mine are safe."

"They'll not carry the war so far into Africa as that," returned Watson; "but I never saw anything like it. Yesterday I had a hundred white friends in the town, or thought I had,—men who spoke pleasantly to me on the street, and sometimes gave me their hands to shake. Not one of them said to me today: 'Watson, stay at home this afternoon.' I might have been killed, like any one of half a dozen others who have bit the dust, for any word that one of my 'friends' had said to warn me. When the race cry is started in this neck of the woods, friendship, religion, humanity, reason, all shrivel up like dry leaves in a raging furnace."

The buggy, into which Watson had climbed, was meanwhile rapidly nearing the town.

"I think I'll leave you here, Miller," said Watson, as they approached the outskirts, "and make my way home by a roundabout path, as I should like to get there unmolested. Home!—a beautiful word that, isn't it, for an exiled wanderer? It might not be well, either, for us to be seen together. If you put the hood of your buggy down, and sit well back in the shadow, you may be able to reach home without interruption; but avoid the main streets. I'll see you again this evening. if we're both alive, and I can reach you; for my time is short. A committee are to call in the morning to escort me to the train. I am to be dismissed from the community with public honors."

Watson was climbing down from the buggy, when a small party of men were seen approaching, and big Josh Green, followed by several other resolute-looking colored men, came up and addressed them.

"Dr. Miller," cried Green, "Mr. Watson,—we're lookin' fer a leader. De w'ite folks are killin' de niggers, an' we ain' gwine ter stan' up an' be shot down like dogs. We're gwine ter defen' ou' lives, an' we ain' gwine ter run away f'm no place where we've got a right ter be; an' woe be ter de w'ite man w'at lays han's on us! Dere's two niggers in dis town to eve'y w'ite man, an' ef we've got ter be killt, we'll take some w'ite folks 'long wid us, ez sho' ez dere's a God in heaven,—ez I s'pose dere is, dough He mus' be 'sleep, er busy somewhar e'se ter-day. Will you-all come an' lead us?"

"Gentlemen," said Watson, "what is the use? The negroes will not back you up. They haven't the arms, nor the moral courage, nor the leadership."

"We'll git de arms, an' we'll git de courage, ef you'll come an' lead us! We wants leaders,—dat's w'y we come ter you!"

"What's the use?" returned Watson despairingly. "The odds are too heavy. I've been ordered out of town; if I stayed, I'd be shot on sight, unless I had a body-guard around me."

"We'll be yo' body-guard!" shouted half a dozen voices.

"And when my body-guard was shot, what then? I have a wife and children. It is my duty to live for them. If I died, I should get no glory and no reward, and my family would be reduced to beggary, —to which they'll soon be near enough as it is. This affair will blow over in a day or two. The white people will be ashamed of themselves tomorrow, and apprehensive of the consequence for some time to come. Keep quiet, boys, and trust in God. You won't gain anything by resistance."

" 'God he'ps dem da he'ps demselves,' " returned Josh stoutly. "Ef Mr. Watson won't lead us, will you, Dr. Miller?" said the spokesman, turning to the doctor.

For Miller it was an agonizing moment. He was no coward, morally or physically. Every manly instinct urged him to go forward and take up the cause of these leaderless people, and, if need be, to defend their lives and their rights with his own—but to what end?

"Listen, men," he said. "We would only be throwing our lives away. Suppose we made a determined stand and won a temporary victory. By morning every train, every boat, every road leading into Wellington, would be crowded with white men,—as they probably will be anyway,—with arms in their hands, curses on their lips, and vengeance in their hearts. In the minds of those who make and administer the laws, we have no standing in the court of conscience. They would kill us in the fight, or would hang us afterwards,—one way or another, we should be doomed. I should like to lead you; I should like to arm every colored man in this town, and have them stand firmly in line, not for attack but for defense; but if I attempted it, and they should stand by me, which is questionable,—for I have met them fleeing from the town,—my life would pay the forfeit. Alive, I may be of some use to you, and you are welcome to my life in that way,—I am giving it freely. Dead, I should be a mere lump of carrion. Who remembers even the names of those who have been done to death in the Southern States for the past twenty years?"

"I members de name er one of 'em," said Josh, "an I 'members de name er de man dat killt 'im, an' I s'pec' his time is mighty nigh come."

"My advice is not heroic, but I think it is wise. In this riot we are placed as we should be in a war: we have no territory, no base of supplies, no organization, no outside sympathy,—we stand in the position of a race, in a case like this, without money and without friends. Our time will come—the time when we can command respect for our rights; but it is not yet in sight. Give it up, boys, and wait. Good may come of this, after all."

Several of the men wavered, and looked irresolute.

"I reckon that's all so, doctah," returned Josh, "an', de way you put it, I don' blame you ner Mr. Watson; but all dem reasons ain't got no weight wid me. I'm gwine in dat town, an' ef any w'ite man 'sturbs me, dere'll be trouble,—dere'll be double trouble,—I feels it in my bones!"

"Remember your old mother, Josh," said Miller.

"Yas, suh, I'll 'member her; dat's all I kin do now. I don' need ter wait fer her no mo', fer she died dis mo'nin'. I'd lack ter see her buried, suh, but I may not have de chance. Ef I gits killt, will you de me a favor?"

"Yes, Josh; what is it?"

"Ef I should git laid out in dis commotion dat's gwine on, will you collec' my wages f'm yo' brother, and see dat de ole 'oman is put away right?"

"Yes, of course."

"Wid a nice coffin, an' a nice fune'al, an' a head-bo'd an' a foot-bo'd?"

"Yes."

"All right, suh! Ef I don' live ter do it, I'll know it'll be 'tended ter right. Now we're gwine out ter de cotton compress, an' git a lot er colored men tergether, an' if de w'ite folks 'sturbs me, I shouldn't be s'prise' ef dere'd be a mix-up;—an' ef dere is, me an *one* w'ite man 'll stan' befo' de jedgment th'one er God dis day; an' it won't be me w'at 'll be 'feared er de jedgment. Come along, boys! Dese gentlemen may have somethin' ter live fer; but ez fer my pa't, I'd ruther be a dead nigger any day dan a live dog!"

JAMES WELDON JOHNSON (1871-1938)

Though well known for his musical-comedy lyrics, James Weldon Johnson (see also pp. 324, 967) reached his first literary distinction with *The Autobiography of an Ex-Colored Man* (1912). Mistakenly considered an autobiography, the novel still leans heavily upon material that Johnson collected in his variegated career. Expository rather than dramatic, the novel has worn very well and has been recently reprinted. It not only is the first of the "passing" novels, the first treatment of the Black Bohemia of New York, and the first novel attempting to give a cross section of Negro life, but it also anticipates much of Johnson's own later work. The selections below are reprinted by permission of Mrs. Grace Nail Johnson and Alfred A. Knopf, Inc., the publishers.

[Camp Meeting]

ALL THIS WHILE I WAS GATHERING material for work, jotting down in my note-book themes and melodies, and trying to catch the spirit of the Negro in his relatively primitive state. I began to feel the necessity of hurrying so that I might get back to some city like Nashville to begin my compositions and at the same time earn at least a living by teaching and performing before my funds gave out. At the last settlement in which I stopped I found a mine of material. This was due to the fact that "big meeting" was in progress. "Big meeting" is an institution something like camp-meeting, the difference being that it is held in a permanent church, and not in a temporary structure. All the churches of some one denomination—of course, either Methodist or Baptist—in a county, or, perhaps, in several adjoining counties, are closed, and the congregations unite at some centrally located church for a series of meetings lasting a week. It is really a social as well as a religious function. The people come in great numbers, making the trip, according to their financial status, in buggies drawn by sleek, fleet-footed mules, in ox-carts, or on foot. It was amusing to see some of the latter class trudging down the hot and dusty road, with their shoes, which were brand-new, strung across their shoulders. When they got near the church, they sat on the side of the road and, with many grimaces, tenderly packed their feet into those instruments of torture. This furnished, indeed, a trying test of their religion. The famous preachers come from near and far and take turns in warning sinners of the day of wrath. Food, in the form of those two Southern luxuries, fried chicken and roast pork, is plentiful, and no one need go hungry. On the opening Sunday the women are immaculate in starched stiff white dresses adorned with ribbons, either red or blue. Even a great many of the men wear streamers of vari-coloured ribbons in the buttonholes of their coats. A few of them carefully cultivate a forelock of hair by wrapping it in twine, and on such festive occasions decorate it with a narrow ribbon streamer. Big meetings afford a fine opportunity to the younger people to meet each other dressed in their Sunday clothes, and much rustic courting, which is as enjoyable as any other kind, is indulged in.

This big meeting which I was lucky enough to catch was particularly well attended; the extra large attendance was due principally to two attractions, a man by the name of John Brown, who was renowned as the most powerful preacher for miles around; and a wonderful leader of singing, who was known as "Singing Johnson." These two men were a study and a revelation to me. They caused me to reflect upon how great an influence their types have been in the development of the Negro in America. Both these types are now looked upon generally with condescension or contempt by the progressive element among the coloured people; but it should never be forgotten that it was they who led the race from paganism and kept it steadfast to Christianity through all the long, dark years of slavery.

John Brown was a jet-black man of medium size, with a strikingly intelligent head and face, and a voice like an organ peal. He preached each night after several lesser lights had successively held the pulpit during an hour or so. As far as subject-matter is concerned, all of the sermons were alike: each began with the fall of man, ran through various trials and tribulations of the Hebrew children, on to the redemption by Christ, and ended with a fervid picture of the judgment-day and the fate of the damned. But John Brown possessed magnetism and an imagination so free and daring that he was able to carry through what the other preachers would not attempt. He knew all the arts and tricks of oratory, the modulation of the voice to almost a whisper, the pause for effect, the rise through light, rapid-fire sentences to the terrific, thundering outburst of an electrifying climax. In addition, he had the intuition of a born theatrical manager. Night after night this man held me fascinated. He convinced me that, after all, eloquence consists more in the manner of saying than in what is said. It is largely a matter of tone pictures.

The most striking example of John Brown's magnetism and imagination was his "heavenly march"; I shall never forget how it impressed me when I heard it. He opened his sermon in the usual way; then, proclaiming to his listeners that he was going to take them on the heavenly march, he seized the Bible under his arm and began to pace up and down the pulpit platform. The congregation immediately began with their feet a tramp, tramp, tramp, in time with the preacher's march in the pulpit, all the while singing in an undertone a hymn about marching to Zion. Suddenly he cried: "Halt!" Every foot stopped with the precision of a company of well-drilled soldiers, and the singing ceased. The morning star had been reached. Here the preacher described the beauties of that celestial body. Then the march, the tramp, tramp, tramp, and the singing were again taken up. Another "Halt!" They had reached the evening star. And so on, past the sun and moon—the intensity of religious emotion all the time increasing—along the milky way, on up to the gates of heaven. Here the halt was longer, and the preacher described at length the gates and walls of the New Jerusalem. Then he took his hearers through the pearly gates, along the golden streets, pointing out the glories of the city, pausing occasionally to greet some patriarchal members of the church, well-known to most of his listeners in life, who had had "the tears wiped from their eyes, were clad in robes of spotless white, with crowns of gold upon their heads and harps within their hands," and ended his march before the great white throne. To the reader this may sound ridiculous, but listened to under the circumstances, it was highly and effectively dramatic. I was a more or less sophisticated and non-religious man of the world, but the torrent of the preacher's words, moving with the rhythm and glowing with the eloquence of primitive poetry, swept me along, and I, too, felt like joining in the shouts of "Amen! Hallelujah!"

John Brown's powers in describing the delights of heaven were no greater than those in depicting the horrors of hell. I saw great, strapping fellows trembling and weeping like children at the "mourners' bench." His warnings to sinners were truly terrible. I shall never forget one expression that he used, which for originality and aptness could not be excelled. In my opinion, it is more graphic and, for us, far more expressive than St. Paul's "It is hard to kick against the pricks." He struck the attitude of a pugilist and thundered out: "Young man, your arm's too short to box with God!"

Interesting as was John Brown to me, the other man, "Singing Johnson," was more so. He was a small, dark-brown, one-eyed man, with a clear, strong, high-pitched voice, a leader of singing, a maker of songs, a man who could improvise at the moment lines to fit the occasion. Not so striking a figure as John Brown, but, at "big meetings," equally important. It is indispensable to the success of the singing, when the congregation is a large one made up of people from different communities, to have someone with a strong voice who knows just what hymn to sing and when to sing it, who can pitch it in the right key, and who has all the leading lines committed to memory. Sometimes it devolves upon the leader to "sing down" a long-winded or uninteresting speaker. Committing to memory the leading lines of all the Negro spiritual songs is no easy task, for they run up into the hundreds. But the accomplished leader must know them all, because the congregation sings only the refrains and repeats; every ear in the church is fixed upon him, and if he becomes mixed in his lines or forgets them, the responsibility falls directly on his shoulders.

For example, most of these hymns are constructed to be sung in the following manner:

Leader. Swing low, sweet chariot.
Congregation. Coming for to carry me home.
Leader. Swing low, sweet chariot.
Congregation. Coming for to carry me home.
Leader. I look over yonder, what do I see?
Congregation. Coming for to carry me home.
Leader. Two little angels coming after me.
Congregation. Coming for to carry me home. . . .

The solitary and plaintive voice of the leader is answered by a sound like the roll of the sea, producing a most curious effect.

In only a few of these songs do the leader and the congregation start off together. Such a song is the well-known "Steal away to Jesus."

> Steal away, steal away,
> Steal away to Jesus;
> Steal away, steal away home,
> I ain't got long to stay here.

Then the leader alone or the congregation in unison:

> My Lord he calls me,
> He calls me by the thunder,
> The trumpet sounds within-a my soul.

Then all together:

> I ain't got long to stay here.

The leader and the congregation again take up the opening refrain; then the leader sings three more leading lines alone, and so on almost *ad infinitum*. It will be seen that even here most of the work falls upon the leader, for the congregation sings the same lines over and over, while his memory and ingenuity are taxed to keep the songs going.

Generally the parts taken up by the congregation are sung in a three-part harmony, the women singing the soprano and a transposed tenor, the men with high voices singing the melody, and those with low voices a thundering bass. In a few of these songs, however, the leading part is sung in unison by the whole congregation, down to the last line, which is harmonized. The effect of this is intensely thrilling. Such a hymn is "Go down, Moses." It stirs the heart like a trumpet-call.

"Singing Johnson" was an ideal leader, and his services were in great demand. He spent his time going about the country from one church to another. He received his support in much the same way as the preachers—part of a collection, food and lodging. All of his leisure time he devoted to originating new words and melodies and new lines for old songs. He always sang with his eyes—or, to be more exact, his eye—closed, indicating the *tempo* by swinging his head to and fro. He was a great judge of the proper hymn to sing at a particular moment; and I noticed several times, when the preacher reached a certain climax, or expressed a certain sentiment, that Johnson broke in with a line or two of some appropriate hymn. The speaker understood and would pause until the singing ceased.

As I listened to the singing of these songs, the wonder of their production grew upon me more and more. How did the men who originated them manage to do it? The sentiments are easily accounted for; they are mostly taken from the Bible; but the melodies, where did they come from? Some of them so weirdly sweet, and others so wonderfully strong. Take, for instance, "Go down, Moses." I doubt that there is a stronger theme in the whole musical literature of the world. And so many of these songs contain more than mere melody; there is sounded in them that elusive undertone, the note in music which is not heard with the ears. I sat often with tears rolling down my cheeks and my heart melted within me. Any musical person who has never heard a Negro congregation under the spell of religious fervour sing these old songs has missed one of the most thrilling emotions which the human heart may experience. Anyone who without shedding tears can listen to Negroes sing "Nobody knows de trouble I see, Nobody knows but Jesus" must indeed have a heart of stone.

As yet, the Negroes themselves do not fully appreciate these old slave songs. The educated classes are rather ashamed of them and prefer to sing hymns from books. This feeling is natural; they are still too close to the conditions under which the songs were produced; but the day will come when this slave music will be the most treasured heritage of the American Negro.

J. A. ROGERS (1883-   )

Joel Augustus Rogers was born in Jamaica. A self-educated man, he has been a journalist traveling in Europe, Asia, and Africa in search of material on the Negro. For four years he served with the British army. His articles have been published in various newspapers and in such magazines as *The American Mercury, The Crisis, The Survey Graphic,* and *The Journal of Negro History. From Superman to Man* (1917 reissued in 1941), *The Maroons of the West Indies and South America* (1921), *The World's Greatest Men of African Descent* (1931) and *Sex and Race* (1941), and articles "Impressions of Dixie," "Jazz at Home," "The American Negro in Europe," and "The Real Facts about Ethiopia," are among his many publications. The passage is from *From Superman to Man* and is reprinted by permission of the author.

[The Porter Debates the Senator]

THE LIMITED WAS SPEEDING to California over the snow-blanketed prairies of Iowa. On car "Bulwer" the passengers had all retired, and Dixon, the porter, his duties finished, sought the more comfortable warmth of the smoker, where he intended to resume the reading of the book he had brought with him, Finot's "Race Prejudice." He had been reading last of the Germans and their doctrine of the racial inferiority of the remainder of the white race. Having found the passage again, he began to read:—"The notion of superior and inferior peoples spread like wildfire through Germany. German literature, philosophy, and politics were profoundly influenced by it——." . . .

The Germans of 1854, he reflected, built up a theory of the inferiority of the other peoples of the white race. Some of these so-called inferior whites have, in turn, built up a similar theory about the darker peoples. This recalled to him some of the many falsities current about his own people. He thought of how in nearly all the large libraries of the United States, which he had been permitted to enter, he had found books advancing all sorts of theories to prove that they were inferior. Some of these theories even denied them human origin. He went on to reflect on the discussions he had heard on the cars and other places from time to time, and of what he called "the heirloom ideas" that many persons had concerning the different varieties of the human race. These discussions, he went on to reflect, had done him good. They had been the means of his acquiring a fund of knowledge on the subject of race, as they had caused him to look up those opinions he had thought incorrect in the works of the standard scientists. Moved by these thoughts he took a morocco-bound notebook from his vest pocket and wrote:—"This doctrine of racial superiority apparently incited the other white peoples, most of whom were enemies to one another, to unite against the Germans, and destroy their empire. Will the doctrine of white superiority over the darker races produce a similar result to white empire?"

But at this juncture his thoughts were interrupted by the entrance of someone. Looking up he saw a man clad in pajamas and overcoat, and with slippered feet, enter the room.

Now Dixon had taken special notice of this man for, during the afternoon, he had been discussing the color question with another passenger in the smoker. From what Dixon had overheard, the man just entering was a Southern senator on his way to California on business. Dixon had occasion to go into the room several times. On one occasion he had heard this man say vehemently "The 'nigger' is a menace to our civilization and should be kept down. I am opposed to educating him, for the educated 'nigger' is a misfit in the white man's civilization. He is a caricature and no good can result from his 'butting in' on our affairs. Would to God that none of the breed had ever set foot on the shores of our country. That's the proper place for a 'nigger,' " he had said quite aloud, on seeing Dixon engaged in wiping out the wash bowls.

At another time he had heard the same speaker deliver himself of this opinion:—"You may say what you please, but I would never eat with a 'nigger.' I couldn't stomach it. God has placed an insuperable barrier between black and white that will ever prevent them from living on the same social plane, at least so far as the Anglo-Saxon is concerned. I have no hatred for the black man—in fact, I could have none, but he must stay in his place."

"That's nothing else but racial antipathy," his opponent had objected.

"You don't have to take my word for it," said the other, snappily. "Didn't Abraham Lincoln say: 'There is a physical difference between the white and black races which, I believe, will forbid the two races living together on terms of social and political equality'? Call it what you will, but there is an indefinable something within me that tells me that I am infinitely better than the best 'nigger' that ever lived. The feeling is instinctive and I am not going to violate nature." . . .

"You, too, had slavery in the North, but it didn't pay and you gave it up. Wasn't your pedantic and self-righteous Massachusetts the first to legalize slavery? You, Northerners, forced slavery on us, and when you couldn't make any more money in it, because England had stopped the slave trade, you made war on us to make us give it up. A matter of climate, that's all. Climes reversed, it would have been the South that wanted abolition. It was a matter of business with you, not sentiment. You Northerners who had an interest in slavery, were bitterly opposed to abolition. It is all very well for you to talk, but if you Yankees had the same percentage of 'niggers' that we have, you would sing a different tune. The bitterest people against the 'nigger' are you Northerners who have come South. You, too, have race riots, lynching and segregation. The only difference between South and North is, that one is frank and the other hypocritical," and he added with vehement sincerity, "I hate hypocrisy."

In spite of this avowed enmity toward his people, Dixon had felt no animosity toward the man. Here, he had thought, was a conscience, honest but uneducated.

All of this ran through the porter's mind when he saw the pajama-clad passenger appear in the doorway. The newcomer, on entering, walked up to the mirror, where he looked at himself quizzically for a moment, then selected a chair and adjusting it to suit his fancy, made himself comfortable in it; next, he took a plain and well-worn gold cigarette case from his pocket, selected a cigarette, and, after tapping it on the chair, began rummaging in his pockets for a match, all in apparent oblivion to the presence of Dixon at the near end of the long cushioned seat. But Dixon had been quietly observing him and deftly presented a lighted match, at the same time venturing to inquire in a respectful and rather solicitous tone, "Can't sleep, sir?"

"No, George," same the reply in an amiable, but condescending tone, "I was awakened at the last stop and can't go back to sleep. I never do very well the first night, anyway."

With this the senator began to talk to Dixon quite freely, telling him of his trip from Oklahoma. They soon began to talk about more personal matters. Into this part of the conversation the senator injected phrases such as "darkies," "niggers" and "coons."

From this he began to tell jokes about chicken-stealing, razor-fights and watermelon feasts. Of such jokes he evidently had an abundant stock. Nearly all of these Dixon had heard time and again. One was the anecdote of a Negro headwaiter in a Northern hotel who, when asked by a Southern guest if he were the head "nigger," indignantly objected to the epithet, but upon the visitor's informing him that it was his custom to give a large tip to the "head-nigger" this head-waiter, so the story goes, effusively retracted, saying, "Yessah, Boss, I'se de' head niggah," and pointing to the waiters, added, "and ef you doan b'leave me ast all dem othah niggahs dah."

The narrator was laughing immoderately, and so was the listener. Had the entertainer been a mind reader, however, he might not have been flattered by his success as a comedian, since it was his conduct, and not his wit, that was furnishing the porter's mirth.

While the senator was still laughing the train began to slow down, and Dixon, asking to be excused, slid to the other end of the seat to look out, thus exposing the book he had placed behind him. The senator saw the volume and his look of laughter was instantly changed to one of curiosity.

The book stood end up on the seat and he could discern from its size and binding that it was a volume that might contain serious thought. He had somehow felt that this Negro was above the ordinary and the sight of the book now confirmed the feeling.

A certain forced quality in the timbre of Dixon's laughter as also the merry twinkle in his eye, had made him feel at times just a bit uncomfortable, and now he wanted to verify the suspicion. His curiosity getting the better of him, he reached over to take the volume, but at the same instant Dixon's slipping back to his former seat caused him to hesitate. Yet he determined to find out. He demanded flippantly, pointing to the book,—"Reading the Bible, George?"

"No, sir."

"What then?"

"Oh, only a scientific work," said the other, carelessly, not wishing to broach the subject of racial differences that the title of the book suggested. Dixon's very evident desire to evade a direct answer seemed to sharpen the other's curiosity. He suggested off-handedly, but with ill-concealed eagerness: "Pretty deep stuff, eh?" Then in the same manner he inquired, "Who's the author?"

Dixon saw the persistent curiosity in the other's eye. Knowing too well the nature of the man before him, he did not want to give him the book, but being unable to find any pretext for further withholding it, he took it from the seat, turned it right side up, and handed it to the senator. The latter took it with feigned indifference. Moistening his forefinger, he began turning over the leaves, then settled down to read the marked passages. Now and then he would mutter: "Nonsense! Ridiculous!" Suddenly in a burst of impatience he turned to the frontispiece, and exclaimed in open disgust: "Just as I thought. Written by a Frenchman." Then, before he could recollect to whom he was talking—so full was he of what he regarded as the absurdity of Finot's view—he demanded—"Do you believe all this rot about the equality of the races?"

Now Dixon's policy was to avoid any topic that would be likely to produce a difference of opinion with a passenger, provided that the avoidance did not entail any sacrifice of his self-respect. In this instance he regarded his questioner as one to be humored, rather than vexed, for just then the following remark, made by this legislator that afternoon, recurred to him:

"The Jew, the Frenchman, the Dago and the Spaniards are all 'niggers' to a greater or lesser extent. The only white people are the Anglo-Saxon, Teutons and Scandinavians."

This, Dixon surmised, had accounted for the remark the other had made about the author's adopted nationality, and it amused him.

As Dixon pondered the question there occurred to him a way by which he could retain his own opinion while in apparent accord with the passenger. He responded accordingly:—

"No, sir, I do not believe in the equality of the races. As you say, it is impossible."

The senator looked up as if he had not been expecting a response, but seemingly pleased with Dixon's acquiescence he continued as he turned the leaves: "Writers of this type don't know what they are talking about. They write from mere theory. If they had to live among 'niggers,' they would sing an entirely different tune."

Dixon felt that he ought not to let this remark go unchallenged. He protested courteously: "Yes, sir, M. Finot has proved his argument admirably. I am sure if you were to read his book you would agree with him, too."

"Didn't you just say you didn't agree with this book?"

"I fear you misunderstood me, sir."

"Didn't you say you did not believe in the equality of the races?"

"Yes, sir."

"Then why?"

"Because as you said, sir, it is impossible."

"Why? Why?"

"Because there is but one race—the human race."

The senator did not respond. Despite his anger at the manner in which Dixon had received and responded to his question, he stopped to ponder the situation in which his unwitting question had placed him.

As he had confessed, he did not like educated Negroes, and had no intention of engaging in a controversy with one. His respect and his aversion for this porter had increased with a bound. Now he was weighing the respective merits of the two possible courses—silence and response. If he remained silent, this Negro might think he had silenced him, while to respond would be to engage in an argument, thus treating the Negro as an equal. After weighing the matter for some time he decided that of the two courses, silence was the less compatible with his racial dignity, and with much condescension, his stiff voice and haughty manner a marked contrast to his jollity of a few minutes past, he demanded:

"You say there is only one race. What do you call yourself?"

"An American citizen," responded the other, composedly.

"Perhaps you have never heard of the word 'nigger'?"

"Couldn't help it, sir," came the reply in the same quiet voice.

"Then do you believe the 'nigger' is the equal of the Anglo-Saxon race?" he demanded with ill-concealed anger.

"I have read many books on anthropology, sir, but I have not seen mention of either a 'nigger' race or an Anglo-Saxon one.

"Very well, do you believe your race—the black race—is equal to the Caucasian?"

Dixon stopped to weigh the wisdom of his answering. What good would it do to talk with a man seemingly so rooted in his prejudices? Then a simile came to him. On a visit to the Bureau of Standards at Washington, D. C., he had seen the effect of the pressure of a single finger upon a supported bar of steel three inches thick. The slight strain had caused the steel to yield one-twenty-thousandth part of an inch, as the delicate apparatus, the interferometer, had registered. Since every action, he went on to reason, produces an effect, and truth, with the impulse of the Cosmos behind it, is irresistible, surely if he advanced his views in a kindly spirit, he must modify the error in this man. But still he hesitated. Suddenly he recalled that here was a legislator: was one of those, who, above all others, ought to know the truth. This thought decided his course. He would answer to the point, resolving at the same time to restrict any conversation that might ensue to the topic of the human race as a whole and to steer clear of the color question in the United States. He responded with soft courtesy:

"I have found, sir, that any division of humanity according to physique can have but a merely nominal value, as differences in physiques are caused by climatic conditions and are subject to rechange by them. As you know, both Science and the Bible are agreed that all so-called races came from a single source. Scientists who have made a study of this question tell us that the Negro and the Yankee are both approaching the Red Indian type. Pigmented humanity becomes lighter in the temperate zone, while unpigmented humanity becomes brown in the tropics. One summer's exposure at a bathing beach is enough to make a life-saver darker than many Indians. The true skin of all human beings is of the same color: all men are white under the first layer.

"Then it is possible by the blending of human varieties to produce innumerable other varities, each one capable of reproducing and continuing itself.

"Again, anthropologists have never been able to classify human varieties. Huxley, as you know, named 2, Blumenbach 5, Burke 63, while others, desiring greater accuracy, have named hundreds. Since these classifications are so vague and changeable, it is evident, is it not, sir, that any division of humanity, whether by color or skin, hair or facial contour, to be other than purely nominal, must be one of mentality? And to classify humanity by intellect, would be, as you know, an impossible task. Nature, so far as we know, made only the individual. This idea has been ably expressed by Lamarck, who, in speaking of the human race, says,—'Classifications are artificial, for nature had created neither classes, nor orders, nor families, nor kinds, nor permanent species, but only individuals.'"

The senator handed back the book to Dixon, huffily. "But, you have not answered my question yet," he insisted, "I asked, do you believe the black race will ever attain the intellectual standard of the Caucasian?"

"Intellect, whether of civilized or uncivilized humanity, as you know, sir, is elastic in quality. That is, primitive man when transplanted to civilization not only becomes civilized, but sometimes excels some of those whose ancestors have had centuries of culture, and the child of civilized man when isolated among primitives becomes one himself. We would find that the differences between a people who had acquired say three or four generations of beneficent culture, and another who had been long civilized would be about the same as that between the individuals in the long civilized group. That is, the usual human differences would exist. To be accurate we would have to appraise each individual separately. Any comparison between the groups would be inexact."

"But," reiterated the other, sarcastically, "you have not answered my question. Do you believe the black man will ever attain the high intellectual standard of the Caucasian? Yes or no?"

"For the most authoritative answer," responded Dixon in the calm manner of the disciplined thinker, "we must look to modern science. If you don't mind, sir, I will give you some quotations from scientists of acknowledged authority, all of your own race."

Dixon drew out his notebook.

"Bah," said the other savagely, "opinions! Mere opinions! I asked you what you think and you are telling me what someone else says. What I want to know is, what do YOU think?"

"Each of us," replied Dixon, evenly, "however learned, however independent, is compelled to seek the opinion of someone else on some particular subject at some time. There is the doctor and the other professionals, for instance. Now in seeking advice one usually places the most reliance on those one considers experts, is it not? This afternoon I overheard you quoting from one of Lincoln's debates with Douglas in order to prove your views."

Silence.

Dixon opened his notebook. After finding the desired passage he said:

"In 1911 most of the leading sociologists and anthropologists of the world met in a Universal Races Congress in London. The opinion of that congress was that all the so-called races of men are essentially equal. Gustav Spiller, its organizer and secretary, voiced the findings of that entire body of experts when, after a careful weighing of the question of superiority and inferiority, he said (here Dixon read from the notebook):

"We are then under the necessity of concluding that an impartial investigator would be inclined to look upon the various important peoples of the world as, to all intents and purposes, essentially equal in intellect, enterprise, morality and physique."

Dixon found another passage and said: "Finot, whose findings ought to be regarded as more valuable than the expressions of those who base their arguments on sentiment or on Hebrew mythology, says,—"All peoples may attain this distant frontier which the brains of the whites have reached." He also says:

"The conclusion, therefore, forces itself upon us, that there are no inferior and superior races, but only races and peoples living outside or within the influence of culture.

"The appearance of civilization and its evolution among certain white peoples and within a certain geographical latitude is only the effect of circumstances."

WALTER WHITE (1893-   )

Walter White (see also p. 1005) was born in Atlanta; he was educated at Atlanta University and the College of the City of New York. His work as secretary of the National Association for the Advancement of Colored People, for which he has investigated lynchings and race riots, and has lobbied unceasingly for the passage of antilynching legislation, is nationally known. In 1927 and 1928 he was a Guggenheim Fellow; in 1937 he won the Spingarn medal. He has written two novels, *Fire in the Flint* (1924) and *Flight* (1926) as well as *Rope and Faggot: A Biography of Judge Lynch* (1929), and articles for the *Bookman, Century, Harper's*, the *American Mercury, The Crisis, Forum, The Nation, The New Republic*, and the *Survey Graphic*. The following is reprinted by permission of the author and of Alfred A. Knopf, Inc.

[A Negro Doctor in the South]

HIS OFFICE COMPLETED, Kenneth began the making of those contacts he needed to secure the patients he knew were coming. In this his mother and Mamie were of invaluable assistance. Everybody knew the

Harpers. It was a simple matter for Kenneth to renew acquaintances broken when he had left for school in the North. He joined local lodges of the Grand United Order of Heavenly Reapers and the Exalted Knights of Damon. The affected mysteriousness of his initiation into these fraternal orders, the secret grip, the passwords, the elaborately worded rituals, all of which the other members took so seriously, amused him, but he went through it all with an outwardly solemn demeanour. He knew it was good business to affiliate himself with these often absurd societies which played so large a part in the lives of these simple and illiterate coloured folk. Along with the strenuous emotionalism of their religion, it served as an outlet for their naturally deep feelings.

In spite of the renewal of acquaintances, the careful campaign of winning confidence in his ability as a physician, Kenneth found that the flood of patients did not come as he had hoped. The coloured people of Central City had had impressed upon them by three hundred years of slavery and that which was called freedom after the Emancipation Proclamation was signed, that no Negro doctor, however talented, was quite as good as a white one. This slave mentality, Kenneth now realized, inbred upon generation after generation of coloured folk, is the greatest handicap from which the Negro suffers, destroying as it does that confidence in his own ability which would enable him to meet without fear or apology the test of modern competition.

Kenneth's youthful appearance, too, militated against him. Though twenty-nine years old, he looked not more than a mere twenty-four or twenty-five. "He may know his stuff and be as smart as all outdoors," ran the usual verdict, "but I don't want no boy treating me when I'm sick."

Perhaps the greatest factor contributing to the coloured folks' lack of confidence in physicians of their own race was the inefficiency of Dr. Williams, the only coloured doctor in Central City prior to Kenneth's return. Dr. Williams belonged to the old school and moved on the theory that when he graduated some eighteen years before from a medical school in Alabama, the development of medical knowledge had stopped. He fondly pictured himself as being the most prominent personage of Central City's Negro colony, was pompous, bulbous-eyed, and exceedingly fond of long words, especially of Latin derivation. He made it a rule of his life never to use a word of one syllable if one of two or more would serve as well. Active in fraternal order circles (he was a member of nine lodges), class-leader in Central City's largest Methodist church, arbiter supreme of local affairs in general, he filled the rôle with what he imagined was unsurpassable éclat. His idea of complimenting a hostess was ostentatiously to loosen his belt along about the middle of dinner. Once he had been introduced as the "black William Jennings Bryan," believed it thereafter, and thought it praise of a high order.

He was one of those who say on every possible occasion: "I am kept so terribly busy I never have a minute to myself." Like nine out of ten who say it, Dr. Williams always repeated this stock phrase of those who flatter themselves in this fashion—so necessary to those of small minds who would be thought great—not because it was true, but to enhance his pre-eminence in the eyes of his hearers—and in his own eyes as well.

He always wore coats which resembled morning coats, known in local parlance as "Jim-swingers." He kept his hair straightened, wore it brushed straight back from his forehead like highly polished steel wires, and, with pomades and hair oils liberally applied, it glistened like the patent leather shoes which adorned his ample feet.

His stout form filled the Ford in which he made his professional calls, and it was a sight worth seeing as he majestically rolled through the streets of the town bowing graciously and calling out loud greetings to the acquaintances he espied by the way. Always his bows to white people were twice as low and obsequious as to those of darker skin. Until Kenneth returned, Dr. Williams had had his own way in Central City. Through his fraternal and church connections and lack of competition, he had made a little money, much of it through his position as medical examiner for the lodges to which he belonged. As long as he treated minor ailments—cuts, colic, childbirths, and the like—he had little trouble. But when more serious maladies attacked them, the coloured population sent for the old white physician, Dr. Bennett, instead of for Dr. Williams.

The great amount of time at his disposal irritated Kenneth. He was like a spirited horse, champing at the bit, eager to be off. The patronizing air of his people nettled him—caused him to reflect somewhat bitterly that "a prophet is not without honour save in his own country." And when one has not the gift of prophecy to foretell, or of clairvoyance to see, what the future holds in the way of success, one is not likely to develop a philosophic calm which enables him to await the coming of long-desired results.

He was seated one day in his office reading when his mother entered. Closing his book, he asked the reason for her frown.

"You remember Mrs. Bradley—Mrs. Emma Bradley down on Ashley Street—don't you, Kenneth?" Without waiting for a reply,

Mrs. Harper went on: "Well, she's mighty sick. Jim Bradley has had Dr. Bennett in to see what's the matter with her but he don't seem to do her much good."

Kenneth remembered Mrs. Bradley well indeed. The most talkative woman in Central City. It was she who had come to his mother with a long face and dolorous manner when he as a youngster had misbehaved in church. He had learned instinctively to connect Mrs. Bradley's visits with excursions to the little back room accompanied by his mother and a switch from the peach-tree in the back yard—a sort of natural cause and effect. Visions of those days rose in his mind and he imagined he could feel the sting of those switches on his legs now.

"What seems to be the trouble with her?" he asked.

"It's some sort of stomach-trouble—she's got an awful pain in her side. She says it can't be her appendix because she had that removed up to Atlanta when she was operated on there for a tumor nearly four years ago. Dr. Bennett gave her some medicine but it doesn't help her any. Won't you run down there to see her?"

"I can't, mamma, until I am called in professionally. Dr. Bennett won't like it. It isn't ethical. Besides, didn't Mrs. Bradley say when I came back that she didn't want any coloured doctor fooling with her?"

"Yes she did, but you mustn't mind that. Just run in to see her on a social call."

Kenneth rose and instinctively took up his bag. Remembering, he put it down, put on his hat, kissed his mother, and walked down to Mrs. Bradley's. Outside the gate stood Dr. Bennett's mud-splashed buggy, sagging on one side through years of service in carrying its owner's great bulk. Between the shafts stood the old bay horse, its head hung dejectedly as though asleep.

Entering the gate held by one hinge, Kenneth made his way to the little three-room unpainted house which served as home for the Bradleys and their six children. On knocking, the door was opened by Dr. Bennett, who apparently was just leaving. He stood there, his hat on, stained by many storms, its black felt turning a greenish brown through years of service and countless rides through the red dust of the roads leading out of Central City. Dr. Bennett himself was large and flabby. His clothes hung on him in haphazard fashion and looked as though they had never been subjected to the indignity of a tailor's iron. A Sherlock Holmes, or even one less gifted, could read on his vest with little difficulty those things which its wearer had eaten for many meals past. Dr. Bennett's face was red through exposure to many suns, and covered with the bristle of a three days' growth of beard. Small eyes set close together, they belied a bluff good humour which Dr. Bennett could easily assume when there was occasion for it. The corners of the mouth were stained a deep brown where tobacco juice had run down the folds of the flesh.

Behind him stood Jim Bradley with worried face, his ashy black skin showing the effects of remaining all night by the bedside of his wife.

Dr. Bennett looked at Kenneth inquiringly.

"Don't you remember me, Dr. Bennett? I'm Kenneth Harper."

"Bless my soul, so it is. How're you, Ken? Let's see—it's been nigh on to eight years since you went No'th, ain't it? Heard you was back in town. Hear you goin' to practice here. Come 'round to see me some time. Right glad you're here. I'll be kinder glad to get somebody t' help me treat these niggers for colic or when they get carved up in a crap game. Hope you ain't got none of them No'the'n ideas 'bout social equality while you was up there. Jus' do like your daddy did, and you'll get along all right down here. These niggers who went over to France and ran around with them French-women been causin' a lot of trouble 'round here, kickin' up a rumpus, and talkin' 'bout votin' and ridin' in the same car with white folks. But don't you let them get you mixed up in it, 'cause there'll be trouble sho's you born if they don't shut up and git to work. Jus' do like your daddy did, and you'll do a lot to keep the white folks' friendship."

Dr. Bennett poured forth all this gratuitous advice between asthmatic wheezes without waiting for Kenneth to reply. He then turned to Jim Bradley with a parting word of advice.

"Jim, keep that hot iron on Emma's stomach and give her those pills every hour. 'Tain't nothin' but the belly-ache. She'll be all right in an hour or two."

Turning without another word, he half ambled, half shuffled out to his buggy, pulled himself up into it with more puffing and wheezing, and drove away.

Jim Bradley took Kenneth's arm and led him back on to the little porch, closing the door behind him.

"I'm pow'ful glad t' see you, Ken. My, but you done growed sence you went up No'th! Befo' you go in dar, I want t' tell you somethin'. Emma's been right po'ly fuh two days. Her stomach's swelled up right sma't and she's been hollering all night. Dis mawning she don't seem jus' right in de haid. I tol' her I was gwine to ast you to come to see her, but she said she didn't want no young nigger doctah botherin' with her. But don't you min' her. I wants you to tell me what to do."

Kenneth smiled.

"I'll do what I can for her, Jim. But what about Dr. Bennett?"

"Dat's a' right. He give her some med'cine but it ain't done her no good. She's too good a woman fuh me to lose her, even if she do talk a li'l too much. You make out like you jus' drap in to pass the time o' day with her."

Kenneth entered the dark and ill-smelling room. Opposite the door a fire smouldered in the fire-place, giving fitful spurts of flame that illumined the room and then died down again. There was no grate, the pieces of wood resting on crude andirons, blackened by the smoke of many fires. Over the mantel there hung a cheap charcoal reproduction of Jim and Emma in their wedding-clothes, made by some local "artist" from an old photograph. One or two nondescript chairs worn shiny through years of use stood before the fire. In one corner stood a dresser on which were various bottles of medicine and of "Madame Walker's Hair Grower." On the floor a rug, worn through in spots and patched with fragments of other rugs all apparently of different colours, covered the space in front of the bed. The rest of the floor was bare and showed evidences of a recent vigorous scrubbing. The one window was closed tightly and covered over with a cracked shade, long since divorced from its roller, tacked to the upper ledge of the window.

On the bed Mrs. Bradley was rolling and tossing in great pain. Her eyes opened slightly when Kenneth approached the bed and closed again immediately as a new spasm of pain passed through her body. She moaned piteously and held her hands on her side, pressing down hard one‑hand over the other.

At a sign from Jim, Kenneth started to take her pulse.

"Go way from here and leave me 'lone! Oh, Lawdy, why is I suff'rin' this way! I jus' wish I was daid! Oh—oh—oh!"

This last as she writhed in agony. Kenneth drew back the covers, examined Mrs. Bradley's abdomen, took her pulse. Every sign pointed to an attack of acute appendicitis. He informed Jim of his diagnosis.

"But, Doc, it ain't dat trouble, 'cause Emma says dat was taken out a long time ago."

"I can't help what she says. She's got appendicitis. You go get Dr. Bennett and tell him your wife has got to be operated on right away or she is going to die. Get a move on you now! If it was my case, I would operate within an hour. Stop by my house and tell Bob to bring me an ice bag as quick as he can."

Jim hurried away to catch Dr. Bennett. Kenneth meanwhile did what he could to relieve Mrs. Bradley's suffering. In a few minutes Bob came with the ice bag. Then Jim returned with his face even more doleful than it had been when Kenneth had told him how sick his wife was.

"Doc Bennett says he don't care what you do. He got kinder mad when I told him you said it was 'pendicitis, and tol' me dat if I couldn't take his word, he wouldn't have anything mo' to do with Emma. He seemed kinder mad 'cause you said it was mo' than a stomach-ache. Said he wa'n't goin' to let no young nigger doctor tell him his bus'ness. So, Doc, you'll have t' do what you thinks bes'."

"All right, I'll do it. First thing, I'm going to move your wife over to my office. We can put her up in the spare room. Bob will drive her over in the car. Get something around her and you'd better come on over with her. I'll get Dr. Williams to help me."

Kenneth was jubilant at securing his first surgical case since his return to Central City, though his pleasure was tinged with doubt as to the ethics of the manner in which it had come to him. He did not let that worry him very long, however, but began his preparations for the operation.

First he telephoned to Mrs. Johnson, who, before she married and settled down in Central City, had been a trained nurse at a coloured hospital at Atlanta. She hurried over at once. Neat, quiet, and efficient, she took charge immediately of preparations, sterilizing the array of shiny instruments, preparing wads of absorbent cotton, arranging bandages and catgut and haemostatics.

Kenneth left all this to Mrs. Johnson, for he knew in her hands it would be well done. He telephoned to Dr. Williams to ask that he give the anaesthesia. In his excitement Kenneth neglected to put in his voice the note of asking a great and unusual favor of Dr. Williams. That eminent physician, eminent in his own eyes, cleared his throat several times before replying, while Kenneth waited at the other end of the line. He realized his absolute dependence on Dr. Williams, for he knew no white doctor would assist a Negro surgeon or even operate with a coloured assistant. There was none other in Central City who could give the ether to Mrs. Bradley. It made him furious that Dr. Williams should hesitate so long. At the same time, he knew he must restrain the hot and burning words that he would have used. The pompous one hinted of the pressure of his own work—work that would keep him busy all day. Into his words he injected the note of affront at being asked—he, *the* coloured physician of Central City—to assist a younger man. Especially on that man's first case. Kenneth swallowed his anger and pride, and pleaded with Dr. Williams at least to come over. Finally, the older physician agreed in a condescending manner to do so.

Hurrying back to his office, Kenneth found Mrs. Bradley arranged on the table ready for the operation. Examining her, he found she was in delirium, her eyes glazed, her abdomen hard and distended, and she had a temperature of 105 degrees. He hastily sterilized his hands and put on his gown and cap. As he finished his preparations, Dr. Williams in leisurely manner strolled into the room with a benevolent and patronizing "Howdy, Kenneth, my boy. I won't be able to help you out after all. I've got to see patients of my own."

He emphasized "my own," for he had heard of the manner by which Kenneth had obtained the case of Mrs. Bradley. Kenneth, pale with anger, excited over his first real case in Central City, stared at Dr. Williams in amazement at his words.

"But, Dr. Williams, you can't do that! Mrs. Bradley here is dying!"

The older doctor looked around patronizingly at the circle of anxious faces. Jim Bradley, his face lined and seamed with toil, the lines deepened in distress at the agony of his wife and the imminence of losing her, gazed at him with dumb pleading in his eyes, pleading without spoken words with the look of an old, faithful dog beseeching its master. Bob looked with a malevolent glare at this pompous sleekness, as though he would like to spring upon him. Mrs. Johnson plainly showed her contempt of such callousness on the part of one who bore the title, however poorly, of physician. In Kenneth's eyes was a commingling of eagerness and rage and bitterness and anxiety. On Emma Bradley's face there was nothing but the pain and agony of her delirious ravings. Dr. Williams seemed to enjoy thoroughly his little moment of triumph. He delayed speaking in order that it might be prolonged as much as possible. The silence was broken by Jim Bradley.

"Doc, won't you please he'p?" he pleaded. "She's all I got!"

Kenneth could remain silent no longer. He longed to punch that fat face and erase from it the supercilious smirk that adorned it.

"Dr. Williams," he began with cold hatred in his voice, "either you are going to give this anaesthesia or else I'm going to go into every church in Central City and tell exactly what you've done here today."

Dr. Williams turned angrily on Kenneth.

"Young man, I don't allow anybody to talk to me like that—least of all, a young whippersnapper just out of school . . ." he shouted.

By this time Kenneth's patience was at an end. He seized the lapels of the other doctor's coat in one hand and thrust his clenched fist under the nose of the now thoroughly alarmed Dr. Williams.

"Are you going to help—or aren't you?" he demanded.

The situation was becoming too uncomfortable for the older man. He could stand Kenneth's opposition but not the ridicule which would inevitably follow the spreading of the news that he had been beaten up and made ridiculous by Kenneth. He swallowed—a look of indecision passed over his face as he visibly wondered if Kenneth really dared hit him—followed by a look of fear as Kenneth drew back his fist as though to strike. Discretion seemed the better course to pursue—he could wait until a later and more propitious date for his revenge—he agreed to help. A look of relief came over Jim Bradley's face. A grin covered Bob's as he saw his brother showing at last some signs of fighting spirit. Without further words Kenneth prepared to operate. . . .

JESSIE FAUSET

Born in Philadelphia, and educated at Cornell, the University of Pennsylvania, and the Collège de France, Jessie Fauset has taught French at Dunbar High School in Washington and in New York City. She has written verse as well as the novels *There is Confusion* (1924), *Plum Bun* (1929), *The Chinaberry Tree* (1932), and *Comedy, American Style* (1933). The selection printed below is from the last-named novel and is here reprinted by permission of the author and of the Frederick A. Stokes Co.

[Color Struck]

Mrs. Olivia Blanchard Cary glanced out of the window of her pleasant residence in West Philadelphia and saw her daughter Teresa, her books under her arm, strolling down the street, with two other little girls similarly laden. One of her companions, a very fair blonde with dark blue eyes and gay gilt hair, Mrs. Cary identified immediately as Phebe Grant. She was not so sure of the identity of the third youngster. Closer inspection revealed to her, however, the dark brown skin, the piquant features, the sparkling black eyes and the abundant, silky and intensely curly locks of Marise Davies. Mrs. Cary frowned. "As often as I've told Teresa to keep away from that Davies child!" she murmured angrily to herself.

She met them at the front door. The countenances of the three children were in striking contrast. Teresa's wore a look of apprehension, Phebe's of bland indifference, Marise's of acute expectancy.

"Good-afternoon, Teresa," Olivia said. "Good-afternoon children. I'm afraid it's not best for Teresa to have so much company today.

She gets excited and worn out and it's hard afterwards for her to settle down to her lessons. I don't mind if one of you stays. Phebe, suppose you come in and play with her a while, and Marise, you can come back another time."

"Tomorrow?" asked Marise, whose black eyes had never left Olivia's face.

"Well, hardly tomorrow," the woman replied, flushing a little. She really disliked this child. "Horrid, little pushing thing," she inwardly apostrophized. But aloud she continued. "Hardly tomorrow, but some other day very soon, I am sure. Come on in, Phebe."

"No, thank you, Mrs. Cary," the child answered, pushing back the thick gilt hair which framed her face. "I was with Marise first, so I'll go on with her. We were just going to ask you to let Teresa come along with us. My mother expects me to be at Marise's if I'm not home." She spoke simply, no trace of the avenging angel about her.

The two children, hand in hand, backed off the bottom step on which they had been precariously teetering. Marise, ignoring Olivia completely, waved a slender hand toward Teresa. "Come on over whenever you can. My mother doesn't mind."

From the pavement both looked back once more to wave a careless farewell to their school-mate. "G'bye, Treesa!"

"Treesa!" Olivia echoed angrily. "Why can't they pronounce your name right?" She glanced sharply at her daughter's tear-stained face. "What's the matter, Teresa?"

The little girl wiped away a tear with the back of her hand.

"Mamma, why, can't I play with Marise? Of course Phebe's all right and I like her very much. But I like Marise best. She's such fun."

Her mother sighed. "I have," she thought, "the stupidest children and husband too in the world. Why can't they see this thing the way I want it?" Not unkindly she took out her handkerchief and wiped the child's eyes.

"Now, Teresa, it isn't worth while going all over this matter again. I don't mind your having Phebe here; in fact I rather like Phebe. But I don't like to have colored people in the house if we can possibly avoid it."

"But, Mamma, Phebe is colored too."

"I know she is but nobody would ever guess it."

"They don't have to guess it; she tells it; she stood right up in class and said so."

"What nonsense!" Olivia countered angrily. "What occasion would a girl, looking like her, have to talk about color?"

"She didn't say it of her own accord, Mamma. The teacher was having a review lesson on races one day and she asked Phebe what race she belonged to and Phebe said: 'I belong to the black or Negro race.'"

"What did the teacher say?"

"She just giggled at first and then she said: 'Well, Phebe, we all know that isn't true. Don't try to be funny. Now tell us what race you do belong to, dear!' And Phebe said it all over again. She said: 'I belong to the black or Negro race.'"

Olivia gasped. "Silly little thing! The idea of a girl as white as she saying that! What happened then?"

"The teacher had her stay after school and Phebe showed her the picture of her mother. She wears it in a locket around her throat all the time. And her mother *is* colored. Not black, you know, Mamma, but real, real brown. Almost as brown as Marise, you know. You should have seen how surprised Miss Packer was!"

In spite of herself the mother was interested. "What did she say then?"

"She looked awful queer and asked Phebe if she looked like her father and Phebe said she looked exactly like him . . . and that he didn't live here and that he was married to someone else. . . . And then Miss Packer turned kind of red and never said another word. . . . How can Phebe's father not be married to her mother, Mamma?"

"Oh, I don't know . . . probably they couldn't get along so they separated. Married people often do that. They call it getting a divorce." Hurriedly she changed the subject: "Did the children act any different to Phebe after that?"

Teresa considered this a moment. "Well, you see, Mamma, the children don't act any special kind of way to Phebe anyway, because Phebe don't care anything about them. The only child Phebe likes a whole lot in school is Marise."

"I thought she liked you."

O she does, but not the same way she likes Marise. Marise is so smart you know. She can think up all the most wonderful things. Why she changed her name herself. It used to be Maria. And she said that was all wrong. She said she didn't look like a Maria person and she didn't feel like a Maria person. . . . Isn't that funny, Mamma? And she can sing and play and dance. You never saw anyone dance like her. And she can think up such smart things to say. I don't see why you don't like her, Mamma."

"I don't dislike her," her mother retorted in exasperation. "You don't understand these things, yet, Teresa. But you will when you're older . . . and you'll be grateful to me. I just don't want you to have Marise and people like that around because I don't want you to grow up among folks who live the life that most colored people have to live . . . narrow and stultified and stupid. Always pushed in the background . . . out of everything. Looked down upon and despised! . . .

"Teresa, how many times must I tell you these things? You and your father and Christopher almost drive me crazy! You're so willfully perverse about it all! Here we could all be as white as the whitest people in Philadelphia. When we moved in this neighborhood not a soul here but thought we were white! And your father is never happy unless he has some typical Negro hanging about. I believe he does it to tease me. And now here you are, all wrapped up in this Davies child!"

"But, Mamma, what difference does it make? And anyway, there's Oliver!"

There indeed was Oliver.

Olivia, with very little love for her husband, Dr. Cary, with no enthusiasm, as such, for the institution of matrimony and with absolutely no urge for the maternal life, had none the less gone cheerfully and willingly into both marriage and motherhood because she believed that through her children she might obtain her heart's desire. She could, she was sure, imbue her offspring with precept and example to such an extent that it would never enter their minds to acknowledge the strain of black blood which in considerable dilution would flow through their veins.

She could be certain of their color. Her twin sister and brother, only two years older than her own children, had. proven that. It was worth every one, she felt, of her labor pains not to hold in her arms little Teresa, her first-born,—but to gaze on that tiny, unremarkable face and note the white skin, the thick, "good" dark hair which covered the frail skull; to note that the tell-tale half-moons of which she had so often read were conspicuously absent. It seemed to her that the tenuous bonds holding her ever so slightly to her group, and its station in America, were perceptibly weakened. Every time she appeared in public with the little girl she was presenting the incontestable proof of her white womanhood. . . .

And when Christopher, the second child was born, she was not the least fraction worried over the closely curling tendency of his slightly reddish hair. She had known Jews with hair much kinkier. Time and care would attend to all that. And meanwhile his skin was actually fairer than that of his little sister, his features finer and better chiselled. He had, she felt, a look of "race," by which she meant of course the only race which God, or Nature, for hidden, inscrutable purposes, meant should rule.

But she had not reckoned with the children's father. Christopher had finally established in his mind the fact of his chaste wife's frigidity. When he fully realized that her much-prized "aloofness," instead of being the *insigne* of a wealth of feeling, was merely the result of an absolute vacuum of passion, young as he was, he resolved not to kick against the pricks.

He had, he told himself, been sold, as many a man before him had; tricked as completely by his deliberate submission to ideals, entirely false to his nature and his desires, as a young girl might be by her first surrender to a passion which her heart tells her is natural, though her mind and breeding might warn her of its inexpediency. The first of that hardening process which was so to change him did have its inception during this period, but as he had some humor and a sense of justice beyond his years he refused to let the iron enter his soul.

Moreover, Olivia, though not a "comfortable" house-keeper, was a clean and considerate one. She really never interfered with his "papers"; she never, even from the beginning, troubled him with the delinquencies of the help. And in those days, and for some years to come, she never exceeded the budget which he allowed her. Also her obvious willingness, even eagerness, to have children pleased and touched him. In his total ignorance of the plans which nestled eternally in the back of her sleek, dark head, he reasoned that a woman so fond of children must by a very natural extension develop eventually a certain tenderness for their father. So he hoped for many things and forgave her much with a somewhat rueful and yet amused indulgence.

Until he found in her the unalterable determination to carry himself and his children definitely across the narrow border-line of race! This too he at first regarded with some indulgence, but her unimaginative persistence finally irritated him. He was too busy to undertake completely the education of the children—he was responsible for their maintenance. But he could let them see his manifest respect and liking for many men who had been his boyhood friends and who bore the badge of their mixed blood plainly upon them.

He told the children every story he knew about the heroes of the race. Olivia would have preferred them to be ignorant of their own remote connection with slavery. But he did strive to make them realize the contrast between their present status and that of their black forebears. He emphasized the racial progress, stressing the brief span of years in which it had been accomplished.

And the children, straightforward, serious little things without an ounce of perversity in their make-up, were entranced, thrilled. Perhaps because they never met with any open expression of prejudice they seemed to find their greatest interest and amusement among the children of their father's friends who most definitely showed color. For a brief while Christopher's hero was Crispus Attucks; Teresa's brave Sojourner Truth. But later, through lack of nourishment, their interest in this phase of history died.

. . . .

When the children were four and a half, and six, respectively, Olivia found she was going to have another baby. She was really very happy about it with a naïvete and a frankness which, Dr. Cary, as before, found inexpressibly moving and charming. Within herself she was making plans. This child should be her very own. She would make her husband believe that she needed a change, she would take the child away and live with him apart for two, three, perhaps for five years. In appearance, in rearing, in beliefs he should be completely, unrelievedly a member of the dominant race. She was a much wiser woman than she had been six years ago. The prospect made her gay and charming, almost girlish; far younger too than her twenty-eight years, younger indeed it seemed to her husband than she had ever been in those remote, so precious years of training.

"This one will be a boy," she told big Christopher gaily. "He'll be the handsomest and most attractive of us all. And I'll name him after myself. An Oliver for your Chrisopher."

Her prophecy was, except in one respect, absolutely true. She had boasted of the ease with which her children had entered the world. But this one she was confident would outstrip them all.

"I'm sure I'll be up very soon, Chris," she told her husband. She adopted one of her rare moods of coquetry. "And when I do get up, you ought to reward a dutiful wife. How would you like to send her and your baby son on a little trip to England?" Her eyes were bright with secrecy. He would, he assured her, do anything, give her anything she wanted within his range.

But the unforseen happened. The baby arrived in due course. "Hale and hearty," said his beaming father. There never was a baby haler and heartier. But Olivia did not fare so well. She had one sinking spell after another. For the first time she was unable to nurse her child. She was to meet with no excitement or shock and as the baby was going very well it was best for her not to be concerned with him for a while. She was to concentrate on recovering her strength. So that it was a full month before the baby was set before her, crowing and laughing and persistently and futilely striking his little hands together.

Olivia sat up, arms outstretched to receive him. Her baby! Her eyes stretched wide to behold every fraction of his tiny person. But the expectant smile faded as completely as though an unseen hand had wiped it off. She turned to her husband sharply:

"That's not my baby!"

But it was her baby. It was a boy, handsomer and more attractive than the other children. He was named Oliver. . . . They had been calling him that for a month, her delighted children assured her . . . his hair was black and soft and curly . . . and he had the exact bronze gold complexion of Lee Blanchard!

She had reckoned without her own father!

. . . .

For the first time since she had known the futile anger of her early childhood she slipped into a black, though silent, rage. Her early anger had been directed against her father. This later ebullition included both her husband and her helpless little boy. She had no special beliefs about prenatal influences but she did observe to herself in the dark and tortuous recesses of her mind that if big Christopher had not been so decidedly a Negrophile, the appearance of their child would have been otherwise.

The little fellow was of a remarkable beauty. Through one pretext and another Olivia contrived not to be seen on the street with him. But the two older children and his father would proudly conduct him anywhere. And wherever he went he attracted attention . . . infinitely more so than his brother and sister had ever earned. Added to this was an undeniable charm of manner and of mind. He possessed not only a winning smile and a genuine sweetness of attitude and conduct but he was unquestionably of remarkable mental endowment. . . . If he had possessed an ounce of self-confidence, or even of the ordinary childish conceit which so often marks the "bright boy," he might easily have become unbearable. But even from babyhood little Oliver sensed in himself one lack which early automatically destroyed any root of undue self-esteem. He knew he did not have his mother's love. . . . Worse than that through some strange childish, unfailing perception he was sure of her active but hidden dislike for him.

When he was home Olivia fed him with the same food, watched

over and satisfied his physical welfare as completely and meticulously as she watched over that of the other members of her household. But she never sought his company, she never took him riding or walking as she did the others, never bestowed on him more than the perfunctory kiss of salutation. . . . When people, struck with his appearance and healthy grace, praised him before his face as so often they did, he would turn sometimes toward her thinking dimly that now she must be proud of this fine little boy who was her son. But he never surprised on her countenance a single flash of delight or pride or love.

It saddened his childish days. . . . As soon as he became old enough to be from under her surveillance Olivia saw to it that he spent most of his time with her own mother in Boston or with her husband's mother in South Philadelphia. In both of these homes he met with the intense affection and generous esteem which his finely keyed little nature so craved. Gradually he became able to adjust himself to the inexplicable phenomenon of a mother who not only did not love with especial signal fondness, but who did not love at all, her youngest son. By sheer strength of will he forced himself to steel his brave and loyal heart against this defection and to crush down his pain.

His father had some sense of what was happening and in his heart he bore his wife a deep and unyielding dislike.

CLAUDE McKAY (1889-   )

Claude McKay (see also p. 348) has written three novels, *Home to Harlem* (1928), *Banjo* (1929), and *Banana Bottom* (1933). The first has its setting in Harlem, the second in Marseilles, and the third in Jamaica. The Harlem which he depicted became for many the overall picture of this Negro metropolis, which he has described more recently in *Harlem: Negro Metropolis* (1940). The selection printed here is from *Home to Harlem;* it is used by permission of the author and of the publishers, Harper and Brothers.

The Treeing of the Chef

PERHAPS THE CHEF of Jake's dining-car was the most hated chef in the service. He was repulsive in every aspect. From the elevated bulk of his gross person to the matted burrs of his head and the fat cigar, the constant companion of his sloppy mouth, that he chewed and smoked at the same time. The chef deliberately increased his repulsiveness of form by the meanness of his spirit.

"I know Ise a mean black nigger," he often said, "and I'll let you all know it on this heah white man's car, too."

The chef was a great black bundle of consciously suppressed desires. That was doubtless why he was so ornery. He was one of the model chefs of the service. His kitchen was well-ordered. The checking up of his provisions always showed a praiseworthy balance. He always had his food ready on time, feeding the heaviest rush of customers as rapidly as the lightest. He fed the steward excellently. He fed the crew well. In a word, he did his duty as only a martinet can.

A chef who is "right-there" at every call is the first asset of importance on an *à la carte* restaurant-car. The chef lived rigidly up to that fact and above it. He was also painfully honest. He had a mulatto wife and a brown boy-child in New York and he never slipped away any of the company's goods to them. Other dining-car men had devised a system of getting by the company's detectives with choice brands of the company's foodstuffs. The chef kept away from that. It was long since the yard detectives had stopped searching any parcel that *he* carried off with him.

"I don't want none o' the white-boss stuff foh mine," he declared. "Ise making enough o' mah own to suppoht mah wife and kid."

And more, the chief had a violent distaste for all the stock things that "coons" are supposed to like to the point of stealing them. He would not eat watermelon, because white people called it "the niggers' ice-cream." Pork chops he fancied not. Nor corn pone. And the idea of eating chicken gave him a spasm. Of the odds and ends of chicken gizzard, feet, head, rump, heart, wing points, and liver—the chef would make the most delicious stew for the crew, which he never touched himself. The Irish steward never missed his share of it. But for his meal the chef would grill a steak or mutton chop or fry a fish. Oh, chef was big and haughty about not being "no regular darky"! And although he came from the Alabama country, he pretended not to know a coon tail from a rabbit foot.

"All this heah talk about chicken-loving niggers," he growled chuckingly to the second cook. "The way them white passengers clean up on mah fried chicken I wouldn't trust one o' them anywheres near mah hen-coop."

Broiling tender corn-fed chicken without biting a leg. Thus, grimly, the chef existed. Humored and tolerated by the steward and hated by the waiters and undercooks. Jake found himself on the side of the waiters. He did not hate the chef (Jake could not hate anybody).

But he could not be obscenely sycophantic to him as the second cook, who was just waiting for the chance to get the chef's job. Jake stood his corner in the coffin, doing his bit in diplomatic silence. Let the chef bawl the waiters out. He would not, like the second cook, join him in that game.

* * * * *

Nothing can be worse on a dining-car than trouble between the pantry and the kitchen, for one is as necessary to the other as oil is to salad. But the war was covertly on and the chef was prepared to throw his whole rhinoceros weight against the pantry. The first waiter had to fight cautiously. He was quite aware that a first-class chef was of greater value than a first-class pantryman.

The trouble had begun through the "mule." The fourth man—a coffee-skinned Georgia village boy, timid like a country girl just come to town—hated the nickname, but the chef would call him nothing else.

"Call him 'Rhinoceros' when he calls you 'Mule,'" Ray told the fourth waiter, but he was too timid to do it. . . .

The dining-car was resting on the tracks in the Altoona yards, waiting for a Western train. The first, third, and fifth waiters were playing poker. Ray was reading Dostoievski's *Crime and Punishment.* The fourth waiter was working in the pantry. Suddenly the restaurant-car was shocked by a terrible roar.

"Gwan I say! Take that theah ice and beat it, you black sissy." . . .

"This ice ain't good for the pantry. You ought to gimme the cleaner one," the timid fourth man stood his ground.

The cigar of the chef stood up like a tusk. Fury was dancing in his enraged face and he would have stamped the guts out of the poor, timid boy if he was not restrained by the fear of losing his job. For on the dining-car, he who strikes the first blow catches the punishment.

"Quit jawing with me, nigger waiter, or I'll jab this heah ice-pick in you' mouf."

"Come and do it," the fourth waiter said, quietly.

"God dam' you' soul!" the chef bellowed. "Ef you doin't quit chewing the rag—ef you git fresh with me, I'll throw you off this bloody car. S'elp mah Gawd, I will. You disnificant down-home mule."

Then the fourth waiter glanced behind him down the corridor and saw Ray, book in hand, and the other waiters, who had left their cards to see the cause of the tumult. Ray winked at the fourth waiter. He screwed up his courage and said to the chef "I ain't no mule, and youse a dirty rhinoceros."

The chef looked apoplectic. . . . "I don't care a dime foh all you done call me? Wha's rhinasras?"

All the waiters laughed. The chef looked ridiculous and Ray said "Why, chef, don't you know? That's the ugliest animal in all Africa."

The chef looked apoplectic. . . . "I don't care a dime foh all you nigger waiters and I ain't joking wif any of you. Cause you manicuring you' finger nails and rubbing up you' stinking black hide against white folks in that theah diner, you all think youse something. But lemme tell you straight, you ain't nothing atall."

"But, chef," cried the pantryman, "why don't you stop riding the fourth man? Youse always riding him."

"Riding who? I nevah rode a man in all mah life. I jest tell that black skunk what to do and him stahts jawing with me. I don't care about any of you niggers, nohow."

"Wese all tiahd of you cussin' and bawking," said the pantryman. "Why didn't you give the boy a clean piece of ice and finish? You know we need it for the water."

"Yaller nigger, you'd better gwan away from here."

"Don't call me no yaller nigger, you black and ugly cotton-field coon."

"Who dat? You bastard-begotten dime-snatcher, you'd better gwan back to you' dining-room or I'll throw this heah garbage in you' crap-yaller face. . . . I'd better git long far away from you all 'foh I lose mah haid." The chef bounced into the kitchen and slammed the door.

* * * * *

The coldness between the kitchen and the pantry continued, unpleasantly nasty, like the wearing of wet clothes, after the fall of a heavy shower, when the sun is shining again. The chef was uncomfortable. A waiter had never yet opposed open hostility to his personality like that. He was accustomed to the crew's surrendering to his ways with even a little sycophancy. It was always his policy to be amicable with the pantryman, playing him against the other waiters, for it was very disagreeable to keep up a feud when the kitchen and the pantry had so many unavoidable close contacts.

So the chef made overtures to the pantryman with special toothsome tidbits, such as he always prepared for the only steward and himself. But the pantryman refused to have any specially-prepared-for-his-Irishness-the-Steward's stuff that the other waiters could not share. Thereupon the chef gave up trying to placate him and started in hating back with profound African hate. African hate is deep down and hard to stir up, but there is no hate more realistic when it is stirred up.

One morning in Washington the iceman forgot to supply ice to the dining-car. One of the men had brought a little brass top on the diner and the waiters were excited over an easy new game called "put-and-take." The pantryman forgot his business. The chef went to another dining car and obtained ice for the kitchen. The pantryman did not remember anything about ice until the train was well on its way to New York. He remembered it because the ice-cream was turning soft. He put his head through the hole and asked Jake for a piece of ice. The chef said no, he had enough for the kitchen only.

With a terrible contented expression the chef looked with malicious hate into the pantryman's yellow face. The pantryman glared back at the villainous black face and jerked his head in rage. The ice-cream turned softer. . . .

Luncheon was over, all the work was done, everything in order, and the entire crew was ready to go home when the train reached New York. The steward wanted to go directly home. But he had to wait and go over to the yards with the keys, so that the pantryman could ice up. And the pantryman was severely reprimanded for his laxity in Washington. . . .

The pantryman bided his time, waiting on the chef. He was cordial. He even laughed at the jokes the chef made at the other waiters' expense. The chef swelled bigger in his hide, feeling that everything had bent to his will. The pantryman waited, ignoring little moments for the big moment. It came.

One morning both the second and the fourth cook "fell down on the job," neither of them reporting for duty. The steward placed an order with the commissary superintendent for two cooks. Jake stayed in the kitchen, working, while the chef and the pantryman went to the store for the stock. . . .

The chef and the pantryman returned together with the large baskets of provisions for the trip. The eggs were carried by the chef himself in a neat box. Remembering that he had forgotten coffee, he sent Jake back to the store for it. Then he began putting away the kitchen stuff. The pantryman was putting away the pantry stuff. . . .

A yellow girl passed by and waved a smile at the chef. He grinned, his teeth champing his cigar. The chef hated yellow men with "cracker" hatred, but he loved yellow women with "cracker" love. His other love was gin. But he never carried a liquor flask on the diner, because it was against regulations. And he never drank with any of the crew. He drank alone. And he did other things alone. In Philadelphia or Washington he never went to a buffet flat with any of the men.

The girls working in the yards were always flirting with him. He fascinated them, perhaps because he was so Congo mask-like in aspect and so duty-strict. They could often wheedle something nice out of other chefs, but nothing out of *the* chef. He would rather give them his money than a piece of the company's raw meat. The chef was generous in his way; Richmond Pete, who owned the saloon near the yards in Queensborough, could attest to that. He had often gossiped about the chef. How he "blowed them gals that he had a crush on in the family room and danced an elephant jig while the gals were pulling his leg."

The yellow girl that waved at the chef through the window was pretty. Her gesture transformed his face into a foolish broadsmiling thing. He stepped outside the kitchen for a moment to have a tickling word with her.

In that moment the pantryman made a lightning-bolt move; and shut down the little glass door between the pantry and the kitchen. . . .

The train was speeding its way west. The first call for dinner had been made and the dining-room was already full. Over half a dozen calls for eggs of different kinds had been bawled out before the chef discovered that the basket of eggs was missing. The chef asked the pantryman to call the steward. The pantryman, curiously preoccupied, forgot. Pandemonium was loose in the pantry and kitchen when the steward, radish-red, stuck his head in.

The chef's lower lip had flopped low down, dripping, and the cigar had fallen somewhere. "Cut them aigs off o' the bill, Sah Farrel. O Lawd!" he moaned, "Ise sartain sure I brought them aiggs on the car mahself, and now I don't know where they is."

"What kind o' blah is that" cried the steward. "The eggs must be there in the kitchen. I saw them with the stock meself."

"And I brought them here hugging them, Boss, ef I ain't been made fool of by something." The rhinoceros had changed into a meek black lamb. "O Lawd! and I ain't been outa the kitchen sence. Ain't no mortal hand could tuk them. Some evil hand. O Lawd!—"

"Hell!" The steward dashed out of the pantry to cut all the egg dishes off the bill. The passengers were getting clamorous. The waiters were asking those who had ordered eggs to change to something else. . . .

The steward suggested searching the pantry. The pantry was ransacked. "Them ain't there, cep'n' they had feets to walk. O Lawd of Heaben!" the chef groaned. "It's something deep and evil, I knows, for I ain't been outa this heah kitchen." His little flirtation with the yellow girl was completely wiped off his memory.

Only Jake was keeping his head in the kitchen. He was acting second cook, for the steward had not succeeded in getting one. The fourth cook he had gotten was new to the service and he was standing, conspicuously long-headed, with gaping mouth.

"Why'n the debbil's name don't you do some'n, nigger?" bellowed the chef, frothy at the corners of his mouth.

"The chef is up a tree, all right," said Ray to the pantryman.

"And he'll break his black hide getting down," the pantryman replied, bitterly.

"Chef!" The yellow pantryman's face carried a royal African grin. "What's the matter with you and them aiggs?"

"I done gived them to you mammy."

"And fohget you wife, ole timer? Ef you ain't a chicken-roost nigger, as you boast, you surely loves the nest."

Gash! The chef, at last losing control of himself, shied a huge ham bone at the pantryman. The pantryman sprang back as the ham bone flew through the aperture and smashed a bottle of milk in the pantry.

"What's all this bloody business today?" cried the steward, who was just entering the pantry. . . . "What nonsense is this, chef? You've made a mess of things already and now you start fighting with the waiters. You can't do like that. You losing your head?"

"Lookahere, Sah Farrel, I jes' want ev'body to leave me 'lone."

"But we must all team together on the dining-car. That's the only way. You can't start fighting the waiters because you've lost the eggs."

"Sah Farrel, leave me alone, I say," half-roared, half moaned the chef, "or I'll jump off right now and let you run you' kitchen you'self."

"What's that?" The steward started.

"I say I'll jump off, and I mean it as Gawd's mah maker."

The steward slipped out of the pantry without another word.

The steward obtained a supply of eggs in Harrisburg the next morning. The rest of the trip was made with the most dignified formalities between him and the chef. Between the pantry and the chef the atmosphere was tenser, but there were no more explosions.

The dining-car went on its next trip with a new chef. And the old chef, after standing a little of the superintendent's notoriously sharp tongue, was sent to another car as second cook.

* * * * *

"Honest, though, how do you think it happened?" persisted Jake. "Did you hoodoo them aiggs, or what did you do?"

"I wouldn't know atall. Better ask them rats in the yards ef they sucked the shells dry. What you' right hand does don't tell it to the left, says I."

"You done said a mou'ful, but how did you get away with it so quiet?"

"I ain't said nothing discrimination and I ain't nevah."

"Don't figure against me. Ise with you, buddy," said Jake, "and now that wese good and rid of him, I hope all we niggers will pull together like civilization folks."

"Sure we will. There ain't another down-home nigger like him in this white man's service. He was riding too high and fly, brother. I knew he would tumble and bust something nasty. But I ain't knowed a thing about it, all the same."

RUDOLPH FISHER (1897-1934)

Rudolph Fisher caught the lighter side of Harlem in his novels *The Walls of Jericho* (1928) and *The Conjure-Man Dies,* as well as in his short stories. But, when working in the larger medium, he is able to portray the diverse types of Harlemites in greater detail. *The Conjure-Man Dies,* while it is a detective story, gives glimpses into the realities of Harlem which many a purpose novel fails to record; *The Walls of Jericho* gives a cross-sectional view of Harlem, from the comic Jinx and Bubber to the professional "uplifter," Miss Cramp. But beneath the comedy and caricature of Fisher, there is a revelation of the truth of Harlem as it was in the late twenties. The following selections from *The Walls of Jericho* are reprinted by permission of the publishers, Alfred A. Knopf, Inc.

[Shine and the Sheba]

"SEE?" [SHINE SAID] TO the cock-eyed world, "that jes' goes to show y', see? One mo' sheba, that's all. Mo' different they look, less different they are. Bet he offered her a stick o' candy or sump'm. . . . And here I come near gettin' excited jes' lookin' at her. Can y' beat it?"

But though this might be only one more instance of a far-reaching general truth, somehow the cynic did not dismiss it with customary casualness. As the evening progressed, he admitted this to himself, indeed could not deny it. For even after he had danced through "Do it, Daddy," with Babe Merrimac, who vamped him desperately with-

out avail, and through a slow and easy, somewhat disturbing "Shake
That Thing" with the voluptuous Lottie Buttsby, the earlier incident
still stuck fast in his mind. Babe and Lottie both complained of finding him even less enthusiastic than usual; he was, they avowed, downright leaden, and Lottie specified where anyone interested could find
the lead. But neither succeeded in bantering him into promising to see
her safely home after the shout.

He caught sight of Linda occasionally, dancing with boys, nice,
Sunday-Schoolish boys he did not know, and he blamed these
occasional views of her for the persistence in his mind of what he had
seen. He began to resent that persistence:

"What the hell I keep thinkin' 'bout *that* for?"

Then, by way of excuse, "Well, she sho' is good to look at. Ain' no
sense in a woman bein' that good-lookin'. Ain' no excuse for it.
Dangerous, what I mean. Ought to be locked up somewheres where
she couldn't do so much harm."

He encountered Jinx and Bubber and they did nothing to help him
forget.

"Boy!" exclaimed Bubber, " 'member that sheba we seen that
mornin' on Court Avenue?"

Shine grunted assent.

"She's right hyeh at d'belly-rub to-night, big boy. Sharp out this
world. We jes' seen 'uh—right over yonder. Great Gordon Gin—talk
about one red hot mamma! Dressed like a fortune-teller—wish she'd
tell mine. Anything she say'd be awright with me. Tell me I go'n' die
tomorrer, I'd go right on and die happy."

"I *mean*," Jinx agreed. "And when I was dead and buried, all she'd
have to do 'd be walk over my grave, see?—and damn if I wouldn't git
up and follow 'uh. Boy, she's got what it takes, and papa don' mean
maybe!"

"She's the owl's bow'ls," Bubber epitomized.

Shine looked at them scornfully. "You guys," he observed, "mus'
both have glass eyes."

When he had glumly departed, they looked at each other a long
time solemnly; then they grinned and finally laughed aloud.

"What's a matter with my boy?" Jinx wanted to know.

"Nothin'. She jes' done put d' locks on 'im, thass all."

"Nothin' different. And then up and gives him lots o' air."

"Seems lak," Bubber grew serious, "our boy has been smote sho'
nuff, though, don' it?"

"Smit," corrected Jinx.

"Smote."

"Smit."

"What you know 'bout language?"

"Mo' 'n you. Don' nobody talk language down yo' home in South Ca'lina."

"What they talk, then?"

"Don' talk 'tall. Jes' grunt."

"Yea—and so did that man grunt what run you out o' Virginia, too."

"Thass aw right 'bout that. Fact is, ev'y time you forgit you up nawth, you start gruntin' in yo' native language."

"Maybe. But what I mean, you don' never *forgit* you up nawth— and ain' nobody never heard you sing that song 'bout 'Carry Me Back to Old Virginny' neither."

"D' word is smit."

"Smote."

"Smit, I say."

"Listen, squirrel-fodder. When you git a letter in yo' mail what somebody *write* y', it's *wrote,* ain't it?"

"You listen, Oscar. When you git a hole in yo' hiney where some dog *bite* y', you *bit*, ain't y'?"

The debate between these two was no more undecided than another, conducted within the mind of Joshua Jones. The question at issue was this: If Henry Patmore had so easily picked up the girl, why should not he pick her up also? Or—why should he?

On the one side were all the customary objections of his avowed attitude toward women. On the other were a number of obscure things, imponderable as vapor, but just as present and annoying: an impulse to win her favor just to have the pleasure of discarding it, compensating somewhat for his own recent disillusion; a plaguing curiosity to observe the girl at close range and satisfy the suspicion that she couldn't be all that she seemed to be at a distance; a thought of riling Patmore by outdoing him at his own game and robbing him of this, his latest triumph; these but the half-conscious excuses, really, for a far simpler, unadmitted urge: the unquestionably compelling attractiveness of the girl herself.

This debate terminated suddenly and decisively. Linda finished a dance with one of the Sunday-School boys, and now, completely bored, shooed him off into the crowd, insisting that otherwise the following dance would begin before he could find his next partner. She came now unaccompanied toward the low terrace, reaching it

just as the orchestra struck up a new number. Here she and Shine
met face to face and the argument was settled; she was alone, she was
at hand, and a new dance was beginning.

Their eyes met and he grinned and said:

"Didn' you promise me this one?"

It was a good grin, wide, honest-looking, a trifle amused, a trifle
audacious. His chin assumed more than its usual challenge, and the
flash of his teeth set up twinkling echoes in his eyes. It was a perfectly spontaneous, disarming grin and it ought to have turned the
trick. But it failed.

The girl looked at him a moment at first surprised, then puzzled;
then with a little smile of comprehension and disdain, brushed past
him without a word.

The superiority of that smile was far and away more telling and
convincing than any scornful toss of the head or sneer or gesture
of anger could have been. It placed the notion of dancing with him
beyond anger, resentment, or contempt. It stamped such a possibility
as too absurd to be aught but a trifle amusing. And it raised Shine's
temperature.

On the impulse of his anger he turned and followed her the short
distance to her table, and when she sat down and looked up, there he
was. She was mildly astonished.

"Wrong number," she said briefly and smiled that smile again.

He sat down and put his arms on the table and leaned forward
as she drew back in surprise. He spoke very gravely, and his voice,
though low, suffered no loss of clarity by reason of the bedlam 'round
about; indeed the merry confusion seemed to lend them a certain
seclusion.

"Listen, Long Distance—who you kiddin'?"

"Wrong number, I said," the girl repeated less generously and
pushed back her chair to rise.

"One moment please, operator," returned Shine. "What number'd
you think I was callin'?"

"The number on that policeman's badge," she said, although "that
policeman" was nowhere in sight.

"Where?" He looked about unconcernedly.

"Or—one of the officials."

"Officials?"

"Yes, officials!"

"Oh. They all friends o' mine."

"Mr. Henry Patmore, I suppose?"

"Who?"

"Henry Patmore." She knew that would settle him.

"Pat? . . . Well I take it back. I know him well but he ain't no friend o' mine."

There was but one way to keep him from imperturbably trailing her the rest of the evening: she had recourse to insult:

"No—he wouldn't be."

That went wide. "What official is he—official bootlegger?"

"He's a judge—and a gentleman."

"Judge? Judge of what?"

"Of costumes—and of people that try to be sheiks."

He looked at her as she sat on the edge of the chair, a bird poised, postponing flight only for one last jab at the snake; and instead of laughing aloud at what she had said about Patmore, he scowled and muttered, "Judge. Humph. So that was his jive. Huh. Judge."

This piqued her curiosity and further delayed her departure. "Yes, judge."

"What else did he tell y'?"

"Nothing else about himself—but a whole lot about you."

"Me?"

"Yes, you."

"Me? How come he to——?"

"I saw you looking and asked him." She rose at last. "I promised him this dance, if"—no missing the sarcasm this time—"if you will excuse me."

"No—wait a minute—listen." He too was standing now, towering over her, leaning a trifle toward her, and perhaps less composed than he'd ever been in his life, in the company of a girl. If she had been interested enough to ask Pat about him, there was no sense in releasing her now so easily, just because she was playing tight. Or maybe she wasn't playing. Maybe she was scared. "Listen—I admit I got you all wrong. But it looked—listen. I'm standin' over there, see? And Pat comes up and puts on his jive—anybody can see you don' know 'im. But you lap it up. You swallow it whole. I mean that's the way it looked. Naturally I figger I can get away too, see? Y' can't kill me f' that, can y'?"

For Shine this was abject apology. Babe would have taken it so, or Lottie, and been delighted and amazed. But Linda, to whom his implication was insult, stiffened as if something unclean had touched her, while her eyes dilated with anger and resentment. Then her body relaxed into an attitude of casual contempt and her look became tranquil scorn. She said quietly, as if verifying a memory:

"Mr. Patmore said you were just a dirty rat."

At first the words merely stuck in his ears unrealized and meaning–
less, like the monotonous pulse of the orchestra's bass drum. Then
suddenly, as if their beating had finally broken through a wall, they
burst full into consciousness and throbbed in his head like pain.

He stood quite still, experiencing new and terrible feelings. Rat.
Well enough from an equal—but from this girl—Rat. Dirty rat. Patmore *said* you were just a dirty rat.

Linda saw the change come over his face; saw the brows contract,
the eyes gleam, the jaws tighten, the lips set; saw his body go taut like
a rope under tension and the bronze skin lose its life and turn dirty
copper. Linda had not the sophistication nor the cultivated self-
protective cruelty of most beautiful women. She did not see that she
had achieved her purpose, had effected a serious wound, and could
now perhaps go on her way unafraid. She saw only that her thrust
had gone too deep and said impulsively:

"Oh, I'm sorry—I didn't really mean that—"

Then in a flutter of contrition and fright she whirled about and
fled.

For yet a while longer he did not move. Music, dancing, laughter—
tumultuous silence, uproarious, crowded solitude. Presently he was
aware of a voice periodically snarling "R-r-rat!" and after a while
realized that the trap-drummer was executing a series of rolls each
swelling to a terminal snap like the epithet. "R-r-rat!"

That woke him. The stupor had been the recession of a wave,
withdrawing only to gather new impetus. Now again it rushed over
him, hot and impelling. He looked about a little madly and very
grimly, and he said aloud:

"Judge. Hmph. Show me that judge. I'm go'n' give 'im sump'm to
judge."

[Miss Cramp and the Function]

MEANWHILE MISS AGATHA CRAMP sat quite overwhelmed at the
strangeness of her situation. This was her introduction to the people
she planned to uplift. True to her word she had personally investigated the G. I. A. and been welcomed with open arms. Certain members of the executive board knew her and her past works—one or two
had been associated with her in other projects—and her experience,
resources, and devotion to service were unanimously acclaimed assets.
And nobody minded her excessively corrective attitude—all new
board members started out revising things. Furthermore, the Costume

Ball was at hand and that would be enough to upset anybody's ideas of revision.

Never had Miss Cramp seen so many Negroes in one place at one time. Moreover, never had she dreamed that so many of her own people would for any reason imaginable have descended to mingle with these Negroes. She had prided herself on her own liberality in joining this company to-night. And so it shocked and outraged her to see that most of these fair-skinned visitors were unmistakably enjoying themselves, instead of maintaining the aloof, kindly dignity proper to those who must sacrifice to serve. And of course little did she suspect how many of the fair-skinned ones were not visitors at all but natives.

When she met Nora Byle, for instance, she was first struck with the beauty of her "Latin type." To save her soul she could not help a momentary stiffening when Buckram Byle, who was a jaundice-brown, was presented as Nora's husband: Intermarriage! She recovered. No. The girl was one of those mulattoes, of course; a conclusion that brought but temporary relief, for the next moment the debonair Tony Nayle had gone off with the "mulatto," both of them flirting disgracefully.

It was all in all a situation which robbed Miss Cramp of words; but she smiled bravely through her distress and found no little relief in sitting beside Fred Merrit, whose perfect manner, cherubic smile and fair skin were highly comforting. She had not yet noticed the significant texture of his hair.

"Well, what do you think of it?" Merrit eventually asked.

"I don't know what to think, really. What do you think?"

"I? Why—it's all too familiar now for me to have thoughts about. I take it for granted."

"Oh—you have worked among Negroes a great deal, then?"

Merrit grinned. "All my life."

"How do you find them?"

That Merrit did not resist temptation and admit his complete identity at this point is easier to explain than to excuse. There was his admitted joy in discomfiting members of the dominant race. Further, however, there was a special complex of reasons closer at hand.

Merrit was far more outraged by the flirtation between Nora Byle and Tony Nayle than had been even Miss Cramp herself, and with greater cause. His own race prejudice was a bitterer, more deep-seated emotion than was hers, and out of it came an attitude that caused him to look with great suspicion and distrust upon all visitors who came to

Harlem "socially." He insisted that the least blameworthy motive that brought them was curiosity, and held that he, for one, was not on exhibition. As for the men who came oftener than once, he felt that they all had but one motive, the pursuit of Harlem women; that their cultivation of Harlem men was a blind and an instrument in achieving this end, and that the end itself was always illicit and therefore reprehensible.

It was withal a terribly serious matter, of which he could see but one side. When Langdon once hinted gently that maybe it was a two-way reaction, he snorted the suggestion away as nonsense. That he should allow it to disturb him so profoundly meant that it went profoundly back into his own life, as it did into the lives of most people of heredity so diverse as his. The everyday difficulty of his own adjustment engendered in him an unforgiving hatred of those past generations responsible for it. Hence every suggestion that history might repeat itself in this particular occasioned revolt. If there could be no fair exchange, let there be no exchange at all.

He knew that no two ardent individuals would ever be concerned with any such formulas, but the very ineffectuality of what seemed to him so just a principle rendered its violation the more irritating. And in the particular case of Tony and Nora—well, he rather liked Nora himself.

And so beneath his pleasant manner, there was a disordered spirit which at this moment almost gleefully accepted the chance to vent itself on Miss Agatha Cramp's ignorance. To admit his identity would have wholly lost him this chance. And as for the fact that she was a woman, that only made the compensation all the more complete, gave it a quality of actual retaliation, of parallel all the more satisfying.

"How do I find Negroes? I like them very much. Ever so much better than white people."

"Oh, Mr. Merrit! Really?"

"You see, they have so much more color."

"Yes. I can see that." She gazed upon the mob. "How primitive these people are," she murmured. "So primeval. So unspoiled by civilization."

"Beautiful savages," suggested Merrit.

"Exactly. Just what I was thinking. What abandonment—what unrestraint——"

"Almost as bad as a Yale-Harvard football game, isn't it?" Merrit's eyes twinkled.

"Well," Miss Cramp demurred, "that's really quite a different thing, you know."

"Of course. This unrestraint is the kind that is hostile to society, hostile to civilization. This is the sort of thing that you and I as sociologists must contend with, must wipe out."

"Yes, indeed. Quite so. This sort of thing is, as you say, quite unfortunate. We must educate these people out of it. There is so much to be done."

"Listen to that music. Savage too, don't you think?"

"Just what has occurred to me. That music is like the beating of— what do they call 'em—dum-dums, isn't it?"

"I was just trying to think what it recalled," mused Merrit with great seriousness. "Tom-toms; that's it—of course. How stupid of me. Tom-toms. And the shuffle of feet——"

"Rain," breathed Miss Cramp, who, since her new interest, had deemed it her duty to read some of Langdon's poetry. "Rain falling in a jungle."

"Rain?"

"Rain falling on banana leaves," said the lady. And the gentleman assented, "I know how it is. I once fell on a banana peel myself."

"So primitive." Miss Cramp turned to Mrs. Dunn, who sat behind and above her. "The throb of the jungle," she remarked.

"Marvelous!" exhaled Mrs. Dunn.

"These people—we can do so much for them—we must educate them out of such unrestraint."

Whereupon Tony and Nora appeared laughing and breathless at the box entrance; and Tony, descendant of Cedrics and Caesars, loudly declared:

"I'm going to get that bump-the-bump dance if it takes me the whole darn night!"

"Bump the what?" Miss Agatha wondered.

"Come on, Gloria," Tony urged Mrs. Dunn. "You ought to know it, long as you've been coming to Harlem. Mrs. Byle gives me up. You try."

Mrs. Dunn smiled and quickly rose. "I'll say I will. Come along. It's perfectly marvelous."

"Furthermore," expounded J. Pennington Potter, "there is a tendency among Negro organizations to incorporate too many words in a single designation with the result that what is intended as mere appellation becomes a detailed description. Take for example the N. O. U. S. E. and the I. N. I. A. W. There can be no excuse for entitlements of such prolixity. They endeavor to encompass a society's past, present and future, embracing as well a description of motive and instrument. There is no call you will agree, no excuse, no justification for delineation, history and prophecy in a single title."

"Quite so, Penny," said Mr. Dunn. "Mrs. Byle, may I have this dance?"

"Certainly," said Nora, smiling a trifle too amusedly.

"We're going home after this one," growled her husband as she passed.

Miss Cramp said in a low voice to Merrit:

"Isn't he a wonderful person?"

"Who?" wondered Merrit.

"Mr. Potter. He talks so beautifully and seems so intelligent."

"He is intelligent, isn't he?" said Merrit, as if the discovery surprised him.

"He must have an awfully good head."

"Unexcelled for certain purposes."

"I had no idea they were ever so cultured. How simple our task would be if they were all like that."

"Like Potter? Heaven forbid!"

"Oh, Mr. Merrit. Really you mustn't let your prejudices prevail. Negroes deserve at least a few leaders like that."

"I don't know what they've ever done to deserve them," he said.

Unable to win him over to her broader viewpoint, she changed the subject.

"Mrs. Byle is very pretty, isn't she?"

"Yes."

"She is so light in complexion for a Negress."

"A what?"

"A Negress. She *is* a Negress, isn't she?"

"Well, I suppose you'd call her that."

"It *is* hard to appreciate, isn't it? It makes one wonder, really. Mrs. Byle is almost as fair as I am, while—well, look at that girl down there. Absolutely black. Yet both——"

"Are Negresses."

"Exactly what I was thinking.—Now how long have there been Negroes in our country, Mr. Merrit?"

"Longer than most one hundred percent Americans, I believe."

"Really?"

"Since around 1500, I understand. And in numbers since 1619."

"How well informed you are, Mr. Merrit. Imagine knowing dates like that—Why that's between three and four hundred years ago, isn't it? But of course four hundred years isn't such a long time if you believe in evolution. I consider evolution very important, don't you?"

"Profoundly so."

"But I was just thinking. These people have been out of their native element only three or four hundred years, and just see what it has done to their complexions! It's hard to believe that just three hundred years in our country has brought about such a great variety in the color of the black race."

"Environment is a powerful influence, Miss Cramp," murmured Merrit.

"Yes, of course. Chiefly the climate, I should judge. Don't you think?"

Merrit blinked, then nodded gravely, "Climate undoubtedly. Climate. Changed conditions of heat and moisture and so on."

"Yes, exactly. Remarkable isn't it? Now just consider, Mr. Merrit. The northern peoples are very fair—the Scandinavians, for example. The tropic peoples, on the other hand are very dark—often black like the Negroes in their own country. Isn't that true?"

"Undeniably."

"Now if these very same people here to-night had originally gone to Scandinavia—three or four hundred years ago, you understand—some of them would by now be as fair as the Scandinavians! Why they'd even have blue eyes and yellow hair!"

"No doubt about that," Merrit agreed meditatively. "Oh yes. They'd have them without question."

"Just imagine!" marveled Miss Cramp. "A Negro with skin as fair as your own!"

"M-m. Yes. Just imagine," said he without smiling.

GEORGE SCHUYLER (1895-)

George S. Schuyler (see also p. 86) wrote the first satirical novel by a Negro, *Black No More* (1931). Schuyler imagines what would result if all Negroes could suddenly change their pigmentation, hair texture, and features until they were indistinguishable from whites. Schuyler lampoons both the intolerance of whites and the demagoguery of Negroes. One of the most uproarious sections shows how high-and-mighty professional race men yield to panic upon hearing that the invention is a success, because they believe that their occupations are gone. The following is reprinted by permission of the author and of the Macaulay Company.

[A World-Shaking Discovery]

MAX'S TELEPHONE WAS RINGING and the late morning sunshine was streaming into his room. He leaped from bed and lifted the receiver.

"Say," shouted Bunny, "did you see this morning's *Times?*"

"Hell no," growled Max, "I just woke up. Why, what's in it?"

"Well, do you remember Dr. Junius Crookman, that colored fellow that went to Germany to study about three years ago? He's just come back and the *Times* claims he's announced a sure way to turn darkies white. Thought you might be interested after the way you fell for that ofay broad last night. They say Crookman's going to open a sanitarium in Harlem right away. There's your chance, Big Boy, and it's your only chance." Bunny chuckled.

"Oh, ring off," growled Max. "That's a lot of hooey."

But he was impressed and a little excited. Suppose there was something to it? He dressed hurriedly, after a cold shower, and went out to the newsstand. He bought a *Times* and scanned its columns. Yes, there it was:

NEGRO ANNOUNCES REMARKABLE DISCOVERY
Can Change Black to White in Three Days.

Max went into Jimmy Johnson's restaurant and greedily read the account while awaiting his breakfast. Yes, it must be true. To think of old Crookman being able to do that! Only a few years ago he'd been just a hungry medical student around Harlem. Max put down the paper and stared vacantly out of the window. Gee, Crookman would be a millionaire in no time. He'd even be a multimillionaire. It looked as though science was to succeed where the Civil War had failed. But how could it be possible? He looked at his hands and felt at the back of his head where the straightening lotion had failed to conquer some of the knots. He toyed with his ham and eggs as he envisioned the possibilities of the discovery.

Then a sudden resolution seized him. He looked at the newspaper account again. Yes, Crookman was staying at the Phyllis Wheatley Hotel. Why not go and see what there was to this? Why not be the first Negro to try it out? Sure, it was taking a chance, but think of getting white in three days! No more jim crow. No more insults. As a white man he could go anywhere, be anything he wanted to be, do most anything he wanted to do, be a free man at last . . . and probably be able to meet the girl from Atlanta. What a vision!

214

He rose hurriedly, paid for his breakfast, rushed out of the door, almost ran into an aged white man carrying a sign advertising a Negro fraternity dance, and strode, almost ran, to the Phyllis Wheatley Hotel.

He tore up the steps two at a time and into the sitting room. It was crowded with white reporters from the daily newspapers and black reporters from the Negro weeklies. In their midst he recognized Dr. Junius Crookman, tall, wiry, ebony black with a studious and polished manner. Flanking him on either side were Henry ("Hank") Johnson, the "Numbers" banker and Charlie ("Chuck") Foster, the realtor, looking very grave, important and possessive in the midst of all the hullabaloo.

"Yes," Dr. Crookman was telling the reporters while they eagerly took down his statements, "during my first year at college I noticed a black girl on the street one day who had several irregular white patches on her face and hands. That intrigued me. I began to study up on skin diseases and found out that the girl was evidently suffering from a nervous disease known as vitiligo. It is a very rare disease. Both Negroes and Caucasians occasionally have it, but it is naturally more conspicuous on blacks than whites. It absolutely removes skin pigment and sometimes it turns a Negro completely white but only after a period of thirty or forty years. It occurred to me that if one could discover some means of artificially inducing and stimulating this nervous disease at will, one might possibly solve the American race problem. My sociology teacher had once said that there were but three ways for the Negro to solve his problem in America," he gestured with his long slender fingers, " 'To either get out, get white or get along.' Since he wouldn't and couldn't get out and was getting along only indifferently, it seemed to me that the only thing for him was to get white." For a moment his teeth gleamed beneath his smartly waxed mustache, then he sobered and went on:

"I began to give a great deal of study to the problem during my spare time. Unfortunately there was very little information on the subject in this country. I decided to go to Germany but I didn't have the money. Just when I despaired of getting the funds to carry out my experiments and studies abroad, Mr. Johnson and Mr. Foster," he indicated the two men with a graceful wave of his hand, "came to my rescue. I naturally attribute a great deal of my success to them."

"But how is it done?" asked a reporter.

"Well," smiled Crookman, "I naturally cannot divulge the secret any more than to say that it is accomplished by electrical nutrition and glandular control. Certain gland secretions are greatly stimulated while others are considerably diminished. It is a powerful and dangerout treatment but harmless when properly done."

"How about the hair and features?" asked a Negro reporter.

"They are also changed in the process," answered the biologist. "In three days the Negro becomes to all appearances a Caucasian."

"But is the transformation transferred to the offspring?" persisted the Negro newspaperman.

"As yet," replied Crookman, "I have discovered no way to accomplish anything so revolutionary but I am able to transform a black infant to a white one in twenty-four hours."

"Have you tried it on any Negroes yet?" queried a sceptical white journalist.

"Why of course I have," said the Doctor, slightly nettled. "I would not have made my announcement if I had not done so. Come here, Sandol," he called, turning to a pale white youth standing on the outskirts of the crowd, who was the most Nordic looking person in the room. "This man is a Senegalese, a former aviator in the French Army. He is living proof that what I claim is true."

Dr. Crookman then displayed a photograph of a very black man, somewhat resembling Sandol but with bushy Negro hair, flat nose and full lips. "This," he announced proudly, "is Sandol as he looked before taking my treatment. What I have done to him I can do to any Negro. He is in good physical and mental condition as you all can see."

The assemblage was properly awed. After taking a few more notes and a number of photographs of Dr. Crookman, his associates and of Sandol, the newspapermen retired. Only the dapper Max Disher remained.

Dr. Junius Crookman, looking tired and worn, poured himself another cup of coffee from the percolator nearby and turning to Hank Johnson, asked "What about that new electrical apparatus?"

"On th' way, Doc. On th' way," replied the former Numbers baron. "Just talkin' to th' man this mornin'. He says we'll get it tomorrow, maybe."

"Well, we certainly need it," said Chuck Foster, who sat beside him on the large leather divan. "We can't handle all of the business as it is."

"How about those new places you're buying?" asked the physician.

"Well, I've bought the big private house on Edgecombe Avenue for fifteen thousand and the workmen are getting it in shape now.

It ought to be ready in about a week if nothing happens," Foster informed him.

"If nuthin' happens?" echoed Johnson. "Whut's gonna happen. We're settin' on th' world, ain't we? Our racket's within th' law, ain't it? We're makin' money faster'n we can take it in, ain't we? Whut could happen? This here is the best and safest graft I've ever been in."

"Oh, you never can tell," cautioned the quondam realtor. "These white newspapers, especially in the South, are beginning to write some pretty strong editorials against us and we've only been running two weeks. You know how easy it is to stir up the fanatical element. Before we know it they're liable to get a law passed against us."

"Not if I c'n git to th' legislature first," interrupted Johnson. "Yuh know, Ah knows how tuh handle these white folks. If yuh 'Say it with bucks, you c'n git anything yuh want."

"There is something in what Foster says, though," Dr. Crookman said. "Just look at this bunch of clippings we got in this morning. Listen to these: 'The Viper in Our Midst,' from the Richmond *Blade;* 'The Menace of Science' from the Memphis *Bugle;* 'A Challenge to Every White Man' from the Dallas *Sun;* 'Police Battle Black Mob Seeking White Skins,' from the Atlanta *Topic;* 'Negro Doctor Admits Being Taught by Germans,' from the St. Louis *North American.* Here's a line from an editorial in the Oklahoma City *Hatchet:* 'There are times when the welfare of our race must take precedence over law. Opposed as we always have been to mob violence as the worst enemy of democratic government, we cannot help but feel that the intelligent white men and women of New York City who are interested in the purity and preservation of their race should not permit the challenge of Crookmanism to go unanswered, even though these black scoundrels may be within the law. There are too many criminals in this country already hiding behind the skirts of the law.'

"And lastly, one from the Tallahassee *Announcer* says: 'While it is the right of every citizen to do what he wants to do with money, the white people of the United States cannot remain indifferent to this discovery and its horrible potentialities. Hundreds of Negroes with newly-acquired white skins have already entered white society and thousands will follow them. The black race from one end of the country to the other has in two short weeks gone completely crazy over the prospect of getting white. Day by day we see the color line which we have so laboriously established being rapidly destroyed. There would not be so much cause for alarm in this, were it not for the fact that this vitiligo is not hereditary. In other words, THE OFF-

SPRING OF THESE WHITENED NEGROES WILL BE
NEGROES! This means that your daughter, having married a supposed white man, may find herself with a black baby! Will the proud
white men of the Southland so far forget their traditions as to remain
idle while this devilish work is going on?"

"No use singin' th' blues?" counseled Johnson. "We ain' gonna be
both'ed heah, even if them crackahs down South do raise a little hell.
Jus' lissen to th' sweet music of that mob out theah! Eve'y scream
means fifty bucks. On'y reason we ain't makin' mo' money is 'cause
we ain't got no mo' room."

"That's right," Dr. Crookman agreed. "We've turned out one hundred a day for fourteen days." He leaned back and lit a cigarette.

"At fifty bucks a th'ow," interrupted Johnson, "that means we've
took in seventy thousand dollahs. Great Day in th' mornin'! Didn't
know tha was so much jack in Harlem."

"Yes," continued Crookman, "we're taking in thirty-five thousand
dollars a week. As soon as you and Foster get that other place fixed
up we'll be making twice that much."

From the hallway came the voice of the switchboard operator
monotonously droning out her instructions: "No, Dr. Crookman
cannot see anyone. . . . Dr. Crookman has nothing to say. . . . Dr.
Crookman will issue a statement shortly. . . . Fifty dollars. . . . No,
Dr. Crookman isn't a mulatto. . . . I'm very sorry, but I cannot answer
that question."

The three friends sat in silence amid the hum of activity around
them. Hank Johnson smiled down at the end of his cigar as he thought
back over his rather colorful and hectic career. To think that today
he was one of the leading Negroes of the world, one who was taking
an active and important part in solving the most vexatious problem
in American life, and yet only ten years before he had been working
on a Carolina chain gang. Two years he had toiled on the roads under
the hard eye and ready rifle of a cruel white guard; two years of being
beaten, kicked and cursed, of poor food and vermin-infested habitations; two years for participating in a little crap game. Then he had
drifted to Charleston, got a job in a pool room, had a stroke of luck with
the dice, come to New York and landed right in the midst of the
Numbers racket. Becoming a collector or "runner," he had managed
his affairs well enough to be able to start out soon as a "banker."
Money had poured in from Negroes eager to chance one cent in the
hope of winning six dollars. Some won but most lost and he had
prospered. He had purchased an apartment house, paid off the police,
dabbled in the bail bond game, given a couple of thousand dollars

to advance Negro Art and been elected Grand Permanent Shogun of the Ancient and Honorable Order of Crocodiles, Harlem's largest and most prosperous secret society. Then young Crookman had come to him with his proposition. At first he had hesitated about helping him but later was persuaded to do so when the young man bitterly complained that the dicty Negroes would not help to pay for the studies abroad. What a stroke of luck, getting in on the ground floor like this! They'd all be richer than Rockefeller inside of a year. Twelve million Negroes at fifty dollars apiece! Great Day in the morning! Hank spat regally into the brass cuspidor across the office and reared back contentedly on the soft cushion of the divan.

Chuck Foster was also seeing his career in retrospect. His life had not been as colorful as that of Hank Johnson. The son of a Birmingham barber, he had enjoyed such educational advantages as that community afforded the darker brethren; had become a schoolteacher, an insurance agent and a social worker in turn. Then, along with the tide of migration, he had drifted first to Cincinnati, then to Pittsburgh and finally to New York. There the real estate field, unusually lucrative because of the paucity of apartments for the increasing Negro population, had claimed him. Cautious, careful, thrifty and devoid of sentimentality, he had prospered, but not without some ugly rumors being broadcast about his sharp business methods. As he slowly worked his way up to the top of Harlem society, he had sought to live down this reputation for double-dealing and shifty practices, all too true of the bulk of his fellow realtors in the district, by giving large sums to the Young Men's and Young Women's Christian Associations, by offering scholarships to young Negroes, by staging elaborate parties to which the dicty Negroes of the community were invited. He had been glad of the opportunity to help subsidize young Crookman's studies abroad when Hank Johnson pointed out the possibilities of the venture. Now, although the results far exceeded his wildest dreams, his natural conservatism and timidity made him somewhat pessimistic about the future. He supposed a hundred dire results of their activities and only the day before he had increased the amount of his life insurance. His mind was filled with doubts. He didn't like so much publicity. He wanted a sort of genteel popularity but no notoriety.

WALLACE THURMAN (1902-1934)

Wallace Thurman, born in Salt Lake City, was educated at the University of Southern California. He served on the editorial staffs of *The Messenger* and of the Macaulay Publishing Company; he helped found the short-lived magazines *Fire* and *Harlem*. His novel, *The Blacker the Berry,* appeared in 1929; his play, *Harlem,* written in collaboration with W. J. Rapp, was produced the same year. *Infants of the Spring,* from which the following selection is taken, appeared in 1932. The selection used here is reprinted by permission of the publishers, the Macaulay Company.

[Niggeratti Manor]

EARLY THE NEXT MORNING, Raymond telephoned Samuel and asked him to come up as soon as possible. Always willing to be of service, and always eager to know just what was going on in Niggeratti Manor, Samuel dropped everything and immediately made his way to Harlem.

"What is it, Ray?" he asked before removing his hat and coat.

"Nothing exciting, Sam. I just want you to see what you can do to help Eustace get an audition downtown. Make him some contacts. Of course he can't sing, but give him a break. I've heard worse, and," he added slyly, "you're always bemoaning the fact that none of us will let you champion our cause. Here's your chance to make an impression."

Samuel set to work immediately. He interviewed many people who were figures in the concert world, and finally located a group who not only promised to grant Eustace an audition, but who also said that if his voice was all Samuel claimed, they, themselves, would present him in a concert of songs at Carnegie Hall.

Exultingly, Samuel rushed back uptown to tell Eustace the good news. Raymond entered the room soon after his arrival, and was startled to find Eustace angrily pacing the room. He had been apprised by telephone of what Samuel had done, and had expected to find Eustace most joyful. It did not take him long to discover what was wrong.

"But I won't sing spirituals," Eustace declared.

"Why won't you sing them?" Samuel asked. "They're your heritage. You shouldn't be ashamed of them."

"What makes you think they're my heritage, Sam? I have no relationship with the people who originated them. Furthermore I'm

220

a musician, and as far as I can see, spirituals are most certainly not music.

"Nonsense."

"It's not nonsense. Aren't there enough people already spurting those bastard bits of doggerel? Must every Negro singer dedicate his life to the crooning of slave songs?"

"But they're beautiful," Raymond interjected.

"Beautiful?" There was scorn in his voice. "Beautiful because they are now the fad. I'm a concert singer, and I won't be untrue to my art."

"Roland Hayes sings them," Samuel announced as if this should put an end to all objections.

"Yes, as a sop. He throws them to his audience because they want them, because they are unwilling to listen to a Negro sing an entire program of classical music. I'm no slave and I won't sing slave music if I never have a concert."

He sat down abruptly at the piano and began striking haphazard chords.

Samuel appealed to Raymond.

"Isn't there anything you can say? These people are most willing to help him. Can't you make him understand that he must make some compromise?"

Raymond shrugged his shoulders. He had done his bit, and he now had little interest in the matter. He was conversant with Eustace's objections to singing spirituals, and to him, these objections were silly, unintelligent, and indefensible. He had no sympathy whatsoever with Negroes like Eustace, who contended that should their art be Negroid, they, the artist, must be considered inferior. As if a poem or a song or a novel by and about Negroes could not reach the same heights as a poem or a song or a novel by or about any other race. Eustace did not realize that by adhering to such a belief, he also subscribed to the theory of Nordic superiority. Yet there was nothing to be done about it. Eustace by refusing to sing spirituals was only hurting himself. And the world would miss nothing if he should die unheard. He had the urge to sing, and he also had a good church choir voice, but on the concert stage he could be at best only one of the mediocre also-rans.

Samuel was irate. "I think you're a damn fool."

"All artists are considered damn fools by Philistines," was the withering retort.

"This argument gets you nowhere," Raymond said. "Both of you are being childish."

"Who wouldn't be childish?" Samuel shouted. "These people have promised to give Eustace an audition. I tooted his horn good and plenty. It may mean the making of him. What I can't make him understand is that he can sing all the Schubert, Schumann, Handel, Brahms, Beethoven or anything else he wishes, but he must expect a request for spirituals. And if he isn't prepared, the whole thing will be called off."

"I have no further interest in the matter. I will not sing spirituals."

And having thus firmly declared himself, he resumed his striking of harmonic chords. These darky folk songs had become his *bête noir*. On several different occasions now, he had been asked to sing before informal gatherings, and each time the crowd had snickered when he had loftily refused to sing spirituals. Moreover, the snickers had continued throughout his repertoire of Schubert, Mozart, Friml, Herbert and Strauss. And even his spirited denunciation of Dvorak's inclusion of a Negro folk song in the *New World Symphony* had provoked not only argument but ridicule. The white people now entering the social world of Negroes were bringing about disturbing changes. Eustace wished to leave these old mammy songs alone; he also wanted to sing in an auspicious downtown auditorium, but it seemed as if no one would back him unless spirituals were listed on the program.

He must, it seemed, capitulate, although in his opinion there was a sufficient number of darkies already shaming contemporary Negroes by singing these barbarous, moaning shouts and too simple melodies. If Robeson, Taylor Gordon, Rosamond Johnson, Roland Hayes, Service Bell, the Hall Johnson Choirs, and many others were all acquiescing to this new demand, why should he not be different and remain the singer of classics he innately was.

Raymond motioned to Samuel. They left the room together and went to Raymond's studio.

"What am I to do, Ray?"

"Leave him alone for a few days. Meanwhile I'll post everyone in the house to keep harping on his good luck in finally finding downtown backing. He'll give in. He's just about at his rope's end now."

"But why should he be so stubborn?"

"Because he was probably brought up to despise anything which reminded his elders of slavery."

"I have no patience with him."

"You should have. That's part of your calling. It is funny, though, and exasperating. I can just picture his family. They're New Englanders, like you. There was probably a grandfather who had been a

WALLACE THURMAN 223

slave. Perhaps he was a free Negro and had migrated north. He probably raised his children to despise anything reminiscent of his days of servitude. Dialect stories were an abomination. Spirituals only to be regarded as unfortunate echoes from the auction block and the whipping post. Came Eustace on the scene. He was destined to become a singer after his primary voice experiments as an adolescent. They probably found him some high-toned white teacher with musty ideas. This teacher probably filled young Eustace's musical craw with pseudo-classical ideals, ideals essentially saccharine and sentimental. Which accounts for what we now have on our hands."

"But he has the audacity to want to sing opera."

"And you know as well as I that he could hardly make it on the concert stage. Negroes, though, have rated him high, higher than Hayes or Robeson. Why? He strives to be a carbon copy of Caruso. He sings at a church or lodge benefit. What does he sing? The aria from Pagliacci. And as an encore renders all the other flashy bits from turgid operas he can learn. You better leave Eustace to me, Sam. You lack tact. I bet you three dinners, I'll have him downtown in time for that audition."

"The bet's on, Ray, but I think you're cuckoo."

Niggeratti Manor was in a ferment. It seemed as if everyone in the house on this particular day was unusually active. From the basement came the lugubrious wailings of Eustace as he finally began the serious practice of spirituals. His conversion had been slow. It had necessitated much cajoling, flattery and diplomatic argument, but he had finally been won over. His piano was now cleared of his beloved classic music which he had tenderly wrapped in luxurious packets of green velvet and laid away in a cedar chest. The time for his audition was approaching rapidly.

"Yes, I'll sing spirituals. And I'll also astound them with the rest of my repertoire. I'll make them appreciate my talent. And I'll sing the classics so much better than spirituals that they'll realize which is my *métier*."

Then with a grimace of distate he had set about learning *Ezekiel Saw the Wheel*.

LANGSTON HUGHES (1903-)

Langston Hughes (see also pp. 89, 366), in *Not Without Laughter* (1930), portrays Negro life in a small Kansas town, a life even more barren than that of Negroes in the South, yet a life "not without laughter." The selection "Guitar," is here used by permission of the author and of the publishers, Alfred A. Knopf, Inc.

Guitar

> Throw yo' arms around me, baby,
> Like de circle round de sun!
> Baby, throw yo' arms around me
> Like de circle round de sun,
> An' tell yo' pretty papa
> How you want yo' lovin' done!

JIMBOY WAS HOME. All the neighborhood could hear his rich low baritone voice giving birth to the blues. On Saturday night he and Annjee went to bed early. On Sunday night Aunt Hager said: "Put that guitar right up, less'n it's hymns you plans on playin'. An' I don't want too much o' them, 'larmin' the white neighbors."

But this was Monday, and the sun had scarcely fallen below the horizon before the music had begun to float down the alley, over back fences and into kitchen-windows where nice white ladies sedately washed their supper dishes.

> Did you ever see peaches
> Growin' on a watermelon vine?
> Says did you ever see peaches
> On a watermelon vine?
> Did you ever see a woman
> That I couldn't get for mine.

Long, lazy length resting on the kitchen-door-sill, back against the jamb, feet in the yard, fingers picking his sweet guitar, left hand holding against its finger-board the back of an old pocket-knife, sliding the knife upward, downward, getting thus weird croons and sighs from the vibrating strings:

> O, I left ma mother
> An' I cert'ly can leave you.
> Indeed I left ma mother
> An' I cert'ly can leave you,
> For I'd leave any woman
> That mistreats me like you do.

Jimboy, remembering brown-skin mamas in Natchez, Shreveport, Dallas; remembering Creole women in Baton Rouge, Louisiana:

> O, yo' windin' an' yo' grindin'
> Don't have no effect on me,
> Babe, yo' windin' an' yo' grindin'
> Don't have no 'fect on me,
> 'Cause I can wind an' grind
> Like a monkey round a cocoanut-tree!

Then Harriet, standing under the ripening apple-tree, in the back yard, chiming in:

> Now I see that you don't want me,
> So it's fare thee, fare thee well!
> Lawd, I see that you don't want me,
> So it's fare—thee—well!
> I can still get plenty lovin',
> An' you can go to—Kansas City!

"O, play it, sweet daddy Jimboy!" She began to dance.

Then Hager, from her seat on the edge of the platform covering the well, broke out: "Here, madam! Stop that prancin'! Bad enough to have all this singin' without turnin' de yard into a show-house." But Harriet kept on, her hands picking imaginary cherries out of the stars, her hips speaking an earthly language quite their own.

"You got it, kid," said Jimboy, stopping suddenly, then fingering his instrument for another tune. "You do it like the stage women does. You'll be takin' Ada Walker's place if you keep on."

"Wha! Wha! . . . You chillen sho can sing!" Tom Johnson shouted his compliments from across the yard. And Sarah, beside him on the bench behind their shack, added: "Minds me o' de ole plantation times, honey! It sho do."

"Unhuh! Bound straight fo' de devil, that's what they is," Hager returned calmly from her place beside the pump. "You an' Harriett both—singin' an' dancin' this stuff befo' these chillens here." She pointed to Sandy and Willie-Mae, who sat on the ground with their backs against the chicken-box. "It's a shame!"

"I likes it," said Willie-Mae.

"Me too," the little boy agreed.

"Naturally you would—none o' you-all's converted yet," countered the old woman to the children as she settled back against the pump to listen to some more.

The music rose hoarse and wild:

> I wonder where ma easy rider's gone?
> He done left me, put ma new gold watch in pawn.

It was Harriett's voice in plaintive moan to the night sky. Jimboy
had taught her that song, but a slight, clay-colored brown boy who had
hopped bells at the Clinton Hotel for a couple of months, on his way
from Houston to Omaha, discovered its meaning to her. Puppy-love,
maybe, but it had hurt when he went away, saying nothing. And
the guitar in Jimboy's hands echoed that old pain with an even
greater throb than the original ache itself possessed.

Approaching footsteps came from the front yard.

"Lord, I can hear you-all two blocks away!" said Annjee, coming
around the house, home from work, with a bundle of food under her
left arm. "Hello! How are you daddy? Hello, ma! Gimme a kiss
Sandy. . . . Lord, I'm hot and tired and almost played out. This late
just getting from work! . . . Here, Jimboy, come on in and eat some
of these nice things the white folks had for supper." She stepped
across her husband's outstretched legs into the kitchen. "I brought a
mighty good piece of cold ham for you, hon', from Mis' Rice's."

"All right, sure, I'll be there in a minute," the man said, but he
went on playing *Easy Rider,* and Harriett went on singing, while the
food was forgotten on the table until long after Annjee had come
outdoors again and sat down in the cool, tired of waiting for Jimboy
to come in to her.

Off and on for nine years, ever since he had married Annjee, Jimboy and Harriett had been singing together in the evening. When they
started, Harriett was a little girl with braided hair, and each time that
her roving brother-in-law stopped in Stanton, he would amuse himself by teaching her the old Southern songs, the popular rag-time
ditties, and the hundreds of varying verses of the blues that he would
pick up in the big dirty cities of the South. The child, with her strong
sweet voice (colored folks called it alto) and her racial sense of
rhythm, soon learned to sing the songs as well as Jimboy. He taught
her the *parse me la,* too, and a few other movements peculiar to
Southern Negro dancing, and sometimes together they went through
the buck and wing and a few taps. It was all great fun, and innocent
fun except when one stopped to think, as white folks did, that some
of the blues lines had, not only double, but triple meanings, and
some of the dance steps required very definite movements of the hips.
But neither Harriett nor Jimboy soiled their minds by thinking. It was
music, good exercise—and they loved it.

"Do you know this one, Annjee?" asked Jimboy, calling his wife's

name out of sudden politeness because he had forgotten to eat her
food, had hardly looked towards her in the darkness where she sat
plump on a kitchen-chair in the yard, apart from the others, with her
back to the growing corn in the garden. Softly he ran his fingers,
light as a breeze, over his guitar strings, imitating the wind rustling
through the long leaves of the corn. A rectangle of light from the
kitchen-door fell into the yard striking sidewise across the healthy
orange-yellow of his skin above the unbuttoned neck of his blue
laborer's shirt.

"Come on, sing it with us, Annjee," he said.

"I don't know it," Annjee replied, with a lump in her throat, and
her eyes on the silhouette of his long, muscular, animal-hard body.
She loved Jimboy too much, that's what was the matter with her! She
knew there was nothing between him and her young sister except the
love of music, yet he might have dropped the guitar and left Harriett
in the yard for a little while to come eat the nice cold slice of ham she
had brought him. She hadn't seen him all day long. When she went to
work in the morning, he was still in bed—and now the blues claimed
him.

In the starry blackness the singing notes of the guitar became a
plaintive hum, like a breeze in a grove of palmettos; became a low
moan, like the wind in a forest of live-oaks strung with long strands
of hanging moss. The voice of Annjee's golden, handsome husband
on the door-step rang high and far away, lonely-like, crying with only
the guitar, not his wife, to understand; crying grotesquely, crying
absurdly in the summer night:

> I got a mule to ride.
> I got a mule to ride.
> Down in the South somewhere
> I got a mule to ride.

Then asking the questions as an anxious, left-lonesome girl-sweet-
heart would ask it:

> You say you goin' North.
> You say you goin' North.
> How 'bout yo' . . . lovin' gal?
> You say you goin' North.

Then sighing in rhythmical despair:

> O, don't you leave me here.
> Babe, don't you leave me here.
> Dog-gone yo' comin' back!
> Said don't you leave me here.

On and on the song complained, man-verses and woman-verses, to the evening air in stanzas that Jimboy had heard in the pine-woods of Arkansas from the lumber-camp workers; in other stanzas that were desperate and dirty like the weary roads where they were sung; and in still others that the singer created spontaneously in his own mouth then and there:

> O, I done made ma bed,
> Says I done made ma bed.
> Down in some lonesome grave
> I done made ma bed.

It closed with a sad eerie twang.

"That's right decent," said Hager. "Now I wish you-all'd play some o' ma pieces like *When de Saints Come Marchin' In* or *This World Is Not Ma Home*—something Christian from de church."

"Aw, mama, it's not Sunday yet," said Harriett.

"Sing *Casey Jones*," called old man Tom Johnson. "That's ma song."

So the ballad of the immortal engineer with another mama in the Promised Land rang out promptly in the starry darkness, while everybody joined in the choruses.

"Aw, pick it, boy," yelled the old man. "Can't nobody play like you."

And Jimboy remembered when he was a lad in Memphis that W. C. Handy had said: "You ought to make your living out of that, son." But he hadn't followed it up—too many things to see, too many places to go, too many other jobs.

"What song do you like, Annjee?" he asked, remembering her presence again.

"O, I don't care. Any ones you like. All of 'em are pretty." She was pleased and petulant and a little startled that he had asked her.

"All right, then," he said. "Listen to me:"

> Here I is in de mean ole jail.
> Ain't got nobody to go ma bail.
> Lonesome an' sad an' chain gang bound—
> Ever' friend I had's done turned me down.

"That's sho it!" shouted Tom Johnson in great sympathy. "Now, when I was in de Turner County Jail . . ."

"Shut up yo' mouth!" squelched Sarah, jabbing her husband in the ribs.

The songs went on, blues, shouts, jingles, old hits: *Bon Bon Buddy,*

*the Chocolate Drop; Wrap Me in Your Big Red Shawl; Under the
Old Apple Tree; Turkey in the Straw*—Jimboy and Harriett breaking
the silence of the small-town summer night until Aunt Hager interrupted:

"Yo-all better wind up, chillens, 'cause I wants to go to bed. I
ain't used to stayin' 'wake so late, nohow. Play something kinder
decent, there, son, fo' you stops."

Jimboy, to tease the old woman, began to rock and moan like an
elder in the Sanctified Church, patting both feet at the same time as
he played a hymn-like lugubrious tune with a dancing overtone:

> Tell me, sister,
> Tell me, brother,
> Have you heard de latest news?

Then seriously as if he were about to announce the coming of
the Judgment:

> A woman down in Georgia
> Got her two sweet-men confused.

How terrible! How sad! moaned the guitar.

> One knocked on de front do',
> One knocked on de back—

Sad, sad . . . sad, sad! said the music.

> Now that woman down in Georgia's
> Door-knob is hung with black.

O, play that funeral march, boy! while the guitar laughed a dirge.

> An' de hearse is comin' easy
> With two rubber-tired hacks!

Followed by a long-drawn-out, churchlike:

> Amen . . .!

Then with rapid glides, groans, and shouts the instrument screamed
of a sudden in profane frenzy, and Harriett began to ball-the-jack,
her arms flopping like the wings of a headless pigeon, the guitar
strings whining in ecstacy, the player rocking gaily to the urgent
music, his happy mouth crying: "Tack 'em down, gal! Tack 'em on
down, Harrie!"

But Annjee had risen.

"I wish you'd come in and eat the ham I brought you," she said as she picked up her chair and started towards the house. "And you, Sandy! Get up from under that tree and go to bed." She spoke roughly to the little fellow, whom the songs had set a-dreaming. Then to her husband: "Jimboy, I wish you'd come in."

The man stopped playing, with a deep vibration of the strings that seemed to echo through the whole world. Then he leaned his guitar against the side of the house and lifted straight up in his hairy arms Annjee's plump, brown-black little body while he kissed her as she wriggled like a stubborn child, her soft breasts rubbing his hard body through the coarse blue shirt.

"You don't like my old songs do you, baby? You don't want to hear me sing 'em," he said, laughing. "Well, that's all right. I like you, anyhow, and I like your ham, and I like your kisses, and I like everything you bring me. Let's go in and chow down." And he carried her into the kitchen, where he sat with her on his knees as he ate the food she so faithfully had brought him from Mrs. J. J. Rice's dinner-table.

Outside, Willie-Mae went running home through the dark. And Harriett pumped a cool drink of water for her mother, then helped her to rise from her low seat, Sandy aiding from behind, with both hands pushing firmly in Aunt Hager's fleshy back. Then the three of them came into the house and glanced, as they passed through the kitchen, at Anjee sitting on Jimboy's lap with both arms tight around his neck.

"Looks like you're clinging to the Rock of Ages," said Harriett to her sister. "Be sure you don't slip, old evil gal!"

But at midnight when the owl that nested in a tree near the corner began to hoot, they were all asleep—Anjee and Jimboy in one room, Harriett and Hager in another, with Sandy on the floor at the foot of his grandmother's bed. Far away on the railroad line a whistle blew, lonesome and long.

GEORGE W. HENDERSON (1904-   )

George Wylie Henderson was born in Warriors Stand, Alabama. A printer—he had learned printing at Tuskegee—he began to write short stories for the New York *Daily News* while working in its plant. His novel of the deep South, *Ollie Miss* (1935), from which the following selection is reprinted, deals with the lives of rural Negroes. The selection below is printed here by permission of the author and of the publishers, Frederick A. Stokes and Company.

[Dance]

OLLIE HAD COME to Alex's on a Monday, and a week from that following Saturday night she attended her first party at Lucy West's. Lucy lived on Phillpott's place. Her two-room shack was perched upon a knoll across the road from Nan's house at the little red hill. One could sit on Nan's doorsteps and watch the "doings" there of a Saturday night. And this Nan usually did, for it provided her with choice and varied bits of news. And Nan liked news, choice or otherwise.

Ollie had gone to the party alone. Slaughter had offered to come by for her. But Ollie had said, "Nuh; no need to come by fer me. Ain't sho I is goin'. An' ef I does, I speck I'll go by myself."

So Ollie had gone, arriving a bit late after things were well under way. There had been a ball game and picnic at the Stand that afternoon, and the boys from Swanson's and Hannon stopped off at Lucy's to have a little fun before returning home.

The yard about the house was well populated with both males and females when Ollie walked up. Slaughter and a man named Boto were making the music with two guitars. Slaughter played the lead part, while Boto added the musical trimmings in a bass tone. And they were breaking down into a fierce sweat now. It was one of those swampy blues pieces, whose words made little or no effort to shield their meaning, and whose music had a slow, artless way of suggesting things that the words might have overlooked. One understood the music completely. All one had to do was listen and keep shuffling. And they were shuffling now. With each vibration of the strings, their lithe, young bodies came closer together, as though harnessed by a fierce, compelling agony. Their laughing eyes were bright and sad-looking. Their faces were sad-looking, too. A liquor-like sadness, as though they knew not what they did—and cared less.

Ollie kicked off her shoes and shuffled in. And little Willie caught her and drew her to him. Ollie heard music. Ollie felt rhythm. So Ollie was ready to go. Slaughter, from the seat where he sat, positively stared; and Willie grinned his surprise at his own boldness. Old men and young swung their partners about to get a look at this girl, and ladies from Black Bottom craned their neck and dilated their black, snapping eyes at the boldness of this creature's hips.

Ollie's eyes began to sparkle; her hair worked loose; and her body might have been one series of hips after another. For, now, it seemed jointless. It moved with a rhythm all its own.

Willie put his best foot forward, and around him her prancing

took shape, and this boy began to feel the weight of his own importance. He could see Shell, standing there in the stag line, his red
eyes staring, his hands doubled into fists and rammed into his
pockets.

Willie swung Ollie around. The music got slower, each bass chord
hitting a deeper note. And one by one the couples dropped out and
gathered there in a semi-circle to watch this boy and girl strut. Hands
and feet beat time to the music, and male voices got loud with praise.
Once, a deep baritone whined, "Tell me, pretty mamma, where did
you stay las' night? . . ."

The music ceased and Ollie sauntered over to a bench beneath
an apple tree to catch her breath and mop her face. The night was hot.
The air was still. And the moon glowed with a fierce, feverish
brilliance.

Ollie sat down, and Willie leaned forward, his hand still in hers,
and said: "I'd lak to hab the next dance too, Miss Ollie, ef you don't
minds."

Ollie said, "I don't minds," and looked up at the boy's face and
smiled. His face, she saw now, was radiant, his dark skin flushed with
a strange warmth.

"You know, I likes dancin' with you," the boy said gleefully,
releasing her hand and dropping into the seat beside her.

Ollie began rolling a cigarette. She said, "Oh, I ain't nuthin' much
to brag about."

"Oh, yes'm you is, too!" Willie said. And the girl, glancing once
again at his face, saw that his eyes danced. She went on rolling her
cigarette.

Young men, minus their escorts, slipped through the shadows and
found their way to the bench where Ollie and Willie were sitting.
Slaughter and Shell came, too. Slaughter's face was wet and smiling.
Shell's hands were still buried deep in his pockets. He didn't look at
Ollie. His eyes, the hot, reddish depth of them, were fixed on Willie.

The group stood there a moment, awkward and silent, and Ollie
went on shaping her cigarette. Willie sat to one side in his seat, his
left arm extended along the back of the bench, and watched Ollie.
Watched the deft movements of her fingers and the bare, brown
surface of her arms and throat, where the v-shaped neck of her waist
came to a point at the junction of her breasts.

Slaughter pushed his way to the front of the group then, and said,
"Thought you'd lak bein' here, Miss Ollie," and grinned.

"Hit's all right, I guess," Ollie said, glancing up with a slow
movement of her eyes. Then she licked her cigarette and caught it fast

between her lips. A man struck a match, dropped quickly to his knees, and held the flame to her cigarette for a light. But Ollie turned her head to one side, lit her own match, and said, "Thank you jes de same, mister, but I has my own matches."

"Sho she has," one of the others said loudly then, "—an' she don't wants you lightin' no cig'ret fer her nohow. . . . Course she wouldn't mind ef it was me, 'cause she gwine give me de next dance anyhow—ain't you, Miss?"

"Who sey so?" the first man said, rising to his feet.

"I sey so—dat's who!" The man speaking was from Hannon, and his young adversary hailed from Swanson's.

Ollie took the cigarette from her lips, and said: "Tain't no use fer you all to start no fightin' about dancin' wid me."

But Ollie's words came a bit late. The man from Swanson's had passed the ugly word then, and the Hannon boy had flung it back into the other's teeth, neatly compounded, with the word "mother" preceding it. The Swanson boy buried his foot in the pit of the Hannon boy's stomach and whipped out his razor. The Hannon boy doubled over and played dead. Then he slid in under the Swanson boy's feet with a catlike movement and dropped him on his head.

They came to grips then, their muscles taut, their bodies rigid, digging their bare fingers into each other's flesh. The razor was lying to one side there on the ground, where it had fallen from the Swanson boy's hand.

Slaughter stepped in and ripped the two men apart, and Lucy West herself shouldered her way through the crowd now, her eyes blazing.

Lucy said, "Who in de hell is dat tryin' to break up my party?"

"Dey was jes scrappin' a l'il bit, Aunt Lucy," Slaughter said. "But dey is all right now."

"Scrappin' a l'il my foot!" Lucy said. "Durn dey souls, ain't none o' dese black devils gwine break up my party!" She glared at the two men standing there, sweating and breathing hard, and said: "Now you two young niggers git you all's mules an' haul yo' rumps on away from here—dat's whut you all do. Now git——"

The two men slunk off and the crowd relaxed. Lucy stood there a moment, looking around. Then she spotted Ollie sitting there on the bench beside Willie, smoking a cigarette. Lucy smiled and said, "Howdy do, daughter? Dem two fools musta been fightin' ovah you, wa'n't day?"

"No'm," Ollie said, smiling back. "Dey wa'n't fightin' ovah me."

"Now course dey was, daughter," Lucy teased, showing her bare gums in a broad, toothless grin. "Dem two bucks was gwine make hash out of one another jes to git de next dance wid you. You know, you is kind o' pretty-lookin', honey, an' de mens sho will fight ovah pretty 'omans."

"They was fightin' 'bout her, all right," somebody said.

"I knowed hit," Lucy said, " 'cause dat's all de mens got to fight about anyhow—de 'omans."

" 'Tain't no use to fight ovah me," Ollie said. "Peoples fight ovah somethin' they owns, an' when they don't owns nuthin' they ain't got nuthin' to fight about."

Lucy looked startled. She said, "Is you tryin' to tell me no man don't owns you, daughter?"

"No'm," Ollie said simply, "I ain't tryin' to tell you nuthin' lak dat. I was jes tryin' to sey they didn't owns nuthin' fer as I was concerned. Dat was all."

Old Lucy savored this with a smack of her lips, but she didn't say anything. The men, huddled there, looked glum, and the women positively stared. Only little Willie smiled to himself, sitting there beside Ollie, his elbows resting on his knees.

Lucy looked at Willie, and said, "Wonder whut dat l'il scamp see to be grinnin' about?" And a smile touched her lips now, made them seem oddly ridiculous, like those of a pouting child.

"He ain't grinnin' 'bout nuthin', Aunt Lucy," Shell said bitterly. Jes' settin' dere grinnin' because he's a fool."

Willie went on smiling, and Lucy turned to Ollie and said, "Daughter, you come on back to de house wid me. I wants to ast you somethin' sort of privately-lak."

So Ollie followed Lucy to the house. Slaughter and Boto returned to their guitars and the dancing went on, it being just a little past midnight now. Willie remained on the bench and Shell stood there watching him, his eyes smoldering like hot embers.

When the others were safely out of hearing, Shell said, "You lay off dat gal, Willie—dat's whut you do! She's a grown 'oman an' you is jes a kid. 'Side o' dat, she ain't none o' you' kind. Don't aim to tell you dat no mo'!"

Willie didn't say anything. He didn't even look up. He simply sat there on the bench, his lips still smiling. He sat there a long time, picking at first this palm and then the other with his finger nails, as though Shell didn't exist at all.

Then he looked up and saw Ollie standing in the doorway, with the firelight behind her, and he got up and walked back to the yard where the dancing was.

GEORGE E. LEE (1894-   )

George E. Lee, born in Indianola, Mississippi, was educated at Alcorn College. He makes his home in Memphis, Tennessee, where he collected materials for his *Beale Street: Where the Blues Began* (1934) and his *River George* (1937). The following is reprinted by permission of the author and of the Macaulay Company.

[Sharecropping]

BY THE END OF NOVEMBER the cotton picking season had ended. The fields that had been alive with gleaners were deserted. The cotton stalks stood brown and bent. But the bales of cotton stood ten tiers high on the platform at Holly Rock, representing months of toil and sweat and aching backs.

The first of December Aaron went to the plantation store for settlement, eagerly speculating on the amount he would bring away with him. He had ginned ten bales of cotton. In the best year Henry had ever known, he had ginned seven.

All morning he waited around in the hot sunshine before the plantation store. The bookkeeper had other matters on his mind. Twice during the morning Aaron reminded the white man that he was waiting there to talk with him and each time he was reminded, none too gently, that he would be called when the bookkeeper was ready for him. At noon the bookkeeper left the store to go to his lunch and Aaron watched him with growing resentment as he walked by with complete unconcern. He was away for three hours and when he came back one of his friends was waiting for him so that Aaron had to sit again and watch while the bookkeeper and his white friend spent an hour in gossip, paying no attention to the waiting black man who had come on business.

It was after 4:30 before the bookkeeper finally called Aaron in. By this time the latter's resentment had resolved itself into a deep bitter silence. He was furiously angry and passionately determined to restrain himself from any violent word or act. He stood silently before the other's desk, still waiting while the bookkeeper slowly glanced over a page of figures before him. Finally, the white man looked up with a leer on his face that was intended to be a smile.

"Well, boy," he said, "you're in fine shape to make some money next year. That crop of yours pays up all of your father's debts and pays for the mule."

Aaron started involuntarily. He knew that, actually, Henry had paid for the mule five or six times over in settlements like this.

"You mean to say that Pa still owed something on old Sally?" he asked. His voice was low and restrained but there was a deep note of anger in it which made the other avert his eyes.

"Sure he did," the bookkeeper said. "Didn't he tell you about it? He made a poor crop last year and we had to advance him something against the mule. But you're all in the clear now."

"And how much money do I get?" Aaron asked.

"Why you don't get any this year," the bookkeeper said. "We got to wipe out old Henry's debts first, but next year, starting out clear like this, you ought to make some money. Of course, if you need a little money for Christmas I'll be glad to help you niggers out, you know."

Hot resentment flared through Aaron's heart and he felt the muscles of his arms and hands contract and a growl rising in his throat. Casually the bookkeeper pushed his chair back from the desk and pulled out his middle desk drawer, opening it wide and displaying an automatic pistol which lay near the front of it handy for reach. Nonchalantly, he reached in and pulled out a plug of tobacco from which he bit off a corner, but when he put it back, he did not close the drawer.

Aaron missed none of the implications of his act.

"You don't have to threaten me with an old 45 pistol, Mr. Martin," he said angrily. "I'm not going to start anything here. Will you let me see your figures? I'd like to know how you arrived at that result."

The agent sprang to his feet, the hot defensive anger of a weak man who was wrong flaming in his eyes, but his hand stayed tensely on the edge of the desk drawer, hovering less than six inches from the butt of the pistol.

"You damn insolent nigger," he cried, "are you intimating that I cheated you?"

Still Aaron restrained himself, standing straight and erect and motionless, the muscles of his mighty arms as tense as coiled springs. When he spoke his voice had sunk lower and each syllable was clipped short through his labored breath.

"I ain't intimating anything, Mr. Martin," he said, slowly. "Only if your figures are fair, there's no reason why you should mind my seeing them. Any man has a right to an accounting for his work." For a moment the two men glared at each other, eye against eye, and then the white man, unable to face the angry, accusing stare of the other, let his eyes drop to Aaron's throat where his pulse was visibly beating.

"Who the hell are you to tell me what your rights are? Get out of here and if you want that $75.00 advance come back tomorrow when you can talk more civil."

George turned and stared sullenly out the window for a moment, fighting hard to control the resentment that flamed through him. He had expected from the beginning that he would be cheated out of a part of his due, but that his entire crop would be taken away from him this way, in payment for debts, the existence of which he greatly doubted, was almost more than he could bear calmly. In the dark recesses of his mind a beautiful vision and a hope suddenly crumbled. Unless he did something, unless he found some way to change the circumstances, which had enslaved his father all of his life, he would have no more freedom than the older man had had. His education would count for nothing and even the little farm, which he had envisioned as a home for his mother, himself, and Ada, would be simply a hopeless dream. Without a word he turned and left the store.

All the rest of the afternoon, he wandered about the streets of Holly Rock half in a daze, unable to orient his thoughts and unwilling to face the prospect of going home and telling his mother what had happened. Finally, late in the evening, mentally exhausted, he rode home, stabled and fed his mule and walked slowly across the yard to his house where he found his mother waiting at the door. Without a word, he walked past her and dropped into a chair.

"What did dey do 'bout de settlemen'?" his mother asked.

"Nothing," said Aaron, "they took everything for the mule and some old debt they claim father owed."

"Henry didn't owe nobody nuthin'; an' he dun paid fuh dat mule hisself. Las' yeah dey tol' him so," she said, glancing up at his face. But when she saw how drawn and pinched it was, and what a fire of hate was suddenly kindled in his eyes, she wanted to recall her words. "Now, 'tain't no need of worryin' 'bout dat," she went on hastily. "We'll get along somehow."

"Get along! Sure we can get along! But why should we let them take everything for debts that have been paid? I won't stand for it. I'm going back down there again tomorrow."

" 'Tain't no need of yuh trying tuh fight back at dem white folks. No nigger kin git nowhere fightin' white folks, less he got some other white folks tuh fight fuh him. Bettuh fergit it, son."

But Aaron knew in his heart that he would never forget it so long as he lived. Wearily he rose to his feet and without another word went to bed.

The next morning he was astride Sally again and on his way, but this time not to Holly Rock. His mother had said that it was no use for a colored man to fight white men unless he had other white men fighting for him. Aaron knew that he would never ask a white man to fight for him but he could ask one to help him. So he was on his way to Indian Mound to see Mr. King, an idea surging through his tired mind, a plan which might still save his cherished dream. He found the old master of Beaver Dam plantation sitting on the broad veranda of his house, as erect and fine as one of the beautiful white columns which supported the veranda roof. He was not surprised to see Aaron George riding up on his mule. In the twenty-five years during which he had owned the plantation the Negroes had come to love him and trust him. Although he had accepted the paternalistic traditions of the south toward his Negroes as incontrovertibly as the truths of the Old Testament, within the frame of those traditions he had treated them with kindliness and fairness. He had never driven them but on days when he felt like going to the fields he would just ride down the turn-rows, basking in their smiling greetings and often say aloud so they could hear him, "I've got the best niggers and the best crop in the Delta bottoms."

When he had sold the plantation and moved to Indian Mound he had not forgotten his Negroes, and it was a common occurrence for one of them, perplexed by a question too difficult for him to decide, or in trouble with the white folks, or needing something he could not get for himself, to come to him for help. As Aaron dismounted and walked up to the porch, the elderly white man smiled a friendly greeting to him.

"Good morning, Aaron," he said. "I'm glad to see you, my boy."

It was strange how this tone and the simple addition of the possessive pronoun took the sting out of that hated word "boy."

"Thank you, sir," Aaron said, standing before him with his hat in his hand. "I thought perhaps I might come and ask you for help."

"Glad to have you," King said. "Sit down."

Aaron looked at him with gratitude in his eyes. To be sure, it was a simple unostentatious courtesy for one man to ask another to be seated, but to have a white man in the south ask a Negro to sit down was so rare an occurrence that Aaron felt a sudden burst of affection for this man who, for twenty-five years, had been his father's master.

"Thank you, sir," he said again, and seated himself on the top step.

"Did you have a good crop, Aaron?" the white man asked.

"Ginned ten bales, Mr. King," the boy answered proudly.

"You don't say," the other cried. "That's more than Henry ever made on that piece."

"Yes, sir," Aaron answered, "but——"

The unspoken words hung between them in the silence that followed. Aaron had decided, before he came, that he would not mention to Mr. King what had happened at the settlement the day before. A matter of pride was involved. If there was any fighting to do he would do it for himself. He was determined to keep his conversation with the white man to its primary purpose, and John King, sensing what was going on in the boy's mind, did not ask for elaboration. He knew too well what went on at the yearly settlements and, although he had a great deal of sympathy for the Negroes and felt that Tyler had carried things a bit too far, he was not eager to seem to set himself against his own race for the sake of a Negro in a land where all tradition was violently against such a course.

"I was thinking, Mr. King," Aaron went on, "that now the farm work is over for a spell, I'd like to get a job in town. I'm strong and can work hard and I could do the work that has to be done on the plantation at night when I get home. I thought maybe you could help me find a job."

The white man looked at him with admiration. It was seldom that any Negro wanted to do more than he had to, he thought.

"Why I reckon I can, Aaron," he said with easy good nature. "Your father, Henry, was one of the best workers I ever saw and you look to me like you was following right in his foot-steps. You wait here while I go in and make a telephone call and I'll see if I can't fix that up for you right now." He rose and went into the house.

In a few minutes he was back, a broad smile on his face.

"I just talked to the superintendent of the oil mill," he smiled. "You go right over there and ask for Mr. Brown. Tell him you are the boy I sent and he'll put you right to work. You can start tomorrow morning. How's that?"

Aaron thanked him and left, his heart suddenly light again. There was some hope after all. He saw the mill superintendent and then went to the bookkeeper at Holly Rock. He would need a little money for clothes, a little money for food, and he would not let Christmas go by without getting at least a new dress for Hannah. He approached the bookkeeper, his face a mask which showed no feeling, reflected none of the anger which had shown in it the day before.

"I'd like to take that $75.00 advance, Mr. Martin," he said quietly. The other looked at him and when he saw the calm black face before him his own face relaxed.

"Come to your senses, did you?" he asked. "Now you're talking like a sensible nigger."   * * * * *

It was about a week after the meeting that he encountered Sam
Turner again. Aaron was jogging home slowly on the back of old
Sally at the end of his day's work at the mill when, coming around a
bend in the road near his home, he found the white riding boss astride
his horse waiting at the side of the road. There was a grim expression
on the agent's face which betokened no friendliness.

As a matter of fact, his meeting with Aaron had come about as a
result of a daily attempt to bring it about for three days. For weeks
the white group who ran the plantation had viewed with annoyance
the exodus of the Negroes from the plantation to jobs in town, knowing
well that knowledge of the wages they could earn in town would soon
open the eyes of many of them to the futility of work on the plantation.
When news of the meeting had reached the white ears, dismay had
turned to fury and they decided to move swiftly against the man whom
they knew instinctively to be the ring-leader.

As Aaron's mule approached, the agent turned his horse into the
road blocking the way.

"Where you been?" he asked gruffly.

Aaron looked at him a moment without replying. He must be careful now. He must watch closely what he said.

"Been up to town," he said quietly.

The agent glared at him with accusing eyes as though he might
have confessed that he had just been out committing a murder.

"They tell me that you got a job in town and that you're using our
mule to ride to work every day. What about it?"

Aaron smiled with a difficult simulation of friendliness.

"Why, yes sir, Mr. Turner, I got a job all right. Thought I'd do
something to help out a little till the planting season. I manage to get
my work around home done all right in the evening. But I ain't been
riding any of your mules. This here is old Sally that my father had
ten years before he died. She's been bought and paid for a dozen times,
I reckon."

Immediately he wished he could recall the last sentence. While he
was sure that what he had said was true, he had been so determined
to say nothing, and do nothing which would arouse the anger of any of
the white folks, and here, in his first encounter, he was encouraging
unpleasantness. The agent glared at him with rising anger.

"You're just crazy as hell," he said. "The mule belongs to the plantation and I'm going to take her along with me right now. If you go
to town again, you'll hoof it."

Aaron felt his body growing tense with fury and it was with difficulty that he restrained himself and spoke calmly.

"That mule is paid for, Mr. Turner," he said. "Whatever the situation was before Pa died, the bookkeeper told me, when we settled this fall, that all the debts were paid and the mule paid for."

"Well you'll give him up, by God," Turner's voice was rising with an angry threat in it. "You think you're a damn smart nigger, but you haven't learned yet to keep your nose out of trouble. The $75.00 advance you got involved the mule and she's our mule until you pay the money back."

Aaron was silent for a moment, fighting hard to control himself. Now, more than ever before, he must be careful. He must not speak the impulsive words of wrath which clamored in his throat for utterance, must not let his great hands double into murderous fists as they were trying to do, must not let his body leave its firm seat on the back of old Sally to fly like a raging fury at the form of the man before him. His eyes wandered off over the fields for a moment to shut out of sight the cause of his wrath. When he spoke again, it was calmly, quietly, but in a low voice.

"The bookkeeper told me," he said slowly, "that the advance of $75.00 was on next year's crop, otherwise I wouldn't have signed the contract to work the land for another year. I have a committee going to see Mr. Tyler and if he says that I should give the mule up, I'll leave it at Holly Rock. Otherwise I won't." His eyes met the agent's unflinchingly, but the other's turned away in evasion, a slow flush of anger running from his neck to his temples. He looked back again, his eyes flaming hate.

"You're telling me what you'll do!" he shouted. "Well I'm in the habit of telling niggers what they're going to do, and if they don't do it I beat the hell out of them. Get down off that mule before I drag you down."

For answer, Aaron's eyes glowered in silent defiance as he sat immobile astride his mule. With a curse, Turner reached behind him and seized a heavy leather strap which hung from his saddle. His arm flashed upward in an ascending arc but the strap never reached Aaron. With the quickness of a cat's paw, his own left hand shot upward and grasped the agent's right wrist, tightening on it with the strength of a steel vise until the white man's face contracted with pain and the strap fell limply to the road, while the eyes of the men fought for supremacy, Aaron's blazing with fury, Turner's smoldering with hate, into which were injected little flashes of fear.

"You ain't gonna whip nobody right now, Mr. Turner," Aaron said tensely and flung the white man's arm from his while his own right hand trembled with its leashed desire to strike. Fearing that he would not be able to control himself, feeling instinctively the need to confine that powerful right arm, Aaron thrust his hand stiffly into his coat pocket, pushing hard against the bottom of it in the need to give it some action which would keep it from the deed it must somehow be restrained from doing.

The agent looked with horror and it was with difficulty that he spoke without letting his voice tremble.

"By God, you dare threaten me with a gun!" he cried. "You dare threaten a white man!"

"No, Mr. Turner, it was you who did the threatening," said Aaron. Taking his hand from his pocket, he let it fall limply to his side, feeling a sudden helpless sense of defeat. He knew that he could crush this white man's body with his bare hands, knew that the white man knew it too and knew equally well that just as such a physical victory that this might be would bring nothing but trouble and further suffering, so the moral victory he had won in this moment had been utterly futile.

"I know better ways to handle a damn nigger like you," the agent snarled, and without further words whirled his horse around and galloped off down the road, leaving the strap he had been unable to use lying where it had fallen.

Late that evening six men gathered in the rear of the plantation store in response to Sam Turner's summons. In addition to Sam Turner, Fred Smith the postmaster, and the clerk, the overseer, the bookkeeper, there was Bud Scott, tall and raw-boned, the leader of the paddy-rollers, that group of ruthless night riders who had put terror into many a cowering Negro's heart, and brought death to not a few, a man who had served a term as Deputy Sheriff, and for twelve years had led every posse that sallied forth in search of desperate characters. His gun had proved more deadly than the gallows on the second floor of the little brown, brick jail up at Indian Mound. There also was Watt Matthews, former boss of a construction gang on the Yellow Dog fifteen years before when Colonel Billie Bob built the road. But Colonel Billie Bob had fired him long before the Yellow Dog was completed. The Colonel had said that he was too hard on his niggers.

The eyes of all the men were turned on Sam Turner.

"Something's got to be done to get rid of Aaron George," he snapped briefly, "and it's got to be done right away. Why this nigger ain't done nothing for months but stir up other niggers, and if he gits away with this, every damned nigger on the plantation will be shipping to town to work; and when they find they can make more money than they git here, they'll be going to other towns and who the hell will work for the farm? An' where'll our jobs be? He's using our mules to ride to town to work and is urging other niggers to do the same. When I tried to stop him this evening and take the mule, he threatened my life."

"I don't know that I've ever liked the looks of this nigger," the bookkeeper, in perfect harmony with the agent, chimed in. "He don't look down at the groun' like the rest of the niggers when a white man is talking to him. Kind of thought he'd git smart when I settled with him last year, but I guess the big forty-five layin' in the open drawer kinda cooled him off."

"Why don't you get a warrant out for him?" the overseer asked, ignoring the bookkeeper and speaking directly to the agent.

"What for?" asked the agent.

"Didn't you say he threatened you? With gun play? Didn't you catch him comin' from town on one of the mules?"

"Yes," the agent replied.

"Well," said the bookkeeper, "he can be indicted. He can be sent to Parchman Farm. No court gwine to decide in no nigger's favor when he threatens a white man."

"That wouldn't work," said the overseer. "That damn' King would step in and spoil everything."

"I guess that's right," the leader of the paddy-rollers said thoughtfully. "It's a damn good thing he ain't got this place no more. I never could understand him. He let the niggers make too much money. That's what's the matter with them now."

Watt Matthews lifted his head and glared at those around the table. There was a look of cold disdain in his eyes. Slowly he drew back his lips revealing a row of teeth stained with tobacco juice.

"You'd think this nigger was somebody the way you all are carrying on," he said in disgust. "Since when did a nigger git so important that you had to stay up all night trying to find a way to deal with him? Why can't you just string him up and then explain afterwards? There ain't gonna be much explaining to do nohow."

"Yes, but he ain't done enough to call for a lynching," said the overseer. "Course he done a lot of talking back to Sam, and I ain't in for letting him get away with that at all, but I—I——"

"But I what? When did you turn into a nigger lover?" the agent cut in coldly. "This nigger ain't no good at all. It ain't gonna be long before he does something sho nuf. If you don't git him now, you gonna have to git him sooner or later. He'll give you plenty reason all right to git him good."

"Well, what do you want us to do, Sam?" the leader of the paddy-rollers asked. The agent was silent for a moment.

"I just wanted to find out and make sure all you boys would be with me if I got something started. Suppose, for instance, this nigger happened to do something that really called for a neck-tie party, would you boys be in on it?"

"Sure, sure!" they chorused, the only dissenting note coming from the overseer who modified, "If it was serious enough."

"All right," Turner said, apparently satisfied. "I guess that's about all then for tonight. I'll let you know when the time comes."

ZORA NEALE HURSTON (1903-   )

Zora Neale Hurston (see also p. 481) was born in Eatonville, Florida. She attended Morgan College and Howard and Columbia Universities. Her short stories, which have appeared in *Opportunity*, *Story*, and *Ebony and Topaz*, have been drawn largely from folk sources. She has also written plays. *Mules and Men* (1935) is a book of folk tales and lore collected in Florida and Louisiana. Miss Hurston has also written two novels, *Jonah's Gourd Vine* (1934) and *Their Eyes Were Watching God* (1937), and a travel book on Jamaica and Haiti, *Tell My Horse* (1938), written while on a Guggenheim Fellowship. Her *Moses, Man of the Mountain* (1931) is a folk rendering of the story of the prophet. The selection below is reprinted by permission of the author and of the J. B. Lippincott Company from *Their Eyes Were Watching God*.

[Hurricane]

Since Tea Cake and Janie had friended with the Bahaman workers in the 'Glades, they, the "Saws," had been gradually drawn into the American crowd. They quit hiding out to hold their dances when they found that their American friends didn't laugh at them as they feared. Many of the Americans learned to jump and liked it as much as the "Saws." So they began to hold dances night after night in the quarters, usually behind Tea Cake's house. Often now, Tea Cake and Janie stayed up so late at the fire dances that Tea Cake would not let her go with him to the field. He wanted her to get her rest.

So she was home by herself one afternoon when she saw a band of Seminoles passing by. The men walking in front and the laden, stolid women following them like burros. She had seen Indians several times in the 'Glades, in twos and threes, but this was a large party. They were headed towards the Palm Beach road and kept moving steadily. About an hour later another party appeared and went the same way.

Then another just before sundown. This time she asked where they were all going and at last one of the men answered her.

"Going to high ground. Saw-grass bloom. Hurricane coming."

Everybody was talking about it that night. But nobody was worried. The fire dance kept up till nearly dawn. The next day, more Indians moved east, unhurried but steady. Still a blue sky and fair weather. Beans running fine and prices good, so the Indians could be, *must* be wrong. You couldn't have a hurricane when you're making seven and eight dollars a day picking beans. Indians are dumb anyhow, always were. Another night of Stew Beef making dynamic subtleties with his drum and living, sculptural, grotesques in the dance. Next day, no Indians passed at all. It was hot and sultry and Janie left the field and went home.

Morning came without motion. The winds, to the tiniest, lisping baby breath had left the earth. Even before the sun gave light, dead day was creeping from bush to bush watching man.

Some rabbits scurried through the quarters going east. Some possums slunk by and their route was definite. One or two at a time, then more. By the time the people left the fields the procession was constant. Snakes, rattlesnakes began to cross the quarters. The men killed a few, but they could not be missed from the crawling horde. People stayed indoors until daylight. Several times during the night Janie heard the snort of big animals like deer. Once the muted voice of a panther. Going east and east. That night the palm and banana trees began that long distance talk with rain. Several people took fright and picked up and went in to Palm Beach anyway. A thousand buzzards held a flying meet and then went above the clouds and stayed.

One of the Bahaman boys stopped by Tea Cake's house in a car and hollered. Tea Cake came out throwin' laughter over his shoulder into the house.

"Hello Tea Cake."

"Hello 'Lias. You leavin', Ah see."

"Yeah man. You and Janie wanta go? Ah wouldn't give nobody else uh chawnce at uh seat till Ah found out if you all had anyway tuh go."

"Thank yuh ever so much, Lias. But we 'bout decided tuh stay."

"De crow gahn up, man."

"Dat ain't nothin'. You ain't seen de bossman go up, is yuh? Well all right now. Man, de money's too good on the muck. It's liable tuh fair off by tuhmorrer. Ah wouldn't leave if Ah wuz you."

"Mah uncle come for me. He say hurricane warning out in Palm

Beach. Not so bad dere, but man, dis muck is too low and dat big lake is liable tuh bust."

"Ah naw, man. Some boys in dere now talkin' 'bout it. Some of 'em been in de 'Glades fuh years. 'Tain't nothin' but uh lil blow. You'll lose de whole day tuhmorrer tryin' tuh git back out heah."

"De Indians gahn east, man. It's dangerous."

"Dey don't always know. Indians don't know much uh nothin', tuh tell de truth. Else dey'd own dis country still. De white folks ain't gone nowhere. Dey oughta know if it's dangerous. You better stay heah, man. Big Jumpin' dance tuhnight right heah, when it fair off."

Lias hesitated and started to climb out, but his uncle wouldn't let him. "Dis time tuhmorrer you gointuh wish you follow crow," he snorted and drove off. Lias waved back to them gaily.

"If Ah never see you no mo' on earth, Ah'll meet you in Africa."

Others hurried east like the Indians and rabbits and snakes and coons. But the majority sat around laughing and waiting for the sun to get friendly again.

Several men collected at Tea Cake's house and sat around stuffing courage into each other's ears. Janie baked a big pan of beans and something she called sweet biscuits and they all managed to be happy enough.

Most of the great flame-throwers were there and naturally, handling Big John de Conquer and his works. How he had done everything big on earth, then went up tuh heben without dying atall. Went up there picking a guitar and got all de angels doing the ring-shout round and round de throne. Then everybody but God and Old Peter flew off on a flying race to Jericho and back and John de Conquer won the race; went on down to hell, beat the old devil and passed out ice water to everybody down there. Somebody tried to say that it was a mouth organ harp that John was playing, but the rest of them would not hear that. Don't care how good anybody could play a harp, God would rather to hear a guitar. That brought them back to Tea Cake. How come he couldn't hit that box a lick or two? Well, all right now, make us know it.

When it got good to everybody, Muck-Boy woke up and began to chant with the rhythm and everybody bore down on the last word of the line:

> Yo' mama don't wear no *Draws*
> Ah seen her when she took 'em *Off*
> She soaked 'em in alco*Hol*

She sold 'em tuh de Santy *Claus*
He told her 'twaw aginst de *Law*
To wear dem dirty *Draws*

Then Muck-Boy went crazy through the feet and danced himself and everybody else crazy. When he finished he sat back down on the floor and went to sleep again. Then they got to playing Florida flip and coon-can. Then it was dice. Not for money. This was a show-off game. Everybody posing his fancy shots. As always it boiled down to Tea Cake and Motor Boat. Motor Boat with his face like a little black cherubim just from a church tower doing amazing things with anybody's dice. The others forgot the work and the weather watching them throw. It was art. A thousand dollars a throw in Madison Square Garden wouldn't have gotten any more breathless suspense. It would have just been more people holding in.

After a while somebody looked out and said, "It ain't gitting no fairer out dere. B'lieve Ah'll git on over tuh mah shack." Motor Boat and Tea Cake were still playing so everybody left them at it.

Sometime that night the winds came back. Everything in the world had a strong rattle, sharp and short like Stew Beef vibrating the drum head near the edge with his fingers. By morning Gabriel was playing the deep tones in the center of the drums. So when Janie looked out of her door she saw the drifting mists gathered in the west—that cloud field of the sky—to arm themselves with thunders and march forth against the world. Louder and higher and lower and wider the sound and motion spread, mounting, sinking, darking.

It woke up old Okechobee and the monster began to roll in his bed. Began to roll and complain like a peevish world on a grumble. The folks in the quarters and the people in the big houses further around the shore heard the big lake and wondered. The people felt uncomfortable but safe because there were the seawalls to chain the senseless monster in his bed. The folks let the people do the thinking. If the castles thought themselves secure, the cabins needn't worry. Their decision was already made as always. Chink up your cracks, shiver in your wet beds and wait on the mercy of the Lord. The bossman might have the thing stopped before morning anyway. It is so easy to be hopeful in the day time when you can see the things you wish on. But it was night, it stayed night. Night was striding across nothingness with the whole round world in his hands.

A big burst of thunder and lightning trampled over the roof of the house. So Tea Cake and Motor stopped playing. Motor looked up in his angel-looking way and said, "Big Massa draw him chair upstairs."

"Ah'm glad y'all stop dat crap-shootin' even if it wasn't for money," Janie said. "Ole Massa is doin' *His* work now. Us oughta keep quiet."

They huddled closer and stared at the door. They just didn't use another part of their bodies, and they didn't look at anything but the door. The time was past for asking the white folks what to look for through that door. Six eyes were questioning *God*.

Through the screaming wind they heard things crashing and things hurtling and dashing with unbelievable velocity. A baby rabbit, terror ridden, squirmed through a hole in the floor and squatted off there in the shadows against the wall, seeming to know that nobody wanted its flesh at such a time. And the lake got madder and madder with only its dikes between them and him.

In a little wind-lull, Tea Cake touched Janie and said, "Ah reckon you wish now you had of stayed in yo' big house 'way from such as dis, don't yuh?"

"Naw."

"Naw?"

"Yeah, naw. People don't die till dey time come nohow, don't keer where you at. Ah'm wid mah husband in uh storm, dat's all."

"Thanky, Ma'am. But 'sposin' yuh wuz tuh die, now. You wouldn't git mad at me for draggin' yuh heah?"

"Naw. We been tuhgether round two years. If you kin see de light at daybreak, you don't keer if you die at dusk. It's so many people never seen de light at all. Ah wuz fumblin' round and God opened de door."

He dropped to the floor and put his head in her lap. "Well then, Janie, you meant whut you didn't say, 'cause Ah never *knowed* you wuz so satisfied wid me lak dat. Ah kinda thought——"

The wind came back with triple fury, and put out the light for the last time. They sat in company with the others in other shanties, their eyes straining against crude walls and their souls asking if He meant to measure their puny might against His. They seemed to be staring at the dark, but their eyes were watching God.

As soon as Tea Cake went out pushing wind in front of him, he saw that the wind and water had given life to lots of things that folks think of as dead and given death to so much that had been living things. Water everywhere. Stray fish swimming in the yard. Three inches more and the water would be in the house. Already in some. He decided to try to find a car to take them out of the 'Glades before worse things happened. He turned back to tell Janie about it so she could be ready to go.

"Git our insurance papers tuhgether, Janie. Ah'll tote mah box mahself and things lak dat."

"You got all de money out de dresser drawer, already?"

"Naw, git it quick and cut uh piece off de tablecloth tuh wrap it up in. Us liable tuh git wet tuh our necks. Cut uh piece uh dat oilcloth quick fuh our papers. We got tuh go, if it ain't too late. De dish can't bear it out no longer."

He snatched the oilcloth off the table and took out his knife. Janie held it straight while he slashed off a strip.

"But Tea Cake, it's too awful out dere. Maybe's it's better tuh stay heah in de wet than it is tuh try tuh——"

He stunned the argument with half a word. "Fix," he said and fought his way outside. He had seen more than Janie had.

Janie took a big needle and ran up a longish sack. Found some newspaper and wrapped up the paper money and papers and thrust them in and whipped over the open end with her needle. Before she could get it thoroughly hidden in the pockets of her overalls, Tea Cake burst in again.

" 'Tain't no cars, Janie."

"Ah thought not! Whut we gointuh do now?"

"We got tuh walk."

"In all dis weather, Tea Cake? Ah don't b'lieve Ah could make it out de quarters."

"Oh yeah you kin. Me and you and Motor Boat kin all lock arms and hold one 'nother down. Eh, Motor?"

"He's asleep on de bed in yonder," Janie said. Tea Cake called without moving.

"Motor Boat! You better git up from dere! Hell done broke loose in Georgy. Dis minute! How kin you sleep at uh time lak dis? Water knee deep in de yard."

They stepped out in water almost to their buttocks and managed to turn east. Tea Cake had to throw his box away, and Janie saw how it hurt him. Dodging flying missiles, floating dangers, avoiding stepping in holes and warmed on the wind now at their backs until they gained comparatively dry land. They had to fight to keep from being pushed the wrong way and to hold together. They saw other people like themselves struggling along. A house down, here and there, frightened cattle. But above all, the drive of the wind and the water. And the lake. Under its multiplied roar could be heard a mighty sound of grinding rock and timber and a wail. They looked back. Saw people trying to run in raging waters and screaming when they found they couldn't. A huge barrier of the makings of the dike to which the cabins had been added was rolling and tumbling forward. Ten feet higher and as far as they could see the muttering wall advanced before the braced-up waters like a road crusher on a cosmic scale. The monstropolous beast had left his bed. The two hundred miles an hour wind had loosed his chains. He seized hold of his dikes and ran forward until he met the quarters; uprooted them like grass and rushed on after his supposed-to-be conquerers, rolling the dikes, rolling the houses, rolling the people in the houses along with other timbers. The sea was walking the earth with a heavy heel.

"De lake is comin'!" Tea Cake gasped.

"De lake!" In amazed horror from Motor Boat, "De lake!"

"It's comin' behind us!" Janie shuddered. "Us can't fly."

"But we kin still run," Tea Cake shouted and they ran. The gushing water ran faster. The great body was held back, but rivers spouted through fissures in the rolling wall and broke like day. The three fugitives ran past another line of shanties that topped a slight rise and gained a little. They cried out as best they could, "De lake is comin'!" and barred doors flew open and others joined them in flight crying the same as they went. "De lake is comin'!" and the pursuing waters growled and shouted ahead, "Yes, Ah'm comin'!", and those who could fled on.

They made it to a tall house on a hump of ground and Janie said, "Less stop heah. Ah can't make it no further. Ah'm done give out."

"All of us is done give out," Tea Cake corrected. "We'se goin' inside out dis weather, kill or cure." He knocked with the handle of his knife, while they leaned their faces and shoulders against the wall. He knocked once more, then he and Motor Boat went round to the back and forced a door. Nobody there.

"Dese people had mo' sense than Ah did," Tea Cake said as they dropped to the floor and lay there panting. "Us oughta went wid 'Lias lak he ast me."

"You didn't know," Janie contended. "And when yuh don't know, yuh just don't know. De storms might not of come sho nuff."

They went to sleep promptly but Janie woke up first. She heard the sound of rushing water and sat up.

"Tea Cake! Motor Boat! De lake is comin'!"

The lake *was* coming on. Slower and wider, but coming. It had trampled on most of its supporting wall and lowered its front by spreading. But it came muttering and grumbling onward like a tired mammoth just the same.

"Dis is uh high tall house. Maybe it won't reach heah at all," Janie counselled. "And if it do, maybe it won't reach tuh de upstairs part."

"Janie, Lake Okechobee is forty miles wide and sixty miles long. Dat uh whole heap uh water. If dis wind is shovin' dat whole lake disa way, dis house ain't nothin' tuh swaller. Us better go. Motor Boat!"

"Whut you want, man?"

"De lake is comin'!"

"Aw, naw it 'tain't."

"Yes, it is *so* comin'! Listen! You kin hear it way off."

"It kin jus' come on. Ah'll wait right here."

"Aw, get up, Motor Boat! Less make it tuh de Palm Beach road. Dat's on uh fill. We'se pretty safe dere."

"Ah'm safe here, man. Go ahead if yuh wants to. Ah'm sleepy."

"Whut you gointuh do if de lake reach heah?"

"Go upstairs."

"S'posing it come up dere?"

"Swim, man. Dat's all."

"Well, uh, good bye, Motor Boat. Everything is pretty bad, yuh know. Us might git missed of one 'nother. You sho is a grand friend fuh uh man tuh have."

"Good bye, Tea Cake. Y'all oughta stay here and sleep, man. No use in goin' off and leavin' me lak dis."

"We don't wanta. Come on wid us. It might be night time when de water hem you up in heah. Dat's how come Ah won't stay. Come on, man."

"Tea Cake Ah got tuh have mah sleep. Definitely."

"Good bye, then, Motor. Ah wish you all de luck. Goin' over tuh Nassau fuh dat visit widja when all dis is over."

"Definitely, Tea Cake. Mah mama's house is yours."

Tea Cake and Janie were some distance from the house before they struck serious water. They had to swim a distance, and Janie could not hold up more than a few strokes at a time, so Tea Cake bore her up till finally they hit a ridge that led on towards the fill. It seemed to him the wind was weakening a little so he kept looking for a place to rest and catch his breath. His wind was gone. Janie was tired and limping, but she had not had to do that hard swimming in the turbulent waters, so Tea Cake was much worse off. But they couldn't stop. Gaining the fill was something but it was no guarantee. The lake was coming. They had to reach the six-mile bridge. It was high and safe perhaps.

Everybody was walking the fill. Hurrying, dragging, falling, crying, calling out names hopefully and hopelessly. Wind and rain beating on old folks and beating on babies. Tea Cake stumbled once or twice in his weariness and Janie held him up. So they reached the bridge at Six Mile Bend and thought to rest.

But it was crowded. White people had preempted that point of elevation and there was no more room. They could climb up one of its high sides and down the other, that was all. Miles further on, still no rest.

They passed a dead man in a sitting position on a hummock, entirely surrounded by wild animals and snakes. Common danger made common friends. Nothing sought a conquest over the other.

Another man clung to a cypress tree on a tiny island. A tin roof of a building hung from the branches by electric wires and the wind swung it back and forth like a mighty ax. The man dared not move a step to his right lest this crushing blade split him open. He dared not step left for a large rattlesnake was stretched full length wth his head in the wind. There was a strip of water between the island and the fill, and the man clung to the tree and cried for help.

"De snake won't bite yuh," Tea Cake yelled to him. "He skeered tuh go intuh uh coil. Skeered he'll be blowed away. Step round dat side and swim off!"

Soon after that Tea Cake felt he couldn't walk anymore. Not right away. So he stretched long side of the road to rest. Janie spread herself between him and the wind and he closed his eyes and let the tiredness seep out of his limbs. On each side of the fill was a great expanse of water like lakes—water full of things living and dead. Things that didn't belong in water. As far as the eye could reach, water and wind playing upon it in fury. A large piece of tar-paper roofing sailed through the air and scudded along the fill until it hung against a tree. Janie saw it with joy. That was the very thing to cover Tea Cake with. She could lean against it and hold it down. The wind wasn't quite so bad as it was anyway. The very thing. Poor Tea Cake!

She crept on hands and knees to the piece of roofing and caught hold of it by either side. Immediately the wind lifted both of them and she saw herself sailing off the fill to the right, out and out over the lashing water. She screamed terribly and released the roofing which sailed away as she plunged downward into the water.

"Tea Cake!" He heard her and sprang up. Janie was trying to swim but fighting water too hard. He saw a cow swimming slowly towards the fill in an oblique line. A massive built dog was sitting on her shoulders and shivering and growling. The cow was approaching Janie. A few strokes would bring her there.

"Make it tuh de cow and grab hold of her tail! Don't use yo' feet. Jus' yo' hands is enough. Dat's right, come on!"

Janie achieved the tail of the cow and lifted her head up along

the cow's rump, as far as she could above water. The cow sunk a
little with the added load and thrashed a moment in terror. Thought
she was being pulled down by a gator. Then she continued on. The
dog stood up and growled like a lion, stiff-standing hackles, stiff
muscles, teeth uncovered as he lashed up his fury for the charge.
Tea Cake split the water like an otter, opening his knife as he dived.
The dog raced down the back-bone of the cow to attack and Janie
screamed and slipped far back on the tail of the cow, just out of
reach of the dog's angry jaws. He wanted to plunge in after her but
dreaded the water, somehow. Tea Cake rose out of the water at the
cow's rump and seized the dog by the neck. But he was a powerful
dog and Tea Cake was over-tired. So he didn't kill the dog with one
stroke as he had intended. But the dog couldn't free himself either.
They fought and somehow he managed to bite Tea Cake high up on
his cheek-bone once. Then Tea Cake finished him and sent him to the
bottom to stay there. The cow, relieved of a great weight, was landing
on the fill with Janie before Tea Cake stroked in and crawled weakly
upon the fill again.

Janie began to fuss around his face where the dog had bitten him
but he said it didn't amount to anything. "He'd uh raised hell though
if he had uh grabbed me uh inch higher and bit me in mah eye.
Yuh can't buy eyes in the store, you know." He flopped to the edge
of the fill as if the storm wasn't going on at all. "Lemme rest awhile,
then us got tuh make it on intuh town somehow."

It was next day by the sun and the clock when they reached Palm
Beach. It was years later by their bodies. Winters and winters of
hardship and suffering. The wheel kept turning round and round.
Hope, hopelessness and despair. But the storm blew itself out as they
approached the city of refuge.

Havoc was there with her mouth wide open. Back in the Ever-
glades the wind had romped among the lakes and trees. In the city
it had raged among houses and men. Tea Cake and Janie stood on
the edge of things and looked over the desolation.

"How kin Ah find uh doctor fuh yo' face in all dis mess?" Janie
wailed.

"Aint got de damn doctor tuh study 'bout. Us needs uh place
tuh rest."

A great deal of their money and perseverance and they found a
place to sleep. It was just that. No place to live at all. Just sleep. Tea
Cake looked all around and sat heavily on the side of the bed.

"Well," he said humbly, "reckon you never 'spected tuh come
tuh dis when you took up wid me, didja?"

"Once upon uh time, Ah never 'spected nothin', Tea Cake, but bein' dead from the standin' still and tryin' tuh laugh. But you come 'long and made somethin' outa me. So Ah'm thankful fuh anything we come through together."

"Thanky, Ma'am."

"You was twice noble tuh save me from dat dawg. Tea Cake, Ah don't speck you seen his eyes lah Ah did. He didn't aim tuh jus' bite me, Tea Cake. He aimed tuh kill me stone dead. Ah'm never tuh fuhgit dem eyes. He wuzn't nothin' all over but pure hate. Wonder where he come from?"

"Yeah, Ah did see 'im too. It wus frightenin'. Ah didn't mean tuh take his hate neither. He had tuh die uh me one. Mah switch blade said it wuz him."

"Po' me, he'd tore me tuh pieces, if it wuzn't fuh you, honey."

"You don't have tuh say, if it wuzn't fuh me, baby, cause Ahm *heah,* and then Ah want youh tuh know it's uh man heah."

ARNA BONTEMPS (1902-

Arna Bontemps (see also p. 379) was born in Alexandria, Louisiana. At twenty he graduated from Pacific Union College in northern California. The following year he came to New York and saw the Negro Renaissance, as he phrases it, "from a grandstand seat." In 1931 he "contributed to it the book that marked the end of that period: *God Sends Sunday* (1931)." Leaving New York, Bontemps taught for a while in a small Alabama college, at the same time writing two of his children's books and gathering material for *Black Thunder* (1936). He returned to Los Angeles in 1934 to complete the latter book. In 1938-39 he was awarded a Rosenwald Fellowship for creative writing. *Drums at Dusk* appeared in 1939. His most recent work has been the editing of *Father of the Blues* (the autobiography of W. C. Handy), which appeared this year. The selections are from *Black Thunder* and are reprinted by permission of the author and The Macmillan Co.

[Conspirators]

Brothers and Friends:

I am Toussaint l'Ouverture; my name is perhaps known to you. I have undertaken to avenge your wrongs. It is my desire that liberty and equality shall reign. I am striving to this end. Come and unite with us, brothers, and combat with us for the same cause.

Your very humble and obedient servant,

Toussaint l'Ouverture,
General for the Public Welfare.

The brown girl curled on the floor in front of the circle of men. Mingo sat on a stool; the others had drawn up benches, work tables and boxes. They were meeting in the saddle-shop because Mingo had said, "Never twice in the same place—on'erstand? Here this time and somewheres else the next."

"That's enough reading this time," Gabriel said. "We going to have all the help we needs once we get our hands in. It's most nigh time to strike, and we got to make haste."

Gabriel, silent and dreamy usually, spoke with a quick excitement these days. There was an urgency in his manner that got under the skin at once. He didn't talk in a loud voice; in fact, he didn't talk at all. He simply whispered. Yet Ditcher's mouth dropped open as he listened; he leaned forward and the muscles tightened on his shoulders. His huge hands, dangling at his sides, closed gradually and gradually opened again. He was ready to strike. Blue, hearing every word, pulled the heavy lips over his large protruding teeth, hunched himself somberly on his box. General John Scott, as scrawny and ragged as a scarecrow, rubbed his brown bark-like hands together, blinked nervously. Ben, wearing gloves, stood with a new Sunday hat in his hand, his head bowed. Some of the group trembled. They were all ready.

They had come into the shop through the back way. They had selected this place for their Sunday gathering because the shops on either side were closed and they were able to feel safely secluded.

"What's going to be the day?" Ditcher said.

"The first day in September," Gabriel told him.

"That falls on a Sad-dy," a pumpkin-colored fellow said quietly.

General John showed his brown fangs without malevolence.

"Sad-dy, hunh?"

"Yes, the first day of September come next Sad-dy," Ben said.

255

"I's just thinking," the yellow Negro muttered. "I's just thinking it might be better to strike on a Sunday."

"Howcome that?" Gabriel asked.

"Well, it's just like today. The country folks can leave home and travel mo' better on a Sunday. Nobody's going to ask where they's going or if they's got a note. That's what I's thinking. Sunday's a mo' better day for the back-country folks to get together."

"We don't need none of them what lives that far in the country—not right now nohow. We done set Sad-dy for the day and Sad-dy it's going to be—hear? We got all the mens we need to hit the first lick round here close."

"Well, I reckon maybe that's right too. That other was just something what come in my head."

"This what *you* got to remember, Pharoah: You's leaving for Caroline County with Ben next Sad-dy evening. You can send word up by the boys going that a-way so everything'll be in shape. We going to write up something like that what Mingo read from Toussaint, soon's we get our power, and you ain't got to do nothing up there but spread the news. Them's all our brothers. I bound you they'll come when they hears the proclamation."

"H'm. They'll come," General John said. "They'll come soon's they hears what we's done."

Ben turned the new Sunday hat round and round in his hands. He was nervous and tremulous again. He turned General John's words in his mind: They'll come. Anything wants to be free. Well, Ben reckoned so; yet and still, it seemed like some folks was a heap mo' anxious about it than others. It was true that they were brothers—not so much because they were black as because they were the outcasts and the unwanted of the land—and for that reason he followed against his will. Then, too, there was old Bundy buried in the low field and that something else that squatted by the hole where he lay.

"They'll come," Ben echoed weakly. "Anything wants to be free—I reckon."

"You mighty right," Gabriel whispered. "Some of y'-all can commence leaving now. Remember just two by two, and don't go till the ones in front of you is had time to get round the square. That's right, Criddle, you and George. You two go first. Ben and Pharoah—you next. Keep moving and don't make no fuss."

Now they were getting away slowly. They were slipping down the alley by twos and the saddle-shop was emptying gradually. Gabriel stood above the thin-waisted brown girl, his foot on the edge of the bench, one elbow on his knee.

"It's a man's doings, Juba. You ain't obliged to keep following along."

"I hears what you say."

"The time ain't long, and it's apt to get worse and worser."

"H'm."

"And it's going to be fighting and killing till you can't rest, befo' it's done."

"I know," she said.

"And you still wants to follow on?"

"Yes."

"Well, it ain't for me to tell you no, gal."

"I'm in it. Long's you's in it, I'm in it too."

"And it's win all or lose all—on'erstand?"

"I'm in it. Win all or lose all."

Mingo stood by listening. His spectacles had slipped down on his nose. He had a thin face for a black and a high receding forehead. He listened to Gabriel's words and Juba's short answers and tried to tear himself away. Somehow he couldn't move. It was win or lose all. He became pale with that peculiar lavender paleness that comes to terrified black men. There was death in the offing, death or freedom, but until now Mingo had thought only in terms of the latter. The other was an ugly specter to meet.

He looked at Gabriel's face, noted the powerful resolution in his expression. Sometimes, he thought, the unlearned lead the learned and teach them courage, teach them to die with a handsome toss of the head. He looked at Juba and saw that she was bewitched. She would indeed follow to the end. He was a free Negro and these were slaves, but somehow he envied them. Suddenly a strange exaltation came to his mind.

"Yes," he said, breaking into their conversation. "It's win all or lose all. It's a game, but it's worth trying and I got a good notion we can win. I'm free now, but it ain't no good being free when all yo' people's slaves, yo' wife and chilluns and all."

"A wild bird what's in a cage will die anyhow, sooner or later," Gabriel said. "He'll pine hisself to death. He just as well to break his neck trying to get out."

[The Trial]

"... and are you the one they call the General?"

"I'm name Gabriel."

"I've heard slaves refer to a General something or other."

"Gen'l John, maybe."

"Didn't they call you General?"

"Some time—not so much."

"Then old John there was the leader, not you?"

"No. I been the leader, *me*. I'm the one. Gen'l John is just named that. I'm the one."

"You *are* the General?"

"I reckon so. Leastwise, I'm the leader. I ain't never turned my back to a nachal man. I don't know if I'm a sure 'nough general or if I ain't."

Gabriel, still in the frayed coachman's clothes, sank back into a lordly slouch. Now, suh, curse they ugly hides, they could make up they own minds about the gen'l part. Is I, or ain't I. One hand clasped the arm of the witness chair; the other hung idly across his knee. His eye kept its penetrating gaze, but now there was a vague sadness on his face. It was as if shadows passed before him now and again. It may have been woe or remorse rising in him, but the look was more like the dark, uncertain torment one sees in the countenance of a crushed beast whose spirit remains unbroken.

Only that morning there had been another execution, a small herd of anonymous field Negroes. The townsfolk were hardened to the spectacle now. Even the customary eyewitnesses were missing. The word had gotten about that these were not the ringleaders, and the mere sight of slaughter for its own sake was no longer attractive or stimulating. So many little groups like this had come to the scaffold since mid-September—five, ten, fifteen at a time—so many. It was a routine. These blacks had contracted a malady, a sort of hydrophobia; they were mad. It was necessary to check the spread of the thing. It was a common-sense matter. Only this morning there had been a difference.

At first no one had seen or heard the wiry old man with the turndown mouth. He had seen the first of the executions, and he raised his voice then.

"You idiots. You're putting them through too fast, I tell you. No sense in killing off a man's live stock in herds like that unless you know for sure what you're doing."

258

He scrambled in the crowd and tried to fight his way through. But they thought he was talking about the blacks being idiots. A chorus of approval rose around him. No one saw him as an individual, only as a part of a snarling crowd.

Today, with things much quieter, they had heard, for he succeeded in delaying the hangings half-an-hour.

"See that long yellow boy there. Well, that's John Thomas. That boy's been to Norfolk for me. He just got back last week. And, by God, if you hang him without proof, you'll pay me his worth. Bloody apes, what's wrong with you? Have you gone stone crazy for life?"

John Thomas did not swing. There was rumor that several other planters had also been to the justices since morning. And already a statement had been issued—some "mistakes" had been made, admittedly. But Gabriel, lying on his face beside Mingo, knew only what the swinging trap indicated. Yet it occurred to him that all this pause, this unhurried questioning, could not possibly have been in keeping with the trials that had preceded his. He concluded at length that the "General" was simply receiving his due recognition, this in spite of the prosecutor's whining, sarcastic voice.

"Here, now, you mean to say you were the one that thought up the whole idea?"

"I was the one. Me."

"Yes, but not all alone, surely——"

"Maybe not all alone."

"Well, then, who were your accomplices? Who helped you think it up?"

Gabriel shrugged.

"You got Ditcher and Mingo and Gen'l John. You done hanged a plenty mo'. I talked to some of them. I told them to come on."

"It's plain that you do not intend to implicate anyone not already in custody. You're not telling all you know."

Gabriel looked at the man long and directly.

"I ain't got cause to talk a heap, suh."

"You haven't?"

"H'm."

Then the prosecutor spun quickly on his heel, barked.

"What do you mean by that, you——"

Gabriel's eyes strayed indolently to the window, to the golden leaves of an oak bough. The court was oppressively rigid, the justices in their wigs and robes, the spectators gaping, straining their necks.

"A man what's booked to hang anyhow——" he mused.

"Oh. So you think——" Then a diplomatic change of tone. "You know, Gabriel, it is not impossible to alter the complexion of things even yet. A—I mean, you have a fine chance to let the court know if you have been made the tool of foreign agitators. If there were white men who talked to you, encouraged——"

That sounded foolish to Gabriel.

"White mens?"

"Yes, men talking about equality, setting the poor against the rich, the blacks against their masters, things like that."

Gabriel was now convinced that the man was resorting to some sort of guile. He fixed his eyes earnestly.

"I tell you. I been studying about freedom a heap, me. I heard a plenty folks talk and I listened a heap. And everything I heard made me feel like I wanted to be free. It was on my mind hard, and it's right there the same way yet. On'erstand? That's all. Something keep telling me that anything what's equal to a gray squirrel wants to be free. That's how it all come about."

"Well, was it necessary to plot such a savage butchery? Couldn't you have contrived an easier way?"

Gabriel shook his head slowly. After a long pause he spoke.

"I ain't got no head for flying away. A man's got a right to have his freedom in the place where he's born. He is got cause to want all his kinfolks free like hisself."

"Oh, why don't you come clean? Don't you realize you're on the verge of hanging? The court wants to know who planted the damnable seeds, what Jacobins worked on you? Were you not treated well by your master?"

Gabriel ignored most of what he said.

"Might just as well to hang."

"That's bravado. You want to live. And the best way for you to——"

"A lion what's tasted man's blood is a caution to keep around after that."

"Don't strut, nigger."

"No, suh, no strutting. But I been free this last four-five weeks. On'erstand? I been a gen'l, and I been ready to die since first time I hooked on a sword. The others too—they been ready. We all knowed it was one thing or the other. The stars was against us, though; that's all."

It was astonishing how the thing dragged on, astonishing how they worried and cajoled, threatened and flattered the captive. "Mistakes" *had* been made, due to haste and excitement, but there was no possibility of a mistake here. Gabriel seemed, if anything, anxious to have them get the thing straight, to have them place responsibility where responsibility belonged.

In another room, under heavy guard and awaiting their call, the last of the accused Negroes sulked. Ditcher's massive head was bowed, his wiry queue curled like a pig's tail. It had never been more apparent that he was a giant. His legs suggested tree stumps. The depth of his chest, the spread of his shoulders seemed unreal. His skin was amber. Now, delaying in the guarded room, he was perfectly relaxed. Indeed, he might have nodded had it not been for the jittery, nervous activity of the armed men around him. They annoyed him.

"We could had them on they knees long ago," he was saying in his mind. "Only that devilish big rain. That's what stopped us. We could all been free as squirrels by now. It wasn't the time to hit. We should had a sign."

Mingo's clothes were better, but his hair had been torn from its braid. He had lost his spectacles. His eyes had an uncertain, watery stare. He was not merely downcast; he looked definitely disappointed. Words were going through his mind, too, but they made a briefer strain. "Toussaint's crowd was luckier. Toussaint's crowd was luckier."

There were others, a dozen or more, unimportant fellows. Then near the door the withered old dead-leaf clad in a rag that had once been an overcoat. He kept licking his white, shriveled lips, kept showing the brown fangs. He was trembling now.

"Somebody's obliged to foot the bill," his mind was saying. "Ne' mind, though. Near about everybody dies *one* time. And there ain't many niggers what gets to cross the river free—not many."

Any one of them would have sped the business along had it been his to do it. No cause for a heap of aggravating questions. Them white mens ought to could see that Gabriel didn't care nothing about them; he was going to tell them just what it was good for them to know, and precious little more. But there was nothing they could do, nothing but wait.

". . . and how did you imagine you'd be able to take the city?"

"We was ready to hit fast. We had three lines, and the one in the middle was going to split in two. They was coming in town from both ends at once. They wasn't going to spare nothing what helt up its hand against us."

"How about the other two?"

"Them's the ones what was ready to take the arsenal and the powder house."

"Which line were you to lead?"

"The one what went against the arsenal."

"What arms had you?"

"We didn't need no guns—us what went against the arsenal there. All we needed was to slip by in the dark with good stout sticks. We could manage them few guards."

"Mad dogs—that's what you are. The audacity! It's inconceivable that well-treated servants like—"

"We was tired being slaves. We never heard tell about no other way."

"You'd take the arsenal and powder house by surprise; then with ample arms, with the city in ashes, with the countryside and crops for your food, you thought you'd be able to stand your ground?"

"H'm."

"How many bullets had you to start with?"

"About a peck."

"And powder?"

" 'Nough for that many bullets."

"Any other arms?"

"Pikes, scythe-swords, knives, clubs, all like of that—'nough to do the work."

"How'd you know it would do the work?"

"There wa'n't but twenty-three muskets in town outside the arsenal."

"You knew that!"

Gabriel felt that it was unnecessary to answer.

There was a hush; a shiver passed over the courtroom.

"It was a diabolical thing. Gentlemen——"

He talked for a time with his back to Gabriel. Later he turned to the prisoner again, but this time he spoke like a changed man, an awakened man who had had an evil dream.

"Did you imagine other well-fed, well-kept slaves would join you?"

"Wouldn't you j'ine us, was you a slave, suh?"

"Don't be impudent. You're still a black——"

"I been a free man—and a gen'l, I reckon."

"And stop saying general, too. Ringleader of mad dogs. That's what you've been. I call on this court of justice——"

Gabriel felt the scene withdrawing. It was almost like a dream, almost mystic. Further and further away it receded. Again there was that insulting mockery of words he could not understand, that babble of legal language and political innuendo. It was all moving away from him, leaving him clinging to an arm of his chair, slouched on one elbow. A lordly insolence rose in him. Suddenly he was vaguely aware of that whiney voice again.

"The only question yet raised, sir, was whether or not the wretch was capable of conceiving such a masterpiece of deviltry, such a demon-inspired——"

It was far away. Gabriel's eyes strayed again. The window—blue. The crisp oak leaves—like gold. Demons. Freedom. Deviltry. Justice. Funny words. All of them sounded like conjure now.

"Maybe we should paid attention to the signs. Maybe we should done that," Gabriel thought.

WATERS E. TURPIN (1910-   )

Waters Edward Turpin was born in Oxford on the Eastern Shore of Maryland, the setting of his novel *These Low Grounds* (1937). He was educated in the public schools of Maryland and New Jersey, at Morgan College, and at Columbia. After working as a porter-clerk in a Harlem delicatessen and as an investigator for a Harlem housing project, he went to Storer College, Harpers Ferry, to teach English and coach football. Later he taught English at Lincoln University, where he won a Rosenwald Fellowship for creative writing. Both *These Low Grounds* (1937) and *O Canaan* (1939) are family chronicles. "Oystering," from *These Low Grounds,* is used by permission of the author and of Harper and Brothers.

[Oystering]

Summer broke abruptly about a week after Carrie's explosion to Jake. The sun tried to hold its own, but there was clear evidence that fall was no longer to be denied. Dropping leaves reddened and yellowed the Public Lot and littered the bricks under the arch of maples down Front Street. Wild geese streamed southward over the Avondale. One by one the crabbers laid aside their lines and took their tong shafts and rusty rakes to young Tom Ridgley, the blacksmith, for repairs. Fewer and fewer crabs came into the wharves until, on the last day of September, the rival houses on the Island and on Town Pier sent no blasts shrieking to the skies. The crabs would have peace until the following summer.

With the crabbing season ended, the oyster season was on, and now the town awoke to full life. For two weeks boats, trains, wagons, and all manner of horse-drawn conveyances brought men and women—

sometimes whole families—to swell the colored population. Most of the incoming oyster-shuckers were men. They came from Virginia and points as far south as North Carolina. And the majority came by way of Baltimore on the steamers *Avalon* and *Talbot*.

One of these boats touched Herdford every night on its way to Eastland Point, which was the last stop on its route. From Monday to Friday the vessel slunk into Town Wharf at about midnight; then, its obligations discharged, departed with expeditious haste. But Saturday night was different. Saturday night was Jug Night.

No matter what the weather, when the first blast of the steamer was heard, nearly all the men of the town who had reached their majority would take themselves hurriedly to the wharf. Here, in the dim light of the kerosene lamps which perched on the walls of the freight-house, they would wait eagerly for the boat to dock with a great splashing of her side wheels.

Their patience was rewarded when, after passengers and merchandise had been transferred, the stevedores would march single file down the gangplank, each swinging a jug in either hand. The jugs were deposited in the freight-house. Then there was a grand rush as the waiting men bore down upon the freight agent, who shouted out the names which tagged the necks of the containers. Every man eventually was awarded a jug. The greedier ones opened theirs on the spot, slung them over the crooks of their arms and gurgled happily—and as they gurgled the trials of the week washed away.

Sunday night also was a gala night at the wharf, for after a day of rest the residents of the sleepy village were prime for any diversion that chance or circumstance offered. A queen and her imperial train could not have received more homage than the side-wheeler from Baltimore as she swung around Tom's Point into the Avondale from Choptank River. Idlers from Front and Tilton streets dashed headlong to the waterfront. Children raced to see who could get to the wharf first. Their elders, out for a walk, accelerated their pace. And as the boat came splashing to rest, with a final shrill blast of her whistle, horses reared and pitched, and the more timid watchers clutched at each other in giggling fright.

Jim Tutley, the shipping agent, his magnificently curled mustachios erect, was a paragon of authoritative pride on such occasions.

"Haul away!" he would bawl after he had slipped the wide nooses of the lead line over stout pilings at each wharf corner.

From that moment until the boat's departure, the proceedings took on a certain ritualistic cast. The roustabouts rushed here and there, clearing a space, removing a bar—every movement an incident in a prearranged plan. Then the gangplank was shot over the boat's side, a waist-high railing was attached, and a resplendent personage in blue uniform advanced to snarl:

"All off 'at's goin' off!"

First the white passengers disembarked, the women throwing timid glances at the water yawning darkly below. After them came the Negro passengers, the oyster-shuckers—swaggering, teeth flashing. Freight was unloaded, outgoing freight was hauled aboard. New passengers arrived. The gangplank was withdrawn. A shrill whistle. The waters churned. And in a minute more the steamer had rounded the bend toward Eastland Point.

Jim Tutley extinguished the lamps and locked the great sliding doors, and once more the wharf was a patch of darkness against the gently swelling river.

The low-raftered oyster-house was a smelly, sloppy place that would have turned the stomachs of the smart people who relished Herdford oysters in the metropolitan restaurants that were their final destination. Four shelf-like, wooden structures, waist-high, ran the length of the room—one on each side, two facing each other down the center. Upon them were distributed heaps of muddy oysters. The shuckers (there were women as well as men) stood in narrow, body-width stalls that reached to the top of the shelves.

A powerful fellow weaved continually up and down the two aisles with a flat-bottomed barrow—bringing fresh supplies of oysters for the shuckers, carrying off shells that the shuckers had cast aside. The shuckers were skilled laborers but this carrier, by comparison, was a menial of the most inferior order. What he had was strength for a strenuous job.

By the dim light struggling through muddy windows Carrie made out the tall form of Grundy leaning industriously over his shucking-board. At the moment he was competing with his neighbor, a wiry little man with the high cheek bones and swarthy coloring that indicated a fusion of Indian and Negro blood. Carrie left Gussie to talk with Bud Saunders and eased over to Grundy's side.

Grundy and the little man were evenly matched but their methods of shucking differed. Grundy used the orthodox oyster-knife, a slender, thin steel blade, about the length and a quarter of the index finger, which he gripped in his right hand. His gloved left hand held the oyster on the board. First he would insert the knife, guiding it with a muslin-stalled forefinger. Then after a preliminary boring effected with his pliant right wrist there would follow a coordinated twisting of oyster and knife—and a juicy grey oyster lay unshelled, to be flipped into one of two pails at the side of the pile. The actual time of this operation was hardly more than five seconds.

His neighbor's methods required more archaic implements—a small hammer and a long-handled knife (originally belonging to a table set) which had been filed down until it resembled a hiltless stiletto. With the hammer the little man broke the mouth of the oyster's shell, temporarily jarring open the two halves. Then he released the hammer with lightning rapidity, the knife fairly leapt into his hand, and the blade darted like the tongue of an aroused serpent between the two shells. With the same twisting motion Grundy practiced he exposed the oyster, and with the same flip he deposited it in its pail.

The movements of the two men were flowing rather than jerky—a symphony in muscular coordination—and Carrie looked on fascinated. The men were not unconscious of their audience.

Finally Grundy jabbed his quivering blade into the soggy board at the base of his oyster pile and turned to his opponent with a broad grin.

"Ah beat you dat time, Sam," he rumbled, good-naturedly.

Sam shrugged his shoulders and spat a stream of tobacco juice onto the discarded shells at the side of his stall, while he continued to ply his knife and hammer.

Grundy swung his two pails down from the shelf, disappeared into the packing-room, and returned. Carrie was still there.

"You sho kin open dem oysters," she smiled.

His gray eyes might have seen her for the first time, but he flashed the whiteness of his teeth.

"Ain't you never seed no fast shuckin' befo'?" he inquired.

"Ah ain't never seed no kind o' shuckin'," answered Carrie.

"Whar you bin at?"

"Ah ain't lived near no water since Ah was a li'l' gal," she explained.

"You watch me an Ah'll show you how it's done," he promised. He took an oyster leisurely. "You see, oysters ain't like humans—dey don't like to open dey mouths 'less'n dey jes' has to. Dat's why dey squeaks an' spits when you sticks 'em wid yo' knife. You gots to twist yo' knife like dis so's to make the jaws tired. See? Den you cuts de muscle off'n de bottom shell easy-like so's you don't mess up his guts. See? Dar he is—a big 'un. Want 'im?"

Carrie took it gingerly, but in a minute her expression of distaste disappeared and her face broke into its most alluring smile.

"Will you shuck me this jar full fo' mah supper, Mr. Grundy?"

"Sho! How'd you know mah name?"

"Oh, Ah larned that when Ah first come to town. Don't you 'member out on the wharf, yonder, an' at the oyster supper?"

Gray eyes met black eyes, smiled, and looked casually away.

The cry of a baby wailed above the buzzing voices and crackling shells. From the side of her husband, felt-booted and mud daubed as was he, a stalwart woman strode to a wooden box by the stove. Catching the kicking infant to her breast, she sat down, crooning softly. But the child's cries shrilled higher and higher.

"Hey thar, Lew Grundy!" called the woman. "Sing dat 'Go Down Moses' fo' dis chile; he's a man-chile efn dey ever was one! He don't like no baby song!"

Coaxing cries came from all quarters:

"Yeah, Lew!"

"Come on, Deacon. We'll help you sing it!"

Without preliminaries, Grundy lifted his head and poured forth the first line in a deeply mellow baritone. He forgot the oysters, and his intensity transmitted itself to Carrie. She found her own mature contralto blending in the refrain. The other shuckers paused in surprise at this duet. A low hum cautiously followed the two leaders. Then, like the burst of an organ, all blazed their voices to the rafters as they leapt into the triumphantly hopeful chorus. Wailing minor chords were woven instinctively into the simple melody until a vibrant fulness blotted out the drab interior of the smelly place of toil.

As the last note slipped away and labor was resumed, Grundy beamed on Carrie.

"You sho can sing, sister!' he exclaimed. His gray-green eyes glowed. "Whyn't you jine de choir?"

Carrie's smile froze abruptly. "Much oblige' fo' shuckin' mah oysters, *Deacon* Grundy!" She snatched the jar and turned to go.

"Hold on!" There was majesty in the boom of his voice. Carrie stopped.

"Wal?" she demanded, impatient at her weakness.

His eyes were wholly green now, and she could not drop hers. His face was expressionless, and so low was his tone it was audible only to Carrie.

"Ah didn't go to say nuffin' to rile you. So you didn't have to be so snappish-like . . . like some spiled young un!"

Carrie whirled away with a toss of her head. His gaze followed her weaving body until she passed through the door. And his hands moved more slowly now.

WILLIAM ATTAWAY (1912-   )

Born in Mississippi, William Attaway was educated in Chicago and at the University of Illinois. He has worked as a seaman, salesman, labor organizer, and has acted in the road company of *You Can't Take It With You*. His *Let Me Breathe Thunder* (1939) was an unusual novel in that it dealt largely with white characters. From his second novel, *Blood on the Forge*, the selection below is taken, by permission of the author and the publishers, Doubleday, Doran and Company.

[Steel Mill Rhythm]

SATURDAY MORNING Big Mat went to the mill a changed man. A-borning in him was a new confidence. He did not sink into himself when O'Casey singled him out as scapegoat for the mistakes of the crew. He looked the little pit boss in the eye. O'Casey knew men. He knew when to let up. The other men were quick to sense the change. They passed little looks among themselves when O'Casey passed by Big Mat. They began to lag in their work. The pit boss had to do something to save face. Luckily, one of the pouring crew failed to show up. And when the call came for a replacement O'Casey recommended Big Mat.

Bo had said that they put the green men on hot jobs before they knew enough to stay alive. That was true. Black George, one of the men from the red hills, had been slow learning. They had put what was left of him in the ground. But Big Mat proved to be a natural hot-job man. After the first turn he did not have as many burns to grease as had the regulars.

The steel pourers' shelf was just a narrow platform high up against a wall. Around it was a rickety iron railing. Big Mat was told about that railing. One of the pourers said, "It was jest put up lately. 'Fore that a guy who faints rolls right into heaven."

They did faint on the shelf—especially on hot spring days like this one. But Big Mat welcomed the heat. Through the long, hot hours he would do twice as much work as anybody else. In competition with white men, he would prove himself.

The Bessemers were directly across from the shelf. Through the blinding heat Big Mat saw them in a haze—the blower on the pulpit, watching the tall air-stretched flames, the flaming air pulsing through the white metal, shimmying thirty feet above the live steel, blowing at the sun through holes in the roof. Once Big Mat had thought the holes were there so the flames could light the sky at night. Once the drone of the Bessemers had frightened him. Now his ears did not hear the drone. The steel began to blow noiselessly after he had been a short turn on the shelf.

The blower was an old Irishman. He knew by the color of the flame when it was time to tip a Bessemer. Now he waved his gloved hand at the shelf. Someone let out a warning "Hallo-o-o-o-o-o!" Big Mat followed the example of the men around him and yanked down his dark glasses. The Bessemer sighed, and the place was full of sparks. The furnace was tilted. And almost before the full ladle could move on its overhead tracks to the pourers' shelf another great Bessemer went into its noiseless song.

Hollow molds were moving beneath the shelf. The pourer signaled when the first was in position. He pulled the lever on the full ladle, releasing the white fire. Through his glasses Big Mat could see the red winking eye growing in the bottom of the mold. The stream that fed that eye threw off curtains of sparks, pinpricking his hands and face. He got his signal and threw strips of manganese into the glowing mold. He was continually dodging, but still the sparks fried in the sweat of his chest where the leather apron sagged. The red stream stopped suddenly. Another mold slid underneath the ladle.

Without slowing between molds, they took tests of the steel. The sweat ran into Big Mat's wide-mouthed gloves and made small explosions when it fell on the hot test steel. Big Mat did not flinch. Alone he held the spoon steady. It took two hunkies to hold up a spoon. He smiled behind his expressionless face. His muscles were glad to feel the growing weight of the steel. The work was nothing. Without labor his body would shrivel and be a weed. His body was happy. This was a good place for a big black man to be.

Melody and Chinatown were helping on the floor underneath the Bessemers. Naked to the waist, they worked hard, cleaning a big ladle for relining. The air was stifling. When Melody raised his lips upward to search the thin air he could see Big Mat high above. Pushing up his glasses, he wiped the sweat out of his eyes. He could see the liquid steel hitting the sides of the test spoon, scattering in clouds of white stars over Mat's gloved hands. Even to his hazed eyes, Mat's muscles sang. His own muscles did not sing. They grew weak and cried for long, slow movement. He could not stop them from twitching. It was not the heat and work alone—the rhythms of the machinery played through his body—the stripper, knocking the hardened steel loose from the molds. He couldn't hear it. It would have been a relief to hear it. He felt it inside himself—the heavy rhythm of the piston that used only a stroke to a mold. That rhythm in his body was like pounding out those ingots with a blow of his fist. And he was tired. Twenty-four hours had to pass before he could stagger away to the bunkhouse. Only a thought kept him on the job; next week end he would pleasure himself in Mex Town while some other bastard was baking on the long shift.

Chinatown was inside the big ladle. He could see the sun lancing through cracks in the ceiling high above. The heat of the sun sitting on the roof was nothing to the temperature inside the ladle. But it was just that little added heat that was too much for him to stand. His clothes were wet to his body. Where he squatted there was a wet spot. He was being smothered in a blanket of heat that pressed in from all sides. His lungs ached for moisture. He would have killed somebody for a drink of water. Yet there was water not far away. He had been told not to drink his fill. They had told him to put a tablet of salt on his tongue. The salt was crusted in his throat. He climbed out of the ladle. O'Casey saw him start for the hydrant.

"Just rinse your mouth and spit," warned O'Casey.

Chinatown fastened his lips to the spigot and turned the water on full force. His lips still clung when the foreman pulled him away. They had to take him out in the yard to untie the knot in his stomach. Then he was sick. Never before had he been so sick. Inside himself he prayed to die if he ever felt like that again.

Between spells Melody and a gray old Slav came out into the yard to watch over Chinatown. The old man's name was Zanski. He looked over the dozing Chinatown to Melody's drooping shoulders.

"You ain't feel so good either?"

"Head turnin'," said Melody.

"Maybe you hold your head far down to the ground . . ."

Melody tried it.

"Do kinda help some."

"Make heat drip out through head."

"Oblidged."

"All feller work in heat know that."

They didn't say any more until it was almost time to get back to the floor.

"Sooner be shot in Kentucky than do another turn," groaned Melody.

The old man smiled.

"Don't nothin' git you guys?" asked Melody. "You jest work and work till it git discouragin' to watch."

Zanski pushed his beard away from his lips and gestured at the two men.

"Colored feller alike. Work in mill but ain't feel happy."

Chinatown raised himself on one elbow. He looked at Zanski and scowled.

"Heat liable to git anybody," he broke in defensively.

"Not heat."

"Well, what then?"

"You fellers don't move out of bunkhouse. You got no kids."

"Jest don't want none," said Melody.

"Yo got no woman. Feller ain't be happy like that."

A thought of Anna flashed into Melody's head. He said nothing.

Chinatown said, "That's where you wrong. You ought to see them boys headed for the cat house of a Saturday."

"That ain't woman."

"You got to git in line for them whores."

"That ain't woman."

"Line reach clear round the mill, I betcha."

"That ain't woman who keep white curtains in a feller's house. Whore girl ain't wash curtains."

Chinatown was puzzled. He did not know what Zanski was talking about. To cover up he said, "Yeah, and they'll roll you if you ain't slick." He settled back to doze again.

The old man went on, "Feller from Ukraine workin'. His woman wash the curtains, and the kids growin' in the yard."

"Hundred o' them," said Melody, because that was the way it looked on washdays.

"Them kids work in the mill sometime. Their kids grow in the yard."

"That makes you feel happy?" mused Melody.

"I think about that when the heat comes," explained Zanski.

"That wouldn't help me none," said Melody.

The old man was silent for a time. Then he spoke as though he knew more than was in a barrelful of books.

"Feller from long way off die like plant put on rock. Plant grow if it get ground like place it come from."

Melody felt the words. But talk faded into nothing in the face of the heat. Under the Bessemers he sweated and gulped the thin air. In his body played the noiseless rhythms of the mill. Before morning he was so worked up that his voice was high and thin, like a knife running over an E string in his throat.

III
POETRY

POETRY

IT IS surprising that while slave ships were still transporting "black ivory" to the American shores, two eighteenth-century Negroes should be publishing poetical works. The first of these was Jupiter Hammon, a slave in Queens Village, Long Island, whose owners were sympathetic to his writing. In 1760 Hammon published "An Evening Thought: Salvation By Christ, with Penitential Cries . . .," in all probability the first poem published by an American Negro. It is something of a shout-hymn, obviously influenced by the Methodist-Dissenter hymnody of the Great Awakening.

> Salvation comes now from the Lord,
> Our victorious King.
> His holy name be well ador'd,
> Salvation surely bring.
> Dear Jesus give thy spirit now,
> Thy grace to every Nation,
> That hasn't the Lord to whom we bow,
> The author of Salvation.
> Dear Jesus, unto Thee we cry,
> Give up the preparation;
> Turn not away thy tender eye;
> We seek thy true Salvation.

In 1778, Hammon published an "Address to Miss Phillis Wheatley"; in 1779 "An Essay on the Ten Virgins"; in 1782 "A Winter Piece," a prose sermon containing at its end "A Poem for Children with thoughts on Death." One of his undated works entitled "An Evening's Improvement" is a poetical dialogue between "The Kind Master and the Dutiful Servant." Hammon's fairly long prose "Address to the Negroes in the State of New York" shows his "dutifulness" even more. As a "literary" slave, Hammon was a curiosity to his age, and he remains a curiosity. His religious doggerel and pious platitudes have no significance other than historical.

The second of these poets, Phillis Wheatley (c. 1753-1784), like Hammon, was influenced by the religious forces of the Wesley-Whitefield revival. Unlike Hammon, however, she was a writer of unusual talent. Though born in Africa, she acquired in an incredibly short time both the literary culture and the religion of her New England masters. Her writings reflect little of her race and much of her age. A typical New Englander of the third quarter of the eighteenth century, she recorded as deftly as any of her literary contemporaries the pious thoughts and poetic conventions of the Boston late Puritans with whom she lived.

Jupiter Hammon died in 1800. It was not until 1829 that a third Negro poet, George Moses Horton, brought out his first volume of poems, though several of them had appeared in print earlier. Even in his first publication, *The Hope of Liberty* (1829), Horton voiced complaint—conventional, to be sure—about his bondage. In the second volume, *Naked Genius* (1865), he expresses his antislavery convictions more clearly. Unlike most of the early poets, Horton possessed a vein of humor, and he becomes effectively satiric on occasions. By nature he was probably better fitted to play the "campus" poet than to write antislavery poetry. He does, however, deserve credit as the first slave poet openly to protest his status, and what personality emerges from his volumes is interesting.

Antislavery propaganda was at its height from 1840 to the Civil War. Like Bryant, Longfellow, and Whittier, Negroes turned to poetry to express their antislavery sentiments. Chief among these were Daniel Payne, Charles L. Reason, George B. Vashon, Elymas Payson Rogers, Frances E. W. Harper, James Madison Bell, and James M. Whitfield. Rogers was a Presbyterian minister who pastored in Newark for a number of years and finally died in Africa, where he had gone in the interest of colonization. His one significant poem, "The Repeal of the Missouri Compromise Considered" (1854), is a twenty-four page political satire, written in conventional verse. Bell's theme is the glory of liberty. His best known work, "The Day and the War," is a long, conventional, uninspired poetical account of the Civil War.

This group of poets suffered from too great decorousness. Their failures as poets may be partly attributed to the strain that color put upon the educated poets of the day. They had to be living proofs that the race was capable of culture. They had to refute the accusation of intrinsic difference. It was therefore only natural that they should imitate too closely the approved American and English writers. Yet, though they have been called the mockingbird school of poets, there was more under the conventional shell of their poetry than mere imitative rhetoric. In their protest against slavery, Harper, Vashon, and Whitfield wrote with genuine passion. These writers were no longer curiosities like Horton and Hammon. They were well trained; two of them (Reason and Vashon) were professors at Central College, an Abolition institution in New York, and Daniel Payne was a scholar. However staid and uninspired their poetry may be, judged by present standards, they have a measure of control over the medium in which they are working. With scorn and denunciation of all halfway measures, they demanded from America full democracy. For them poetry had one main purpose: to serve as an instrument to hasten the unshackling of their enslaved brethren. But they struggled to make their use of that instrument skillful.

Before the Civil War, the poetry of American Negroes conformed to the prevailing modes of poetry. Negro life and character were naturally not the concerns of the poets; when they did write of the Negro they used the abstractions: freedom and slavery, liberty and bondage, virtue and villainy. The few Negro characters shown were almost always pathetic victims rather than dimensional people. Technically, however, these poets showed ability that is striking when one considers the educational difficulties they encountered.

It was only after the Civil War that American poets began to deal with Negro experience in any other ways than as material for proslavery or antislavery argumentation. During the Reconstruction period there arose a strong school of Southern white "local color" writers, sectional apologists who seized upon the Negro question and the Negro character as their major theme for purposes of propagandizing America. Irwin Russell, Sidney Lanier, Thomas Nelson Page, A. C. Gordon, and others wrote nostalgic poems of the Old South peopled with indelible stereotypes of the plantation Negro, docile, contented, and comic.

The Negro writer in the closing years of the century, then, was confronted with a nice problem. Yeats has explained how Irish writers, smarting at the "stage Irishman" which the English, or an English-inspired taste, had foisted upon them, followed two ways: one of denying the stereotype by setting up his opposite as the true Irishman; the other of deepening the characterization by careful, sympathetic realism. Both courses have been taken by Negro writers when confronted with stereotypes strikingly similar to the "stage Irish." Albery Whitman, a self-educated minister with a passion for poetry, took the way of swinging the pendulum to the opposite extreme. Against the dialect lyrics about naïve, cute-talking folks (they were *not* the folk), he set up long narratives of idealized heroes and heroines. *Not A Man and Yet A Man* (1877), the longest poem ever published by a Negro, tells of a heroic mulatto slave; *Rape of Florida, or Twasinta's Seminoles* (1884) tells of that tragic chapter in American history, the removal of the Seminoles and their Negro comrades, kinsmen, and wives from Florida to the West; *The Octoroon* (1901) repeats the sad story of the love of a beautiful octoroon and her noble master. Whitman's intentions were epic; he took poetry seriously as an art. But his poems send back echoes of poets as various as Goldsmith, Longfellow, Whittier, Scott, and Byron. Whitman's militancy is pronounced, except for a late poem, "The Southland's Charms and Freedom's Magnitude," which is conciliatory.

A poet of much greater ability, Paul Laurence Dunbar, took the second way, displacing comic posters with sympathetic photography. But there was much to overcome in the habitual concepts of publishers and public and in the conciliatory spirit dictated by the vexatious times. Dunbar's first poems came out when he was very young; he did not live to be old. His temperament was that of a humorous observer, not of a reformer. In his poems of the Old South, he gave substantially the apologia of Irwin Russell and Page. In his poems of his own times he was better, but since the bucolic tradition of James Whitcomb Riley and Will Carleton was strong in America, Dunbar's dialect poetry is largely pastoral. Because he wrote of his own, however, for whom he had genuine affection, his portraiture is more dimensional than Irwin Russell's; and his poems of rural Negro life strike many readers as more memorable than those of Riley's gentle Hoosiers. Praised by William Dean Howells as the first American Negro "to feel the Negro life aesthetically and express it lyrically," Dunbar has long been the best-known American Negro poet. His best dialect poetry has kept a charming freshness over the years; his picture of rural Negro life, though it may seem idyllic, is peopled with likable human beings, not with clowns.

Dunbar wrote more poems in standard English than he did in dialect, and much has been made over his being forced by the American public to turn from his "deeper notes" to write "a jingle in a broken tongue." Dunbar's standard English poems, however, do not always strike "deeper notes"; many are conventional and sentimental. More often, however, he goes beneath the surface in poems that catch the bitterness of his tragically short life. Though Dunbar shied away from direct protest, coming nearest to it in such poems as "We Wear the Mask" and "The Haunted Oak," some of his sonnets, such as those to Frederick Douglass, Harriet Beecher Stowe, and Robert Gould Shaw show a really deep love and aspiration for his people.

Dunbar had many imitators in the dialect tradition. James Edwin Campbell, who wrote dialect about Gullah life; James David Corrothers; Daniel Webster Davis, long popular as a reader and lecturer in Virginia; J. Mord Allen, who approached Dunbar in his mastery of the dialect medium; John Wesley Holloway, whose "Calling the Doctor" is well known; and others down to J. Mason Brewer's *Negrito*

(1933) have carried on the tradition with varying degrees of popularity. These handled the church life, the courtships, the big dinners, the gossip, the hunting and fishing of rural Negroes. It is not truly folk stuff, because of its sentimentality and often forced comedy. It was a step away from minstrelsy, however, and was once very popular.

But the spirit of protest was very much alive, and even writers who, like Dunbar, worked principally in the plantation tradition could produce on occasion realistic evaluations of the Negro's status in post-Civil War America. The almost total disfranchisement of the black man and the increasing violence that the first decade of the twentieth century brought forth jolted many a Negro writer into denunciation of America's treatment.

The most bitter and at the same time the most influential of these writers was the young W. E. B. DuBois, then professor at Atlanta University. Though not primarily a poet, his *Darkwater* (1919) contains several pieces in verse form, the best of which is the passionate "A Litany at Atlanta" (see p. 321), occasioned by the Atlanta Riot of 1906. DuBois has other poems in a similar vein, and though his feeling often carries him into farfetched imagery, one senses in all of these pieces the burning hatred of racial injustice that has characterized all of his works. Other poets, before the New Negro movement, who applied their poetry to race defense or protest are the Cotters, father and son, Roscoe Jamison, Carrie W. Clifford, and Kelly Miller.

The first decades of the twentieth century produced yet another type of Negro poet—the type which, for want of a better name, may be called "literary." These poets had learned to respect poetry that was romantically detached from the hurly-burly of life, and they could hardly be expected to see how poetry could stoop to the ugly and grim realities of the race problem in America. With metrical and lyrical dexterity they showed the influence of various English masters from Elizabethans to Pre-Raphaelites; American poets, except for the belated American Tennysonians, were not influential. In *Along This Way,* James Weldon Johnson tells of Dunbar's discomfiture at reading *Leaves of Grass.* Rossetti, Swinburne, Ernest Dowson, Richard Le Gallienne, and Thomas Bailey Aldrich were more important poetic mentors than Walt Whitman, as they were to most American poets in the first years of the century. George McClellan, Leslie Pinckney Hill, Benjamin Brawley, all wrote correct poems that show their passion for books and the quiet groves of academe. William Stanley Braithwaite's polished lyrics are on the immemorial themes of love and death; his later work is decidedly mystical. Such writers as these found poetry an escape from the harshness of living in a world of prejudice, discrimination, and mob violence. Perhaps the best informed of any Negroes on poetry, and perhaps those who loved it best, they confined their writing to poetry of retreat, or rebuilding through dreams a world "nearer to the heart's desire."

James Weldon Johnson's services to Negro poets are much more valuable. In his earliest poems he refused to dodge the fact of race, preferring to capitalize upon it in poems that carry "messages" much better than the earlier race poetry, though they are rhetorical, judged by present standards. Johnson's "Fifty Years" is better "race" poetry than earlier odes to Emancipation, Lincoln, or Ethiopia. Johnson's early "Jingles and Croons," influenced by Dunbar and musical comedy, fall under his own censure of dialect poetry as "limited to two stops—pathos and humor." He experimented with new ways to get the true Negro idiom and cadence, which he rightly felt was far from the stage corruption of dialect. As a critic he was congenial to efforts at recording true folk speech. His own poetry is transitional: from rhetorical race defense, romantic lyricism, and conventional dialect it has gone to the dramatic portraiture of *God's Trombones,* in the idiom of the people. To contrast the techniques of "Brothers" (see p. 326) and of "St. Peter Relates an Incident" (see pp. 333) will indicate the growth in subtlety and depth in the protest poetry of the New Negro.

During the first World War and in the postwar years, many social forces altered the general contours of Negro life in America. There were extensive migrations from the South to such cities as New York, Pittsburgh, Detroit, Chicago, St. Louis, and Kansas City. There arose a new consciousness of the rights and power of labor; a growing aware-ness of the importance of organization, generally on the basis of race (though a few advanced thinkers saw the Negro problem as essentially a working-class problem); a greater racial self-respect, fostered by both Garveyite oratory and sober scholarship; and increased militancy, springing from several factors such as participation in the war and in key industries, the change from the confining pressures of the South to the comparative freedom of the North, and the growth of postwar liberalism, which was more than humanitarian in its support of the Negro's cause.

Negro expression reflected all of this, and poetry by Negroes was a fairly sensitive barometer of the changes. Delicate lyricism was still present in the works of such poets as Georgia Douglass Johnson and Angelina Grimké, but in general a more vigorous, socially aware poetry was produced. Though Fenton Johnson wrote in the old vein of race defense and praise, his more important work, after the models of Sand-burg and Masters, was in "African Nights," a series of portraits of characters caught in the meshes of poverty, ignorance, and prejudice. In grim understanding these exceed any earlier poetry, and they anticipate the social realism of Langston Hughes and Sterling Brown.

The New Poetry Movement, sponsored by critics like Amy Lowell, Harriet Monroe, and Louis Untermeyer, anthologized by Untermeyer and Braithwaite, and producing such important poets as Edwin Arlington Robinson, Robert Frost, Vachel Lindsay, Edgar Lee Masters, and Carl Sandburg, had a nationwide influence. The movement repudiated sentimentality, didacticism, optimism, romantic escape, and "poetic" diction. The lessons it taught were beneficial to Negro poets.

Claude McKay's *Harlem Shadows* (1922) was the first volume by a Negro in the new tradition. Trenchant poems of social and economic injustice, brooding poems like the title poem and "Harlem Dancer," and lyrics of love and nostalgia, candid and impassioned, revealed an originality and power that made McKay a poetic force to be reckoned with. His well-known "If We Must Die" was something of a rallying cry in the perilous postwar days, when bloody riots were started to put Negroes back "in their place," and when Negroes were striking back. No poem of similar defiance had ever been written by a Negro, and it is still one of the most-quoted. Jean Toomer's few but startling poems in *Cane* (1924) were also presages and influences; his sketches and stories in the same volume, of lyrical beauty and deep understanding, were also influential upon poets who followed him.

Neither of these poets has written much poetry since, which is a decided loss. The poems in Alain Locke's *New Negro* (1925) revealed that since Johnson's *Book of American Negro Poetry* (1922) several promising young poets had arisen. Countee Cullen had made quite a name for himself by winning nationwide poetry contests in his high school and college days; in 1925, when the poet was only twenty-two years old, his first volume, *Color,* was received by the critics and the reading public with enthusiasm. *Color* bore witness to a fine free lyrical gift and to surprising technical mastery. By many it is still considered the author's best book, though he has published four others since (see p. 357). Cullen insists that he be not considered a "Negro" poet, wanting "no racial consideration to bolster up his reputation"; and of course he is not a Negro poet, but an American poet who happens to be a Negro. And yet James Weldon Johnson is right when he says that Cullen's finest poems are those "motivated by race." Cullen's wide public, nevertheless, can find many lyrics on the ageless and raceless themes of love and disappointed youth and death. In form he is a poetic conservative, respecting the tradition of "the measured line and the skillful rhyme"; he is far closer to Keats, Housman, and

Edna St. Vincent Millay than to the vanguard figures of twentieth-century American poetry.

Almost of the same age and appearing as a poet at almost the same time as Cullen, Langston Hughes is his opposite in many respects. He is unconventional in form, and less lyrically subjective. He is a constant experimenter, writing in the blues form, in regular stanzas, and in free verse. His subject matter is not the time-honored themes of love and death, but the gay abandon of cabarets, the weary blues of a wandering piano plunker, of a woman deserted by a no-good man, or the stoicism of a mother trying to keep up the spirits of her son. At times he writes, briefly, symbolically, of his people as a whole as in "The Negro Speaks of Rivers" and "Minstrel Man." Generally his poetry is simple and direct; he consciously tries to reach the hearts of the people whose lives he interprets. He has been an influential figure.

Both Cullen and Hughes, for all of their differences, expressed ideas that were cardinal in the New Negro movement. Africa was looked upon atavistically with a sort of literary Garveyism more romantic than convincing; race pride was sponsored by celebrating brown beauty and by recounting Negro history. Many poets—Jessie Fauset, Waring Cuney, Gwendolyn Bennett, Lewis Alexander, Frank Horne, Helene Johnson, and Lucy Ariel Williams among them—wrote effective single poems that showed the new poetic interests. None of these poets, however, has published a volume.

Arna Bontemps, a writer of skill whether in the field of the short story, novel, children's books, drama, or poetry, is one of the most finished poetic craftsmen. His poems are generally mystical, philosophical, with an elegiac quality. Anne Spencer is an individualist, following her own poetic road regardless of schools, writing poetry of refreshing candor and sincerity. A great lover of Browning, her poetry is closer to the metaphysical than that of any other American Negro poet. Volumes from Bontemps and Mrs. Spencer would be welcome.

That Harlem was the Mecca of the New Negro movement is only natural, just as New York is the publishing capital of the nation. Literary contests conducted by *Opportunity Magazine,* under the editorship of Charles S. Johnson, and by *The Crisis,* under the editorship of W. E. B. DuBois, attracted the aspiring writers. And yet, as Charles S. Johnson pointed out, the New Negro poets were by no means a Harlem school. Only McKay and Cullen were really Harlemites, and McKay was in Russia at the height of the movement.

All over the country, Negro poets were writing: Jonathan Brooks in Mississippi; George Leonard Allen in North Carolina; Anne Spencer in Virginia; Sterling Brown in Virginia, Missouri, and Tennessee;

Frank Marshall Davis in Atlanta and Chicago. Sterling Brown's *Southern Road* (1932) was a book consisting chiefly of portraiture of Southern characters and scenes. One of the aims of the poet was to record in the language and idiom of the people the comedy and tragedy of their lives. Brown's work belongs to the new regionalism in American literature; regionalism and social protest characterize his later poems, which have not yet been published in a volume.

Recent poets of promise are Frank Marshall Davis, Richard Wright, M. B. Tolson, and Robert Hayden. Davis has published two collections of powerful social criticism in *Black Man's Verse* (1935) and *I Am the American Negro* (1937). Similar social understanding and radical protest are in the poems of Tolson and Wright. Hayden's first book, *Heart Shape In the Dust* combines technical aptitude of high quality with social realism. Waring Cuney has turned from the charming lyrics he wrote during the New Negro movement to poems that document proletarian tragedies and protest, some of which have been sung by Joshua White in an album of records called "Southern Exposure." David Wadsworth Cannon, Jr., who before his early death had written *Black Labor Chant* (1939), Margaret Walker, and Owen Dodson are the most recent newcomers to the ranks of poets who are socially aware.

Far more books of poetry have been published by Negroes than of any other type of literature. Writing poetry is still popular among Negroes, but it is largely occasional verse, derivative, and escapist. Part of a large company of readers who believe that poetry should be divorced from reality, many Negroes resent what they consider the Negro poet's preoccupation with Negro subject matter. But poetry is not solely lyrical subjectivity; it can also give a poet's view of his world in dramatic, narrative, and philosophical poetry. Negro poets have concentrated upon protest poetry more than upon poetry of interpretation and illumination, but Negro poets have often had more to protest than others. The Negro poet seems to be learning that propaganda cannot make poetry, any more than it must necessarily mar poetry. In view of the present status of Negro life in America, however, it is likely that Negro poets will for a long time write of what they know best, and that is, what it means to be a Negro in America. Some are sure to follow the lyrical tradition of expressing their personal emotions; others, more objective, will render characters and situations. Whichever they do, if they learn craftsmanship from the best poetry of the past and present without slavish imitation, if they write with sincerity and understanding and passion, American poetry will be the better for them.

PHILLIS WHEATLEY (c. 1753-1784)

Kidnapped in her native Senegal when she was about seven, Phillis was brought to Boston in 1761 and sold to John Wheatley, a tailor of that city, who bought the girl to be a special servant for his wife. Mrs. Wheatley and her daughter, Mary, soon noted the quickness of the young African girl, and encouraged her efforts to acquire learning. Within sixteen months Phillis was reading the Bible with ease. She also soon acquired a knowledge of the elementary sciences and of English and Latin literature. Becoming especially fond of the poetry of Pope, she learned to imitate that author with such proficiency that she became "a kind of poet laureate in the domestic circles of Boston." Her first publication, "A Poem, by Phillis, A Negro Girl in Boston, on the death of the Reverend George Whitefield," appeared in 1770. It was addressed to the Countess of Huntingdon, Whitefield's patroness.

In 1771, Phillis was allowed to become a communicant of the Old South Meeting House in Boston, a unique privilege for a slave. When her health began to show signs of decline, she was advised by her doctors to take a sea voyage. The kindly mistress, however, manumitted the slave before she sailed for England. Her poem on Whitefield opened to her the doors of the influential Countess of Huntingdon. The Countess was to present her at the court of George III, but, her mistress falling ill in Boston, Phillis hurried back to be with her. Before she left London, however, she arranged for the publication of her only volume of collected verses, *Poems on Various Subjects, Religious and Moral* (1773).

The end of Phillis Wheatley's life was not without bitterness; her patrons died, her marriage turned out unhappily; and her three children did not survive infancy. She ended her days as a servant in a cheap lodging house.

Most of Phillis Wheatley's poetry is occasional. Nearly half of her poems are elegies. Six treat public events of importance, the best-known being that on the appointment of George Washington as Commander-in-Chief of the Continental Army, for which Washington sent her a letter of thanks and received her at his headquarters. There are also paraphrases from the Bible and translations from the classics. Very seldom are there any references to her own experience. "To the University of Cambridge, in New England" contains the lines:

> 'Twas not long since I left my native shore,
> The land of errors and Egyptian gloom:
> Father of mercy! 'twas thy gracious hand
> Brought me in safety from those dark abodes.

In only one poem, that addressed to the Earl of Dartmouth (see below) does she express any resentment, and then fairly detached, against slavery. This was of course in line with her neoclassic models. Just as Phillis Wheatley shared their preference for the elegant and ornate, so she shared their dislike for self-revelation. Phillis Wheatley seemed to shrink from this even more shyly, however, than even Pope her master, and certainly more than such American contemporaries as Freneau and John Trumbull. Her life was interesting, full of contrasts, triumph, and sorrow, but she did not seem to think it worthy of poetic treatment.

To the Right Honorable William, Earl of Dartmouth, His Majesty's Principal Secretary of State for North America, Etc.

Hail, happy day, when, smiling like the morn,
Fair *Freedom* rose New-England to adorn:
The northern clime beneath her genial ray,
Dartmouth, congratulates thy blissful sway:
Elate with hope her race no longer mourns,
Each soul expands, each grateful bosom burns,
While in thine hand with pleasure we behold
The silken reins, and *Freedom's* charms unfold.
Long lost to realms beneath the northern skies
She shines supreme, while hated *faction* dies:
Soon as appear'd the *Goddess* long desir'd,
Sick at the view, she languish'd and expir'd;
Thus from the splendors of the morning light
The owl in sadness seeks the caves of night.
    No more *America* in mournful strain
Of wrongs, and grievance unredress'd complain,
No longer shalt thou dread the iron chain,
Which wanton *Tyranny* with lawless hand
Had made, and which it meant t' enslave the land.
    Should you, my lord, while you pursue my song,
Wonder from whence my love of *Freedom* sprung,
Whence flow these wishes for the common good,
By feeling hearts alone best understood,
I, young in life, by seeming cruel fate
Was snatch'd from *Afric's* fancy'd happy seat:
What pangs excruciating must molest,
What sorrows labour in my parent's breast?
Steel'd was the soul and by no misery mov'd
That from a father seiz'd his babe belov'd
Such, such my case. And can I then but pray
Others may never feel tyrannic sway?
    For favours past, great Sir, our thanks are due,
And thee we ask thy favours to renew,

Since in thy pow'r, as in thy will before,
To sooth the griefs,. which thou did'st once deplore.
May heav'nly grace the sacred sanction give
To all thy works, and thou for ever live
Not only on the wings of fleeting *Fame,*
Though praise immortal crowns the patriot's name,
But to conduct to heav'n's refulgent fane,
May fiery coursers sweep th' ethereal plain,
And bear thee upwards to that blest abode,
Where, like the prophet, thou shalt find thy God.

His Excellency General Washington

Celestial choir! enthron'd in realms of light,
Columbia's scenes of glorious toils I write.
While freedom's cause her anxious breast alarms,
She flashes dreadful in refulgent arms.
See mother earth her offspring's fate bemoan,
And nation's gaze at scenes before unknown!
See the bright beams of heaven's revolving light
Involved in sorrows and the veil of night!
The goddess comes, she moves divinely fair,
Olive and laurel binds her golden hair:
Wherever shines this native of the skies,
Unnumber'd charms and recent graces rise.
Muse! how propitious while my pen relates
How pour her armies through a thousand gates;
As when Eolus heaven's fair face deforms,
Enwrapp'd in tempest and a night of storms;
Astonish'd ocean feels the wild uproar,
The refulgent surges beat the sounding shore,
Or thick as leaves in Autumn's golden reign,
Such, and so many, moves the warrior's train.
In bright array they seek the work of war,
Where high unfurl'd the ensign waves in air.
Shall I to Washington their praise recite?
Enough thou know'st them in the fields of fight.
Thee, first in peace and honours,—we demand
The grace and glory of thy martial band.
Fam'd for thy valour, for thy virtues more,
Hear every tongue thy guardian and implore!

One century scarce perform'd its destined round,
When Gallic powers Columbia's fury found;
And so may you, whoever dares disgrace
The land of freedom's heaven defended race!

Fir'd are the eyes of nations on the scales,
For in their hopes Columbia's arm prevails.
Anon Britannia droops the pensive head,
While round increase the rising hills of dead.
Ah! cruel blindness to Columbia's state!
Lament thy thirst of boundless power too late.
    Proceed, great chief, with virtue on thy side,
Thy ev'ry action let the goddess guide.
A crown, a mansion, and a throne that shine,
With gold unfading, *Washington!* be thine.

Liberty and Peace
(1784)

Lo! freedom comes. Th' prescient muse foretold,
All eyes th' accomplish'd prophecy behold:
Her port describ'd, "She moves divinely fair,
Olive and laurel bind her golden hair."
She, the bright progeny of Heaven, descends,
And every grace her sovereign step attends;
For now kind Heaven, indulgent to our prayer,
In smiling peace resolves the din of war.
Fix'd in Columbia her illustrious line,
And bids in thee her future council shine.
To every realm her portals open'd wide,
Receives from each the full commercial tide.
Each art and science now with rising charms,
Th' expanding heart with emulation warns.
E'en great Britannia sees with dread surprise,
And from the dazzling splendors turns her eyes.
Britain, whose navies swept th' Atlantic o'er,
And thunder sent to every distant shore;
E'en thou, in manners cruel as thou art,
The sword resign'd, resume the friendly part.
For Gallia's power espous'd Columbia's cause,
And new-born Rome shall give Britannia laws,
Nor unremember'd in the grateful strain,
Shall princely Louis' friendly deed remain;
The generous prince th' impending vengeance eyes,
Sees the fierce wrong and to the rescue flies.
Perish that thirst of boundless power, that drew
On Albion's head the curse to tyrants due.
But thou appeas'd submit to heaven's decree,
That bids this realm of freedom rival thee.
Now sheath the sword that bade the brave atone '

With guiltless blood for madness not their own.
Sent from th' enjoyment of their native shore,
Ill-fated—never to behold her more.
From every kingdom on Europe's coast
Throng'd various troops, their glory, strength, and
    boast.
With heart-felt pity fair Hibernia saw
Columbia menac'd by the Tyrant's law:
On hostile fields fraternal arms engage,
And mutual deaths, all dealt with mutual rage:
The muse's ear hears mother earth deplore
Her ample surface smoke with kindred gore:
The hostile field destroys the social ties,
And everlasting slumber seals their eyes.
Columbia mourns, the haughty foes deride,
Her treasures plunder'd and her towns destroy'd:
Witness how Charlestown's curling smokes arise,
In sable columns to the clouded skies.
The ample dome, high-wrought with curious toil,
In one sad hour the savage troops despoil.
Descending peace the power of war confounds;
From every tongue celestial peace resounds:
As from the east th' illustrious king of day,
With rising radiance drives the shades away,
So freedom comes array'd with charms divine,
And in her train commerce and plenty shine.
Britannia owns her independent reign,
Hibernia, Scotia, and the realms of Spain;
And great Germania's ample coast admires
The generous spirit that Columbia fires.
Auspicious Heaven shall fill with fav'ring gales,
Where'er Columbia spreads her swelling sails:
To every realm shall peace her charms display,
And heavenly freedom spread her golden ray.

GEORGE MOSES HORTON (1797-c. 1883)

Born in Northampton County, North Carolina, the slave of the
Horton family, George Moses was passed from member to member of
that family until he obtained his freedom in 1865. His master allowed
him to hire himself out at Chapel Hill, and it was while working
there in the home of the president of the university that he learned
to read and write. Horton was for many years a campus "character"
at Chapel Hill. He wrote love poems for the students at twenty-five
or fifty cents a-piece, according to the degree of ardor desired. Fugi-

tive poems of Horton's crept into print. It is somewhat interesting
to find two of Byron's lines as the last in Horton's "To Eliza" (see
below). In 1829, his first volume, *The Hope of Liberty,* was published in Raleigh. The poet hoped to gain enough from the sale of
this work to buy his liberty, but he was disappointed. The same
work was reissued in Philadelphia in 1837 as *Poems by a Slave.*
When the Northern troops occupied Raleigh in 1865, Horton escaped
to their lines and became a free man, and in the same year his
second work, *Naked Genius,* appeared. Not much is known concerning Horton's life after this period. He presumably lived in
Philadelphia until his death, which occurred probably in 1883.

George Moses Horton, Myself

I feel myself in need
    Of the inspiring strains of ancient lore,
My heart to lift, my empty mind to feed,
    And all the world explore.

I know that I am old
    And never can recover what is past,
But for the future may some light unfold
    And soar from ages blast.

I feel resolved to try,
    My wish to prove, my calling to pursue,
Or mount up from the earth into the sky,
    To show what Heaven can do.

My genius from a boy,
    Has fluttered like a bird within my heart;
But could not thus confined her powers employ,
    Impatient to depart.

She like a restless bird,
    Would spread her wings, her power to be
        unfurl'd,
And let her songs be loudly heard,
    And dart from world to world.

On Liberty and Slavery

Alas! and am I born for this,
    To wear this slavish chain?
Deprived of all created bliss,
    Through hardship, toil and pain!

How long have I in bondage lain,
   And languished to be free!
Alas! and must I still complain—
   Deprived of liberty.

Oh, Heaven! and is there no relief
   This side the silent grave—
To soothe the pain—to quell the grief
   And anguish of a slave?

Come Liberty, thou cheerful sound,
   Roll through my ravished ears!
Come, let my grief in joys be drowned,
   And drive away my fears.

Say unto foul oppression, Cease:
   Ye tyrants rage no more,
And let the joyful trump of peace,
   Now bid the vassal soar.

Soar on the pinions of that dove
   Which long has cooed for thee,
And breathed her notes from Afric's grove,
   The sound of Liberty.

Oh, Liberty! thou golden prize,
   So often sought by blood—
We crave thy sacred sun to rise,
   The gift of nature's God!

Bid Slavery hide her haggard face,
   And barbarism fly:
I scorn to see the sad disgrace
   In which enslaved I lie.

Dear Liberty! upon thy breast,
   I languish to respire;
And like the Swan unto her nest,
   I'd to thy smiles retire.

Oh, blest asylum—heavenly balm!
   Unto thy boughs I flee—
And in thy shades the storm shall calm,
   With songs of Liberty!

To Eliza

Eliza, tell thy lover why
Or what induced thee to deceive me?
Fare thee well—away I fly—
I shun the lass who thus will grieve me.

Eliza, still thou art my song,
Although by force I may foresake thee;
Fare thee well, for I was wrong
To woo thee while another take thee.

Eliza, pause and think awhile—
Sweet lass! I shall forget thee never:
Fare thee well! although I smile,
I grieve to give thee up for ever.

Eliza, I shall think of thee—
My heart shall ever twine about thee;
Fare thee well—but think of me,
Compell'd to live and die without thee.
"Fare thee well!—and if for ever,
Still for ever fare thee well!"

JAMES M. WHITFIELD (1830-1870)

Born in Boston, James M. Whitfield moved to Buffalo, New York,
when he was a young man and probably spent most of his life in
the latter city. He was a barber by trade, but, according to Loggins,
probably gave up this work after his *America, and Other Poems*
appeared in 1853. Because of the favorable reception to this work,
Whitfield was enabled to leave the shop for the public platform.
Associated with Martin R. Delany, Whitfield became an ardent
advocate of emigration as the solution to America's race problem.
He attended the National Emigration Convention of Colored Men
called by Delany in 1854. Attacked by Douglass because of this
affiliation, Whitfield vigorously defended the convention's program
against Douglass' charges. It seeems that Whitfield's mission was to
promote emigration to Central America. The scheme was never
carried out, however, and Whitfield dropped from public notice.

America

America, it is to thee,
Thou boasted land of liberty,—
It is to thee I raise my song,
Thou land of blood, and crime, and wrong.

It is to thee my native land,
From which has issued many a band
To tear the black man from his soil,
And force him here to delve and toil;
Chained on your blood-bemoistened sod,
Cringing beneath a tyrant's rod,
Stripped of those rights which Nature's God
   Bequeathed to all the human race,
Bound to a petty tyrant's nod,
   Because he wears a paler face.
Was it for this that freedom's fires
Were kindled by your patriot sires?
Was it for this they shed their blood,
On hill and plain, on field and flood?
Was it for this that wealth and life
Were staked upon that desperate strife,
Which drenched this land for seven long years
With blood of men, and women's tears?
When black and white fought side by side,
   Upon the well-contested field,—
Turned back the fierce opposing tide,
   And made the proud invader yield—
When, wounded, side by side they lay,
   And heard with joy the proud hurrah
From their victorious comrades say
   That they had waged successful war,
The thought ne'er entered in their brains
That they endured those toils and pains,
To forge fresh fetters, heavier chains
For their own children, in whose veins
Should flow that patriotic blood,
So freely shed on field and flood.
Oh, no; they fought, as they believed,
   For the inherent rights of man;
But mark, how they have been deceived
   By slavery's accursed plan.
They never thought, when thus they shed
   Their heart's best blood, in freedom's cause,
That their own sons would live in dread,
   Under unjust, oppressive laws:
That those who quietly enjoyed
   The rights for which they fought and fell,
Could be the framers of a code,
   That would disgrace the fiends of hell!
Could they have looked, with prophet's ken,
   Down to the present evil time,

Seen free-born men, uncharged with crime,
Consigned unto a slaver's pen,—
Or thrust into a prison cell,
With thieves and murderers to dwell—
While that same flag whose stripes and stars
Had been their guide through freedom's wars
As proudly waved above the pen
Of dealers in the souls of men!
Or could the shades of all the dead,
    Who fell beneath that starry flag,
Visit the scenes where they once bled,
    On hill and plain, on vale and crag,
By peaceful brook, or ocean's strand,
    By inland lake, or dark green wood,
Where'er the soil of this wide land
    Was moistened by their patriot blood,—
And then survey the country o'er,
    From north to south, from east to west,
And hear the agonizing cry
Ascending up to God on high,
From western wilds to ocean's shore,
    The fervent prayer of the oppressed;

* * *

And manhood, too, with soul of fire,
And arm of strength, and smothered ire,
Stands pondering with brow of gloom,
Upon his dark unhappy doom,
Whether to plunge in battle's strike,
And buy his freedom with his life,
And with stout heart and weapon strong,
Pay back the tyrant wrong for wrong
Or wait the promised time of God,
    When his Almighty ire shall wake,
And smite the oppressor in his wrath,
And hurl red ruin in his path,
And with the terrors of his rod,
    Cause adamantine hearts to quake.
Here Christian writhes in bondage still,
    Beneath his brother Christian's rod,
And pastors trample down at will,
    The image of the living God.

* * *

Almighty God! thy aid impart,
And fire anew each faltering heart,

And strengthen every patriot's hand,
Who aims to save our native land.
We do not come before thy throne,
  With carnal weapons drenched in gore,
Although our blood has freely flown,
  In adding to the tyrant's store.
Father! before thy throne we come,
  Not in panoply of war,
With pealing trump, and rolling drum,
  And cannon booming loud and far;
Striving in blood to wash out blood,
  Through wrong to seek redress for wrong;
For while thou'rt holy, just and good,
  The battle is not to the strong;
But in the sacred name of peace,
  Of justice, virtue, love and truth,
We pray, and never mean to cease,
  Till weak old age and fiery youth
In freedom's cause their voices raise,
And burst the bonds of every slave;
Till, north and south, and east and west,
The wrongs we bear shall be redressed.

FRANCES E. W. HARPER (1825-1911)

Easily the most popular American Negro poet of her time, Frances
Ellen Walkins Harper was also a popular lecturer. Intimately connected with the Abolitionist movement, the Underground Railroad,
the Women's Christian Temperance Union, and the A. M. E. Church,
she led a busy and purposeful life. Her able public reading contributed
to the popularity of her poetry. Born in Baltimore, Mrs. Harper was
educated in that city and lived there until 1850. She moved to Ohio
and taught for a while at Union Seminary in Columbia. In 1853
she went to Little York, Pennsylvania, to work with the Underground
Railroad. Her work becoming known, Mrs. Harper was engaged as a
permanent lecturer by the Anti-Slavery Society of Maine on September 28, 1854. After the Civil War she worked as a representative
of the Women's Christian Temperance Union, traveling widely
throughout the South. She died February 22, 1911. Her first volume,
Poems on Various Subjects was published in 1854, but there were
several later editions. She also published *Moses: A Story of the Nile*
(1869), *Poems* (1871), and *Sketches of Southern Life* (1872). William
Still asserted that fifty thousand copies of Mrs. Harper's first two
volumes were sold.

Eliza Harris

Like a fawn from the arrow, startled and wild,
A woman swept by us, bearing a child;
In her eye was the night of a settled despair,
And her brow was o'ershaded with anguish and care.

She was nearing the river—in reaching the brink,
She heeded no danger, she paused not to think;
For she is a mother—her child is a slave—
And she'll give him his freedom, or find him a grave!

It was a vision to haunt us, that innocent face—
So pale in its aspect, so fair in its grace;
As the tramp of the horse and the bay of the hound,
With the fetters that gall, were trailing the ground!

She was nerv'd by despair, and strengthened by woe,
As she leap'd o'er the chasms that yawn'd from below;
Death howl'd in the tempest, and rav'd in the blast,
But she heard not the sound till the danger was past.

Oh! how shall I speak of my proud country's shame?
Of the stains on her glory, how give them their name?
How say that her banner in mockery waves—
Her "star spangled banner"—o'er millions of slaves?

How say that the lawless may torture and chase
A woman whose crime is the hue of her face?
How the depths of the forest may echo around,
With the shrieks of despair, and the bay of the hound?

With her step on the ice, and her arm on her child,
The danger was fearful, the pathway was wild;
But, aided by Heaven, she gained a free shore,
Where the friends of humanity open'd their door.

So fragile and lovely, so fearfully pale,
Like a lily that bends to the breath of the gale,
Save the heave of her breast, and the sway of her hair,
You'd have thought her a statue of fear and despair.

In agony close to her bosom she press'd
The life of her heart, the child of her breast:—
Oh! love from its tenderness gathering might,
Had strengthen'd her soul for the dangers of flight.

But she's free!—yes, free from the land where the slave
From the hand of oppression must rest in the grave;
Where bondage and torture, where scourges and chains
Have plac'd on our banner indelible stains.

The bloodhounds have miss'd the scent of her way;
The hunter is rifled and foil'd of his prey;
Fierce jargon and cursing, with clanking of chains,
Make sounds of strange discord on Liberty's plains.

With the rapture of love and fulness of bliss,
She placed on his brow a mother's fond kiss:—
O poverty, danger and death she can brave,
For the child of her love is no longer a slave!

The Slave Auction

The sale began—young girls were there,
  Defenceless in their wretchedness,
Whose stifled sobs of deep despair
  Revealed their anguish and distress.

And mothers stood with streaming eyes,
  And saw their dearest children sold;
Unheeded rose their bitter cries,
  While tyrants bartered them for gold.

And woman, with her love and truth—
  For these in sable forms may dwell—
Gaz'd on the husband of her youth,
  With anguish none may paint or tell.

And men, whose sole crime was their hue,
  The impress of their Maker's hand,
And frail and shrinking children, too,
  Were gathered in that mournful band.

Ye who have laid your love to rest,
  And wept above their lifeless clay,
Know not the anguish of that breast,
  Whose lov'd are rudely torn away.

Ye may not know how desolate
  Are bosoms rudely forced to part,
And how a dull and heavy weight
  Will press the life-drops from the heart.

Bury Me In a Free Land

Make me a grave where'er you will,
In a lowly plain, or a lofty hill;
Make it among earth's humblest graves,
But not in a land where men are slaves.

I could not rest if around my grave
I heard the steps of a trembling slave;
His shadow above my silent tomb
Would make it a place of fearful gloom.

I could not rest if I heard the tread
Of a coffle gang to the shambles led,
And the mother's shriek of wild despair
Rise like a curse on the trembling air.

I could not sleep if I saw the lash
Drinking her blood at each fearful gash,
And I saw her babes torn from her breast,
Like trembling doves from their parent nest.

I'd shudder and start if I heard the bay
Of bloodhounds seizing their human prey,
And I heard the captive plead in vain
As they bound afresh his galling chain.

If I saw young girls from their mothers' arms
Bartered and sold for their youthful charms,
My eye would flash with a mournful flame,
My death-paled cheek grow red with shame.

I would sleep, dear friends, where bloated might
Can rob no man of his dearest right;
My rest shall be calm in any grave
Where none can call his brother a slave.

I ask no monument, proud and high,
To arrest the gaze of the passers-by;
All that my yearning spirit craves,
Is bury me not in a land of slaves.

Let the Light Enter
(The dying words of Goethe)

"Light! more light! the shadows deepen,
And my life is ebbing low,
Throw the windows widely open:
Light! more light! before I go.

"Softly let the balmy sunshine
   Play around my dying bed,
E'er the dimly lighted valley
   I with lonely feet must tread.

"Light! more light! for Death is weaving
   Shadows 'round my waning sight,
And I fain would gaze upon him
   Through a stream of earthly light."

Not for greater gifts of genius;
   Not for thoughts more grandly bright,
All the dying poet whispers
   Is a prayer for light, more light.

Heeds he not the gathered laurels,
   Fading slowly from his sight;
All the poet's aspirations
   Centre in that prayer for light.

Gracious Saviour, when life's day-dreams
   Melt and vanish from the sight,
May our dim and longing vision
   Then be blessed with light, more light.

ALBERY A. WHITMAN (1851-1902)

Born in Kentucky in 1851, Albery A. Whitman was a slave until 1863. By the time he was twenty-five he had taught school and had become a fairly well-known A. M. E. minister. Most of his years were spent as an itinerant preacher in Ohio and Kansas. He was another of the many beneficiaries of Bishop Payne (see p. 732). His narrative, "Not a Man and Yet a Man," the longest poem written by a Negro, was published in 1877. His best-known work, *The Rape of Florida,* appeared in 1884, but was reprinted with slight alterations the following year as *Twasinta's Seminoles; or The Rape of Florida.* In 1890 both poems were again reprinted along with some short poems. In 1893 he composed and read "The Freedman's Triumphant Song" at the Chicago World's Fair. *The Octoroon, An Idyl of the South,* his last publication, came out in 1901.

From *Twasinta's Seminoles; or, Rape of Florida*
Canto I

I

The negro slave by Swanee river sang;
Well-pleased he listened to his echoes ringing;
For in his heart a secret comfort sprang,
When Nature seemed to join his mournful singing.
To mem'ry's cherished objects fondly clinging;
His bosom felt the sunset's patient glow,
And spirit whispers into weird life springing,
Allured to worlds he trusted yet to know,
And lightened for awhile life's burdens here below.

II

The drowsy dawn from many a low-built shed,
Beheld his kindred driven to their task;
Late evening saw them turn with weary tread
And painful faces back; and dost thou ask
How sang these bondmen? how their suff'rings mask?
Song is the soul of sympathy divine,
And hath an inner ray where hope may bask;
Song turns the poorest waters into wine,
Illumines exile hearts and makes their faces shine.

III

The negro slave by Swanee river sang,
There soon the human hunter rode along;
And eagerly behind him came a gang
Of hounds and men,—the bondmen hushed his song—
Around him came a silent, list'ning throng;
"Some runaway!" he muttered; said no more,
But sank from view the growing corn among;
And though deep pangs his wounded spirit bore,
He hushed his soul, and went on singing as before.

IV

So fared the land where slaves were groaning yet—
Where beauty's eyes must feed the lusts óf men!
'Tis as when horrid dreams we half forget,
Would then relate, and still relate again—
Ah! cold abhorrence hesitates my pen!

The heavens were sad, and hearts of men were faint;
Philanthropy implored and wept, but then
The wrong, unblushing trampled on Restraint,
While feeble Law sat by and uttered no complaint.

V

"Fly and be free!" a whisper comes from heaven,
"Thy cries are heard!" the bondman's up and gone!
To grasp the dearest boon to mortals given,
He frantic flies, unaided and alone.
To him the red man's dwellings are unknown;
But he can crave the freedom of his race,
Can find his harvests in the desert sown,
And in the cypress forest's dark embrace
A pathway to his lonely habitations trace.

VI

The sable slave, from Georgia's utmost bounds,
Escapes for life into the Great Wahoo.
Here he has left afar the savage hounds
And human hunters that did late pursue;
There in the hommock darkly hid from view,
His wretched limbs are stretched awhile to rest,
Till some kind Seminole shall guide him thro'
To where by hound nor hunter more distrest,
He in a flow'ry home, shall be the red man's guest.

VII

If tilled profusion does not crown the view,
Nor wide-ranged farms begirt with fences spread;
The cultivated plot is well to do;
And where no slave his groaning life has led,
The songs of plenty fill the lowliest shed.
Who could wish more, when Nature, always green,
Brings forth fruit-bearing woods and fields of bread?
Wish more, where cheerful valleys bloom between,
And herds browse on the hills, where winter ne'er has been? . . .

X

Fair Florida! whose scenes could so enhance—
Could in the sweetness of the earth excel!
Wast thou the Seminole's inheritance?
Yea, it was thee he loved, and loved so well!
'Twas 'neath thy palms and pines he strove to dwell.

Not savage, but resentful to the knife,
For these he sternly struggled—sternly fell!
Thoughtful and brave, in long uneven strife,
He held the verge of manhood mid the heights of life.

XI

A wild-born pride endeared him to thy soil!
When roamed his herds without a keeper's care—
Where man knew not the pangs of slavish toil!
And where thou didst not blooming pleasures spare,
But well allotted each an ample share,
He loved to dwell: Oh! isn't the goal of life·
Where man has plenty and to man is fair?
When free from avarice's pinch and strife,
Is earth not like the Eden-home of man and wife? . . .

XIX

Oh! sing it in the light of freedom's morn,
Tho' tyrant wars have made the earth a grave;
The good, the great, and true, are, if so, born,
And so with slaves, *chains do not make the slave!*
If high-souled birth be what the mother gave,—
If manly birth, and manly to the core,—
Whate'er the test, the man will he behave!
Crush him to earth and crush him o'er and o'er,
A man he'll rise at last and meet you as before.

XX

So with our young Atlassa,[1] hero-born,—
Free as the air within his palmy shade,
The nobler traits that do the man adorn,
In him were native: Not the music made
In Tampa's forests or the everglade
Was fitter than in this young Seminole
Was the proud spirit which did life pervade,
And glow and tremble in his ardent soul—
Which, lit his inmost-self, and spurned all mean control.

[1]"Atlassa," was Wild Cat, or Cooacoochee—an eminent Seminole chieftain. He went with his people to Fort Smith and the Indian Territory and thence to South Rosa, Mexico, where [he] died at a very advanced age, not long ago. I had the honor of meeting two of his nephews, very intelligent gentlemen, in 1884.—The Author.

XXI

Than him none followed chase with nimbler feet,
None readier in the forest council rose;
To speak for war, e'er sober and discreet,
In battle stern, but kind to fallen foes;
He led the *charge,* but halted,—slow to close
The vexed retreat: In front of battle he,
Handsome and wild his proud form would expose;
But in the cheering van of victory,
Gentle and brave he was the real chief to see.

XXII

Lo! mid a thousand warriors where he stands,
Pride of all hearts and idol of his race!
Look how the chieftains of his war-tried bands
Kindle their courage in his valiant face!
And as his lips in council open, trace
How deep suspense her earnest furrows makes
On ev'ry brow! How rings the forest-place
With sounding cheers! when native valor wakes
His dark intrepid eyes, and he their standard takes!

XXIII

Proud spirit of the hommock-bounded home
Well wast thy valor like a buckler worn!
And when the light of other times shall come,—
When history's muse shall venture to adorn
The brow of all her children hero-born,—
When the bold truth to man alike assigns
The place he merits, of no honor shorn;
The wreath shall be, that thy proud brow entwines,
As green as Mickasukie's everlasting pines!

XXIV

Well bled thy warriors at their leader's side!
Well stood they the oppressor's wasting fire;
For years sweep on, and in their noiseless tide,
Bear down the mem'ries of the past! The dire
And gloomful works of tyrants shall expire,
Till naught survives, save truth's great victories;
Then shall the voyager on his way aspire
To ponder what vast wrecks of time he sees,
And on Fame's temple columns read their memories!

xxv

Not so with Osceola, thy dark mate;
The hidden terror of the hommock, he
Sat gloomily and nursed a bitter hate,—
The white man was his common enemy—
He rubbed the burning wounds of injury,
And plotted in his dreadful silent gloom;
As dangerous as a rock within the sea.
And when in fray he showed his fearless plume,
Revenge made sweet the blows that dealt the white man's doom.

xxvi

The pent-up wrath that rankled in his breast,
O'er smould'ring embers shot a lurid glare,
And wrongs that time itself had not redrest,
In ghost-like silence stalked and glimmered there.
And from the wizard caverns of despair,
Came voice and groan, reminding o'er and o'er
The outrage on his wife so young and fair;
And so, by heaven and earth and hell he swore
To treat in council with the white man never more.

xxvii

Such were the chiefs who led their daring braves
In many a battle nobly lost or won,
And consecrated Mickasukie's graves
To that sweet province of the summer sun!
And still shall history forgetful run?
Shall legend too be mute? then Poesy,
Divinest chronicler of deeds well done,
From the blest shrine and annals of the free,
Sing forth thy praise and man shall hear attentively.

xxviii

The poorest negro coming to their shore,
To them was brother—their own flesh and blood,—
They sought his wretched manhood to restore,—
They found his hidings in the swampy wood,
And brought him forth—in arms before him stood,—
The citizens of God and sovran earth,—
They shot straight forward looks with flame imbued,
Till in him manhood sprang, a noble birth,
And warrior-armed he rose to all that manhood's worth.

XXIX

On the dark front of battle often seen,
Or holding dang'rous posts through dreadful hours,—
In ranks obedient, in command serene,
His comrades learn to note the tested powers
Which prove that valor is not always ours,
Be whomsoever we: A common race
Soon from this union flows—soon rarest flowers
Bloom out and smile in beauty's blending grace,
And rivals they become for love's sublimest place.

XXX

The native warrior leads his ebon maid,
The dark young brave his bloom-hued lover wins;
And where soft spruce and willows mingle shade,
Young life mid sunniest hours its course begins:
All Nature pours its never-ending dins
In groves of rare-hued leaf without'n end,—
'Tis as if Time, forgetting Eden's sins,
Relents, and spirit visitors descend
In love's remembered tokens, earth once more to blend.

XXXI

The sleepy mosses wave within the sun,
And on the dark elms climbs the mistletoe;
Great tangled vines through pendant branches run,
And hang their purple clusters far below;
The old pines wave their summits to and fro,
And dancing to the earth, impatient light
Touches the languid scene, to quickly go,
Like some gay spirit in its sunny plight,
That, visiting the earth, did glance and take its flight. . . .

PAUL LAURENCE DUNBAR (1872-1906)

Paul Laurence Dunbar has been the one Negro poet that all America
has accepted wholeheartedly. Born in Dayton, Ohio, he was educated in that city. His formal education ended with graduation from
high school. Unable to go to college, he worked as an elevator
operator, but continued his versifying, which he had begun as far
back as grammar school. His first book, *Oak and Ivy,* appeared in
1893. The second volume, *Majors and Minors* (1895), attracted the
notice of William Dean Howells, under whose sponsorship *Lyrics
of Lowly Life,* made up of the best from the first two volumes, was

published in 1896. The commendatory preface by Howells helped
to make Dunbar a national literary figure. From that time on his
success was assured. The best magazines of the country accepted
his contributions, and he worked feverishly to supply the ever-increas-
ing demand for his poems. Other volumes followed in quick succession: *Lyrics of the Hearthside* (1899), *Lyrics of Love and Laughter*
(1903), *Lyrics of Sunshine and Shadow* (1905), four collections of
short stories, and four novels. In spite of domestic troubles and
rapidly failing health, Dunbar turned out a great deal of work in
his last years. He died at the age of thirty-four, at the height of his
literary popularity. The poems in this selection are used by permission of Dodd, Mead, and Company.

Ere Sleep Comes Down to Soothe the Weary Eyes

Ere sleep comes down to soothe the weary eyes,
Which all the day with ceaseless care have sought
The magic gold which from the seeker flies;
Ere dreams put on the gown and cap of thought,
And make the waking world a world of lies,—
Of lies most palpable, uncouth, forlorn,
That say life's full of aches and tears and sighs,—
Oh, how with more than dreams the soul is torn,
Ere sleep comes down to soothe the weary eyes.

Ere sleep comes down to soothe the weary eyes,
How all the griefs and heartaches we have known
Come up like pois'nous vapors that arise
From some base witch's caldron, when the crone,
To work some potent spell, her magic plies.
The past which held its share of bitter pain,
Whose ghost we prayed that Time might exorcise,
Comes up, is lived and suffered o'er again,
Ere sleep comes down to soothe the weary eyes.

Ere sleep comes down to soothe the weary eyes,
What phantoms fill the dimly lighted room;
What ghostly shades in awe-creating guise
Are bodied forth within the teeming gloom.
What echoes faint of sad and soul-sick cries,
And pangs of vague inexplicable pain
That pay the spirit's ceaseless enterprise,
Come thronging through the chambers of the brain,
Ere sleep comes down to soothe the weary eyes.

Ere sleep comes down to soothe the weary eyes,
Where ranges forth the spirit far and free?
Through what strange realms and unfamiliar skies
Tends her far course to lands of mystery?
To lands unspeakable—beyond surmise,
Where shapes unknowable to being spring,
Till, faint of wing, the Fancy fails and dies
Much wearied with the spirit's journeying,
Ere sleep comes down to soothe the weary eyes.

Ere sleep comes down to soothe the weary eyes,
How questioneth the soul that other soul,—
The inner sense which neither cheats nor lies,
But self exposes unto self, a scroll
Full writ with all life's acts unwise or wise,
In characters indelible and known;
So, trembling with the shock of sad surprise,
The soul doth view its awful self alone,
Ere sleep comes down to soothe the weary eyes.

Ere sleep comes down to soothe the weary eyes,
The last dear sleep whose soft embrace is balm,
And whom sad sorrow teaches us to prize
For kissing all our passions into calm,
Ah, then, no more we heed the sad world's cries,
Or seek to probe th' eternal mystery,
Or fret our souls at long-withheld replies,
At glooms through which our visions cannot see,
Ere sleep comes down to soothe the weary eyes.

The Party

Dey had a gread big pahty down to Tom's de othah night;
Was I dah? You bet! I nevah in my life see sich a sight;
All de folks f'om fou' plantations was invited, an' dey come,
Dey come troopin' thick ez chillun when dey hyeahs a fife
        an' drum.
Evahbody dressed deir fines'—Heish yo' mouf an' git away,
Ain't seen no sich fancy dressin' sence las' quah'tly meetin'
        day;
Gals all dressed in silks an' satins, not a wrinkle ner a crease,
Eyes a-battin', teeth a-shinin', haih breshed back ez slick
        ez grease;
Sku'ts all tucked an' puffed an' ruffled, evah blessed seam
        an' stitch;

Ef you'd seen 'em wif deir mistus, couldn't swahed to which
    was which.
Men all dressed up in Prince Alberts, swallertails 'u'd tek
    you' bref!
I cain't tell you nothin' 'bout it, yo' ought to seen it
    fu' yo'se'f.
Who was dah? Now who you askin'? How you 'spect I gwine
    to know?
You mus' think I stood an' counted evahbody at de do'.
Ole man Babah's house boy Isaac, brung dat gal, Malindy Jane,
Huh a-hangin' to his elbow, him a struttin' wif a cane;
My, but Hahvey Jones was jealous! seemed to stick him lak
    a tho'n;
But he laughed with Viney Cahteh, tryin' ha'd to not let on,
But a pusson would'a' noticed f'om de d'rection of his look,
Dat he was watchin' ev'ry step dat Ike an' Lindy took.
Ike he foun' a cheer an' asked huh: "Won't you set down?"
    wif a smile,
An' she answe'd up a-bowin', "Oh, I reckon 'tain't wuth while."
Dat was jes' fu' style, I reckon, 'cause she sot down jes'
    de same,
An' she stayed dah 'twell he fetched huh fu' to jine some
    so't o' game;
Den I hyeahd huh sayin' propah, ez she riz to go away,
"Oh, you raly mus' excuse me, fu' I hardly keers to play."
But I seen huh in a minute wif de othahs on de flo',
An' dah wasn't any one o' dem a-playin' any mo';
Comin' down de flo' a-bowin' an' a-swayin' an' a-swingin',
Puttin' on huh high-toned mannahs all de time dat she was
    singin':
"Oh, swing Johnny up an' down, swing him all aroun',
Swing Johnny up an' down, swing him all aroun',
Oh, swing Johnny up an' down, swing him all aroun',
Fa' you well, my dahlin'."
Had to laff at ole man Johnson, he's a caution now you bet—
Hittin' clost onto a hunderd, but he's spry an' nimble yet;
He 'lowed how a-so't o' gigglin', "I ain't ole, I'll let you see,
D'ain't no use in gettin' feeble, now you youngstahs jes'
    watch me,"
An', he grabbed ole Aunt Marier—weighs th'ee hunderd
    mo'er less,
An' he spun huh 'roun' de cabin swingin' Johnny lak de res'.
Evahbody laffed an' hollahed: "Go it, swing huh, Uncle Jim!"
An' he swung huh too, I reckon, lak a youngstah, who but him.
Dat was bettah'n young Scott Thomas, tryin' to be so awful
    smaht.

You know when dey gits to singin' an' dey comes to dat ere
    paht:
      "In some lady's new brick house,
    In some lady's gyahden.
        Ef you don't let me out, I will jump out,
    So fa' you well, my dahlin'."
Den dey's got a circle 'roun' you, an' you's got to break
    de line;
Well, dat dahky was so anxious, lak to bust hisse'f a-tryin';
Kep' on blund'rin' 'round' an' foolin' 'twell he giv' one
    great big jump,
Broke de line, an' lit head-fo'most in de fiahplace right
    plump;
Hit 'ad fiah in it, mind you; well, I thought my soul I'd
    bust,
Tried my best to keep f'om laffin', but hit seemed like
    die I must!
Y' ought to seen dat man a-scramblin' f'om de ashes an'
    de grime.
Did it bu'n him! Sich a question, why he didn't give it time;
Th'ow'd dem ashes and dem cindahs evah which-a-way I guess,
An' you nevah did, I reckon, clap yo' eyes on sich a mess;
Fu' he sholy made a picter an' a funny one to boot,
Wif his clothes all full o' ashes an' his face all full o' soot.
Well, hit laked to stopped de pahty, an' I reckon lak ez not
Dat it would ef Tom's wife, Mandy, hadn't happened on de spot,
To invite us out to suppah—well, we scrambled to de table,
An' I'd lak to tell you 'bout it—what we had—but I ain't
    able,
Mention jes' a few things, dough I know I hadn't orter,
Fu' I know 'twill staht a hank'rin' an' yo' mouf'll 'mence
    to worter.
We had wheat bread white ez cotton an' a egg pone jes'
    like gol',
Hog jole, bilin' hot an' steamin' roasted shoat an' ham
    sliced cold—
Look out! What's de mattah wif you? Don't be fallin' on
    de flo';
Ef it's go'n to 'fect you dat way, I won't tell you nothin' mo'.
Dah now—well, we had hot chittlin's—now you's tryin'
    ag'in to fall,
Cain't you stan' to hyeah about it? S'pose you'd been an'
    seed it all;
Seed dem gread big sweet pertaters, layin' by de possum's side,
Seed dat coon in all his gravy, reckon den you'd up and died!
Mandy 'lowed "you all mus' 'scuse me, d' wa'n't much upon
    my she'ves,

But I's done my bes' to suit you, so set down an' he'p
yo'se'ves."
Tom, he 'lowed: "I don't b'lieve in 'pologizin' an' perfessin',
Let 'em tek it lak dey ketch it. Eldah Thompson, ask de
blessin' ".
Wish you'd seed dat colo'ed preachah cleah his th'oat an'
bow his head;
One eye shet an' one eye open,—dis is evah wud he said:
"Lawd, look down in tendah mussy on sich generous hea'ts
ez dese;
Makes us truly thankful, amen. Pass dat possum, ef you
please!"
Well, we eat and drunk ouah po'tion, 'twell dah wasn't
nothin' lef',
An' we felt jes' like new sausage, we was mos' nigh stuffed
to def!
Tom, he knowed how we'd be feelin', so he had de fiddlah
'roun',
An' he made us cleah de cabin fu' to dance dat suppah down.
Jim, de fiddlah, chuned his fiddle, put some rosum on his bow,
Set a pine box on de table, mounted it an' let huh go!
He's a fiddlah, now I tell you, an' he made dat fiddle ring,
'Twell de ol'est an' de lamest had to give deir feet a fling.
Jigs, cotillions, reels an' break-downs, cordrills an' a waltz
er two;
Bless yo' soul, dat music winged 'em an' dem people lak to
flew.
Cripple Joe, de ole rheumatic, danced dat flo' f'om side to
middle,
Th'owed away his crutch an' hopped it, what's rheumatics
'ginst a fiddle?
Eldah Thompson got so tickled dat he lak to lo' his grace,
Had to tek bofe feet an' hol' dem so's to keep 'em in deir
place.
An' de Christuns an' de sinnahs got so mixed up on dat flo',
Dat i don't see how dey'd pahted ef de trump had chanced
to blow.
Well, we danced dat way an' capahed in de mos' redic'lous
way,
'Twell de roostahs in de bahnyard cleahed deir th'oats an'
crowed fu' day.
Y' ought to been dah, fu' I tell you evahthing was rich an'
prime,
An' dey ain't no use in talkin', we jes' had one scrumptious
time!

At Candle-Lightin' Time

When I come in f'om de co'n-fiel' aftah wo'kin' ha'd all day,
It's amazin' nice to fin' my suppah all erpon de way;
An' it's nice to smell de coffee bubblin' ovah in de pot,
An' it's fine to see de meat a-sizzlin' teasin'-lak an' hot.

But when suppah-time is ovah, an' de t'ings is cleahed away;
Den de happy hours dat foller are de sweetes' of de day.
When my co'ncob pipe is sta'ted, an' de smoke is drawin' prime,
My ole 'ooman says, "I reckon, Ike, it's candle-lightin' time."

Den de chillun snuggle up to me, an' all commence to call,
"Oh, say, daddy, now it's time to mek de shadders on de wall."
So I puts my han's togethah—evah daddy knows de way,—
An' de chillun snuggle closer 'roun' ez I begin to say:—

"Fus' thing, hyeah come Mistah Rabbit; don' you see him
    wo'k his eahs?
Huh, uh! dis mus' be a donkey,—look, how innercent
    he 'pears!
Dah's de ole black swan a'swimmin'—ain't she got a' awful
    neck?
Who's dis feller dat's a-comin'? Why, dat's ole dog Tray,
    I 'spec'l"

Dat's de way I run on, tryin' fu' to please 'em all I can;
Den I hollahs, "Now be keerful—dis hyeah las's de buga-man!"
An' dey runs an' hides dey faces; dey ain't skeered—dey's
    lettin' on:
But de play ain't really ovah twell dat buga-man is gone.

So I jes' teks up my banjo, an' I plays a little chune,
An' you see dem haids come peepin' out to listen mighty soon,
Den my wife says, "Sich a pappy fu' to give you sich a fright!
Jes' you go to baid, an' leave him: say yo' prayers an' say
    good-night."

Sympathy

I know what the caged bird feels, alas!
When the sun is bright on the upland slopes;
When the wind stirs soft through the springing grass
And the river flows like a stream of glass;
When the first bird sings and the first bud opes,
And the faint perfume from its chalice steals—
I know what the caged bird feels!

I know why the caged bird beats his wing
Till its blood is red on the cruel bars;
For he must fly back to his perch and cling
When he fain would be on the bough a-swing;
And a pain still throbs in the old, old scars
And they pulse again with a keener sting—
I know why he beats his wing!

I know why the caged bird sings, ah me,
When his wing is bruised and his bosom sore,—
When he beats his bars and would be free;
It is not a carol of joy or glee,
But a prayer that he sends from his heart's deep core,
But a plea, that upward to Heaven he flings—
I know why the caged bird sings!

We Wear the Mask

We wear the mask that grins and lies,
It hides our cheeks and shades our eyes,—
This debt we pay to human guile;
With torn and bleeding hearts we smile,
And mouth with myriad subtleties.

Why should the world be over-wise,
In counting all our tears and sighs?
Nay, let them only see us, while
        We wear the mask.

We smile, but, O great Christ, our cries
To thee from tortured souls arise.
We sing, but oh the clay is vile
Beneath our feet, and long the mile;
But let the world dream otherwise,
        We wear the mask.

Forever

I had not known before
  Forever was so long a word.
The slow stroke of the clock of time
  I had not heard.

'Tis hard to learn so late;
  It seems no sad heart really learns,
But hopes and trusts and doubts and fears,
  And bleeds and burns.

The night is not all dark,
  Nor is the day all it seems,
But each may bring me this relief—
  My dreams and dreams.

I had not known before
  That Never was so sad a word,
So wrap me in forgetfulness—
  I have not heard.

Robert Gould Shaw[1]

Why was it that the thunder voice of Fate
  Should call thee, studious, from the classic groves,
  Where calm-eyed Pallas with still footstep roves,
And charge thee seek the turmoil of the state?
What bade thee hear the voice and rise elate,
  Leave home and kindred and thy spicy loaves,
  To lead th' unlettered and despised droves
To manhood's home and thunder at the gate?

Far better the slow blaze of Learning's light,
  The cool and quiet of her dearer fane,
Than this hot terror of a hopeless fight,
  This cold endurance of the final pain,—
Since thou and those who with thee died for right
  Have died, the Present teaches, but in vain!

---

[1] See below, George Williams, "Negro Troops in the Civil War," page 869.

Harriet Beecher Stowe

She told the story, and the whole world wept
    At wrongs and cruelties it had not known
    But for this fearless woman's voice alone.
    She spoke to consciences that long had slept:
Her message, Freedom's clear reveille, swept
    From heedless hovel to complacent throne.
    Command and prophecy were in the tone
    And from its sheath the sword of justice leapt.
Around two peoples swelled a fiery wave,
    But both came forth transfigured from the flame.
Blest be the hand that dared be strong to save,
    And blest be she who in our weakness came—
    Prophet and priestess! At one stroke she gave
    A race to freedom and herself to fame.

A Song

Thou art the soul of a summer's day,
Thou art the breath of the rose.
    But the summer is fled
    And the rose is dead.
Where are they gone, who knows, who knows?

Thou art the blood of my heart o' hearts,
Thou art my soul's repose,
    But my heart grows numb
    And my soul is dumb.
Where art thou, love, who knows, who knows?

Thou art the hope of my after years—
Sun for my winter snows
    But the years go by
    'Neath a clouded sky.
Where shall we meet, who knows, who knows?

The Debt

This is the debt I pay
Just for one riotous day,
Years of regret and grief,
Sorrow without relief.

Pay it I will to the end—
Until the grave, my friend,
Gives me a true release—
Gives me the clasp of peace.

Slight was the thing I bought,
Small was the debt I thought,
Poor was the loan at best—
God! but the interest!

Signs of the Times

Air a-gittin' cool an' coolah,
    Frost a-comin' in de night,
Hicka'nuts an' wa'nuts fallin',
    Possum keepin' out o' sight.
Tu'key struttin' in de ba'nya'd,
    Nary step so proud ez his;
Keep on struttin', Mistah Tu'key,
    Yo' do' know whut time it is.

Cidah press commence a-squeakin'
    Eatin' apples sto'ed away,
Chillun swa'min' 'roun' lak ho'nets,
    Huntin' aigs ermung de hay.
Mistah Tu'key keep on gobblin'
    At de geese a-flyin' souf,
Oomph! dat bird do' know whut's comin'
    Ef he did he'd shet his mouf.

Pumpkin gittin' good an' yallah
    Mek me open up my eyes;
Seems lak it's a-lookin' at me
    Jes' a-lai'n' dah sayin' "Pies."
Tu'key gobbler gwine 'roun' blowin'
    Gwine 'roun' gibbin' sass an' slack;
Keep on talkin', Mistah Tu'key,
    You ain't seed no almanac.

Fa'mer walkin' th'oo de ba'nya'd
    Seein' how things is comin' on,
Sees ef all de fowls is fatt'nin'—
    Good times comin' sho's you bo'n.
Hyeahs dat tu'key gobbler braggin',
    Den his face break in a smile—
Nebbah min', you sassy rascal,
    He's gwine nab you atter while.

Choppin' suet in de kitchen,
   Stonin' raisins in de hall,
Beef a-cookin' fu' de mince meat,
   Spices groun'—I smell 'em all.
Look hyeah, Tu'key, stop dat gobblin',
   You ain' luned de sense ob feah,
You ol' fool, yo' naik's in dangah,
   Do' you know Thanksgibbin's hyeah?

A Christmas Folksong

De win' is blowin' wahmah,
   An hit's blowin' f'om de bay;
Dey's a so't o' mist a-risin'
   All erlong de meddah way;
Dey ain't a hint o' frostin'
   On de groun' ner in de sky,
An' dey ain't no use in hopin'
   Dat de snow'll 'mence to fly.
     It's goin' to be a green Christmas,
     An' sad de day fu' me.
     I wish dis was de las' one
     Dat evah I should see.

Dey's dancin' in de cabin,
   Dey's spahkin' by de tree;
But dancin' times an' spahkin'
   Are all done pas' fur me.
Dey's feastin' in de big house,
   Wid all de windahs wide—
Is dat de way fu' people
   To meet de Christmas-tide?
     It's goin' to be a green Christmas,
     No mattah what you say.
     Dey's us dat will remembah
     An' grieve de comin' day.

Dey's des a bref o' dampness
   A-clingin' to my cheek;
De aih's been dahk an' heavy
   An' threatenin' fu' a week,
But not wid signs o' wintah,
   Dough wintah'd seem so deah—
De wintah's out o' season,
   An' Christmas eve is heah.

It's goin' to be a green Christmas,
  An' oh, how sad de day!
Go ax de hongry chu'chya'd,
  An' see what hit will say.

Dey's Allen on de hillside,
  An' Marfy in de plain;
Fu' Christmas was like spring-time,
  An' come wid sun an' rain.
Dey's Ca'line, John, an' Susie,
  Wid only dis one lef':
An' now de curse is comin'
  Wid murder in hits bref.
    It's goin' to be a green Christmas,
    Des hyeah my words an' see:
    Befo' de summah beckons
    Dey's many'll weep wid me.

Itching Heels

Fu' de peace o' my eachin' heels, set down;
  Don' fiddle dat chune no mo'.
Don' you see how dat melody. stuhs me up
  An' baigs me to tek to de flo'?
You knows I's a Christian, good an' strong;
  I wusship f'om June to June;
My pra'ahs dey ah loud an' my hymns ah long:
  I baig you don' fiddle dat chune.

I's a crick in my back an' a misery hyeah
  Whaih de j'ints's gittin' ol' an' stiff,
But hit seems lak you brings me de bref o' my youf;
  W'y, I's suttain I noticed a w'iff.
Don' fiddle dat chune no mo', my chile,
  Don' fiddle dat chune no mo';
I'll git up an' taih up dis groun' fu' a mile,
  An' den I'll be chu'ched fu' it, sho'.

Oh, fiddle dat chune some mo', I say,
  An' fiddle it loud an' fas':
I's a youngstah ergin in de mi'st o' my sin;
  De p'esent's gone back to de pas'.
I'll dance to dat chune, so des fiddle erway;
  I knows how de backslidah feels;
So fiddle it on 'twell de break o' de day
  Fu' de sake o' my eachin' heels.

A Death Song

Lay me down beneaf de willers in de grass,
Whah de branch'll go a-singin' as it pass.
    An' w'en I's a-layin' low,
    I kin hyeah it as it go
Singin', "Sleep, my honey, tek yo' res' at las.' "

Lay me nigh to whah hit meks a little pool,
An' de watah stan's so quiet lak an' cool,
    Whah de little birds in spring,
    Ust to come an' drink an' sing,
An' de chillen waded on dey way to school.

Let me settle w'en my shouldahs draps dey load
Nigh enough to hyeah de noises in de road;
    Fu' I t'ink de las' long res'
    Gwine to soothe my sperrit bes'
Ef I's layin' 'mong de t'ings I's allus knowed.

JAMES EDWIN CAMPBELL (c. 1860-c. 1905)

James Edwin Campbell, one of the first Negroes to write dialect poetry, was born in Pomeroy, Ohio, where he received his early education. He spent some time in Miami College and during the 1880-1900 period was a journalist in Chicago. His volume *Echoes from the Cabin and Elsewhere* (1905) contains poems in Gullah dialect.

Ol' Doc' Hyar

Ur ol' Hyar lib in ur house on de hill,
He hunner yurs ol' an' nebber wuz ill;
He yurs dee so long an' he eyes so beeg,
An' he laigs so spry dat he dawnce ur jeeg;
He lib so long that he know ebbry tings
'Bout de beas'ses dat walks an' de bu'ds dat sings—
        Dis Ol' Doc' Hyar,
        Whar lib up dar
Een ur mighty fine house on ur mighty high hill.

He doctah fur all de beas'ses an' bu'ds—
He put on he specs an' he use beeg wu'ds,
He feel dee pu's' den he look mighty wise,
He pull out he watch an' he shet boofe eyes;
He grab up he hat an' grab up he cane,

Den—"blam!" go de do'—he gone lak de train,
            Dis Ol' Doc' Hyar,
            Whar lib up dar
Een ur mighty fine house on ur mighty high hill.

Mistah B'ar fall sick—dee sont fur Doc' Hyar,
"Oh, Doctah, come queeck, an' see Mr. B'ar;
He mighty nigh daid des sho' ez you b'on!"
"Too much ur young peeg, too much ur green co'n,"
Ez he put on he hat, said Ol' Doc' Hyar;
"I'll tek 'long meh lawnce, an' lawnce Mistah B'ar,"
            Said Ol' Doc' Hyar,
            Whar lib up dar
Een ur mighty fine house on ur mighty high hill.

Mistah B'ar he groaned, Mistah B'ar he growled,
W'ile de ol' Miss B'ar an' de chillen howled;
Doctah Hyar tuk out he sha'p li'l lawnce,
An' pyu'ced Mistah B'ar twel he med him prawnce
Den grab up he hat an' grab up he cane
"Blam!" go de do' an' he gone lak de train,
            Dis Ol' Doc' Hyar,
            Whar lib up dar
Een ur mighty fine house on ur mighty high hill.

But de vay naix day Mistah B'ar he daid;
Wen dee tell Doc' Hyar, he des scratch he haid:
"Ef pahsons git well ur pahsons git wu's,
Money got ter come een de Ol' Hyar's pu's;
Not wut folkses does, but fur wut dee know
Does de folkses git paid"—an' Hyar larfed low,
            Dis sma't Ol' Hyar,
            Whar lib up dar
Een de mighty fine house on de mighty high hill!

When Ol' Sis' Judy Pray

When ol' Sis' Judy pray,
De teahs come stealin' down my cheek,
De voice ur God widin me speak';
I see myse'f so po' an' weak,
Down on my knees de cross I seek,
When ol' Sis' Judy pray.

When ol' Sis' Judy pray,
De thun'ers ur Mount Sin-a-i

Comes rushin' down f'um up on high—
De Debbil tu'n his back an' fly
While sinnahs loud fur pa'don cry,
When ol' Sis' Judy pray.

When ol' Sis' Judy pray,
Ha'd sinnahs trimble in dey seat
Ter hyuh huh voice in sorro' 'peat:
(While all de chu'ch des sob an' weep)
"O Shepa'd, dese, dy po' los' sheep!"
When ol' Sis' Judy pray.

When ol' Sis' Judy pray,
De whole house hit des rock an' moan
Ter see huh teahs an' hyuh huh groan;
Dar's somepin' in Sis' Judy's tone
Dat melt all ha'ts dough med ur stone
When ol' Sis' Judy pray.

When ol' Sis' Judy pray,
Salvation's light comes pourin' down—
Hit fills de chu'ch an' all de town—
Why, angels' robes go rustlin' 'roun,
An' hebben on de yurf am foun',
When ol' Sis' Judy pray.

When ol' Sis' Judy pray,
My soul go sweepin' up on wings,
An' loud de chu'ch wid "Glory!" rings,
An' wide de gates ur Jahsper swings
Twel you hyuh ha'ps wid golding strings,
When ol' Sis' Judy pray. . . .

W. S. BRAITHWAITE (1878-   )

Born in Boston of West Indian parentage, William Stanley Braithwaite (see also p. 773) has been largely self-educated. For several
years he was on the editorial staff of the *Boston Transcript,* and
from 1913 to 1929 he published a yearly *Anthology of Magazine
Verse.* In addition, Braithwaite has edited the following anthologies:
The Book of Elizabethan Verse (1906), *The Book of Georgian
Verse* (1908), and *The Book of Restoration Verse* (1909). He was
awarded the Spingarn Medal in 1918. At present he is professor of
creative literature at Atlanta University. Braithwaite's original poetry
has appeared in two volumes: *Lyrics of Life* (1904), and *The House*

of Falling Leaves (1908). Of his poems written since then only a few have appeared in anthologies. Though Braithwaite actively sponsors the New Poetry movement in America, his own work is in the tradition of the late nineteenth-century poets. The poems included in this collection are reprinted by permission of the author.

The Watchers

Two women on the lone wet strand,
  (The wind's out with a will to roam)
The waves wage war on rocks and sand,
  (And a ship is long due home.)

The sea sprays in the women's eyes—
  (Hearts can writhe like the sea's wild foam)
Lower descend the tempestuous skies,
  (For the wind's out with a will to roam.)

"O daughter, thine eyes be better than mine,"
  (The waves ascend high as yonder dome)
"North or south is there never a sign?"
  (And a ship is long due home.)

They watched there all the long night through—
  (The wind's out with a will to roam)
Wind and rain and sorrow for two,—
  (And heaven on the long reach home.)

Sandy Star

I
Sculptured Worship

The zones of warmth around his heart,
  No alien airs had crossed;
But he awoke one morn to feel
  The magic numbness of autumnal frost.

His thoughts were a loose skein of threads,
  And tangled emotions, vague and dim;
And sacrificing what he loved
  He lost the dearest part of him.

In sculptured worship now he lives,
  His one desire a prisoned ache;
If he can never melt again
  His very heart will break.

II
Laughing It Out

He had a whim and laughed it out
  Upon the exit of a chance;
He floundered in a sea of doubt—
  If life was real—or just romance.

Sometimes upon his brow would come
  A little pucker of defiance;
He totalled in a word the sum
  Of all man made of facts and science.

And then a hearty laugh would break,
  A reassuring shrug of shoulder;
And we would from his fancy take
  A faith in death which made life bolder.

III
Exit

No, his exit by the gate
  Will not leave the wind ajar;
He will go when it is late
  With a misty star.

One will call, he cannot see;
  One will call, he will not hear;
He will take no company
  Nor a hope or fear.

We shall smile who loved him so—
  They who gave him hate will weep;
But for us the winds will blow
  Pulsing through his sleep.

IV
The Way

He could not tell the way he came,
  Because his chart was lost:
Yet all his way was paved with flame
  From the bourne he crossed.

He did not know the way to go,
  Because he had no map:
He followed where the winds blow—
  And the April sap.

He never knew upon his brow
The secret that he bore,—
And laughs away the mystery now
The dark's at his door.

V

Onus Probandi

No more from out the sunset,
No more across the foam,
No more across the windy hills
Will Sandy Star come home.

He went away to search it
With a curse upon his tongue:
And in his hand the staff of life,
Made music as it swung.

I wonder if he found it,
And knows the mystery now—
Our Sandy Star who went away,
With the secret on his brow.

W. E. B. DuBOIS (1868-   )

Several free-verse poems by William E. Burghardt DuBois (see also p. 763) are scattered throughout his works, such as "The Riddle of the Sphinx," "Children of the Moon," and "The Prayers of God." "A Litany at Atlanta," one of the earliest poems by a Negro in free verse, is the author's impassioned prose at its most typical, prose that has crossed the tenuous line dividing it from poetry. This work is reprinted by permission of the author and of Harcourt, Brace and Company, publishers of *Darkwater*.

A Litany at Atlanta

Done at Atlanta, in the Day of Death, 1906.
O Silent God, Thou whose voice afar in mist and mystery hath left our ears an-hungered in these fearful days—
Hear us, good Lord!

Listen to us, Thy children: our faces dark with doubt are made a mockery in Thy sanctuary. With uplifted hands we front Thy heaven, O God, crying:
We beseech Thee to hear us, good Lord!

We are not better than our fellows, Lord, we are but weak and human men. When our devils do deviltry, curse Thou the doer and the deed: curse them as we curse them, do to them all and more than ever they have done to innocence and weakness, to womanhood and home.
Have mercy upon us, miserable sinners!

And yet whose is the deeper guilt? Who made these devils? Who nursed them in crime and fed them on injustice? Who ravished and debauched their mothers and their grandmothers? Who bought and sold their crime, and waxed fat and rich on public iniquity?
Thou knowest, good God!

Is this Thy justice, O Father, that guile be easier than innocence, and the innocent crucified for the guilt of the untouched guilty?
Justice, O judge of men!

Wherefore de we pray? Is not the God of the fathers dead? Have not seers seen in Heaven's halls Thine hearsed and lifeless forms stark amidst the black and rolling smoke of sin, where all along bow bitter forms of endless dead?
Awake, Thou that sleepest!

Thou art not dead, but flown afar, up hills of endless light through blazing corridors of suns, where worlds do swing of good and gentle men, of women strong and free—far from the cozenage, black hypocrisy, and chaste prostitution of this shameful speck of dust!
Turn again, O Lord, leave us not to perish in our sin!

From lust of body and lust of blood,
Great God, deliver us!

From lust of power and lust of gold,
Great God, deliver us!

From the leagued lying of despot and of brute,
Great God, deliver us!

A city lay in travail, God our Lord, and from her loins sprang twin Murder and Black Hate. Red was the midnight; clang, crack and cry of death and fury filled the air and trembled underneath the stars when church spires pointed silently to Thee. And all this was to sate the greed of greedy men who hide behind the veil of vengeance!
Bend us Thine ear, O Lord!

In the pale, still morning we looked upon the deed. We stopped our ears and held our leaping hands, but they—did they not wag their

heads and leer and cry with bloody jaws: *Cease from Crime!* The word
was mockery, for thus they train a hundred crimes while we do cure
one.

    Turn again our captivity, O Lord!

    Behold this maimed and broken thing; dear God, it was an humble
black man who toiled and sweat to save a bit from the pittance paid
him. They told him: *Work and Rise.* He worked. Did this man sin?
Nay, but some one told how some one said another did—one whom he
had never seen nor known. Yet for that man's crime this man lieth
maimed and murdered, his wife naked to shame, his children, to
poverty and evil.

    Hear us, O heavenly Father!

    Doth not this justice of hell stink in Thy nostrils, O God? How long
shall the mounting flood of innocent blood roar in Thine ears and
pound in our hearts for vengeance? Pile the pale frenzy of blood-crazed
brutes who do such deeds high on Thine altar, Jehovah Jireh, and burn
it in hell forever and forever.

    Forgive us, good Lord; we know not what we say!

    Bewildered we are, and passion-tost, mad with the madness of a
mobbed and mocked and murdered people; straining at the armposts
of Thy Throne, we raise our shackled hands and charge Thee, God,
by the bones of our stolen fathers, by the tears of our dead mothers, by
the very blood of Thy crucified Christ: *What meaneth this?* Tell us the
Plan; give us the Sign!

    Keep not Thou silence, O God!

    Sit no longer blind, Lord God, deaf to our prayer and dumb to our
dumb suffering. Surely Thou too art not white, O Lord, a pale, bloodless,
heartless thing?

    Ah! Christ of all the Pities!

    Forgive the thought! Forgive these wild, blasphemous words. Thou
art still the God of our black fathers, and in Thy soul's soul sit some
soft darkenings of the evening, some shadowings of the velvet night.

    But whisper—speak—call, great God, for Thy silence is white terror
to our hearts! The way, O God, show us the way and point us the path.

    Whither? North is greed and South is blood; within, the coward,
and without the liar. Whither? To Death?

    Amen! Welcome dark sleep!

    Whither? To life? But not this life, dear God, not this. Let the
cup pass from us, tempt us not beyond our strength, for there is that

clamoring and clawing within, to whose voice we would not listen, yet
shudder lest we must,—and it is red, Ah! God! It is a red and awful shape.
  Selah!

> In yonder East trembles a star.
>   *Vengeance is mine; I will repay, saith the Lord!*

> Thy will, O Lord, be done!
>   *Kyrie Eleison!*

> Lord, we have done these pleading, wavering words.
>   *We beseech Thee to hear us, good Lord!*

> We bow our heads and hearken soft to the sobbing of
>   women and little children.
>   *We beseech Thee to hear us, good Lord!*

> Our voices sink in silence and in night.
>   *Hear us, good Lord!*

> In night, O God of a godless land!
>   *Amen!*

> In silence, O silent God.
>   *Selah!*

JAMES WELDON JOHNSON (1871-1938)

Born in Jacksonville, Florida, James Weldon Johnson (see also
pp. 168, 967) received his early education there, subsequently going
to college at Atlanta University. He began his career as a teacher in
his native city. Not content, however, to remain a public-school principal, Johnson read law and passed the Florida bar. Law was also
found prosaic, and in 1901 he and his brother, Rosamond, went to
New York and entered the field of musical comedy with almost
immediate success. At the same time, Johnson continued his studies
in literature and drama at Columbia University. From 1906 to 1913
Johnson was United States Consul, first in Venezuela and later in
Nicaragua. While in the consular service, he wrote his well-known
novel, *The Autobiography of an Ex-Colored Man* (1912). On his
return to America, he became connected with the N. A. A. C. P.,
serving from 1916 to 1920 as field secretary, and from 1920 to 1930
as general secretary. In 1925 he was awarded the Spingarn Medal.
He became professor of creative literature at Fisk University in
1930; he also served as visiting professor at New York University.

He was killed in an automobile accident in the summer of 1938.
Johnson published the following volumes of poetry: *Fifty Years and
Other Poems* (1917), *God's Trombones* (1927), and *St. Peter Relates
an Incident of the Resurrection Day* (1930). His *Book of American
Negro Poetry* (1922) was a pioneer effort in anthologies, serving as
an interpreter of Negro artistic achievement and as a stimulus to
young Negro writers. One of his best-known earlier poems, "Lift
Every Voice and Sing," was set to music by his brother J. Rosamond
Johnson; it is widely known as the National Negro Anthem. "O
Black and Unknown Bards," "Brothers," and "Sence You Went
Away" are reprinted by permission of Mrs. Grace Nail Johnson and
of the Cornhill Publishing Co.; the remaining poems by permission of
Mrs. Johnson and of the Viking Press.

O Black and Unknown Bards

O black and unknown bards of long ago,
How came your lips to touch the sacred fire?
How, in your darkness, did you come to know
The power and beauty of the minstrel's lyre?
Who first from midst his bonds lifted his eyes?
Who first from out the still watch, lone and long,
Feeling the ancient faith of prophets rise
Within his dark-kept soul, burst into song?

Heart of what slave poured out such melody
As "Steal away to Jesus"? On its strains
His spirit must have nightly floated free,
Though still about his hands he felt his chains.
Who heard great "Jordan roll"? Whose starward eye
Saw chariot "swing low"? And who was he
That breathed that comforting, melodic sigh,
"Nobody knows de trouble I see"?

What merely living clod, what captive thing,
Could up toward God through all its darkness grope,
And find within its deadened heart to sing
These songs of sorrow, love and faith, and hope?
How did it catch that subtle undertone,
That note in music heard not with the ears?
How sound the elusive reed so seldom blown,
Which stirs the soul or melts the heart to tears.

Not that great German master in his dream
Of harmonies that thundered amongst the stars

At the creation, ever heard a theme
Nobler than "Go down, Moses." Mark its bars
How like a mighty trumpet-call they stir
The blood. Such are the notes that men have sung
Going to valorous deeds; such tones there were
That helped make history when Time was young.

There is a wide, wide wonder in it all,
That from degraded rest and servile toil
The fiery spirit of the seer should call
These simple children of the sun and soil.
O black slave singers, gone, forgot, unfamed,
You—you alone, of all the long, long line
Of those who've sung untaught, unknown, unnamed,
Have stretched out upward, seeking the divine.

You sang not deeds of heroes or of kings;
No chant of bloody war, no exulting paean
Of arms-won triumphs; but your humble strings
You touched in chord with music empyrean.
You sang far better than you knew; the songs
That for your listeners' hungry hearts sufficed
Still live,—but more than this to you belongs:
You sang a race from wood and stone to Christ.

Brothers

See! There he stands; not brave, but with an air
Of sullen stupor. Mark him well! Is he
Not more like brute than man? Look in his eye!
No light is there; none, save the glint that shines
In the now glaring, and now shifting orbs
Of some wild animal caught in the hunter's trap.

How came this beast in human shape and form?
Speak, man!—We call you man because you wear
His shape—How are you thus? Are you not from
That docile, child-like, tender-hearted race
Which we have known three centuries? Not from
That more than faithful race which through three wars
Fed our dear wives and nursed our helpless babes
Without a single breach of trust? Speak out!

I am, and am not.

Then who, why are you?

I am a thing not new, I am as old
As human nature. I am that which lurks,
Ready to spring whenever a bar is loosed;
The ancient trait which fights incessantly
Against restraint, balks at the upward climb;
The weight forever seeking to obey
The law of downward pull;—and I am more:
The bitter fruit am I of planted seed;
The resultant, the inevitable end
Of evil forces and the powers of wrong.

Lessons in degradation, taught and learned,
The memories of cruel sights and deeds,
The pent-up bitterness, the unspent hate
Filtered through fifteen generations have
Sprung up and found in me sporadic life.
In me the muttered curse of dying men,
On me the stain of conquered women, and
Consuming me the fearful fires of lust,
Lit long ago, by other hands than mine.
In me the down-crushed spirit, the hurled-back prayers
Of wretches now long dead,—their dire bequests,—
In me the echo of the stifled cry
Of children for their bartered mothers' breasts.

I claim no race, no race claims me; I am
No more than human dregs; degenerate;
The monstrous offspring of the monster, Sin;
I am—just what I am. . . . The race that fed
Your wives and nursed your babes would do the same
Today, but I—

Enough, the brute must die!
Quick! Chain him to that oak! It will resist
The fire much longer than this slender pine.
Now bring the fuel! Pile it 'round him! Wait!
Pile not so fast or high, or we shall lose
The agony and terror in his face.
And now the torch! Good fuel that! the flames
Already leap head-high. Ha! hear that shriek!
And there's another! wilder than the first.
Fetch water! Water! Pour a little on
The fire, lest it should burn too fast. Hold so!
Now let it slowly blaze again. See there!
He squirms! He groans! His eyes bulge wildly out,
Searching around in vain appeal for help!

Another shriek, the last! Watch how the flesh
Grows crisp and hangs till, turned to ash, it sifts
Down through the coils of chain that hold erect
The ghastly frame against the bark-scorched tree.

Stop! to each man no more than one man's share.
You take that bone, and you this tooth; the chain—
Let us divide its links; this skull, of course,
In fair division, to the leader comes.

And now his fiendish crime has been avenged;
Let us back to our wives and children.—Say,
What did he mean by those last muttered words,
"Brothers in spirit, brothers in deed are we"?

Sence You Went Away

Seems lak to me de stars don't shine so bright,
Seems lak to me de sun done loss his light,
Seems lak to me der's nothin' goin' right,
        Sence you went away.

Seems lak to me de sky ain't half so blue,
Seems lak to me dat ev'ything wants you,
Seems lak to me I don't know what to do,
        Sence you went away.

Seems lak to me dat ev'ything is wrong,
Seems lak to me de day's jes twice as long,
Seems lak to me de bird's forgot his song,
        Sence you went away.

Seems lak to me I jes can't he'p but sigh,
Seems lak to me ma th'oat keeps gittin' dry,
Seems lak to me a tear stays in my eye,
        Sence you went away.

The Prodigal Son

Young man—
Young man—
Your arm's too short to box with God.

But Jesus spake in a parable, and he said:
A certain man had two sons.
Jesus didn't give this man a name,

But his name is God Almighty.
And Jesus didn't call these sons by name,
But ev'ry young man,
Ev'rywhere,
Is one of these two sons.

And the younger son said to his father,
He said: Father, divide up the property,
And give me my portion now.
And the father with tears in his eyes said: Son,
Don't leave your father's house.
But the boy was stubborn in his head,
And haughty in his heart,
And he took his share of his father's goods,
And went into a far-off country.

There comes a time,
There comes a time
When ev'ry young man looks out from his father's house,
Longing for that far-off country.

And the young man journeyed on his way,
And he said to himself as he travelled along:
This sure is an easy road,
Nothing like the rough furrows behind my father's plow.

Young man—
Young man—
Smooth and easy is the road
That leads to hell and destruction.
Down grade all the way,
The further you travel, the faster you go.
No need to trudge and sweat and toil,
Just slip and slide and slip and slide
Till you bang up against hell's iron gate.

And the younger son kept travelling along,
Till at night-time he came to a city.
And the city was bright in the night-time like day,
The streets all crowded with people,
Brass bands and string bands a-playing,
And ev'rywhere the young man turned
There was singing and laughing and dancing.
And he stopped a passer-by and he said:

Tell me what city is this?
And the passer-by laughed and said: Don't you know?
This is Babylon, Babylon,
That great city of Babylon.
Come on, my friend, and go along with me.
And the young man joined the crowd.

Young man—
Young man—
You're never lonesome in Babylon.
You can always join a crowd in Babylon.
Young man—
Young man—
You can never be alone in Babylon,
Alone with your Jesus in Babylon.
You can never find a place, a lonesome place,
A lonesome place to go down on your knees,
And talk with your God, in Babylon.
You're always in a crowd in Babylon.

And the young man went with his new-found friends,
And bought himself some brand new clothes,
And he spent his days in the drinking dens,
Swallowing the fires of hell.
And he spent his nights in the gambling dens,
Throwing dice with the devil for his soul.
And he met up with the women of Babylon.
Oh, the women of Babylon!

Dressed in yellow and purple and scarlet,
Loaded with rings and earrings and bracelets,
Their lips like a honeycomb dripping with honey,
Perfumed and sweet-smelling like a jasmine flower;
And the jasmine smell of the Babylon women
Got in his nostrils and went to his head,
And he wasted his substance in riotous living,
In the evening, in the black and dark of night,
With the sweet-sinning women of Babylon.
And they stripped him of his money,
And they stripped him of his clothes,
And they left him broke and ragged
In the streets of Babylon.

Then the young man joined another crowd—
The beggars and lepers of Babylon.
And he went to feeding swine,
And he was hungrier than the hogs;

He got down on his belly in the mire and mud
And ate the husks with the hogs:
And not a hog was too low to turn up his nose
At the man in the mire of Babylon.
Then the young man came to himself—
He came to himself and said:
In my father's house are many mansions,
Ev'ry servant in his house has bread to eat,
Ev'ry servant in his house has a place to sleep;
I will arise and go to my father.

And his father saw him afar off,
And he ran up the road to meet him.
He put clean clothes upon his back,
And a golden chain around his neck,
He made a feast and killed the fatted calf,
And invited the neighbors in.

Oh-o-oh, sinner,
When you're mingling with the crowd in Babylon—
Drinking the wine of Babylon—
Running with the women of Babylon—
You forget about God, and you laugh at Death.
Today you've got the strength of a bull in your neck
And the strength of a bear in your arms,
But some o' these days, some o' these days,
You'll have a hand-to-hand struggle with bony Death,
And Death is bound to win.

Young man, come away from Babylon,
That hell-border city of Babylon.
Leave the dancing and the gambling of Babylon,
The wine and whiskey of Babylon,
The hot-mouthed women of Babylon;
Fall down on your knees,
And say in your heart:
I will arise and go to my Father.

Go Down Death

A Funeral Sermon

Weep not, weep not,
She is not dead;
She's resting in the bosom of Jesus.
Heart-broken husband—weep no more;
Grief-stricken son—weep no more;
She's only just gone home.

Day before yesterday morning,
God was looking down from his great, high heaven,
Looking down on all his children,
And his eye fell on Sister Caroline,
Tossing on her bed of pain.
And God's big heart was touched with pity,
With the everlasting pity.

And God sat back on his throne,
And he commanded that tall, bright angel standing at his
      right hand:
Call me Death!
And that tall, bright angel cried in a voice
That broke like a clap of thunder:
Call Death!—Call Death!
And the echo sounded down the streets of heaven
Till it reached away back to that shadowy place,
Where Death waits with his pale, white horses.

And Death heard the summons,
And he leaped on his fastest horse,
Pale as a sheet in the moonlight.
Up the golden street Death galloped,
And the hoof of his horse struck fire from the gold,
But they didn't make no sound.
Up Death rode to the Great White Throne,
And waited for God's command.

And God said: Go down, Death, go down,
Go down to Savannah, Georgia,
Down in Yamacraw,
And find Sister Caroline.
She's borne the burden and heat of the day,
She's labored long in my vineyard,
And she's tired—
She's weary—
Go down, Death, and bring her to me.

And Death didn't say a word,
But he loosed the reins on his pale, white horse,
And he clamped the spurs to his bloodless sides,
And out and down he rode,
Through heaven's pearly gates,
Past suns and moons and stars;
On Death rode,

And the foam from his horse was like a comet in the sky;
On Death rode,
Leaving the lightning's flash behind;
Straight on down he came.

While we were watching round her bed,
She turned her eyes and looked away,
She saw what we couldn't see;
She saw Old Death. She saw Old Death.
Coming like a falling star.
But Death didn't frighten Sister Caroline;
He looked to her like a welcome friend.
And she whispered to us: I'm going home,
And she smiled and closed her eyes.

And Death took her up like a baby,
And she lay in his icy arms,
But she didn't feel no chill.
And Death began to ride again—
Up beyond the evening star,
Out beyond the morning star,
Into the glittering light of glory,
On to the Great White Throne.
And there he laid Sister Caroline
On the loving breast of Jesus.

And Jesus took his own hand and wiped away her tears,
And he smoothed the furrows from her face,
And the angels sang a little song,
And Jesus rocked her in his arms,
And kept a-saying: Take your rest,
Take your rest, take your rest.

Weep not—weep not,
She is not dead;
She's resting in the bosom of Jesus.

Saint Peter Relates an Incident of the Resurrection Day

Eternities—now numbering six or seven—
Hung heavy on the hands of all in heaven.
Archangels tall and fair had reached the stage
Where they began to show some signs of age.

The faces of the flaming seraphim
Were slightly drawn, their eyes were slightly dim.
The cherubs, too, for now—oh, an infinite while
Had worn but a wistful shade of their dimpling smile.

The serried singers of the celestial choir
Disclosed a woeful want of pristine fire;
When they essayed to strike the glad refrain,
Their attack was weak, their tone revealed voice strain.

Their expression seemed to say, "We must! We must!" though
'Twas more than evident they lack the gusto;
It could not be elsewise—that fact all can agree on—
Chanting the selfsame choral aeon after aeon.
Thus it was that Saint Peter at the gate
Began a brand new thing in heaven: to relate
Some reminiscences from heavenly history,
Which had till then been more or less a mystery.

So now and then, by turning back the pages,
Were whiled away some moments from the ages,
Was gained a respite from the monotony
That can't help settling on eternity.

II

Now, there had been a lapse of ages hoary,
And the angels clamored for another story.
"Tell us a tale, Saint Peter," they entreated;
And gathered close around where he was seated.

Saint Peter stroked his beard,
And "Yes," he said
By the twinkle in his eye
And the nodding of his head.

A moment brief he fumbled with his keys—
It seemed to help him call up memories—
Straightway there flashed across his mind the one
About the unknown soldier
Who came from Washington.

The hosts stood listening,
Breathlessly awake;
And thus Saint Peter spake:

III

'Twas Resurrection morn,
And Gabriel blew a blast upon his horn
That echoed through the arches high and vast
Of Time and Space—a long resounding blast.

To wake the dead, dead for a million years;
A blast to reach and pierce their dust-stopped ears;
To quicken them, wherever they might be,
Deep in the earth or deeper in the sea.

A shudder shook the world, and gaping graves
Gave up their dead. Out from the parted waves
Came the prisoners of old ocean. The dead belonging
To every land and clime came thronging.

From the four corners of all the earth they drew,
Their faces radiant and their bodies new.
Creation pulsed and swayed beneath the tread
Of all the living, and all the risen dead.

Swift-winged heralds of heaven flew back and forth,
Out of the east, to the south, the west, the north,
Giving out quick commands, and yet benign,
Marshaling the swarming milliards into line.

The recording angel in words of thundering might,
At which the timid, doubting souls took fright,
Bade all to await the grand roll-call; to wit
To see if in the Book their names were writ.

The multitudinous business of the day
Progressed, but naturally, not without delay.
Meanwhile, within the great American border
There was the issuance of a special order.

IV

The word went forth, spoke by some grand panjandrum,
Perhaps, by some high potentate of Klandom,
That all the trusty patriotic mentors,
And duly qualified Hundred-Percenters

Should forthwith gather together upon the banks
Of the Potomac, there to form their ranks,
March to the tomb, by orders to be given,
And escort the unknown soldier up to heaven.

Compliantly they gathered from each region,
The G. A. R., the D. A. R., the Legion,
Veterans of wars—Mexican, Spanish, Haitian—
Trustees of the patriotism of the nation;

Key Men, Watchmen, shunning circumlocution,
The Sons of This and That and of the Revolution;
Not to forget, there gathered every man
Of the Confederate Veterans and the Ku-Klux Klan.

The Grand Imperial Marshal gave the sign;
Column on column, the marchers fell in line;
Majestic as an army in review,
They swept up Washington's wide avenue.

Then, through the long line ran a sudden flurry,
The marchers in the rear began to hurry;
They feared unless the procession hastened on,
The unknown soldier might be risen and gone.

The fear was groundless; when they arrived, in fact,
They found the grave entirely intact.
(Resurrection plans were long, long past completing
Ere there was thought of re-enforced concreting.)

They heard a faint commotion in the tomb,
Like the stirring of a child within the womb;
At once they saw the plight, and set about
The job to dig the unknown soldier out.

They worked away, they labored with a will,
They toiled with pick, with crowbar, and with drill
To cleave a breach; nor did the soldier shirk;
Within his limits, he helped to push the work.

He, underneath the debris, heaved and hove
Up toward the opening which they cleaved and clove;
Through it, at last, his towering form loomed big and bigger—
"Great God Almighty! Look!" they cried, "he is a nigger!"

Surprise and consternation and dismay
Swept over the crowd; none knew just what to say
Or what to do. And all fell back aghast.
Silence—but only an instant did it last.

Bedlam: They clamored, they railed, some roared, some bleated;
All of them felt somehow they'd been cheated.
The question rose: What to do with him, then?
The Klan was all for burying him again.

The scheme involved within the Klan's suggestion
Gave rise to a rather nice metaphysical question:
Could he be forced again through death's dark portal,
Since now his body and soul were both immortal?

Would he, forsooth, the curious-minded queried,
Even in concrete, re-entombed, stay buried?
In a moment more, midst the pile of broken stone,
The unknown soldier stood, and stood alone.

V

The day came to a close.
And heaven—hell too—was filled with them that rose.
I shut the pearly gate and turned the key;
For Time was now merged into Eternity.

I gave one last look over the jasper wall,
And afar described a figure dark and tall:
The unknown soldier, dust-stained and begrimed,
Climbing his way to heaven, and singing as he climbed:
    Deep river, my home is over Jordan,
    Deep river, I want to cross over into camp-ground.
Climbing and singing—
    Deep river, my home is over Jordan,
    Deep river, I want to cross over into camp-ground.
Nearer and louder—
    Deep river, my home is over Jordan,
    Deep river, I want to cross over into camp-ground.

At the jasper wall—
    Deep river, my home is over Jordan.
    Deep river,
    Lord,
    I want to cross over into camp-ground.

I rushed to the gate and flung it wide,
Singing, he entered with a loose, long stride;
Singing and swinging up the golden street,
The music married to the tramping of his feet.

Tall, black soldier—angel marching alone,
Swinging up the golden street, saluting at the great white throne.
Singing, singing, singing, singing, clear and strong.
Singing, singing, singing, till heaven took up the song:
  Deep river, my home is over Jordan,
  Deep river, I want to cross over into camp-ground.

VI

The tale was done,
The angelic hosts dispersed,
    but not till after
There ran through heaven
Something that quivered
    'twixt tears and laughter.

LESLIE PINCKNEY HILL (1880-   )

Born in Lynchburg, Virginia, and educated at Harvard, Leslie Pinckney Hill has had a varied experience as an educator. He is at present
principal of the Cheyney State Teachers College in Pennsylvania. Hill
has published two volumes: *The Wings of Oppression* (1921) and
Toussaint L'Ouverture—A Dramatic History (1928), a blank-verse
drama in five acts. "Tuskegee" and "So Quietly" appear in *Wings
of Oppression* (Stratford Co., Boston, 1921) and are reprinted by
permission of the publishers.

"So Quietly"

News item from the *New York Times* on the lynching of a Negro at Smithville,
Ga., December 21, 1919.
  "The train was boarded so quietly . . . that members of the train crew
did not know that the mob had seized the Negro until informed by the prisoner's
guard after the train had left the town. . . . . A coroner's inquest held immediately
returned the verdict that West came to his death at the hands of unidentified men."

        So quietly they stole upon their prey
        And dragged him out to death, so without flaw
        Their black design, that they to whom the law
        Gave him in keeping, in the broad, bright day,
        Were not aware when he was snatched away;
        And when the people, with a shrinking awe,
        The horror of that mangled body saw,
        "By unknown hands!" was all that they could say.

So, too, my country, stealeth on apace
The soul-blight of a nation. Not with drums
Or trumpet blare is that corruption sown,
But quietly—now in the open face
Of day, now in the dark—and when it comes,
Stern truth will never write, "By hands unknown."

Tuskegee

Wherefore this busy labor without rest?
Is it an idle dream to which we cling,
Here where a thousand dusky toilers sing
Unto the world their hope? "Build we our best.
By hand and thought," they cry, "although unblessed."
So the great engines throb, and anvils ring,
And so the thought is wedded to the thing;
But what shall be the end, and what the test?
Dear God, we dare not answer, we can see
Not many steps ahead, but this we know—
If all our toilsome building is in vain,
Availing not to set our manhood free,
If envious hate roots out the seed we sow,
The South will wear eternally a stain.

GEORGIA DOUGLASS JOHNSON (1886-   )

Georgia Douglass Johnson was the first Negro woman after Frances
Harper to gain general recognition as a poet. Born in Atlanta, Georgia,
she was educated at Atlanta University and at Oberlin. At present she
lives in Washington, D. C. Mrs. Johnson has published three volumes
of poems: *The Heart of a Woman* (1918). *Bronze* (1922), and *An
Autumn Love Cycle* (1928). The poems included below are reprinted
by permission of the author.

The Heart of a Woman

The heart of a woman goes forth with the dawn,
As a lone bird, soft winging, so restlessly on,
Afar. o'er life's turrets and vales does it roam
In the wake of those echoes the heart calls home.

The heart of a woman falls back with the night,
And enters some alien cage in its plight,
And tries to forget it has dreamed of the stars
While it breaks, breaks, breaks on the sheltering bars.

The Suppliant

Long have I beat with timid hands upon life's leaden
    door,
Praying the patient, futile prayer my fathers prayed
    before,
Yet I remain without the close, unheeded and unheard,
And never to my listening ear is borne the waited word.

Soft o'er the threshold of the years there comes this
    counsel cool:
The strong demand, contend, prevail; the beggar is a
    fool!

I Closed My Shutters Fast Last Night

I closed my shutters fast last night,
Reluctantly and slow,
So pleading was the purple sky
With all the lights hung low;
I left my lagging heart outside
Within the dark alone,
I heard it singing through the gloom
A wordless, anguished tone.
Upon my sleepless couch I lay
Until the tranquil morn
Came through the silver silences
To bring my heart forlorn,
Restoring it with calm caress
Unto its sheltered bower,
While whispering: "Await, await
Your golden, perfect hour."

I Want to Die While You Love Me

I want to die while you love me,
    While yet you hold me fair,
While laughter lies upon my lips
    And lights are in my hair.

I want to die while you love me
    And bear to that still bed
Your kisses—turbulent, unspent,
    To warm me when I'm dead.

I want to die while you love me,
Oh, who would care to live,
'Til love has nothing more to ask
And nothing more to give?

I want to die while you love me,
And never, never see
The glory of this perfect day
Grow dim, or cease to be!

ANGELINA W. GRIMKÉ (1880-   )

Born in Boston, Angelina Weld Grimké (see also p. 804) was educated in various Northern schools, including the Girls' Latin School
and the Boston Normal School of Gymnastics. For a number of years
she taught English at Dunbar High School in Washington, D. C.
She is now living in New York City. Miss Grimké is the author
of *Rachel,* a problem drama produced in 1916 and published in 1921,
but her poems have never been collected. The poems included below
are reprinted by permission of the author.

Hushed By the Hands of Sleep
(To *Dr. George F. Grant*)

I

Hushed by the hands of Sleep,
By the beautiful hands of Sleep.
Very gentle and quiet he lies,
With a little smile of sweet surprise,
Just softly hushed at lips and eyes,
Hushed by the hands of Sleep,
By the beautiful hands of Sleep.

II

Hushed by the hands of Sleep,
By the beautiful hands of Sleep.
Death leaned down as his eyes grew dim,
And his face, I know, was not strange, not grim,
But oh! it was beautiful to him,
Hushed by the hands of Sleep,
By the beautiful hands of Sleep.

Surrender

We ask for peace. We, at the bound
O life, are weary of the round
In search of Truth. We know the quest
Is not for us, the vision blest
Is meant for other eyes. Uncrowned,
We go, with heads bowed to the ground,
And old hands, gnarled and hard and browned.
Let us forget the past unrest,—
        We ask for peace.

Our strainéd ears are deaf,—no sound
May reach them more; no sight may wound
Our worn-out eyes. We gave our best,
And, while we totter down the West,
Unto that last, that open mound,—
        We ask for peace.

When the Green Lies Over the Earth

When the green lies over the earth, my dear,
A mantle of witching grace,
When the smile and the tear of the young child year
Dimple across its face,
And then flee, when the wind all day is sweet
With the breath of growing things,
When the wooing bird lights on restless feet
And chirrups and trills and sings
        To his lady-love
        In the green above,
Then oh! my dear, when the youth's in the year,
Yours is the face that I long to have near,
        Yours is the face, my dear.

But the green is hiding your curls, my dear,
Your curls so shining and sweet;
And the gold-hearted daisies this many a year
Have bloomed and bloomed at your feet,
And the little birds just above your head
With their voices hushed, my dear,
For you have sung and have prayed and have pled
        This many, many a year.

And the blossoms fall,
On the garden wall,
And drift like snow on the green below.
But the sharp thorn grows
On the budding rose,
And my heart no more leaps at the sunset glow.
For oh! my dear, when the youth's in the year,
Yours is the face that I long to have near,
Yours is the face, my dear.

A Winter Twilight

A silence slipping around like death,
Yet chased by a whisper, a sigh, a breath;
One group of trees, lean, naked and cold,
Inking their crests 'gainst a sky green-gold;
One path that knows where the corn flowers were;
Lonely, apart, unyielding, one fir;
And over it softly leaning down,
One star that I loved ere the fields went brown.

JOSEPH SEAMON COTTER, SR. (1861-   )

Joseph Seamon Cotter, Sr., was born in the historic year, 1861, at the historic Bardstown, Kentucky, where Stephen Foster wrote "My Old Kentucky Home." He was forced to leave school in the third grade. Before he could return to his schooling at the age of twenty-two, he had worked as ragpicker, tobacco stemmer, brickyard hand, whiskey distiller, teamster, and prize fighter. When he did complete his education, he became a schoolteacher in Louisville. In 1938, as he writes in the dedication of his *Collected Poems*, he was elected by the Louisville Board of Education to serve as teacher and principal for his fiftieth year. He has been a great educational influence. Some of his poetry is that of the schoolmaster, some that of the teller of tales for children, some that of the race leader. His dialect poetry, though in the Dunbar tradition phonetically, is more racially critical than Dunbar's. His earliest work, *A Rhyming* (1895), is contemporary with Dunbar's poetry; his modern "Tragedy of Pete" won a prize in an *Opportunity* prize contest in the twenties; his *Collected Poems* appeared in 1938. The following is reprinted by permission of *Opportunity: Journal of Negro Life.*

The Tragedy of Pete

There was a man
    Whose name was Pete,
And he was a buck
    From his head to his feet.

He loved a dollar,
    But hated a dime;
And so was poor
    Nine-tenths of the time.

The judge said "Pete,
    What of your wife?"
And Pete replied
    "She lost her life."

"Pete," said the Judge,
    "Was it lost in a row?
Tell me quick,
    And tell me how."

Pete straightened up
    With a hic and a sigh,
Then looked the Judge
    Full in the eye.

"O, Judge, my wife
    Would never go
To a Sunday dance
    Or a movie show.

"But I went, Judge,
    Both day and night,
And came home broke
    And also tight.

"The moon was up,
    My purse was down,
And I was the bully
    Of the bootleg town.

"I was crooning a lilt
    To corn and rye
For the loop in my legs
    And the fight in my eye.

"I met my wife;
    She was wearing a frown,
And catechising
    Her Sunday gown.

" 'O Pete, O Pete'
    She cried aloud,
'The Devil is falling
    Right out of a cloud.'

"I looked straight up
    And fell flat down
And a Ford machine
    Pinned my head to the ground.

"The Ford moved on,
    And my wife was in it;
And I was sober,
    That very minute.

"For my head was bleeding,
    My heart was a-flutter;
And the moonshine within me
    Was tipping the gutter.

"The Ford, it faster
    And faster sped
Till it dipped and swerved
    And my wife was dead.

"Two bruised men lay
    In a hospital ward—
One seeking vengeance,
    The other the Lord.

"He said to me:
    'Your wife was drunk,
You are crazy,
    And my Ford is junk.'

"I raised my knife
    And drove it in
At the top of his head
    And the point of his chin.

"O Judge, O Judge,
        If the State has a chair,
Please bind me in it
        And roast me there."

There was a man
        Whose name was Pete,
And he welcomed death
        From his head to his feet.

JOSEPH SEAMON COTTER, JR. (1895-1919)

The precocious son of a well-known father, the young Cotter was
born in Louisville, Kentucky, September 2, 1895. Delicate from childhood, he had to end his college career at Fisk in his second year
when he developed tuberculosis. In 1918 Cotter published a thin
volume of thirty pages entitled *The Band of Gideon*. For a boy of
twenty-three this work showed great promise. The following are
reprinted by permission of the Cornhill Publishing Company.

And What Shall You Say?

Brother, come!
And let us go unto our God.
And when we stand before Him
I shall say—
"Lord, I do not hate,
I am hated.
I scourge no one,
I am scourged.
I covet no lands,
My lands are coveted.
I mock no peoples,
My people are mocked."
And, brother, what shall you say?

Rain Music

On the dusty earth-drum
        Beats the falling rain;
Now a whispered murmur,
        Now a louder strain.

Slender, silvery drumsticks,
On an ancient drum,
Beat the mellow music
Bidding life to come.

Chords of earth awakened,
Notes of greening spring,
Rise and fall triumphant
Over every thing.

Slender, silvery drumsticks
Beat the long tattoo—
God, the Great Musician,
Calling life anew.

FENTON JOHNSON (1888-   )

Fenton Johnson was born in Chicágo and educated in the public
schools of that city and at the University of Chicago. At nineteen
he produced some of his original plays at the old Pekin Theater in
his native city. His first volume of poems, *A Little Dreaming,* was
published in 1914. In 1915 appeared *Visions of the Dusk,* and one year
later, *Songs of the Soil.* He has also edited magazines and published
a volume of short stories, *Tales of Darkest America* (1920). His
works have appeared in numerous anthologies of American poetry.
Fenton Johnson writes in two traditions. Most of his earlier poetry
was influenced by the spirituals and by the dialect school; his later
poems, written under the influence of Sandburg and Masters, are
his most significant work. The following are reprinted by permission
of the author.

Tired

I am tired of work; I am tired of building up somebody
    else's civilization.
Let us take a rest, M'Lissy Jane.
I will go down to the Last Chance Saloon, drink a gallon
    or two of gin, shoot a game or two of dice and
    sleep the rest of the night on one of Mike's barrels.
You will let the old shanty go to rot, the white people's
    clothes turn to dust, and the Calvary Baptist Church
    sink to the bottomless pit.
You will spend your days forgetting you married me and
    your nights hunting the warm gin Mike serves the
    ladies in the rear of the Last Chance Saloon.

Throw the children into the river; civilization has given
    us too many. It is better to die than to grow up
    and find that you are colored.
Pluck the stars out of the heavens. The stars mark our
    destiny. The stars marked my destiny.
I am tired of civilization.

The Scarlet Woman

Once I was good like the Virgin Mary and the Minister's wife.
My father worked for Mr. Pullman and white people's tips;
    but he died two days after his insurance expired.
I had nothing, so I had to go to work.
All the stock I had was a white girl's education and a
    face that enchanted the men of both races.
Starvation danced with me.
So when Big Lizzie, who kept a house for white men,
    came to me with tales of fortune that I could reap
    from the sale of my virtue I bowed my head to Vice.
Now I can drink more gin than any man for miles around.
Gin is better than all the water in Lethe.

CLAUDE McKAY (1889-   )

Poet, novelist, short-story writer, Claude McKay (see also p. 196)
has been a versatile figure in the literary world. Born in the parish
of Clarendon in Jamaica, British West Indies, he was taught by his
freethinking brother, the schoolmaster of his home town. When he
was seventeen he won a Jamaica Government trade scholarship, but
after a short apprenticeship to a cabinetmaker, he joined the island
constabulary. In 1911 he published his first book, *Songs of Jamaica*.
Soon after he left the West Indies and came to America to study.
After a few months at Tuskegee, he left to study agriculture at Kansas
State University. He remained in Kansas two years. Inheriting a
legacy of a few thousand dollars, he came to New York and quickly
disposed of it through bad investments. He then went to work at
anything that came to hand, writing all the while. The year 1919
found him living abroad. In 1920 he published *Spring in New
Hampshire* while in London. On his return to America he become
associate editor under Max Eastman of the *Liberator*. *Harlem Shadows*,
his first American publication, came out in 1922. In the same year,
he visited Russia. In 1923 he lived in Berlin; leaving there he moved
to France, where he lived and wrote for several years. At present he
is back in New York City. The poems in this collection, with the

exception of "White Houses," are reprinted by permission of the
author and Harcourt, Brace, and Co., publishers of *Harlem Shadows*.
Permission to print "White Houses" was granted by the author and
the Survey Associates, publishers of *The Survey Graphic*.

Baptism

Into the furnace let me go alone;
Stay you without in terror of the heat.
I will go naked in—for thus 'tis sweet—
Into the weird depths of the hottest zone.
I will not quiver in the frailest bone,
You will not note a flicker of defeat;
My heart shall tremble not its fate to meet,
Nor mouth give utterance to any moan.
The yawning oven spits forth fiery spears;
Red aspish tongues shout wordlessly my name.
Desire destroys, consumes my mortal fears,
Transforming me into a shape of flame.
I will come out, back to your world of tears,
A stronger soul within a finer frame.

America

Although she feeds me bread of bitterness,
And sinks into my throat her tiger's tooth,
Stealing my breath of life, I will confess
I love this cultured hell that tests my youth!
Her vigor flows like tides into my blood,
Giving me strength against her hate.
Her bigness sweeps my being like a flood.
Yet as a rebel fronts a king in state,
I stand within her walls with not a shred
Of terror, malice, not a word of jeer.
Darkly I gaze into the days ahead,
And see her might and granite wonders there,
Beneath the touch of Time's unerring hand,
Like priceless treasures sinking in the sand.

White Houses

Your door is shut against my tightened face,
And I am sharp as steel with discontent;
But I possess the courage and the grace
To bear my anger proudly and unbent.

The pavement slabs burn loose beneath my feet,
A chafing savage, down the decent street;
And passion rends my vitals as I pass,
Where boldly shines your shuttered door of glass.
Oh, I must search for wisdom every hour,
Deep in my wrathful bosom sore and raw,
And find in it the superhuman power
To hold me to the letter of your law!
Oh, I must keep my heart inviolate
Against the potent poison of your hate.

If We Must Die

If we must die, let it not be like hogs
Hunted and penned in an inglorious spot,
While round us bark the mad and hungry dogs,
Making their mock at our accurséd lot.
If we must die, O let us nobly die,
So that our precious blood may not be shed
In vain; then even the monsters we defy
Shall be constrained to honor us though dead!
O kinsmen! we must meet the common foe!
Though far outnumbered let us show us brave,
And for their thousand blows deal one deathblow!
What though before us lies the open grave?
Like men we'll face the murderous, cowardly pack,
Pressed to the wall, dying, but fighting back!

The Lynching

His Spirit in smoke ascended to high heaven.
His father, by the cruelest way of pain,
Had bidden him to his bosom once again;
The awful sin remained still unforgiven.
All night a bright and solitary star
(Perchance the one that ever guided him,
Yet gave him up at last to Fate's wild whim)
Hung pitifully o'er the swinging char.
Day dawned, and soon the mixed crowds came to view
The ghastly body swaying in the sun:
The women thronged to look, but never a one
Showed sorrow in her eyes of steely blue;
And little lads, lynchers that were to be,
Danced round the dreadful thing in fiendish glee.

Flame-Heart

So much have I forgotten in ten years,
    So much in ten brief years! I have forgot
What time the purple apples come to juice,
    And what month brings the shy forget-me-not.
I have forgot the special, startling season
    Of the pimento's flowering and fruiting;
What time of year the ground doves brown the fields
    And fill the noonday with their curious fluting.
I have forgotten much, but still remember
The poinsettia's red, blood-red in warm December.

I still recall the honey-fever grass,
    But cannot recollect the high days when
We rooted them out of the ping-wing path
    To stop the mad bees in the rabbit pen.
I often try to think in what sweet month
    The languid painted ladies used to dapple
The yellow by-road mazing from the main,
    Sweet with the golden threads of the rose-apple.
I have forgotten—strange—but quite remember
The poinsettia's red, blood-red in warm December.

What weeks, what months, what time of the mild year
    We cheated school to have our fling at tops?
What days our wine-thrilled bodies pulsed with joy
    Feasting upon blackberries in the copse?
Oh some I know! I have embalmed the days,
    Even the sacred moments when we played,
All innocent of passion, uncorrupt,
    At noon and evening in the flame-heart's shade.
We were so happy, happy, I remember,
Beneath the poinsettia's red in warm December.

ANNE SPENCER (1882-   )

Anne Spencer was born in Bramwell, West Virginia, and was educated at Virginia Seminary in Lynchburg, Virginia, in which city she has spent practically all of her life. At present she is the librarian of the Dunbar High School there. Her poems have frequently appeared in anthologies, but have not yet been collected in a volume. The poems of Mrs. Spencer are reprinted by permission of the author.

Life-Long, Poor Browning . . .

Life-Long, poor Browning never knew Virginia,
Or he'd not grieved in Florence for April sallies
Back to English gardens after Euclid's linear:
Clipt yews, Pomander Walks, and pleachéd alleys;

Primroses, prim indeed, in quiet ordered hedges,
Waterways, soberly, sedately enchanneled,
No thin riotous blade even among the sedges,
All the wild country-side tamely impaneled . . .

Dead, now, dear Browning, lives on in heaven,—
(Heaven's Virginia when the year's at its Spring)
He's haunting the byways of wine-aired leaven
And throating the notes of the wildings on wing;

Here canopied reaches of dogwood and hazel,
Beech tree and redbud fine-laced in vines,
Fleet clapping rills by lush fern and basil,
Drain blue hills to lowlands scented with pines . . .

Think you he meets in this tender green sweetness
Shade that was Elizabeth . . . immortal completeness!

At the Carnival

Gay little Girl-of-the-Diving-Tank,
I desire a name for you,
Nice, as a right glove fits;
For you—who amid the malodorous
Mechanics of this unlovely thing,
Are darling of spirit and form.
I know you—a glance, and what you are
Sits-by-the-fire in my heart.
My Limousine-Lady knows you, or
Why does the slant-envy of her eye mark
Your straight air and radiant inclusive smile?
Guilt pins a fig-leaf; Innocence is its own adorning.
The bull-necked man knows you—this first time
His itching flesh sees form divine and vibrant health
And thinks not of his avocation.
I came incuriously—
Set on no diversion save that my mind
Might safely nurse its brood of misdeeds
In the presence of a blind crowd.

The color of life was gray.
Everywhere the setting seemed right
For my mood.
Here the sausage and garlic booth
Sent unholy incense skyward;
There a quivering female-thing
Gestured assignations, and lied
To call it dancing;
There, too, were games of chance
With chances for none;
But oh! Girl-of-the-Tank, at last!
Gleaming Girl, how intimately pure and free
The gaze you send the crowd,
As though you know the dearth of beauty
In its sordid life.
We need you—my Limousine-Lady,
The bull-necked man and I.
Seeing you here brave and water-clean,
Leaven for the heavy ones of earth,
I am swift to feel that what makes
The plodder glad is good; and
Whatever is good is God.
The wonder is that you are here;
I have seen the queer in queer places,
But never before a heaven-fed
Naiad of the Carnival-Tank!
Little Diver, Destiny for you,
Like as for me, is shod in silence;
Years may seep into your soul
The bacilli of the usual and the expedient;
I implore Nepture to claim his child to-day!

Before the Feast of Shushan

Garden of Shushan!
After Eden, all terrace, pool, and flower recollect thee:
Ye weavers in saffron and haze and Tyrian purple,
Tell yet what range in color wakes the eye;
Sorcerer, release the dreams born here when
Drowsy, shifting palm-shade enspells the brain;
And sound! ye with harp and flute ne'er essay
Before these star-noted birds escaped from paradise awhile
  to
Stir all dark, and dear, and passionate desire, till mine

Arms go out to be mocked by the softly kissing body of
    the wind—
Slave, send Vashti to her King!

The fiery wattles of the sun startle into flame
The marbled towers of Shushan:
So at each day's wane, two peers—the one in
Heaven, the other on earth—welcome with their
Splendor the peerless beauty of the Queen.

Cushioned at the Queen's feet and upon her knee
Finding glory for mine head,—still, nearly shamed
Am I, the King, to bend and kiss with sharp
Breath the olive-pink of sandaled toes between;
Or lift me high to the magnet of a gaze, dusky,
Like the pool when but the moon-ray strikes to its depth;
Or closer press to crush a grape 'gainst lips redder
Than the grape, a rose in the night of her hair;
Then—Sharon's Rose in my arms.

And I am hard to force the petals wide;
And you are fast to suffer and be sad.
Is any prophet come to teach a new thing
Now in a more apt time?
Have him 'maze how you say love is sacrament;
How says Vashti, love is both bread and wine;
How to the altar may not come to break and drink,
Hulky flesh nor fleshly spirit!

I, thy lord, like not manna for meat as a Judahn;
I, thy master, drink, and red wine, plenty, and when
I thirst. Eat meat, and full, when I hunger.
I, thy King, teach you and leave you, when I list.
No woman in all Persia sets out strange action
To confuse Persia's lord—
Love is but desire and thy purpose fulfillment;
I, thy King, so say!

Lines to a Nasturtium
(A lover muses)

Flame-flower, Day-torch, Mauna Loa,
I saw a daring bee, today, pause and soar,
    Into your flaming heart;
Then did I hear crisp, crinkled laughter

As the furies after tore him apart?
   A bird, next, small and humming,
Looked into your startled depths and fled . . .
Surely, some dread sight, and dafter
   Than human eyes as mine can see,
Set the stricken air waves drumming
   In his flight.

Day-torch, Flame-flower, cool-hot Beauty,
I cannot see, I cannot hear your flutey
Voice lure your loving swain,
But I know one other to whom you are in beauty
Born in vain:
Hair like the setting sun,
Her eyes a rising star,
Motions gracious as reeds by Babylon, bar
All your competing;
Hands like, how like, brown lilies sweet,
Cloth of gold were fair enough to touch her feet . . .
Ah, how the sense floods at my repeating,
As once in her fire-lit heart I felt the furies
Beating, beating.

JEAN TOOMER (1894-)

Jean Toomer (see also p. 41) has contributed to several magazines,
most of them experimental, such as *The Dial, Double Dealer, Broom,
Little Review, S4N, The Liberator, The Crisis,* and *Prairie*. One of
his most recent poems, "Blue Meridian," appeared in *The New Caravan* 1936). The following two poems are taken from *Cane* and are
reprinted by the permission of the author and the Horace Liveright
Publishing Corporation.

Song of the Son

Pour O pour that parting soul in song,
O pour it in the saw-dust glow of night,
Into the velvet pine-smoke air to-night,
And let the valley carry it along.
And let the valley carry it along.

O land and soil, red soil and sweet-gum tree,
So scant of grass, so profligate of pines,
Now just before an epoch's sun declines

Thy son, in time, I have returned to thee,
Thy son, I have, in time, returned to thee.

In time, for though the sun is setting on
A song-lit race of slaves, it has not set;
Though late, O soil, it is not too late yet
To catch thy plaintive soul, leaving, soon gone,
Leaving, to catch thy plaintive soul soon gone.

O Negro slaves, dark purple ripened plums,
Squeezed, and bursting in the pine-wood air,
Passing, before they strip the old tree bare
One plum was saved for me, one seed becomes

An everlasting song, a singing tree,
Caroling softly souls of slavery,
What they were, and what they are to me,
Caroling softly souls of slavery.

Georgia Dusk

The sky, lazily disdaining to pursue
    The setting sun, too indolent to hold
    A lengthened tournament for flashing gold,
Passively darkens for night's barbecue,

A feast of moon and men and barking hounds,
    An orgy for some genius of the South
    With blood-hot eyes and cane-lipped scented mouth,
Surprised in making folk-songs from soul-sounds.

The sawmill blows its whistle, buzz-saws stop,
    And silence breaks the bud of knoll and hill,
    Soft settling pollen where plowed lands fulfill
Their early promise of a bumper crop.

Smoke from the pyramidal sawdust pile
    Curls up, blue ghosts of trees, tarrying low
    Where only chips and stumps are left to show
The solid proof of former domicile.

Meanwhile, the men, with vestiges of pomp,
    Race memories of king and caravan,
    High-priests, an ostrich, and a juju-man,
Go singing through the footpaths of the swamp.

Their voices rise . . . the pine trees are guitars,
   Strumming, pine-needles fall like sheets of rain . . .
   Their voices rise . . . the chorus of the cane
Is caroling a vesper to the stars . . .

O singers, resinous and soft your songs
   Above the sacred whisper of the pines,
   Give virgin lips to cornfield concubines,
Bring dreams of Christ to dusky cane-lipped throngs.

COUNTEE CULLEN (1903-   )

Countee Cullen's metrical skill attracted attention even when he was
a high school student; as a student at New York University he won
the Witter Bynner Poetry Prize for undergraduates in American
colleges. He received his master's degree from Harvard in 1926. At
present he is a teacher in the New York public schools. In 1925, when
the poet was only twenty-two years old, his first volume, *Color,*
appeared, winning the Harmon Gold Award for literature as well as
great critical acclaim. His other volumes are *The Ballad of the Brown
Girl* (1927); *Copper Sun* (1927); *The Black Christ* (1929), written
while on a Guggenheim Fellowship; *One Way to Heaven* (1932), a
novel: *The Medea and Other Poems* (1935), and *The Lost Zoo*
(1940). Cullen served as assistant editor of *Opportunity,* and in
1927 edited *Caroling Dusk,* an anthology of verse by Negroes. Of
the poems included, "Heritage," "To John Keats," "Incident," and
"A Brown Girl Dead" come from *Color;* "From the Dark Tower"
and "Youth Sings a Song of Rosebuds" are from *Copper Sun.* All
are reprinted by permission of the author and Harper and Brothers.

Heritage

What is Africa to me:
Copper sun or scarlet sea,
Jungle star or jungle track,
Strong bronzed men, or regal black
Women from whose loins I sprang
When the birds of Eden sang?
*One three centuries removed
From the scenes his fathers loved,
Spicy grove, cinnamon tree,
What is Africa to me?*

So I lie, who all day long
Want no sound except the song

Sung by wild barbaric birds
Goading massive jungle herds,
Juggernauts of flesh that pass
Trampling tall defiant grass
Where young forest lovers lie
Plighting troth beneath the sky.
So I lie, who always hear
Though I cram against my ear
Both my thumbs, and keep them there,
Great drums beating through the air.
So I lie, whose fount of pride,
Dear distress, and joy allied,
Is my sombre flesh and skin,
With the dark blood dammed within
Like great pulsing tides of wine
That, I fear, must burst the fine
Channels of the chafing net
Where they surge and foam and fret.

Africa? A book one thumbs
Listlessly, till slumber comes.
Unremembered are her bats
Circling through the night, her cats
Crouching in the river reeds,
Stalking gentle flesh that feeds
By the river brink; no more
Does the bugle-throated roar
Cry that monarch claws have leapt
From the scabbards where they slept.
Silver snakes that once a year
Doff the lovely coats you wear,
Seek no covert in your fear
Lest a mortal eye should see;
What's your nakedness to me?
Here no leprous flowers rear
Fierce corollas in the air;
Here no bodies sleek and wet,
Dripping mingled rain and sweat,
Tread the savage measures of
Jungle boys and girls in love.
What is last year's snow to me,
Last year's anything? The tree
Budding yearly must forget
How its past arose or set—
Bough and blossom, flower, fruit,
Even what shy bird with mute

Wonder at her travail there,
Meekly labored in its hair.
One three centuries removed
From the scenes his fathers loved,
Spicy grove, cinnamon tree,
What is Africa to me?

So I lie, who find no peace
Night or day, no slight release
From the unremittent beat
Made by cruel padded feet
Walking through my body's street.
Up and down they go, and back,
Treading out a jungle track.
So I lie, who never quite
Safely sleep from rain at night—
I can never rest at all
When the rain begins to fall;
Like a soul gone mad with pain
I must match its weird refrain;
Ever must I twist and squirm,
Writhing like a baited worm,
While its primal measures drip
Through my body, crying, "Strip!
Doff this new exuberance.
Come and dance the Lover's Dance!"
In an old remembered way
Rain works on me night and day.

Quaint, outlandish heathen gods
Black men fashion out of rods,
Clay, and brittle bits of stone,
In a likeness like their own,
My conversion came high-priced;
I belong to Jesus Christ,
Preacher of humility;
Heathen gods are naught to me.

Father, Son, and Holy Ghost,
So I make an idle boast,
Jesus of the twice turned cheek,
Lamb of God, although I speak
With my mouth thus, in my heart
Do I play a double part.
Ever at thy glowing altar
Must my heart grow sick and falter,

Wishing He I served were black,
Thinking then it would not lack
Precedent of pain to guide it,
Let who would or might deride it;
Surely then this flesh would know
Yours had borne a kindred woe.
Lord, I fashion dark gods, too,
Daring even to give to You
Dark despairing features where,
Crowned with dark rebellious hair,
Patience wavers just so much as
Mortal grief compels, while touches
Quick and hot, of anger, rise
To smitten cheek and weary eyes.
Lord, forgive me if my need
Sometimes shapes a human creed.

All day long and all night through,
One thing only must I do:
Quench my pride and cool my blood,
Lest I perish in the flood.
Lest a hidden ember set
Timber that I thought was wet
Burning like the dryest flax,
Melting like the merest wax,
Lest the grave restore its dead.
Not yet has my heart or head
In the least way realized
They and I are civilized.

To John Keats, Poet. At Springtime

I cannot hold my peace, John Keats;
There never was a spring like this;
It is an echo, that repeats
My last year's song and next year's bliss.
I know, in spite of all men say
Of Beauty, you have felt her most.
Yea, even in your grave her way
Is laid. Poor, troubled, lyric ghost,
Spring never was so fair and dear
As Beauty makes her seem this year.

I cannot hold my peace, John Keats,
I am as helpless in the toil
Of Spring as any lamb that bleats

To feel the solid earth recoil
Beneath his puny legs. Spring beats
Her tocsin call to those who love her,
And lo! the dogwood petals cover
Her breasts with drifts of snow, and sleek
White gulls fly screaming to her, and hover
About her shoulders, and kiss her cheek,
While white and purple lilacs muster
A strength that bears them to a cluster
Of color and odor; for her sake
All things that slept are now awake.

And you and I, shall we lie still,
John Keats, while Beauty summons us?
Somehow I feel your sensitive will
Is pulsing up some tremulous
Sap road of a maple tree, whose leaves
Grow music as they grow, since your
Wild voice is in them, a harp that grieves
For life that opens death's dark door.
Though dust, your fingers still can push
The Vision Splendid to a birth,
Though now they work as grass in the hush
Of the night on the broad sweet page of the earth.

"John Keats is dead," they say, but I
Who hear your full insistent cry
In bud and blossom, leaf and tree,
Know John Keats still writes poetry.
And while my head is earthward bowed
To read new life sprung from your shroud,
Folks seeing me must think it strange
That merely spring should so derange
My mind. They do not know that you,
John Keats, keep revel with me, too.

Incident

Once riding in Old Baltimore,
  Heart-filled, head-filled with glee,
I saw a Baltimorean
  Keep looking straight at me.

Now I was eight and very small,
  And he was no whit bigger,

And so I smiled, but he poked out
　　His tongue and called me, "Nigger."

I saw the whole of Baltimore
　　From May until December;
Of all the things that happened there
　　That's all that I remember.

A Brown Girl Dead

With two white roses on her breasts,
　　White candles at head and feet,
Dark Madonna of the grave she rests;
　　Lord Death has found her sweet.

Her mother pawned her wedding ring
　　To lay her out in white;
She'd be so proud she'd dance and sing
　　To see herself tonight.

From the Dark Tower

We shall not always plant while others reap
The golden increment of bursting fruit,
Not always countenance, abject and mute,
That lesser men should hold their brothers cheap;
Not everlastingly while others sleep
Shall we beguile their limbs with mellow flute,
Not always bend to some more subtle brute;
We were not made eternally to weep.

The night whose sable breast relieves the stark
White stars is no less lovely being dark,
And there are buds that cannot bloom at all
In light, but crumple, piteous, and fall;
So in the dark we hide the heart that bleeds,
And wait, and tend our agonizing seeds.

Youth Sings a Song of Rosebuds
(To *Roberta*)

Since men grow diffident at last,
And care no whit at all,
If spring be come, or the fall be past,
Or how the cool rains fall,

I come to no flower but I pluck,
I raise no cup but I sip,
For a mouth is the best of sweets to suck;
The oldest wine's on the lip.

If I grow old in a year or two,
And come to the querulous song
Of "Alack and aday" and "This was true,
And that, when I was young,"

I must have sweets to remember by,
Some blossom saved from the mire,
Some death-rebellious ember I
Can fan into a fire.

GEORGE LEONARD ALLEN (1905-1935)

Born in Lumberton, North Carolina, Allen was educated in the public schools of his home town and at Johnson C. Smith University. After a brief career as a teacher, Allen died prematurely in 1935. His verses have appeared in *Opportunity, American Life, The South-western Christian Advocate,* and *The Lyric West.* In 1927, Allen's poem, "To Melody," won first prize in a state-wide poetry contest conducted by the North Carolina chapter of the United Daughters of the Confederacy. It is reprinted by permission of Countee Cullen, editor of *Caroling Dusk,* and Harper and Brothers; "Pilate in Modern America" is reprinted from *The Church School Journal.*

Pilate In Modern America

Lord, 'twas not I that slew my guiltless brother
    Without a cause, save that his skin was black!
Not my fierce hate, but that of many another
    Stole what man's puny strength cannot give back!
My hands are clean. Though it was in my city,
    To what avail could I have said a word
For him, or given aught but helpless pity?
    How, in that crowd, could one man's voice be heard?

Why am I troubled still? With those who trifle
    With human life—God's gift—I have no part.
And yet, try as I will, I cannot stifle
    The voice that whispers, deep within my heart,
"Though thou has sworn the sin is theirs alone,
Their guilt is no whit greater than thine own."

To Melody

The hands of man hath wrought no beauteous thing
More lovely than a glorious melody
That soars aloft in splendor, full and free,
And graceful as a swallow on the wing!
A melody that seems to move, and sing
And quiver, in its radiant ecstasy,
That bends and rises, like a slender tree
Which sways before the warm, sweet winds of spring!
Ah, men will ever love thee, holy art!
For thou, of all the blessings God hath given,
Canst best revive and cheer the wounded heart,
And nearest bring the weary soul to Heaven.
Of all God's precious gifts, it seems to me,
The choicest is the gift of Melody.

JONATHAN BROOKS (1904-)

Jonathan Brooks was born on a farm "twelve miles southwest of
Lexington, Mississippi." His father and mother parting, Jonathan
stayed with the latter, and the two of them worked in the community on "half shares" until he was fourteen. The mother had
somehow saved enough money to send him to Jackson College for
four months. While there he won the first prize in a short-story
contest with his entry, "The Bible in the Cotton Field." With frequent interruptions to farm and to teach, Brooks finally made his
way through high school at Lincoln University (Missouri). From
there he went to college at Tougaloo, Mississippi. His uncollected
poems show him to be of a deeply religious nature. The following is
reprinted by permission of the author.

The Resurrection

His friends went off and left Him dead
In Joseph's subterranean bed,
Embalmed with myrrh and sweet aloes,
And wrapped in snow-white burial clothes.

Then shrewd men came and set a seal
Upon His grave, lest thieves should steal
His lifeless form away, and claim
For Him an undeserving fame.

"There is no use," the soldiers said,
"Of standing sentries by the dead."
Wherefore, they drew their cloaks around
Themselves, and fell upon the ground,
And slept like dead men, all night through,
In the pale moonlight and chilling dew.

A muffled whiff of sudden breath
Ruffled the passive air of death.

He woke, and raised Himself in bed;
   Recalled how He was crucified;
Touched both hands' fingers to His head,
   And lightly felt His fresh-healed side.

Then with a deep, triumphant sigh,
He coolly put His grave-clothes by—
Folded the sweet, white winding sheet,
   The toweling, the linen bands,
   The napkin, all with careful hands—
And left the borrowed chamber neat.

His steps were like the breaking day:
   So soft across the watch He stole,
   He did not wake a single soul,
Nor spill one dewdrop by the way.

Now Calvary was loveliness:
   Lilies that flowered thereupon
Pulled off the white moon's pallid dress,
   And put the morning's vesture on.

"Why seek the living among the dead?
He is not here," the angel said.

The early winds took up the words,
And bore them to the lilting birds,
The leafing trees, and everything
That breathed the living breath of spring.

The Last Quarter Moon of the Dying Year

The last quarter moon of the dying year,
Pendant behind a naked cottonwood tree
On a frosty, dawning morning
With the back of her silver head

Turned to the waking sun.
Quiet like the waters
Of Galilee
After the Lord had bid them
"Peace, be still."
O silent beauty, indescribable!

Dead, do they say?
Would God that I shall seem
So beautiful in death.

LANGSTON HUGHES (1902-   )

The best-known and most versatile writer produced by the New
Negro movement, Langston Hughes (see also pp. 89, 224) has
lived a life which is a modern odyssey. He has rubbed shoulders
with all kinds of people in all corners of Africa, Asia, Europe, and
America. In poem, novel, short story, drama, essay, and autobiography
he has recorded his wide, adventurous experience.

Hughes was born in Joplin, Missouri, in 1902. Because of the separation of his parents his childhood was spent in several places. Part
of the time he lived in Lawrence, Kansas, with his maternal grandmother, the widow of Lewis Sheridan Leary, one of the five Negroes
with John Brown at Harper's Ferry (see p. 641). Moving to Cleveland when he was fourteen, he finished high school there. After
graduation, he lived for fifteen months with his father in Mexico. It
was at this time that he wrote his first published poem, "The Negro
Speaks of Rivers." In 1921 Hughes matriculated at Columbia University. He remained in school a full year, but breaking with his
father, he went on "his own." Working on freight steamers, he saw
West Africa and Europe. He spent the winter of 1924 in Paris, working as doorman and second cook in Montmartre cabarets. Then followed a summer in Italy. He spent a year in Washington, working
first in Carter Woodson's office and later as bus boy at Wardman
Park Hotel, where he was "discovered" by Vachel Lindsay. In
1925 he won first prize in the *Opportunity* poetry contest. Hughes
completed his formal education at Lincoln University, where he was
graduated in 1929. While there he won the Witter Bynner Prize for
undergraduate poetry and wrote his novel, *Not Without Laughter*.
Since then he has traveled to Russia and to Loyalist Spain during
the Civil War. He has published numerous plays, poems, and one
section of his autobiography, *The Big Sea* (1940). He won the
Harmon Award in 1931 and a Guggenheim Fellowship in 1935.
Among Hughes' published works are the following volumes of poetry:
The Weary Blues (1926), *Fine Clothes to the Jew* (1927), *Dear Lovely*

Death (1931), *The Dream Keeper* (1932), *and A New Song* (1938). His next volume, scheduled to appear in 1941, is entitled *Shakespeare in Harlem*. Separate pieces have appeared in many of the important dailies, periodicals, and anthologies of the nation. Of the poems included below, "The Negro Speaks of Rivers," "The Weary Blues," "To Midnight Nan at Leroy's," and "Minstrel Man" come from *The Weary Blues;* "Young Gal's Blues" and "Song for a Dark Girl" are from *Fine Clothes;* "Let America Be America Again" from *A New Song*. All are reprinted by permission of the author, of Alfred A. Knopf, publisher of *The Big Sea, The Weary Blues,* and *Fine Clothes to the Jew,* and of the International Workers Order, publishers of *A New Song*.

The Negro Speaks of Rivers
(To W. E. B. DuBois)

I've known rivers:
I've known rivers ancient as the world and older than the
    flow of human blood in human veins.

My soul has grown deep like the rivers.

I bathed in the Euphrates when dawns were young.
I built my hut near the Congo and it lulled me to sleep.
I looked upon the Nile and raised the pyramids above it.
I heard the singing of the Mississippi when Abe Lincoln
    went down to New Orleans, and I've seen its muddy
    bosom turn all golden in the sunset.

I've known rivers:
Ancient, dusky rivers.

My soul has grown deep like the rivers.

The Weary Blues

Droning a drowsy syncopated tune,
Rocking back and forth to a mellow croon,
    I heard a Negro play.
Down on Lenox Avenue the other night
By the pale dull pallor of an old gas light
        He did a lazy sway . . . .
        He did a lazy sway . . . .
To the tune o' those Weary Blues.

With his ebony hands on each ivory key
He made that poor piano moan with melody.
  O Blues!
Swaying to and fro on his rickety stool
He played that sad raggy tune like a musical fool.
  Sweet Blues!
Coming from a black man's soul.
  O Blues!
In a deep song voice with a melancholy tone
I heard that Negro sing, that old piano moan—
  "Ain't got nobody in all this world,
  Ain't got nobody but ma self.
  I's gwine to quit ma frownin'
  And put ma troubles on the shelf."
Thump, thump, thump, went his foot on the floor.
He played a few chords then he sang some more—
  "I got the Weary Blues
  And I can't be satisfied.
  Got the Weary Blues
  And can't be satisfied—
  I ain't happy no mo'
  And I wish that I had died."
And far into the night he crooned that tune.
The stars went out and so did the moon.
The singer stopped playing and went to bed
While the Weary Blues echoed through his head.
He slept like a rock or a man that's dead.

To Midnight Nan at Leroy's

Strut and wiggle,
Shameless gal.
Wouldn't no good fellow
Be your pal.

Hear dat music. . . .
Jungle night.
Hear dat music. . . .
And the moon was white.

Sing your Blues song,
Pretty baby.
You want lovin'
And you don't mean maybe.

Jungle lover. . . .
Night black boy. . . .
Two against the moon
And the moon was joy.

Strut and wiggle,
Shameless Nan.
Wouldn't no good fellow
Be your man.

Young Gal's Blues

I'm gonna walk to de graveyard
'Hind ma friend, Miss Cora Lee.
Gonna walk to de graveyard
'Hind ma dear friend Cora Lee.
Cause when I'm dead some
Body'll have to walk behind me.

I'm going to de po' house
To see ma old Aunt Clew.
Goin' to de po' house
To see ma old Aunt Clew.
When I'm old an' ugly
I'll want to see somebody, too.

De po' house is lonely
An' de grave is cold.
O, de po' house is lonely,
De graveyard grave is cold.
But I'd rather be dead than
To be ugly an' old.

When love is gone what
Can a young gal do?
When love is gone, O,
What can a young gal do?
Keep on a-lovin' me, daddy,
Cause I don't want to be blue.

Song for a Dark Girl

Way Down South in Dixie
     (Break the heart of me)
They hung my black young lover
     To a cross roads tree.

Way Down South in Dixie
      (Bruised body high in air)
I asked the white Lord Jesus
      What was the use of prayer.

Way Down South in Dixie
      (Break the heart of me)
Love is a naked shadow
      On a gnarled and naked tree

Minstrel Man

Because my mouth
Is wide with laughter
And my throat
Is deep with song,
You do not think
I suffer after
I have held my pain
So long.

Because my mouth
Is wide with laughter
You do not hear
My inner cry;
Because my feet
Are gay with dancing
You do not know
I die.

Let America Be America Again

Let America be America again.
Let it be the dream it used to be.
Let it be the pioneer on the plain
Seeking a home where he himself is free.

(America never was America to me.)

Let America be the dream the dreamers dreamed—
Let it be that great strong land of love
Where never kings connive nor tyrants scheme
That any man be crushed by one above.

(It never was America to me.)

O, let my land be a land where Liberty
Is crowned with no false patriotic wreath,
But opportunity is real, and life is free,
Equality is in the air we breathe.

(There's never been equality for me,
Nor freedom in this "homeland of the free.")

Say who are you that mumbles in the dark?
And who are you that draws your veil across the stars?

I am the poor white, fooled and pushed apart,
I am the Negro bearing slavery's scars.
I am the red man driven from the land,
I am the immigrant clutching the hope I seek—
And finding only the same old stupid plan.
Of dog eat dog, of mighty crush the weak.

I am the young man, full of strength and hope,
Tangled in that ancient endless chain
Of profit, power, gain, of grab the land!
Of grab the gold! Of grab the ways of satisfying need!
Of work the men! Of take the pay!
Of owning everything for one's own greed!
I am the farmer, bondsman to the soil.
I am the worker sold to the machine.
I am the Negro, servant to you all.
I am the people, humble, hungry, mean—
Hungry yet today despite the dream.
Beaten yet today—O, Pioneers!
I am the man who never got ahead,
The poorest worker bartered through the years.

Yet I'm the one who dreamt our basic dream
In that Old World while still a serf of kings,
Who dreamt a dream so strong, so brave, so true,
That even yet its mighty daring sings
In every brick and stone, in every furrow turned
That's made America the land it has become.
O, I'm the man who sailed those early seas
In search of what I meant to be my home—
For I'm the one who left dark Ireland's shore,
And Poland's plain, and England's grassy lea,
And torn from Black Africa's strand I came
To build a "homeland of the free."

The free?

Who said the free? Not me?
Surely not me? The millions on relief today?
The millions shot down when we strike?
The millions who have nothing for our pay?
For all the dreams we've dreamed
And all the songs we've sung
And all the hopes we've held
And all the flags we've hung,
The millions who have nothing for our pay—
Except the dream that's almost dead today.

O, let America be America again—
The land that never has been yet—
And yet must be—the land where *every* man is free.
The land that's mine—the poor man's, Indian's, Negro's, ME—
Who made America,
Whose sweat and blood, whose faith and pain,
Whose hand at the foundry, whose plow in the rain,
Must bring back our mighty dream again.

Sure, call me any ugly name you choose—
The steel of freedom does not stain.
From those who live like leeches on the people's lives,
We must take back our land again,
America!

O, yes,
I say it plain,
America never was America to me,
And yet I swear this oath—
America will be!

Out of the rack and ruin of our gangster death,
The rape and rot of graft, and stealth, and lies,
We, the people, must redeem
The land, the mines, the plants, the rivers,
The mountains and the endless plain—
All, all the stretch of these great green states—
And make America again!

Song to a Negro Wash-Woman

Oh, wash-woman,
Arms elbow-deep in white suds,
Soul washed clean,
Clothes washed clean,
I have many songs to sing you
Could I but find the words.

Was it four o'clock or six o'clock on a winter afternoon,
    I saw you wringing out the last shirt in Miss White
    Lady's kitchen? Was it four o'clock or six o'clock?
    I don't remember.

But I know, at seven one spring morning you were on
    Vermont Street with a bundle in your arms going to
    wash clothes.

And I know I've seen you in the New York subway in
    the late afternoon coming home from washing
    clothes.

Yes, I know you, wash-woman.

I know how you send your children to school, and
    high-school, and even college.
I know how you work to help your man when times are
    hard.
I know how you build your house up from the washtub
    and call it home.
And how you raise your churches from white suds for
    the service of the Holy God.

I've seen you singing, wash-woman. Out in the backyard
    garden under the apple trees, singing, hanging white
    clothes on long lines in the sunshine.
And I've seen you in church on Sunday morning singing,
    praising your Jesus because some day you're going to
    sit on the right hand side of the Son of God and
    forget you ever were a wash-woman.
And the aching back and the bundles of clothes will be
    unremembered then.

Yes, I've seen you singing.

So for you,
O singing wash-woman,

For you, singing little brown woman,
Singing strong black woman,
Singing tall yellow woman,
Arms deep in white suds,
Soul washed clean,
Clothes washed clean,
For you I have
Many songs to sing
Could I but find the words.

WARING CUNEY (1906-   )

Born in Washington, D. C., Waring Cuney was educated in the
public schools there, at Howard, at Lincoln, and at the New England
Conservatory of Music, Boston, and in Rome, where he studied
voice. He first won recognition as a student poet at Lincoln. His
poem "No Images" received first prize in the *Opportunity* poetry
contest of 1926. Since that time his works have appeared in several
national magazines and standard anthologies. Some of his later poems
of protest, sung by Joshua White, have been recorded and issued
as an album under the title *Southern Exposure*. The poems included
below are reprinted by permission of the author.

The Death Bed

All the time they were praying
He watched the shadow of a tree
Flicker on the wall.

There is no need of prayer
He said,
No need at all.

The kin-folk thought it strange
That he should ask them from a dying bed.
But they left all in a row
And it seemed to ease him
To see them go.

There were some who kept on praying
In a room across the hall,
And some who listened to the breeze
That made the shadows waver
On the wall.

He tried his nerve
On a song he knew
And made an empty note
That might have come,
From a bird's harsh throat.

And all the time it worried him
That they were in there praying,
And all the time he wondered
What it was they could be saying.

No Images

She does not know
Her beauty,
She thinks her brown body
Has no glory.

If she could dance
Naked,
Under palm trees
And see her image in the river
She would know.

But there are no palm trees
On the street,
And dish water gives back no images.

Hard Time Blues

I went down home
About a year ago
Things looked so bad
My heart was sore.
People had nothing
It was a sinning shame,
Everybody said
Hard times was to blame.

Great-God-A-Mighty
Folks feeling bad,
Lost all they ever had.

Sun was shining fourteen
Days and no rain,
Hoeing and planting
Was all in vain.
It was hard times, Lawd,
All around,
Meal barrels empty,
Crops burnt to the ground.

Great-God-A-Mighty
Folks feeling bad,
Lost all they ever had.

Skinny looking children
Bellies poking out,
Old pellagra
Without a doubt,
Old folks hanging 'round
The cabin door
Aint seen things
This bad before.

Great-God-A-Mighty
Folks feeling bad,
Lost all they ever had.

Went to the Boss
At the Commissary Store,
Folks all hungry
Please don't close the door,
Want more food, little time to pay.
Boss Man laughed
And walked away.

Great-God-A-Mighty
Folks feeling bad,
Lost all they ever had.

Landlord coming 'round
When the rent's due,
Aint got the money
Take your home from you.
Takes your mule and horse
Even take your cow,
Says get off this land
You no good no how.

Great-God-A-Mighty
Folks feeling bad,
Lost all they ever had.

LUCY ARIEL WILLIAMS (1905-   )

Born March 3, 1905, in Mobile, Alabama, Lucy Ariel Williams was
educated there and at Talladega. Her poem "Northboun'" won first
prize in the *Opportunity* poetry contest for 1926. It is reprinted by
permission of the author and of *Opportunity: Journal of Negro Life.*

Northboun'

O' de wurl' ain't flat,
An' de wurl' ain't roun',
Hits one long strip
Hangin' up an' down—
Jes' Souf an' Norf;
Jes' Norf an' Souf.

Talkin' 'bout sailin' 'round de wurl'—
Huh! I'd be so dizzy my head 'ud twurl.
If dis heah earf wuz jes' a ball
You know the people all 'ud fall.

O' de wurl' ain't flat,
An' de wurl' ain't roun',
Hits one long strip
Hangin' up an' down—
Jes' Souf an' Norf;
Jes' Norf an' Souf.

Talkin' 'bout the City whut Saint John saw—
Chile you oughta go to Saginaw;
A nigger's chance is "finest kind,"
An' pretty gals ain't hard to find.

Huh! de wurl' ain't flat .
An' de wurl' ain't roun'
Jes' one long strip
Hangin' up an' down.
Since Norf is up,
An' Souf is down,
An' Hebben is up,
I'm upward boun'.

FRANK HORNE (1899-)

Born in New York, Frank Horne was educated at the College of the City of New York, the Northern Illinois College of Opthalmology, Columbia University, and at the University of Southern California. He has taught at Fort Valley Normal and Industrial School (Georgia) and has contributed to *Opportunity, The Crisis,* and *Carolina* magazines. At present he is with the United States Housing Authority in Washington. The following is reprinted by permission of the author.

Nigger

Little Black boy
Chased down the street—
"Nigger, nigger, never die
Black face an' shiny eye,
Nigger . . . nigger . . . nigger."

Hannibal . . . Hannibal
Bangin' thru the Alps
Licked the proud Romans,
Ran home with their scalps—
"Nigger . . . nigger . . . nigger . . ."

Othello . . . black man
Mighty in war
Listen to Iago,
Called his wife a whore—
"Nigger . . . nigger . . . nigger . . ."

Crispus . . . Attucks
Bullets in his chest
Red blood of freedom
Runnin' down his vest
"Nigger . . . nigger . . . nigger . . ."

Toussaint . . . Toussaint
Made the French flee
Fought like a demon
Set his people free—
"Nigger . . . nigger . . . nigger . . ."

Jesus . . . Jesus
Son of the Lord
—Spit in his face
—Nail him on a board
"Nigger . . . nigger . . . nigger . . ."

Little Black boy
Runs down the street—
"Nigger, nigger never die
Black face an' shiny eye,
Nigger . . . nigger . . . nigger."

ARNA BONTEMPS (1902-   )

Though better known now as a novelist, Arna Bontemps (see also
p. 254) is also a poet of distinction. His first recognition was in the
latter field. In 1926 "Golgotha is a Mountain" won the Alexander
Pushkin Award for Poetry offered by *Opportunity*. In the following
year that achievement was repeated, and "Nocturne at Bethesda"
took first place in the *Crisis* poetry contest. "Nocturne at Bethesda"
is reprinted by permission of the author and *Crisis;* "A Black Man
Talks of Reaping," by permission of the author.

Nocturne At Bethesda

I thought I saw an angel flying low,
I thought I saw the flicker of a wing
Above the mulberry trees; but not again.
Bethesda sleeps. This ancient pool that healed
A host of bearded Jews does not awake.
This pool that once the angels troubled does not move.
No angel stirs it now, no Saviour comes
With healing in His hands to raise the sick
And bid the lame man leap upon the ground.

The golden days are gone. Why do we wait
So long upon the marble steps, blood
Falling from our open wounds? and why
Do our black faces search the empty sky?
Is there something we have forgotten? some precious thing
We have lost, wandering in strange lands?

There was a day, I remember now,
I beat my breast and cried, "Wash me God,
Wash me with a wave of wind upon
The barley; O quiet One, draw near, draw near!
Walk upon the hills with lovely feet
And in the waterfall stand and speak.

"Dip white hands in the lily pool and mourn
Upon the harps still hanging in the trees
Near Babylon along the river's edge,
But, oh, remember me, I pray, before
The summer goes and rose leaves lose their red."

The old terror takes my heart, the fear
Of quiet waters and of faint twilights.
There will be better days when I am gone
And healing pools where I cannot be healed.
Fragrant stars will gleam forever and ever
Above the place where I lie desolate.

Yet I hope, still I long to live.
And if there can be returning after death
I shall come back. But it will not be here;
If you want me you must search for me
Beneath the palms of Africa. Or if
I am not there then you may call to me
Across the shining dunes, perhaps I shall
Be following a desert caravan.

I may pass through centuries of death
With quiet eyes, but I'll remember still
A jungle tree with burning scarlet birds.
There is something I have forgotten, some precious thing.
I shall be seeking ornaments of ivory,
I shall be dying for a jungle fruit.

You do not hear, Bethesda.
O still green water in a stagnant pool!
Love abandoned you and me alike.
There was a day you held a rich full moon
Upon your heart and listened to the words
Of men now dead and saw the angels fly.
There is a simple story on your face;
Years have wrinkled you. I know, Bethesda!
You are sad. It is the same with me.

A Black Man Talks of Reaping

I have sown beside all waters in my day.
I planted deep, within my heart the fear
That wind or fowl would take the grain away.
I planted safe against this stark, lean year.

I scattered seed enough to plant the land
In rows from Canada to Mexico,
But for my reaping only what the hand
Can hold at once is all that I can show.

Yet what I sowed and what the orchard yields
My brother's sons are gathering stalk and root,
Small wonder then my children glean in fields
They have not sown, and feed on bitter fruit.

STERLING A. BROWN (1901-)

Sterling A. Brown was born in Washington, D. C. Educated in the Washington schools, at Williams College and Harvard University, he has taught at Virginia Seminary, at Fisk, and at Lincoln University (Missouri), as visiting lecturer at Atlanta University, and at New York University, and at Howard University, where he is now associate professor of English. From 1936 to 1939 he served as Editor on Negro Affairs for the Federal Writers' Project; in 1939 he was a staff member of the Carnegie-Myrdal Study of the Negro. He was a Guggenheim Fellow in 1937-1938. He has contributed poetry, reviews, and essays to numerous publications. His books are *Southern Road* (1932), *The Negro in American Fiction* (1938), and *Negro Poetry and Drama* (1938). "Long Gone," "Southern Road," and "Strong Men" are from *Southern Road* and are published by permission of Harcourt Brace and Co. "Slim in Hell" is reprinted by permission of the editor of *Folk-Say IV;* "Old Lem" by permission of the editor of *New Challenge;* and "Break of Day" by permission of *The New Republic.* The last three poems appeared in *This Generation,* edited by George Anderson and Eda Lou Walton.

Long Gone

I laks yo' kin' of lovin',
    Ain't never caught you wrong,
But it jes' ain' nachal
Fo' to stay here long;

It jes' ain' nachal
 Fo' a railroad man,
With a itch fo' travelin'
 He cain't understan'. . . .

I looks at de rails,
 An' I looks at de ties,
An' I hears an ole freight
 Puffin' up de rise,

An' at nights on my pallet,
 When all is still,
I listens fo' de empties
 Bumpin' up de hill;

When I oughta be quiet,
 I is got a itch
Fo' to hear de whistle blow
 Fo' de crossin' or de switch,

An' I knows de time's a-nearin'
 When I got to ride,
Though it's homelike and happy
 At yo' side.

You is done all you could do
 To make me stay;
'Tain't no fault of yours I've leavin'—
 I'se jes dataway.

I is got to see some people
 I ain't never seen,
Gotta highball thu some country
 Whah I never been.

I don't know which way I'm travelin'—
 Far or near,
All I knows fo' certain is
 I cain't stay here.

Ain't no call at all, sweet woman,
 Fo' to carry on—
Jes' my name and jes' my habit
 To be Long Gone. . . .

Slim In Hell

I

Slim Greer went to heaven;
　　St. Peter said, "Slim,
You been a right good boy."
　　An' he winked at him.

　　　　"You been a travelin' rascal
　　　　　　In yo' day.
　　　　You kin roam once mo';
　　　　　　Den you comes to stay.

"Put dese wings on yo' shoulders,
　　An' save yo' feet."
Slim grin, and he speak up,
　　"Thankye, Pete."

　　　　Den Peter say, "Go
　　　　　　To Hell an' see,
　　　　All dat is doing, and
　　　　　　Report to me.

"Be sure to remember
　　How everything go."
Slim say, "I be seein' yuh
　　On de late watch, bo."

　　　　Slim got to cavortin'
　　　　　　Swell as you choose,
　　　　Like Lindy in de Spirit
　　　　　　Of St. Louis Blues.

He flew an' he flew,
　　Till at last he hit
A hangar wid de sign readin'
　　DIS IS IT.

　　　　Den he parked his wings,
　　　　　　An' strolled aroun',
　　　　Gittin' used to his feet
　　　　　　On de solid ground.

II

Big bloodhound came aroarin'
      Like Niagry Falls,
Sicked on by white devils
      In overhalls.

Now Slim warn't scared,
      Cross my heart, it's a fac',
An de dog went on a bayin'
      Some po' devil's track.

            Den Slim saw a mansion
                  An' walked right in;
            De Devil looked up
                  Wid a sickly grin.

"Suttinly didn't look
      Fo' you, Mr. Greer,
How it happen you comes
      To visit here?"

            Slim say—"Oh, jes' thought
                  I'd drop by a spell."
            "Feel at home, seh, an' here's
                  De keys to hell."

Den he took Slim around
      An' showed him people
Rasin' hell as high as
      De First Church Steeple.

            Lots of folks fightin'
                  At de roulette wheel,
            Like old Rampart Street,
                  Or leastwise Beale.

Showed him bawdy houses
      An' cabarets,
Slim thought of New Orleans
      An' Memphis days.

            Each devil was busy
                  Wid a devilish broad,
            An' Slim cried, "Lawdy,
                  Lawd, Lawd, Lawd."

Took him in a room
    Where Slim see
De preacher wid a brownskin
    On each knee.

        Showed him giant stills,
            Going everywhere,
        Wid a passel of devils
            Stretched dead drunk there.

Den he took him to de furnace
    Dat some devils was firing,
Hot as hell, an' Slim start
    A mean presspirin'.

        White devils wid pitchforks
            Threw black devils on,
        Slim thought he'd better
            Be gittin' along.

An' he say—"Dis makes
    Me think of home—
Vicksburg, Little Rock, Jackson,
    Waco and Rome."

        Den de devil gave Slim
            De big Ha-Ha;
        An' turned into a cracker,
            Wid a sheriff's star.

Slim ran fo' his wings,
    Lit out from de groun'
Hauled it back to St. Peter,
    Safety boun'.

III

        St. Peter said, "Well,
            You got back quick.
        How's de devil? An' what's
            His latest trick?"

An' Slim say, "Peter,
    I really cain't tell,
The place was Dixie
    That I took for hell."

Then Peter say, "You must'
Be crazy, I vow,
Where'n hell dja think Hell *was*,
Anyhow?

"Git on back to de yearth,
Cause I got de fear,
You'se a leetle too dumb,
Fo' to stay up here . . ."

Southern Road

Swing dat hammer—hunh—
Steady, bo';
Swing dat hammer—hunh—
Steady, bo';
Ain't no rush, bebby,
Long ways to go.

Burner tore his—hunh—
Black heart away;
Burner tore his—hunh—
Black heart away;
Got me life, bebby,
An' a day.

Gal's on Fifth Street—hunh—
Son done gone;
Gal's on Fifth Street—hunh—
Son done gone;
Wife's in de ward, bebby,
Babe's not bo'n.

My ole man died—hunh—
Cussin' me;
My ole man died—hunh—
Cussin' me;
Ole lady rocks, bebby,
Huh misery.

Doubleshackled—hunh—
Guard behin';
Doubleshackled—hunh—
Guard behin';
Ball and chain, bebby,
On my min'.

White man tells me—hunh--
Dam yo' soul;
White man tells me—hunh—
Dam yo' soul;
Got no need, bebby,
To be tole.

Chain gang nevah—hunh—
Let me go;
Chain gang nevah—hunh—
Let me go;
Po' los' boy, bebby,
Evahmo' . . .

Old Lem

I talked to old Lem
And old Lem said:
   "They weigh the cotton
They store the corn
     We only good enough
     To work the rows;
They run the commissary
They keep the books
     We gotta be grateful
     For being cheated;
Whippersnapper clerks
Call us out of our name
     We got to say mister
     To spindling boys
They make our figgers
Turn somersets
We buck in the middle
     Say, "Thankyuh, sah.'
       They don't come by ones
       They don't come by twos
       But they come by tens.

"They got the judges
They got the lawyers
They got the jury-rolls
They got the law
       They don't come by ones
They got the sheriffs
They got the deputies
       They don't come by twos

They got the shotguns
They got the rope
    We git the justice
    In the end
       And they come by tens.

"Their fists stay closed
Their eyes look straight
    Our hands stay open
    Our eyes must fall
       They don't come by ones
They got the manhood
They got the courage
       They don't come by twos
    We got to slink around,
    Hangtailed hounds.
They burn us when we dogs
They burn us when we men
       They come by tens. . . .

"I had a buddy
Six foot of man
Muscled up perfect
Game to the heart
       They don't come by ones
Outworked and outfought
Any man or two men
       They don't come by twos
He spoke out of turn
At the commissary
They gave him a day
To git out the county.
He didn't take it.
He said "Come and get me."
They came and got him.
       And they came by tens.
He stayed in the county—
He lays there dead.

       They don't come by ones
       They don't come by twos
       But they come by tens."

Break of Day

Big Jess fired on the Alabama Central,
Man in full, babe, man in full.
Been throwing on coal for Mister Murphy
From times way back, baby, times way back.

Big Jess had a pleasing woman, name of Mamie,
Sweet-hipted mama, sweet-hipted Mamie;
Had a boy growing up for to be a fireman,
Just like his pa, baby, like his pa.

Out by the roundhouse Jess had his cabin,
Longside the tracks, babe, long the tracks,
Jess pulled the whistle when they highballed past it
"I'm on my way, baby, on my way."

Crackers craved the job what Jess was holding,
Times right tough, babe, times right tough,
Warned Jess to quit his job for a white man,
Jess he laughed, baby, he jes' laughed.

He picked up his lunch-box, kissed his sweet woman,
Sweet-hipted mama, sweet-hipted Mame,
His son walked with him to the white-washed palings,
"Be seeing you soon, son, see you 'soon."

Mister Murphy let Big Jess talk on the whistle,
"So long sugar baby, so long babe";
Train due back in the early morning
Breakfast time, baby, breakfast time.

Mob stopped the train crossing Black Bear Mountain
Shot rang out, babe, shot rang out.
They left Big Jess on the Black Bear Mountain,
Break of day, baby, break of day.

Sweet Mame sits rocking, waiting for the whistle
Long past due, babe, long past due.
The grits are cold, and the coffee's boiled over,
But Jess done gone, baby; he done gone.

Strong Men

The strong men keep coming on.
                                   —Sandburg.

They dragged you from homeland,
They chained you in coffles,
They huddled you spoon-fashion in filthy hatches,
They sold you to give a few gentlemen ease.

They broke you in like oxen,
They scourged you,
They branded you,
They made your women breeders,
They swelled your numbers with bastards. . .
They taught you the religion they disgraced.

You sang:
  Keep a-inchin' along
  Lak a po' inch worm. . . .

You sang:
  Bye and bye
  I'm gonna lay down dis heaby load. . . .

You sang:
  Walk togedder, chillen,
  Dontcha git weary. . . .

      The strong men keep a-comin' on
      The strong men git stronger.

They point with pride to the roads you built for them,
They ride in comfort over the rails you laid for them.
They put hammers in your hands
And said—Drive so much before sundown.

You sang:
  Ain't no hammah
  In dis lan',
  Strikes lak mine, bebby,
  Strikes lak mine.

They cooped you in their kitchens,
They penned you in their factories,
They gave you the jobs that they were too good for,
They tried to guarantee happiness to themselves
By shunting dirt and misery to you.

You sang:
>   *Me an' muh baby gonna shine, shine*
>   *Me an' muh baby gonna shine.*
>   The strong men keep a-comin' on
>   The strong men git stronger. . . .

They bought off some of your leaders
You stumbled, as blind men will . . .
They coaxed you, unwontedly soft-voiced. . . .
You followed a way.
Then laughed as usual.
They heard the laugh and wondered;
Uncomfortable;
Unadmitting a deeper terror. . . .
>   The strong men keep a-comin' on
>   Gittin' stronger. . . .

What, from the slums
Where they have hemmed you,
What, from the tiny huts
They could not keep from you—
What reaches them
Making them ill at ease, fearful?
Today they shout prohibition at you
"Thou shalt not this"
"Thou shalt not that"
"Reserved for whites only"
You laugh.

One thing they cannot prohibit—
>   The strong men . . . coming on
>   The strong men gittin' stronger.
>   Strong men. . . .
>   Stronger. . . .

FRANK MARSHALL DAVIS (1905-)

Frank Marshall Davis was born in Arkansas City, Kansas, December 31, 1905. After studying journalism two years at Kansas State College he left for Chicago to do newspaper work. Awarded the first Sigma Delta Chi Perpetual Scholarship ever given at Kansas State College, he returned to school in 1929, but this time remained only one year. He went to Georgia in 1931 to help start the *Atlanta Daily World*. Returning in Chicago, he became affiliated with the

Associated Negro Press and has remained with that organization
up to the present time. In 1937 Davis was awarded a Julius Rosenwald Fellowship for work in the field of poetry. *Black Man's Verse,*
his first book of poems, appeared in 1935; the second, *I Am the
American Negro,* in 1937. His third book, *47th Street,* is scheduled
for early publication. Reprinted by permission of the author.

Snapshots of the Cotton South

Listen, you drawing men
I want a picture of a starving black
I want a picture of a starving white
Show them bitterly fighting down on the dark soil
Let their faces be lit by hate
Above there will stand
The rich plantation owner, holder of the land
A whip in his red fist
Show his pockets bulging with dollars spilled
From the ragged trousers of the fighting men
And I shall call it
"Portrait of the Cotton South."

* * *

Co'n pone, collard greens, side meat
Sluggish sorghum and fat yams
Don't care who eats them.
The popping bolls of cotton
Whiter than the snobbish face
Of the plantation owner's wife
Never shrink in horror
At the touch of black croppers' hands.
And when the weevils march
They send no advance guard
Spying at doors, windows
Reporting back
"This is a privileged place
We shall pass it by
We want only nigger cotton."
Death
Speeding in a streamlined racing car
Or hobbling on ancient crutches
Sniffs at the color line;
Starvation, privation, disease, disaster
Likewise embarrass Social Tradition
By indiscriminately picking victims

Instead of arranging
Black folk later—
But otherwise
Life officially flows
In separate channels.

* * *

Chisel your own statute of God.
Have him blonde as a Viking king
A celestial czar of race separation
Roping off a jim crow section
On the low lying outskirts of heaven
Hard by the platinum railroad tracks
Where there will dwell for eternity
Good darkies inferiority-conscious
Of their brothers and sisters
In the Methodist Episcopal Church, South
Or
Have him a dealer of vengeance
Punishing in hell's hot fires
Lynchers, quick trigger sheriffs,
Conniving land owners, slave driving overseers
While today's black Christians
Look down at their endless torture
Then travel the golden streets of paradise
To the biggest mansions
In the best districts
And there feast themselves
On milk and honey
As say the preachers
In the little colored churches.
Of course
There is no intermingling socially
Between the races
Such is absolutely unthinkable
Oh my yes
Still
At regular intervals
The wife of Mobtown's mayor
Sees an Atlanta specialist
For syphillis contracted from her husband
Who got it from their young mulatto cook
Who was infected by the chief of police
Who received it from his washerwoman
Who was made diseased by the shiftless son
Of the section's richest planter

One night before
He led the pack that hanged
The black bastard who broke into
A farm woman's bedroom—
But
As was mentioned before
There is no intermingling socially . . . . .

*   *   *

Neither Socialist nor Communist lingers here.
The Southern Tenant Farmers Union
Is officially a Grave Menace
Here we have Democracy at its best
Amid "native American"
"Bedrock of the nation"
Untouched by "The Foreign Element"
They have "Rugged Individualism"
"Any man may be President"
"Equality of Opportunity"
Which, translated, means
The rich men grow richer
Big planters get bigger
Controlling the land and the towns
Ruling their puppet officials
Feeding white croppers and tenant farmers
Banquets of race hate for the soul
Sparse crumbs for their thin bodies
Realizing
The feast of animosity
Will dull their minds
To their own plight

So the starving po' whites
Contemptuous of neighboring blacks
Filled with their pale superiority
Live in rotting cabins
Dirt floored and dirty
Happy hunting ground of hookworm and vermin
Overrun with scrawny children
Poverty sleeping on the front stoop
Enslaved on islands of rundown clay
And to the planter-owned commissaries;
Dying, then dumped into the grinning graves
Their worm-picked bones resting silently
In a white burial ground

Separated even in death
As were their fathers before them.

No matter what the cost in taxes
Sacrificed by penniless croppers
Unmissed by money-grabbing land owners
There must be separate accommodations
And public institutions
For each race.
Impoverished white schools
Loosing tidewaters
Of anti-Negro propaganda
While the fallen-in buildings
For black children
Have course in Manual Arts,
Writing, and a little figuring
In between cotton picking and sowing
And of course
Care must be taken
By public officials
Not to make jails too strong
And thus inconvenience
The hungry lynchers.
Now
There are some who say
Voteless blacks never get
A proportionate return of taxes paid
But since so many
Land in the hoosegow
On copyrighted charges
And the county pays their keep
In stockade, on chain gang,
They really use their share
Of public funds—
The arithmetic and logic
Are indisputable.

* * *

At sunrise
Into the broad fields they go—
Cropper, tenant, day laborer
Black and white—
Leaving behind
Shacks of logs and rough planks.
Arching their crooked backs
Slowly, like long mistreated cats,

They throttle the living cotton,
Hustle it, dead and grayish white,
Into the gaping sacks
Portable tombs
For the soft body
Of the South's Greatest Industry—
While, nearby
Overseers stand
Throttling the living souls
Of the broken workers
Choking their spirit
Until
Worn out and useless
They are crammed into
The waiting earth—
Another industry
Of the Cotton South.

* * *

Well, you remakers of America
You apostles of Social Change
Here is pregnant soil
Here are grass roots of a nation.
But the crop they grow is Hate and Poverty.
By themselves they will make no change
Black men lack the guts
Po' whites have not the brains
And the big land owners want Things As They Are.
You disciples of Progress
Of the Advancing Onward
Communist, Socialist, Democrat, Republican
See today's picture—
It is not beautiful to look upon.
Meanwhile paints pots drip over
There is fresh canvas for the asking.
Will you say,
"But that is not my affair"
Or will you mold this section
So its portrait will fit
In the sunlit hall
Of Ideal America?

Robert Whitmore

Having attained success in business
possessing three cars
one wife and two mistresses
a home and furniture
talked of by the town
and thrice ruler of the local Elks
Robert Whitmore
died of apoplexy
when a stranger from Georgia
mistook him
for a former Macon waiter.

Arthur Ridgewood, M.D.

He debated whether
as a poet
to have dreams and beans
or as a physician
have a long car and caviar.
Dividing his time between both
he died from a nervous breakdown
caused by worry
from rejection slips
and final notices from the finance company.

Giles Johnson, Ph.D.

Giles   Johnson
had four college degrees
knew the whyfore of this
the wherefore of that
could orate in Latin
or cuss in Greek
and, having learned such things
he died of starvation
because he wouldn't teach
and he couldn't porter.

MELVIN B. TOLSON (1908-   )

Born in Moberly, Missouri, Melvin B. Tolson was educated in the public schools of Kansas and Missouri. He took his A.B. at Lincoln University and his M.A. at Columbia. Tolson has been the recipient of numerous prizes and awards for speech and creative writing. He was the first to receive the Omega Fellowship in Creative Literature. His poem, "Dark Symphony," won the national poetry prize at the Negro American Exposition in Chicago. Tolson is the author of two full-length plays: *Southern Front,* which deals with the unionizing of the Arkansas sharecroppers, and *The Moses of Beale Street* (in collaboration with Edward Boatner), a Negro miracle play. At present Tolson teaches at Wiley College, Texas, and conducts a column, "Caviar and Cabbage," in the *Washington Tribune.* Reprinted by permission of the author and the *Atlantic Monthly.*

Dark Symphony

I

Allegro Moderato

Black Crispus Attucks taught
       Us how to die
Before white Patrick Henry's bugle breath
Uttered the vertical
       Transmitting cry:
"Yea, give me liberty, or give me death."

And from that day to this
       Men black and strong
For Justice and Democracy have stood,
Steeled in the faith that Right
       Will conquer Wrong
And Time will usher in one brotherhood.

No Banquo's ghost can rise
       Against us now
And say we crushed men with a tyrant's boot,
Or pressed the crown of thorns
       On Labor's brow,
Or ravaged lands and carted off the loot.

II
Lento Grave

The centuries-old pathos in our voices
Saddens the great white world,
And the wizardry of our dusky rhythms
Conjures up shadow-shapes of ante-bellum years:

Black slaves singing *One More River to Cross*
In the torture tombs of slave-ships,
Black slaves singing *Steal Away to Jesus*
In jungle swamps,
Black slaves singing *The Crucifixion*
In slave-pens at midnight,
Black slaves singing *Swing Low, Sweet Chariot*
In cabins of death,
Black slaves singing *Go Down, Moses*
In the canebrakes of the Southern Pharaohs.

III
Andante Sostenuto

They tell us to forget
The Golgotha we tread . . .
We who are scourged with hate,
A price upon our head.
They who have shackled us
Require of us a song,
They who have wasted us
Bid us o'erlook the wrong.

They tell us to forget
Democracy is spurned.
They tell us to forget
The Bill of Rights is burned.
Three hundred years we slaved,
We slave and suffer yet:
Though flesh and bone rebel,
They tell us to forget!

Oh, how can we forget
Our human rights denied?
Oh, how can we forget
Our manhood crucified?
When Justice is profaned
And plea with curse is met,
When Freedom's gates are barred,
Oh, how can we forget?

IV

Tempo Primo

The New Negro strides upon the continent
In seven league boots . . .
The New Negro
Who sprang from the vigor-stout loins
Of Nat Turner, gallows-martyr for Freedom,
Of Joseph Cinquez, Black Moses of the Amistad Mutiny,
Of Frederick Douglass, oracle of the Catholic Man,
Of Sojourner Truth, eye and ear of Lincoln's legions,
Of Harriet Tubman, St. Bernard of the Underground
    Railroad.

V

Larghetto

None in the Land can say
To us black men Today:
You send the tractors on their bloody path,
And create Oakies for *The Grapes of Wrath*.
You breed the slum that breeds a *Native Son*
To damn the good earth Pilgrim Fathers won.

None in the Land can say
To us black men Today:
You dupe the poor with rags-to-riches tales,
And leave the workers empty dinner pails.
You stuff the ballot-box, and honest men
Are muzzled by your demagogic din.

None in the Land can say
To us black men Today:
You smash stock markets with your coined blitzkriegs,
And make a hundred million guinea pigs.
You counterfeit our Christianity,
And bring contempt upon Democracy.

None in the Land can say
To us black men Today:
You prowl when citizens are fast asleep,
And hatch Fifth Column plots to blast the deep
Foundations of the State and leave the Land
A vast Sahara with a Fascist brand.

None in the Land can say
To us black men Today:
You send flame-gutting tanks, like swarms of flies,
And plump a hell from dynamiting skies.
You fill machine-gunned towns with rotting dead—
A No Man's Land where children cry for bread.

VI
Tempo di Marcia

Out of abysses of Illiteracy,
Through labyrinths of Lies,
Across wastelands of Disease . . .
We advance!

Out of dead-ends of Poverty,
Through wildernesses of Superstition,
Across barricades of Jim Crowism . . .
We advance!

With the Peoples of the World . . .
We advance!

RICHARD WRIGHT (1909-)

Richard Wright (see also pp. 105, 1050) has published verse in such magazines as *International Literature, New Masses, Anvil, Midland,* and *Left.* This poem is reprinted by permission of *New Masses.*

I Have Seen Black Hands

I am black and I have seen black hands, millions and millions
      of them—
Out of millions of bundles of wool and flannel tiny black
      fingers have reached restlessly and hungrily for life.
Reached out for the black nipples at the black breasts of black
      mothers,
And they've held red, green, blue, yellow, orange, white, and
      purple toys in the childish grips of possession,
And chocolate drops, peppermint sticks, lollypops, wineballs,
      ice cream cones, and sugared cookies in fingers sticky
      and gummy,
And they've held balls and bats and gloves and marbles and
      jack-knives and sling-shots and spinning tops in the
      thrill of sport and play,

And pennies and nickels and dimes and quarters and some-
    times on New Year's, Easter, Lincoln's Birthday, May
    Day, a brand new green dollar bill,
They've held pens and rulers and maps and tablets and books
    in palms spotted and smeared with ink,
And they've held dice and cards and half-pint flasks and cue
    sticks and cigars and cigarettes in the pride of new
    maturity . . .

II

I am black and I have seen black hands, millions and millions
    of them—
They were tired and awkward and calloused and grimy and
    covered with hangnails,
And they were caught in the fast-moving belts of machines and
    snagged and smashed and crushed,
And they jerked up and down at the throbbing machines
    massing taller and taller the heaps of gold in the banks
    of bosses,
And they piled higher and higher the steel, iron, the lumber,
    wheat, rye, the oats, corn, the cotton, the wool, the
    oil, the coal, the meat, the fruit, the glass, and the
    stone until there was too much to be used,
And they grabbed guns and slung them on their shoulders
    and marched and groped in trenches and fought and
    killed and conquered nations who were customers for
    the goods black hands had made.
And again black hands stacked goods higher and higher until
    there was too much to be used,
And then the black hands held trembling at the factory
    gates the dreaded lay-off slip,
And the black hands hung idle and swung empty and grew
    soft and got weak and bony from unemployment and
    starvation,
And they grew nervous and sweaty, and opened and shut in
    anguish and doubt and hesitation and irresolution . . .

III

I am black and I have seen black hands, millions and millions
    of them—
Reaching hesitantly out of days of slow death for the goods
    they had made, but the bosses warned that the goods
    were private and did not belong to them,
And the black hands struck desperately out in defence of life

and there was blood, but the enraged bosses decreed
that this too was wrong,

And the black hands felt the cold steel bars of the prison they
had made, in despair tested their strength and found
that they could neither bend nor break them,

And the black hands fought and scratched and held back but
a thousand white hands took them and tied them,

And the black hands lifted palms in mute and futile
supplication to the sodden faces of mobs wild in the
revelries of sadism,

And the black hands strained and clawed and struggled in
vain at the noose that tightened about the black throat,

And the black hands waved and beat fearfully at the tall
flames that cooked and charred the black flesh . . .

IV

I am black and I have seen black hands
Raised in fists of revolt, side by side with the white fists of
white workers,
And some day—and it is only this which sustains me—
Some day there shall be millions and millions of them,
On some red day in a burst of fists on a new horizon!

OWEN DODSON (1914-   )

Owen Dodson (see also p. 543) has contributed poems in both traditional and experimental verse forms to *New Masses, Opportunity,*
and *Phylon*. The following are used by permission of the author.

Cradle Song

Sleep late with your dreams:
The morning has a scar
To mark on the horizon
With the death of the morning star.

The color of blood will appear
And wash the morning sky,
Aluminum birds flying with fear
Will scream to your waking,
Will send you to die;

Sleep late with your dream;
Pretend that the morning is far;
Deep in the horizon country,
Unconcerned with the morning star.

Miss Packard and Miss Giles

(Two New England Women Who Founded the School for Negro
Women in Georgia, Spelman College)

Two Women, here in April, prayed alone
And saw again their vision of an altar
Built for mind and spirit, flesh and bone.
They never turned away; they never said:
"This dream is air, let us go back to our New England spring
And cultivate an earth that is not dead;

"Let dark mothers weep, dark children bleed,
This land is barren land
Incapable of seed."
They made their crucifix far more
Than ornament; they wrestled with Denial
And pinned him to the floor.

They made defeat an exile:
And year by year their vision shed its mist:
And still they smiled their Noah smile,

Knowing that they had no death to fear,
Knowing that their future would be now
And all the Aprils we assemble here.

ROBERT E. HAYDEN (1913-)

Certainly one of the most promising of the younger poets, Robert
E. Hayden was born in Detroit, Michigan, in 1913. He attended
Wayne University and in 1936, to use his own phrase, "graduated
to the Federal Writers' Project," where he had charge of research
into local Negro history and the collection of folklore. In 1938
Hayden did advanced work in English, play production, and creative writing at the University of Michigan. While there he won
the Jule and Avery Hopwood Prize for poetry. Hayden has written
radio scripts and *Go Down Moses,* a play about the Underground
Railroad. His first book of poems, *Heart-Shape in the Dust,* was
published in 1940. At present he is music and drama critic for the
Michigan Chronicle. The poems in this collection are reprinted by
permission of the author.

Prophecy

And in the end he wept like a child.
There were no drums. There were no flags.
The morning was final and anonymous.
They could not keep them out of the great castle
With its guards and its gates,
Its secret rooms and hidden stairways that morning.
The leaves were yellow on the twisted trees,
Fog rolled hoarse elegies over the ruins
Of the gutted city in the valley below.
They took him into the dying gardens,
And he wept like a child. The rifles cried,
"Gotterdamerung." He fell with his mouth
Crushing into the cold earth
And lay unharming at last
Under the falling leaves and the fog. . . .

They returned to the ruined city
And began to build again.

Gabriel
(Hanged for leading a slave-revolt)

Black Gabriel, riding
To the gallows tree,
In this last hour
What do you see?

I see a thousand
Thousand slaves
Rising up
From forgotten graves,
And their wounds drip flame
On slavery's ground,
And their chains shake Dixie
With a thunder sound.

Gabriel, Gabriel,
The end is nigh,
What is your wish
Before you die?

That rebellion suckle
The slave-mother's breast
And black men
Never, never rest

Till slavery's pillars
Lie splintered in dust
And slavery's chains
Lie eaten with rust.

Gabriel, Gabriel,
This is the end,
Your barbarous soul,
May God befriend.

The blow I struck
Was not in vain,
The blow I struck
Shall be struck again.

Gabriel hangs
Black-gold in the sun,
Flame-head of
Rebellion.

The black folk weep,
The white folk stare:
Gabriel is
A sword in the air.

His spirit goes flying
Over the land
With a song in his mouth
And a sword in his hand.

Speech

Hear me, white brothers,
Black brothers, hear me:

I have seen the hand
Holding the blowtorch
To the dark, anguish-twisted body;
I have seen the hand
Giving the high-sign
To fire on the white pickets;
And it was the same hand,
Brothers, listen to me,
It was the same hand.

Hear me, black brothers,
White brothers, hear me:

I have heard the words
They set like barbed-wire fences
To divide you,
I have heard the words—
Dirty nigger, poor white trash—
And the same voice spoke them;
Brothers, listen well to me,
The same voice spoke them.

Obituary

My father's hands
Were gnarled and hard,
The fruits of their labor
He shared with the Lord.
His roots sat deep
In the rock of the Word,
In Abraham's bosom
He nestled like a bird.
When I was a child,
I sat at his knee,
He opened The Book
And read to me
Of Salome dancing
Columnar and faulty
And Lot's wife standing
Forlorn and salty;
Of Salome dancing
For the head of the evangel
And Jacob wresting
Blessings from an angel.
Cymbals and roses
And bronze and myrrh,
Flame and thunder
Those stories were. . . .
And closing The Book
With gaze stern and level
My father would counsel,
"My son, shun evil."
Though life was marshes
And dark journeyings,
He lived as one
Prepared for wings.

He died quietly
One sun-white morn,
Just as spring was
Being born.
He died serenely,
Having found
God's footprints flowering
On mortal ground.

Bacchanal

Gonna git high,
High's a Georgia pine,
Can't laugh,
Don't wanna cry:
Gonna git high.

Factory closed this mawnin,
Done drawed that last full pay;
One of these Hastings studs
Done coaxed ma brown away.

A little likker,
O a little gin
Makes you fergit
The fix you in.

What the hell's the use'n
Miseryin on? . . .
Wonder what I'll do when
Ma lush-money's gone.

There must be joy,
There's gotta be joy somewhere
For a po colored boy
This side the sky.

Gonna git high.

MARGARET WALKER (1915-   )

Margaret Walker was born in Birmingham, Alabama. She was educated in the public schools of Mississippi, Alabama, and Louisiana, at Northwestern University, and at the University of Iowa. She has done social service work in Chicago and in New Orleans and has been a member of the Chicago Writers' Project. "For My People" appeared in *Poetry: a Magazine of Verse* in 1937 and is here printed by permission of the author and the editors of the magazine.

For My People

For my people everywhere singing their slave songs repeatedly: their
dirges and their ditties and their blues and jubilees, praying their
prayers nightly to an unknown god, bending their knees humbly to
an unseen power;

For my people lending their strength to the years: to the gone years
and the now years and the maybe years, washing ironing cooking
scrubbing sewing mending hoeing plowing digging planting pruning
patching dragging along never gaining never reaping never knowing and never understanding;

For my playmates in the clay and dust and sand of Alabama backyards
playing baptizing and preaching, and doctor and jail and soldier
and school and mama and cooking and playhouse and concert and
store and Miss Choomby and hair and company;

For the cramped bewildered years we went to school to learn to know
the reasons why and the answers to and the people who and the
places where and the days when, in memory of the bitter hours
when we discovered we were black and poor and small and different
and nobody wondered and nobody understood;

For the boys and girls who grew in spite of these things to be Man
and Woman, to laugh and dance and sing and play and drink their
wine and religion and success, to marry their playmates and bear
children and then die of consumption and anemia and lynching;

For my people thronging 47th Street in Chicago and Lenox Avenue in
New York and Rampart Street in New Orleans, lost disinherited
dispossessed and HAPPY people filling the cabarets and taverns and
other people's pockets needing bread and shoes and milk and land
and money and Something—Something all our own;

For my people walking blindly, spreading joy, losing time being lazy,
sleeping when hungry, shouting when burdened, drinking when
hopeless, tied and shackled and tangled among ourselves by the
unseen creatures who tower over us omnisciently and laugh;

For my people blundering and groping and floundering in the dark
of churches and schools and clubs and societies, associations and
councils and committees and conventions, distressed and disturbed
and deceived and devoured by money-hungry glory-craving leeches,
preyed on by facile force of state and fad and novelty by false
prophet and holy believer;

For my people standing staring trying to fashion a better way from confusion from hypocrisy and misunderstanding, trying to fashion a
world that will hold all the people all the faces all the adams and
eves and their countless generations;

Let a new earth rise. Let another world be born. Let a bloody peace
be written in the sky. Let a second generation full of courage issue
forth, let a people loving freedom come to growth, let a beauty full
of healing and a strength of final clenching be the pulsing in our
spirits and our blood. Let the martial songs be written, let the
dirges disappear. Let a race of men now rise and take control!

IV
FOLK LITERATURE

FOLK LITERATURE

TRAVELERS through the antebellum South were struck by the singing and dancing of the slaves. Some dismissed these as uncouth barbarism, others were stirred by the vigor of the dancing and the weird sadness of the songs. Report of these reached the North in travelers' accounts, published journals, novels, and the narratives of fugitive slaves. Southern authors, in the main, did not consider the songs and dances worth mentioning, except, strangely, as proofs of the slave's contentment.

It was not until the Civil War that any of these songs were collected. In 1864, Charlotte Forten (see below p. 649) wrote down a few songs that she heard the new freedmen sing on Saint Helena Island. Thomas Wentworth Higginson, moved greatly as the black soldiers of his regiment sang in the evenings about the campfires, recorded several spirituals for an article in *The Atlantic Monthly* (1867) and included a chapter on them in his *Army Life in a Black Regiment* (1870). The first systematic collection was made by three Northerners, William F. Allen, Charles P. Ware, and Lucy McKim Garrison, in their *Slave Songs of the United States* (1867). This book, sympathetically edited, is an important landmark in American musical history.

The wider introduction of these songs to the world came a few years later in 1871, when a group of Fisk University students, under the leadership of George White, started on tour, singing the songs that they had learned from their slave parents. They had to struggle for a hearing. One tavern keeper, astounded that real Negroes and not burnt-cork singers were advertised to sing Negro songs, drove them out of his tavern. In Brooklyn they were scoffed at as Beecher's Nigger Minstrels. But they packed churches there and in New York and went on to Europe on a truly triumphal tour. When they left Fisk, the school was in straitened circumstances; when they returned, they had enough money to construct a new building, Jubilee Hall. Their example has been followed even until the present by a large number of colleges that send out choral groups that specialize in spirituals.

Fisk University's part in establishing the spirituals is definite. The origins of the type of songs that the young college group sang is less definite. Whether they are of individual or group authorship, for instance, is one problem. An early collector heard a slave tell how the songs were made:

> I'll tell you, it's dis way. My master call me up and order me a short peck of corn and a hundred lash. My friends see it, and is sorry for me. When dey come to de praise-meeting dat night dey sing about it. Some's very good singers and know how; and dey work it in—work it in, you know, till they get it right; and dat's de way.

Higginson found a young oarsman who boasted that

> Once we boys went for tote some rice, and de nigger-driver, he keep a-callin' on us, and I say, "O de ole nigger-driver." Den anudder said, "Fust ting my mammy told me was, nothin' so bad as nigger-drivers." Den I made a sing, just puttin' a word, and den anudder word.

When this poet started singing, however, the other oarsmen, after listening a moment joined in the chorus "as if it were an old acquaintance though they evidently had never heard it before."

James Weldon Johnson, who called the makers of spirituals "black and unknown bards of long ago" (see p. 324), believed that many spring from highly gifted individuals (see p. 171). Robert W. Gordon, according to his *Folk Songs of America,* discovered in the isolated Low Country of South Carolina a type of spiritual that in its primitive structure (single line of recitative alternating with simple line refrain) is probably closest to the earliest spirituals sung. For their "recitative" these spirituals demanded a highly special sort of singer:

> He was not an "author" in the ordinary sense, for he did not himself create new lines. He merely put together traditional lines in new forms, adding nothing of his own . . . He gathered together and held in his memory countless scraps and fragments, and had the ability to sew or patch them together as occasion demanded.

One of the present groups most productive of new spirituals, The Golden Gate Quartet, works similarly, according to report. Willie Johnson, their talented poet and leader, with an enormous stock of folk idioms and lines, reworks these into new and original patterns. Yet the songs that this quartet sings, though obviously showing a creative gift, are not so "original" that the folk would not recognize them as theirs. "Composers" of the best of present-day blues likewise levy upon the folk storehouse, turning out products that are close to authentic folk stuff.

Something of this sort is meant by the folk origin of the spirituals. It is unlikely that any group of worshipers and singers, as a group, composed spirituals. Single individuals with poetic ingenuity, a rhyming gift, or a good memory "composed" or "remembered" lines, couplets, or even quatrains out of a common storehouse. The group would join in with the refrain or the longer chorus. When one leader's ingenuity or memory was exhausted, another might take up the "composition." About two matters of origin, however, there is more certainty than about method of composition. The first is that stories purporting to tell the circumstances and dates of individual spirituals are more fanciful than accurate. This is true of all folk song. The claims of ex-slaves that they were present at the creation of well-known spirituals are to be trusted no more than the claims of many yarn-spinners that they worked side by side with John Henry or were shot at by Stackalee. The second is that the spirituals are genuinely folk products, regardless of the fact that gifted individuals may have played leading roles in their composition. From the folk storehouse came the ideas, the vocabulary, the idioms, the images. The folk approved the song or rejected it, as it squared with folk knowledge, memory, and vision. The folk changed lines that were not easily understood, inserted new stanzas, sometimes bringing the songs up to date, and transmitted them orally to the next generation. In the long journey, stanzas were lost or imperfectly remembered; and new and often incoherent interpolations took their places. But the folk kept a very large number of the songs alive and in a rather sound condition.

A second problem of origin: whether the spirituals were derived from African music or European music, whether they were "original" with the Negro or imitations, started its controversial course at the end of the nineteenth century. In a period when the glorification of the Aryan by Gobineau and Houston Stewart Chamberlain was popular, the attribution of artistic capacity to the Negro seemed presumptuous. In 1893 Richard Wallaschek, a German musicologist, attacked the songs of the Negro as "very much overrated," "mere imitations of European compositions," "ignorantly borrowed." Certain musical critics, irritated by the praise of the spirituals, and especially by Dvořák's use of Negro melodies in his symphony *From The New World,* gladly made use of Wallaschek's dicta. In 1915, Henry E. Krehbiel, an American musical critic of high repute, answered Wallaschek's charges.

This was not difficult, since Wallaschek had included many spurious minstrel melodies in the "Negro" songs he studied. Krehbiel set out to prove, in a discriminating analysis, that the Negro songs were the only indigenous body of folk songs in America, and that these songs were the Negro's own.

John W. Work, James Weldon Johnson, R. Nathaniel Dett, N. Ballanta-Taylor, and several other Negroes allied themselves with Krehbiel. Naturally sensitive about the aspersion on the originality of their race, some of these at times overstated their argument and stressed not only the complete originality of the songs, but also their Africanism.

A cogent attack on the Africanism of the songs came from Guy B. Johnson, one of the most sympathetic and informed students of Negro folklore. In *Folk Culture on St. Helena Island* (1930) Johnson approached the Negro spiritual as a problem in anthropology: "What happened when the Negro slave, possessing a system of music admittedly different from European or Western music, came into contact with the American white man's music?" Johnson established definite points of contact between the slave and "white music," which the defenders of the originality of the spirituals had scouted. He found both musical and textual similarities in white revival hymns and Negro spirituals. Newman White in *American Negro Folk Songs* (1928) adduced proof of the slaves' participation in the camp meetings of the South, and of the similarity of white and Negro religious primitivism. He found a large number of close textual resemblances in white revival hymns and the spirituals. George Pullen Jackson in *White Spirituals of the Southern Uplands* (1934) illustrates melodic and textual similarities between white and Negro spirituals. A large school of commentators now accepts the conclusions of these scholars.

Extremists have set up the controversy as between Africanism, or complete originality, and white camp-meeting derivation, or complete unoriginality. This oversimplification does injustice to the careful scholarship of some of the men on both sides.

As far as the music is concerned, this is not the place to enter the controversy, since the spirituals have to be represented in this anthology solely as folk literature. Certain observations, however, may be useful, since they pertain to the whole picture of the Negro in American culture. Few of the disputants know all three of the musics involved: African music (if the music of an entire continent of different peoples can be so simply categorized); Southern white music of the slavery period with which the slave might have come into contact; and the spirituals themselves. Collections of slave songs were made very late; they are at best only approximations, in a system of notation that is admittedly skeletal. Analyzing the songs collected by Allen, Ware, and Garrison is a long way from analyzing the songs as sung by folk Negroes, either then or now. That the slave had contact with white religious folk and minstrel music is no less undebatable than that whites had contact with Negro music. A give-and-take seems logical to expect. Correspondences between white and Negro melodies have been established. The complete Africanism of the spirituals was never tenable. The spirituals are obviously not in an African musical idiom, not even so much as the music of Haiti, Cuba, and Brazil. But all of this does not establish the Negro spiritual, and most certainly not hot jazz, the blues, and boogie-woogie, as imitative of white music, or as unoriginal, or as devoid of traces of the African idiom. Believing one's ears, especially where folk-music is concerned, is probably better than believing the conventional notation of that music; believing phonograph records, as recent scholars are doing, is even better. The obstinate fact of a great difference between Negro folk-songs and the white camp-meeting hymns exists. Even the strongest adherents of the view that the origin of the Negro spirituals is in white music, agree that now the spiritual is definitely the Negro's own and, regardless of birthplace, is stamped with originality. The conclusions of Milton Metfessel, derived from a use of "phonophotography" in music, are that

> In bridging the gap between civilized and primitive music, the Negro sings some songs in which the analyzed elements are probably more often European than African, others in which the two are equally present, and others still in which the African element predominates. In our present group, the work songs seem to have more of the latter elements, the blues and workaday religious songs partake of both, while the formal spirituals appear to lean toward Europe.

The present state of scholarship on the subject is summarized by George Herzog:

> It becomes more and more clear that Southern Negro folk music does not furnish a chapter in the rigid survival of original musical features, but an equally fascinating chapter in the recreation of musical forms. European folk song, in the hands of the Negro, achieved special forms and idiosyncrasies, one step further removed from the European prototypes and from the old European background.

To many this step is a good long one. Lovers of Negro folk songs need not fear either its detractors or the students of origins. Neither European nor African, but partaking of elements of both, the result is a new kind of music, certainly not mere imitation, but more creative and original than any other American music.

The resemblance of words and ideas in white hymns and Negro spirituals is not of such great moment. The slaves, accepting Christianity, naturally accepted the vocabulary and subject matter of Christianity; and, liking a good song wherever they heard it, they sang church hymns as well as spirituals. Jupiter Hammon (see p. 274) used the common evangelical currency. Exact correspondences between lines in white hymns and spirituals have been discovered; Guy Johnson found such lines as "Ride on, Jesus"; "O, Lord, remember me"; "I am bound for the land of Canaan"; "O, could I hear some sinner pray"; "Lay this body down"; and "You will see the graves a-bursting" in a single white songbook, *The Millenial Harp* (published in 1843). Both Negro and white religious songs tell of "poor, wayfaring strangers," "a union band," on "a pilgrimage to heaven."

But, as Guy Johnson states, the line, or at most the stanza, seems to be the unit of transfer; there are not many instances (though more than generally suspected) "in which a white song was taken over in its entirety by Negroes." This fact should be considered with the fact that some of the correspondences are forced. For instance, George Pullen Jackson cites the following lines:

> At his table we'll sit down,
> Christ will gird himself and serve us with sweet
>   manna all around. (white)

as parallel with

> Gwine to sit down at the welcome table,
> Gwine to feast off milk and honey. (Negro)

and

> To hide yourself in the mountaintop
> To hide yourself from God. (white)

as parallel with

> Went down to the rocks to hide my face,
> The rocks cried out no hiding place. (Negro)

These are similar only in general idea, certainly not in the poetry. Newman White believes that white songs in "crossing over" are greatly transformed. Samuel Asbury believes "the words of the best white spirituals," cannot compare as poetry with the words of the best Negro spirituals and Carl Engel sees the spirituals as amazingly profound and beautiful verse, unlike anything in "the Bay Psalm Book or its numerous successors," though both men deny "complete originality" to the music. Louis Untermeyer writes that the slaves, having absorbed the Christianity to which they were exposed, repeated it in a highly original way:

> Only those who have heard the *cadences* can appreciate the originality of the Negro's contribution . . . The magic emanates from the unaffected nobility of the themes, the teasing-shifting rhythms, so simple on the surface, so intricately varied beneath; it rises from a deep emotional sincerity in every beat.

Where suspicions of the new scholarship were justified was in the interpretation of the spirituals, based on the verbal similarities between white hymns and Negro spirituals. Finding that white camp-meeting hymns spoke of "freedom" and of "hard trials," Newman White argued against the "abolitionist use of the spirituals as an instrument of propaganda," as sorrow songs produced by the oppression of slavery. He bases his argument upon the paucity of songs containing "unequivocal references to the desire for freedom," and upon his assumption that the Negro "seldom contemplated his low estate in slavery." According to White, the spirituals of the slaves, when referring to freedom mean exactly what the camp-meeting hymns of slaveholders mean by their references to freedom: namely, freedom from the oppression of sin. This is ingenious but unconvincing reasoning.

There are not many spirituals that speak openly of a love for freedom and a determination to be free. The slaves were not so naïve as that; they knew, better than several of their historians, how close to hysteria the slaveholders really were, how rigid the control could be. The very fact of a group of slaves meeting and singing and praying together was cause of anxiety to many masters, even if the slaves were singing of Jordan or Jericho.

If we can believe several fugitive slave autobiographies, however, there were many not so indirect references to physical bondage and freedom. It required no stretch of imagination to see the trials of the Israelites as paralleling the trials of the slaves, Pharaoh and his army as oppressors, and Egyptland as the South. "Go Down, Moses" was a censored song, according to fugitive slaves. "O Mary don't you weep, don't you mourn; Pharaoh's army got drowned, O Mary don't you weep" is less direct, but expresses the same central idea. Douglass tells us not only of the doubletalk of the slaves' songs, but also sees the whole body of spirituals as reflecting a desire for freedom.

Nevertheless, the spirituals which without ingenious forcing are seen to have double meanings: "Didn't my Lord deliver Daniel, and why not every man?" "Rich man Dives, he lived so well—When he died he found a home in hell"; the challenging "Go Down, Moses"; the shouts of jubilee possible under the banners of a liberating army: "O Freedom, befo' I'd be a slave, I'd be buried in my grave!" are numerically in the minority. The slaves sang songs expressing Christianity, and then not as "Christian soldiers, marching on to war," but as lost sheep, all crying for a shepherd.

Yet Newman White goes too far in stating that the slave "never contemplated his low estate," and that because few outspoken abolitionist spirituals can be found, the slave's references to freedom connote only freedom from sin, from the bonds of the flesh and the world. Analysis of the body of white camp-meeting "spirituals" reveals fairly perfunctory references to heaven as freedom; but in Negro spirituals references to trouble here below are far more numerous, and are poignant rather than perfunctory, springing from a deep need, not from an article of faith. Such lines as

> Bye and bye, I'm gonna lay down dis heavy load.
>
> ---
>
> De blind man stood on de road, and cried
> Crying Lord, my Lord, save-a po' me.
>
> ---
>
> Keep a-inchin' along, lak a po' inchworm.
>
> ---
>
> I don't know what my mother wants to stay here fuh,
> Dis ole worl' ain't been no friend to huh.
>
> ---
>
> I'm rolling through an unfriendly worl'.
>
> ---
>
> Lord, keep me from sinking down.

surely reflect the slave's awareness of his bitter plight more than his consciousness of the oppression of sin.

The spirituals tell of hard trials, great tribulations; or wanderings in some lonesome valley, or down some unknown road, a long ways from home, with brother, sister, father, mother gone. It is only a half-truth to see the spirituals as otherworldly. "You take dis worl', and give me Jesus" is certainly one of the least of the refrains. In the spirituals the slave took a clear-eyed look at this world, and he revealed in tragic poetry what he saw:

> O I been rebuked, and I been scorned,
> Done had a hard time sho's you born.

There are spirituals, many of them well known, that spring with joy. The convert shouts when he gets out of the wilderness. The true believer sees heaven as a welcome table, a feasting place; quite as often, significantly, as a place of rest where the worn out ones can sit down, for once at their ease. The saved dilate on the activities of that great "gittin' up morning" with greater zeal and trust than that with which Michael Wigglesworth foresaw his Day of Doom. But even in heaven, life on earth is not forgotten:

> I'm gonna tell God all my troubles,
> When I get home. . . .

> I'm gonna tell Him the road was rocky
> When I get home. . . .

> I'm gonna tell Him I had hard trials
> When I get home. . . .

> I'm gonna tell God how you're doing
> When I get home.

If the spirituals that talk about heaven are often joyful, it should be remembered that the joy is a joy at escape.

The spirituals were born of suffering. Yet Zora Neale Hurston is right when, thinking of their rendition, she refuses the inclusive title "Sorrow Songs." Negro folk singers, certainly today, sing spirituals with great gusto. There is much more than melancholy in their singing; there is a robustness, vitality, a fused strength. The singing serves as a release; the fervor of the release indicates something of the confining pressure that folk Negroes know too well and have known too long.

Musicologists find in the spiritual singing of today a musical relative of the wild free improvisations of hot jazz. The resemblance is seen especially in the singing of such groups as the Golden Gate Quartet and the Mitchell Christian Singers. The spirituals that they sing are often of recent origin, frequently narratives of Biblical characters, and their arrangements of the older spirituals are probably more dynamic and less restrained than their forefathers' singing in the old brush arbors. With some pronounced exceptions, the new spirituals seem more evangelical in nature and less the outpourings of "a

troubled sperrit." Besides the new spirituals springing up in the rural
churches of the South, evangelists sell hymns, printed as broadsides,
as their own compositions, though many of the lines seem lifted from
hymnbooks.

Newman White states that there was a time "when most of the
literate and semi-literate members of the Negro race were desirous
of forgetting [the spiritual]." This is only a half-truth. Many Negroes
in the upper strata did so, some because of what James Weldon Johnson
calls "second-generation respectability," some because of the dubious
uses to which spirituals were put, some because of the interpretations
of them as plantation songs, reminiscent of the good ole days befo'
de war, which is exactly what they are not. Some Negro college
students have refused to sing them, but more colleges have stressed
them in the repertoires of their choral groups, not only because of
their value in gaining finances and prestige. Most of the leading race
interpreters: Frederick Douglass (p. 725 f.), Booker T. Washington,
Paul Laurence Dunbar, W. E. B. DuBois, Kelly Miller, Carter G.
Woodson, and Alain Locke have paid honor to them. Leading musical
scholars such as those mentioned earlier have praised them even
extremely; leading musicians like Harry T. Burleigh, R. Nathaniel
Dett, Hall Johnson, Eva Jessye, W. C. Handy, Charles Cooke, William
Grant Still, and William Dawson have interpreted and arranged them;
leading artists like Marian Anderson, Dorothy Maynor, Roland Hayes,
and Paul Robeson sing them with utmost respect.

For nearly a century, articulate Negroes have recognized the
spirituals as the Negro's first important cultural gift to America. Folk
Negroes have nourished them for longer than that, and are still creating
new ones, hoarding a treasure though unconscious of its value.

SLAVE SECULARS

The first collectors of Negro folk song were New Englanders, of
abolitionist background, seriously concerned with the grave problems
facing the newly freed. The first use of the folk songs in the colleges
was to foster race pride. Naturally, therefore, the secular songs of the
slaves were considered least worthy of collection. Their appropriation
by blackface minstrelsy, the ribaldry of some of the verses, their
overuse by writers to show the Negro's carefree nature, were other
forces militating against them. One early commentator, John Mason
Brown in *Lippincott's Magazine* (1868), included a few secular songs,
but collectors generally neglected them.

But slaves did not sing sorrow songs only. There were many dance

songs, children's play songs, humorous songs. These are by no means
merely nonsense songs of giddy clowns. American counterparts to
the stylized Calypso songs of Trinidad were to be found chiefly in
New Orleans, but there were many satiric songs elsewhere. In terse
stanzas the folk Negro carries his irony as far as he can:

> Naught's a naught, figger's a figger,
> All for de white man, an' none fo' de nigger.

> When dey gits old and gray,
> When dey gits old and gray,
> White folks looks like monkeys,
> When dey gits old and gray.

Many seculars were good-humoredly irreverent of religion. These
songs, called "upstart crows" by Newman White, and other "fiddle-
sings," "cornfield hollers," and "jig-tunes" were considered "devil
tunes." Though well known by many true-believing Negroes, they
are not easily surrendered to collectors.

> Our Father, who art in heaven
> White man owe me 'leven, and pay me seven,
> Thy kingdom come, thy will be done
> And ef I hadn't tuck that, I wouldn't a got none.

The slave seculars afford many realistic glimpses of slavery:

> Old master bought a yaller gal,
> He bought her from the South.

The tussles with "pattyrollers," the contempt for "po' white trash,"
the complaints at short rations and tough masters, appear in swift
biting lines. There is very little in the seculars like Stephen Foster's
gentle "Massa's In De Cold, Cold Ground." The spirit is closer to
Louis Armstrong's "I'll be Glad When You're Dead, You Rascal,
You."

J. A. Macon and Joel Chandler Harris collected several slave songs,
but in rendering them to the public, they forced them into patterns
of standard versifying. Thomas W. Talley's *Negro Folk Rhymes*
(1922) was the first collection of the secular songs of the Negro, a
valuable pioneering work. Odum and Johnson, Newman White, John
and Alan Lomax, Carl Sandburg, and Zora Neale Hurston are recent
collectors of seculars. But the songs they collect are not chiefly slave
seculars, many of which must be lost beyond recovery.

APHORISMS

Like all folk groups, the folk Negro has a store of aphorisms or proverbs expressing his weather lore, love lore, medicinal lore, and general wisdom about life. In the early years of the discovery of the Negro folk, Joel Chandler Harris and J. A. Macon collected many of these pithy sayings. The folk Negro's gift of compressing much into a little space is found in the spirituals:

> Better mind dat sun, and see how she run,
> And don't let him catch you wid yo' work undone.

> Better look out, sister, how you walk on de cross
> Yo' foot might slip and yo' soul git lost.

> See dat sister, dressed so fine,
> She ain't got Jesus on her mind.

in the blues:

> Every shut-eye ain't sleep, every good-bye ain't gone.

> My mammy tole me, my pappy tole me too,
> Everybody grin in yo' face, son, ain't no friend to you.

> You never miss de water till de well goes dry
> You'll never miss yo' baby till she says good-bye.

and in the ballads:

> Never drive a stranger from your do'
> He may be yo' best friend; you never know.

Not the concern of collectors today, aphorisms are still abundantly used by the old folk to hand down to the young ones what they have learned of life by the hard way:

> De ole sheep dey knows de road
> Young lambs gotta find de way.

BALLADS

Ballad collectors have found many variants of English and Scotch ballads among folk Negroes. This is not so strange as it may seem. The social isolation of southern folk Negroes, like the physical isolation of the mountain folk in Kentucky, Tennessee, North Carolina, and the Ozarks, has made for the preservation of older English dialects, lore, and songs. "Barbara Allen," "The Briary Bush," "Lady Isabel and the Elf Knight," and "Lord Lovell" are examples of traditional ballads that the Negro has helped to preserve.

The charming lullaby that has been sung by so many Negroes, with such lines as:

> Mister Frog went a-courting, he did ride
> Unh-hunh, unh-hunh,
> Mister Frog went a-courting, he did ride,
> Sword and pistol by his side
> Unh-hunh, unh-hunh.
>
> Said Miss Mousie, will you marry me?
> Unh-hunh, unh-hunh, [etc.]
>
> Not without Uncle Rat's consent
> Unh-hunh, unh-hunh
> Not without Uncle Rat's consent
> Would I marry de President,
> Unh-hunh, unh-hunh.

first appeared in London in 1580 as "A Moste Strange Weddinge of the Frogge and the Mouse." Stanzas like

> There was a tall an' handsome man,
> Who came a-courtin' me,
> He said "Steal out atter dark tonight,
> An' come a-ridin' with me,
> An' come a-ridin' with me;"

from "Lady Isabel and The Elf Knight," and

> Hangman, hangman, slack on the line,
> Slack on the line a little while;
> For I think I see my brother coming
> With money to pay my fine.

from "The Briary Bush," show that the stuff of the old ballads was not too remote from Negro folk experience. The question

> Who's gonna shoes yo' little feet
> Who's gonna glove yo' hand

which is asked of John Henry's little woman (p. 455, stanza 2) has come down the long years from the old Scottish ballad called "The Lass of Roch Royal."

Native American ballads also have been altered in Negro versions. Among these are "Casey Jones," of sure appeal to working-class Negroes because of its railroading heroism, and "Frankie and Johnny," not certainly of white or Negro origin, and probably partaking of both. An interesting example of how a Negro guitar player builds up a "symphonic drama" out of Frankie and Johnny is given in John and Alan Lomax's *Negro Folk Songs As Sung By Leadbelly*. "Careless Love," originally a mountain ballad, has been added to so often by Negro troubadours that there is now a new song, definitely Negro.

But preserving traditional ballads or altering other American ballads that strike their fancy are not the chief pursuits of Negro balladeers. They create ballads narrating the exploits of their own heroes and lives. They have contributed some of the finest ballads to America's "songbag," such as "John Henry," "Stackalee," "Uncle Bud," "Railroad Bill," and "Po' Lazarus." The corrupt condition of some of these leads to the fear that ballad making and singing are on the decline. Yet the assiduous efforts of such collectors as the Lomaxes are uncovering fine ballads still—as their versions of "Poor Lazarus" (see p. 457) and of "De Grey Goose" indicate. Like all folk ballads, Negro ballads celebrate the outlaw as in "Railroad Bill" and "Stackalee," or the swift fugitive as in "Long Gone Lost John" and "The Travellin' Man," or the hero of strength, courage, and endurance as in "John Henry." Spectacular events like the sinking of the Titanic, the death of Floyd Collins in the cave, the Mississippi River on a grand rampage, and a tornado's "busting loose" call for ballads. Negro folk ballads tell a story with economy, without sentimentality, and very often with the tragic sense of life characteristic of the best ballads of all lands.

WORK SONGS, SOCIAL SONGS, SONGS OF PROTEST

On many jobs—chopping cotton, roustabouting on the levees, "coonjining" on the gangplank, laying ties and rails on the railroad, driving spikes, swinging picks—the working-class Negro sings in rhythm with his labor. Higginson found examples of rowing songs in South Carolina. These work-songs are generally remembered or improvised stanzas strung together on the thread of melody, not of narrative. Timed with the swinging of his pick, a Negro laborer may sing

> Lawdy, lawdy,—hunh—
> Think I will—hunh—

> Make my home—hunh—
> In Jacksonville.

Many of the stanzas are thrusts at the captain or boss, sometimes good-humored, sometimes—when he is far enough away—frankly rebellious:

> If I'd had—hunh—
> My weight in lime—
> I'd a-whupped my captain—
> Till he went stone-blind.

There are also a large number of social songs, differing from the ballads in that they deal with personal emotions (see p. 467, "Death Letter") and differing from the blues in their stanzaic form.

The Lomaxes, Lawrence Gellert, and Joshua White have recently brought to light many songs of strong social protest. These are censored songs, to be discovered in prison construction camps and on chain gangs only by collectors who have won the confidence of the singers. They express a bitterness, not new to the Negro folk, but fairly new in song collections. Lawrence Gellert, who has garnered the richest yield of such songs in *Negro Songs of Protest* and *Me and My Captain,* realized the need of "cultivating and cementing confidences with individual Negroes" in order to get to the "core of living folklore." At that core he found an "otherwise inarticulate resentment against injustice, a part of the unrest stirring the South." Joshua White's "Silicosis Blues" is the creation of an individual folk singer who phrases the bitter awareness of many industrial workers.

THE BLUES

Among Negro folk songs the blues are second in importance only to the spirituals. In contrast to the spirituals, which were originally intended for group singing, the blues are sung by a single person. They express his feelings and ideas about his experience, but they do this so fundamentally, in an idiom so recognizable to his audience, that his emotion is shared as theirs. The mood is generally a sorrowful one; the word "blues" is part of the American vocabulary now as a synonym for melancholy, for unhappy moodiness.

Most blues use a fairly strict form: a leading line, repeated (sometimes with slight variations), and generally a rhyming third line. Sometimes the first line is repeated twice; in the less developed blues, sometimes the last line does not rhyme. The form is simple, but well adapted to express the laments of folk Negroes over hard luck, "careless" or unrequitted love, broken family life, or general dissatisfaction with a cold and trouble-filled world. The standard form of the blues stanza is as follows:

> I went down to the depot; I looked upon the board;
> It say: There's good times here, they's better up the road.

The blues go far back in time probably in their most rudimentary form to slavery. John and Alan Lomax trace them to the "hollers," the mournful line sung over and over again by a man or woman at work, the brief phrasing of some line sharply meaningful:

> Oh I ain't gonna stay here no mo!

or

> Sometimes I think my woman, she too sweet to die;
> Den sometimes I think she ought to be buried alive.

"Jelly Roll" Morton, while playing piano in the sporting houses of New Orleans, heard Mamie Desdunes play and sing the "first blues I no doubt heard in my life:"

> De 219 took my baby away
> 219 took my babe away
> 217 bring her back someday.

"Ma" Rainey heard the blues while trouping up and down her native southland, and started singing them herself to audiences that were spellbound as her deep husky voice gave them back their songs. W. C. Handy's quick ear heard them on the levees, outside of country railroad depots, and in the streets of southern towns. He recognized their value, and in 1909 wrote "Memphis Blues," and in 1912, the most widely known blues of all, "St. Louis Blues." Handy is called the "Father of the Blues." As "the first musician of creative and analytical powers to appreciate the possibilities of the blues, and the writer of the first published blues," Handy is credited by Abbe Niles with "commencing a revolution in the popular tunes of this land comparable only to that brought about by the introduction of ragtime."

The blues are recognized as indubitably the Negro's. Many songs that have come out of Tin Pan Alley are called blues with very dubious warrant. Irving Berlin's "Schoolhouse Blues," Jerome Kern's "Left All Alone Again Blues," Braham's "Limehouse Blues," Hess's "Homesickness Blues," and "Blues My Naughty Sweetie Gave to Me" are examples of these pseudo blues. As one critic summarizes it, in the blues by Tin Pan Alley composers the grief is feigned, but in genuine Negro blues the gayety is feigned. The musical influence upon jazz of the genuine blues is great; the "blue note" is one of the most significant developments in jazz, and it is entering "serious" American music. Certain bands are advertised as bands that play the blues as they should be played; certain white singers, such as Dinah Shore and Jack Teagarden, are famous for the way they sing the blues. One music critic points to a hillbilly's singing of a Negro blues with Swiss yodeling added, as a good instance of the hybridization of American popular music. The blues are now an inseparable part of that music. But they are still, almost entirely, of Negro origin, and at their best are close to folk sources.

Because of the enormous popularity on phonograph records of women blues singers such as Ma Rainey, Mamie Smith, Bessie Smith (the "Blues Empress"), Clara Smith, Trixie Smith, Ida Cox, and Billy Holiday, the blues are frequently thought of as a woman's plaint for her departed or departing lover. Not so widely known to America are the many male blues singers such as Jim Jackson, Lonnie Johnson, Leroy Carr, Leroy's Buddy (Bill Gaither), Peetie Wheatstraw, Hound Head Henry, Big Bill, and Huddie Ledbetter (Leadbelly), but they are enthusiastically received by the Negro masses.

The commercial recording companies issue more blues about love than any other kind. Love is looked upon with shrewd cynicism or irony or self-pity or sincere despair:

> Love is like a faucet, you can turn it off or on,
> But when you think you've got it, done turned off and gone.

> All you men, sho' do make me tired,
> You gotta hand full of gimme, mouthful of much obliged.

> Soon dis morning, 'bout de break of day,
> Laid my head on de pillow, where my mamma used to lay.

> If you don't want me, you don't have to carry no stall,
> I can git mo' women than a passenger train can haul.

> If you don't want me, why don't you tell me so,
> I'm little and low, can get a man anywhere I go.

> I stay drunk so much, I cain't tell night from day,
> But the woman I love, she treat me any way.

If you don't think I'm sinking, look what a hole I'm in,
If you don't think I love you, look what a fool I've been.

I hear my daddy calling some other woman's name
I know he don't mean me; I'm gonna answer jes' de same.

Many a long day I sit and watch de sun,
Thinking about de good things you and I have done.

Some blues celebrate the charms of the loved one, in imagery related
to that of the American tall tale:

De train I ride is sixteen coaches long,
De gal I love is chocolate to de bone.

Big fat mamma wid de meat shaking on her bones,
Everytime she shakes, some skinny gal done lost her home.

My gal's got teeth like a lighthouse on de sea,
Everytime she smile, she throw a light on me.

A good-looking woman make a cow forget her calf.

A good-looking woman make a rabbit chase a hound.

A good-looking woman make a bulldog gnaw his chain.

But love is not the sole subject of the blues. A general vague dissatisfaction, romantic longing for other people and places, fills many
of them. The road, the train, and recently the bus are the metaphors
of escape, or sometimes of forces of separation:

I'd rather drink muddy water, sleep in a hollow log,
Dan to stay in dis town, treated like a dirty dog.

Going to Chicago where de water drinks like cherry wine,
Cause dis Birmingham water drinks like turpentine.

I'm going to leave here tomorrow, if I have to ride de blinds.

I'm got a mind to ramble, a mind for to leave dis town.

How long, how long, has dat evenin' train been gone?

Sitting here wondering would a matchbox hold my clothes,
I ain't got so many, and I got so far to go.

I'd rather be a catfish swimming in dat deep blue sea,
Dan to stayed in Texas, treated like dey wanted to do po' me.

———————

I'm going where the Southern cross de Yellow Dog.

———————

Did you ever ride on dat Mobile Central Line?
Dat's the road to ride to ease yo' troublin' mind.

———————

I went down to de depot, I looked up on de board,
Couldn't see no train, couldn't hear no whistle blow.

———————

Greyhound, Greyhound, I heard you when you blowed yo' horn,
Well, I knew it was yo' warning that my baby was long gone.

Many blues deal with the social life of "folk" Negroes. Not so commercially rewarding as the love blues, they still exist in large numbers, as the large Library of Congress collection bears witness. Blues have sprung up in the wake of such disasters as the boll-weevil plague, the Mississippi in flood, tornadoes, and fires. "Backwater Blues," composed during the tragic flood of 1927, and the "St. Louis Cyclone Blues" (see pp. 478, 480) are examples. Several WPA blues have been recorded; the "Pink Slip Blues" and the "304 Blues" tell of the hardships of WPA cuts.

The examples already given show something of the poetic imagery of the blues, which is often of a high order. Honest, elemental, sometimes frank to the point of starkness, the blues are welcome to many because of their contrast to the saccharine and insincere lyrics too often produced in Tin Pan Alley. The blues are valuable, also, as shedding a great deal of light on the social experience of the Negro masses. The smutty variants sung in cabarets and on best-selling records should not be allowed to blur the real qualities of this important folk poetry.

FOLK TALES

The most widely known examples of the folk tales of slavery are the Brer Rabbit stories of Joel Chandler Harris. A good listener to the taletellers of the slave quarters, friendly to plantation Negroes and artistically sensitive, Harris was well fitted to become what Alain Locke calls him: "a kindly amanuensis for the illiterate Negro peasant." Harris deserves great credit for recognizing the worth of the Negro fables about Brer Rabbit, Brer Terrapin, Brer Bear, Brer Fox, Brer Wolf, and the others of that fine company. His handling of southern Negro speech was superior to that of any writer preceding him. Yet, as Arthur

Huff Fauset points out in *The New Negro,* his Uncle Remus stories are not folk tales, but adaptations:

> In true folk tales, the story teller himself was inconsequential . . . The Uncle Remus stories break this tradition, however; instead the story teller plays an important, a too important role. By that very fact, this type of story ceases to be a folk tale and becomes in reality a product of the imagination of the author . . . These stories cannot present Negro folk life and feeling seen and felt on its own level. Enough has been said, perhaps, to show, without in any way detracting from the true service and real charm of the Harris stories, that there are enough incongruous elements insinuated into the situation to make it impossible to accept them as a final rendering of American Negro folklore.

Fauset blames the Harris variety of the Negro folk tale for assuming to interpret Negro character instead of simply telling stories. Harris shows Uncle Remus telling the stories for the entertainment of his little white master, and Uncle Remus too often conforms to the plantation tradition. Finally, the Uncle Remus stories are considered children's classics; the stark and almost cynical qualities of genuine folklore, especially that of rural Negroes, are deleted in favor of gentility and sentiment. A whole school of reminiscent writers gave stories as told by faithful uncles and aunties. But their purpose was more to cast a golden glow over the antebellum South than to set forth authentic Negro folklore.

Of the numerous collectors of folklore essentially in the Uncle Remus tradition, the following did work interesting to the general reader and of some usefulness for the student: C. C. Jones, Jr., whose *Negro Myths From the Georgia Coast* (1888) are renderings of Negro tales, closer than Harris' to the genuine, in the Gullah dialect of the coast; and Virginia Frazer Boyle, whose *Devil Tales* (1900) are able transcripts of superstitions.

William Wells Brown, as he was the first Negro in so many fields, was the first to publish folk anecdotes, in *My Southern Home* (1880). Much more informed and artistically handled are the tales in *The Conjure Woman* (1899) by Charles W. Chesnutt. These seven tales, rich in folklore, were compared favorably with the work of Harris and Thomas Nelson Page. The dialect is meticulous, almost to a fault. The narrator of the tales is Uncle Julius, an ex-slave Munchausen, who differs from Harris' and Page's Uncles by being sarcastic about the "good ole days." Uncle Julius tells his stories with cunning, leading up to morals that benefit his designs.

For a long time, Brown and Chesnutt were the only Negroes to publish folktales. But white folklorists have been assiduous. Ambrose Gonzales' *With Aesop Along the Black Border* (1922) is a rendering of fables in carefully phonetic dialect. Here is a sample from "The Fox and the Grapes":

> Bumbye 'e git up 'en 'e walk off, 'en 'e walk berry sedate. Attuwhile 'e biggin fuh grin. 'E suck 'e teet, en' 'e say to 'eself, 'e say, "Me yent hab time fuh w'ary me bone en' t'ing fuh jump attuh no sour grape lukkuh dem. Soon es Uh smell 'um Uh know dem *done* fuh sour! No, suh! Ef Uh haffuh chaw t'ing lukkuh dat, Uh gwine hunt green possimun . . ." Buh Fox sma'at!

Other collections from South Carolina are Elsie Clews Parson's *Folklore of the Sea Islands, South Carolina* (1923); Stoney and Shelby's *Black Genesis* (1930), a collection of what are said to be Negro biblical tales; and Guy Johnson's *Folk Culture on St. Helena Island* (1930), which includes typical folk tales, riddles, and superstitions. Guy Johnson takes the common-sense approach of the observer of social reality, rather than that of the seeker for the picturesque and quaint:

> To the student of folklore, this vast body of stories is something to be collected, preserved, studied, compared, analyzed, something which it would be a shame to let die out. But to the Negroes these stories are like any other stories. They lie tucked away in memory most of the time . . . New stories, perhaps cheap stories, are constantly crowding in upon them, and if some of the old-time ones which go back almost to Adam slip out of memory through disuse, no tears are shed. Finding a rare tale may thrill the collector, but the islander may think something else is far more valuable. To them the story of a stuttering slave's being beaten up by a stuttering Irish patrol because the Irishman thought the Negro was mocking him may be more attractive than Buh Rabbit's victory over Buh Lion.

Julia Peterkin, in *Roll, Jordan, Roll* (1933) and Carl Carmer in *Stars Fell on Alabama* (1934) include good Negro yarns. John Sale's *The Tree Named John* (1929) is a valuable collection of Mississippi lore and tales. Howard Odum's trilogy about Left Wing Gordon: *Rainbow Round My Shoulder* (1928); *Wings On My Feet* (1929); and *Cold Blue Moon* (1930) are a sociologist's collections of living folklore rendered almost as creative literature. E. C. L. Adams in *Congaree Sketches* (1927) and *Nigger to Nigger* (1928) combines the abilities of folklorist and short-story writer. More than anyone else he catches the truth about folk Negroes when talking to each other. The humor of some of Adams' sketches is uproarious, but the bitter irony of some goes deeper than any other treatment of the Negro folk had ever gone before. B. A. Botkin's critical articles sponsoring the new regionalism as opposed to the old local color, and his creative editing of *Folk-Say* from 1929 to 1932, were spurs to understanding studies and re-creations of Negro folk stuff.

Whether familiarity has bred contempt, or whether there has been too great a sensitivity toward folk expression, Negroes have lagged behind whites in the gathering of folk tales. Without Joel Chandler Harris, it is likely that the Uncle Remus stories, which now belong with the minor masterpieces of American literature, would have been lost. Awareness of the importance of a study of the folk is increasing among Negroes, but still slowly. Under the auspices of the American Folk Lore Society, Arthur Huff Fauset studied Nova Scotian folklore in 1923 and the Mississippi Delta folklore in 1925. In 1932 J. Mason Brewer made a small collection of slave tales under the title *Juneteenth*. The first substantial collection of folk tales by a Negro scholar is *Mules and Men* (1935) by Zora Neale Hurston. Miss Hurston is a trained anthropologist, who brings a great zest to both the collecting and the rendering of the "big old lies" of her native South. Onah L. Spencer's tales of John Henry and Stackalee are the first ventures of a new writer in the field. Charles S. Johnson has amassed a large collection of folk-lore, as yet unpublished, at Fisk University.

Whether laughing at the mishaps of his master or of a fellow slave; whether siding with Brer Rabbit while he checkmates stronger opponents with cunning and deceit, or with the Tar-Baby while he foils Brer Rabbit; whether telling about John Henry defeating the steam drill, or Railroad Bill outshooting the sheriff and his deputies, oral telling of tales has been a favorite occupation of American Negroes. Down by the big gate, at the store or cotton gin, at the end of the row at lunch time, in poolroom, barbershop, fraternal lodge, college dormitory, railroad depot, railroad coach, the Negro has told his tall tales and anecdotes, now sidesplitting, now ironic, now tragic. Though it is an art not likely to die out, it certainly deserves more serious attention than it has received.

FOLK SERMONS

The Negro folk preacher has long been burlesqued; Roark Bradford's *Ol' Man Adam and His Chillun,* from which *The Green Pastures* was derived, is a well known example. Beginning with James Weldon Johnson's "The Creation," to which Johnson added the other

sermons that went to make up *God's Trombones,* a different attitude
to "folk" sermons has developed. Vachel Lindsay and E. C. L. Adams,
white authors, and Arthur Huff Fauset and Zora Neale Hurston,
Negro authors, in their recreations of Negro folk sermons, have definitely caught something of their eloquence, essential dignity, and poetic
picturesqueness.

SPIRITUALS

(The following spirituals are derived from the *Book of American Negro Spirituals*
by James Weldon Johnson and J. Rosamond Johnson, *Religious Folk-Songs of the
American Negro* by R. Nathaniel Dett, *Slave Songs of the United States* by Allen,
Ware, and Garrison, *American Folk Songs* by John Lomax and Alan Lomax, *Songs
of Our Fathers* by Willis James, the repertory of the Golden Gate Quartette, and
from the collections of the editors of *The Negro Caravan.*)

Sometimes I Feel Like a Motherless Child

Sometimes I feel like a motherless child,
Sometimes I feel like a motherless child,
Sometimes I feel like a motherless child,
A long ways from home;
A long ways from home.

Sometimes I feel like I'm almost gone,
Sometimes I feel like I'm almost gone,
Sometimes I feel like I'm almost gone,
A long ways from home;
A long ways from home.

Swing Low, Sweet Chariot

Swing low, sweet chariot,
Coming for to carry me home,
Swing low, sweet chariot,
Coming for to carry me home.

I looked over Jordan and what did I see
Coming for to carry me home,
A band of angels, coming after me,
Coming for to carry me home.

If you get there before I do,
Coming for to carry me home,
Tell all my friends I'm coming too,
Coming for to carry me home.

Swing low, sweet chariot,
Coming for to carry me home,
Swing low, sweet chariot,
Coming for to carry me home.

Steal Away

Steal away, steal away, steal away to Jesus,
Steal away, steal away home,
I ain't got long to stay here.

My Lord, He calls me,
He calls me by the thunder,
The trumpet sounds within-a my soul,
I ain't got long to stay here.

Steal away, steal away, steal away to Jesus,
Steal away, steal away home,
I ain't got long to stay here.

Green trees a-bending,
Po' sinner stands a-trembling
The trumpet sounds within-a my soul,
I ain't got long to stay here.

Steal away, steal away, steal away to Jesus,
Steal away, steal away home,
I ain't got long to stay here.

Deep River

Deep river, my home is over Jordan,
Deep river, Lord; I want to cross over into camp ground.

O children, O, don't you want to go to that gospel feast,
That promised land, that land, where all is peace?

Deep river, my home is over Jordan,
Deep river, Lord; I want to cross over into camp ground.

I Got a Home in Dat Rock

I got a home in dat rock,
Don't you see?
I got a home in dat rock,
Don't you see?

Between de earth an' sky,
Thought I heard my Saviour cry,
You got a home in dat rock,
Don't you see?

Poor man Laz'rus, poor as I,
Don't you see?
Poor man Laz'rus, poor as I,
Don't you see?
Poor man Laz'rus, poor as I,
When he died he found a home on high,
He had a home in dat rock,
Don't you see?

Rich man Dives, he lived so well,
Don't you see?
Rich man Dives, he lived so well,
Don't you see?
Rich man Dives, he lived so well,
When he died he found a home in Hell,
He had no home in dat rock,
Don't you see?

God gave Noah de Rainbow sign,
Don't you see?
God gave Noah de Rainbow sign,
Don't you see?
God gave Noah de Rainbow sign,
No more water but fire next time,
Better get a home in dat rock,
Don't you see?

I Been Rebuked and I Been Scorned

I been rebuked and I been scorned,
I been rebuked and I been scorned,
Chillun, I been rebuked and I been scorned,
I'se had a hard time, sho's you born.

Talk about me much as you please,
Talk about me much as you please,
Chillun, talk about me much as you please,
Gonna talk about you when I get on my knees.

De Hammer Keeps Ringing

Oh, de hammer keeps ringing
On somebody's coffin,
Oh, de hammer keeps ringing
On somebody's coffin,
Oh, de hammer keeps ringing
On somebody's coffin:
Good Lord, I know my time ain't long.

Oh, de wagon keeps rolling
Somebody to de graveyard,
Oh, de wagon keeps rolling
Somebody to de graveyard,
Oh, de wagon keeps rolling
Somebody to de graveyard:
Good Lord, I know my time ain't long.

Oh, de preacher keeps preaching
Somebody's funeyal,
Oh, de preacher keeps preaching
Somebody's funeyal,
De preacher keeps preaching
Somebody's funeyal:
Good Lord, I know my time ain't long.

De Ole Sheep Dey Know De Road

Oh, de ole sheep, dey know de road,
De ole sheep, dey know de road,
De ole sheep, dey know de road,
De young lambs must find de way.

My brother, better mind how you walk on de cross,
    De young lambs must find de way,
For your foot might slip, and yo' soul git lost,
    De young lambs must find de way.

Better mind dat sun, and see how she run,
    De young lambs must find de way,
And mind, don't let her catch you wid yo' work undone,
    De young lambs must find de way.

Oh, de ole sheep, dey know de road,
De ole sheep, dey know de road,
De ole sheep, dey know de road,
Young lambs must find de way.

De Blind Man Stood on De Road

O, de blind man stood on de road and cried
O, de blind man stood on de road and cried
Crying "O, my Lord, save-a me;"
De blind man stood on de road and cried.

Crying dat he might receive his sight
Crying dat he might receive his sight
Crying "O, my Lord, save-a me;"
De blind man stood on de road and cried.

He Never Said a Mumbaling Word

Oh, dey whupped him up de hill, up de hill, up de hill,
Oh, dey whupped him up de hill, and he never said a mumbaling word,
Oh, dey whupped him up de hill, and he never said a mumbaling word,
He jes' hung down his head, and he cried.

Oh, dey crowned him wid a thorny crown, thorny crown, thorny crown,
Oh, dey crowned him wid a thorny crown, and he never said a
    mumbaling word,
Oh, dey crowned him wid a thorny crown, and he never said a
    mumbaling word,
He jes' hung down his head, and he cried.

Well, dey nailed him to de cross, to de cross, to de cross,
Well, dey nailed him to de cross, and he never said a mumbaling word,
Well, dey nailed him to de cross, and he never said a mumbaling word,
He jes' hung down his head, and he cried.

Well, dey pierced him in de side, in de side, in de side,
Well, dey pierced him in de side, and de blood come a-twinkling down,
Well, dey pierced him in de side, and de blood come a-twinkling down,
Den he hung down his head, and he died.

Joshua Fit De Battle of Jericho

Joshua fit de battle of Jericho,
Jericho, Jericho,
Joshua fit de battle of Jericho,
And de walls come tumbling down.

You may talk about yo' king of Gideon
Talk about yo' man of Saul,
Dere's none like good old Joshua
At de battle of Jericho.

Up to de walls of Jericho,
He marched with spear in hand;
"Go blow dem ram horns," Joshua cried,
"Kase de battle am in my hand."

Den de lamb ram sheep horns begin to blow,
Trumpets begin to sound,
Joshua commanded de chillen to shout,
And de walls come tumbling down.

Dat morning,
Joshua fit de battle of Jericho,
Jericho, Jericho,
Joshua fit de battle of Jericho,
And de walls come tumbling down.

Oh, Mary, Don't You Weep

Oh Mary, don't you weep, don't you moan,
Oh Mary, don't you weep, don't you moan,
Pharaoh's army got drownded,
Oh Mary, don't you weep.

One of dese mornings, bright and fair,
Take my wings and cleave de air,
Pharaoh's army got drownded,
Oh Mary, don't you weep.

One of dese mornings, five o'clock,
Dis ole world gonna reel and rock,
Pharaoh's army got drownded,
Oh Mary, don't you weep.

Don't know what my mother wants to stay here fuh,
Dis ole world ain't been no friend to huh,
Pharaoh's army got drownded,
Oh Mary, don't you weep.

Oh Mary, don't you weep, don't you moan,
Oh Mary, don't you weep, don't you moan,
Pharaoh's army got drownded,
Oh Mary, don't you weep.

Go Down, Moses

Go down, Moses,
Way down in Egyptland
Tell old Pharaoh
To let my people go.

When Israel was in Egyptland
Let my people go
Oppressed so hard they could not stand
Let my people go.

Go down, Moses,
Way down in Egyptland
Tell old Pharaoh
"Let my people go."

"Thus saith the Lord," bold Moses said,
"Let my people go;
If not I'll smite your first-born dead
Let my people go.

"No more shall they in bondage toil,
    Let my people go;
Let them come out with Egypt's spoil,
    Let my people go."

The Lord told Moses what to do
    Let my people go;
To lead the children of Israel through,
    Let my people go.

Go down, Moses,
    Way down in Egyptland,
Tell old Pharaoh,
    "Let my people go!"

Slavery Chain

Slavery chain done broke at last, broke at last, broke at last,
Slavery chain done broke at last,
Going to praise God till I die.

Way down in-a dat valley,
Praying on my knees;
Told God about my troubles,
And to help me ef-a He please.

I did tell him how I suffer,
In de dungeon and de chain,
And de days I went with head bowed down,
And my broken flesh and pain.

Slavery chain done broke at last, broke at last, broke at last,
Slavery chain done broke at last,
Going to praise God till I die.

I did know my Jesus heard me,
'Cause de spirit spoke to me,
And said, "Rise my child, your chillun,
And you too shall be free.

"I done 'p'int one mighty captain
For to marshall all my hosts,
And to bring my bleeding ones to me,
And not one shall be lost."

Slavery chain done broke at last, broke at last, broke at last,
Slavery chain done broke at last,
Going to praise God till I die.

No More Auction Block

No more auction block for me,
No more, no more,
No more auction block for me,
Many thousand gone.

No more peck of corn for me,
No more, no more,
No more peck of corn for me,
Many thousand gone.

No more pint of salt for me,
No more, no more,
No more pint of salt for me,
Many thousand gone.

No more driver's lash for me,
No more, no more,
No more driver's lash for me,
Many thousand gone.

Noah

(From the Golden Gate Quartet, Bluebird B-8160. Printed by permission of the quartet and the RCA Manufacturing Company, Inc.)

Oh Noah; Oh, oh Noah; Oh, oh Noah,
God's gonna ride on de rain and de tide. (2)
Oh Noah, Brother Noah, my God's talking,
He's gonna ride on the rain and tide.

Children stop still, listen to me:
God walked down by the briny sea,
Beheld the evil of sinful man,
Declared that he would 'stroy the land,
He spoke to Noah, Noah stopped,
He said "Look-a-here Noah, build me a ark,
I want you to build it big and strong,
Build it three hundred cubits long,
Thirteen high and fifteen wide,
I want it to stand the rain and the tide."

Oh Noah, Brother Noah heard God talking,
He's gonna move on the rain and tide.

Well, after God told him what to do
Noah began to cut and to hew
The ringing of the hammer was judge-a-ment
The ringing of the saw cried, "Sinner, repent."
A hundred years they hammered and sawed,
Built the ark by the Grace of God,
After the foundation was laid,
Hewed the timber, the ark was made,
They called in the animals two by two
The ox, the camel, and the kangaroo,
Then he called in Japheth, Shem and Ham,
And God began to flood the land,
He raised His hand to Heaven on high,
Knocked the sun and moon from the skies,
Shook the mountains and disturbed the seas,
Hitched the winds to His chariot wheel,
He stood on the land and stepped on the shore
And declared that time would be no more.

Oh Noah; Oh, oh Noah; Oh, oh Noah;
God's gonna ride on the rain and the tide.

If I Had My Way

(From the Golden Gate Quartet. Bluebird B-8306. Printed by permission of the quartet and the RCA Manufacturing Company, Inc.)

If I had-a my way,
If I had-a my way, little children,
If I had-a my way,
I'd tear this buildin' down.
Great God, then, if I had-a my way,
If I had-a my way, little children,
If I had-a my way,
I'd tear this buildin' down.

Well you read in the Bible, you will understand
Samson was the strongest man,
Tell me God moved on the wings of the wind
He saw old Samson and he called to him,
Whispered low into Samson's mind
Said "Deliver my children from the Philistines."

Well, If I had-a my way
If I had-a my way, little children,
If I had-a my way,
I'd tear the buildin' down.

Great God, then, Samson went down and he wandered about,
Tell me that his strength was never found out,
They tell us down in Chapter Nine,
That he killed three thousand Philistines.
Then Samson's wife she sat on his knees,
Said "Tell me Samson where your strength lies please";
Samson's wife she talked so fair,
That Sampson told her to cut his hair,
Said "You shave my head as clean as your hand,
Then my strength gonna come like a natural man."

He said-a "If I had-a my way,
If I had-a my way, little children,.
If I had-a my way,
I'd tear the buildin' down."

Great God, they shaved his head just as clean as the hand,
They took him on down in a strange land,
They led him on down to the judgment hall
Blinded him and chained him to the wall,

But he called on his God and he called him low,
They tell me that his hair begin to grow,
Then he called a kid about three feet tall
He said "You place my hands up against the wall";
Then they placed his hands up against the wall,
And he tore that buildin' down.

Great God, then, Samson had-a his way,
Samson had-a his way, little children,
Samson had-a his way,
He tore the buildin' down.

Job

(From the Golden Gate Quartet. Bluebird B-73776. Printed by permission of the quartet and the RCA Manufacturing Company, Inc.)

I'm on my way to the Kingdom Land,
I'm on my way to the Kingdom Land,
If you don't go, I'll journey on,
I'm on my way, Lord, Lord, I'm on my way.

You know Job was the richest man that lived in the land of Nod,
He was the only man for miles around to get the commandments
    of God,
Well the devil he got jealous of Job and he came to God one day,
Said "If you move your hand from around the man,
He's gonna curse you to your face."

He said, "There's nothing you can do to turn him around,
There's nothing you can do to turn him around,
'Cause he's done signed up, made up his mind,
He's on his way, Lord, Lord, he's on his way."

Then the devil laid his fingers on Job, and Job fell down right
    weak,
He got in the bed of afflictitude, got sores from his head to
    his feet,
Old Job's friends started to kneel to Heaven, along about one
    to five,
They said, "Job's he's sick and he won't get well,
And I believe he's going to die."

Yes, I'm on my way to the Kingdom Land,
Yes, I'm on my way to the Kingdom Land,
If you don't go, I'll journey on,
I'm on my way, Great God, I'm on my way.

Then old Job's wife she came a-truckin' to him, wid de devil
    right in her eyes,
    She said, "Fool you're sick and you won't get well, you'd
      better curse your God and die;"
Old Job looked right straight at the woman, then he looked
    up in the skies,
He said, "Woman you talk like the foolish one,
Well you don't sound like the wise.

"There's nothing you can do to turn me around,
There's nothing you can do to turn me around,
'Cause I done signed up, made up my mind,
I'm on my way, Lord, Lord, I'm on my way."

Then old Job's servant came a-runnin' to him, said, "Job I
    got something to say,
You know the fire done come from Heaven last night, and
    carried your cattle away,"
Old Job looked right straight at the man and said "I don't
    have anything to say,
'Cause the Lord God in Heaven giveth,
And the Lord God taketh away.

"I'm on my way to the Kingdom Land,
I'm on my way to the Kingdom Land,
If you don't go, I'll journey on,
I'm on my way, Lord, Lord, I'm on my way."

My God Is a Rock

(From the collection of Willis James. Reprinted by his permission.)

Oh look-a-yonder at Mary and Joseph
An de young child, King Jesus
On de journey to Jerusalem
For to pay their poll taxes;
On de way back dey miss de young child
And dey went to Jerusalem
For to search for the young child, Jesus.

Where'd dey fin' him?
In de temple wid de lawyers an' de doctors
An' de elders
Ask'n questions one to another.

Den he turn to de doctor
Said, "Doctor, state and county doctor,
Can you heal some sin sick soul, suh?"
Oh no, oh no, dat's a question he could not answer.

Den he turned to de lawyer,
"Oh lawyer, oh lawyer,
You a lawyer, state and county lawyer, suh
Can you plead some sinners cause, suh?"
Oh no, oh no, dat's a question he could not answer.

Den he turned to de judge
"Oh judge, oh judge, you the judge, suh,
State and county judge, suh,
Can you judge their righteous souls, suh?"
Oh no, oh no, that's a question he couldn't answer.

Chorus

My God is a rock in a weary lan', weary lan', weary lan'
My God is a rock in a weary lan',
Shelter in de time of storm.

SLAVE SECULARS

Song

(From Frederick Douglass, *My Bondage and My Freedom*, 1853)

We raise de wheat,
Dey gib us de corn:
We bake de bread,
Dey gib us de crust;
We sif de meal,
Dey gib us de huss;
We peel de meat,
Dey gib us de skin;
And dat's de way
Dey take us in;
We skim de pot,
Dey gib us de liquor,
And say dat's good enough for nigger.

Song

(From Martin R. Delany, "Blake; or, The Huts of America."
in *The Anglo-African Magazine,* June 1859)

Come all my brethren, let us take a rest,
While the moon shines bright and clear;
Old master died and left us all at last,
And has gone at the bar to appear!
Old master's dead and lying in his grave;
And our blood will now cease to flow;
He will no more tramp on the neck of the slave,
For he's gone where slave-holders go!
Hand up the shovel and the hoe-o-o-o!
I don't care whether I work or no!
Old master's gone to the slave-holders rest—
He's gone where they all *ought* to go!"

Promises of Freedom

(This and the following two songs are from Thomas W. Talley's *Negro Folk
Rhymes*. They are published by permission of the collector and of The Macmillan Co.,
publishers of the book.)

My ole Mistiss promise me,
W'en she died, she'd set me free,
She lived so long dat 'er head got bal',
An' she give out'n de notion a-dyin'
    at all.

My ole Mistiss say to me:
"Sambo, I'se gwine ter set you free."
But w'en dat head git slick an' bal',
De Lawd couldn't a' killed 'er wid
    a big green maul.

My ole Mistiss never die,
Wid 'er nose all hooked an' skin all
    dry.
But my ole Miss, she's somehow gone,
An' she lef' Uncle Sambo a-hillin'
    up co'n.

Ole Mosser lakwise promise me,
W'en he died, he'd set me free.
But ole Mosser go an' make his will
Fer to leave me a-plowin' ole Beck
    still.

Yes, my ole Mosser promise me;
But "his papers" didn' leave me free.
A dose of pizen he'ped 'im along.
May de Devil preach 'is funer'l song.

He Is My Horse

One day as I wus a-ridin' by,
Said dey: "Ole man, yo' hoss will die."
    "If he dies, he is my loss;
    An' if he lives, he is my hoss."

Nex' day w'en I come a-ridin' by,
Dey said: "Ole man, yo' hoss may die."
    "If he dies, I'll tan 'is skin;
    An' if he lives, I'll ride 'im ag'in."

Den ag'in w'en I come a-ridin' by,
Said dey: "Ole man, yo' hoss mought
        die."
    "If he dies, I'll eat his co'n;
    An' if he lives, I'll ride 'im on."

Did You Feed My Cow?

"Did yer feed my cow?" "Yes, Mam!"
"Will yer tell me how?" "Yes, Mam!"
"Oh, w'at did yer give 'er?" "Cawn an hay."
"Oh, w'at did yer give 'er?" "Cawn an hay."

"Did yer milk 'er good?" "Yes, Mam!"
"Did yer do lak yer should?" "Yes, Mam!"
"Oh, how did yer milk 'er?" "Swish! Swish!
        Swish!"
"Oh, how did yer milk 'er?" "Swish! Swish!
        Swish!"

"Did dat cow git sick?" "Yes, Mam!"
"Wus she kivered wid tick?" "Yes, Mam!"
"Oh, how wus she sick?" "All bloated up."
"Oh, how wus she sick?" "All bloated up."

"Did dat cow die?" "Yes, Mam!"
"Wid a pain in 'er eye?" "Yes, Mam!"
"Oh, how did she die?" "Uh—! Uh—! Uh—!"
"Oh, how did she die?" "Uh—! Uh—! Uh—!"

"Did de Buzzards come?" "Yes, Mam!"
"Fer to pick 'er bone?" "Yes, Mam!"
"Oh, how did they come?" "Flop! Flop! Flop!"
"Oh, how did they come?" "Flop! Flop! Flop!"

Folk Song

(This song is reprinted from Joel Chandler Harris' *Uncle Remus, His Songs and His Sayings,* and is reprinted by permission of Houghton Mifflin Company, the publishers of the book.)

De ole bee make de honey-comb,
　　De young bee make de honey,
De niggers make de cotton en co'n,
　　En de w'ite folks gits de money.

De raccoon he's a cu'us man,
　　He never walk twel dark,
En nuthin' never 'sturbs his mine,
　　Twel he hear ole Bringer bark.

De raccoon totes a bushy tail,
　　De 'possum totes no ha'r,
Mr. Rabbit, he come skippin' by,
　　He ain't got none ter spar'.

Monday mornin' break er day,
　　W'ite folks got me gwine,
But Sat'dy night, w'en de sun goes down,
　　Dat yaller gal's in my mine.

Run, Nigger, Run

(This song is reprinted from Dorothy Scarborough's *On the Trail of Negro Folk-Songs* [1925], and is reprinted by permission of The Harvard University Press, the publishers of the book.)

Run, nigger run; de patter-roller catch you;
Run, nigger, run, it's almost day.
Run, nigger, run; de patter-roller catch you;
Run, nigger, run, and try to get away.

Dis nigger run, he run his best,
Stuck his head in a hornet's nest,
Jumped de fence and run fru de paster;
White man run, but nigger run faster.

Dat nigger run, dat nigger flew,
Dat nigger tore his shirt in two.

Raise a Rukus Tonight

(This song is reprinted from Howard Odum's and Guy Johnson's *The Negro and His Songs* by permission of the authors and the University of North Carolina Press, the publishers of the book.)

My ol' master promise me,
Raise rukus tonight;
Before he died he'd set me free,
Raise rukus tonight.

Chorus

Come along, chillun, come along,
While the moon is shining bright,
Get on board, down the river float,
'Cause we gonna raise a rukus tonight.

His hair come out and his head turned bal',
Raise rukus tonight;
He got out o' notion dyin' at all,
Raise rukus tonight.
'Scuse me, mister, don't get mad,
Raise rukus tonight;
'Cause you look sumpin the buzzards had,
Raise rukus tonight.

Look at that nigger, ain't he black?
Raise rukus tonight;
Got hair on his head like a carpet tack,
Raise rukus tonight.

Black cat settin' on chimney jam,
Raise rukus tonight;
If that ain't hot place, I'll be damn,
Raise rukus tonight.

Way down yonder on chit'lin' switch,
Raise rukus tonight;
Bull frog jump from ditch to ditch,
Raise rukus tonight.

Bull frog jump from bottom of well,
Raise rukus tonight;
Swore, by God, he jumped from hell,
Raise rukus tonight.

APHORISMS

It's hard to make clothes fit a miserable man.

De stopper get de longest rest in de empty jug.

De church bells sometimes do better work dan de sermon.

De price of your hat ain't de measure of your brain.

Ef your coat-tail catch a-fire, don't wait till you kin see de blaze 'fo' you put it out.

De graveyard is de cheapes' boardin'-house.

Dar's a fam'ly coolness 'twix' de mule an' de single-tree.

It pesters a man dreadful when he git mad an' don' know who to cuss.

Buyin' on credit is robbin' next year's crop.

Christmas without holiday is like a candle without a wick.

De crawfish in a hurry look like he tryin' to git dar yesterday.

Lean hound lead de pack when de rabbit in sight.

Little flakes make de deepest snow.

Knot in de plank will show through de whitewash.

Dirt show de quickest on de cleanest cotton.

De candy-pulling can call louder dan de log-rolling.

De right sort of religion heaps de half-bushel.

De steel hoe dat laughs at de iron one is like de man dat is shamed of his grand-daddy.

A mule can tote so much goodness in his face that he don't have none left for his hind legs.

De cow-bell can't keep a secret.

Ripe apples make de tree look taller.

Blind horse knows when de trough is empty.

De noise of de wheels don't measure de load in de wagon.

Last year's hot spell cools off mighty fast.

Little hole in your pocket is worse than a big one at de knee.

Appetite don't regulate de time of day.

He drinks so much whisky that he staggers in his sleep.

De rich git richer and de po' git children.

Watch out when you're gettin' all you want. Fattenin' hogs ain't in luck.

Persimmons ain't no good until dey're frost-bit.

Man who gits hurt working oughta show de scars.

Life is short and full of blisters.

If you want to see how much folks is goin' to miss you, just stick your finger in de pond den pull it out and look at de hole.

De quagmire don't hang out no sign.

One person can thread a needle better than two.

De point of de pin is de easiest end to find.

451

Muzzle on de yard dog unlocks de smokehouse.

It's hard for de best and smartest folks in de world to git along
    without a little touch of good luck.

De billy-goat gets in his hardest licks when he looks like he's
    going to back out of de fight.

In God we trust, all others cash.

He may mean good, but he *do* so doggone po'.

A whistling woman and a crowing hen,

Don't never come to no good end.

BALLADS

John Henry

(The following ballad is pieced together from stanzas assembled in Guy Johnson's *John Henry* and from the editor's collections. The stanzas from *John Henry*
are reprinted by permission of Guy Johnson and the University of North Carolina
Press, the publishers.)

When John Henry was a little fellow,
    You could hold him in the palm of your hand,
He said to his pa, "When I grow up
    I'm gonna be a steel-driving man.
    Gonna be a steel-driving man."

When John Henry was a little baby,
    Setting on his mammy's knee,
He said "The Big Bend Tunnel on the C. & O. Road
    Is gonna be the death of me,
    Gonna be the death of me."

One day his captain told him,
    How he had bet a man
That John Henry would beat his steam-drill down,
    Cause John Henry was the best in the land,
    John Henry was the best in the land.

John Henry kissed his hammer,
    White man turned on steam,
Shaker held John Henry's trusty steel,
    Was the biggest race the world had ever seen,
    Lord, biggest race the world ever seen.

John Henry on the right side
    The steam drill on the left,
"Before I'll let your steam drill beat me down,

I'll hammer my fool self to death,
        Hammer my fool self to death."

John Henry walked in the tunnel,
    His captain by his side,
The mountain so tall, John Henry so small,
    He laid down his hammer and he cried,
        Laid down his hammer and he cried.

Captain heard a mighty rumbling,
    Said "The mountain must be caving in,
John Henry said to the captain,
    "It's my hammer swinging in de wind,
        My hammer swinging in de wind."

John Henry said to his shaker,
    "Shaker, you'd better pray;
For if ever I miss this piece of steel,
    Tomorrow'll be your burial day,
        Tomorrow'll be your burial day."

John Henry said to his shaker,
    "Lordy, shake it while I sing,
I'm pulling my hammer from my shoulders down,
    Great Gawdamighty, how she ring,
        Great Gawdamighty, how she ring!"

John Henry said to his captain,
    "Before I ever leave town,
Gimme one mo' drink of dat tom-cat gin,
    And I'll hammer dat steam driver down,
        I'll hammer dat steam driver down."

John Henry said to his captain,
    "Before I ever leave town,
Gimme a twelve-pound hammer wid a whale-bone handle,
    And I'll hammer dat steam driver down,
        I'll hammer dat steam drill on down."

John Henry said to his captain,
    "A man ain't nothin' but a man,
But before I'll let dat steam drill beat me down,
    I'll die wid my hammer in my hand,
        Die wid my hammer in my hand."

The man that invented the steam drill
    He thought he was mighty fine,
John Henry drove down fourteen feet,
    While the steam drill only made nine,
        Steam drill only made nine.

"Oh, lookaway over yonder, captain,
    You can't see like me,"
He gave a long and loud and lonesome cry,
    "Lawd, a hammer be the death of me,
        A hammer be the death of me!"

John Henry had a little woman,
    Her name was Polly Ann,
John Henry took sick, she took his hammer,
    She hammered like a natural man,
        Lawd, she hammered like a natural man.

John Henry hammering on the mountain
    As the whistle blew for half-past two,
The last words his captain heard him say,
    "I've done hammered my insides in two,
        Lawd, I've hammered my insides in two."

The hammer that John Henry swung
    It weighed over twelve pound,
He broke a rib in his left hand side
    And his intrels fell on the ground,
        And his intrels fell on the ground.

John Henry, O, John Henry,
    His blood is running red,
Fell right down with his hammer to the ground,
    Said, "I beat him to the bottom but I'm dead,
        Lawd, beat him to the bottom but I'm dead."

When John Henry was laying there dying,
    The people all by his side,
The very last words they heard him say,
    "Give me a cool drink of water 'fore I die,
        Cool drink of water 'fore I die."

John Henry had a little woman,
    The dress she wore was red,
She went down the track, and she never looked back,
    Going where her man fell dead,
        Going where her man fell dead.

John Henry had a little woman,
    The dress she wore was blue,
De very last words she said to him,
    "John Henry, I'll be true to you,
        John Henry, I'll be true to you."

"Who's gonna shoes yo' little feet,
    Who's gonna glove yo' hand,
Who's gonna kiss yo' pretty, pretty cheek,
    Now you done lost yo' man?
        Now you done lost yo' man?"

"My mammy's gonna shoes my little feet,
    Pappy gonna glove my hand,
My sister's gonna kiss my pretty, pretty cheek,
    Now I done lost my man,
        Now I done lost my man."

They carried him down by the river,
    And buried him in the sand,
And everybody that passed that way,
    Said, "There lies that steel-driving man,
        There lies a steel-driving man."

They took John Henry to the river,
    And buried him in the sand,
And every locomotive come a-roaring by,
    Says "There lies that steel-drivin' man,
        Lawd, there lies a *steel*-drivin' man."

Some say he came from Georgia,
    And some from Alabam,
But its wrote on the rock at the Big Bend Tunnel,
    That he was an East Virginia man,
        Lord, Lord, an East Virginia man.

Bad Man Ballad[1]

Late las' night I was a-makin' my rounds,
Met my woman an' I blowed her down,
Went on home an' I went to bed,
Put my hand cannon right under my head.

[1]Words and air from a tongue-tied Negro convict at Parchman, Mississippi.

Early nex' mornin' 'bout de risin' o' de sun,
I gets up-a for to make-a my run.
I made a good run but I made it too slow,
Got overtaken in Mexico.

Standin' on de corno', readin' of a bill,
Up step a man name o' Bad Texas Bill:
"Look here, bully, ain' yo' name Lee Brown?
B'lieve you are de rascal shot yo' woman down."

"Yes, oh, yes," says. "This is him.
If you got a warrant, jes' read it to me."
He says: "You look like a fellow that knows what's bes'.
Come 'long wid me—you're under arres'."

When I was arrested, I was dressed in black;
Dey put me on a train, an' dey brought me back.
Dey boun' me down in de county jail;
Couldn' get a human for to go my bail.

Early nex' mornin' 'bout half pas' nine,
I spied ol' jedge drappin' down de line.
I heered ol' jailer when he cleared his th'oat,
"Nigger, git ready for de deestreec' cote."

Deestreec' cote is now begin,
Twelve big jurymen, twelve hones' men.
Five mo' minutes up step a man,
He was holdin' my verdic' in his right han'.

Verdic' read murder in de firs' degree.
I said, "O Lawd, have mercy on me."
I seed ol' jedge when he picked up his pen,
Say, "I don' think you'll ever kill a woman ag'in.

"This here killin' of women natchly got to stop,
I don't know whether to hang you er not.
Ninety-nine years on de hard, hard groun',
'Member de night you blowed de woman down."

Here I is, bowed down in shame,
I got a number instead of a name.
Here for de res' of my nachul life,
An' all I ever done is kill my wife. . . .

Poor Lazarus [2]

("Bad Man Ballad," "Poor Lazarus," and "De Ballit of De Boll Weevil" are taken from *American Folk Songs* by John and Alan Lomax, and are reprinted by permission of the collectors and of The Macmillan Co., the publishers.)

High sheriff tol' de deputy, "Go out an' bring me Laz'us."
High sheriff tol' de deputy: "Go out an' bring me Laz'us.
Bring him dead or alive, Lawd, Lawd, bring him dead or alive."

Oh, bad man Laz'us done broke in de commissary winder,
Oh, bad man Laz'us done broke in de commissary winder,
He been paid off, Lawd, Lawd, he been paid off.

Oh, de deputy 'gin to wonder, where in de worl' he could fin' him;
Oh, de deputy 'gin to wonder, where in de worl' he could fin' him;
Well, I don' know, Lawd, Lawd, I jes' don' know.

Oh, dey found po' Laz'us way out between two mountains,
Oh, dey found' po' Laz'us way out between two mountains,
An' dey blowed him down, Lawd, Lawd, an' dey blowed him down.

Ol' Laz'us tol' de deputy he had never been arrested,
Ol' Laz'us tol' de deputy he had never been arrested,
By no one man, Lawd, Lawd, by no one man.

So dey shot po' Laz'us, shot him wid a great big number,
Dey shot po' Laz'us, shot him wid a great big number,
Number 45, Lawd, Lawd, number 45.

An' dey taken po' Laz'us an' dey laid him on de commissary county,
Dey taken po' Laz'us an' dey laid him on de commissary county,
An' dey walked away, Lawd, Lawd, an' dey walked away.

Laz'us tol' de deputy, "Please gimme a cool drink o' water,
Laz'us tol' de deputy, "Please gimme a cool drink o' water,
Jes' befo' I die, Lawd, Lawd, jes' befo' I die."

Laz'us' sister run an' tol' her mother,
Laz'us' sister run an' tol' her mother,
Dat po' Laz'us dead, Lawd, Lawd, po' Laz'us dead.

Laz'us' mother, she laid down her sewin',
Laz'us' mother, she laid down her sewin',
'Bout de trouble, Lawd, Lawd, she had wid Laz'us.

[2]Some of the verses of this ballad worksong we have taken from *Negro Workaday Songs*. The rest of the words and the tune were recorded in Southern prison camps. (Collectors' note.)

Laz'us' mother she come a-screamin' an' a-cryin',
Laz'us' mother she come a-screamin' an' a-cryin',
"Dat's my only son, Lawd, Lawd, dat's my only son."

De Ballit of De Boll Weevil[3]

Oh, have you heard de lates',
De lates' of de songs?
It's about dem little Boll Weevils,
Dey's picked up bofe feet an' gone
A-lookin' for a home,
Jes a-lookin' for a home.

De Boll Weevil is a little bug
F'um Mexico, dey say,
He come to try dis Texas soil
En thought he better stay,
A-lookin' for a home,
Jes a-lookin' for a home.

De nigger say to de Boll Weevil
"Whut makes yo' head so red?"[4]
"I's been wanderin' de whole worl' ovah
Till it's a wonder I ain't dead,
A-lookin' for a home,
Jes a-lookin' for a home."

First time I saw Mr. Boll Weevil,
He wuz on de western plain;
Next time I saw him,
He wuz ridin' on a Memphis train,
A-lookin' for a home,
Jes a-lookin' for a home. . . .

De fus' time I saw de Boll Weevil
He wuz settin' on de square,
De nex' time I saw de Boll Weevil
He had all his family dere—
Dey's lookin' for a home,
Jes a-lookin' for a home. . . .

[3]Words from Texas and Mississippi; tune from Texas. Text largely collected in 1909.

[4]The Negro must have his rhyme. He is thinking of the red-headed peckerwood. (Collectors' notes.)

De Farmer took de Boll Weevil
An' buried him in hot san';
De Boll Weevil say to de Farmer,
"I'll stan' it like a man,
Fur it is my home,
It is my home."

Den de Farmer took de Boll Weevil
An' lef' him on de ice;
Says de Boll Weevil to de Farmer,
"Dis is mighty cool an' nice.
Oh, it is my home,
It is my home."

Mr. Farmer took little Weevil
And put him in Paris Green;
"Thank you, Mr. Farmer;
It's the best I ever seen.
It is my home,
It's jes my home."

Den de Farmer say to de Merchant:
"We's in an awful fix;
De Boll Weevil's et all de cotton up
An' lef' us only sticks.
We's got no home,
Oh, we's got no home." . . .

Oh, de Farmer say to de Merchant,
"I ain't made but only one bale,
An' befo' I bring yo' dat one
I'll fight an' go to jail,
I'll have a home,
I'll have a home." . . .

De Boll Weevil say to de Farmer,
"You better lemme alone,
I've et up all yo' cotton
An' now I'll begin on de co'n,
I'll have a home,
I'll have a home."

Boll Weevil say to de Doctor,
"Better po' out all yo' pills,
When I git through wid de Farmer,
He cain't pay no doctor's bills.
He'll have no home,
He'll have no home."

Boll Weevil say to de Preacher,
"You better close yo' chu'ch do',
When I git through wid de Farmer,
He cain't pay de Preacher no mo',
Won't have no home,
Won't have no home."

De Merchant got half de cotton,
De Boll Weevil got de res';
Didn't leave de nigger's wife
But one old cotton dress.
And it's full of holes,
Oh, it's full of holes. . . .

If anybody axes you
Who wuz it writ dis song,
Tell 'em 'twuz a dark-skinned nigger
Wid a pair o' blue duckins on,
A-lookin' for a home,
Jes a-lookin' for a home.

Old Dog Blue

Had ole dog his name was Blue,
You know Blue was mighty true,
You know Blue was a good ole dog,
Blue treed a possum in a hollow log;
You can know from dat, he was a good ole dog.

Blue treed a possum out on a limb
Blue looked at me, and I looked at him,
Grabbed dat possum, put him in a sack,
Suits me and Blue till I git back.
Hyeah Ring, hyeah Ring, hyeah
Hyeah Ring, hyeah Ring, hyeah.

Who been here since I been gone?
Little bitty girl wid de red dress on.
Who been here since I been gone?
Little bitty girl wid de red dress on.

Ole Blue's feet was big and round,
Ole Blue's feet was big and round,
Never 'lowed a possum to tetch the ground.

Me and Blue went out on a hunt,
Blue treed a possum in a hollow stump,
You know Blue was a good ole dog
Blue treed a possum in a hollow log,
You can know from dat he's a good ole dog.

Now ole Blue died and I dug his grave,
I dug his grave wid a silver spade,
I let him down wid a golden chain,
And every link I called his name:
"Go on Blue, you good dog you,
Go on Blue, you good dog you."

Blue laid down and died like a man,
Blue laid down and died like a man,
Now he's treein' possums in de promised lan'.

I'm gonna tell you dis to let you know,
Ole Blue's gone where de good dogs go.

When I hear ole Blue bark,
When I hear ole Blue bark,
Blue treed a possum in Noah's ark,
Blue treed a possum in Noah's ark.

Frankie and Johnny

Frankie and Johnny were lovers,
    Lordy, how they could love,
Swore to be true to each other,
    True as the stars up above,
        He was her man, but he done her wrong.

Frankie went down to the corner,
    To buy her a bucket of beer,
Frankie says "Mister Bartender,
    Has my lovin' Johnnie been here?
        He is my man, but he's doing me wrong."

"I don't want to cause you no trouble
    Don't want to tell you no lie,
I saw your Johnnie half-an-hour ago
    Making love to Nelly Bly.
        He is your man, but he's doing you wrong."

Frankie went down to the hotel
    Looked over the transom so high,
There she saw her lovin' Johnnie
    Making love to Nelly Bly
        He was her man; he was doing her wrong.

Frankie threw back her kimono,
    Pulled out her big forty-four;
    Rooty-toot-toot: three times she shot
    Right through that hotel door,
        She shot her man, who was doing her wrong.

"Roll me over gently,
    Roll me over slow,
Roll me over on my right side,
    Cause these bullets hurt me so,
        I was your man, but I done you wrong."

Bring all your rubber-tired hearses
    Bring all your rubber-tired hacks,
They're carrying poor Johnny to the burying ground
    And they ain't gonna bring him back,
        He was her man, but he done her wrong.

Frankie says to the sheriff,
    "What are they going to do?"
The sheriff he said to Frankie,
    "It's the 'lectric chair for you.
        He was your man, and he done you wrong."

"Put me in that dungeon,
    Put me in that cell,
Put me where the northeast wind
    Blows from the southeast corner of hell,
        I shot my man, 'cause he done me wrong."

Stackalee

(Collected and arranged by Onah L. Spencer. Reprinted by his permission.)

It was in the year of eighteen hundred and sixty-one
In St. Louis on Market Street where Stackalee was born.
Everybody's talkin about Stackalee.
It was on one cold and frosty night
When Stackalee and Billy Lyons had one awful fight,
Stackalee got his gun. Boy, he got it fast!

He shot poor Billy through and through;
Bullet broke a lookin glass.
Lord, O Lord, O Lord!
Stackalee shot Billy once; his body fell to the floor.
He cried out, Oh, please, Stack, please don't shoot me no more.

The White Elephant Barrel House was wrecked that night;
Gutters full of beer and whiskey; it was an awful sight.
Jewelry and rings of the purest solid gold
Scattered over the dance and gamblin hall.
The can-can dancers they rushed for the door
When Billy cried, Oh, please, Stack, don't shoot me no more.
Have mercy, Billy groaned, Oh, please spare my life;
I've got two little babies and an innocent wife.

Stack says, God bless your children, damn your wife!
You stold my magic Stetson; I'm gonna steal your life.
But, says Billy, I always treated you like a man.
'Tain't nothin to that old Stetson but the greasy band.
He shot poor Billy once, he shot him twice,
And the third time Billy pleaded, please go tell my wife.
Yes, Stackalee, the gambler, everybody knowed his name;
Made his livin hollerin high, low, jack and the game.
Meantime the sergeant strapped on his big forty-five,
Says now we'll bring in this bad man, dead or alive.
And brass-buttoned policemen all dressed in blue
Came down the sidewalk marchin two by two.
Sent for the wagon and it hurried and come
Loaded with pistols and a big gatling gun.
At midnight on that stormy night there came an awful wail
Billy Lyons and a graveyard ghost outside the city jail.
Jailer, jailer, says Stack, I can't sleep,
For around my bedside poor Billy Lyons still creeps.
He comes in shape of a lion with a blue steel in his hand,
For he knows I'll stand and fight if he comes in shape of man.
Stackalee went to sleep that night by the city clock bell,
Dreaming the devil had come all the way up from hell.
Red devil was sayin, you better hunt your hole;
I've hurried here from hell just to get your soul.

Stackalee told him yes, maybe you're right,
But I'll give even you one hell of a fight.
When they got into the scuffle, I heard the devil shout,
Come and get this bad man before he puts my fire out.
The next time I seed the devil he was scramblin up the wall,
Yellin, come and get this bad man fore he mops up with us all.

Then here come Stack's woman runnin, says, daddy, I love you true;
See what beer, whiskey, and smokin hop has brought you to.
But before I'll let you lay in there, I'll put my life in pawn.
She hurried and got Stackalee out on a five thousand dollar bond.
Stackalee said, ain't but one thing that grieves my mind,
When they take me away, babe, I leave you behind.
But the woman he really loved was a voodoo queen
From Creole French market, way down in New Orleans.

He laid down at home that night, took a good night's rest,
Arrived in court at nine o'clock to hear the coroner's inquest.
Crowds jammed the sidewalk, far as you could see,
Tryin to get a good look at tough Stackalee.
Over the cold, dead body Stackalee he did bend,
Then he turned and faced those twelve jury men.
The judge says, Stackalee, I would spare your life,
But I know you're a bad man; I can see it in your red eyes.
The jury heard the witnesses, and they didn't say no more;
They crowded into the jury room, and the messenger closed the door.

The jury came to agreement, the clerk he wrote it down,
And everybody was whisperin, he's penitentiary bound.
When the jury walked out, Stackalee didn't budge,
They wrapped the verdict and passed it to the judge.
Judge looked over his glasses, says, Mr. Bad Man Stackalee,
The jury finds you guilty of murder in the first degree.
Now the trial's come to an end, how the folks gave cheers;
Bad Stackalee was sent down to Jefferson pen for seventy-five years.

Now late at night you can hear him in his cell,
Arguin with the devil to keep from goin to hell.
And the other convicts whisper, whatcha know about that?
Gonna burn in hell forever over an old Stetson hat!
Everybody's talkin bout Stackalee.

[*Chorus or Refrain:*]

> Everybody's talkin bout Stackalee
> That bad man Stackalee,
> Oh, tough man Stackalee.
>
> Oh, oh, Lord, Lord, Lord,
> All about an old Stetson hat.[1]

[1] The variation in length of stanza is explained by the fact that a folk singer shortens, slurs, or gives beats to a measure according to his particular mood. (Collector's note.)

WORK SONGS AND SOCIAL SONGS

John Henry Hammer Song

Dis is de hammer
Killt John Henry,
Twon't kill me, baby,
Twon't kill me.

Take dis hammer,
Carry it to de captain
Tell him I'm gone, baby,
Tell him I'm gone.

Ef he axe you,
Was I running
Tell him how fast, baby,
Tell him how fast.

Ef he axe you,
Any mo' questions,
Tell him you don't know, baby,
You don't know.

Every mail day,
Gits a letter,
"Son, come home, baby,
Son come home."

Been all night long
Backing up timber,
Want to go home, baby,
Want to go home.

Jes' wait till I make
Dese few days I started
I'm going home, baby,
I'm going home.

Everywhere I
Look dis morning
Look lak rain, baby,
Look lak rain.

I got a rainbow
Tied 'round my shoulder,
Ain't gonna rain, baby,
Ain't gonna rain.

Dis ole hammer
Ring lak silver,
Shine lak gold, baby,
Shine lak gold.

Take dis hammer
Throw it in de river,
It'll ring right on, baby,
Ring right on.

Captain, did you hear
All yo' men gonna leave you,
Next pay day, baby,
Next pay day?

Hammer Song

Well she ask me—hunh—
In de parlor—hunh;
And she cooled me—hunh—
Wid her fan—hunh;
An' she whispered—hunh—
To her mother—hunh:
"Mamma, I love dat—hunh—
Dark-eyed man"—hunh.

Well I ask her—hunh—
Mother for her—hunh;
And she said she—hunh
Was too young—hunh;
Lord, I wished I'd—hunh—
Never seen her—hunh;
And I wished she'd—hunh—
Never been born—hunh.

Well, I led her—hunh—
To de altar—hunh;
And de preacher—hunh—
Give his command—hunh—
And she swore by—hunh—
God that made her—hunh;
That she'd never—hunh—
Love another man—hunh.

Death Letter

Got me a letter,
What you think it read:
"Come home, come home,
Yo' mammy's dead."

Grabbed me a train,
Then I went home flyin';
Now she weren't dead,
But slowly dying.

She said, "My son,
Git down upon yo' knees,
And sing me a
Good old hymn tune, please."

De only song,
Dat seemed to come to me,
Was "Nearer,
Nearer, My God to Thee."

"Nearer my God to thee,
Nearer to thee,
Ever my song shall be
Nearer to thee."

De tears run down my cheeks
Like showers of falling rain,
"Good-bye, see you
No more again."

Tears run down my cheeks,
Like showers of falling rain,
"Good-bye, see you
No more again."

Roberta Lee

(This and the following two songs are from the collection of Willis James, professor of Music at Spelman College, who has been collecting Negro songs for twenty years. They are reprinted by his permission.)

Chorus

I cried, Oh pity, a pity an' a shame
It's jes' a pity an' a shame—
An' if dis trouble don't stop worrin' me
I'll lay down an' die like 'Berta Lee,
Lawd, I'll lay down an' die like 'Berta Lee.

De longes' day I ever did see
Was de day dat Roberta died;
I got de news ten miles from home
An' I walked back dat road an' I cried.

I been aroun' from town to town
From Texas to Santah Fee,
I done been dis worl' aroun',
But I can't find no Roberta Lee.

I dreamed las' night an' de night befo'
I was on my way back home,
But since I heard Roberta died
I got a mind to roam.

Roberta lived in Tennessee
Befo' she came to town,
There never was a girl like her
I been dis whole worl' roun'.

Dis worl' is high
Dis worl' is low
Dis worl' is deep and wide;
But de longes' road I ever did see
Was de one I walked an' cried.

It Sound Like Thunder

(By permission of Willis James.)

I'm a man tall like a mountain
I'm a man steddy like a fountain
Folks all wonder what makes it thunder
When dey hear, Lawd, my hammer fall.

Chorus

An' hit sound like thunder
Lawd, hit sound like thunder
When my hammer fall.

Did yo' read it in de paper
'Bout de gov'nor an his family,
Dey am 'cided to come to de new road
Jes' to hear, Lawd, my hammer fall.

Boss got money—mo den de government
Come to town ridin' a chariot
Drivin' forty big, fine race horses
Jes' to hear, Lawd, my hammer fall.

Hyah Come De Cap'm

(By permission of Willis James.)

Hyah come de cap'm
Stan' right steddy
Walkin' lak Samson,
Stan' right steddy.
A big Goliath
Stan' right steddy
He totin' his talker
Stan' right steddy.

Lookin' fer Jimbo
Don' say nothin'
Go 'head Jimbo
Don' say nothin'
Run in de bushes
Don' say nothin'
Cap'm cain't fin' you
Don' say nothin'.

De houn' dawgs come
Oh! hab mercy
Start to runnin'
Dey cain't fin' you
Oh, hab mercy
Good ol' Jimbo
Lawd, Lawd.

Boy you mus' be flyin'
Lawd, Lawd.
Some good day
Lawd, Lawd,
Ef ah git de drop,
Lawd, Lawd,
Ah'm goin' on
Lawd, Lawd,
Dat same good way
Lawd, Lawd,
Dat Jimbo gone
Lawd, Lawd.

Good ol' Jimbo
Lawd, Lawd,
He done gone,
Lawd, Lawd.
He done gone.

SOCIAL PROTEST SONGS

Standin' on De Corner

(This and the following two songs are from Lawrence Gellert's *Negro Songs of Protest*. They are reprinted by permission of the collector.)

Standin' on de corner, weren't doin' no hahm,
Up come a 'liceman an' he grab me by de ahm.
Blow a little whistle an' ring a little bell
Heah come patrol wagon runnin' like hell.

Judge he call me up an' ast mah name.
Ah tole him fo' sho' Ah weren't to blame.
He wink at 'liceman, 'liceman wink too;
Judge say, "Nigger, you get some work to do."

Workin' on ol' road bank, shackle boun'.
Long, long time 'fo' six months roll aroun'.
Miserin' fo' my honey, she miserin' fo' me,
But, Lawd, white folks won't let go holdin' me.

Lay Down Late

Lay down late, gettin' up soon,
Twelve o'clock an' ah has no noon.
All ah want's dese cold iron shackles off mah leg.

Diggin' in de road bank, diggin' in de ditch,
Chain gang's got me, boss got de switch.
All ah want's dese cold iron shackles off mah leg.

Judge say, "Three days!" Ah turn aside.
"An' ninety nine more years!" Ah hung mah head an' cried.
All ah want's dese cold iron shackles off mah leg.

Golly, judge, you done me wrong.
Ninety nine years in jail too long.
All ah want's dese cold iron shackles off mah leg.

Poor ol' pris'ner blind an' can't see
Why de whole world look down on me.
All ah want's dese cold iron shackles off mah leg.

Me and My Captain

(This song is from Lawrence Gellert's *Me And My Captain*, 1939. It is reprinted by permission of the collector.)

Me an my captain don't agree,
But he don't know, 'cause he don't ask me;
He don't know, he don't know my mind,
When he see me laughing
Just laughing to keep from crying.

Oh what's the matter now,
Me and my captain can't get along nohow;
He don't know, he don't know my mind,
When he see me laughing
Just laughing to keep from crying.

He call me low down I just laugh,
Kick seat of my pants and that ain't half;
He don't know, he don't know my mind,
When he see me laughing
Just laughing to keep from crying.

Got one mind for white folks to see,
'Nother for what I know is me;
He don't know, he don't know my mind,
When he see me laughing
Just laughing to keep from crying.

Told My Cap'n

(This song is from Joshua White's *Chain Gang Album*, Columbia Records, Set C-22. It is reprinted by permission of the collector and the Columbia Recording Corporation.)

Told my Cap'n my hands was cold,
Said "Damn your hands, boy;
    Let de wheelin' roll."

Ask my Cap'n to give me my time,
Damn ol' Cap'n wouldn't pay me no mind.

Raised my hand, wiped de sweat off my head;
Cap'n got mad, Lord, shot my buddy dead.

Cap'n walkin' up an' down
Buddy layin' there dead, Lord,
On de burnin' ground.

It I'd a-had my weight in lime
I'd a-whup dat Cap'n till he went stone blind.

If you don't believe my buddy is dead,
Jus look at dat hole in my buddy's head.

Buzzard circlin' round de sky,
Knows dat Cap'n sure is bound to die.

Silicosis Blues

(By Joshua White. Reprinted by permission of the author.)

Now, silicosis, you made a mighty bad wreck of me,
I said, silicosis, you made a mighty bad wreck of me,
Robbed me of my right to live and I'm worried as I can be.

Now I'm digging in that tunnel, making only six bits a day,
I'm digging in that tunnel, making only six bits a day,
Didn't know I was digging my grave, silicosis eating my lungs away.

Now, mamma, mamma, mamma, cool my fevered head,
I says, mamma, mamma, mamma, cool my fevered head,
I'm gonna see my Jesus, God knows I'll soon be dead.

If you see my buddies, and if you see all my friends,
If you see my buddies, tell 'em don't weep for me,
Cause I'm going way up yonder, please don't weep for me.

BLUES

St. Louis Blues

(By W. C. Handy. Reprinted by permission of the author and of the Handy Brothers Music Co. Inc.)

I hate to see de evenin' sun go down
I hate to see de evenin' sun go down
Cause mah baby, he done lef' dis town

Feelin' tomorrow lak I feel today
Feelin' tomorrow lak I feel today
I'll pack mah trunk, an' make mah getaway

St. Louis woman wid her diamon' rings
Pulls dat man aroun' by her apron strings
'Twant for powder an' for store-bought hair
De man I love would not gone nowhere

Got de St. Louis blues, jes as blue as I can be
Dat man got a heart lak a rock cast in de sea
Or else he wouldn't have gone so far from me

Been to de gypsy to get mah fortune tol'
To de gypsy, done got mah fortune tol'
Cause I'm most wild 'bout mah jelly roll

Gypsy done tol' me, "Don't you wear no black"
Yes, she done tol' me, "Don't you wear no black.
Go to St. Louis, you can win him back"

Help me to Cairo; make St. Louis by mahself
Git to Cairo, find mah ol' frien', Jeff
Gwine to pin mahself close to his side
If I flag his train, I sho can ride

I loves dat man lak a schoolboy loves his pie
Lak a Kentucky Colonel loves his mint an' rye
I'll love mah baby till de day I die

You ought to see dat stovepipe brown o' mine
Lak he owns de Dimon' Joseph line
He'd make a cross-eyed 'oman go stone blind

Blacker than midnight, teeth lak flags of truce
Blackest man in de whole St. Louis
Blacker de berry, sweeter is de juice. . . .

* * * *

A black headed gal make a freight train jump de track
Said, a black headed gal make a freight train jump de track
But a long tall gal makes a preacher "Ball de Jack"

Lawd, a blond headed woman makes a good man leave the town
I said, blond headed woman makes a good man leave the town
But a red headed woman make a boy slap his papa down. . . .

Dink's Blues

(From John A. and Alan Lomax, *American Ballads and Folk Songs*, 1935. Reprinted by permission of the editors and the publishers, the Macmillan Company.)

Some people say dat de worry blues ain' bad
Some people say dat de worry blues ain' bad
It's de wors' o' feelin' I ever had

Git you two, three men, so one won't worry you' min'
Git you two, three men, so one won't worry you' min'
Don't,—dey'll keep you worried an' bothered all de time

I wish to God eas'-boun' train would wreck
I wish to God eas'-boun' train would wreck
Kill de engineer, break de fireman's neck

I'm gwine to de river, set down on de groun'
I'm gwine to de river, set down on de groun'
Ef de blues overtake me, I'll jump overboard an' drown

Ef trouble was money I'd be a millioneer
Ef trouble was money I'd be a millioneer
Ef trouble was money I'd be a millioneer. . . .

* * * *

Come de big *Kate Adam* wid headlight turn down de stream
Come de big *Kate Adam* wid headlight turn down de stream
An' her side-wheel knockin', "Great-God-I-been-redeemed"

Ef I feels tomorrow like I feels today
Ef I feels tomorrow like I feels today
Stan' right here an' look ten-thousan' miles away

My mother tol' me when I was a chil'
My mother tol' me when I was a chil'
Bout de mens an' whiskey would kill me after while

Ef I gets drunk, wonder who's gwine carry me home
Ef I gets drunk, wonder who's gwine carry me home
Ef I gets drunk, wonder who's gwine carry me home

I used to love you, but, oh, God damn you, now
I used to love you, but, oh, God damn you, now
I used to love you, but, oh, God damn you, now

De worry blues ain' nothin' but de heart disease
De worry blues ain' nothin' but de heart disease
De worry blues ain' nothin' but de heart disease

Jes as soon as de freight train make up in de yard
Jes as soon as de freight train make up in de yard
Some poor woman got an achin' heart

Tol' my mother not to weep an' moan
Tol' my mother not to weep an' moan
I do de bes' I can, cause I's a woman grown

I flag de train an' it keep on easin' by
I flag de train an' it keep on easin' by
I fold my arms; I hang my head an' cry

When my heart struck sorrow de tears come rollin' down
When my heart struck sorrow de tears come rollin' down
When my heart struck sorrow de tears come rollin' down

Worry now an' I won't be worry long
Worry now an' I won't be worry long
Take a married woman to sing de worry song

Ef I leave here walkin', it's chances I might ride
Ef I leave here walkin', it's chances I might ride
Ef I leave here walkin', it's chances I might ride

Mamie's Blues

(By Jelly Roll Morton. General 40001. Printed by permission of Consolidated Records, Inc. Introductory line, spoken: "This is the first blues I, no doubt, heard in my life.")

De Two-Nineteen done took mah baby away
Two-Nineteen took mah babe away
Two-Seventeen bring her back some day

Stood on the corner with her feets soakin' wet
Stood on the corner with her feets soakin' wet
Beggin' each an' every man that she met

If you can't give me a dollar, give me a lousy dime
Can't give a dollar, give me a lousy dime
I wanna feed that hongry man of mine

Grievin' Hearted Blues

(By Ma Rainey. Paramount 12419.)

You'll find you love me daddy, some sweet day
You'll find you love me daddy, some sweet day
It's true I love you, but I can't take mistreatment this-a-way

All I want's mah ticket; show me mah train
All I want's mah ticket; show me mah train
I'm gonna ride till I can't hear dem call yo' name

I'm gonna start cryin'; mah love been refused
I'm gonna start cryin'; mah love been refused
Goan keep on cryin'; lose dese grievin' hearted blues

Dirty No-Gooder's Blues

(By Bessie Smith. Columbia 14476. Printed by permission of the Columbia
Recording Corporation.)

Did you ever fall in love wid a man that was no good
Did you ever fall in love wid a man that was no good
No matter what you did fo' him he never understood

De meanest things he could say would thrill you through an' through
Meanest things he could say would thrill you through an' through
An' there wasn't nothin' too dirty fo' dat man to do

He treat you nice an' kind till he win yo' heart an' hand
Treat you nice an' kind till he win yo' heart an' hand
Den he git so cruel, dat man you jes could not stand

Lawd, I really think no man's love can last
Lawd, I really think no man's love can last
Dey'll love you to death den treat you lak a thing of de past

There's nineteen men livin' in mah neighborhood
Nineteen men livin' in mah neighborhood
Eighteen of them are fools an' de other ain' no doggone good

Law-w-w-wd; Law-w-w-wd; Lawd, Lawd, Lawd, Lawd
Law-w-w-wd; Law-w-w-wd; Lawd, Lawd, Lawd, Lawd
Dat dirty no-good man treats me jes lak I'm a dog

The Southern Blues

(By Willard "Big Bill" Broonzy. Bluebird B-6964. Printed by permission of the
author and the RCA Manufacturing Company.)

When I got up this mornin', I heah'd de ol' Southern whistle blow
When I got up this mornin', I heah'd de ol' Southern whistle blow
I was thinkin' 'bout my baby; Lawd, I sho did want to go

I was standin', lookin' an' listenin', watchin' de Southern cross
    de Dog
I was standin', lookin' an' listenin', watchin' de Southern cross
    de Dog
If my baby didn't catch dat Southern, she musta caught dat Yellow
    Dog

Down at de station, looked up on de board, waitin' fo' de conductor
    jes to say "all aboard"
Down at de station, Lawd, I looked up on de board
I don't know my baby left from here, oh, but I was told

I'm goin' to Moorhead, get me a job on de Southern Line
I'm goin' to Moorhead, get me a job on de Southern Line
So that I can make some money, jes to send fo' dat brown o' mine

De Southern cross de Dog at Moorhead, mama, Lawd, an' she keeps
    on throo
De Southern cross de Dog at Moorhead, mama, Lawd, an' she keeps
    on throo
I swear my baby's gone to Georgia, I believe I go to Georgia too

She's My Mary

(By Lonnie Johnson. Bluebird Record B-8322. Used by permission of the RCA
Manufacturing Co., Inc.)

My friends all scorn us, talk all over town,
They try to make trouble for us, the news is out all around,
But after all she's still my Mary, and will be until the deal goes
    down.

She was my Mary, when this whole world turned me down,
She was my father, mother, sister, brother; she helped me to carry
    on
And she will still be my Mary, when everything goes wrong.

She's so sweet to me when everything goes wrong;
She's so consolation; she helps me to carry on,
That's why I know she'll still be my Mary, when this rotten deal
    goes down.

I know I can find a woman, each and every day that bright sun
    shine,
I know I can find a woman, each and every day that bright sun
    shine,
But after all she's still my Mary, and there's nothing else can ever
    change my mind.

People say that I'm a fool, cause I don't git out and chase around,
People say that I'm a fool, cause I don't git out and chase around,
I still can find the consolation that I need, and she'll still be my
    Mary, when the deal goes down.

Backwater Blues

(By Bessie Smith. Columbia 3176. Printed by permission of the Columbia
Recording Corporation.)

When it rain five days an' de skies turned dark as night
When it rain five days an' de skies turned dark as night
Then trouble taken place in the lowland that night

I woke up this mornin', can't even get outa mah do'
I woke up this mornin', can't even get outa mah do'
That's enough trouble to make a po' girl wonder where she wanta go

Then they rowed a little boat about five miles 'cross the pond
They rowed a little boat about five miles 'cross the pond
I packed all mah clothes, th'owed 'em in, an' they rowed me along

When it thunder an' a-lightnin', an' the wind begin to blow
When it thunder an' a-lightnin', an' the wind begin to blow
An' thousan' people ain' got no place to go

Then I went an' stood up on some high ol' lonesome hill
I went an' stood up on some high ol' lonesome hill
An' looked down on the house where I used to live

Backwater blues done cause me to pack mah things an' go
Backwater blues done cause me to pack mah things an' go
Cause mah house fell down an' I cain' live there no mo'

O-o-o-oom, I cain' move no mo'
O-o-o-oom, I cain' move no mo'
There ain' no place fo' a po' ol' girl to go

When the Levee Breaks

(By Kansas Joe and Memphis Minnie. Columbia 14439-D. Printed by permission of the Columbia Recording Corporation.)

If it keeps on raining, levee's going to break
If it keeps on raining, levee's going to break
An' de water goan come, an' you'll have no place to stay

Well, all last night I sat on de levee an' moaned
Well, all last night I sat on de levee an' moaned
Thinkin' 'bout my baby an' my happy home

If it keeps on raining, levee's going to break
If it keeps on raining, levee's going to break
An' all dese people won't have no place to stay

Now, look here, mama, what am I to do?
Now, look here, mama, what am I to do?
I ain' got nobody tell my troubles to

I worked on de levee, mama, both night an' day
I worked on de levee, mama, both night an' day
I ain' got nobody to keep the water away

Cryin' won't help you, prayin' won't do no good
Cryin' won't help you, prayin' won't do no good
When de ol' levee breaks, mama, you got to move

I worked on de levee, mama, both night an' day
I worked on de levee, mama, both night an' day
Had to work so hard to keep that water away

I had a woman, she wouldn't do fo' me
I had a woman, she wouldn't do fo' me
I goin' back to my use-to-be

It's that mean ol' levee, cause me to to weep an' moan
It's that mean ol' levee, cause me to to weep an' moan
Cause me to leave my baby an' my happy home

St. Louis Cyclone Blues

(By Elzadie Robinson. Paramount 12573.)

I was sitting in my kitchen, looking out across the sky
I was sitting in my kitchen, looking out across the sky
I thought the world was ending, I started in to cry

The wind was howling, the buildings began to fall
The wind was howling, the buildings began to fall
I seen dat mean ol' twister comin' jes like a cannon ball

De world was black as midnight, I never heard such a noise before
De world was black as midnight, I never heard such a noise before
Like a million lions, when turned loose, dey all roar

De people was screamin', runnin' eve'y which-a-way (Lord, help
    us, help us)
De people was screamin', runnin' eve'y which-a-way
I fell down on my knees an' began to pray

De shack where we were livin' reeled an' rocked but never fell
De shack where we were livin' reeled an' rocked but never fell
How de cyclone started, nobody but de Lawd can tell

Hard Times Blues

(By Ida Cox. Vocallon 05293. Printed by permission of the author and the
Columbia Recording Corporation.)

I never seen such real hard times befo'
Says, I never seen such real hard times befo'
De wolf keeps walkin' all aroun' mah do'

Dey howl all night long, an' dey moan till de break of day
Howl all night long, an' dey moan till de break of day
Dey seems to know mah good man gone away

I cain' go outside to mah grocery sto'
I cain' go outside to mah grocery sto'
I ain' got no money, an' mah credit doan go no mo'

Won't somebody please try an' find mah man fo' me
Won't somebody please try an' find mah man fo' me
Tell him I'm broke an' hongry, lonely as I can be. . . .

FOLK TALES

From Mules and Men

(The following tales are from Zora Neale Hurston's *Mules and Men*. They are reprinted by permission of the author and of J. B. Lippincott Co., the publishers of the book.)

You know befo' surrender Ole Massa had a nigger name John and John always prayed every night befo' he went to bed and his prayer was for God to come git him and take him to Heaven right away. He didn't even want to take time to die. He wanted de Lawd to come git him just like he was—boot, sock and all. He'd git down on his knees and say: "O Lawd, it's once more and again yo' humble servant is knee-bent and body-bowed—my heart beneath my knees and my knees in some lonesome valley, crying for mercy while mercy kin be found. O Lawd, Ah'm astin' you in de humblest way I know how to be *so* pleased as to come in yo' fiery chariot and take me to yo' Heben and its immortal glory. Come Lawd, you know Ah have such a hard time. Old Massa works me *so* hard, and don't gimme no time to rest. So come, Lawd, wid peace in one hand and pardon in de other and take me away from this sin-sorrowing world. Ah'm tired and Ah want to go home."

So one night Ole Massa passed by John's shack and heard him beggin' de Lawd to come git him in his fiery chariot and take him away; so he made up his mind to find out if John meant dat thing. So he goes on up to de big house and got hisself a bed sheet and come on back. He throwed de sheet over his head and knocked on de door.

John quit prayin' and ast: "Who dat?"

Ole Massa say: "It's me, John, de Lawd, done come wid my fiery chariot to take you away from this sin-sick world."

Right under de bed John had business. He told his wife: "Tell him Ah ain't here, Liza."

At first Liza didn't say nothin' at all, but de Lawd kept right on callin' John: "Come on, John, and go to Heben wid me where you won't have to plough no mo' furrows and hoe no mo' corn. Come on, John."

Liza says: "John ain't here, Lawd, you hafta come back another time."

Lawd says: "Well, then Liza, you'll do."

Liza whispers and says: "John, come out from underneath dat

bed and g'wan wid de Lawd. You been beggin' him to come git you. Now g'wan wid him."

John back under de bed not saying a mumblin' word. De Lawd out on de door step kept on callin'.

Liza says: "John, Ah thought you was so anxious to get to Heben. Come out and go on wid God."

John says: "Don't you hear him say 'You'll do?' Why don't you go wid him?"

"Ah ain't a goin' nowhere. Youse de one been whoopin' and hollerin' for him to come git you and if you don't come out from under dat bed Ah'm gointer tell God youse here."

Ole Massa makin' out he's God, says: "Come on, Liza, you'll do."

Liza says: "Oh, Lawd, John is right here underneath de bed."

"Come on, John, and go to Heben wid me and its immortal glory."

John crept out from under de bed and went to de door and cracked it and when he seen all dat white standin' on de doorsteps he jumped back. He says: "O, Lawd, Ah can't go to Heben wid you in yo' fiery chariot in dese ole dirty britches; gimme time to put on my Sunday pants."

"All right, John, put on yo' Sunday pants."

John fooled around just as long as he could, changing them pants, but when he went back to de door, de big white glory was still standin' there. So he says agin: "O, Lawd, de Good Book says in Heben no filth is found and I got on dis dirty sweaty shirt. Ah can't go wid you in dis old nasty shirt. Gimme time to put on my Sunday shirt!"

"All right, John, go put on yo' Sunday shirt."

John took and fumbled around a long time changing his shirt, and den he went back to de door, but Ole Massa was still on de door step. John didn't had nothin' else to change so he opened de door a little piece and says:

"O, Lawd, Ah'm ready to go to Heben wid you in yo' fiery chariot, but de radiance of yo' countenance is so bright, Ah can't come out by you. Stand back jus' a l'il way please."

Ole Massa stepped back a li'l bit.

John looked out agin and says: "O, Lawd, you know dat po' humble me is less than de dust beneath yo' shoe soles. And de radiance of yo' countenance is so bright Ah can't come out by you. Please, please, Lawd, in yo' tender mercy, stan back a li'l bit further."

Ole Massa stepped back a li'l bit mo'.

John looked out agin and he says: "O, Lawd, Heben is so high and wese so low; youse so great and Ah'm so weak and yo' strength is too much for us poor sufferin' sinners. So once mo' and again yo' humble servant is knee-bent and body-bowed askin' you one mo' favor befo' Ah step into yo' fiery chariot to go to Heben wid you and wash in yo' glory—be so pleased in yo' tender mercy as to stand back jus' a li'l bit further."

Ole Massa stepped back a step or two mo' and out dat door John come like a streak of lightning. All across de punkin patch, thru de cotton over de pasture—John wid Ole Massa right behind him. By de time dey hit de cornfield John was way ahead of Ole Massa.

Back in de shack one of de children was cryin' and she ast Liza: "Mama, you reckon God's gointer ketch papa and carry him to Heben wid him?"

"Shet yo' mouf, talkin' foolishness!" Liza clashed at de chile. "You know de Lawd can't outrun yo' pappy—specially when he's barefooted at dat."

* * * * *

Jim Allen laughed just as loud as anybody else and then he said: "We better hurry on to work befo' de buckra[1] get in behind us."

"Don't never worry about work," says Jim Presley. "There's more work in de world than there is anything else. God made de world and de white folks made work."

"Yeah, dey made work but they didn't make us do it," Joe Willard put in. "We brought dat on ourselves."

"Oh, yes, de white folks did put us to work too," said Jim Allen.

"Know how it happened? After God got thru makin' de world and de varmints and de folks, he made up a great big bundle and let it down in de middle of de road. It laid dere for thousands of years, then Ole Missus said to Ole Massa: 'Go pick up dat box, Ah want to see whut's in it.' Ole Massa look at de box and it look so heavy dat he says to de nigger, 'Go fetch me dat big ole box out dere in de road.' De nigger been stumblin' over de box a long time so he tell his wife:

" 'Oman, go git dat box.' So de nigger 'oman she runned to git de box. She says:

" 'Ah always lak to open up a big box 'cause there's nearly always something good in great big boxes.' So she run and grabbed a-hold of de box and opened it up and it was full of hard work.

"Dat's de reason de sister in black works harder than anybody else in de world. De white man tells de nigger to work and he tells his wife."

* * * * *

[1] West African word meaning white people.

During slavery time two ole niggers wuz talkin' an' one said tuh de other one, "Ole Massa made me so mad yistiddy till Ah give 'im uh good cussin' out. Man, Ah called 'im everything wid uh handle on it."

De other one says, "You didn't cuss *Ole Massa,* didja? Good God! Whut did he do tuh you?"

"He didn't do *nothin',* an' man, Ah laid one cussin' on 'im! Ah'm uh man lak dis, Ah won't stan' no hunchin'. Ah betcha he won't bother *me* no mo'.'"

"Well, if you cussed 'im an' he didn't do nothin' tuh you, de nex' time he make me mad Ah'm goin' tuh lay uh hearin' on him."

Nex' day de nigger did somethin'. Ole Massa got in behind 'im and he turnt 'round an' give Ole Massa one good cussin' an Ole Massa had 'im took down and whipped nearly tuh death. Nex' time he saw dat other nigger he says tuh 'im. "Thought you tole me, you cussed Ole Massa out and he never opened his mouf."

"Ah did."

"Well, how come he never did nothin' tuh yuh? Ah did it an' he come nigh uh killin' *me.*"

"Man, you didn't go cuss 'im tuh his face, didja?"

"Sho' Ah did. Ain't dat whut you tole me you done?"

"Naw, Ah didn't say Ah cussed 'im tuh his face. You sho is crazy. Ah thought you had mo' sense than dat. When Ah cussed Ole Massa he wuz settin' on de front porch an' Ah wuz down at de big gate."   *   *   *   *   *

. . . Ole Massa said: "Well John, . . . I goin' to Philly-Me-York and won't be back in three weeks. I leave everything in yo' charge."

So Ole Massa and his wife got on de train and John went to de depot with 'em and seen 'em off on de train bid 'em goodbye. Then he hurried on back to de plantation. Ole Massa and Ole Miss got off at de first station and made it on back to see whut John was doin'.

John went back and told de niggers, "Massa's gone to Philly-Me-York and left eve'ything in my charge. Ah want one of you niggers to git on a mule and ride three miles north, and another one three miles west and another one three miles south and another one three miles east. Tell everybody to come here—there's gointer be a ball here tonight. The rest of you go into the lot and kill hogs until you can walk on 'em."

So they did. John goes in and dressed up in Ole Massa's swaller-tail clothes, put on his collar and tie; got a box of cigars and put under his arm, and one cigar in his mouth.

When the crowd come John said: "Y'all kin dance and Ah'm goin' to call figgers."

So he got Massa's biggest rockin' chair and put it up in Massa's bed and then he got up in the bed in the chair and begin to call figgers.

"Hands up!" "Four circle right." "Half back." "Two ladies change." He was puffing his cigar all de time.

'Bout this time John seen a white couple come in but they looked so trashy he figgered they was piney woods crackers, so he told 'em to g'wan out in de kitchen and git some barbecue and likker and to stay out there where they belong. So he want to callin' figgers again. De git Fiddles[2] was raisin' cain over in de corner and John was callin' for de new set:

"Choose yo' partners." "Couples to yo' places like horses to de traces." "Sashay all." "Sixteen hands up." "Swing Miss Sally 'round and 'round and bring her back to me!"

Just as he went to say "Four hands up," he seen Ole Massa comin' out de kitchen wipin' the dirt off his face.

Ole Massa said: "John, just look whut you done done! I'm gointer take you to that persimmon tree and break yo' neck for this—killing up all my hogs and havin' all these niggers in my house."

John ast, "Ole Massa, Ah know you gointer kill me, but can Ah have a word with my friend Jack before you kill me?"

"Yes, John, but have it quick."

So John called Jack and told him; says: "Ole Massa is gointer hang me under that persimmon tree. Now you get three matches and get in the top of the tree. Ah'm gointer pray and when you hear me ast God to let it lightning Ah want you to strike matches."

Jack went on out to the tree. Ole Massa brought John on out with the rope around his neck and put it over a limb.

"Now, John," said Massa, "have you got any last words to say?"

"Yes sir, Ah want to pray."

"Pray and pray damn quick. I'm clean out of patience with you, John."

So John knelt down. "O Lord, here Ah am at de foot of de persimmon tree. If you're gointer destroy Old Massa tonight, with his wife and chillun and everything he got, lemme see it lightnin'."

Jack up the tree, struck a match. Ole Massa caught hold of John and said: "John, don't pray no more."

John said: "Oh yes, turn me loose so Ah can pray. O Lord, here

[2]Guitars.

Ah am tonight callin' on Thee and Thee alone. If you gointer destroy Ole Massa tonight, his wife and chillun and all he got, Ah want to see it lightnin' again."

Jack struck another match and Ole Massa started to run. He give John his freedom and a heap of land and stock. He run so fast that it took a express train running at the rate of ninety miles an hour and six months to bring him back, and that's how come niggers got they freedom today.

* * * * *

Well, when God made de snake he put him in de bushes to ornament de ground. But things didn't suit de snake so one day he got on de ladder and went up to see God.

"Good mawnin', God."

"How do you do, Snake?"

"Ah ain't so many, God, you put me down there on my belly in de dust and everything trods upon me and kills off my generations. Ah ain't got no kind of protection at all."

God looked off towards immensity and thought about de subject for awhile, then he said, "Ah didn't mean for nothin' to be stompin' you snakes lak dat. You got to have some kind of a protection. Here, take dis poison and put it in yo' mouf and when they tromps on you, protect yo' self."

So de snake took de poison in his mouf and went on back.

So after awhile all de other varmints went up to God.

"Good evenin', God."

"How you makin' it, varmints?"

"God, please do somethin' 'bout dat snake. He' layin' in de bushes there wid poison in his mouf and he's strikin' everything dat shakes de bush. He's killin' up our generations. Wese skeered to walk de earth."

So God sent for de snake and tole him:

"Snake, when Ah give you dat poison, Ah didn't mean for you to be hittin' and killin' everything dat shake de bush. I give you dat poison and tole you to protect yo'self when they tromples on you. But you killin' everything dat moves. Ah didn't mean for you to do dat."

De snake say, "Lawd, you know Ah'm down here in de dust. Ah ain't got no claws to fight wid, and Ah ain't got no feets to git me out de way. All Ah kin see is feets comin' to tromple me. Ah can't tell who my enemy is and who is my friend. You gimme dis protection in my mouf and Ah uses it."

God thought it over for a while then he says:

"Well, snake, I don't want yo' generations all stomped out and I don't want you killin' everything else dat moves. Here, take dis bell and tie it to yo' tail. When you hear feets comin' you ring yo' bell and if it's yo' friend, he'll be keerful. If it's yo' enemy, it's you and him."

So dat's how de snake got his poison and dat's how come he got rattles.

Biddy, biddy, bend my story is end.

Turn loose de rooster and hold de hen.

*   *   *   *   *

Well, you know when de Flood was and dey had two of everything in de ark—well, Ole Nora[3] didn't take on no trees, so de woodpecker set 'round and set 'round for a week or so then he felt like he just had to peck himself some wood. So he begin to peck on de Ark. Ole Nora come to him and tole him, "Don't peck on de Ark. If you peck a hole in it, we'll all drown."

Woodpecker says: "But Ah'm hungry for some wood to peck."

Ole Nora says, "Ah don't keer how hongry you gits don't you peck on dis ark no mo. You want to drown everybody and everything?"

So de woodpecker would sneak 'round behind Ole Nora's back and peck every chance he got. He'd hide hisself way down in de hold where he thought nobody could find him and peck and peck. So one day Ole Nora come caught him at it. He never opened his mouth to dat woodpecker. He just 'hauled off and give dat peckerwood a cold head-whipping wid a sledge hammer, and dat's why a peckerwood got a red head today—'cause Ole Nora bloodied it wid dat hammer. Dat's how come Ah feel like shootin' every one of 'em Ah see. Tryin' to drown *me* before Ah was born.

"A whole lot went on on dat ole Ark," Larkins White commented. "Dat's where de possum lost de hair off his tail."

"Now don't you tell me no possum ever had no hair on dat slick tail of his'n," said Black Baby, "'cause Ah know better."

Yes, he did have hair on his tail one time. Yes, indeed. De possum had a bushy tail wid long silk hair on it. Why, it useter be one of de prettiest sights you ever seen. De possum struttin' 'round wid his great big ole plumey tail. Dat was 'way back in de olden times before de big flood.

But de possum was lazy—jus' like he is today. He sleep too much.

[3]Noah.

You see Ole Nora had a son name Ham and he loved to be playin'
music all de time. He had a banjo and a fiddle and maybe a guitar
too. But de rain come up so sudden he didn't have time to put 'em
on de ark. So when rain kept comin' down he fretted a lot 'cause
he didn't have nothin' to play. So he found a ole cigar box and
made hisself a banjo, but he didn't have no strings for it. So he
seen de possum stretched out sleeping wid his tail all spread 'round.
So Ham slipped up and shaved de possum's tail and made de strings
for his banjo out de hairs. When dat possum woke up from his
nap, Ham was playin' his tail hairs down to de bricks and dat's
why de possum ain't got no hair on his tail today. Losin' his pretty
tail sorta broke de possum's spirit too. He ain't never been de same
since. Dat's how come he always actin' shame-faced. He know his
tail ain't whut it useter be; and de possum feel mighty bad about it.

De dog is sho hot after [de rabbit]. Run dem doggone rabbits
so that they sent word to de dogs dat they want peace. So they had a
convention. De rabbit took de floor and said they was tired of runnin',
and dodgin' all de time, and they asted de dogs to please leave rabbits
alone and run somethin' else. So de dogs put it to a vote and 'greed
to leave off runnin' rabbits.

So after de big meetin' Brer Dog invites de rabbit over to his
house to have dinner wid him.

He started on thru de woods wid Brer Dog but every now and
then he'd stop and scratch his ear and listen. He stop right in his
tracks. Dog say:

"Aw, come on Brer Rabbit, you too suscautious. Come on."

Kept dat up till they come to de branch just 'fore they got to
Brer Dog's house. Just as Brer Rabbit started to step out on de foot-
log, he heard some dogs barkin' way down de creek. He heard de
old hound say, "How o-l-d is he?" and the young dogs answer him:
"Twenty-one or two, twenty-one or two!" So Brer Rabbit say, "Excuse
me, but Ah don't reckon Ah better go home wid you today, Brer
Dog."

"Aw, come on, Brer Rabbit, you always gitten scared for nothin'.
Come on."

"Ah hear dogs barkin', Brer Dog."

"Naw, you don't Brer Rabbit."

"Yes, Ah do. Ah know, dat's dogs barkin'."

"S'posin' it is, it don't make no difference. Ain't we done held
a convention and passed a law dogs run no mo' rabbits? Don't pay
no 'tention to every li'l bit of barkin you hear."

Rabbit scratch his ear and say,

"Yeah, but all de dogs ain't been to no convention, and anyhow some of dese fool dogs ain't got no better sense than to run all over dat law and break it up. De rabbits didn't go to school much and he didn't learn but three letters, and that's trust no mistake. Run every time de bush shake."

So he raced on home without breakin' another breath wid de dog.

* * * * *

Somebody tole one on de snail.

"You know de snail's wife took sick and sent him for de doctor.

"She was real low ill-sick and rolled from one side of de bed to de other. She was groanin', 'Lawd knows Ah got so much misery Ah hope de Doctor'll soon git here to me.'

"After seben years she heard a scufflin' at de door. She was real happy so she ast, 'Is dat you baby, done come back wid de doctor? Ah'm so glad!'

"He says, 'Don't try to rush me—Ah ain't gone yet.' He had been seben years gettin' to de door."

"Yeah, Ah was over there too," said Larkins White, "and somebody else tole a lie on de snail. A snail was crossin' de road for seben years. Just as he got across a tree fell and barely missed him 'bout a inch or two. If he had been where he was six months before it would er kilt him. De snail looked back at de tree and tole de people, 'See, it pays to be fast.' "

FOLK SERMON

From Jonah's Gourd Vine

(From a sermon in Zora Neale Hurston's *Jonah's Gourd Vine*, 1934. Reprinted by permission of the author and the publishers, J. B. Lippincott and Co.)

Faith hasn't got no eyes, but she long-legged
But take de spy-glass of Faith
And look into dat upper room
When you are alone to yourself
When yo' heart is burnt with fire, ha!
When de blood is lopin' thru yo' veins
Like de iron monasters (monsters) on de rail
Look into dat upper chamber, ha!
We notice at de supper table
As He gazed upon His friends, ha!
His eyes flowin' wid tears, ha! He said
"My soul is exceedingly sorrowful unto death, ha!
For this night, ha!
One of you shall betray me, ha!

It were not a Roman officer, ha!
It were not a centurion
But one of you
Who I have chosen my bosom friend
That sops in the dish with me shall betray me."
I want to draw a parable.
I see Jesus
Leaving heben with all of His grandeur
Dis-robin' Hisself of His matchless honor
Yielding up de scepter of revolvin' worlds
Clothing Hisself in de garment of humanity
Coming into de world to rescue His friends.
Two thousand years have went by on their rusty ankles
But with the eye of faith, I can see Him
Look down from his high tower of elevation
I can hear Him when He walks about the golden streets
I can hear 'em ring under His footsteps
Sol me-e-e, Sol do
Sol me-e-e, Sol do
I can hear Him step out upon the rim bones of nothing
Crying I am de way
De truth and de light
Ah!
God A'mighty!
I see Him grab de throttle
Of de well ordered train of mercy
I see kingdoms crush and crumble
Whilst de archangels held de winds in de corner chambers
I see Him arrive on dis earth
And walk de streets thirty and three years
Oh-h-hhh!
I see Him walking beside de sea of Galilee wid His disciples
This declaration gendered on His lips
"Let us go on to the other side."
God A'mighty!
Dey entered de boat
Wid their oarus (oars) stuck in de back
Sails unfurled to de evenin' breeze
And de ship was now sailin'
As she reached de center of de lake
Jesus was sleep on a pillow in de rear of de boat
And de dynamic powers of nature became disturbed
And de mad winds broke de heads of de Western drums
And fell down on de lake of Galilee
And buried themselves behind de gallopin' waves
And de white-caps marbilized themselves like an army

And walked out like soldiers goin' to battle
And de zig-zag lightning
Licked out her fiery tongue
And de flying clouds
Threw their wings in the channels of the deep
And bedded de waters like a road-plow
And faced de current of de chargin' billows
And de terrific bolts of thunder—they bust in de clouds
And de ship begin to reel and rock
God A'mighty!
And one of de disciples called Jesus
"Master!! Carest Thou not that we perish?"
And He arose
And de storm was in its pitch
And de lightnin' played on His raiments as He stood on
      de prow of the boat
And placed His foot upon de neck of the storm
And spoke to the howlin' winds
And de sea fell at His feet like a marble floor
And de thunders went back in their vault
Then He set down on de rim of de ship
And took de hooks of His power
And lifted de billows in His lap
And rocked de winds to sleep on His arm
And said, "Peace, be still."
And de Bible says there was a calm.

V
DRAMA

DRAMA

"WHEN Shakespeare wrote *Othello*," one critic has aptly stated, "he also wrote the birth certificate of the Negro actor." It might be added that the Negro actor has had to wait for over three hundred years for another role as great and as sympathetic as that of the tragic Moor. The Negro's place in the field of drama has been rigidly circumscribed. In the earliest American theatre he was relegated to the role of clown, and even today the moving pictures keep him there. As a consequence both the Negro actor and the Negro playwright have had a one-sided development. Once they stepped out of the character assigned to them they found an audience only with difficulty.

And yet the experience of the Negro has been the material for many of America's best known plays. *Uncle Tom's Cabin, The Emperor Jones,* and *The Green Pastures* have been internationally known. Scores of other dramas about Negroes have raised their authors from obscurity. It is noteworthy that the three plays named, and several of the others, have been melodrama, or spectacle, or fantasy, definitely removed from the normal experience of Negro life in America. It is the way of drama to heighten reality, but in plays of Negro life the heightening is greater than usual.

The Negro playwright has so far contributed little to the drama of his people, as that drama is known in America. With the exception of the writers of musical comedies, there are only a few Negroes whose plays have appeared on Broadway. Garland Anderson's *Appearances* had little if any pertinence to Negro life or to American life in general. Hall Johnson's *Run, Little Chillun* is the only play of Negro life of complete Negro authorship to have had a Broadway run. Three plays of part Negro authorship had successful runs: *Harlem* by Wallace Thurman in collaboration with William Rapp; *Mulatto* by Langston Hughes and Martin Jones; and *Native Son* by Richard Wright and Paul Green. These plays are discussed below. The Federal Theatre Project (also discussed below) introduced several plays by Negro authors to fairly large audiences. In the main, however, since serious plays of Negro life are considered to be "box-office poison," the Negro playwright is at best a stepchild of Broadway.

But that does not mean that the story of the Negro playwright can

494

be easily dismissed. Because Broadway has been a closed thoroughfare to him, he has taken to the tributary streets, sometimes as a detour, hoping to get to the main street later. Quite as often, however, like so many fellow theatre lovers, he believes that the American theatre is too large to be encompassed by the Broadway area. He shares the belief that "footlights over America" promise more dramatically than do the white lights of Broadway.

It is certain that Broadway, *i.e.,* the commercial theatre, has little connection with Negro life in America. Comparatively few Negroes, for instance, are among New York's theatregoers. Even if commercial producers had the best will in the world toward plays presenting "inside" views of Negro life, it is hardly likely that many such plays could pay their way in New York theatres. For a Negro author to place a play on Broadway is an individual achievement undoubtedly to be cherished. If the play is a good one it will do good, as a contributor to truth and understanding. But many Negro playwrights want to do more. They want to write drama in terms of their people's own lives, and they want to carry drama to the people. Their audiences are to be found over the land among people whose experience has been rife with elements of comedy and melodrama and tragedy, but who have had little if any chance to see those elements shaped into meaningful patterns.

The selections in this anthology, then, must be considered as belonging to the "tributary theatre" of America, a theatre still in its apprenticeship but full of promise. Special problems for the Negro playwright have arisen from the history of the Negro as character and as actor or, more exactly, entertainer. A brief survey of the Negro's association with the theatre should clarify these problems. For convenience this survey is divided into three periods; in each period the Negro as subject matter, the Negro performer, and the Negro playwright are discussed.

In 1795 James Murdock, seeking comic effect for his *The Triumph of Love,* introduced a Negro character named Sambo. Sambo has been with us ever since. Earlier plays had used the subsidiary servant, but Sambo's name and lengthy treatment are significant, and he was to come in for ample development in the minstrel show.

The origins of minstrelsy are obscure, but its great popularity at home and abroad is undisputed. Prominent in its beginnings was Thomas D. (Daddy Jim Crow) Rice, whose mimicry of a Negro hostler's grotesque song and dance started a vogue that has not yet disappeared. By 1850 the chicken-stealing, watermelon-eating, razor-wielding, bombastic comical "darkey" had become a stage convention. It should always be remembered that the first and probably greatest blackface minstrels were white and not Negro; the composers of their songs and skits were white; and the audiences were white. In its later, ritualized period, minstrelsy plagiarized gags, quizzes, and wheezes of the "Joe Miller" stripe more than it explored Negro life. Some of the material, however, had a rudimentary realism, and some of it has permeated Negro folklore.

Blackface comedy has been lucrative on the American stage, but Negro actors have not shared the wealth. Only after emancipation could Negroes become blackface minstrels. In the twentieth-century continuation of the stereotype, two white comedians, Amos an' Andy, have had a fabulous radio run at a fabulous salary, but there is no similar Negro team. There are a few individual Negro comic performers like Eddie Green and Rochester and a few teams in Negro vaudeville. In the moving pictures the comic Negro stereotype is steady, almost inevitable whenever a Negro appears on the screen. Taken by and large, however, Negroes themselves have had a minor role in creating what passes for "Negro" humor.

From the earliest, Negro actors fought against the comic circumscription. The first group of Negro actors of which there is any record was organized as The African Company in New York in 1821. This group presented Shakespeare and other classics at their theatre "in Mercer Street in the rear of 1 Mile Stone, Broadway," until, partly because of the boisterous behavior of white patrons, civil authorities closed the theatre. James Hewlett was the leader and principal actor of this company.

A greater actor was his contemporary, Ira Aldridge (1807-1867), who played Othello to Charles Kean's Iago in the leading European theatres. There was no place in the United States for his great abilities which European dramatic critics uniformly praised. Aldridge was the first talented American Negro to take Europe by storm. The career of Paul Robeson has much in common with that of Aldridge, the "African Roscius."

Although Aldridge's career was European and not American, it is probable that some of his prestige came as a result of the interest in talented Negroes that the Abolition Movement sponsored. Plays centered about the slavery controversy were Mrs. Stowe's *Uncle Tom's Cabin* (dramatized without her permission) and *Dred* (based upon her second novel), J. T. Trowbridge's *Neighbor Jackwood* (1857), Mrs. J. C. Swayze's topical *Ossawatomie Brown* (1859), and Dion

Boucicault's *The Octoroon* (1859). Though these plays were generally antislavery in purpose, they helped to fix the Negro character. The heroic, or nobly forgiving black and the pathetic victim appear fleetingly, but the comic Negro and that most woeful of heroines, the beautiful octoroon, are recurring characters, and have remained as hardy perennials on the stage and in the moving pictures.

William Wells Brown, who ventured into almost all of the literary fields, was the first Negro to write a play, *The Escape, or a Leap for Freedom* (1858). This was probably never staged, but Brown gave numerous readings from it. Even for nineteenth-century drama *The Escape* is a bad play. The central plot, based on the old triangle, involves a beautiful and innocent slave heroine, a lustful master, and a heroic slave lover. For *deus ex machina* there is an abolitionist who aids the two lovers to escape across the river into Canada in the last scene. The language is drawn out of the old stock:

> Sir, I am your slave, you can do as you please with the avails of my labor, but you shall never tempt me to swerve from the path of virtue.

There is also consciously intended humor in the play. Comic skits are interspersed among the lugubrious and elegant passages. It is interesting that Brown fell right into the prevailing minstrel tradition when he attempted comedy. His letters as antislavery worker (see pages 625 ff.) show that Brown could be humorous in an unforced and untraditional way, but when he attempted playwriting, it seems that he had to imitate blackface minstrelsy.

After emancipation a few Negro minstrel companies barnstormed over the nation. Noted among these Negro minstrels were Billy Kersands, Sam (Dad) Lucas, the Grand Old Man of the Negro stage, and Jim Bland, the composer of "Carry Me Back to Old Virginny" and "In De Evenin' by De Moonlight." The first successful Negro company was the Georgia Minstrels, later Callender's Original Georgia Minstrels; and there were other large companies. Even with the backing of such astute promoters as the Frohmans, however, Negro minstrel companies were not serious competitors to the established white companies. Though no longer a monopoly, blackface minstrelsy, the creation of the whites, remained largely theirs. Cutting monkeyshines as "comic darkeys" on the stage existed then, as it does now, largely for the release, the sport, and the profit of white people.

The first steps away from the minstrel show pattern have been told

of by James Weldon Johnson in his *Black Manhattan*. (See p. 967.)
The comic scenes played by Ernest Hogan, the teams of Bert Williams
and George Walker, and Bob Cole and J. Rosamond Johnson, were
somewhat smoother than blackface minstrelsy, with more of the genuine flavor of Negro folk humor. But as the coon songs indicate, minstrelsy still was influential. The greatest difference lay elsewhere. As
indicated by such names as "The Creole Girl" and "The Octoroons,"
producers definitely aimed at "glorifying" the colored girl, lining up
leading ladies and choruses famed for attractiveness and grace. In 1898
Will Marion Cook and Paul Laurence Dunbar collaborated on *Clorindy—The Origin of the Cakewalk,* a musical comedy which opened
to Broadway the possibilities of syncopated Negro music and dancing.
Between the ludicrous clog dancing started by Daddy Rice and the
pirouetting and prancing of the cakewalking choruses, there was a
marked difference. By 1909 the Great White Way had seen and
enjoyed *Jes Lak White Folks, The Policy Players, the Sons of Ham,
In Dahomey, Bandana Land, The Shoofly Regiment, Rufus Rastus,*
and *Red Moon.*

Occasionally the early Negro troupes would interrupt their buffoonery and high-spirited dancing to attempt something of a more
aspiring or serious nature. Black Patti's Troubadours, for instance,
opened with minstrelsy to clear the way for Black Patti's rendition of
operatic arias. Even her grand voice was thought to need a minstrel
introduction. The tradition of easing in aspiration or protest after
disarming an audience with the expected song and dance has persisted
until the present, though it generally achieves little more than artistic
incongruity.

But such subterfuges were necessary. Veterans recall an old theatrical commandment: "Never let a nigger say a line"; *i.e.,* confine his
performance to song and dance, unless in an all-Negro show playing
in an all-Negro house. Whether this reminiscence is completely accurate or not, it is certain that this era of Negro shows belongs to the
realm of entertainment, not of drama. The leading figures: Bert Williams, George Walker, Ada Overton, Stella Wiley, Ernest Hogan, Bob
Cole, J. Rosamond Johnson, Alex Rogers, Jesse Shipp, and S. H. Dudley, were either masters of blackface drollery, or singers and dancers.

The legitimate plays of the period included the Negro only incidentally. Even these roles, with very rare exceptions, were played by
whites. It is noteworthy that when Gustave Frohman asked "Why not
have a real Negro play Uncle Tom?" the idea was considered a stroke
of theatrical genius. The few roles of mammy, butler, and clown were
probably played just as well by white actresses and actors, since the

plays, almost all of them glorifications of the Old South, were even
less related to Negro life than were the musical comedies. With very
few exceptions, no plays of this period touched upon the seriousness
of Negro life in America. About a half century after the dramas of
antislavery propaganda, Thomas Dixon's *Clansman* (1905), a dramatization of his hate-filled novel, agitated against the free Negro as a
menace. *The Nigger* (1909) by Edward Sheldon tells of a supposedly
white candidate for governor of a Southern state who learned on the
eve of his election that he was partly Negro. The dramatist points out
to him the proper course of renunciation and devotion to his people
(*i.e.,* Negroes, though in appearance he was white). Both the problem
and the "tragedy" were certainly far removed from Negro life.

Kept out of the American theatre as performers, except in music
comedies, and unwanted generally in the audiences, Negroes struggled
to start their own theatres and acting companies. Between 1900 and
1915 Negro theatres were built in many Northern cities. The first of
these theatres to organize a stock company was the old Pekin in Chicago. In New York groups were organized at the Lincoln Theatre
and the Lafayette Theatre. The Lafayette Players, sometimes called
The Quality Amusement Company, was the best known and most
productive stock company. At one time the Lafayette Players had four
companies on the road playing to Negro audiences. Their plays were,
naturally enough in the circumstances, melodramatic Broadway successes like *Kick In, Madame X, Dr. Jekyll and Mr. Hyde,* and *The
Count of Monte Cristo.* Though unrelated to Negro life, these plays
satisfied an audience hungry for drama, and they furnished an apprenticeship for such actors as Charles Gilpin, Rose McClendon, Abbie
Mitchell, Edna Thomas, Jack Carter, and Frank Wilson, who were
later to be successful in very different kinds of drama. Amateurs,
organized in churches or community groups, also attempted to give
plays, very often by Shakespeare.

The Negro was eager to play serious drama, but there was almost
no effort on his part to write it. The first published serious drama of
the period is *Caleb, The Degenerate,* a poetical closet play dealing
with the problem of industrial versus liberal education. The author,
Joseph S. Cotter, Sr., apparently knew little of the theatre; *Caleb,
The Degenerate* is even less actable than William Wells Brown's *The
Escape.* A much better play was Angelina Grimké's *Rachel,* produced
by the Drama Committee of the N. A. A. C. P. under the direction
of Nathaniel Guy at the Neighborhood Theater in New York and in
Cambridge, Massachusetts. A story of a sensitive young Negro woman
whose life is ruined by American racial injustice, it courageously entered

a field of dramatic possibilities. As pioneering work, as the first successful drama written and interpreted by Negroes, it is significant; as drama it is not too convincing.

In 1917 when Ridgely Torrence, a distinguished white poet, produced three one-act plays of Negro life: *The Rider of Dreams, Granny Maumee,* and *Simon the Cyrenian,* he revitalized the whole field of Negro drama. No comedy—even in the sketches by Dunbar, Williams and Walker, or Cole and Johnson—was as authentic as *The Rider of Dreams;* no tragedy such as that in *Granny Maumee* had even been approached. Showing the dramatic possibilities of the folk, doing for Negro life something of what Synge and Lady Gregory had done for Irish peasants, Torrence laid a healthy and sound basis for plays of Negro life.

Torrence's plays were modest but significant contributions to the new realism in American drama. In his earlier period, Eugene O'Neill explored Negro life; giving the first tragedy of urban life in *The Dreamy Kid* (1919); creating in 1920 what some consider his greatest play, *The Emperor Jones*; and in 1924, probing the problem of intermarriage in *All God's Chillun Got Wings*. Ernest Culbertson's *Goat Alley* (1922), a naturalistic play of the slums; Du Bose Heyward's and Dorothy Heyward's magical *Porgy* (1927), based upon life in Charleston's Cat-Fish Row; and Paul Green's Pulitzer play *In Abraham's Bosom* (1926), bitterly depicting a Negro's unavailing struggle to educate his people, were significant works. Paul Green has done many of the best plays of Negro life, from the poetic *No 'Count Boy,* the farcical *The Man Who Died At Twelve O'Clock,* and the brooding *White Dresses,* to the symphonic *Roll, Jordan, Roll,* and his collaboration with Richard Wright on *Native Son*. The miracle play *The Green Pastures* (1930), a poetic reworking of what purported to be the naïve aspects of Negro folk religion, was immensely successful. The folk opera *Porgy and Bess* by the Heywards and the Gershwins, *Mamba's Daughters* by the Heywards, Roark Bradford's *John Henry,* and *Cabin In The Sky* by John Latouche and Vernon Duke continue the folk tradition without deepening it.

Later plays by white authors have concentrated less upon the naïve and the "folksy" and include more social protest. James Knox Millen's *Never No More* (1932), a powerful play about a lynching; Frederick Schlick's *Bloodstream* (1932), about industrial workers; and John Wexley's *They Shall Not Die* (1934), about the Scottsboro case, opened the way for Paul Peters' and George Sklar's *Stevedore,* the most effective drama so far to protest the injustice that is the American Negro's daily lot and to urge the unity of black and white workers. This trend, though apparently a reversion to the problem drama, is really different, because it removes the Negro character from a narrow racial groove, and shows the social causes of his problem, as well as his fellowship with others who are oppressed.

For the Negro actor, the coming of realism to the American theatre was good fortune. Plays such as the above obviously had to be performed by Negroes. Suddenly Negro actors were discovered: among them Charles Gilpin, Paul Robeson, Jules Bledsoe, Frank Wilson, Leigh Whipper, Rose McClendon, Abbie Mitchell, Georgette Harvey, Todd Duncan, Anne Wiggins Brown, Fredi Washington, Rex Ingram, Ethel Waters, Canada Lee, and last, but not least, Richard Harrison, whose performance as De Lawd in *The Green Pastures* was one of the causes of the play's phenomenal run.

The rise of these plays coincided with a flourishing period in Negro musical shows. As part of the discovery of Harlem in the jazz age, Negro tap dancers, choruses, jazz bands, and comedies were brought from comparative obscurity in Negro theatres and cabarets down to Broadway. *Shuffle Along* (1921), the work of Miller and Lyles, Sissle and Blake, started the ball rolling. In quick succession came such shows as *Liza, Runnin' Wild, Chocolate Dandies, From Dixie to Broadway, Hot Chocolates, Brown Buddies,* Lew Leslie's *Blackbirds,* and *Rhapsody in Black.* Here the brown girl was definitely glorified. The outstanding characteristics of these shows were their infectious gayety, the swift tempo and the excellence of their dancing (the influence outlasting the performers on Broadway), and the stirring music. Bill "Bojangles" Robinson, Florence Mills, and Ethel Waters made their reputations in such shows. Once considered to be good medicine for an ailing Broadway, these shows have since lost favor for many reasons, chief among them being an unwillingness to vary the old patterns, and the skillful appropriation of their best features by white musical shows.

Negro playwrights were heartened when the new realism about Negro life gained a hearing on the American stage. Coincidentally, the "Negro Renaissance" was encouraging Negroes to write, and prize contests were conducted by *The Crisis* and *Opportunity* magazines. Frank Wilson heads Negro dramatists in point of time. His *Sugar Cane,* written in 1920, won the *Opportunity* prize contest for 1925. With a varied experience as an actor in all types of shows, Frank Wilson has the "feel" of the theatre. His *Brother Mose* (1928) and *Walk Together Children* (1936) were produced by the Federal Theatre Project. Influenced by the Torrence-Green tradition were Georgia Douglass Johnson's tragedy *Plumes* and many of the plays of Willis Richardson. Richardson won *The Crisis* play contest with *The Broken Banjo* in 1925. He has edited *Plays and Pageants of Negro Life* (1930) and in collaboration with May Miller, *Negro History in Thirteen Plays* (1935). May Miller has written folk-plays such as *Riding The Goat,* a humorous play of lodge life. Eulalie Spence is concerned with urban life in *Undertow* and *The Starter.* James W. Butcher, Jr., whose *The Seer* (see p. 520) and *Milk and Honey* effectively make capital out of the mine of folk humor; John F. Matheus, whose *'Cruiter* and *Black Damp* showed great promise; and Zora Neale Hurston, whose *Great Day* was a loose dramatic arrangement of her collected lore, are also in the folk tradition. One of the most influential figures in the creation of a body of Negro plays is Randolph Edmonds, whose work is discussed below.

As stated earlier, few Negro playwrights have had plays produced on Broadway. Wallace Thurman and William Rapp, a white writer, coproduced *Harlem,* a highly sensational melodrama which in 1929 had a fairly successful run on Broadway, since it capitalized on the Harlem-mania. It combined, in smart theatrical fashion, the thrills of a Harlem rent party and a murder play. Much more sincere was Hall Johnson's *Run, Little Chillun* (1933), the most brilliant play by a Negro author to get to Broadway. Its church scenes were truer to Negro folk experience than the more successful *The Green Pastures.* *Run, Little Chillun* was part opera, part ballet, and part drama, including the frenzied dancing and the ecstatic singing of a weird Negro cult; the authentic preaching, swinging, and shouting of an orthodox Negro church; and a melodramatic story of illicit love. It had magnificent moments, but it was spectacle rather than drama. Nevertheless, it had one quality that Kenneth Burke points out in comparing it with *The Green Pastures*:

> *The Green Pastures* was a canny theatre production staged by white men who thoroughly knew their stage. *Run, Little Chillun* is a sincere but in many respects a laborious and untutored effort by a Negro at welding music and drama into one performance. But the difference goes deeper than that. *The Green Pastures* was . . . essentially a white man's play . . . not the Negro telling of the Old Testament, but rather the white man's amused retelling . . . For all the honest pleasantness of its dialogue, it did contrive to exploit the old minstrel show conception of the Negro (naïve, good-natured, easily put upon) . . . an endearing symbol for the eliciting of white warmth . . . [*Run, Little Chillun*

emphasizes] an aspect of the Negro symbol with which our theatre going public is not theatrically at home: the power side of the Negro.

The most versatile Negro dramatist has been Langston Hughes. Whether in folk play, social satire, problem drama or mass chant, he is daring and provocative. His *Mulatto* (1935) (done in collaboration with Martin Jones), a crudely effective but sensational dramatization of interracial mixture in the deep South, had a long run. His *Scottsboro, Limited* is a skillful mass chant; *Don't You Want To Be Free?* is a militant propaganda play. Hughes's best dramatic work is probably in the folk plays which have been performed by the Gilpin Players of Cleveland.

The last play partly of Negro authorship to be successful in New York is *Native Son,* the collaboration of Richard Wright and Paul Green, and directed by Orson Welles. With almost as much smashing impact as Wright's powerful novel, *Native Son* was considered to be one of the finest plays of the year.

One of the best services of The Federal Theatre Project was the invaluable apprenticeship and encouragement it gave to Negro actors, technicians, and playwrights. Its successes were not only the Haitian *Macbeth,* or *Haiti,* or the *Swing Mikado,* in spite of the contributions of these to the gayety of the nation. Its sponsorship of plays by Negro authors looms large—and if the Project had not been condemned to an untimely death would have loomed larger. Before it closed, however, it produced, besides the plays of Frank Wilson mentioned earlier, Arna Bontemps' and Countee Cullen's dramatization of Rudolph Fisher's *The Conjure Man Dies;* Hughes Allison's *The Trial of Dr. Beck;* J. A. Smith's and Peter Morell's *Turpentine;* and Theodore Brown's *Natural Man,* a folk opera version of the John Henry legend. Theodore Ward's *Big White Fog* (1938) was the strongest play by a Negro produced by the Project. Concerned with the problems of poverty, unemployment, and prejudice, and such solutions as Garveyism and communism, the play was recognized both in Chicago, where it first appeared, and in New York as a work worthy of serious attention. Langston Hughes called it the best Negro play that had appeared. It was presented in New York by the Negro Playwrights Group at the same time as *Cabin In The Sky.* Most critics used the two plays as symbols: *Cabin In The Sky* as the white man's version of Negro life in America: naïve, amusing, bordering on the fantastic; and *Big White Fog,* as the Negro's inside version: grim and purposeful, kept very close to the real.

These Federal Theatre plays differed in their dramatic qualities, but by and large they deserved what one critic said of *Turpentine*: "The downtown public will not be interested in *Turpentine* because in the production the Negro is not 'exotic.' Plain working people and their problems are movingly dramatized." For allowing such an emphasis, the Federal Theatre Project deserves credit, as it does for presenting the largest number of serious, ambitious plays by Negro authors ever to be presented on the professional stage, and for giving the best productions that Negro playwrights have ever been afforded.

Keeping pace with the national movement, Little Theatre groups among Negroes have sprung up at intervals, and though many have been short-lived, they have contributed to the growth of a drama consciousness. The Krigwa Players were sponsored by W. E. B. DuBois in the early twenties in several Northern cities, but could not survive as a serious artistic movement. The Boston Players, and groups in Baltimore, Philadelphia, and Washington have appeared sporadically. Much sturdier, and one of the most effective little theatre groups in America, is The Gilpin Players of Cleveland, a group which, under the direction of Rowena Jelliffe, has produced a surprising number of plays of Negro life. Two recent New York groups—resembling working-class theatres—were The Suitcase Theatre, which, founded in 1937, produced Langston Hughes's *Don't You Want To Be Free?* and The Negro Playwrights Company, which produced *Big White Fog* as its first play. The status of both of these is uncertain. Two other New York groups less concerned with propaganda are The Rose McClendon Players, which, under the direction of Dick Campbell, has played for several seasons, and The American Negro Theatre, which created a hit with Abram Hill's *On Strivers' Row*. This play, a satire of bourgeois affectation, is one of the first social comedies of middle-class Negro life by a Negro playwright. Much of its appeal to Harlem audiences came from a character who was a past master of the "jumping jive" argot of Harlem "hep-cats."

Most of these amateur or semiprofessional groups are well disposed toward Negro playwrights. But they are few in number and poor in purse. With the death of the Federal Theatre Project the Negro playwright's opportunities for genuine apprenticeship in his craft and for professional productions dwindled. It is likely that, as Randolph Edmonds suggests, the hope of a genuine Negro theatre is to be found in the "organizational" approach of the associations of Negro colleges. From the founding of the first college dramatic group, The Howard Players, by Montgomery Gregory and Alain Locke in 1921, to the present, drama has been increasingly fostered at Negro colleges. Ran-

dolph Edmonds deserves great credit for his efforts in the founding
of the Negro Intercollegiate Drama Association, which now comprises
The North Carolina Agricultural and Industrial College, Hampton
Institute, Howard University, Lincoln University, Morgan College,
Shaw University, Virginia State College, and Virginia Union University. Edmonds, now professor of drama at Dillard University, has since
organized The Southern Association of Drama and Speech Arts. At
Atlanta University a thriving university theatre is directed by Anne
Cooke, assisted by Owen Dodson. John M. Ross, at Fisk University, and
Fannin Belcher, at West Virginia State College, bring a high grade of
technical training to their work of instruction in dramatic arts. Such
college teachers work strenuously to train actors and technicians and
to build that most necessary of adjuncts to a little theatre—an intelligent audience.

All of these realize the paucity of plays about Negro life. Many,
seeing the dearth, write plays themselves. Some of the best plays about
Negro life are the works of men engaged in teaching dramatics.
Randolph Edmonds has listed what he feels to be the necessities for
plays that will take with theatrically unsophisticated Negro audiences:
"worthwhile themes, sharply drawn conflict, positive characters, and
a melodramatic plot." His *Seven Plays For A Negro Theatre,* the first
book of Negro folk plays to be published, include these necessities,
and the success of his plays with Negro audiences has been definite.
(See *Bad Man,* below, pp. 506-520.) Other instructors of dramatics—
John M. Ross, James W. Butcher, Jr., Owen Dodson, and Thomas D.
Pawley—have all turned out plays of Negro life that warrant attention.
Shirley Graham, with experience in the Federal Theatre Project and
training at the Yale Drama School, is the author of the opera *Tom-
Tom,* and plays and radio scripts of Negro life.

These instructors have been well trained in schools of drama, and
though denied the more thoroughgoing apprenticeship of the professional stage, they do have something of a stage and an acting company to work with, and they study their medium closely. Pawley's play
Jedgement Day, produced in the drama department of the University
of Iowa, and Owen Dodson's *Divine Comedy,* produced at the Yale
Theatre, were highly praised. Owen Dodson is interested in the experimental, poetic drama; his first plays hold fine artistic promise.

Playwriting is at best one of the most arduous of writing skills.
The Negro playwrights find aggravated difficulties. Just as the Irish
playwrights found a time-honored stage Irishman bossing the boards,
so Negro playwrights find many stereotypes endeared to the American
public. They must loosen the hold of these before closer resemblances

to the truth will be accepted. There are other complicating factors. Broadway can accommodate only a few Negro plays at best, and many white playwrights, experienced in technique, are considered the final interpreters of Negro life and character. The Negro audience is as yet unformed; its theatrical experience is too often limited to song and dance, or church pageants, or fashion shows. The Negro writers' enforced separation from collaboration with acting companies, technicians, directors, and producers is bound to reflect itself in insecure, inept work. How far this can be counterbalanced by whole-hearted devotion to the little theatre movement is uncertain. But dramatic enthusiasm, kept alive in the colleges, is higher today than ever. Negro playwrights, though still few and young, seem to be aware of what Hallie Flanagan pointed out in *Arena*: "The theatre, often regarded even by members of its own profession as dead or dying, still has tremendous power to stir up life and infuse it with fire." There is fine dramatic material in Negro life in America; there is abundant reason why dramatists should be developed capable of rendering that material.

RANDOLPH EDMONDS (1900-   )

Born in Lawrenceville, Virginia, Randolph Edmonds was educated in the St. Paul Normal and Industrial School of that city and at Oberlin College. He received his master's degree from Columbia and in 1934 was awarded a General Education Board Fellowship to study in the Department of Drama at Yale University. Another fellowship, granted him by the Rosenwald Fund in 1938, enabled him to study drama organizations in Ireland and Great Britain and to observe the production methods of the Abbey Theater in Dublin. Randolph Edmonds is the author of two books: *Shades and Shadows,* six imaginative stories in dramatic form, and *Six Plays for a Negro Theatre,* a book of folk plays. He has also been an important figure in the Negro little theatre movement, founding both the Negro Intercollegiate Drama Association and the Southern Association of Drama and Speech Arts. At present he is professor of drama at Dillard University. *Bad Man* comes from *Six Plays for a Negro Theatre* and is reprinted by permission of the author and Walter H. Baker Co., publishers. All rights are reserved by the author.

Bad Man

CAST OF CHARACTERS

Tom Joiner
Ted James
Hubbard Bailey
Percy Hardy

Jack Burchard
Burt Ross
Maybelle Joiner
Thea Dugger

Scene.—*The interior of a shanty house located at a sawmill camp in a remote section of Alabama. The walls are very rough and crude, giving the impression of weather boards nailed up on the outside without any finishing material on the inside.*

The furniture is very crude and primitive. There are two home-made cots, one along the side to the left and another on the right. The rest of the furniture consists of a crude table, several dilapidated chairs and home-made stools. An upright home-made box is placed conveniently with cooking utensils on top of it.

One door in the back, left, leads to the outside, and another, on the right side, leads to another room in the shanty. One window is in the back, right, and another on the left side. Both have dirty, ragged curtains hung before them. Old coats and overalls hang on nails on the wall, and everything is in an untidy condition.

The people who inhabit these shanties are peasant Negroes who work at the sawmill. Many types are usually found at these camps, ranging from pious church goers to gamblers, murderers, and escaped convicts. All are, generally speaking, illiterate; but some possess a keen native wit, and worthy ambitions.

[*The opening curtain shows* Tom, Maybelle, *and* Ted. Tom *is a typical sawmill hand, just under forty, and a hard worker. He is dressed in dirty blue overalls, and a ragged shirt.* Ted, *who is about twenty, is dressed in dirty, dark trousers, and a white shirt which is beginning to get dirty.* Maybelle *is dressed in a loud checked calico dress in rural style. She is about eighteen and is inclined somewhat to coquetry.* Tom *has been looking anxiously out of the window in the rear.* Maybelle *was seated at the crude table downstage, somewhat to the left. An oil lamp in the middle shines in her face.* Ted *is seated on a bench on the right trying to read a book, and is eating peanuts. The season is early fall, and the time is early dusk.*]

Tom [*turning away from the window*]. Hit don't look like Pa is comin' back fuh yuh. Hit's dust o' dark now.

Maybelle [*anxiously*] He said he would be back at least an hour befo' sunset.

Tom. Ah hopes he hurries up and come on.

Maybelle. He's bound to be 'long in a little while. Don't worry yose'f so much.

507

Tom. Dat's easy tuh say; but shanty houses at sawmill camps ain't no place fuh women, least of all ma own sister.

Maybelle. Hit don't seem all dat bad.

Tom [*earnestly*]. Yuh never can tell whut is gwine tuh happen, and anyt'ing is liable tuh happen 'tween sundown and sunup. Ah don't see why Pa left yuh heah nohow.

Maybelle. Ah wanted tuh see de place, so he left me heah while he druv five miles out in de country tuh git a possum dawg.

Ted [*looking up*]. Ah noticed dat one wheel on de buggy was bad. Maybe he gut broke down.

Tom [*moving about anxiously*]. Hit would be jes' lak dat ole buggy tuh break down on a night when hit shouldn't.

Maybelle. Well, ef he don't git back tonight, maybe yuh can find me a place tuh stay.

Tom. Naw! Dere ain't no place 'round heah fuh women tuh stay. Ef he don't come back soon we starts walkin'.

Maybelle [*looking at her shoes*]. Dese shoes don't want me tuh do no walkin'. Dese men heah ain't so bad Ah's gut tuh walk ten miles in de dark.

Tom. Yuh don't know whut yuh is talkin' 'bout. A sawmill camp is de worse place in de world. Somepen bad is always happenin' heah. A man gits killed in de woods or at de mill, or gits shot or cut tuh death each an' every month. We's gut men heah dat will stay 'round de shanty house and gamble from de time de whistle blow Sattiday at noon, 'til Monday mawning. Plenty dese men heah done 'scaped from de chain gang, or killed one or two men. And de white folks dat live up de road at dat little village is wus dan poisen. Ah tells yuh too much happen roun' heah fuh a ooman tuh be mixed up in hit.

Maybelle. Maybe nothin' won't happen tonight.

Tom [*slightly peeved*]. Yuh nevah can tell when hit's gwine tuh happen. Ah told yuh not tuh stay heah nohow. Yuh should 'a' gone on wid him tuh git dat dawg. Well, ef he don't come pretty soon, we starts walkin'.

Ted [*looking up again*]. Ah wouldn't walk way home tonight in de dark, Tom. Ef yo' pa don't come back, Hubbard and me can make a pallet on de floor, and stay in heah wid yuh and Thea.

Tom. Ah'll think 'bout hit. Ef yuh is gwine tuh be in heah a minute, Ted, Ah'se gut tuh go over to de commissary and git some Blood Hound chewin' tobacca. When Ah gits back Ah'll decide what tuh do.

Ted. Ah'll be heah. Ah ain't gwine nowhar. [Tom *goes out.* Ted *throws the book aside and comes over to where* Maybelle *is.*] Well, yuh might got Tom worried, but yuh ain't got me. Yuh could stay heah a whole week, and Ah'd see dat nothin' bothers yuh.

Maybelle [*coquettishly*]. Dat's sweet of yuh tuh say so anyhow.

Ted [*trying to put his arms around her*]. Dat ain't nothin'. Ah wish Ah could say sompen sweet, as Ah is crazy 'bout yuh.

MAYBELLE [*pulling away*]. Not now. Ah want yuh tell me sompen 'bout de place heah. Tom is always telling me 'bout how bad de men is. Ah saw some by de commissary, and dey didn't look so bad tuh me.

TED. Dey is bad enough. Tom told yuh 'bout right. All dey do jes' as soon as de whistle blow is tuh eat, shoot crap or play gawgie skin. Dey is shootin' and cuttin' all de time. Dey kill a man pretty often heah. Sometime dey git killed in de log woods or at de mill shad.

MAYBELLE. Whar is Thea Dugger? Ah's heard Tom talk so much 'bout how bad he is.

TED. He is a bad man in many ways all right. He's done killed six men in gamblin' games. He always keep five or six pistols, and five or ten boxes of cottriges. He won't run from nobody. He ain't scared o' de debbil. Ah ain't never seed a man who wa'n't scared of nobody like he.

MAYBELLE. He mus' be brave all right.

TED. He is. Dey say once when he was workin' in a steel mill in Birmingham, he went into a pool parlor where dey was gamblin'. One man started tuh pull a gun on him. He picked up a cue ball and hit him in de temple and killed him daid as a goat. Den he picked up de man's Smith and Weston and shot up de place. Everybody ran out in de street. Thea ran out arter dem but didn't see nothin' but a mule. So he poured de lead into de mule. Dey say de mule jumped up and fell down daid.

MAYBELLE. Hit's a wonder dey didn't 'rest him way up dere in de city.

TED [*proudly*]. De police ain't gwine bother Thea Dugger. Nobody 'round heah ain't neither. Dey all giv' him plenty o' elbow room. He kinder like me dough.

MAYBELLE. Will Ah git a chance tuh see him?

TED. Ef yuh pa don't come 'long pretty quick. He and some de boys is over at de slab fire cookin' and eatin'. Dey'll drift up heah in a little while tuh play gawgie skin or shoot dice.

MAYBELLE. Ah's glad Ah is gwine tuh git a chance tuh see him. Ah always wanted to see an honest tuh goodness bad man.

TED [*moving closer*]. Ain't Ah bad nuff fuh yuh?

MAYBELLE [*smiling*]. Yuh ain't jealous, is yuh?

TED [*putting his arm around her waist*]. Who wouldn't be jealous of a fine lookin' gal lak yuh?

MAYBELLE [*pushing him away*]. Don't Ted. Not in heah. Tom will be back in a minute.

TED [*slightly crestfallen*]. Is yo' pa softened up on yuh any? Ah'd lak tuh see yuh at yo' house some time.

MAYBELLE. Naw, not a bit. He is so set on my gwine away tuh boardin' school nex' week. He don't want me tuh marry no sawmill han'. He wants me tuh marry a school teacher or doctor or sompen.

TED. Well, Ah hopes yuh don't think Ah is gwine be a sawmill han' all ma life. Ah's readin books. Ah's gwine away tuh de city and be a business man. Ah's already done saved fifty dollars.

MAYBELLE. Dat sure is good.

TED [*meditating*]. Ah 'spect we's gut tuh run away ef we ever gits married.

MAYBELLE. Maybe so.

TED. Ah's started many times tuh tell Tom 'bout our love. Ah'se tired of meetin' yuh in secret.

MAYBELLE [*alarmed*]. Don't do dat. He'd git mad as de debbil. Tom is jes' as bad as Pa 'bout ma goin' tuh school. Ef he thought Ah stopped heah mainly tuh see yuh, he'd have a fit.

TED [*pulling her to him*]. Fit or no fit, Ah's gwine tuh kiss yuh, dat's all.

[*She pulls away but he manages to kiss her.*]

MAYBELLE. Don't Ted! Ah's scared in heah.

TED. Wid yuh in ma arms, Ah ain't scared of nobody. Yuh don't realize how yuh makes me feel.

MAYBELLE [*coquettishly*]. How does Ah makes yuh feel, Ted?

TED. Ah don't know. Ah can't tell yuh. Ah'se gut tuh read many mo' books befo' Ah'll be able tuh find words 'nuff. All Ah knows is dat when Ah's wid yuh dere is some kind of feelin' dat runs through me dat makes me feel glad. Sometimes ma heart seems lak hit's gwine tuh bust; other times Ah feel lak shoutin' lak dey do at de Sanctified Church. Ah can't keep meetin' yuh in secret, and den come way up heah in de woods and leave yuh fuh a week. Ah can't do hit much longer, Maybelle. Let's run away and git married.

MAYBELLE. Sometime, maybe.

TED. Let's make hit next week when yuh is supposed tuh go off tuh boardin' school. We could both go tuh de city, and wurk and go tuh night school. Ah could open up some kind of business. Ah'd do anyt'ing in de wurld ef Ah had yuh wid me all de time.

MAYBELLE. All right. Next week, den.

TED. Yuh really mean dat?

[MAYBELLE *shakes her head in the affirmative. He pulls her to him; but before he can kiss her,* TOM *comes in. They look confused and break away.*]

TOM [*scowling*]. Whut yuh all doin' in heah?

MAYBELLE. Ah . . . ah . . . was jes' showin' Ted ma ring. [*Holding it up for him to see.*]

TOM [*not looking*]. Hit looked mighty lak yuh was kissin'.

MAYBELLE. Naw we wa'n't. Honest we wa'n't.

TOM [*glaring at* TED, *slowly*]. Dis is ma youngest sis, Ted; Ah laks yuh all right, but ef Ah catches any sawmill han' kissin' huh, dat man don't live no mo'. Do yuh understand?

TED [*sulkily*]. Ah heah yuh. 'Tain't no use tuh git so mad 'bout hit, dough.

MAYBELLE [*excited and wishing to change the subject*]. Ain't yuh seed pa, yit?

TOM. Naw, so Ah s'pose we'd better start walkin'.

MAYBELLE [*pouting*]. Ah don't feel lak walkin' no ten miles.

TOM. Ah done tell yuh, yuh can't stay heah!

TED. Yuh'd save yose'f a lot o' trouble ef yuh let huh sleep in de next room. Ah'm sure Hubbard don't mind sleepin' on a pallet heah on de floor, and Ah know Ah don't mind.

[*Before* TOM *can answer,* HUBBARD BAILEY *and* JACK BURCHARD *enter. They are typical sawmill workers, dirty, grimy and unkempt.* HUBBARD *has on blue overalls spotted with resin, a tattered khaki shirt, and a dirty grey cap.* JACK *has on a pair of grey trousers and a tan shirt. He wears a cap with the brim turned around in the back. A red bandana handkerchief is tied around his neck.*]

HUBBARD [*before he enters*]. Comin' in, Tom.

TOM. Come on in ef yuh nose is clean.

JACK. Hit ain't clean 'cause hit's full o' sawdust.

[*Both are surprised when they see a woman in the shanty.*]

HUBBARD. Didn't know yuh had company, Tom.

TOM. Jes' mah sistah. Set down, we's gwine in a minute.

TED. Whar's Thea?

JACK. Comin' up de path right right behind us. Heah he is now.

THEA [*as he opens the door*]. Back up in heah everybody, Thea Dugger comin' in! [*He opens the door and lumbers in, but stops suddenly when he sees a girl in the shanty.* THEA *is a veritable giant, mean and hard looking. He is dressed in brown overalls, and a dirty white shirt. A crumpled brown hat sets on a head of hair that has needed cutting for a month. Long sideburns come down his jaws. He is a domineering type, and everybody is afraid of him. They hasten to do whatever he says. In a slow draggy manner.*] So we's gut a gal visitin' us tonight. Whut she doin' heah, Tom?

TOM [*apologetically*]. Dis is ma youngest sistah, Miss Maybelle Joiner, Mr. Thea Dugger. And Ah forgot, Mr. Jack Burchard and Mr. Hubbard Bailey.

MAYBELLE. Ah'm glad tuh meet yuh gentlemen.

THEA. Ah'm surprised at yuh, Tom, bringin' yo' sistah into a hell hole lak dis.

TOM. Ah didn't exactly bring huh. She jes' stopped off heah. Pa was s'posed tuh have been heah and gut huh. We was jes' startin' tuh leave when yuh come in.

THEA. Well, don't let me stop yuh. A skin game is gwine on heah tonight, not no Sunday School fuh no ooman tuh teach.

TOM [*hurrying* MAYBELLE]. All right, Thea. Come on, Maybelle! Let's git gwine.

TED [*coming up to* THEA]. Listen, Thea. Ah thought, or er was thinkin' dat since Tom's pa's buggy 'bout broke down, and dey would hab tuh walk 'bout ten miles befo' dey gits home, maybe, somehow we could fix hit up so Maybelle could stay heah.

THEA. Ah don't git yo' drift, kid. Yuh is gut tuh th'ow again. What does yuh want me tuh do? Give up ma bunk?

TED [backing away]. Naw, not yuh, Thea. Ah thought ef hit's all right wid Hubbard, we could bring some quilts in from de other room and make a pallet on de floor when we git ready tuh go tuh bed, and let huh have our room.

THEA. Dat suits me ef hit's all right wid de res'. [To MAYBELLE.] But, Miss, yuh had better stop yo' ears up wid cotton, 'cause Ah can't play gawgie skin and talk Sunday School talk.

HUBBARD. Hit's all right wid me, Tom.

MAYBELLE. Ah thank yuh all, and 'tickler yuh, Mr. Thea.

[TOM, TED and MAYBELLE go into the next room. JACK and HUBBARD look at the door through which they have departed.]

JACK. Ain't she a good looker, dough?

HUBBARD. She's a peach all right. Ef Ah was ten years younger, Ah'd give all de boys a run fuh dere money.

THEA. Whut yuh two dumb bells standin' dere fuh? Git de cards and de table. 'Tain't no usen lettin' yo' mouth water 'cause Tom would kill both yuh ef yuh made one pass tuh git huh.

HUBBARD. He can't stop us from lookin', dough.

THEA [yelling]. Come on, git de things straight and stop talkin' so much wid yo' mouth. [THEA pulls out a pack of worn cards from under his bunk. They sit around the table and HUBBARD starts to deal.] Dis deck is too thick. Git de other deck, Hubbard; you'll find hit right under de bunk dere.

HUBBARD. Dis deck is all right.

THEA. Ah ain't never had no luck wid a thick deck.

HUBBARD. We'll play wid dis one jes a little while anyway.

THEA [standing up and looking at HUBBARD]. Git dat deck, Ah say! [HUBBARD doesn't move fast enough. THEA knocks him out of his chair to the floor.] Is yuh gwine tuh git dat deck?

HUBBARD [getting up submissively]. All right, Thea.

[Before he can sit down, PERCY HARDY comes in. He is very nervous and excitable. He is dressed in a pair of patched overalls with a grey shirt.]

JACK. Yuh is jes' in time fuh a lil game, Percy. Dat is, providin' yuh is gut some money.

PERCY. Ah's gut a little left.

HUBBARD [sitting down dealing. Money is put up]. Ah thought we cleaned yuh out las' night.

PERCY [sitting down nervously]. Aw, yuh didn't clean me out. Luck was runnin' 'gainst me so Ah left.

JACK. Well, yuh won't hab hit long, 'cause Ah's gwine tuh carry de cub tuh everybody.

[TED comes into the room and walks around meditatively as if in deep thought.]

THEA. Whut's de matter, kid? Sompen on yo' mind?

TED. Nothin' in particler, Thea. Ma mind mus' be wanderin' round, dat's all.

JACK [*teasing him*]. Mus' be de swell gal in de next room?

THEA. Lay off dat kid, Jack. Nobody is s'pose tuh bother him 'long as Thea Dugger is 'round.

JACK [*submissively*]. All right, Thea.

PERCY [*he takes a deck and starts to deal. He is nervous and fidgety. His card turns up quickly*]. Well, Ah'll be—

THEA [*sternly*]. Hold dat, Percy. Dere ain't gwine to be no cussin' in heah tonight. Dere is a ooman in de next room.

PERCY [*submissively*]. Well, Ah'll carry de deal on down.

THEA [*pointing to his card*]. Well, dis king will go on down tuh de bottom wid yuh.

[*Money changes hands several times.* THEA *changes cards, too.*]

PERCY. Wal, Ah sho' lost on dat deal.

HUBBARD. Aw, stop belly achin'.

THEA. Deal Jack! Maybe Percy'll do better.

[TED *sits down hard on one of the bunks,* PERCY *jumps.*]

JACK. Whut yuh jumpin' 'bout? Yuh seems mighty nervous tonight.

PERCY. Ah ain't felt right ever since Ah heard old man Sam was killed.

HUBBARD. Any time a white man lives out in de woods by hisse'f, somebody ought tuh knock him in de haid.

PERCY. Ah don't know nothin' 'bout hit; but Ah don't believe we's heard de las' of hit yit.

JACK. Naw, don't know nothin' 'bout hit, so we ain't gut nothin' tuh worry 'bout.

THEA. Gimme dem pasteboards. Lemme deal. [THEA *takes the cards and shuffles them expertly.*] Cut dem, Jack.

HUBBARD. Ef Ah don't win dis time Ah gives up.

THEA [*dealing*]. Don't give up. Nobody never win nothin' by givin' up. [*He plucks them off one by one.*] Fall card, fall jes' lak de leaves in de winter time.

[*Everybody is tense.* THEA *takes the money from first one of them then the other. They select other cards and lose again. The deal goes down.*]

HUBBARD. Ah's never seen de beat. Two nights in a row he done carried de cub tuh us.

THEA. Jes' a little streak o' luck, boys. Yuh'll do de same thing in a minute.

JACK [*disgusted. Gets up*]. Ah'm stoppin'. Ah'm through playin' cards when dey fall lak dat.

THEA [*glaring sternly at* JACK]. Whut do yuh mean fallin' lak dat? Yuh ain't hintin' dat Ah fixed de cards, is yuh?

JACK [*becoming reckless because of his luck*]. Well dey fell mighty funny!

THEA [*rising*]. Den yuh is meanin' Ah's cheated.

JACK. Ah ain't saying nothin'.

[*The others spring up and back away to the wall expecting a fight.* PERCY *is frightened throughout.*]

THEA. Oh, yes yuh is; and nobody never said dat Thea Dugger cheated at cards and lived.

[JACK *reaches in his pocket for his gun. Before he can bring it out,* THEA *hits him and knocks him down. He springs up and holds the gun on* THEA.]

JACK. Yuh's been bullyin' us long 'nuff now; and Ah fuh one ain't gwine tuh stand hit no mo'.

THEA [*glancing at the drawn gun*]. Well, go on and shoot, yuh white livered chicken; Ah don't believe yuh'se got nerve 'nuff.

HUBBARD. Don't shoot, Jack!

THEA. Yuh needn't say nothin'. He ain't gut guts 'nuff tuh shoot. [*He walks toward* JACK. JACK *backs away.*]

JACK. Don't yuh come any closer! Don't yuh come any closer, Ah'll shoot!

THEA [*laughing and going toward him*]. Yuh wouldn't shoot ef yuh had de nerve.

JACK. Don't yuh come any closer or Ah'll shoot!

[*Suddenly* THEA *makes a spring forward and knocks* JACK'S *arm up.* MAYBELLE *and* TOM *come in just in time to see* THEA *wrench the gun from* JACK. *Then he covers* JACK. MAYBELLE *screams, but is quickly stopped by* TOM.]

THEA [*holding the gun on* JACK]. Six men has tried tuh draw guns on me in ma life, and six men is layin' somewhar in de graveyard,— yuh is de seventh one. Ef yuh knows any prayers tuh say, yuh'd better start sayin' dem.

JACK [*getting down on his knees, moaning*]. Have mercy, Thea! Have mercy, Ah didn't mean nothin'.

THEA. Yes, yuh did too. Yuh mean Ah cheated at cards. No man is gwine tuh say dat and live.

JACK. Ah takes hit back, Thea. Ah takes hit back. Ah didn't mean nothin'.

THEA. Ef dere's anything in dis wurl Ah hates, hit's a coward. Since yuh is down on yo' knees, yuh'd better say yo' prayers, 'cause when Ah counts three Ah's gwine tuh shoot.

JACK. Please spare ma life, Thea! For Gawd's sake don't shoot me!

THEA. One!

JACK [*looking around wildly*]. He'p me! He'p me somebody!

THEA. Two!

JACK. For Gawd's sake don't shoot, think whut yuh is doin'!

[*As* THEA *is about to say three* MAYBELLE *screams.*]

MAYBELLE. For Gawd's sake don't shoot dat man in cold blood!

THEA. Yuh'd better keep outer dis, lady. Don't yuh meddle wid things dat don't concern yuh.

Tom. Don't say anything tuh him, Maybelle.

Maybelle [*getting down on her knees and pulling on* Thea's *free arm*]. Please! Please! Don't shoot him fuh mah sake!

Thea [*gun still drawn on* Jack]. Yuh is in de wrong place, lady. Women ain't gut no business 'round sawmill camps; but since yuh is heah, yuh will have de pleasure of seein' yo' fust man die.

Maybelle. Please, please don't shoot him!

Thea. Yuh don't understand, Miss. Ef a man draws a gun on yuh and yuh let him off 'cause he ain't got de nerve tuh shoot, de next time he will git dat nerve. Well, if yuh kill him, dere can't be no next time.

Maybelle [*pleading*]. Tom always told me how bad yuh was, and Ah always wanted tuh see yuh 'cause Ah didn't believe him. Ah knows dere is a good streak in yuh somewhar. Yuh ain't never 'lowed.hit tuh come out. Ah believes yuh is a good man, and won't shoot nobody down in cold blood.

Thea. Me a good man! Nobody never told me dat befo'. Me, a good man! Dat's funny. [*He lowers his gun, speaks to* Jack] Aw, git up offen yo' knees, and thank dis gal fuh savin' yo' life.

Jack [*profuse in his thanks*]. Thank yuh, Miss. Thank yuh. Ah thank yuh, too, Thea. Ah didn't mean no harm. Losin' ma money jes' made me furgit.

Thea [*handing the gun back*]. Don't do hit no mo', 'cause de next time, dis good man won't be so good. Let's furgit whut happened.

Jack. Hit's furgottened.

Percy. Ah's glad dat's over.

[Burt Ross *breaks into the door hurriedly. He is the foreman of the mills. He has on dirty wrinkled trousers and a clean blue shirt.*]

Burt [*excitedly*]. Run for your lives everybody! Be quick about it. I've warned the other shanties and they've already gone.

Hubbard. Whut's matter, Cap'n Ross?

Burt. Somebody found old man Sam, the old white man who lives by himself over on the hill, with his head split in two with an axe. They said somebody working at the mill did it. The mob is coming down here to get somebody. You'd all better scatter to the woods. I'll join the mob and do what I can to save you.

Percy [*general confusion*]. Oh, my Gawd!

Maybelle. Whut'll we do, Tom? Whut'll we do, Ted?

Tom. Come on, let's make a break fuh de woods.

Percy. Ah knowed sompen would happen. Ah jes' knowed hit. Let's git gwine befo' hit's too late. [*Goes out.*]

Jack. Yes, let's git gwine. Ef dey catch us in dis shanty we ain't gut a chance wid a river in de back, a marsh on one side, and a steep hill on de other.

Tom. Come on, Maybelle. Let's git goin'.

Maybelle. Come on, Ted! [*They hurry out.*]

Jack. Come along, Hubbard. Dey'll be heah in a minute.

HUBBARD. Ain't yuh comin' long, Thea?

THEA [*calmly looking out the window*]. Naw!

JACK. Ah'll see yuh later. [*He starts to go out, but stops.*]

HUBBARD. Why ain't yuh goin' tuh de woods, Thea?

THEA. Yuh go on, Hubbard, ef yuh wants tuh. All ma life Ah's hated a coward, folks dat run away. When Ah was ten years old Ah made up ma mind dat Ah wa'n't gwine tuh run from nothing dat lives, man nor beast; and I ain't never did hit yit, and Ah's too old tuh change. Ain't no man livin' gwine make me run nowhar.

HUBBARD. Dese po' whites will shoot yuh down lak a dog.

THEA. Ef dey shoot me, dey is gwine tuh shoot me standin' up and facin' dem. Dey ain't gwine tuh shoot me runnin' through no bushes lak no rabbit.

HUBBARD. Ah'll stay heah wid yuh, Thea.

JACK. Ah s'pose Ah'd jes' as well stay, too.

[TED, MAYBELLE, *and* TOM *come back.*]

TOM. We heard dem comin'! We was scared tuh cut across de clearin' tuh git tuh de woods.

TED. All de other shanty houses is empty. Cap'n Ross told dem befo' he did us.

MAYBELLE. Ef Pa had only come back Ah wouldn't 'a' been in all dis.

[PERCY *comes crawling in like a whipped dog.*]

PERCY. Dey done reached de upper end ob de clearin'. We is cut off from de woods. Dey is gut blood hounds wid dem, too.

HUBBARD. Whut'll we all do? . . . Dem po' whites will stop at nothin'.

JACK. Whut is we tuh do, Thea? Yuh is de boss.

THEA [*calmly*]. We'd better prepare to die.

MAYBELLE. Ain't dere nothing we can do? Is we all gut tuh die heah lak rats in a trap?

TED. Dat's de way hit looks.

THEA. Naw, we don' exactly has tuh die lak no rats. How many gut guns?

JACK. I has.

THEA [*gets his box*]. Nobody but Jack. Ah'se gut six guns in dis box. Each one has already killed da man who tried to draw hit on me. Each one ought to do some mo' du'ty work. [*He gives one to* TOM, HUBBARD, TED, *and* PERCY.] Yuh's gut tuh take one, too, Miss, dis small one.

MAYBELLE. Ah's skeered of dem pistols.

THEA. Hit's too small tuh be skeered of. Yuh'd better tak hit, Miss.

[MAYBELLE *reluctantly takes it.*]

TED. Dat's right, take hit.

[*The barking of dogs can be heard far off through the woods. Everyone becomes tense.* THEA *tries to break it.*]

THEA. Ah wonder who killed de old man anyhow.

PERCY [*hysterically*]. Nobody knows; hit's certain nobody heah killed him.

[*The barking of the dogs is very near now. Confused voices are also heard.* THEA *is the only one who appears calm. He is looking out of the window.*]

TOM [*nervously*]. Well, dey is gittin' near heah.

TED [*to* MAYBELLE]. Since we don't know whut's gwine tuh happen, don't yuh think we ought tuh tell Tom?

MAYBELLE. Umph, humph, yuh tell him.

TED. Tom, we's gut sumpin' tuh tell yuh. Wal, er . . . since we don't know whut might happen, we thought—er—would, er . . . tell yuh dat Maybelle and Ah love each other, and we had planned tuh git married sometime even ef we had tuh run away.

TOM. I sorta suspicioned dat; but ef yuh'd told me dat four hours ago, Ah would 'a' knocked de daylight outer yuh. We wanted Maybelle tuh go tuh school and git some larnin' and not marry no sawmill han'; but now when hit seems—— Well, hit jes' don't matter now 'bout yo' love.

TED [*softly*]. Thank yuh, Tom.

[*Noise from the mob and a crash of broken glass*].

MAYBELLE [*running to* TED]. Ah's skeeered! Whut is we gwine do? [*Puts her arms around his neck.* THEA *looks at them.*]

TED. Don't git skeered, honey. Try tuh be brave lak Thea.

MAYBELLE. Don't mind me when Ah say things. Ah really don't mind dying jes' so Ah is wid yuh.

[*Barking dogs.* THEA, *who has been watching the windows, wheels around.*]

THEA [*wheeling and taking on new life*]. Ah thought maybe dey wouldn't come up heah, but heah dey come!

[*Groans. A tense strain is evident.*]

PERCY [*whining*]. My Gawd! Whut is we gwine tuh do?

THEA. We's gwine tuh fight and fight lak hell! Yuh, Tom, and Jack, go into de next room, rip off a board in de back so yuh can see ef anybody comes up from de river. Yuh can see who's coming from de swamp through de window. Shoot if yuh see anybody sneakin' up. Ted, yuh and Hubbard guard dat window. [*One to left.*] Shoot ef you see anyone sneakin' up. Me and Percy'll take dis one. [*He goes back to window in the rear.*]

TED [*shouting*]. Dere dey come 'round de front, Thea.

THEA. Let dem come, Ah's ready!

MAYBELLE. Ted! [*going over to him*].

TED. Git away from befo' dat window! Do yuh want tuh git shot? Git back over dere in de corner!

THEA [*raising his pistol, shouting*]. Don't come any further up dat path or Ah'll shoot.

VOICE. They're in there, fellows!

ANOTHER VOICE. Burn the shanty down!

[*A rock comes in through the window at the left.* MAYBELLE *screams.*]

VOICES. Get the niggers! Lynch 'em.

PERCY [*crawling away down stage*]. Ah's skeered, Thea. Ah's skeered tuh death.

THEA [*angrily*]. Git back up dere and help me guard dat window or I'll plug yuh mase'f.

VOICE. Come on, fellows, let's get 'em.

[*Barking of dogs.*]

ANOTHER VOICE. All right, let's go!

[THEA *raises his gun and fires.*]

VOICES. Get de niggers! Burn de shanty! They got guns. Get dem!

THEA. Don't come no closer. De next time I ain't goin' tuh miss. Ah's goin' tuh shoot tuh kill.

VOICE. They got guns!

ROSS. *Listen!* You're destroying my property. Don't kill all my men; they didn't do it.

VOICE. Kill all the niggers! Burn them up!

ROSS [*shouting*]. Let's tell them that if the one that did it comes out, we'll let the others go. I can't run my mill if you kill all my hands.

VOICE [*shouting above the noise*]. If the one that did the murder comes out we won't do nothin' to the rest. We'll give you five minutes to make up your mind.

ANOTHER VOICE. If you don't come out by then we'll burn the shanty down on top of you.

THEA [*walking over to the door on the right*]. Tom, Jack, did yuh hear whut dey said?

TOM *and* JACK *come in.* THEA *goes up center.*

TOM. Yeah. Dey's give us five minutes.

JACK. Dey said de one dat done hit. Who is de one dat done hit, Ah'd lak tuh know.

HUBBARD. Dey don't care who done hit jes' so dey git one man.

PERCY [*whining*]. But who is goin' tuh be dat one man?

THEA [*in middle of stage*]. Heah's yo' chance, boys. One man's gut to go out dere and die. Speak up. We ain't gut long.

TOM. Ah would go but Ah's gut tuh he'p pay off Pa's mortgage, and he'p Maybelle heah tuh go tuh school.

JACK. Ef Ah had ever seed de old man, Ah wouldn't mind.

PERCY [*whining*]. Ah can't go! Ah can't, dat's all! Ah's scared.

HUBBARD. Ain't nobody done nothin' heah. Ah don't see why dey have tuh go.

TED. Ah suppose. Ah's de only one left.

MAYBELLE [*throwing her arms around him*]. Ah can't let yuh go! Ah jes' can't!

THEA. Ah wouldn't let yuh go, neither, kid. Dat's all right, Ah'll go!

TOM. Yuh can't go out dere, Thea.

THEA [*changing tone*]. 'Tain't no usen all us gittin' killed; and somebody gut tuh go.

Tom. Yuh can't go, Thea! Let's cut de cards. Dat'll settle 'bout who is to go.

Thea. 'Tain't no usen doin' dat. All o' yuh gut fam'lies tuh look out fuh. Ah ain't gut nobody but mase'f; and when Ah'm gone, nothin' much'll be lost.

Ted. Dat don't make no diff'rence. Yuh has as much right tuh live as any of us.

Thea. Hit do make a diff'rence. All ma life Ah's been a bad man, driftin' from one camp tuh another, and one mill tuh another, shootin' and cuttin' and fightin'. Ah s'pose Ah wasn't cut out tuh mount tuh much. [To Maybelle.] Young miss, yuh said Ah had a good streak in me somewhar. Maybe ef yuh wasn't heah, Ah'd feel better and know better whut tuh do. Ah's killed many men in ma life, but Ah ain't never stood 'round and seed no ooman die. Somehow Ah can't bring mase'f tuh do hit. Ah hopes yuh and de kid will be happy. Tom ain't gwine do nothin' tuh stop yuh. [He wheels and walks out of the house leaving everybody stunned and tense.]

Tom. Thea! Thea! Come back!

Voice. Here he is, fellows! Grab him!

Voice. Burn him.

[Dogs bark.]

Ross. You didn't do it, Thea! I've seen you all day.

Thea. Ah did hit all right.

Voice. He's confessed! That's enough.

Voice. String him up!

Voice. Make a fire!

[Voices and barking of the dogs.]

Tom [looking out of the window at the blazing fire]. Dey is tying him up . . . and he ain't doing nothing. . . . Dey is lighting a fire to him now. He's burning! [In wild agony.] He's burning! And he ain't even groaning!

[Dogs bark. There is a confusion of voices.]

Percy [coming back from peeping out of the window. He swings wildly and sinks on the bed]. Ah'se gwine crazy!

Ted [rushing toward the door]. Let me outer heah! Ah can't stand hit!

Tom [grabbing him and holding him back]. Yuh can't do nothing, Ted. Yuh might as well stay on de inside!

Ted [shouting]. But Thea is burning up out dere, Ah'm tellin' yuh!

Tom. Yuh can't do nothin' 'bout hit! None of us can't do nothin' 'bout hit!

Ted [turning dejectedly]. Yuh is right, dead right. We ain't nothin' but sawmill hands. All we is s'posed tuh do is to cut logs, saw lumber, live in dingy shanties, cut, fight, and kill each other. We ain't s'posed tuh pay no 'tention tuh a burnin' man . . . but ef de people wid larnin' can't do nothin' 'bout hit 'taint nothin' we can do. 'Taint nothing we can do. [He lowers his head in dejection.]

[MAYBELLE *bursts into tears and faints in a chair. The others are staring wildly or swaying with tears. Outside the fire is burning and the dogs are barking. Voices of the mob come in confused sounds as they ask for souvenirs, and ask each other to pile wood upon the burning body.*]

[CURTAIN]

JAMES W. BUTCHER, JR. (1909-   )

Born in Washington, D. C., James W. Butcher, Jr., was educated in the public schools of that city. He attended Howard University for three years but took his A. B. degree at the University of Illinois in 1932. He received his M. A. from the University of Iowa in 1941. Butcher has acted with the Morningside Players of Columbia University and with the University Players at the University of Iowa; he has taught for three years at the Atlanta University Summer School of the Theatre; he helped to organize and directed the Negro Repertory Theatre of Washington; and at the present time he is Director of the Howard University Players. "The Seer" is reprinted by permission of the author, who has reserved all rights.

The Seer

THE CAST

BUCEPHALUS WILSON, *the* SEER, *a "mysterious" Negro, about forty years old.*
IVORY TOLES, *a superstitious Negro, about forty-five years old.*
LUCY TOLES, *his niece.*
WILLIE GORDON, *a young Negro in love with* LUCY.
JOSH, *an old roustabout.*

PLACE: *A Negro settlement in the hills of Virginia.*
TIME: *Contemporary.*

THE SCENE *is a room in Ivory's home, an old ramshackle house, ghostly and deserted in appearance. The house sits in a clump of straggly trees a few yards back from the wagon road. In the back of the room are two windows looking out on the lawn. On the right is a door leading to the kitchen. On the left is a similar door to opening into the hall, which in turn, leads to an outer door. The walls are adorned with the usual portraits of a "dear departed." An old-fashioned sofa is jammed against the center of the right wall. On the other side are two old chairs; in the middle of the room is a little center table on which sits an old kerosene lamp with a fancy shade.*

When the curtain rises, LUCY *and* IVORY *are in the center of the room arguing.*

LUCY. But, Uncle, I wants to marry Willie. We got it all planned. You said I could, too. Said I ought to, up till dis even'.

IVORY. I knows dat, chile. I did think dat way, but I'se changed my min'.

LUCY. Well, what's de matter? Is Willie done something' bad?

IVORY. Naw, tain't dat. Willie's 'n awright boy. I likes him good 'nough. I jes ain't so sot on you marryin' him. Dat's all.

LUCY. But I loves him, Uncle. An' he's workin' steady an' he doan run aroun' wid no goodtimers. Dey's a hunnerd gals over in town would give dere right arms fo' a chance at Willie but he doan pay 'em no min'. He's de bes' man in dis section.

IVORY. I knows all dat, chile. Dat ain't de point. De point is you jes cain't marry him.

LUCY. But why, Uncle Ivory?

IVORY. Cause de sperrits says you cain't, dats why.

LUCY. De sperrits! Ain't no sech things. If dey is, what dey got to do wid us? Willie ain't never done nothin' to none of dem.

IVORY. Doan you talk lak dat gal. Somethin' turble liable to happen to you. Dey kin hyuh you right dis minit.

LUCY. I doan care. Willie say Mr. Mackey tole him dey wasn't no sech things, an he's a perfesser.

IVORY. Humph! Mr. Mackey. What does white folks know 'bout sperrits an' sech things? Seer Bucephalus say dey ain't got de right kin' of eyes to see sperrits.

LUCY. Dat lyin' ole fool! He's a fake. Dat's what he is. He cain't no mo' see sperrits dan you kin.

IVORY. Is you losin' yo' min'? Who was it took de spell off ole man Brown's chickens when dey wouldn't eat? Who was it tole me somebody gonna steal my pig de night befo' he was stole? Who was it? Seer Bucephalus, dat's who. He got de powers. Dat's all dere is to it.

LUCY. Betcha he stole dat pig hisself. He ain't no good I tells you. Willie say he used to peddle some kin' of medicine. Sold some to ole crazy Bill over in Branchville an' it killed him. Dat's how he started dis Seer business.

IVORY. Dat may be de reason an' it may not be. I doan care. One thing sho'; he got de power now.

LUCY. I wish he'd stay 'way from hyuh wid his power. He got you most as bad as he is. Be talkin' 'bout seein' ghosts yo'self nex'.

IVORY. Naw, Naw, chile. Not me. Dey's awright, I reckon, but I doan wanna see none of 'em. I'se satisfied to hyuh tell 'bout 'em. Dat's plenty good 'nough fo' me.

LUCY. You'se scairt of 'em jes lak I thought. Scairt of de Seer too, ain't you?

IVORY. Maybe I is an' maybe I ain't. Anyway we ain't gonna talk 'bout dem no mo'. We jes gonna do what dey says an' we'll be awright.

LUCY. Deed we ain't gonna do what dey says. Not if dey says I cain't marry Willie. Dat's sho'.

IVORY. I'se tole you befo' gal, what we gonna do an' we gonna do jes dat. You knows well 'nough dat I'se always done my bes' fo' you. I ain't gonna quit now. De sperrits say you be ruint if you marries dat Willie an' I be ruint fo' lettin' you do it. Now dat's dat.

LUCY. Well den, I ain't gonna marry nobody.

IVORY. Oh yeah you is too.

LUCY. Who?

IVORY. Doan know yet. Gonna find out tonight. De Seer say he comin' up hyuh an' hol' a seeaunce. I'se got to help him.

LUCY. You gotta hep him do what?

IVORY. I gotta he'p him hol' de seeaunce. He say dat'll tell us who you gotta marry. 'Spect you better stay wid Mis' Williams tonight. De Seer say we gotta have it very quiet. Now you goan down dere soon's you kin. I'se goin' down to de sto' an' git a plug of tobacco. I guess you better leave de do' open so de Seer kin git in effin he comes befo' I gits back. [He exits at left.]

LUCY [pacing up and down nervously for a minute]. You'se a fool dat's what you is, a sof' easy fool. Stan' up dere an' doan say nothin'. When dat man comes back hyuh I'se gonna haul him out. Le's see now. [She faces the sofa as if there is someone seated at it.] I ain't gonna do it. Dat's dat. I ain't gonna do it. [WILLIE comes in from the left carrying a little package.] I'se gonna marry who I wants, an' dat ain't nobody but Willie, so dere. I is—

WILLIE. Honey, you done spoke a gospel.

LUCY [turning in surprise]. Oh gee, sugar, you sho' did give me a turn. [She runs over to him and embraces him.] Why didn't you knock.

WILLIE. I did. You so busy in here preachin' I guess you didn't hyuh me.

LUCY. I sho' didn't.

WILLIE. Must be gittin' batty. Prancin' roun' hyuh talkin' to yo' self. Be scairt to marry you; you keep dat up.

LUCY. Hyuh, now, doan you start talkin' lak dat. I'se mad and I'se rehearsin'.

WILLIE. Rehearsin' what?

LUCY. Rehearsin' what I'se gonna say to Uncle IVORY when he gits back.

WILLIE. You talks lak he doan wan' us to git married.

LUCY. Dat's 'xactly it. He doan. He jes say so five minits ago.

WILLIE. Aw, he mus' be kiddin'. Me an' him jes lak dis. [Holds up two fingers.]

LUCY. You mean you an' him was jes lak dat. He say he lak you all right but dat we cain't git married. He say de sperrits say somethin' turble gonna happen to all of us if we do. He's scairt, dat's what.

WILLIE. He so scairt of sperrits how come dey got close 'nough to tell him all dat mess.

LUCY. Dey ain't. You know he been runnin' 'round wid dat ol' Seer Bucephalus. He de one tol' him. He sposed to come up hyuh in a few minits an' hold' a seeance. Uncle IVORY doan know what dat is, I'se sho'. He say de seeance gonna tell him who I gotta marry.

WILLIE. But I'se tol' yo' Uncle dat dat ole man is a fake. Sides he oughta know dat dere ain't no sperrits.

LUCY. I know, but he jes doan believe it. He say you doan know what you'se talkin' 'bout. De Seer done fed him up wid all dem lies, 'bout sperrits till he's scairt not to believe him. I'se talked till my teeth rattled an' it ain't done no good. [Sits.] Dat man leads him aroun' jes lak a lamb.

WILLIE. Well, ef he thinks he gonna stop me from marryin' you he got another think comin':

LUCY. I ain't eighteen yit.

WILLIE. We'll wait till you is. Dat won't be long.

LUCY. But spose he make me marry somebody befo' den. How 'bout dat?

WILLIE. Dat's right. Dat's right. We gotta do somethin'.

LUCY. Yeah, we gotta do somethin' awright, but what?

WILLIE. You say dey's holdin' a seeance up hyuh tonight?

LUCY. Yeah, in a few minutes. You know what dat is.

WILLIE. I got a pretty good idea.

LUCY. Miss Williams was tellin' me 'bout 'em. De sperrits spose to come in an' walk an' talk an' everythin'. I ain't tole Uncle what it is cause I thought maybe we could scare him or somethin'. Den I thought too dat ef de Seer couldn't make no ghosts come in, why maybe Uncle would believe dat he really is a fake.

WILLIE. Unhunh. You say ghosts is sposed to come in an' walk an' talk?

LUCY. Yeah.

WILLIE. Well, de dirty rascal!

LUCY. What's de matter?

WILLIE. Listen. Dat Seer Bucephalus is fixin' to marry you hisself.

LUCY. What you mean?

WILLIE. I mean jes dat.

LUCY. How you know?

WILLIE. I was down to de sto' dis mawnin' an' I met dat ole no good Josh dere. He was drunk an' wanted to buy me a drink. I tole him he bedder save his money. He say he had plenty an' pulled out a five-spot an' waved it 'roun'. Say de Seer give it to him to play he was a ghost an' help him git a wife tonight. He wouldn't tell me no mo'. Got mad cause I wouldn't drink an' went up de road to de Seer's house.

LUCY. I sees what you mean. De Seer gonna have ole Josh come in an' tell Uncle dat I gotta marry de Seer.

WILLIE. Dat's right.

LUCY. Oh, Willie, dat's turble. What we gonna do? Uncle will sho'ly b'lieve all dat mess. We gotta do somethin' real quick.

WILLIE. Wait a minute. Lemme think. Huh. I got it.

LUCY. What is it? Tell me quick.

WILLIE. Dey's gonna be two ghosts at de seeance tonight.

LUCY. What you mean? One ghost is too many.

WILLIE. Yeah, too many fo' de Seer. Now lissen. Dis hyuh's what I mean. I'se gonna be a ghost. Gonna scare bofe dem ole fools back into dere right min's.

LUCY. You cain't do dat. De Seer ain't gonna be scared.

WILLIE. Oh, yeah he is too. He been talkin' 'bout sperrits so much he really believes in 'em hisself. 'Sides he knows dat he ain't paid but one ghost so dey couldn't be but one. How he gonna feel when he see two?

LUCY. Maybe you'se right, honey. We kin try anyway. We gotta hurry though.

WILLIE [*opening his package*]. See dis paint? Dis what Mr. Mackey paint house numbers on wid so dey shine in de dark. Well, dis is one can what he won't git in de mawnin'. You git a sheet an' I'll paint it up wid dis stuff. Hurry up now.

LUCY. I sho' will. [*She runs off right.* WILLIE *reaches into his pocket and pulls out an old canvass work glove. Out of another pocket he takes a little paint brush and begins to paint the glove.*]

LUCY. [*reentering with sheet*]. Hyuh, Willie. Dis all right?

WILLIE. Yeah, dat's fine. Hyuh, hol' dis glove. Now, after dey start dis ghost mess you go out in de yard an' knock on de window an' wave de glove. Doan let dem see de rest of you. Jes de glove. Unnerstan'? Humph, we gonna fix 'em dis night.

LUCY. Boy, you is a wizard. I jes hope it works. We gonna . . .

[*Footsteps are heard approaching.*]

WILLIE. Sh, sh. Somebody comin'. We'll have to fix dis somewhere else.

LUCY. Go out to de kitchen. We kin go up de back steps an' finish it upstairs. Hurry.

WILLIE [*starting off right*]. Awright, come on. Bring de glove.

LUCY [*following him off*]. I got it.

[*The stage is empty for a minute as the footsteps and voices come nearer. In a moment the* SEER *comes in, followed by* JOSH *who is carrying a bundle.*]

SEER. Is you sho' Ivory didn't see you?

JOSH. Sho' I'se sho'. When I seed you two talkin' I snuck 'roun' de brickyard an' waited at de corner where you jes met me.

SEER. Dat's good. Got everything?

JOSH. Everything. Sheet, devil costume, basin, matches, powder.

SEER. Take 'em out. Can't take no chances at de last minute. Take 'em out.

JOSH. [*Undoing the bundle and showing each article as he names it*]. Sheet, devil costume, basin, matches, powder. All dere.

SEER. Where's de incense an' de turban?

JOSH. You got dem. Sho', look in yo' pockets.

SEER. Yeah, dat's right, so I has. Well, lets start gittin' ready. Ivory be hyuh in a minit. I tol' him I'd take 'bout five minits to fix things up. [*He puts the basin on the table and places some incense in it which he lights. This finished, he wraps his turban around his head.*] You unnerstan's what you's sposed to do?

JOSH. Yeah, I goes in dis room an' puts on de sheet an' when you say, "Now Look" I walks real slow an' quiet an' bows to you an' answers de questions you axes me. . . .

SEER. Dat's right. An' doan fo'git to talk kinda low-like.

JOSH. Naw, I knows. Den when you sends me back, I goes into dat same room an' puts on de devil's suit an' you knocks on de table three times. I runs in an' tells Ivory dat de gal has got to marry you.

SEER. Dat's right. An' doan you fo'git to call me "Mos' Powerful." Boy, I sho' be glad when dis mess is ovuh wid. I gotta have dat gal tho' an' dis is de only way I can git her.

JOSH. I be glad when its ovuh wid too. Ain't none too crazy 'bout dis job nohow. Spose you makes a mistake an' really does call in a sperrit. We be ruint fo' sho'.

SEER. Aint gonna be no mistake. 'Sides, Josh you cain't call in no real sperrit. Dey does jes what dey pleases. Mos' de time dey jes haunts folks which has killed somebody. Aint never seen one but onct.

JOSH. What he look lak?

SEER. I doan know. Was too scairt to think. It was kinda big an' whitish an' shiny-like all ovuh. Gimme de creeps to think 'bout it. Aint nothin' gonna happen to-night though. Go in dere an' git ready. (Exit Josh). [*Turning the lamp down a little lower after glancing around nervously.*] Ghosts! Boo! Caint hurt nobody nohow . . . bet dey'd run if you jes holler at 'em. Never was scairt much nohow. [JOSH *pokes his head around door with sheet on.*]

JOSH. S-s-s-s-s.

SEER. What dat? [*Looks around and sees head*] Lordy me . . . Hey! Dat you Josh?

JOSH. Sho', it's me. Who you think it is? You aint fo'git to bring my other five spot, is you?

SEER. No, you gits it soon's we leave. An' lissen, doan you never stick your head out dat door lak dat no mo'. Wait till I calls yo' so I'll know what's goin' on. [*Someone is heard coming up the road.*] Git back; hyuh comes Ivory. [JOSH *goes into kitchen.* SEER *becomes very dignified. In a minute* IVORY *comes in.*]

IVORY. Well Seer, got everything ready? [SEER *bows gravely.*]

Whooee! Somethin' sho' smells funny. Smell lak sweet pertaters burnin'. You been cookin' sweet pertaters, Seer?

SEER. Sh. You smells de magic incense dat I burns to draw de sperrits.

IVORY. Never min' 'bout drawin' de sperrits. We doan need none of dem, I reckon. Where is de seeance?

Seer [*making a sweeping gesture with his arms*]. It is hyuh.

IVORY. Well, let's hurry up an' hol' it.

[*He starts toward a chair. The* SEER *stops him, pulls him aside and bows to the empty space.*]

SEER. Howdedo, suh. [IVORY *looks at the* SEER *and then at the empty space. He looks around and then starts for another chair without saying anything. He starts to sit down. Stopping* IVORY.] Wait a minit. Doan sit on de gentleman.

IVORY [*Jumping as if burnt*]. Hunh?

SEER. Doan sit on de gentleman.

IVORY [*Looking frightened at the chair*]. Is dey, is dey somebody dere?

SEER [*puts finger to his lips in a gesture of silence. He goes over to the chair and bows low*]. De gentleman begs yo' pardon. [*He comes back to* IVORY *and leads him over to the sofa, bowing occasionally and weaving his way as if the room were full of people*] De sperrits has very tender feelin's, IVORY. Yo' has to be very perlite to dem. [*He steps down and shakes hands with the air*] Howdedo. Dis is Ivory Toles.

IVORY [*Groping about with his hand, which the* SEER *finally puts in an imaginary hand directly in front of him.* IVORY *shakes*]. Howdedo, uh uh, Mr., Mr. uh suh. [*To the* SEER] Is he gone, Seer?

SEER. Yeah, he's ovah dere by de table talkin' wid some friends. Fo' of dem dere. Jes lak bees 'roun' dat incense.

IVORY. Cain't we put dat incense out in de yard somewhere?

SEER. Naw, we gotta keep de sperrits hyuh fo' de seeance. Dat's what makes a seeance.

IVORY. What? De sperrits? An' we gonna hol' it? Naw suh. Naw suh! I doan want nothin' to do wid it. Yo' kin hol' it. Not me. Send dem sperrits on home.

SEER. Cain't. Wouldn't never have no peace if I do. Call 'em way up hyuh fo' nothin'. Dey's ovah dere now arguin' 'bout you an' Lucy.

IVORY. Arguin' 'bout me an' Lucy? What dey sayin'?

SEER. Dey tryin' to decide who dey wants her to marry. Come on now let's start dis seeance. Dey'll be ready pretty soon, I reckon. You sit ovah hyuh between dese two gentlemans. [*He pushes* IVORY *over to the sofa.*]

IVORY. What me? Nawsuh! Not me!

SEER. You got to. Hurry up now, we'se wastin' time. [*He pushes* IVORY *into the seat.* IVORY *is too terrified to move. He rolls his eyes from one corner to the other, trying to see who his imaginary companions are, as the* SEER *goes over to the table, makes some passes over the incense and begins chanting.*]

I is de power, I is de king,
I makes de sperrits do anything.
When I calls dey comes a'jumpin', . . .
[*There is a low wail under the window. The* SEER *stops, rather startled.* IVORY *rolls his eyes in the direction of the window. The* SEER *clears his throat nervously, and begins again.*]

When I calls dey comes a'jumpin' . . .
[*There is a louder wail from the window. The hand appears, waves for a second, and disappears.*]

IVORY [*starting out of his seat*]. Se-Se-Seer, uh, uh, I seed somethin'.

SEER. Not yit, not yit. You couldn't see nothin' yit. I ain't finished the spell yit. Now sit down an' keep quiet.

IVORY. Wait a minit, wait a minit. I seed somethin', I tells you.
[*He starts out of door at right.*]

SEER. Hyuh, where you goin'?

IVORY. I be back. I'm goin' to git some salt.

SEER. Salt?

IVORY. Yeah, salt, salt. [*He exits right, going into the kitchen. The wailing begins under the window again. The hand reappears. The* SEER *stares at it, rubs his eyes. He turns away, then looks back quickly. The hand is still there. He turns his back on the window.*]

SEER [*fervently*]. I makes de sperrits do anything.

I makes de sperrits do anything.

Now go 'way from hyuh. Scat! Go on. [*He slowly turns and looks at the window. The hand is still there. He mops his brow. He looks out into the kitchen and calls.*] Ivory, Ivory, come on! Quick. [IVORY *comes in from the kitchen with a salt shaker. The hand has disappeared.*]

IVORY. What's de matter?

SEER. [*Glancing toward the window*] Nothin'. I jes wanted you to hurry up and git this thing ovuh wid.

IVORY. Awright, le's go. [*He goes over to the sofa and sprinkles salt all around his seat.*]

SEER. What's dat fo'.

IVORY. What's it fo'? It's to keep dem sperrits from techin' me, dat's what it's fo'.

SEER. How kin it do dat?

IVORY. I doan know how it does it, but it do it. Dey jes cain't pass cross a line o' salt, dat's all.

SEER. Sho' dat's right?

IVORY. Sho' it's right.

SEER. Maybe I bedder try some too. [*He takes the shaker and sprinkles salt around the table making the circle large enough for him to stand in*]. Now I feels bedder. Le's git on wid de seeance. [IVORY *sits down once more, a little more confidently though still not completely at ease. The* Seer *resumes his chanting*].

I is de power, I is de king.
I makes de sperrits do anything;
When I calls dey comes a'jumpin',
Po'k chops, pig feet, chicken, punkin!

[*There is a loud moan from the window. Both men watch window intently*].

Seer. Uh-uh—Ivory, did you hyuh somethin'?

Ivory. D-d-did I hyuh somethin'? You knows I hyuhed somethin'.

Seer. I was jes wonderin' . . . [*The hand appears and knocks loudly on the window*].

Ivory. D-d-dere 'tis agin, Seer. Oh me, oh . . .

Seer. 'Tain't nothin' but yo' 'magination, man. Dat's all. Now you go on ovuh dere an' pull down de shade. Maybe dat make you feel bedder.

Ivory. Who me? Me pull down dat shade? Naw suh. You'se de one. You pull it down.

Seer. No, Ivory, I cain't. You knows I cain't leave dis hyuh incense. I gotta stay ovuh hyuh and make de charm. Go on now an' pull it down.

Ivory. Deed I ain't. Dat thing might jump up dere an' grab me. You'se de one, Seer, ain't you? You do it.

Seer. Well no, Ivory, I'se done tol' you how it is. Go 'head an' do it.

Ivory. Naw suh, not me.

Seer. You don't have to be scairt. Go on an' do it now. I'se right hyuh wid you.

Ivory. I doan have to be scairt, but I *is* scairt. Dat thing would ruin me 'fo' you could think.

Seer. Well, since you'se scairt let's both go ovuh dere. We'll pull it down together. Dat's all right, ain't it?

Ivory. Yeah, I guess so. Only you bedder go in front.

Seer. Awright. Come on.

[*They join hands and start towards the window, each trying to get the other in front. The wail from the window grows louder. They make a step. The wail stops*].

Seer. [*With meek bravado*] Huh, guess it ain't nothin' but a dog howlin'. I bedder go back an' min' dis incense though. Gittin' kinda low. Go on, Ivory, pull de shade down.

Ivory. I reckon we both bedder min' dat incense.

Seer. Naw, doan need but me fo' dat. You pull down dat shade. Wasn't nothin' but a dog howlin' I tells you.

Ivory. Dat mighta been a dog howlin', but dat wasn't no dog wavin' his han' at you.

Seer. Dat's yo' 'magination I tells you. I know I didn't see no han'.

I jes couldn't see no han'. Ain't no way in de worl' . . . [*The hand appears and points at the* SEER].

IVORY. D-d-dere goes my 'magination again. Looks lak it's pointin' at you too.

SEER. Yeah, yeah. [*He turns his head and walks toward* IVORY. *He quickly turns to see if the hand is still following him. It is*] Lordy, Lordy. It do kinda look lak dat thing's pointin' at me. Lordy.

IVORY. Kinda? Sho' it's pointin' at you. Hyuh, doan git so close to me. Go on way from hyuh. Do somethin'. You got de power, ain't you? Git de salt. Chase dat thing way from hyuh.

SEER. Dat's it, de salt. Guess dat'll git him. [*He takes up the salt shaker and throws some salt at the window*] I hope dis gits him. I sho' does. [*He throws some more salt and the hand disappears*]. It got him awright. It sho' got him. [*He continues to sprinkle salt in front of him and walks up to the window and pulls down the shade*] Dere now. I feels better. Not dat I was scairt, you unnerstands. I jes doan want no foreign sperrits 'roun' hyuh buttin' into my seeance.

IVORY. You mean you gonna have de seeance anyhow?

SEER. Sho' we gonna have it. We got plenty salt ain't we? 'Sides, my sperrits is peaceful sperrits. You'll see in a minit.

IVORY. Naw I won't see neither. I'se had 'nough already—too much. I'se through.

SEER. Naw you ain't. 'Member what I tole you befo'. S'pose all dem good sperrits gits mad. I couldn't hol' 'em off you. Dey's too many of dem. Dey'd tear you to pieces. Come on now, sit down in dat chair an' we'll git started.

IVORY. Well, le's hurry an' git dis foolishness ovuh wid. [*He glances about nervously and then sits down on the sofa*]

SEER. [*Beginning his incantations*].

Moonbeams and rats' teeth. Chicken combs an' fishes' scales, berried in de groun' fo'teen yeahs. Dig 'em up, dig 'em up. Bats' eahs, black cats' tails, dig 'em up, dig 'em up, dig 'em up. Haaaaaaaaaaaaaaa aaaaaaaaah. Haaaaaaaaaaaaaaaaaaaah, I feels de power, de power, haaaaaaaaaaaaah, dig, 'em up, dig 'em up, dig 'em up, haaaaaaaah, de power, dig 'em up, haaaaah, sperrits, appear, appear, appear, haaaaah, dey come. I feels de presence, haaaa dey is hyuh. [*He turns to the door*] Aaah, hyuh you is come to do de master's biddin'. Aaah. Step up and repo't. Aaaah, . . . yeah . . . yeah dat's good. You'se sorry you'se late, hunh? Awright, I 'scuse you dis time.

Yeah. [*To* IVORY] Kin you see him?

IVORY. Naw, I doan see him. Doan wanna see him.

SEER. Wait a minit. I'll fix yo' eyes so you kin. Come on now. Doan be scairt. I'se hyuh. Come on, we'se wastin' time [*To the imaginary spirit*] Hey sperrit! Go into dat room an' wait till I calls you. Now hurry up. [*He pauses a minute, then comes close to* IVORY *and starts rubbing his eyes. Then he chants*].

I is de power, I is de king,
I makes yo' eyes see everything.
When I tells you look again
You will see de sperrit men.
[*He leaves* Ivory *and walks over to table, takes his package of gun-powder out of his pocket and holds it over the incense*]
Now I lights dis magic powder
An' I calls de sperrits louder
Ivory Toles you jes keep steady
Cause I feels de hants is ready.
[*He drops the whole package on the incense. There is a puff of flame as it ignites. The* Seer *claps his hand and points to the door as* Josh *enters dressed in the sheet.* Ivory *stares in amazement*]

Ivory. Uh-uh-uh-uh-uh Seer, Seer. Take dat thing . . .

Seer. Sh . . . sh . . . sperrit approach.

Josh. [*Approaching*] Most Powerful, I approaches.

Seer. Is you ready to do my biddin'?

Josh. I is ready, Most Powerful.

Seer. Good. Last week you gave me some advice 'bout Ivory hyuh an' Lucy. Does yo' 'member?

Josh. I 'members everything, Most Powerful. I sees everything. Dere is a great danger, suh, a great danger.

Seer. Who is de danger fo'? Quick! Who is it fo'?

Josh. [*Turning suddenly and pointing at* Ivory] Dis man. Dis turble man. Aaaaaaaaaaaaaah . . . An' dat gal Lucy. Whoooooeeee turble.

Seer. Sh. Sh. Now sperrit, what mus' we do to save dese people?

Josh. Most Powerful, dat gal must git married tomorrer.

Seer. Married?

Josh. Married. Uh-uh, I smell smoke.

Seer. [*Surprised*] What? What's de matter wid you? [Josh *notices the table which is smouldering from the sparks of some of the powder which have dropped on it. He jumps up in the air and waves his arms about wildly*]

Josh. FYuh! Fyuh! Fyuh, hey fyuh! [*He rushes into the kitchen*]

Ivory. Seer, Seer, de table's on fyuh! Do something'. Hurry up! Beat it out!

Seer. I *is* doin' somethin'. You do somethin'. [*They beat out the fire as* Josh *rushes in with a pail of water, which he trips over as soon as he gets well into room*]

Josh. Help! Somebody help me. [*He scrambles up*] Is de fyuh out yit?

Seer. Yeah, de fyuh's out. You'se a hell of a sperrit. What's de matter wid you? Doan you know dat ain't no way fo' a sperrit to act? Come on now. Let's git dis mess ovuh wid. Sperrit ef you messes up now, you know what's gonna happen to you. [*To* Ivory] See, dats how I runs my sperrits. Now where was we?

Josh. Le's see, we was uh, we was . . .

Ivory. We was where dat gentleman was tellin' us dat Lucy had to marry sombody tomorrer.

Seer. Yeah, dat's right. Now sperrit, what we wants to know is who is Lucy got to marry?

Josh. She got to marry . . . [*There is a loud wail from the window*] Uh-uh-Most Powerful, I'se awful tired. Cain't think right now. 'Spect dey's evil sperrits 'roun' hyuh.

Ivory. See dere, I tole you so. He kin see 'em.

Seer. Well you go on back in dat room an' res'. Tell de devil I say to come up hyuh. He kin tell us how to git out'n dis danger. Tell him to hurry too. Go on now, git out.

Josh. Yassuh, yassuh. I'll tell him. Think it'll take him a few minits to git hyuh though. He's powerful busy.

Seer. I'll give him 'bout five minits. Den I'm gonna call fo' him. We gotta do what we kin to git Ivory safe out'n his danger.

Josh. [*As he goes into kitchen*] De devil. He'll tell awright. He'll tell you quick.

Ivory. Seer, how much longer dis mess gonna las'? I'se gittin' kinda jumpy.

Seer. Won't be long now. Jes soon's we fin' out 'bout Lucy, we's through.

Ivory. Cain't we do dat widout callin' in de devil. He liable to git bad.

Seer. Naw, naw. You doan have to be scairt of him. I runs my sperrits, I tells you. [*There is another wail from the window*]

Ivory. Wish you'd run dat one way from dat window. Look like he want somebody in hyuh.

Seer. Uh-uh-uh-. Doan talk lak dat. He's jes lonesome, I reckon. I know dat's all it is.

Ivory. Seem lak dat other sperrit wasn't so crazy 'bout dis one either.

Seer. Jes fo'git 'bout it, Ivory. You kinda upsets my min' when yo' talks so much. I'll be as bad as you . . .

[*There is a noise in the kitchen of someone running about and falling over the chairs and furniture.* Josh *can be heard shouting and pleading. Above this is the sound of a deep moan which rises and falls with a hollow sound*]

Ivory. What dat, Seer? Dat de devil comin'? [*The* Seer *is too terrified to speak. He watches the kitchen door. In a minute,* Josh *with a sheet about him and the devil's costume in his hand, rushes across the stage*]

Josh. Look out de way. Lemme go. Dis place is haunted. De spooks is after me. It's de devil. Run, run!

[*He rushes out of the door, left, and can be heard running down the road still yelling*]

Ivory. What he say, Seer? What he say 'bout spooks?

Seer. He say we better git outta hyuh. I'se goin', I'se goin' now. Somethin' turble don' happen. [*He starts out of the door, left, followed by* Ivory *as* Willie *appears at the kitchen door, unseen by them, of course*]

Willie. Stop! Stop! Come back hyuh. [*The two men stop and turn around slowly. When they see* Willie *they are literally frozen with fear*]

Ivory. Oh me, me, me. What does I see? Lawdy, Seer, Seer, take dat thing out'n hyuh.

Willie. Ooooooooooooooooooh, aaaaaaaaaaaaaah. I gotcha. Haaaah.

Seer. Oh, oh, oh, Mr. Sperrit, I'se sorry. I begs yo' pardon. I-I-I-I didn't mean no harm suh.

Willie. Bucephalus, you is doomed. I is come fo' you, haaaaaaah.

Seer. Oh, don't bother me. Please doan bother me this time. Ivory, kin you see him? Ain't I jes 'maginin?

Ivory. I doan know. I cain't see nothin'.

Seer. You cain't see nothin'?

Ivory. No. I'se got my eyes shet.

Seer. Well open 'em. Look quick. Is dere anything dere?

Ivory. [*Looking at* Willie *and then covering his eyes*] Oh me, oh me.

Seer. He's really dere?

Willie. Yeah I'se hyuh. I'se staying too. When I goes you goes wid me. First I'se gonna tear you up lak a piece of paper. Hyuh I pulls you to pieces. Haaaaaah. [*Takes a step towards* Seer]

Seer. Please doan, Mr. Sperrit. Please doan. I ain't never bothered you.

Willie. Oh yeah you is. Yo' 'members old crazy Bill what you killed wid dat fake medecin? Haaaaaaah, well I'se crazy Bill an' I'se come fo' my revenge. [*Creeps slowly up to the* Seer *who backs toward table.* Ivory, *who is not being bothered, now creeps up to and under table*]

Seer. Oh please gimme a little time to think, please. I didn't know de medecin' would hurt you. I didn't mean no harm, suh. I'se sorry. Deed I is.

Willie. Bucephalus, dat ain't all. You'se a fake, ain't you? Speak up fo' I gits really mad.

Seer. Yassuh, I'se a fake. I'se sorry. Please go way an' leave me alone now.

Willie. Go way an' leave you 'lone. Why didn't you leave dat gal Lucy alone an' dis ole man hyuh? Why didn't you?

Seer. I wanted Lucy an' dat was de only way I could make dem agree.

Willie. Haaaaaah. I pull off yo' ears right now. Haaaaah.

Seer. Oh nawsuh, please don't bodder me. I'se sorry I played dis trick, hones' I is. I wont never bodder dese people no mo.

Willie. Will you git out of dis town an' never come back?

SEER. Yassuh, YASSUH . . .

WILLIE. Will you ever tell people you got power over de sperrits again?

SEER. Oh no suh, no suh. Jes lemme go now. I'll go way right dis minit.

WILLIE. Bucephalus, I is gonna let you go. But I'se gonna foller you, see? I'se gonna watch you close and de firs' time you slip, I'se gonna git you sho'. I'se gonna foller you all yo' days. Now git. Quick. Haaaaaah. I kin hardly keep from follerin' yo' anyhow. Aaaaaaaaaaah. [SEER *looks about for a second and then goes out the door.* IVORY *tries to scurry after him on all fours.* WILLIE *blocks the door*] Aaaaaaah, you ole fool, gonna give dat gal to de Seer fake.

IVORY. I didn't know he was a fake, hones' I didn't.

WILLIE. You should uv had bedder sense dan to believe dat man. I got you now. Aaaaaaaah. [*He creeps up toward* IVORY *who is in the corner of the room*]

IVORY. Oh Lordy. He'p! He'p! Lucy, he'p me.

WILLIE. [*Coming closer*] I teach you to play wid de sperrits. Cain't nothin' he'p you now. Aaaaaaaaaaaaaah.

IVORY. He'p, he'p, he'p! Whoooooooo, he'p, he'p! [LUCY *comes in from the door left*]

LUCY. What's de matter, Uncle?

IVORY. What's de matter? Come hyuh and git dis ghost out hyuh chile. He'p, he'p!

LUCY. Ghost! Dat ain't no ghost Uncle Ivory, dat's Willie.

IVORY. Willie! Naw dat ain't Willie neither.

WILLIE. Aaaaaaah, dat's right.

LUCY. Aw, Willie, stop now. We'd had enough ghosts tonight. [*She pulls sheet off of him*] See dere, what did I tell you?

IVORY. Well—well I do declare. 'Tis Willie sho' 'nough. Whooeee. Boy I sho' is glad to see you. —Lemme sit down. Feels kinda weak in de knees.

WILLIE. You aint scairt is yo', Uncle?

LUCY. Sho' he's scairt. Tremblin' lak a leaf.

IVORY. I reckon I aint scairt now, I kinda was a minit back tho'. Whee, doan you all never do dat again. Mighta kilt me.

LUCY. We wasn't gonna do nothin' lak dat Uncle. Had to do somethin' tho'. You was gonna make me marry dat ole Seer.

IVORY. Well, you doan have to worry about dat ole rascal no' mo'. I was scairt of him, chile. I thought he really did have de power. Dat's ovuh tho'. You an' Willie is gonna git married tomorrer. I aint gonna have no mo' trouble lak dis.

WILLIE. You means dat really?

IVORY. Sho' I means it. Tomorrer.

LUCY. [*Embracing* IVORY *happily*] Oh, Uncle. I'se so happy. I'se so glad. I knowed you was gonna do dat.

IVORY. Yeah, yeah, dat's all right chile. Yo'll go on out on de po'ch an' talk. I'se awful tired, dat I is. Think I go to bed.

WILLIE. I reckon you is tired, Uncle. I reckon yo' is. Come on, Lucy, I cain't stay long.

LUCY. Awright honey. [*They go out left*]

IVORY. Sperrits, aint no sech things. Sperrits! [*He starts towards kitchen*] Lucy, Lucy! Reckon you bedder light de light in de kitchen chile.

[CURTAIN]

THOMAS D. PAWLEY, JR. (1917-   )

Born in Jackson, Mississippi, Thomas D. Pawley, Jr., was educated at Virginia State College and at the State University of Iowa. He has been director of dramatics at Prairie View State College and is now on the staff of the Atlanta University Summer Theatre and director of dramatics at Lincoln University (Missouri). In addition to *Jedgement Day* (1938), he has written *Smokey* (1938), *Freedom in My Soul* (1938), all one-act plays, and *Son of Liberty* (1938), a three-act play. The following is reprinted by permission of the author. Acting rights, professional and amateur, are reserved by the author.

Jedgement Day

THE CAST

ZEKE	PLUTO
MINERVA	HANNABELLE LEE
REV'M BROWN	SOLOMON JONES
GABRIEL	CATO
MEPHISTOPHELES	

SCENE. *The plainly furnished home of* ZEKE *and* MINERVA PORTER. *Its appointments include an old dresser, a water basin and white pitcher, a double bed, chairs and a table. In the left wall there is a window through which can be seen a street sign marked "Plum Street" and a few feet beyond a grayish frame church. In the center, a door which opens on a porch. On the other side of the room, two doors, one of which leads into the kitchen, the other to a clothes closet. (These doors in the scene of the "jedgement" represent Paradise and Club Hades).*

TIME. *One Sunday Morning.*

As the scene opens, ZEKE *is lying asleep on the bed with his feet extended toward the audience. He is dressed only in his shirt and long drawers and is snoring contentedly. Through the kitchen door, which stands partly open, MINERVA is heard singing in a rich alto voice:*

> "I looked over Jordan
> An' what did I see,
> Comin' fo' to carry me—"

Suddenly the singing stops and MINERVA begins calling ZEKE.

MINERVA. ZEKE! You up yit? ZEKE!

ZEKE [*sleepily*]. Huh?

MINERVA. I say, it's time to git up!

ZEKE. Un-huh.

[*ZEKE turns over as MINERVA enters the room completely dressed for church. She is halfway across before she realizes that ZEKE is still in bed.*]

MINERVA. Well, if'n you ain't de laziest man what ever lived! Here I'se all ready to go an' you ain't started to git dressed! ZEKE! Git up from dere! Don't you know its mos' time fo' church, huh?

[*ZEKE merely stirs and grunts sleepily*].

Well! If talkin' ain't enough to git you up, I know what will!

[*She turns abruptly and seizes the water pitcher. Returning to the bed she empties its contents on the sleeping black man. ZEKE sits up immediately, fighting off an imaginary foe.*]

ZEKE. Cut it out! You don' push me right into de river!

MINERVA. Ain't nobody don' push you into no river. You's only dreamin'.

ZEKE. Den if I'se only dreamin' what's de whole ocean doin' on me!

MINERVA. Dat ain't no ocean—dat water come from de water company!

ZEKE. Den somebody musta poured it on me.

MINERVA. They sho' did. [*Grasping the pitcher*]. An' if you don' git out'n dat bed somebody's gon' pour some mo' on you.

ZEKE. Hey, waita minute . . . I'se up! What's de matter wif' you, anyhow? When I don' come home an' go to bed you raise hell; an' when I do, damn if you don' try to run me out agin'. Now, I asks you, what's a man gon' do wif a woman like you?

MINERVA. Don' you know it's mos' 'leven? Church's gon' be startin' in a few minutes. Look yonder—some of de sisters is already goin' in. Laws' a mussy—Hannabelle Lee's got on a new bonnet, too!

ZEKE. You know dis ain't my mornin' to go to church.

MINERVA. How come it ain't? Zeke Porter, you better watch out befo' de Lawd strike you stone dead.

ZEKE. He ain't got no time to be bothered with me. Not today, He ain't!

MINERVA [*shocked*]. You's blasphemin'!

ZEKE. Naw I ain't, I'se tellin' de truth. Don' de Lawd listen to everybody's prayers? Sho' he do. An' ain't dere 'bout a million people a-prayin' to Him dis Sunday morning all over de worl'? Sho' dey is. Den how you figure He's gon' to take time out to see what I'm doin'?

MINERVA. You's crazy, dat's what you is—But what you mean by sayin' dis ain't yo' mornin'?

ZEKE. Well, it ain't. Dis ain't communion day, is it?

MINERVA. What difference dat make?

ZEKE. Well, it ain't no us'n my goin' to church when it's right across de street. 'Sides, I c'n lie here in bed an' shout 'n sing jus' as loud as I could over dere any day. Den I c'n do it lyin' down an' dat's easier on my feet.

MINERVA. What's de communion got to do with it?

ZEKE. Well, dey gives away free wine on dat day. So when I gits thirsty from shoutin', all I'se gotta do is step up to de rail an' ask fo' communion.

MINERVA. You's a sinner! Oh, Lawd have mercy on him! He don' know what he's a-sayin'!

ZEKE. Minerva, ain't no us'n you botherin' Him—I tell you He's too dawgone busy.

MINERVA. Oh, what's I'm gonna do 'bout you. De devil'll git you sho' if I don' do sump'n!

ZEKE. Listen, honey. If dat devil come at me wif his pitchfork, I'm goin' right back at him wif my razor.

[MINERVA *begins to wail in despair.*]

MINERVA. Oh Lawd! What's I'm gonna do?

[*At this moment a kindly looking old colored gentleman enters. His hair is grey and he wears a long frock tail coat. Among other things he wears a pair of grey spats on spotless brown shoes.*]

BROWN. What's the matter, sister?

[MINERVA *looks up, sees the minister, and runs toward him.*]

MINERVA. Oh, I'se sho' glad you come in, Rev'm Brown!

ZEKE [*standing up*]. Mornin' Rev'm.

BROWN. Mornin' Zeke. I was jus' passin' on my way to church when I heard Minerva shoutin'. So I come in to see what's the matter. Is there anything I can do?

MINERVA. There sho' is, Rev'm.

BROWN. Zeke, you ain't been beatin' Minerva, has you?

ZEKE. Naw, Rev'm. Do it look like I been beatin' anybody?

BROWN. No, it don't. What's the matter with you anyhow? You look like you'd gone swimmin' with all your clothes on.

ZEKE. Ask her. She done it.

BROWN. Minerva?

MINERVA. Rev'm, I hadda do sump'm. Him sleepin' when its mos' time fo' church.

BROWN. Oh!

MINERVA. Den after I gits him up he come tellin' me dat he ain't goin' 'cause it ain't communion day.

[ZEKE *turns sheepishly.*]

BROWN. What's all this, Zeke?

ZEKE. Well, Rev'm, I jus' can't see why I'se got to go to church when she's jus' across de street.

BROWN. That's jus' why you should go. Look at me—I come all the way 'cross town jus' to give you people the gospel—simply 'cause I know it's my duty.

MINERVA. Amen!

ZEKE. I ain't got nothin' 'gainst goin'. But it ain't no use if I c'n hear everything here jus' as plain as day.

BROWN [pleased]. Can you?

ZEKE. Sho' I can! When dem brothers 'n sisters gits to shoutin' it's a wonder de whole town don' hear 'em!

BROWN [catching himself]. Even so, it's—it's the spirit of goin' that counts.

ZEKE. Maybe—but I ain't got the spirit today. 'Cose I'll be over on communion day like I said.

BROWN. It might be too late then. Besides, you should come every Sunday. Remember, He said, "Six days shalt thou labor and on the seventh." . . .

ZEKE [sitting on the bed]. "Rest." An' dat's jus' what I'm gonna do!

BROWN [confused]. But—but that ain't what He meant—

ZEKE. Well, dat's sho' enough what He said, ain't it?

BROWN [grudgingly]. Ye-yes.

ZEKE. Well, now, ain't no us'n you tryin' to git me to go 'gainst de Bible. 'Cause when de Bible tell me to res', I'm a sho' gonna do it!

BROWN [approaching]. Zeke Porter, I command you in the name a' Gawd to get off of that bed and go into church and ask fo'giveness for yours sins!

ZEKE. Now, Rev'm you's gettin' just like Minerva.

BROWN. If you don't, I'll call down the wrath-a Gawd on you. Your soul will burn forever. You'll never see the gates-a paradise.

ZEKE. What's all dat you talkin' 'bout?

BROWN. On the day of jedgement when Gabriel gits to blowin' his trumpet an' the dry bones rise outa the valley, yours'll sink deep into the depths of Hell!

MINERVA. Oh, Lawd, Lawd. Save him befo' it's too late! [She falls to her knees.]

ZEKE [frightened]. Cut out all dat moanin', Minerva! Now Rev'm you know nothin' like dat ain't a gonna happen!

BROWN. I leave the matter in the hands-a Gawd—I wash my hands of it. I can't 'low the sacred garment of the min'stry to be soiled by a disciple of the devil!

MINERVA. Save him—save him!

BROWN. Come, sister, there ain't nothin' more we can do. It's up to him now. If you want to be saved an' enter them green fields when you come befo' Him for jedgement, get down on your knees an' ask Him for fo'giveness. Then come into His church an' be baptised of your sins.

MINERA. Come on, Zeke, befo' it's too late!

ZEKE. I ain't a comin' nowhere. Y'all jus' tryin' to scaire me, dat's all—an' it ain't gonna work. Now git!

[MINERVA *and* BROWN *move towards the door. As they reach the threshold* BROWN *turns, shakes his head sadly, then points at* ZEKE.]

BROWN. Your soul belongs to the devil!

[*They go out.* ZEKE *watches them for a moment and then falls back on the bed and starts mumbling to himself.*]

ZEKE. Dey's both crazy—don't know what dey's talkin' about—tryin' to scaire me—Gawd, I'se some sleepy!

[*He lies still for a moment and the service across the street is heard to begin with a jubilant spiritual.*]

> "I got shoes,
>   You got shoes,
>   All God's chillun' got shoes,
>   When I gits to Hev'm
>   Gon' put on my shoes
>   An' gon' shout all over God's Hev'm."

[ZEKE *begins to mutter sleepily as the spiritual dies.*]

ZEKE. Dey's tryin' to scaire me. Ain't nothin' goin to happen . . . jedgement.

[*His voice trails off as the lights fade on the bed and come up slowly on the far side of the room. Immediately two brown angels appear through the doors.*]

GABRIEL. Well, this is the day.

MEPHISTOPHELES. It sho' is.

GABRIEL. I suppose we might as well get started. The chiefs'll be out in a minute.

MEPHISTOPHELES. Yeah, might as well.

[*At this point they take out signs from under their garments. Gabriel takes out one marked "Paradise," dusts it off, and nails it over the kitchen door. Mephistopheles takes out another marked "Club Hades" and nails it over the closet. As they finish both stand back to admire their work.*]

GABRIEL. Pretty smooth, huh?

MEPHISTOPHELES. Nothing like it—nowhere! Say ain't you Gabriel?

GABRIEL. That's right, an' you?

MEPHISTOPHELES. Well, they call me Mephistopheles.

GABRIEL. Mephistopheles! Well! Ain't seen you since the boss kicked you an' Pluto into Hades.

MEPHISTOPHELES [*as they shake hands*]. Yeah, it's been a hell of a long time, ain't it? Reckon you'll be sort of glad to blow your trumpet too.

GABRIEL. Yeah, I've been practicin' a pretty long time now. Well, what do we need?

MEPHISTOPHELES. A table for one thing.

GABRIEL. What's the matter with this one? [*He indicates a table which stands between the two doors.*] Just pull her out a bit.

MEPHISTOPHELES. There, that don't look so bad, do it Gabe?

GABRIEL. No, it don't, but let's hurry on an' get the chairs. [*Looking at his wrist watch.*] It's almost time for me to sound the call.

MEPHISTOPHELES. Okay.

[*Each picks up a chair and places it behind the table.*]

GABRIEL. I 'spose the chief'll lay me out for not havin' his throne ready on time. But I been so devilish busy that judgment was here before I knew it. [*Looking around.*] I guess that's all. You think of anything else?

MEPHISTOPHELES. No, I don't. An' now I got to beat it an' get things ready on the inside.

GABRIEL. Me, too! So long Mephistopheles.

MEPHISTOPHELES. I'll be seein' you, Gabriel.

[*They both go out through their respective entrances. For a moment* ZEKE *is heard snoring gently, then* GABRIEL *returns with a silver trumpet. He pauses, looks at his trumpet, takes a deep breath and blows a terrific blast. Startled, he examines the instrument; then decides that it must be all right.*]

GABRIEL. Hear ye, hear ye, ye descendents of Cain! Draw nigh on this day of judgment so that the Lords of Heaven an' Hell may pass judgment upon ye.

[*With this he blows the trumpet once more. Again there is a discordant blast and he walks off, giving up the whole thing as a bad job. Almost immediately* PLUTO *appears out of Hades wearing a top hat and evening clothes. From Paradise Minister* BROWN *appears attired as before. He carries a huge black book which he places before him. He and* PLUTO *do not greet each other, but merely bow. Minister* BROWN *motions with his hands and a church choir begins humming softly. Simultaneously the devil motions and a familiar swing band begins jamming the same air. After a moment the music fades and they sit. Then the Minister, after much ado, pronounces the first name.*]

BROWN. Hannabelle Lee!

[*The front door opens and the over-dressed Miss* LEE *primps up before them.*]

HANNABELLE. Howdy, Rev'm. [*The minister draws himself up haughtily.*] Hi ya, Pluto.

PLUTO. Hi, ya, babe!

HANNABELLE. How's things doin'? [PLUTO *starts to get up.*] Never mind, I'll be over soon enough to find out.

BROWN. Well, since this woman had already made up her mind, I see no need for proceeding further in *this* case.

PLUTO. Okay by me! Over here, Hannabelle!

HANNABELLE. Better come on down tonight, Rev'm. [*To* PLUTO] Well, where do I go from here?

PLUTO. Mephistopheles is waitin' on the inside. He'll take care of you. See you later!

HANNABELLE. Okay. So long boys! [*She goes out.*]

BROWN. Solomon Jones!

[*The front door opens again and an old man enters. He walks reverently up before the judgment.*]

PLUTO. You're Solomon Jones?

JONES. Yessuh!

PLUTO. Want to join up with me? We're goin' to have a big time on the inside.

JONES [*shaking his head*]. No, I'se had my fling. All I wants to do now is res'.

PLUTO. Okay, gran'pop. [*To* BROWN] Your man.

BROWN. Over here, Solomon. Now jus' go straight ahead an' don't be afraid. Nothin' ain't goin' to harm you now.

JONES. Yessuh! [*He goes out.*]

BROWN. Cato!

[*The door opens again and a flashily dressed Harlem pimp comes in.*]

BROWN. What's your last name—we don't have no record of it.

CATO. Cato!

BROWN. What's your first name?

CATO. Julius Caesar—

BROWN [*writing*]. Julius Caesar Cato! Well, Cato, you're charged with cheating at cards, shootin' dice, cuttin', an' livin' unmarried with women. What you got to say for yourself?

CATO. Nothin'.

BROWN. Don't you know you'll burn forever if you don't ask for fo'giveness?

CATO. Sho'.

BROWN. Don't you want to be fo'given?

CATO. Don't make a damn bit a difference to me.

BROWN. You'd better take him.

PLUTO. Okay. [*He motions to* CATO *who comes over to him.*] Listen, there's a dame inside named Hannabelle Lee. Go on in an' tell her I sent you.

CATO. Hannabelle Lee! Say, this ain't gonna be half bad! [*He enters "Club Hades."*]

PLUTO. Who's next?

BROWN. Minerva Porter! [MINERVA *enters. She has been weeping.*]

BROWN. What's the matter, Minerva?

MINERVA. Nothin'.

BROWN. What're you cryin' for then?

MINERVA. Well, I'm worried 'bout Zeke. Please let him come with me. I don' want him to go one way an' me another.

PLUTO. Well, from what I hear about this guy if you'll come on in with me, you'll be sho' to be with him!

MINERVA. No—I'se a good Christian, I is. An' I want Zeke to be with me.

PLUTO. Ain't much chance of that, sister.

BROWN. Yes, he's got a mighty bad record.

MINERVA. But ain't there nothin' you can do?

BROWN. I don't know. If he wa'nt such a good fo' nothin', maybe I could set him off on a star for a couple of thousand years—an' than after that maybe I could let him come to see you once in a while. But as it is—[*He shakes his head.*]

MINERVA. Den if he can't come I guess I'se got to go on by myself.

BROWN. You go on in—I'll do what I can. But I think his case is pretty hopeless. [MINERVA *enters "Paradise."*]

BROWN. Zeke Porter!

[*The door doesn't open.* PLUTO *and* BROWN *look at each other.*]

PLUTO. Louder, maybe he didn't hear you.

BROWN. Zeke Porter! [ZEKE *begins to stir.*]

ZEKE. Who dat call me?

BROWN. Zeke Porter, come to judgment!

ZEKE. Jedgement! How come it come so soon? I ain't ready to go yit.

PLUTO. Maybe I'd better send Mephistopheles after him.

ZEKE. Dat's all right. Dat's all right. I'se comin'.

[*He approaches the table.*] So dis is jedgement? It sho' looks familiar!

BROWN. Zeke Porter, of all the souls that have come before us, yours is the worse. Of all those we shall yet judge, not one approaches such a record as yours.

ZEKE. Is I—all dat bad?

BROWN. You mean, were you all dat bad. 'Cause you no longer exist as you were. Do you realize that you can't enter Paradise, and Hades don't want you?

ZEKE. But I gotta go somewhere. I can't jus' wander 'bout 'mong de stars.

BROWN. That's jus' the trouble.

PLUTO. Well, what're we going to do with him?

BROWN. I don't know. He's so lazy that he didn't even get to judgment on time!

PLUTO [*after a pause*]. I got it. We'll draw cards. The one that pulls the ace of spades don't have to take him.

BROWN. Good enough! Hand me the cards. I'll shuffle them.

PLUTO. Say—don't you trust me none?

BROWN. Sho' I trust you, but not on this deal.

[*He shuffles them.*] Now cut!

[PLUTO *reaches for the deck which* BROWN *hands him. He looks at it for a moment, then draws a card which he looks at but keeps covered.*

BROWN *then places the deck in front of him, spreads the cards out, and picks one.*]

BROWN. All right. Show your card.

[PLUTO *does so. It is the ace of spades.* BROWN *looks at it for a moment then turns up his card, also the ace of spades.*]

PLUTO. I oughta known it'd turn out this way. You musta stacked the deck.

BROWN. I didn't do nothin' of the kind.

PLUTO. Well, them two aces didn't jus' walk into that deck.

BROWN. How you know they didn't?

PLUTO. Huh?

BROWN. I say, mine did.

PLUTO. You mean—

BROWN. Has you forgotten who I am? All I'se got to do is wish for something to be, an' by the time I finish it shall have been!

PLUTO. Well, this don't get us nowhere.

BROWN. No, it don't.

PLUTO. Then there ain't but one thing to do.

BROWN. What's that?

PLUTO. Divide him up between us.

ZEKE. No—no—don't do that! Please Mr. Devil!

BROWN. That's the only way—cut him up between us—half an' half.

PLUTO. Mephistopheles! Bring me the butcher knife!

MEPHISTOPHELES. Yes, sire!

ZEKE. Fo' Gawd's sake, don' cut me up!

BROWN. What you mean by calling on God? Maybe we oughta cut him up in quarters!

ZEKE. I'll do anything, anything you say! But don't cut me up!

BROWN. You oughta thought about that when you were alive on earth.

MEPHISTOPHELES [*entering*]. The butcher knife, sire. [*He presents the knife to* PLUTO *and then goes out.*]

ZEKE. Keep dat butcher knife away from me! Stay back I tell you!

PLUTO [*hypnotically*]. Come here, Zeke.

ZEKE. Wha-what?

PLUTO. Come here, Zeke!

ZEKE. Yessuh, yessuh, I'se comin'.

[PLUTO *advances with the butcher knife while* ZEKE *crawls tremblingly forward. They stand facing one another.*]

PLUTO. Take off your shirt and prepare to die.

ZEKE. Yessuh, Mr. Devil! [*He does so.*]

PLUTO. Hurry!

ZEKE. I'se hurrin' as fas' as I can.

PLUTO. Now say your prayers.

ZEKE. Oh, Lawd have mercy on me! Have mercy! Fo'give me, Lawd. Fo'give me.

[*The lights begin to fade; then they come up again on* ZEKE *tossing on the bed.*]

ZEKE [*sitting up*]. Dey's gone! An' I'se saved! I'se saved!

[*At this moment the choir across the street begins singing.*]

ZEKE. An' dey's still over dere singin'! Maybe I'd better git over dere befo' it's too late.

[*He begins pulling on his shoes hastily. His movements become slower and slower until finally he emits a huge yawn.*]

Golly, I'se *so* sleepy. I reckon I'll jus' take a little nap befo' I go—

[CURTAIN]

OWEN DODSON (1914-   )

Owen Dodson (see also p. 403) was born in Brooklyn, New York. He received his college training at Bates College and a Master of Fine Arts degree from Yale. Two of his plays—*Divine Comedy* and *Garden of Time*—were given as major productions at Yale. Dodson's plays have been performed in little theatre groups at Howard, Atlanta, and Brooklyn College. Talladega College commissioned him to write a play on the Amistad mutiny. At present he is an instructor at Spelman College, Atlanta University. *Divine Comedy,* first produced at the Yale University Theatre, Feb. 16-22, 1938, is perhaps the first serious play to exploit the dramatic possibilities of the Father Divine Movement. It is one of the few poetic dramas yet produced by an American Negro. The scenes from *Divine Comedy* are reprinted by permission of the author. All rights are reserved by the author.

From Divine Comedy

The stage should be divided into five distinct areas: the stained-glass window place, the street, the Jackson home area, the church area, the Apostle's domain.

Up center a stained-glass window extends from the center level up as far into the proscenium as possible. In deep purple glass a cross with a halo in golden glass dominates. The cross shaft should be slanted; its head leaning to one side, one arm drooped, the other raised. It represents Christ's body. There is no figure. The rest of the window is in deep red and blue. Stage left of the cross is the street area. This area is raised about nine feet above the stage level proper. Below the street area, on the stage proper is the Apostle's domain. Steps connect the two. Stage right of the cross is the church area. It is raised about ten feet above the stage level proper. Steps lead from the street area down to a platform below the cross and up to the church area. Below the church level is the Jackson home place. Steps lead from the Jackson home place onto the platform before the cross and onto the church area.

Before the curtain rises the music of the chorus is heard; slow, despairing, desolate, hollow music. Several of the chorus are on the stage as the curtain rises. A mother is sitting on a step rocking a baby; a bum is sprawled on the floor; a group is huddled on the church area, etc. More ragged people come in from every entrance. They form the chorus of the poor: Negro and white.

The choral speeches are for the most part compact. But sometimes they speak individually, sometimes in a mass, sometimes contrapuntally, sometimes they chant. The director may break up the choral speeches almost anyway he wishes. At the beginning, however, the choral speech should be broken up into individual speeches.

The sky is dimly lit at the beginning. It is gray purple. The cross is only faintly lighted. There should be enough light for the audience to see without difficulty. The action of each act should be continuous.

ACT I

First Chorus.

Two winters come in one this year:
The wind thrusts fingers through our fear,
Curves its palm into our walls,
And whistles and rumbles along the halls.

Where grass was feathers for our beds,
The snow makes pillows for our heads:
We are Winter worn,
Wind torn.

Despair
Leaps in the air,
Falls down
Like a clown
We saw at a fair
Long, long ago.

Second Chorus.

Our bellies are large with wind in them;
Our children are giddy for the taste of bread;
Our tables and chairs are thrown on the street:
And we walk with winter shoes on our feet.

We are winter worn,
Wind torn,
Despair
Leaps in the air.

BOTH.

> "The Lord will provide" is only an echo
> Whispering in and out of these winter branches,
> Where are the fertile days?

FIRST CHORUS.

> Have the orchards gone to seed?

SECOND CHORUS.

> Have the storehouses burned to ashes on the ground?
> How long shall our feet bleed?

FIRST CHORUS.

> How long shall our feet bleed and change
> The color of the city snow?

SECOND CHORUS.

> How long shall our children cry out
> In the night with hunger awake in their bellies?
> Where is bread?

FIRST CHORUS.

> Where is shelter?

BOTH.

> Where is Christ?

FIRST CHORUS.

> We are winter worn,
> All doors are shut in our faces:
> The thud is a burning in our ears:
> We wander the streets like rats in a moldy church.

BLIND MAN.

> The blind in the haunted places
> Without fire to warm the hands they've never seen,
> What shall they do?

SECOND CHORUS.

> Who shall lift a hand to help us?
> Who shall find bread for our children?
> Death comes blowing darkness into our hearts.

FIRST CHORUS.

> He is a little man. Death is a little man.
> Who will grapple with him and win?

SECOND CHORUS.

> Where is Christ?

FIRST CHORUS.

    Death is a little man:
    A little, little man:
    A runt and an ugly dwarf,
    Who will grapple with him and win?

SECOND CHORUS.

    Where is Christ?
    Where is Christ?

[*From behind the cross a Priest appears in full regalia. He makes the sign of the cross and swings incense. The* CHORUS *now is grouped about him on the cross level, on the steps. A tattered army of the Poor.*]

ONE.

    We come asking for simple bread
    And fire to ease the coldness in our bodies.
    We have seen the blue flame of death lighting our streets,
    And we are afraid and alone.
    Where is our Master, Christ?

PRIEST.

    Christ is here and in your homes.
    Go home now and pray.
    Take the dusty hymnal down from the dusty shelf.
    Polish the silver rosaries again,
    Reset the crooked cross,
    Re-clothe the naked Christ.
    Go back to your homes and light the flameless candle.

CHORUS.

    The candle is guttered.
    Where is Christ?
    Our feet are cold,
    The skin is frozen to the bone;
    Two winters come in one this year.

PRIEST.

    The Lord's children are never alone or cold.
    Go home and pray. Prayer changes things.

CHORUS.

    We have prayed in the bitter night,
    We have prayed, but still the hunger needles
    Press, press inward.
    We are too weak to pray;
    Too desolate to hope;
    Give us bread,
    Give us shelter;
    Re-clothe our bodies.

PRIEST.

> Go home and pray!

CHORUS.

> We have no home!

PRIEST.

> Go home and pray!

[PRIEST *disappears after he has made the cross sign and swung incense.*]
[*Exit* PRIEST.]

CHORUS.

> [*In group, mumbling.*]
> We cannot go home when poverty leaks
> Down the gutters and cannot be drained.
> We cannot go home, we cannot go home:
> The fires are out,
> The children are crying.
> Death is eating our faith.

CHORUS LEADER.

> Incense swung by a bony hand,
> The sign of the cross traced in the air,
> The unctuous chant of a faith-ridden priest,
> Is not fire to offset the winter in our flesh,
> Is not manna for our children or ourselves.
> Where shall we turn for a half-chewed crust of bread?
> Where shall we turn?
> Call up the government on the telephone,
> Ask for Congress, tell them we're alone.

A Mother [*singing to an infant in her arms.*]
> Sleep darling sleep,
> Sleep darling sleep,
> There will be milk in the morning and bread:
> There will be blankets to cover your bed.
> Sleep darling sleep,
> There will be toys to play with and keep,
> Sleep darling sleep,
> Sleep darling sleep,

[*Mother hums tune during next lines.*]

MOTHER.

> What shall we do with our children asleep
> Dreaming the promise we never can keep.

LEADER.

> Call up the government on the telephone;
> Ask for Congress, tell them we're alone.

CHORUS.
>We have called again and again,
>We get no answer from the silk-hat men.

SEMI-CHORUS.
>At the bottom of the river
>Salvation lies.
>They have tossed away food
>Right under our eyes.
>We have called again and again;
>We are forgotten, the empty men.

MOTHER [*singing*].
>Sleep darling sleep,
>Sleep darling sleep,
>There will be milk in the morning and bread;
>There will be blankets to cover your bed.
>Sleep darling sleep,
>There will be toys—

[*Screams as she realizes she has been rocking a dead child. She says flatly:*]
>Burn the blanket;
>The promise I said,
>Let it be forgotten:
>My baby is dead.

MOTHERS [*echoing. The background music emphasizes the words here.*]
>Her baby is dead.
>Dead.
>The promise she said
>Let it drift away,
>Her baby is dead.
>Husbands,
>Sons,
>Brothers,
>Fathers, ·
>Nephews,
>Uncles,
>Men who walk meekly in this winter,
>See what has come
>To the golden-haired child,
>And now it will go:
>Be buried in snow,
>When the sun shines hot
>The baby will rot.

SEMI-CHORUS [*moaning*].
>Where is Christ?
>Where is Christ?

He has not come in our sorest hour.
Even to bring a faith blooming flower.

[*Confusion and desolation. They go up the stairs, wander out. The background music continues low and empty. The lights all dim out and as the music fades on the crowd, a light comes up slowly in* MRS. RACHAEL's *home area. The stage is now empty except for* RACHAEL. *She is dressing. The stained-glass window is bright. The sky is deep purple shading to gray.* MRS. CORA JENKINS *enters from the street place and goes slowly down the steps to* RACHAEL's *home. She stands outside the light and calls.*]

CORA.

Rachael. Oh, Rachael, comin' to de meetin'?

RACHAEL.

Come right in, Cora. I didn't 'spect you so soon.

[CORA *passes into the light and sits on a chair that has been placed there during the darkness.*]

Come in an' rest your rheumatism and your heart whilst I finishes dressin'. How you tonight?

CORA.

Ma knees been kinda stiff dese last few months. Lawd only knows how much longer I kin stand dis scrubbin' floors and clothes for the white folks. It near kill me every time I get near water. In fact everytime it rains ma knees twitches lak kingdom come. It's all tight in here. [*Hand on breast.*] I gets tired so easy. Ma heart pounds lak a hammer.

RACHAEL.

I can't complain none. Ma children takes care of me right well. Sometimes I feels bad, but it's mostly that I gets lonely. Don't know what I'd do without you Cora. You're a comfort.

CORA.

Thank you Rachael. [*Breathing heavily all the while.*]

RACHAEL.

Now that I don't work, the Church meetin's the only things I goes to. Ain't got no trouble so I only prays sunshine to the Lawd and wait for death. I'm just wore out waiting for something to happen. Folks don't come to Church much now. Church ain't got the old spirit.

CORA.

You shouldn't complain none. No ma'am you got de blessin's right here. I have to scratch 'bout for food and a place to lay dis head. Hit ain't no paradise, I tells you. Hit sure ain't no paradise.

RACHAEL.

One way or the other it ain't no Eden. You'se right there.

[*Pause.*]

Ought to see 'bout that heart.

CORA.

Hit come and go.

RACHAEL.

Better see to it just the same.

[*Pause.*]

CORA.

Suppose you heard 'bout dat new man—calls himself de Apostle of Light. Some folks calls him Christ come back. Say he's healing folks.

RACHAEL.

Lawd, Lawd, what is we comin to?

CORA.

He's givin out food an' shelter sure 'nough. Yes ma'm, dey say he's Christ come back, walkin' right here on earth, givin' out pieces of Heaven if you'll only believe in him.

RACHAEL.

Seems like I heard Sister Maria Lee talkin' 'bout him. But I don't set no store by these new-fangled prophets. I puts ma trust in the Lawd. He's takin' care of me so far. I can trust him for the future.

CORA.

He's a-given me life dats all. I'se had to drag all de rest of de way alone.

RACHAEL.

The Lawd works in a mysterious way, His wonders to perform.

CORA.

He ain't worked no wonders on me. How you know dis Apostle ain't what dey say he is? T'would be a sorry thing if he really was Christ come back an' none of us knowed it. 'T'would be a sorry thing, yes ma'm. An' they say he's givin' out food free, an' healin' the sick, yes my gracious. Healin' the sick and givin' out food.

RACHAEL.

I put ma trust in the Lawd; that's all I got to say 'bout it. Guess we'd better be gettin' along.

CORA.

Guess we'd better.

[*They get up and go out of light. They pass up the street level and talk as they go.*]

Did you hear 'bout Sister Ruby Howard's chile died? Undernourishment dey say.

Don't know what things a-comin to. Folks dyin' all 'bout, an' losin' jobs. Near time for the depression to be over an' some folks just feelin' it.

CORA.

Dat ole depression lak a black snake, you drive him away wid a stick an' he still come back.

[*A few of the chorus come in wearily and wander about on the stage level or just sit. They should not, however, detract from the two talking women. They are a background. As they come in the choral background music begins; hollow, despairing. When the chorus speaks their speech sounds far off; like an echo of their first lines.*]

RACHAEL.

My children manage to keep their jobs; praise His name.

CORA.

Wish ma little ones hadn't died. Two inside one year. Tu-ber-culosis of the lung so the doctor say. Been a long time but I remember well, yes ma'm. An' since dat time I been knockin' from pillar to post, an' every pillar bin stone an' every post bin iron.

RACHAEL.

The Lawd will protect his own.

CORA.

. . . Some in Park Avenue an' some in de slums of Harlem. De Lawd protects his own all right.

RACHAEL.

That's mighty bitter talk, Sister, for a church member.

CORA.

Yeh. You know I got to thinkin'. The Church ain't doin' nothin' for me. It's me been doin' for the church.

RACHAEL.

If you would have your life, you must lose it first.

CORA.

I've done givin' ma life an' got nothin' 'cept rags an' poverty an' left-overs from de white folks, an' those I work for ain't got much.

RACHAEL.

De Lawd works in a mysterious way his wond. . . .

CORA.

He ain't worked wonders on me. I'se sick an' tired of hell on earth, an' kingdom after I'm cold and dust. I'se sick an' tired of prayin' an' gettin' only silence. I'se sick of de left-overs an' the cold-cellar nights, an' only rags for ma back, I'se tired, tired, I tells you, waitin' for the sky to rain manna. I wants heaven here. Here on dis earth. O Lawd, Lawd I wants to keep faith but I'se tired of tryin' wid only dese two po' hands. I wants heaven now, an' I don't want to die to get it.

RACHAEL.

I knows. But you gotta have patience; you gotta keep the faith. Wait Cora, wait, I say, on the Lawd.

[*The music of the chorus has faded into the music of the Apostle of Light. It is way off but comes nearer. Cora begins to walk toward it.*]

CORA.

De music of de new Apostle. Listen, Listen
Ain't it sweet an' nice soundin'?

[*She talks as if in her sleep.*]

RACHAEL.

Come back, Cora, come back.

CORA.

Listen to that music. Listen! It's wonderful.
It make me feel spry again. Ain't it blessed.
Ain't it sweet.

[*Her voice takes on a new, happy quality.*]

RACHAEL.

Cora, come back. I knows whereof I speak. Don't go off to no man who calls himself Christ. Cora, Cora!

CORA.

Oh, Rachael this music fills de lonely places.
Yes, Jesus, ahm a-comin'. Yes, Lawd, ahm a-comin', Jesus, to lay ma troubles at yo' breast and take yo' song for mine. I'se waited so long in de cold an' de blackness not to come Lawd. Ahm comin' as fast as Ah kin. Ahm a-comin' Jesus.
Dat music sure is blessed; that music sho is sweet.
Halleluiah!! Ahm so glad.

[*Cora walks into the music and is lost in blackness and the music. RACHAEL stands with her hands stretched out to where CORA has gone.*]

RACHAEL.

Come back, Cora, come back. The Lawd sees. Give him a chance. Remember Job. Come back, Cora, come back.

[*The music trails off and comes back with the Chorus melody. The slow, empty music that swells while RACHAEL prays later on.*]

CHORUS.

> We are winter worn,
> Wind torn,
> Despair
> Leaps in the air.
>
> Falls down
> Like a clown,
> We saw at a fair,
> Long, long, ago.
> Two winters come in one this year,
> The wind thrusts fingers through our fear,
> Curves its palm into our walls
> And whistles and rumbles along the walls.
>
> Where is Christ?
> Where is Christ?

[*Rachael walks down from the street level, through the* CHORUS *and into her lighted home area. As she prays the stained-glass window lights up.*]

RACHAEL.

> It's many times I come to you, Jesus, my hands stretched in pain and prayer, askin' for some of Your sunshine.

CHORUS.

> Where is Christ?

RACHAEL.

> Beggin' that ma children might be raised up in Thy light. Seekin' more faith to follow the road.

CHORUS.

> Where is Christ?

RACHAEL.

> I come askin' in the dead of winter when dere was no food, no coal for the fire.

CHORUS.

> Have the storehouses burned to ashes on the ground?

RACHAEL.

> An' You answered, Jesus, You answered this po' sinner's prayer.

CHORUS.

> How long will our children cry out,
> In the night with hunger awake in their bellies?

RACHAEL.

Now I come, my ole knees creakin' an' sore, my ole heart full of gratitude for what you done for me an' mine, seekin' sunshine for another lost soul, Cora Jenkins.

CHORUS.

Where is Christ?

RACHAEL.

She's wandered away cause' she's sick of waitin' for thy mercy. She She don't understand, Jesus. She don't know. Give her strength, Jesus. She don't understand Thy ways an' Thy power.

CHORUS.

Where is Christ?

RACHAEL.

For Thy sweet blessin's and Thy pain remembered, I ask that this my humble prayer be acceptable in Thy sight, O my redeemer, Amen.
[*The stained-glass window sends a glow down onto* RACHAEL. *The* CHORUS *is gone.* RACHAEL *is still on her knees.*]

* * * * *

[*During the last few speeches between* RACHAEL *and her daughter* NORMA *the Apostle's Music has begun and now begins to swell.* RACHAEL *stands up, is impelled toward the music. By a terrific grip of her will, she does not go toward it. She goes back and sits. The music becomes syncopated and she stands: goes a step or two and turns back, falls in her chair murmuring.*]

RACHAEL.

Help me Jesus, help me.
[*Blackout.*]

* * * *

[*She is alone now. The large light about her home space gets smaller and smaller. There is a pause.* RACHAEL *looks terribly alone. She gets up and starts to walk from her space to the church level singing:*]
Sometimes I feel like a motherless child,
Sometimes I feel like a motherless child,
Sometimes I feel like a motherless child,
A long way from home,
A long way from home,
A long way from home.
[*The light in the Church area comes dimly on as she mounts the stairs. Several men and women on their knees, standing up and sitting on chairs, swaying: their shadows huge against the backdrop. They have taken up her song even before she gets there. Now* RACHAEL *kneeling*

*makes another shadow. The cross has grown bright. Just below the street
area on the stage proper a light comes on. This is the Apostle's space.
Several people are sitting about, but in contrast to the Church group,
they seem happy, supremely content. They exchange such greetings as
"Ain't you glad," "He's come," "Joy, joy, Sister," "Joy, Brother," "Ain't
He Sweet," "Bless His name." They are also singing but with a softer
tone than the others so that the spiritual music is predominant.*]

FOLLOWERS.

    He gave us all our tickets,
    The train arrived on time,
    O, He gave us all our tickets,
    The train arrived on time.
    Now, we are in heaven
    An' didn't spend a dime.

    He's come to us at last,
    Now ain't you mighty glad.
    O, he's come to us at last,
    Now ain't you mighty glad.
    He's brung the warmin' sunshine
    Forgivin' good and bad.

    I think my heart will burst
    With joy at seein' him.
    I think my heart will burst
    With joy at seein' him.
    He looked on me an' "pop"
    My soul was free of sin.

[*To the tune of "There is Power."*]
    He has come, come,
    Oh yes, he has come
    Bringin' light,
    Bringin' light,
    Bringin' light,
    Bringin' light to all the earth.

[*Now some of the church people begin creeping down the stage to the
Apostle's area. The cross light is dimming, the Church light is dimming.
The preacher tries to keep them from going.*]
PREACHER [*in church area*].
    Comes death, the invader,
    Pacing through the sky scatterin'
    The planets and the lesser stars,
    O, my people.
    When he comes,

When death, the invader comes,
An' you have to stand before His great white throne,
What shall you say?
Shall you say you have deserted His Church?
O, my people!
When the red hot tongs of death,
You know what tongs are,
Tongs handle fire.
When the tongs of retribution grasp you,
O, my people!
What shall you say?
Come back, come back!
Death will ride over you,
One of these days!
Shall you be ready?
He'll scorch the sinners; singe the bone:
Tear the heart.
O, my people!
Come back!
Repent!
Wait for the Lord!
Repent, Come back!
Don't follow this false God!
Don't worship the golden calf.
God will smite you sure.
Pray, pray . . .

[*But they have all gone to the Apostle of Light except* RACHAEL. *The* PREACHER *goes to* RACHAEL *and lays a hand on her shoulder.*]

Sister, your faith is still strong. Don't let dat music an' dat dancin' turn you from yo' Christ. He still watchin' from above.

RACHAEL.

Dey're all gone now. All those I loved have gone. Jesus has left me alone. Alone!! Oh Christ, I'm alone. I've gotta go. The church has done closed, dere ain't no one here.

PREACHER.

This is the real test, Sister. Christ never deserts his people.

RACHAEL.

Cora was right: I done given all for the church an' what happens? Ma son is gone, ma girl is gone, ma friend is gone. I wants some joy. Some little joy, not loneliness, not death.

PREACHER.

If you would have your life, you must lose it first.

RACHAEL.

I said that once. İt don't sound so good now.

[*The music becomes louder.* RACHAEL *stands deciding. The* APOSTLE *music impels her. As it swells up she begins to go down. Slowly, not sure of her ground, but slowly she goes down. The* PREACHER *is the only one left and he kneels. His figure is a silhouette against the backdrop and finally the church area light goes out and the light behind the stained-glass window goes out. Only the Apostle area is lighted. As more people enter this light, it begins to spread.*]

FOLLOWERS [*singing*].

When we were lost in a forest of pain,
He came back to us bringing sunshine and rain.
All our pain was washed away,
All our sin is dried today.
How shall we praise him
The Apostle of Light,
Jesus come back,
When even the night
Was starless.
Put ribbons in your hair,
Rejoice!
Cast off all despair,
Rejoice!
Be clothed all in white
He came when our night
Was starless.

[*This ends with "Ain't you glad," "Hallelujah," "It's Wonderful," "Thank you, God Almighty," etc.*]

VOICE.

My children, are you there?

FOLLOWERS.

Yes, God Almighty.

VOICE.

Will you follow me?

FOLLOWERS.

Yes, my Jesus!
Please your Grace!
All the Way!
Tell us what!
Yes, my Savior!
Oh how sweet!!

[*They sing hoarsely, blatantly.*]

He has come, come
O yes, he has come,
Bringin' light,
Bringin' light,
Bringin' light,
Bringin' light,
Bringin' light to all the earth.

MOTHER HUMILITY.

I wuz starvin; ma husband left me with two children, but dey
died of Tu-ber-cu-losis of the lung, so the doctor say. Ma heart
pounded lak a hammer. I strained it every time I walked upstairs. I
kept praisin' a Gawd I thought wuz beyond the sky. I emptied my
pennies in a red plush plate. One evenin' I heard His music an'
come an' wuz made well in mind an' body. There ain't no Gawd
beyond the clouds. He's right here with us. Ain't you glad. Ma
redeemer is right here. Praise his name. An' there ain't no death
for me, but only eternal life. It's so sweet. Thank you Apostle.
Thank you GOD.

[*The usual "amens," "Ain't it the truth," "Thank you, God Almighty,"
etc. Brief song. During* MOTHER HUMILITY'S *speech and as she begins, the
followers accompany her with such phrases as . . .*]

FOLLOWERS.

Listen at Mother Humility.
Did he do dat sho 'nough?
My, ain't he de Savior dough.
Tell us more, mother.
Preach it, Sister.
Ain't it grand.
Blessed Lover.
Blessed Teacher.
Blessed Father.
Blessed Gawd.

[*As she finishes they say such phrases as:*]
Yes praise him.
I knowed he could do all dat, etc.

MOTHER HUMILITY.

I praised Him. An' the more I praised Him the more blessings He
showered on me. He's a-givin' me new life. Two months ago I had
only one lung an' the other was just a little piece. He cured that. I
would sleep with any man who would pay me enough for liquor.
He cured that. It's truly grand. I know He's God. He didn't only
help me, he's raised the dead and cured the dyin' from cancer.
He's the true an' livin' God. He don't need money to carry on His
work. Ain't He God? He don't need money.

FOLLOWERS.

My Lord's treasury never run dry,
A-never run dry,
My Lord's treasury never run dry,
A-never run dry,
It's everlastin' as the stars on high.
A-never run dry,
A-never run dry.
My Lord's treasury like stars in the sky.

He's given me a blank check,
Ain't a-gonna die.
He's given me a blank check,
Ain't a-gonna die.
He's given me a blank check,
Ain't a-gonna die.
Ain't a-gonna die.
He's given me a blank check an' that's a-why.

RACHAEL

I can testify to His goodness tonight 'cause He's helped me. I
wrestled with the Angel of our Lord here, seekin' to stay bound to
earth. I struggled, but one night I commenced to feel lifted up and
that Angel spread out his wings and carried me up here to Beulah
Land. That Angel was robed all in white an' his wings was sparklin'.
He was the Apostle. He was the Apostle. I was lonely but now I'm
full. I saw Death comin' once but he been struck down, an' I'm
with my God. I was all alone but now I'm full. An' I'll never be
lonely again. Neber again. I have my Jesus.
[*Usual answers, exclamations, etc.*]

VOICE.

Are you there, my children? I'm coming down.
[*The usual answers.*]

* * * *

[*Where the Priest stood at the beginning of the act, the* APOSTLE OF LIGHT
*stands now. He is in ordinary business clothes, A light illumines him.
As he speaks the followers bow down. The whole stage is full of kneeling
people, as he speaks . . .*]

APOSTLE.

I come to earth because dust has blown into my people's eyes and
blinded them: shut out my eternal light. O my people. I come
because there's been iron resting on your hearts, with no one to
lift the weight but me. I come because there's been a wall between

my peoples an' I gotta hew it down; pick axe this wall of oppression and prejudice and hate. O my people. I come with my body before you but I've been with you. I'm with you always. I'm in your heart. Ain't you glad? O my people. Ain't you glad? Are you with me? Will you follow me? I've come because too long my prophets have preached death and pain, instead of joy and life. I come bringing a kingdom where you are. O my people. Ain't you glad? I come bringing light. Pray because prayer changes things. Don't have to pray out loud, I hear you when your mind talks. Ain't you glad? Pray in darkness, I see you. Pray with your mouth shut, I hear you. I see things you see and things you don't see. I hear the same. Ain't you glad? O my people, joy, joy, joy. The kingdom is here. Manna is here. Shelter and guidance is here. Ain't you glad? I come down because dust has blown into my people's eyes and blinded them. Joy, joy, joy.

[*His voice trails off, the light about him fades. He is gone. The followers begin to sing softly and then louder and louder, tambourines. Women prance up and down. Some of the men "truck" in time to the music. Some sway or move their shoulders rhythmically. A piano jazzes up the song, etc.*]

FOLLOWERS [*singing*].

    He's hitched our wagon to a star:
    Ain't you glad,
    Ain't you glad,

    He's hitched our wagon to a star:
    Ain't you glad,
    Ain't you glad?

    He's made this earth a paradise:
    Ain't you glad,
    Ain't you glad?

    He's made this earth a paradise:
    Ain't you glad,
    Ain't you glad?

[*The curtain slowly falls on a mass of ecstatic worshippers.*]

THEODORE WARD (1908-   )

Born in Thibodeaux, Louisiana, Theodore Ward received his early education there and for short periods in New Orleans and St. Louis. He ran away from home at the age of thirteen, making his way finally to Chicago, where he lived for several years working as bellhop, errand boy, and bootblack. Wanderlust carried him to the West Coast, where a streak of luck in a Chinese gambling house in Seattle changed the course of his life by making education possible. From the University of Utah, where he won the Zona Gale Scholarship in creative writing, he went to the University of Wisconsin, where he continued his work in creative writing and in speech. Since then Ward has been staff artist of Station WIDA, Madison, instructor of dramatics for the WPA, and an actor in *Swing Mikado*. Ward's *Big White Fog* was first produced at the Great Northern Theatre, Chicago. Feeling that Negroes should have their own people's theatre, Ward, when he came to New York, helped organize The Negro Playwrights Company in 1940. *Big White Fog* is significant as the first play to deal with the Garvey movement. The selection given below can of course do no justice to the play, but it is given as a narrative unit and should within limits be self-explanatory. The play centers about a Negro family in Chicago in the depression years, struggling against the fog of poverty and prejudice. The selection is reprinted by permission of the author. All rights are reserved by the author.

From Big White Fog

A Negro Tragedy

ACT III

SCENE I. *The same [i.e. the home of the Masons.]*
TIME. *A late afternoon, nine years later.*
Ostensibly, the living room of the Masons has not changed. Its furnishings are the same. But there is no longer that brightness and orderliness which characterized it when we saw it last. Poverty, brought on by world wide depression broods over all. . . .

* * * *

CLAUDINE. Is there anything I can do for you, Mrs. Mason?
ELLA [*rising slowly*]. No, Claudine. [*Going.*] I guess I'll just have to let them set us out and make the best of it. [*She ascends stairs.*]
CLAUDINE [*taking out cigarette and coming around left end of couch*]. So you all going to be evicted, too, huh?
WANDA [*as* CLAUDINE *sits on couch*]. I guess so. [*Taking chair center.*] Papa's gone to Court now.

561

CLAUDINE. *Well,* [*lighting cigarette*] that's too bad—But it's your own fault!

WANDA. [*huskily*] Where do you get that stuff; it's my own fault?

CLAUDINE [*coolly*]. If you had any sense you wouldn't be in this trouble.

WANDA. Oh, yeah!

CLAUDINE. You're damn right—I wish I could get a break with an old chump like Hogan. I'd show you something. I'd take his sugar so quick he'd think I was a gangster!

WANDA [*firmly*]. I've told you, I don't go for that!

CLAUDINE. No, you're too dumb. Here you are with your Mama about to be set out in the street and all you've got to do is ask that old sucker for the money to save her—crazy as he is about you!

WANDA [*rising*]. I know. [*Crossing to window seat.*] In fact, I already have.

CLAUDINE [*rising surprised*]. You have? [*Crossing slowly toward her.*] Then you've got more sense than I gave you credit for!

WANDA. I just thought I'd ask him last night to see what he'd say.

CLAUDINE. Sweet Patootee! And he shelled right out, didn't he?

WANDA. No, there's a catch in it. He said he'd be glad to help me if I'd promise to be nice to him—

CLAUDINE [*strolling behind rocker*]. Well . . .?

WANDA. I can't stomach that.

CLAUDINE. Don't talk foolish, Wanda. There won't be nothing to it. Hogan's not so bad; he's just old—Anyway, you're no virgin, you know!

WANDA. No. But I'm no whore!

CLAUDINE [*emphatically*]. You're a fool, if you ask me. [*Suddenly crossing to ash tray on end table to snuff cigarette.*] But she's your mother, Kiddo. If you don't care whether they set her out in disgrace before all the neighbors, that's your business. [*Turning.*] But I'll tell you one thing; you'd never catch me turning my mother down for the sake of such a flimsy idea. [*Going.*] But I've got to get home. [*In door.*] You'd better think it over like you got some sense. [*Exit.*]

WANDA. Think it over—[*Burying her face in her hands and lap.*] God! [*For a moment she sits thus, but shortly hearing her mother descending, she straightens up with an air of ease.*] I thought you were going to lie down for a while?

ELLA. My pillow's like a bag of rocks. [*As she reaches floor.*] Claudine gone?

WANDA. Yes.

ELLA. Isn't it time for you to be going to work?

WANDA. What time is it?

ELLA. My clock had five-thirty. But I wouldn't trust it.

WANDA [*rising*]. I guess I'd better get ready.

ELLA. I guess you'd better.

DAN [*entering with* LES—*no longer the cocksure business man and seedily dressed*]. Well, what'd they do?

ELLA [*as he hangs his hat*]. I don't know. Vic's still downtown.

LES [*noticing her eyes*]. You've been crying!

WANDA. Marx upset her.

LES. Marx—what Marx?

WANDA. The furniture man. [*Going above.*] You should've heard what he offered her for that couch and chair—six fifty! [*Exit above.*]

DAN. Can you beat it? [*Going down right.*] But it's no more than you can expect from a Jew!

LES. That's prejudice, Uncle Dan.

DAN [*heatedly*]. Call it what you like. But I'm sick of them. They're all alike!

LES [*coolly, his development into full manhood showing itself in a total aspect of quiet strength*]. The white man says the same thing about us. But the Jews are no different from any other people. If anything, they've contributed a damn sight more.

DAN. Oh, yeah—another of your communistic ideas, eh?

LES [*taking a pamphlet from his pocket and taking seat down left*]. It didn't take the Communists to find that out. The whole world's been aware of it ever since the coming of Christ—And look at Marx, Einstein, Spinoza—

ELLA. Oh, for God's sake, let the Jews rest! [*Seeing* CAROLINE *enter.*] I thought you went to Juanita's?

CAROLINE [*putting hat on table—a young woman of 20 now.*] I just left her.

ELLA [*suspiciously*]. You didn't stay long.

CAROLINE [*searching mail on table*]. She acted so funny I decided not to stay—[*Coming down to couch and finding book there.*] I can't understand her any more.

ELLA. What do you mean, she acted funny?

CAROLINE. Oh, I don't know, Mama— [*Glancing at* DAN *and noticing that he has grown nervous.*] Did Papa get back?

ELLA [*persisting*]. It's mighty strange you can't explain what you mean—

CAROLINE. [*looking at* DAN]. I don't know what to think, Mama. But every time I go there lately, she watches me and Grandma like a hawk.

DAN [*uneasily, with a glance at* LES *who sits watching him and smiling knowingly*]. That's just your imagination.

CAROLINE. Maybe so. But she made me feel so much like I was in the way, [*Crossing to rocker,*] I just told her goodbye and came on home.

DAN [*defensively*]. Juanita's just worried like everybody else over these hard times.

ELLA. I wish your father would come on!

LES [*reading again*]. The courts are packed, Mama. They're evicting right and left.

DAN [*seizing the new subject with relief*]. They have to protect people's property.

LES. Yeah. Protect the property and to hell with the people!

ELLA. For fifteen years Cochrane never missed a month getting his rent on this house.

DAN. Yeah. But what can you expect when nine renters out of ten are nothing but dead beats?

LES. That's a lot of hooey. Anyway, if the Big Dogs can't give us work, they've no right to expect any rent. Furthermore, a just government would make them bear their part of the responsibility.

DAN [*bitterly*]. Yeah! I bore my part and you see what it got me!

LES. It serves you right for kidding yourself.

DAN. Oh, yeah!

LES [*Rising and coming into center*]. You doggone tooting! You've never been more than a Negro *striver* trying to go big. And now that you've been wiped out, you haven't got sense enough to see what hit you!

DAN [*Rising and coming in shaking his finger*]. You rattle-brained, young snipe; if you weren't my own nephew——

ELLA. Now, Dan, is that necessary?

LES [*Patting her shoulder*]. Don't mind us, Mama.

ELLA. [*Going around behind chair*] We've all made mistakes enough—

DAN. Mistake nothing. Suppose I had kept my money in the bank, would I have it?

LES. That's just another contradiction in the present rotten order. You and Papa were both wrong—You for putting faith in it. Papa for thinking the Garvey Movement anything more than an impractical and chauvinistic dream.

DAN. You wise punk! You're just like your Daddy. You think you see everything. Nobody can't——

ELLA [*exploding and striking the back of the chair with both hands*]. Oh, for God's sake, *stop* it! I'm sick of listening to nothing but talk, talk! For twenty years that's all we've had in this house—and ain't nobody done nothing yet! [LES *returns to his former seat.*]

DAN [*cooled by the outburst*]. I guess you're right, Ella. [*For a moment he stands searching his pockets then approaching* LES.] Gimme a cigarette?

LES [*smiling*]. I can't afford them!

DAN [*going up to hall tree*]. I guess not. [*Turning with his hat.*] But maybe you Reds'll include them in the rations when you get in power.

LES [*rising and going up toward him*]. At least you can bet everybody'll be *able* to smoke them!

DAN [*ironically*]. Oh, absolutely. [*In door.*] I'll be back Ella. I'm just going to the corner. [*Exit.*]

ELLA. [*Going as* LES *is seen near the newel post flipping a coin*] I guess I'll go put the little we got on the stove. [*Exit right.*]

CAROLINE [*Over her shoulder to* LES *who stands with his back toward her*]. I think you are foolish to argue with him, Les. [*He turns.*] You'll never recruit him in a thousand years.

Les. Yeah. I may not, but the times will. [*Hearing* Wanda *descending behind him and turning.*] I've been waiting for a chance to see *you*.

Wanda [*Halting*]. Yeah. [*Following a pause in which she eyes him coming down.*] Well, you'll have to do it later.

Les. [*Catching her arm as she attempts to pass*]. Oh, no you don't. I said I wanted to talk to you, and I don't mean tomorrow. [*To* Caroline *as he releases her and she goes into corner for umbrella.*] Excuse us will you, Caroline?

Caroline [*rising and going above*]. Of course. [*Going above reluctantly, she hesitates on stairs until a glance from* Les *drives her out of sight.*]

Wanda [*meanwhile turning*]. But I tell you—I've got to get to the drugstore.

Les. I can't help that. [*Going down to companion piece he turns it around, placing the back of it toward the spectator, obliquely.*] Sit down!

Wanda. I won't sit down. You can't bully me. I've got to—

Les [*ominously*]. Mama's in the kitchen—perhaps you'd rather I spoke to her?

Wanda [*frightened*] What'd you mean?

Les. You know what I mean.

Wanda [*in a low belligerent voice*]. You haven't got anything on me!

Les. No? But let's not be melodramatic. *Sit down and talk low.*

Wanda [*after measuring him a moment*]. All right. [*She eases herself into chair, and for a moment waits as he walks toward window, evidently trying to collect his thoughts.*] Well, why don't you say what you're going to say?

Les. [*turning and facing her*]. I don't suppose you realize it, Wanda. But it's been pretty painful to me and Papa, sitting around here day after day, allowing you to bear the burden of the whole house.

Wanda. When have you heard me complaining?

Les. Never. But it's begun to look as if it's about to get you down. Isn't that so?

Wanda [*rising*]. No. Who said it was?

Les. Nobody. But the facts seem to indicate it.

Wanda [*braving him*]. Come to the point!

Les [*decisively*]. All right, I will. I saw you get out of that car around the corner last night!—You're slipping!

Wanda [*stepping back speechless*]. What— [*Then desperately.*] But it was nothing like that, Les. Honest! He was just an old drug salesman who always comes into the store.

Les. Then, why didn't you let him bring you to the door?

Wanda. Because I knew you or some of the rest would misunderstand, that's why.

Les [*quietly*]. Don't lie, Wanda. You're a grown woman and don't have to tell me anything. But you know damn well, when a white man begins to take a Nigger girl riding, it can't mean but one thing!

WANDA. But you're wrong, though.

LES. I'm not. You're trifling with him. [*Menacingly*] Aren't you?

WANDA [*fending him off*]. No, no!

LES. I say you are!

WANDA [*controlling herself*]. Oh, all right. Have it your way.

LES. You little bum!

WANDA [*whirling*]. You lie! Hogan never touched me.

LES. Oh, no. And I suppose he didn't even try— That he had nothing but a wish to assist the poor little Nigger gal home?

WANDA [*turning down left*]. Am I responsible for what a man thinks?

LES [*snatching her around*] That's a convenient little subterfuge!

WANDA [*huskily*]. I've got as much right to use it as any other woman.

LES. Oh, you have? Well, what was the purpose of it here, may I ask?

WANDA [*turning away*]. You know as well as I do what we're up against!

LES [*turning toward table and walking away*]. Ugh humn! [*She whirls. Darkly.*] Just as I thought.

WANDA [*Coming up behind him appealing for an understanding*]. We've got to have some place to stay, haven't we? I thought I might be able to borrow a few dollars from him.

LES [*turning*]. You got them, I suppose?

WANDA [*turning and starting out*]. That's my business.

LES [*bitterly*] You dirty little chippy!

WANDA [*whirling in pain as though he had plunged a knife between her ribs*]. Les!

LES. [*His voice low but vibrant with intense bitterness*] You're not as good as a chippy—[*She retreats backwards down left.*] Any girl that'd stoop to such a thing and call herself decent—

WANDA [*growing hysterical*]. That's right, wipe your feet on me. Drag me in the dirt!

LES. Sh! Mama'll hear you.

WANDA. Let her. I don't care. [*Going down left wildly.*] I don't care about nothing!

LES [*following her*]. Hush, I tell you!

WANDA. I won't hush. You can tell the whole damn world for all I care. You think I'm nothing but a whore, why shouldn't she?

ELLA [*rushing in*]. For God's sake, what's going on in here?

LES. Nothing, Mama.

WANDA [*stepping forward. Wildly*]. Oh, yes there is. Come on in. You'll get the thrill of your life. Les's got a little story to tell you. [*Going*] Go on, Les. Tell her. Tell it to Mama. Give her your spicy little tale. [*She exits running*]

ELLA [*following her up to landing. But halts as she disappears into street and turns back to* LES.] What in the world is it?

LES. Nothing I tell you.

ELLA. Don't lie to me. What is it?

LES. She's just hysterical.

ELLA. Hysterical—hysterical about what?

LES. The house, I guess. She's worried about getting money for another place.

ELLA [*sitting on edge of couch*]. Yes; go on!

LES [*Starts toward door*]. There isn't anything else to say.

ELLA. Don't tell me—what about this spicy tale business?

LES [*turning back to her*]. Nothing you'd be interested in—She came up with a wild scheme to raise money for another place—

ELLA. A wild scheme?

LES [*placing one foot on edge of couch and leaning on his knee toward her confidentially*]. Yes, but don't let it bother you. I've already put my foot down on it—Anyway, I intended to tell you when I came in: I think we're going to get relief in another week or so.

ELLA. What do you mean—"relief"?

LES. We're moving in on Governor Emerson— Going to Springfield tomorrow.

ELLA. Who's we?

LES. Oh, [*Going toward door,*] just a bunch of folks like myself who're sick of waiting for "prosperity to turn the corner," while their folks starve and their sisters creep into the gutter.

ELLA [*as* DAN *is seen entering*]. And you're going with them?

LES. Yes, I am.

DAN [*hanging hat*]. Going where?

LES. To Springfield to see the governor about conditions.

ELLA. Have you said anything to your father?

LES. No, not yet.

DAN. I guess not. [*Threateningly.*] You haven't forgotten what the police did to that mob in Ohio the other day, have you?

LES. I'm not worrying about that.

DAN. No, you're not. You and that bunch of riff-raff I see you with don't give a damn about nothing—But I warn you, you're headed for trouble!

LES [*casually leaning back against the wall and folding his arms*] I'm already in trouble, and so's the rest of us. But you can't understand that.

DAN. I can't eh? Well, there's one thing I do understand, and so will you Reds before long!

LES. [*smiling*]. Yeah. What's that?

DAN. You can't beat the government.

LES [*contemptuously*]. You and your blind pessimism!

DAN. But you'll learn when the rifles begin to talk!

LES. Let them. The quicker the better.

ELLA. Lester!

DAN. [*Going down left*]. You young fool!

LES. The disinherited will never come to power without bloodshed!

ELLA. [*turning to face him*]. Les, don't say such things!

DAN. Let him rave on. He'll wake up one of these days.

LES. It's you who're asleep, not me. Your world has crashed, but you're so full of capitalist dope, you don't even know we're building a new one.

DAN. [*turning and facing him and shaking his finger, his outstretched hand seeming to pin the youth against the wall, despite his distance away*]. Building a new world. You're building a wall to be put up against and shot!

LES. I'd rather look forward to that than a pauper's grave. [*Turning, he goes above leaving them dumfounded*].

ELLA. [*finally breaking the silence, with a shake of her head*]. I don't know what in the world's come over him!

DAN [*wearily sitting in window*]. That's what you get for letting him raise himself.

ELLA. Don't blame me. I've done the best I could by him.

DAN. Yes you have. [*Heatedly.*] For eight years all you and Vic 've done is sit around here like a pair of petrified mummies and let him go straight to the dogs!

VOICE [*in street, singing brokenly*]. "Is there anybody here wants to buy a lil dog . . . Buy a lil dog . . ." [LES *reenters above as* PERCY *appears in doorway to stand there singing and swaying drunkenly*.] "Is there anybody here want to buy a lil dog . . . I got one for to sell!"

DAN [*disgusted*]. Just look at that!

LES [*running down and going to his uncle's assistance*]. Come on in Uncle Percy and sit down before you fall.

DAN [*watching them as* LES *tries to take* PERCY *to rocker*]. A regular bum!

PERCY [*breaking away from* LES]. What you mean, I'm a bum? [*Swaying.*] Whatcha mean?

DAN. You'd better sit down and try to sober up.

PERCY. Sober up—Do I look like I'm drunk to you? Do I, hunh? [*He begins to fumble in his back pocket.*]

ELLA [*to* LES]. You'd better take him back and put him in Mama's room. He may get sick in here.

LES [*as* PERCY *fishes out a flask of whiskey*]. Come on, Uncle Percy. I'll put you to bed.

DAN [*seeking bottle*]. Gimme that!

PERCY [*as* VIC *appears in doorway behind him. Withdrawing his bottle and clutching it to his bosom*]. Oh, no you don't, Big Shot. No, you don't. This is my moon.

VIC [*framed in doorway, his face grim with care and his frame clothed in his old Garvey uniform which is now faded and bedraggled—as* DAN *tries to take liquor from* PERCY.] Let him alone, Dan.

DAN [*snappingly*]. Can't you see he's drunk?

VIC [*entering*]. What difference does it make?

PERCY [*happily, as* PHILLIP *enters behind hem*]. That a boy, Vic, old man. Get him told.

VIC [*to* LES]. Take him somewhere and put him to bed—Go on, now, Percy. Let him put you to bed.

PERCY [*going across to right with* LES]. Awh right, Vic. Anything you say, old man. [*Halting near end of couch and turning.*] I know you wouldn't tell me nothin wrong. And if you say I'm drunk and ought to go to bed, well . . . well, I'm drunk and ought to go to bed. [LES *leads him out, a ragged, broken, pathetic figure with one foot in the grave. As he exits.*] I know I must be drunk if you say so . . . [*Exit.*]

DAN. He's going to keep on fighting that stuff until it kills him.

VIC [*taking rocker*]. Maybe he'd be better off dead.

DAN [*glancing at him sharply*]. I judge you didn't come out so well?

VIC [*his gaze avoiding* ELLA's *with whom he has never achieved a reconciliation and to whom he never speaks directly*]. No, I didn't.

DAN [*sympathetically*]. How much time did the judge give you?

VIC [*as* LES *reenters*]. Twenty days.

ELLA [*gasping*]. Twenty days!

DAN. That all?

PHILLIP. I guess Papa was lucky to get that, after the judge noticed that uniform—[*Indicates* VIC's.]

VIC [*angrily*]. Will you never learn to hold your tongue!

PHILLIP [*going behind couch, a young man of 20*]. I didn't mean no harm, Papa. I just—

VIC. Dry up! You never do!

DAN [*as* LES *joins* PHILLIP *and pats his hand as it rests on back of couch*]. There's no use hiding anything from us, Vic. We're all in the family.

VIC. I ain't got nothing to hide. He just got tough when I admitted I used to be a Garveyite.

DAN. No!

LES. What did he say, Papa?

VIC [*quoting*]. "Oh, so you're one of the Niggers who think this country isn't good enough for you, eh? Well, well, and yet you've got the nerve to appeal to this court for leniency?"—As if that wasn't enough, he went on to rub it in by telling me how thankful we ought to be to his people for bringing us out of savagery—but I couldn't say anything.

DAN [*thoughtlessly*]. You had no business wearing it down there.

VIC [*bitterly*]. What was I going in, my ragged drawers?

DAN. I'm sorry, Vic. I wasn't thinking. [*Pause as the spirit of dejection hovers over all.*] Have you any idea what you're going to do?

VIC. Move to Hooverville, I guess.

DAN. Don't be sardonic, Vic.

VIC. If you think I don't mean it, find me a truck!

LES [*coming in. Easily*]. Forget it, Papa. We're not going anywhere.

VIC. Eh?

LES. I said we're not going to have to move a step!

VIC. What're you talking about?

BROOKS [*offstage*]. Les! Les! [*Entering in a huff with a bundle of clothes under her arm, almost out of breath.*] Where's Les? [*Seeing him as he joins her.*] Les, I want you to go yonder to Juanita's and bring me the rest of mah things, cause I ain't fixin to stay there another blessed night.

ELLA [*as* LES *brings his Grandmother down to chair center*]. For God's sake, Mama. What happened?

BROOKS [*easing herself into companion chair*]. That hussy done come up heah and forgot her raisin', dat's what—But if she thinks I'm goin live in sich dirt, she never was so wrong in her life—[LESTER *stands behind her smiling and watching* DAN.] Mah garment's clean and spotless fore the Savior, and she and nobody else ain't goin chainge it.

ELLA [*to* DAN *who is quite perturbed*]. What in the world's she talking about?

DAN [*evasively*]. You can search me— But it sounds like she's losing her mind!

BROOKS [*turning toward him angrily*]. Don't you try to call me crazy, you sneakin blackguard! Don't you dare try it! If you don't want me to lay you out, don't you open your mouth!

DAN [*attempting to placate her*]. Aw, go on, Mama. Whatever it is forget it. [*Suddenly, cunningly.*] Ella and Vic don't want to hear that stuff! They've got troubles enough of their own. Here they are about to be evicted, kicked out in the street—

ELLA [*interposing*]. Never mind, Dan. There must be something wrong or she wouldn't be here—go on, Mamma. What is it?

BROOKS. You bet your bottom dollar there is. [*To* DAN.] And you needn't think you can shut me up, neither, cause—

DAN [*sharply*]. Shut you up? [*Rising.*] Why should I want to shut you up. [*To others.*] If you all want to listen to her crazy tales, go ahead. [*Going upstage.*] It doesn't make a damn bit of difference what she says!

ELLA. Go on, Mama, what happened?

BROOKS. I got after her bout rentin rooms and havin all kinds o low-down good-for-nothin tramps laying up in her house—[*Glancing around at* DAN *who moves further upstage.*] while some folks I ain't mentionin kept duckin in and out and makin out they can't see what's goin on. And, she say, "Mama, do you know how you're livin? Do you know who's takin care o you? Do you know nobody's givin me a dime to look after this house? Where you think I'm goin git rent to keep a roof ovuh yo head?— Like as if I never kept a roof ovuh bofe o you all's heads for twenty years without spottin mah garment—But ask me if

I didn't bless her out. I bet you she'll remember what I told her to her dyin day! After that, I just got mah things together and come on to you cause I know you'd give me a clean place to lay mah weary head, even if we did fall out bout the chillun and Vic and me had a word or two. Cause I know Vic ain't goin hold no more malice agin me for what I said bout him, than I'm goin hold against him for what he said bout me—[*Turning to* Vic.] Now ain't that right, Vic?

Vic. Of course, Mama. Though I'm sorry to say things ain't like they used to be here. We're just about to be kicked into the street, and if something don't happen in the next twenty days we will be. But you're welcome to come back if you want to.

Brooks. Twenty days!

Ella. Twenty days!

Brooks. Lawd, Lawd, Lawd! [*Glancing at* Dan *who has come down to eye her gleefully.*] But I'd heap rather sleep in the street with you all than to spot mah garment in the *wallow* they got over there.

Les [*laughing*]. Don't worry, Grandma—a lot of things can happen in twenty days!

[CURTAIN]

VI
SPEECHES, PAMPHLETS, AND LETTERS

SPEECHES, PAMPHLETS, AND LETTERS

IN 1855 a series of newspaper sketches was republished as *Black Diamonds: or Humor, Satire, and Sentiment, Treated Scientifically by Professor Julius Caesar Hannibal in A Series of Burlesque Lectures Darkly Colored.* The author did not sign his name. A literary ancestor of such writers as Octavus Roy Cohen and E. K. Means, he hoped to "brush away the cobwebs of care from the brow of the most learned, and carry smiles into the homes of all classes" by burlesquing Negroes.

> I hab come, as you all know, from 'way down in Ole Warginna, whar I studded edicashun and siance all for myself, to gib a corse of lectures on siance gineraly, an events promiscuously, as dey from time to time occur. De letter ob invite I receibed from de komitee from dis unlitened city, 'was as full ob flattery as a gemman ob my great desernment, edication, definement, and research could wish.

The author praised this as "genuine."

Black Diamonds is negligible as American humor, a straining imitation of minstrel lectures. It is considered here because it is an early expression of the popular derision of a Negro "speechyfyin'" on "Sykeology," "Siance," "Pollyticks," and "Filossofy." Touching gingerly on the slavery controversy and then attacking abolitionists for encouraging "stealin' from your Souffern brudren . . . braking up de homony ob de country," *Black Diamonds* shows Negro life in the North to be ludicrous and carefree.

In the year that *Black Diamonds* appeared, Frederick Douglass published *My Bondage and My Freedom,* with an introduction by James McCune Smith, a Negro graduate of the University of Glasgow; Samuel Ringgold Ward published *The Autobiography of a Fugitive Slave;* William Wells Brown published *St. Domingo: Its Revolutions and Its Patriots* and *The American Fugitive in Europe: Sketches of Places and People Abroad;* and William C. Nell published *The Colored Patriots of the American Revolution.* Finally, not to extend the list, in 1855 John Mercer Langston, a young Negro lawyer who, like "Professor Hannibal," was originally from Virginia, addressed the American Antislavery Society in New York, displaying a mastery of both the allusive rhetoric and the genuine eloquence of nineteenth-century oratory.

Douglass, Langston, and these others, though exceptional men for any people and any time, belong to history. "Professor Julius Caesar Hannibal" is the figment of a mediocre imagination. But the latter (helped by his many brethren) has probably been more influential in governing beliefs about the Negro in America than Douglass, Ward, Brown, and Langston, whose records today are generally forgotten, and were never fully known.

The free Negroes of antebellum America have too often been dismissed as wretched anomalies. Suffering in the South from ever increasing restrictions and in the North from difficulties in employment and schooling, they certainly had no easy time. Many were beaten down and defeated; some were even renegades to their people's cause. Nevertheless, struggle rather than wretchedness was the theme of their story. Free Negroes were among the bravest and shrewdest antislavery fighters. They were important in organizing and conducting the Underground Railroad, and in resisting the kidnapping of fugitives; they were vigorous and effective in speech-making, pamphleteering, and journalism. Their literary record is highly creditable. It consists almost entirely of propaganda, but this fact does them honor; free themselves, they did not forget their brothers below the line.

From the day when John Quincy Adams first spoke against "gag rule" in Congress, the slavery controversy challenged the efforts of many of America's best orators. The classic debates of Webster and Calhoun, of Lincoln and Douglas, the brilliant rationalization of slavery by Jefferson Davis and Robert Toombs, and the antislavery attacks of Seward, Joshua Giddings, and Sumner were centered in the controversy. Salmon P. Chase and Thaddeus Stevens started their vigorous forensic careers defending fugitive slaves. In this "golden day" of oratory, antislavery orators loomed large: William Ellery Channing, Wendell Phillips, William Lloyd Garrison, Theodore Parker, Stephen S. Foster, Theodore Weld, Angelina and Sarah Grimké, Abby Kelly, and Lucretia Mott. Negro orators belong with this fine company, fellows in effectiveness if not always in rhetorical skill.

Chief among these is Frederick Douglass. "Few orators among us surpass him," wrote Harriet Beecher Stowe, whose brother, Henry Ward Beecher, was himself a resounding trumpet of freedom. Thomas Wentworth Higginson had "hardly heard his equal, in grasp upon an audience, in dramatic presentation, in striking at the pith of an ethical question, and in single illustrations and images." Contemporary judgment ranked Douglass, the self-educated ex-slave, with Phillips and Parker, the finest products of New England culture. During his two-year tour of England, Scotland, and Ireland, Douglass was a potent force in stirring British antislavery feeling. In the United States he was frequently handled roughly by mobs; he was segregated, insulted, threatened, and pelted with rotten eggs. At one meeting he was so badly beaten that the mob left him for dead.

In a New York meeting, when tempers were rasped by the Fugitive Slave Bill controversy, Douglass was set upon by a gang of ruffians led by Isaiah Rynders, a Tammany desperado. When Douglass answered Rynders' taunts with the proud question, "Am I a man?" Rynders roared, "You're not a black man; you're only half a nigger!" Douglass turned this off with "Then I am a half brother to Captain Rynders." At the end of his speech he gestured to a black man at the rear of the stage. This man came forward and asked Rynders, "Am I black enough?" and then launched into a speech that, according to one observer, "established a grand triumph of intelligence over brute force." This man was Samuel Ringgold Ward, described by his friend Wendell Phillips as so black that "when he closed his eyes you could not see him." A preacher, Samuel Ringgold Ward found his calling too tame and indulged in strenuous antislavery activity.

Another fearless orator was Charles Lenox Remond, a free Negro of Massachusetts, whose spirit was expressed in a speech on the eve of the Anthony Burns rendition:

> I know, Mr. Chairman, that I am not, as a general thing a peacemaker. I am irritable, excitable, quarrelsome—and I confess it, Sir, and my prayer to God is, that I may never cease to be irritable, that I may never cease to be excitable, that I may never cease to be quarrelsome, until the last slave shall be made free in our country, and the colored man's manhood acknowledged.

Other speakers of note were James McCune Smith, of New York, educated at the University of Glasgow, and generally considered to be the most learned Negro of the antebellum period; William Whipper, an Underground agent of Columbia, Pa., and Frances Ellen Watkins Harper, who lectured and gave public readings of her poetry around the antislavery circuit.

When Douglass made his first speeches, he was generally introduced as a "chattel"—a "thing"—"a piece of Southern property." Douglass believed that he was the first fugitive slave lecturer. There were many to follow, among them Lewis and Milton Clarke, George

Latimer, Josiah Henson, William and Ellen Craft, and Anthony Burns. Ambition and good training enabled many to leave the status of "Exhibit A," however, and William Wells Brown, Jermain W. Loguen, and Sojourner Truth became drawing cards for audiences, not as curiosities, but as speakers with something to say. Public appearances for Harriet Tubman were naturally unwise, but according to Thomas Wentworth Higginson, she told of her amazing adventures to private audiences, in a graphic manner that was hard to equal.

The pulpits in Negro churches of the North were often turned into forums concerned with antislavery protest, or at least with race defense. In 1786 the Negro communicants of St. George's in Philadelphia left the church in protest at their treatment, and founded a church of their own. Their leaders were Richard Allen (later the first bishop of the African Methodist Episcopal Church) and Absalom Jones (later the first rector of the African Episcopal Church). In New York such preachers as the Reverends Peter Williams, Theodore Wright, and Nathaniel Paul gave wise counsel to their congregations, and persuasively pointed out to America the Negro's disabilities, achievements, and rights. In one of the earliest printed orations, "An Address Delivered on the Celebration of the Abolition of Slavery in the State of New York July 5, 1827," Nathaniel Paul equated Christianity with abolitionism, anticipating the religious arguments of men like his friend, Garrison, Theodore Parker, Frederick Douglass, and Whittier. According to Paul, if he was ever forced to believe that slavery could not be destroyed, such belief would lead him to "disallow submission" to the laws of his country, and to "deny the superintending powers of divine Providence in the affairs of this life . . . treat as the worst of men the ministers of the everlasting gospel . . . and consider my Bible as a book of false and delusive fables. . . ." Other forceful antislavery preachers were the Reverend J. W. C. Pennington, "the fugitive blacksmith," a Doctor of Divinity from the University of Heidelberg; Henry Highland Garnet, whom Vernon Loggins calls "a sort of political Thomas Paine for Negroes"; and Leonard Grimes of Boston, whose apprenticeship for preaching included a prison term for Underground Railroad activities. The Reverend Theodore Holly in the interim of preaching vindicated "the capacity of the Negro race for self-government" by pointing to the Haitian Republic. Lemuel Haynes is interesting because he served as pastor to white churches in Connecticut, Vermont, and upstate New York. Unlike Samuel Ringgold Ward, who likewise preached to white congregations, Haynes took no part in antislavery activities. His character and attainments, however, were good propaganda.

Pamphleteering is the literary weapon for critical periods and for embattled peoples. Among American Negroes, certainly an embattled people, whose critical periods are practically coextensive with their history, pamphleteers have therefore been numerous. The first pamphlet by an American Negro, however, was more lay preaching than anti-slavery propaganda. It was Jupiter Hammon's *Address to the Negroes in the State of New York* (1787), which speaks only guardedly for gradual emancipation, but urges the slaves to good conduct. In contrast, several Negroes who at the end of the eighteenth century attained a prestige superior to that of their fellows spoke out for greater justice to their people. "An Essay on Slavery" by "Othello" is strongly anti-slavery, but cannot be unquestionably attributed to a Negro. Benjamin Banneker, whose scientific mind ranged in such fields as astronomy, clockmaking, mechanics, zoology, and botany, wrote a notable letter to the like-minded Thomas Jefferson deploring the "general prejudice and prepossession . . . so prevalent in the world against those of my complexion." Paul Cuffe, a self-made shipowner and trader, sponsored colonization as the way out for his oppressed people. Richard Allen and Absalom Jones collaborated on *A Narrative of the Proceedings of the Black People during the Late Awful Calamity in Philadelphia; and a Refutation of Some Censures Thrown upon Them in Some Late Publications* (1794), a needed defense of the Negro's services in the yellow fever epidemic.

In the same city in 1813, *Letters from a Man of Colour* appeared in protest against a bill prohibiting "further immigration of free persons of color." This has been attributed inconclusively to James Forten, a native of Philadelphia, who is definitely known to have collaborated with Russell Parrott on *An Address to the Humane and Benevolent Inhabitants of the City and County of Philadelphia* (1818). Forten's son-in-law, Robert Purvis, one of the organizers of the Philadelphia branch of the Underground Railroad, continued the family tradition of pamphleteering in his *Appeal of Forty Thousand Citizens Threatened With Disfranchisement to the People of Pennsylvania* (1838).

The above pamphlets were most concerned with the local problems of free Negroes in Northern cities. Purvis, for instance, qualified his *Appeal* by pleading for "the industrious, peaceable, and useful part of the colored race." A heated attack upon slavery in general came early from a free Negro in Boston, David Walker, whose *Appeal* (1829) was correctly reported by a Southern police magistrate as expressing "sentiments totally subversive of all subordination in our slaves." The *Appeal* caused consternation in the South; it certainly seemed incendiary to Southern oligarchs, who believed that the tinder for slave revolt was plentiful and dry. The Nat Turner revolt occurred in 1831, less than two years after the *Appeal,* but attempts to put the two together fail for lack of evidence. Both were powerful signs of how the wind was blowing. Garrison deprecated the spirit of rebellion in the *Appeal,* but his nonresistance appeals shared the wrath stirred up by Walker's bitter words.

In David Ruggles New York had a pamphleteer as bold as David Walker, and a greater master of biting invective. Ruggles enjoyed a good fight, whether against "blackbirders" stalking and capturing fugitives and free Negroes in the slums of New York, or against "doughfaces," *i.e.,* proslavery Northerners. His two pamphlets are counterattacks upon denouncers of the New York Antislavery Society.

A later work by a Boston Negro, *A Treatise on the Intellectual Character and Civil and Political Condition of the Coloured People of the United States, and the Prejudice Exercised Towards Them,* by the Reverend Hosea Eaton, was also defiant. Like many later racialists of all types, Eaton turned accepted ideas "topsy-turvy." Arguing for the African's cultural past, he belittled the European's and white American's: "The Egyptians have done more to cultivate such improvements as comport to the happiness of mankind than all the descendants of Japhet put together." The treatise received far less attention than Walker's *Appeal.*

In 1831, a Boston woman, Maria W. Stewart, surprised Garrison with a manuscript of devotional thoughts and essays, which he promptly printed as the tract *Religion and the Pure Principles of Morality.* A second similar work came out the next year; in 1879 a selection of her works was reissued as *Meditations From the Pen of Mrs. Maria W. Stewart.* Written in the style of religious apostrophes, Mrs. Stewart's subject matter was by no means conventional for her day: she was a great admirer of David Walker, and a denouncer of slavery and racial prejudice; she spoke out for Negroes to develop education, business enterprise, and race pride; and she insisted that Negro women were not born for menial drudgery, "to bury their minds and talents beneath a load of iron pots and kettles!" Mrs. Stewart was probably the first Negro woman to work publicly for her people's cause.

Ruggles and Walker departed from the main line of abolitionist pamphleteers. Lydia Maria Child in *An Appeal in Favor of That Class of Americans Called Africans* (1833) and James Forten and Robert Purvis wished greater recognition of the achievements of Negroes and the injustices done them. Walker's intransigency was continued by his eulogist, Henry Highland Garnet, in *An Address to the Slaves of the United States of America.* It is significant that this address was rejected by a small majority of a convention of Negroes in Buffalo because it "encouraged insurrection." Slave insurrections, which were far more numerous than popular historians have cared to record, were nurtured by the secret meetings, the "grapevine telegraph," and clandestine boring, not by pamphlets and orations.

The radical and the less radical trends clashed at the historical meeting of John Brown and Frederick Douglass at Chambersburg, Pennsylvania. For all of his personal courage, Douglass could not see wisdom in John Brown's course. The bloody and fairly easy way in which the insurrections of Nat Turner and Vesey had been put down was grim warning. Though uprisings occurred after Nat Turner's and were rumored until Appomattox, most Negroes, as so many oppressed people before and since have done, believed that the "underground" route, instead of revolts, promised freedom.

Negroes did not urge insurrection, but they did urge escape and even violent defense of liberty. Thirty fugitive slaves in Cazenovia, New York, on the eve of the passage of the Fugitive Slave Bill drew up the following advice for their slave brothers:

> We cannot furnish you with weapons; some of us are not inclined to carry arms; but if you can get them, take them, and, before you go back into bondage, use them . . . The slaveholders would not hesitate to kill you.

The slaves were also urged to take the masters' fastest horses, and even money.

It is hardly necessary to point out that these pamphlets were produced by free Negroes in the North. Free Negroes in the South, too close to the powder keg, were silent. Had they written, where could their works have been published, and where read? The ban on "incendiary" publications was severe. Once in the North, however, and to a slight measure safe, Negroes became strongly articulate.

In a different pamphleteering tradition was Martin R. Delany's *The Condition, Elevation, Emigration, and Destiny of the Colored People of the United States* (1852). Delany felt that "we have speculated and moralized much about equality, claiming to be as good as our neighbors, and everybody else—all of which may do very well in ethics, but not in politics." Speculating was not enough for Delany, who wanted practical measures for reform. In something of a spirit of defeatism brought on by the passage of the Fugitive Slave Bill, Delany favored emigration. But he was not absolutely devoted to his proposal, and after abolitionists attacked it as impeding emancipation, he stopped the sale of the book.

Closely related to pamphleteering is the early journalism of American Negroes. This was begun in the crusading spirit. Samuel E. Cornish, a preacher in New York, and John B. Russwurm, the first Negro college graduate in the United States, started *Freedom's Journal* in 1827, nearly four years before *The Liberator*. Cornish took over the paper as *Rights For All* in 1829 and continued it for nearly a year. *The Colored American* ran from 1837 to 1841, having as its editors such men as Cornish, James McCune Smith, and Charles B. Ray. The last named was another of the Negro preachers in the North who were tireless workers on the Underground Railroad. John G. Stewart's *African Sentinel and Journal of Liberty* appeared early and very briefly in Albany; Stephen Myers, backed by Horace Greeley and Gerrit Smith, published *The Elevator* there for a longer run. In neighboring Troy, Henry Highland Garnet and William G. Allen published *The National Watchman*. Journals in New York City were David Ruggles' *The Genius of Freedom,* Willis A. Hodges' *The Ram's Horn* and Thomas Hamilton's *The People's Press*. Samuel Ringgold Ward "sank every shred of his property" in two newspaper ventures, *The Impartial Citizen* and *The Northern Star and Colored Farmer,* published in Syracuse. Martin Delany's *The Mystery* was issued regularly between 1843 and 1847, when Delany joined Frederick Douglass' *North Star*. The files of Ruggles' and Delany's journals are lost. In 1855 James McCune Smith estimated that not less than one hundred newspaper enterprises had been started by Negroes in the United States. Almost all were short-lived, but the number is surprising.

A few magazines were ventured. Ruggles' *The Mirror of Liberty* and William Whipper's *National Reformer* ran for only a few issues. More successful and significant was the *Anglo-African Magazine,* edited and published by Thomas Hamilton. This was the first "literary" magazine, including fiction, poetry, and essays of many types, from such contributors as Martin Delany, Edward Blyden, Alexander Crummell, James McCune Smith, and Frances Watkins.

The first financial support of Garrison's *Liberator* came from Negroes. William C. Nell, a Negro, was Garrison's editorial associate. Negroes supported the *Liberator* so staunchly, and Garrison presented the Negroes' cause so well, that Garrisonians frowned on Douglass' decision to publish a paper of his own. But Douglass was convinced that he could increase his effectiveness by agitation through the press in addition to the platform. In 1847 he founded *The North Star* in Rochester, with funds contributed in England. This paper, a weekly, lasted from 1847 to 1860 (from 1850 being known as *Frederick Douglass' Paper*). From 1860 until the Emancipation Proclamation Douglass published *Douglass' Monthly*. His purposes were "to attack slavery in all its forms and aspects; advocate universal emancipation; exalt the standard of public morality; promote the moral and intellectual improvement of the Colored People; and hasten the day of Freedom to the Three Millions of our enslaved Fellow Countrymen." If a single editor could accomplish such great purposes, Douglass was probably the man. He surmounted grave problems of finance and sectarian battles. In longevity and content, Douglass' is the most important of all Negro antebellum journalism. A disastrous fire in his Rochester home in 1872 destroyed the only complete files known to have been preserved of his two journals and magazine.

One of the features of antislavery journalism was the open letter attacking slavery. Often these were written by fugitive slaves, such as Douglass' letter to Auld, "Jarm" Loguen's to his slave mistress, and Anthony Burnes's to his persecutors. William Wells Brown wrote numerous breezy letters on his experiences on the antislavery circuit in England and in America.

The style of this pamphleteering and journalism is often turgid, as in Walker, often pedantic, as in Forten with his historic allusiveness, or labored, as in Ruggles. Such defects, however, place these Negro writers in the mainstream of the slavery controversy. They were writing propaganda in the heat of the battle, and their faults are the faults of such propaganda. The real cause for surprise is the general high caliber of the writing. Whether freeborn Negroes, whether brought as children to the North by their fugitive parents, whether they reached the North only when grown men, they had all won book learning the hardest way. If many were overliterary and addicted to purple passages, others practiced their craft better and wrote with moving directness; if some repeated Jeremiads, others varied what might have been monotony with skillful use of humor and wit. What all contributed is courageous and strong pleading for a cause close to their hearts. Though this cause has been, in a measure, achieved, they still deserve to be better known.

At the passing of the Fifteenth Amendment, Frederick Douglass sadly quoted "Othello's occupation's gone!" But this quotation was more poetry than truth. The problems of Reconstruction were soon challenging the intelligence and vigor of the antislavery workers. Douglass quickly threw over his feeling of being at a loss, and began a distinguished career of statesmanship. Delany went to South Carolina to serve in the reconstruction of that state. Charlotte Forten and Frances Watkins Harper entered enthusiastically into educational work for the freedmen. Daniel Payne, finding the fields less bounded, set determinedly to his chosen tasks in religion and education. Younger figures appeared, most of them turning naturally to the new and alluring field of politics.

The traditional view of Negro politicians in Reconstruction is that they were ignorant and venal. Partisan scholarship has labored to establish this view, but thorough investigation seems to discount it. Taken by and large, Negro legislators and officeholders in Reconstruction were neither ignorant nor venal; they accomplished valuable purposes, not all of them confined to their own race's welfare. They would compare favorably with any random sampling of United States politicians. Even James S. Pike, whose tirades are so often repeated, admitted that in South Carolina, "all of the best speakers in the House are quite black" and that one state senator had "more native ability than half the white men in the Senate." W. E. B. DuBois, their best defender, says that

> It is impossible to be convinced that the people who gave South Carolina so excellent a constitution, who founded good social legislation, a new system of public schools, and who were earnest in their general demeanor, could at the same time in all cases be stealing, carousing, and breaking every law of decency.

Without doubt some Negro officeholders spoke ludicrously, and "feathered their nests," just as so many other politicians have done before and since. But in the main it was not bad government that irritated the denouncers of Negro legislators. It was Negro participation in any government at all. The worst crime of Negro Reconstruction politicians is that too often they spoke out bluntly for the rights of their people, and for social reform in general. To many that is one of the major tragedies of the era.

Hiram R. Revels and B. K. Bruce, both of Mississippi, served in the United States Senate. By an irony of history, Revels was elected to fill the place of Jefferson Davis. Both Revels and Bruce were educated men, the former studying at a Quaker Seminary in Indiana and at Knox College in Illinois, and the latter at Oberlin. From among the many members of the Lower House, several might be singled out. John Willis Menard of Louisiana was the first Negro to speak in Congress. Although his election was rejected, he was allowed full pay as Congressman. John R. Lynch of Mississippi, who served in three Congresses and was elected though counted out from the fourth, later wrote a book refuting James Ford Rhodes's errors about Reconstruction. Robert Brown Elliott of South Carolina, a high-ranking graduate of Eton, was considered the most learned and eloquent Negro Congressman; Robert Smalls, also of South Carolina, was a Civil War hero who, during the blockade of Charleston, delivered a Confederate vessel to the Federal fleet. Richard H. Cain, a third member from South Carolina, was later bishop of the A. M. E. Church. John Mercer Langston was a distinguished lawyer long before his election to Congress from Virginia. The last Negro member of Congress from a Southern state was George H. White of North Carolina.

The oratory of these Negro legislators conforms to the pattern of congressional oratory of the times. The faults are stodginess, repetitiveness, and bombast; the virtues are sincerity and courage. Knowing that their race was on trial, these men, all of whom had struggled against great odds to improve themselves, put forth their best efforts. The storm and stress of their own people did not, however, blind them to the needs of America as a whole. Many spoke out forcefully for causes only generally related to the Negro problems. It is not unnatural, in the light of historic events, that they spoke as partisans of the Republican Party. In this period they had reason to agree with Frederick Douglass that "The Republican Party is the deck, all else the sea."

A new spirit toward Negro leadership was expressed by Richard T. Greener when he said:

> The convention was the favorite resort of the leading Negro of ten years ago. He convened and resolved, resolved and convened—read his own speeches, was delighted with his own frothy rhetoric, and really imagined himself a great man. He talked eloquently then, it must be granted, because he spoke of his wrongs; but when the war overturned the edifice of slavery, "Othello's occupation was gone," indeed . . . The question is: Will the young men of color . . . resolve to begin now to take part in public affairs, asserting their claim wherever it is denied, maintaining it wherever contested, and show that the young may be safe in counsel as well as good for war?

In the flush of youth, of an unusually good education, and of opening opportunities, Greener spoke brave words. The bugle call of reveille to the young men of his race, however, was soon to change to taps. The fight for the suffrage and civil rights, the participation in public affairs, though ostensibly won, were, in the late years of the nineteenth century, seen to be gains on paper only, not actualities.

The strategy of attack, started by the antislavery movement and continued by Negro congressmen and such allies as Charles Sumner and Thaddeus Stevens, was altered into the tactics of consolidating positions, of compromise, of retreating. It was only thus, in a period of conciliation between North and South with the Negro omitted, that Negro spokesmen believed that even scant gains could be kept. The greatest speaker (oratory had changed to speechmaking) for compromise and interracial cooperation was Booker T. Washington. Considerably astute, a master of parry and defense, seasoning bitterness with good humor, Washington fell in with the conciliatory trend, satisfying a goodly portion of both North and South, Negroes and whites. Washington urged forgiving and forgetting, the opportunities rather than the grievances of the Negro. He was an optimistic Benjamin Franklin rather than a battling Thomas Paine. When he said "In all things that are purely social we can be as separate as the fingers, yet one as the hand in all things essential to mutual progress," he sounded a keynote that has been struck since by many spokesmen on the race problem. Of the Negroes in Washington's tradition, Robert Russa Moton has received the widest hearing.

Opposition to the gradualism of Booker T. Washington was naturally most articulate among Negroes in the North. Chief among these were William Monroe Trotter, a fearless journalist in Boston; Kelly Miller, who, though finding much to praise in Washington, spoke out constantly on the Negro's need for higher education; and W. E. B. DuBois, who in speeches and journalism attacked the weak points in Washington's program. The National Association for the Advancement of Colored People, with such speakers as William Dean Pickens, James Weldon Johnson, Walter White, Charles Houston, Andrew Ransom, and William Hastie, has continued DuBois' fight for civil and political equality for the Negro.

Though there is little evidence on the radio in spite of its numerous forums on national problems, the Negro problem is one which, as one historian blithely puts it, "we always have with us." There is still "much talk about it and about." A great deal of this talk has fallen into deserved disrepute. Clichés abound—from white speakers: "I personally have no prejudice, but"; "Some of my best friends are Negroes"; "I had a dear old colored mammy"; "Your music and rhythm are what we sorely need"; from Negro speakers: "No race in an equal span of time (50 years, 60 years, 75 years as the case may be) has ever accomplished so much as the American Negro"; "Ethiopia stretches forth her hands unto God"; "No Negro has ever turned his back upon Old Glory"; and from both: "This isn't the time, the time isn't ripe." There are professional race men of both races, some whites viewing the Negro as a menace, some Negroes their equals in race chauvinism, both making capital out of demagoguery. Much speechmaking on the Negro, however, by both Negroes and whites, is sound and informed. The stress today is on reason more than arousement. Against the spellbinders should be set such lecturers as social scientists, journalists, college professors, and labor organizers whose speeches shed more light and less heat. They interpret the Negro in America, evaluate his achievements and point out his disabilities in a way that deserves and will most likely get a hearing. The best work of these last named, however, appears in the essay form, and it is thus that several are represented in this anthology.

Pamphleteering seems to be coming back into favor as the Negro wakes to the power of mass pressure. The National Association for the Advancement of Colored People, the National Urban League, the National Negro Congress, and many other organizations are increasing the use of educational and agitational pamphleteering. Popular causes have been the Elaine, Arkansas, Sharecroppers' Case, the Antilynching Bill; the American Occupation of Haiti; the Scottsboro case; and the Negro's part in National Defense. Open letters, such as those by Kelly Miller to Thomas Dixon (see p. 884), are still an occasional literary weapon.

Negro journalism is now a thriving business. Its editorial spirit is still one of crusading, not very different from the pioneering journalism of Russwurm, Cornish, and Douglass. Prominent in the history of Negro journalism in America are T. Thomas Fortune, W. Monroe Trotter, Robert Abbot, founder and editor of the *Chicago Defender,* Robert Vann, founder and editor of the *Pittsburgh Courier,* Carl Murphy, of the Baltimore *Afro-American,* Robert Pelham, of the *Washington Tribune,* P. B. Young, of the *Norfolk Journal and Guide,* and Roscoe Dungee, editor of the Oklahoma *Black Dispatch.* The above newspapers, only a few of the many scattered about the country, are all weeklies; the only Negro daily is the *Atlanta World.* All of these propagandize the Negro's cause and publish news about Negroes and "race-angled" general news.

There have been many Negro magazines, but only a few have survived. Like their ancestors a century ago, most have run for only one or two issues. *The Messenger,* edited by A. Philip Randolph and Chandler Owen in the years of the first World War and shortly thereafter, was the first Negro publication to espouse economic radicalism. *The Crisis,* now edited by Roy Wilkins, and *Opportunity,* edited by Elmer A. Carter, have had the longest records among Negro magazines. Though organs of the N. A. A. C. P. and the National Urban League, respectively, they have both given encouragement to Negro writers and artists. *The Interracial Review* presents the position of the Catholic Church toward the Negro. Negro scholarly journals are *The Journal of Negro History,* edited by Carter G. Woodson; *The Journal of Negro Education,* edited by Charles Thompson at Howard University; *The Quarterly Review of Higher Education Among Negroes,* edited by Henry L. McCrory at Johnson C. Smith University; the Florida *A. and M. Quarterly,* edited by Isaac Fisher at Tallahassee; and *Phylon,* edited by W. E. B. DuBois at Atlanta University. Though these journals are well disposed to Negro creative writers, it is still a matter of moment that there is no magazine published by Negroes that is devoted solely to literature.

It is true that many Negro clergymen pride themselves on preaching only "Christ and him crucified." Many others, however, stemming from the abolitionist tradition really make their pulpits social forums. It is probable that larger bodies of Negroes are reached by pulpit discussion of the social problems than by any other agency except Negro journalism. Nor are such "social" preachers confined to the intellectual class; many who might be called "folk" preachers increase the social awareness of their congregations. The sermons in this anthology were not selected as representative of the style and content of the innumerable sermons of Negro preachers, but for their bearing upon Negro life in America and their pertinence to the historic lines of pamphleteering and oratory.

DAVID WALKER (1785-1830)

In 1829 the South was restive under rumors of slave revolts in tidewater Virginia and reports of serious fires in Augusta. Then in Savannah a copy of David Walker's *Appeal* was found upon a luckless slave, and sixty copies were discovered in the possession of a Negro preacher. Two missionaries to the Cherokee Indians were arrested for owning copies. An alleged letter from Walker to a Georgia printer fell into the hands of the authorities; the printshop was searched and twenty pamphlets found. The South was thrown into commotion. Two states promptly "enacted laws prohibiting the circulation of incendiary publications and forbidding the teaching of slaves to read and write." In North Carolina a person found guilty of writing or circulating publications which might "excite insurrection, conspiracy, or resistance in the slaves or free Negroes" was to be "imprisoned for not less than a year and be put in the pillory and whipped at the discretion of the court." For the second offense he should "suffer death without benefit of clergy." A reward of $1,000 was placed on Walker dead, a reward of $10,000 on Walker alive.

David Walker was born free, since he was the son of a free mother and a slave father. In his teens he left his native North Carolina, which he hated, and settled in Boston. He was truly a self-made man, earning his living as a dealer in old clothes, but little known until he published *Walker's Appeal in Four Articles Together With a Preamble to the Colored Citizens of the World, But in Particular and Very Expressly to Those of the United States* (1829). Two other editions were published in the following year in spite of the furore created by the first edition. When the mayor of Savannah requested the mayor of Boston to arrest Walker, the latter replied that Walker had not violated any law of the state. He added that Walker intended "to circulate his pamphlets by mail, at his own expense, if he [could not] otherwise effect his object."

Walker refused to run away to Canada, telling his wife and friends: "Somebody must die in this cause. I may be doomed to the stake and the fire, or to the scaffold tree, but it is not in me to falter if I can promote the work of emancipation." In the *Appeal* Walker wrote: "I expect some will try to put me to death, to strike terror to others." When he died, shortly afterwards, this prophecy increased the suspicion of abolitionists that he had been murdered. The Negroes of Boston considered him a martyr to their cause.

The effect of Walker's *Appeal* on the South is discussed in Clement Eaton's "A Dangerous Pamphlet in the Old South," *Journal of Southern History*, August, 1936. The selection printed here is from Article II, "Our Wretchedness in Consequence of Ignorance," of the second edition of the *Appeal*.

[Attack Upon Abjectness and Ignorance]

IGNORANCE AND TREACHERY ONE AGAINST THE OTHER—a grovelling servile and abject submission to the lash of tyrants, we see plainly, my brethren, are not the natural elements of the blacks, as the Americans try to make us believe; but these are the misfortunes which God has suffered our fathers to be enveloped in for many ages, no doubt in consequence of their disobedience to their Maker, and which do, indeed, reign at this time among us, almost to the destruction of all other principles: for I must truly say, that ignorance, the mother of treachery and deceit, gnaws into our very vitals. Ignorance, as it now exists among us, produces a state of things, Oh my Lord! too horrible to present to the world. Any man who is curious to see the full force of ignorance developed among the coloured people of the United States of America, has only to go to the southern and western states of this confederacy, where, if he is not a tyrant, but has the feelings of a human being, who can feel for a fellow creature, he may see enough to make his very heart bleed! He may see there, a son take his mother, who bore almost the pains of death to give him birth, and by the command of a tyrant, strip her as naked as she came into the world, and apply the cow-hide to her, until she falls a victim to death in the road! He may see a husband take his dear wife, not unfrequently in a pregnant state, and perhaps far advanced, and beat her for an unmerciful wretch, until his infant falls a lifeless lump at her feet! Can the Americans escape God Almighty? If they do, can he be to us a God of Justice? God is just, and I know it—for he has convinced me to my satisfaction—I cannot doubt him. My observer may see fathers beating their sons, mothers their daughters, and children their parents, all to pacify the passions of unrelenting tyrants. He may also see them telling news and lies, making mischief one upon another. These are some of the productions of ignorance, which he will see practiced upon my dear brethren, who are held in unjust slavery and wretchedness, by avaricious and unmerciful tyrants, to whom, and their hellish deeds, I would suffer my life to be taken before I would submit. And when my curious observer comes to take notice of those who are said to be free, (which assertion I deny) and who are making some frivolous pretentions to common sense he will see that branch of ignorance among the slaves assuming a more cunning and deceitful course of procedure. —He may see some of my brethren in league with tyrants, selling their own brethren into *hell upon earth,* not dissimilar to the exhibitions in Africa, but in a more secret, servile, and abject manner. Oh Heaven! I am full!!! I can hardly move my pen!!! and as I expect some will try to put me to death, to strike terror into others, and to obliterate from their minds the notion of freedom, so as to keep my brethren the more secure in wretchedness where they will be permitted to stay but a short time (whether tyrants believe it or not)—I shall give the world a development of facts, which are already witnessed in the court of heaven. My observer may see some of those ignorant and treacherous creatures (coloured people) sneaking about in the large cities, endeavoring to find out all strange coloured people, where they work and where they reside, asking them questions, and trying to ascertain whether they are runaways or not, telling them, at the same time, that they always have been, are, and always will be, friends to their brethren, whom they scandalously delivered into the hands of our *natural enemies!*

Oh! coloured people of these United States, I ask you, in the name of that God who made us, have we, in consequence of our oppression, nearly lost the spirit of man, and, in no very trifling degree, adopted that of brutes? Do you answer, no?—I ask you, then, what set of men can you point me to, in all the world, who are so abjectly employed by their oppressors, as we are by our *natural enemies*? How can, Oh! how can those enemies but say that we and our children are not of the HUMAN FAMILY, but were made by our Creator to be an inheritance to them and theirs for ever? How can the slave holders but say that they can bribe the best coloured person in the country, to sell his brethren for a trifling sum of money, and take that atrocity to confirm them in their avaricious opinion, that we were made to be slaves to them and their children? How could Mr. Jefferson but say,[1] "I advance it therefore as a suspicion only, that the blacks, whether originally a distinct race, or made distinct by time and circumstances, are *inferior* to the whites in the endowments both of body and mind?"—"It," says he, "is not against experience to suppose, that the different species of the same genus, or varieties of the same species may present different qualifications." [Here, my brethren, listen to him.]] "Will not a lover of natural history, then, one who views the gradations in all the races of *animals* with the eye of philosophy, excuse an effort to keep those in the department of MAN as *distinct* as nature has formed them?"—I hope you will try to find out the meaning of this verse—its widest sense and all its bearings: whether you do or not, remember the whites do. This very verse, brethren, having emanated from Mr. Jefferson, a much greater philosopher the world never afforded, has in truth injured us more, and has been as great a barrier to our emancipation as any thing that has ever been advanced against us. He goes on further and says, "This *unfortunate* difference of colour, and *perhaps* of *faculty*, is a powerful obstacle to the emancipation of these people. Many of their advocates, while they wish to vindicate the liberty of human nature, are also anxious to preserve its *dignity* and beauty. Some of these, embarrassed by the question, 'What further is to be done with them?' join themselves in opposition with those who are actuated by sordid avarice only." Now I ask you candidly, my suffering brethren in time, who are candidates for the eternal worlds, how could Mr. Jefferson but have given these remarks respecting us, when we are so submissive to them, and so much servile deceit prevails among ourselves—when we so *meanly* submit to their murderous lashes, to which neither the Indians nor any other people under Heaven would submit? No, they would rather die to a man, before they would suffer such things from men who are no better than themselves, and *perhaps not as good*. Yes, how can our friends but be embarrassed, as Mr. Jefferson says, by the question,

---

[1] See his *Notes on Virginia,* page 213.

"What further is to be done with these people?" For while they are working for our emancipation, we are, by our treachery, wickedness and deceit, working against ourselves and our children—helping ours, and the enemies of God, to keep us and our dear little children in their infernal chains of slavery!!! Indeed, our friends cannot but relapse and join themselves "with those who are actuated by sordid avarice only!!!" For my own part, I am glad Mr. Jefferson has advanced his positions for your sake; for you will either have to contradict or confirm him by your own actions, and not by what our friends have said or done for us; for those things are other men's labours, and do not satisfy the Americans, who are waiting for us to prove to them ourselves, that we are MEN, before they will be willing to admit the fact; for I pledge you my sacred word of honour, that Mr. Jefferson's remarks respecting us, have sunk deep into the hearts of millions of the whites, and will never be removed this side of eternity.—For how can they, when we are confirming him every day, by our *groveling submissions* and *treachery?* I aver, that when I look over these United States of America, and the world, and see the ignorant deceptions and consequent wretchedness of my brethren, I am brought ofttimes solemnly to a stand, and in the midst of my reflections I exclaim to my God, "Lord didst thou make us to be slaves to our brethren, the whites?" But when I reflect that God is just, and that millions of my wretched brethren would meet death with glory—yea, more, would plunge into the very mouths of cannons and be torn into particles as minute as the atoms which compose the elements of the earth, in preference to a mean submission to the lash of tyrants, I am with streaming eyes, compelled to shrink back into nothingness before my Maker, and exclaim again, Thy will be done, O Lord God Almighty.

Men of colour, who are also of sense, for you particularly is my APPEAL designed. Our more ignorant brethren are not able to penetrate its value. I call upon you therefore to cast your eyes upon the wretchedness of your brethren, and to do your utmost to enlighten them —*go to work and enlighten your brethren!*—Let the Lord see you doing what you can to rescue them and yourselves from degradation. Do any of you say that you and your families are free and happy, and what have you to do with the wretched slaves and other people? So can I say, for I enjoy as much freedom as any of you, if I am not quite as well off as the best of you. Look into our freedom and happiness, and see of what kind they are composed!! They are of the very lowest kind—they are the very *dregs!*—they are the most servile and abject kind, that ever a people was in possession of! If any of you wish to know how FREE you are, let one of you start and go through the southern and western States of this country, and unless you travel as a slav~ to a white man (a servant is a *slave* to the man whom he serves) or have your free papers, (which if you are not careful they will get from you) if they do not take you up and put you in jail, and if you cannot give good evidence of your freedom, sell you into eternal slavery, I am not a living man: or any man of colour, immaterial who he is, or where he came from, if he is not *the fourth from the negro race!!* (as we are called) the white Christians of America will serve him the same; they will sink him into wretchedness and degradation for ever while he lives. And yet some of you have the hardihood to say that you are free and happy! May God have mercy on your freedom and happiness!! I met a coloured man in the street a short time since, with a string of boots on his shoulders; we fell into a conversation, and in course of which, I said to him, what a miserable set of people we are! He asked, why?—Said I, we are so subjected under the whites, that we cannot obtain the comforts of life, but by cleaning their boots and shoes, old clothes, waiting on them, shaving them, etc. Said he, (with the boots on his shoulders) "I am completely happy!!! I never want to live any better or happier than when I can get a plenty of boots and shoes to clean!!!" Oh! how can those who are actuated by avarice only, but think, that our Creator made us to be an inheritance to them for ever, when they see that our greatest glory is centered in such mean and low objects? Understand me, brethren, I do not mean to speak against the occupations by which we acquire enough and sometimes scarcely that, to render ourselves and families comfortable through life. I am subjected to the same inconvenience, as you all.—My objections are, as to our *glorying* and being *happy* in such low employments; for if we are men, we ought to be thankful to the Lord for the past, and for the future. Be looking forward with thankful hearts to higher attainments than *wielding the razor* and *cleaning boots and shoes.* The man whose aspirations are not *above,* and even *below* these, is indeed, ignorant and wretched enough. I advance it therefore to you, not as *problematical,* but as an unshaken and for ever immovable *fact,* that your full glory and happiness, as well as all other coloured people under Heaven, shall never be fully consummated, but with the *entire emancipation of your enslaved brethren all over the world.* You may therefore, go to work and do what you can to rescue, or join in with tyrants to oppress them and yourselves, until the Lord shall come upon you all like a thief in the night. For I believe that it is the will of the Lord that our greatest happiness shall consist in working for the salvation of our whole body. When this is accomplished a burst of glory will shine upon you, which will indeed astonish you and the world. Do any of you say this will never be done? I assure you that God will accomplish it—if nothing else will answer, he will hurl tyrants and devils into *atoms* and make way for his people. But O my brethren! I say unto you again, you must go to work and prepare the way of the Lord.

There is a great work for you to do, as trifling as some of you may think of it. You have to prove to the Americans and the world, that we are MEN, and not *brutes,* as we have been represented, and by millions treated. Remember, to let the aim of your labours among your brethren, and particularly the youths, be the dissemination of education and religion.[2] It is lamentable, that many of our children go to school, from four until they are eight or ten, and sometimes fifteen years of age, and leave school knowing but a little more about the grammar of their language than a horse does about handling a musket —and not a few of them are really so ignorant, that they are unable to answer a person correctly, general questions in geography, and to hear them read, would only be to disgust a man who has a taste for reading; which, to do well, as trifling as it may appear to some, (to the ignorant in particular) is a great part of learning. Some few of them, may make out to scribble tolerably well, over half a sheet of paper, which I believe has hitherto been a powerful obstacle in our way, to keep us from acquiring knowledge. An ignorant father, who knows no more than what nature has taught him, together with what little he acquires by the senses of hearing and seeing, finding his son able to write a neat hand, sets it down for granted that he has as good learning as any body; the young, ignorant gump, hearing his father or mother, who perhaps may be ten times more ignorant, in point of literature, than himself, extolling his learning, struts about, in the full assurance, that his attainments in literature are sufficient to take him through the world, when in fact, he has scarcely any learning at all! . . .

Most of the coloured people, when they speak of the education of one among us who can write a neat hand, and who perhaps knows nothing but to scribble and puff pretty fair on a small scrap of paper, immaterial whether his words are grammatical, or spelt correctly, or not; if it only looks beautiful, they say he has as good an education as

[2] Never mind what the ignorant ones among us may say, many of whom when you speak to them for their own good, and try to enlighten their minds, laugh at you, and perhaps tell you plump to your face, that they want no instruction from you or any other Nigger, and all such aggravating language. Now if you are a man of understanding and sound sense, I conjure you in the name of the Lord, and of all that is good, to impute their actions to ignorance, and wink at their follies, and do your best to get around them some way or other, for remember they are your brethren; and I declare to you that it is for your interests to teach and enlighten them.

any white man—he can write as well as any white man, etc. The poor, ignorant creature, hearing this, he is ashamed, forever after, to let any person see him humbling himself to another for knowledge but going about trying to deceive those who are more ignorant than himself, he at last falls an ignorant victim to death in wretchedness. I pray that the Lord may undeceive my ignorant brethren, and permit them to throw away pretensions, and seek after the substance of learning. I would crawl on my hands and knees through mud and mire, to the feet of a learned man, where I would sit and humbly supplicate him to instil into me, that which neither devils nor tyrants could remove, only with my life—for coloured people to acquire learning in this country, makes tyrants quake and tremble on their sandy foundations. Why, what is the matter? Why, they know that their infernal deeds of cruelty will be made known to the world. Do you suppose one man of learning and good sense would submit himself, his father, mother, wife, and children, to be slaves to a wretched man like himself, who, instead of compensating him for his labours, chains, hand-cuffs and beats him and his family almost to death, leaving life enough in them, however, to work for, and call him master? No! no! he would cut his devilish throat from ear to ear, and well do the slave-holders know it. The bare name of educating the coloured people, scares our cruel oppressors almost to death. But if they do not have enough to be frightened for yet, it will be, because they can not always keep us ignorant, and because God approbates their cruelties, with which they have been for centuries murdering us. The whites shall have enough of the blacks, yet, as true as God sits on his throne in Heaven.

DAVID RUGGLES (?-1849)

David Ruggles would be a significant figure if for no other reason than that he aided Frederick Douglass' escape from slavery. But he also stands on his own feet. Ruggles was a Jack-of-all-trades, but master of antislavery devices. He referred to himself as a minister; he had considerable information on all sorts of subjects, though his formal training is unknown and probably was nil; he opened a reading room exclusively for Negroes in New York; he was Secretary of the Committee of Vigilance of New York; he ran a magazine, wrote antislavery letters to the press and two pamphlets, and was the proprietor of a water-cure resort. His two books are *The "Extinguisher" Extinguished, or David M. Reese, M.D., Used Up* (1834) and *An Antidote for a Poisonous Combination Recently Prepared by a "Citizen of New York," alias Dr. Reese*. These are in the polemical tradition of antislavery journalism, but their pedantry and logic-chopping cannot conceal Ruggles' great gusto, information, and debating skill.

[Extinguishing an Extinguisher]

DR. REESE COMMENCES his *extinguisher* by stating that he is "going at once to the fountain head of the Anti-Slavery Society," that he is going to be very fair—to treat that society "according to the principles of their constitution, and to judge of these principles from their report, and to censure no man except when sustained in that publication." This is very nice and fair. In the next place he avows himself to be "the uncompromising enemy of slavery," etc.; he disclaims the allegation of being "either an advocate or apologist for slavery," etc.; but he says that "slavery exists in our land, and its existence is provided for by the Constitution of the Union," and it is plainly inferred from what follows that he considers slavery no crime or sin, from the fact that it "is provided for by the Constitution." What does he say? Why he censures the abolitionists for saying that "slave holding is a heinous crime or sin in the sight of God." The exordium concludes by inviting attention to the report itself, which he attempts to stigmatize by a host of epithets, which I have not time or patience to mention.

After inserting a long paragraph from the Anti-Slavery Report, he proceeds—"Such presumptuous effrontery on the part of these novices in philanthropy—of these raw recruits in the cause of emancipation, if their insignificance did not forbid it, it would subject them to the derision of the universe." It is truly ludicrous to hear such a man as David M. Reese call Arthur Tappan a "novice in philanthropy," etc. I hold truth to be sacred by all men, and when I hear professors of religion and ministers of the gospel trifle with it, it really makes me sad. Now, Dr. Reese knows very well that most of these men whom he calls "novices in philanthropy," &c. have been philanthropists for years, and are celebrated for their benevolence and philanthropy. But that is one way of choking the truth. Now, after all, what is the obnoxious mass? Why it appears there is only one exceptionable sentiment; it is as follows: *"Till the organization of the New England Anti-Slavery Society in 1832, there was scarcely a rill of pity for the slave."* Is this consummate arrogance? Try it. Abolitionists and the framers of the Anti-Slavery Constitution, and the writers of the report were not ignorant of the names and deeds of the illustrious worthies mentioned by Dr. R. They were intimately acquainted with their history; their memory was dear and their works remembered and appreciated by them; but, after all, considering the small amount of good effected for the people of color, compared with our sufferings, and what has been done since '32 for our elevation, it may truly be said, that "scarcely a rill of pity" has been felt for the *slave;* and the pity that the colonizationists have for the *"free"* is like the pity of the *spider* for the *fly.* The Doctor makes a grand parade of the public schools in the Free States for the *free,* to prove the amount of *"pity for the slave"* prior to 1832. What a logician! To know the amount of pity toward the colored population of this country, let the colonization riots and mobs of New York and Philadelphia speak for the *free!* Let the iron that enters into the soul of the slave; let the bloody whip of the cruel taskmaster; let the cries, tears, groans and blood of three millions of American bondmen tell how large is the stream of pity that flows in America to wash the wounds of bleeding humanity! Dr. R. confounds the deeds of statesmen and the designs of politicians with pity, as if nothing had been done for the colored population which did not originate in pity, or was incorporated with it. This is another instance of his admirable logic.

"Such shameless extravagance and brazen untruths would indicate the charitable imputation of insanity upon its authors, &c." One scarcely knows how to restrain his indignation when reading such fulsome railing. Dr. R. speaks here of insanity, and truly if insanity exists in extravagance of expression, he is entitled to that epithet most richly. How different is the style of Heman Howlett, with all becoming modesty,—he says, in the very commencement of his address—"Fellow citizens—it is with no small degree of diffidence that I address you on this important subject, a diffidence in my abilities to do justice to such an important question, while my finer feelings of sensibility vibrate from my heart" and so forth; and then after finishing his introduction, he gravely (not in a sneering ridiculous manner) asks the question—"is colonization and gradual emancipation preferable to immediate emancipation?" and then like a man who sets his work before him, he describes the whole condition of Africa, in all its several bearings to the four cardinal points; he tells of its history since the world began, its civil, moral, and religious condition both now and for time past; dwells with pathos upon its animal kingdom—"its lion, leopard, and tiger," and charms by his mellifluous strains in describing the "sweet melody of the nightingale, the lark, and the robin." But what of this description, the geography, &c. of Africa? These are but preliminary remarks used as a scholium or something of that kind they say in logic—something from which a whole gang of sweeping inferences are to be drawn. Next follows a description of the inhabitants—the inhabitants, yes, of Africa! Hear! The original inhabitants of Africa (says Heman) were the posterity of Ham, and settled in the country which the negroes now inhabit. It seems there was a curse pronounced against this said Ham and his posterity by his father Noah, which reads as follows, (9th chap. Genesis, 24th, 25th, 26th, and 27th verses) "And Noah awoke from his wine, and knew what his youngest son had done unto him, and he said 'cursed be Canaan, a servant of servants shall he be unto his brethren, &c.'" After several texts, he proceeds:—"now these passages appear perfectly clear that Ham and his posterity are cursed by the 9th chapter of Genesis." Here is demonstration work for you—the Old Book for it! Now in view of all these "facts and arguments," Howlett infers very logically that the "African, when enslaved in this country, is better off than he is in his own;" and Mr. H. superadds many powerful reasons. This is a strong argument in favor of colonization!! Dr. Reese, in page 13 says, "Here it cannot be denied that the doctrine of the amalgamation of the races so frequently disclaimed is manifestly broached." What is the *here* at which the Dr. starts? I cannot insert the whole, but take what appears the most appropriate to the Dr.'s position. "Let some of our higher institutions *trample on the cord* of caste! open their doors to all, *without distinction of complexion*. We trust that the friends of the oppressed will not be slow to support an institution which promises so much to the cause of humanity in its struggle with prejudice and the foul spirit of *caste*." If Dr. Reese has seen or perceived any thing in the paragraph cited which inculcated the doctrine of amalgamation, I would be glad were he to set it forth. The truth is, his assertion is blank and unsupported, and he leaves it so and goes on with a passage of the most silly trash that can be thought of, first quoting a long paragraph from the A. S. Report and then declaring—this is amalgamation. He says, "hereafter it will be utterly vain for the society, or any of its officers or members to enter a disclaimer of any design to promote or encourage amalgamation by intermarriages, unless they disclaim marriage as being among those happy and elevating institutions which are open to others, &c." Here is a contemptible begging of the question. Will it not satisfy a man if he be told in the language of the disclaimer, *"that no amalgamation by intermarriage is intended?"*

* * * * *

Abolitionists do not wish "amalgamation." I do not wish it, nor does any colored man or woman of my acquaintance, nor can instances be adduced where a desire was manifested by any colored person; but I deny that "intermarriage" between the "whites and blacks are unnatural," and hazard nothing in giving my opinion that if *"amalgamation"* should become popular Dr. R. would not be the last to vindicate it, practically too if *expedient*. How utterly vain and futile are the following remarks, (page 16). "The fact that no white person ever did consent to marry a negro without having previously forfeited all character with the whites, and that even profligate sexual intercourse between the races, everywhere meets with the execration of the respectable and virtuous among the whites, as the most despicable form of licentiousness; is of itself irrefragable proof that *equality* in any aspect in this country, is neither practicable nor desirable. Criminal amalgamation may and does exist among the most degraded of the species, but Americans (what a patriot!) will never yield the sanction of law and religion to an equality so incongruous and unnatural" . . . .

"Would you be willing to marry a black wife," is a question often asked by colonizationists to members of the A. S. Society. Were I a white man, and was the question reversed and put to me, my reply would be—you had better put your question to colonizationists at the south, who have been so long in a process of training. Why insult gentlemen with a silly "quirkish" nonsensical interrogative, loped off from the fag ends of extremity? Every man that can read and has sense enough to put two ideas together without losing one, knows what the abolitionists mean when they speak of elevating us "according to our equal rights." But why is it that it seems to you so "repugnant" to marry your sons and daughters to colored persons? Simply because public opinion is against it. *Nature* teaches no such "repugnance," but experience has taught me that education only does. Do children feel and exercise that prejudice towards colored persons? Do not colored and white children play together promiscuously until the white is taught to despise the colored? How old are children, I mean white children, before this *"natural repugnance"* shows itself? Just old enough to receive the elements of an inculcated repugnance, perhaps from five to fifteen years of age. In *by-gone* days in New England, the land of steady habits, where my happiest hours were spent with my playmates, in her schools—in her churches—treading my little pathway over her broad hills and through her deep valleys. When we waded and swam her beautiful silver streams—when we climbed her tall pines and elms and oaks—when we rambled thro' her fine orchards, and partook of sweet fruits—when we followed our hoops and our balls—when we wended our way from the top of the snowy white hills to the valley. When on the icy pond we skated till the school-bell would bid us "retire!" Then—then, her morals were rich—she taught us sweet virtue! Then Connecticut, indeed, was the queen of our land!—then *nature* never, *never,* taught us such sinful "repugnance!" She was *strong* to the contrary. It took the most powerful efforts of a sophisticated education to weaken her hold—

> Fleecy locks and black complexion
> Did not forfeit nature's claim;
> Skins did "differ," but affection
> Dwelt "in black and white the same."

How could "nature" excite such "repugnance," and uneducated children know it not? The southern infant, I mean the white infant, is suckled at slavery's breast, and dandled on black slavery's knee, and if it was here that nature excited a repugnance in the white against the colored child, could they both suck at one breast? Now all this "repugnance" about which such repugnant ideas are entertained, is identified with public opinion. Let it become fashionable (God grant it never may) for white and colored persons to intermarry and the "repugnance" will vanish like dew before the rising sun; and those who were loudest in the cry against "amalgamation" will be the first to advocate it both by precept and example. In South America, white and colored persons live together on terms of perfect equality, no "repugnance" exists natural or artificial; and certainly nature is true to herself. If the "repugnance" of N. America is natural, why is it not natural in S. America? The Dr.'s logic on this subject is as false as I believe his heart to be, and just so far as such logic excludes the offices of Christian benevolence, it is sinful in the sight of God.

The recklessness of consequences with which the abolitionists are charged in this *extinguishing* book, seem to imply a dread (in the author's mind) that in somehow or other, at some future time, prejudice will wear away, and amalgamation in every aspect will predominate. Here the Doctor's logic is itself *extinguished*. If prejudice is invincible, amalgamation can never take place by intermarriages between white and colored persons. Why then is all this rout and poetry about amalgamation, if the *"races do not and will not incorporate."* Now as amalgamation seems to be the only bugbear that can be held up against abolitionists, let every candid man ask himself this question—What is the cause of amalgamation between white and colored persons? and after reviewing the North and South he must come to the conclusion that *slavery* is the cause. Then if he wished to check that base and damning prostitution that is fast making the United States "a NATION OF MULATTOES AND MONGRELS," would he not *annihilate* slavery? To me nothing is more disgusting than to see my race bleached to a pallid sickly hue by the lust of those cruel and fastidious white men whose prejudices are so strong that they can't come in sight of a colored skin; ah no! his natural "prejudices" forbid it! Oh delicacy thou hast run mad, and chased thy sister chastity out of the bounds of the Southern States! Thou hast frightened the Doctor too, for not a word does he say about the virtue of ebon virgins—virgins reared for—. But I forbear, God knows the truth is appalling enough to make a devil start; disgraceful enough to crimson the face of the whole heavens and make the angels blush!

HENRY HIGHLAND GARNET (1815-1881)

Henry Highland Garnet was born on a plantation on the eastern shore of Maryland, the birthplace of such noted fugitives as Frederick Douglass and Harriet Tubman. Garnet's father, using the ruse of attending a funeral, drove his family and several other slaves in a covered wagon to Wilmington, where they were sheltered by Thomas Garrett, the Quaker Underground Railroad stationmaster. In New York City, Garnet received a fair education, having as his classmates Patrick Reason, who was to be one of the earliest Negro painters, Charles L. Reason, later a poet and teacher, Ira Aldridge, later to be the famous actor, James McCune Smith, and Samuel Ringgold Ward. Garnet was one of the Negro students at the school at Canaan, New Hampshire, which was broken up by irate farmers. He finished his higher education at Oneida Institute, New York. The Reverend Theodore Wright inspired Garnet to enter the ministry. An able and scholarly preacher, Garnet, like Ward, was bent toward preaching abolition rather than more orthodox gospel. His hatred of slavery was intensified by the blackbirders who broke up his New York home, searching for his fugitive father. After this event, Garnet walked Broadway, nearly crazed, armed with a clasp knife.

Garnet was frail and sickly; in later life his leg had to be amputated. His spirit, however, was indomitable. He printed an edition of David Walker's *Appeal* in 1848, containing a eulogistic biography of Walker, whose radicalism he had already favored in *An Address to the Slaves of the United States of America* (1843). This oration excited much antagonism among less radical abolitionists. Even Douglass thought it spoke "too much of physical force." Garnet defended himself bluntly to Mrs. Maria W. Chapman: " . . . the address to the slaves you seem to doom to the most fiery trials. And yet, madam, you have not seen that address—you have merely *heard* of it; nevertheless, you criticized it very severely . . . In a few days I hope to publish the address, then you can judge how much treason there is in it. In the meantime, be assured that there is one black

American who dares to speak boldly on the subject of universal liberty." Garnet died in Monrovia, Liberia, in 1881. Alexander Crummell, one of Garnet's classmates at the ill-fated New Hampshire school, wrote *The Eulogy of Henry Highland Garnet* (1882), a valuable biographical source.

An Address to the Slaves of the United States of America

BRETHREN AND FELLOW CITIZENS: Your brethren of the North, East, and West have been accustomed to meet together in National Conventions, to sympathize with each other, and to weep over your unhappy condition. In these meetings we have addressed all classes of the free, but we have never, until this time, sent a word of consolation and advice to you. We have been contented in sitting still and mourning over your sorrows, earnestly hoping that before this day your sacred liberties would have been restored. But, we have hoped in vain. Years have rolled on, and tens of thousands have been borne on streams of blood and tears to the shores of eternity. While you have been oppressed, we have also been partakers with you; nor can we be free while you are enslaved. We, therefore, write to you as being bound with you.

Many of you are bound to us, not only by the ties of a common humanity, but we are connected by the more tender relations of parents, wives, husbands, and sisters, and friends. As such we most affectionately address you.

Slavery has fixed a deep gulf between you and us, and while it shuts out from you the relief and consolation which your friends would willingly render, it afflicts and persecutes you with a fierceness which we might not expect to see in the fiends of hell. But still the Almighty Father of mercies has left us a glimmering ray of hope, which shines out like a lone star in a cloudy sky. Mankind are becoming wiser, and better—the oppressor's power is fading, and you, every day, are becoming better informed, and more numerous. Your grievances, brethren, are many. We shall not attempt, in this short address, to present to the world all the dark catalogue of the nation's sins, which have been committed upon an innocent people. Nor is it indeed necessary, for you feel them from day to day, and all the civilized world looks upon them with amazement.

Two hundred and twenty-seven years ago the first of our injured race were brought to the shores of America. They came not with glad spirits to select their homes in the New World. They came not with their own consent, to find an unmolested enjoyment of the blessings of this fruitful soil. The first dealings they had with men calling themselves Christians exhibited to them the worst features of corrupt and sordid hearts: and convinced them that no cruelty is too great, no villainy and no robbery too abhorrent for even enlightened men to perform, when influenced by avarice and lust. Neither did they come flying upon the wings of Liberty to a land of freedom. But they came with broken hearts, from their beloved native land, and were doomed to unrequited toil and deep degradation. Nor did the evil of their bondage end at their emancipation by death. Succeeding generations inherited their chains, and millions have come from eternity into time, and have returned again to the world of spirits, cursed and ruined by American slavery.

The propagators of the system, or their immediate successors, very soon discovered its growing evil, and its tremendous wickedness, and secret promises were made to destroy it. The gross inconsistency of a people holding slaves, who had themselves "ferried o'er the wave" for freedom's sake, was too apparent to be entirely overlooked. The voice of Freedom cried, "Emancipate your slaves." Humanity supplicated with tears for the deliverance of the children of Africa. Wisdom urged her solemn plea. The bleeding captive plead his innocence, and pointed to Christianity who stood weeping at the cross. Jehovah frowned upon the nefarious institution, and thunderbolts, red with vengeance, struggled to leap forth to blast the guilty wretches who maintained it. But all was vain. Slavery had stretched its dark wings of death over the land, the Church stood silently by—the priests prophesied falsely, and the people loved to have it so. Its throne is established, and now it reigns triumphant.

Nearly three millions of your fellow-citizens are prohibited by law and public opinion (which in this country is stronger than law) from reading the Book of Life. Your intellect has been destroyed as much as possible, and every ray of light they have attempted to shut out from your minds. The oppressors themselves have become involved in the ruin. They have become weak, sensual, and rapacious—they have cursed you—they have cursed themselves—they have cursed the earth which they have trod.

The colonies threw the blame upon England. They said that the mother country entailed the evil upon them, and they would rid themselves of it if they could. The world thought they were sincere, and the philanthropic pitied them. But time soon tested their sincerity. In a few years the colonists grew strong, and severed themselves from the British Government. Their independence was declared, and they took their station among the sovereign powers of the earth. The declaration was a glorious document. Sages admired it, and the patriotic of every nation reverenced the God-like sentiments which it contained. When the power of Government returned to their hands, did they emancipate the slaves? No; they rather added new links to our chains. Were they ignorant of the principles of liberty? Certainly they were not. The sentiments of their revolutionary orators fell in burning eloquence upon their hearts, and with one voice they cried, LIBERTY OR DEATH. Oh, what a sentence was that! It ran from soul to soul like electric fire, and nerved the arms of thousands to fight in the holy cause of Freedom. Among the diversity of opinions that are entertained in regard to physical resistance, there are but a few found to gainsay the stern declaration. We are among those who do not.

SLAVERY! How much misery is comprehended in that single word. What mind is there that does not shrink from its direful effects? Unless the image of God be obliterated from the soul, all men cherish the love of liberty. The nice discerning political economist does not regard the sacred right more than the untutored African who roams in the wilds of Congo. Nor has the one more right to the full enjoyment of his freedom than the other. In every man's mind the good seeds of liberty are planted, and he who brings his fellow down so low, as to make him contented with a condition of slavery, commits the highest crime against God and man. Brethren, your oppressors aim to do this. They endeavor to make you as much like brutes as possible. When they have blinded the eyes of your mind—when they have embittered the sweet waters of life—when they have shut out the light which shines from the word of God—then, and not till then, has American slavery done its perfect work.

TO SUCH DEGRADATION IT IS SINFUL IN THE EXTREME FOR YOU TO MAKE VOLUNTARY SUBMISSION. The divine commandments you are in duty bound to reverence and obey. If you do not obey them, you will surely meet with the displeasure of the Almighty. He requires you to love Him supremely, and your neighbor as yourself—to keep the Sabbath day holy—to search the Scriptures—and bring up your children with respect for His laws, and to worship no other God but Him. But slavery sets all these at nought, and hurls defiance in the face of Jehovah. The forlorn condition in which you are placed does not destroy your obligation to God. You are not certain of heaven, because you allow yourselves to remain in a state of slavery, where you cannot obey the commandments of the Sovereign of the universe. If the ignorance of slavery is a passport to heaven, then it is a blessing, and no curse, and you should rather desire its perpetuity than its abolition. God will not receive slavery, or ignorance, nor any other state of mind, for love and obedience to Him. Your condition does not absolve you from moral obligation. The diabolical injustice by which your liberties are cloven down, NEITHER GOD NOR ANGELS, OR JUST MEN, COMMAND YOU TO SUFFER FOR A SINGLE MOMENT. THEREFORE IT IS YOUR SOLEMN AND IMPERATIVE DUTY TO USE EVERY MEANS, BOTH MORAL, INTELLECTUAL, AND PHYSICAL, THAT PROMISES SUCCESS. If a band of heathen men should attempt to enslave a race of Christians, and to place their children under the influence of some false religion, surely Heaven would frown upon the men who would not resist such aggression, even to death. If, on the other hand, a band of Christians should attempt to enslave a race of heathen men, and to entail slavery upon them, and to keep them in heathenism in the midst of Christianity, the God of heaven would smile upon every effort which the injured might make to disenthral themselves.

Brethren, it is as wrong for your lordly oppressors to keep you in slavery as it was for the man thief to steal our ancestors from the coast of Africa. You should therefore now use the same manner of resistance as would have been just in our ancestors when the bloody footprints of the first remorseless soul-thief was placed upon the shores of our fatherland. The humblest peasant is as free in the sight of God as the proudest monarch that ever swayed a sceptre. Liberty is a spirit sent out from God, and like its great Author, is no respecter of persons.

Brethren, the time has come when you must act for yourselves. It is an old and true saying that, "if hereditary bondmen would be free, they must themselves strike the blow." You can plead your own cause, and do the work of emancipation better than any others. The nations of the Old World are moving in the great cause of universal freedom, and some of them at least will, ere long, do you justice. The combined powers of Europe have placed their broad seal of disapprobation upon the African slave-trade. But in the slaveholding parts of the United States the trade is as brisk as ever. They buy and sell you as though you were brute beasts. The North has done much—her opinion of slavery in the abstract is known. But in regard to the South, we adopt the opinion of the *New York Evangelist*—"We have advanced so far, that the cause apparently waits for a more effectual door to be thrown open than has been yet." We are about to point you to that more effectual door. Look around you, and behold the bosoms of your loving wives heaving with untold agonies! Hear the cries of your poor children! Remember the stripes your father bore. Think of the torture and disgrace of your noble mothers. Think of your wretched sisters, loving virtue and purity, as they are driven into concubinage and are exposed to the unbridled lusts of incarnate devils. Think of the undying glory that hangs around the ancient name of Africa—and forget not that you are native-born citizens, and as such you are justly entitled to all the rights that are granted to the freest. Think how many tears you have poured out upon the soil which you have cultivated with unrequited toil and enriched with your blood; and then go to your lordly enslavers and tell them plainly, that you *are determined to be free*. Appeal to their sense of justice, and tell them that they have no more right to oppress you than you have to enslave them. Entreat them to remove the grievous burdens which they have imposed upon you, and to remunerate you for your labor. Promise them renewed diligence in the cultivation of the soil, if they will render to you an equivalent for your services. Point them to the increase of happiness and prosperity in the British West Indies since the Act of Emancipation. Tell them in language which they cannot misunderstand of the exceeding sinfulness of slavery, and of a future judgement, and of the righteous retributions of an indignant God. Inform them that all you desire is FREEDOM, and that nothing else will suffice. Do this, and forever after cease to toil for the heartless tyrants, who give you no other reward but stripes and abuse. If they then commence work of death, they, and not you, will be responsible for the consequences. You had far better all die—*die immediately,* than live slaves, and entail your wretchedness upon your posterity. If you would be free in this generation, here is your only hope. However much you and all of us may desire it, there is not much hope of redemption without the shedding of blood. If you must bleed, let it come at once—rather *die freemen than live to be the slaves*. It is impossible, like the children of Israel, to make a grand exodus from the land of bondage. The Pharaohs are on both sides of the blood-red waters! You cannot move *en masse* to the dominions of the British Queen—nor can you pass through Florida and overrun Texas, and at last find peace in Mexico. The propagators of American slavery are spending their blood and treasure that they may plant the black flag in the heart of Mexico and riot in the halls of the Montezumas. In language of the Reverend Robert Hall, when addressing the volunteers of Bristol, who were rushing forth to repel the invasion of Napoleon, who threatened to lay waste the fair homes of England, "Religion is too much interested in your behalf not to shed over you her most gracious influences."

* * * * *

It is in your power so to torment the God-cursed slaveholders that they will be glad to let you go free. If the scale was turned, and black men were the masters and white men the slaves, every destructive agent and element would be employed to lay the oppressor low. Danger and death would hang over their heads day and night. Yes, the tyrants would meet with plagues more terrible than those of Pharaoh. But you are a patient people. You act as though you were made for the special use of these devils. You act as though your daughters were born to pamper the lusts of your masters and overseers. And worse than all, you tamely submit while your lords tear your wives from your embraces and defile them before your eyes. In the name of God, we ask, are you men? Where is the blood of your fathers? Has it all run out of your veins? Awake, awake; millions of voices are calling you! Your dead fathers speak to you from their graves. Heaven, as with a voice of thunder, calls on you to arise from the dust.

Let your motto be resistance! *resistance!* RESISTANCE! No oppressed people have ever secured their liberty without resistance. What kind of resistance you had better make you must decide by the circumstances that surround you, and according to the suggestion of expediency. Brethren, adieu! Trust in the living God. Labor for the peace of the human race, and remember that you are FOUR MILLIONS!

FREDERICK DOUGLASS (1817-1895)

Shortly after his escape from Maryland, Frederick Douglass (see also pp. 17, 719) addressed a large antislavery meeting at Nantucket in 1841. His book learning was still meager and his only experience in public speaking had been before gatherings of New Bedford Negroes, Nevertheless his speech was electrifying. Parker Pillsbury wrote of the occasion: "When the young man closed, late in the evening though none seemed to know nor to care for the hour, Mr. Garrison rose to make the concluding address. I think he never before nor afterwards felt more profoundly the sacredness of his mission . . . I surely never saw him more deeply, more divinely inspired. His last question was this: 'Shall such a man ever be sent back to slavery from the soil of old Massachusetts?'—this time uttered with all the power of voice of which Garrison was capable . . . Almost the whole assembly sprang with one accord to their feet, and the walls and roof of the Athenaeum seemed to shudder with the 'No, No!' loud and long-continued . . ."

So began Douglass' long oratorical career which was to rank him with the greatest of nineteenth-century orators. So began, also, his alliance with Garrison. This was to last until he differed from his tutor, refusing to believe that the Constitution was proslavery and that politics was futile in the antislavery struggle. Douglass' secession from the Garrisonians came in 1847 when he started his own weekly, *The North Star.* In spite of journalistic quarrels between the two men, both masters of the sharp attack, Douglass retained his friendship and admiration for Garrison. Though first introduced to American audiences as "a graduate from the peculiar institution with his diploma written on his back," Douglass had been advised to stick to the facts and let his abolitionist white friends "take care of the philosophy." But since he was doing his own reading and thinking, it was not long before he was stating both fact and philosophy, and was denouncing wrongs as well as narrating them.

During his first sojourn of two years in the British Isles Douglass was much in demand as an orator. Contact with leading liberals awoke a consciousness of his own powers. Among the English he made many converts to abolition and many personal friends who raised money to ransom him from slavery and to enable him to publish his own journal.

There is no collected edition of Douglass' numerous speeches, though many were issued. His first published speech was printed by proslavery men as *Abolition Fanaticism in New York* (1847). Typical of his speeches are *Lectures on American Slavery* (1851); the Fourth of July *Oration* (1852); *Two Speeches of Frederick Douglass* (one of them on the Dred Scott case) (1857); two speeches defending himself against Garrisonians, *The Anti-Slavery Movement* (1855) and *The Constitution of the United States: Is It Pro-Slavery, or Anti-Slavery?* (1860); a speech appealing for Negro enlistments in the Civil War, in 1863; *What the Black Man Wants* (1865); *Oration Delivered on the Occasion of the Unveiling of the Freedmen's Monument. In Memory of Abraham Lincoln, in Lincoln Park, Washington, D. C., April 14, 1876; and John Brown* (1881).

By the time of his open letter to Auld, Douglass had written his *Narrative* (1845) and had spoken over the length and breadth of the British Isles and the northern United States. The second selection, the Speech at Faneuil Hall (1849), was one of Douglass' successful thrusts at colonization. It is of interest to compare the bold conclusion of this speech with Garnet's *Address* (see p. 601), which Douglass had criticized as extreme.

Garrison spoke of Douglass as "one in physical proportions and stature commanding and exact—in intellect richly endowed—in natural eloquence a prodigy." As an orator, Douglass was master of a powerfully moving style. He told of events of slavery with startling vividness. His indignation seldom got out of control; his invective was not so melodramatic as that of many of his fellows. He made frequent use of irony and sarcasm; at times he burlesques his opponents with apt mimicry. He knew the inside of slavery better than any other Negro orator, and he could drive home his message as well as any white orator. The sonority of his eloquence is out of fashion today, but the logic and power remain as literary excellences. The following appeared in the *Liberator,* Sept. 22, 1848.

Letter to His Master

THOMAS AULD:

Sir—The long and intimate, though by no means friendly relation which unhappily subsisted between you and myself, leads me to hope that you will easily account for the great liberty which I now take in addressing you in this open and public manner. The same fact may possibly remove any disagreeable surprise which you may experience on again finding your name coupled with mine, in any other way than in an advertisement, accurately describing my person, and offering a large sum for my arrest. In thus dragging you again before the public, I am aware that I shall subject myself to no inconsiderable amount of censure. I shall probably be charged with an unwarrantable, if not a wanton and reckless disregard of the rights and proprieties of private life. There are those North as well as South who entertain a much higher respect for rights which are merely conventional, than they do for rights which are personal and essential. Not a few there are in our country, who, while they have no scruples against robbing the laborer of the hard earned results of his patient industry, will be shocked by the extremely indelicate manner of bringing your name before the public. . . .

I have selected this day on which to address you, because it is the anniversary of my emancipation; and knowing of no better why, I am led to this as the best mode of celebrating that truly important event. Just ten years ago this beautiful September morning, yon bright sun beheld me a slave—a poor, degraded chattel—trembling at the sound of your voice, lamenting that I was a man, and wishing myself a brute. The hopes which I had treasured up for weeks of a safe and successful escape from your grasp, were powerfully confronted at this last hour by dark clouds of doubt and fear, making my person shake and my bosom to heave with the heavy contest between hope and fear. I have no words to describe to you the deep agony of soul which I experienced on that never to be forgotten morning—(for I left by daylight). I was making a leap in the dark. The probabilities, so far as I could by reason determine them, were stoutly against the undertaking. The preliminaries and precautions I had adopted previously, all worked badly. I was like one going to war without weapons—ten chances of defeat to one of victory. One in whom I had confided, and one who had promised me assistance, appalled by fear at the trial hour, deserted me, thus leaving the responsibility of success or failure solely with myself. You, sir, can never know my feelings. As I look back to them, I can scarcely realize that I have passed through a scene so trying. Trying however as they were, and gloomy as was the prospect, thanks be to the Most High, who is ever the God of the oppressed, at the moment which was to determine my whole earthly career. His grace was sufficient, my mind was made up. I embraced the golden opportunity, took the morning tide at the flood, and a free man, young, active and strong, is the result. . . .

Since I left you, I have had a rich experience. I have occupied stations which I never dreamed of when a slave. Three out of the ten years since I left you, I spent as a common laborer on the wharves of New Bedford, Massachusetts. It was there I earned my first free dollar. It was mine. I could spend it as I pleased. I could buy hams or herring with it, without asking any odds of any body. That was a precious dollar to me. You remember when I used to make seven or eight, or even nine dollars a week in Baltimore, you would take every cent of it from me every Saturday night, saying that I belonged to you, and my earnings also. I never liked this conduct on your part—to say the best, I thought it a little mean. I would not have served you so. But let that pass. I was a little awkward about counting money in New England fashion when I first landed in New Bedford. I like to have betrayed myself several times. I caught myself saying phip, for fourpence; and at one time a man actually charged me with being a runaway, whereupon I was silly enough to become one by running away from him, for I was greatly afraid he might adopt measures to give me again into slavery, a condition I then dreaded more than death.

I soon, however, learned to count money, as well as to make it, and got on swimmingly. I married soon after leaving you: in fact, I was engaged to be married before I left you; and instead of finding my companion a burden, she was truly a helpmeet. She went to live at service, and I to work on the wharf, and though we toiled hard the first winter, we never lived more happily. After remaining in New Bedford for three years, I met with Wm. Lloyd Garrison, a person of whom you have *possibly* heard, as he is pretty generally known among slave-holders. He put it into my head that I might make myself serviceable to the cause of the slave by devoting a portion of my time to telling my own sorrows, and those of other slaves which had come under my observation. This was the commencement of a higher state of existence than any to which I had ever aspired. I was thrown into society the most pure, enlightened and benevolent that the country affords. Among these I have never forgotten you, but have invariably made you the topic of conversation—thus giving you all the notoriety I could do. I need not tell you that the opinion formed of you in these circles, is far from being favorable. They have little respect for your honesty, and less for your religion.

But I was going on to relate to you something of my interesting experience. I had not long enjoyed the excellent society to which I have referred, before the light of its excellence exerted a beneficial influence on my mind and heart. Much of my early dislike of white persons was removed, and their manners, habits and customs, so entirely unlike what I had been used to in the kitchen-quarters on the plantations of the South, fairly charmed me, and gave me a strong disrelish for the coarse and degrading customs of my former condition. I therefore made an effort so to improve my mind and deportment, as to be somewhat fitted to the station to which I seemed almost providentially called. The transition from degradation to respectability was indeed great, and to get from one to the other without carrying some marks of one's former condition, is truly a difficult matter. I would not have you think that I am now entirely clear of all plantation peculiarities, but my friends here, while they entertain the strongest dislike to them, regard me with that charity to which my past life somewhat entitles me, so that my condition in this respect is exceedingly pleasant. So far as my domestic affairs are concerned, I can boast of as comfortable a dwelling as your own. I have an industrious and neat companion, and four dear children—the oldest a girl of nine years, and three fine boys, the oldest eight, the next six, and the youngest four years old. The three oldest are now going regularly to school—two can read and write, and the other can spell with tolerable correctness words of two syllables: Dear fellows! they are all in comfortable beds, and are sound asleep, perfectly secure under my own roof. There are no slaveholders here to rend my heart by snatching them from my arms, or blast a mother's dearest hopes by tearing them from her bosom. These dear children are ours—not to work up into rice, sugar and tobacco, but to watch over, regard, and protect, and to rear them up in the nurture and admonition of the gospel—to train them up in the paths of wisdom and virtue, and, as far as we can to make them useful to the world and to themselves. Oh! sir, a slaveholder never appears to me so completely an agent of hell, as when I think of and look upon my dear children. It is then that my feelings rise above my control. I meant to have said more with respect to my own prosperity and happiness, but thoughts and feelings which this recital has quickened unfit me to proceed further in that direction. The grim horrors of slavery rise in all their ghastly terror before me, the wails of millions pierce my heart, and chill my blood. I remember the chain, the gag, the bloody whip, the death-like gloom overshadowing the broken spirit of the fettered bondman, the appalling liability of his being torn away from wife and children, and sold like a beast in the market. Say not that this is a picture of fancy. You well know that I wear stripes on my back inflicted by your direction; and that you, while we were brothers in the same church, caused this right hand, with which I am now penning this letter, to be closely tied to my left, and my person dragged at the pistol's mouth, fifteen miles, from the Bay side to Easton to be sold like a beast in the market, for the alleged crime of intending to escape from your possession. All this and more you remember, and know to be perfectly true, not only of yourself, but of nearly all of the slaveholders around you.

At this moment, you are probably the guilty holder of at least three of my own dear sisters, and my only brother in bondage. These you regard as your property. They are recorded on your ledger, or perhaps have been sold to human flesh mongers, with a view to filling your own ever-hungry purse. Sir, I desire to know how and where these dear sisters are. Have you sold them? or are they still in your possession? What has become of them? are they living or dead? And my dear old grand-mother, whom you turned out like an old horse, to die in the woods—is she still alive? Write and let me know all about them. If my grandmother be still alive, she is of no service to you, for by this time she must be nearly eighty years old—too old to be cared for by one to whom she has ceased to be of service, send her to me at Rochester, or bring her to Philadelphia, and it shall be the crowning happiness of my life to take care of her in her old age. Oh! she was to me a mother, and a father, so far as hard toil for my comfort could make her such. Send me my grandmother! that I may watch over and take care of her in her old age. And my sisters, let me know all about them. I would write to them, and learn all I want to know of them, without disturbing you in any way, but that, through your unrighteous conduct, they have been entirely deprived of the power to read and write. You have kept them in utter ignorance, and have therefore robbed them of the sweet enjoyments of writing or receiving letters from absent friends and relatives. Your wickedness and cruelty committed in this respect on your fellow-creatures, are greater than all the stripes you have laid upon my back, or theirs. It is an outrage upon the soul—a war upon the immortal spirit, and one

for which you must give account at the bar of our common Father
and Creator. . . .

I will now bring this letter to a close, you shall hear from me again
unless you let me hear from you. I intend to make use of you as a
weapon with which to assail the system of slavery—as a means of concentrating public attention on the system, and deepening their horror
of trafficking in the souls and bodies of men. I shall make use of you
as a means of exposing the character of the American church and
clergy—and as a means of bringing this guilty nation with yourself
to repentance. In doing this I entertain no malice towards you personally. There is no roof under which you would be more safe than
mine, and there is nothing in my house which you might need for
your comfort, which I would not readily grant. Indeed, I should esteem
it a privilege, to set you an example as to how mankind ought to treat
each other.

I am your fellow man, but not your slave,

FREDERICK DOUGLASS.

Speech in Faneuil Hall, June 8, 1849 [1]

MR. CHAIRMAN, LADIES AND GENTLEMEN: I never rise to speak in
Faneuil Hall without a deep sense of my want of ability to do justice
to the subject upon which I undertake to speak. I can do a pretty
good business, some have said, in the country school houses in Western
New York and elsewhere; but when I come before the people of Boston in Faneuil Hall, I feel my exceeding weakness. I am all the more
embarrassed this evening, because I have to speak to you in respect
to a subject concerning which an apology seems to be demanded. I
allude to the subject of the American Colonization Society—a subject
which has had a large measure of anti-slavery attention, and been long
since disposed of at the hands of Wm. Lloyd Garrison. The only
apology that I can make for calling attention to it this evening is that
it has had a sort of "revival" of late, through the agency of a man whom
I presume a large portion of this audience esteem and admire. I allude
to the Honorable Henry Clay of Kentucky. (Applause.) Though not
a Yankee, you see I guessed correctly. I have presumed rightly that
you esteem and admire that gentleman. Now, if you admire Mr. Clay,
of course you would like to know all about him. You would like, of
course, to hear whatever can be said of him, and said fairly, although
a black man may presume to say it.

[1] *Liberator,* June 8, 1849.

Mr. Clay has recently given to the world a letter, purporting to advocate the emancipation of the slaves of Kentucky. That letter has been extensively published in New England as well as other parts of the United States; and in almost every instance where a Whig paper has spoken of the letter it has done so in terms of high approval. The plan which Mr. Clay proposes is one which seems to meet almost the universal assent of the Whig party at the North; and many religious papers have copied the article, and spoken in terms of high commendation of the humanity, of the clear-sightedness and philanthropy of Henry Clay. Now, my friends, I am going to speak to you in a manner that, unless you allow your reason and not your prejudice to prevail, will provoke from you demonstrations of disapprobation. I beg of you, then, to hear me calmly—without prejudice or opposition. You, it must be remembered, have in your hands all the power in this land. I stand here not only in a minority, but identified with a class whom everybody can insult with impunity. Surely, the ambition for superiority must be great indeed in honorable men to induce them to insult a poor black man, whom the basest fellow in the street can insult with impunity. Keep this in mind, and hear what I have to say with regard to Mr. Clay's letter, and his position as a slaveholder.

The letter of Mr. Clay commences in a manner that gives promise to the reader that he shall find it a consistent, straightforward anti-slavery document. It commences by refuting, with one or two strokes of the pen, the vast cart-loads of sophistry piled up by Mr. Calhoun and others in favor of perpetual slavery. He shows clearly that Mr. Calhoun's theory of slavery, if admitted to be sound, would enslave the whites as readily as it enslaves the blacks—this would follow necessarily. Glancing at the question of the natural inferiority of the colored man, he says: "Admitting a question he does not raise—admitting that the whites of this country are superior to the blacks, the fact devolves upon the former the duty of enlightening, instructing and improving the condition of the latter." These are noble sentiments, worthy of the heart and head of a great and good man. But how does Mr. Clay propose to carry out this plan? He goes on to state that, in carrying out his proposed plan of gradual emancipation, great care should be taken that the rights and interests of the slaveholder should not be jeopardized. He proceeds to state that the utmost caution and prudence should guide the hand that strikes down slavery in Kentucky. With reference to emancipation, he affirms that it should not commence until the year 1885. The plan is that all children born of slave parents in Kentucky after the year 1860 shall be free after arriving at the age of twenty-five. He sets, therefore, the day of emancipation beyond the average length of the slave's life, for a generation of slaves in the far South dies out in seven years. But how would he have these children of slave parents free? Not free to work for themselves—not free to live on the soil that they have cultivated with their own hard hands—that they have nourished with their best blood, and toiled over and beautified and adorned—but that then they shall be let out under an agent of the State for three long years, to raise one hundred and fifty dollars with which to pay the price of their own expatriation from their family and friends. (Voices—"Shame!")

I hear the cry of shame—yes, it is a deep and damning shame. He declares in that letter that not only shall these emancipated slaves work three years, but that he, Mr. Clay, will oppose any measure for emancipation without the expatriation of the emancipated slaves. Just look at the peculiar operation of this plan. Let us suppose that it is adopted, and that in the year 1860 it commences. All children born of slave parents are to be free in the year 1888. It is well known that all persons in the South have contracted marriages long before this period, and have become parents, some having children from one to four years of age. Henry Clay's plan is that when these persons arrive at the age of twenty-eight, these parents shall be torn away from their tender children, and hurried off to Liberia or somewhere else; and that the children taken from these parents, before they have become acquainted with the paternal relation, shall remain another twenty-eight years; and when they have remained that period, and have contracted matrimonial alliances, and become fathers and mothers, they, too, shall be taken from their children, the slaveholders having kept them at work for twenty-eight years, and hurried off to Liberia.

But a darker, baser feature than all these appears in this letter of Mr. Clay. It is this: He speaks of the loss which the slaveholder will be called on to experience by the emancipation of his slaves. But he says that even this trifling expenditure may be prevented by leaving the slaveholder the right to sell—to mortgage—to transfer his slave property any time during the twenty-five years. Only look at Henry Clay's generosity to the slaveholders of Kentucky. He has twenty-five long years during which to watch the slave markets of New Orleans, of Memphis, of Vicksburg and other Southern cities, and to watch the prices of cotton and rice and tobacco on the other side of the Atlantic, and as the prices rise there in these articles, he may expect a corresponding rise in the price of flesh in the slave markets, and then he can sell his slaves to the best advantage. Thus it is that the glorious State of Kentucky shall be made free, and yet her purse be made the heavier in consequence of it. This is not a proposition for emancipation, but

a proposition to Kentucky to sell off into the far Southern States—
and then hypocritically boast of being a free State, while almost every
slave born upon her soil remains a slave. And this is the plan of the
good Henry Clay, whom you esteem and admire so much. (Applause
and hisses.) You that like to hiss, if you had the chain on your own
limbs, and were pent up in Henry Clay's own quarter, and had free
access to Henry Clay's own meal-tub, I think would soon change your
tune. (Laughter.)

I want to say a word about the Colonization Society, of which
Henry Clay is President. He is President of nothing else. (Laughter.)
That Society is an old enemy of the colored people in this country.
Almost every respectable man belongs to it, either by direct membership
or by affinity. I meet with colonizationists everywhere; I met with a
number of them the other day, on board the steamer *Alida,* going f.om
Albany to New York. I wish to state my experience on board of that
steamer, and as it is becoming a subject of newspaper remark, it may
not be out of place to give my version of the story:—On Thursday
last, I took my passage on board the steamer *Alida,* as I have stated,
to go from Albany to New York. I happened to have, very contrary
to American taste and American prejudices and customs, in my company, a couple of friends from England—persons who had not been
ashamed—nor had they cause to be ashamed from any feeling that
exists in that country against the colored man—of being found on equal
social terms with him in the city of London. They happen now to be
sojourning in this country; and as if unaware of the prejudice existing
in this country, or, if aware, perfectly regardless of it, they accompanied
me on the steamer, and shared, of course, my society, or permitted me
to share theirs on the passage to New York. About noon, I went into
the cabin, and inquired of one of the waiters if we could have dinner.
The answer was, we could. They had on a sign on each side of the
captain's office words to this effect: "Meals can be received in the cabin
at any hour during the day, by application to the steward." I made the
application, and expected, of course, that dinner would be forthcoming
at the time appointed. The bell rung—and though I do not know as it
was altogether wise and prudent, I took a lady on each arm—for my
friends were white ladies, you must know—and moved forward to the
cabin. The fact of their being white ladies will enable you more readily
to understand the cause of the intensity of hate displayed towards me.
I went below forgetting all about my complexion, the curl of my hair,
or the flatness of my nose, only remembering I had two elbows and a
stomach, and was exceedingly hungry. (Laughter.) I walked below, as
I have said, and took my seat at the table, supposing that the table was
the place where a man should eat.

I had been there but a few moments, before I observed a large number of American gentlemen rising up gradually—for we are gradualists in this country—and moving off to another table, on the other side. But feeling I was there on my own responsibility, and that these gentlemen could not eat dinner for me, and I must do it for myself, I preferred to sit still, unmoved by what was passing around me. I had been there but a few moments, when a white man—after the order of American white men—for I would say, for your consolation, that you are growing darker and darker every year—the steward came up to me in a very curious manner, and said, "Yer must get up from that table." (Laughter.) I demanded by what authority he ordered me from the table. "Well," said he, "yer know the rule?" "Sir," said I, "I know nothing of your rules. I know that the rule is, that the passengers can receive their meals at any hour of the day on applying to the steward." Says he, "Now, it is no use for yer to talk, yer must leave." (Laughter.) "But where is the rule?" "Well," said he, "yer cannot get dinner on any boat on this river." I told him I went up the river in the *Confidence,* and took dinner, and no remark had been made. "Well," said he, "what yer can do on the *Confidence,* yer can't do on the *Alida.* (Laughter.) Are yer going to get up?" "No, sir," said I. "Well," says he, "I will have you up." So off he goes to the upper deck, and brings down the captain, mate, clerk, and two or three hands. I sat still during the time of his absence; but finding they were mustering pretty strong, and remembering I had but one coat, and not caring to have it torn, and feeling I had borne a sufficient testimony against their unrighteous treatment, I arose from the table, and walked to the other end of the cabin, in company with my friends. A scene then occurred which I shall never forget; not because of its impudence, but because of its malignity. A large number of American ladies and gentlemen, seated around the table on the other side of the cabin, the very moment we walked away, gave three cheers for the captain, and applauded in the most uproarious manner the steward, for having driven two ladies and one gentleman from the table, and deprived them of dinner.

Mr. Garrison—That is a fact for Europe.

Mr. Douglass—They drove us from the table, and gave three cheers for the captain for driving us away. I looked around on the audience there assembled, to see if I could detect one line of generous magnanimity on any face—any indignation manifested against the outrage that had been perpetrated upon me and my friends. But not a look, not a word, not the slightest expression of disapprobation in any part of the vessel. Now, I have traveled in England, Ireland, and Scotland—I mention this, not by way of boast, but because I want to contrast the freedom of our glorious country—and it is a glorious one, after all—with that of other countries through which I have traveled—by railroads, in highways and byways, steamboats, stagecoaches, and every imaginable kind of vehicle—I have stayed at some of the first hotels in London, Liverpool, Edinburgh, Glasgow, Dublin, and elsewhere—and I must say to you, good Americans, that I never, in any of those cities or towns, received the first mark, or heard the first word of disapprobation on account of the color of my skin. I may tell you that one of the ladies with me on the steamboat, though not a believer in the right of women to speak in public, was so excited and so indignant at the outrage perpetrated, that she went to the American captain and told him she had heard much of the country, much of the gallantry of American gentlemen—that they would be willing to rise from their seats to allow a lady to be seated—and she was very happy in having the opportunity of witnessing a manifestation of American gallantry and American courtesy. I do think I saw one neck hang when this rebuke was administered. (Applause.)

Most of the passengers were of the baser sort, very much like some Western men—dark-complexioned, lean, lank, pinched up, about the ugliest set of men I ever saw in my life. (Laughter.) I went to the steward about two hours after they had cleared off the dinner table for those hungry, wolfish-looking people. (Laughter.) My dear friends, if you had seen them, you would have agreed with me. I then inquired of the steward if now, after this hungry multitude had been fed, we could have a cup of coffee and a biscuit. Said he—"Who are you? If you are the servant of those ladies, you shall have what you want." I thought that was kind, anyhow. "Yes," said I, "I am their most humble servant." (Great laughter.) "Well," said he, "what are you walking about on deck with them for, if you are their servant?" I told him they were very courteous to me—putting him off in that way. He then told me if I did not get out of the cabin, he would split my head open. He was rather a diminutive being, and would not have been a mouthful for anything like a Tom Hyer man. (Applause.) However, seeing his Anglo-Saxon blood was up, I thought I would move off; but tapping him on the shoulder, I told him I wanted to give him a piece of advice: "I am a passenger, you are a servant; and therefore you should always consult the wants of the passengers." (Laughter.) He finally told me he was ready to give me my dinner in the capacity of a servant, but not otherwise. This acknowledgment told the whole story of American prejudice. There were two or three slaveholders on board. One was a lady from New Orleans; rather a dark-looking person—for individuals from that quarter are dark, except the blacks, and they are getting lighter. (Laughter.) This woman was perfectly horrified with my appearance, and she said to gentlemen standing by, that she was really afraid to be near me, and that I would draw a bowie knife. Indeed, she had liked to have fainted. This woman, I learned from good authority, owned three hundred slaves in Louisiana; and yet she was afraid of a black man, and expected every moment I would attempt to commit violence on her. At the time she was affecting this horror of a Negro, she was being waited on at the table by colored men. It was, "Waiter, come here!" and "Waiter, go there!" and there they were actually, cutting up the meat, standing right over it, quite near those white persons who really shouted when I was driven out.

This tells the whole story. You have no prejudice against blacks— no more than against any other color—but it is against the black man appearing as the colored gentleman. He is then a contradiction of your theory of natural inferiority in the colored race. It was not in consequence of my complexion that I was driven out of the cabin, for I could have remained there as a servant; but being there as a gentleman, having paid my own passage, and being in company with intelligent, refined persons, was what awakened the hatred, and brought down upon me the insulting manifestations I have alluded to.

It is because the American Colonization Society cherishes and fosters this feeling of hatred against the black man, that I am opposed to it. And I am especially disposed to. speak out my opposition to this colonization scheme to-night, because not only of the renewed interest excited in the colonization scheme by the efforts of Henry Clay and others, but because there is a lecturer in the shape of the Rev. Mr. Miller, of New Jersey, now in England, soliciting funds for our expatriation from this country, and going about trying to organize a society, and to create an impression in favor of removing us from this country. I would ask you, my friends, if this is not mean and impudent in the extreme, for one class of Americans to ask for the removal of another class?

I feel, sir, I have as much right in this country as any other man. I feel that the black man in this land has as much right to stay in this land as the white man. Consider the matter in the light of possession in this country. Our connection with this country is contemporaneous with your own. From the beginning of the existence of this people, as a people, the colored man has had a place upon the American soil. To be sure, he was not driven from his home in pursuit of a greater liberty than he enjoyed at home, like the Pilgrim fathers; but in the same year that the Pilgrims were landing in this State, slaves were landing on the James River, in Virginia. We feel on this score, then, that we have as much right here as any other class of people.

We have other claims to being regarded and treated as American citizens. Some of our number have fought and bled for this country, and we only ask to be treated as well as those who have fought against it. We are lovers of this country, and we only ask to be treated as well as the haters of it. We are not only told by Americans to go out of our native land to Africa, and there enjoy our freedom—for we must go there in order to enjoy it—but Irishmen newly landed on our soil, who know nothing of our institutions, nor of the history of our country, whose toil has not been mixed with the soil of the country as ours —have the audacity to propose our removal from this, the land of our birth. For my part, I mean, for one, to stay in this country; I have made up my mind to live among you. I had a kind offer, when I was in England, of a little house and lot, and the free use of it, on the banks of the river Eden. I could easily have stayed there, if I had sought for ease, undisturbed, unannoyed by American skin-aristocracy; for it is an aristocracy of skin (applause)—those passengers on board the *Alida* only got their dinners that day in virtue of color; if their skins had been of my color, they would have had to fast all day. Whatever denunciations England may be entitled to on account of her treatment of Ireland and her own poor, one thing can be said of her, that no man in that country, or in any of her dominions, is treated as less than a man on account of his complexion. I could have lived there; but when I remembered this prejudice against color, as it is called, and slavery, and saw the many wrongs inflicted on my people at the North that ought to be combated and put down, I felt a disposition to lay aside ease, to turn my back on the kind offer of my friends, and to return among you—deeming it more noble to suffer along with my colored brethren, and meet these prejudices, than to live at ease, undisturbed, on the other side of the Atlantic. (Applause.) I had rather be here now, encountering this feeling, bearing my testimony against it, setting it at defiance, than to remain in England undisturbed. I have made up my mind wherever I go, I shall go as a man, and not as a slave. When I go on board of your steamboats, I shall always aim to be courteous and mild in my deportment towards all with whom I come in contact, at the same time firmly and constantly endeavoring to assert my equal rights as a man and a brother.

But the Colonization Society says this prejudice can never be overcome—that it is natural—God has implanted it. Some say so; others declare that it can only be removed by removing the cause, that is, by removing us to Liberia. I know this is false, from my own experience in this country. I remember that, but a few years ago, upon the railroads from New Bedford and Salem and in all parts of Massachusetts, a most unrighteous and proscriptive rule prevailed, by which colored men and women were subjected to all manner of indignity in the use of these conveyances. Antislavery men, however, lifted up their testimony against this principle from year to year; and from year to year, he whose name cannot be mentioned without receiving a round of applause, Wendell Phillips (applause) went abroad, exposing this proscription in the light of justice. What is the result? Not a single railroad can be found in any part of Massachusetts, where a colored man is treated and esteemed in any other light than that of a man and a traveller. Prejudice has given way and must give way. The fact that it is giving way proves that this prejudice is not invincible. The time was when it was expected that a colored man, when he entered a church in Boston, would go into the Jim Crow pew—and I believe such is the case now, to a large extent; but then there were those who would defend the custom. But you can scarcely get a defender of this proscription in New England now.

The history of the repeal of the intermarriage law shows that the prejudice against color is not invincible. The general manner in which white persons sit with colored persons shows plainly that the prejudice against color is not invincible. When I first came here, I felt the greatest possible diffidence of sitting with whites. I used to come up from the shipyard, where I worked, with my hands hardened with toil, rough and uncomely, and my movements awkward (for I was unacquainted with the rules of politeness), I would shrink back, and would not have taken my meals with the whites had they not pressed me to do so. Our president, in his earlier intercourse with me, taught me, by example, his abhorrence of this prejudice. He has, in my presence, stated to those who visited him, that if they did not like to sit at the table with me, they could have a separate one for themselves.

The time was, when I walked through the streets of Boston, I was liable to insult if in company with a white person. To-day I have passed in company with my white friends, leaning on their arm and they on mine, and yet the first word from any quarter on account of the color of my skin I have not heard. It is all false, this talk about the invincibility of prejudice against color. If any of you have it, and no doubt some of you have, I will tell you how to get rid of it. Commence to do something to elevate and improve and enlighten the colored man, and your prejudice will begin to vanish. The more you try to make a man of the black man, the more you will begin to think him a man. . . .

A word more. There are three millions of slaves in this land, held by the United States Government, under the sanction of the American Constitution, with all the compromises and guaranties contained in that instrument in favor of the slave system. Among those guaranties and compromises is one by which you, the citizens of Boston, have sworn, before God, that three millions of slaves shall be slaves or die—that your swords and bayonets and arms shall, at any time at the bidding of the slaveholder, through the legal magistrate or governor of a slave State, be at his service in putting down the slaves. With eighteen millions of freemen standing upon the quivering hearts of three millions of slaves, my sympathies, of course, must be with the oppressed. I am among them, and you are treading them beneath your feet. The weight of your influence, numbers, political combinations and religious organizations, and the power of your arms, rest heavily upon them, and serve at this moment to keep them in their chains. When I consider their condition—the history of the American people—how they bared their bosoms to the storm of British artillery, in order to resist simply a three-penny tea tax, and to assert their independence of the mother country—I say, in view of these things, I should welcome the intelligence to-morrow, should it come, that the slaves had risen in the South, and that the sable arms which had been engaged in beautifying and adorning the South were engaged in spreading death and devastation there. (Marked sensation.) There is a state of war at the South at this moment. The slaveholder is waging a war of aggression on the oppressed. The slaves are now under his feet. Why, you welcomed the intelligence from France, that Louis Phillippe had been barricaded in Paris—you threw up your caps in honor of the victory achieved by Republicanism over Royalty—you shouted aloud—"Long live the republic!"—and joined heartily in the watchword of "Liberty, Equality, Fraternity"—and should you not hail, with equal pleasure, the tidings from the South that the slaves had risen, and achieved for himself, against the iron-hearted slaveholder, what the republicans of France achieved against the royalists of France? (Great applause and some hissing.)

SAMUEL RINGGOLD WARD (1817-c. 1864)

When Samuel Ringgold Ward was three years old, his parents escaped from Maryland and brought him to New York. There he received something of an education, taught school a while, and became a preacher. One of his charges was a congregation of white worshipers in South Butler, N. Y. He was a tireless antislavery agent, a co-worker with Gerrit Smith. In 1851, because of his inflammatory speech-making at the rescue of the fugitive Jerry McHenry in Syracuse, even New York State became too hot a place for him, and he was forced to follow Jerry into Canada. He was thus lost to the anti-slavery movement in America, but continued to lecture in Canada and England. He died in Jamaica. His many orations were not printed completely; his only book is *The Autobiography of a Fugitive Slave* (1855). Ward's power was helped by humor and satire; Frederick Douglass was the only Negro orator who was considered to be his superior. Douglass said of him: "In depth of thought, fluency of speech, readiness of wit, logical exactness, and general intelligence, Samuel R. Ward has left no successor among the colored men amongst us . . ."

Speech on the Fugitive Slave Bill [1]

I AM HERE TO-NIGHT as a guest. You have met here to speak of the sentiments of a Senator of your State whose remarks you have the honor to repudiate. In the course of the remarks of the gentleman who preceded me, he has done us the favor to make honorable mention of a Senator of my own State—William H. Seward. (Three hearty cheers .were given for Senator Seward.)

I thank you for this manifestation of approbation of a man who has always stood head and shoulders above his party, and who has never receded from his position on the question of slavery. It was my happiness to receive a letter from him a few days since, in which he said he never would swerve from his position as the friend of freedom. (Applause.)

To be sure, I agree not with Senator Seward in politics, but when an individual stands up for the rights of men against slaveholders, I care not for party distinctions. He is my brother. (Loud cheers.)

We have here much of common cause and interest in this matter. That infamous bill of Mr. Mason, of Virginia, proves itself to be like all other propositions presented by Southern men. It finds just

[1] *Liberator,* April 5, 1850.

enough of Northern dough-faces who are willing to pledge themselves, if you will pardon the uncouth language of a backwoodsman, to lick up the spittle of the slavocrats, and swear it is delicious. (Applause.)

You of the old Bay State—a State to which many of us are accustomed to look as to our fatherland, just as we look back to England as our mother country—you have a Daniel who has deserted the cause of freedom. We, too, in New York, have a "Daniel who has come to judgment," only he don't come quite fast enough to the right kind of judgment. (Tremendous enthusiasm.) Daniel S. Dickinson represents some one, I suppose, in the State of New York; God knows, he doesn't represent me. I can pledge you that our Daniel will stand cheek by jowl with your Daniel. (Cheers.) He was never known to surrender slavery, but always to surrender liberty.

The bill of which you most justly complain, concerning the surrender of fugitive slaves, is to apply alike to your State and to our State, if it shall ever apply at all. But we have come here to make a common oath upon a common altar, that that bill shall never take effect. (Applause.) Honorable Senators may record their names in its behalf, and it may have the sanction of the House of Representatives; but we, the people, who are superior to both Houses and the Executive, too (hear! hear!), we, the people, will never be human bipeds, to howl upon the track of the fugitive slave, even though led by the corrupt Daniel of your State, or the degraded one of ours. (Cheers.)

Though there are many attempts to get up compromises—and there is no term which I detest more than this, it is always the term which makes right yield to wrong; it has always been accursed since Eve made the first compromise with the devil. (Repeated rounds of applause.) I was saying, sir, that it is somewhat singular, and yet historically true, that whensoever these compromises are proposed, there are men of the North who seem to foresee that Northern men, who think their constituency will not look into these matters, will seek to do more than the South demands. They seek to prove to Northern men that all is right and all is fair; and this is the game Webster is attempting to play.

"Oh," says Webster, "the will of God has fixed that matter, we will not re-enact the will of God." Sir, you remember the time in 1841, '42, '43 and '44, when it was said that Texas could never be annexed. The design of such dealing was that you should believe it, and then, when you thought yourselves secure, they would spring the trap upon you. And now it is their wish to seduce you into the belief that slavery never will go there, and then the slaveholders will drive slavery there as fast as possible. I think that this is the most contemptible proposition of the whole, except the support of that bill which would attempt to make the whole North the slave-catchers of the South.

You will remember that that bill of Mr. Mason says nothing about color. Mr. Phillips, a man whom I always loved (applause), a man who taught me my horn-book on this subject of slavery, when I was a poor boy, has referred to Marshfield. There is a man who sometimes lives in Marshfield, and who has the reputation of having an honorable dark skin. Who knows but that some postmaster may have to sit upon the very gentleman whose character you have been discussing to-night? (Hear! hear!) "What is sauce for the goose is sauce for the gander." (Laughter.) If this bill is to relieve grievances, why not make an application to the immortal Daniel of Marshfield? (Applause.) There is no such thing as complexion mentioned. It is not only true that the colored men of Massachusetts—it is not true that the fifty thousand colored men of New York may be taken—though I pledge you there is one, whose name is Sam Ward, who will never be taken alive. (Tremendous applause.) Not only is it true that the fifty thousand black men of New York may be taken, but any one else also can be captured. My friend Theodore Parker alluded to Ellen Craft. I had the pleasure of taking tea with her, and accompanied her here to-night. She is far whiter than many who come here slave-catching. This line of distinction is so nice that you cannot tell who is white or black. As Alexander Pope used to say, "White and black soften and blend in so many thousand ways, that it is neither white nor black." (Loud plaudits.)

This is the question. Whether a man has a right to himself and his children, his hopes and his happiness, for this world and the world to come. That is a question which, according to this bill, may be decided by any backwoods postmaster in this State or any other. Oh, this is a monstrous proposition; and I do thank God that if the Slave Power has such demands to make on us, that the proposition has come now—now, that the people know what is being done—now that the public mind is turned toward this subject—now that they are trying to find what is the truth on this subject.

Sir, what must be the moral influence of this speech of Mr. Webster on the minds of young men, lawyers and others, here in the North? They turn their eyes towards Daniel Webster as towards a superior mind, and a legal and constitutional oracle. If they shall catch the spirit of this speech, its influence upon them and upon following generations will be so deeply corrupting that it never can be wiped out or purged.

I am thankful that this, my first entrance into Boston, and my first introduction to Faneuil Hall, gives me the pleasure and privilege of uniting with you in uttering my humble voice against the two Daniels, and of declaring, in behalf of our people, that if the fugitive slave is traced to our part of New York State, he shall have the law of Almighty God to protect him, the law which says, "Thou shalt not return to the master the servant that is escaped unto thee, but he shall dwell with thee in thy gates, where it liketh him best." And if our postmasters cannot maintain their constitutional oaths, and cannot live without playing the pander to the slave-hunter, they need not live at all. Such crises as these leave us the right of Revolution, and if need be, that right we will, at whatever cost, most sacredly maintain.

WILLIAM WELLS BROWN (1816-1884)

When Douglass parted company with the Garrisonians, William Wells Brown was groomed to take his place. Though he delivered well over a thousand speeches in America and Great Britain, few have been printed. He is more interesting as a contributor of open letters to antislavery periodicals. He was much-traveled, as attested by his *Three Years in Europe: or, Places I Have Seen and People I Have Met* (1852). Like many fellow fugitives, Brown found Europe to be a scene of both duty and pleasure, where he could further the antislavery campaign and also live the kind of life denied to him in America. Unlike most antislavery agents, Brown was not lost in righteous indignation. His gossipy letters showed how he savored experience. He writes humorously, often with ingenuous but pardonable pride at being lionized.

Letters

DEAR FRIEND GARRISON:

I have not forgotten the promise that I made you, before leaving America, to give you a letter occasionally for the Liberator. You have doubtless learned, ere this, that the steamer in which I came over made the shortest passage ever known. This, I need not inform you, added much to the pleasure of the voyage. Among the unusually large number of passengers on board were four or five slaveholders, and among these was a Judge Chinn, a Louisiana slaveholder, who had been appointed by our democratic government as Consul to Naples, and who was on his way to occupy his post. The steamer had scarcely left the shore, before it was rumored that an American slave was on board, and that he was going out as a delegate to the Peace Congress at Paris. The latter part of the rumor gave additional interest to it, and soon there was no little anxiety manifested on the part of the passengers to know something of the history of the fugitive. My Narrative, —a few copies of which I had with me,—was sought after, and extensively read, the reading of which produced considerable sensation among the passengers, especially the slaveholding and pro-slavery portion of them. This Judge Chinn had with him a free colored man as servant, and I was somewhat anxious to know what kind of protection he was to receive in travelling in this country, for you will recollect that I made application to the Hon. John M. Clayton, before leaving America, for a passport, which was refused me. So, upon inquiring of this servant, he showed me his passport, which proved to be nothing less than a regular passport from the hand of the Secretary of State. True, it was not from Mr. Clayton, but it was from his immediate predecessor, Mr. Buchanan. This proves conclusively, that if a colored person wishes the protection of the U. S. government in going into any foreign country, he must not think of going in any other capacity than that of a boot-black. Wherever the colored man goes, he must carry with him the badge of slavery to receive the protection of the Americans. The act of the government, in denying to its colored citizens the same protection that it extends to the whites, is more cowardly and mean, if possible, than any act committed for years. But it is entirely in keeping with American republicanism. I am glad to see that the English press generally has denounced this act of high-handed injustice and oppression.

After a pleasing passage of only nine days and twenty-two hours, we arrived at Liverpool. I remained there only long enough to take a view of the place, and then proceeded to Dublin, where I met with a warm reception from the Webbs, the Haughtons, and many other friends of the cause. I have become acquainted with none, since my arrival in this country, to whom I am more attached, than the hospitable family of Richard D. Webb. I remained in Dublin twenty days, but the friends of the slave there would not permit me to leave without adding to their many private manifestations of kindness that of a public welcome, an account of which you must gather from the newspapers.

On the 19th of August, I left Dublin, in company with R. D. Webb, for Paris, to attend the Peace Congress. So much has been said and written about the Congress, that I suppose any thing from me, at this late hour, would be considered stale, to say the least; but I will, however, venture to mention a circumstance or two, that may not have reached you through any other channel. As you are aware, the Congress met on Wednesday, the 23d, at 12 o'clock, and, strange to say, among the first that I saw entering the hall, were three slaveholders, who came over in the same steamer with me, one of whom was Judge Chinn; but whether they were members of the Congress or not, I am unable to say. At any rate, they were supplied with the same card of admission that members were. However, they did not show any symptoms of color-phobia so natural to the American taste. A circumstance occurred at the close of the first session, which shows how easily Americans can lay aside their prejudices when they reach this country. While I was in conversation with Richard Cobden, Esq., member of the British Parliament, and Victor Hugo, the President of the Congress, I observed a man standing near us, whom I recognized as one of the passengers in the same steamer with me from America, and who during the voyage was not at all backward in expressing his belief in the inferiority of the 'niggers,' and who would not deign to speak to me during the whole passage. At the close of the conversation, and as I was leaving the parties with whom I had been talking, this man advanced towards me with his hat in one hand and the other extended out, and addressed me with, 'How do you do, Mr. Brown? I hope I find you well, Sir.' 'Why, Sir, you have the advantage of me—I do not know you.' 'Why, Sir,' said he, 'don't you know me? I was a fellow-passenger with you from America. I wish you would introduce me to Mr. Cobden.' I felt so indignant at the downright impudence of the fellow, that I left him without making any reply. The change from an American to an European atmosphere makes a wonderful change in the minds of Americans. The man who would not have shaken hands with me in the city of New York or Boston, with a pair of tongs ten feet long, comes to me in the metropolis of France, and claims that we were 'fellow-passengers from America.' M. de Tocqueville, Minister of Foreign Affairs, gave a splendid Soirée to the members of the Congress. I perceived no difference whatever in the attention paid to those of a fairer complexion than that paid me. I could but contrast the feeling that pervaded that assembly of men and women from all parts of the globe, to the low, mean and contemptible prejudices so common in the U. S. Here were representatives and Ministers Plenipotentiary from all governments, including the United States. Messrs. Walsh and Rush were there, and you know that they are proverbial for their pro-slavery feeling. The whites and blacks were all together, and I did not hear the word 'nigger' once. If there was any difference paid to one more than to another, that difference was certainly paid to myself, not on account of my complexion, but on account of my identity with the oppressed millions in America. On being presented to Madame de Tocqueville, I was received with the same courtesy that characterized the reception of others; but as soon as it was mentioned to the distinguished lady that I was an American slave, all conventionalities were laid aside by a cordial shake of the hand, that gave me double assurance that I was not only safe from the slave-hunter in Paris, but that I was a welcome guest in the saloon of the French Minister of Foreign Affairs. While there, I could but think of the bitter cold night in the winter of 1840, when I was compelled to walk the deck of the steamer Swallow on the Hudson river, on account of my complexion. I could but think of my being excluded from the saloon of the steamer Huntress, on the passage from Portland to Bath, in the State of Maine, but a few days before I left America, by which exclusion I was compelled to fast twelve hours.

The Peace Congress, though entirely different from our New England Conventions, was nevertheless a pleasant meeting, and was made doubly so to me by the appearance, at every session, of that noble band of abolitionists, the Chapmans and Westons. It was really pleasant to see six of them in the Congress at one time. I felt myself fortunate in being known as an abolitionist in America, if for no other purpose than that of sharing their society in France. At the close of the Congress, I paid them a visit at their summer residence at Versailles, and often while there, fancied myself in Boston. But a walk to the window, or the appearance of a French visitor, reminded me that I was in Versailles, and not Boston—in France, and not America. After remaining in France ten days, the most of which time I spent in visiting the monuments and public buildings for which Paris is so noted, I returned to London; where, for the first time, I had the pleasure of seeing that world-renowned philanthropist, George Thompson, Esq. I did not have to wait till he had read the letter of introduction that you were kind enough to furnish me with, before he knew who I was. He had read of the farewell meeting given to me by my colored friends in Boston, together with the announcement in the Liberator that I had left for England, and colored men are so scarce here, that as soon as I entered his room, he arose, and smilingly approaching me said—"I presume this is William W. Brown"; and answering him affirmatively, he gave me a hearty shake of the hand, and bade me welcome to the soil of old England. His first inquiry was about yourself and family, and then about the progress of the anti-slavery cause in America. Mr. Thompson has rendered me signal service since my arrival in this country. You will see by the papers that I am overwhelmed with welcome meetings. I have just attended a very large meeting in the London Tavern, to consider the proposition of the government of Austria for a loan to enable her to pay off the vast debt caused by the late war with the Hungarians. I had been furnished with a ticket for the 'reserved seats' before I went to the meeting; but on entering the hall, instead of being shown to the reserved seats, I was conducted to the platform, and soon found myself surrounded by such men as Lord Dudley Coutts Stewart, M. P., Richard Cobden, Esq., M. P., J. Williams, Esq., M. P., &c. &c. If such a meeting had been held in New York or Philadelphia, I could only have gained access to it by appearing there with a pitcher of water or some stationery in my hands for the use of the meeting, and as soon as that had been deposited on the platform, I would have been saluted with the familiar American phrase, 'I say, nigger, it's time for you to be off.' Here the man is measured by his moral worth, and not by the color of the skin or the curl of the hair.

I forgot to mention to you, that the Rev. Wm. Allen, D.D., of Northampton, made a speech at the breakfast given to the American delegates at Versailles, and in his speech he apologized for our slave-holding government, declaring that it had nothing to do with slavery. His speech, instead of gaining applause for him, brought down the condemnation of nearly the whole audience upon his own head. It is too late in the nineteenth century for men coming from America to attempt to whitewash her slaveholding institution. I am more than ever convinced, that some sterling abolitionist should be in this country at all times, if for no other purpose, to watch American Doctors of Divinity, who may happen to be here.

Yours for the slave,
Wm. Wells Brown.

London, October 12, 1849.

Dear Mr. Garrison:

I forward to you, by this day's mail, the papers concerning accounts of the great meeting held in Exeter Hall last night. No meeting during this anniversary has caused so much talk and excitement as this gathering. No time could possibly have been more appropriate for such a meeting than the present. Uncle Tom's Cabin has come down upon the dark abodes of slavery like a morning's sunlight, unfolding to view its enormities in a manner which has fastened all eyes upon the "peculiar institution," and awakening sympathy in hearts that never before felt for the slave. Had Exeter Hall been capable of holding fifty thousand instead of five thousand, it would no doubt have been filled to its utmost capacity. For more than a week before the meeting came off, the tickets were all disposed of, and it was understood that hundreds were applying every day. With those who may be classed as Mrs. Stowe's converts, that lady was the center of attraction for them; while the elder abolitionists came for the sake of the cause. I entered the great Hall an hour before the time, and found the building filled, there scarcely being standing room, except on the platform, which was in charge of the officials, to keep places for those who had tickets to that part of the house. At half-past six, the Earl of Shaftesbury appeared upon the platform, followed by the Committee and speakers, amid the most deafening applause. The Noble Earl, who has many more noble qualities than that of a mere nobleman, made the opening speech, and, as you will see, a good one. While his lordship was speaking, Her Grace, the Duchess of Sutherland, came in, and took her seat in the balcony on the right of the platform, and an half hour after, a greater lady (the authoress of Uncle Tom) made her appearance, and took her seat by the side of the Duchess. At this stage of the meeting, there was a degree of excitement in the room that can better be imagined than described. The waving of hats and handkerchiefs, the clapping of hands, the stamping of feet, and the screaming and fainting of ladies, went on as if it had been in the programme, while the thieves were at work helping themselves out of the abundance of the pockets of those who were most crowded. A few arrests by the police soon taught the latter that there was no room there for pick-pockets. Order was once more restored, and the speaking went on. Many good things were said by different speakers, who were mostly residents of the metropolis. Professor Stowe, as you might expect, was looked upon as the lion of the speakers; but his speech disappointed all, except those of us who knew enough of American divines not to anticipate much from them on the subject of slavery. For my own part, I was not disappointed, for I have long since despaired of anything being done by clergymen; and the Professor's speech at Glasgow, and subsequent addresses, had prepared me to look for but little from him. He evidently wishes for no agitation on the subject, and said it would do no good as long as England purchased America's cotton. I look upon this cotton question as nothing more than to divert the public from the main subject itself. Mr. Stowe is not very young, yet he is only a child in the anti-slavery movement. He is now lisping his A, B, C, and if his wife succeeds in making him a good scholar, she will find it no easy thing.

The best speech of the evening was made by our countryman, Samuel R. Ward. Mr. Ward did himself great credit, and exposed the hypocrisy of the American pro-slavery churches in a way that caused Professor Stowe to turn more than once upon his seat. I have but little faith in the American clergy—either colored or white; but I believe Ward to be not only one of the most honest, but an uncompromising and faithful advocate of his countrymen. He is certainly the best colored minister that has yet visited this country.

I recognized in the audience several of our American friends. Among them was Mrs. Follen, Miss Cabot, J. Miller M'Kim, Miss Pugh, Professor Wm. G. Allen and lady, and Wm. and Ellen Craft. Upon the whole, the anti-slavery cause is in a more healthy state than it ever was before, and from all appearance much good will be done by the present excitement. The fact that no American clergyman has dared to appear at any of the anniversary meetings without professing anti-slavery principles, and that one at least (Rev. Mr. Prime) was denied a seat as a delegate at one of these meetings, shows the feeling already created in Great Britain; and I hope it will soon be understood in America, that no man will be welcomed here, unless he is an out-and-out abolitionist; and then the days of the slave's deliverance will be close at hand.

Yours, very sincerely,
Wm. Wells Brown.

22 Cecil Street, Strand, London, May 17th, 1853.

Dear Mr. Garrison:

After attending the New York State Fair at Buffalo, on the 9th instant, and lecturing in the Rev. Dr. Prime's church, on Sunday evening the 11th, I visited Cataraugus county, and held meetings at Bagdad and Cataraugus, where I had large audiences. From the latter place I made my way to Girard, a village in one of the extreme counties in Western Pennsylvania, where Miss Anthony, Mr. Powell and myself were to attend a Convention. For want of interest in Girard, our friends changed the arrangements, and advertised us to lecture in separate places, which, upon the whole, worked well, for we found crowded houses and willing listeners in all of the gatherings. The strictest attention was paid to the most radical doctrines upon the Government and the Church. Although settled several years, this seems a comparatively new country, the log cabins of the early settlers still being occupied. To a New Englander, this part of our 'glorious Union' appears very strange. The people are generally kind and hospitable, but wonderfully green. But the oddest feature in our meetings is the swarms of little ones. O, the children! I never beheld so many babies in so short a time, since the commencement of my anti-slavery labors. At one meeting last week, I counted *twenty-seven* babies in their mothers' arms or in their laps. And such music I never before heard. Take an untuned piano, a cornstalk fiddle, a Swiss hurdy-gurdy, and a

Scotchman with his bag-pipes, put them all in one room, and set them agoing, and you will have but a faint idea of the juvenile concert we had that evening. I waited till a late hour before commencing the meeting, with the hope that the little ones would stop; but I waited in vain. After being reminded by the dusty clock on the wall that it was ten minutes past seven, I counted five babies, whose open mouths were sending forth delicious music, and then commenced my lecture. I raised my voice to the highest note, and the little ones and I had it, 'which and tother,' for some time. At last, I was about giving it up as a bad job, when an elderly gentleman near me said, 'Keep on, sir, the babies will get tired bye and bye, and will go to sleep.' This encouraged me, and I continued with renewed vigor; and sure enough, a half an hour more, and I realized the advice of the old man; for, as the clock struck 8, I found the babies all asleep, and I master of the field. It is astonishing how little the people out here are disturbed by the noise of the children; but I presume they have become used to it.

Mr. Isaac Brooks, one of the most devoted friends of freedom in this section, met us at Lockport, and took Mr. Powell and Miss Anthony to Linesville, some twenty-five miles, while I remained and lectured a second time. We could not have wished for a more enthusiastic or better attended meeting than we had at Linesville. The place of meeting was a double school-house, with the partition opened, and the two rooms thrown into one. The Baptist church, the only religious building in the town, was shut against us. The Convention commenced on Saturday morning, and continued till Sunday night at half past 10, and was addressed by Miss Anthony, Mr. Powell and Myself.

At Linesville, we found another large crop of children. The scene on Sunday beggars description. The house where we held the meeting was jammed in every part, except a small space in the centre of the room, where there were no seats. On their mothers' laps lay a dozen or two babies, while five or six who were old enough to run alone were let loose on the unseated spot on the floor. The latter were suplied with various articles to keep them quiet. One had his father's cane; a second a tin horn; a third its mother's bonnet; and a fourth its father's jacknife. One little boy, seven or eight years old, was lying on the floor, nibbling at his younger brother's toes, while the latter lay in its mother's arms, nibbling at something more substantial. One bright-eyed boy was chasing a dog about the floor; while another, with two caps on his head, was sailing about to the amusement of the other little ones. In different sections of the room were children standing on the tops of desks, or hanging around their fathers' or mothers' necks. At this juncture, the house looked as if Barnum's baby show had adjourned to our meeting. Miss Anthony seemed very much amused at a little woman in a pink bloomer, seated on the front bench, with her feet, not long enough to reach the floor, hanging down, while a child a few weeks old, in her arms, nibbled away at its *dinner*.

O, the noise! I will not attempt to describe it. Suffice it to say, that some babies were crowing, some crying, and some snoring, while mothers were resorting to all sorts of means to keep their babies quiet. One was throwing her child up, and catching it; another patting her foot, and another singing 'bi-lo-baby.' You may guess how difficult it was to be heard in such an assembly. My head aches now, from the great exertion that I made to be heard above the noise of the children. And poor Powell, I pitied him, from the bottom of my heart, for he had not strength to speak to a still audience, to say nothing of such a noisy one as this; and while he was speaking, as if to make the scene more ridiculous, a tall, brawny man walked in, and, the benches being full, seated himself on the stove, which he thought had no fire in it,—but he soon found it too *peppery* for comfort. Just then, a child tumbled from the top of one of the desks, and Mr. Powell made his bow and retired. But they give us rice pudding out here for breakfast, and that gives me strength to meet the babies.

We are to hold meetings at Albion, Lockport, Coneautville, and one other place, the name of which I have forgotten, and then we go to Painesville. The people here are all alive for the Cleveland Convention, and we anticipate a large gathering and a glorious time.

Yours, truly,
W. W. Brown.

Linesville, Oct. 20, 1857.

MARTIN R. DELANY (1812-1885)

Martin R. Delany (see also p. 152) was born in Charlestown, Virginia. A man of great physical and mental energy, he was proud of his blackness, tracing his lineage to African chieftains with probably more accuracy than many later Negroes have done. His first teacher was a Yankee peddler. When his family stole away from Virginia to western Pennsylvania, Martin was enabled to go to school. He later studied medicine at the Harvard University Medical School. While practicing in Pittsburgh he was one of the physicians who put down an epidemic of cholera.

Delany was somewhat like Banneker in his deep interest in science and invention. In 1853, he was one of the prime movers for an industrial college to train Negro mechanics and artisans, anticipating Booker T. Washington. In 1859, because of his interest in colonization (he did not, however, approve of the Liberian experiment), he led an investigation into the Niger Valley in Africa. In 1861, his presence as a delegate to the International Statistical Congress in London was the cause of the withdrawal of the other Americans, led by Judge Augustus Baldwin Longstreet, the famed author of *Georgia Scenes*. Longstreet considered the introduction of Delany and his remarks "an ill-timed assault upon our country, a wanton indignity offered to our ministry, and a pointed insult offered to me."

Delany's political writings include his newspaper *The Mystery*, which he edited in Pittsburgh from 1843 to 1847, and *The Condition, Elevation, Emigration, and Destiny of the Colored People of the United States, Politically Considered* (1852). *The Official Report of the Niger Valley Exploring Party* appeared in 1861.

Delany served as a medical officer in the Civil War, and was commissioned major at its close. He was an important political figure in Reconstruction in South Carolina, serving in the Freedmen's Bureau for three years, then as a customhouse inspector and a trial justice in Charleston. In 1874 he was the unsuccessful Independent Republican candidate for Lieutenant Governor of South Carolina. His closing years were spent in preparing his most ambitious work, *Principia of Ethnology* (1879). He died in Xenia, Ohio, the home of Wilberforce University in 1885.

[Condition of Free Negroes]

We have no fault to find with our Anti-Slavery friends, and here wish it to be understood, that we are not laying anything to their charge as blame, neither do we desire for a moment to reflect on them, because we heartily believe that all that they did at the time, they did with the purest and best of motives, and further believe that they now are, as they then were, the truest friends we have among the whites in this country. And hope, and desire, and request, that our people should always look upon *true* anti-slavery people, Abolitionists we mean, as their friends, until they have just cause for acting otherwise. It is true, that the Anti-Slavery, like all good causes, has produced some recreants, but the cause itself is no more to be blamed for that, than Christianity is for the malconduct of any professing hypocrite, nor the society of Friends, for the conduct of a broad-brimmed hat and shad-belly coated horse-thief, because he spoke *thee* and *thou* before stealing the horse. But what is our condition even amidst our Anti-Slavery friends? And here, as our sole intention is to contribute to the elevation of our people, we must be permitted to express our opinion freely, without being thought uncharitable.

In the first place, we should look at the objects for which the Anti-Slavery cause was commenced, and the promises or inducements it held out at the commencement. It should be borne in mind, that Anti-Slavery took its rise among *colored men,* just at the time they were introducing their greatest projects for their own elevation, and that our Anti-Slavery brethren were converts of the colored men, in behalf of their elevation. Of course, it would be expected that being baptized into the new doctrines, their faith would induce them to embrace the principles therein contained, with the strictest possible adherence.

The cause of dissatisfaction with our former condition, was, that we were proscribed, debarred, and shut out from every respectable position, occupying the places of inferiors and menials.

It was expected that Anti-Slavery, according to its professions, would extend to colored persons, as far as in the power of its adherents, those advantages nowhere else to be obtained among white men. That colored boys would get situations in their shops and stores, and every other advantage tending to elevate them as far as possible, would be extended to them. At least, it was expected, that in Anti-Slavery establishments, colored men would have the preference. Because, there was no other ostensible object in view, in the commencement of the Anti-Slavery enterprise, than the *elevation* of the *colored man,* by facilitating his efforts in attaining to equality with the white man. It was urged, and it was true, that the colored people were susceptible of all that the whites were, and all that was required was to give them a fair opportunity, and they would prove their capacity. That it was unjust, wicked, and cruel, the result of an unnatural prejudice, that debarred them from places of respectability, and that public opinion could and should be corrected upon this subject. That it was only necessary to make a sacrifice of feeling, and an innovation on the customs of society, to establish a different order of things,— that as Anti-Slavery men, they were willing to make these sacrifices, and determined to take the colored man by the hand, making common cause with him in affliction, and bear a part of the odium heaped upon him. That his cause was the cause of God—that "In as much as ye did it not unto the least of my little ones, ye did it not unto me," and that as Anti-Slavery men, they would "do right if the heavens fell." Thus, was the cause espoused, and thus did we expect much. But in all this, we were doomed to disappointment, sad, sad, disappointment. Instead of realizing what we had hoped for, we find ourselves occupying the very same position in relation to our Anti-Slavery friends, as we do in relation to the pro-slavery part of the community—a mere secondary, underling position, in all our relations to them, and anything more than this, is not a matter of course affair—it comes not by established anti-slavery custom or right, but like that which emanates from the proslavery portion of the community, by mere sufferance.

It is true, that the "Liberator" office, in Boston, has got Elijah Smith, a colored youth, at the cases—the "Standard," in New York, a young colored man, and the "Freeman," in Philadelphia, William Still, another, in the publication office, as "packing clerk;" yet these are but three out of the hosts that fill these offices in their various departments, all occupying places that could have been, and as we once thought, would have been, easily enough, occupied by colored men. Indeed, we can have no other idea about anti-slavery in this country, than that the legitimate persons to fill any and every position about an anti-slavery establishment are colored persons. Nor will it do to argue in extenuation, that white men are as justly entitled to them as colored men; because white men do not from *necessity* become anti-slavery men in order to get situations; they being white men, may occupy any position they are capable of filling—in a word, their chances are endless, every avenue in the country being opened to them. They do not therefore become abolitionists, for the sake of employment—at least, it is not the song that anti-slavery sung, in the first love of the new faith, proclaimed by its disciples.

And if it be urged that colored men are incapable as yet to fill these positions, all that we have to say is, that the cause has fallen far short; almost equivalent to a failure, of a tithe, of what it promised to do in half the period of its existence, to this time, if it have not as yet, now a period of twenty years, raised up colored men enough, to fill the offices within its patronage. We think it is not unkind to say, if it had been half as faithful to itself, as it should have been—its professed principles we mean; it could have reared and tutored from childhood, colored men enough by this time, for its own especial purpose. These we know could have been easily obtained, because colored people in general, are favorable to the anti-slavery cause, and wherever there is an adverse manifestation, it arises from sheer ignorance; and we have not but comparatively few such among us. There is one thing certain, that no colored person, except such as would reject education altogether, would be adverse to putting their child with an anti-slavery person, for educational advantages. This then, could have been done. But it has not been done, and let the cause of it be whatever it may, and let whoever may be to blame, we are willing to let all that pass, and extend to our anti-slavery brethren the right-hand of fellowship, bidding them God-speed in the propagation of good and wholesome sentiments—for whether they are practically carried out or not, the professions are in themselves all right and good. Like Christianity, the principles are holy and of divine origin. And we believe, if ever a man started right, with pure and holy motives, Mr. Garrison did; and that, had he the power of making the cause what it should be, it would all be right, and there never would have been any cause for the remarks we have made, though in kindness, and with the purest of motives. We are nevertheless, still occupying a miserable position in the community, wherever we live; and what we most desire is, to draw the attention of our people to this fact, and point out what, in our opinion, we conceive to be a proper remedy.

[Practical Efforts]

MORAL THEORIES HAVE LONG BEEN RESORTED TO by us, as a means of effecting the redemption of our brethren in bonds, and the elevation of the free colored people in this country. Experience, has taught us, that speculations are not enough; that the *practical* application of principles adduced, the thing carried out, is the only true and proper course to pursue.

We have speculated and moralized much about equality—claiming to be as good as our neighbors, and everybody else—all of which, may do very well in ethics—but not in politics. We live in society among men, conducted by men, governed by rules and regulations. However arbitrary, there are certain policies that regulate all well organized institutions and corporate bodies. We do not intend here to speak of the legal political relations of society, for those are treated on elsewhere. The business and social, or voluntary and mutual policies, are those that now claim our attention, society regulates itself—being governed by mind, which like water, finds its own level. "Like seeks like," is a principle in the laws of matter, as well as of mind. There is such a thing as inferiority of things, and positions; at least society has made them so; and while we continue to live among men, we must agree to all *just* measures—all those we mean, that do not necessarily infringe on the rights of others. By the regulations of society, there is no equality of persons, where there is not an equality of attainments. By this, we do not wish to be understood as advocating the actual equal attainments of every individual; but we mean to say, that if these attainments be necessary for the elevation of the white man, they are necessary for the elevation of the colored man. That some colored men and women, in a like proportion to the whites, should be qualified in all the attainments possessed by them. It is one of the regulations of society the world over, and we shall have to conform to it, or be discarded as unworthy of the associations of our fellows. . . .

White men are producers—we are consumers. They build houses, and we rent them. They raise produce, and we consume it. They manufacture clothes and wares, and we garnish ourselves with them. They build coaches, vessels, cars, hotels, saloons, and other vehicles and places of accommodation, and we deliberately wait until they have got them in readiness, then walk in, and contend with as much assurance for a "right," as though the whole thing was bought by, paid for, and belonged to us. By their literary attainments, they are the contributors to, authors and teachers of, literature, science, religion, law, medicine, and all other useful attainments that the world now makes use of. We have no reference to ancient times—we speak of modern things.

These are the means by which God intended man to succeed; and this discloses the secret of the white man's success with all of his wickedness, over the head of the colored man, with all of his religion. We have been pointed and plain, on this part of the subject, because we desire our readers to see persons and things in their true position. Until we are determined to change the condition of things, and raise ourselves above the position in which we are now prostrated, we must hang our heads in sorrow, and hide our faces in shame. It is enough to know that these things are so; the causes we care little about. Those we have been examining, complaining about, and moralising over, all our life time. This we are weary of. What we desire to learn now is, how to effect a *remedy;* this we have endeavored to point out. Our elevation must be the result of *self-efforts,* and work of our *own hands.* No other human power can accomplish it. If we but determine it shall be so, it will be so. Let each one make the case his own, and endeavor to rival his neighbor, in honorable competition.

. . . . Let our young men and women prepare themselves for usefulness and business; that the men may enter into merchandise, trading, and other things of importance; the young women may become teachers of various kinds, and otherwise fill places of usefulness. Parents must turn their attention more to the education of their children. We mean, to educate them for useful practical building purposes. Educate them for the store and the counting house—to do everyday practical business. Consult the children's propensities, and direct their education according to their inclinations. It may be that there is too great a desire on the part of parents to give their children a professional education, before the body of the people are ready for it. A people must be a business people, and have more to depend upon than mere help in people's houses and hotels, before they are either able to support, or capable of properly appreciating the services of professional men among them. This has been one of our great mistakes—we have gone in advance of ourselves. We have commenced at the superstructure of the building instead of the foundation—at the top instead of the bottom. We should first be mechanics and common tradesmen, and professions as a matter of course would grow out of the wealth made thereby. Young men and women must now prepare for usefulness—the day of our elevation is at hand—all the world now gazes at us—and Central and South America, and the West Indies, bid us come and be men and women, protected, secure, beloved and Free.

WILLIAM C. NELL (1816-1874)

William C. Nell was one of the hardest antislavery workers among Boston Negroes. He was closely associated with William Lloyd Garrison in the publication of the *Liberator*. A man of little formal education, he struggled for self-improvement. Upon the suggestion of Whittier, Nell gathered the facts for a pamphlet, *Services of Colored Americans in the Wars of 1776 and 1812* (1851), which he enlarged into *The Colored Patriots of the American Revolution* (1855). Wendell Phillips and Harriet Beecher Stowe prepared introductions to this work, one of the best examples of early historical writing by American Negroes. The following letter was printed in the *Liberator,* December 16, 1853.

Letter to Garrison

Southfield, Oakland Co., Mich.,
Sept. 6th, 1858.

DEAR FRIEND GARRISON:

The papers have already, I presume, informed you somewhat of the recent kidnapping case, and the consequent excitement in Cincinnati. I happened to be in Detroit, where the betrayer and his two victims (all colored men) resided, and when the news reached there, you can easily imagine the effect produced upon the colored men and women, many of whom were acquainted with all the parties.

Miss Francis E. Watkins already had a meeting announced for Thursday evening, Sept. 2d, in the Croghan Street Baptist Church, but the arrival of Rev. Henry Garnet, fresh from Cincinnati, prompted an attempt to secure the City Hall for a large gathering of the citizens to protest against kidnapping in Detroit; but the Buchanan Democratic Convention being held there, was of itself sufficient to put a veto upon any hope of ingress for an anti-Fugitive Slave Law demonstration.

The Colored Methodist Conference adjourned its evening session, and thus augmented the numbers which crowded the meeting. The exercises commenced at an early hour by Mr. Garnet's reading the appropriate hymn of Mr. Follen, commencing, 'What mean ye that ye bruise and bind?' This was sung with thrilling effect; after which a fervent prayer was offered by Rev. J. P. Campbell, in which every reference to the traitor, his deserved punishment, his victims and their sad fate, elicited heart-moving responses from various parts of the house.

Rev. Mr. Davis, Chairman, then introduced Rev. H. H. Garnet, who in a graphic and eloquent manner detailed the history of the kidnapping case, tracing Brodie's connection with it under written instructions from the slaveholders, until the imprisonment of the two captives in the jail at Covington, Ky. They had accepted Brodie's pledge to assist their return to the South, with a view to secure the liberation of some of their relatives from slavery. Instead of this blissful realization of their hopes, they were delivered into the hands of their self-styled owners, and by the very man in whom they had most implicitly trusted, receiving each one hundred lashes, and ordered to be sold further South, expressly to cut off all future chances of escape to the North. Mr. Garnet exhibited a pair of manacles, such as were worn by them on their way to jail, and a bull whip, as used in their severe flogging.

The young men of Cincinnati, on learning the facts, with that 'eternal vigilance' which is 'the price of liberty,' succeeded in getting possession of the traitor, and instituted measures for his trial. This occupied two hours, during most of which time Mr. Garnet was present, and it was mainly owing to his intercession that Brodie was not torn limb from limb. He escaped with life, after the infliction of three hundred blows with a paddle—one blow for each dollar of blood money which he had received for doing the infamous work of these Kentucky hunters of men. Two white men, in sympathy with the right, though pretending otherwise to him, acted as police men, and removed him from immediate danger of being killed. He breathed vengeance upon the colored people, threatened to expose the operations of the Underground Railroad, &c. &c.; but when a committee of colored men started for the purpose of hurrying him from Cincinnati, it was found that his gold had bribed the white men, who were endeavoring to screen him from further molestation. But the colored men were determined, and his whereabouts were made known. Brodie delivered himself into the hands of the authorities, who put him in jail to save his life.

It has since turned out that the slaveholding influences united for his defense. State warrants have been issued for the arrest of several colored men charged with participating in his trial and punishment; and the day I left Detroit, some of them had arrived there, to avoid that liability.

But to return to the meeting. Miss Watkins, in the course of one of her very best outbursts of eloquent indignation, charged the treachery of this colored man upon the United States Government, which is the arch traitor to liberty, as shown by the Fugitive Slave Law and the Dred Scott decision. A discussion ensued on the pertinent question, submitted by Mr. Garnet, what shall be done with the traitor on his arrival in Detroit? A resolution embodying their detestation of the man was passed, and at a late hour, the meeting adjourned.

One of these betrayed men has left a wife in Detroit, and a babe born since his departure. A committee of ladies have called to administer to her wants, and to do what in them lies to save her from the clutches of the kidnapper.

Yours, for the speedy downfall of slavery,

Liberator, Sept. 11, 1858.   WILLIAM C. NELL.

CHARLES LANGSTON (1817-1892)

Charles Langston's memory has been overshadowed by the career of his half-brother, John Mercer Langston, but one speech of his should certainly not be forgotten. Students of Oberlin College and citizens of the town banded together to rescue a Negro who had been kidnapped and was being held in the neighboring town of Wellington. Among the rescuers was Charles Langston. He was the second to be tried in the famous case. His speech struck the court so favorably that he was given a much lighter sentence than his white predecessor, although his actions were equally "criminal." John Mercer Langston wrote an account of the Oberlin-Wellington rescue in *The Anglo-African* magazine of July, 1859, printing his brother's speech to the court. Charles Langston married the widow of Sheridan Leary, one of John Brown's men. His daughter, Caroline, is the mother of Langston Hughes (see pp. 89, 224, 366).

[Speech Before Sentence]

. . . I AM FOR THE FIRST TIME IN MY LIFE before a court of justice, charged with the violation of law, and am now to be sentenced. But before receiving that sentence I purpose to say one or two words in regard to the mitigation of that sentence, if it may be so construed. I cannot, and of course do not expect, that anything I shall say will in any way change your predetermined line of action. I ask no such favor at your hands. I know that the courts of this country, that the laws of this country, that the governmental machinery of the country are so constituted as to oppress and outrage the colored men: men of my own complexion. I cannot, then, of course, expect, judging from the past history of the country, any mercy from the laws, from the Constitution, or from the courts of the country.

Some days prior to the 13th of September, 1858, happening to be in Oberlin on a visit, I found the country round about there and the village itself filled with alarming rumors as to the fact that slave-catchers, kidnappers, Negro-stealers, were lying hidden and skulking about, waiting some opportunity to get their bloody hands on some helpless creature, to drag him back, or drag him for the first time, into hopeless and life-long bondage. These reports becoming current all over that neighborhood, old men and women and innocent children became exceedingly alarmed for their safety. It was not uncommon to hear mothers say that they durst not send their children to school, for fear they would be caught up and carried off by the way. Some of these people had become free by long and patient toil at night, after working the long, long day for cruel masters, and then, at length, getting money enough to buy their liberty. Others had become free by means of the good will of their masters. And there were others who had become free—to their everlasting honor do I say it—by the exercise of their God-given powers, by escaping from the plantation of their masters, eluding the blood-thirsty patrols and sentinels so thickly scattered all along their path, outrunning bloodhounds and horses, swimming rivers, and fording swamps, and reaching at last, through incredible difficulties, what they, in their delusion, supposed to be free soil. These three classes were in Oberlin, trembling alike for their safety, because they knew well their fate should these men-hunters get their hands on them.

In the midst of such excitement the 13th of September was ushered in—a day ever to be remembered in the history of that place, and I am sure, no less in the history of this court—in which these men, by lying devices, decoyed into a place, where they could get their hands on him—I will not say a slave, for I do not know that; but a man, a brother, who had a right to his liberty under the law of God, under the laws of Nature, and under the Declaration of Independence.

Many of us believed there would not be courage to make a seizure; but in the midst of all the excitement the news came to us like a flash of lightning that an actual seizure, by means of fraudulent pretenses, had been made.

Being identified with that man by color, by race, by manhood, by sympathies such as God has implanted in us all, I felt it my duty to go and do what I could toward liberating him. I had been taught by my Revolutionary father, and by his honored associates, that the fundamental law of this Government is, that all men have a right to life and liberty, and coming from the Old Dominion, I brought into Ohio these sentiments deeply impressed on my heart. I went to Wellington, and having learned from the men themselves by what authority they held this boy in custody, I conceived from what knowledge I had of law that they had no right to hold him. And as your honor has repeatedly laid down the law in this court, that in the State of Ohio a man is presumed to be free until he is proved to be legally restrained of his liberty, I believed that upon that principle of law those men were bound to take their prisoner before the first magistrate they found, and there establish the facts set forth in their warrant, and that until they did this, every man had a right to presume their claim was unfounded, and to institute such proceedings for the purpose of receiving such an investigation as he might find warranted by the laws of this State. Now, sir, if that is not plain, common sense, and a correct view of the law, then I have been misled by your honor, and by the prevalent received opinion. . . .

The law under which I am arraigned is an unjust one, one made to crush the colored man, and one that outrages every feeling of humanity, as well as every rule of right. I have nothing to do with its constitutionality; and about it I care a great deal less. I have often heard it said by learned and good men that it is unconstitutional; I remember the excitement that prevailed throughout all the free States when it was passed; and I remember how often it has been said by individuals, conventions, communities, and legislatures, that it never could be, never should be, never was meant to be enforced. I had always believed, until the contrary appeared in the actual institution of proceedings, that the provisions of this odious statute would never be enforced within the bounds of this State.

But I have another reason to offer why I should not be sentenced, and one which I think pertinent to the case. I have not had a trial before a jury of my peers. The common law of England—and you will excuse me for referring to that, since I am but a private citizen, and not a lawyer—was that every man should be tried before a jury of men occupying the same position in the social scale as himself. That lords should be tried before a jury of lords; that peers of the realm should be tried before peers of the realm; vassals before vassals, and aliens before aliens, and they must not come from the district where the crime was committed, lest the prejudice of either personal friends or foes should affect the accused. The Constitution of the United States guarantees, not merely to its citizens, but to all persons, a trial before an impartial jury. I have had no such trial.

The colored man is oppressed by certain universal and deeply fixed prejudices. Those jurors are well-known to have shared largely in these prejudices, and I therefore consider they were neither impartial, nor were they a jury of my peers. And the prejudices which white people have against colored men grow out of this fact: that we have, as a people, consented for two hundred years to be slaves of the whites. We have been scourged, crushed, and cruelly oppressed, and have submitted to it all tamely, meekly, peaceably; I mean as a people, and with rare individual exceptions; and today you see us thus; meekly submitting to the penalties of an infamous law. Now the Americans have this feeling, and it is an honorable one, that they will respect those who will rebel at oppression, but despise those who tamely submit to outrage and wrong; and while our people as a people submit, they will as a people be despised. Why, they will hardly meet on terms of equality with us in a whiskey shop, in a car, at a table, or even at the altar of God. So thorough and hearty a contempt have they for those who will meekly lie still under the heel of the oppressor. The jury came into the box with that feeling. They knew they had that feeling, the court itself has that feeling, and even the counsel who defended me have that feeling.

I was tried before a jury who were prejudiced; prosecuted by an officer who was prejudiced, and defended, though ably, by counsel that were prejudiced. And therefore it is, your honor, that I urge by all that is good and great in manhood, that I should not be subjected to the pains and penalties of this oppressive law, when I have not been tried, either by a jury of my peers, or by a jury that were impartial.

One more word, sir, and I have done. I went to Wellington, knowing that colored men have no rights in the United States which white men are bound to respect; that the courts had so decided; that Congress had so enacted; that the people had so decreed.

There is not a spot in this wide country, not even by the altars of God, nor in the shadow of the shafts that tell the imperishable fame and glory of the heroes of the Revolution; no, nor in the old Philadelphia hall, where any colored man may dare to ask mercy of a white man. Let me stand in that hall, and tell a United States marshal that my father was a Revolutionary soldier; that he served under Lafayette, and fought through the whole war; and he told me that he fought for my freedom as much as for his own; and he would sneer at me, and clutch me with his bloody fingers, and say he had a right to make me a slave! And when I appeal to Congress, they say he has a right to make me a slave; when I appeal to the people, they say he has a right to make me a slave, and when I appeal to your honor, your honor says he has a right to make me a slave, and if any man, white or black, seeks an investigation of that claim, he makes himself amenable to the pains and penalties of the Fugitive Slave Act; for black men have no rights which white men are bound to respect. (Great applause.) I, going to Wellington with the full knowledge of all this, knew that if that man was taken to Columbus, he was hopelessly gone, no matter whether he had ever been in slavery before or not. I knew that I was in the same situation myself, and that by the decision of your honor, if any man whatever were to claim me as his slave and seize me, and my brother, being a lawyer, should seek to get out a writ of *habeas corpus* to expose the falsity of the claim, he would be thrust into prison under one provision of the Fugitive Slave Law, for interfering with the man claiming to be in pursuit of a fugitive; and I, by the perjury of a solitary wretch, would, by another of its provisions, be helplessly doomed to life-long bondage, without the possibility of escape.

Some persons may say there is no danger of free persons being seized and carried off as slaves. No one need labor under such a delusion. Sir, four of the eight persons who were first carried back under the act of 1850 were afterwards proved to be free men. The pretended owner declared they were not his, after his agent had 'satisfied the commissioner' that they were, by his oath. They were free persons, but wholly at the mercy of one man. And but last Sabbath afternoon a letter came to me from a gentleman in St. Louis, informing me that a young lady, who was formerly under my instruction at Columbus, a free person, is now lying in the jail at that place, claimed as the slave of some wretch who never saw her before, and waiting for testimony from relatives at Columbus to establish her freedom. I could stand here by the hour and relate such instances. In the very nature of the case they must be constantly occurring. A letter was not long since found upon the person of a counterfeiter when arrested, addressed to him by some Southern gentleman in which the writer says:

"*Go among the niggers; find out their marks and scars; make good descriptions and send to me, and I'll find masters for them.*"

That is the way men are carried "back" to slavery.

But in view of all the facts I say, that if ever a man is seized near me, and is about to be carried Southward as a slave before any legal investigation has been had, I shall hold it to be my duty, as I held it that day, to secure for him, if possible, a legal inquiry into the claim by which he is held. And I go farther; I say that if it is adjudged illegal to procure even such an investigation, then we are thrown back upon those last defenses of our rights, which cannot be taken from us, and which God gave us that we need not be slaves. I ask your honor, while I say this, to place yourself in my situation, and you will say with me that if your brother, if your friend, if your wife, if your child, had been seized by men who claimed them as fugitives, and the law of the land forbade you to ask any investigation, and precluded the possibility of any legal protection or redress—then you will say with me, that you would not only demand the protection of the law, but you would call in your neighbors and your friends, and would ask them to say with you, that these your friends would not be taken into slavery.

And now I thank you for this little leniency, this indulgence, in giving a man unjustly condemned, by a tribunal before which he is declared to have no rights, the privilege of speaking in his own behalf. I know that it will do nothing toward mitigating your sentence, but it is a privilege to be allowed to speak, and I thank you for it. I shall submit to the penalty, be it what it may. But I stand up here to say, that if for doing what I did on that day at Wellington, I am to go to jail for six months, and pay a fine of a thousand dollars, according to the Fugitive Slave Law, and such is the protection the laws of this country afford me, I must take upon myself the responsibility of self-protection; and when I come to be claimed by some perjured wretch as his slave, I shall never be taken into slavery. And as in that trying hour I would have others do to me, as I would call upon my friends to help me; as I would call upon you, your honor, to help me, as I would call upon you (to the district attorney) to help me; and upon you (to Judge Bliss), and upon you (to his counsel), so help me God! I stand here to say that I will do all I can, for any man thus seized and held, though the inevitable penalty of six months' imprisonment and one thousand dollars fine for each offence hangs over me! We have a common humanity. You would do so; your manhood would require it; and no matter what the laws might be, you would honor yourself for doing it; your children to all generations would honor you for doing it; and every good and honest man would say you had done right!" (Great and prolonged applause in spite of the efforts of the court and the marshal.)

JERMAIN W. LOGUEN (1814-1871)

Tiring of bondage, "Jarm" Loguen rode one of his master's mares away from Tennessee to the free North. He became a noted Underground Railroad agent in upper New York. With Gerrit Smith and Samuel Ward he participated in the Jerry McHenry rescue. After the Civil War he became a bishop in the African Methodist Episcopal Church. His biography, *The Reverend J. W. Loguen, as a Slave and As a Freeman* (published anonymously 1859) is far more stilted than his own interesting open letters.

Reply to His Old Mistress

Syracuse (N. Y.), March 28, 1860.

MRS. SARAH LOGUE: Yours of the 20th of February is duly received, and I thank you for it. It is a long time since I heard from my poor old mother, and I am glad to know that she is yet alive, and, as you say, 'as well as common.' What that means, I don't know. I wish you had said more about her.

You are a woman; but had you a woman's heart, you never could have insulted a brother by telling him you sold his only remaining brother and sister, because he put himself beyond your power to convert him into money.

You sold my brother and sister, Abe and Ann, and twelve acres of land, you say, because I ran away. Now you have the unutterable meanness to ask me to return and be your miserable chattel, or, in lieu thereof, send you $1000 to enable you to redeem the *land*, but not to redeem my poor brother and sister! If I were to send you money, it would be to get my brother and sister, and not that you should get land. You say you are a *cripple*, and doubtless you say it to stir my pity, for you knew I was susceptible in that direction. I do pity you from the bottom of my heart. Nevertheless, I am indignant beyond the power of words to express, that you should be so sunken and cruel as to tear the hearts I love so much all to pieces; that you should be willing to impale and crucify us all, out of compassion for your poor *foot* or *leg*. Wretched woman! Be it known to you that I value my freedom, to say nothing of my mother, brothers and sisters, more than your whole body; more, indeed, than my own life; more than all the lives of all the slaveholders and tyrants under heaven.

You say you have offers to buy me, and that you shall sell me if I do not send you $1000, and in the same breath and almost in the same sentence, you say, 'You know we raised you as we did our own children.' Woman, did you raise your *own children* for the market? Did you raise them for the whipping-post? Did you raise them to be driven off, bound to a coffle in chains? Where are my poor bleeding brothers and sisters? Can you tell? Who was it that sent them off into sugar and cotton fields, to be kicked and cuffed, and whipped, and to groan and die; and where no kin can hear their groans, or attend and sympathize at their dying bed, or follow in their funeral? Wretched woman! Do you say *you* did not do it? Then I reply, your husband did, and *you* approved the deed—and the very letter you sent me shows that your heart approves it all. Shame on you!

But, by the way, where is your husband? You don't speak of him. I infer, therefore, that he is dead; that he has gone to his great account, with all his sins against my poor family upon his head. Poor man! gone to meet the spirits of my poor, outraged and murdered people, in a world where Liberty and Justice are *Masters*.

But you say I am a thief, because I took the old mare along with me. Have you got to learn that I had a better right to the old mare, as you call her, than Mannasseth Logue had to me? Is it a greater sin for me to steal his horse, than it was for him to rob my mother's cradle, and steal me? If he and you infer that I forfeit all my rights to you, shall not I infer that you forfeit all your rights to me? Have you got to learn that human rights are mutual and reciprocal, and if you take my liberty and life, you forfeit your own liberty and life? Before God and high heaven, is there a law for one man which is not a law for every other man?

If you or any other speculator on my body and rights, wish to know how I regard my rights, they need but come here, and lay their hands on me to enslave me. Did you think to terrify me by presenting the alternative to give my money to you, or give my body to slavery? Then let me say to you, that I meet the proposition with unutterable scorn and contempt. The proposition is an outrage and an insult. I will not budge one hair's breadth. I will not breathe a shorter breath, even to save me from your persecutions. I stand among a free people, who, I thank God, sympathize with my rights, and the rights of mankind; and if your emissaries and venders come here to re-enslave me, and escape the unshrinking vigor of my own right arm, I trust my strong and brave friends, in this city and State, will be my rescuers and avengers.

Yours, &c.,

J. W. LOGUEN.

CHARLOTTE FORTEN (1837-1914)

Charlotte Forten, granddaughter of James Forten, Revolutionary War veteran and abolitionist of Philadelphia, left her home in 1854 to go to Salem, Massachusetts, to enter school, since she was unable to obtain an education in her native Philadelphia. There she went to the Higginson Grammar School, winning applause for her poetry. Upon graduation from the State Normal School, she taught in white grammar schools until the Civil War when, as an agent of the Freedmen's Aid Society, she went to Port Royal, St. Helena Island, to teach. After the war she moved to Boston, where she worked with the New England Freedmen's Aid Society. Later she taught in Charleston, S. C., and in Washington, D. C., where, in 1878, she married Francis J. Grimké. For the *National Anti-Slavery Standard* she wrote a series of sketches, *Glimpses of New England,* and in 1864 she contributed to the *Atlantic Monthly* two sketches drawn from her experiences on the Sea Islands. The following selection is reprinted by permission of Mrs. Anna J. Cooper whom Dr. Grimké appointed literary executor of his wife's and his own works. Mrs. Cooper is completing a book of reminiscences of the Grimkés and an edition of Miss Forten's writings.

Life on the Sea Islands

IT WAS ON THE LATE AFTERNOON of a warm, murky day late in October that our steamer, the United States, touched the landing at Hilton Head. A motley assemblage had collected on the wharf,—officers, soldiers, and "contraband" of every size and hue: black was, however, the prevailing color. The first view of Hilton Head is desolate enough,— a long, low, sandy point, stretching out into the sea, with no visible dwellings upon it, except the rows of small white-roofed houses which have lately been built for the freed people.

After signing a paper wherein we declared ourselves loyal to the Government, and wherein, also, were set forth fearful penalties, should we ever be found guilty of treason, we were allowed to land, and immediately took General Saxton's boat, the Flora, for Beaufort.

The General was on board, and we were presented to him. He is handsome, courteous, and affable, and looks—as he is—the gentleman and the soldier.

From Hilton Head to Beaufort the same long, low line of sandy coast, bordered by trees; formidable gunboats in the distance, and the gray ruins of an old fort, said to have been built by the Huguenots more than two hundred years ago. Arrived at Beaufort, we found that we had not yet reached our journey's end. While waiting for the boat which was to take us to our island of St. Helena, we had a little time to observe the ancient town. The houses in the main street, which fronts the "Bay," are large and handsome, built of wood, in the usual Southern style, with spacious piazzas, and surrounded by fine trees. We noticed in one yard a magnolia, as high as some of our largest shade-maples, with rich, dark, shining foliage. A large building which was once the Public Library is now a shelter for freed people from Fernandina. Did the Rebels know it, they would doubtless upturn their aristocratic noses, and exclaim in disgust, "To what base uses," etc. We confess that it was highly satisfactory to us to see how the tables had turned, now that "the whirligig of time has brought about its revenges." We saw the market-place, in which slaves were sometimes sold; but we were told that the buying and selling at auction were usually done in Charleston. The arsenal, a large stone structure, was guarded by cannon and sentinels. The houses in the smaller streets had mostly a dismantled, desolate look. We saw no one in the streets but soldiers and freed people. There were indications that already Northern improvements had reached this Southern town. Among them was a wharf, a convenience that one wonders how the Southerners could so long have existed without. The more we know of their mode of life, the more are we inclined to marvel at its utter shiftlessness.

Little colored children of every hue were playing about the streets, looking as merry and happy as children ought to look,—now that the evil shadow of Slavery no longer hangs over them. Some of the officers we met did not impress us favorably. They talked flippantly, and sneeringly of the negroes, whom they found we had come down to teach, using an epithet more offensive than gentlemanly. They assured us that there was great danger of Rebel attacks, that the yellow fever prevailed to an alarming extent, and that, indeed, the manufacture of coffins was the only business that was at all flourishing at present. Although by no means daunted by these alarming stories, we were glad when the announcement of our boat relieved us from their edifying conversation.

We rowed across to Ladies Island, which adjoins St. Helena, through the splendors of a grand Southern sunset. The gorgeous clouds of crimson and gold were reflected as in a mirror in the smooth, clear waters below. As we glided along, the rich tones of the negro boatmen broke upon the evening stillness,—sweet strange, and solemn:—

> Jesus make de blind to see,
> Jesus make de cripple walk,
> Jesus make de deaf to hear.
> Walk in, kind Jesus!
> No man can hender me.

It was nearly dark when we reached the island, and then had a three-miles' drive through the lonely roads to the house of the superintendent. We thought how easy it would be for a band of guerrillas, had they chanced that way, to seize and hang us; but we were in that excited, jubilant state of mind which makes fear impossible, and sang "John Brown" with a will, as we drove through the pines and palmettos. Oh, it was good to sing that song in the very heart of Rebeldom! Harry, our driver, amused us much. He was surprised to find that we had not heard of him before. "Why, I thought eberybody at de Nort had heard o' me!" he said, very innocently. We learned afterward that Mrs. F., who made the tour of the islands last summer, had publicly mentioned Harry. Some one had told him of it, and he of course imagined that he had become quite famous. Notwithstanding this little touch of vanity, Harry is one of the best and smartest men on the island.

Gates occurred, it seemed to us, at every few yards' distance, made in the oldest fashion,—opening in the middle, like folding doors, for the accommodation of horsemen. The little boy who accompanied us as gate-opener answered to the name of Cupid. Arrived at the headquarters of the general superintendent, Mr. S., we were kindly received by him and the ladies, and shown into a large parlor, where a cheerful wood-fire glowed in the grate. It had a home-like look; but still there was a sense of unreality about everything, and I felt that nothing less than a vigorous "shaking-up," such as Grandfather Smallweed daily experienced, would arouse me thoroughly to the fact that I was in South Carolina.

The next morning L. and I were awakened by the cheerful voices of men and women, children and chickens, in the yard below. We ran to the window, and looked out. Women in bright-colored handkerchiefs, some carrying pails on their heads, were crossing the yard, busy with their morning work; children were playing and tumbling around them. On every face there was a look of serenity and cheerfulness. My heart gave a great throb of happiness as I looked at them, and thought, "They are free! so long down-trodden, so long crushed to the earth, but now in their old homes, forever free!" And I thanked God that I had lived to see this day.

After breakfast Miss T. drove us to Oaklands, our future home. The road leading to the house was nearly choked with weeds. The house itself was in a dilapidated condition, and the yard and garden had a sadly neglected look. But there were roses in bloom; we plucked handfuls of feathery, fragrant acacia-blossoms; ivy crept along the ground and under the house. The freed people on the place seemed glad to see us. After talking with them, and giving some directions for cleaning the house, we drove to the school, in which I was to teach. It is kept in the Baptist Church,—a brick building, beautifully situated in a grove of live-oaks. These trees are the first objects that attract one's attention here: not that they are finer than our Northern oaks, but because of the singular gray moss with which every branch is heavily draped. This hanging moss grows on nearly all the trees, but on none so luxuriantly as on the live-oak. The pendants are often four or five feet long, very graceful and beautiful, but giving the trees a solemn, almost funereal look. The school was opened in September. Many of the children had, however, received instruction during the summer. It was evident that they had made very rapid improvement, and we noticed with pleasure how bright and eager to learn many of them seemed. They sang in rich, sweet tones, and with a peculiar swaying motion of the body, which made their singing the more effective. They sang "Marching Along," with great spirit, and then one of their own hymns, the air of which is beautiful and touching:

> My sister, you want to git religion,
>   Go down in de Lonesome Valley;
> My brudder, you want to git religion,
>   Go down in de Lonesome Valley.

Chorus

> Go down in de Lonesome Valley,
> Go down in de Lonesome Valley, my Lord,
> Go down in de Lonesome Valley,
>   To meet my Jesus dere!

> Oh, feed on milk and honey,
> Oh, feed on milk and honey, my Lord,
> Oh, feed on milk and honey,
>   Meet my Jesus dere!

Oh, John he brought a letter,
Oh, John he brought a letter, my Lord,
Oh, Mary and Marta read 'em,
    Meet my Jesus dere!

Chorus

Go down in de Lonesome Valley, etc.

They repeat their hymns several times, and while singing keep perfect time with their hands and feet.

On our way homeward we noticed that a few of the trees were beginning to turn, but we looked in vain for the glowing autumnal hues of our Northern forests. Some brilliant scarlet berries—the cassena—were growing along the road-side, and on every hand we saw the live-oak with its moss-drapery. The palmettos disappointed me; stiff and ungraceful, they have a bristling, defiant look, suggestive of Rebels starting up and defying everybody. The land is low and level,—not the slightest approach to a hill, not a rock, nor even a stone to be seen. It would have a desolate look, were it not for the trees, and the hanging moss and numberless vines which festoon them. These vines overrun the hedges, form graceful arches between the trees, encircle their trunks, and sometimes cling to the topmost branches. In February they begin to bloom, and then throughout the spring and summer we have a succession of beautiful flowers. First comes the yellow jessamine, with its perfect, gold-colored, and deliciously fragrant blossoms. It lights up the hedges, and completely canopies some of the trees. Of all the wild-flowers this seems to me the most beautiful and fragrant. Then we have the snow-white, but scentless Cherokee rose, with its lovely, shining leaves. Later in the season come the brilliant trumpet-flower, the passion flower, and innumerable others.

The Sunday after our arrival we attended service at the Baptist Church. The people came in slowly; for they have no way of knowing the hour, except by the sun. By eleven they had all assembled, and the church was well filled. They were neatly dressed in their Sunday attire, the women mostly wearing clean, dark frocks, with white aprons and bright-colored hand-handkerchiefs. Some had attained to the dignity of straw hats with gay feathers, but these were not nearly as becoming nor as picturesque as the handkerchiefs. The day was warm, and the windows were thrown open as if it were summer, although it was the second day of November. It was very pleasant to listen to the beautiful hymns, and look from the crowd of dark, earnest faces within, upon the grove of noble oaks without. The people sang, "Roll, Jordan, Roll," the grandest of all their hymns. There is a great, rolling wave of sound through it all.

> Mr. Fuller settin' on de Tree ob Life,
> Fur to hear de Jordan roll.
> Oh, roll, Jordan! roll, Jordan! roll, Jordan roll!

Chorus

> Oh, roll, Jordan, roll! oh, roll, Jordan, roll!
> My soul arise in heab'n, Lord,
> Fur to hear de Jordan roll!

> Little chil'en, learn to fear de Lord,
> And let your days be long.
> Oh, roll, Jordan! roll, Jordan roll!

Chorus

> Oh, march, de angel, march! oh, march, de angel, march!
> My soul arise in heab'n, Lord,
> Fur to hear de Jordan roll!"

The "Mr. Fuller" referred to was their former minister, to whom they seem to have been much attached. He is a Southerner, but loyal, and is now, I believe, living in Baltimore. After the sermon the minister called upon one of the elders, a gray-headed old man, to pray. His manner was very fervent and impressive, but his language was so broken that to our unaccustomed ears it was quite intelligible. After the services the people gathered in groups outside, talking among themselves, and exchanging kindly greetings with the superintendents and teachers. In their bright handkerchiefs and white aprons they made a striking picture under the gray-mossed trees. We drove afterward a mile farther, to the Episcopal Church, in which the aristocracy of the island used to worship. It is a small white building, situated in a fine grove of live-oaks, at the junction of several roads. On one of the tombstones in the yard is the touching inscription in memory of two children,—"Blessed little lambs, and *art thou* gathered into the fold of the only true shepherd? Sweet *lillies* of the valley, and *art thou* removed to a more congenial soil?" The floor of the church is of stone, the pews of polished oak. It has an organ, which is not so entirely out of tune as are the pianos on the island. One of the ladies played, while the gentlemen sang,—old-fashioned New-England church-music, which it was pleasant to hear, but it did not thrill us as the singing of the people had done.

During the week we moved to Oaklands, our future home. The

house was of one story, with a low-roofed piazza running the whole length. The interior had been thoroughly scrubbed and whitewashed; the exterior was guiltless of whitewash or paint. There were five rooms, all quite small, and several dark little entries, in one of which we found shelves lined with old medicine-bottles. These were a part of the possessions of the former owner, a Rebel physician, Dr. Sams by name. Some of them were still filled with his nostrums. Our furniture consisted of a bedstead, two bureaus, three small pine tables, and two chairs, one of which had a broken back. These were lent to us by the people. The masters, in their hasty flight from the islands, left nearly all their furniture; but much of it was destroyed or taken by the soldiers who came first, and what they left was removed by the people to their own houses. Certainly, they have the best rights to it. We had made up our minds to dispense with all luxuries and even many conveniences; but it was rather distressing to have no fire, and nothing to eat. Mr. H. had already appropriated a room for the store which he was going to open for the benefit of the freed people, and was superintending the removal of his goods. So L. and I were left to our own resources. But Cupid the elder came to the rescue,— Cupid, who, we were told, was to be our right-hand man, and who very graciously informed us that he would take care of us; which he at once proceeded to do by bringing in some wood, and busying himself in making a fire in the open fire-place. While he is thus engaged, I will try to describe him. A small, wiry figure, stockingless, shoeless, out at the knees and elbows, and wearing the remnant of an old straw hat, which looked as if it might have done good service in scaring the crows from a cornfield. The face nearly black, very ugly, but with the shrewdest expression I ever saw, and the brightest, most humorous twinkle in the eyes. One glance at Cupid's face showed that he was not a person to be imposed upon, and that he was abundantly able to take care of himself, as well as of us. The chimney obstinately refused to draw; in spite of the original and very uncomplimentary epithets which Cupid heaped upon it,—while we stood by, listening to him in amusement, although nearly suffocated by the smoke. At last perseverance conquered, and the fire began to burn cheerily. Then Amaretta, our cook,—a neat-looking black woman, adorned with the gayest of head-handkerchiefs,—made her appearance with some eggs and hominy, after partaking of which we proceeded to arrange our scanty furniture, which was soon done. In a few days we began to look civilized, having made a table-cover of some red and yellow handkerchiefs which we found among the store-goods,—a carpet of red and black woolen plaid, originally intended for frocks and shirts,—

a cushion, stuffed with corn-husks and covered with calico, for a lounge, which Ben, the carpenter, had made for us of pine boards,— and lastly some corn-husk beds, which were an unspeakable luxury, after having endured agonies for several nights, sleeping on the slats of a bedstead. It is true, the said slats were covered with blankets, but these might as well have been sheets of paper for all the good they did us. What a resting-place it was: Compared to it, the gridiron of St. Lawrence—fire excepted—was a bed of roses.

The first day at school was rather trying. Most of my children were very small, and consequently restless. Some were too young to learn the alphabet. These little ones were brought to school because the older children—in whose care their parents leave them while at work—could not come without them. We were therefore willing to have them come, although they seemed to have discovered the secret of perpetual motion, and tried one's patience sadly. But after some days of positive, though not severe treatment, order was brought out of chaos, and I found but little difficulty in managing and quieting the tiniest and most restless spirits. I never before saw children so eager to learn, although I had had several years' experience in New-England schools. Coming to school is a constant delight and recreation to them. They come here as other children go to play. The older ones, during the summer, work in the fields from early morning until eleven or twelve o'clock, and then come into school, after their hard toil in the hot sun, as bright and as anxious to learn as ever.

Of course there are some stupid ones, but these are the minority. The majority learn with wonderful rapidity. Many of the grown people are desirous of learning to read. It is wonderful how a people who have been so long crushed to the earth, so imbruted as these have been—and they are said to be among the most degraded negroes of the South,—can have so great a desire for knowledge, and such a capability for attaining it. One cannot believe that the haughty Anglo-Saxon race, after centuries of such an experience as these people have had, would be very much superior to them. And one's indignation increases against those who, North as well as South, taunt the colored race with inferiority while they themselves use every means in their power to crush and degrade them, denying them every right and privilege, closing against them every avenue of elevation and improvement. Were they, under such circumstances, intellectual and refined, they would certainly be vastly superior to any other race that ever existed.

After the lessons, we used to talk freely to the children, often giving them slight sketches of some of the great and good men. Before teaching them the "John Brown" song, which they learned to sing with great spirit, Miss T. told them the story of the brave old man who had died for them. I told them about Toussaint, thinking it well they should know what one of their own color had done for his race. They listened attentively, and seemed to understand. We found it rather hard to keep their attention in school. It is not strange, as they have been so entirely unused to intellectual concentration. It is necessary to interest them every moment, in order to keep their thoughts from wandering. Teaching here is consequently far more fatiguing than at the North. In the church, we had of course but one room in which to hear all the children; and to make one's self heard, when there were often as many as a hundred and forty reciting at once, it was necessary to tax the lungs very severely.

My walk to school, of about a mile, was part of the way through a road lined with trees,—on one side stately pines, on the other noble live-oaks, hung with moss and canopied with vines. The ground was carpeted with brown, fragrant pine-leaves; and as I passed through in the morning, the woods were enlivened by the delicious songs of mocking-birds, which abound here, making one realize the truthful felicity of the description in "Evangeline,"—

> The mocking-bird, wildest of singers,
> Shook from his little throat such floods of delirious music
> That the whole air and the woods and the waves seemed to listen.

The hedges were all aglow with the brilliant scarlet berries of the cassena, and on some of the oaks we observed the mistletoe, laden with its pure white, pearl-like berries. Out of the woods the roads are generally bad, and we found it hard work plodding through the deep sand.

* * * * *

In the evenings, the children frequently came in to sing and shout for us. These "shouts" are very strange,—in truth, almost indescribable. It is necessary to hear and see in order to have any clear idea of them. The children form a ring, and move around in a kind of shuffling dance, singing all the time. Four or five stand apart, and sing very energetically, clapping their hands, stamping their feet, and rocking their bodies to and fro. These are the musicians, to whose performance the shouters keep perfect time. The grown people on this plantation did not shout, but they do on some of the other plantations. It is very comical to see little children, not more than three or four years old, entering into the performance with all their might. But the shouting of the grown people is rather solemn and impressive than otherwise.

We cannot determine whether it has a religious character or not. Some of the people tell us that it has, others that it has not. But as the shouts of the grown people are always in connection with their religious meetings, it is probable that they are the barbarous expression of religion, handed down to them from their African ancestors, and destined to pass away under the influence of Christian teachings.[1] The people on this island have no songs. They sing only hymns, and most of these are sad. Prince, a large black boy from a neighboring plantation, was the principal shouter among the children. It seemed impossible for him to keep still for a moment. His performances were most amusing speciments of Ethiopian gymnastics. Amaretta the younger, a cunning, kittenish little creature of only six years old, had a remarkably sweet voice. Her favorite hymn, which we used to hear her singing to herself as she walked through the yard, is one of the oddest we have heard:—

> What makes ole Satan follow me so?
> Satan got nuttin' 't all fur to do wid me.

Chorus

> Tiddy Rosa, hold your light!
> Brudder Tony, hold your light!
> All de member, hold bright light
> On Canaan's shore!

This is one of the most spirited shouting tunes. "Tiddy" is their word for sister.

A very queer-looking old man came into the store one day. He was dressed in a complete suit of brilliant Brussels carpeting. Probably it had been taken from his master's house after the "gun-shoot"; but he looked so very dignified that we did not like to question him about it. The people called him Doctor Crofts,—which was, I believe, his master's name, his own being Scipio. He was very jubilant over the new state of things, and said to Mr. H.,—"Don't hab me feelins hurt now. Used to hab me feelins hurt all de time. But don't hab 'em hurt now no more." Poor old soul! We rejoiced with him that he and his brethren no longer have their "feelins" hurt, as in the old time.

On the Sunday before Thanksgiving, General Saxton's noble Proclamation was read at church. We could not listen to it without emotion. The people listened with the deepest attention, and seemed to understand and appreciate it. Whittier has said of it and its writer,—

---

[1] See below, Katherine Dunham, "The Negro Dance," pp. 990 ff.

"It is the most beautiful and touching official document I ever read. God bless him! 'The bravest are the tenderest.' "

General Saxton is truly worthy of the gratitude and admiration with which the people regard him. His unfailing kindness and consideration for them—so different from the treatment they have sometimes received at the hands of other officers—have caused them to have unbounded confidence in General *"Saxby,"* as they call him.

After the service, there were six couples married. Some of the dresses were unique. One was particularly fine,—doubtless a cast-off dress of the bride's former mistress. The silk and lace, ribbons, feathers and flowers, were in a rather faded condition. But, comical as the costumes were, we were not disposed to laugh at them. We were too glad to see the poor creatures trying to lead right and virtuous lives. The legal ceremony, which was formerly scarcely known among them, is now everywhere consecrated. The constant and earnest advice of the minister and teachers has not been given in vain; nearly every Sunday there are several couples married in church. Some of them are people who have grown old together.

Thanksgiving-Day was observed as a general holiday. According to General Saxton's orders, an ox had been killed on each plantation, that the people might that day have fresh meat, which was a great luxury to them, and, indeed, to all of us. In the morning, a large number—superintendents, teachers, and freed people—assembled in the Baptist Church. It was a sight not soon to be forgotten,—that crowd of eager, happy black faces, from which the shadow of Slavery had forever passed. "Forever free! forever free!" those magical words of the Proclamation were constantly singing themselves in my soul. After an appropriate prayer and sermon by Mr. P., and singing by the people, General Saxton made a short, but spirited speech, urging the young men to enlist in the regiment then forming under Colonel Higginson. Mrs. Gage told the people how the slaves in Santa Cruz had secured their liberty. It was something entirely new and strange to them to hear a woman speak in public; but they listened with great attention, and seemed much interested. Before dispersing, they sang "Marching Alone," which is an especial favorite with them. It was a very happy Thanksgiving-Day for all of us. The weather was delightful; oranges and figs were hanging on the trees; roses, oleanders, and japonicas were blooming out-of-doors; the sun was warm and bright; and over all shone gloriously the blessed light of Freedom,— Freedom forevermore! . . .

GEORGE H. WHITE (1852-1918)

George H. White, last of the post-Civil War congressmen, was born a slave at Rosindale, North Carolina. He was educated in the North Carolina public schools and at Howard University, from which he was graduated in 1877. Admitted to the bar in 1879, he was elected in 1880 to the state legislature of North Carolina. From 1886 to 1894 he was solicitor of the Second Judicial District. In 1896 he was elected to Congress, where he served two terms. White was considered the successor to Langston, and, as the only Negro member of the House, protested against increasing racial discrimination, introducing the first of a series of antilynching bills. During the Spanish-American War period he advocated the formation of new Negro regiments. His farewell speech to Congress, delivered January 29, 1901, was quoted widely in the early years of the century.

Defense of the Negro Race

I WANT to enter a plea for the colored man, the colored woman, the colored boy, and the colored girl of this country. I would not thus digress from the question at issue and detain the House in a discussion of the interests of this particular people at this time but for the constant and the persistent efforts of certain gentlemen upon this floor to mold and rivet public sentiment against us as a people and to lose no opportunity to hold up the unfortunate few who commit crimes and depradations and lead lives of infamy and shame, as other races do, as fair specimens of representatives of the entire colored race. And at no time, perhaps, during the Fifty-sixth Congress were these charges and countercharges, containing, as they do, slanderous statements, more persistently magnified and pressed upon the attention of the nation than during the consideration of the recent reapportionment bill, which is now a law. As stated some days ago on this floor by me, I then sought diligently to obtain an opportunity to answer some of the statements made by gentlemen from different States, but the privilege was denied me; and I therefore must embrace this opportunity to say, out of season, perhaps, that which I was not permitted to say in season.

In the catalogue of members of Congress in this House perhaps none has been more persistent in his determination to bring the black man into disrepute and, with a labored effort, to show that he was unworthy of the right of citizenship than my colleague from North Carolina, Mr. Kitchin. During the first session of this Congress, while the constitutional amendment was pending in North Carolina, he labored long and hard to show that the white race was at all times and under all circumstances superior to the Negro by inheritance if not otherwise, and the excuse for his party supporting that amendment, which has since been adopted, was that an illiterate Negro was unfit to participate in making the laws of a sovereign State and the administration and execution of them; but an illiterate white man living by his side, with no more or perhaps not so much property, with no more exalted character, no higher thoughts of civilization, no more knowledge of the handicraft of government, had by birth, because he was white, inherited some peculiar qualification, clear, I presume only in the mind of the gentleman who endeavored to impress it upon others, that entitled him to vote, though he knew nothing whatever of letters. It is true, in my opinion, that men brood over things at times which they would have exist until they fool themselves and actually, sometimes honestly, believe that such things do exist.

I would like to call the gentleman's attention to the fact that the Constitution of the United States forbids the granting of any title of nobility to any citizen thereof, and while it does not in letters forbid the inheritance of this superior caste, I believe in the fertile imagination of the gentleman promulgating it, his position is at least in conflict with the spirit of that organic law of the land. He insists and, I believe, has introduced a resolution in this House for the repeal of the fifteenth amendment to the Constitution. As an excuse for his peculiar notions about the exercise of the right of franchise by citizens of the United States of different nationality, perhaps it would not be amiss to call the attention of this House to a few facts and figures surrounding his birth and rearing. To begin with, he was born in one of the counties in my district, Halifax, a rather significant name.

I might state as a further general fact that the Democrats of North Carolina got possession of the State and local government since my last election in 1898, and that I bid adieu to these historic walls on the fourth day of next March, and that the brother of Mr. Kitchin will succeed me. Comment is unnecessary. In the town where this young gentleman was born, at the general election last August for the adoption of the constitutional amendment, and the general election for the state and county officers, Scotland Neck had a registered white vote of 395, most of whom of course were Democrats, and a registered colored vote of 534, virtually if not all of whom were Republicans, and so voted. When the count was announced, however, there were 831 Democrats to 75 Republicans; but in the town of Halifax, the same county, the result was much more pronounced.

In that town the registered Republican vote was 345, and the total registered vote of the township was 539, but when the count was announced it stood 990 Democrats to 41 Republicans, or 492 more Democratic votes counted than were registered votes in the township. Comment here is unnecessary, nor do I think it necessary for anyone to wonder at the peculiar notion my colleague has with reference to the manner of voting and the method of counting these votes, nor is it to be a wonder that he is a member of this Congress, having been brought up and educated in such wonderful notions of dealing out fair-handed justice to his fellow-man.

It would be unfair, however, for me to leave the inference upon the minds of those who hear me that all the white people of the State of North Carolina hold views with Mr. Kitchin and think as he does. Thank God, there are many noble exceptions to the example he sets, that, too, in the Democratic party; men who have never been afraid that one uneducated, poor, depressed Negro could put to flight and chase into degradation two educated, wealthy, thrifty white men. There never has been, nor ever will be, any Negro domination in that State, and no one knows it any better than the Democratic party. It is a convenient howl, however, often resorted to in order to consummate a diabolical purpose by scaring the weak and gullible whites into support of measures and men suitable to the demagogue and the ambitious office seeker, whose crave for office overshadows and puts to flight all other considerations, fair or unfair.

As I stated on a former occasion, this young statesman has ample time to learn better and more useful knowledge than he has exhibited in many of his speeches upon this floor, and I again plead for him the statute of youth for the wild and spasmodic notions which he has endeavored to rivet upon his colleagues and this country. But I regret that Mr. Kitchin is not alone upon this floor in these peculiar notions advanced.

It is an undisputed fact that the Negro vote in the State of Alabama, as well as most of the other Southern States, has been effectively suppressed, either one way or the other—in some instances by constitutional amendment and State legislation, in others by cold-blooded fraud and intimidation, but whatever the method pursued, it is not denied, but frankly admitted in the speeches in this House, that the black vote has been eliminated to a large extent. Then, when some of us insist that the plain letter of the Constitution of the United States, which all of us have sworn to support, should be carried out, as expressed in the second section of the fourteenth amendment thereof, to wit:

"Representatives shall be apportioned among the several States according to their respective numbers, counting the whole number of persons in each State, excluding Indians not taxed. But when the right to vote at any election for the choice of electors for President and Vice-President of the United States, Representatives in Congress, the executive and judicial officers of a State, or the members of a legislature thereof, is denied to any of the male inhabitants of such State, being twenty-one years of age, and citizens of the United States, or in any way abridged, except for participation in rebellion, or other crime, the basis of representation therein shall be reduced in proportion which the number of such male citizens shall bear to the whole number of male citizens twenty-one years of age in such State."

That section makes the duty of every member of Congress plain, and yet the gentleman from Alabama (Mr. Underwood) says that the attempt to enforce this section of the organic law is the throwing down of firebrands, and notifies the world that this attempt to execute the highest law of the land will be retaliated by the South, and the inference is that the Negro will be even more severely punished than the horrors through which he has already come.

Let me make it plain: The divine law, as well as most of the State laws, says in substance: "He that sheddeth man's blood, by man shall his blood be shed." A highwayman commits murder, and when the officers of the law undertake to arrest, try, and punish him commensurate with the enormity of his crime, he straightens himself up to his full height and defiantly says to them: "Let me alone; I will not be arrested, I will not be tried, I'll have none of the execution of your laws, and in the event you attempt to execute your laws upon me, I will see to it that many more men, women, or children are murdered."

Here's the plain letter of the Constitution, the plain, simple, sworn duty of every member of Congress; yet these gentlemen from the South say, "Yes, we have violated your Constitution of the nation; we regard it as a local necessity; and now, if you undertake to punish us as the Constitution prescribes, we will see to it that our former deeds of disloyalty to that instrument, our former acts of disfranchisement and opposition to the highest law of the land will be repeated many fold."

Not content with all that has been done to the black man, not because of any deeds that he has done, Mr. Underwood advances the startling information that these people have been thrust upon the whites of the South, forgetting, perhaps, the horrors of the slave trade, the unspeakable horrors of the transit from the shores of Africa by means of the middle passage to the American clime; the enforced bondage of the blacks and their descendants for two and a half centuries in the United States, now, for the first time perhaps in the history of our lives, the information comes that these poor, helpless, and in the main inoffensive people were thrust upon our Southern brethren.

Individually, and so far as my race is concerned, I care but little about the reduction of Southern representation, except in so far as it becomes my duty to aid in the proper execution of all the laws of the land in whatever sphere in which I may be placed. Such reduction in representation, it is true, would make more secure the installment of the great Republican party in power for many years to come in all its branches, and at the same time enable the great party to be able to dispense with the further support of the loyal Negro vote; and I might here parenthetically state that there are some members of the Republican party today—"lily whites," if you please—who, after receiving the unalloyed support of the Negro vote for over thirty years, now feel that they have grown a little too good for association with him politically, and are disposed to dump him overboard. I am glad to observe, however, that this class constitutes a very small percentage of those to whom we have always looked for friendship and protection.

I wish to quote from another Southern gentleman, not so young as my other friends, and who always commands attention in this House by his wit and humor, even though his speeches may not be edifying and instructive. I refer to Mr. Otey, of Virginia, and quote from him in a recent speech on this floor, as follows:

"Justice is merely relative. It can exist between equals. It can exist among homogeneous people—among equals. Among heterogeneous people it never has and, in the very nature of things, it never will obtain. It can exist among lions, but between lions and lambs, never. If justice were absolute, lions must of necessity perish. Open his ponderous jaws and find the strong teeth which God has made expressly to chew lamb's flesh! When the Society for the Prevention of Cruelty to Animals shall overcome this difficulty, men may hope to settle the race question along sentimental lines, not sooner.

"These thoughts on the Negro are from the pen, in the main, of one who has studied the Negro question, and it was after I heard the gentleman from North Carolina, and after the introduction of the Crumpacker bill, that they occurred to me peculiarly appropriate."

I am wholly at sea as to just what Mr. Otey had in view in advancing the thoughts contained in the above quotation, unless he wished to extend the simile and apply the lion as a white man and the Negro as a lamb. In that case we will gladly accept the comparison, for of all animals known in God's creation the lamb is the most inoffensive, and has been in all ages held up as a badge of innocence. But what will my good friend of Virginia do with the Bible, for God says that He created all men of one flesh and blood? Again, we insist on having one race—the lion clothed with great strength, vicious, and with destructive propensities, while the other is weak, good natured, inoffensive, and useful—what will he do with all the heterogeneous intermediate animals, ranging all the way from the pure lion to the pure lamb, found on the plantations of every Southern State in the Union?

I regard his borrowed thoughts, as he admits they are, as very inaptly applied. However, it has perhaps served the purpose of which he intended it—the attempt to show the inferiority of the one and the superiority of the other. I fear I am giving too much time in the consideration of these personal comments of members of Congress, but I trust I will be pardoned for making a passing reference to one more gentleman—Mr. Wilson of South Carolina—who, in the early part of this month, made a speech, some parts of which did great credit to him, showing, as it did, capacity for collating, arranging, and advancing thoughts of others and of making a pretty strong argument out of a very poor case.

If he had stopped there, while not agreeing with him, many of us would have been forced to admit that he had done well. But his purpose was incomplete until he dragged in the reconstruction days and held up to scorn and ridicule the few ignorant, gullible, and perhaps purchasable Negroes who served in the State legislature of South Carolina over thirty years ago. Not a word did he say about the unscrupulous white men, in the main bummers who followed in the wake of the Federal Army and settled themselves in the Southern States, and preyed upon the ignorant and unskilled minds of the colored people, looted the States of their wealth, brought into lowest disrepute the ignorant colored people, then hied away to their Northern homes for ease and comfort the balance of their lives, or joined the Democratic party to obtain social recognition, and have greatly aided in depressing and further degrading those whom they had used as tools to accomplish a diabolical purpose.

These few ignorant men who chanced at that time to hold office are given as reason why the black man should not be permitted to participate in the affairs of the Government which he is forced to pay taxes to support. He insists that they, the Southern whites, are the black man's best friend, and that they are taking him by the hand and trying to lift him up; that they are educating him. For all that he and all Southern people have done in this regard, I wish in behalf of the colored people of the South to extend our thanks. We are not ungrateful to friends, but feel that our toil has made our friends able to contribute the stinty pittance which we have received at their hands.

I read in a Democratic paper a few days ago, the Washington *Times*, an extract taken from a South Carolina paper, which was intended to exhibit the eagerness with which the Negro is grasping every opportunity for educating himself. The clipping showed that the money for each white child in the State ranged from three to five times as much per capita as was given to each colored child. This is helping us some, but not to the extent that one would infer from the gentleman's speech . . . . With all these odds against us, we are forging our way ahead, slowly, perhaps, but surely. You may tie us and then taunt us for lack of bravery, but one day we will break the bonds. You may use our labor for two and a half centuries and then taunt us for our poverty, but let me remind you we will not always remain poor. You may withhold even the knowledge of how to read God's word and learn the way from earth to glory and then taunt us for our ignorance, but we will remind you that there is plenty of room at the top, and we are climbing.

After enforced debauchery, with the many kindred horrors incident to slavery, it comes with ill grace from the perpetrators of these deeds to hold up the shortcomings of some of our race to ridicule and scorn.

JOHN MERCER LANGSTON (1829-1897)

John Mercer Langston, like so many American Negroes, was of Negro, Indian, and Anglo-Saxon ancestry. His white father's will liberally provided for his education, and he studied at Oberlin College and in the law office of Philemon Bliss. Langston was admitted to the bar in 1855, the first Negro to practice law in the West. His examination for admission turned on the question, "Shall a Negro or mulatto be admitted to the Ohio bar?" and not on his evident legal knowledge. He was, however, admitted to the bar, since he "had more white than Negro blood." Langston tried both civil and criminal cases with a clientele that was largely white. But he served often in fugitive slaves cases, and with his brother Charles, was a dominant figure in the antebellum Negro conventions. He was elected several times to township offices, twice to the Oberlin council, served eleven years as member of the board of education of Oberlin, and supervised the schooling of Negro youth in Ohio. During the Civil War Langston helped recruit Negro troops, and at the close of the war was inspector-general of the freedmen's schools. He served as dean of the Law Department and as acting president of the newly established Howard

University. In 1877 he was appointed minister-resident and consul-general to Haiti. When Grover Cleveland was elected president, Langston, a dyed-in-the-wool Republican, returned to the United States. He was soon elected to the presidency of the Virginia Normal and Collegiate Institute. In 1888 he was elected to Congress from the state of Virgina. *From the Virginia Plantation to the National Capitol* (1894) is generally considered to be his autobiography, although written in the third person.

From The Exodus

. . . . IN THE DISCUSSIONS had in regard to the non-extension of slavery, the distinctive principles of the Republican party and its purposes should it come into power, nothing had been said with reference really, to the immediate abolition of slavery in the several States where it existed, and no well-defined position had been taken, no measures suggested for ameliorating the condition of the slave in such States should he be emancipated. Indeed, the one great purpose, the sole object which the most advanced leader of the Republican party advocated and expected to realize, was the prevention of the spread of slavery into territory then free. But it was discovered in the midst of our war against the rebellion, that the abolition of slavery, as just indicated, was a fitting and necessary war measure; and the brave and true Lincoln, with one mighty stroke of his pen, decreed the emancipation of the Negro, who went out from his prison-house of enslavement, but in the poverty bequeathed by centuries of hard and cruel oppression. He was landless; he was homeless. Destitute mainly of those things which distinguish the humblest life, he has been battling for the past seventeen years of his freedom, in a material sense, for the merest, simplest necessities of a lowly condition. In fact, the merest emancipation of person and body has been practically the only thing, up to this hour, which has been guaranteed him. In this connection it is our duty to discriminate between simple emancipation, accompanied by a destitution characteristic of slave existence, and practical freedom, in which such destitution does not ordinarily exist; for its provision is not made for the newly emancipated by State or national regulation, opportunity, with fair wages, ought to be given for regular and remunerative labor, with intelligent investment of its proceeds in those things which are indispensable to well-ordered and prosperous life.

This brings me directly to the consideration of the condition of the American ex-slave as we find him today, struggling for life, with its common, usual rewards, in the South. This condition ought to be considered in its several relations of protection, industry, and politics. In dwelling on this branch of the subject we are not to forget that our national constitution has been amended so as to guarantee freedom, civil rights, and the ballot to the freedman; that Congress has legislated in support of any rights, immunities, and privileges claimed by this class of our citizens; and that it is true that generally in the States of the South laws have been enacted the purpose and object of which seem to be the protection and conservation of the rights, civil and other, which belong to the same class. In a word, as far as mere legislation is concerned, the condition of the freedman seems to be altogether tolerable—indeed good. In a material and industrial point of view, however, as well as political, the difficulty in his case seems to be even more deep-rooted and hard of management. His real condition is described and appreciated only when we recollect that although emancipated and legislation has been had in this case, as stated, still he has not been given *practical independence* of the old slave-holding class, constituting the land-proprietors and the employers in the section where he lives and labors for daily support. And besides this, he is left to seek existence in the midst of those classes who of all others are most interested in demonstrating that emancipation is a failure; that the freedman is incapable of cultivating those things that pertain to dignified, honorable life; and that slavery is his natural and normal condition. Not only holding the lands, the old slave-holding class control the wealth and intelligence, as well as the social and governmental appliances of that section. They are masters in the church, masters in the courts, masters in the schools, masters in politics, masters at the polls, and masters of the legislatures, as well as the plantations, directing and controlling according to their caprices, their interests, their prejudices, and their predilections. The non-land-holding white of the South must do their bidding; and the non-landholding Negro, also, occupies a subservient position to them. Depending, then, upon his former master—the property holder—who is his abusive, tyrannical employer, making even harder exactions than he was wont to make of him when a slave, the condition of the freedman is certainly sad. . . .

*   *   *   *   *

The facts that bear upon this point are clear, positive, and undeniable. The freedman is without protection. His condition as a laborer, whether he work for wages, as a share-farmer, or a renter, is not favorable; indeed, it is lamentable; while as a voter, it is well known that he cannot safely cast a free ballot according to the dictates of a wise and patriotic judgment. The "bull-dozing" record of the South is well understood, and the knowledge of the bloody deeds of its instigators and supporters is widespread and fully appreciated by the people of our country. Nor do his appeals to the courts of justice for redress of wrong meet with any success. If he make an appeal on law and fact to a jury of his fellow-citizens, who should, even from their own interests, if from no other and higher consideration, do him justice, what is the result? Even if the facts be plain and the law clear in support of his claim, the jury disagree ordinarily, and the judicial remedy which would naturally work him justice is defeated in its operation. This is true in civil as well as criminal proceedings, especially where the interests of the landed class as against the freedman are involved. In this regard the black man seems to have no rights which the white man is bound to respect.

After seventeen years of emancipation, in a condition of life even worse than that of serfage, in struggles against want and hardship, taxing his utmost endurance, the freedman has at least discovered his real situation and necessities, and has resolved, if possible, to relieve himself by escaping thence. What more natural than his efforts in this regard, what more manly, what more worthy of him? What effort is better calculated to relieve him of his servile dependence? The movement is a declaration of the purpose of the freedman to assert and maintain that independence in his own behalf, without which no individual and no people can rise to the level of dignified and honorable manhood. His exodus, if justified on no other ground, is justified thoroughly and entirely by the fact that it is, on his part, an effort to relieve himself of his present condition of utter dependence upon the old slave-holding class which he has served so faithfully in the past, and thus secure for himself the fact as well as the consciousness of real freedom.

The history of the emancipated classes of the world, whether they have been serfs or slaves, abundantly sustain the assertion that in most cases in which emancipation has occurred, and the emancipated class has been left under the control of the former master class, in the midst of the old associations of its slavery, upon the plantations or estates where it was wont to labor, such class thus situated and thus controlled does not and cannot rise until by some means it has freed itself from the dependence connected with such condition. It remains, in fact, in a servile position, without self-control, self-reliance, or independent character; without the purpose to make earnest, courageous effort to accomplish those things which are worthy of manhood.

It is not astonishing that centuries of slavery imbued in the very soul of the enslaved the spirit of servility and dependence; nor is it astonishing that this feeling once mastering the soul of man, holds it chained to those things which work degradation and ruin to freedom. The soul of man is only relieved of this feeling as it becomes conscious of its own power in the assertions and maintenance of its own purposes in the struggles and achievements of life. And until the soul is emancipated from this freedom, man does not enjoy real, substantial freedom. While one man leans against another, or in his soul fears him, he is subservient; and in his subserviency loses his freedom as he does the real dignity of his manhood. And this is especially true of a class once enslaved.

To really comprehend the condition of the freed class, it is necessary to understand and appreciate that on the part of the ex-master class there still exists the feeling of superiority; the feeling of the right to rule, direct, and, in fact, to own, if not the body and soul, certainly the services of its former slaves; while on the part of the dependent and serving class, there exists, from long habit connected with its slave condition, the sense of inferiority, of subserviency—a disposition to go and come as commanded. Either the relations of the two classes must be changed entirely, and the change thoroughly recognized and admitted by both; or the former masters will attempt the continuance of their old conduct and ways of mastership; while the other class, not conscious of its freedom, will continue to serve as formerly from fear and force of habit, their freedom being only recognized as something ideal, without the practical benefits which it should bring.

If there be any doubt in the mind of any intelligent person in regard to this matter, he has only to read carefully the history of the emancipation of the serf of Russia and consider his present condition; the history of the West India bondman and consider his situation, to be entirely convinced that the statement is true. Wallace, in dwelling upon the emancipation of the serfs in Russia, and in considering the question as to how their condition may be improved, states, in addition to other considerations offered, that "it would be well to organize an extensive system of emigration by which a portion of the peasantry would be transferred from the barren soil of the North and West to the rich fertile lands of the Eastern provinces." . . .

* * * * *

How shall the American ex-slave, who has served for two hundred and forty-five years under the influence of which I speak, be relieved of the presence and control of a class heretofore his masters? The history of the world offers but one solution of this question, and that solution is found in his exodus. Let him go forth; and where sympathy and the recognition of liberty and equal rights are accorded him; where labor is to be performed; where struggle is to be made; where the stern realities of life are to be met, there let him demonstrate his courage, his self-reliance, his manly independence. Under such new conditions his capacities, his powers, and his efforts will win the crown which befits the brow of noble manhood.

The exodus of the Colored American is intimately connected with and inseparable from the continued existence of the old order of things in the South. Up to this time there seems to have been in this regard practically little, if any, change. It is very true that a few plantations, comparatively speaking, have changed hands; a few even of the former slave class have here and there possessed themselves of small homes, have bought small pieces of land, and erected thereon small houses, but the "the great house" has not disappeared, nor has the old Negro quarter; and in some of the Southern States the old whipping-post, with its proverbial thirty-nine lashes, is still recognized as a judicial institution. Nor have the modes of industry, or the crops grown in that section, been materially changed. Cotton and sugar are the chief products of the South to-day, as they were a half century ago. Nor has there been any change, certainly no general and fundamental change, in the feelings and purposes of the old slave-holding class as to their right to work, drive, and scourge the Negro laborer. Having been his master once, their conduct would indicate that they believe, even in spite of the action of the General Government and the results of our great war, that their mastership is to continue forever. Nor has the feeling of the non-slaveholding class of the South undergone any material change with respect to the freedman. Indeed, it seems to be true that this class hates the colored man more now than when he was a slave; and stands ready at the command of the aristocratic class to do its bidding, even to the shedding of his blood. As showing that this condition of affairs is true and that little advancement has been made, one has only to pronounce in your hearing certain terrible words coined in connection with the barbarous, cruel treatment that has been meted out to the emancipated class of Mississippi, Louisiana, and other States formerly slaveholding. What is the meaning of the frightful words, "Ku-Klux," "Bull-dozers;" and the terrible expression, "the shot-gun or Mississippi policy?" The meaning is clear. It is that neither the old slaveholding spirit, nor the old slaveholding purpose or control is dead in the South; that plantocracy, with its fearful power and influences, has not passed away; that the colored American under it is in a condition of practical enslavement, trodden down and outraged by those who exercise control over him. Such things will continue so long as the spirit of slavery exists in the South, so long as the old master class is in power; so long as the freedman consents to remain in a condition more terrible than any serfage of which history gives account. How can this condition of things be broken up? How can the planter-rule be changed? How can the master class be made to realize that it is no longer slaveholding, and that the slave has been set free. And how can the freedman be made to feel and realize that having been emancipated, practical liberty is within his reach, and that it is his duty to accept and enjoy it in its richest fruits; fearing neither the responsibilities of enfranchised manhood, nor trembling as a coward in the presence of trials and dangers?

To the intelligent and sagacious inquirer, who, without feeling, without passion, but philosophically and in a statesman-like manner considers this matter, there can be, it seems to me, but a single answer. It is this: Let the freedman of the South, as far as practicable, take from the old plantocracy, by his exodus, the strong arms, broad shoulders, stalwart bodies, which by compulsion, have been made to prop and sustain such system too long already in this day of freedom. Let him stand from beneath and the fabric will fall, and a new and necessary reconstruction will follow.

* * * * *

In view then of the considerations presented; to secure the highest good of all the parties concerned by the overthrow of the plantocracy of the South and the reconstruction of the industrial system of that section, on the basis of free labor, justice, and fair dealing; to relieve the ex-slave from his dependent and practical slavery, and while giving him the fact and consciousness of his freedom and independence, furnish him the opportunity to cultivate, not only ordinary labor, but to build up his present interests, industrial, material, educational, and moral, with reference to that future of which his past conduct, his capabilities and powers, his loyal and Christian devotion, give such reasonable promise, I do most reverently and heartily accept the lesson contained in the words—

"I have surely seen the affliction of my people which are in Egypt, and have heard their cry by reason of their taskmasters; for I know their sorrows; and I am come down to deliver them out of the hand of the Egyptians and to bring them up out of that land into a good land, and large, a land flowing with milk and honey."

BOOKER T. WASHINGTON (1858-1915)

Booker T. Washington (see also p. 742), whose work as principal of Tuskegee Institute, public lecturer, and spokesman of the doctrine of interracial co-operation made him famous, was born in Hales Ford, Virginia. His *Up from Slavery,* one of the most widely known of American autobiographies, tells a story of success which ranks with that of Benjamin Franklin and Edward Bok in its adherence to the best in American democratic tradition. From the time of his historic speech at the opening of the Cotton States Exposition at Atlanta to his death, Washington lectured tirelessly, advocating industrial education for the Negro, collecting funds for the work at Tuskegee, helping organize such projects as the National Negro Business League. His published speeches, the best known of which are the Atlanta Exposition Address, printed here, the "Harvard Alumni Dinner Address," delivered June 24, 1896, upon the occasion of Harvard's awarding him an honorary Master of Arts degree, and the "Robert Gould Shaw Monument Address," delivered in Boston on May 31, 1897, run into the hundreds. Typical of the sentiments contained in his best speeches is the "message to Harvard" and her dead sons who aided the Negro's struggle: "Tell them that the sacrifice was not in vain. Tell them that by habits of thrift and economy, by way of the industrial school and college, we are coming. We are crawling up, working up, yea, bursting up. Often through oppression, unjust discrimination, and prejudice, but through them all we are coming up, and with proper habits, intelligence, and property, there is no power on earth that can stop us."

Speech at the Atlanta Exposition

MR. PRESIDENT AND GENTLEMEN of the Board of Directors and Citizens: One-third of the population of the South is of the Negro race. No enterprise seeking the material, civil, or moral welfare of this section can disregard this element of our population and reach the highest success. I but convey to you, Mr. President and Directors, the sentiment of the masses of my race when I say that in no way have the value and manhood of the American Negro been more fittingly and generously recognized than by the managers of this magnificent Exposition at every stage of its progress. It is a recognition that will do more to cement the friendship of the two races than any occurrence since the dawn of freedom.

Not only this, but the opportunity here afforded will awaken among us a new era of industrial progress. Ignorant and inexperienced, it is not strange that in the first years of our new life we began

673

at the top instead of at the bottom; that a seat in Congress or the State Legislature was more sought than real estate or industrial skill; that the political convention or stump speaking had more attractions than starting a dairy farm or truck garden.

A ship lost at sea for many days suddenly sighted a friendly vessel. From the mast of the unfortunate vessel was seen a signal: "Water, water; we die of thirst!" The answer from the friendly vessel at once came back: "Cast down your bucket where you are." A second time the signal, "Water, water; send us water;" ran up from the distressed vessel, and was answered: "Cast down your bucket where you are." The captain of the distressed vessel, at last heeding the injunction, cast down his bucket, and it came up full of fresh, sparkling water from the mouth of the Amazon River. To those of my race who depend upon bettering their condition in a foreign land, or who underestimate the importance of cultivating friendly relations with the Southern white man, who is his next door neighbor, I would say: "Cast down your bucket where you are"—cast it down in making friends in every manly way of the people of all races by whom we are surrounded.

Cast it down in agriculture, mechanics, in commerce, in domestic service, and in the professions. And in this connection it is well to bear in mind that whatever other sins the South may be called to bear, when it comes to business, pure and simple, it is in the South that the Negro is given a man's chance in the commercial world, and in nothing is this Exposition more eloquent than in emphasizing this chance. Our greatest danger is, that in the great leap from slavery to freedom we may overlook the fact that the masses of us are to live by the productions of our hands, and fail to keep in mind that we shall prosper in proportion as we learn to draw the line between the superficial and the substantial, the ornamental geegaws of life and the useful. No race can prosper till it learns that there is as much dignity in tilling a field as in writing a poem. It is at the bottom of life we must begin, and not at the top. Nor should we permit our grievances to overshadow our opportunities.

To those of the white race who look to the incoming of those of foreign birth and strange tongue and habits for the prosperity of the South, were I permitted I would repeat what I say to my own race, "Cast down your bucket where you are." Cast it down among the 8,000,000 Negroes whose habits you know, whose fidelity and love you have tested in days when to have proved treacherous meant the ruin of your firesides. Cast down your bucket among these people who have, without strikes and labor wars, tilled your fields, cleared your forests, builded your railroads and cities, and brought forth treasures from the bowels of the earth, and helped make possible this magnificent representation of the progress of the South. Casting down your bucket among my people, helping and encouraging them as you are doing on these grounds, and, with education of head, hand and heart, you will find that they will buy your surplus land, make blossom the waste places in your fields, and run your factories. While doing this, you can be sure in the future, as in the past, that you and your families will be surrounded by the most patient, faithful, law-abiding, and unresentful people that the world has seen. As we have proved our loyalty to you in the past, in nursing your children, watching by the sick bed of your mothers and fathers, and often following them with tear-dimmed eyes to their graves, so in the future, in our humble way, we shall stand by you with a devotion that no foreigner can approach, ready to lay down our lives, if need be, in defense of yours, interlacing our industrial, commercial, civil, and religious life with yours in a way that shall make the interests of both races one. In all things that are purely social we can be as separate as the fingers, yet one as the hand in all things essential to mutual progress.

There is no defense or security for any of us except in the highest intelligence and development of all. If anywhere there are efforts tending to curtail the fullest growth of the Negro, let these efforts be turned into stimulating, encouraging, and making him the most useful and intelligent citizen. Effort or means so invested will pay a thousand per cent interest. These efforts will be twice blessed— blessing him that gives and him that takes.

There is no escape through law of man or God from the inevitable:

> "The laws of changeless justice bind
> Oppressor with oppressed;
> And close as sin and suffering joined
> We march to fate abreast."

Nearly sixteen millions of hands will aid you in pulling the load upwards, or they will pull against you the load downwards. We shall constitute one-third and more of the ignorance and crime of the South, or one-third its intelligence and progress; we shall contribute one-third to the business and industrial prosperity of the South, or we shall prove a veritable body of death, stagnating, depressing, retarding every effort to advance the body politic.

Gentlemen of the Exposition, as we present to you our humble effort at an exhibition of our progress, you must not expect overmuch. Starting thirty years ago with ownership here and there in a few quilts and pumpkins and chickens (gathered from miscellaneous sources), remember the path that has led from these to the invention and production of agricultural implements, buggies, steam engines, newspapers, books, statuary, carving, paintings, the management of drug stores and banks has not been trodden without contact with thorns and thistles. While we take pride in what we exhibit as a result of our independent efforts, we do not for a moment forget that our part in this exhibition would fall far short of your expectations but for the constant help that has come to our educational life, not only from the Southern States, but especially from Northern philanthropists, who have made their gifts a constant stream of blessing and encouragement.

The wisest among my race understand that the agitation of questions of social equality is the extremest folly, and that progress in the enjoyment of all the privileges that will come to us must be the result of severe and constant struggle rather than of artificial forcing. No race that has anything to contribute to the markets of the world is long in any degree ostracized. It is important and right that all privileges of the law be ours, but it is vastly more important that we be prepared for the exercise of those privileges. The opportunity to earn a dollar in a factory just now is worth infinitely more than the opportunity to spend a dollar in an opera house.

In conclusion, may I repeat that nothing in thirty years has given us more hope and encouragement, and drawn us so near to you of the white race, as this opportunity offered by the Exposition; and here bending, as it were, over the altar that represents the results of the struggles of your race and mine, both starting practically empty-handed three decades ago, I pledge that, in your effort to work out the great and intricate problem which God has laid at the doors of the South, you shall have at all times the patient, sympathetic help of my race; only let this be constantly in mind that, while from representations in these buildings of the products of field, of forest, of mine, of factory, letters, and art, much good will come, yet far above and beyond material benefits will be the higher good, that let us pray God will come, in a blotting out of sectional differences and racial animosities and suspicions, in a determination to administer absolute justice, in a willing obedience among all classes to the mandates of law. This, coupled with our material prosperity, will bring into our beloved South a new heaven and a new earth.

MARCUS GARVEY (1887-1939)

Marcus Garvey was the most magnetic leader produced by Negroes during the twenties. His resounding addresses, his grandiosely conceived United Africa, with its red, black, and green flag, its hierarchy of dukes and duchesses, knights and ladies, its Black Star Line, its Black Cross nurses, and its newspaper, *The Negro World,* captured the imaginations of countless American Negroes, who were ready to follow their leader back to Africa. Garvey was born in St. Anne's Parish, Jamaica, and was educated for the printer's trade. He went to England studying at night at the University of London; later he worked at the ports of Central America, in the West Indies, and in the United States, which he finally made the headquarters of his movement. The Universal Negro Improvement Association flourished in the postwar years, starting business enterprises, raising money for ships, and saving funds to return to Africa. The movement was broken when Garvey was sentenced to Atlanta for using the mails to defraud; after his release from prison, he was deported. Garvey's speeches and writings, no matter how unrealistic, had an appeal to the urban Negro mass mind; they are skilled examples of propaganda designed for a minority people. The *Philosophy and Opinions of Marcus Garvey,* compiled by Amy Jacques-Garvey, was published in 1925. The following selection is used by permission of Mrs. Garvey.

The Negro's Place in World Reorganization

GRADUALLY WE ARE APPROACHING the time when the Negro peoples of the world will have either to consciously, through their own organization, go forward to the point of destiny as laid out by themselves, or must sit quiescently and see themselves pushed back into the mire of economic serfdom, to be ultimately crushed by the grinding mill of exploitation and be exterminated ultimately by the strong hand of prejudice.

There is no doubt about it that we are living in the age of world reorganization out of which will come a set program for the organized races of mankind that will admit of no sympathy in human affairs, in that we are· planning for the great gigantic struggle of the survival of the fittest group. It becomes each and every one engaged in this great race for place and position to use whatsoever influence possible to divert the other fellow's attention from the real object. In our own sphere in America and the western world we find that we are being camouflaged, not so much by those with whom we are competing for our economic, political existence, but by men from within our own race, either as agents of the opposition or as unconscious fools who are endeavoring to flatter us into believing that our future should rest with chance and with Providence, believing that through these agencies will come the solution of the restless problem. Such leadership is but preparing us for the time that is bound to befall us if we do not exert ourselves now toward our own creative purpose. The mission of the Universal Negro Improvement Association is to arouse the sleeping consciousness of Negroes everywhere to the point where we will, as one concerted body, act for our own preservation. By laying the foundation for such we will be able to work toward the glorious realization of an emancipated race and a constructed nation. Nationhood is the strongest security of any people and it is for that the Universal Negro Improvement Association strives at this time. With the clamor of other peoples for a similar purpose, we raise a noise even to high heaven for the admission of the Negro into the plan of autonomy.

On every side we hear the cry of white supremacy—in America, Canada, Australia, Europe, and even South America. There is no white supremacy beyond the power and strength of the white man to hold himself against the others. The supremacy of any race is not permanent; it is a thing only of the time in which the race finds itself powerful. The whole world of white men is becoming nervous as touching its own future and that of other races. With the desire of self-preservation, which naturally is the first law of nature, they raise the hue and cry that the white race must be first in government and in control. What must the Negro do in the face of such a universal attitude but to align all his forces in the direction of protecting himself from the threatened disaster of race domination and ultimate extermination?

Without a desire to harm anyone, the Universal Negro Improvement Association feels that the Negro should without compromise or any apology appeal to the same spirit of racial pride and love as the great white race is doing for its own preservation, so that while others are raising the cry of a white America, a white Canada, a white Australia, we also without reservation raise the cry of a "Black Africa." The critic asks, "Is this possible?" and the four hundred million courageous Negroes of the world answer, "Yes."

Out of this very reconstruction of world affairs will come the glorious opportunity for Africa's freedom. Out of the present chaos and European confusion will come an opportunity for the Negro never enjoyed in any other age, for the expansion of himself and the consolidation of his manhood in the direction of building himself a national power in Africa.

The germ of European malice, revenge and antagonism is so deeply rooted among certain of the contending powers that in a short while we feel sure they will present to Negroes the opportunity for which we are organized.

No one believes in the permanent disablement of Germany, but all thoughtful minds realize that France is but laying the foundation through revenge for a greater conflict than has as yet been seen. With such another upheaval, there is absolutely no reason why organized Negro opinion could not be felt and directed in the channel of their own independence in Africa.

To fight for African redemption does not mean that we must give up our domestic fights for political justice and industrial rights. It does not mean that we must become disloyal to any government or to any country wherein we were born. Each and every race outside of its domestic national loyalty has a loyalty to itself; therefore, it is foolish for the Negro to talk about not being interested in his own racial, political, social and industrial destiny. We can be as loyal American citizens or British subjects as the Irishman or the Jew, and yet fight for the redemption of Africa, a complete emancipation of the race.

Fighting for the establishment of Palestine does not make the American Jew disloyal; fighting for the independence of Ireland does not make the Irish-American a bad citizen. Why should fighting for the freedom of Africa make the Afro-American disloyal or a bad citizen?

The Universal Negro Improvement Association teaches loyalty to all governments outside of Africa; but when it comes to Africa, we feel that the Negro has absolutely no obligation to any one but himself.

Out of the unsettled state and condition of the world will come such revolutions that will give each and every race that is oppressed the opportunity to march forward. The last world war brought the opportunity to many heretofore subject races to regain their freedom. The next world war will give Africa the opportunity for which we are preparing. We are going to have wars and rumors of wars. In another twenty or thirty years we will have a changed world, politically, and Africa will not be one of the most backward nations, but Africa shall be, I feel sure, one of the greatest commonwealths that will once more hold up the torchlight of civilization and bestow the blessings of freedom, liberty and democracy upon all mankind.

Generally the public is kept misinformed of the truth surrounding new movements of reform. Very seldom, if ever, reformers get the truth told about them and their movements. Because of this natural attitude, the Universal Negro Improvement Association has been greatly handicapped in its work, causing thereby one of the most liberal and helpful human movements of the twentieth century to be held up to ridicule by those who take pride in poking fun at anything not already successfully established.

The white man of America has become the natural leader of the world. He, because of his exalted position, is called upon to help in all human efforts. From nations to individuals the appeal is made to him for aid in all things affecting humanity, so, naturally, there can be no great mass movement or change without first acquainting the leader on whose sympathy and advice the world moves.

It is because of this, and more so because of a desire to be Christian friends with the white race, why I explain the aims and objects of the Universal Negro Improvement Association.

The Universal Negro Improvement Association is an organization among Negroes that is seeking to improve the condition of the race, with the view of establishing a nation in Africa where Negroes will be given the opportunity to develop by themselves, without creating the hatred and animosity that now exists in countries of the white race through Negroes rivaling them for the highest and best positions in government, politics, society and industry. The organization believes in the rights of all men, yellow, white and black. To us, the white race has a right to the peaceful possession and occupation of countries of its own and in like manner the yellow and black races have their rights. It is only by an honest and liberal consideration of such rights can the world be blessed with the peace that is sought by Christian teachers and leaders.

The following preamble to the constitution of the organization speaks for itself:

"The Universal Negro Improvement Association and African Communities' League is a social, friendly, humanitarian, charitable, educational, institutional constructive, and expansive society, and is founded by persons, desiring to the utmost to work for the general uplift of the Negro peoples of the world. And the members pledge themselves to do all in their power to conserve the rights of their noble race and to respect the rights of all mankind, believing always in the Brotherhood of Man and the Fatherhood of God. The motto of the organization is: One God! One Aim! One Destiny! Therefore, let justice be done to all mankind, realizing that if the strong oppresses the weak confusion and discontent will ever mark the path of man, but with love, faith and charity toward all the reign of peace and plenty will be heralded into the world and the generation of men shall be called Blessed."

The declared objects of the association are:

"To establish a Universal Confraternity among the race; to promote the spirit of pride and love; to reclaim the fallen; to administer to and assist the needy; to assist in civilizing the backward tribes of Africa; to assist in the development of Independent Negro Nations and Communities; to establish a central nation for the race; to establish Commissaries or Agencies in the principal countries and cities of the world for the representation of all Negroes; to promote a conscientious Spiritual worship among the native tribes of Africa; to establish Universities, Colleges, Academies and Schools for the racial education and culture of the people; to work for better conditions among Negroes everywhere."

MORDECAI W. JOHNSON (1890-   )

Mordecai W. Johnson, one of the most distinguished of today's pulpit speakers, was born in Paris, Tennessee. He was educated at Morehouse (A. B., 1913), Rochester Theological Seminary (B. D., 1919) and at Harvard (S. T. M., 1922). He has been pastor of the First Baptist Church, Charleston, W. Va., Student Secretary of the International Committee of the Y. M. C. A., and professor of English and, later, of economics and history at Morehouse College. In 1926 he was elected president of Howard University. In 1929 he was awarded the Spingarn Medal. The following is reprinted by permission of the author.

The Faith of the American Negro

SINCE THEIR EMANCIPATION from slavery the masses of American Negroes have lived by the strength of a simple but deeply moving faith. They have believed in the love and providence of a just and holy God; they have believed in the principles of democracy and in the righteous purpose of the Federal Government, and they have believed in the disposition of the American people as a whole and in the long run to be fair in all their dealings.

In spite of disfranchisement and peonage, mob violence and public contempt, they have kept this faith and have allowed themselves to hope with the optimism of Booker T. Washington that in proportion as they grew in intelligence, wealth, and self-respect they should win the confidence and esteem of their fellow white Americans, and should gradually acquire the responsibilities and privileges of full American citizenship.

In recent years, and especially since the Great War, this simple faith has suffered a widespread disintegration. When the United States Government set forth its war aims, called upon Negro soldiers to stand by the colors and Negro civilians, men, women, and children, to devote their labor and earnings to the cause, and when the war shortage of labor permitted a quarter million Negroes to leave the former slave States for the better conditions of the North, the entire Negro people experienced a profound sense of spiritual release. For the first time since emancipation they found themselves bound with other Americans in the spiritual fellowship of a common cause.

When they stood on the height of this exalted experience and looked down on their pre-war poverty, impotence, and spiritual isolation, they realized as never before the depth of the harm they had suffered, and there arose in them a mighty hope that in some way the war would work a change in their situation. For a time indeed it seemed that their hope would be realized. For when the former slave States saw their labor leaving for the North, they began to reflect upon the treatment they had been accustomed to give the Negro, and they decided that it was radically wrong, Newspapers and public orators everywhere expressed this change of sentiment, set forth the wrongs in detail, and urged immediate improvement. And immediate improvement came. Better educational facilities were provided here and there, words of appreciation for the worth and spirit of the Negro as a citizen began to be uttered, and public committees arose to inquire into his grievances and to lay out programs for setting these grievances right. The colored people in these States had never experienced such collective good-will, and many of them were so grateful and happy that they actually prayed for the prolongation of the war.

At the close of the war, however, the Negro's hopes were suddenly dashed to the ground. Southern newspapers began at once to tell the Negro soldiers that the war was over and the sooner they forgot it the better. "Pull off your uniform," they said, "find the place you had before the war, and stay in it." "Act like a Negro should act," said one newspaper, "work like a Negro should work, talk like a Negro should talk, study like a Negro should study. Dismiss all ideas of independency or of being lifted up to the plane of the white man. Understand the necessity of keeping a Negro's place." In connection with such admonitions there came the great collective attacks on Negro life and property in Washington, Chicago, Omaha, Elaine, and Tulsa. There came also the increasing boldness of lynchers who advertised their purposes in advance and had their photographs taken around the burning bodies of their victims. There came vain appeals by the colored people to the President of the United States and to the houses of Congress. And finally there came the reorganization and rapid growth of the Ku Klux Klan.

The swift succession and frank brutality of all this was more than the Negro people could bear. Their simple faith and hope broke down. Multitudes took weapons in their hands, and fought back violence with bloody resistance. "If we must die," they said, "it is well that we die fighting." And the Negro American world, looking on their deed with no light of hope to see by, said: "It is self-defense; it is the law of nature, of man, and of God; and it is well."

From those terrible days until this day the Negro's faith in the righteous purpose of the Federal Government has sagged. Some have laid the blame on the parties in power. Some have laid it elsewhere. But all the colored people, in every section of the United States, believe that there is something wrong, and not accidentally wrong, at the very heart of the Government.

Some of our young men are giving up the Christian religion, thinking that their fathers were fools to have believed it so long. One group among us repudiates entirely the simple faith of former days. It would put no trust in God, no trust in democracy, and would entertain no hope for betterment under the present form of government. It believes that the United States Government is through and through controlled by selfish capitalists who have no fundamental good-will for Negroes or for any sort of laborers whatever. In their publications and on the platform the members of this group urge the colored man to seek his salvation by alliance with the revolutionary labor movement of America and the world.

Another and larger group among us believes in religion and believes in the principles of democracy. It believes that the creed of the former slave States is the tacit creed of the whole nation, and that the Negro may never expect to acquire economic, political, and spiritual liberty in America. This group has held congresses with representatives from the entire Negro world, to lay the foundations of a black empire, a black religion, and a black culture; it has organized the provisional Republic of Africa, set going a multitude of economic enterprises, instituted branches of its organization wherever Negroes are to be found, and binds them together with a newspaper ably edited in two languages.

Whatever one may think of these radical movements and their destiny, one thing is certain: they are home-grown fruits, with roots deep sprung in a world of black American sufferings. Their power lies in the appeal which they make to the Negro to find a way out of his trouble by new and self-reliant paths. The larger masses of the colored people do not belong to these more radical movements. They retain their belief in the Christian God, they love their country, and hope to work out their salvation within its bounds. But they are completely disillusioned. They see themselves surrounded on every hand by a sentiment of antagonism which does not intend to be fair. They see themselves partly reduced to peonage, shut out from labor unions, forced to an inferior status before the courts, made subjects of public contempt, lynched and mobbed with impunity, and deprived of the ballot, their only means of social defense. They see this antagonistic sentiment consolidated in the places of power in the former slave States and growing by leaps and bounds in the North and West. They know that it is gradually reducing them to an economic, political, and social caste. And they are now no longer able to believe with Dr. Booker T. Washington, or with any other man, that their own efforts after intelligence, wealth, and self-respect can in any wise avail to deliver them from these conditions unless they have the protection of a just and beneficent public policy in keeping with American ideals. With one voice, therefore, from pulpit and from press, and from the humblest walks of life, they are sending up a cry of pain and petition such as is heard today among the citizens of no other civilized nation in the world. They are asking for the protection of life, for the security of property, for the liberation of their peons, for the freedom to sell their labor on the open market, for a human being's chance in the courts, for a better system of public education, and for the boon of the ballot. They ask, in short, for public equality under the protection of the Federal Government.

Their request is sustained by every sentiment of humanity and by every holy ideal for which this nation stands. The time has come when the elemental justice called for in this petition should be embodied in a public policy initiated by the Federal Government and continuously supervised by a commission of that Government representing the faith and will of the whole American people.

The Negro people of America have been with us here for three hundred years. They have cut out forests, tilled our fields, built our railroads, fought our battles, and in all of their trials until now they have manifested a simple faith, a grateful heart, a cheerful spirit, and an undivided loyalty to the nation that has been a thing of beauty to behold. Now they have come to the place where their faith can no longer feed on the bread of repression and violence. They ask for the bread of liberty, of public equality, and public responsibility. It must not be denied them.

We are now sufficiently far removed from the Civil War and its animosities to see that such elemental justice may be given to the Negro with entire good-will and helpfulness toward the former slave States. We have already had one long attempt to build a wealth and culture on the backs of slaves. We found that it was a costly experiment, paid for at last with the blood of our best sons. There are some among our citizens who would turn their backs on history and repeat that experiment, and to their terrible heresy they would convert our entire great community. By every sacred bond of love for them we must not yield, and we must no longer leave them alone with their experiment. The faith of our whole nation must be brought to their support until such time as it is clear to them that their former slaves can be made both fully free and yet their faithful friends.

Across the seas the darker peoples of the earth are rising from their long sleep and are searching this Western world for light. Our Christian missionaries are among them. They are asking these missionaries: Can the Christian religion bind this multi-colored world in bonds of brotherhood? We of all nations are best prepared to answer that question, and to be their moral inspiration and their friend. For we have the world's problem of race relationships here in crucible, and by strength of our American faith we have made some encouraging progress in its solution. If the fires of this faith are kept burning around that crucible, what comes out of it is able to place these United States in the spiritual leadership of all humanity. When the Negro cries with pain from his deep hurt and lays his petition for elemental justice before the nation, he is calling upon the American people to kindle anew about the crucible of race relationships the fires of American faith.

HOWARD THURMAN (1899-   )

Howard Thurman, born in Florida, was educated at the Florida Baptist Academy at Jacksonville, which was removed to St. Augustine and renamed the Florida Normal Institute before he completed his training; at Morehouse (A. B., 1923), Rochester Theological Seminary (B. D., 1926), the Oberlin Divinity School, and at Haverford, where, as a Kent Fellow, he studied with Rufus Jones. In 1935 he was the leader of a "pilgrimage of friendship" of students of religion to the colleges of Burma, India, and Ceylon. For two years he was a pastor in Oberlin; in 1929 he went to Morehouse as student religious adviser. Since 1932 he has been at Howard in a similar capacity and as dean of the Chapel and professor of Christian theology. He has contributed to *The Christian Century, The World Tomorrow, The Southern Workman, Christendom,* and *The Journal of Religion.* "Good News for the Underprivileged," orginally published in *Religion and Life,* is here reprinted by permission of the author.

Good News for the Underprivileged

THERE IS NO MORE SEARCHING QUESTION that the individual Christian should ask himself than this: What is the message, the good news, that Christianity has to give to the poor, the disinherited, the dispossessed? In seeking an answer certain basic historical facts must be taken into account. First, Christianity is an historical faith, the result of a movement that was started in time, by an individual located in history. Setting aside for the moment all metaphysical and theological considerations, simply stated, this individual was a Jew. That mere fact is arresting. Did it simply happen that as a result of some accidental collocation of atoms, this human being came into existence so conditioned and organized within himself that he was a perfect instrument for the embodiment of a set of ideals of such alarming potency that they were capable of changing the calendar, redirecting the thought of the world, and placing a new sense of the rhythm of life in a weary nerve-broken civilization? Or was there something basic in the great womb of the people out of which he sprang that made of him the logical founding of a long development of race experience, ethical in quality and spiritual in tone? Doubtless there is widespread agreement with the latter position.

He was a poor Jew—so poor that his family could not afford a lamb for the birth presentation to the Lord, but had to secure doves instead (Leviticus 12.8). Is it too daring to suggest that in his poverty he was the symbol of the masses of men so that he could truly be Son of Man more naturally and accurately than if he had been a rich Jew?

As a poor Jew, Jesus was a member of a minority race, underprivileged and to a great degree disinherited. The Jews were not citizens of the Roman Empire and hence were denied the rights and privileges such citizenship guaranteed. They were a captive group, but not enslaved.

There were exceptions. The first great creative interpreter of the Christian religion was a Jew, but a Roman citizen. This fact is instructive in enabling us to understand the psychology of this flaming, mystic tent-maker with his amazing enthusiasm. It is demanding too much of human nature to expect that a man who was by blood and ties deeper than blood—religion—a member of a despised group, could overcome that fact and keep it from registering in the very ground of his underlying interpretation of the meaning of existence. No matter where Paul happened to be located within the boundaries of the then all inclusive Roman Empire, he could never escape the consciousness of his citizenship. Whenever he was being beaten by a mere Roman soldier, doubtless hired to be the instrument of discipline and imperialism of the Empire, he knew that in the name of the Emperor he could demand the rights of citizenship of the Empire. He could appeal to Caesar in his own right and be heard. It is to his great credit and a decided tribute to the "fragrance of Christ," of which he called himself the essence, that he did not resort to this more frequently. But there it stands, a distinguishing mark setting him off from his group in no uncertain fashion. Do we wonder then that he could say: "Every subject must obey the government authorities, for no authority exists apart from God, the existing authorities have been constituted of God, hence any one who resists authority is opposing the divine order, and the opposition will bring judgment on themselves . . . If you want to avoid being alarmed at the government authorities lead an honest life, and you will be commended for it; the magistrate is God's servant for your benefit. . . . You must be obedient, therefore, not only to avoid the divine vengeance but as a matter of conscience, for the same reason that you pay taxes. Since magistrates are God's offering bent upon the maintenance of order and authority" (Romans 13). Or again: "Slaves, be obedient to those who are your masters, saith the Lord, with reverence and trembling, with singleness of heart, as to Christ himself" (Ephesians 6.5). Other familiar references could be quoted. Why Paul could feel this way is quite clear, when we remember that he was a Jew—yes, but a free Jew. But Jesus was not a free Jew. If a Roman soldier kicked Jesus into a Galilean ravine, it was merely a Jew in the ravine. He could not appeal to Caesar. Jesus was compelled to expand the boundaries of his citizenship out beyond the paltry political limitations of a passing Empire, and establish himself as a Lord of Life, the Son of God, who caused his sun to shine upon Roman and Jew, free and bond. The implications of his insight had to be worked out on a narrow stage in the agonizing realities of the struggle of his people against an over-arching mighty power—the Roman Empire. *Christianity, in its social genesis, seems to me to have been a technique of survival for a disinherited minority.*

The meaning of his public commitment in the little Nazareth

synagogue, when he felt himself quickened into dedication by the liquid words of the prophet of Deutero-Isaiah, is much to the point:

> "The Spirit of the Lord is upon me:
> For he has consecrated me to preach the gospel to the poor,
> He has sent me to proclaim release for captives
> And recovery of sight for the blind, to set free the oppressed,
> To proclaim the Lord's year of favor." (Moffatt.)

What, then, is the gospel that this underprivileged One would proclaim to the poor and the disinherited? The first demand it makes is that fear should be uprooted and destroyed, so that the genuine power of the dominant group may not be magnified or emphasized. Fear is the lean, hungry hound of hell that rarely ever leaves the track of the dispossessed.

The dispossessed are a minority, sometimes a minority as to numbers, always a minority as to economic power, but even then, it is a matter of playing one element of the powerful over against the other. Because of the insecure political and economic position of the dispossessed, they are least able to protect themselves against violence and coercion on the part of the powerful. The fear of death is ever present. Men with healthy minds and fairly adequate philosophies do not fear death as an orderly process in the scheme of life. But it is exceedingly difficult for individuals to accommodate themselves to cataclysmic death at the hands of other men, not nature, without associating it with some lofty ideal or great cause. This is the lot of the dispossessed. Without a moment's notice any one of them may be falsely accused, tried, sentenced without adequate defense and certainly without hope of justice. This is true because the dispossessed man is without political and economic status as a psychological *fact,* whatever the idea of the state may specify to the contrary.

Fear becomes, therefore, a safety valve which provides for a release of certain tensions that will ordinarily be released in physical resistance. Physical resistance is almost always suicidal, because of a basic lack in the tools of violence and the numbers to use them. Fear is a natural defense because it acts as a constant check on the activities which may result in clashes and subsequent reprisals. Psychologically, it makes certain costly errors impossible for the individual and thereby becomes a form of normal insurance against violence. But it disorganizes the individual from within. It strikes continually at the basic ground of his self-estimate, and by so doing makes it impossible for him to live creatively and to function effectively even within the zones of agreement.

Religion undertakes to meet this situation in the life of the dispossessed by seeking to establish for the individual a transcending basis of security which locates its center in the very nature of life. Stated in conventional religious terminology, it assures the individual that he is a child of God. This faith, this confidence, this affirmation has a profound effect upon the individual's self-estimate. It assures him of a basic status that his environment cannot quite undermine. "Fear not, those who can kill the body, but rather fear him who can destroy both soul and body," says Jesus. To say that this is merely a defense mechanism is not to render it invalid. Granted that it may be, although I do not think so, the practical results of such a conception are rich and redemptive.

This kind of self-estimate makes for an inner-togetherness, carrying within it the moral obligation to keep itself intact. It gives to the inner life a regulation that is not conditioned by external forces. In its most intensified form it makes of men martyrs and saints. Operating on the lower reaches of experience, it gives to them a wholeness and a simple but terrible security that renders fear of persons and circumstances ridiculous.

Again, this kind of relaxation at the center of life, growing out of a healthy self-estimate, gives to the individual an objectivity and detachment which enable him to seek fresh and unsuspecting ways for defeating his environment. "Behold, I send you out as lambs among wolves, you must be wise as serpents and as harmless as doves." Often there are things on the horizon that point logically to a transformation of society, especially for the underprivileged, but he cannot cooperate with them because he is spiritually and intellectually confused. He mistakes fear for caution and caution for fear. Now, if his mind is free and his spirit unchained, he can work intelligently and courageously for a new day. Yes, with great calmness and relaxation, as sons of God, the underprivileged may fling their defiance into the teeth of circumstances as they work out their salvation with fear and trembling *as to God*.

Religion also insists upon basic sincerity and genuineness as to attitude and character. Let your words be yes and no; you must be clear and transparent, and of no harm to any one; have your motive so single that your purpose is clear and distinct—such are the demands of religion.

This emphasis in Christianity creates the most difficult problem for the weak. It is even more difficult than the injunction to love your enemies. This is true because it cuts the nerve of the most powerful defense that the weak have against the strong—deception. In the world of nature, the weak survive because in the regular process of natural selection ways of deceiving the enemy have been determined upon and developed. Among some lower animals and birds the techniques are quite uncanny. The humble cuttlefish is supplied with a tiny bag of sepia fluid, and when beset by an enemy he releases the fluid into the water, making it turn murky and cloudy. Under the cover of this smoke screen he disappears, to the utter confusion of his enemy.

Among many American Negroes, self-deception has been developed into an intricate subtle defense mechanism. This deception is often worked out with deliberate unerring calculation. A classic example is to be found in the spiritual, "All God's Chillun." The slave heard his master's minister talk about heaven as the final abode of those who had lived the good life. Naturally, the terror of his present existence made him seek early to become a candidate for a joyous to-morrow, under a very different order of existence. Knowing how hard and fast the lines were drawn between him and his master in this world, he decided that there must be two heavens; but no, for there is but one God. Then an insight occurred to him. While on earth, his master was having his heaven; when he died, he would have his hell. The slave was having his hell now; when he died, he would have his heaven. As he worked the next day chopping cotton, he sang to his fellow-slave: "I got shoes, you got shoes, all God's chillun got shoes (pointing to the rest of the slaves); when we get to heaven we're goin' to put on our shoes, and shout all over God's heaven. (No lines, no slave row there.) But everybody talking 'bout heaven (pointing to the big house where the master lives) ain't goin' there."

There are three possible solutions to the dilemma of genuineness as the underprivileged man faces it. First, deliberate deception and a naive confidence that God will understand the tight place in which the individual is caught and be merciful. It is needless to point out what such a course may do to the very foundation of moral values. Traffic along this avenue leads to the quicksand of complete moral breakdown and ineffectiveness. The second possibility is an open frankness and honesty of life projecting itself in a world-society built upon subterfuge and deceit. It is the way that is taken by the rare spirit in response to the highest demands of his nature without regard to consequences; for the average individual completely outside of the range of his powers as yet developed. It will mean stretching himself out of shape for the sake of ends that are neither clear nor valid. The third means accepting an attitude of compromise. The word is a bad one. No man can live in a society of which he does not approve without some measure of compromise. The good man is one who often with studied reflection seeks to reduce steadily to a vanishing point the areas of compromise without and within. The third attitude stated categorically is, absoluteness as to the ideal; compromise in achievement. This means that the battle must be fought to the limit of one's power in areas not fundamental to one's self-estimate and integrity. A line must be drawn beyond which the underprivileged man cannot go in compromising. Religion, with its cardinal virtue, sincerity, inspires the individual to become increasingly aware of, and sensitive to, the far-reaching significance of many of his simplest deeds, making it possible for him to act, in time, as though his deeds were of the very essence of the eternal. This type of action inspires courage and makes for genuineness at increasingly critical points. He is made to know that out of the heart are the issues of life and that life is its own restraint. With an insight overmastering and transcending, he becomes spiritually and practically convinced that *vengeance belongeth to God*. It becomes clear to him that there are some things in life that are worse than death.

The third demand that religion makes upon the underprivileged is that they must absorb violence directed against them by the exercise of love. No demand has been more completely misused. The keenest discrimination is quite necessary in the exercise of this prerogative of the spirit. It belongs in the same category as grace, the outpouring of unasked for and unobligated kindness without chartering it on the basis of objective merit. For the underprivileged man this often seems to mean cowardice and treason to his own highest group and personal interest. This particular emphasis of Christianity has many times been used by the exploiters of the weak to keep them submissive and subservient. For the man of power to tell the powerless to love is like the Zulu adage which says: "Full belly child says to empty belly child, be of good cheer!"

In examining the basic roots of the concept there are revealed three elements which are fundamental. Love always implies genuine courage. It is built upon an assumption of individual spiritual freedom that knows not the limitations of objective worthiness and merit. It means acting contrary to the logical demands of objective worthiness and character—hence the exercise of a kind of bold power, vast and overwhelming!

It means the exercise of a discriminatory understanding which is based upon the inherent worth of the other, unpredictable in terms of external achievement. It says, meet people where they are and treat them as if they were where they ought to be. Here we are dealing with something more than the merely formal and discursive, rational demand. It is the functioning of a way of knowing that Paul aptly describes as "having a sense of what is vital." Love of this sort places a crown over the head of another who is always trying to grow tall enough to wear it. In religion's profoundest moments it ascribes to God this complete prerogative.

It widens the foundations of life so that one's concept of self increasingly includes a larger number of other individual units of life. This implies the dramatic exercise of simple, direct, thoroughgoing imaginativeness rooted in an experience of life as one totality. Years ago, I encountered this quotation: "The statement, 'know thyself,' has been taken more mystically from the statement, 'thou hast seen thy brother, thou hast seen thy God.' "

In this third demand religion gives to the underprivileged man no corner for individual hatred and isolation. In complete confidence it sends him forth to meet the enemy upon the highway; to embrace him as himself, understanding his limitations and using to the limit such discipline upon him as he has discovered to be helpful in releasing and purifying his own spirit.

Only the underprivileged man may bring the message to the underprivileged. No other can without the penalty of the Pharisee. Jesus, the underprivileged One of Palestine, speaks his words of power and redemption across the ages to all the disinherited:

> "Come to me, all who are laboring and burdened,
> And I will refresh you.
> Take my yoke upon you and learn from me, for I am gentle
> and humble in heart, and you will find your souls
> refreshed;
> My yoke is kindly and my burden light."

VII
BIOGRAPHY

BIOGRAPHY

AUTOBIOGRAPHIES BY Negroes outnumber biographies, although collections of biographical sketches nearly bring the balance even. The curiosity concerning outstanding personalities from Gustavus Vassa, the educated African, to George Washington Carver, the wizard of Tuskegee, assures a wide audience for their life stories. For the sake of convincing immediacy, such stories should be told by the individuals themselves; but since the heroes are seldom literary figures, verisimilitude is attempted by having a sympathetic editor tell the story as far as possible in the individual's own words. Many autobiographies of Negroes, therefore, range from the "ghosted" to the "slightly revised," in the way of much autobiography of outstanding figures. Many, of course, are purely autobiography.

The earliest prose writing by an American Negro was an autobiographic pamphlet, *A Narrative of the Uncommon Sufferings and Surprising Deliverance of Briton Hammon, a Negro Man* (1760). Loggins characterizes *A Narrative of The Lord's Wonderful Dealings With J. Marrant, a Black...Taken Down from His Own Relation* (1785) as a more colorful work than its predecessor, "most unbelievable and most readable." These works resemble Defoe's adventure tales, without his magic, rather than the later antislavery autobiographies.

Much better as writing and more widely known was the first real autobiography attributed to a Negro, *The Interesting Narrative of the Life of Olondah Equiano, or Gustavus Vassa, the African* (1789). Though Vassa probably received editorial assistance and spent comparatively little time in America, his narrative is of definite importance in American literature as the forerunner of a long line of ex-slave autobiographies. It is a vivid story of adventure, carrying strong antislavery arguments.

From the end of the eighteenth century to the 1830's, there was little autobiographical writing. Richard Allen wrote a brief story of his life, but it was not printed until 1880. There were autobiographies of oddities: a Negro murderer, who made a sort of Newgate confession; a three-hundred-pound native African "measuring six feet around the waist"; James Albert Ukawsaw Gronniosaw, an African prince. *The*

Confessions of Nat Turner, obviously doctored by Thomas R. Gray, the editor, appeared in 1832.

In the thirties, however, a new literary form sprang into popularity. This was the autobiographic narrative of a fugitive slave, written for antislavery propaganda. Slavery as a subject fascinated the American public on both sides of the Mason and Dixon line. Above the line, however, the public was readier to listen to the slaves themselves than to their owners. Isaac Hopper, in his work with the Underground Railroad, was excited by the stories he heard from the lips of escaping slaves, and he set some of these down as *Tales of Oppression* (1853), which had been previously published in Northern newspapers. Levi Coffin, Harriet Beecher Stowe, and William Still were later Underground agents who did the same. But the sensationalism of *Slavery in the United States: A Narrative of the Life and Adventures of Charles Ball, A Black Man* (1836) awoke a realization of the value of the type to the antislavery cause and also to publishers. Charges of falsity naturally came from the South. Whittier is alleged to have been misled into serving as amanuensis for the dictation of the *Narrative of James Williams*; after evidence from the South disproved many of the statements in the book, the American Antislavery Society stopped its circulation, feeling rightly that their cause "needed no support of a doubtful character." There is no doubt that some refugees would draw the long bow; others would refuse complete accuracy for obvious reasons of shielding kinsfolk and abettors left behind. It is likely that certain zealous abolitionists would ask leading questions, and would heighten that which helped their cause. But the tendency to reject the entire body of fugitive slave narratives is unsound.

There were three classes of such narratives: the fictionalized, the dictated and edited, and the genuine autobiographies. To the first class belong the works of Ball and James Williams; to the second belong *The Narrative of the Life and Adventure of Henry Bibb, Written By Himself,* the editor of which insisted that he only corrected spelling and punctuation, and arranged the chapters and the table of contents, and *Running a Thousand Miles For Freedom* (1860), the life of William and Ellen Craft; to the third belong Samuel Ringgold Ward's *The Autobiography of a Fugitive Negro* and the *Narrative of William Wells Brown.*

One of the most popular of these narratives, the *Narrative of the Sufferings of Lewis and Milton Clarke* [etc.] is supposed to be a dictated joint autobiography. *Incidents in the Life of a Slave Girl* was dictated by "Linda Brent," really Mrs. Harriet Jacobs, to Lydia Maria Child. Linda Brent admits concealing names of places, and giving per-

sons fictitious names, but insists that her "descriptions fall far short
of the facts." Lydia Maria Child admitted to condensation and orderly
arrangement, but adds that with "trifling exceptions, both the ideas
and the language are [Linda's] own." Mrs. Child was confident of
Linda's veracity and attributed Linda's superior education to a kindly
mistress who taught her to read and spell and to her favorable circumstances on escaping from slavery.

Twelve Years A Slave: The Narrative of Solomon Northup (1853)
was a dictated autobiography. The editor, David Wilson, writes that
many of the statements are corroborated by abundant evidence. He is
satisfied with the reliability of Northup, who often repeated the same
story without deviating in the slightest particular, and who dictated
alterations "wherever the most trivial inaccuracy appeared." *Twelve
Years A Slave* seems less like a novel than *Incidents in the Life of
a Slave Girl*; it is one of the most readable of these autobiographies,
going into its twenty-seventh thousand in its second year. Northup was
kidnapped and sold to many masters in the deep South; his memories
of the cotton plantations of Louisiana are rich in material of social
interest.

Less spectacular than these is Josiah Henson's *Truth Is Stranger
Than Fiction: Father Henson's Story of His Life* (1858). His first
autobiographic pamphlet, *The Life of Josiah Henson...as Narrated by
Himself* (1849) was edited anonymously, but his second book, frequently enlarged, was his own work, as he had applied himself diligently to educational improvement in the intervening years. The
identification of Henson as the model for Uncle Tom has done some
disservice to Henson's proved manliness and ability to get along in this
world.

The autobiographies of William Wells Brown, Samuel Ringgold
Ward, and Frederick Douglass were unquestionably written by themselves. It is regrettable that the *Narrative of William Wells Brown*
(1847) and Ward's *Autobiography of a Fugitive Slave* are not longer,
because of the personalities of the authors. Douglass' growth as a
writer is traceable in his several autobiographies from the crude though
powerful *Narrative of the Life of Frederick Douglass* (1845), through
My Bondage and My Freedom (1855), which many consider his most
rewarding autobiographic work, to *The Life and Times of Frederick
Douglass* (1881). The last two belong definitely in the ranks of important American autobiographies.

Mrs. Keckley's *Behind the Scenes: or Thirty Years a Slave, and
Four Years in the White House* (1868) is said to be a dictated work,
but the truth of Mrs. Keckley's experiences has been vouched for.

Gamaliel Bradford, in his psychograph of Mary Todd Lincoln, considers Mrs. Keckley's book to be one of his best sources. Though an addition to Lincolniana and to the intimate history of Washington during the war years, it was never widely circulated and suspicions have been voiced that it was censored. Daniel Payne's *Recollections of Seventy Years* (1888) are drawn from his voluminous notebooks and journals. Since Payne was one of the best-educated Negroes of his day, the editorial assistance he received was only one of compilation and arrangement that a busy man in his declining years might fall back upon.

Though the last two books were published after the war, and are little concerned with slavery, they have been included with the fugitive slave autobiographies because they resemble them in spirit and cover the same period. These autobiographies have been unduly neglected. Though they contain the sentimentality and sensationalism of antislavery propaganda, they contain many glimpses of social reality valuable to the student. That in certain instances their status of autobiography is open to question should not weigh too heavily against them; if one dismisses all autobiographies that could be suspected of being "ghosted," autobiographic writing would surely dwindle in amount. A dictated autobiography can be essentially true. These autobiographies were the only written records of men who had undergone slavery. Why the eyewitness of the enslaved is inferior to the eyewitness of the slaveholder, why the anger and reproach of the one are to be rejected while the self-satisfaction of the other is to be trusted, are not clear. The fugitive slave autobiography was a popular literary type of the American romantic movement. Harriet Beecher Stowe's *Uncle Tom's Cabin* would not have been the same but for the early narratives of the Clarkes, Josiah Henson, and Frederick Douglass. They should not be considered useless merely because they do not present slavery as the "most gracious civilization ever found in America."

John Mercer Langston's purported autobiography (it was written in the third person, like *The Education of Henry Adams*) *From the Virginia Plantation to the National Capitol* (1894) is something of a bridge from the fugitive slave autobiography to a new type. Whereas the earlier type generally gave a picture of the harshness of slavery with the climax coming when the fugitive reached the free North, the later type showed the struggle to achieve status in the postwar world. Yet both types agree in showing struggle over great odds, ending with victory. Even though showing the bitter reality and incidental tragedies of slavery, the fugitive autobiographies were essentially optimistic: the hero won through, the cause would triumph. The postwar autobiographies are even more optimistic, even closer to the American dream, to the Horatio Alger formula that pervades so much American writing. The titles of the autobiographies of racial leaders are indicative: Booker T. Washington's *Up From Slavery* (1900), Robert Russa Moton's *Finding a Way Out* (1920), Kelly Miller's *Out of The House of Bondage* (1914), William Pickens' *Bursting Bonds* (1923), James Corrother's *In Spite of Handicap* (1916), Benjamin Brawley's *The Lower Rungs Of The Ladder* (1925), and A. Clayton Powell's *Against The Tide* (1939). Since these men lived American success stories, since all rose over such obstacles as prejudice, poverty, and lack of privilege, they are entitled to write American success stories. What is worth pointing out, however, is that the tradition whose motto is *ad astra per aspera* is not genuinely autobiographical. These books served for race edification and encouragement; they serve less as revelations of personalities.

The form and content of these autobiographies are therefore added instances of how the pressure of the Negro problem in America affects Negro writing. These works are not solely "success stories"; they are also valuable reflectors of social conditions, which appear more candidly than do the real selves of the authors. Since all deepen or repudiate superficial estimates of Negro character, they have an added value. None rises, however, to the stature of Douglass' later autobiographies, though *Up From Slavery* is more popular, because of the author's viewpoint and style.

The various recent trends in autobiographical writing have influenced Negro writers. James Weldon Johnson's *Along This Way* is less a divulging of personality than a social commentary, with swift but clear sketches of many of the personalities with whom he was in contact in his variegated career; W. E. B. DuBois' *Dusk of Dawn* (1940), as indicated by the subtitle "An Autobiography of a Race Concept," is a tracing of ideas; Claude McKay's *A Long Way From Home* (1937) and Langston Hughes's *The Big Sea* (1940) are in the tradition of the personal records of globe-trotting journalists. Taylor Gordon's *Born To Be* (1929) is a lighthearted, frank story of a Negro singer of widely varied experiences; Juanita Harrison's *My Great Wide Beautiful World* (1938) is similar. Both strain for humor. In almost direct contrast is Angelo Herndon's *Let Me Live* (1937), in the tradition of earlier autobiographies, a new abolitionist attack upon that slavery which was never abolished. Mary Church Terrell's *A Colored Woman in a White World* (1940) is the first full autobiography of an educated, leading Negro woman. The most recent autobiography is W. C. Handy's *Father of the Blues* (1941), the life story of a man who was closely associated with both the Southern milieu producing Negro folk song and Tin Pan Alley, which plays such a part in popular music.

The elder autobiographers were probably reticent as a mark of being well-bred. But they also had to consider their positions as leaders of a struggling minority, which they felt must always put its best foot forward. In line with the realistic movement, later autobiographers show more candor, both in social criticism and self-analysis. But not yet have there been autobiographies that achieve the highest virtue of autobiography: not race edification or defense, not social documentation, but truth about personality. Edgar Johnson writes in *One Mighty Torrent, The Drama of Biography:*

> Honesty is the greatest stumbling block of the autobiographer. The resolution to tell the truth about oneself takes a Spartan rigor of character, and the ability to do so requires a more than common insight. There have been few if any autobiographers who have told no untruths . . . If the autobiographer has purity of purpose, he wants to tell us the story of his life and to paint a portrait of his character as it appears to him . . . How deep the man's insight into himself goes, then, will determine the fundamental truth of his self-portrayal. Only those autobiographers that have purity of purpose and depth, as here defined, are of the highest quality.

BIOGRAPHY

Biographical writing by Negroes has been slight in quantity and quality. As with much of the autobiography by Negroes, inspirational stories of "beacon lights of history" are more common than explorations and revelations of character.

The first biographer of any note, William Wells Brown, takes as his models Henri Grégoire's *De la littérature des nègres* (1808) and Lydia Maria Child's *An Appeal in Favor of That Class of Americans called Africans* (1836), each of which is a series of sketches of Negroes who had risen above the average. Brown's biographical sketches were included in *The Black Man: His Antecedents, His Genius, and His Achievements* (1863), which was enlarged into *The Rising Son* (1874), a work of considerable popularity.

Brown's biographies of such figures as Phillis Wheatley, Toussaint L'Ouverture (whose story he told at some length), and Nat Turner are naturally propaganda of the Negro's achievement. These works held the field for quite some time; Negro writers were attracted to other fields than biography. But Brown's daughter, Josephine Brown, compiled from her father's autobiographical sketches a narrative of her father, *Biography of an American Bondman* (1856), and "Frank A. Rollin" (really Frances Rollin Whipper) recorded the life and services of Martin Delany. The life stories of the outstanding antislavery heroes and heroines, Jermain W. Loguen, Lunsford Lane, Harriet Tubman, and Sojourner Truth, were told by white biographers.

The tradition in which Brown wrote was continued in William J. Simmon's *Men of Mark* (1887). This is a large book of numerous short sketches, uniformly approving and optimistic. The sketches follow the straight-line plot: from poverty and hardship to achievement. G. F. Riching's *Evidences of Progress among Colored People* (1902) and J. W. Gibson's and William F. Crogman's *The Remarkable Achievement of the Afro-American* (1902) (still being sold in 1920 in slightly altered form as Crogman's *The New Progress of a Race*) are other attempts at "Who's Who in Colored America." All of these books contain useful facts, but little biography. All were popular and reached many editions. Generally privately printed, sold by subscriptions or by door-to-door canvassing, they appealed to the rising race consciousness of people who were sorely tried by the usual literary caricature and libel. They were dedicated to Negroes "that they might come to a wholesome understanding and appreciation of what has been accomplished in spite of the handicap"; their spirit was that of one of Booker T. Washington's favorite sentences: "No matter how poor you are, how black you are, or how obscure your present work and position, I want each one to remember that there is a chance for him, and the more difficulties he has to overcome, the greater will be his success."

This spirit seemed so valuable to the rising interracial cooperation program that white authors compiled similar books. *The Negro in Revelation, in History, and in Citizenship* (1902) by the Reverend J. J. Pipkin, Texan, avowedly a Democrat of the old school, with an introduction by John B. Gordon, then commander of the United Confederate Veterans, celebrated "What the Race Has Done and is Doing in Arms, Arts, Letters, The Pulpit, the Forum, the School, the Marts of Trade, and With Those Mighty Weapons in the Battle of Life, The Shovel and The Hoe," certainly an interesting example of climax. W. D. Weatherford's *Present Forces in Negro Progress* (1912) and L. H. Hammond's *In The Vanguard of a Race* (1922) are more carefully written, but essentially in the Booker T. Washington tradition.

The purposes behind most of the biographical sketches in these books, whether by Negro or white, are praiseworthy. They were to instil race pride, keep up race courage, and advertise good points of

the race to white America. The assumption was that all that was necessary for justice to the Negro in America was a knowledge of his
achievements. But, though Washington's apothegm: that a man should
be judged not so much by the heights he had reached as by the depths
from which he had come, was valuable in its recognition of the
Negro's obstacles, it often meant actually a magnifying of mediocrities,
a holding up of partial achievement for real. This is of course an old
story both in biographical writing by members of a minority group and
in the sentimental attitudes of a safely powerful majority towards
minorities. But unfailing and uncritical praise can be as dangerous
to a struggling minority as undue blame, and often the recitals of race
achievement, whether by chauvinist Negro biographers or condescending white sentimentalists, are depressing rather than stimulating.

Differing in method of presentation, though still by a race fighter,
are the biographical notes that William Still jotted down hurriedly
upon the arrival of fugitive slaves at his Philadelphia office. Naturally
informal, they have, because of their immediacy, a life to them that
is lacking in the more pretentious sketches, which sometimes resemble
funeral eulogies. The first Negro biographer who really belongs in the
history of American biography is Archibald H. Grimké, whose *William Lloyd Garrison, the Abolitionist* (1891) and *The Life of Charles
Sumner, The Scholar in Politics* (1892) appeared in a series on American reformers. Much briefer but similarly able was Charles W.
Chesnutt's *Frederick Douglass* (1899). Booker T. Washington's
Frederick Douglass (1907) is a useful but secondary biography. Washington naturally stresses such elements in Douglass as his sponsoring
industrial education, his disapproval of the exodus of Negroes from
the South, and his forgiveness of his old master. But he gives a rather
unrestricted account of the antislavery movement. It is likely that of
Washington's several audiences, he had his Northern audience in mind
for this work.

The development of race pride seems to remain the purpose of
twentieth-century Negro biographers. John W. Cromwell used the
biographical method chiefly in *The Negro in American History* (1915).
As secretary of the American Negro Academy and as a practising
journalist Cromwell had access to valuable sources. Hallie Q. Brown's
Homespun Heroines (1926), Sadie Daniel's *Women Builders* (1931),
and Wendell P. Dabney's *Maggie L. Walker* (1927) tell the story of the
Negro woman's achievement. Dabney has included in *Cincinnati's
Colored Citizens* (1926) more spice and flavor than generally appears
in biographies of Negroes; his occasional memoirs of the great and the
near great and the not great whom he has known in his long crowded

life show the fine qualities of wit, a point of view, and the ability to
re-create living persons and scenes. But there are not many biographers
like the raconteur Dabney.

Typical of the many factually valuable, conventional success stories
of Negro church leaders and business men are R. McCants Andrews'
John Merrick: A Biographical Sketch (1926), Ralph W. Bullock's *In
Spite of Handicaps* (1927), George F. Bragg's *Men of Maryland*
(1914), and Raleigh Merritt's *From Captivity to Fame, or the Life
of George Washington Carver* (1938).

Benjamin Brawley has published more biography than any other
Negro writer. His *Women of Achievement* (1919), *Paul Laurence
Dunbar, Poet of His Race* (1936), *The Negro Genius* (1937), which
is biographical as much as critical, and *Negro Builders and Heroes*
(1937) are written to inspire Negro youth with pride and white
America to recognition and consequently to just dealings. Dunbar
"struggled against the most grinding poverty...yet became famous
when just twenty-four years of age." The closing paragraph of *Negro
Builders and Heroes* illustrates both the racial and the interracial
purposes:

> What this man did could be multiplied many times. Hundreds
> of helping hands, white and black, have reached across the color
> line. Thousands of Negro men have died for their country in
> battle. In view of the record, their people hope for fair dealing,
> especially in the courts. Less than this they should not expect,
> more than this they do not want. In the words of Joseph B.
> Foraker, "They ask no favors because they are Negroes, but
> only justice because they are men."

A series of which Brawley was editor was planned to supply biographies
of noted Negroes, in a style suitable for young people as well as adults.
Brawley's *Dunbar* and Arthur Huff Fauset's *Sojourner Truth* (1938)
were published in this series before the death of the editor. Fauset had
already written *For Freedom* (1927), a book of biographical sketches
for children.

Several able biographical essays have been published in *The
Journal of Negro History,* edited by Carter G. Woodson, who has
himself done occasional biographies. Charles Wesley's *Richard Allen,
Apostle of Freedom* (1935) tells the story of the noted churchman.
In *William A. Hunton, A Pioneer Prophet of Young Men* (1938),
Addie W. Hunton recorded the life of her husband, who was impor-
tant in the work of the Y. M. C. A. In 1930 Eslanda Goode Robeson
wrote the biography of her husband in *Paul Robeson, Negro.* This was

the sole biography produced by the New Negro movement. Robeson's career has been a most interesting one; unfortunately this biography was written at a sort of midway point. There is an attempt at conveying the personality of the scholar-athlete-singer-ambassador of his people to Europe, and in this respect *Paul Robeson, Negro,* differs from almost all preceding biographies.

The rise of biography in popularity, second only to that of novels, has seemed to be a matter of indifference to Negro writers. There is certainly no lack of suitable subjects, from such antislavery heroes as Harriet Tubman, Martin Delany, William Wells Brown (even the better known Frederick Douglass deserves a twentieth-century biography) down to the prominent figures in many fields of present-day achievement. The records are available, though frightening instances of neglect and even destruction of documents are reported.

There is an inviting field open. But there are risks involved. Since there are so many blank spaces in the story of the Negro in America, biographies may be inclined to overestimate the material that they dig up out of the research mine. They also run the risk, mentioned above, that minority biographers run: the tendency to glorify achievement. Their theme need not be, should not be: "A poor thing but mine own," but it should as certainly not be: "Mine own, and therefore a great thing." A sense of proportion, based upon standards derived from careful study of history and biography, should hold in check both racial belittling and aggrandizement. Negro biographers undoubtedly run the risk of being declared treasonous if they show weaknesses in accepted heroes. They run an equal risk of being bad writers if they show only plaster saints. They must make a choice. Undeniably their problems are aggravated because of their minority status. But there is no reason today why Negro biographers cannot forego indiscriminate race praise in favor of the revelations of the personalities of Negroes who definitely deserve mature biographies.

MILTON CLARKE (c. 1817- ?)

A year after Lewis Clarke escaped from slavery, his brothers, Cyrus and Milton, followed. All engaged in antislavery work. In 1846 Lewis Clarke's *Narrative,* originally published in 1845, was enlarged to include an account of Milton's life. The following selection is from the *Narratives of the Sufferings of Lewis and Milton Clarke, Sons of a Soldier of the Revolution, during a Captivity of more than Twenty Years among the Slave-Holders of Kentucky, One of the so-called Christian States of North America; Dictated by Themselves.*

[Abolitionist Rescue]

DURING THE SUMMER OF 1841, the emigration to Canada, through Oberlin, was very large. I had the pleasure of giving the "right hand of fellowship" to a goodly number of my former acquaintances and fellow-sufferers. The masters accused me of *stealing* several of them. This is a great lie. I never stole one in my life. I have assisted several to get into possession of the true owner, but I never assisted any man to steal another away from himself. God has given every man the true title-deed to himself, written upon his face. It cannot be blotted entirely out. The slaveholders try hard to do it, but it can yet be read; all other titles are shams and forgeries. Among others, I assisted a Mrs. Swift, and her two children, to get over to Canada, where they can read titles more clearly than they do in some of the states. This was brought up as a heavy charge against me by Mr. Postlewaite, the illustrious catchpole of the slaveholders.

In the autumn of this year, I was delighted to meet brother Lewis at Oberlin. The happiness which we both experienced at meeting each other, as we supposed, securely free, in a free state, may be well imagined.

In 1842, there were nine slaves reached Oberlin by one arrival, all from one plantation. A Mr. Benningale, of Kentucky, was close upon them, impiously claiming that he had property in these images of God; ay, that they were *property,* and entirely his, to all intents and purposes. This is not the doctrine taught by a great many good men in Ohio. These men came to Oberlin. The next day, Benningale arrived. He lined the lake with watchmen. **Benedict** of Illyria was on the alert; thirty pieces of silver were always the full price of innocent blood with him. Benningale, finding they were hid in the village, threatened to burn the town. The colored people were on guard all night. They met two persons, whom they suspected as spies of the kidnappers. They told him, if they caught them out again, they should be hung right up, as spies against liberty. The fugitives at length were put into a wagon, carried to the lake, and shipped for Canada. The pursuers offered a thousand dollars for their arrest. No one was found sufficiently enterprising to claim the reward. They landed safe upon the other side. Soon after this, there were seven more slaves arrived at Oberlin. The miserable **Benedict,** assisted by the Chapmans, set their traps around the village. Seven hundred dollars reward was offered for their arrest. Power of attorney had been sent on to the traitor **Benedict.** The slaves were kept concealed, till, as in the

case of Moses, it was no longer safe for them. There were six men
and one woman in the company. A plan was contrived to put the kidnappers upon a false scent. Six colored men were selected to
personate the men, and I was dressed in female attire, to be passed
off for the woman. A telltale was informed that the slaves would
start for the lake at such a time, and go in a certain direction. He
was solemnly enjoined not to tell a word of it. Those who knew him
understood what he would do. The secret was too precious for him
to keep. He ran right to **Benedict** with it. We left Oberlin in one
direction, and the real objects of pursuit started, soon after, upon
another road. The *ruse* took; **Benedict** and Company were in full pursuit, with sheriff, writ, and all the implements of kidnapping. We
selected one of our number, George Perry, to act as spokesman for the
gang. Just as we arrived at the village of Illyria, eight miles from
Oberlin, **Benedict** and Company surrounded our carriage, and ordered
the driver to stop. Platt, the driver, challenged his authority. **Benedict**
pulled out his advertisement, six men and one women, with the
description of their persons. Platt told him he thought they were not
the persons he was after. The traitor affirmed he knew they were.
The driver turned to his passengers, and said he could do no more for
them. George then began to play his part: "Well, 'den, 'dis nigger must
get out." We accordingly left the carriage, and were conducted into
the tavern. In the tavern were two travellers, who were very inquisitive.
"Where are you from?" George answered, "Don't care where I from."
Benedict when he began to suspect that all was not exactly right,
came up to me for a more minute examination of my person. I had
kept my head and face under my hood and cloak. He ordered me to
hold up my head. George says, "Let 'dat gal alone, Mr. white man;
de nigger gal plague enough in slave state—you just let her alone,
here, if you please." One of the travellers called for cider; George
stepped up and drank it for him. The table was furnished for some of
the guests, and George, without any ceremony, declared " 'Dis nigger
hungry," and swept the table for himself and comrades. The landlord
threatened to flog him. The colored men all spoke up together, "You
strike 'dat nigger if you dare." At last, they got a justice of the peace;
but he had been let into the whole secret. **Benedict** began his plea;
produced his evidence; said that ungrateful girl (pointing to me) had
left a kind mistress, right in the midst of a large ironing!!! The justice
finally said, he did not see but he must give up to **Mr. Benedict** as
slaves, fugitives from their service. Our friends then gave the signal,
and I threw off my bonnet and cloak, and stood up a man. Such a
shout as the spectators raised would do the heart of freedom good.

"Why, your woman has turned into a man, Mr. **Benedict**." "It may be these others, that appear to be men, are all women." **Benedict** saw through the plot, and took his saddle without any rejoinder to his plea. The tavern-keeper ordered us out of the house, and we took carriage for Oberlin. Meanwhile the real objects of pursuit were sailing on the waters of the blue lake.

Benedict was terribly angry at me. He swore he would have me captured. He wrote immediately to Deacon Logan, that no slaves could be captured there while Milton Clarke was at large.

The slaveholders of Lexington had a meeting, and determined to send a Mr. Postlewaite, a crack slave-breaker, and a Mr. McGowan, after me. They came and lingered about Oberlin, watching their opportunity. They engaged two wretches named Chapman, of Illyria, to assist in the capture. Brother Lewis and I went up to Madison, Lake country, to spend a few days. We had a meeting on Sabbath evening, at which we addressed the people. There was a traitor there named Warner, from Lexington, who told Postlewaite where we were. Monday morning, my brother and myself rode up to Dr. Merriam's, accompanied by two or three of Mr. Winchester's family, with whom we had spent the Sabbath. I sat a few minutes in the carriage; and a little girl out of health, the niece of Dr. Merriam, and his own daughter, came out and wanted to ride. I took them in, and had not driven a mile when a close carriage overtook and passed me, wheeled right across the road, and four men leaped out of it and seized my horse. I had no conjecture who they were. I asked them what they wanted—"if money, I have only fifty cents in the world; you are welcome to that." "We want no *money,* but *you!*" The truth then flashed upon my mind in a moment—"They are kidnappers."

I jumped from the carriage for the purpose of running for life. My foot slipped, and I fell. In a moment, four men were upon me. They thrust my head down upon the ground, bound me hand and foot, put me into the carriage, and started for Judge Page's; a judge prepared beforehand for their purposes. Soon after we started, we met a man in the road. I spoke to him, and asked him to take care of the girls in the buggy, and tell Lewis the kidnappers from Kentucky had got me. Postlewaite and McGowan took off my hat, and gave me a beating upon the head. One of the Chapmans spoke and said, "Now we have got you, my good fellow; you are the chap that has enticed away so many slaves; we will take care of you; we will have Lewis soon." They then took me to Mr. Judge Page. The sheriff of the county was there. He asked me what I had done, that they had tied me up so close. "Have you murdered anybody?" I said, "No." "Have you been stealing?" "No, sir." "What have you done?" "Nothing, sir." "What have they tied you for, then?" Postlewaite told him it was none of his business. The sheriff said it was his business, and, "if he has committed no crime, you must untie him." He then came up to take off the cords from me. Postlewaite drew his pistols, and threatened to shoot him. Judge Page told the sheriff he had better not touch the gentleman's *property*. The sheriff said he would see whose property he was. By this time the alarm was spread, and a large company had gathered around the tavern. The sheriff told the people to see that that man was not removed till he came back. He went out, and summoned the posses of farmers in every direction. They left their ploughs, and jumped upon their horses, with the collars yet on their necks, and rode with all speed for the scene of action. "The kidnappers had got the white nigger," was the watchword.

Postlewaite began to be alarmed. He asked Mr. Page which was the best way for him to go. Could he go safely to the lake, and take a steamboat for Cleveland? "Why, no, the abolitionists watch all the landing places." Could he go to Painesville? "Why, no, General Paine, a red-hot abolitionist, is there." Postlewaite asked for a place to take me, where I should be secure. They carried me to the counting room of the judge. They then began to coax. The judge said, "You better go back, Clarke, willingly; it will be better for you, when you get there." "Did not your master treat you well?" asked the very gracious Mr. Postlewaite. "Yes," I said, "he treated me well; no fault to find with him on that score." "What did you run away for, then?" "I came, sir, to get my freedom. I offered him eight hundred dollars for my liberty, and he would not take it. I had paid him about that much for my time, and I thought I might as well have what I earned, as to pay it to him." "Well, sir, if you had come off alone, the deacon would not have cared so much about it; but you led others off; and now we are going to carry you back, and whip you, on the public square in Lexington." . . .

Dinner came on, at length, and I was moved back into the tavern. Postlewaite had a rope around me, which he kept in his hand all the time. They called for dinner for six—the driver and myself among the number. When they sat down, I was placed at a short distance from the table. The landlady asked if I was not to sit down, Postlewaite said, no nigger should sit at table with him. She belabored him in good womanly style; told him he was a thief, and a scoundrel, and that, if she was a *man,* he should never carry me away. The people were gathered, all this time, around the windows, and in the road, discussing the matter, and getting up the steam, to meet the

Kentucky bowie knives and pistols. Postlewaite sent out, and got a man to come in and watch me, while he eat his dinner. The people at the windows were preparing to take me out. He watched the movement, and had me brought up nearer to the table.

At three o'clock, my trial came on. My friends claimed, that I should have a trial as a *white* man. Robert Harper pleaded for the oppressors, assisted by another, whose name is unknown to me. For me, lawyer Chase, and another, appeared. To these gentlemen, and all others, who were friendly to me on this occasion, I feel an obligation which I can never express. It was to me, indeed, a dark hour, and they were friends in time of need. General Paine arrived about the commencement of the trial, and presented a firm front to the tyrants. My lawyer asked by what law they claimed me. They said, under the black law of Ohio. The reply was, that I was not a black man. Postlewaite said he arrested me, as the property of Archibald Logan, under the article of the constitution, that persons *"owing service,"* and fleeing from one state to another, shall be given up to the person to whom such service is due. He then read the power of attorney, from Deacon Logan to him, authorizing him to seize one Milton Clarke—describing me as a person five feet two and a half inches tall, probably trying to pass myself off as white. "His hair is straight, but curls a little at the lower end." After reading this, he read his other papers, showing that I was the slave of Logan. He produced a bill of sale, from Joseph to Deacon Logan. He then asked me if I had not lived, for several years, with Deacon Logan. General Paine said, if I spoke at all, I might tell the whole story—that I had a free pass to go where I chose, (and this was the fact.) The suggestion of General Paine frightened Postlewaite; he told me to shut up my jaws, or he would smash my face in for me. The people cried out, "Touch him if you dare; we will string you up, short metre." He then said to me, "D--n you; we will pay you for all this, when we get home." The anxiety on my part, by this time, was beyond any thing I ever felt in my life. I sometimes hoped the people would rescue me, and then feared they would not. Many of them showed sympathy in their countenances, and I could see that the savageism of Postlewaite greatly increased it. My lawyer then asked, for what I *owed* service to Deacon Logan; told Harper & Co., if Mr. Clarke owed the deacon, present his bill, and, if it is a reasonable one, his friends will pay it. He then asked me if I owed Deacon Logan, of Kentucky. I told him no— the deacon owed me about eight hundred dollars; I owed him nothing. Postlewaite said, then, he arrested me as the *goods* and *chattels* of Logan. Mr. Chase said, "Mr. Clarke had permission to come into the free states." "Yes," said Postlewaite, "but not to *stay* so long." Finally, Mr. Chase asked, "Where did Joseph Logan get *his* right to Clarke?" On this point, he had no specific evidence. . . . Judge Page had received his fee, as I verily believe, before he gave judgment; and he very soon came to the conclusion, that Deacon Logan had proved his claim. I was delivered over to the tender mercies of Postlewaite & Co. Just as we were going out at the door, the sheriff met us, and arrested Postlewaite, McGowan and the Chapmans, for assault and battery on the person of Milton Clarke. They were told, their trial would come on the next day, at ten o'clock, before Justice Cunningham. Postlewaite swore terribly at this; said it was abolition concern. Some one asked the sheriff what should be done with me. He said he did not want me— it was the others that he had arrested. I was then tied to Postlewaite. Some one said, "Cut him loose." Postlewaite replied, "The first that attempts to touch him, I will blow him through." I asked the people if I should be carried back, as I had committed no crime. They said, "No, no; never." General Paine said he would call out the militia, before I should be carried back.

. . . The people had fixed their carriages so that ours must pass upon the Ashtabula side. Soon as the wheels passed the border of this county, the carriage was stopped, and the sheriff of Ashtabula demanded the body of Milton Clarke. The people shouted, came up and unhitched the horses, and turned them face to the carriage. Postlewaite cried out, "Drive on." Driver replied, "The horses are faced about." P. began to be very angry. The people asked the driver what he was there for, assisting in such business as this. The poor fellow begged they would not harm his horses; he did not know what they wanted him for, or he never would have come. He begged for his horses, and himself. Postlewaite said, if they meddled with the horses, he would shoot a hundred of them. The people told him, if he put his head out of that carriage, he would never shoot again. At this stage of the business, Robert Harper, Esq., came up, to read the riot act. The people were acting under a charter broader and older than any statutes passed on earth. Harper was glad to escape himself, or justice would have speedily been meted out to him. The friends came up to the carriage, and told me not to be alarmed; they would have me, at any rate. Among others in the crowd, was a huge Buckeye blacksmith, six feet tall. At first, he took sides with the thieves; said he wanted no niggers there. My friends told him to come up to the carriage, and pick out the nigger, it there was any there. He came, and pointing to Postlewaite, said, "that is the nigger." The chivalric Mr. P. told him no man called him nigger with impunity. The Buckeye insisted upon it he was the nigger. P. told him he lied, three times. The northern lion was waked up, and he slapped the armed knight in the face. Postlewaite drew his bowie knife, and threatened to cut him. The Ohioan asked him what it was. He said, a bowie knife. "What are you going to do with it?" "Put it into you, if you put your head in here again." "Ay, ay, you are going to booy me, are you? Then I'll booy you." He ran to the fence, and seized a sharp rail, and said he was going to booy, too. The sheriff, that had the writ to take me, let down the steps; and the people called out, "Let us kill them." The man armed with the rail, began to beat the door, and told them to let me out. General Paine spoke, and urged the multitude not to proceed to violence. Judge Page began to feel quite uneasy, in his new position. He exhorted me to keep still, or they would kill us all. The sheriff then gave Postlewaite and Company five minutes' time to release me, or take the consequences; said the carriage would be demolished in two minutes, when he spoke the word to the people. The pistols and bowie knives were quietly put away, and the tone of the stationary passengers, inside the carriage, very suddenly changed. Judge Page said, "Better let Clarke get out; they will kill us, if you don't." The cowardly Chapmans began to plead for mercy: "You can't say that we touched you, Clarke." "Yes you did," I told them; "you all jumped on me at once." The people became more and more clamorous outside the carriage—those inside more and more uneasy. They at length were more eager to get rid of me than they ever had been to catch me. "Get out; get out, Clarke," rung round on every side of me.

Soon as my feet touched the ground, the rope was cut, and once more I felt free. I was hurried into a wagon, and, under the care of the sheriff, driven off toward Austinburg, while the other sheriff took the kidnappers in another direction into Lake county. They soon stopped to give me something to eat; but I had no appetite for food, either then or for a week afterwards. . . .

JOSIAH HENSON (1789-1881)

Josiah Henson, famous as the original of Harriet Beecher Stowe's Uncle Tom, published several versions of his story from 1849 to 1878. Henson, a member of the fugitive slave colony at Dawn, Canada, made frequent trips back to the States, working with the Underground Railroad and soliciting funds from sympathizers, among them Mrs. Stowe and Longfellow.

[Home at Dawn]

I DID NOT FIND that our prosperity increased with our numbers. The mere delight the slave took in his freedom, rendered him, at first, contented with a lot far inferior to that which he might have attained. Then his ignorance led him to make unprofitable bargains, and he would often hire wild land on short terms, and bind himself to clear a certain number of acres; and by the time they were clear and fitted for cultivation, his lease was out, and his landlord would come in, and raise a splendid crop on the new land; and the tenant would, very likely, start again on just such another bargain, and be no better off at the end of ten years than he was at the beginning. Another way in which they lost the profits of their labor was by raising nothing but tobacco, the high price of which was very tempting, and the cultivation of which was a monopoly in their hands, as no white man understood it, or could compete with them at all. The consequence was, however, that they had nothing but tobacco to sell; there was rather too much of it in the market, and the price of wheat rose, while their commodity was depressed; and they lost all they should have saved, in the profit they gave the trader for his corn and stores.

I saw the effect of these things so clearly that I could not help trying to make my friends and neighbors see it too; and I set seriously about the business of lecturing upon the subject of crops, wages, and profit, just as if I had been brought up to it. I insisted on the necessity of their raising their own crops, saving their own wages, and securing the profits of their own labor, with such plain arguments as occurred to me, and were as clear to their comprehension as to mine. I did this very openly; and, frequently, my audience consisted in part of the very traders whose inordinate profits upon individuals I was trying to diminish, but whose balance of profit would not be ultimately lessened, because they would have so many more persons to trade with, who would be able to pay them a reasonable advance in cash, or its equivalent, on all their purchases. The purse is a tender part of the system; but I handled it so gently, that the sensible portion of my natural opponents were not, I believe, offended; while those whom I wished to benefit saw, for the most part, the propriety of my advice, and took it. At least, there are now great numbers of settlers, in this region of Canada, who own their farms, and are training up their children in true independence, and giving them a good elementary education, who had not taken a single step toward such a result before I began to talk to them.

While I remained at Colchester, I became acquainted with a Congregational missionary from Massachusetts, by the name of Hiram Wilson, who took an interest in our people, and was disposed to do what he could to promote the the the cause of improvement which I had so much at heart. He coöperated with me in many efforts, and I was associated with him for upwards of thirty years. He was a faithful friend, and continued his important labors of love in our behalf. Among other things which he did for us then, he wrote to a Quaker friend of his, an Englishman, by the name of James C. Fuller, residing at Skaneateles, New York, and endeavored to interest him in the welfare of our struggling population.

He succeeded so far, that Mr. Fuller, who was going on a visit to England, promised to do what he could among his friends there, to induce them to aid us. He came back with fifteen hundred dollars which had been subscribed for our benefit. It was a great question how this sum, which sounded vast to many of my brethren, should be appropriated. I had my opinion pretty decidedly as to what it was best for us all to do with it. But, in order to come to a satisfactory conclusion, the first thing to be done was to call a convention of delegates from every settlement of blacks that was within reach; that all might see that whatever was decided on, was sanctioned by the disinterested votes of those who were thought by their companions, best able to judge what was expedient. Mr. Wilson and myself called such a convention, therefore, to meet in London, Upper Canada, and it was held in June, 1838.

I urged the appropriation of the money to the establishment of a manual-labor school, where our children could be taught those elements of knowledge which are usually the occupations of a grammar-school; and where the boys could be taught, in addition, the practice of some mechanic art, and the girls could be instructed in those domestic arts which are the proper occupation and ornament of their sex. Such an establishment would train up those who would afterwards instruct others; and we should thus gradually become independent of the white man for our intellectual progress, as we might be also for our physical prosperity. It was the more necessary, as in many districts, owing to the insurmountable prejudices of the inhabitants, the children of the blacks were not allowed to share the advantages of the common school. There was some opposition to this plan in the convention; but in the course of the discussion, which continued for three days, it appeared so obviously for the advantage of all to husband this donation, so as to preserve it for a purpose of permanent utility, that the proposal was, at last, unanimously adopted;

and a committee of three was appointed to select and purchase a site for the establishment. Mr. Wilson and myself were the active members of this committee, and after traversing the country for several months, we could find no place more suitable than that upon which I had had my eye for three or four years, for a permanent settlement, in the town of Dawn.

We therefore bought two hundred acres of fine rich land, on the river Sydenham, covered with a heavy growth of black walnut and white wood, at four dollars the acre. I had made a bargain for two hundred acres adjoining this lot, on my own account; and circumstances favored me so, that the man of whom I purchased was glad to let me have them at a large discount from the price I had agreed to pay, if I would give him cash for the balance I owed him. I transferred a portion of the advantage of this bargain to the institution, by selling to it one hundred acres more, at the low price at which I obtained them.

In 1842 I removed with my family to Dawn, and as a considerable number of my friends were there about me, and the school permanently fixed there, the future importance of this settlement seemed to be decided. There were many other settlements which were considerable; and, indeed, the colored population was scattered over a territory which did not fall far short of three hundred miles in extent, in each direction, and probably numbered not less than twenty thousand persons in all. We looked to the school, and the possession of landed property by individuals, as two great means of the elevation of our oppressed and degraded race to a participation in the blessings, as they had hitherto been permitted to share only the miseries and vices, of civilization.

My efforts to aid them, in every way in my power, and to procure the aid of others for them, were very constant. I have made many journeys into New York, Connecticut, Massachusetts, and Maine, in all of which States I found or made some friends to the cause, and, I hope, some personal friends. I received many liberal gifts, and experienced much kindness of treatment; but I must be allowed to allude particularly to the donations received from Boston—by which we were soon enabled to erect a saw-mill, and thus to begin in good earnest the clearing of our lands, and to secure a profitable return for the support of our school—as among those which were most welcome and valuable to us. . . .

SOLOMON NORTHUP (1807-)

Little is known of Solomon Northup except what he tells in the book *Twelve Years a Slave* (1893). The title page announces him as "a citizen of New York, kidnapped in Washington City in 1841 and rescued in 1853, from a cotton plantation near the Red River in Louisiana." In the year of his rescue David Wilson took down his story as "a correct picture of slavery." An appendix contains letters establishing the authenticity of Solomon Northup's kidnapping and of the many efforts, finally successful, to redeem him from the Red River plantation.

[Christmas on Bayou Boeuf]

THE ONLY RESPITE from constant labor the slave has through the whole year, is during the Christmas holidays. Epps allowed us three—others allow four, five and six days, according to the measure of their generosity. It is the only time to which they look forward with any interest or pleasure. They are glad when night comes, not only because it brings them a few hours repose, but because it brings them one day nearer Christmas. It is hailed with equal delight by the old and the young; even Uncle Abram ceases to glorify Andrew Jackson, and Patsy forgets her many sorrows, amid the general hilarity of the holidays. It is the time of feasting, and frolicking, and fiddling—the carnival season with the children of bondage. They are the only days when they are allowed a little restricted liberty, and heartily indeed do they enjoy it.

It is the custom for one planter to give a "Christmas supper," inviting the slaves from neighboring plantations to join his own on the occasion; for instance, one year it is given by Epps, the next by Marshall, the next by Hawkins, and so on. Usually from three to five hundred are assembled, coming together on foot, in carts, on horseback, on mules, riding double and triple, sometimes a boy and girl, at others a girl and two boys, and at others again a boy, a girl and an old woman. Uncle Abram astride a mule, with Aunt Phebe and Patsy behind him, trotting towards a Christmas supper, would be no uncommon sight on Bayou Boeuf.

Then, too, "of all days i' the year," they array themselves in their best attire. The cotton coat has been washed clean, the stump of a tallow candle has been applied to their shoes, and if so fortunate as to possess a rimless or a crownless hat, it is placed jauntily on the head.

They are welcome with equal cordiality, however, if they come bare-headed and bare-footed to the feast. As a general thing, the women wear handkerchiefs tied about their heads, but if chance has thrown in their way a fiery red ribbon, or a cast-off bonnet of their mistress' grandmother, it is sure to be worn on such occasions. Red—the deep blood red—is decidedly the favorite color among the enslaved damsels of my acquaintance. If a red ribbon does not encircle the neck, you will be certain to find all the hair of their woolly heads tied up with red strings of one sort or another.

The table is spread in the open air, and loaded with varieties of meat and piles of vegetables. Bacon and corn meal at such times are dispensed with. Sometimes the cooking is performed in the kitchen on the plantation, at others in the shade of wide branching trees. In the latter case, a ditch is dug in the ground, and wood laid in and burned until it is filled with glowing coals, over which chickens, ducks, turkeys, pigs, and not unfrequently the entire body of a wild ox, are roasted. They are furnished also with flour, of which biscuits are made, and often with peach and other preserves, with tarts, and every manner and description of pies, except the mince, that being an article of pastry as yet unknown among them. Only the slave who has lived all the years on his scanty allowance of meal and bacon, can appreciate such suppers. White people in great numbers assemble to witness the gastronomical enjoyments.

They seat themselves at the rustic table—the males on one side, the females on the other. The two between whom there may have been an exchange of tenderness, invariably manage to sit opposite; for the omnipresent Cupid disdains not to hurl his arrows into the simple hearts of slaves. Unalloyed and exulting happiness lights up the dark faces of them all. The ivory teeth, contrasting with their black complexions, exhibit two long, white streaks the whole extent of the table. All around the bountiful board a multitude of eyes roll in ecstacy. Giggling and laughter and the clattering of cutlery and crockery succeed. Cuffee's elbow hunches his neighbor's side, impelled by an involuntary impulse of delight; Nelly shakes her finger at Sambo and laughs, she knows not why, and so the fun and merriment flows on.

When the viands have disappeared, and the hungry maws of the children of toil are satisfied, then, next in the order of amusement, is the Christmas dance. My business on these gala days always was to play on the violin. The African race is a music-loving one, proverbially; and many there were among my fellow-bondsmen whose organs of tune were strikingly developed, and who could thumb the banjo with dexterity; but at the expense of appearing egotistical, I must, nevertheless, declare, that I was considered the Ole Bull of Bayou Boeuf. My master often received letters, sometimes from a distance of ten miles, requesting him to send me to play at a ball or festival of the whites. He received his compensation, and usually I also returned with many picayunes jingling in my pockets—the extra contributions of those to whose delight I had administered. In this manner I became more acquainted than I otherwise would, up and down the bayou. The young men and maidens of Holmes-ville always knew there was to be a jollification somewhere, whenever Platt Epps was seen passing through the town with his fiddle in his hand. "Where are you going now, Platt?" and "What is coming off to-night, Platt?" would be interrogations issuing from every door and window, and many a time when there was no special hurry, yielding to pressing importunities, Platt would draw his bow, and sitting astride his mule, perhaps, discourse musically to a crowd of delighted children, gathered around him in the street.

Alas! had it not been for my beloved violin, I scarcely can conceive how I could have endured the long years of bondage. It introduced me to great houses—relieved me of many days' labor in the field—supplied me with conveniences for my cabin—with pipes and tobacco, and extra pairs of shoes, and oftentimes led me away from the presence of a hard master, to witness scenes of jollity and mirth. It was my companion—the friend of my bosom—trumphing loudly when I was joyful, and uttering its soft, melodious consolations when I was sad. Often, at midnight, when sleep had fled affrighted from the cabin, and my soul was disturbed and troubled with the contemplation of my fate, it would sing me a song of peace. On holy Sabbath days, when an hour or two of leisure was allowed, it would accompany me to some quiet place on the bayou bank, and, lifting up its voice, discourse kindly and pleasantly indeed. It heralded my name round the country—made me friends, who, otherwise would not have noticed me—gave me an honored seat at the yearly feasts, and secured the loudest and heartiest welcome of them all at the Christmas dance. The Christmas dance! Oh, ye pleasure-seeking sons and daughters of idleness, who move with measured step, listless and snail-like, through the slow winding cotillon, if ye wish to look upon the celerity, if not the "poetry in motion"—upon genuine happiness, rampant and unrestrained—go down to Louisiana, and see the slaves dancing in the starlight of a Christmas night.

On that particular Christmas I have now in my mind, a description whereof will serve as a description of the day generally, Miss

Lively and Mr. Sam, the first belonging to Stewart, the latter to Roberts, started the ball. It was well known that Sam cherished an ardent passion for Lively, as also did one of Marshall's and another of Carey's boys; for Lively was *lively* indeed, and a heartbreaking coquette withal. It was a victory for Sam Roberts, when, rising from the repast, she gave him her hand for the first "figure" in preference to either of his rivals. They were somewhat crestfallen, and, shaking their heads angrily, rather intimated they would like to pitch into Mr. Sam and hurt him badly. But not an emotion of wrath ruffled the placid bosom of Samuel as his legs flew like drum-sticks down the outside and up the middle, by the side of his bewitching partner. The whole company cheered them vociferously, and, excited with the applause, they continued "tearing down" after all the others had become exhausted and halted a moment to recover breath. But Sam's superhuman exertions overcame him finally, leaving Lively alone, yet whirling like a top. Thereupon one of Sam's rivals, Pete Marshall, dashed in, and, with might and main, leaped and shuffled and threw himself into every conceivable shape, as if determined to show Miss Lively and all the world that Sam Roberts was of no account.

Pete's affection, however, was greater than his discretion. Such violent exercise took the breath out of him directly, and he dropped like an empty bag. Then was the time for Harry Carey to try his hand; but Lively also soon out-winded him, amidst hurrahs and shouts, fully sustaining her well-earned reputation of being the "fastest gal" on the bayou.

One "set" off, another takes its place, he or she remaining longest on the floor receiving the most uproarious commendation, and so the dancing continues until broad daylight. It does not cease with the sound of the fiddle, but in that case they set up a music peculiar to themselves. This is called "patting," accompanied with one of those unmeaning songs, composed rather for its adaption to a certain tune or measure, than for the purpose of expressing any distinct idea. The patting is performed by striking the hands on the knees, then striking the hands together, then striking the right shoulder with one hand, the left with the other—all the while keeping time with the feet, and singing, perhaps, this song:

> "Harper's creek and roarin' ribber,
> Thar, my dear, we'll live forebber;
> Den we'll go to de Ingin nation,
> All I want in dis creation,
> Is pretty little wife and big plantation.

> *Chorus.* Up dat oak and down dat ribber,
>   Two overseers and one little nigger."

Or, if these words are not adapted to the tune called for, it may be that "Old Hog Eye" *is*—a rather solemn and startling specimen of versification, not, however, to be appreciated unless heard at the South. It runneth as follows:

> "Who's been here since I've been gone?
> Pretty little gal wid a josey on.
>   Hog Eye!
>   Old Hog Eye!
>   And Hosey too!
>
> Never see de like since I was born,
> Here comes a little gal wid a josey on.
>   Hog Eye!
>   Old Hog Eye!
>   And Hosey too!"

Or, may be the following, perhaps, equally nonsensical, but full of melody, nevertheless, as it flows from the negro's mouth:

> "Ebo Dick and Jurdan's Jo,
> Them two niggers stole my yo'.
>
>   *Chorus.* Hop Jim along,
>   Walk Jim along,
>   Talk Jim along," &c.
>
> Old black Dan, as black as tar,
> He dam glad he was not dar.
>   Hop Jim along," &c.

During the remaining holidays succeeding Christmas, they are provided with passes, and permitted to go where they please within a limited distance, or they may remain and labor on the plantation, in which case they are paid for it. It is very rarely, however, that the latter alternative is accepted. They may be seen at these times hurrying in all directions, as happy looking mortals as can be found on the face of the earth. They are different beings from what they are in the field; the temporary relaxation, the brief deliverance from fear, and from the lash, producing an entire metamorphosis in their appearance and demeanor. In visiting, riding, renewing old friendships, or, perchance, reviving some old attachment, or pursuing whatever pleasure may suggest itself, the time is occupied. Such is "southern life as it is," *three days in the year,* as I found it—the other three hundred and sixty-two being days of weariness, and fear, and suffering, and unremitting labor.

Marriage is frequently contracted during the holidays, if such an institution may be said to exist among them. The only ceremony required before entering into that "holy estate," is to obtain the consent of the respective owners. It is usually encouraged by the masters of female slaves. Either party can have as many husbands or wives as the owner will permit, and either is at liberty to discard the other at pleasure. The law in relation to divorce, or to bigamy, and so forth, is not applicable to property, of course. If the wife does not belong on the same plantation with the husband, the latter is permitted to visit her on Saturday nights, if the distance is not too far. Uncle Abram's wife lived seven miles from Epps', on Bayou Huff Power. He had permission to visit her once a fortnight, but he was growing old, as has been said, and truth to say, had latterly well nigh forgotten her. Uncle Abram had no time to spare from his meditations on General Jackson—connubial dalliance being well enough for the young and thoughtless, but unbecoming a grave and solemn philosopher like himself.

FREDERICK DOUGLASS (1817-1895)

Frederick Douglass, (see also pp. 17, 606) the foremost Negro in the antislavery movement, was born a slave in Eastern Shore Maryland. In his first autobiography he tells of his slave childhood, of his work as family servant for the Aulds in Baltimore, where his kindly mistress awakened his desire for learning; of his labor as a plantation field hand and as a skilled ship caulker hiring his own time, and of his attempts to escape to the North. The slavery experiences of Douglass were so varied, and he was so clear-sighted, that his autobiographies give one of the most convincing and deeply moving accounts to be had of the "peculiar institution." He did much more than narrate incidents of violence: "My feelings were not the result of any marked cruelty in the treatment I received . . . It was slavery—not its mere incidents—that I hated." Upon his escape to the North, he dedicated his energies to the destruction of what he hated. (For his career as antislavery propagandist, see pp. 575f.) He struggled to improve his learning at every opportunity. His first book was the *Narrative of the Life of Frederick Douglass* (1845); ten years later his much enlarged and improved *My Bondage and My Freedom* was published.

His third autobiography, *Life and Times of Frederick Douglass* (1881), enlarged in 1892, naturally compressed the material on slavery to include the events and opinions of his later years. He fought for civil rights and denounced not only lynching and the Ku Klux Klan but also less flagrant and insidious injustices of the color line. He urged his own people to develop industry, education, and character. Though generally considered a spokesman for the Republican Party, he nevertheless warned that any political party was unavailing and would be indifferent if Negroes did not have sufficient spirit and wisdom to organize themselves for defense "from outrage, discrimination, and oppression."

Douglass was active in urging the use of Negro troops in the Civil War and helped recruit two Negro regiments in Massachusetts, two of his sons enlisting. He was successively appointed United States Marshal for the District of Columbia, Recorder of Deeds, and Minister to Haiti. The honors that came to him did not blind him to the gravity of his people's position in America. But he insisted that the Negro problem was really the white man's problem: "The question is whether the white man can ever be elevated to that plane of justice, humanity, and Christian civilization which will permit Negroes, Indians, and Chinamen, and other darker colored races, to enjoy an equal chance in the race of life."

Treatment of Slaves on Lloyd's Plantation

THE HEART-RENDING INCIDENTS, related in the foregoing chapter, led me, thus early, to inquire into the nature and history of slavery. *Why am I a slave? Why are some people slaves, and others masters? Was there ever a time when this was not so? How did the relation commence?* These were the perplexing questions which began now to claim my thoughts, and to exercise the weak powers of my mind, for I was still but a child, and knew less than children of the same age in the free states. As my questions concerning these things were only put to children a little older, and little better informed than myself, I was not rapid in reaching a solid footing. By some means I learned from these inquiries, that *"God, up in the sky,"* made everybody; and that he made *white* people to be masters and mistresses, and *black* people to be slaves. This did not satisfy me, nor lessen my interest in the subject. I was told, too, that God was good, and that He knew what was best for me, and best for everybody. This was less satisfactory than the first statement; because it came, point blank, against all my notions of goodness. It was not good to let old master cut the flesh off Esther, and make her cry so. Besides, how did people know that God made black people to be slaves? Did they go up in the sky and learn it? or, did He come down and tell them so. All was dark here. It was some relief to my hard notions of the goodness of God, that, although he made white men to be slaveholders, he did not make them to be *bad* slaveholders, and that, in due time, he would punish the bad slaveholders; that he would, when they died, send them to the bad place, where they would be "burnt up." Nevertheless, I could not reconcile the relation of slavery with my crude notions of goodness.

Then, too, I found that there were puzzling exceptions to this theory of slavery on both sides, and in the middle. I knew of blacks who were *not* slaves; I knew of whites who were *not* slaveholders; and I knew of persons who were *nearly* white, who were slaves. *Color,* therefore, was a very unsatisfactory basis for slavery.

Once, however, engaged in the inquiry, I was not very long in finding out the true solution of the matter. It was not *color,* but *crime,* not *God,* but *man,* that afforded the true explanation of the existence of slavery; nor was I long in finding out another important truth, viz: what man can make, man can unmake. The appalling darkness faded away, and I was master of the subject. There were slaves here, direct from Guinea; and there were many who could say that their fathers and mothers were stolen from Africa—forced from their homes, and compelled to serve as slaves. This, to me, was knowledge; but it was a kind of knowledge which filled me with a burning hatred of slavery, increased my suffering, and left me without the means of breaking away from my bondage. Yet it was knowledge quite worth possessing. I could not have been more than seven or eight years old, when I began to make this subject my study. It was with me in the woods and fields; along the shore of the river, and wherever my boyish wanderings led me; and although I was, at that time, quite ignorant of the existence of the free states, I distinctly remember being, *even then,* most strongly impressed with the idea of being a free man some day. This cheering assurance was an inborn dream of my human nature— a constant menace to slavery—and one which all the powers of slavery were unable to silence or extinguish.

Up to the time of the brutal flogging of my Aunt Esther—for she was my own aunt—and the horrid plight in which I had seen my cousin from Tuckahoe, who had been so badly beaten by the cruel Mr. Plummer, my attention had not been called, especially, to the gross features of slavery. I had, of course, heard of whippings, and of savage *rencontres* between overseers and slaves, but I had always been out of the way at the times and places of their occurrence. My plays and sports, most of the time, took me from the corn and tobacco fields, where the great body of the hands were at work, and where scenes of cruelty were enacted and witnessed. But, after the whipping of

Aunt Esther, I saw many cases of the same shocking nature, not only in my master's house, but on Col. Lloyd's plantation. One of the first which I saw, and which greatly agitated me, was the whipping of a woman belonging to Col. Lloyd, named Nelly. The offense alleged against Nelly, was one of the commonest and most indefinite in the whole catalogue of offenses usually laid to the charge of slaves, viz: "impudence." This may mean almost anything, or nothing at all, just according to the caprice of the master or overseer, at the moment. But, whatever it is, or is not, if it gets the name of "impudence," the party charged with it is sure of a flogging. This offense may be committed in various ways; in the tone of an answer; in answering at all; in not answering; in the expression of countenance; in the motion of the head; in the gait, manner and bearing of the slave. In the case under consideration, I can easily believe that, according to all slave-holding standards, here was a genuine instance of impudence. In Nelly there were all the necessary conditions for committing the offense. She was a bright mulatto, the recognized wife of a favorite "hand" on board Col. Lloyd's sloop, and the mother of five sprightly children. She was a vigorous and spirited woman, and one of the most likely, on the plantation, to be guilty of impudence. My attention was called to the scene, by the noise, curses and screams that proceeded from it; and, on going a little in that direction, I came upon the parties engaged in the skirmish. Mr. Sevier, the overseer, had hold of Nelly, when I caught sight of them; he was endeavoring to drag her towards a tree, which endeavor Nelly was sternly resisting; but to no purpose, except to retard the progress of the overseer's plans. Nelly—as I have said—was the mother of five children; three of them were present, and though quite small, (from seven to ten years old, I should think), they gallantly came to their mother's defense, and gave the overseer an excellent pelting with stones. One of the little fellows ran up, seized the overseer by the leg and bit him; but the monster was too busily engaged with Nelly, to pay any attention to the assaults of the children. There were numerous bloody marks on Mr. Sevier's face, when I first saw him, and they increased as the struggle went on. The imprints of Nelly's fingers were visible, and I was glad to see them. Amidst the wild screams of the children—*"Let my mammy go"*—*"let my mammy go"*—there escaped, from between the teeth of the bullet-headed overseer, a few bitter curses, mingled with threats, that "he would teach the d—d b—h how to give a white man impudence." There is no doubt that Nelly felt herself superior, in some respects, to the slaves around her. She was a wife and mother; her husband was a valued and favorite slave. Besides, he was one of the first hands on board of the sloop, and the sloop hands—since they had to represent the plantation abroad —were generally treated tenderly. The overseer never was allowed to whip Harry; why then should he be allowed to whip Harry's wife? Thoughts of this kind, no doubt, influenced her; but, for whatever reason, she nobly resisted, and, unlike most of the slaves, seemed determined to make her whipping cost Mr. Sevier as much as possible. The blood on his (and her) face, attested her skill, as well as her courage and dexterity in using her nails. Maddened by her resistance, I expected to see Mr. Sevier level her to the ground by a stunning blow; but no; like a savage bull-dog—which he resembled both in temper and appearance—he maintained his grip, and steadily dragged his victim toward the tree, disregarding alike her blows, and the cries of the children for their mother's release. He would, doubtless, have knocked her down with his hickory stick, but that such act might have cost him his place. It is often deemed advisable to knock a *man* slave down, in order to tie him, but it is considered cowardly and inexcusable, in an overseer, thus to deal with a *woman*. He is expected to tie her up, and to give her what is called, in southern parlance, a "genteel flogging," without any very great outlay of strength or skill. I watched, with palpitating interest, the course of the preliminary struggle, and was saddened by every new advantage gained over her by the ruffian. There were times when she seemed likely to get the better of the brute, but he finally overpowered her, and succeeded in getting his rope around her arms, and in firmly tying her to the tree, at which he had been aiming. This done, and Nelly was at the mercy of his merciless lash; and now, what followed, I have no heart to describe. The cowardly creature made good his every threat; and wielded the lash with all the hot zest of furious revenge. The cries of the woman, while undergoing the terrible infliction, were mingled with those of the children, sounds which I hope the reader may never be called upon to hear. When Nelly was untied, her back was covered with blood. The red stripes were all over her shoulders. She was whipped—severely whipped; but she was not subdued, for she continued to denounce the overseer, and to call him every vile name. He had bruised her flesh, but had left her invincible spirit undaunted.

Such floggings are seldom repeated by the same overseer. They prefer to whip those who are most easily whipped. The old doctrine that submission is the best cure for outrage and wrong, does not hold good on the slave plantation. He is whipped oftenest, who is whipped easiest; and that slave who has the courage to stand up for himself against the overseer, although he may have many hard stripes at the first, becomes, in the end, a freeman, even though he sustain the formal relation of a slave. "You can shoot me but you can't whip me," said a slave to Rigby Hopkins; and the result was that he was neither whipped nor shot. If the latter had been his fate, it would have been less deplorable than the living and lingering death to which cowardly and slavish souls are subjected. I do not know that Mr. Sevier ever undertook to whip Nelly again. He probably never did, for it was not long after his attempt to subdue her, that he was taken sick, and died. The wretched man died as he had lived, unrepentant; and it was said—with how much truth I do not know—that in the very last hours of his life, his ruling passion showed itself, and that when wrestling with death, he was uttering horrid oaths, and flourishing the cowskin, as though he was tearing the flesh off some helpless slave. One thing is certain, that when he was in health, it was enough to chill the blood, and to stiffen the hair of an ordinary man, to hear Mr. Sevier talk. Nature, or his cruel habits, had given to his face an expression of unusual savageness, even for a slave-driver. Tobacco and rage had worn his teeth short, and nearly every sentence that escaped their compressed grating, was commenced or concluded with some outburst of profanity. His presence made the field alike the field of blood, and of blasphemy. Hated for his cruelty, despised for his cowardice, his death was deplored by no one outside his own house—if indeed it was deplored there; it was regarded by the slaves as a merciful interposition of Providence. Never went there a man to the grave loaded with heavier curses. Mr. Sevier's place was promptly taken by a Mr. Hopkins, and the change was quite a relief, he being a very different man. He was, in all respects, a better man than his predecessor; as good as any man can be, and yet be an overseer. His course was characterized by no extraordinary cruelty; and when he whipped a slave, as he sometimes did, he seemed to take no especial pleasure in it, but, on the contrary, acted as though he felt it to be a mean business. Mr. Hopkins stayed but a short time; his place—much to the regret of the slaves generally—was taken by a Mr. Gore, of whom more will be said hereafter. It is enough, for the present, to say, that he was no improvement on Mr. Sevier, except that he was less noisy and less profane.

I have already referred to the business-like aspect of Col. Lloyd's plantation. This business-like appearance was much increased on the two days at the end of each month, when the slaves from the different farms came to get their monthly allowance of meal and meat. These were gala days for the slaves, and there was much rivalry among them as to *who* should be elected to go up to the great house farm for the allowance, and, indeed, to attend to any business at this, (for them), the capital. The beauty and grandeur of the place, its numerous slave population, and the fact that Harry, Peter and Jake—the sailors of the sloop—almost always kept, privately, little trinkets which they bought at Baltimore, to sell, made it a privilege to come to the great house farm. Being selected, too, for this office, was deemed a high honor. It was taken as a proof of confidence and favor; but, probably, the chief motive of the competitors for the place, was, a desire to break the dull monotony of the field, and to get beyond the overseer's eye and lash. Once on the road with an ox team, and seated on the tongue of his cart, with no overseer to look after him, the slave was comparatively free; and, if thoughtful, he had time to think. Slaves are generally expected to sing as well as to work. A silent slave is not liked by masters or overseers. "Make a noise," "make a noise," and "Bear a hand," are the words usually addressed to the slaves when there is silence amongst them. This may account for the almost constant singing heard in the southern states. There was, generally, more or less singing among the teamsters, as it was one means of letting the overseer know where they were, and that they were moving on with the work. But, on allowance day, those who visited the great house farm were peculiarly excited and noisy. While on their way, they would make the dense old woods, for miles around, reverberate with their wild notes. These were not always merry because they were wild. On the contrary, they were mostly of a plaintive cast, and told a tale of grief and sorrow. In the most boisterous outbursts of rapturous sentiment, there was ever a tinge of deep melancholy. I have never heard any songs like those anywhere since I left slavery, except when in Ireland. There I heard the same *wailing notes,* and was much affected by them. It was during the famine of 1845-6. In all the songs of the slaves, there was ever some expression in praise of the great house farm; something which would flatter the pride of the owner, and, possibly, draw a favorable glance from him.

> "I am going away to the great house farm,
>   O yea! O yea! O yea!
> My old master is a good old master,
>   Oh yea! O yea! O yea!"

This they would sing, with other words of their own improvising— jargon to others, but full of meaning to themselves. I have sometimes thought, that the mere hearing of those songs would do more to impress truly spiritual-minded men and women with the soul-crushing and death-dealing character of slavery, than the reading of whole volumes of its mere physical cruelties. They speak to the heart and to the soul of the thoughtful. I cannot better express my sense of them

now, than ten years ago, when, in sketching my life, I thus spoke of
this feature of my plantation experience:

"I did not, when a slave, understand the deep meanings of those
rude, and apparently incoherent songs. I was myself within the circle,
so that I neither saw nor heard as those without might see and hear.
They told a tale which was then altogether beyond by feeble comprehension; they were tones, loud, long and deep, breathing the
prayer and complaint of souls boiling over with the bitterest anguish.
Every tone was a testimony against slavery, and a prayer to God for
deliverance from chains. The hearing of those wild notes always
depressed my spirits, and filled my heart with ineffable sadness. The
mere recurrence, even now, afflicts my spirit, and while I am writing
these lines, my tears are falling. To those songs I trace my first glimmering conceptions of the dehumanizing character of slavery. I can
never get rid of that conception. Those songs still follow me, to deepen
my hatred of slavery, and quicken my sympathies for my brethren
in bonds. If any one wishes to be impressed with a sense of the soul-
killing power of slavery, let him go to Col. Lloyd's plantation, and,
on allowance day, place himself in the deep, pine woods, and there
let him, in silence, thoughtfully analyze the sounds that shall pass
through the chambers of his soul, and if he is not thus impressed, it will
only be because 'there is no flesh in his obdurate heart.' "

The remark is not unfrequently made, that slaves are the most contented and happy laborers in the world. They dance and sing, and
make all manner of joyful noises—so they do; but it is a great mistake
to suppose them happy because they sing. The songs of the slave represent the sorrows, rather than the joys, of his heart; and he is relieved
by them, only as an aching heart is relieved by its tears. Such is the
constitution of the human mind, that, when pressed to extremes, it
often avails itself of the most opposite methods. Extremes meet in mind
as in matter. When the slaves on board of the "Pearl" were overtaken,
arrested, and carried to prison—their hopes for freedom blasted—as
they marched in chains they sang, and found (as Emily Edmundson
tells us) a melancholy relief in singing. The singing of a man cast
away on a desolate island, might be as appropriately considered an
evidence of his contentment and happiness, as the singing of a slave.
Sorrow and desolation have their songs, as well as joy and peace.
Slaves sing more to *make* themselves happy, than to express their
happiness.

It is the boast of slaveholders, that their slaves enjoy more of the
physical comforts of life than the peasantry of any country in the
world. My experience contradicts this. The men and the women slaves

on Col. Lloyd's farm, received, as their monthly allowance of food, eight pounds of pickled pork, or their equivalent in fish. The pork was often tainted, and the fish was of the poorest quality—herrings, which would bring very little if offered for sale in any northern market. With their pork or fish, they had one bushel of Indian meal—unbolted —of which quite fifteen per cent. was fit only to feed pigs. With this, one pint of salt was given; and this was the entire monthly allowance of a full grown slave, working constantly in the open field, from morning until night, every day in the month except Sunday, and living on a fraction more than a quarter of a pound of meat per day, and less than a peck of corn-meal per week. There is no kind of work that a man can do which requires a better supply of food to prevent physical exhaustion, than the field-work of a slave. So much for the slave's allowance of food; now for his raiment. The yearly allowance of clothing for the slaves on this plantation, consisted of two tow-linen shirts—such linen as the coarsest crash towels are made of; one pair of trowsers of the same material, for summer, and a pair of trowsers and a jacket of woolen, most slazily put together, for winter; one pair of yarn stockings, and one pair of shoes of the coarsest description. The slave's entire apparel could not have cost more than eight dollars per year. The allowance of food and clothing for the little children, was committed to their mothers, or to the older slave-women having care of them. Children who were unable to work in the field, had neither shoes, stockings, jackets nor trowsers given them. Their clothing consisted of two coarse tow-linen shirts—already described—per year; and when these failed them, as they often did, they went naked until the next allowance day. Flocks of little children from five to ten years old, might be seen on Col. Lloyd's plantation, as destitute of clothing as any little heathen on the west coast of Africa; and this, is not merely during the summer months, but during the frosty weather of March. The little girls were no better off than the boys; all were nearly in a state of nudity.

As to beds to sleep on, they were known to none of the field hands; nothing but a coarse blanket—not so good as those used in the north to cover horses—was given them, and this only to the men and women. The children stuck themselves in holes and corners, about the quarters; often in the corner of the huge chimneys, with their feet in the ashes to keep them warm. The want of beds, however, was not considered a very great privation. Time to sleep was of far greater importance, for, when the day's work is done, most of the slaves have their washing, mending and cooking to do; and, having few or none of the ordinary facilities for doing such things, very many of their sleeping hours are consumed in necessary preparations for the duties of the coming day.

The sleeping apartments—if they may be called such—have little regard to comfort or decency. Old and young, male and female, married and single, drop down upon the common clay floor, each covering up with his or her blanket,—the only protection they have from cold or exposure. The night, however, is shortened at both ends. The slaves work often as long as they can see, and are late in cooking and mending for the coming day; and, at the first gray streak of morning, they are summoned to the field by the driver's horn.

ELIZABETH KECKLEY (1825-1905)

Madame Keckley, as Abraham Lincoln called her, was born a slave in Virginia. In *Behind the Scenes: or Thirty Years a Slave,* and *Four Years in the White House* (1868) she told a story of a life replete with unusual experiences. As a slave in Virginia, North Carolina, and St. Louis, who bought freedom for herself and her son through her skill as a dressmaker, as "modiste" to the high officials in Washington, among them Mrs. Jefferson Davis, Mrs. Stephen A. Douglass, Mrs. E. M. Stanton, and, later, Mrs. Abraham Lincoln, she was able to observe closely the lives of widely contrasting types of people. Her account of Mrs. Lincoln, especially her chapters relating her experiences in New York when Mrs. Lincoln tried to auction off her White House wardrobe, and her account of Washington during the war years, are filled with shrewd observations. Mrs. Keckley, after serving as director of domestic art at Wilberforce, died in Washington, where her funeral services were conducted by the Reverend Francis J. Grimké (see p. 804). When the authorship of her book was attacked in 1936, the Reverend Mr. Grimké, along with others who knew her, vouched for its authenticity. Mrs. Keckley herself often expressed her gratefulness to G. W. Carleton, her publisher, for helping her with grammatical constructions, but insisted that the book itself was her own. John E. Washington's *They Knew Lincoln* casts much light upon Mrs. Keckley's autobiography.

[The Death of Lincoln]

THE DAYS PASSED without any incident of particular note disturbing the current of life. On Friday morning, April 14th—alas! what American does not remember the day—I saw Mrs. Lincoln but for a moment. She told me that she was to attend the theatre that night with the

President, but I was not summoned to assist her in making her toilette. Sherman had swept from the northern border of Georgia through the heart of the Confederacy down to the sea, striking the death-blow to the rebellion. Grant had pursued General Lee beyond Richmond, and the army of Virginia, that had made such stubborn resistance, was crumbling to pieces. Fort Sumter had fallen;—the stronghold first wrenched from the Union, and which had braved the fury of Federal guns for so many years, was restored to the Union; the end of the war was near at hand, and the great pulse of the loyal North thrilled with joy. The dark warcloud was fading, and a white-robed angel seemed to hover in the sky, whispering "Peace—peace on earth, good-will toward men!" Sons, brothers, fathers, friends, sweethearts were coming home. Soon the white tents would be folded, the volunteer army disbanded, and tranquillity again reign. Happy, happy day!—happy at least to those who fought under the banner of the Union. There was great rejoicing throughout the North. From the Atlantic to the Pacific, flags were gayly thrown to the breeze, and at night every city blazed with tens of thousand lights. But scarcely had the fireworks ceased to play, and the lights been taken down from the windows, when the lightning flashed the most appalling news over the magnetic wires. "The President has been murdered!" spoke the swift-winged messenger, and the loud huzza died upon the lips. A nation suddenly paused in the midst of festivity, and stood paralyzed with horror—transfixed with awe.

Oh, memorable day! Oh, memorable night! Never before was joy so violently contrasted with sorrow.

At 11 o'clock at night I was awakened by an old friend and neighbor, Miss M. Brown, with the startling intelligence that the entire Cabinet had been assassinated, and Mr. Lincoln shot, but not mortally wounded. When I heard the words I felt as if the blood had been frozen in my veins, and that my lungs must collapse for the want of air. Mr. Lincoln shot! the Cabinet assassinated! What could it mean? The streets were alive with wondering, awe-stricken people. Rumors flew thick and fast, and the wildest reports came with every new arrival. The words were repeated with blanched cheeks and quivering lips. I waked Mr. and Mrs. Lewis, and told them that the President was shot, and that I must go to the White House. I could not remain in a state of uncertainty. I felt that the house would not hold me. They tried to quiet me, but gentle words could not calm the wild tempest. They quickly dressed themselves, and we sailed out into the street to drift with the excited throng. We walked rapidly towards the White House, and on our way passed the residence of Secretary

Seward, which was surrounded by armed soldiers, keeping back all intruders with the point of the bayonet. We hurried on, and as we approached the White House, saw that it too was surrounded with soldiers. Every entrance was strongly guarded, and no one was permitted to pass. The guard at the gate told us that Mr. Lincoln had not been brought home, but refused to give any other information. More excited than ever, we wandered down the street. Grief and anxiety were making me weak, and as we joined the outskirts of a large crowd, I began to feel as meek and humble as a penitent child. A gray-haired old man was passing. I caught a glimpse of his face, and it seemed so full of kindness and sorrow that I gently touched his arm, and imploringly asked: "Will you please, Sir, to tell me whether Mr. Lincoln is dead or not?"

"Not dead," he replied, "but dying. God help us!" and with a heavy step he passed on.

"Not dead, but dying! then indeed God help us!"

We learned that the President was mortally wounded—that he had been shot down in his box at the theatre, and that he was not expected to live till morning; when we returned home with heavy hearts. I could not sleep. I wanted to go to Mrs. Lincoln, as I pictured her wild with grief; but then I did not know where to find her, and I must wait till morning. Never did the hours drag so slowly. Every moment seemed an age, and I could do nothing but walk about and hold my arms in mental agony.

Morning came at last, and a sad morning was it. The flags that floated so gayly yesterday now were draped in black, and hung in silent folds at half-mast. The President was dead, and a nation was mourning for him. Every house was draped in black, and every face wore a solemn look. People spoke in subdued tones, and glided whisperingly, wonderingly, silently about the streets.

About eleven o'clock on Saturday morning a carriage drove up to the door, and a messenger asked for "Elizabeth Keckley."

"Who wants her?" I asked.

"I come from Mrs. Lincoln. If you are Mrs. Keckley, come with me immediately to the White House."

I hastily put on my shawl and bonnet, and was driven at a rapid rate to the White House. Everything about the building was sad and solemn. I was quickly shown to Mrs. Lincoln's room, and on entering, saw Mrs. L. tossing uneasily about upon a bed. The room was darkened, and the only person in it besides the widow of the President was Mrs. Secretary Welles, who had spent the night with her. Bowing to Mrs. Welles, I went to the bedside.

"Why did you not come to me last night, Elizabeth—I sent for you?" Mrs. Lincoln asked in a low whisper.

"I did try to come to you, but I could not find you," I answered, as I laid my hand upon her hot brow.

I afterwards learned, that when she had partially recovered from the first shock of the terrible tragedy in the theatre, Mrs. Welles asked:

"Is there no one, Mrs. Lincoln, that you desire to have with you in this terrible affliction?"

"Yes, send for Elizabeth Keckley. I want her just as soon as she can be brought here."

Three messengers, it appears, were successively despatched for me, but all of them mistook the number and failed to find me.

Shortly after entering the room on Saturday morning, Mrs. Welles excused herself, as she said she must go to her own family, and I was left alone with Mrs. Lincoln.

She was nearly exhausted with grief, and when she became a little quiet, I asked and received permission to go into the Guests' Room, where the body of the President lay in state. When I crossed the threshold of the room, I could not help recalling the day on which I had seen little Willie lying in his coffin where the body of his father now lay. I remembered how the President had wept over the pale beautiful face of his gifted boy, and now the President himself was dead. The last time I saw him he spoke kindly to me, but alas! the lips would never move again. The light had faded from his eyes, and when the light went out the soul went with it. What a noble soul was his—noble in all the noble attributes of God! Never did I enter the solemn chamber of death with such palpitating heart and trembling footsteps as I entered it that day. No common mortal had died. The Moses of my people had fallen in the hour of his triumph. Fame had woven her choicest chaplet for his brow. Though the brow was cold and pale in death, the chaplet should not fade, for God had studded it with the glory of the eternal stars.

When I entered the room, the members of the Cabinet and many distinguished officers of the army were grouped around the body of their fallen chief. They made room for me, and approaching the body, I lifted the white cloth from the white face of the man that I had worshipped as an idol—looked upon as a demi-god. Notwithstanding the violence of the death of the President, there was something beautiful as well as grandly solemn in the expression of the placid face. There lurked the sweetness and gentleness of childhood, and the stately grandeur of god-like intellect. I gazed long at the face, and turned away with tears in my eyes and a choking sensation in my throat. Ah! never was man so widely mourned before. The whole world bowed their heads in grief when Abraham Lincoln died.

Returning to Mrs. Lincoln's room, I found her in a new paroxysm of grief. Robert was bending over his mother with tender affection, and little Tad was crouched at the foot of the bed with a world of agony in his young face. I shall never forget the scene—the wails of a broken heart, the unearthly shrieks, the terrible convulsions, the wild, tempestuous outbursts of grief from the soul. I bathed Mrs. Lincoln's head with cold water, and soothed the terrible tornado as best I could. Tad's grief at his father's death was as great as the grief of his mother, but her terrible outbursts awed the boy into silence. Sometimes he would throw his arms around her neck, and exclaim, between his broken sobs, "Don't cry so, Mamma! don't cry, or you will make me cry, too! You will break my heart."

Mrs. Lincoln could not bear to hear Tad cry, and when he would plead to her not to break his heart, she would calm herself with a great effort, and clasp her child in her arms.

Every room in the White House was darkened, and every one spoke in subdued tones, and moved about with muffled tread. The very atmosphere breathed of the great sorrow which weighed heavily upon each heart. Mrs. Lincoln never left her room, and while the body of her husband was being borne in solemn state from the Atlantic to the broad prairies of the West, she was weeping with her fatherless children in her private chamber. She denied admittance to almost every one, and I was her only companion, except her children, in the days of her great sorrow.

DANIEL A. PAYNE (1811-1893)

Daniel A. Payne, a bishop of the African Methodist Episcopal Church, was born in Charleston, South Carolina. He was educated in the school of the Miner's Moralist Society in Charleston and at the Gettysburg Lutheran Seminary. From the beginning his efforts were directed into two channels: the education of Negroes and the expansion and improvement of the Negro church. He conducted a private school in antebellum Charleston until, in 1835, the state law against schools for Negro children went into effect. He then started a private school in Philadelphia. As a bishop he traveled widely in both slave and free territory, prescribing for his ministers systematic study, lecturing on the need for education, and establishing literary societies and groups for the self-improvement of Negroes. In 1862, in the company of Carl

Schurz, Payne visited the White House and urged Lincoln to sign the bill for emancipation in the District of Columbia. In 1863 he persuaded the A. M. E. church to purchase Wilberforce, a school established in 1856 by the M. E. church for the education of colored youth. He was elected president of Wilberforce, the first Negro to be a college president, and served for sixteen years. *The History of the A. M. E. Church* (1891), occasional poetry, and tracts on education are his chief works aside from published sermons. A biography, *Daniel Alexander Payne, Christian Educator,* by Josephine R. Coam, was published in 1935. The following selections are taken from *Recollections of Seventy Years* (1888).

[Young Schoolmaster]

MY FIRST SCHOOL was opened in 1829 in a house on Tradd Street occupied by one Caesar Wright. It consisted of his three children, for each of whom he paid me fifty cents a month. I also taught three adult slaves at night, at the same price, thus making my monthly income from teaching only three dollars. This was not sufficient to feed me, but a slave-woman, Mrs. Eleanor Parker, supplied many of my wants. I was happy in my humble employment, but at the end of the year I was so discouraged at the financial result, and by the remarks expressed by envious persons, that I decided to seek some other employment which would yield better pay.

At this juncture a wealthy slave-holder arrived in Charleston, *en route* to the West Indies for his health. Knowing that British law emancipated every slave that put his foot on British soil, he desired to obtain the services of a free young man of color sufficiently intelligent to do his out-of-door business. I was commended to him, and called upon him at the Planters' Hotel. Among the inducements he offered he said: "If you will go with me, the knowledge that you will acquire of men and things will be of far more value to you than the wages I will pay you. Do you know what makes the difference between the master and the slave? *Nothing but superior knowledge.*"

This statement was fatal to his desire to obtain my services, for I instantly said to myself: "If it is true that there is nothing but superior knowledge between the master and the slave, I will not go with you, but will rather go and obtain that knowledge which constitutes the master." As I politely took my leave these words passed through my mind:

> He that flies his Saviour's cross
> Shall meet his Maker's frown.

Then these reflections followed. "In abandoning the school-room am I not fleeing from the cross which the Saviour has imposed upon me? Is not the abandonment of the teacher's work in my case a sin?" The answer was easily found, and I resolved to reopen my school and to inform my patrons to that effect.

On the first of the year 1830 I re-opened my school, which continued to increase in numbers until the room became too small, and I was constrained to procure a more commodious place. This in turn became too small, and one was built for me on Anson Street, by Mr. Robert Howard, in the rear of his yard. This house is still standing (1886). Here I continued to teach until April, 1835.

During the three years of my attendance at the school of Mr. Thomas S. Bonneau I learned how to read, write, and spell; also arithmetic as far as the "Rule of Three." Spelling was a delightful exercise of my boyhood. In this I excelled. Seldom did I lose my place at the head of my class, and he who won it did not occupy it long. History was my great delight. Of geography and map-drawing, English grammar and composition, I knew nothing, because they were not taught in any of the schools for colored children. I therefore felt the need of knowledge in these directions; but how was I to obtain it?

I had a geography, but had never seen an atlas, and what was more, I knew not how or where to get one. Fortunately for me, one day as I was sitting on the piazza endeavoring to learn some lesson, a woman entered the gate and approached me with a book in her hand. Said she: "Don't you want to buy this book?" Taking it, I opened it, and to my great joy I beheld the colored maps of an atlas—the very thing I needed. Said I: "What will you take for it?" The woman had found it on the street, and replied: "Whatever you choose to give." All that I could command at the time was a York shilling (twelve and one-half cents in silver coin), so I gave it to her, and rejoiced over my prize. Immediately I went to work with my geography and atlas, and in about six months was able to construct maps on the Mercator's and globular projection. After I had acquired this ability I introduced geography and map-drawing into my school. At the same time with geography I studied and mastered English grammar. I began with "Murray's Primary Grammar," and committed the entire book to memory, but did not understand it; so I reviewed it. Then light sprung up; still I felt like one in a dungeon who beheld a glimmer of light at a distance, and with steady but cautious footsteps moved toward it, inspired by the hope that I would soon find its source and come out into the full blaze of animated day. I then made a second review of it, and felt conscious of my power to teach it. I therefore added that to my curriculum.

Having now the groundwork, I began to build the superstructure. I commenced with "Playfair's Euclid," and proceeded as far as the first five books. The next thing which arrested my attention was botany. The author and her specimens enchanted me; my progress was rapid, and the study became to me a source of great happiness and an instrument of great usefulness. Descriptive chemistry, natural philosophy, and descriptive astronomy followed in rapid succession.

"Burret's Geography of the Heavens" was my text-book in the last-named science. Stimulated by this interesting guide, I watched the total eclipse of 1832 from its commencement to its completion with my *naked eye;* but I paid dear for my rash experiment. The immediate result was a partial loss of sight. No book could be read for about three weeks. Whenever I opened a book the pages had the appearance of *black sheets*. From this injury I have never fully recovered. Up to that time my eyes were like those of the eagle; ever since they have been growing weaker and weaker.

Then, on a Thursday morning, I bought a Greek grammar, a lexicon, and a Greek Testament. On the same day I mastered the Greek alphabet; on Friday I learned to write them; on Saturday morning I translated the first chapter of Matthew's Gospel from Greek into English. My very soul rejoiced and exulted in this glorious triumph. Next came the Latin and the French. Meanwhile I was pushing my studies in drawing and coloring till I was able to produce a respectable flower, fruit, or animal on paper and on velvet.

My researches in botany gave me a relish for zoology; but as I could never get hold of any work on this science I had to *make books* for myself. This I did by killing such insects, toads, snakes, young alligators, fishes, and young sharks as I could catch. I then cleaned and stuffed those that I could, and hung them upon the walls of my school-room. The following fact will give the index of my methods. I bought a live alligator, made one of my pupils provoke him to bite, and whenever he opened his mouth I discharged a load of shot from a small pistol down his throat. As soon as he was stunned I threw him on his back, cut his throat, ripped open his chest, hung him up and studied his viscera till they ceased to move. The flesh of all that I killed I cooked and tasted. I excepted nothing but the toad and snake. My detestations for these was too intense to allow me to put their flesh into my mouth.

My enthusiasm was the inspiration of my pupils. I used to take my first class of boys into the woods every Saturday in search of insects, reptiles, and plants, and at the end of five years I had accumulated some fine speciments of each of these. I had also taken a fatherless boy to educate gratuitously. This lad's sister one day found a large caterpillar on an elderberry tree. This worm she sent to me. It was the length and thickness of a large laboring-man's middle finger. Its color was that of gold blended with azure. It had four rows of horns running the whole length of its body; these horns were made up of golden and ebony-like points; its head was also circled with a crown of these horns.

Not being able to determine the species or genus of this worm, I took it to Mrs. Ferguson, the sister of Judge Colcox, who was unable to give me any information in regard to it; but she advised me to take it to Dr. Bachman, who was then the most distinguished naturalist in South Carolina. I little knew what that visit was to bring about ultimately.

The Doctor received me kindly, and gave its classification. He also instructed me in its nature and habits, and how to carry it through its different stages of existence. This, however, I preferred him to do, allowing me at the same time to visit his studio and observe the transformations. This request was kindly complied with by the learned divine and naturalist. On my second visit he took me into his garden and showed me his fine collections of flowers. He also exhibited to me his herbarium and his valuable collection of insects from different parts of the world. On my last visit he took me into his parlor and introduced me to his wife and daughters as "the young philosopher." There I sat and conversed with his family as freely as though all were of the same color and equal rank; and by my request his daughter skillfully performed several pieces upon the piano. A remark of his at that visit has occurred to me many times through life. There was upon the center-table, protected by a large glass globe, an artificial tree bearing a collection of beautifully-mounted birds. My attention was drawn to them, and I expressed myself to the effect that he had about him every thing to make his home pleasant. His reply was substantially this: "Yes; I feel it my duty to throw around my home every possible attraction for my daughters, so that they may never have occasion to seek elsewhere for forbidden pleasures." . . .

In the prosecution of my studies in zoology I desired to obtain a highland moccasin, which was then considered a species of rattlesnake, and whose bite was deadly. Therefore I engaged the services of a slave of lawyer Lionel Kennedy, who was at that time an alderman of the city of Charleston. The plantation of this gentleman was about one mile distant from the city. On the appointed Saturday I dispatched three of my advanced class (John Lee, Robert Wishan, and Michael Eggart) with a large glass bottle, in order that they might bring me the viper alive. On their arrival at the plantation they found Lawyer Kennedy and his son, Dr. Kennedy, overlooking the work of the slaves. They knew me and knew the boys' parents. Calling the lads to them, they demanded the reason of their appearance on the plantation. A direct answer was given. They then inquired after my motives for buying this serpent from their slaves; to which a direct answer was also given. Then they asked the lads to tell them what were the different things taught them, and they also examined them in their studies. The boys answered every question put to them except one. Then said the young doctor: "Why, pa, Payne is playing hell in Charleston." This occurred about the middle of the summer of 1834.

[Called to Preach]

. . . I COMMENCED MY CAREER as a pastor at a little more than twenty-six years of age. With no pastoral experience, I deeply felt my own insufficiency and need of more than human counsel, of more than human aid, and found it necessary to spend much time on my knees both in praying and studying out my sermons.

There were about forty or fifty members in the Church in East Troy when I became its pastor *pro tempore*. Among my friends and helpers were two noble women: Aunt Peggy, an aged woman who was beyond fifty years before she knew how to read the Bible, but who was strong in faith, full of prayer, and could almost always tell when a season of revival was approaching. She was of great aid to me. Then there was that godly heroine, Miss Hannah Hubbard, an educated white lady, who shrunk not from the lowest of God's poor because they were of African descent, but mingled with them in their social circles, in the Sunday-school, and in the prayer-meeting. It was there that her communion and power with God was manifest. I think it was in the summer of 1839 that she married Rev. Hiram Wilson, who was then agent for some anti-slavery society to care for the varied interests of the fugitives from American slavery in Canada. She was of great aid to her self-sacrificing husband, and for many years made her personal influence felt as a blessing to our unfortunate brethren in Canada. She died at Dawn, Canada West, in the house of Mrs. Stowe's "Uncle Tom."[1]

In the autumn of 1851, in company with others, I visited Dawn,

[1] Mr. Josiah Henson.

Canada, in search of material for the history of the A. M. E. Church, and to see if Canada would be a safe asylum for our people.[2] As "Uncle Tom" was conducting us down toward the banks of the River Thames, I noticed in a field at the left a grave encompassed by a newly-whitewashed paling. Its neatness aroused my curiosity to know whose grave it was. In answer to my question came the response: "It is the grave of Mrs. Hiram Wilson." In an instant I was there, and found a beautiful rose blooming at the head. This rose I plucked, with some leaves, and on my return to the house of "Uncle Tom" his daughter gave me a lock of the hair of Mrs. Wilson, which is still in my possession as a relic of that godly heroine.

Shortly after I had entered upon my work at East Troy I was sent by the citizens to represent them in the meeting of the National Moral Reform Society held in Philadelphia. Among the distinguished delegates were the Rev. Samuel E. Cornish, editor of the *Colored American*, and Rev. Joshua Leavitt, then of the *New York Evangelist*. On my return I stopped in New York at Mrs. Asenath Nicholson Graham's boarding-house. This lady was a devout Christian, in deep sympathy with every movement leading to the amelioration of the condition of the colored people and to the uplifting of humanity in general. She was also a woman of intellect and culture, and had written a biography of the first pioneer in the efforts to reform the abandoned women of New York. She was, as might be expected, in deep sympathy with the Oberlin movement of that day. At her boarding-house I met that gifted man, Theodore Weld, one of the most eloquent of the anti-slavery lecturers. He invited me to the Shiloh Presbyterian Church, where, at the request of the pastor, I preached. Lewis Tappan and oth rs of the Executive Committee of the Anti-Slavery Society were present. Soon after my return to Troy I received a commission from the committee to be one of its public lecturers, with a salary of $300 per year and traveling expenses. Here was an inducement— an inviting field, yet as laborious and dangerous as it was flattering to the pride and ambition of a young man twenty-seven years old. In those days heroism and consequent fame offered their laurels to any young man of talent and intelligence who might be willing to become the fearless and successful opponent of American slavery, and the eloquent defender of liberty and human rights. But I had consecrated myself to the pulpit and the work of salvation. Could I turn aside from so high a position and so holy a calling? Inclined to refuse, yet mistrusting my own judgment, I submitted the question

[2] In 1851 the fugitive slave bill was then affecting our people, and all felt unsafe in the United States.

to a friend—Lawyer Yates. His advice was put in these words: "I turned aside from my chosen profession to engage in work which others had marked out for me, and now I repent that I did. I think God has called you to the pulpit, and therefore advise that you stick to theology and the work of the Christian ministry." This advice determined my choice, and I respectfully declined the position offered me by the Executive Committee of the Anti-slavery Society. I have never regretted the decision.

When God has a work to be executed he also chooses the man to execute it. He also qualifies the workman for the work. Frederick Douglas was fitted for his specialty; Daniel Alexander Payne for his. Frederick Douglass could not do the work which was assigned to Daniel Alexander Payne, nor Daniel Alexander Payne the work assigned to Frederick Douglass. "The hour for the man, and the man for the hour." He who undertakes, through envy, jealousy, or any other motive or consideration, to reverse this divine law resists the purpose of the Almighty and brings misfortune, sometimes ruin, upon himself. . . .

. . . In May it was my privilege to visit the Sunday-school of Old Bethel, in Philadelphia, and at a meeting of the Sunday-school teachers I conducted responsive reading of the First and Second Psalms of David. I showed them how England had become great by habitually making her people read the Scriptures on Sunday in the great congregations; and how the colored race, who had been oppressed for centuries through ignorance and superstition, might become intelligent, Christian, and powerful through the enlightening and sanctifying influences of the word of God. I also stated that thereafter, by my orders, every pastor occupying the pulpit of Bethel should make responsive readings of the Holy Scriptures a part of the public worship. Bethel Church about this time had set about furnishing the music-room at our university, which they completed by June.

I have mentioned the "Praying and Singing Bands" elsewhere. The strange delusion that many ignorant but well-meaning people labor under leads me to speak particularly of them. About this time I attended a "bush meeting," where I went to please the pastor whose circuit I was visiting. After the sermon they formed a ring, and with coats off sung, clapped their hands and stamped their feet in a most ridiculous and heathenish way. I requested the pastor to go and stop their dancing. At his request they stopped their dancing and clapping of hands, but remained singing and rocking their bodies to and fro. This they did for about fifteen minutes. I then went, and taking their leader by the arm requested him to desist and to sit down and sing in a rational manner. I told him also that it was a heathenish way to worship and disgraceful to themselves, the race, and the Christian name. In that instance they broke up their ring; but would not sit down, and walked sullenly away. After the sermon in the afternoon, having another opportunity of speaking alone to this young leader of the singing and clapping ring, he said: "Sinners won't get converted unless there is a ring." Said I: "You might sing till you fell down dead, and you would fail to convert a single sinner, because nothing but the spirit of God and the word of God can convert sinners." He replied: "The Spirit of God works upon people in different ways. At camp-meeting there must be a ring here, a ring there, a ring over yonder, or sinners will not get converted." This was his idea, and it is also that of many others. These "Bands" I have had to encounter in many places, and, as I have stated in regard to my early labors in Baltimore, I have been strongly censured because of my efforts to change the mode of worship or modify the extravagances indulged in by the people. In some cases all that I could do was to teach and preach the right, fit, and proper way of serving God. To the most thoughtful and intelligent I usually succeeded in making the "Band" disgusting; but by the ignorant masses, as in the case mentioned, it was regarded as the essence of religion. So much so was this the case that, like this man, they believed no conversion could occur without their agency, nor outside of their own ring could any be a genuine one. Among some of the songs of these "Rings," or "Fist and Heel Worshipers," as they have been called, I find a note of two in my journal, which were used in the instance mentioned. As will be seen, they consisted chiefly of what are known as "corn-field ditties:"

> "Ashes to ashes, dust to dust;
> If God won't have us, the devil must.

> "I was way over there where the coffin fell;
> I heard that sinner as he screamed in hell."

To indulge in such songs from eight to ten and half past ten at night was the chief employment of these "Bands." Prayer was only a secondary thing, and this was rude and extravagant to the last degree. The man who had the most powerful pair of lungs was the one who made the best prayer, and he could be heard a square off. He who could sing loudest and longest led the "Band," having his loins girded and a handkerchief in hand with which he kept time, while his feet resounded on the floor like the drumsticks of a bass drum. In some places it was the custom to begin these dances after every night service and keep it up till midnight, sometimes singing and dancing alternately—a short prayer and a long dance. Some one has even called it the "Voudoo Dance." I have remonstrated with a number of pastors for permitting these practices, which vary somewhat in different localities, but have been invariably met with the response that he could not succeed in restraining them, and an attempt to compel them to cease would simply drive them away from our Church. I suppose that with the most stupid and headstrong it is an incurable religious disease, but it is with me a question whether it would not be better to let such people go out of the Church than remain in it to perpetuate their evil practice and thus do two things: disgrace the Christian name and corrupt others. Any one who knows human nature must infer the result after such midnight practices to be that the day after they are unfit for labor, and that at the end of the dance their exhaustion would render them an easy prey to Satan. These meetings must always be more damaging physically, morally, and religiously than beneficial. How needful it is to have an intelligent ministry to teach these people who hold to this ignorant mode of worship the true method of serving God. And my observations lead me to the conclusion that we need more than an intelligent ministry to cure this religious fanaticism. We need a host of Christian reformers like St. Paul, who will not only speak against these evils, but who will also resist them, even if excommunication be necessary. The time is at hand when the ministry of the A. M. E. Church must drive out this heathenish mode of worship or drive out all the intelligence, refinement, and practical Christians who may be ·in her bosom.

So far from being in harmony with the religion of the Lord Jesus Christ, it antagonizes his holy religion. And what is most deplorable, some of our most popular, and powerful preachers labor systematically to perpetuate this fanaticism. Such preachers never rest till they create an excitement that consists in shouting, jumping, and dancing. I say systematically do they preach to produce such results, and just as systematically do they avoid the trial of persons accused of swindling, drunkenness, embezzling, and the different forms of adultery. I deliberately record that which I know, and am prepared if necessary to prove.

To these sensational and recreant preachers I recommend the careful and prayerful study of the text: "To the unknown God, whom ye ignorantly worship, him declare I unto you." (Acts xvii. 23.) The preachers against whom I make this record are intensely religious, but grossly immoral. "By their fruits ye shall know them."

BOOKER T. WASHINGTON (1859-1915)

Up From Slavery (1901) (see p. 673) has been more frequently reprinted than any other book by a Negro author. A note to the Pocket Book Edition states that the Doubleday, Doran volume went into at least forty-one editions, and there have been three other reprints. The work grew out of a series of articles in the *Outlook*. Coming at a crucial period in race relations, it attracted and has continued to attract readers by its message of interracial good will and success over obstacles. In his preface Washington says that he tried to write straightforwardly "with no attempt at embellishment." But *Up From Slavery* is skillfully adapted to its ends: it is filled with modesty and Christian forbearance; it deprecates bitterness, praises Southern whites for their friendship to Negroes, sets forth the maxims of the American dream, and is unfailingly optimistic. The same qualities are in *The Story of My Life and Work* (1900), an earlier version. Washington's later autobiographical works celebrate his work as executive of Tuskegee and as ambassador of interracial good will more than they reveal Washington's good nature. The following selections are from *The Story of My Life and Work*.

Birth and Early Childhood

I WILL NOT TROUBLE those who read these lines with any lengthy historical research concerning my ancestry, for I know nothing of my ancestry beyond my mother. My mother was a slave on a plantation near Hale's Ford, in Franklin County, Virginia, and she was, as I now remember it, the cook for her owners as well as for a large part of the slaves on the plantation. The first time that I got a knowledge of the fact that my mother and I were slaves, was by being awakened by my mother early one morning, while sleeping in a bed of rags, on the clay floor of our little cabin. She was kneeling over me, fervently praying as was her custom to do, that some day she and her children might be free. The name of my mother was Jane. She, to me, will always remain the noblest embodiment of womanhood with which I have come in contact. She was wholly ignorant, as far as books were concerned, and, I presume, never had a book in her hands for two minutes at a time. But the lessons in virtue and thrift which she instilled into me during the short period of my life that she lived will never leave me. Some people blame the Negro for not being more honest, as judged by the Anglo-Saxon's standard of honesty; but I can recall many times when, after all was dark and still, in the late hours of the night, when her children had been without sufficient food during the day, my mother would awaken us, and we would find that she had gotten from somewhere something in the way of eggs or chickens and cooked the food during the night for us. These eggs and chickens were gotten without my master's permission or knowledge. Perhaps, by some code of ethics, this would be classed as stealing, but deep down in my heart I can never decide that my mother, under such circumstances, was guilty of theft. Had she acted thus as a free woman she would have been a thief, but not so, in my opinion, as a slave. After our freedom no one was stricter than my mother in teaching and observing the highest rules of integrity.

Who my father was, or is, I have never been able to learn with any degree of certainty. I only know that he was a white man.

As nearly as I can get at the facts, I was born in the year 1858 or 1859. At the time I came into the world no careful registry of births of people of my complexion was kept. My birthplace was near Hale's Ford, in Franklin County, Virginia. It was about as near to Nowhere as any locality gets to be, so far as I can learn. Hale's Ford, I think, was a town with one house and a postoffice, and my birthplace was on a large plantation several miles distant from it.

I remember very distinctly the appearance of the cabin in which I was born and lived until freedom came. It was a small log cabin about 12 x 16 feet, and without windows. There was no floor except one of dirt. There was a large opening in the center of the floor, where sweet potatoes were kept for my master's family during the winter. In this cabin my mother did the cooking, the greater part of the time, for my master's family. Our bed, or "pallet," as we called it, was made every night on the dirt floor. Our bed clothing consisted of a few rags gathered here and there.

One thing I remember more vividly than any other in connection with the days when I was a slave was my dress, or, rather, my lack of dress.

The years when the war was in progress between the States were especially trying to the slaves, so far as clothing was concerned. The Southern white people found it extremely hard to get clothing for themselves during that war, and, of course, the slaves underwent no little suffering in this respect. The only garment that I remember receiving from my owners during the war was a "tow shirt." When I did not wear this shirt I was positively without any garment. In Virginia, the tow shirt was quite an institution during slavery. This shirt was made of the refuse flax that grew in that part of Virginia, and it was a veritable instrument of torture. It was stiff and coarse.

Until it had been worn for about six weeks it made one feel as if a thousand needle points were pricking his flesh. I suppose I was about six years old when I was given one of these shirts to wear. After repeated trials the torture was more than my childish flesh could endure and I gave it up in despair. To this day the sight of a new shirt revives the recollection of the tortures of my first new shirt. In the midst of my despair, in connection with this garment, my brother John, who was about two years older than I, did me a kindness which I shall never forget. He volunteered to wear my new shirt for me until it was "broken in." After he had worn it for several weeks I ventured to wear it myself, but not without pain.

Soon after my shirt experience, when the winter had grown quite cold, I received my first pair of shoes. These shoes had wooden bottoms, and the tops consisted of a coarse kind of leather. I have never felt so proud since of a pair of shoes.

As soon as I was old enough I performed what, to me, was important service, in holding the horses, and riding behind the white women of the household on their long horseback rides, which were very common in those days. At one time, while holding the horses and assisting quite a party of visiting ladies to mount their horses, I remember that, just before the visitors rode away, a tempting plate of ginger cakes was brought out and handed around to the visitors. This, I think, was the first time that I had ever seen ginger cakes, and a very deep impression was made upon my childish mind. I remember I said to myself that if I ever could get to the point where I could eat ginger cakes as I saw those ladies eating them, the height of my ambition would be reached.

When I grew to be still larger and stronger the duty of going to the mill was intrusted to me; that is, a large sack containing three or four bushels of corn was thrown across the back of a horse and I would ride away to the mill, which was often three or four miles distant, wait at the mill until the corn was turned into meal, and then bring it home. More than once, while performing this service, the corn or meal got unevenly balanced on the back of the horse and fell off into the road, carrying me with it. This left me in a very awkward and unfortunate position. I, of course, was unable, with my small strength, to lift the corn or meal upon the horse's back, and therefore would have to wait, often for hours, until someone happened to be passing along the road strong enough to replace the burden for me.

My owner's name was Jones Burroughs, and I am quite sure he was above the average in the treatment of his slaves. That is, except in a few cases, they were not cruelly whipped. Although I was born a slave, I was too young to experience much of its hardships. The thing in connection with slavery that has left the deepest impression on me was the instance of seeing a grown man, my uncle, tied to a tree early one morning, stripped naked, and someone whipping him with a cowhide. As each blow touched his back the cry, "Pray, master! Pray, master!" came from his lips, and made an impression upon my boyish heart that I shall carry with me to my grave.

When I was still quite a child, I could hear the slaves in our "quarter" whispering in subdued tones that something unusual—the war—was about to take place, and that it meant their freedom. These whispered conferences continued, especially at night, until the war actually began.

While there was not a single slave on our plantation that could read a line, in some way we were kept informed of the progress of the war almost as accurately as the most intelligent person. The "grapevine" telegraph was in constant use. When Lee surrendered all of the plantation people knew it, although all of them acted as if they were in ignorance of the fact that anything unusual had taken place.

Early one morning, just after the close of the war, word was sent around to the slave cabins that all the slaves must go to the "big house," the master's house; and in company with my mother and a large number of other slaves, including my sister Amanda and brother John, I went to the "big house," and stood by the side of my mother, and listened to the reading of some papers and a little speech made by the man who read the papers. This was the first public address I had ever heard, and I need not add that it was the most effective one to which it had ever been my privilege to listen. After the reading of the paper, and the speech, my mother leaned over and whispered, "Now, my children, we are free." This act was hailed with joy by all the slaves, but it threw a tremendous responsibility upon my mother, as well as upon the other slaves. A large portion of the former slaves hired themselves to their owners, while the others sought new employment; but, before the beginning of the new life, most of the ex-slaves left the plantation for a few days at least, so as to get the "hang" of the new life, and to be sure that they were free. My mother's husband, my stepfather, had in some way wandered into West Virginia during the war, and had secured employment in the salt furnace near Malden, in Kanawha County. Soon after freedom was declared he sought my mother and sent a wagon to bring her and her children to West Virginia. After many days of slow, tiresome traveling over the mountains, during which we suffered much, we finally reached Malden, and my mother and her husband were united after a long enforced separation. . . .

ROBERT RUSSA MOTON (1867-1940)

Born at Rice, Prince Edwards County, Virginia, Robert Russa Moton was the successor to Booker T. Washington as principal of Tuskegee Institute; as such he inherited his predecessor's position as spokesman for industrial education. He was educated at Hampton Institute, where he was commandant from 1890 until 1915, when he went to Tuskegee. In 1930 he received the Harmon Award for bettering race relations and in 1932 he received the Spingarn Medal. He was the author of *Racial Good Will* (1916), *Finding a Way Out* (1920), and *What the Negro Thinks* (1929). The following selection is from *Finding a Way Out* (1920) and is used by permission of Doubleday, Doran and Company, Inc.

War Activities

ON THE 2ND OF DECEMBER, 1918, at the request of President Wilson and Secretary of War Newton D. Baker, I went to France to look into conditions affecting Negro soldiers, many of whom were undergoing hardships of one kind and another. Secretary Baker said that he and President Wilson felt that my going to France would be encouraging to the men, and that the presence and words of a member of their own race would be particularly helpful, in view of all circumstances under which they were serving the nation, at the same time inviting me to make any suggestions that might in my judgment help the situation. In spite of pressing matters in connection with the Institute, I felt it was the school's duty to do anything possible to help our Negro soldiers, and decided to make the trip.

While in France, I visited nearly every point where Negro soldiers were stationed. At most of them I spoke to the men, and at each place I was most cordially welcomed by the officers and men. I also had the privilege of conferring with Col. E. M. House; Bishop Brent, senior chaplain of the American Expeditionary Forces; General Pershing, and many other high officials of the American and French governments, all of whom I consulted with reference to the record which had been made by Negro troops, and received only words of very highest praise and commendation on their character and conduct in all branches of the service.

During the late summer and early fall of 1918 there were a great many rumors, in and outside of official circles in this country, to the effect that, morally, the Negro soldier in France had failed and that the statement sometimes made that "the Negro is controlled by brutal instincts" was justified. The report was current in France that the "unmentionable crime" was very common; and according to the rumors, Negro officers, as well as privates, in all branches and grades of the service, were guilty of this crime.

A letter I saw that had been written by a lady overseas to another lady in the United States stated that the writer had been told by the colonel of a certain unit, whose guest she was, that he would not feel it safe for her to walk, even with him, through his camp of Negro soldiers. Another letter from a high official in a very important position with the Negro troops overseas, written unofficially to a prominent official on this side, stated that in the 92nd Division alone there had recently been at least thirty cases of the "unmentionable crime."

Another rumor, equally prevalent and damaging, was to the effect that the fighting units which were commanded by Negro officers had been a failure. In other words, the "whispering gallery," which was very active in France on most phases of life overseas, said that the 92nd Division, in which the Negroes of America took special pride, had failed utterly; that, wherever they had been engaged, the Negro officers had gone to pieces; that in some cases the men had to pull themselves together after their officers had shown "the white feather"; and other statements of similar import.

I went to France with authority to go anywhere and get any information from any source, so far as the American Expeditionary Force was concerned. It so happened that I went on the steamer assigned to the newspaper correspondents, a steamer which was one of the convoy ships for the President's party, on which Dr. W. E. B. DuBois, editor of the *Crisis,* was also a passenger. Mr. Lester A. Walton, of the *New York Age;* Mr. Nathan Hunt, of Tuskegee, together with Dr. DuBois and myself, occupied the same very comfortable stateroom. We had many frank and pleasant talks, both on the ship and in Paris, where we occupied opposite rooms in the same hotel. The subject that we discussed most often was, of course, some phase of the Negro question, always with a view to helping the situation.

I was accompanied on the trips out from Paris, as well as at many interviews in Paris, by two coloured and two white men—one white newspaper man, Mr. Clyde R. Miller, of the Cleveland *Plaindealer,* and Mr. Lester A. Walton, of the *New York Age*. I also asked to go with me, Dr. Thomas Jesse Jones, of the United States Bureau of Education and the Phelps-Stokes Foundation, and Mr. Nathan Hunt, of Tuskegee Institute.

I realized that the mission was a delicate one, and that questions which I might ask and the things which I would say might probably be misunderstood or misinterpreted. My purpose, however, was to get at the facts and to stop untruthful rumours. In order to ascertain the facts, I made extended inquiries of all those with whom I came in contact. I asked many questions with relation to the conduct and character of the coloured soldiers as compared with other soldiers.

When I reached General Headquarters of the American Expeditionary Force I found that, a few days before my arrival, a young white soldier had been sentenced to be hanged for the "unmentionable crime," but because of his previous good record in every other way the sentence was finally commuted to life imprisonment. The opinion at General Headquarters was that the crime to which I have referred was no more prevalent among coloured soldiers than among white, or any other soldiers.

From Chaumont we went immediately to Marbache, the Headquarters of the 92nd Division. I asked the general then in command of this division about the prevalence of the crime in question. He said that it was very prevalent, and that there had been a great many cases over which he was very much disturbed. This statement was corroborated by conversation with two of his white staff officers, who were present. I courteously asked if he would mind having one of his aides get the records. I said that I thought general statements were often very damaging, and that, inasmuch as the reputation of a race was at stake, I was very anxious to get the facts in order to make an accurate report, and, if possible, to stop the damaging rumors which were becoming more and more prevalent in America and were already prevalent in France, especially among Americans, including military circles, the Young Men's Christian Association, the Red Cross, and other organizations.

When the records were brought in and examined, seven cases where this crime had been charged were found in the entire division of more than twelve thousand. *Of these charged, only two had been found guilty and convicted, and one of the two convictions had been "turned down" at General Headquarters.*

In other fighting units, as well as the units of the Service of Supply at Bordeaux, Saint Nazaire, and Brest, and other places, I made the same investigations. I interviewed American and French commanding officers; I talked, as well, with scores of American and French officials of lower rank. When the records were taken, as with the 92nd Division, the number of cases charged was very few and the number of convictions fewer still. I likewise took much time with certain members of the Peace Conference, and with Americans engaged in various branches of war activity, in an effort to disprove and set at rest this awful slander upon the Negro race. I spared no pains or effort to do this, and it would appear, from subsequent investigations on this side of the water and from reports which have come to me from overseas, that the momentum of these damaging rumours perceptibly lessened.

There was apparently no doubt in anybody's mind in France, so far as I was able to find out among the French or the Americans, as to the excellent qualities of the American Negro as a soldier, when led by white officers. There was also little question about the fighting record of four Negro regiments—the 369th, 370th, 371st, and 372nd—which had been brigaded with French divisions; but when it came to the 92nd Division, there was a subtle and persistent rumor in Paris and in other places in France, apparently substantiating the rumour which was prevalent in America—only in France it was much more generally accepted as true; namely, that Negro officers "had been practically a failure," and that it was a mistake ever to have attempted to form a division with Negroes as officers.

I took a great deal of pains and care, as did also the gentlemen with me, to run down every rumour. We spent much time in and out of Paris ferreting out every statement that came from the "whispering gallery." We finally found that, so far as the 92nd Division was concerned, only a very small detachment of a single battalion of one regiment had failed.

Later, talking with General Pershing in France, regarding this story of the failure of Negro officers, he said that the probabilities were that any officers, white or black, under the same adverse circumstances that these men faced, would have failed. A few officers of the battalion were sent before a court martial for trial for having shown cowardice. Not all of them, however, were found guilty. And since then, these cases have been reviewed by the War Department, and the President, on the recommendation of the Secretary of War, has disapproved the proceedings involving the four officers of the 368th Infantry convicted by court martial abroad. After thorough investigation the War Department issued the following statement with regard to this one battalion of the 368th Regiment:

"The 368th Regiment had not had battle experience prior to its assignment to the French brigade. It was expected to operate as a liaison organization, maintaining contact with combat forces on either side, but not itself as an attacking force. In the development of the battle it became necessary to use the regiment in attack.

"The ground over which the 368th Regiment advanced was extremely difficult. It had been fought over and fortified for four years, and consisted of a dense belt of intricate barbed wire, through which in four years underbrush had grown, concealing the wire and making any advance most difficult. The section in which the regiment was engaged developed at times intense shell, machine-gun, and rifle fire and subjected those troops to a severe test.

"The regiment was not fully supplied with wire cutters, maps, and signalling devices. This was in part due to the fact that the troops were serving at the time with the French, from whom the supply was finally received, the delay being caused doubtless by the hurried movement of the regiment and the assumption on the part of the French that it would be supplied from American depots, and on the part of the Americans that it would be supplied by the French, with whom it was serving—a misunderstanding explained only by the confusion and emergencies of battle."

It was gratifying even then to find that the commanding general, who knew all phases of the affair, did not take this failure nearly so seriously as the rumour about it seemed to suggest. The facts in the case in no sense justified the common report.

In talking with the commanding general at Le Mans, I referred to the fact that something like fifteen Negro officers had been sent back as "inefficient." He said to me: "If it is any comfort to you, I will tell you this: we sent back through Blois to America, in six months, an average of one thousand white officers a month, who failed in one way or another in this awful struggle. I hope, Doctor Moton," he added, "that you won't lose your faith in my race because of this, and certainly I am not going to lose my faith in your race because of the record of a few coloured soldiers who failed."

We talked with Colonel House, Mr. Ray Stannard Baker, Captain Walter Lippman, leading Y. M. C. A. workers, and many others. All assured me that they were glad to get the facts, and that, so far as they were able, they would stop the slanderous rumours concerning our Negro soldiers. I spoke to white officers in a number of places—at one place to two hundred of them—and candidly stated the facts in the case. I raised the question, if they did not think it was a good and fair thing to stop this rumor of the "whispering gallery," which was defaming a race, which threatened to cut down the efficiency of Negro troops, and was, of course, putting America in a bad light before the world.

Many of the difficulties and troubles among the officers and men of the 92nd Division, as well as other coloured units, could have been avoided if we had had at General Headquarters in France a coloured man to render the same wise, dignified, and efficient help as Mr. Emmett J. Scott, secretary of Tuskegee Institute, so splendidly rendered in the War Department at Washington to both the race and the nation. President John Hope, of Morehouse College, Atlanta, Georgia, who under many and trying conditions had done excellent work overseas in connection with the Y. M. C. A., felt this need very much. General Pershing would gladly have had such a man if it had previously occurred to any of us to suggest it.

In almost every instance I found the commanding officers open to suggestions with a view to relieving the needless embarrassment of the coloured soldiers. I found in the Service of Supply that coloured stevedores were working twelve and sixteen hours a day, and sometimes more, which made it impossible for the Y. M. C. A. to do any effective work along educational lines with the thousands of coloured soldiers in this branch of the service. I took this matter up with the commanding general, and within three days orders had been given to reduce the time of work to eight hours. At several places the quarters of the coloured men seemed unfavorably located. In various instances changes were soon made.

I took up with care also, going to the source of the trouble, the matter of excluding coloured women from France. Here, again, I found that there seemed to be no justification for the general exclusion of women of our race from overseas service. This I took up with the proper authorities, military and otherwise, and before I left arrangements had been made to send for more of our coloured women, and men also. The best Y. M. C. A. hut I saw, from every point of view, was the one where Mrs. W. A. Hunton, Mrs. J. L. Curtis, and Miss Katherine Johnson were located. There was here a very fine spirit of coöperation between the white and coloured workers. Mr. Wallace, the manager of the district, whom I later met in Paris, was warm in his praise of Secretary Nichols, Secretary Whiting, Chaplain Oveltrea, and other coloured workers.

I took the opportunity wherever it presented itself to speak to our men about the splendid record which they were making and of the danger that would attend any failure on their part to maintain their record untarnished. I said:

"The record you have made in this war, of faithfulness, bravery, and loyalty, has deepened my faith in you as men and as soldiers, as well as in my race and country. You have been tremendously tested. You have suffered hardships and many privations. You have been called upon to make many sacrifices. Your record has sent a thrill of joy and satisfaction to the hearts of millions of black and white Americans, rich and poor, high and low. Black mothers and wives, sweethearts, fathers, and friends have rejoiced with you and with your country in your record.

"You will go back to America heroes, as you really are. You will go back as you have carried yourselves over here—in a straightforward, manly and modest way. If I were you, I would find a job as soon as possible and get to work. To those who have not already done so, I would suggest that you get hold of a piece of land and a home as soon as possible, and marry and settle down. . . . Save your money, and put it into something tangible. I hope no one will do anything in peace to spoil the magnificent record you have made in war."

In the same way I took advantage of many opportunities to speak to white soldiers, officers and men, about their duty to their coloured comrades who were sharing with them the hardships of the war. I said in my talk:

"These black soldiers, officers and men, have with you willingly and gladly placed their lives at the disposal of their country, not only 'to make the world safe for democracy,' but, of equal importance, 'to make democracy safe for mankind,' black and white. You and they go back to America as heroes, brave and modest, of course, but there is a difference; you go back without let or hindrance with every opportunity our beloved country offers open to you. You are the heirs of all the ages. God has never given any race more than he has given to you. The men of my race who return will have many unnecessary hardships and limitations along many lines. What a wonderful opportunity you have, therefore, and what a great responsibility for you, to go back to America resolved that so far as in your power lies you are going to see that these black men and the twelve millions of people whom they represent in our great country, who have stood so loyally by you and America in peace and in war, shall have a fair and absolutely equal chance with every other American citizen, along every line. This is your sacred obligation and duty. They ask only fair play and, as loyal American citizens, they should have it."

I cannot conclude without again mentioning the heroic record of all of our men in France, especially the Negro officers, who, in spite of hardships and discrimination from sources which should have accorded them much encouragement, went into battle with dash, and courage, and an absolutely unshaken and undisturbed morale. I do not believe that men of any other race, under similarly trying circumstances, could have retained more self-possession and made a more glorious record than did our Negro soldiers, officers and men. I am glad that most of those from Tuskegee Institute have returned and taken up their work as before. We cherish, however, the memory of Lieut. Henry H. Bogar, one of our teachers, who, with many other brave Americans, sleeps beneath the sacred soil of France.

Before leaving France for London, President Wilson sent me the following letter:

Paris, January 1, 1919.

"Dear Principal Moton: I wish to express my appreciation for the service you have rendered during the past few weeks in connection with our coloured soldiers here in France. I have heard, not only of the wholesome advice you have given them regarding their conduct during the time they will remain in France but also of your advice as to how they should conduct themselves when they return to our own shores. I very much hope, as you have advised, that no one of them may do anything to spoil the splendid record that they, with the rest of our American forces, have made.

"Cordially and sincerely yours,
"Woodrow Wilson."

WILLIAM PICKENS (1881-)

William Pickens was born in Anderson County, South Carolina. Educated at Talladega, Yale, and Fisk, he has taught at Talladega, Wiley, and Morgan, where he was dean of the college. He has been field secretary of the N. A. A. C. P. since 1920; he is now on the Defense Savings Staff of the United States Treasury Department. Besides *Bursting Bonds* (1923), from which the following selections are taken, he has written *Abraham Lincoln, Man and Statesman* (1909), *Frederick Douglass and the Spirit of Freedom* (1912), *Fifty Years of Emancipation* (1913), and *American Aesop; Negro and Other Humor* (1926). The following selection is used by permission of the author.

A Christian Missionary College

I REACHED TALLADEGA at night and went early the next morning to the home of the college president, to try my fate again as I had tried it three years before with the high school authorities in Little Rock. He had forgotten me, but remembered when I mentioned the "card of hope." With the coolness and slowness of one who has prepared to look fate in the face I said: "Not hearing any more from you I decided to come and see. And"—drawing something slowly from my pocket—"and I have here *three ten* dollar bills." I noticed the change in the good man's countenance between the words *three* and *ten;* too often had he faced the difficulty of finding a way for apparently worthy students who brought less than a tenth part of their year's expenses. When he learned that I had come five hundred miles on faith, the smile that lit his countenance was auspicious. My star of "hope" had not misled me. He said that he would give the thirty dollars to the treasurer, and asked if I could hitch a horse, milk a cow and work a garden. I replied that I could learn to do any kind of work.

My faith and adventure evidently made a great impression on this man. In his chapel talk that morning, without calling names or making indications, he told a story to the assembled students, how a young man had written from a distant state; how the correspondence had been lost and forgotten; how the fellow had based his hope on a rather indefinite proposition, had worked hard all summer to earn a few dollars, had come many miles. He described the coolness with which this young man had faced him and his own shifting emotions between the words "three" and "ten."

I had not seen a school test all summer, and in my entrance examinations I learned what an excellent preparation it is *not to prepare* for an examination, but to learn each daily lesson and then take a period of rest and not of cramming just before the test. And for the remainder of my school life I prepared for the examination of tomorrow by retiring at eight or nine o'clock the night before.

First the Latin teacher started in to test me in Cicero, which I read so easily that he closed it and opened Vergil's "Aeneid," asking me to scan and read. I announced that I could read the first six books, and he turned from book to book, forwards and backwards, but I always "scanned and read." I was then passed on to the teacher of mathematics. Many white people have an honest opinion that the Negro mind is characteristically unmathematical. The teacher asked

754

me to draw the figure and demonstrate the proposition that the sum of three angles of a triangle is equal to two right angles. He added that he would go about some desk work and that I might call attention when I was ready. As a good-natured resentment to this statement I called his attention at once, drawing the figure "freehand" as I did so, and announced that I was "ready." It is a simple and easy proposition, and it was so clearly demonstrated that this teacher, who was the college dean, gave me no further examinations and enrolled me in the sophomore class. So I never was a *freshman*.

I noticed that I was not put to milking cows and hitching teams, willing as I was, but was given work in the college library. In the first of January came the annual week "of prayer," and I joined the little Congregational church which is fostered in connection with the college. I was just about nineteen years old. Why had I not become a church member before this time? That is a thing worth explaining in the interest of the younger generation of Negroes. I believed in God and the church, and had always been a most faithful worshiper, but I could not dream dreams and see visions. Without dreams and visions no one was allowed to join the average Negro church of the past. The cause that produced many of the Negro songs was the fact that the candidate was required to bring and sing a "new song" to prove that he was really converted by God, for the doctrine was that "the devil can convert you, but he can't give you a new song." Rather suggestive, this idea of the unpoeticalness of the devil. It would amuse more than it would instruct for me to relate some of the ridiculous stories which I have heard accepted in church as convert's "experiences." At last I had found a church which did not require that I visit hell, like Dante, in a dream, to be chased by the hounds of the devil and make a narrow, hair-raising escape. And I have been a member of this church since my first college year.

Talladega College is a typical monument of unselfishness. There is nothing in the annals of human history that outrivals the unselfishness that founded and has maintained these institutions for half a century. When the institution was founded in 1867 practically the whole Negro population was illiterate and penniless. It is on record that many workers gave their services absolutely free. The sentiment of the South was naturally opposed to Negro education, especially at the hands of its late enemies. The early workers had to face something more than mere social ostracism: the Ku Klux Klan did not stop with that barbarity of civilization, but often adopted real barbarities, terrifying, banishing, whipping and killing. It is interesting to note what an *evolutionary* influence a school like Talladega has on the sentiment of its neighborhood; white people of the town are now among its chief defenders whenever danger is threatened, and are among its best donors when a new building is to be erected.

And oh, the developments of Father Time! The building which has been the main educational hall of the institution for forty years, was erected by slave labor in 1852-53 as a college for white boys. One of the slaves who toiled at the work has since had his many children and grandchildren educated in it.

In my first winter at Talladega I won the college oratorical contest and several other literary prizes. This suggested to the president and faculty the idea of sending me to the North in the following summer with a party of four other students and a teacher on a campaign in the financial interest of the college. The teacher, who has since become President Metcalf, presented the work, the aims and the needs of the institution, the quartet of boys sang and I delivered an address which I prepared especially for the campaign. That speech and that campaign proved to be the doorway of my future, as will appear.

It was in the summer of 1900, and it was my first time north of the Ohio and the Potomac. We went northward in the month of·June through Tennessee and Kentucky into Ohio, thence eastward, visiting Niagara and the summer haunts of the rich in the Adirondacks and concluding our campaign in the New England States in September.

It was Commencement time when we reached Oberlin, and the class of 1875 was celebrating its twenty-fifth anniversary. Professor Scarborough of Wilberforce University, the Negro scholar who is a member of this class, was present at an impromptu parlor entertainment by the five boys of our party, and he so much liked a recitation which I combined from Spartacus to the Gladiators and The Christian Gladiator that when we parted he gave me in the act of handshaking a silver half dollar. I noticed what he did not notice, that the coin bore the date of "1875," the year of his class—and I have it now, black with age and non-use in my purse.

At Akron, O., an event happened on which hangs a chain of circumstances; the people requested that my speech be printed in pamphlets so that copies could be purchased. Copies were sent to Dr. G. W. Andrews, the head of Talladega College, the author of my "card of hope." He marked a copy and sent it to Dr. A. F. Beard, the senior secretary of the American Missionary Association.

This trip impressed me with the unselfish spirit of the Christian people of the North—and also showed me that the good people of the North had a very inadequate idea of the real capacity of the American Negro. When we visited the summer camp of Mr. Harrison, ex-president of the United States, members of his party expressed frank surprise that a party of Negro college students could sing and speak and deport themselves so well—and I myself was scrutinized with a most uncomforting curiosity.

Our little campaign paid expenses and brought back a thousand dollars for the college—a small sum of money but a big experience. Moreover I had seen Yale, had actually looked upon its elms, its ivies and its outer walls. From that day the audacious idea began to take me that I must push my educational battles into its gates.

BENJAMIN G. BRAWLEY (1882-1939)

Benjamin Griffith Brawley (see also p. 793) was born in Columbia, South Carolina, and was educated at Morehouse, Chicago, and Harvard. He taught English at Morehouse, Shaw, and Howard, and was a minister in the Baptist church. He produced a number of essays, short stories, poems, and literary and social histories, among them: *A Short History of the American Negro* (1913), *The Negro in Literature and Art* (1918), *Your Negro Neighbor* (1918), *A Social History of the American Negro* (1921), *A Short History of the English Drama* (1921), *A New Survey of English Literature* (1925), *Doctor Dillard and the Jeanes Fund* (1930), *Early Negro American Writers* (1935), *The Negro Genius* (1937), and *Negro Builders and Heroes* (1937). The following autobiographical selection appeared in 1925 in *The Reviewer,* a Southern magazine edited by Paul Green. "From the Lower Rungs of the Ladder" is reprinted by permission of *The Daily Tar Heel.*

From The Lower Rungs of the Ladder

AT LAST I WAS GRADUATED at the institution that is now Morehouse College. There followed an uncertain summer. I was hoping to go to a Northern university to continue my studies; but the weeks passed, the way did not seem to open, and at the first of September I found myself in Florida, without any immediate prospect. An examination for teachers being announced, I decided to enter, and the superintendent for the county offered me such schools as he had. The better-paying ones had all been taken, and the best that he could suggest was that at Georgetown, about forty miles below Palatka on the St. John's. It paid only thirty dollars a month, running for five months;

but I decided to take it, as the situation was becoming desperate. Within five minutes after I left the office I had in hand a letter from Mr. Bert Fish, of Deland, offering me a place in a school that ran for a longer term and paid a much better salary; but I decided not to begin my career as a teacher by breaking a contract.

It was on Saturday, September 14, 1901, the day on which President McKinley died, that I left for my school in the country. The river was as beautiful as ever, and on the shore the Spanish moss hung dreamily from the treetops. When I reached my destination late at night, however, I found not even a village, and the forest loomed in the background menacingly. Then it was that a young man with whom I had talked on the boat, the older brother of some of the pupils in the school, went a mile out of his way to take me to the home of the supervisor. Over the years I remember what he did as but one of many acts of kindness with which my path has been strewn.

While I still waited in the front room the lady of the house called out to me from the next, "Is you Baptis' or Methodis'?" "I'm a Baptist," I replied; "are you?" "No," she said, "I'm Methodis' root an' branch." I found out a little later that she could not give me any special reason why she was Methodist, but I also learned that she was not the only person in the community with strong denominational feeling.

On the first night I became aware of some strange sounds that were later to be very familiar. It seemed that not far away there was something panting, panting, panting with low steady grunts. The next morning I was informed that often an alligator in a creek near the house would rest on the bank and make the noise I heard. On the whole I had no reason to complain of my boarding place. The house was small but very clean, and I found only two elderly people in the home, as their only child, a grown son, was living elsewhere. Everything seemed adjusted to the scale of my finances. The board was about eight dollars a month. The good people said that they would not take more, as they could give only very simple fare. It was indeed simple, but well-cooked and varied, and the gopher as prepared by Mrs. Johnson on a cool evening was always appetizing.

The schoolhouse, however, was a very different thing from my home. It contained only one room and it was so old and feeble that the roof swayed back and forth whenever the wind rose. Lizards with red and blue streaks down the back ran across the floor every day. Sometimes Mr. Johnson would come and try to place special props on the side of the structure, but nothing seemed to do any good. The Methodists had just recently erected a neat little church, and one of the words of warning given me was that under no circumstances was I to hold school in it. The Baptist edifice was much nearer, however; the few members gave me full freedom of the place; and to it we repaired whenever the swaying of the school-house became suggestive of danger.

I began with fourteen pupils, but when the Manuels came the enrollment rose to twenty. The children ranged from the first grade to the eighth, though there were none in either the fourth or the seventh grade. There were only a few weeks of cold weather; but one day about the middle of December I observed that little Andy Gordon was shivering and that his feet were still bare. Nothing made me more happy than that he was able to get a pair of shoes in time for the Christmas exercises.

Thus the weeks passed, and before long we had come to the end of February and the closing of the term. I had had a season of most valuable experience, though never again was I to teach ten miles from a railroad. From that time forward, with school work and study and writing, the years were very crowded.

By early spring the skies had brightened, and the first week in May found me in Boston with the intention of studying at the School of Expression. I took lessons for two months, but I soon realized that I was learning little more than Miss Bemus had taught me in rehearsals. Accordingly when a request came for me to return to Atlanta as a teacher I decided that it would be more to my advantage to go over to the Summer School at Harvard and take some work more definitely in line with my plans.

It was early this summer also that I first sought and found employment in Boston as a printer. For two days I looked for a job. At the close of the second day of effort the foreman at the Library Bureau on Atlantic Avenue told me that he had nothing in the composing line but that if I could run a small press he could use me. At the beginning of still another summer I again looked for work. This time I walked for three days and visited more than forty places. I knew it was a season of general depression, and I was not sure just which one of three things was standing in my way, whether it was simply that there was little work to be done, or that I was not a union man, or that I was a Negro. Seeming to make no headway, I asked the manager of the Farrington Press, whom I happened to find alone, if he thought it likely that I should get anything to do in Boston. He told me that the beginning of the summer was always a dull season, but that there was one man who happened to have a rush of work, Mr. Gould at the Bartlett Press on Beach Street, and that if I went there I might be taken on. I did as he suggested and was told to report at eight o'clock the next morning.

I shall not soon forget my experience in a typical industrial plant in the North. As never before I saw life from the standpoint of the man with whom every dollar counts. There were about thirty persons in the composing room and just as many in the pressroom and bindery on the floor below. Sometimes the inks used in fancy printing made it necessary for the men in the pressroom to work in a torrid temperature; then again it was important that the room should be almost cold. In the composing room the cases of type stretched away in row after row, and it would all have been very bewildering if the firm had not had the good custom of placing a new man with one of the older workers for a week. Everybody seemed to feel for everybody else; at the same time the spirit of the place required that no one do anything to make anyone else lose time. One old woman could do only very simple tasks and seemed to be in the way; but Mr. Gould told me that he did not want to discharge her, for even if she could make only five or six dollars a week, so much would help to keep her going. One of the younger women, I understood, was the mainstay of a family in which the father had died and in which there were several small children. At the close of the summer I was told that I might come back the next year if I wished; and while I did not return, never in recent years, in catching an early morning train in Boston, have I been able to pass the *Globe* office and see men scanning the Want Ads without just a little clutch at the heart. I too have been there in the early dawn, and I know.

In my first years as a teacher in Atlanta I learned the rudiments of my profession, and it was there that I tried out many things for myself and profited by my mistakes. I can not now wish that any of those days were back. The work was very hard and the salary not much more than enough to pay the board bill. We taught six classes a day, and there was no end of duties outside the classroom. In the first year I taught English, Latin, Algebra, and Geometry. Somewhat later I was relieved of the Mathematics, but I had to take the Greek. After five years, however, I passed over from the Academy to the College, and more and more, as the institution grew, I was able to restrict myself to my own field of English.

I soon perceived that the nature of my task made it necessary for me to be independent in my methods. The books we used were all written for young people who were moving along normally but not for young men who were fairly mature in some ways but whose early training had been defective. In the first class I taught, a group that numbered fifteen, every man except one was older than I. Almost all were unnaturally serious-minded. They were self-supporting, and even if they could not spell and punctuate, they demanded of education some very real values. One day a stolid young man who had been looking out of the window while we were reading the *Idylls,* turned suddenly upon me. "This is all very good," he said, "but what has it to do with that man who was lynched at Newnan last week?" Then, and on many other occasions, I had to show that literature is not something extraneous but a part of life, and that just as Arthur's knights went forth to make a better world, so did we have our tasks to do. This high purpose that governs all our teaching came to me with renewed force a few years ago when I was called upon to conduct the War Aims Course for the Students' Army Training Corps, and when each morning there sat before me a crowd of young men in uniform who expected at any moment to be summoned to France.

The matter of the race problem, however, was ever present. In 1906, at the close of a hectic summer, came the Atlanta Massacre, in which nearly a score of Negroes lost their lives. Two of our students who happened to be down town came very near to being killed. This was only the worst of many events, for in Georgia life was always at fever heat. Perhaps one of the ways in which I was most handicapped by the artificial restrictions was in the matter of the use of the Public Library. We had our little store of books at the College, and on a neighboring hill was Atlanta University; but again I knew that I could have been helped if I had had access to the central library. I never entered its portal, however, and I either bought my own books or waited until I could get away again to Boston or Chicago.

I soon saw that for a Negro to win recognition in any field he would need to hold before him an unusual standard of excellence. Where discount had to be made for prejudice, he had often to do a task even better than anybody else. I regretted accordingly to see that many teachers put forth little real effort for self-improvement, that they had no reserve power, and that in writing they were often guilty of the most flagrant errors. I resolved forthwith to learn with the utmost detail any subject that I approached. Somehow I had the feeling that if a man made himself the most efficient electrician or dentist in a community, he would not have to wait long before people turned to him for help.

Because I had this feeling I wanted to continue my studies just as far as possible, and I did so at the University of Chicago and at Harvard. It was both expensive and physically taxing to study for three months summer after summer, and naturally I was happy when I could arrange to take a whole year off. I tried always to place myself with only teachers of unquestioned efficiency. I probably owe most to William Allan Neilson, now president of Smith, who gave to me a sense of the larger meaning of scholarship. I first worked with Dr. Neilson in a summer term while he was still an instructor at Harvard. He was considerate of my shortcomings but severe in his standards, and I resolved that as soon as I could spend a whole year in Cambridge he would have to be one of my chief teachers. Professor Bliss Perry, with the keen sense of a famous editor, at once saw clearly both my strong and weak points, and he warned me accordingly. I have always honored him for the deep interest he has ever taken in my people. I also came in contact with the deep scholarship of Professor Kittredge; and about Professor Kittredge especially I have regretted that many who know him as a leader in learning do not also seem to know how broadly humane his real interests are. My experience with the late Barrett Wendell was of course different from that with any-one else. I too can join in the paean of praise that has recently been accorded this eminent critic of life. He was still in his prime when I knew him. He said very frankly that he was no scholar, and often an individual lecture was demoralizing; but I found at the end of the year that he had stimulated me quite as much as anybody else. I made my highest grades with him, and I still cherish some papers on which he wrote his characteristic comment. They are among my most prized possessions.

At Chicago I had numerous instructors, but the most important to me were Professor Manly in English and Professor Dodd in History, both of whom happened to be Southern men. I have often been asked about the attitude of the Southern teacher at a Northern university toward the Negro student; and I can only say that, while I do not doubt that there has sometimes been a display of feeling, I have never had one such instructor who did not endeavor to be fair. With Professor Manly the only ideal in the classroom is Truth, and any earnest student will find in him a most helpful mentor. Professor Dodd has been especially helpful to me in my more independent work. He made me feel from the first that I might consult him about any point on which I was in doubt, and I have availed myself fully of his broad acquaintance with the newer phases of our country's life.

Chicago, however, for most of the time that I was there, was a battleground. Questions involving the race problem were constantly coming up, and even when I was not in residence some summers different persons would write and say that I ought to have been there. Sometimes it was a matter of living in the dormitories, or it was an attempt at segregation, or something affecting the Commons. We hardly felt that President Judson was our friend, and if any matter was referred to him as final arbiter, we generally knew that we had lost. Accordingly we were always very happy when something in Europe or Asia demanded his presence and when Professor Burton was left in charge. I lived in Snell Hall for some time, but later, after I had arranged for one of my students to live there, he was put out, the explanation from the office being that the composition of the halls was democratic (!) and that no man could stay if the other residents voted against him. At another time one of the instructors in Public Speaking gave a series of readings from Southern authors that the Negro students considered an unnecessary affront; but protest was of little avail. On still another occasion, however, before the cafeteria system was installed, a young waiter in the Commons with something of an air refused to take my order for lunch. I took up the matter in the office and was referred to the Acting President. All that Dr. Burton told me was that while he could not account for some individuals, it was not the policy of the University to encourage discrimination; but I later learned that as soon as he received my letter he walked across the quadrangle to the Commons to tell the steward one or two things that he needed to know.

It was just a few months ago that Ernest DeWitt Burton died. All of us who were made happy by his becoming president regretted that so soon he was forced to lay down the burden. But this one thing we know, and it is deeply engraved on our hearts: Here at least was one man who feared only God and who loved his neighbor as himself.

W. E. B. DuBOIS (1868-   )

In the earlier years of the twentieth century W. E. B. DuBois (see also p. 974) and Booker T. Washington (see pp. 673, 742) were the leaders of the two chief schools of thought on the solution of the Negro's problem. Here DuBois discusses the controversy between the two leaders, one the editor of *The Crisis,* publication of the N. A. A. C. P. (see p. 585), and the other the principal of Tuskegee Institute, Alabama's center for the industrial education of Negro youth. This selection, from *Dusk at Dawn,* is here reprinted by permission of the author and of Harcourt, Brace and Company.

[The DuBois-Washington Controversy]

SINCE THE CONTROVERSY between myself and Mr. Washington has become historic, it deserves more careful statement than it has had hitherto, both as to the matters and the motives involved. There was first of all the ideological controversy. I believed in the higher education of a Talented Tenth who through their knowledge of modern culture could guide the American Negro into a higher civilization. I knew that without this the Negro would have to accept white leadership, and that such leadership could not always be trusted to guide this group into self-realization and to its highest cultural possibilities. Mr. Washington, on the other hand, believed that the Negro as an efficient worker could gain wealth and that eventually through his ownership of capital he would be able to achieve a recognized place in American culture and could then educate his children as he might wish and develop his possibilities. For this reason he proposed to put the emphasis at present upon training in the skilled trades and encouragement in industry and common labor.

These two theories of Negro progress were not absolutely contradictory. I recognized the importance of the Negro gaining a foothold in trades and his encouragement in industry and common labor. Mr. Washington was not absolutely opposed to college training, and sent his own children to college. But he did minimize its importance, and discouraged the philanthropic support of higher education; while I openly and repeatedly criticized what seemed to me the poor work and small accomplishment of the Negro industrial school. Moreover, it was characteristic of the Washington statesmanship that whatever he or anybody believed or wanted must be subordinated to dominant public opinion and that opinion deferred to and cajoled until it allowed a deviation toward better ways. This is no new thing in the world, but it is always dangerous.

But beyond this difference of ideal lay another and more bitter and insistent controversy. This started with the rise at Tuskegee Institute, and centering around Booker T. Washington, of what I may call the Tuskegee Machine. Of its existence and work, little has ever been said and almost nothing written. The years from 1899 to 1905 marked the culmination of the career of Booker T. Washington. In 1899 Mr. Washington, Paul Laurence Dunbar, and myself spoke on the same platform at the Hollis Street Theatre, Boston, before a distinguished audience. Mr. Washington was not at his best and friends immediately raised a fund which sent him to Europe for a three months' rest. He was received with extraordinary honors; he had tea with the aged Queen Victoria, but two years before her death; he was entertained by two dukes and other members of the aristocracy; he met James Bryce and Henry M. Stanley; he was received at the Peace Conference at The Hague and was greeted by many distinguished Americans, like ex-President Harrison, Archbishop Ireland and two justices of the Supreme Court. Only a few years before he had received an honorary degree from Harvard; in 1901, he received a LL.D. from Dartmouth and that same year he dined with President Roosevelt to the consternation of the white South.

Returning to America he became during the administrations of Theodore Roosevelt and William Taft, from 1901 to 1912, the political referee in all Federal appointments or action taken with reference to the Negro and in many regarding the white South. In 1903 Andrew Carnegie made the future of Tuskegee certain by a gift of $600,000. There was no question of Booker T. Washington's undisputed leadership of the ten million Negroes in America, a leadership recognized gladly by the whites and conceded by most of the Negroes.

But there were discrepancies and paradoxes in this leadership. It did not seem fair, for instance, that on the one hand Mr. Washington should decry political activities among Negroes, and on the other hand dictate Negro political objectives from Tuskegee. At a time when Negro civil rights called for organized and aggressive defense, he broke down that defense by advising acquiescence or at least no open agitation. During the period when laws disfranchising the Negro were being passed in all the Southern states, between 1890 and 1909, and when these were being supplemented by "Jim Crow" travel laws and other enactments making color caste legal, his public speeches, while they did not entirely ignore this development, tended continually to excuse it, to emphasize the shortcomings of the Negro, and were interpreted widely as putting the chief onus for his condition upon the Negro himself.

All this naturally aroused increasing opposition among Negroes and especially among the younger classes of educated Negroes, who were beginning to emerge here and there, especially from Northern institutions. This opposition began to become vocal in 1901 when two men, Monroe Trotter, Harvard 1895, and George Forbes, Amherst 1895, began the publication of the Boston *Guardian*. The *Guardian* was bitter, satirical, and personal; but it was well-edited, it was earnest, and it published facts. It attracted wide attention among colored people; it circulated among them all over the country; it was quoted and discussed. I did not wholly agree with the *Guardian*, and indeed only a few Negroes did, but nearly all read it and were influenced by it.

This beginning of organized opposition, together with other events, led to the growth at Tuskegee of what I have called the Tuskegee Machine. It arose first quite naturally. Not only did presidents of the United States consult Booker Washington, but governors and congressmen; philanthropists conferred with him, scholars wrote to him. Tuskegee became a vast information bureau and center of advice. It was not merely passive in these matters but, guided by a young unobtrusive minor official who was also intelligent, suave and far-seeing, active efforts were made to concentrate influence at Tuskegee. After a time almost no Negro institution could collect funds without the recommendation or acquiescence of Mr. Washington. Few political appointments were made anywhere in the United States without his consent. Even the careers of rising young colored men were very often determined by his advice and certainly his opposition was fatal. How much Mr. Washington knew of this work of the Tuskegee Machine and was directly responsible, one cannot say, but of its general activity and scope he must have been aware.

Moreover, it must not be forgotten that this Tuskegee Machine was not solely the idea and activity of black folk at Tuskegee. It was largely encouraged and given financial aid through certain white groups and individuals in the North. This Northern group had clear objectives. They were capitalists and employers and yet in most cases sons, relatives, or friends of the abolitionists who had sent teachers into the new Negro South after the war. These younger men believed that the Negro problem could not remain a matter of philanthropy. It must be a matter of business. These Negroes were not to be encouraged as voters in the new democracy, nor were they to be left at the mercy of the reactionary South. They were good laborers and they might be better. They could become a strong labor force and properly guided they would restrain the unbridled demands of white labor, born of the Northern labor unions and now spreading to the South.

One danger must be avoided and that was to allow the silly idealism of Negroes, half-trained in Southern missionary "colleges," to mislead the mass of laborers and keep them stirred-up by ambitions incapable of realization. To this school of thought, the philosophy of Booker Washington came as a godsend and it proposed by building up his prestige and power to control the Negro group. The control was to be drastic. The Negro intelligentsia was to be suppressed and hammered into conformity. The process involved some cruelty and disappointment, but that was inevitable. This was the real force back of the Tuskegee Machine. It had money and it had opportunity, and it found in Tuskegee tools to do its bidding.

There were some rather pitiful results in thwarted ambition and curtailed opportunity. I remember one case which always stands in my memory as typical. There was a young colored man, one of the most beautiful human beings I have ever seen, with smooth brown skin, velvet eyes of intelligence, and raven hair. He was educated and well-to-do. He proposed to use his father's Alabama farm and fortune to build a Negro town and independent economic unit in the South. He furnished a part of the capital but soon needed more and he came North to get it. He struggled for more than a decade; philanthropists and capitalists were fascinated by his personality and story; and when, according to current custom, they appealed to Tuskegee for confirmation, there was silence. Mr. Washington would not say a word in favor of the project. He simply kept still. Will Benson struggled on with ups and downs, but always balked by a whispering galley of suspicion, because his plan was never endorsed by Tuskegee. In the midst of what seemed to us who looked on the beginnings of certain success, Benson died of overwork, worry, and a broken heart.

From facts like this, one may gauge the bitterness of the fight of young Negroes against Mr. Washington and Tuskegee. Contrary to most opinion, the controversy as it developed was not entirely against Mr. Washington's ideas, but became the insistence upon the right of other Negroes to have and express their ideas. Things came to such a pass that when any Negro complained or advocated a course of action, he was silenced with the remark that Mr. Washington did not agree with this. Naturally the bumptious, irritated, young black intelligentsia of the day declared, "I don't care a damn what Booker Washington thinks! This is what I think, and *I have a right to think*."

It was this point, and not merely disagreement with Mr. Washington's plans, that brought eventually violent outbreak. It was more than opposition to a program of education. It was opposition to a system and that system was part of the economic development of the United States at the time. The fight cut deep: it went into social relations; it divided friends; it made bitter enemies. I can remember that years later, when I went to live in New York and was once invited to a social gathering among Brooklyn colored people, one of the most prominent Negroes of the city refused to be present because of my former attitude toward Mr. Washington.

When the *Guardian* began to increase in influence, determined effort was made to build up a Negro press for Tuskegee. Already

Tuskegee filled the horizon so far as national magazines and the great newspapers were concerned. In 1901 the *Outlook,* then the leading weekly, chose two distinguished Americans for autobiographies. Mr. Washington's "Up from Slavery" was so popular that it was soon published and circulated all over the earth. Thereafter, every magazine editor sought articles with his signature and publishing houses continued to ask for books. A number of talented "ghost writers," black and white, took service under Tuskegee, and books and articles poured out of the institution. An annual letter "To My People" went out from Tuskegee to the press. Tuskegee became the capital of the Negro nation. Negro newspapers were influenced and finally the oldest and largest was bought by white friends of Tuskegee. Most of the other papers found it to their advantage certainly not to oppose Mr. Washington, even if they did not wholly agree with him. Negroes who sought high positions groveled for his favor.

I was greatly disturbed at this time, not because I was in absolute opposition to the things that Mr. Washington was advocating, but because I was strongly in favor of more open agitation against wrongs and above all I resented the practical buying up of the Negro press and choking off of even mild and reasonable opposition to Mr. Washington in both the Negro press and the white.

Then, too, during these years there came a series of influences that were brought to bear upon me personally, which increased my discomfort and resentment. I had tried to keep in touch with Hampton and Tuskegee, for I regarded them as great institutions. I attended the conferences which for a long time were held at Hampton, and at one of them I was approached by a committee. It consisted of Walter Hines Page, editor of the *Atlantic Monthly;* William McVickar, Episcopal bishop of Rhode Island; and Dr. Frissel, principal of Hampton. They asked me about the possibilities of my editing a periodical to be published at Hampton. I told them of my dreams and plans, and afterwards wrote them in detail. But one query came by mail: that was concerning the editorial direction. I replied firmly that editorial decisions were to be in my hands, if I edited the magazine. This was undiplomatic and too sweeping; and yet, it brought to head the one real matter in controversy: would such a magazine be dominated by and subservient to the Tuskegee philosophy, or would it have freedom of thought and discussion? Perhaps if I had been more experienced, the question could have been discussed and some reasonable outcome obtained; but I doubt it. I think any such magazine launched at the time would have been seriously curtailed in its freedom of speech. At any rate, the project was dropped.

Beginning in 1902 considerable pressure was put upon me to give up my work at Atlanta University and go to Tuskegee. There again I was not at first adverse in principle to Tuskegee, except that I wanted to continue what I had begun and if my work was worth support, it was worth support at Atlanta University. Moreover, I was unable to be assured that my studies would be continued at Tuskegee, and that I would not sink to the level of a "ghost writer." I remember a letter came from Wallace Buttrick late in 1902, asking that I attend a private conference in New York with Felix Adler, William H. Baldwin, Jr., George Foster Peabody, and Robert Ogden. The object of the conference was ostensibly the condition of the Negro in New York City. I went to the conference and I did not like it. Most of the more distinguished persons named were not present. The conference itself amounted to little, but I was whisked over to William H. Baldwin's beautiful Long Island home and there what seemed to me to be the real object of my coming was disclosed. Mr. Baldwin was at that time president of the Long Island Railroad and slated to be president of the Pennsylvania. He was the rising industrial leader of America; also he was a prime mover of the Tuskegee board of trustees. Both he and his wife insisted that my place was at Tuskegee; that Tuskegee was not yet a good school, and needed the kind of development that I had been trained to promote.

This was followed by two interviews with Mr. Washington himself. I was elated at the opportunity and we met twice in New York City. The results to me were disappointing. Booker T. Washington was not an easy person to know. He was wary and silent. He never expressed himself frankly or clearly until he knew exactly to whom he was talking and just what their wishes and desires were. He did not know me, and I think he was suspicious. On the other hand, I was quick, fast-speaking and voluble. I found at the end of the first interview that I had done practically all the talking and that no clear and definite offer or explanation of my proposed work at Tuskegee had been made. In fact, Mr. Washington had said about as near nothing as was possible.

The next interview did not go so well because I myself said little. Finally, we resorted to correspondence. Even then I could get no clear understanding of just what I was going to do at Tuskegee if I went. I was given to understand that the salary and accommodations would be satisfactory. In fact, I was invited to name my price. Later in the year I went to Bar Harbor for a series of speeches in behalf of Atlanta University, and while there met Jacob Schiff, the Schieffelins and Merriam of Webster's dictionary. I had dinner with the Schieffelins and again was urged to go to Tuskegee.

Early the next year I received an invitation to join Mr. Washington and certain prominent white and colored friends in a conference to be held in New York. The conference was designed to talk over a common program for the American Negro and evidently it was hoped that the growing division of opinion and opposition to Mr. Washington within the ranks of Negroes would thus be overcome. I was enthusiastic over the idea. It seemed to me just what was needed to clear the air.

There was difficulty, however, in deciding what persons ought to be invited to the conference, how far it should include Mr. Washington's extreme opponents, or how far it should be composed principally of his friends. There ensued a long delay and during this time it seemed to me that I ought to make my own position clearer than I had hitherto. I was increasingly uncomfortable under the statements of Mr. Washington's position: his depreciation of the value of the vote; his evident dislike of Negro colleges; and his general attitude which seemed to place the onus of blame for the status of Negroes upon the Negroes themselves rather than upon the whites. And above all, I resented the Tuskegee Machine.

I had been asked sometime before by A. M. McClurg and Company of Chicago if I did not have some material for a book; I planned a social study which should be perhaps a summing up of the work of the Atlanta Conferences, or at any rate, a scientific investigation. They asked, however, if I did not have some essays that they might put together and issue immediately, mentioning my articles in the *Atlantic Monthly* and other places. I demurred because books of essays almost always fall so flat. Nevertheless, I got together a number of my fugitive pieces. I then added a chapter, "Of Mr. Booker T. Washington and Others," in which I sought to make a frank evaluation of Booker T. Washington. I left out the more controversial matter: the bitter resentment which young Negroes felt at the continued and increasing activity of the Tuskegee Machine. I concentrated my thought and argument on Mr. Washington's general philosophy. As I read that statement now, a generation later, I am satisfied with it. I see no word that I would change. The "Souls of Black Folk" was published in 1903 and is still selling today.

My book settled pretty definitely any further question of my going to Tuskegee as an employee. But it also drew pretty hard and fast lines about my future career. Meantime, the matter of the conference in New York dragged on until finally in October, 1903, a circular letter was sent out setting January, 1904, as the date of meeting. The conference took place accordingly in Carnegie Hall, New York. About fifty persons were present, most of them colored and including many well-known persons. There was considerable plain speaking but the whole purpose of the conference seemed revealed by the invited guests and the tone of their message. Several white persons of high distinction came to speak to us, including Andrew Carnegie and Lyman Abbott. Their words were lyric, almost fulsome in praise of Mr. Washington and his work, and in support of his ideas. Even if all they said had been true, it was a wrong note to strike in a conference of conciliation. The conferences ended with two speeches by Mr. Washington and myself, and the appointment of a Committee of Twelve in which we were also included.

The Committee of Twelve which was thus instituted was unable to do any effective work as a steering committee for the Negro race in America. First of all, it was financed, through Mr. Washington, probably by Mr. Carnegie. This put effective control of the committee in Mr. Washington's hands. It was organized during my absence and laid down a plan of work which seemed to me of some value but of no lasting importance and having little to do with the larger questions and issues. I, therefore, soon resigned so as not to be responsible for work and pronouncements over which I would have little influence. My friends and others accused me of refusing to play the game after I had assented to a program of co-operation. I still think, however, that my action was wise.

Meantime, the task of raising money for Atlanta University and my work became increasingly difficult. In the fall of 1904 the printing of our conference report was postponed by the trustees until special funds could be secured. I did not at the time see the handwriting on the wall. I did not realize how strong the forces were back of Tuskegee and how they might interfere with my scientific study of the Negro. My continuing thought was that we must have a vehicle for both opinion and fact which would help me carry on my scientific work and at the same time be a forum less radical than the *Guardian,* and yet more rational than the rank and file of Negro papers now so largely arrayed with Tuskegee. With this in mind, as early as 1904, I helped one of the Atlanta University graduates, who was a good printer, to set up a job office in Memphis.

In 1905 I wrote to Jacob Schiff, reminding him of having met him in Bar Harbor in 1903: "I want to lay before you a plan which I have and ask you if it is of sufficient interest to you for you to be willing to hear more of it and possibly to assist in its realization.

The Negro race in America is today in a critical condition. Only united concerted effort will save us from being crushed. This union must come as a matter of education and long continued effort. To this end there is needed a high class of journal to circulate among the intelligent Negroes, tell them of the deeds of themselves and their neighbors, interpret the news of the world to them, and inspire them toward definite ideals. Now we have many small weekly papers and one or two monthlies, and none of them fill the great need I have outlined. I want to establish, therefore, for the nine million American Negroes and eventually for the whole Negro world, a monthly journal. To this end I have already in Memphis a printing establishment which has been running successfully at job work a year under a competent printer—self-sacrificing educated young man. Together we shall have about $2,000 invested in this plant by April 15."

Mr. Schiff wrote back courteously, saying: "Your plans to establish a high class journal to circulate among the intelligent Negroes is in itself interesting, and on its face has my sympathy. But before I could decide whether I can become of advantage in carrying your plans into effect, I would wish to advise with men whose opinion in such a matter I consider of much value." Nothing ever came of this, because, as I might have known, most of Mr. Schiff's friends were strong and sincere advocates of Tuskegee.

It was with difficulty that I came fully to realize the situation that was thus developing: first of all, I could not persuade myself that my program of solving the Negro problem by scientific investigation was wrong, or that it could possibly fail of eventual support when once it was undertaken; that it was understood in widening circles of readers and thinkers, I was convinced, because of the reception accorded the Atlanta University Studies. When, however, in spite of that, the revenue of the University continued to fall off, and no special support came for my particular part of its work, I tried several times by personal effort to see if funds could not be raised.

In 1906 I made two appeals: first and boldly, I outlined the work of the Atlanta Conference to Andrew Carnegie, reminding him that I had been presented to him and Carl Schurz some years before. I hoped that despite his deep friendship for Mr. Washington and the Tuskegee idea, he would see the use and value of my efforts at Atlanta. The response was indirect. At the time a white Mississippi planter, Alfred W. Stone, was popular in the North. He had grave doubts about the future of the Negro race, widely criticized black labor, and once tried to substitute Italians on his own plantations, until they became too handy with the knife. To his direction, Mr. Carnegie and others entrusted a fund for certain studies among Negroes. Why they selected him and neglected an established center like Atlanta University, I cannot imagine; but at any rate, Stone turned to me and offered to give the University a thousand dollars to help finance a special study of the history of economic co-operation among Negroes. I had planned that year, 1907, to study the Negro in politics, but here was needed support and I turned aside and made the study asked for.

W. S. BRAITHWAITE (1878-   )

William Stanley Braithwaite (see p. 318) published his autobiography, *House Under Arcturus,* in *Phylon* in 1941; the selection here printed is used by permission of the author and of the magazine.

[Search for Employment]

MOTHER TOOK THE CHILDREN and departed early in September for Boston and home, leaving me behind at my job with Pusey. I felt a sense of abandonment at this separation, which was decided upon as an economic necessity. My earnings for the time of my stay were needed, she said, to support the readjustment compelled by the change back to the city and the demands preparatory to the forthcoming winter. I was to stay in Newport until late in October. But unhappy among strangers, and separated from the other children, the autumnal mood and temper affected me deeply with nostalgia for home, and without warning I suddenly left Newport. Mother was angrily displeased when I arrived at Pleasant Street, and to appease her displeasure, I went immediately in search for work.

I obtained a position with Ginn and Company, the school and text-book publishers, at their press which was then located at the corner of Pearl and Purchase streets. I was engaged by a Mr. Wienshank, superintendent of the composition room, and it was my duty to make four trips a day, two in the morning and two in the afternoon, between the press and publishing offices on Tremont Place, taking proofs and other matter from the press and returning with authors' corrected proofs, correspondence, and other items for the various departments at the press which I distributed.

Between these regular errands to the editorial offices, I had nothing to do. A chair and table were mine just outside Mr. Wienshank's office where four or five women were busily engaged reading proofs. Seated in the chair I idled for the first two weeks, watching the compositors as with nimble fingers they picked the type letters from the case following the copy before them, and setting up for printing the manuscripts of many books. There were thirty or forty of the compositors, mostly Germans, handsetting the type for the text-books used by practically all the leading colleges and most of the public schools in America, for at that time Ginn and Company possessed almost a monopoly of the college and school book business.

Observing how quietly I sat at my table unoccupied, Mr. Weinshank asked me one day if I did not like to read. He thought it a good way to pass the time between my errands and taking me into his office showed me the shelves of books with the privilege of reading any that might interest me. He did not attempt to suggest any selections nor to guide my reading. I remember the first book I read was Church's *Greek Gods and Heroes*. I must have read some ten or twelve books when Mr. Wienshank came to me again with a proposal which had a profound effect upon my future. "Willie," he asked, "would you like to learn the trade of a compositor?" Before, in my surprise and pleasure, I could reply, he continued, "I've noticed that while you are out here between your errands to the office, you are studious, and do not annoy the compositors as the other boys I've had working here used to do."

I told him "Yes, I would like to learn the trade of a compositor." He then told me to get my mother's consent to become an apprentice. She gave it, and I began laying the foundation for both my education and the vocation I was to follow.

I was first set the task of learning the "case" by distributing the type from the page-forms that had returned from the foundry after the "plates" had been made. The case, now that the linotype and monotype machines in modern printing have rendered them useless—was a square, shallow box about three feet long and two feet wide, with spaces of unequal sizes, holding the alphabetical letters in type cast in lead. The alphabetical boxes did not run successively, but like the keys on a typewriter, were arranged so that the letters most frequntly used in words were nearer the hand of the compositor, as he stood at the center of the case, for rapid pick-up.

When I had mastered the case Mr. Wienshank gave me my first text to set up, and I have never lost the savor of this triumph, for the mechanical skill which won it was glorified by the acquaintance I made with the story of England's greatest naval hero. I was given a reprint of Robert Southey's *Life of Lord Nelson,* to set for a new edition of that famous work.

It was in early December that I began setting type, and in January the press moved into its new home the firm had built in Cambridge, on First Street, which was then but a river road along the banks of the Charles River basin between the old Longfellow and East Cambridge bridges. The Athenaeum Press was the name of the manufacturing branch of Ginn and Company, and it was the first of the many large structures in the industrial development of those marshy regions, which Mr. Howells has so picturesquely described in a familiar essay, along the banks of the Charles River in lower Cambridge.

When I began setting type I was given the additional duty of taking the galley proofs of the type set by all the compositors. My interest in books was beginning to develop into a passion, and to possess reading matter which I could not afford to buy, I used surreptitiously to make an extra impression of every galley of straight text that I proved, taking them home when I left work. I accumulated a good many works in this way, those galleys forming the first library I owned. The most precious of that early reading which I recall, was La Fayette's *La Princesse de Clèves,* the galley proofs of which I read with fascinating interest.

Mr. Wienshank made use of me in a variety of odd tasks until the composition room was equipped and in order; new mechanical devices were installed, the first linotype machine, a new-fangled proof operator, new cases, etc., and when all was in readiness, I was given a case by a window (we were on the top floor of the building) overlooking the Charles River basin, and across the river Beacon Hill with its terraced houses rising to the State House and its gilded dome.

The morning I stood by that window before my case waiting for copy, I did not know it was a day of annunciation, and that my spirit would magnify the Lord for making me a chosen vessel! Mr. Wienshank came with an innocent-looking sheaf of printed pages in his hand and left them with me with instructions as to the character of type and size of type pages. I set to work, and with an instantaneous transformation wandered into a world of magical beauty!

When I had fixed the pages in the copy-holder, seized the stick, and began to pick the type-letters from the case, I was setting the line.

Thou still unravish'd bride of quietness

beginning a poem that ended with lines that broke upon both my sense and spirit with the flush of a sunrise—

"Beauty is truth, truth beauty,"—that is all
  Ye know on earth, and all ye need to know.
Here was the spirit of a man flaming with a strange, new mystery
of life and nature!

Keats' poems were followed with reprints of selections from Wordsworth and Burns, and from both these poets I received communi-
cations, impressions, and revelations, which transported me into
realms, and awakened sensibilities, that remade my world in terms of
poignant imaginative desires. Keats had created in me an aspiration
that became the most passionate urgency in my life, and Wordsworth
and Burns nourished it into an ambition that developed into a fanatical determination.

I began composing verses, pitiful attempts, as I have since known
them to be, but which nothing could restrain, for the need of expression was as inevitable as the natural force of birth following conception. Croce's aesthetic concept of the identity of intuition and expression had a confirming experience in my case, however mediocre the
character of the product.

As I composed these early verses I would put them into type,
and again surreptitiously place the type on the end of a galley of
composition, and striking off the proof beheld the first printings of
my poetic effusions. I made scores of these "privately printed" verses
of mine, which in the shuffle of time and movement were lost as was
also my first "library" made of the galley proofs of the Ginn publications. No printing of anything I've written, with few exceptions,
has given me the thrill and excitement of these early verses, for whatever the verbal and rhythmical merits they had, there was the odor
of fresh ink and damp paper in making the impressions, which
transferred to the words and the memory an indefinable but persuasive flavor abiding with the senses and the memory forever.

The passion which I now was driven by for a poetic and literary
career, made me sensible of the cultural training necessary for an
artist before he could hope to realize his ambitions. Keats was my
master, nay, more, I worshipped him as a god! From his poems I
turned to his life and read such biographies and studies as I could
obtain from the Boston Public Library. The deeper I read the more,
and often discouragingly I realized the difficulties confronting me of
time and opportunity to acquire the knowledge and to cultivate the
faculties necessary in mastering an education for the pursuit of a
literary career.

ANGELO HERNDON (1913-   )

Angelo Herndon was born in Wyoming, Ohio, a steel and coal-mining town. He first became acquainted with the terrorism of the South when organizing sharecroppers and leading demonstrations for the Scottsboro boys. In the 1932 presidential campaign he was arrested for leading a protest march of nearly a thousand unemployed whites and Negroes in Atlanta, Georgia. Under the antislave insurrection law of 1861 he was sentenced to prison for eighteen to twenty years for distributing incendiary literature. The Angelo Herndon case, like the *causes célèbres* of Tom Mooney, Sacco and Vanzetti, and the Scottsboro boys, rallied liberal and radical support. Fifteen thousand dollars bail was "raised in pennies, nickels, and dimes by workers and sympathizers throughout the world pending the decision of the Supreme Court." This decision set aside the sentence as unconstitutional. The following selection is from chapter nineteen of Herndon's autobiography, *Let Me Live* (1937). It is reprinted by permission of the author and Random House, the publishers.

[Georgia Trial]

MY DEFENSE SUFFERED many setbacks on the second day of the trial. The judge saw fit to overrule every motion or objection that my defense counsel raised. Mr. Davis moved for a *prima facie* case in my favor because the state had admitted that there were no names of Negroes in the Grand Jury box from which the Grand Jury that indicted me was drawn, and because the state did not think it necessary to offer any evidence that Negroes were not excluded from the jury.

Curtly Judge Wyatt overruled the motion.

Mr. Davis then called Professor Mercer G. Evans to the witness stand. He wished to qualify him as an expert on Communism. Professor Evans recited his pedigree:

"I am a teacher at Emory University, in the Department of Economics. I have the Bachelor of Science (B.S.) degree from Emory University, and the Master of Arts (A. M.) and Doctor of Laws (LL.D.) degrees from the University of Chicago. I have been a teacher of economics at Emory University for nine years. I have read widely in the field of theoretical economics, including a good deal of Anarchistic and sociological or Communist literature, which is, of course, of an economic nature. Some of the magazines that have carried my articles of an economic nature are: *The Annals of the American*

Academy of Social and Political Science, The American Federationist.
I have read the books stated in this indictment."

During the state's cross-examination of Professor Evans and over
the objection of defense counsel, the court allowed him to testify as
follows:

"I am acquainted with what is known as the Communism of Soviet
Russia or the Soviet Union, of the present form of government in the
nation of Russia, that it is a government which succeeded the Kerensky government, which succeeded the former Czarist government;
that was brought about by a revolution, putting out the Czar and the
assassination of the Czar and his family came later, not necessarily
as the result of a revolution. As to the Russian Revolution, history so
regards it, that there was a revolution. The Czarist government over-
thrown, the Kerensky government took charge, and after about six
months another revolution of bloodless character in which the present
regime succeeded the Kerensky government. I wouldn't attempt to
dispute that as an historical fact."

The Reverend Hudson then interjected:

"Have you ever been to Russia, Doctor?"

"Yes, I have been to Russia. I was over there this summer. I spent
about two weeks in Russia, I think."

The second expert for the defense, Professor T. J. Corley, also of
Emory University, next took the witness stand. The Reverend Hudson
asked him:

"Doctor, are you familiar with the Communist platform in the
1932 election?"

Professor Corley replied: "Yes, parts of it."

"Do you agree with the full platform?"

Mr. Davis objected to this question as irrelevant. Judge Wyatt
overruled him and Professor Corley was obliged to answer:

"Most of it."

The prosecutor continued:

"Did you know that the platform demands the right of self-
determination for the niggers in the Black Belt?"

"Yes."

"Would you want a nigger to marry your daughter?"

Mr. Davis jumped to his feet:

"Your Honor, I object," he said.

"Objection overruled," snapped back the judge.

"Excuse me, Your Honor," said the Prosecutor, as he resumed
his questioning of the witness, "I will re-frame the question: Do you
understand the Communist position on the Negro question to mean

the right of a colored boy to marry your daughter, if you have one?"

Mr. Davis was on his feet again.

"Your Honor," he remonstrated, "we object to the question on the ground that it is irrelevant and immaterial and calls for a conclusion of the witness."

Tiresomely as well as tirelessly Judge Wyatt droned:

"I overrule the objection."

Professor Corley then answered the question put to him:

"That is against the laws of the State of Georgia."

To this the Prosecutor answered with the following question:

"Did you know that there are twenty states in the United States where the two races (white and Negro) can intermarry or mix?"

"I do not know how many states there are in the union where they have that right," answered Professor Corley. "I only know that a Negro doesn't happen to have the right to marry my daughter under the laws of this state."

Judge Wyatt now interrupted in a manner which appeared to me, to my counsel and to the court audience as rather "irrelevant and immaterial:"

"If Emory University is guilty of anything, we will try them; I think even if Emory University had actually attempted to incite riot, it wouldn't be material in this case; it is a question of what this defendant has done. If the defendant attempted to overthrow the government he is an anarchist. The defense has failed to qualify the professors as experts on the question of economics. I, therefore, overrule the motion as experts on the ground that Communism has nothing to do with economics. Of course, I don't deny that the defendant might not be an economical man."

The spectators doubled up with laughter and the judge again brought his gavel down with a bang. He ranted:

"I am not going to have any demonstration in this court room. A man is on trial for his life, and I am going to see that justice is done. The next one I catch demonstrating, I am going to have the bailiff bring you up here, and I will send you where you can't demonstrate."

What did the hypothetical question of a white woman marrying a Negro, put to Professors Corley and Evans by the Prosecutor, have to do with my attempt to incite insurrection in the incomparable State of Georgia? Was I mad or were they mad? It was all gibberish to me. I just could not make head or tail of it. Nor could anybody else, for that matter.

The Reverend Hudson finally called his star witness for examination. He was E. A. Stephens, one of the assistant prosecutors. It was he who was supposed to have "investigated" me and obtained a "confession."

Confession? What confession? Had I ever confessed?

Mr. Stephens testified:

"I called on the chief of police to have that box [1] watched and the man who got the mail out of there taken in charge and questioned; the same day, Officer Watson or Mr. W. B. Martin, I don't recollect which, brought this darkey, Angelo Herndon, to the solicitor's office, and I talked to him in the Grand Jury room."

When Mr. Davis objected to the use of the word "darkey" on the ground that it was an insulting and prejudicial name, Judge Wyatt drawled:

"I don't know whether it is or not; but suppose you refer to him as the defendant."

Thereupon my counsel moved for a directed verdict in my favor on the ground that it was impossible for me to receive a fair trial because of the race prejudice exhibited throughout the trial by the court, the prosecutors and the state's witnesses.

Judge Wyatt looked surprised. Apparently he had never heard of a directed verdict issued on such grounds and he overruled the motion.

Mr. Davis knew that I did not have a ghost of a chance for acquittal. If he made so many exceptions, it was with an appeal to the higher courts in mind.

At last I was called to testify. I was very calm and collected. I felt that the worst that my legal inquisitors could do to me they had already done. Any statement I could make to the jury seemed superfluous, as it was altogether obvious that the jurymen had already made up their minds to render a verdict of guilty against me. Taking this into consideration, I decided not to mince my words and speak what I thought. At least I could let people know what kind of justice was being given me and for what reasons.

I did not address myself to the judge nor, for that matter, to the prosecutors nor to the jurors who were deciding my fate. Far beyond them I saw a vision of millions of white and Negro workers, oppressed and hungry, listening to every word I was saying. It was they who were going to be my jury. By them I wished to be judged. I knew that my case was a challenge to them and to their right to organize into labor unions and to live in peace and security. In their name I accepted this challenge and spoke, not as if I were in a court room, but as if I were addressing my fellow-workers at one of our educational meetings.

[1] My mail box in the post office.

There was great silence as I spoke. Men and women sat pale and tense. I looked at them and they looked at me, and I felt that we were fused together by the deepest bonds of sympathy. A warm glow shot through my body and I tingled with the joy of it. The hard cruel faces of the state's instruments of class injustice receded from me. The walls of the court house seemed to melt away and I walked the earth erect and free. I thought of the rugged beauty and greatness of heart of the American people. It was to them that I was now speaking. Yet what I was saying could not be in the nature of a defense. Quite the contrary. It was a scathing indictment of the system. It was also a plea to the workers to rise and change the world. My words sprang from the heart and I directed them to the heart and the conscience of my fellowmen.

To disprove the charges that I had made in my address to the jury that I had been persecuted and mistreated in Fulton Tower, the state brought forward Chief Jailer Bob Holland to testify. He lied like a Trojan. His childish chatter amused the court audience very much. He was a little shamefaced and angry when Mr. Davis in his cross-examination exposed the contradictions of his denials. He did not dare look in my direction because he knew he was lying.

Very remarkable is the fact that the two principal witnesses against me were the Assistant Prosecutor and the Chief Jailer, as if my "crime of insurrection" was committed after my arrest!

The defense finally rested.

The following day, January 18, 1933, Mr. Davis made his summary before the jury. It was clear that he was under a great mental and emotional strain. He knew the jury that he was appealing to, but this knowledge did not prevent him from fighting as gamely and as long as it was possible. Although he was the son of a wealthy Negro politician, a National Republican Committeeman, and had been educated at Harvard, he felt that all that separated us were merely surface differences; that in reality he and I and millions of disenfranchised and exploited Negroes shared the same rotten fate. I looked at him and I felt wretched for his sake. He was tense and his voice shook. It was one of the most moving addresses I have ever heard. He spoke with the dignity of a man belonging to a despised race and who has the courage to assert his manhood in the face of his people's oppressors. The audience of black and white workers thrilled to his words.

The Reverend Hudson followed with his final summary for the state. He looked like the avenging angel. The court room was filled with the thunder of his eloquence. He went through the most incredible antics. This was the final curtain, and he was going to perform his level best. For this purpose the role of man of God would suit him best. So he fell on his knees before the jury box, just as if he were before a church altar and, with tears in his eyes, pleaded in the holy name of God that such a fiend as I should be electrocuted and wiped off the face of the earth. Folding his hands piously he outstretched them to the gentlemen of the jury, beseeching hoarsely:

"Gentlemen of the jury: You have heard the defendant lay down his defy to the State of Georgia. He is a confirmed revolutionist, with an unbreakable soul. But we accept his challenge. Gentlemen, when you go into the box, I expect you to arrive at a verdict that will automatically send this damnable anarchistic Bolsheviki to his death by electrocution, and God will be satisfied that justice has been done and the daughters of the state officials can walk the streets safely. Stamp this thing out now with a conviction."

As I listened to him, it struck me with full force that he had made a sensational impression with his speech upon both judge and jury. It became very clear to me why that was so. He spoke their language. He interlarded his lynch frenzy with goodly sprinklings from Holy Writ. Blood and piety, these are the two principal ingredients of boasted Southern civilization. Murder is perfumed with the altar incense of religion to hide its rotten stench.

When the Reverend Hudson had concluded, the judge gave his instructions to the jury. He said:

"You are the sole judges of all the facts, and the court can express no opinion, and does express no opinion as to what has or has not been proven; it is for you to determine whether or not any of these things that I have charged you upon have been proven."

At eight o'clock that night the jury sent word that it had reached a verdict. When they filed into the jury box the silence in the court room became painful. Now, by nature I am an optimist. One might say it is a strange sort of optimism. It largely consists of a realistic expectation of the worst that can possibly happen. The optimism part of it is that in expecting the worst there is no longer any room for suspense. Therefore, there is no more cause for anxiety or inner conflict. For this reason I imagine that I was the jolliest person in the court room that day, with the possible exception of that man of God, the Reverend Hudson, who knew what was coming.

"Gentlemen," said the Clerk of the Court, "have you arrived at a verdict, and if you have will you please read it to the court?"

Judge Wyatt ordered all doors locked, and, glaring at the court audience, he warned:

"While the verdict is being read there must not be any demonstrating to indicate your approval or disapproval of the verdict. The jurors have arrived at a verdict and no one knows whether it is in favor or against the defendant."

The foreman of the jury then rose and read from a little piece of paper:

"We, the jury, find the defendant, Angelo Herndon, guilty as charged, but recommend that mercy be shown and fix his sentence at from eighteen to twenty years."

At this a great commotion rose in the court room. Men and women of both races and belonging to all classes sprang to their feet and raised a clamor of protest. Some pounded on the benches and others cried out. In the general hubbub it was not clear what they were saying except that they were registering general disapproval of the verdict.

A bright newspaper reporter leaned over and asked me:

"How do you feel, Angelo; are you scared?"

As if he cared a lot whether I was or not! But it might make good reading copy.

"No," I answered. "I am feeling fine. This verdict is the surprise of my life. I expected the electric chair, but these fine gentlemen of the jury have made me a Christmas present. They have recommended mercy, and so I am getting away with only twenty years on the chain gang. Am I not lucky?"

The newspaper man looked bewildered at me. He could not make up his mind whether I was crazy or just a simpleton. Maybe, he will find out some day. Who knows?

Judge Wyatt called me to the bar. He was almost fatherly to me now. So much "mercy" had softened his heart toward me. He could well afford it now. The show was all over except for the applause. And he was sure to get the lion's share of it from the newspapers and all good citizens. Almost benignly he smiled at me as he said:

"Angelo, the jury has found you guilty of attempting to incite to insurrection and fixed the sentence. I think they are justified in doing so. Have you anything to say before I pass sentence upon?"

"Yes, Your Honor," I answered, "I have this to say:

"You may do what you will with Angelo Herndon. You may indict him. You may put him in jail. But there will come other thousands of Angelo Herndons. If you really want to do anything about the case, you must go out and indict the social system. But this you will not do, for your role is to defend the system under which the toiling masses are robbed and oppressed. You may succeed in killing one, two, even a score of working-class organizers. But you cannot kill the working class."

Judge Wyatt then passed sentence upon me:

"Whereupon, it is ordered and adjudged by the court that the defendant, Angelo Herndon, be taken from the bar of this court to the jail of Fulton County, and be there safely kept until a sufficient guard is sent for him from the Georgia Penitentiary, and be then delivered to, and be by said guard taken to said penitentiary, or to such other place as the Governor may direct, where he, the said Angelo Herndon, be confined at hard labor for the full term of not less than eighteen (18) years, and not more than twenty (20) years, to be computed as provided in the Act approved August 27, 1931."

Again a commotion was raised in the audience. The judge pounded his gavel, but the noise would not subside. One Negro woman cried out in a ringing voice:

"It's a damn shame! If they ever get him on that chain gang, they will sure kill him!"

A policeman clapped handcuffs on me and led me out through the rear entrance of the court to a waiting automobile. Outside a large crowd of Negro and white spectators crowded around us to bid me good-bye. Men and women shouted encouragement to me. Their cries were indistinct. I could not make out what they were saying. But their eyes were more eloquent than words could be. With earnest, tense faces they clenched their fists in farewell salute.

My class brothers! I knew they would never forget me and would fight tirelessly for my freedom.

Tranquilly, in a gravely reflective mood, I followed my jailer as he led me back into Fulton Tower.

It was a clear mild night although in mid-winter. The only things that looked fresh and green were the magnolia trees stirring in the wind at the entrance of the jail. I looked at them long and yearningly with a last caress of the eyes as the heavy prison gates swung close behind me.

Would I ever see those wonderful magnolia trees again? I wondered! ...

WILLIAM STILL (1821-1902)

When William Still, serving as clerk in the Philadelphia antislavery office, was asking routine questions of a Negro newly arrived from Alabama, he was suddenly amazed by certain replies. Further questioning established beyond any doubt that the stranger and he were brothers. This dramatic event struck so closely home that Still was prompted to keep records of the Underground Railroad. "Thousands of escapes, harrowing separations, dark gropings after lost parents, brothers, sisters, and identities, seemed ever to be pressing on my mind. While I knew the danger of keeping strict records, and while I did not then dream that in my day slavery would be blotted out, or that the time would come when I could publish these records, it used to afford me great satisfaction to take them down fresh from the lips of fugitives on the way to freedom, and to preserve them as they had given them." Still kept these records from 1850 to 1860. Knowing the danger to all concerned—the fugitives and their rescuers—he secreted these voluminous records in the loft of a cemetery building. In 1872 he compiled *Underground Railroad Records*.

Still's parents had escaped separately from Eastern Shore Maryland to New Jersey. His brother, Peter Still, who finally reached him in Philadelphia, was the hero of Mrs. Kate Pickard's biography *The Kidnapped and the Ransomed*. William Still was born free, in Burlington County, New Jersey, since his fugitive parents had guarded their secret closely. Ingenious, thorough, methodical, and courageous, Still not only forwarded numberless Negro passengers on the Underground but also aided the escape of several of John Brown's men after Harper's Ferry. Nineteen out of twenty fugitives stopped at Still's house on their way through Philadelphia. The original notes were set down in haste, often late at night, as the "trains" were waiting for "the passengers." Sometimes the notes were scanty; the fugitives had more to think about than their past, or they were reticent and suspicious. Even collected in such fashion, *Underground Railroad Records* is a storehouse of good things, little advertised but vouched for as authenic.

In 1861 Still organized a social, civil, and statistical association to collect and preserve data on the Negro. After the war he was engaged in antidiscrimination work, welfare work and in religious activities. In 1880 he founded the first colored Young Men's Christian Association.

Captain F. and the Mayor of Norfolk

CAPTAIN F. WAS certainly no ordinary man. Although he had been living a seafaring life for many years, and the marks of this calling were plainly enough visible in his manners and speech, he was, nevertheless, unlike the great mass of this class of men, not addicted to intemperance and profanity. On the contrary, he was a man of thought, and possessed, in a large measure, those humane traits of character which lead men to sympathize with suffering humanity wherever met with.

It must be admitted, however, that the first impressions gathered from a hasty survey of his rough and rugged appearance, his large head, large mouth, large eyes, and heavy eye-brows, with a natural gift at keeping concealed the inner-workings of his mind and feelings, were not calculated to inspire the belief, that he was fitted to be entrusted with the lives of unprotected females, and helpless children; that he could take pleasure in risking his own life to rescue them from the hell of Slavery; that he could deliberately enter the enemy's domain, and with the faith of a martyr, face the dread slave-holder, with his Bowie-knives and revolvers—Slave-hunters, and blood-hounds, lynchings, and penitentiaries, for humanity's sake. But his deeds proved him to be a true friend of the Slave; whilst his skill, bravery, and success stamped him as one of the most daring and heroic Captains ever connected with the Underground Rail Road cause.

At the time he was doing most for humanity in rescuing bondsmen from Slavery, Slave-laws were actually being the most rigidly executed. To show mercy, in any sense, to man or woman, who might be caught assisting a poor Slave to flee from the prison-house, was a matter not to be thought of in Virginia. This was perfectly well understood by Captain F.; indeed he did not hesitate to say, that his hazardous operations might any day result in the "sacrifice" of his life. But on this point he seemed to give himself no more concern than he would have done to know which way the wind would blow the next day. He had his own convictions about dying and the future, and he declared, that he had "no fear of death," however it might come. Still, he was not disposed to be reckless or needlessly to imperil his life, or the lives of those he undertook to aid. Nor was he averse to receiving compensation for his services. In Richmond, Norfolk, Petersburg, and other places where he traded, many slaves were fully awake to their condition. The great slave sales were the agencies that served to awaken a large number. Then the various mechanical trades were necessarily given to the Slaves, for the master had no taste for "greasy, northern mechanics." Then, again, the stores had to be supplied with porters, draymen, etc., from the slave population. In the hearts of many of the more intelligent amongst the slaves, notwithstanding all opposition and hard laws, the spirit of Freedom was steadily burning. Many of the slaves were half brothers, and sisters, cousins, nephews, and nieces to their owners, and of course "blood would tell."

It was only necessary for the fact to be made known to a single reliable and intelligent slave, that a man with a boat running North had the love of Freedom for all mankind in his bosom to make that man an object of the greatest interest. If an angel had appeared amongst them doubtless his presence would not have inspired greater anxiety and hope than did the presence of Captain F. The class most anxious to obtain freedom could generally manage to acquire some means which they would willingly offer to captains or conductors in the South for such assistance as was indispensable to their escape. Many of the slaves learned if they could manage to cross Mason and Dixon's line, even though they might be utterly destitute and penniless, that they would then receive aid and protection from the Vigilance Committee. Here it may be well to state that, whilst the Committee gladly received and aided all who might come or be brought to them, they never employed agents or captains to go into the South with a view of enticing or running off slaves. So when captains operated, they did so with the full understanding that they alone were responsible for any failures attending their movements.

The way is now clear to present Captain F. with his schooner lying at the wharf in Norfolk, loading with wheat, and at the same time with twenty-one fugitives secreted therein. While the boat was thus lying at her mooring, the rumor was flying all over town that a number of slaves had escaped, which created a general excitement a degree less, perhaps, than if the citizens had been visited by an earthquake. The mayor of the city with a posse of officers with axes and long spears repaired to Captain F.'s boat. The fearless commander received his Honor very coolly, and as gracefully as the circumstances would admit. The mayor gave him to understand who he was, and by what authority he appeared on the boat, and what he meant to do. "Very well," replied Captain F., "here I am and this is my boat, go ahead and search. His Honor with his deputies looked quickly around, and then an order went forth from the mayor to "spear the wheat thoroughly." The deputies obeyed the command with alacrity. But the spears brought neither blood nor groans, and the sagacious mayor obviously concluded that he was "barking up the wrong tree." But the mayor was not there for nothing. "Take the axes and go to work," was the next order; and the axe was used with terrible effect by one of the deputies. The deck and other parts of the boat were chopped and split; no greater judgment being exercised when using an axe than when spearing the wheat; Captain F. all the while wearing an air of utter indifference or rather of entire composure. Indeed every step they took proved conclusively that they were wholly ignorant with regard to boat searching. At this point, with remarkable shrewdness, Captain F. saw wherein he could still further confuse them by a bold strategical move. As though about out of patience with the mayor's blunders, the captain instantly reminded his Honor that he had "stood still long enough" while his boat was being "damaged, chopped up," etc. "Now if you want to search," continued he, "give me the axe, and then point out the spot you want opened and I will open it for you very quick." While uttering these words he presented, as he was capable of doing, an indignant and defiant countenance, and intimated that it mattered not where or when a man died provided he was in the right, and as though he wished to give particularly strong emphasis to what he was saying, he raised the axe, and brought it down edge foremost with startling effect, at the same time causing the splinters to fly from the boards. The mayor and his posse seemed, if not dreadfully frightened, completely confounded, and by the time Captain F. had again brought down his axe with increased power, demanding where they would have him open, they looked as though it was time for them to retire, and in a few minutes after they actually gave up the search and left the boat without finding a soul. Daniel in the lions' den was not safer than were the twenty-one passengers secreted on Captain F.'s boat. The law had been carried out with a vengeance, but did not avail with this skilled captain. The "five dollars" were paid for being searched, the amount which was lawfully required of every captain sailing from Virginia. And the captain steered direct for the City of Brotherly Love. The wind of heaven favoring the good cause, he arrived safely in due time, and delivered his precious freight in the vicinity of Philadelphia within the reach of the Vigilance Committee. . . .

Samuel Green

THE PASSENGER ANSWERING to the above name, left Indian Creek, Chester Co., Md., where he had been held to service or labor, by Dr. James Muse. One week had elapsed from the time he set out until his arrival in Philadelphia. Although he had never enjoyed school privileges of any kind, yet he was not devoid of intelligence. He had profited by his daily experience as a slave, and withal, had managed to learn to read and write a little, despite law and usage to the contrary. Sam was about twenty-five years of age and by trade, a blacksmith. Before running away, his general character for sobriety, industry, and religion, had evidently been considered good, but in coveting his freedom and running away to obtain it, he had sunk far below the utmost limit of forgiveness or mercy in the estimation of the slave-holders of Indian Creek.

During his intercourse with the Vigilance Committee, while rejoicing over his triumphant flight, he gave, with no appearance of excitement, but calmly, and in a common-sense like manner, a brief description of his master, which was entered on the record book substantially as follows: "Dr. James Muse is thought by the servants to be the worst man in Maryland, inflicting whipping and all manner of cruelties upon the servants."

While Sam gave reasons for this sweeping charge, which left no room for doubt, on the part of the Committee, of his sincerity and good judgment, it was not deemed necessary to make a note of more of the doctor's character than seemed actually needed, in order to show why "Sam" had taken passage on the Underground Rail Road. For several years, "Sam" was hired out by the doctor at blacksmithing; in this situation, daily wearing the yoke of unrequited labor, through the kindness of Harriet Tubman (sometimes called "Moses"), the light of the Underground Rail Road and Canada suddenly illuminated his mind. It was new to him, but he was quite too intelligent and liberty-loving, not to heed the valuable information which this sister of humanity imparted. Thenceforth he was in love with Canada, and likewise a decided admirer of the U. R. Road. Harriet was herself, a shrewd and fearless agent, and well understood the entire route from that part of the country to Canada. The spring previous, she had paid a visit to the very neighborhood in which "Sam" lived, expressly to lead her own brothers out of "Egypt." She succeeded. To "Sam" this was cheering and glorious news, and he made up his mind, that before a great while, Indian Creek should have one less slave and that Canada should have one more citizen. Faithfully did he watch an opportunity to carry out his resolution. In due time a good Providence opened the way, and to "Sam's" satisfaction he reached Philadelphia, having encountered no peculiar difficulties. The Committee, perceiving that he was smart, active, and promising, encouraged his undertaking, and having given him friendly advice, aided him in the usual manner. Letters of introduction were given him, and he was duly forwarded on his way. He had left his father, mother, and one sister behind. Samuel and Catharine were the names of his parents. Thus far, his escape would seem not to affect his parents, nor was it apparent that there was any other cause why the owner should revenge himself upon them.

The father was an old local preacher in the Methodist Church—much esteemed as an inoffensive, industrious man; earning his bread by the sweat of his brow, and contriving to move along in the narrow road allotted colored people bond or free, without exciting a spirit of ill will in the pro-slavery power of his community. But the rancor awakened in the breast of slave-holders in consequence of the high-handed step the son had taken, brought the father under suspicion and hate. Under the circumstances, the eye of Slavery could do nothing more than watch for an occasion to pounce upon him. It was not long before the desired opportunity presented itself. Moved by parental affection, the old man concluded to pay a visit to his boy, to see how he was faring in a distant land, and among strangers. This resolution he quietly carried into effect. He found his son in Canada, doing well; industrious; a man of sobriety, and following his father's footsteps religiously. That the old man's heart was delighted with what his eyes saw and his ears heard in Canada, none can doubt. But in the simplicity of his imagination, he never dreamed that this visit was to be made the means of his destruction. During the best portion of his days he had faithfully worn the badge of Slavery, had afterwards purchased his freedom, and thus became a free man. He innocently conceived the idea that he was doing no harm in availing himself not only of his God-given rights, but of the rights that he had also purchased by the hard toil of his own hands. But the enemy was lurking in ambush for him—thirsting for his blood. To his utter consternation, not long after his return from his visit to his son "a party of gentlemen from the New Market district, went at night to Green's house and made search, whereupon was found a copy of Uncle Tom's Cabin, etc." This was enough— the hour had come, wherein to wreak vengeance upon poor Green. The course pursued and the result, may be seen in the following statement taken from the Cambridge (Md.), "Democrat," of April 29th, 1857, and communicated by the writer to the "Provincial Freeman."

Sam Green

"The case of the State against Sam Green (free Negro) indicted for having in his possession, papers, pamphlets and pictorial representations, having a tendency to create discontent, etc., among the people of color in the State, was tried before the court on Friday last.

"The case was of the utmost importance, and has created in the public mind a great deal of interest—it being the first case of the kind ever having occurred in our country.

"It appeared, in evidence, that this Green has a son in Canada, to whom Green made a visit last summer. Since his return to this county, suspicion has fastened upon him, as giving aid and assisting slaves who have since absconded and reached Canada, and several weeks ago, a party of gentlemen from New Market district, went at night, to Green's house and made search, whereupon was found a volume of 'Uncle Tom's Cabin,' a map of Canada, several schedules of routes to the North, and a letter from his son in Canada, detailing the pleasant trip he had, the number of friends he met with on the way, with plenty to eat, drink, etc., and concludes with a request to his father, that he shall tell certain other slaves, naming them, to come on, which slaves, it is well known, did leave shortly afterwards, and have reached Canada. The case was argued with great ability, the counsel on both sides displaying a great deal of ingenuity, learning and eloquence. The first indictment was for the having in possession the letter, map and route schedules.

"Notwithstanding the mass of evidence given, to show the prisoner's guilt, in lawfully having in his possession these documents, and the nine-tenths of the community in which he lived, believed that he had a hand in the running away of slaves, it was the opinion of the court, that the law under which he was indicted, was not applicable to the case, and that he must, accordingly, render a verdict of not guilty.

"He was immediately arraigned upon another indictment, for having in possession 'Uncle Tom's Cabin,' and tried; in this case the court has not yet rendered a verdict, but holds it under *curia* till after the Somerset county court. It is to be hoped, the court will find the evidence in the case sufficient to bring it within the scope of the law under which the prisoner is indicted (that of 1842, chap. 272), and that the prisoner may meet his due reward—be that what it may.

"That there is something required to be done by our Legislators, for the protection of slave property, is evident from the variety of constructions put upon the statute in this case, and we trust, that at the next meeting of the Legislature there will be such amendments, as to make the law on this subject, perfectly clear and comprehensible to the understanding of every one.

"In the language of the assistant counsel for the State, 'Slavery must be protected or it must be abolished.' "

From the same sheet, of May 20th, the terrible doom of Samuel Green, is announced in the following words:

"In the case of the State against Sam Green, (free negro) who was tried at the April term of the Circuit Court of this county, for having in his possession abolition pamphlets, among which was 'Uncle Tom's Cabin,' has been found guilty by the court, and sentenced to the penitentiary for the term of ten years—until the 14th of May, 1867."

The son, a refugee in Canada, hearing the distressing news of his father's sad fate in the hands of the relentless "gentlemen," often wrote to know if there was any prospect of his deliverance. The subjoined letter is a fair sample of his correspondence:

Salford, 22, 1857

"Dear Sir I take my pen in hand to request a favor of you if
you can by any means without duin InJestus to your self or your
Bisness to grant it as I Bleve you to be a man that would Sympathize
in such a ones Condition as my self I Reseved a letter that Stats to
me that my Fater has ben Betraed in the act of helping sum frend
to Canada and that law has Convicted and Sentanced him to the
Stats prison for 10 yeares his White Frands ofered 2 thousen Dollers
to Redem him but they would not short three thousen. I am in Canada
and it is a Dificult thing to get a letter to any of my Frands in Maryland so as to get prop per infermation abot it—if you can by any
means get any in telligence from Baltimore City a bot this Event
Plese do so and Rit word and all so all the inform mation that you
think prop per as Regards the Evant and the best mathod to Redeme
him and so Plese Rite soon as you can You will oblige your sir Frand
and Drect your letter to Salford P. office C. W."

Samuel Green.

In this dark hour the friends of the Slave could do but little more
than sympathize with this heart-stricken son and the grey-headed
father. The aged follower of the Rejected and Crucified had like
Him to bear the "reproach of many," and make his bed with the
wicked in the Penitentiary. Doubtless there were a few friends in
his neighborhood who sympathized with him, but they were powerless to aid the old man. But thanks to a kind Providence, the great
deliverance brought about during the Rebellion by which so many
captives were freed, also unlocked Samuel Green's prison-doors and
he was allowed to go free.

After his liberation from the Penitentiary, we had from his own
lips narrations of his years of suffering—of the bitter cup, that he was
compelled to drink, and of his being sustained by the Almighty Arm
—but no notes were taken at the time, consequently we have nothing
more to add concerning him, save quite a faithful likeness.

BENJAMIN G. BRAWLEY (1882-1939)

Benjamin G. Brawley (see p. 757) in *The Negro Genius* (1937) and *Negro Builders and Heroes* (1937) produced two volumes of sketches of Negro notables. The first book deals largely with men and women whose endeavors were in art and literature; the second, covering a wider field, he described as "an introduction to Negro biography." Figures discussed vary as widely as Crispus Attucks, Benjamin Banneker, Paul Cuffe, John Chavis, Daniel Payne (see above p. 732), Blanche K. Bruce, and John Merrick. The selection, "John Jasper: 'The Sun Do Move,'" from the latter volume, is used by permission of the University of North Carolina Press and of Mrs. Brawley.

John Jasper: "The Sun Do Move"

JOHN JASPER STAMPED HIMSELF so indelibly on those among whom he moved in his later years that there are still many who have memories of his presence. In temper and outlook, however, he was of the period before the Civil War. He grew up in slavery, had lived more than half of his long life when the war came, and was as crude in his old age as in his youth; but in one sphere at least, that of imaginative and pictorial expression, he has seldom been equaled. In this his ability amounted to genius.

He was born on a plantation in Fluvanna County, Virginia, in July, 1812, the youngest of the several children of Philip Jasper, a slave preacher, and his wife, Nina. The mother was the head of the force of working women on the farm and later became the chief servant in a rich family. As Philip Jasper had died, she took full charge of the training of her son John, and endeavored to lead him into righteous paths. As the youth grew into manhood, he was a tall ungainly figure, with a small body and long swinging limbs; but he had a dashing and self-confident manner, was full of life and humor, and was quite a beau in the neighborhood. While still a young man he went to Richmond and worked in the tobacco factory of Samuel Hargrove.

On the Fourth of July, 1837, which seems to have been his twenty-fifth birthday, Jasper passed by Capitol Square in Richmond and witnessed a holiday demonstration. Something in the scene awoke his deeper self. He realized as never before the vanity of the world, and for weeks thereafter his spirit was heavy. On the morning of July 25 the tobacco was harder to stem than usual; his sins seemed piled on him like mountains, and he felt that of all who had broken the law of God he was the worst. He thought he would die, and sent to heaven a cry for mercy. Before he knew it, the clouds vanished and he felt light as a feather. As he later said, his feet were on the mountain, salvation rolled like a flood through his soul, and he thought he could blow the factory roof off with his shouts.

He thought it best to restrain himself until the noon hour; so he cried and laughed and tore up the tobacco. Then he saw not far away an old man who had tried to lead him from darkness to light. Jasper stepped over to him and said, "Hallelujah! my soul is redeemed." Then he saw a good old woman who knew of his striving and had been praying for him. He had to speak to her too; but what was intended as a whisper became a great shout, and soon the whole room was in commotion. The overseer came to see the cause of the disturbance and was told that Jasper had "got religion." His word was short and to the effect that the new convert had better get back to work. Then Mr. Hargrove himself stepped from the office to make inquiry. He was a man of benevolent spirit, a member of the First Baptist Church. In a few minutes he sent for Jasper. "His voice," said the preacher later, "was sof' like, an' it seemed to have a little song in it that played into my soul like an angel's harp." When he learned that Jasper had told his story with such power, he said: "Go back in there and go up and down the tables, and tell all of them. You needn't work any more to-day. After you get through here at the factory, go up to the house and tell your folks; go around to your neighbors and tell them; go anywhere you want to, and tell the good news. It'll do you good, do them good, and help to honor your Lord and Savior."

Jasper joined the church and immediately began to preach. Realizing the need of acquaintance with the Scriptures, he studied hard for seven months with another slave, William Jackson, in order to learn how to read. Thenceforth he was a man of one book. He read the Bible again and again, comparing passages and lingering upon the noble diction of the King James version. In a moment he grasped the essential elements of a story, and his ability to visualize some scenes was overpowering. Without the slightest regard for grammar, he would sometimes use dialogue, and he would make a scene like that of the coming forth of Lazarus from the grave so vivid that the congregation was transfixed with terror. Again, in a funeral sermon, he would give such a picture of the great white throne and the King in his beauty that all would be sent into the wildest enthusiasm.

Preaching thus, Jasper was not long in becoming known; his fame soon spread to other cities and the country districts. One day he had to be in Farmville to officiate on an occasion when a number of the dead were to have their virtues celebrated. A great throng assembled to hear him. As was usual at the time, a white minister was present to see that the proprieties were observed. This man as master of ceremonies thought to dispose of the visitor by asking him to lead in prayer. That was all Jasper needed; he had proven to be as capable in talking to heaven as to men on earth. The congregation was carried away with his eloquence and, when the white minister had concluded his rather tame address, cried out for Jasper. The visitor, now on fire and emboldened by the disposition of the presiding officer to shut him out, responded to the call and gave an address so brilliant that all who heard it remembered it to the end of their lives.

In the course of the Civil War Jasper often preached to the Confederate soldiers in hospitals. The fall of Richmond found him with seventy-three cents in his pocket and forty-two dollars in debt. Undaunted, he began to preach to a little group on an island in the James River, and baptized scores of converts in the river. The crowds increased and it was soon necessary to move to a deserted building not far away. Then, as conditions improved, a number of the people went to live in the northern part of the city. Their preacher went with them and led in the purchase of an old brick building formerly used by a Presbyterian mission. The cost was $2,025, but it was not long before $6,000 had to be spent to remodel the edifice. At length Jasper came to the church home that he knew and loved best, the Sixth Mount Zion, and there he was working at the height of his fame, about 1880. Multitudes came to hear him preach "De Sun Do Move," a sermon he is said to have delivered two hundred and fifty times.

One of Jasper's church members said that the sermon was called forth by an argument between Woodson, the sexton of the church, and another man as to whether or not the sun went around the earth. As was usual with the parishioners, the dispute was referred to the pastor. Jasper studied and used many texts, but the one upon which he chiefly rested was Exodus xv. 3: "The Lord is a man of war; the Lord is his name." It took him half an hour to roam over the Old Testament for examples of the power of God, and even longer to develop his theory. Naturally he gave much attention to Joshua's commanding the sun to stand still. At the height of his discourse he spoke somewhat as follows:

"But I ain't done wid yer yit. As de song says, dere's mo' to foller. I invite yer to hear de fus' verse in de sev'nth chapter of de book of Reverlations. What do John, under de power of de Spirit say? He say he saw fo' angels standin' on de fo' corners of de earth, holdin' de fo' corners of de earth, an' so fo'th. 'Low me to ax ef de earth is roun', whar do it keep its corners? Er flat, squar thing has corners, but tell me whar is de corner of a apple, er a marble, er a cannon ball, er a silver dollar. Ef dere is any of dem pherloserphers whar's been takin' so many cracks at my ol' haid 'bout here, he is corjully invited to step for-'ward an' squar up dis vexin' business. I here tell yer dat yer carn't squar a circle, but it looks lak dese great scholers done learn how to circle de squar. Ef dey kin do it, let 'em step front an' do de trick. But, mer brutherin, in my po' judgment, dey carn't do it; tain't in 'em to do it. Dey is on de wrong side of de Bible; dat's on de outside of de Bible, an' dere's whar de trouble comes in wid 'em. Dey done got out of de bres'wuks of de truf, an' ez long ez dey stay dere, de light of de Lord will not shine on deir path. I ain't keerin' so much 'bout de sun, tho' it's mighty convenient to have it, but my trus' is in de Word of de Lord. Long ez my feet is flat on de solid rock, no man kin move me. I's gettin' my orders f'om de Gawd of my salvation."

One of the white ministers of Richmond well known at the time was the Reverend Dr. William E. Hatcher, pastor of Grace Street Baptist Church. To him we are indebted for the fullest account yet given of the life and work of Jasper. He has told how legislators, ladies of fashion, visitors from out of town, all flocked to hear the famous preacher. One day as he was still some blocks from the church, he was met by the returning tide. "No use of going," he was told; "house already packed, streets full, men fighting and women fainting."

Even with such success Jasper was not a sensationalist. He was ever simple and unaffected, an earnest minister of the gospel, rightly dividing the word of truth. He loved little children and was a comfort to those in sorrow. At the height of career, when the gifts of visitors multiplied the sums in the collection plates, his officers pressed upon him to increase his salary. He finally agreed to accept $62.50 a month and no more.   * * * * *

Jasper knew nothing of homiletics. His sermons were all delivered extemporaneously, though this does not mean that he did not meditate long upon their content. He was chiefly drawn to subjects that gave scope for imagery, such as "Joseph and his Brethren," "Daniel in the Lion's Den," "The Stone Cut out of the Mountain," and "The Raising of Lazarus"; and he had no hesitation about using a theme more than once. He was meticulously careful about the faith of those received into the church; yet, beginning on the island in the James River with nine persons, he closed his ministry with a membership of two thousand. One Sunday he baptized three hundred persons in two hours.

He died at his home in Richmond, 1112 St. James Street, Saturday morning, March 30, 1901, and was buried the following Thursday. On Wednesday the body lay in state in the church. All day long and far into the night a steady line passed in silence. Those who thus did him honor were estimated at about eight thousand. To-day a magnificent monument with a tall shaft is over his grave.

On the day that John Jasper died, one of the landmarks of Richmond, the Jefferson Hotel, was destroyed by fire. The next morning the *Times,* the daily paper of the city, said in an editorial: "It is a sad coincidence that the destruction of the Jefferson Hotel and the death of the Rev. John Jasper should have fallen upon the same day. John Jasper was a Richmond institution, as surely as was Major Ginter's fine hotel. He was a national character, and he and his philosophy were known from one end of the land to the other. Some people have the impression that John Jasper was famous simply because he flew in the face of the scientists and declared that the sun moved. In one sense that is true, but it is also true that his fame was due, in great measure, to a strong personality, to a deep, earnest conviction, as well as to a devout Christian character. Some preachers might have made this assertion about the sun's motion without having attracted any special attention. The people would have laughed over it, and the incident would have passed by as a summer breeze. But John Jasper made an impression on his generation because he was sincerely and deeply in earnest in all that he said. No man could talk with him in private, or listen to him, from the pulpit, without being thoroughly convinced of that fact. His implicit trust in the Bible and everything in it, was beautiful and impressive. He had no other lamp by which his feet were guided. He had no other science, no other philosophy. He took the Bible in its literal significance; he accepted it as the inspired word of God; he trusted it with all his heart and soul and mind; he believed nothing that was in conflict with the teachings of the Bible—scientists and philosophers and theologians to the contrary notwithstanding. . . .He followed his divine calling with faithfulness, with a determination, as far as he could, to make the ways of God known unto men, his saving health among all nations. And the Lord poured upon his servant, Jasper, 'the continual dew of his blessing.' "

ARTHUR HUFF FAUSET (1899-)

Arthur Huff Fauset, born in Flemington, New Jersey, was educated in the Philadelphia public schools, the Philadelphia School of Pedagogy, and the University of Pennsylvania. Since 1918 he has been a teacher in the Philadelphia public schools. He has collected folklore in Nova Scotia and in the Mississippi Delta. He is the author of the prize-winning short story "Symphonesque" (1926), which was republished in the O. Henry Memorial Award volume, *For Freedom: A Biographical Story of the American Negro* (1927), *Folklore from Nova Scotia* (1931), and *Sojourner Truth: God's Faithful Pilgrim* (1938). "Sojourner Truth" is reprinted by permission of the University of North Carolina Press.

Sojourner Truth

SHE WAS A CURIOSITY wherever she went. Her color was both an asset and a liability. People flocked to hear her, because it was such an unusual thing for them to hear a Negro speak; but they were often rude even when they did not mean to be.

One night, after she had spoken in one of the halls in Rochester, she was returning to the home of a friend. A policeman, of small stature, stopped her on the street and demanded her name. This was a surprising request and, coming from this little man, it annoyed her. She paused an instant, then struck the ground firmly with the walking stick she was carrying, and then replied deliberately, in that loud, deep voice which few could imitate, "I am that I am."

Did the policeman really get frightened and imagine that she was some unearthly creature? He hurriedly vanished in the night. Sojourner strode majestically homeward.

She was on one of her many forages into the Middle West. At the close of a meeting in northern Ohio, where she had made some slashing attacks against slave-holding classes, a man approached her and said, "Old woman, do you think that your talk about slavery does any good? Do you suppose that people care what you say? . . . .Why," he went on, "I don't care any more for your talk than I do for the bite of a flea."

That was her opening.

"Perhaps not," she replied, "but the Lord willing, I'll keep you scratching!"

She is addressing a temperance gathering in a town in Kansas. All the while she is speaking she hears dull thud of tobacco juice being spit upon the floor. Her habits of orderliness, developed years ago in the time when she had been a slave, have made her extremely sensitive to this form of slovenliness.

She pauses a moment and looks at the pools of tobacco juice scattered round about the place.

"When I attended the Methodist Church," she tells her audience, "we used to kneel down in the house of God during prayers. Now I ask you, how could anyone kneel down on these floors?"

She gives a vicious look at the offenders and says, "IF Jesus were here he would scourge you from this place."

She has herself to defend on this score, however.

In Iowa, an antitobacco advocate, learning about her own addiction to the weed, propounds a question.

"Do you believe in the Bible?" he asks.

"Of course," she replies.

"Well," says the man, "the Bible tells us that 'no unclean thing can enter the kingdom of Heaven'. Now what can be more filthy than the breath of a smoker?"

Sojourner realizes that she is caught, but her keen mind quickly seizes upon a fitting response.

"Yes, chile," she answers, "but when I goes to Heaven I 'spects to leave my breff behind me."

Sometime later, however, she decided to give up the habit, if only to seem consistent in her own temperance stand.

Some of her roughest experiences were in Indiana. Here was a state which was undecided about the slave issue, but had strong leanings in favor of the institution. Laws were passed forbidding Negroes to enter the state, much less remain or attempt to speak there. Laws, however, unless they originated in Heaven, had no terror for Sojourner.

A group of ruffians had it all arranged to frustrate her attempts to hold meetings. They spread about the town the rumor that Sojourner was an imposter, and that all her anti-slavery activity was a sham to assist the Republicans, which was anathema in that section. Furthermore, they stated that she was not a woman, but a man disguised in woman's clothing!

Sojourner nevertheless attempted to hold a meeting in the meeting-house of the United Brethren, a sect in Indiana. The atmosphere was quite hostile. In the middle of her attempts to speak, a local physician arose and cried out to her, "Hold on. There is a doubt existing in the minds of many persons present respecting the sex of the speaker. My impression is that the majority of the persons present believe the speaker to be a man. I know that this speaker's friends do not think so, but it really is for the speaker's own benefit that I demand that if she is a woman, she submit her breast to the inspection of some of the ladies present, that the doubt may be removed by their testimony.

The wildest confusion ensued.

Many of the ladies in the house were indignant at such a proposal. It had taken most people by surprise, and enemies of the Negro woman felt as highly incensed as her friends. The suggestion was preposterous.

But Sojourner was in complete control of her emotions. She stood quietly and addressed the group once more.

"Why do you suspect me of being a man?" she asked.

"Your voice is not the voice of a woman. It is the voice of a man, and we believe you are a man." A chorus of voices had responded to her inquiry.

The meeting, thus rudely interrupted, was taken over completely by the physician and his mob.

"Let us have a vote on the proposition," he shouted—as if in a democracy even the sex of an individual could be established by means of a majority vote!

"Aye," was the boisterous response.

"The ayes have it!" and thus Sojourner was voted into the male sex.

Sojourner leaped to battle.

"My breasts," she shouted, "have suckled many a white babe, even when they should have been suckling my own. Some of those white babes are now grown men and even though they have suckled my Negro breasts, they are in my opinion far more manly than any of you appear to be.''

Then she disrobed her bosom, and showed her breasts to the public gaze.

"I will show my breasts to the entire congregation," she shouted out to them. "It is not my shame but yours that I should do this. Here, then," she cried, "see for yourselves."

And then as a parting thrust at the rude men, she exclaimed with fiery indignation, "Do you wish also to suck!"

She traveled to another place in Indiana, where the noted abolitionist, Parker Pillsbury, was speaking on the slavery issue. A big thunderstorm overtook the meeting. Outside, the rain beat upon the roof of the church; the wind blew with great violence, crashing the branches of trees against the church edifice.

Between two mammoth peals of thunder, a young Methodist arose and interrupted Pillsbury, who had continued speaking despite the fury of the elements. The young man was very much perturbed. Probably he knew of Pillsbury's atheistic leanings.

"I am alarmed," he said, "I feel as if God's judgment is about to fall upon me for daring to sit and hear such blasphemy. It makes my hair almost rise from terror."

And then a voice, sounding above the rain and all the noise of the violent storm, shouted over to him, "Chile, don't be skeered; you are not going to be harmed. I don't spec' God's even hearn tell on ye!"

Fort Sumter is history.

A rather cynical friend approaches her and asks, "What business are you now following?"

Quick as a flash she retorts, "Years ago, when I lived in New York City, my occupation was scouring brass door knobs; but now I go about scouring copperheads!"

Sojourner Truth may have been the direct cause of the change in attitude towards "Jim Crow" in the street cars of Washington.

She was out with a white friend, Mrs. Laura Haviland, who proposed that they ride in the cars. Both of them understood that a Negro and a white person could not ride in the same car; therefore, when Mrs. Haviland signalled for the approaching vehicle, Sojourner stepped over to one side as if she were going to continue walking but when the car stopped, she ran and jumped aboard.

The conductor pushed her back.

"Get out of the way," he yelled at her, "and let the lady come aboard."

"I am a lady, too," remonstrated Sojourner.

The conductor made no reply to this remark, and Sojourner remained on the car.

A little later it was necessary to change cars. A man was coming out of the second car as Sojourner and her friend jumped aboard. He turned to the conductor and asked, "Are niggers allowed to ride?"

The conductor grabbed Sojourner by the shoulder, and jerked her around, at the same time ordering her to get off of the car.

Sojourner said, "I will not."

The conductor started to put her off.

Mrs. Haviland said, "Don't put her out of the car."

"Does she belong to you?" asked the conductor.

"No," replied Sojourner's friend, "she belongs to humanity."

"Then take her and go," the irate official said, as he pushed Sojourner up against the door.

Sojourner was furious.

"I will let you know," she said, "whether you can treat me like a dog."

Then turning to her friend, she continued, "Take the number of this car."

This surprise remark by Sojourner frightened the conductor, and he did not utter another word.

But when Sojourner returned to the hospital, it was discovered that a bone in her shoulder was dislocated as a result of the conductor's rude treatment.

Sojourner made a complaint to the president of the car line, and he advised her to have the conductor arrested. This she did, and the Freedmen's Bureau provided her with a lawyer to argue the case. The conductor was dismissed.

Not long after this incident, the Jim Crow rule was abolished in street cars, and there was a noticeable difference in the attitude of most of the conductors towards Negro riders.

Nevertheless, the possibility of trouble was already present. For instance, not long after the Jim Crow cars were removed, she signalled for a car, but the motorman, observing that she was black, pretended not to see her, and went on. The same thing occurred when a second car approached. By this time the enraged Sojourner with typical ingenuity cried out as loudly as her bellowing voice would carry, "I want to ride! I want to ride!"

At the sound of this unusual noise, all traffic in the very congested street stopped. People blocked the side-walks to see what was happening, and carriages halted in the middle of the street. Before the trolley car could proceed on its way any farther, Sojourner had jumped aboard.

The conductor was furious.

"Go forward with the horses," he shouted at the now gloating woman, "or I will put you out."

Sojourner sat herself calmly down, then replied with all the queenliness of a visitor from heaven, "I am a passenger."

"Go forward where the horses are," the conductor thundered, "or I will throw you out."

The intrepid battler rose in all the proud dignity of a member of one of the first families of New York.

"I am no Marylander," she retorted, "nor Virginian. I am not afraid of your threats. I am from the Empire State of New York and I know the laws as well as you."

The astonished conductor retreated at this display of self-assurance, but some soldiers who were on the car taunted him, and made a point of informing every passenger who entered the car, "You should have heard that old woman talk to the conductor."

Sojourner rode even farther than she needed to, thinking that she might as well make the most of her disputed ride. As she alighted from the car she cried, "Bless God! I have had a ride!" . . .

One day Sojourner was returning from Georgetown with one of the hospital nurses. They boarded an empty car at the station, and waited for it to leave. A little while later two white women came in and sat opposite Sojourner. On observing the Negro couple, they began to whisper to each other, looking scornfully in Sojourner's direction. The nurse, who still entertained illusions about white folks, became frightened, and hung her head almost to her lap; but Sojourner gazed fearlessly in front of her.

A few minutes later, one of the white women faintly called to the conductor and asked, "Conductor, does niggers ride in these cars?"

The conductor looked about him hesitatingly.

"Ye-e-s," he replied.

" 'Tis a shame and a disgrace," the woman said. "They ought to have a nigger car on this track."

Sojourner interrupted at this point, saucily and regally.

"Of course colored people ride in the cars," she said. "Street cars are made for poor white and colored folks. Carriages are for ladies and gentlemen."

Through the window she discerned a carriage. Pointing to it she remarked scornfully, "See those carriages. They will take you three or four miles for six pence—and then you talk of a nigger car!"

The women were more embarrassed than they cared to admit. They abruptly left their seats and alighted from the car.

"Ah," Sojourner shouted at them gleefully, "now they are going to take a carriage. . . . Good bye, ladies!"

ANGELINA W. GRIMKÉ (1880-)

Angelina Weld Grimké (see also p. 341) here describes her father in
one of the few intimate biographical sketches in the
literature of the Negro.

A Biographical Sketch of Archibald H. Grimke

SEVENTY-FIVE YEARS AGO, the seventeenth of last August [1925], my
father was born on his father's plantation, "Caneacre," thirteen miles
out of Charleston, S. C. He was the eldest of three sons. Henry
Grimké, his father, was a member of one of Charleston's aristocratic
families; Nancy Weston Grimké, his mother, was a slave by birth,
but a most remarkable woman. I knew her for the only time, the last
year of her life (she lived to be eighty-four) and though I was a child,
then, I can remember her perfectly. She spent her days, sitting in a
large rattan rocker in her sunny room on the second floor back of
my uncle's Washington home. She moved about seldom and then
with the greatest effort, leaning on a cane; but there was something
unconquerable, indomitable in that bent, gaunt body and in that clean-
cut, eagle-like face. If she yielded to age it was only inch by inch.
Her keen old eyes could flash and I never heard her speak in uncertain tones. Once she had been beautiful. My father has a picture of
her in her early forties, I should say, and there is that in her face
and her bearing that is truly regal. Doubters in reincarnation should
have known her. Sometime, somewhere, that spirit must have lived in
the body of a great queen or an empress. How else explain her? But
the most beautiful thing about her was her motherly love. It was the
guiding passion, the driving force in her long life. There was literally
no sacrifice she would not have made for her children. In defense of
them she would have torn an enemy to pieces. I never saw my Uncle
John, until I looked down at his dead face in his coffin; but often and
often, I have heard both my father and my uncle pay respect and
the highest and finest tribute that can be paid to any woman—that
what they are they owe mainly to her, her teachings and her love. A
vivid, powerful, unselfish personality. . . .

When my father was three or four years old, my grandmother
moved to a little house on Cummings Street in Charleston. It was
simple, crude even, for they were very poor; but when did poverty
even bother boys much? These were mainly happy years for them,

the source, now, of many a pleasant and laugh provoking recollection. Here the little family lived until 1865.

I have never seen a picture of my father as a little boy but he has been described to me. He was not robust in appearance (he was too sensitive, too highly-strung to be that) but he was wiry and possessed that indispensable quality, vitality. His face framed in auburn curls had the deceiving gentleness, I have been told, of a young angel's. I use the expression "deceiving gentleness" advisedly, as shall be seen.

As the years passed, Cummings Street came to know the three Grimké boys. No, not because they loved church and Sunday school and washed their faces and hands and behind their ears and kept their clothes clean and in spotless condition, but because of all the fighters in the street, they were the greatest. Each was an adept in his line and invincible in it. My uncle John was the champion "butter"; my uncle Frank the champion "biter" and my father the champion "kicker." The trio always fought in unison, an attack on one being an attack on all. Against such a versatile Grimké army what could the other boys do? Nothing on the street dared to appear aggressive even. A good many years have passed since then, but the Grimké brothers are fighters to this day, pens and tongues proving as efficient weapons as teeth and feet.

Before the Civil War, the three brothers learnt their "Three R's" in a sedate little school conducted by some white southern gentlemen of Charleston for the children of free colored people. After the war, as was to be expected, a great change came into the lives of the little family. It began in this way. Gilbert Pillsbury, the brother of the famous abolitionist, Parker Pillsbury, and himself an abolitionist, came to Charleston from the North to be its first mayor during the Reconstruction Period. With him came his wife, Frances, who opened, for the colored youth of the city, what was known as the Morris Street School. To this school went the three boys. They were good students and successful, but the most important part of this experience was that they gained a lasting and powerful friend in Mrs. Pillsbury. So interested did she become that she finally determined that the two boys who were the eldest, Archibald and Francis, should go North to get their education.

My father was sixteen, then, and my uncle Frank fifteen, when after many prayers and much heartbreak and the final consent of the ambitious, self-sacrificing mother, they set their faces toward the North and went eagerly to seek their Great Adventure. There is always something pathetic about confident youth setting forth to conquer the world, their trust in themselves and in their stars is so high and they never, never suspect that sooner or later just around some innocently appearing corner, Disappointment is lying in wait. It was "sooner" rather than "later" for the two boys. Mrs. Pillsbury had sent them, as she supposed, into families where in return for work done by them they would be educated. My father spent six months in Peacedale, R. I., in a pleasant enough family and my uncle in Stoneham, Mass., but the longed for opening to their education never appeared. In the meantime, the mother feeling, as it seemed to her, that she had made the sacrifice of separation for nothing, from her children, went to see Mrs. Pillsbury. The result of this visit was, that Mrs. Pillsbury took up the cudgels again for them and, although President Isaac N. Rendall felt they were entirely too young, she was finally instrumental in getting them into Lincoln University.

The four years which followed were happy enough for the two boys. A new universe was theirs, a new outlook on life and lasting friendships. It was not always that it was an easy matter to make both ends meet: they had to work during their summers either at waiting or teaching little country schools in the South, but all this seemed merely to add a zest to their happiness. They enjoyed their studies to the full; they enjoyed all the school activities and, of course, all the usual horse play and fun of college boys. Here they had their first lessons in leadership. At first President Rendall watched the boys from afar. What he saw interested him. Soon interest became love and between them, on the one hand, and the dear old gentleman on the other, there grew up a most beautiful friendship. Whenever and wherever he could, he helped them. Through him they became student-teachers and my father was made the only colored librarian Lincoln ever had, for Lincoln is the sole colored university with neither a colored professor nor a colored trustee [1925].

In Hyde Park, Mass., at this time, were living two sisters, Angelina and Sarah Grimké, sisters also of Henry Grimké, the father of these boys. Angelina was married to the brilliant anti-slavery orator, Theodore D. Weld. Sarah, the elder sister, felt exactly as she did, and these two utterly inexperienced women, carefully sheltered from birth, broke without a qualm with their traditions and their family, came North and joined themselves to the abolitionists. A correspondence began between Angelina and the boys and, in their junior year, accompanied by her son, Stuart, she came to visit them. She now did a thing that seems well nigh unbelievable. Becoming convinced that these boys were her brother's children, she acknowledged them as her nephews! More, upon their graduation she invited them to visit her and her family in Hyde Park.

They went. They often laugh, now, over the picture they must have made to the astonished eyes of the Weld family that was the simplest of the simple in manner, dress and living. To the boys this was a great occasion, the greatest in all their lives and, cost what it might, they were determined to live up to it. They were virtually penniless, but each carried a cane, wore a high silk hat which had been made to order, and boots that were custom-made. Whatever the aunts and the Welds thought, they were welcomed with wide open arms and hearts and made at home. The simplicity here soon taught them their lesson.

But this Boston experience had a much more far-reaching effect upon the life of my father. At the end of their visit they both returned to Lincoln where my father took both his A.B. and M.A., but a love for Boston and the North had entered into his blood, and he was happy enough when his Aunt Sarah decided in 1872 that he should return and attend Harvard Law School. His second and last year, for the course then was two years, he won a scholarship. Upon his graduation in 1874 there came a slight rift between him and the aunts over where he should practice. They believed his chances would be much better in the South; but he, knowing what it meant to be, for the first time, a free man, was not a bit inclined to leave Boston. Luckily for him, at this time, a Mrs. Walling, with whom he had lived in Cambridge while a student, came to his rescue and interested the well-known lawyer, William I. Bowditch, in him, who, from the goodness and kindness of a big heart, admitted the young man into his office.

Those first years, after graduation, were hard ones. The practice of law, at best, for a beginner is not an easy matter. When richer in knowledge, he left Mr. Bowditch, he made his start in partnership with James H. Wolff. Later on he formed a new alliance with Butler R. Wilson, but it was hard sledding, indeed, those early days. In 1879 he married and beginning with 1883, for two years he published and edited, with the aid of Butler R. Wilson, a colored newspaper called "The Hub." It was in 1884 that he was sent to the Republican National Convention as Henry Cabot Lodge's alternate delegate at large. This was the convention where both Lodge and Roosevelt, as young men, were winning their spurs.

In 1882, he had moved from Boston and gone to live in Hyde Park, then a suburb, but now a part of greater Boston. It is here that my own memories of my father begin. "Tanglewood" was the name of the modest two-story grey house owned by a couple in their way as lovable as any I have known. Their name was Leverett. They lived down stairs and we, up. Some of my pleasantest recollections are of what would be called now, our living room—the drawn shades, the yellow lamp light, the big coal stove, the wind or rain or snow without pounding against the six windows and our "reading-time."

It was at the big table in the center of this room that he wrote his articles for "The Boston Herald" and "The Boston Traveller"; and it was here that he wrote, for the "True Reformer Series," published by Funk and Wagnalls, his two books, "The Life of William Lloyd Garrison" and "The Life of Charles Sumner."

In 1894 all these pleasant days came to an end, for it was at this time that President Cleveland appointed him as Consul to Santo Domingo. Four years he was in Santo Domingo. Of that time personally, I know nothing, as I was too young to be taken with him; but I do not know whether he enjoyed the tropics as much as his days which were busy, eventful and happy ones. His one big achievement was the settling of a law suit over a bridge in favor of an American citizen named McKay, a suit that had been pending for years and a source of great annoyance to this government. In 1898 he returned to this country and has been here ever since.

In 1919, at Cleveland, he received the "Spingarn Medal," awarded him for a life long service to his race. President Thwing of Western Reserve College made the speech and presented the medal and Oswald Garrison Villard came the whole way to Cleveland to be present, as a friend, at the ceremony.

As I said in the beginning, he is seventy-five years old now. He thinks his work is over. I do not agree with him. Perhaps he may come to agree with me. Many men have done things and great things after seventy-five. He spends his days sitting in the sunlight. He reads and he thinks. Whatever else may be said about him he has the satisfaction of knowing that his life is open to the inspection of any man; that he has been a consistent and uncompromising fighter, all his life, for the welfare of his race as he has seen it; that the fight has been a good one, a clean one and above board, unmarred by any pettiness and treachery; that he has never turned a deaf ear to anyone who has come to him with a just cause; that as a true friend, himself, he has made true friends; and if all men do not love him, they respect him. Pleasant, pleasant thoughts these.

As his daughter, it is not for me to say whether what he has said or done or written is going to live—but I know what I think.

EDWARD ARNOLD (1863-)

One of Dunbar's staunchest friends in Washington was Edward Arnold, who, at the time, was in the service of the United States Government. His reminiscences of his gifted friend are an example of a type of writing strangely neglected by Negroes. A large number of anecdotes about such figures as Frederick Douglass, Booker T. Washington, Bert Williams, and Paul Laurence Dunbar are told by men who knew them well, but few of these get into print. They would help greatly in rounding out the pictures we have of such men. "Some Reminiscences of Paul Laurence Dunbar" was first printed in *The Journal of Negro History,* from which it is reprinted by the permission of the author and Carter G. Woodson, the editor.

Some Personal Reminiscences of Paul Laurence Dunbar

IT HAS BEEN SAID by some one that "to grow great, to bring out the best in ourselves, a knowledge of the lives of the great is imperative." They give us a sense of direction through life's wilderness as well as the courage to press on. This has been the experience of our race. The race had proven itself gifted in music, oratory and in some other arts, but as William Dean Howells expresses it, Paul Dunbar was the only man of pure African blood and of American civilization to feel the Negro life aesthetically and to express it lyrically; and that a race which had come to this effect in any member of it, had attained civilization in him. His poem "Ere Sleep Comes down to Soothe the Weary Eye" is a production worthy of the greatest. And as Col. Robert Ingersoll says,—It is as profound as "Thanatopsis" and as musical as "Hiawatha."

As an educator, Dunbar taught the world the essential unity of the human race, which does not think or feel black in one and white in another, but humanly in all. He gave our poetry which had hitherto been faintly expressed in music a full and complete literary interpretation.

At one time he had thought of taking up the law as a profession and also that of the ministry as a calling; but later in writing to a friend of his great aspiration he said, "My all absorbing desire is to be a worthy singer of the songs of God and of nature. To be able to interpret my own people through song and story, and to prove to the many that after all we are more human than African." He discussed such things with me. In this paper, then, I want to speak of Paul

Dunbar as I knew him, as I knew of his bigness of heart, his gentleness of soul and his everlasting gratitude to those who helped him in any way as he struggled onward and upward. A simple act of kindness on my part in the loan of a paltry sum of money, when he was friendless, poor and unknown, was the beginning of a friendship that lasted until the day of his death. It was the greatest investment I ever made in all my life.

To be able to stand up and talk and at the same time to think clearly while on your feet, to be able to sit down and write and at the same time to think through while writing is a gift as rare as it is unusual. Paul Dunbar had this gift. I once saw in a barber shop a sign— "Hair cuts while you wait." Mr. Dunbar could have written a sign somewhat similar to this. "Poems while you wait." I can better illustrate this by telling the following story.

I remembered being at Paul's home one afternoon, when an old ante-bellum friend of his who lived in the "Camp," a Negro settlement at the foot of Howard University, came in. He was very fond of these old-timers, and often used to invite them in when passing his home, give them a glass of beer, and listen to their stories about times down South "Before the War."

On this occasion this old man told a story of how down in Alabama where he was born, a nephew of his had been falsely accused of rape; how the "night riders" took him from jail and strung him up on a limb of a giant oak that stood by the side of the road. In a few weeks thereafter the leaves on this limb turned yellow and dropped off, and the bough itself gradually withered and died while the other branches of the tree grew and flourished. For years in that section this tree was known as the "haunted oak." The story so impressed Paul that when the old man had finished telling it he exclaimed, "That is too good a story to be forgotten! I am going to write a poem on the 'Haunted Oak.'"

Immediately drawing up his chair to his desk he picked up a lead pencil and commenced to scribble on a piece of paper. This interesting and beautiful poem, "The Haunted Oak," was the result of that effort.

It has been frequently said of Dunbar that on more than one occasion he was under the influence of liquor while giving a recital. This is true. It is also true that there was a real cause behind this drinking, a cause beyond that which actuates the ordinary drinker. This gifted man had lung trouble. Often he had severe hemorrhages which he concealed from his family and friends. At such times he drank, especially if he had an engagement, with the hope that the stimulants would bolster him up and enable him to go through with his program.

On several occasions this method failed and caused him a great deal
of embarrassment, humiliation, and shame. In this connection, I am
reminded of an incident that occurred in February, 1900. At that time
the *Philadelphia Press* engaged him to go to the Tuskegee Institute
and report the proceedings of the annual conference of Negro farmers.
When the time came for him to leave for the South, he was in a pretty
bad condition, in no condition to go—in fact, did not and could not
attend this conference. Getting himself together two days later, he sat
down in his library and wrote up that conference and sent it on to
the *Philadelphia Press.* Fortunately for him he had attended this annual
Negro conference the previous year and so with the assistance of the
printed program which had been sent him his imagination did the
rest. . . .

In the spring of 1898 Paul received from a wealthy society woman
of Albany, New York, a very flattering offer to give a recital. This
was the first time he had asked and received $100.00 and expenses for
an evening's reading.

He told me of arriving on this occasion in Albany about six o'clock
in the evening, of the funny experience he had with the colored bus
driver of the Kenmore Hotel where a reservation had been made for
him, how when he stepped in the bus, the driver asked him what he
was going there for, whether he was going there to work. When Paul
told him that he was not going there to work, that he was going there
to stop, the old fellow with a grunt and a shake of his head drew the
reins on his horses and started up the street.

Arriving at the place, Paul walked up to the desk, picked up a
pen, and attempted to register.

"Hold on there!" the clerk said to him, "what are you going
to do?"

"To register, of course," Paul replied.

"You can't register here; we have no rooms for you in this hotel."

"Oh yes you have. A reservation has been made for me in this hotel.
I am Paul Laurence Dunbar."

That was at a time when outside of the literary world Paul was
scarcely known, and his name conveyed nothing to the hotel clerk.
However, turning to his files, the clerk found that Mrs. X, one of
the wealthiest society women of the city, had engaged the most expensive suite of rooms in the hotel for Paul Laurence Dunbar, poet, with
no reference to his race, color, or previous condition. Puzzled, the clerk
rushed back to the manager's office to explain the situation. The manager came to the front and looking Paul up and down said, "This
Negro is crazy, telephone to the police station and let them come up

and get him." At this juncture Mrs. X. arrived on the scene and relieved him from further embarrassment.

Paul was married March 6, 1898, in New York City by Bishop Potter of the Episcopal Church to Miss Alice Ruth Moore of New Orleans, a handsome talented young school teacher, who had attained some distinction in letters. His announcement cards were sent out April 18. Two days later April 20, 1898, my marriage took place in Baltimore, and at my reception that night we decided to "turn out" the following Sunday morning by going together to St. Luke's Episcopal Church in Washington.

In the old days your first public appearance with your bride was called your "turning out," giving the public a chance to look you and your bride over. In front of the church, as we passed out that Sunday morning, was a young fellow well known about town, who facetiously remarked: "There go the two ugliest grooms with the two prettiest brides I have seen in many a day."

Paul was a great lover of children; he had the child heart. During the weeks and months that went by after our marriage, we often talked about our hoped-for sons and daughters, and what we desired them to be. So when I became an expectant father, I told him I was sure it was going to be a boy, and his name was to be Paul Laurence Arnold. "And I am going to be his god-father," he laughingly replied. But alas! the boy was a girl, and so we consoled ourselves by naming her Sara Pauline.

Dunbar was fond of society. He loved music and dancing. I recall how glad he was to have me present his name for membership in the Bachelor-Benedict Club. This was in 1899 when the late Dr. M. O. Dumas was president of the club. But the dance he loved best was his "war dance" which he would stage occasionally at his home. This dance would come after a buffet supper to eight or ten of his close friends. When everything was in readiness, he would stand in the center of the floor, his friends would circle about him and commence to clap, pat, shout and chant to the tune of the "Georgia Camp Meeting." Paul would remain motionless for a few seconds, suddenly he would leap into the air and then the "dance was on." It was a sight never to be forgotten to see his lithe slender form, his wonderful eyes as they gave expression to the emotions of his heart—to see him jump up and down with an abandon, a rhythm of movement which showed that his very soul responded to the music of the claps and shouts about him.

In the fall of 1899 Paul was in such a bad condition that his doctor advised him to go to Denver, Colorado. He did so; his wife and mother accompanied him. Although he went to Colorado for rest and recreation—went, where he hoped, for balmy days and peaceful nights, he was destined to face disappointment. That feverish desire to write came over him and gave him no rest. It was while in Denver he wrote his novel, *The Love of Landry*. I treasure this novel very highly. One of the reasons is that he sent me one of the first copies off the press and wrote on the fly leaf, "To my friend Ed. from Paul."

I also treasured very highly the beautiful letters he used to write me while in Denver. This wonderful country, as he described it, "with great rolling illimitable plains, and bleak mountains standing up like hoary sentinels guarding the land" was beautiful beyond description. Speaking of Denver he wrote, "The city where so many hopes are blighted, where so many dreams come true, where so many fortunes go up and so many lives go down. Denver, over which nature broods with mystic calm, and through which humanity struggles with hot strenuous life." . . .

When Paul and his wife were out of town, as they were a great deal, it was my custom to go by and spend some time with his mother. I remember calling there one morning and found her busy ironing. The first thing she said was, "My! Mr. Arnold, I must hurry and get this ironing out of the way, for I have a hard day's work before me. I must write to my boy Paul." When I saw her sit down and struggle with that pen trying to put her thoughts on paper with beads of perspiration rolling down her kindly face, I fully realized what she meant by saying, "I have a hard day's work before me."

When Paul returned to the city, he thanked me for addressing the letter to him from his mother and then smilingly said, "Nobody on earth but me could read that letter; yet I can decipher what she is trying to write me."

What a beautiful relationship existed between mother and son. And as expressed by one writer, "No good Angel in human guise ever more faithfully fulfilled a heavenly mission than did she through all the weary years of her son's long illness."

Despite his weaknesses, Paul Dunbar had a deep religious nature. He loved to sit in the evenings at twilight and join in when his mother sang, "When Malindy Sings," and the good old hymns in the the good old way. It was in this vein that two or three months before his death he wrote this beautiful little poem—

> Lead gently Lord and Slow
> For fear that I may fall
> I know not where to go
> Unless I hear Thy call.

> My fainting soul doth yearn
> For thy green hills afar—
> So let thy mercy burn—
> My greater guiding Star.

His friends were legion; the rich and the poor, the high and the low, all loved him alike. Numbered among his friends were statesmen, authors, poets, orators, doctors, preachers, inventors, lawyers, and men and women in the lowly walks of life. But to my mind there are two men who stand out above all the rest, who had possibly the greatest influence of any upon his life and work. I refer to Dr. H. A. Tobey and Hon. Brand Whitlock. Dr. Tobey was Superintendent of the State Hospital at Toledo, and Mr. Whitlock was Mayor of that city.

During my years of close friendship with Dunbar, I listened to him talk of these two men over and over again. He told me of the personal interest they took in all his affairs, how they helped him financially, how they helped him socially, and gave him the inspiration to struggle on. It was to them that Paul went in all his troubles. "But for them," he said, "I fear I could never have made it; we have walked and talked and drunk and eaten together for nights and days at a time." These three men lived in a world all of their own making, far removed from the ken of ordinary mortals.

On February 10, 1906, this short overshadowed life came to an end. At the funeral of Paul Dunbar Dr. Tobey said, "I never loved a man so much. Golden Rule Jones, Brand Whitlock and myself, we three were great cronies, because we were cranks, I suppose, but we took Paul in and made him one of us." Dr. Tobey then read a letter written him by Mr. Whitlock who was unable to attend the funeral on account of the serious illness of his aged mother. Let me quote some messages from that remarkable letter as it reveals the close tie that bound these men together.

Dear Dr. Tobey:

I wish I could be with you all tomorrow to pay my tribute to poor Paul. If friendship knew obligation, I would acknowledge my debt to you for the boon of knowing Paul Dunbar. It is one of the countless good deeds to your credit that you were among the first to recognize the poet in him and help him to a larger and freer life.

You and I know something of his deeper sufferings, something of the disease that really killed him. I can never forget the things he said about this that last evening we spent together. That last evening he recited his "Ships that Pass in the Night." You will remember I sat and listened sadly conscious that I would not hear him often again, knowing that voice would soon be mute. I can hear him now and see the expression on his fine face as he said "Passing! Passing!" It was prophetic.

Dunbar sleeps in the beautiful Woodland Cemetery, overlooking the city of Dayton which he loved so well. God keeps his gentle soul and may he find in that world where the "spirits of just men are made perfect" that rest which on earth he never knew!

Ella Wheeler Wilcox loved Dunbar's "the Warrior's Prayer," and he considered it one of his best poems. At the close of a delightful interview with Mrs. Wilcox she asked Paul to recite "The Warrior's Prayer." He graciously complied. At the conclusion of the performance she threw her left arm across his shoulders and with her right arm raised high above her head she cried, "Go on, Paul, go on."

ESLANDA GOODE ROBESON

In 1930 Eslanda Goode Robeson, herself a scholar, wrote a biography of her husband, *Paul Robeson, Negro,* which narrates all phases of Robeson's career. Much, of course, has happened in the decade since 1930, but the biography is a good introduction to one of the best-known American Negroes. Robeson was born in Princeton, New Jersey, in 1898. At Rutgers, from which he was graduated in 1919, he took honors in oratory and debating, was a member of the Glee Club and of Phi Beta Kappa, and was a four-letter man, winning a place on Walter Camp's All-American team. In 1923 he was graduated from the Columbia Law School; however, he turned to the theatre and the concert stage for a career. The selection below, printed here by permission of the author, and of Harper & Brothers, treats of the beginning of this career. Since then he has played *Othello* in London and *John Henry* in New York; he has also played in many motion pictures, a Hollywood version of *The Emperor Jones* among them.

[Paul Robeson and the Provincetowners]

. . . THE "something that turned up" this time was an invitation to play Eugene O'Neill's *All God's Chillun Got Wings* and *The Emperor Jones* at the Provincetown Theatre. The Provincetown Players were really responsible for Paul's choice of the stage as a career. They form one of the most intelligent, sincere, and non-commercial of the artistic groups in America. The group is made up of some of the most interesting figures in the American Theatre: George Cram Cook and Susan Glaspell, the founders, Eugene O'Neill, Robert Edmond Jones, Eleanor

Fitzgerald, James Light, John Reed, Edna St. Vincent Millay, Theodore Dreiser, Harry Kemp, Cleon Throckmorton were some of its first members. The group was originated at a wharf in Provincetown, Massachusetts, by a small number of people who wanted to write, produce, and act their own plays. "To-day, after twelve years," says the manifesto of the Provincetown Players for 1929, "it still continues its original policy, and has successfully established and maintained a stage where playwrights of sincere, poetic, literary and dramatic purposes can see their plays in action and superintend their production without submitting to the commercial managers' interpretation of public taste. Equally it has afforded an opportunity for actors, producers, scenic and costume designers to experiment with a stage of extremely simple resources—it being the idea of the Players that elaborate settings are unnecessary to bring out the essential qualities of a good play. The Provincetowners wrote and produced plays entirely for intellectual and artistic self-expression and experiment, and all the group fell to work to get the most good and the most fun out of each experiment. They have maintained this enthusiasm for their experiment throughout twelve years of their existence." They naturally attracted people like themselves to their little group. It is small wonder that when Paul Robeson came to work with them he fell under their spell, and through them has remained under the spell of the theatre ever since.

When he began rehearsals, during the spring of 1924, in the famous little theatre in Macdougal Street, his first friends were James Light, Eugene O'Neill, Eleanor Fitzgerald, and Harold McGhee. At Jimmy's or Fitzy's or Gig's he had long talks with O'Neill about *Jones* and *Chillun,* about the meaning of the plays, about the purpose of the theatre. As he knew them better the talk drifted to the theatre in general, to life in general. They felt the existing commercial theatre, with its stock ways of presenting its unimaginative material, had nothing to give—except perhaps a superficial kind of entertainment. They felt a truly important and artistic theatre should not only present life, but should interpret it, should help people know and understand each other, should introduce people to atmospheres, human beings, and emotions they had not known before—thus widening their intellectual, emotional, and spiritual experience and colouring their lives; should help people find more things of beauty in the world and in life. They were deeply interested in the modern expressionistic theatre of the Germans. "Why must a play be necessarily confined to three acts," protested Gene, "when the life you are thinking about may happen in scenes, or in many long acts?" Gene broke away from the conventional rules of playwrighting in many of his experiments. When he wrote *The Emperor Jones,* in eight powerful staccato scenes, the Provincetowners enthusiastically produced it. It was much shorter than the usual play, lasting only one hour and a half in all. "Too short," said the commercial managers. When he wrote *Strange Interlude,* in nine long acts, the commercial managers protested that the public would never sit through a play lasting nearly five hours. "Too long," they said. Both these plays have achieved world-wide artistic and financial success.

Paul began to sense vaguely how great plays were written. When a sensitive, gifted artist like Gene went into a community, or witnessed a human experience, or felt the powerful influences of nature, he reacted emotionally to them; because of his great gift he could go back to the theatre, and, with characters, conversation, scenes, and acts re-create that community, or person, or feeling of the sea so successfully that he could make the people who saw his play know and understand and sympathise with that community, or person, or the sea as he did; and perhaps feel, according to their sensitivity, at least some of the emotional reactions he felt. This knowledge gave Paul an entirely new conception of the theatre. As a spectator and as an actor it meant infinitely more to him. He could now get more from a play and give more to a play.

There were many long, lazy, fascinating talks. Gene had been nearly all over the world, had seen and done many interesting things; they all knew many interesting people—among them some of the great personalities of the present. Paul would listen eagerly for hours, for days, for weeks. Meantime they worked on the plays. Jimmy was vastly different from the usual director: he never told Paul what to do nor showed him how to do it. He never told him what to say; he merely sat quietly in the auditorium and let him feel his way; he often helped him, of course. When Paul had trouble with a speech Jimmy would sit down on a soap-box beside him on the empty stage, and they would analyse the speech thought by thought, word by word. "I think Gene means so and so," Jimmy would say, and they would argue and discuss. Very often Gene himself would come in to help them. Again Jimmy would call out, "Let yourself go, Paul. Don't hold yourself in; you look as though you're afraid to move." "I am," Paul would answer; "I'm so big I feel if I take a few steps I'll be off this tiny stage." "Then just take two steps, but make them fit you. You must have complete freedom and control over your body and your voice, if you are to control your audience," explained Jimmy. They tore the lines to pieces and Paul built them up again for himself, working out his own natural movements and gestures with Jimmy's watchful help.

"I can't tell you what to do," said Jimmy, "but I can help you find what's best for you." Paul was able to bring to both *Chillun* and *Jones* not only a thorough understanding of the script itself and its intent, given him by Gene and Jimmy, but also further racial understanding of the characters. When he came at last to the performance, he never had to *remember* anything; he went freely and boldly ahead, secure in the knowledge that he knew and understood the character he was portraying. So that, at the age of twenty-six and very inexperienced, he was immediately acclaimed by the leading dramatic critics in New York as one of America's finest actors.

* * * * *

Even more gratifying and encouraging than the generous praise of the critics was a note written by his friend on the fly-leaf of the book containing his plays:

"In gratitude to Paul Robeson, in whose interpretation of Brutus Jones I have found the most complete satisfaction an author can get— that of seeing his creation born into flesh and blood; and in whose creation of Jim Harris in my *All God's Chillun Got Wings* I found not only complete fidelity to my intent under trying circumstances, but, beyond that, true understanding and racial integrity. Again with gratitude and friendship.—EUGENE O'NEILL, 1925."

This book is now one of Paul's most treasured possessions.

With his success in the plays Paul's interest in the theatre grew. He loved the life and the spirit of the group in Macdougal Street. Their freedom of mind, their friendliness, their informality, their complete lack of any kind of routine or system or efficiency in its irritating sense, charmed him at first and then appealed to him deeply. Their leisurely, lazy life suited his own temperament perfectly. Their lives seemed to be one long round of lunches or dinners or suppers in the little food shops in "The Village," where prices were very moderate and the food and wine or beer excellent, and where one could sit indefinitely and talk, and greet friends and talk some more—sometimes even the proprietor joining in the discussion; and innumerable parties in the theatre sitting-room, or in the studio or flat of one of "the crows." Yet how they worked when anything was to be done. Gene would disappear completely while he was writing a play. When a play was to be put on, all hands galvanised into action; every member of the group would report personally, and perhaps bring friends to help do the work; everyone lent a hand wherever he or she could; circulars were planned, printed, addressed, and mailed; mailing lists checked over; scenery constructed and painted; lighting systems

worked out; costumes planned and executed; the box office and telephones attended regularly. No one was too unimportant to give valuable suggestions. Sewing machines hummed, telephones rang, gay
voices buzzed all day and evening for weeks in the theatre before an
opening. Jimmy worked relentlessly whipping the play into shape;
everyone reported promptly for rehearsals and worked seriously and
eagerly. Then, after the successful opening, everyone would join in the
inevitable party of celebration; the round of sociable meals, parties, and
long, lazy talks about everything under the sun would begin again.

VIII
ESSAYS

ESSAYS

NEGROES AND their defenders in the early nineteenth century naturally considered the first use of history to be the stirring of race pride. American analogues to the Henri Grégoire's *De la littérature des nègres* (translated in 1810) sketched the careers of Negro notables, and were essentially biographical rather than historical. It might be stated that this was the period when many historians wrote as if history consisted chiefly of the biographies of distinguished men.

Many years went by before a Negro could be found able and willing to do the requisite research and interpretation of the historian. Acting upon a suggestion of Whittier, William C. Nell (see p. 639) published a pamphlet, *Services of Colored Americans in the Wars of 1776 and 1812* (1851). In 1855 he brought out a larger work, *The Colored Patriots of the American Revolution, with Sketches of Several Distinguished Colored Persons: to Which is Added a Brief Survey of the Condition and Prospects of Colored Americans*. The long title is indicative of what was to be for a long time the concern of the Negro historian, namely, the Negro's military service, biographical sketches of the few Negroes who had risen out of the rut, and a discussion of the "race problem."

In 1841, James McCune Smith wrote on subjects that were to be high favorites with Negro historians in a *Lecture on the Haytien Revolution With a Sketch of Touissant L' Ouverture*. Early church history was written by William T. Catto, who in 1857 recorded the history of the Presbyterian movement among Philadelphia Negroes, and by William Douglass, who in 1862 recorded the Annals of the First African Church in the United States of America. J. W. C. Pennington's earliest work was a history for school children, arranged in question-answer form, called *A Text Book of the Origin and History of the Colored People* (1841).

William Wells Brown early turned his versatile pen to the writing of history. He published a historical lecture, *St. Domingo: Its Revolutions and Its Patriots*, in 1855, concentrating upon Touissant L' Ouverture. Brown's *The Black Man: His Antecedents, His Genius and Achievements,* is more biographical than historical. *The Negro in the*

American Rebellion (1867) was a timely work, struck off while the iron was hot. The first of the records of Negro troops, contrabands, and slaves during wartime, it is still readable and useful to the historian. *The Rising Son* (1874), a more ambitious venture, includes much that had appeared in the preceding works. Brown's activities as propagandist before the war were not good training for a historian. His love of the sensational militated against his accuracy, although it helped to guarantee large sales (e.g., *The Rising Son* sold over 10,000 copies in its first year).

Nell, Pennington, and Brown were more prominent as antislavery figures than as historians. Edward Wilmot Blyden had the requisite scholarship for writing sound history, but confined his writing largely to the problems of the Liberian colonists and of Africa. The first Negro historian whose scholarship made him worthy of serious consideration is George Washington Williams. Industrious in the garnering of facts and aware of the importance of structure, Williams is certainly one of the first Negroes to win recognition from the literary world. His reasons for writing his *History of the Negro Race in America* (1833) were: that though the material was ample, no such history had been written; that the Negro has been the "vexatious problem in North America"; that the Negro has "always displayed matchless patriotism and incomparable heroism"; that the world needed "more correct ideas of the Negro"; and that "the Negro needed to be incited to greater effort in the struggle for citizenship and manhood." His work therefore pleads a cause, though much less obviously than the earlier histories of Brown and Pennington. Unwieldy, with some padding of unessentials and some strange gaps (the Underground Railroad, for instance, is skimpily treated), written in an emotionally charged style, *The History of the Negro Race in America* is nevertheless a landmark in historical writing, packed with valuable documents, and still useful. Williams' great interest in the record of Negro troops, apparent in this work, is continued in *A History of the Negro Troops in the War of the Rebellion* (1888). Written with far more racial glorification is Joseph T. Wilson's *The Black Phalanx* (1888), which contains much interesting material. Chosen as historian by the Grand Army of the Republic, Wilson writes in spread-eagle style with the enthusiasm of a recent veteran. Yet his idealization, exceptionable as history, is something of a corrective to the neglect or belittling of the Negro's services in winning his own freedom.

The Story of the Negro (1909) written by Booker T. Washington with the assistance of a staff of trained investigators, has been popular for a long time, a reprint having appeared in 1940. It is a readable running account. Worthy of notice as other histories by writers whose eminence lay in fields other than historical research are T. G. Steward's serviceable histories from the Negro's viewpoint of the Haitian Revolution, and Archibald Grimké's *Right On the Scaffold, or the Martyrs of 1822,* an account of the Denmark Vesey plot in Charleston, South Carolina. These were by members of the Negro American Academy, an organization of Negro scholars founded by Alexander Crummell. John W. Cromwell's *The Negro in American History* (1914), by the secretary of the Negro American Academy, is chiefly biographical. Emmett Scott's *The Negro in the World War* (1919) is an account taken from the records that Scott had access to as special assistant to the Secretary of War. Joseph C. Carroll's *Slave Insurrections in the United States, 1800-1865* (1939), is the only history by a Negro treating this neglected phase of American history.

Scientific history of the Negro appeared first in W. E. B. DuBois's *The Suppression of the African Slave Trade to the United States of America, 1638-1870* (1896), the first monograph of the Harvard Historical Studies. This is the work of sound scholarship, authoritative in its field. After a long period as a crusading editor, DuBois returned to history with *The Negro* (1915), a volume in The Home University Library, enlarged and altered to *Black Folk, Then and Now* (1939), a study of the Negro in Africa and the Americas. *Black Reconstruction* (1935) is a comprehensive defense of the role of Negroes and Radical Republicans in Reconstruction. It repudiates the widespread opinion of Reconstruction as a "tragic era," productive only of evil.

The second Negro to be trained in the scientific scholarship of history was Carter G. Woodson, now generally considered to be the dean of American Negro historians. The author of *The History of the Negro Church* (1915), *The Education of the Negro Prior to 1861* (1919), *A Century of Negro Migration* (1918), *The Negro in Our History* (latest edition 1940), *The African Background Outlined* (1936), and many other books, Woodson was the pioneering force in the founding of the Association for the Study of Negro Life and History and *The Journal of Negro History.* The purposes of the Association are to conduct research that will uncover the neglected or unknown facts of the history of the Negro, to correct prevalent historical bias, and to increase race pride. Professor W. B. Hesseltine of the University of Wisconsin writes of this program:

> To the historical purist, believing that the study of history should serve no useful purpose, such a mission may be anathema. Yet from such motives have sprung most of the historical societies

of the United States. State historical societies recount the proud deeds of the states' citizens . . . Other societies study and extol the contributions of the Irish, Jews, Germans, Scotch-Irish, or Norwegians to American culture . . . In seeking to promote race pride through preserving and teaching racial history, the Association for the Study of Negro Life and History is engaged in no unusual enterprise.

The Journal of Negro History has been quite useful to younger Negro historians who often have published the first products of their research in its pages. Charles H. Wesley has been a frequent contributor to the Journal, publishing there his studies of the Negro in the abolition movement and of the downfall of the Confederacy. James Hugo Johnston and Luther P. Jackson have published able studies of the Negro in antebellum Virginia, Johnston writing especially of Negro-white relationships and Jackson especially of the free Negro. Other historians closely affiliated with the Association are Alrutheus A. Taylor, the author of The Negro in South Carolina During The Reconstruction (1924), The Negro in the Reconstruction of Virginia (1926), and The Negro in Tennessee 1865-1880 (1941); and W. Sherman Savage, author of The Controversy over the Distribution of Abolition Literature 1830-1860 (1938). Rayford Logan, the author of The Diplomatic Relations of the United States with Haiti (1941), was for a time engaged in research for the Association, as was Lorenzo Greene, co-author with Woodson of The Negro Wage Earner (1930). White scholars interested in phases of the history of the Negro in America, the West Indies, South America, Europe, and Africa have been frequent contributors to the Journal.

With the New Negro movement interest was kindled in the African background of the American Negro (see p. 957). Partly responsible for this was the bibliophile, Arthur Schomburg, who discovered many curiosa about African, South American, and Caribbean Negroes. This type of research has been continued with zeal by J. A. Rogers, who turns up little known facts about unusual Negroes all over the world. But the writings of American Negroes on Africa has been more often romantic and chauvinistic than informed.

Many Negro historians believe that what is called Negro history should be approached as the history of the Negro in America, not as a separate entity. They insist that the Negro has been an integral part of American life, however grudgingly received, a participant quite as much as a contributor.

In its many state guides the Federal Writers' Project attempted to show this integration of the Negro in the American milieu. Occasionally, as in *The Mississippi Guide,* the Negro was handled with condescension, but in other Southern states (e.g., North Carolina, Georgia, and Virginia) the Negro's participation in the history of the state was amply recognized. Material on *The Negro in Virginia* (1940) was collected by Negro project workers under the direction of Roscoe E. Lewis, who was responsible for the final draft. Though the research was not by trained history students, and the organization and writing were not by a professional historian, *The Negro in Virginia* was praised by Jonathan Daniels as one of the most significant books to come from the Federal Writers' Project, "a grand book . . . which no longer feels the need to make all the Negroes out as angels in chains and no longer the need to take the white South's story without scrutinizing it."

Like the historians of all minority groups, the Negro historian runs the risk of chauvinism. He has not always been able to evade this risk. Conscious of the inadequate presentation of the Negro in orthodox American histories, inadequate because of ignorance, or indifference, or design, the Negro historian has to be careful lest he overstress the Negro's contribution to history, and idealize rather than present the true account. On the other hand, shying away from chauvinism, he sometimes takes timorous refuge in the amassing of factual material without interpretation.

But the present trend in historical writing is neither rash race idealization nor unfocused, unselective collection of facts, and this is fine warrant that the history of the Negro in America will get the hearing that it deserves.

Much of the best historical writing by American Negroes naturally does not lend itself to the purposes of this anthology. Some of the selections are chapters from books and are therefore inaccurately called essays, but it is believed that they can stand as units. After the selections from the nineteenth-century historians, the remaining selections are arranged according to the period with which they deal, and not in chronological order of publication.

Social Essays

In 1902 a book was published with the title *Twentieth-Century Literature.* The title is strange in another instance than the date: of the one hundred contributors, only three treat creative literature. The rest write about politics, civil rights, education, religion, business, health, crime, agriculture, industry, invention, and the professions. These were crucial matters then as they are now, and they were approached soberly and frankly, though generally optimistically. The book is mentioned here as an instance of the articulate Negro's concentration upon social writing and of his conception of literature.

From the days of Martin Delany and William C. Nell, Negroes have attempted social description and analysis. As in the field of history, many took up social interpretation with no other warrants than wide experience, common sense, and prominence. Frederick Douglass candidly admits nearly falling into the same trap when he was invited to speak upon ethnology. He "boned up" on the subject but discovered that in delivery his "carefully-studied and written address, full of learned quotations, fell dead at [his] feet." He was warier thereafter.

Ethnology attracted such men as William Wells Brown, Martin Delany, and James McCune Smith. Smith, the best equipped, refuted Calhoun's theories of the physiology of the Negro from the vantage point of knowledge of both science and the Negro. The ethnology that these men propounded is antislavery rather than scientific in emphasis. That it is generally superior to the proslavery ethnology is not high praise. Not much higher praise can be given the later race "ethnologists" who prefer propaganda to science; ethnology has rather strangely been little studied by Negroes.

In the late years of the nineteenth century, social writing was directed toward reform. A clear-sighted observer, T. Thomas Fortune, spoke sharply against the wiles of carpetbaggers, urged Negro independence in politics as a protest against the "broken promises, the sugar-coated capsules, of political mountebanks" in the Republican party, and, in the spirit of the early Populist movement, urged the union of the Negro and white working classes. After his first "socialism," however, he became one of Booker T. Washington's right-hand men, helping to organize the National Negro Business League. Throughout his long journalistic career, he stood for Negro nonpartisanship in politics, belaboring both Republicans and Democrats for abuses against his people, and praising them for their occasional services.

William Hannibal Thomas considered his *The American Negro* (1901) to be the first sociological treatise on the subject. He is incorrect. Though professing to be carefully documented, *The American Negro* is still subjective, a tirade against what is called "Negroism," the disillusionment of an idealist whose training and character made him see the "shadow of slavery" as almost impenetrably dark. The reality that Thomas looked upon with dismay: the sloth, vice, improvidence, and ignorance were present in as full measure as he stated, but his explanation of these on biological instead of historical and social grounds does not hold. Thomas was naturally relied upon by those seeking to estab-

lish the belief of Negro inferiority, and he was just as naturally repudiated by Negroes. Sociologically discounted today, Thomas is still
important as one of the first Negroes to point out weaknesses in Negro
life and character, to convey a harsh social reality without sentimental-
izing. His pessimism was at least less immature than the optimism of
many professional race men.

Booker T. Washington shared Thomas' dismay at the grimness
of the Negro's condition. He was a social pragmatist, however, recognizing the value of a slow pull for a long haul. *The Future of the
American Negro* (1899), *Education of the Negro* (1900), and *The
Negro in the South, His Economic Progress in Relation to His Moral
and Religious Development* (1907) of which W. E. B. DuBois was
co-author, all illustrate Washington's concern with industrial education, interracial good will, and the Negro's need for thrift, business
enterprise, and efficiency. As Kelly Miller wrote to him during his
heyday:

> You are not only the foremost man of the Negro race, but
> one of the foremost men of all the world. We American Negroes
> did not give you that "glad eminence" and we cannot take it
> away, but we would utilize and appropriate it to the good of the
> race . . . Sir, if you will . . . pursue policies that are commensurate
> with the entire circle of our needs . . . and advocate the fullest
> opportunity of Negro youth to expand and exploit their facilities,
> if you will stand as the fearless champion of the Negro's political
> rights before the law and behind the law, then a united race will
> rise up and join in gladsome chorus: "Only thou our leader be . . ."

There were many, however, who refused to consider Washington
a fearless champion, or an advocate of full opportunity for Negroes.
Debates pro and con Washington's policies were numerous, as were
such books as *The Negro Problem* (1903), to which Chesnutt, Dunbar, Fortune, Washington, and DuBois contributed, and *How to Solve
the Race Problem* (1904), the findings of a conference held in Washington, D. C., in 1903 under the auspices of the National Sociological
Society.

In addition to the opponents of Washington mentioned in the discussion of speeches, pamphleteering, and journalism, numerous pub-
licists attacked the Tuskegee idea. In *The African Abroad* (1913) William H. Ferris attributes Washington's great popularity to the fact that
"his devotion to industrial education brings him special favor with

nearly all the representatives of Southern sentiment[1] and culture, and also with a large part of our Northern people, who unconsciously sympathize with the idea that manual labor is as much as the Negro can properly aspire to." *The African Abroad* seems encyclopedic in scope, embracing ethnology, history, biography, astronomy, literary criticism, philosophy, and theology. It contains many facts not easily found elsewhere on interesting people and periods. Despite its prolixity and pedantry, it is useful for its sharp insight and intimate details. Typical of the time, its discussion of the Negro problem shoves the more grandiose erudition into the background.

In 1924 Alain Locke wrote:

> For nearly a generation Kelly Miller has been the Negro's chief intellectual protagonist. Others have formulated programs, peddled nostrums, and elaborated panaceas; but he, dealing with the concrete issues, has conducted our defenses.

Kelly Miller stands halfway between Booker T. Washington and his detractors, applauding the sanity and common sense of the one and the insistence of the others upon "fullest opportunities." Miller was energetic in sponsoring higher education among Negroes, utilizing Booker T. Washington himself as an example of the leadership that higher education should make possible. Miller also stands halfway between the social reformer and the objective social analyst. He wrote propaganda, as in his open letters to Thomas Dixon, to John Temple Graves, and to Woodrow Wilson; but there he tried to convince by style and argument that were temperate and logical rather than denunciatory.

W. E. B. DuBois was the first scientific scholar of social affairs, as he was the first scientific historian. *The Philadelphia Negro* (1899), a publication of the University of Pennsylvania, was the first of a series of careful monographs on aspects of racial life, including the Atlanta University Studies. DuBois's work has been praised as monumental, and as the first genuine social science to appear in the South whether by white or Negro. More pertinent to this anthology, however, is *The Souls of Black Folk* (1902). Here are essays in which he stated the shortcomings of Booker T. Washington's philosophy, praised the achievement and spirit of Alexander Crummell, wrote autobiographically of his early teaching years, and set forth the cultural gifts of the Negro to America. *The Gift of Black Folk* (1924) elaborates the last subject.

[1] See Kelly Miller, *As to the Leopard's Spots*, p. 889f.

At Fisk University, George E. Haynes pursued social research, his early study of the Negro migrant in New York leading to the foundation of the National Urban League. In 1922 appeared *The Negro in Chicago,* a work produced by the Chicago Commission on Race Relations as an aftermath of the Chicago race riots. Prominent in the preparation of this book was Charles S. Johnson, a young sociologist. In 1928, after a period of editing *Opportunity, A Journal of Negro Life,* he became the head of the Department of Social Science at Fisk University. Johnson has been the most productive of the Negro social scientists. The *Negro in American Civilization* (1930), *The Shadow of the Plantation* (1934), *The Negro College Graduate* (1938), *Growing Up in the Black Belt* (an American Youth Commission Study, 1941), *A Statistical Atlas* (1941), *Race Relations* (in collaboration with W. D. Weatherford, 1936), and *The Collapse of Cotton Tenancy* (in collaboration with Will Alexander and Edwin Embree, 1937), have all been needed and influential works.

For over a decade E. Franklin Frazier has been publishing provocative essays: his books, important to American sociology, are *The Negro Family in Chicago* (1932), *The Negro Family in the United States* (1939), and *Negro Youth at the Crossways* (1940). Ira DeA. Reid of Atlanta University has done important work in his *The Negro Immigrant* (1938), *In a Minor Key* (1940), and *Sharecroppers All* (in collaboration with Arthur Raper, 1941). Also of Atlanta University, Walter Chivers was of valuable assistance to Arthur Raper in Raper's *The Tragedy of Lynching* (1933). Allison Davis is, with John A. Dollard of the Yale Institute of Human Relations and W. Lloyd Warner of the University of Chicago, one of the expounders of a new theory of "class and caste." This theory is illustrated in *Children of Bondage* (1940), a Youth Commission Study done in collaboration with John Dollard, and in the *Deep South* (1941), a cultural anthropological study of Southern urban life.

Except for studies of Negro banking and business by George Hines in 1914 and 1915, little was written by Negroes in the field of economics until the last decade. Charles H. Wesley's *Negro Labor in the United States* (1927) was the first to record this important chapter in history. In 1931 appeared Abram L. Harris' and Sterling Spero's significant *The Black Worker* (1931), describing and analyzing "the relation of the dominant section of the working class to the segregated, circumscribed, and restricted Negro minority." Harris conceived a larger study to cover (1) Africa and the rise of capitalism, (2) the accumulation of wealth among Negroes prior to 1860, and (3) the economic basis of the Negro middle class. Harris covers the third phase in *The Negro as Capitalist* (1936), Monograph No. 2 of the American Academy of Political and Social Science.

Other works dealing with Negro labor are a socio-economic study, *Black Workers and the New Unions* (1939), the joint work of Horace Cayton, a sociologist, and George Mitchell, a white economist, and *The Negro Labor Unionist of New York* (1936), by Lionel Franklin.

Political science has not been a stressed subject in Negro colleges, especially those located in the South. Many professional Negro politicians deride the notion of political science, preferring to look at politics as a gamble or a barter. Ralph J. Bunche of Howard University, however, has brought scientific training to the subject, not only of the Negro in American politics, but of the Negro in world politics. Max Yergan, director of the International Committee on African Affairs and now president of the National Negro Congress, has bitterly indicted imperialism on the basis of his acquaintance with the political, economic, and social conditions of the South African native.

In the field of education the studies have been numerous. Those of more general interest have been Dwight O. W. Holmes's *The Evolution of the Negro College* (1934), Horace Mann Bond's *The Education of the Negro in the American Social Order* (1934) and *Negro Education in Alabama (A Study in Cotton and Steel)* (1939), Charles H. Thompson's trenchant essays, and Doxey Wilkerson's *Special Problems on Negro Education* (1939). All of these are insistent upon the necessity of genuinely democratic education.

Differing in approach, temper, interpretation, and conclusions, these social scientists agree in their determination to shed light where there has been darkness. Many Americans are not only ignorant of facts about the American Negro, but worse, too many are like the man to whom Josh Billings said "You'd better not know so much, than know so many things that ain't so." No reader with an open mind could review the work of these scholars and retain the stereotyped concepts of Negro life and character. Whether dealing with the shadow of the plantation lying darkly over Negro sharecroppers, or the hardships of families congested in Northern slums, or the frustrated lives of Negro youth from Natchez to Harlem, or the struggle of Negro laborers against unemployment and prejudice, or the pitiful inadequacies of schools for Negroes in the South, or the chicanery of white voting officials, all of these have added enormously to the new realism about Negro life of which America is becoming aware and must become even more aware. These men have won respect in the world of scholarship. They are social analysts rather than solvers of a race problem—

indeed several have been accused of too great an unconcern by impatient propagandists—but diagnosis is the first step in any cure.

It is worth pointing out that the Negro social scientist confronts many of the problems of the creative writer. His racial audience turns a readier ear to race praise or complaints of race victimization than to analyses of racial shortcomings, the scholarly documentation of which it considers race treason. His wider American audience is often readier to receive description than interpretation. "Objectivity" of a doubtful validity is urged upon him. Nevertheless, Negro social scientists, taken by and large, have been neither aloof nor timid, but have shown themselves ready to interpret their facts, to generalize, to set forth points of view, to make of their social science a tool as well as a measuring rod. Though the eldest of these social scientists are not old as scholars go, they have already written much, and they give promise of a great deal more that the democratic planning of the future must take into serious account.

Cultural Essays

In his *Letters and Leadership* (1918) Van Wyck Brooks deplored the ineffectuality of American critics who were never "on terms of intimacy with the real conditions of our life."

> For Ireland and America really are alike in that they inherit a dominant academic tradition colonial in essence, having its home in centers of civilization remote from the springs of a national life which has only of late come into its own consciousness. For the shaping of that consciousness, therefore, we cannot look to our critics for any assistance. Not guides and friends of the creative spirit about them, but incredulous pedagogues by necessity, they have been really driven to destroy in others the poet that has died in themselves.

This was a true bill against the American critics of the early twentieth century.

In exaggerated form the weaknesses that Van Wyck Brooks diagnosed in American culture afflicted the writing of Negroes. If American literature and criticism suffered from a "colonial" complex, literature by American Negroes suffered from the complex of a minority within that colony. Negro writers too were "strangled by practicality." If Americans in general were concerned with "getting on," Negroes even after Emancipation were concerned with getting free.

Creative efforts were few and far between. Literary criticism was even more infrequent. Comment on Negro writers in the nineteenth century was largely biographical and almost always laudatory. Pushkin in Russian poetry and Dumas in French fiction were pointed to as beacons. Cataloguing of American Negro writers with monotonous, indiscriminate words of praise is about all the literary criticism that existed. Writers were respected as they echoed the English and occasionally the American "greats." For a Negro to get a book into print seemed sufficient achievement; what else was there to say? Many critics showed more acquaintance with the approved list of famous literary names than with the works they were commenting upon.

Even in the present century, literary criticism has not kept pace with the advancing creative work that it should serve and guide. The standards have been academic, moralistic, racialistic. A book may be judged on its resemblance to established or purported masterpieces, or on its "moral" tone, or on its effect on race relations; much more seldom it is judged for its veracity, its insight, its power. There has been little criticism that considered the Negro writer as integrally related to American literature. Many Negro critics apparently considered intimacy with the living literature of the present and with the real conditions of American life in general and Negro life in particular to be less valuable than an acquaintance with a book of readings from Beowulf to Bennett, or a five-foot shelf of culture.

In 1910, Benjamin Brawley's *The Negro in Literature and Art* appeared. This pioneer booklet has been twice enlarged under the same title; in final and revised form, it was published as *The Negro Genius* (1937). A sign of growing race consciousness when it first appeared, Brawley's history of the Negro's artistic achievements is less critical than biographical. The criticism is academic and genteel. Brawley is unsympathetic with realism or with modern literature in general; basic among his criteria seems to be "race aspiration," and the authors are frequently considered as symbols of race achievement over difficulties, rather than as craftsmen. Nevertheless, Brawley was a pioneer, and several essays on the Negro in American literature for *The Dial, The Bookman,* and *The English Journal,* and his *Early Negro American Writers* are useful works.

William Stanley Braithwaite's critical career started at about the same time as Brawley's. As a contributor to *The Boston Evening Transcript* and an anthologist, he had wider concerns than the Negro's literary performance. His *Anthology of Magazine Verse* (appearing annually from 1913 to 1929) has been praised for the "stubborn self-effacing enthusiasm" with which he worked to create the American "poetic renaissance" and its audience. He published anthologies of

Elizabethan, Restoration, and Georgian Verse, and *The Poetic Year,* a series of critical articles on the poetry that appeared in 1916. Several Negro poets enjoyed the hospitality of his anthologies. His essay on "The Negro in American Literature" was published in *The New Negro* (1925), and an essay in praise of Jessie Fauset's novels appeared in *Opportunity,* but he has written little else on the Negro in American literature.

More robustly rooted in the life of American Negroes, James Weldon Johnson was a better intermediary than Brawley or Braithwaite. In 1923 he published *The Book of American Negro Poetry* with a revealing prefatory essay on the Negro's creative genius. Of this he spoke out boldly and incautiously, considering the Negro to be the creator of the "only things artistic that have yet sprung from native soil and been universally acknowledged as distinctive American products." The four creations are the Uncle Remus stories, the spirituals, the cakewalk, and ragtime. It is easy today to see the inaccuracy and incompleteness of Johnson's claim. Distinctive American folklore—even Negro folklore—abounds with so many more heroes than Uncle Remus; the cakewalk is not the first nor the last of the many American dances derived from Negroes; and ragtime is no longer made synonymous, as Johnson sometimes makes it, with the blues and with jazz. Nevertheless, Johnson's refusal, because of his own experience in musical comedy, to accept the genteel disdain of popular arts was refreshing. His attack on traditional dialect was influential. The anthology was something of a cause pleader, but the general American ignorance of the Negro as a writer forced it to be. By his interpretations of Negro poetry and music, by occasional essays on the problems of Negro writers, and by his own creative work, Johnson succeeded more than any predecessor in furthering the cause of the Negro artist. The enlarged *Book of American Negro Poetry* (1931) contained better poetry and better criticism. *Black Manhattan,* a chronicle of the Negro in New York, and the autobiography, *Along This Way,* devote much space to Negro musicians, dancers, actors, painters, sculptors, and writers.

In 1924, W. E. B. DuBois published *The Gift of Black Folk,* a conventional account of the Negro's cultural achievement in the past; in 1925 *The New Negro* appeared, a much less conventional account and an earnest plea for the future. The editor of the latter volume was Alain Locke, who has been unceasing in his efforts for the Negro in art, music, and literature. An artistic ferment had been going on, chiefly in Harlem. Evidences had been seen in *Opportunity, A Journal of Negro Life,* then edited by Charles S. Johnson, and in *The Crisis,* then edited by W. E. B. DuBois, both friendly toward aspiring Negro artists. *The New Negro* was the distillation of this ferment.

The best statement of the aims of the New Negro movement is to be found in Locke's several essays in *The New Negro*. In spite of certain hopes that were to fail and certain emphases later abandoned, this volume performed valuable services. It focussed attention upon the creditable works of Negro artists, it placed creative writing among Negroes in a position of self-respect, it gave something of a unifying bond to struggling Negro artists, whose loneliness is even greater than the proverbial loneliness of the artist in America. The writers of the antislavery campaign had been united in a common purpose, but their work had not been creative; later artists—Dunbar, Chesnutt, Braithwaite, James Weldon Johnson—had achieved individually, but there had been no organized artistic movement before. For a while the New Negro movement thrived in Harlem. True to the general New York literary scene, however, most of the best writers were visitors, not natives. Walrond was a West Indian; McKay, another West Indian, was a member *in absentia;* Jean Toomer was from Washington, Langston Hughes from Missouri, Zora Neale Hurston from Florida, Alain Locke, the spokesman of the group, was a professor at Howard University in Washington. As a semiorganized group, the "New Negroes" declined into the ineffectual Bohemianism caricatured in Thurman's *Infants of The Spring* (see above, p. 220). The influence of Locke's essays, however, and of the movement in general, spread over the country, touching writers in Missouri and Mississippi, in Boston, Philadelphia, Washington, and Chicago. Since 1929 Alain Locke has continued his literary criticism with annual "Retrospective Reviews" of books about and by Negroes in *Opportunity*.

Book reviewing in *The Crisis* and *Opportunity* has been a natural accompaniment to the Negro's steady work in the creative fields. Allison Davis wrote some of the soundest literary criticism in these magazines; Countee Cullen and Gwendolyn Bennett conducted literary columns in the earlier *Opportunity;* and Sterling Brown wrote a monthly "Chronicle and Comment" for several years in *Opportunity*. James W. Ivy in *The Crisis,* Ulysses Lee in *Opportunity,* Theophilus Lewis in *The Interracial Review,* and George S. Schuyler in the *Pittsburgh Courier* are doing the best of the current book reviewing. Books of literary criticism are still few and far between.

Early comment on Negro painters and plastic artists, such as Brawley's *The Negro in Literature and Art* and DuBois's *The Gift of Black Folk,* were merely short biographies, instances of "race" achievement over adversities. Only in recent years has a basis for criticism of Negro artists been laid in Alain Locke's occasional essays, his *Negro Art: Past and Present,* and his portfolio *The Negro in Art,* and in essays by James A. Porter.

There has been much writing on Negro music. James M. Trotter's *Music and Some Highly Musical People,* appearing in 1878, was naturally an aid to race pride more than to musicology, but its biographical sketches contain valuable information. Maud Cuney Hare's *Negro Musicians and Their Music* (1936) is similarly biographical rather than critical. In a few essays Clarence Cameron White has listed the achievements of Negroes in classical music. Alain Locke's *The Negro and His Music* (1936) was the first book to interpret the entire range of Negro music without apologizing for the folk and popular types.

The spirituals have been expounded frequently by race leaders, literary men, folklorists, less frequently by musicologists. Booker T. Washington stressed their forgivingness, W. E. B. DuBois their deep grief; Zora Neale Hurston has stated that the name "sorrow songs" is a misnomer, and John Lovell has urged their hidden militancy. In 1915, John W. Work's *Folk Song of The American Negro* was put forth as an ally to H. E. Krehbiel's *Afro-American Folk Songs* (1914), a strong defense of the originality and merit of the spirituals. Work went even farther than Krehbiel, however, in urging the Africanism of the spirituals, a quality that such white scholars as Guy Johnson, Newman White, and George Pullen Jackson have cast much doubt upon (see above, p. 415). R. Nathaniel Dett's preface to *Religious Folk Songs of the Negro* (1927) is the attempt of a highly trained and gifted musician to overthrow this school which finds the source of the Negro spiritual in the white camp-meeting hymn. James Weldon Johnson's introductions to his two *Books of American Negro Spirituals* make occasional overstatements, but they contain much information on the method of composition and singing (see above, p. 171.) J. Rosamond Johnson's *Rolling Along in Song* is a collection of songs with descriptive comment. Recently younger Negro students, such as John W. Work, Jr., in his *American Negro Folk-Songs* and Willis James, are bringing serious scholarship to the collecting, interpreting, and analyzing of Negro folk song.

The interest of these younger men in work songs, blues, and jazz is gratifying. So far, the artistic fields in which the Negro has shown the greatest originality and the greatest influence upon American culture have been disdainfully skirted by Negro interpreters. In *The Negro Genius,* Brawley refused to discuss jazz because it "raised questions of musical value." Others have written of the Negro in American music without once mentioning jazz. W. C. Handy has given incidental information of value concerning the blues in his most interesting auto-biography, but the best musical analysts of the blues are Abbe Niles and Winthrop Sargeant, two white men. Similarly, the best work on jazz has been done by such white critics as Frederic Ramsey and Charles Smith, the editors of *Jazzmen,* and such of their collaborators as William Russell, Stephen Smith, and Otis Ferguson; Wilder Hobson in *American Jazz Music;* Winthrop Sargeant in *Jazz: Hot and Hybrid;* and John Hammond in numerous articles. Negro writing on jazz has been almost confined to the musical pages of weekly newspapers.

The activity of the dance among Negroes has seen no correspond-ing activity among Negro interpreters. Katherine Dunham has written on the folk dances of the West Indies, and has lectured on the evolu-tion of the Negro dance, but there has been little other writing on this amazing art. Too frequently, Negro writers on "cultural" subjects have spelled "culture" with a capital C. The lively arts of the Negro have not appealed to them, in spite of their overwhelming appeal to the rest of the world. That this is understandable as the sensitivity of a minority group does not keep it from being unfortunate.

Personal Essays

The delight of more leisurely, bookloving times and places, the per-sonal essay has declined in favor in twentieth-century America. Among Negro writers it was never a favored form. Antislavery authors would have considered it to be fiddling while Rome burned; the later practi-cal preachers of social reform would consider it to be dillydallying. A leisure-class audience, sensitive to the cadence of sentences and para-graphs, the nuances of words, the interplay of personality and subject matter, has not been one of the blessings of the American Negro.

Autobiographical writing among Negroes is common enough, but more often it is like an object lesson or ego gratification, rather than the ego exploration of Montaigne, Lamb, or Hazlitt. Even where the personal essay is attempted, the "problem" raises its head; the personal essay becomes a social analysis, a complaint, an indictment. It might be added that if the virtues of the personal essay reflect the virtues of conversation, the few personal essays by Negro authors reflect the con-versation of intelligent Negroes, for there the race problem is not long absent. Constant pressure hardly makes for the imaginative freedom requisite to personal essayists.

Nevertheless, several of the writers most socially aware have a fund of revelatory anecdotes that, told with ironic twists, stud their conver-sations. Though the personal essay is a declining literary form, it is quite likely that a new type of essay will evolve, namely, social commentary individually told. Several of the essays below may be considered to be examples of the emergence of this type.

CARTER G. WOODSON (1875-   )

Carter G. Woodson was born in Buckingham County, Virginia. He was educated at Berea College, Kentucky, the University of Chicago, the Sorbonne, and Harvard. Before retiring from the educational field to devote his full time to the work of the Association for the Study of Negro Life and History, which he, with five others, founded in 1915, he had taught in the public schools of West Virginia and the District of Columbia and had been dean of the College of Liberal Arts at Howard University and dean of West Virginia Collegiate Institute. Since 1916, Dr. Woodson has been editor of *The Journal of Negro History;* under his direction, the Associated Publishers have issued a list of notable books, monographs, and bulletins that have made the Association for the Study of Negro Life and History the outstanding organization in research in the Negro past. In 1926 he was awarded the Spingarn Medal. Among the score of books written by Dr. Woodson are: *The Education of the Negro Prior to 1861* (1915), *A Century of Negro Migration* (1918), *The History of the Negro Church* (1924), *Free Negro Heads of Families in the United States in 1830* (1925), *Negro Makers of History* (1928), *The Miseducation of the Negro* (1933), *The Negro Professional Man and the Community* (1934), and *The Negro in Our History,* a textbook that has gone through several editions.

Carter Woodson combines the interest of a scholar with that of an organizer and a journalist. Ever on the alert to detect historical inaccuracies, especially concerning the Negro in history, he found fair game in G. D. Eaton, a magazine editor, who had delivered himself of the usual attack upon abolitionists coupled with a defense of the plantation tradition. "History Made to Order," published in the *Journal of Negro History* in 1927, is a good example of Woodson's grasp of subject matter and controversial gusto. The selection is used by permission of the author.

History Made to Order

Mr. G. D. Eaton,
204 West 13th St.,
New York City.

My dear Mr. Eaton:

I have read your article on slavery and abolition entitled "Horrors Made to Order," which appeared in the February issue of *McNaught's Monthly*. Inasmuch as I am quoted in support of your unwarranted deductions and distortion of facts, I consider it my duty to address you this open letter.

The most flagrant errors which you made in your paper are an exaggeration of the number of slaves who had to return from persecution in the North to yield to slavery in the South, too much emphasis on the isolated cases of the interest of Southerners in emancipation, a minimization of the horrors of slavery, a misrepresentation of the church as it developed in the slaveholding South, and an unwarranted attack on the abolitionists. Considered in detail, however, your errors are too numerous to be mentioned in a letter; and, since some of your statements refute themselves, they require no answer from the undersigned.

You are unfortunate in failing to understand that slavery differed from period to period in this country, and differed further in its aspects from country to country during the same period. In fact, the first Negroes brought to this country were not slaves. They were indentured servants and became gradually debased to the lower status. At that time, slavery was unknown to English law. Slavery in the West Indies was not the same as slavery in the colonies along the Atlantic Coast, and slavery in its beginnings in America differed widely from what it was when it was finally abolished. Slavery differed from plantation to plantation, too, because each slaveholder was a law unto himself and could make it anything he wanted. Like the six men who visited the elephant, then, one can make almost any sort of argument with respect to slavery.

At this point uninformed writers do the cause of truth unusual harm. Finding a few treatises on slavery during the earliest period, they refer to the institution as strictly patriarchal and wonder why abolitionists were so unwise as to attack it. On the other hand, other unfortunates may discover treatises dealing with the institution during its most cruel development and may radically denounce it in terms more scathing than it is portrayed in abolition literature. An historical student, however, understands how to consider an institution according to its cycles of development and the standard of its time.

The question as to whether or not slavery in the United States was cruel, moreover, results merely from the difference in points of view. Pagan historians of our time insist that slavery was a benevolent institution. The god of race superiority ordained that the one race should be subjugated to serve the other. The Negro, therefore, was at fault in resisting his enslavement. His master in whipping him or even killing him if he resisted was doing no wrong, for slavery could not have been maintained any other way, and it had to be maintained. Classifying Negroes as animals, too, such authors find that the masters were often indulgent and kind to the slaves. The slaves cost more to support and caused so much more trouble than horses and mules. Yet the slaves were given more consideration. Whereas the resistance of the horses and mules never got beyond that of a little kicking back, the slaves sometimes fought their masters or started insurrections among their fellows. These writers naturally think that the masters did unusually well under the circumstances.

Enlightened people, however, do not understand how there can be any justice in enslaving one race to another to establish its monopoly of all the good things of this world. Civilized people can see no justice in beating or killing a man because he will not do the will of another. Man should not exercise power over another except for altruistic purposes. There was no wisdom in keeping the Negro in drudgery and darkness under the false notion of keeping the white man in a higher realm, for ultimately the system meant ruin to the white man as well. To maintain the institution there must be some one brutal enough to beat and kill an unoffending people. To have slavery there must be an enslaver. To have murder there must be a murderer. The reform element insisted that we should not have either.

Your misuse of facts becomes decidedly astounding when one reads that 40,000 free Negroes owned nearly 100,000 slaves. I doubt that a more mischievous exaggeration has ever been written. Some years ago, the Association for the Study of Negro Life and History made a careful study of the Negro ownership of slaves in the United States, recorded in the Census Reports of 1830, and found that 3,777 free Negroes actually owned 12,920 slaves, an average of less than 4 to each Negro slaveholder. Unless these numbers increased by leaps and bounds during the next three decades, they could not have reached the estimate you have made. As a matter of fact, the number of Negro slaveholders tended to decrease proportionately after 1830. Laws made it more difficult for Negroes to acquire slave property because it brought such Negroes too near to the status of white men.

Most of these cases of Negro slaveholding, moreover, were not primarily for the purpose of exploitation. There were a few Southern Negroes who had considerable land. To develop this land they had to use laborers and the easiest way to supply the demand was through the purchase of slaves. The large majority of Negroes who owned slaves, however, were engaged in it from a benevolent point of view. Free Negroes often purchased slaves to make their lot easier by granting them their freedom for a nominal sum or by permitting them to work it out on liberal terms. In many cases, a husband purchased the wife or vice versa. The children of such unions, therefore, became slaves. After the reactionary measures in the South made it unlawful for a free Negro to remain in certain States unless he could give bond or by special act of the State legislature had been permitted to remain, it was deemed unwise for Negro slaveholding husbands or wives to manumit their own relatives. If they had done so, these slaves on becoming free would have been compelled to leave the State. They could not easily establish themselves in strange communities. In treating this exceptional history of the Negro, therefore, you have made the blunder of emphasizing the exception rather than the rule.

It is true that at the time of the immigration of the Germans and Scotch-Irish into this country during the thirties, forties, and fifties, it was difficult for the free Negroes migrating from the South to the North to find employment. Most of these foreigners were common laborers. Competing with these elements in menial service, the Negro migrants became an object of attacks by mobs and some few of them found it so unpleasant that they had to return to the land of slavery. However, it is a misrepresentation to refer to these unfortunates as an unusual number. The actual figures published by the Census Bureau showing the large number of free Negroes who, in spite of this condition, moved to the North and settled there is ample refutation of your statement. They could easily find labor in the South inasmuch as the Southern whites were trying to make their living from the labor of others rather than indulge in drudgery hemselves. After all, moreover, our history shows that the economic actor is the most important one in determining whether persecuted people will bear the ills they have rather than fly to those they know not of.

You are wrong in your estimate of the Southern sentiment in behalf of abolition after the rise of the cotton kingdom. You do not seem to know that such abolition sentiment as is usually accredited to the South was restricted largely to the Appalachian Highland, which extended like a Northern peninsula into a pro-slavery South. This section of the South was settled by Scotch-Irish Presbyterians and Germans, who, in coming to the South after the slaveholders had preempted the fertile lands in the tidewater district had to settle in the uplands and in the mountains of the seaboard states. Having come from Europe, where they had struggled against the aristocracy, they found themselves easily arrayed against the rich planters near the coast. Inasmuch as the planters in control of the seaboard slave States administered government in the interests of the slaveholders, a class to which the mountaineers did not belong, the newcomers politically opposed the planters of the lowlands and sometimes promoted the cause of abolition. It required considerable time before they could be indoctrinated in the pro-slavery propaganda in the proportion as slavery extended into the valley between the Blue Ridge and Allegheny Mountains, and even across the more westerly highland. This was gradually brought about, however, and before the Civil War, the small slaveholders of the upland and trans-Allegheny districts who had increased their acreage and their number of slaves grew so lukewarm on the question of abolition that abolition in those parts became unpopular and even dangerous by 1840.

If, however, as you have said, the planters of the South realized that slavery was doomed, why did they wage war for the right to perpetuate the institution? Why did they practically re-establish slavery through the vagrancy acts immediately after the Civil War in their first effort at reconstruction? And why do parts of that section still practice slavery in the form of peonage? There are in the South today intelligent white people who say that slavery was wrong, but there are few of them who do not still give unstinted praise to their leaders who fought, bled, and died for the right to perpetuate the institution.

The churches for which you make the excuse of having remained pro-slavery until insurrectionists like Nat Turner forced them the other way hardly changed their attitude altogether on account of the deeds of such men. The evangelical denominations like the Methodists and Baptists were anti-slavery in the beginning because they were not tolerated prior to the American Revolution; and, in certain parts, existed on sufferance even after religious freedom had been legally established. Slaveholders and aristocratic people in general did not as a rule belong to these churches. The Baptists and Methodists, therefore, made their appeal directly to poor whites and Negroes. Negroes were welcomed not only as communicants but even as ministers preaching to both races. As American people became further removed from the traditional attitude toward these evangelical sects, however, there was less stigma attached to membership therein; and the well-to-do began to join the ranks. Furthermore, some of the very poor whites who had at first connected with these churches became slaveholders as they developed in the economic world. This was the easiest way an employer could obtain labor in a slaveholding section. When slavery thus crept into these popular churches, therefore, the anti-slavery element in the congregations in the South tended to diminish until the national churches finally divided as a result of a contest during the crisis. Southern communicants had some serious fears of servile insurrection; but this was not sufficient to break the tie, for the Northern churches which denounced slavery denounced also servile insurrection.

Your contention that the South would have probably granted civic rights to the Negroes and would have liberated the slaves, if it had not been for insurrections like that of Nat Turner, cannot be proved. Uprisings like these help rather than hinder reform movements. While they may cause the lukewarm to shift from one side to another, they usually result in more sharply defining the issue and in forcing an immediate decision of the tremendously important question. The main reason for considering the emancipation of the slaves in those Southern States which did not produce sugar and cotton was that slavery was becoming economically impossible. Slavery can exist as a society only when the slave can produce sufficient for himself and for his master. This was gradually ceasing to be the case in the Southern States which produced neither sugar nor cotton. Furthermore, because of a lack of knowledge as to fertilization and rotation of crops, the land in the declining States had been worn out. Capital from these States, then, tended to go to the more promising cotton States along the Gulf of Mexico, where young men from the declining section found it possible to retrieve their lost fortunes. The idea of emancipating slaves for this economic reason, however, soon passed from the minds of the slaveholders in the seaboard States when their problem was to some extent solved by the employment of slaves in railroad construction and in the breeding of slaves to supply the market in the lower South. Negro men and women were mated and matched for the purpose of breeding. Negro women in these selfsame States, moreover, were hired out and disposed of to lustful white men for sexual purposes; and some of these owners actually sold their own blood to supply the interstate slave trade.

The statement as to the benevolent aspect of slavery is a self-refutable contention. There were kind slaveholders who treated their slaves as human beings. But these men stood out exceptionally like shining lights after a prolonged darkness had covered the land. Some of the benevolent masters were silent abolitionists, for a few of them moved North, freed their slaves, and joined the antislavery crusade. If slavery was such an ideal situation, however, why was it necessary for slaveholding States to maintain a patrol system for slave control and devise all sorts of laws to prevent the slaves from escaping? And why did an average of a thousand slaves a year risk their lives in making the dash for liberty across the border and into Canada? If the slaves were so much better fed and clothed and had less to do than the free laborers of the North, why did not they take the places made vacant by the slaves who escaped to the North? The white laborers of the North could have come South much more easily than the slaves could go North; and the recent migration proves that free labor goes where it can do best in economic improvement.

You make yourself facetious in referring to such a work as *Uncle Tom's Cabin* as being untrue. This is a novel and in no sense a treatise like those referred to elsewhere in your paper. I have never heard of a literary man expressing surprise that such literature cannot be supported by documentary evidence. On such a basis the Bible itself would be condemned. *Uncle Tom's Cabin* met the test of realism. While Mrs. Stowe did not live in the South, she lived in Cincinnati right across the river where she had every opportunity to learn what was going on in slaveholding Kentucky. No single slave ever had exactly the same experience as that of Uncle Tom, but there were numbers of slaves whose hardships all but paralleled what is set forth in this narrative. The story of Josiah Henson is very much like it. George Woodson, an uncle of the undersigned, held as a slave in Fluvanna County, Virginia, went through most of such hardships. He was cruelly whipped from time to time because he would not be a good slave. He was finally beaten almost to death, then washed down in salt and water, and sold south where, like many other slaves, he was driven to death in the land of cotton.

* * * * *

You make another error in questioning the abolitionists' contention that Negroes in the South were cruelly beaten and killed. I do not believe that you will find in abolition literature a sweeping statement that slaveholders made a business of killing Negroes. No reformer would have had such little common sense as to think that slaveholders could have profited by their slaves if they killed them for slight offenses. But you do find evidence to the effect that Negroes were unnecessarily beaten and killed. The facts collected by an unbiased investigator in Southern history will prove this. John Spencer Bassett's apology for the cruelties of slavery may have some justification in the enlightened parts of the slave States among the few liberal masters, some of whom became abolitionists. No such favorable conditions generally obtained on the large tobacco, sugar and cotton plantations. There are thousands of witnesses to the contrary, and some of them slaveholders themselves. . . .

The Negroes naturally recoiled from slavery. They had to be "broken in." To reduce them to servitude, their owners resorted to harsh measures. If they did not submit, the masters considered them better off when dead, for the owners could not support them in the capacity of free men from whom no profit could be derived. I have personally talked with hundreds of slaves who passed through the ordeals which are in no sense exaggerated by most of the abolition treaties which you question. I do think that the slaves who felt the lash upon their backs and saw their fellowmen killed should be permitted to testify in their own behalf, even if you do rule out of court the abolitionists who were the only persons who had the moral courage to speak out in their behalf. The victims of the lash knew more about these cruelties than post bellum observers.

Furthermore, there are court records which prove that masters were punished for cruelly beating and killing slaves. (See B. T. Catterall's *Judicial Cases concerning American Slavery and the Negro* . . .) These Court records restricted to Virginia, West Virginia, and Kentucky where slavery existed in a milder form than in the lower South, moreover, show cases of the killing of Negroes by being "fired upon by patrols," "through abuse under hire," "by exposure," and "by cruel and excessive punishment." The causes adjudicated were evidently a small fraction of such offenses; for, as in the case of Virginia, states had positive laws exonerating masters from punishment of their slaves and even from killing them in the act if the offender could hide behind the pretext of resistance or accident. . . .

Propaganda writers are accustomed to refer to the abolitionists as unusually excited persons who by their radicalism did the cause of freedom more harm than good. These authors contend that slavery would have eventually come to an end as a result of the logical arraignment of it through spokesmen of Southern poor whites and Northern free laborers, but the abolitionists climaxing their efforts with such uprisings as those of Nat Turner and John Brown, precipitated the Civil War. Writers of this type, however, manifest just about as much reason as the man who, finding his friend decided to have an incurably diseased limb amputated, advised him not to undergo such a painful operation because the limb would eventually rot off. The work of Abraham Lincoln would have been impossible if he had not been preceded by the abolitionists. In the crisis he had to come to the position of instant abolition, for his plan was to get rid of the institution through gradual and compensated emancipation by 1900. The conflict of antislavery and proslavery forces became inevitable. The abolitionists kept the question before the country. They actually excited the South and forced it to the position of militantly defending mediaevalism. The moral and spiritual cost of the conflict which ensued was tremendous, but it had to come. History shows that the human family is still too spiritually weak to work out such problems by peaceful means.

To undertake to discredit the unselfish work of the abolitionists exhibits a rather unfortunate state of mind. To ignore the record of these men and women of vision would be merely omitting a most interesting part of our history. These reformers worked jointly for temperance, legal reform, woman suffrage, and the rights of labor. If you eliminate their record, then, our history will become an artless tale which few will care to read. People will not eternally delight in the vices, follies, and quarrels of those who contend for power to oppress the weak. The public will not always recite the exploits of the oppressor nor idolize the man who "wrings his bread from the sweat of another's brow." We shall some day appreciate these reformers who were so far ahead of their time. They endeavored to lift man above selfishness into an altruism of a regenerated universe. They labored to realize the ideals for which Socrates, Jesus Christ and John Brown died. Following the examples of the martyrs of old, some of these lived up to the ideal of the great Nazarene who said: "Greater love hath no man than this, that a man lay down his life for his friends."

Respectfully yours,

C. G. Woodson.

THE FEDERAL WRITERS' PROJECT

There were several Negroes on the Federal Writers' Project in Washington and the various states, but there were none in Virginia until in 1936 a Negro unit was set up under Roscoe E. Lewis as supervisor. One of the ambitions of Henry G. Alsberg, then national director of the Federal Writers' Project, was to supply a series of studies of Negro life in America. Local studies and essays on the Negro in city and state guides appeared, but only one of the several books planned. *The Negro in Virginia* owes much to Roscoe E. Lewis. He drew up the original plan, after the assignment was given him to prepare a history of the Virginia Negro. He directed the research, doing a great deal of it himself, and wrote the drafts, from the first to the final one. Checking and revision of the manuscript were done in the Richmond office and in Washington, but *The Negro in Virginia* is essentially a one-man job.

The significance of *The Negro in Virginia* is that it is an instance of a governmental cultural agency's sponsorship of a serious history of a minority group. It has been praised as one of the finest productions of the Federal Writers' Project. It is the first state history of the Negro ever published. Not the work of a professional historian, its approach—through anecdote, interview, and documents—makes for good social history.

Roscoe E. Lewis was born in Washington, D. C., in 1904; he was educated at Brown University, Howard, and Columbia. Though trained in the natural sciences he has long had a great interest in American history. He is at present assembling interviews with all of the living ex-slaves he can find. The following selections are reprinted by permission of the author, of Hampton Institute, which sponsored the publication of *The Negro in Virginia,* and of Hastings House, the publishers.

The Narrators

Jesus gonna make up my dyin' bed.

THREE QUARTERS OF A CENTURY have passed since the Emancipation Proclamation ended legal slavery in America. Of some 500,000 Virginia slaves to whom the act applied, there were in 1930, according to the United States Census, 8,058 Negroes 75 years of age or older, a higher old-age percentage than obtained in any of the former slave-holding states south of Virginia. Of the 300 or more elderly Negroes interviewed in connection with this work—*The Negro in Virginia*—perhaps 250 had lived long enough as slaves to offer credible testimony about life during slavery. Of the 250 whose accounts seem trustworthy, about two-score died within a year of the time they were interviewed. Soon the last person who has known what it meant to be a slave will have died.

There are questions about the slave system that can be answered only by one who has experienced slavery. How did it "feel" to be owned? What were the pleasures and sufferings of the slave? What was the slave's attitude toward his owner, toward the white man's assumption of superiority, toward the white man's God? Did the slaves want to be free? Did they feel that it was their right to be free? Seventy-five years after Lincoln signed the Emancipation Proclamation, ex-slaves now approaching the grave have perhaps an objectiveness in their retrospection that only time could supply.

"What form of questionnaire are you going to use in talking with these old folks?" we were asked. Though we had not thought of preparing a formal guide for our interviews, we drew up a tentative list of questions and sought to find our way through trial and error. The results were discouraging. Aunt Eliza Sparks of Mathews County, who doesn't know how old she is but had two babies living when the War came, had no ear or mind for questions. "Lemme tell you 'bout the time ole Marse Shep took me on his knee . . . ," she began. After two hours, we came away with a vivid picture of slave life in Mathews County. Talks with other ex-slaves convinced us that what many had to tell was infinitely more important than what they were asked. They needed no prompting or interviewing; all they desired was an audience that would not interrupt. Relatives have been for the most part unsympathetic listeners, especially those who have heard the same stories over and over. "Gramma, quit talking 'bout that ole back-stuff," complained one house-wife. "Don't no one want to hear 'bout that slavery business no more," declared another of Gramma's younger relatives. But we were eager listeners. As these old people delved into the recesses of their memories and recreated the "back days," we began to get a picture of the plantation as seen from slave row—a picture that too often has been neglected in accounts of the period.

To those who would question what the ex-slaves have told us, we can only say, "Believe it or not." We have attempted to record their stories as faithfully as possible. We have tried neither to add to nor detract from the flavor of the telling. The old people perhaps have mixed fact and fancy, have sometimes related others' experiences as their own and have tended now and then to exercise the best of their histrionic talents in playing up to the most appreciative audience that has ever sat before them. All in all, however, the sum total of the ex-slave stories re-creates a picture without which posterity would have been the poorer.

We cannot hope to do full justice to the ex-slaves we have interviewed. One must look into their eyes, hear their voices, watch their gestures, to appreciate them and their stories. Spry and voluble, or feeble and pain-ridden, they reveal a single common outlook. They are certain that the next day or week or month will deliver them into the promised land that their forebears, less fortunate than they, first revealed to them. They look forward to that day with a serenity and faith that marks the true believer. "Been ready to die so long," admitted the Reverend John Brown, "that I don't worry no more 'bout it." And sometime during the night of January 20, 1938, 86-year-old John Brown passed in his sleep to the reward that he knew awaited him. Long-suffering, patient, and blind, John Brown had been a familiar figure along Petersburg streets, tapping his way from curb to curb with the long white cane that white folks had given him. Hardly five feet tall, an over-sized black preacher's suit draped around him, he presented to jeering children a ludicrous figure, but to those who knew him, a pathetic one. Sister 'Liza, his 75-year-old wife, had supported her aged husband for many years by working in a Petersburg tobacco factory. When they told her she was too old, she managed to keep herself and husband going by odd jobs of washing and cooking. "Guess I ought to go 'haid an' die, 'Liza," John Brown used to say, "so's you won't have to work so hard." "Shet yo' mouf," she would answer. "You gonna bury me yet." But Sister 'Liza still sits patiently in her little shack on Wallace Street, waiting for the day when she will join her husband.

"Are these actually ex-slaves?" we have been asked many times. "They couldn't remember all these fanciful stories." We should be delighted, of course, if slaveowners and county clerks had kept a record of slave ages, for the Virginia Bureau of Vital Statistics was not established until 1912. City records, property and tax lists afford scanty information. Where tales seem patently fantastic or where appearance does not seemingly indicate an age comparable with that claimed, we have, of course, placed no dependence on the story. It was not until we had questioned William Brooks over and over, attempting to find some basis for the graphic picture of slave days on his old plantation (he could not remember his owner's name) that neighbors finally admitted that he was better known as "Lying Brooks." Relatives and neighbors usually offered doubtful approximations of the "community Methuselah's" true age. "Sure, Grandpa's well over a hundred," declares one member of a family, while Grandpa himself thinks he was born in the forties. "Will Gramma get old-age pension if she's a hundred years old?" parries another offspring. "Sure, she's a hundred, but we ain't got no way of provin' it." The old folks themselves offer more likely approximations. Mildred Graves of Hanover County, feeble but sharp-tongued, reckons she is about a hundred because she "married de year de war started and was long out of cotton-shirts" at the time. Eliza Ann Taylor is willing to swear she was 95 years old on February 14, 1938, because her father told her how old she was before he died, and she hasn't "lost nary a letter of her age." Beverly Jones of Gloucester says he is 90 years old, and "if you don't believe it, look at the list of seamen that served in the Civil War. They got my age on the pension list." Nelson Hammock, who died in January, 1938, declared that he was born on October 10, 1844, in Brunswick County. Horace Muse thinks he is 103 years old, and an admiring neighbor, feeble at 65, is sure that Muse is about 110. Horace Muse himself says he was married and had two children "long 'fore de Yanks an' de Reb's started thinkin' 'bout goin' to war."

The Civil War is the never-to-be-forgotten date from which many ex-slaves reckon their age. Della Harris—small, wiry, and wrinkled— declares she was 13 years old at Lee's surrender. "I know," she states, "because ole Marse Peter Turnbull tole us all how ole we was when we lef' de plantation to go to Petersburg at surrender time." Placid and kindly, Frank Bell of Bailey's Cross Roads, ten miles below Alexandria, learned his age when the Civil War started. He explains:

"Here's how I know how old I is. De rebel troops come to Vienna an' tole Marse John Fallons to git ready to fight. Said dey'd give him three days, an' he'd better come; else dey'd come an' git him. De night fo' he was to go he called me to de front porch an' give me a long talkin' to. He made me promise to look arter Missus an' de younguns an' not to run away. Den he say: 'Frank, you know how ole you is?' 'No, sir, Marse John,' I answer. 'Well, Frank, on de fifth of March you were twenty-six years old. Now what year was you born?' 'Deed, Marse John, I don't know. I know dat I'll be twenty-seven on de fifth of March next year.' Ole Marse laughed an' clumped me on de shoulder. 'Well, you was born in 1835,' he tole me. 'When I git back fum whuppin' de Yanks, I'm goin' to teach yo' figgers.' "

"Marse John Fallons" never did get back from the war, says Frank Bell, for he was killed at the battle of Fredericksburg and buried where he fell.

More valuable even than the War as a guage of the ages of ex-slaves was Cox's Snow, a notable event that occurred on the ninth, tenth, and eleventh of February, 1857, and covered all Virginia and most of North Carolina. Records support ex-slaves in the assertion that Cox's Snow was the worst snow that ever hit the Old Dominion. Tissie White of Newport News, who lived on the Turner place in Dinwiddie County, says she was about 14 years old when the big snow "frez" Doctor Cox to death.

"It started on a Friday morning, an' mama had a stack of pies in de oven she was bakin' for de quiltin' bee on Saddy. Never did have dat party, though. It snowed all day Friday, all night Friday night, all day Sadday, all Sadday night, all day Sunday, all Sunday night, all day Monday, all Monday night, an' it didn't stop Tuesday 'til 'bout five o'clock. Twarn't no drift snow. Twas' jus' a ordinary fallin' snow, an' de sky must of been packed tight wid it. When it finally stopped, you couldn't see out an' you couldn't git out. Snow was way up level wid de roof top. Father couldn't git out to go to de house, an' he made all of us shove 'gainst de do' tell we pushed it open a little bit. I 'member I was skeered de snow was goin' to run in an' fill up de cabin. Arter while Dad got a path beat down to de barn, en' he fed de stock. De hogs was all daid. Snow done covered up dere pen an' buried 'em 'neath it.

"An' here's how dat come to be called Cox's Snow. Write it down 'cause it ain't never been in no hist'ry books. Ole Doc Phillip Cox was de medicine doctor dat come round to deliver all de slave babies. Mama say he done helped bring me into de worl'. Well, he was a great drinkin' man. Some sick person in de country sent fo' him, an' he went out into dat snow, though his folks tole him he hadn't ought to. Never did see him no more alive. Dey found him arter de snow was over settin' in his buggy on de country road, holdin' his reins like he was drivin', frez to death. De news dat ole Doc Cox done died went roun' like de wind. Arter dat dey called de big snow Cox's Snow."

The Reverend Israel Massie of Petersburg also judges his age by Cox's Snow. "Now Cox's Snow was in fifty-seven, and I was eight years ole at de time. How ole is I?" he asks. Small, dark, and slender, Israel Massie has a low-pitched, resonant voice, which he uses to good advantage. For many years he preached at various country churches; he still preaches at any church that will grant him the privilege. He has never married. "I'm waitin' fo' de right girl to come along," he declares. He needs a wife, he says, because he is tired of living at the City Home in Petersburg. His task is to dig graves for his fellow-inmates when they die and to preach their funeral sermons. "I reckon I'll dig my own grave," he suggests with a wry smile, "but I don't figger to preach my own fun'ral. Jim Boatman will have to do that fo' me."

Cornelius Garner, 91-year-old Civil War veteran, lives in a section of Norfolk by no means as inviting as his small, neat two-story frame house, built across the street from one of the war-time monstrosities for Negro shipyard workers. It is "not much," Garner explains, "but it's home enough for me." Standing but an inch or two over five feet, Cornelius Garner has the torso of a prize-fighter and the mind of a lawyer. His small beady eyes and scornful mouth hardly prepare one for his crisp half-amused voice. He loves to talk, admits that talking and his lodge meetings are his two remaining interests in life.

Every sunshiny day he steps down from his rickety stoop and parades up and down the uneven brick sidewalk, disdaining a cane and pausing at intervals to lean against a fence post. His frayed, faded bathrobe, the gift of a friend twenty years ago, is worn everywhere except to lodge meetings. He has a special uniform for such occasions, one befitting his position as oldest member and Past Grand Master. His failing strength is a constant worry, but it is not so much death he fears as missing his lodge meetings. "When my legs go, I hope I die," he declares with a sudden seriousness. "I ain't aimin' to pass away slowly lyin' in bed. Want to die on my feet, widdout knowin' nothin' 'bout it."

Charles Grandy, living on Smith Street in Norfolk, is Cornelius Garner's closest friend. He has two ages, he declares; his "war age" lists him as born January 31, 1842, and his slave age a year younger. "Used to set slaves' ages back in Virginia," he asserts. "Dat's so dey bring a better price if dey sell 'em." Charles Grandy, his mother, and six brothers and sisters belonged to Doctor William Wood on a plantation across from the town of Hampton, now part of the grounds of Hampton Institute. He was promised his freedom, he says, when he became 21, but the war interrupted. Thereupon he and two other slaves paddled across the river one night to Norfolk and were taken on as cooks in Company E of the 19th Wisconsin Volunteers. Seeking more active service, he enlisted at the expiration of his term in the Navy at $6.00 a month on the *U. S. Lawrence,* his official designation "Captain of the cutter," his duty to row officers from the gunboat to the shore and back. Charles Grandy lives comfortably on the pension he receives.

Ella Williams, shriveled and emaciated, clings to life with a tenacity that amazes her neighbors. She believes she is about 101 years old— although her owner, Henry Wilson, "never bothered 'bout no ages." Encased in a Victorian dress, with voluminous skirts revealing patches that have overlapped with the years, Ella Williams does her own shopping, for she lives on Wilson Street alone. "Got a bad misery in dis leg," she explains, as she hobbles up to her door. "Stuck a nail in dis foot a while back, an' it hurt fearful sometime. Went to de drug store to git some goose-grease to rub it. Pained so much I had to stop on de street an' pray fo' strength to git home. Gawd is awful kind to me when I need Him."

West Turner lives in the backwoods of Nansemond County, near Whaleyville. He stands six feet two inches in his stocking feet, he declares. As a matter of fact, he wears no shoes. "Cain't git none to fit so easy," he explains. "De sto' man say I wear size fo'teen, but de pair I got is too tight."

West Turner was born on Fayette Jackson's place near Danville in the tobacco and cotton country, " 'bout ninety-six years ago near as I can figger," he says. "Was strong as an ox when I was a boy. Could h'ist up on en' a hogshead of tobacco, an' spec' I could carry it if someone put it on my back. Cain't do it now. Old age got me good. Ain't got no kick comin' wid life, dough. My grandson an' his wife is good to me. Give me a room to myself an' plenty to eat. Used to git day work wid de white farmers up to a year or two ago. Cain't no mo,' dough. Death's creepin' up on me, an' my time ain't long. Might live to be a hundred, but I ain't figgerin' hard on it. Mighty hard on de young folks havin' me to look arter. Reckon it be better fo' 'em effen I die."

Far back in the woods of the Wilderness, close to the spot where Stonewall Jackson was accidentally shot by one of his own soldiers, lives aged Mildred Fowler who, in 1863, "saw de troops runnin' helter-skelter, an' shootin' at each other." For a week after the fighting she "couldn't git nothin' but red water from de spring," she insists. Partly deaf, she explains in an off-key voice that the huge goiter on her neck was "sposed to kill me fo'ty years ago. It come soon arter my husband died, an' de doctor say I would die effen he didn't cut it off. Well, it's still dere, an' I'm still livin', but de doctor's dead."

Out in Poquoson, a community of mixed Indian-Negro and white residents, lives Uncle Mobile Hopson, barely able to walk and totally blind. Uncle Mobile was free-born. He used to "see de black men workin' in de fields but never was allowed to talk to 'em." Grecian-featured, with skin as "white as a white man's," Uncle Mobile explains that he actually was white until the "Kluxers" reconstructed things after the war.

"We used to go to de white churches fo' de war; an' arter dey started schools, dey say we was Injuns. Well, we was, too, partly. But we wasn't no Negroes. First dey say we couldn't go in de white church no more. Well, we stopped goin'. Den when dey start de schools, dey say we couldn't go to de white schoolhouse. Some wouldn't go to de colored school-house, an' some would. My dad wouldn't let us go to school wid de

Negroes, so we didn't git no schoolin'. When it come to marryin' we was in a worse fix. Couldn't marry white an' we wasn't aimin' to marry colored. Started in to marryin' each other an' we been marryin' close cousins ever since."

In Norfolk in a neat comfortable house on one of the better residential streets lives 83-year-old Virginia Hayes Sheppard. Born on December 21, 1856, she knows more than most ex-slaves about her family history.

"My mother was a slave. Mamma was hired out to work for Doctor Howey King, who came down from the North and started practicing in Churchland. The master, a bachelor, allowed his two hundred and fifty slaves to do pretty much as they pleased. He let them hire themselves out, and consequently, when emancipation came, many of them had considerable savings stored away."

Stately and gentle, wearing her years lightly, Virginia Hayes Sheppard hardly fits the current conception of one who has experienced slavery. Her schooling began at seven under her mistress and continued until she graduated from Hampton Institute in 1877. She needs no one to care for her—does her own cooking, tends house, and looks after her precious flowers. More fortunate than most old folks of her age, she retains excellent eyesight, sews, and reads the newspapers each day. "It gives me a wonderful feeling," she says, "to see what our people are doing in these times. Only one who has been in slavery can appreciate how they have progressed since emancipation."

While some are humbled with the years, others still retain the fire of younger days. Meek little Georgianna Preston, timid and cowed, is one extreme; Anna Harris, proud and fiery, is another. Anna Harris says she has lived 92 years, and in her 73 years of freedom "no white man ever been in my house."

"Don't 'low it. Dey sole my sister Kate. I saw it wid dese here eyes. Sole her in 1860, and I ain't seed nor heard of her since. Folks say white folks is all right dese days. Maybe dey is, maybe dey isn't. But I can't stand to see 'em. Not on my place."

For many ex-slaves, the years have softened the memories of slavery. Some tell of playing with young Massa, of running all over the big house, of games and dances and parties. Others, however, recall their days in the fields, the lash, the slave auctions, the runaways.

They are an impressive group. Having lived beyond their allotted three-score years and ten, they cling to life, helpless and bedridden, or spry and gay, still looking forward to each numbered day as a new experience to be treasured the more, because it may be the last. Many express their determination to live to be a hundred. Dependent in many cases upon unsympathetic relatives of sub-marginal economic status, they "try not to be no trouble," for their creed through the years has uniformly been to look after themselves. Occasionally some of them speak of the relief that their death will bring to the household but the tone is more of apology than of conviction. They are ready for death when it comes, serenely confident that they have "lived right with God." Having witnessed the miracle of freedom, they believe that God has other miracles awaiting them.

From Slave Row

A little streak o' lean, an' a little streak o' fat,
Ole massa grumble ef you eat much o' dat.

FREDERICK LAW OLMSTEAD, visiting Virginia in 1853, saw "large and comfortable negro quarters . . . built of logs," which made slave row in Virginia far superior to its counterparts in the cotton and rice countries. Other observers, comparing slave quarters with the houses of the working classes in New England, found the Virginia variety "miserable hovels . . . no more habitable than the quarters afforded the plantation stock." Slave quarters yet standing and statements of ex-slaves support both views. "Us had a two-story house wid three rooms and floors upstairs and down," says Levi Pollard. "Us lived in a shack worse dan what de hogs lived in," declares Georgianna Gibbs, 89-year-old ex-slave of Portsmouth. Probably the key to the whole question is furnished in the penetrating comment of genial Beverly Jones:

"Now you see, dar was good marsas an' bad marsas. Marsas what was good saw dat slaves lived decent an' got plenty to eat. Marsas what was mean an' skinflinty throw em' scraps like dey feed a dog an' don' care what kind of shack dey live in. Warn't no law sayin' dey got to treat slaves decent."

A fair assumption is that among the landed aristocracy conditions were superior to those prevailing among the poor white class. Striving to wring from the exhausted lands a living, the poor whites of the pre-war days lived amid conditions as desolate as did the slave families. The contempt for poor whites was shared by blacks, as well as by white members of the "aristocracy," and Negroes so unfortunate as to labor for "poor-whites" were pitied and scorned. Slave row on some plantations consisted of pleasant, vine-covered cottages with windows and floors, and on others of broken down "log and daub" cabins with the sky visible through the roofs. Some were neat white-washed houses, weather and rain-proofed, while others were patched lean-tos, resting on the north side of "marsa's" house, providing support as well as protection.

The slave cabin was a haven of rest and sleep. Ex-slaves tell of the old folks, who at sundown would stretch their weary bodies on the bed, fully clothed, and remain motionless until the dreaded notes of the "conker-shell" blew them out at sunrise. Frequently a bed for the grown-ups and cots for the children were the only pieces of furniture. On some places discarded broken furniture from the plantation house was given the slaves, but more often they improvised their own furnishings. In slave row, where all slept and ate in the same room, canopies were rather necessary for modesty. Limitations of space led to other elaborations; children's cots were constructed to slide under the big bed. Slaves came to confuse such trundle beds with "tester" beds.

"Tester bed?" repeated Cecelia Tyler with surprise. "You don't know what a tester bed is? Tester bed is a big bed wid a little one 'neath it. Little one fo' de chillun an' it slide up under de big one. Had to stay there tell mama pulled us out in de mornin'—me, Lilly, and Prudence. Prudence was de baby an' whatever she got to do she got to do right in de bed."

Food allotments varied as widely as living conditions. In the 1830's John Taylor of Caroline County, president of the Agricultural Society of Virginia, wrote in his Agricultural Essays:

"Bread alone ought never to be considered a sufficient diet for slaves except as a punishment . . . Give our slaves . . . in addition to bread, salt meat and vegetables, and . . . we shall be astonished to discover upon trial, that this great comfort to them is a profit to the master."

About the same time the Reverend Mr. C. S. Renshaw reported that Virginia slaves were commonly fed "two meals a day—breakfast at from ten to eleven a. m. and supper at from six to nine or ten at night." The general allowance was a pint of corn meal and a salt herring, or in lieu of the herring, a "dab" of fat meat. Sour milk or clabber was occasionally added when there was an excess supply, but it was "a luxury not often afforded." In harvest time, meat rations were commonly increased, but, observes the Reverend Renshaw, slaves could "use more bacon."

Ex-slaves offer varied testimony. Susan Maberry, 95 years old, says her master gave his slaves "plenty to eat," while Horace Muse says he got "only one good meal a day an' dat was a measly ash cake an' cup o' buttermilk." Other accounts list a "family man" as receiving two and a half pounds of salt meat, a quart of molasses, and two pecks of corn. On most plantations provisions were apportioned according to the size of the family, with a half-ration given to each child.

Frederick Olmstead found that "drawings" of rations were on Saturday nights in the country, a custom that changed in urban areas to Wednesdays in order to prevent slaves from bartering food for whiskey. Allowances varied with the section of the state, the type of work done, and especially with the disposition of the master.

Food was commonly cooked in the fireplace, on "spiders." West Turner describes a spider as "Sompin' like a fryin' pan, ceptin' it got a long handle so's you kin pull it out de fire. Got long legs on it, too, so's it stand up 'tweenst de logs."

Most regular diet of slaves was hoe-cake—meal and water mixed to a thick dough, patted into a cake, and fried on the flat edge of an ordinary hoe that rested in the ashes. Says Marinder Singleton, listed in the Norfolk City records as 97 years old:

"Hoe-cakes was made of meal. You mix a cup of meal wid water an' pat it into small cakes. Grease it if you got grease—dat keep it from stickin'. Den you rake out de ashes an' stick it on de hoe into de bottom of de fire an' cover it up. Let it cook 'bout five minutes, den take it out, rub de ashes off an' pick out de splinters. Wash it off wid warm water an' eat it fo' it cools. Don't taste like nothin' if you let it get cold."

Occasionally the housewives would hold the hoe above the fire to avoid burning. Fannie Nicholson, 89 years old, asserts, however: "Twarn't no hoe-cake lessen de ashes burned it."

On some plantations a special kitchen was built in slave row with a huge brick oven lined with clay. In hog-killing time slave row would be presented with a hog, which was no less appreciated than the fat shoat Virginia slaveowners generally gave as a Christmas present. Those who experienced slavery say they were really "livin' good" when they had a clay oven equipped with "hand-irons" on which a hog or turkey could be roasted.

It was the unusual Virginia slaveowner who did not grant his slaves the privilege of raising pigs, chickens, and vegetables. "Missus used to give us seed ev'y spring fo' our own garden," recalls Aunt Lize Sparks. "Wasn't no starvin' on our place." And Virginia has always been a difficult place in which to starve. Its broad rivers with their many tributaries abounding in seafood, fish, crabs, and oysters, provided important supplements to the slave diet. Ex-slaves say that sometimes seafood was more than supplementary fare. "Us slaves lived off fish," asserts Archie Booker, 90-year-old inmate of the Elizabeth City County Poorhouse. " 'Feed yo' selves,' old Marsa Tabb used to tell us. 'You stealin' all my oysters anyway. Don't look fo' me to issue you no rations.' "

Corn, the major crop raised in slaves' gardens, required a minimum of cultivating and was a basic food. With no mill convenient, slaves ground the corn themselves, using an oak mortar with stone pestle, or a hand-mill clamped to the well-post. Coarse meal was sifted, "poured" to remove the chaff, then mixed with water, or buttermilk, if available, and cooked. The concoction called "hog and hominy" was the most tasty form in which the coarse meal could be used. Bacon and greens, enjoying equal favor, were considered a "proper food for gentlemen." The combination was natural in more ways than one. When hog pens became saturated with waste matter, the swine were turned out and the fertile soil was planted in turnip seed that soon sprang up luxuriantly. The tender tops—turnip salad—mixed with bacon, furnished welcome relief from the regular fare.

Clothes presented more of a problem than food. T. T. Bouldin, a slaveholder and congressman from Virginia, told Congress in 1835 "Many negroes had died from exposure as a consequence of flimsy fabric, that will turn neither wind nor weather."

On the larger plantations slave clothing was woven from home-grown cotton. Short-staple Virginia cotton, grown especially for slave garments, was loomed and fashioned into jackets, pants, and dresses by the slaves themselves. Georgianna Gibbs states that her mistress had three slaves who did nothing but weave and sew, while Arthur Greene, 86-year-old ex-slave of Petersburg, reports that his fellow laborers wrought their clothing from the first stage to the last.

"De women folks would spin de cotton, card it and weave it. Den dey could cut it an' sew it. Had to turn everything dey made over to marsa—warn't 'lowed to take nothin' fo' yo'self. Couldn't spin nuf clothes for ev'body. All dat didn't git homespun got guano bags."

New England cotton mills developed a special "Negro-cloth," a very coarse mixture of cotton and hemp, which went far towards outmoding homespun. The English variety of slave cloth, osnaburgh, or "fearnought"—a heavy coarse cloth—made a durable, if uncomfortable, garment. According to ex-slaves, there were but two sizes—large and small. The man who required a woman's size jacket had to "live humble," before the jibes of his fellows. George White of Lynchburg says slaves seldom enjoyed getting a new suit of osnaburgh.

"Dat ole nigger-cloth was jus' like needles when it was new. Never did have to scratch our back. Jus' wiggle yo' shoulders an' yo' back was scratched."

The usual dress for a man was canvas trousers and a cotton shirt with half-elbow length sleeves. Women wore a cotton "shift" and a heavier dress over it. Children wore a simple "tow" shirt, the discarded apparel of grown-ups, or a guano bag with arm-holes cut in the corners.

There was usually cast-off clothing from the big house to supplement "Negro cloth." "Missus" would donate old dresses and torn petticoats; "Marsa" would send each year a bundle of old clothes down to slave row, to be given out by his body servant. Ex-slaves tell of difficulties arising from such "dispensing."

Nancy Williams recalls such occasions:

"Missus would clean out de house each spring, an' Ant Emma would come puffin' down to de quarters totin' 'cross her back a big bundle of clothes tied up in Missus' ole petticoat. Spread 'em out an' all de niggers scramble fo' 'em. Never could git nothin' to fit you. After de scramble de slaves go round tradin' each other, tryin' to git fittin's."

Shoes and hats, say ex-slaves, were reserved for field work. The broiling sun was unbearable without protection, and the baked jagged clods of the tobacco fields were hard on bare feet. When children were issued shoes they knew that field work was about to begin for them. On some places the plantation shoemaker, commonly a Negro slave, could give a decent fit. But manufactured shoes, bought usually in the large sizes, gave sores and callouses. Home-cured leather was designed for wear rather than comfort. Slaves preferred these, however, to "bought" shoes, which were not built to stand service in the field.

Ex-slaves assert that the shoemaker of the plantation frequently shod both horses and slaves. West Turner says the blacksmith on his place, old Black Jack Fly, would "trace yo' foot in de dirt wid a stick, but it didn't do no good, 'cause he ain't never made de shoes like de dirt say."

Slaves' shoes were commonly high-topped boots with a double layer sole a half inch thick. Those who have worn them say that at no time of the year did they feel "right." In warm weather they chafed and blistered; in winter the poorly-cured leather stiffened to board-like hardness. Horace Muse recalls the care with which his mother tended his boots.

"No matter what tasks mother got to do, fo' she go to bed she clean dem shoes an' grease 'em wid tallow grease. Git stiff as a board in cold weather, an' lessen you grease 'em dey burn your feet an' freeze 'em too."

Children, too young to work, were the only happy ones in slave row, say many ex-slaves. "Aunty," ex-slaves say, was the common designation of the slave who nursed black children, while the title "Mammy," was reserved for the white children's nurse.

Nannie Williams, of Petersburg, who claims one hundred and two years, says she was brought up by Aunt Hannah who must have weighed "nigh onto three hundred pounds."

"I was Ant Hannah's helper, and each mornin' mama would drap me past Ant Hannah's house. Guess dey was 'bout fo'teen chillun she had to look arter, all of 'em black babies. Deed, chile, you ain't gonna believe dis but it's de gospel truf. Ant Hannah had a trough in her back yard— jus' like you put in a pig pen. Well, Ant Hannah would just po' dat trough full of milk an' drag dem chillun up to it. Chillun slop up dat milk jus' like pigs."

Sometimes "Aunty" took care of all babies, white and black, fed them from the same breast and put them to bed for "naps" together. Larger plantations had nurseries and a separate "mother" for the big house.

When a slave died, the quarters became mourners' row. Every one came quietly to pay his respects to the bereaved family. All night long friends would "set" with the family and sing and chant over the body. "Used to comfort 'em bes' you could," says Mariah Hines. "Wasn't much said. People nowadays talk wid dey tongues; us slaves used to talk wid our hearts."

Proper respect to the departed required that the body not be left unattended until burial. On the door of the bereaved family was hung some article of the dead person's clothing, a hat, a sock, or a coat—a custom that was possibly adopted from the hatchments that gentlemen farmers displayed in Colonial days to announce a death. In the "death wakes" of slave row were possibly conceived the hauntingly mournful spirituals voicing the hope of Death as the Great Deliverer: "Lord, Am I Born to Die;" "Come Down, Death, Right Easy;" and "Goin' to See Jesus in the Morning." The mourning period was a single night, for work had to go on without interruption. Besides, death was but one form of separation, perhaps the easiest; sale of loved ones effected a separation that had to be borne without even the solace of ceremony.

In rural areas and on larger plantations burial societies were common. Pennies were laid aside and turned over to the "treasurer," who recorded the payments by code in a book kept well-hidden. When a member died, the others would build or purchase a coffin, clothe their departed brother decently, and accompany him to the Negro burying ground, chanting hymns along the way. When the deceased was an old, respected family retainer, burial would possibly be in the family plot, and master and mistress would attend. In such cases the sorrow of whites would be as pronounced as that of blacks. A prominent tombstone in Old Bruton Parish churchyard is inscribed to "Mammy Sarah, devoted servant of the family who died aged sixty years." The tombstone was erected by Mammy Sarah's mistress, Mrs. James A. Semple, daughter of President Tyler. All of Mrs. Semple's children had been nursed and "reared" by the faithful old black woman, who died in 1863. For such occasions a regular service would be held with a minister to pray at the graveside. However, the deceased was often consigned to the earth in the manner described by West Turner.

"Now on our place when a slave die, 'ole overseer would go to de saw mill an' git a twelve inch board, shape it wid a point head and foot, an' dig a grave to fit it. Slaves tie de body to de board dressed in all de puhson's clothes 'cause wouldn't no one ever wear 'em. Whoever wear a dead man's clothes gonna die hisself real soon, dey used to say."

Most slaves were buried without benefit of clergy. Black preachers were banned after 1831; in their place black laymen would pray at the graveside, holding forth the palm of the hand as symbol of "God's book."

But many relatives were not satisfied until a Christian service was held, however long they must wait. Ex-slaves say the visit of the parish minister to the plantation would always be welcomed; then a "Bible" service would be said for all who had died since his last visit. And, in spite of the law, there were black preachers who traveled through the countryside "preachin' black men into their graves." Tom Stokes of Henrico County, who thinks he is getting near ninety, recalls John Jasper as such a preacher;

"John Jasper would go from place to place preachin' funerals fo' slaves. Sometimes dem slaves been daid an' buried a year or mo'. Den one Sunday ole Jasper would preach one big sermon over dem all."

Slave row had its brighter moments also. It was the one place where black men and women were free from supervision, where they

could "lower the mask," which a good servant must always wear
before master and mistress. There bantering and mimicry, gossiping
and laughter could be unrestrained, even if there were tragic under-
tones. House servant and field hand might meet there, and the testimony of the living ex-slaves does not support the tradition of animosity between the two. House servants would regale other members
of the "row," some of whom had never set foot in the "big house,"
with tales of "master" and "missus," would "take them off" in speech
and gesture so faithful that the less-privileged would shake with
laughter. They would "discuss their master or overseer, with a keen
freedom, a critical observation, and an irony as bitter as it is just."
And although slaves were great listeners at keyholes, they did not
always have to stoop so for inside information. In the cool of the evening—the tables cleared, the silver polished and put away, the children
in bed, the old clocks wound, the mules and horses watered, curried
down and fed, hoes and ploughs and harrows laid aside for the night—
house servants, stable-boys, and field hands would gather and tune in
upon the "grapevine telegraph." Perhaps the news was of old Nat
Turner on his wild revolt or of a "niggerbuyer" back on his Virginia
rounds or of a fugitive who had slipped away. Perhaps old and young
chuckled over Brer Rabbit's cunning or over John's fooling ole Marsa
out of a whipping, or perhaps they puzzled over the meaning of the
Good Book or sang in the moonlight, their blending voices plaintive
and compellingly beautiful. Or they would sit in their doorways,
their pipes glowing dully in the darkness, "puffin' old trouble away,"
finding solace in the very reason for their being in slave row.

And there were other pleasures—harvest, festivals, cornshuckings,
barbecues, Christmas, and Whitsuntide. These were times for general
celebration; old ones sang and prayed, while the younger and more
active would gather in the biggest cabin and "dance ole Jennie down."
And to break the monotony of the week, there was the welcome
although frequently unannounced ceremony that attended slave nup-
tials when, during a precious half-hour taken from the noonday period
or from the evening's rest, boys and girls in their Sunday best, would
parade down the "line" of cheering well-wishers, join hands, and
"jump the broomstick."

GEORGE WASHINGTON WILLIAMS (1849-1891)

George Washington Williams was born in Bedford Spring, Pennsylvania. He enlisted in the Union Army at the age of fourteen, serving through the War and becoming later a lieutenant-colonel in the Mexican army. After the fall of Maximillian, he re-enlisted in the United States Army, serving in several Indian campaigns. He entered Howard University and later, having decided upon the ministry as a career, he entered Newton Theological Seminary. Williams had a variegated career, conducting two newspapers, *The Commoner* in Washington and *The Southwestern Review* in Cincinnati, practicing law in Ohio and serving in the Ohio state legislature and as minister to Haiti. He developed an interest in the Congo and entered the service of the Belgian government. He died in Blackpool, England, while still in the Belgian service. His *The History of the Negro Race in America from 1819 to 1880* (1883) and *A History of the Negro Troops in the War of the Rebellion* (1888) were recognized in their day as the most authoritative accounts of the Negro that had appeared. In 1890, Williams published his denunciatory *An Open Letter . . . to Leopold II.*

[Negro Troops in the Civil War]

It was a question of grave doubt among white troops as to the fighting qualities of Negro soldiers. There were various doubts expressed by the officers on both sides of the line. The Confederates greeted the news that "niggers" were to meet them in battle with derision, and treated the whole matter as a huge joke. The Federal soldiers were filled with amazement and fear as to the issue.

It was the determination of the commanding officer at Port Hudson to assign this Negro regiment to a post of honor and danger. The regiment marched all night before the battle of Port Hudson, and arrived at one Dr. Chamber's sugar house on the 27th of May, 1863. It was just 5 A. M. when the regiment stacked arms. Orders were given to rest and breakfast in one hour. The heat was intense and the dust thick, and so thoroughly fatigued were the men that many sank in their tracks and slept soundly.

Arrangements were made for a field hospital, and the drum corps instructed where to carry the wounded. Officers' call was beaten at 5:30, when they received instructions and encouragement. "Fall in" was sounded at 6 o'clock, and soon thereafter the regiment was on the march. The sun was now shining in his full strength upon the field where a great battle was to be fought. The enemy was in his stronghold, and his forts were crowned with angry and destructive guns. The hour to charge had come. It was 7 o'clock. There was a feeling of anxiety among the white troops as they watched the movements of these Blacks in blue. The latter were anxious for the fray. At last the command came, "Forward, double-quick, march!" and on they went over the field of death. Not a musket was heard until the command was within four hundred yards of the enemy's works, when a blistering fire was opened upon the left wing of the regiment. Unfortunately Companies A, B, C, D, and E wheeled suddenly by the left flank. Some confusion followed, but was soon over. A shell— the first that fell on the line—killed and wounded about twelve men. The regiment came to a right about, and fell back for a few hundred yards, wheeled by companies, and faced the enemy again with the coolness and military precision of an old regiment on parade. The enemy was busy at work now. Grape, canister, shell, and musketry made the air hideous with their noise. A masked battery commanded a bluff, and the guns could be depressed sufficiently to sweep the entire field over which the regiment must charge. It must be remembered that this regiment occupied the extreme right of the charging line. The masked battery worked upon the left wing. A three-gun battery was situated in the centre, while a half dozen large pieces shelled the right, and enfiladed the regiment front and rear every time it charged the battery on the bluff. A bayou ran under the bluff, immediately in front of the guns. It was too deep to be forded by men. These brave colored soldiers made six desperate charges with indifferent success, because

> "Cannon to right of them,
> Cannon to left of them,
> Cannon in front of them,
> Volleyed and thundered;
> Stormed at with shot and shell."

The men behaved splendidly. As their ranks were thinned by shot and grape, they closed up into place, and kept a good line. But no matter what high soldierly qualities these men were endowed with, no matter how faithfully they obey the oft-repeated order to "charge," it was both a moral and physical impossibility for these men to cross the deep bayou that flowed at their feet—already crimson with patriot blood—and capture the battery on the bluff. Colonel Nelson, who commanded this black brigade, despatched an orderly to General Dwight, informing him that it was not in the nature of things for his men to accomplish anything by further charges. "Tell Colonel

Nelson," said General Dwight, "I shall consider that he has accomplished nothing unless he takes those guns." This last order of General Dwight's will go into history as a cruel and unnecessary act. He must have known that three regiments of infantry, torn and shattered by about fifteen or twenty heavy guns, with an impassable bayou encircling the bluff, could accomplish nothing by charging. But the men, what could they do?

> "Theirs not to make reply,
> Theirs not to reason why,
> Theirs but to do and die."

Again the order to charge was given, and the men, worked up to a feeling of desperation on account of repeated failures, raised a cry and made another charge. The ground was covered with dead and wounded. Trees were felled by shell and solid shot; and at one time a company was covered with the branches of a falling tree. Captain Callioux was in command of Company E, the color company. He was first wounded in the left arm—the limb being broken above the elbow. He ran to the front of his company, waving his sword and crying, "Follow me." But when within about fifty yards of the enemy he was struck by a shell and fell dead in front of his company.

Many Greeks fell defending the pass at Thermopylae against the Persian army, but history has made peculiarly conspicuous Leonidas and his four hundred Spartans. In a not distant future, when a calm and truthful history of the battle of Port Hudson is written, notwithstanding many men fought and died there, the heroism of the "Black Captain," the accomplished gentleman and fearless soldier, Andre Callioux, and his faithful followers, will make a most fascinating picture for future generations to look upon and study.

"Colonel, I will bring back these colors to you in honor, or report to God the reason why." It was now past 11 A. M., May 27, 1863. The men were struggling in front of the bluff. The brave Callioux was lying lifeless upon the field, that was now slippery with gore and crimson with blood. The enemy was directing his shell and shot at the flags of the First Regiment. A shell, about a six-pounder, struck the flag-staff, cut it in two, and carried away part of the head of Planciancois. He fell, and the flag covered him as a canopy of glory, and drank of the crimson tide that flowed from his mutilated head. Corporal Heath caught up the flag, but no sooner had he shouldered the dear old banner than a musket ball! went crashing through his head and scattered his brains upon the flag, and he, still clinging to it, fell dead upon the body of Sergeant Planciancois. Another corporal caught up the banner and bore it through the fight with pride.

This was the last charge—the seventh; and what was left of this gallant Black brigade came back from the hell into which they had plunged with so much daring and forgetfulness seven times.

They did not capture the battery on the bluff it's true, but they convinced the white soldiers on both sides that they were both willing and able to help fight the battles of the Union. And if any person doubts the abilities of the Negro as a soldier, let him talk with General Banks, as we have, and hear "his golden eloquence on the black brigade at Port Hudson."

A few days after the battle a "New York Times" correspondent sent the following account to that journal:

". . . Hearing the firing apparently more fierce and continuous to the right than anywhere else, I hurried in that direction, past the sugar house of Colonel Chambers, where I had slept, and advanced to near the pontoon bridge across Big Sandy Bayou, which the negro regiments had erected, and where they were fighting most desperately. I had seen these brave and hitherto despised fellows the day before as I rode along the lines, and I had seen General Banks acknowledge their respectful salute as he would have done that of any white troops; but still the question was—with too many,—'Will they fight?' The black race was, on this eventful day, to be put to the test, and the question to be settled—now and forever,—whether or not they are entitled to assert their right to manhood. Nobly, indeed, have they acquitted themselves, and proudly may every colored man hereafter hold up his head, and point to the record of those who fell on that bloody field. . . .

"The deeds of heroism performed by these colored men were such as the proudest white men might emulate. Their colors are torn to pieces by shot, and literally bespattered by blood and brains. The color-sergeant of the 1st La., on being mortally wounded, hugged the colors to his breast, when a struggle ensued between the two color-corporals on each side of him, as to who should have the honor of bearing the sacred standard, and during this generous contention one was seriously wounded. One black lieutenant actually mounted the enemy's works three or four times, and in one charge the assaulting party came within fifty paces of them. Indeed, if only ordinarily supported by artillery and reserve, no one can convince us that they would not have opened a passage through the enemy's works.

"Capt. Callioux of the Ist La., a man so black that he actually prided himself upon his blackness, died the death of a hero, leading on his men in the thickest of the fight. One poor wounded fellow came along with his arm shattered by a shell, and jauntily swinging it with the other, as he said to a friend of mine: 'Massa, guess I can fight no more.' I was with one of the captains, looking after the wounded going in the rear of the hospital, when we met one limping along toward the front. On being asked where he was going, he said: 'I been shot bad in the leg, captain, and dey want me to go to de hospital, but I guess I can gib 'em some more yet.' I could go on filling your columns with startling facts of this kind, but I hope I have told enough to prove that we can hereafter rely upon black arms as well as white in crushing this infernal rebellion. I long ago told you there was an army of 250,000 men ready to leap forward in defence of freedom at the first call. You know where to find them and what they are worth.

"Although repulsed in an attempt which—situated as things were —was all but impossible, these regiments, though badly cut up, are still on hand, and burning with a passion ten times hotter from their fierce baptism of blood. Who knows but that it is a black hand which shall first plant the Standard of the Republic upon the doomed ramparts of Port Hudson?" [1]

The official report of Gen. Banks. . . . applauds the valor of the Colored regiments:

". . . On the extreme right of our line I posted the first and third regiments of negro troops. The First Regiment of Louisiana Engineers, composed exclusively of colored men, excepting the officers, was also engaged in the operations of the day. The position occupied by these troops was one of importance, and called for the utmost steadiness and bravery in those to whom it was confided.

"It gives me pleasure to report that they answered every expectation. Their conduct was heroic. No troops could be more determined or more daring. They made, during the day, three charges upon the batteries of the enemy, suffering very heavy losses, and holding their position at nightfall with the other troops on the right of our line. The highest commendation is bestowed upon them by all the officers in command on the right. Whatever doubt may have existed before as to the efficiency of organizations of this character, the history of this day proves conclusively to those who were in a condition to observe the conduct of these regiments, that the Government will find in this class of troops effective supporters and defenders.

"The severe test to which they were subjected, and the determined

[1] New York Times, June 13, 1863.

manner in which they encountered the enemy, leave upon my mind no doubt of their ultimate success. They require only good officers, commands of limited numbers, and careful discipline, to make them excellent soldiers.

"Our losses from the 23d to this date, in killed, wounded, and missing, are nearly 1,000, including, I deeply regret to say, some of the ablest officers of the corps. I am unable yet to report them in detail.

"I have the honor to be, with much respect

"Your obedient servant,

"N. P. Banks,
            "Major-General   Commanding."

The effect of this battle upon the country can scarcely be described. Glowing accounts of the charge of the Black Regiments appeared in nearly all the leading journals of the North. The hearts of orators and poets were stirred to elegant utterance. The friends of the Negro were encouraged, and their number multiplied. The Colored people themselves were jubilant. Mr. George H. Boker, of Philadelphia, the poet friend of the Negro, wrote "The Black Regiment" on the gallant charge of the 1st Louisiana. . . .

The month of July, 1863, was memorable. Gen. Meade had driven Lee from Gettysburg, Grant had captured Vicksburg, Banks had captured Port Hudson, and Gillmore had begun his operations on Morris Island. On the 13th of July the New York Draft Riot broke out. The Democratic press had advised the people that they were to be called upon to fight the battles of the "Niggers" and "Abolitionists"; while Gov. Seymour *"requested"* the rioters to await the return of his adjutant-general whom he had despatched to Washington to have the President suspend the draft. The speech was either cowardly or treasonous. It meant, when read between the lines, it is unjust for the Government to draft you men; I will try and get the Government to rescind its order, and until *then* you are respectfully requested to suspend your violent acts against *property*. But the riot went on. When the troops under Gen. Wool took charge of the city, thirteen rioters were killed, eighteen wounded, and twenty-four made prisoners. The rioters rose ostensibly to resist the draft, but there were three objects before them: robbery, the destruction of the property of the rich sympathizers with the Union, and the assassination of Colored persons wherever found. They burned the Colored Orphans' Asylum, hung Colored men to lamp posts, and destroyed the property of this class of citizens with impunity.

During these tragic events in New York a gallant Negro regiment was preparing to lead an assault upon the rebel Fort Wagner on Morris Island, South Carolina. On the morning of the 16th of July, 1863, the 54th Massachusetts—first Colored regiment from the North —was compelled to fall back upon Gen. Terry from before a strong and fresh rebel force from Georgia. This was on James Island. The 54th was doing picket duty, and these early visitors thought to find Terry asleep; but instead found him awaiting their coming with all the vigilance of an old soldier. And in addition to the compliment his troops paid the enemy, the gunboats "Pawnee," "Huron," "Marblehead," "John Adams," and "Mayflower" paid their warmest respects to the intruders. They soon withdrew, having sustained a loss of 200, while Gen. Terry's loss was only about 100. It had been arranged to concentrate the Union forces on Morris Island, open a bombardment upon Fort Wagner, and then charge and take it on the 18th. The troops on James Island were put in motion to form a junction with the forces already upon Morris Island. The march of the 54th Mass., began on the night of the 16th and continued until the afternoon of the 18th. Through ugly marshes, over swollen streams, and broken dykes—through darkness and rain, the regiment made its way to Morris Island where it arrived at 6 A. M. of the 18th of July. The bombardment of Wagner was to have opened at daylight of this day; but a terrific storm sweeping over land and sea prevented. It was 12:30 P. M. when the thunder of siege guns, batteries, and gun-boats announced the opening of the dance of death. A semi-circle of batteries, stretching across the island for a half mile, sent their messages of destruction into Wagner, while the fleet of iron vessels battered down the works of the haughty and impregnable little fort. All the afternoon one hundred great guns thundered at the gates of Wagner. Toward the evening the bombardment began to slacken until a death-like stillness ensued. To close this part of the dreadful programme Nature lifted her hoarse and threatening voice, and a severe thunder-storm broke over the scene. Darkness was coming on. The brave Black regiment had reached Gen. Strong's headquarters fatigued, hungry, and damp. No time could be allowed for refreshments. Col. Shaw and Gen. Strong addressed the regiment in eloquent, inspiring language. Line of battle was formed in three brigades. The first was led by Gen. Strong, consisting of the 54th Massachusetts (Colored), Colonel Robert Gould Shaw; the 6th Connecticut, Col. Chatfield; the 48th New York, Col. Barton; the 3d New Hampshire, Col. Jackson;

the 76th Pennsylvania, Col. Strawbridge; and the 9th Maine. The
54th was the only regiment of Colored men in the brigade, and to it
was assigned the post of honor and danger in the front of the
attacking column. The shadows of night were gathering thick and
fast. Gen. Strong took his position, and the order to charge was given.
On the brave Negro regiment swept amid the shot and shell of
Sumter, Cumming's Point, and Wagner. Within a few minutes the
troops had double-quicked a half mile; and but few had suffered
from the heavy guns; but suddenly a terrific fire of small arms was
opened upon the 54th. But with matchless courage the regiment
dashed on over the trenches and up the side of the fort, upon the
top of which Sergt. Wm. H. Carney planted the colors of the regiment. But the howitzers in the bastions raked the ditch, and hand-
grenades from the parapet tore the brave men as they climbed the
battle-scarred face of the fort. Here waves the flag of a Northern
Negro regiment; and here its brave, beautiful, talented young colonel,
Robert Gould Shaw, was saluted by death and kissed by immortality!
Gen. Strong received a mortal wound, while Col. Chatfield and
many other heroic officers yielded a full measure of devotion to the
cause of the Union. Three other colonels were wounded,—Barton,
Green, Jackson. The shattered brigade staggered back into line under
the command of Major Plympton, of the 3d New Hampshire, while
the noble 54th retired in care of Lieutenant Francis L. Higginson.
The second brigade, composed of the 7th New Hampshire, Col. H.
S. Putnam; 62d Ohio, Col. Steele; 67th Ohio, Col. Vorhees; and
the 100th New York, under Col. Danby, was led against the fort,
by Col. Putnam, who was killed in the assault. So this brigade was
compelled to retire. One thousand and five hundred (1,500) men were
thrown away in this fight, but one fact was clearly established, that
Negroes could and would fight as bravely as white men. The following letter, addressed to the Military Secretary of Gov. Andrew, of
Massachusetts, narrates an instance of heroism in a Negro soldier
which deserves to go into history:

> "Headquarters 54th Massachusetts Vols.,
>   "Morris Island, S. C., Oct. 15, 1863.

"Colonel: I have the honor to forward you the following letter,
received a few days since from Sergeant W. H. Carney, Company C,
of this regiment. Mention has before been made of his heroic conduct
in preserving the American flag and bearing it from the field, in the
assault on Fort Wagner on the 18th of July last, but that you may
have the history complete, I send a simple statement of the facts as I

have obtained them from him, and an officer who was an eye-witness:

"When the Sergeant arrived to within about one hundred yards of the fort—he was with the first battalion, which was in the advance of the storming column—he received the regimental colors, pressed forward to the front rank, near the Colonel, who was leading the men over the ditch. He says, as they ascended the wall of the fort, the ranks were full, but as soon as they reached the top, 'they melted away' before the enemy's fire 'almost instantly.' He received a severe wound in the thigh, but fell only upon his knees. He planted the flag upon the parapet, lay down on the outerslope, that he might get as much shelter as possible; there he remained for over half an hour, till the 2d brigade came up. He kept the colors flying until the second conflict was ended. When our forces retired he followed, creeping on one knee, still holding up the flag. It was thus that Sergeant Carney came from the field, having held the emblem of liberty over the walls of Fort Wagner during the sanguinary conflict of the two brigades, and having received two very severe wounds, one in the thigh and one in the head. Still he refused to give up his sacred trust until he found an officer of his regiment.

"When he entered the field hospital, where his wounded comrades were being brought in they cheered him and the colors. Though nearly exhausted with the loss of blood, he said: 'Boys, the old flag never touched the ground.'

"Of him as a man and soldier, I can speak in the highest of praise.

"I have the honor to be, Colonel, very respectfully,

Your most obedient servant,

"M. S. Littlefield,
Col. Comd'g 54th Reg't Mass. Vols."

Col. A. G. Brown, Jr., Military Secretary to his Excellency John A. Andrews, Mass.

CHARLES H. WESLEY (1891-   )

Charles Harris Wesley, born in Louisville, Kentucky, was educated at Fisk University, Yale, the Guild Internationale, and Harvard. He has been a minister of the African Methodist Episcopal Church and, since 1913, a member of the faculty of Howard University, where he became head of the department of history in 1921 and where he is now dean of the Graduate School. Wesley has been a Guggenheim Fellow. He has written many articles and monographs on phases of

Negro history, and four books: *Negro Labor in the United States,
1850-1925*, a pioneering study; *The Collapse of the Confederacy*
(1937), the first book to summarize the internal causes of the decline
of Southern resistance; *The History of Alpha Phi Alpha: a Development in Negro College Life* (1929); and *Richard Allen, Apostle of
Freedom* (1935). The following is Chapter 3, "Popular Morale," of *The
Collapse of the Confederacy,* with a section omitted which deals with
the widespread desertions. This is reprinted by permission of the
author and of The Associated Publishers, Inc.

From The Collapse of the Confederacy

The Decline of Enthusiasm

THE FIRST YEARS OF THE WAR were marked by the enthusiasm of
those who were influenced by the secessionists. Nevertheless, there
had been opposition to the Confederate program of secession from
the beginning of the conflict, and there were those who had never
been enthusiastic in their support of it. The movement for secession
had been opposed by the representatives of the up-country interests in
many of the seceding states. In Alabama, thirty-nine delegates voted
against the ordinance of secession, and more than one-third of the
secession convention in Georgia registered their opposition to the
movement.[1] In Mississippi fifteen of the ninety-nine members of the
convention voted against secession, and in Texas there was much
opposition although secession was finally carried with only eight
votes against it. Secession was successfully fought in Virginia, North
Carolina, Arkansas and Tennessee until it was shown to the people
of these states that coercion was being exerted by the North. In
Louisiana, the popular vote for delegates to the convention showed
that 20,448 had voted for secession delegates and 17,296 had voted
against them. Reluctantly the opposition yielded its position in state
after state. This group of the Southern population grew resentful
at the invasion of their territory and the probability that the slaves
would be placed upon a plane of equality with them if the North
should be victorious. The secession movement gathered momentum
as the news of its victories passed from one state to the other; and,
following the votes of the seven states of the lower South, a united
front seemed to be presented to the North. A rapid victory would
have satisfied the people, but when this did not come disappointment

[1] W. L. Fleming, *Civil War and Reconstruction in Alabama,* pp. 53, 55; *Tribune
Almanac,* 1862, p. 42; *Annual Cyclopedia,* 1861, pp. 9-10; E. M. Coulter, *Short History
of Georgia,* p. 200; U. B. Phillips, *Georgia and States Rights,* p. 203.

began to appear. Defeatism slowly undermined the foundations of an apparently united resistance.

After 1861 there was a gradual decline in popular enthusiasm. The discontented class grew in numbers and power, so that by February, 1863, the *Richmond Dispatch* was forced to ask, "Can it be that after all, we are not in earnest?" Governor Vance pleaded for "the stern and determined devotion to our cause which alone can sustain a revolution." "Let us remember," he said, "that it is the spirit of the people which tyrants cannot subdue. On this depends all. So long as they continue harmonious, willing, self-sacrificing, the united armies of the continent may be hurled against us in vain."[2] Again and again, he urged that the spirit of the people should be sustained by every act of the General Assembly. Jefferson Davis traveled into many camps and cities, and endeavored to renew the courage of the despondent element. His speeches were given wide publicity. Some of the newspapers joined in the campaign to keep alive the zeal of the people. But despondency and discontent continued to reign.

From the beginning of the year 1863, the President of the Confederacy seemed to be discounted with Congress and the military leadership. The Congress appeared to be equally discontented with the President; and the majority of the people continued to be dissatisfied with both. Several observers stated that the turning point in Southern morale during the war seemed to have come in 1863. Judah P. Benjamin wrote to R. T. Hubard on August 8, 1863, "The disasters at Vicksburg and Port Hudson produced for the time being a general depression and despondency of which none but those of firm purpose and resolute spirit were wholly free."[3] There is no evidence that the people believed that they were beaten from the time of these events to the end of the war, but there was developed a gradual sentiment which manifested a change in popular morale. Jones, of the Surrey Light Artillery, wrote at this time that "our losses have been great but there is yet hope for us"—which was only a half-hearted consolation.

Another observer, Jonathan Worth, of North Carolina, declared in August, 1863, that the war could not last much longer. "The want of subsistence," wrote he, "and the returning sanity of our women will contribute much to close it. The last-dollar and the last-man men abuse Holden's peace article, but the fact that he has the largest and most rapidly increasing circulation of any other journal in the state

[2] *Off. Reds. Rebell.*, Ser. IV, Vol. II, pp. 180-190.
[3] *Confederate State Department*, Benjamin to Hubard, Aug. 8, 1863.

indicated the current of public opinion." It was said that Holden's subscription list had increased 25 per cent within a very short time. The situation in this state was described as a sense of insecurity which presaged an appeal to arms, and the root of the whole matter was "a deadly hostility to our cause and our Government." It was in this year that Vance and Holden parted company. Vance had been brought forward as a gubernatorial candidate in 1862, and in 1863 the split came over the issues of the war. Governor Vance continued to work for the Southern cause while Holden worked for peace. Worth also expected that at the expiration in 1864 of the three-year term of service of the men of 1861, they would not re-enlist, and that no member of Congress would dare require a longer service. Worth concluded that "the masses are for peace on any terms . . . they are determined the war shall cease. . . . As soon as this spirit extends from the people to the army, the end will come."[4]

Additional testimony concerning this condition among the people is given by J. E. Joyner, a citizen of Henry Court-House, Virginia, who had been traveling about the upper counties of Virginia in 1863. He reported that he had discovered an unfortunate condition of affairs in this section of the state. He stated that in parts of Bedford, portions of Botecourt, Roanoke, Montgomery, Giles, Floyd, Franklin, Patrick Henry, and portions of Pittssylvania counties, the people seemed completely demoralized. He found that this state of mind existed to a great extent among the best citizens. He stated further, "They think and say that we are whipped, and are bound to be overrun and subjugated. The impression has very extensively obtained that our army is disspirited and is deserting by hundreds and whole regiments have left at a time." He added, the upper counties of North Carolina were much worse than those that he had mentioned and that "the deserters are accumulating a vast number of muskets in all the country and avow that they shall be used against the Confederacy if there is any attempt to arrest them. There are hundreds of men throughout this country, aye, I may say thousands, who ought to be in the service, but there is not moral force enough in the country to bring them out."[5]

Throughout the first years of the war, when the Confederate armies were successful in the majority of battles, enthusiasm had run high. General Lee was then able to withstand the onslaughts of the Union forces although his army was from one-half to one-third as large as his opponents. This fact had verified the secessionists' belief that one

---

[4] *Correspondence of Jonathan Worth*, Vol. I, pp. 251, 256.
[5] *Off. Reds Rebell.*, Ser. IV, Vol. II, pp. 721-723.

Confederate soldier could whip several Yankees sent against the South. As it became apparent that such bravery was not accomplishing a permanent victory over the North, the defeatist attitude became still more pronounced. . . .

"Rich Man's War"

Many people in the South had only an academic interest in the continuance of slavery and the success of secession. As has been noted, most slaves were owned by a relatively small group of slave-holders, who were in the Black Belt, the tide-water and river valley sections. The white population of the seceded states by the census of 1860 was 5,447,219. Of this number, 384,000 owned slaves. These were distributed among 1,733 who owned one hundred or more slaves, 10,781 who owned fifty or more slaves, 107,950 who possessed ten or more slaves and the remaining number of owners holding less than ten slaves. Since these slaves belonged to the slave-holding families and not always to an individual slaveholder, it is probable that the actual number of slaveholders was larger than the census enumerations indicates. These slave capitalists exerted an influence far exceeding their number over the majority of the people who had no direct connection with slavery or did not profit by the system. It was inevitable that this large number would be led to the conclusion that the war was "a Poor Man's Fight." One group of these was composed of small farmers and artisans. Another group known as the "poor whites," the crackers and the backwoodsmen, was very numerous and formed through their active opposition a menace to the existing social order in the Confederacy.

The exemption of slave-owners and overseers led to much disaffection in the army and among the people. The cry became widespread that the conflict was a "Rich Man's War" and a "Poor Man's Fight." General Ruggles of Mississippi wrote in 1863 that "the people assumed that if the more wealthy portion of our population, the slave-owners, will not enter the ranks to defend their property, it was not incumbent on those who had no such large interests at stake. The argument received greater force by the number of substitutes employed by the more wealthy." He concluded that "unless something is done to correct this growing spirit of discontent, we shall cease to have that cordial support of the citizens who constitute the majority of our fighting forces."[6] Senator Phelen of the same state wrote President Davis, giving the opinion that "never did a law meet with more

[6] *Publications, Mississippi Historical Society*, Centenary Ser. Vol. II, p. 181.

universal odium than the exemption of slaveowners." "Its gross injustice," he added, was denounced "even by those whose position enables them to take advantage of its privileges—its influence upon the poor is most calamitous and has awakened a spirit and elicted a discussion of which we may safely predict unfortunate results.[7]

There was no solidarity of interest among the Southern people. Class antagonisms and class conflicts were inevitable. The South was a stratified society based mainly upon two sharp class lines, those who owned slaves and those who did not own slaves. The owners of slaves constituted the ruling class. Jealous of the security of the ruling class, the common folk shirked the call to war. . . .

The Will to Fight

The last six months of the Confederacy, so far as the populace was concerned, were months of sham. The will to fight had been broken. In May, 1864, General Sherman left Chattanooga for Georgia. Governor Brown issued a series of appeals to Georgians to arise and repel the invaders. They were urged to come in squads or singly, to bring such weapons as they could find and to bush-whack the invaders without mercy.[8] Senator Hill of Georgia fervently appealed, saying, "Every citizen with his gun and every Negro with his spade and axe, can do the work. Georgians, be firm, act promptly and fear not." The delegation from Georgia in the Confederate House sent the state the urgent message, "Let every man fly to arms—remove provisions and Negroes. Burn all bridges and block up the road in his route. Assail the invader by day and night—let him have no rest." General Beauregard also sought to arouse the state to danger. Said he, "Arise for the defense of your native soil. Obstruct and destroy all roads in Sherman's front, flank and rear, and his army will soon starve in your midst."[9] The *Richmond Dispatch* reported the response to these appeals. It stated that the planters stayed at home, awaiting the invaders approach, "nor did they destroy any property or drive away their cattle." It concluded that there was only one interpretation, that "confidence in the success of the rebellion no longer exists anywhere outside of the official class and the army."[10]

Other contemporaries voiced the same defeatist spirit. Senator Foote, writing early in 1864, stated that by December of that year, "to all men in Richmond, the collapse of the Confederate cause

---

[7] *Ibid.*, p. 182.
[8] *Off. Reds. Rebell.*, Ser. I, Vol. IIII, pt. II, pp. 673-674.
[9] *Charleston Mercury*, November 22, 1864.
[10] *Richmond Dispatch*, February 14, 1865.

appeared inevitable." Mrs. Chesnut wrote in September 1864 that the end had come—"since Atlanta fell, I have felt as if all were dead within me forever."[11] Another observer, De Leon, stated in *Four Years in Rebel Capitals* that the fall of Atlanta was a terrible shock to the people of the South. "A sullen and increasing gloom," said he, "seemed to settle over the majority of the people With a base of communication five hundred miles in Sherman's rear, through our own country, not a bridge has been burned, nor a car thrown from its track, nor a man shot by the people whose country he has desolated. They seem everywhere to submit when our armies are withdrawn. What does this show, my dear Sir? It shows what I have always believed, that the great popular heart is not now, and never has been in this war. It was a revolution of the politicians, not the people; and was fought at first by the natural enthusiasm of our young men, and has been kept going by state and sectional pride, assisted by that bitterness of feeling produced by the cruelties and brutalities of the enemy.[12] Edmund Ruffin wrote on November 18, 1864, "If the residents and proprietors have the patriotism to burn and destroy all provisions ahead of the army's advance it would be the surest mode of defense. But I fear this cannot be hoped for, and if enough provisions were found along the line of march, I do not see why Sherman may not successfully pass through any extent of Georgia, South Carolina, and Alabama, finding a country hitherto undepleted of its supplies on either route." . . .

As the year 1865 dawned, there was an absence of the enthusiasm of 1861 among many of the Southern people. The events of 1865 seemed to contribute to this alarming change. At Salisbury and Charlotte, North Carolina, there were two destructive fires which consumed great quantities of stores, and there was a great freshet on January 10, which carried away bridges, mills, fences and tore up railroads all through the central part of the state. Mrs. Spencer in the *Last Ninety Days of the War* declared that these happenings added to the general gloom and depression and that "the very elements seemed to have enlisted against us."[13] From Georgia, Howell Cobb wrote that "gloom and despondency rule the hour and bitter opposition to the administration mingled with dissatisfaction and disloyalty is manifesting itself."[14] A correspondent of the *Richmond Dispatch*,

[11] Chestnut, p. 327.
[12] *Last Ninety Days*, pp. 27-28.
[13] *Last Ninety Days*, p. 29.
[14] *Southwestern Historical Quarterly*, Vol. XIX, p. 229; Jones, *War Clerk*, Vol. II, p. 393.

in January, 1865, told of the contrast in Charleston between 1860 and 1865; that those who were the most furious advocates of secession in 1860-61 as well as many of the most confident and resolute supporters of the cause were in 1865 the most despondent; that the city which had been "the cradle of rebellion and the hot-bed of secession no longer presented the bold front with which it entered the conflict and the men who would not stop to count the cost four years ago and who inaugurated the secession movement, now think of another revolution."[15]

Evidences of this new revolutionary spirit were not entirely absent. In Georgia there were stationed near Dalton troops who threatened to lay down their arms and refuse to fight. The demand for an end of the war was said to have continued among some of the companies of soldiers in the state until its close.[16] In Florida, was held a meeting in which loyalty to the Union was proclaimed.[17] Similar incidents occurred in other states, especially during the last six months of the war.

Several manifestations of the state of the public mind, revealing still further the declining spirit of the Southern people and showing a gradual loss of faith and confidence in the future were recorded during these months. Thomas Bocock wrote President Davis on January 21, 1865, that there was a rapid change for the worse in the public sentiment of the country, "not only in other states but here in our loved and honored Virginia"; and he urged that something should be done "to restore confidence and revive hopes or else we may look for the worst results." As one writer interpreted the situation, "The people are not only weary of the war, but they have no longer any faith in the President, his Cabinet, Congress, the Commissaries, quartermasters, enrolling officers and most of the Generals." Finally he was led to cry out, "God save us! We seem incapable of saving ourselves." [18] Edmund Ruffin declared that he hoped to live to see the triumph of the Confederate cause but that "every passing month seems to leave the attainment less hopeful—I cannot die too soon." Even General Lee realized the condition. He wrote to General Wise in February 1865, "We have strength enough left to win it, if the people will not give way to foolish despair.[19] A few days before, he had thus addressed W. G. Rives, emphasizing, "If the people will

---

[15] *Richmond Dispatch,* January 20, 1865.

[16] *Off. Reds. Rebell.,* Ser. I, Vol. XXXII, pt. I, p. 13; Vol. XXXV, pt. I, p. 531.

[17] Moore, *Rebellion Record, Vol.* VI, p. 484.

[18] Jones, *War Clerk,* Vol. II, p. 391.

[19] *Richmond Dispatch,* February 17, 1865.

sustain the soldiers and evince the same resolution as the army," he felt no apprehension about the issue of the contest.[20] Again in March, he wrote to Secretary Breckinridge, "Everything, in my opinion, has depended and still depends upon the disposition and feelings of the people." Reagan, the Post Master-General, informed President Davis on April 22, 1865, "It is also for me to say that much as we have been exhausted in men and resources, I am of the opinion that if our people continue the contest with the spirit which animated them during the first years of the war, our independence might yet be in our reach. But I see no reason for that now."[21]

Confidence was thus rapidly passing away. "Reestablish confidence," said the *Daily South Carolinian,* a Columbia weekly, "and our greatest victory is won."[22] Ex-Governor Graham of North Carolina stated that he left Richmond in the evacuation movement, convinced of three things, (1) that independence for the Southern Confederacy was perfectly hopeless; (2) that through the administration of Jefferson Davis they could not expect peace, so long as he was supplied with the resources of war; and (3) that it was the duty of the state Government to adjust the quarrel with the United States.[23]

While much depended upon the people, almost as much depended upon the army. Straggling bodies of Confederate soldiers hurried through North Carolina and Georgia. In some of the armies discipline seemed to have broken down. There were those who saw that the subjugation of the Confederacy would be a matter of years. The extensive territory of the South, if the soldiers could be kept fighting, would make immediate subjugation impossible. Warfare by detached parties who knew the country could have been carried on for years. Small bands of soldiers could have existed where large armies would starve. But the will to fight was gone, and the Confederacy was growing weaker with the passing days.

Two days before General Lee's surrender, April 7, 1865, Mrs. Andrews wrote in her diary, "The war is closing in upon us from all sides. I am afraid there are rougher times ahead than we have ever known yet!" On April 18, while in the streets, she learned of rumors of the surrender, and she wrote, "nobody seems to doubt it and everybody feels ready to give up hope." When the confirmation of Lee's surrender was brought, she wrote, "There is a complete revulsion

[20] *Ibid.,* February 9, 1865.
[21] Reagan, *Memoirs,* p. 204.
[22] *Daily South Carolinian,* February 12, 1865.
[23] *Last Ninety Days,* pp. 137-141.

in public feeling. No more talk about help from France and England, but all about emigration to Mexico and Brazil. We are irretrievably ruined."[24]

T. THOMAS FORTUNE (1856-1928)

T. Thomas Fortune was born in Florida, the son of a Reconstruction politician. Fortune was one of the leading Negro journalists, in 1882 editing the *Globe*, a Negro daily, and later *The New York Age*. In the twenties he was connected with *The Negro World*. *Black and White: Land, Labor, and Politics in the South* (1884) and *The Negro in Politics* (1885), both written before Fortune was thirty years old, show him to be a fearless thinker in advance of his times and worthy of more than the neglect that has befallen him. In 1900 he joined Booker T. Washington in organizing the National Negro Business League. The selection reprinted is the conclusion of *Black and White: Land, Labor, and Politics in the South.*

Land and Labor in the South

I KNOW IT IS NOT FASHIONABLE for writers on economic questions to tell the truth, but the truth should be told, though it kill. When the wail of distress encircles the world, the man who is linked by "the one touch of nature" which "makes the whole world kin" to the common destiny of the race universal; who hates injustice wherever it lifts up its head; who sympathizes with the distressed, the weak, and the friendless in every corner of the globe, such a man is morally bound to tell the truth as he conceives it to be the truth. . . .

In these times, when the law-making and enforcing authority is leagued against the people; when great periodicals—monthly, weekly and daily—echo the mandates or anticipate the wishes of the powerful men who produce our social demoralization, it becomes necessary for the few men who do not agree to the arguments advanced or the interests sought to be bolstered up, to "cry aloud and spare not." The man who with the truth in his possession flatters with lies, that "thrift may follow fawning" is too vile to merit the contempt of honest men.

The government of the United States confiscated as "contrabrand of war" the slave-population of the South, but it left to the portion

[24] Andrews, *Diary,* pp. 136, 153-155. These sentiments are directly opposed to the sentiment of Colonel Freemantle, who stated in his *Three Months in the Southern States* in 1863 that the devotion of South would not witness the destruction of "such a gallant race."

of the unrepentent rebel a far more valuable species of property. The slave, the perishable wealth, was confiscated to the government and then manumitted; but property in land, the wealth which perishes not nor can fly away, and which had made the institution of slavery possible, was left as the heritage of the robber who had not hesitated to lift his iconoclastic hand against the liberties of his country. The baron of feudal Europe would have been paralyzed with astonishment at the leniency of the conquering invader who should take from him his slave, subject to mutation, and leave him his landed possessions which are as fixed as the Universe of Nature. He would ask no more advantageous concession. But the United States took the slave and left the thing which gave birth to *chattel slavery* and which is now fast giving birth to *industrial slavery*; a slavery more excruciating in its exactions, more irresponsible in its machinations than that other slavery, which I once endured. The chattel slave-holder must, to preserve the value of his property, feed, clothe and house his property, and give it proper medical attention when disease or accident threatened its life. But industrial slavery requires no such care. The new slave-holder is only solicitous of obtaining the maximum of labor for the minimum of cost. He does not regard the man as of any consequence when he can no longer produce. Having worked him to death, or ruined his constitution and robbed him of his labor, he turns him out upon the world to live upon the charity of mankind or to die of inattention and starvation. He knows that it profits him nothing to waste time and money upon a disabled industrial slave. The multitude of laborers from which he can recruit his necessary laboring force is so enormous that solicitude on his part for one that falls by the wayside would be a gratuitous expenditure of humanity and charity which the world is too intensely selfish and materialistic to expect of him. Here he forges wealth and death at one and the same time. He could not do this if our social system did not confer upon him a monopoly of the soil from which subsistance must be derived, because the industrial slave, given an equal opportunity to produce for himself, would not produce for another. On the other hand the large industrial operations, with the multitude of laborers from which Adam Smith declares employers grow rich, as fast as this applies to the soil, would not be possible, since the vast volume of increased production brought about by the industry of the multitude of co-equal small farmers would so reduce the cost price of food products as to destroy the incentive to speculation in them, and at the same time utterly destroy the necessity or the possibility of famines, such as those which have from time to time come upon the Irish people. There could be no famine, in the natural course of things, where all had an opportunity to cultivate as much land as they could wherever they found any not already under cultivation by some one else. It needs no stretch of the imagination to see what a startling tendency the announcement that all vacant land was free to settlement upon condition of cultivation would have to the depopulation of overcrowded cities like New York, Baltimore and Savannah, where the so-called pressure of population upon subsistence has produced a hand-to-hand fight for existence by the wage-workers in every avenue of industry.

This is no fancy picture. It is a plain, logical deduction of what would result from the restoration to the people of that equal chance in the race of life which every man has a right to expect, to demand, and to exact as a condition of his membership of organized society.

The wag who started the "forty acres and a mule" idea among the black people of the South was a wise fool; wise in that he enunciated a principle which every argument of sound policy should have dictated, *upon the condition that the forty acres could in no wise be alienated,* and that it could be regarded *only* as *property* as *long as it was cultivated;* and a fool because he designed simply to impose upon the credulity and ignorance of his victims. But the justness of the "forty acre" donation cannot be controverted. In the first place, the slave had earned this miserable stipend from the government by two hundred years of unrequited toil; and, secondly, as a free man, he was inherently entitled to so much of the soil of his country as would suffice to maintain him in the freedom thrust upon him. To tell him he was a free man, and at the same time shut him off from free access to the soil upon which he had been reared, without a penny in his pocket, and with an army of children at his coat-tail—some of his reputed wife's children being the illegitimate offspring of a former inhuman master—was to add insult to injury, to mix syrup and hyssop, to aggravate into curses the pretended conference of blessings.

When I think of the absolutely destitute condition of the colored people of the South at the close of the Rebellion; when I remember the moral and intellectual enervation which slavery had produced in them; when I remember that not only were they thus bankrupt, but that they were absolutely and unconditionally cut off from the soil, with absolutely no right or title in it, I am surprised,—not that they have already got a respectable slice of landed interests; not that they have taken hold eagerly of the advantages of moral and intellectual opportunities of development placed in their reach by the charitable philanthrophy of good men and women; not that they have bought homes and supplied them with articles of convenience and comfort, often of luxury,—but I am surprised that the race did not turn robbers and highwaymen, and, in turn, terrorize and rob society as society had for so long terrorized and robbed them. The thing is strange, marvelous, phenomenal in the extreme. Instead of becoming outlaws, as the critical condition would seem to have indicated, the black men of the South *went manfully to work* to better their own condition and the crippled condition of the country which had been produced by the ravages of internecine rebellion; *while the white men of the South, the capitalists, the land-sharks, the poor white trash, and the nondescripts, with a thousand years of Christian civilization and culture behind them, with "the boast of chivalry, the pomp of power," these white scamps, who had imposed upon the world the idea that they were paragons of virtue and the heaven-sent vicegerents of civil power, organized themselves into a band of outlaws, whose concatenative chain of auxiliaries ran through the entire South, and deliberately proceeded to murder innocent men and women for POLITICAL REASONS and to systematically rob them of their honest labor because they were too accursedly lazy to labor themselves.* ...

But this highly abnormal, unnatural condition of things is fast passing away. The white man having asserted his superiority in the matters of assassination and robbery, has settled down upon a barrel of dynamite, as he did in the days of slavery, and will await the explosion with the same fatuity and self-satisfaction true of him in other days. But as convulsions from within are more violent and destructive than convulsions from without, being more deep-seated and therefore more difficult to reach, the next explosion will be more disastrous, more far-reaching in its havoc than the one which metamorphosed social conditions in the South, and from the dreadful reactions of which we are just now recovering.

As I have said elsewhere, the future struggle in the South will be, not between white men and black men, but between capital and labor, landlord and tenant. Already the cohorts are marshalling to the fray; already the forces are mustering to the field at the sound of the slogan.

The same battle will be fought upon Southern soil that is in preparation in other states where the conditions are older in development but no more deep-seated, no more pernicious, no more blighting upon the industries of the country and the growth of the people.

It is not my purpose here to enter into an extended analysis of the foundations upon which our land system rests, nor to give my views as to how matters might be remedied. I may take up that question at some future time. It is sufficient for my purposes to have indicated that the social problems in the South, as they exfoliate more and more as resultant upon the war, will be found to be the same as those found in every other section of our country; and to have pointed out that the questions of "race," "condition," "politics," etc., will all properly adjust themselves with the advancement of the people in wealth, education, and forgetfulness of the unhappy past.

The hour is approaching when the laboring classes of our country, North, East, West and South, will recognize that they have a *common cause,* a *common humanity* and a *common enemy*; and that, therefore, if they would triumph over wrong and place the laurel wreath upon triumphant justice, without distinction of race or of previous condition, *they must unite!* And unite they will, for "a fellow feeling makes us won'drous kind." When the issue is properly joined, the rich, be they black or be they white, will be found upon the same side; and the poor, be they black or be they white, will be found on the same side.

Necessity knows no law and discriminates in favor of no man or race.

KELLY MILLER (1863-1939)

Kelly Miller, born in Winnsboro, South Carolina, was for many years a member of the faculty of Howard University, which he served as professor of mathematics, professor of sociology, dean of the College of Arts and Sciences, and dean of the Junior College. Educated at Howard and Johns Hopkins, he became one of the best-known lecturers of the early years of the twentieth century. His pamphlets on controversial subjects were widely distributed. He was the author of *Race Adjustment* (1908), *Out of the House of Bondage* (1914), *An Appeal to Conscience* (1918), *History of the World War and the Important Part Taken by the Negroes* (1919), and *The Everlasting Stain* (1924). His "As to the Leopard's Spots: an Open Letter to Thomas Dixon, Jr." was occasioned by the publication of Dixon's *The Leopard's Spots,* a novel attacking the Negro race. The following is reprinted by permission of Mrs. Kelly Miller.

An Open Letter to Thomas Dixon, Jr.

September, 1905.

Mr. Thomas Dixon, Jr.,

Dear Sir:—

I am writing you this letter to express the attitude and feeling of ten millions of your fellow citizens toward the evil propagandism of race animosity to which you have lent your great literary powers. Through the widespread influence of your writings you have become the chief priest of those who worship at the shrine of race hatred and wrath. This one spirit runs through all your books and published utterances, like the recurrent theme of an opera. As the general trend of your doctrine is clearly epitomized and put forth in your contribution to the *Saturday Evening Post* of August 19, I beg to consider chiefly the issues therein raised. You are a white man born in the midst of the civil war, I am a Negro born during the same stirring epoch. You were born with a silver spoon in your mouth, I was born with an iron hoe in my hand. Your race has inflicted accumulated injury and wrong upon mine, mine has borne yours only service and good will. You express your views with the most scathing frankness; I am sure, you will welcome an equally candid expression from me.

Permit me to acknowledge the personal consideration which you have shown me. You will doubtless recall that when I addressed The Congregational Ministers, of New York City, some year or more ago, you asked permission to be present and listened attentively to what I had to say, although as might have been expected, you beat a precipitous retreat when luncheon was announced. In your article in the *Post* you make several references to me and to other colored men with entire personal courtesy. So far as I know you have never varied from this rule in your personal dealings with members of my race. You are merciless, however, in excoriating the race as a whole, thus keenly wounding the sensibilities of every individual of that blood. I assure you that this courtesy of personal treatment will be reciprocated in this letter, however sharply I may be compelled to take issue with the views you set forth and to deplore your attitude. I shall endeavor to indulge in no bitter word against your race nor against the South, whose exponent and special pleader you assume to be.

I fear that you have mistaken personal manners, the inevitable varnish of any gentleman of your antecedents and rearing, for friendship to a race which you hold in despite. You tell us that you are kind and considerate to your personal servants. It is somewhat strange that you should deem such assurance necessary, any more than it is necessary for us to assure us that you are kind to and fond of your horse or your dog. But when you write yourself down as "one of their best friends," you need not be surprised if we retort the refrain of the ritual: "From all such proffers of friendship, good Lord deliver us."

*　　*　　*　　*　　*

Your fundamental thesis is that "no amount of education of any kind, industrial, classical or religious, can make a Negro a white man or bridge the chasm of the centuries which separates him from the white man in the evolution of human history." This doctrine is as old as human oppression. Calhoun made it the arch stone in the defense of Negro slavery—and lost.

This is but a recrudescence of the doctrine which was exploited and exploded during the antislavery struggle. Do you recall the school of proslavery scientists who demonstrated beyond doubt that the Negro's skull was too thick to comprehend the substance of Aryan knowledge? Have you not read in the discredited scientific books of that period, with what triumphant acclaim it was shown that the Negro's shape and size of skull, facial angle, and cephalic configuration rendered him forever impervious to the white man's civilization? But all enlightened minds are now as ashamed of that doctrine as they are of the onetime dogma that the Negro had no soul. We become aware of mind through its manifestations. Within forty years of only partial opportunity, while playing as it were in the back yard of civilization, the American Negro has cut down his illiteracy by over fifty per cent; has produced a professional class, some fifty thousand strong, including ministers, teachers, doctors, lawyers, editors, authors, architects, engineers, and all higher lines of listed pursuits in which white men are engaged; some three thousand Negroes have taken collegiate degrees, over three hundred being from the best institutions in the North and West established for the most favored white youth; there is scarcely a first-class institution in America, excepting some three or four in the South, that is without colored students who pursue their studies generally with success, and sometimes with distinction; Negro inventors have taken out four hundred patents as a contribution to the mechanical genius of America; there are scores of Negroes who, for conceded ability and achievements, take respectable rank in the company of distinguished Americans.

It devolves upon you, Mr. Dixon, to point out some standard, either of intelligence, character, or conduct to which the Negro can not conform. Will you please tell a waiting world just what is the psychological difference between the races? No reputable authority, either of the old or the new school of psychology, has yet pointed out any sharp psychic discriminant. There is not a single intellectual, moral, or spiritual excellence attained by the white race to which the Negro does not yield an appreciative response. If you could show that the Negro was incapable of mastering the intricacies of Aryan speech, that he could not comprehend the intellectual basis of European culture, or apply the apparatus of practical knowledge, that he could not be made amenable to the white man's ethical code or appreciate his spiritual motive, then your case would be proved. But in default of such demonstration, we must relegate your eloquent pronouncement to the realm of generalization and prophecy, an easy and agreeable exercise of the mind in which the romancer is ever prone to indulge.

The inherent, essential, and unchangeable inferiority of the Negro to the white man lies at the basis of your social philosophy. You disdain to examine the validity of your fondly cherished hope. You follow closely in the wake of Tom Watson, in the June number of his homonymous magazine. You both hurl your thesis of innate racial inferiority at the head of Booker T. Washington. You use the same illustrations, the same arguments, set forth in the same order of recital, and for the most part in identical language. This seems to be an instance of great minds, or at least of minds of the same grade, running in the same channel.

These are your words: "What contribution to human progress have the millions of Africa who inhabit this planet made during the past four thousand years? Absolutely nothing." These are the words of Thomas Watson spoken some two months previous: "What does civilization owe to the Negro race? Nothing! Nothing!! Nothing!!!" You answer the query with the most emphatic negative noun and the strongest qualifying adjective in the language. Mr. Watson, of a more ecstatic temperament, replies with the same noun and six exclamation points. One rarely meets, outside of yellow journalism, with such lavishness of language, wasted upon a hoary dogma. A discredited dictum that has been bandied about the world from the time of Canaan to Calhoun, is revamped and set forth with as much ardor and fervency of feeling as if discovered for the first time and proclaimed for the illumination of a waiting world.

But neither boastful asseveration on your part nor indignant denial on mine will affect the facts of the case. That Negroes in the average are not equal in developed capacity to the white race, is a proposition which it would be as simple to affirm as it is silly to deny. The Negro represents a backward race which has not yet taken a commanding part in the progressive movement of the world. In the great cosmic scheme of things, some races reach the limelight of civilization ahead of others. But that temporary forwardness does not argue inherent superiority is as evident as any fact of history. An unfriendly environment may hinder and impede the one, while fortunate circumstances may quicken and spur the other. Relative superiority is only a transient phase of human development. You tell us that "The Jew had achieved a civilization—had his poets, prophets, priests, and kings, when our Germanic ancestors were still in the woods cracking cocoanuts and hickory-nuts with the monkeys." Fancy some learned Jew at that day citing your query about the contribution of the Germanic races to the culture of the human spirit, during the thousands of years of their existence! Does the progress of history not prove that races may lie dormant and fallow for ages and then break suddenly into prestige and power? Fifty years ago you doubtless would have ranked Japan among the benighted nations and hurled at their heathen heads some derogatory query as to their contribution to civilization. But since the happenings at Mukden and Port Arthur, and Portsmouth, I suppose that you are ready to change your mind. Or maybe since the Jap has proved himself "a first-class fighting man," able to cope on equal terms with the best breeds in Europe, you will claim him as belonging to the white race, notwithstanding his pig eye and yellow pigment.

*   *   *   *   *

The Negro enters into the inheritance of all the ages on equal terms with the rest, and who can say that he will not contribute his quota of genius to enrich the blood of the world?

The line of argument of every writer who undertakes to belittle the Negro is a well-beaten path. Liberia and Haiti are bound to come in for their share of ridicule and contemptuous handling. Mr. Watson calls these experiments freshly to mind, lest we forget. We are told all about the incapacity of the black race for self-government, the relapse into barbarism and much more of which we have heard before; and yet when we take all the circumstances into account, Haiti presents to the world one of the most remarkable achievements in the annals of human history. The panegyric of Wendell Phillips on Toussaint L'Ouverture is more than an outburst of rhetorical fancy; it is a just measure of his achievements in terms of his humble environment and the limited instrumentalities at his command. Where else in the course of history has a slave, with the aid of slaves, expelled a powerfully intrenched master class, and set up a government patterned after civilized models and which without external assistance or reinforcement from a parent civilization, has endured for a hundred years in face of a frowning world? When we consider the difficulties that confront a weak government, without military or naval means to cope with its more powerful rivals, and where commercial adventurers are ever and anon stirring up internal strife, thus provoking the intervention of stronger governments, the marvel is that the republic of Haiti still endures, the only self-governing state of the Antilles. To expect as effective and proficient government to prevail in Haiti as at Washington would be expecting more of the black men in Haiti than we find in the white men of South America. And yet, I suspect that the million Negroes in Haiti are as well governed as the corresponding number of blacks in Georgia, where only yesterday eight men were taken from the custody of the law and lynched without judge or jury. It is often charged that these people have not maintained the pace set by the old master class, that the plantations are in ruin and that the whole island wears the aspect of dilapidation. Wherever a lower people overrun the civilization of a higher, there is an inevitable lapse toward the level of the lower. When barbarians and semi-civilized hordes of northern Europe overran the southern peninsulas, the civilization of the world was wrapped in a thousand years of darkness. Relapse inevitably precedes the rebound. Is there anything in the history of Haiti contrary to the law of human development?

You ask: "Can you change the color of the Negro's skin, the kink of his hair, the bulge of his lip, or the beat of his heart, with a spelling book or a machine?" This rhetorical outburst does great credit to your literary skill, and is calculated to delight the simple; but analysis fails to reveal in it any pregnant meaning. Since civilization is not an attribute of the color of skin, or curl of hair, or curve of lip, there is no necessity for changing such physical peculiarities, and if there was, the spelling book and the machine would be very unlikely instruments for its accomplishment. But why, may I ask, would you desire to change the Negro's heart throb, which already beats at a normal human pace? You need not be so frantic about the superiority of your race. Whatever superiority it may possess, inherent or acquired, will take care of itself without such rabid support. Has it ever occurred to you that the people of New England blood, who have done and are doing most to make the white race great and glorious in this land, are the most reticent about extravagant claims to everlasting superiority? You protest too much. Your loud pretensions, backed up by such exclamatory outbursts of passion, make upon the reflecting mind the impression that you entertain a sneaking suspicion of their validity.

Your position as to the work and worth of Booker T. Washington is pitiably anomalous. You recite the story of his upward struggle with uncontrolled admiration: "The story of this little ragged, barefooted pickaninny, who lifted his eyes from a cabin in the hills of Virginia, saw a vision and followed it, until at last he presides over the richest and most powerful institution in the South, and sits down with crowned heads and presidents, has no parallel even in the Tales of the Arabian Nights." You say that his story appeals to the universal heart of humanity. And yet in a recent letter to the *Columbia States,* you regard it as an unspeakable outrage that Mr. Robert C. Ogden should walk arm in arm with this wonderful man who "appeals to the heart of universal humanity," and introduce him to the lady clerks in a dry goods store. Your passionate devotion to a narrow dogma has seriously impaired your sense of humor. The subject of your next great novel has been announced as "The Fall of Tuskegee." In one breath you commend the work of this great institution, while in another you condemn it because it does not fit into your preconceived scheme in the solution of the race problem. The Tuskegee ideal: "to make Negroes producers, lovers of labor, independent, honest, and good" is one which you say that only a fool or a knave can find fault with, because, in your own words, "it rests squarely upon the eternal verities." Over against this you add with all the condemnatory emphasis of italics and exclamation point: *"Tuskegee is not a servant training school!"* And further: "Mr. Washington is not training Negroes to take their places in the industries of the South in which white men direct and control them. He is not training students to be servants and come at the beck and call of any man. He is training them to be masters of men, to be independent, to own and operate their own industries, plant their own field, buy and sell their own goods." All of which you condemn by imperative inference ten times stronger than your faint and forced verbal approval. It is a heedless man who wilfully flaunts his little philosophy in the face of "the eternal verities." When the wise man finds that his prejudices are running against fixed principles in God's cosmic plan, he speedily readjusts them in harmony therewith. Has it never occurred to you to reexamine the foundation of the faith, as well as the feeling, that is in you, since you admit that it runs afoul of the "eternal verities?"

Mr. Washington's motto, in his own words, is that "the Negro has been worked; but now he must learn to work." The man who works for himself is of more service to any community than the man whose labor is exploited by others. You bring forward the traditional bias of the slave regime to modern conditions, viz.: that the Negro did not exist in his own right and for his own sake, but for the benefit of the white man. This principle is as false in nature as it is in morals. The naturalists tell us that throughout all the range of animal creation, there is found no creature which exists for the sake of any other, but each is striving after its own best welfare. Do you fear that the Negro's welfare is incompatible with that of the white man? I commend to you a careful perusal of the words of Mr. E. Gardner Murphy who, like yourself, is a devoted Southerner, and is equally zealous to promote the highest interest of that section: "Have prosperity, peace and happiness ever been successfully or permanently based upon indolence, inefficiency, and hopelessness? Since time began, has any human thing that God has made taken damage to itself or brought damage to the world through knowledge, truth, hope, and honest toil?" Read these words of your fellow Southerner, Mr. Dixon, meditate upon them; they will do you good as the truth doeth the upright heart.

You quote me as being in favor of the amalgamation of the races. A more careful reading of the article referred to would have convinced you that I was arguing against it as a probable solution of the race problem. I merely stated the intellectual conviction that two races cannot live indefinitely side by side, under the same general regime without ultimately fusing. This was merely the expression of a belief, and not the utterance of a preference nor the formulation of a policy. I know of no colored man who advocates amalgamation as a feasible policy of solution. You are mistaken. The Negro does not "hope and dream of amalgamation." This would be self-stultification with a vengeance. If such a policy were allowed to dominate the imagination of the race, its women would give themselves over to the unrestrained passion of white men, in quest of tawny offspring, which would give rise to a state of indescribable moral debauchery. At the same time you would hardly expect the Negro, in derogation of his common human qualities, to proclaim that he is so diverse from God's other human creatures as to make the blending of the races contrary to the law of nature. The Negro refuses to become excited or share in your frenzy on this subject. The amalgamation of the races is an ultimate possibility, though not an immediate probability. But what have you and I to do with ultimate questions, anyway? Our concern is with duty, not destiny.

*   *   *   *   *

But do you know, Mr. Dixon, that you are probably the foremost promoter of amalgamation between the two races? Wherever you narrow the scope of the Negro by preaching the doctrine of hate, you drive thousands of persons of lighter hue over to the white race carrying more or less Negro blood in their train. The blending of the races is less likely to take place if the self-respect and manly opportunity of the Negro are respected and encouraged, than if he is to be forever crushed beneath the level of his faculties for dread of the fancied result. Hundreds of the composite progeny are daily crossing the color line and carrying as much of the despised blood as an albicant skin can conceal without betrayal. I believe that it was Congressman Tillman, brother of the more famous Senator of that name, who stated on the floor of the constitutional convention of South Carolina, that he knew of four hundred white families in that State who had a taint of Negro blood in their veins. I personally know, or know of, fifty cases of transition in the city of Washington. It is a momentous thing for one to change his caste. The man or woman who affects to deny, ignore, or scorn the class with whom he previously associated is usually deemed deficient in the nobler qualities of human nature. It is not conceivable that persons of this class would undergo the self-degradation and humiliation of soul necessary to cross the great "social divide" unless it be to escape for themselves and their descendants an odious and despised status. Your oft expressed and passionately avowed belief that the progressive development of the Negro would hasten amalgamation is not borne out by the facts of observation. The refined and cultivated class among colored people are as much disinclined to such unions as the whites themselves. I am sorry that you saw fit to characterize Frederick Douglass as "a bombastic vituperator." You thereby gave poignant offense to ten millions of his race who regard him as the best embodiment of their possibilities. Besides millions of your race rate him among the foremost and best beloved of Americans. How would you feel if some one should stigmatize Jefferson Davis or Robert E. Lee in such language, these beau ideals of your Southern heart? But I will not undertake to defend Frederick Douglass against your calumniations. I am frank to confess that I do not feel that he needs it. The point I have in mind to make about Mr. Douglass is that he has a hold upon the affection of his race, not on account of his second marriage, but in spite of it. He seriously affected his standing with his people by that marriage.

*   *   *   *   *

It seems to me, Mr. Dixon, that this frantic abhorrence of amalgamation is a little late in its appearance. Whence comes this stream of white blood, which flows with more or less spissitude, in the veins of some six out of ten million Negroes? The Afro-American is hardly a Negro at all, except constructively; but a new creature. Who brought about this present approachment between the races? Do you not appreciate the inconsistency in the attitude and the action on the part of many of the loudmouthed advocates of race purity? It is said that old Father Chronos devoured his offspring in order to forestall future complications. But we do not learn that he put a bridle upon his passion as the surest means of security. The most effective service you can render to check the evil of amalgamation is to do missionary work among the males of your own race. This strenuous advocacy of race purity in face of proved proneness for miscegenation affords a striking reminder of the lines of Hudibras:—

> The self-same thing they will abhor,
> One way, and long another for.

Again, you say that "we have spent about $800,000,000 on Negro education since the war." This statement is so very wide of the mark, that I was disposed to regard it as a misprint, if you had not reinforced it with an application implying a like amount. In the report of the Bureau of Education for 1901, the estimated expenditure for Negro education in all the former slave States since the Civil War was put down at $121,184,568. The amount contributed by Northern philanthropy during that interval is variously estimated from fifty to seventy-five millions. Your estimate is four times too large. It would be interesting and informing to the world if you would reveal the source of your information. These misstatements of fact are not of so much importance in themselves, as that they serve to warn the reader against the accuracy and value of your general judgments. It would seem that you derive your figures of arithmetic from the same source from which you fashion your figures of speech. You will not blame the reader for not paying much heed to your sweeping generalizations, when you are at such little pains as to the accuracy of easily ascertainable data.

Your proposed solution of the race problem by colonizing the Negroes in Liberia reaches the climax of absurdity. It is difficult to see how such a proposition could emanate from a man of your reputation. Did you consult Cram's Atlas about Liberia? Please do so. You will find that it has an area of 48,000 square miles and a population of 1,500,000, natives and immigrants. The area and population are about the same as those of North Carolina, which, I believe, is your native State. When you tell us that this restricted area, without commerce, without manufacture, without any system of organized industry, can support every Negro in America, in addition to its present population,

I beg mildly to suggest that you recall your plan for revision before submitting it to the judgment of a critical world. Your absolute indifference to and heedlessness of the facts, circumstances, and conditions involved in the scheme of colonization well befit the absurdity of the general proposition.

The solution of the race problem in America is indeed a grave and serious matter. It is one that calls for statesmanlike breadth of view, philanthropic tolerance of spirit, and exact social knowledge. The whole spirit of your propaganda is to add to its intensity and aggravation. You stir the slumbering fires of race wrath into an uncontrollable flame. I have read somewhere that Max Nordau, on reading *The Leopard's Spots,* wrote to you suggesting the awful responsibility you had assumed in stirring up enmity between race and race. Your teachings subvert the foundations of law and established order. You are the high priest of lawlessness, the prophet of anarchy. Rudyard Kipling places this sentiment in the mouth of the reckless stealer of seals in the Northern Sea: "There's never a law of God nor man runs north of fifty-three." This description exactly fits the brand of literature with which you are flooding the public. You openly urge your fellow citizens to override all law, human and divine. Are you aware of the force and effect of these words? "Could fatuity reach a sublimer height than the idea that the white man will stand idly by and see the performance? What will he do when put to the test? He will do exactly what his white neighbor in the North does when the Negro threatens his bread—kill him!" These words breathe out hatred and slaughter and suggest the murder of innocent men whose only crime is quest for the God-given right to work. You poison the mind and pollute the imagination through the subtle influence of letters. Are you aware of the force and effect of evil suggestion when the passions of men are in a state of unstable equilibrium? A heterogeneous population, where the elements are, on any account, easily distinguishable, is an easy prey for the promoter of wrath. The fuse is already prepared for the spark. The soul of the mob is stirred by suggestion of hatred and slaughter, as a famished beast at the smell of blood. The rabble responds so much more readily to an appeal to passion than to reason. To wantonly stir up the fires of race antipathy is as execrable a deed as flaunting a red rag in the face of a bull at a summer's picnic, or raising a false cry of "fire" in a crowded house. Human society could not exist one hour except on the basis of law, which holds the baser passions of men in restraint.

In our complex situation it is only the rigid observance of law re-enforced by higher moral restraint that can keep these passions in bound.

You speak about giving the Negro a "square deal." Even among gamblers, a "square deal" means to play according to the rules of the game. The rules which all civilized States have set for themselves are found in the Ten Commandments, the Golden Rule, the Sermon on the Mount, and the organic law of the land. You acknowledge no such restraints when the Negro is involved, but waive them all aside with frenzied defiance. You preside at every crossroad lynching of a helpless victim; wherever the midnight murderer rides with rope and torch, in quest of the blood of his black brother, you ride by his side; wherever the cries of the crucified victim go up to God from the crackling flame, behold you are there; when women and children, drunk with ghoulish glee, dance around the funeral pyre and mock the death groans of their fellow man and fight for ghastly souvenirs, you have your part in the inspiration of it all. When guilefully guided workmen in mine and shop and factory, goaded by a real or imaginary sense of wrong, begin the plunder and pillage of property and murder of rival men, your suggestion is justifier of the dastardly doings. Lawlessness is gnawing at the very vitals of our institutions. It is the supreme duty of every enlightened mind to allay rather than spur on this spirit. You are hastening the time when there is to be a positive and emphatic show of hands—not of white hands against black hands, God forbid; not of Northern hands against Southern hands, heaven forfend; but a determined show of those who believe in law and God and constituted order, against those who would undermine and destroy the organic basis of society, involving all in a common ruin. No wonder Max Nordau exclaimed: "God, man, are you aware of your responsibility!"

But do not think, Mr. Dixon, that when you evoke the evil spirit, you can exorcise him at will. The Negro in the end will be the least of his victims. Those who become inoculated with the virus of race hatred are more unfortunate than the victims of it. Voltaire tells us that it is more difficult and more meritorious to wean men of their prejudices than it is to civilize the barbarian. Race hatred is the most malignant poison that can afflict the mind. It freezes up the fount of inspiration and chills the higher faculties of the soul. You are a greater enemy to your own race than you are to mine.

I have written you thus fully in order that you may clearly understand how the case lies in the Negro's mind. If any show of feeling or bitterness of spirit crops out in the treatment or between the lines, it is wholly without vindictive intent; but is the inevitable outcome of dealing with issues that verge upon the deepest human passion.

Yours truly,
KELLY MILLER.

CHARLES S. JOHNSON (1893-   )

Charles S. Johnson (see above p. 924), born in Bristol, Virginia, in 1893, was educated at Virginia Union University and the University of Chicago. He has been associate executive secretary of the Chicago Race Relations Commission, director of research for the National Urban League, and a member of a number of committees on racial problems. As founder and editor of *Opportunity: Journal of Negro Life* his service to Negro expression has been great. At present he is director of the Department of Social Sciences at Fisk University. He has contributed to *Survey, The Modern Quarterly, The World Tomorrow, The Journal of Negro Education,* and *The Journal of Negro History.* Among his books are *The Negro in American Civilization* (1930), *The Economic Status of the Negro* (1933), *The Shadow of the Plantation* (1934), *Race Relations* with W. D. Weatherford, (1934), *The Collapse of Cotton Tenancy* (with Edwin R. Embree and W. W. Alexander, 1935), *A Preface to Racial Understanding* (1936), *The Negro College Graduate* (1938), which won the Annisfield Award, and *Growing Up in the Black Belt* (1940). The following is used by permission of the author and of the University of Chicago Press.

From The Shadow of the Plantation

TENANTS

THE FIRST DISTINCTION which should be made clear in regard to the tenants is that between those who have made arrangements for cash payments and those who have contracted to pay a stipulated amount of cotton. Usually these tenants paid forty or fifty dollars for one-horse horse farms. The tenants seem to have no definite idea concerning the actual number of acres in a one-horse farm, but from the best available sources it seemed that a one-horse farm was from fifteen to twenty acres in extent. Tenants who pay their rental usually give a bale and a half for a one-horse farm. Here, again, the arrangement varies according to custom, or the terms of the landlord. The tenant may pay rent in cash, or in cotton and other produce; he may or may not receive advances from the landlord in the form of cash or rations. A renter may subrent. Again, he may apply for a government loan or borrow from the bank.

"(a) We pay 400 pounds of lint cotton. We made nearly 6 bales last year and he sold it hisself, but we still owe 'bout $50. We ain't got no advance, but we borrows from the bank. I think we pay 10 cents on the dollar. We sold cotton for 9 cents last year. We could a got 10 but just kept holding it. Old man J—— (landlord) won't do a thing. He come by here five years ago and said he was going to fix this house up. All he's give us since then is a few planks to fix the porch. It's rotting down. We're just living outdoors. We rents out our ox for $12 a year, and the folks feed him.

"(b) I aint' got no children and me and my husband works a one-horse farm and we got 'bout thirty acres. Last year we made 6 bales of cotton and rented the thirty acres for $60; fifteen acres we used for cotton, the rest for corn. We kept the corn and didn't sell none hardly. At ten cents a pound the six bales would bring $300. We had $10 advanced for four months. We turned it all over, and they took out the $40 advanced, $30 for fertilizer, and $60 rent. We got through and then they say we come out $72.43 in the hole.

"(c) Tenant received no advance, but paid 400 pounds of cotton as rent. He raised 3 bales of cotton (around 800 lbs.), sold the other, and received 10 cents a pound ($40). He also grew 3 bushels of potatoes, 16 rows of sugar cane, and 4 loads of corn.

"(d) Tenant received no advances. He raised 2½ bales of cotton and paid 1 bale for rent. He cleared $25 on the sale of 1½ bales. He also raised 12½ bushels of corn, 1 bank of potatoes, and 6 gallons of syrup."

In more prosperous times when there is a reasonable assurance of returns, the landowners made advances both to tenants and to share-croppers. It is a most frequent complaint of the tenants now that they cannot get advances. One said: "I ask Mr. —— to 'vance me jest nuff for a pair of overalls. He tell me he needs overalls hisself." In other cases advances to tenants have merely been reduced.

"Last year I drawed $10 to the plow (meaning $10 a month for from four to six months for each 20 acres cultivated) but I ain't getting but $7 this year. I rents the whole place (400 acres) and then subrents it, and pays four (4) bales of cotton for rent. But I don't never make nothing offen it. Didn't clear nothing last year. I paid out $200 last year. Interest steps on me time I pay my rent (for money borrowed from the bank) and interest cost 15 cents on the dollar. I haven't made nothing since 1927. I clears $210 then and ain't cleared nothing since. I got 21 cents for cotton that year."

Another explained:

"They don't give nothing now. Use to 'low us $10 provisions a month, but dey done cut us way down. The white folks say some of these banks done fell in; dere ain't no money to be got. That's all. Said this is the suppression time."

Another type of tenant pays a good rental in cash and receives advances.

"We farms 60 acres and pays $150 for rent. That's $75 to the plow.

They 'vances us $15 a month for five months. I come out jest $175 in the hole.

"We run a two-horse farm. We was due to pay $150 rent last year, but I don't know what us is paying this year. We cut down on the land we was using. We made 22 bales of cotton last year, and it was selling at 8, 9, and 10 cents when we turned it in to the man. We didn't git nothing back. You see, the man had been carrying us for two years. I took 'sponsibility for the whole patch and let some of it out to three other parties, and stood for them. Besides the cotton the men took 13 loads of corn, but I saved about 200 bushels for myself to live on, and I sold some peanuts and corn."

The normal earnings of a man and wife, if both work as tenants on a one-horse cotton farm, would probably average $260 a year in cash value. However, they pay about half of their cotton in rent, use the corn for their stock, and eat the potatoes, peas, and sorghum which they grow along with the cotton. As a result very little cash is handled. They manage to live on the advances, or by borrowing for food and clothing and permitting their crop to be taken in satisfaction of the debt. It becomes very largely a paper loss or gain. In the case of loss the tenant may move away, leaving his debt. In the latter case he may be conscious of having earned more than he got, or of paying for some other Negro tenant's default.

"We got right 'round sixty acres and one-half of it is cotton. We working on halves. We got a two-horse farm. My daughter got one and I got one. I farmed with Mr. P—— last year. We had thirty acres over there and made 5 bales of cotton and paid $100 for rent. We gits $2 a month in cash and $10 in rations. We came out $200 in the hole last year. *I don't have to pay that off 'cause I let that went when I come here* (he had to give up farm tools, etc). I been farming all my life 'cept two years when we went to Virginia . . . I worked in the coke field out there. That was the year the war was."

One daughter lived at home. Four boys were away living in cities in Alabama. One grown daughter lived in the county and worked with them. One grown son was dead—"got knocked in the head"; seven little children had died between the ages of two and four.

There is another type of farmer, the share-cropper, who, without tools or any form of capital, farms on the condition that he give the landlord one-half of the crop. There were ninety-eight families working on this arrangement besides one woman who gave a fourth of the crop for the rental of her small farm. The arrangement varies with the landlord and the condition of the tenant. When the tenant is furnished tools and work animals in addition to ʰhe land, he may get only a third of the cotton raised. Most commonly, however, it is halves, and he may find it necessary to rent a mule for his plowing.

The share-croppers frequently are subtenants for small white and Negro tenant farmers, or for their relatives. It is at least a means of beginning, and a good share-cropper can, with good fortune, place himself in position to undertake the responsibilities of full tenant later.

"I works a one-horse farm on halves. I get 'bout $12 a month in rations. Last year (1930) I worked for the Tallahassee Mill Company, and made $9.75 a week. My wife was working by the day for 50 cents a day. We been married 'bout four years now. I moved here from Tallahassee 'cause I was lacking for sense. The white folks liked me down there and everything, and I moved. I called myself liking ter farm best."

FARM LABORERS

Seventy heads of families were farm laborers who worked on other people's farms for a stipulated wage. Eleven of these farm laborers had small patches of their own which they were permitted to cultivate rent free. The wage usually paid these laborers was 50-65 cents a day, the women receiving more often 40 cents. The following statement of a farm laborer indicates the conditions under which this class works.

"We jest work by the day and pay $1.50 a month for this house. It's jest a piece of house. I gits 50 cents a day and my husband and the boy gits 65 cents each. We have to feed ourselves and pay rent out of that. My husband is pretty scheming, but sometimes he can't git nothing to do. I don't know how much time we lose, but he works most of the time. Course the boy stops and goes to school in the winter sometimes, but if he can git work to do, he works too."

The husband lives with his wife and her sixteen-year-old illegitimate boy. The boy was caught with whiskey on him and stayed in jail a month before his aunt could bail him out. He is only in the third grade in school, and his mother gives this as the reason for his retardation. He had to work out the $105 bail which his aunt paid.

Among these families there were also laborers who were working on railroads, logging, and on county roads. There were eighteen of these laborers, including seven whose wives managed a small farm or a patch as a means of contributing to the family support. The wife of one of these laborers related the following history:

"My husband and me married eight years. He works at the Hardaway log mill and makes $7.00 a week. He been working there four years now . . . We don't have to pay no rent. The man he works for pays for hit. I don't do nothing but stay home . . . My husband was in debt when we left Millstead but he ain't much in debt now. He don't owe but 'bout a dollar or two. He don't lack this man he's working for 'cause he don't pay him but $1.10 a day. The man's name is Mr. S—— and he is mean to work for. He got 14 or 15 working for him down there at the log mill 'sides my husband. If we git hard up and want some money, he don't help us. He don't do nothing but run you away from there . . . My husband goes ter work wid sunrise every morning and works till dark. I git up day and cooks his breakfast. He don't come back home ter dinner cause hit's so far. Hit's 'bout seven miles from here."

CASUALS

Probably the lowest class of farm laborers was made up of the four farm hands who did not receive a stipulated monetary wage, but were to get what was known as a "hand's share." This, seemingly, just amounts to enough to keep them living. One old woman who lives by herself in a one-room shack and works for a hand's share told the following story:

"I works for a hand's share in the crop with the folks cross dere. My husband *been* dead. I ain't never had but one child and dat's de son what's down there . . . I been up north in Birmingham with my sister . . . but I come back here, 'cause dese chillun kept worrying me to come on here to live wid them. It's mighty tight on me to have to go working in dese fields half starved, and I ain't had a bit of money to buy a piece of cloth as big as my hand since I been back. I washed fer white people in Birmingham, and dey was good to me. I am jest gitting long by the hardest. I works for dese people for a hand's share in the crop. Dey gives me a load of corn and a load of potatoes. I gits some of all the other stuff what's made, and when selling cotton dey give you a little money out of the seed. I don't see no money on time. Dey gives me a little something to eat 'cause I works wid dem and dey gives me a little groceries. I never was in this fix before in my life. I had good money when I come from Birmingham. I had two fives and five single dollahs. I sho' gonna git what I works for dis year."

Eight women who were heads of families were employed in domestic service, and one of these women had a small patch which she cultivated. There were twenty-two persons, some of them very old, in other cases dependent relatives and in a few cases children, who were living on their parents' or relatives' farms, without being required to pay any rent. Two very old couples were living in this manner on white men's places, where they were permitted to sustain themselves on small plots of ground without having to pay rent. One old couple, now too old for much work, had been given a place by a white landlord. The man said, rather wearily:

"I jest got a little patch, 'bout an acre. The people plows it for me, and I works it. I could work more (land) but I jest ain't able to plow it. He lets me have what I make. I don't raise no cotton, jest corn. You see I got hogs and I have to feed 'em and we have to have bread. When the corn gives out I works 'bout by the day, and git meal that way.

"I used to be doing well; I used to rent a great big farm and rent it out. I had lots of stock. Oh, they died. I had to git rid of some. I had plows, hands, and everything. Oh, they ruint me, just making one bale when they coulda made five, and me standing fer it. It jest broke me."

The old man is eighty-four years old and has been married twice. His wife is seventy-two years old. A white landowner allows them to live in the house and work the patch free. This white man and his wife often bring food to the old couple. . . .

THE DREARY CYCLE OF LIFE

The weight of generations of habit holds the Negro tenant to his rut. Change is difficult, even in the face of the increasing struggle for survival under the old modes. One intelligent old farmer had sensed an important element of the natural conservation of these tenants. He said:

"Farming is like gambling. If I get out I ought to get back and work a smaller farm next year. But you take an old farmer and if he ever gets out the hole with a good-size farm, instead of cutting down he'll get him another mule and take on some more. That's what keeps us down."

Such philosophy is for the man who retains some hope for improvement. The most dismal aspect of this situation is the air of resignation everywhere apparent.

"If it wasn't the boll weevil it was the drought; if it wasn't the drought it was the rains.

"One thing, we ain't got proper tools we ought to have. If you git any good land you have to buy things to make it good, and that takes lots of money, and if we had money to buy these things we wouldn't be so hard up.

"What kills us here is that we jest can't make it cause they pay us nothing for what we give them, and they charge us double price when they sell it back to us."

Year after year of this experience for many of them and the hopelessness crystallizes itself at times into despair. "Ain't make nothing, don't speck nothing no more till I die. Eleven bales of cotton and man take it all. We jest work for de other man. He git everything." Mysticism and religion come to the rescue of some who add to hopelessness a fear of the future. "I axed Jesus to let me plant a little more. Every time I plant anything I say, 'Jesus, I ain't planting this for myself; I'm planting this for you to increase.'"

It is evident that all is not exploitation. The high level of illiteracy at times fuses its weight with a diffidence and ignorance which not only invite exploitation but make misunderstandings inevitable. Some families did not know the acreage they were working; the work to be done; the terms under which they accepted the land; the weight of their cotton yield. They were just working; if they came out they would spend the money from the very novelty of having it; if they stayed in the hole, it was only what they expected. "We always owe money and going to owe it, too; jest one month after another always something. That's the way it goes."

The plantation in theory was a capital investment for large-scale production under a continuing routine. Its purpose was not the encouragement of peasant proprietorship. The social relations, labor, mentality, and discipline fostered by it are at the same time reflected in its surviving forms and traditions, and in the continuing selection and molding of its tenant types. It demands an unquestioning obedience to its managerial intelligence; it demands the right to dictate and control every stage of cultivation; it cannot and does not tolerate a suggestion of independent status. Those Negro tenants who have in spirit revolted against its implication, or who have with praiseworthy intent sought to detach themselves from its grip by attaining an independent status, have felt the full force of its remaining strength. Nothing remains but to succumb or to migrate.

"I am working myself to death, mighty near; been working mighty hard. I am trying to get straight. I made a bale and a half last year, but never got nothing out of it. I stayed in that little house over there and paid $60 and never got nothing last year, I worked and dug and never got a thing, and when I told him I wasn't making nothing he said, "Well, you are making money for me, ain't you?' And I said, 'Well, I can quit.' I moved from there, and he didn't know it. Folks went up there looking for Dick Richards and Dick Richards done moved."

Henry Robinson had been living in the same place for nineteen years, paying $105 a year rent for his land. He raises three bales of cotton a year, turns it all over, and continues to go deeper in debt. He said:

"I know we been beat out of money direct and indirect. You see, they got a chance to do it all right, 'cause they can overcharge us and I know its being done. I made three bales again last year. He said I owed $400 t the beginning of the year. Now you can't dispute his word. When I said

'Suh?' he said 'Don't you dispute my word; the book says so.' When the book says so and so you better pay it, or they will say 'So, I'm a liar, eh?' You better take to the bushes too if you dispute him, for he will string you up for that.

"I don't want them to hurt my feelings and I just have to take what they say, 'cause I don't want to go to the mines (convict labor) and I do want to live."

Another man complained:

"I tried keeping books one year, and the man kept worrying me about it, saying his books was the ones he went by anyhow. And nothing you can do but leave. He said he didn't have no time to fool with no books. He don't ever give us no rent notes all the time. They got you 'cause you have to carry your cotton to his mill to gin and you better not carry your cotton nowhere else. I don't care how good your cotton is, a colored man's cotton is always second- or third-grade cotton if a colored man sells it. The only way you can get first prices for it is to get some white man to sell it for you in his name. A white man sold mine once, and got market price for it.

"We haven't paid out to Mr. —— in twelve years. Been in debt that long. See, when a fella's got a gun in your face you gotter take low or die."

To the Negro tenant the white landlord is the system; to the white landlord the capital of the banks is the system. The landlord needs credit by which to advance credit to the tenants. The security of the landlord is in the mortgages on his land; the security of the tenant is the mortgage on the crops which he will raise. Because cotton lends itself best to this arrangement, cotton is overproduced and debts descend to obscure still another year of labor, and the vicious circle continues. In the desperate struggle both may lose, but the advantage is always with the white landlord. He dictates the terms and keeps the books. The demands of the system determine the social and economic relations, the weight of which falls heaviest upon those lowest down. There was a song which old women hummed as they hacked the earth with their hoes. The words were almost always indistinct but the mood of the tune, dreary and listless, fitted as naturally to the movement of their bodies as it did to the slick and swish of the earth under the blows of their hoes. One verse only was remembered by one of them, and it ran so:

> Trouble comes, trouble goes.
> I done had my share of woes.
> Times get better by 'n' by,
> But then my time will come to die.

E. FRANKLIN FRAZIER (1894-   )

E. Franklin Frazier was born in Baltimore and educated at Howard University, Clark University, the New York School of Social Work (on a research fellowship), the University of Copenhagen, and the University of Chicago. Besides teaching in many colleges, he has directed the Atlanta School of Social Work and has been professor of sociology at Fisk University and, since 1934, at Howard University, where he is now chairman of the department. He has contributed to several American periodicals and learned journals. Among his books are *The Negro Family in Chicago* (1932), *The Negro Family in the United States* (1938), which received the Annisfield award for the best book on race relations of that year, and *Negro Youth at the Crossways* (1940), an American Youth Commission study. In 1940-1941, Frazier studied in Brazil and the West Indies on a Guggenheim fellowship. "The Pathology of Race Prejudice" was first published in the *Forum* magazine in 1927. It is here reprinted by permission of the author and of the Events Publishing Company.

The Pathology of Race Prejudice

"The Negro-in-America, therefore, is a form of insanity that overtakes white men." (*The Southerner,* by Walter Hines Page.)

ALTHOUGH THE STATEMENT ABOVE makes no claim to technical exactness, it is nevertheless confirmed by modern studies of insanity. If, in developing this thesis, we consider some of the newer conceptions of mental processes as they apply to abnormal behaviour, we shall find in each case that the behavior motivated by race prejudice shows precisely the same characteristics as those ascribed to insanity. This does not refer, of course, to those phenomena of insanity due to abnormalities of the actual structure of the brain nor does it refer to the changes that come in dementia. We are concerned here chiefly with the psychological approach to the problem of insanity—for race prejudice is an acquired psychological reaction, and there is no scientific evidence that it represents the functioning of inherited behaviour patterns. Even from a practical viewpoint, as we shall attempt to show, we are forced to regard certain manifestations of race prejudice as abnormal behaviour.

The conception used to explain abnormal behaviour which we shall consider first is dissociation of conciousness. Normally, the mental life appears to be a "homogeneous stream progressing in a definite direction toward a single end," as Dr. Hart puts it. That this apparent homogeneity is deceptive, even in normal minds, is shown by a little observation. Every one has had the experience of performing a task while engaged in an unrelated train of thought. In cases such as this the dissociation is temporary and incomplete, while in insanity the dissociation is relatively permanent and complete. Automatic writing in cases of hysteria, somnambulism, dual personality, and delusions are cases of the splitting off of whole systems of ideas. The conclusion of Hart that "this dissociation of the mind into logic-tight compartments is by no means confined to the population of the asylum" will lead us to those manifestations of race prejudice that show the same marked mental dissociation found in the insane. Herbert Seligman, in his book on the Negro, suggests the insane nature of Southern reactions to the blacks when he says, "The Southern white man puts certain questions beyond discussion. If they are pressed he will fight rather than argue." Southern white people write and talk about the majesty of the law, the sacredness of human rights, and the advantages of democracy—and the next moment defend mob violence, disfranchisement, and jim-crow treatment of the Negro. White men and women who are otherwise kind and law-abiding will indulge in the most revolting forms of cruelty towards black people. Thus the whole system of ideas respecting the Negro is dissociated from the normal personality, and—what is more significant for our thesis—this latter system of ideas seems exempt from the control of the personality.

These dissociated systems of ideas generally have a strong emotional component and are known as complexes. The Negro-complex—the designation which we shall give the system of ideas which most Southerners have respecting the Negro—has the same intense emotional tone that characterises insane complexes. The prominence of the exaggerated emotional element has been noted by Josiah Royce in contrasting with the American attitude the attitude of the English in the West Indies, who are "wholly without those painful emotions, those insistent complaints and anxieties, which are so prominent in the minds of our own Southern brethren." Moreover, just as in the insane, any pertinent stimulus may arouse the whole complex, so any idea connected with the Negro causes the whole Negro-complex to be projected into consciousness. Its presence there means that all thinking is determined by the complex. For example, a white woman who addresses a colored man as Mister is immediately asked whether she would want a Negro to marry her sister, and must listen to a catologue of his sins. How else than as the somnambulism of the insane and almost insane are we to account for the behaviour of a member of a school board who jumps up and paces the floor, cursing and accusing Negroes, the instant the question of appropriating money for Negro schools is raised? Likewise, the Negro-complex obtrudes itself on all planes of thought. Health programs are slighted because it is argued Negroes will increase; the selective draft is opposed because the Negro will be armed; woman suffrage is fought because colored women will vote. In many other cases the behaviour of white people toward life in general is less consciously and less overtly influenced by the Negro-complex. Bitter memories quite often furnish its emotional basis while the complex itself is elaborated by ideas received from the social environment.

There is a mistaken notion, current among most people, that the insane are irrational, that their reasoning processes are in themselves different from those of normal people. The insane support their delusions by the same mechanism of rationalisation that normal people employ to support beliefs having a non-rational origin. The delusions of the insane, however, show a greater imperviousness to objective fact. The delusions of the white man under the Negro-complex show the same imperviousness to objective facts concerning the Negro. We have heard lately an intelligent Southern woman insisting that nine-tenths of all Negroes have syphilis, in spite of statistical and other authoritative evidence to the contrary. Moreover, just as the lunatic seized upon every fact to support his delusional system, the white man seizes myths and unfounded rumors to support his delusion about the Negro. When the lunatic is met with ideas incompatible with his delusion he distorts facts by rationalisation to preserve the inner consistency of his delusions. Of a similar nature is the argument of the white man who declares that white blood is responsible for character and genius in mixed Negroes, and at the same time that white blood harms the Negroes! Pro-slavery literature denying the humanity of the Negro, as well as contemporary Southern opinion supporting lynching and oppression, utilises the mechanism of rationalisation to support delusions.

Race prejudice involves the mental conflict, which is held to be the cause of the dissociation of ideas so prominent in insanity. The Negro-complex is often out of harmony with the personality as a whole and therefore results in a conflict that involves unpleasant emotional tension. In everyday life such conflicts are often solved by what—in those following contradictory moral codes—is generally known as hypocrisy. When, however, the two systems of incompatible ideas cannot be kept from conflict, the insane man reconciles them through the process of rationalisation. Through this same process of rationalisation, the Southern white man creates defenses for his immoral acts, and lynching becomes a holy defense of womanhood. That the alleged reasons for violence are simply defense mechanisms for unacceptable wishes is shown by a case in which a juror was lynched for voting to exonerate a Negro accused of a crime! The energetic measures which Southerners use to prevent legal unions of white with colored people look suspiciously like compensatory reactions for their own frustrated desires for such unions. Other forms of defence mechanisms appear in the Southerner's sentimentalising over his love for the Negro and the tendency in the South to joke about him—which has a close parallel in the humor of the alcoholic. At the basis of these unacceptable ideas, requiring rationalisations and other forms of defense mechanisms to bring them into harmony with the personality, we find fear, hatred and sadism constantly cropping out.

When one surveys Southern literature dealing with the Negro, one finds him accused of all the failings of mankind. When we reflect, however, that the Negro, in spite of his ignorance and poverty, does not in most places contribute more than his share to crime, and—even in the opinion of his most violent disparagers—possesses certain admirable qualities, we are forced to seek the cause of these excessive accusations in the minds of the accusers themselves. Here, too, we find striking similarities to the mental processes of the insane. Where the conflict between the personality as a whole and the unacceptable complex is not resolved within the mind of the subject, the extremely repugnant system of dissociated ideas is projected upon some real or imaginary individual. Except in the case of those who, as we have seen, charge the Negro with an inherent impulse to rape as an unconscious defense of their own murderous impulses, the persistence—in the face of contrary evidence—of the delusion that the Negro is a ravisher can only be taken as a projection. According to this view, the Southern white man, who has—arbitrarily without censure—enjoyed the right to use colored women, projects this insistent desire upon the Negro when it is no longer socially approved and his conscious personality likewise rejects it. Like the lunatic, he refuses to treat the repugnant desire as a part of himself and consequently shows an exaggerated antagonism toward the desire which he projects upon the Negro. A case has come to the attention of the writer which shows clearly the projection of the unacceptable wish. A telephone operator in a small Southern city called up a Negro doctor and told him that someone at his home had made an improper proposal to her. Although the physician protested that the message could not have come from his house the sheriff was sent to arrest him. His record in the town had been conspicuously in accord with the white man's rule about the color line. He had consistently refused to attend white men, not to mention white women, who had applied to him for treatment. Unable, in spite of his record, to escape arrest, he sought the aid of a white physician. The whole matter died down suddenly, the white physician explaining to his colored colleague that he had gone to the operator and found that she was only "nervous" that day. To those who are acquainted with the mechanism of projecting, such a word as "nervous" here has a deeper significance.

The mechanism of projection is also seen in the general disposition of Southern white men to ascribe an inordinate amount of fear to Negroes. That the Negro has no monoply of fear was admirably demonstrated in Atlanta, where, a year or so ago, white people were fleeing from a haunted road while Negroes were coolly robbing graveyards! This same mental process would explain why white men constantly lay crimes onto Negroes when there is no evidence whatever to indicate the race of the criminal. Can we not find here also an explanation of the unwarranted anxiety which white men feel for their homes because of the Negro? Is this another projection of their own unacceptable complexes? In the South the white man is certainly a greater menace to the Negro's home than the latter is to his.

We must include in our discussion two more aspects of the behaviour of the insane that find close parallels in the behaviour of those under the influence of the Negro-complex. We meet in the insane with a tendency on the part of the patient to interpret everything that happens in his environment in terms of his particular delusion. In the case of those suffering from the Negro-complex we see the same tendency at work. Any recognition accorded the Negro, even in the North, is regarded as an attempt to give him "social equality," the personal connotations of which are familiar to most Americans. In the South, Negroes have been lynched for being suspected of such a belief. Misconstructions such as are implied in the Southern conception of social equality are so manifestly absurd that they bear a close resemblance to the delusions of reference in the insane. Perhaps more justly to be classed as symptoms of insanity are those frequent hallucinations of white women who complain of attacks by Negroes when clearly no Negroes are involved. Hallucinations often represent unacceptable sexual desires which are projected when they can no longer be repressed. In the South a desire on the part of a white woman for a Negro that could no longer be repressed would most likely be projected—especially when such a desire is supposed to be as horrible as incest. It is not unlikely, therefore, that imaginary attacks by Negroes are often projected wishes.

The following manifestation of race prejudice shows strikingly its pathological nature. Some years ago a mulatto went to a small Southern town to establish a school for Negroes. In order not to become *persona non grata* in the community, he approached the leading white residents for their approval of the enterprise. Upon his visit to one white woman he was invited into her parlor and treated with the usual courtesies shown visitors; but when this woman discovered later that he was colored, she chopped up the chair in which he had sat, and, after pouring gasoline over the pieces, made a bonfire of them. The pathological nature of a delusion is shown by its being out of harmony with one's education and surroundings. For an Australian black fellow to show terror when he learns that his wife has touched his blanket would not evince a pathological state of mind; whereas it did indicate a pathological mental state for this woman to act as if some mysterious principle had entered the chair.

From a practical viewpoint, insanity means social incapacity. Southern white people afflicted with the Negro-complex show themselves incapable of performing certain social functions. They are, for instance, incapable of rendering just decisions when white and colored people are involved; and their very claim that they "know" and "understand" the Negro indicates a fixed system of ideas respecting him—whereas a sane and just appraisal of the situation would involve the assimilation of new data. The delusions of the sane are generally supported by the herd, while those of the insane are often anti-social. Yet—from the point of view of Negroes, who are murdered if they believe in social equality or are maimed for asking for an ice cream soda, and of white people, who are threatened with similar violence for not subscribing to the Southerner's delusions —such behaviour is distinctly anti-social. The inmates of a madhouse are not judged insane by themselves, but by those outside. The fact that abnormal behaviour towards Negroes is characteristic of a whole group may be an example illustrating Nietzsche's observation that "insanity in individuals is something rare—but in groups, parties, nations, and epochs it is the rule."

ABRAM L. HARRIS (1899-   )

Born in Richmond, Virginia, Abram L. Harris was educated at Virginia Union University, the New York School of Social Work, New York University, University of Pittsburgh, and Columbia. He has worked with the National Urban League and has taught at West Virginia State College and at Howard University, where he is now head of the department of economics. He has contributed to *Current History, The Modern Quarterly, Social Forces, The Nation, The New Republic, The Journal of Political Economy, Opportunity, The Crisis. The Black Worker* was written with Sterling D. Spero in 1931 and *The Negro as Capitalist* in 1936. "The Economics of the Founding Fathers" is here reprinted by permission of the author and of *Harper's Magazine.*

The Economics of the Founding Fathers

THE DEFEAT OF PRESIDENT ROOSEVELT'S PROGRAM of judicial reform has brought a temporary lull in the long tireless fight of liberals and progressives to curb the power of the United States Supreme Court. Many persons looked upon the proposal as an artfully disguised attempt to "pack the court." Others supported the measure on the basis of their conception of the original function of the Supreme Court. According to this view, popularized by some liberal thinkers in the past, the founding fathers never intended to give the Supreme Court the power to void the acts of Congress. The Court, so the legend runs, beginning with John Marshall, first Chief Justice, usurped this power, and by so doing has been able persistently to nullify the will of the people as expressed through their representatives. Even though the plan to reform the Supreme Court is no longer a political issue it calls up for re-examination of not merely the founding fathers' views of judicial control but their fundamental economic and political ideas.

The question of the Supreme Court's power was not one of the issues that divided the founding fathers into hostile political parties at the end of the Revolutionary War. Jefferson and his democratic followers differed in no essential respect from Hamilton, Marshall, and the rest of the Federalists in their idea of the Court's function. The view of some historians that Jefferson championed the cause of the "people" against "judicial oligarchy" is wholly unsupportable. The causes of the bitter war waged by Jefferson and his party against Marshall and the Court after the former became President are to be found in partisan politics and not in conflicting theories of constitutional government.

What each party, Federalist and Republican alike, feared was the depotism of unbridled majority rule. This common anxiety was stated in its classic form by Madison, the Federalist. In a letter to Jefferson, he said: "Whatever the real power in government lies, there is the danger of oppression. In our Government, real power lies in the majority of the community, and the invasion of private rights is chiefly to be apprehended, not from acts of Government contrary to the sense of its constituents, but from acts in which the government is the mere instrument of the major number of constituents." Fearing this danger as much as the most "aristocratic" of his opponents in the Federalist party, Jefferson, as is shown by his private correspondence and by his proposed constitutions of Virginia, was in complete agreement with Hamilton that the judiciary should have express power to void acts of Congress. Indeed, the plan of judicial control sanctioned by him before he became President was far more reactionary than anything Hamilton had to say on the subject. In this plan the Supreme Court was to be given power to invalidate legislation on grounds not only of law but also of policy.

Thus it is impossible to attribute the deep-seated antagonism of Jefferson and the Republican party to Hamilton and the Federalists to the belief of the former in "rule by the people" and to the belief of the latter in an independent judiciary able to check this rule. Both political factions and their leaders desired a government of checks and balances in which the Supreme Court was to be firmly established as the bulwark against legislative depotism. Neither faction looked with favor upon "pure democracy" with its "leveling spirit." Like the Father of the Country, both parties felt that "the tumultuous populace of the large cities are ever to be dreaded," because "their indiscriminate violence prostrates for the time all public authority." In consequence, the Federalists and the Republicans were agreed not only on the necessity of controlling the expression of public will but also on the necessity of limiting the suffrage by property qualifications.

Notwithstanding their agreement on these issues, the gulf that separated the Jeffersonian Democrats and the Federalists was wide and far from imaginary. The antagonism between them was rooted in the economic soil of the country. It dated back to colonial times and still exerts an incalculable influence over the social thought of this country. Jefferson and Hamilton, as the learned historians have so often told us, represented the divergent economic interests of two social groups, the agrarian, on the one hand, and the commercial

and financial, on the other. This conflict between the forces of
agrarianism and of finance and commerce had flared up from time
to time in the colonies. There, enmity between the back-country folk
—frontiersmen and small farmers—and the mercantile and financial
families of the seaboard towns had been provoked by their opposing
interests in taxation, paper money, and military protection from the
Indians. Stifled by the struggle for national independence, the hostilities
between these contending groups broke out with renewed vigor and
became crystallized by new issues at the end of the war. To the old
issues that had tended from the beginning to divide American society
into agrarians and debtors, on the one side, and into a creditor
aristocracy of wealth and commerce, on the other, were now added
the funding of the debt incurred by the war, the protection of nascent
industries from foreign competition, and the establishment of a
national bank. In this conflict Hamilton championed the cause of the
future captains of industry and finance while Jefferson espoused
that of the small landed proprietors.

The economic rivalries of which Hamilton and Jefferson were
the political symbols emanated from no struggle between propertyless proletarians, on one hand, and the owners of land and capital,
on the other. Had industrial conditions permitted such a struggle
at that time, it is most improbable that Jefferson would have been
found in the camp of the proletariat. His ideas were cast in a
different economic mold. He no less than Hamilton was a champion
of the rights of private property. His allegiance to the institution of
private property was hardly less deep than that of Hamilton. Jefferson
thought that "a right to private property is founded in our natural
wants, in the means with which we are endowed to satisfy these
wants, and the right to what we acquire by those means without
violating the similar rights of other sensible beings." What Hamilton
and Jefferson represented was the rivalry of different fractions of the
propertied class, not the conflict between distinct classes playing
different roles in the process of production. Although the conflict
took the form of an alignment of agrarianism against finance and
commerce, at bottom it was a struggle of small property-owners
against relatively greater wealth.

Viewed in the perspective of the 18th-century political struggle,
Jefferson, the political leader of the small property interests, represented the radical wing of bourgeois democracy, while Hamilton,
the ideologist of a rising capitalist class, represented the conservative
wing. Conservative democracy drew its inspiration from the middle-
class liberalism of England. Radical democracy was inspired by the

petty bourgeois radicalism of the leaders of the French Revolution. Believing in the rights of private property, both groups, in this country as well as in England and France, were individualistic and accepted a laissez-faire economics. It was into these two camps, both representing property, that the founding fathers became divided.

II

To Benjamin Franklin and not to Jefferson belongs the distinction of being the first great exponent of petty bourgeois democracy with its agrarian foundation, and thus the earliest symbol of the common man tradition in this country. This self-made democrat and spokesman for the colonial cause on the eve of the American Revolution, entered politics in his adopted Pennsylvania as a leader of the back-country yeomanry and small men against the wealthy town gentry. In the conflict between agrarian-debtors and the town merchants and money lenders over the issue of paper money, Franklin, a leader in the anti-Proprietary party, naturally sided with the agrarians and in his first economic treatise defended the issue of paper money as indispensable to the farmer and small business man. Accepting the liberal economic doctrines of free trade, laissez-faire, and competition, like the French Physiocrats with whom he later came in contact, he considered land to be the sole source of wealth. He expounded this Physiocratic doctrine of the basic importance of land with as great clarity as the French economist, Quesnay, ever did. He said: "There seem to be but three ways for a nation to acquire wealth. The first is by *war,* as the Romans did, in plundering their neighbors. This is *robbery.* The second by *commerce,* which is generally *cheating.* The third by *agriculture,* the only *honest way,* wherein man receives a real increase of the seed thrown into the ground, in a kind of continued miracle, wrought by the hand of God in his favor."

As a forerunner of Jefferson, Franklin profoundly distrusted industrialism, which, he held, depends on the destruction of the independent farmer and small property-owner and on the cheap labor of a landless proletariat. But he was too firmly wedded to laissez-faire politics and economics to advocate the preservation of his democracy of agrarian freeholders by prohibitions against manufactures and trade. The only effective barrier to the factory system and its wage-earning proletariat was free land. When this disappeared, manufacturing and a wage-earning class would inevitably appear.

"Unprejudiced men well know," Franklin wrote in 1760, "that all penal and prohibitory laws that were ever thought on will not be sufficient to prevent manufacturers in a country, whose inhabitants surpass the number who can subsist by the husbandry of it. Manufacturers are founded in poverty. It is the number of poor without land in a country and who must work for others at low wages or starve, that enables undertakers to carry on a manufacture, and afford it cheap enough to prevent the importation of the same kind from abroad, and to bear the expense of its own exportation. But no man, who can have a piece of land of his own, sufficient by his labor to subsist his family in plenty, is poor enough to be a manufacturer, and work for a master. Hence while there is land in America for our people, there can never be manufacturers to any amount or value."

Franklin was of course correct in basing the growth of industrialism and a wage-earning proletariat upon the disappearance of free land. But although he looked upon industrialism as inevitable, he thought that it would be ages before a decline in free land and the evil consequence of it would occur in the United States. On the basis of a theory of population which Malthus at a later date worked out more systematically, he pictured the country enjoying a long reign of peace and happiness under the regime of an equalitarian democracy of free holders and small property-owners. This theory of society was the only one in which he could have faith. His belief in such a society limited his intellectual horizon and caused him to underestimate the tempo of economic forces. But in steadfastly adhering to it to the end of his life he came nearer than any other revolutionary father to advocating a "pure democracy." A government of checks and balances was repugnant to his conception of democracy. And, as a representative at the Constitutional Convention, but one who was too old to exert much influence, he was unmoved by "aristocratic" opposition to his belief in an unrestricted manhood suffrage, annual parliaments, and a single-chamber legislature representing a democratic electorate.

III

Neither Franklin's "pure democracy" nor his optimistic forecast of the economic future of the country was shared by Jefferson. This slaveholding liberal and Virginia planter in espousing the cause of the "people" never permitted his frequently expressed belief in a "general suffrage"—or for that matter his opposition to slavery—to transcend the sphere of thought and become an issue in the world of political fact. It is true that he proclaimed: "All power is inherent in the people. Nothing is unchangeable but the inherent and inalienable rights of man." But, according to his conception, the people on whose will the authority of government should rest were property owners, and, by property he meant primarily landed property. Thus the constitution which he proposed for his native State provided that only those males who had paid taxes for two years prior to election or those "having a freehold estate in one quarter of an acre of land in any town or twenty-five acres in the country" should have the right to vote for members of the lower house of the legislature. Though much broader than the suffrage actually adopted by the State, Jefferson's plan of limiting the vote to freeholders and taxpayers meant the disfranchisement of the propertyless.

This proposed plan of suffrage stemmed directly from his economic and political philosophy. The fact that his plan would have eventually amounted to manhood suffrage, since it required the State to grant non-landholders small estates out of the public domain, does not in the least contradict his philosophy. According to Jefferson the economic foundation of democracy consisted of small land-owning farmers supported by the mass of talents—petty merchants, tradesmen, and independent handicraftsmen. The future of democracy depended upon the preservation of these economic units. "We shall remain virtuous," he wrote Madison, "as long as agriculture is our principal object, which will be the case while there remain vacant lands in any part of America. When we get piled upon one another in large cities, as in Europe, we shall become corrupt as in Europe, and go to eating one another as they do there."

What in Jefferson's estimation threatened to destroy this democracy of small farmers and property holders was the emerging system of manufacturing, banking, and commerce which the policies of Hamilton and the Federalists tended to hasten. Even though he naturally shared Franklin's distrust of industrialism and abhorred the growth of an urban working class, he was under no illusion about the economic tendencies of the country. Manufacturing industry, he counseled, should be resorted to out of necessity and not from choice. He thought that it should be opposed as long as possible but that eventually it would have to be resorted to as a means of absorbing the surplus population for which there would be no free land. And while in Jefferson's opinion it would be some time before the country would have to make the choice, he did not place this probable contingency in Franklin's distant age.

When Jay questioned him on the advisability of encouraging manufacturing, Jefferson replied: "Were we perfectly free to decide this question, I should reason as follows. We have now lands enough to employ an infinite number of people in their cultivation. Cultivators of the earth are the most valuable citizens. They are the most virtuous, and they are tied to their country, and wedded to its liberty and interests, by most lasting bonds. As long, therefore, as they can find employment in this line, I would not convert them into mariners, artisans, or anything else. But our citizens will find employment in this line, till their numbers, and of course their productions, become too great for the demand, both internal and foreign. This is not the case yet, and probably will not be for a considerable time. As soon as it is, the surplus of hands must be turned to something else. I should then, perhaps, wish to turn them to the sea in preference to manufactures; because, comparing the characters of the two classes, I find the former most valuable citizens. I consider the class of artificers [the working class] as the panders of vice, and the instruments by which the liberties of a country are generally overturned."

It was indeed strange that for all of his astute reasoning on the future development of the country, Jefferson never saw that his democracy of independent farmers and small property-owners was threatened by the slaveholding planters of the South as much as it was by Hamilton's system of finance and industry. Even in Jefferson's day it was becoming evident that Southern tobacco and cotton farming was causing rapid exhaustion of soil, and making it necessary for the slaveocracy to bring fresh territories of virgin land under its control. Under these conditions any proposal such as he made to carve up the public domain into small estates for the non-landholders was foredoomed by the adamant opposition and superior political power of the planter aristocracy. This failure to see the incompatibility, in a democracy, of small farmers and slaveholding aristocrats has often been ascribed to the fact that Jefferson himself owned slaves. But in weighing his personal motives it ought to be borne in mind that in spite of his expressed belief in the inherent inferiority of the Negro race, he was true to his profession of humanitarian and liberal principles and advocated the manumission of the slaves. He said that when he thought of slavery and remembered that liberty, the gift of God, is not to be violated but with his wrath, he trembled for his country. However, Jefferson was dependent upon the planter aristocracy for political support. This, rather than his membership in the slaveholding caste, was the reason why his theoretical strictures against the slave regime remained politically sterile.

The conflict between Jefferson's principles and his actions in practical politics led his chief adversary, Hamilton, to characterize him as a "contemptible hypocrite." In urging the Federalists to support Jefferson rather than Aaron Burr for the presidency, Hamilton argued that Jefferson would not do "anything in pursuance of his

principles which would contravene his popularity or his interest."
We must leave it to the historians and biographers to decide the
correctness of Hamilton's appraisal. Nevertheless, we must admit that
Jefferson's willingness to ride to power on the shoulders of a democracy
which was committed, in principle, to the interests of small farmers
and property holders but was dominated and controlled, in fact, by a
slaveholding aristocracy, epitomized the greatest paradox in the
history of left-wing American liberalism. The persistence of the
vestiges of this paradox has prevented a rational alignment of economic
forces in present-day American party politics. Today, Jeffersonian
democracy is nothing more than an unstable union of dissident groups
in pursuit of conflicting if not altogether irreconcilable ends.

This failure to recognize the inherent antipathy between the
interests of small farmers and the large slaveholding planters was
not the least of Jefferson's shortcomings as an analyst of economic
and political forces. He was too occupied with the question of how
to postpone the evil day of industrialism to speculate on the possibility
of a surplus population which could be absorbed neither by maritime
occupations, his first alternative, nor by manufactures, his last resort.
His forecast of the future was blurred by his conception of what was
socially desirable and good. But the picture drawn by two gentlemen
on the other side of the political fence, Madison and Adams, was
painted with cold-blooded deftness and with an insight almost
prophetic.

IV

With a concern equal to that of Jefferson over the disposal of the
country's future surplus population, Madison concluded that "a certain
degree of misery seems inseparable from a high degree of populous-
ness." He thought that Malthus' foreboding of increasing poverty
applied to "a state of things inseparable from old countries, and
awaiting younger ones." Although he advocated the parceling up of
the hunting and other unproductive lands of the idle rich as a means
of absorbing surplus population, he felt that this was simply a palliative
which could not forever banish the specter of poverty. "Let the lands,"
he maintained, "be shared among them ever so wisely, and let them
be supplied with laborers ever so plentifully; as there must be a
surplus of subsistence, there will also remain a great surplus of
inhabitants, a greater number by far than will be employed in clothing
both themselves and those who feed them. . . . What is to be
done with this surplus? Hitherto, we have seen them distributed
into manufactures of superfluities, idle proprietors of productive lands,

domestics, soldiers, merchants, mariners, and a few other less numerous classes. All these classes, notwithstanding, have been found insufficient to absorb the redundant members of a populous society." Thus Madison's view was that whether society is organized on an agrarian or manufacturing basis, poverty will always be the fate of a large part of the population. In this he had the concurrence of his fellow Federalist, Adams.

To Adams the disproportionate growth of food supply and population was a law of nature. He said: "That the first want of man is his dinner, and the second his girl, were truths well known to every democrat and aristocrat, long before the great philosopher Malthus arose, to think he enlightened the world by the discovery. It has been equally well known that the second want is frequently so impetuous as to make men and women forget the first, and rush into rash marriages, leaving both the first and the second wants, their own as well as those of their children and grand children, to the chapter of accidents." The unavoidable consequence of this, he concluded, is "that the multiplication of the population so far transcends the multiplication of the means of subsistence, that the constant labor of nine-tenths of our species will forever be necessary to prevent all of them from starving with hunger, cold, and pestilence."

In Adams's hands this dismal theory of population became organically integrated with a theory of government and of class differentiation. Adams saw no reason to bemoan the fate to which the vast majority of mankind are consigned by their improvidence and their inability to restrain the sexual impulse. On the contrary, he thought that poverty was in one fundamental respect highly advantageous to society. "The great question," he argued, "will forever remain, *who shall work?* Our species cannot all be idle. Leisure for study must ever be the portion of the few. The number employed in government must forever be very small. Food, raiment, and habitations, the indispensable wants of all, are not to be obtained without the continual toil of ninety-nine in a hundred of mankind. As rest is rapture to the weary man, those who labor little will always be envied by those who labor much, though the latter in reality be probably the most enviable. With all encouragements, public and private, which can ever be given to general education, and it is scarcely possible they should be too many or too great, the laboring part of the people can never be learned."

According to Adams, then, whatever form government may take, society will always be divided into rich and poor, into those who work and those who do not. Out of this class division will arise mutual suspicions and rivalries. "The controversy between the rich and the poor, the laborious and the idle, the learned and the ignorant, distinctions which no art or policy, no degree of virtue or philosophy can ever wholly destroy, will continue, and rivalries will arise out of them." The main function of government is to balance these rivalries. Otherwise liberty can not be maintained and property, the foundation of liberty, will become insecure. Neither democracy, aristocracy, nor monarchy, in their *simple forms,* can achieve the ends of a balanced government. It is only a constitutional democracy based upon an adequate system of checks and balances that is competent to hold the different orders of mankind and their mutual antipathies in equilibrium.

In terms of his social theory and of his conception of the function of government, Adams's ideas varied only in minor details from those of other leading Federalists. He agreed with Madison, first, that uniformity of interests is impossible in society because of "diversity in the faculties of men, from which the rights of property originate"; and, second, that "the protection of these faculties is the first object of government." His thesis that society naturally divides itself into superiors and inferiors is identical with Hamilton's that "all communities divide themselves into the few and the many," "the rich and the well born," and "the mass of people." While Adams believed it indispensable that every man should know his place, and be made to keep it, he could not accept Hamilton's view that the natural guardians of good government are the "rich and well born." He thought that the rich no less than the poor had to be watched. Without adequate checks the rich would crush the liberties of the poor and the poor would despoil the rich. Mankind, he said, "are governed by the teeth." And, in the words of Machiavelli, he admonished, "Whoever would found a state, and make proper laws for the government of it, must presume that all men are bad by nature." Power, unbalanced and unchecked, cannot therefore be entrusted to kings, to noblemen, or to popular assembly.

But in rejecting Hamilton's naïve faith in the "rich and well born" Adams did not deny that society is ruled in final analysis by the men of birth and wealth. This he thought was self-evident and as it should be. All society, he reasoned, even under his "balanced" republican government, is ruled by a *natural aristocracy* of wealth and talents.

By *natural aristocracy,* Adams said he meant "those superiorities of influence which grow out of the constitution of human nature." He also spoke of an *artificial aristocracy* which arises from "those inequalities of weight and superiorities of influence which are created and established by civil laws." But the distinction which Adams made between the two types of aristocracy can be ignored because he himself did not adhere to it. The sources of aristocracy, he stated, are to be found in the inequality of wealth and property, the inequality of birth, and the inequalities of merit and talents. These inequalities "are common to every people" and "can never be altered by any, because they are founded in the constitution of nature."

To John Taylor, the most systematic thinker among the Jeffersonian democrats, Adams's *natural aristocracy* was a social rather than a natural invention. It was the product of the profits derived from paper money, banking, corporations, and unequal education. Taylor thought that the proper diffusion of property, the only basis of a true democracy, could be brought about by prohibitions against banking and charters of incorporation, by equal education, and by the reform of the inheritance laws. To this argument Adams replied that as long as the institution of private property remained, and he thought that man's inherent love of riches would always preserve it, Taylor's proposals would merely transfer property from one set of hands to another, and as a result the concentration of wealth would begin anew, and a *natural aristocracy* would thereby arise.

Adams reasoned as follows: "Suppose congress should, at one vote, or by one act, declare all negroes in the United States free, in imitation of that great authority, the French sovereign legislature, what would follow? Would the democracy, nine in ten, among the negroes, be gainers? Would not nine in ten, perhaps ninety-nine in a hundred of the rest, petition their old aristocratical masters to receive them again, to protect them, to feed them, to clothe them, and to lodge and shelter them as usual? Would not some of the most thinking and philosophical among the aristocratical negroes ramble in to distant states, seeking a poor and precarious subsistence by daily labor? Would not some of the most enterprising aristocrats allure a few followers into the wilderness, and become squatters? or, perhaps, incorporate with Indians? . . . Will the poor, simple, democratical part of the people gain any happiness by such a rash revolution? . . . When the national convention in France voted all the negroes in St. Domingo, Martinique, Gaudaloupe, St. Lucia, etc., free, at a breath, did the poor democracy among the negroes gain anything by the change? Are they more free from Toussaint to Pétion and Christophe? Do they live better? Bananas and water they still enjoy, and a whole regiment would follow a leader who should hold a salt-fish to their noses. . . . I hope, sir, that all these considerations will convince you that property has been, is, and everlastingly will be a natural and unavoidable cause of aristocracy, and God Almighty has made it such by the water, and the fire, among which he has placed it."

Adams's *natural aristocracy* may have been anathema to the liberty-loving advocates of agrarian democracy, Taylor and Jefferson. But neither Jeffersonian democrats nor Hamiltonian Federalists disagreed with Adams's fundamental thesis that economic power determines the political. To the leading thinkers in each party, this was self-evident.

But it was Madison who formulated in a definitive way this commonly shared view of the determinism of economics upon politics. Writing in Number 10 of the *Federalist,* he said: "The most common and durable source of factions has been the various and unequal distribution of property. Those who hold and those who are without property have ever formed distinct interests in society. Those who are creditors and those who are debtors, fall under a like discrimination. A landed interest, a manufacturing interest, a mercantile interest, a moneyed interest, with many lesser interests, grow up of necessity in civilized nations, and divide them into different classes, actuated by different sentiments, and views. The regulation of these various and interfering interests forms the principal task of modern legislation, and involves the spirit of party and faction in the necessary and ordinary operations of the government."

In thus founding his political theory upon an economic basis Madison was not unique. At a much earlier date the English thinker, Harrington, had held that "empire follows the balance of property." Both he and Locke had sought to discover the secrets of politics and history in a form of economic determinism. Nevertheless, Madison does enjoy the distinction of being the first political thinker in this country to accept the doctrine and to apply it rigorously to American conditions. It would be wrong of course to impute to him an acceptance of the theory of class struggle or to conclude that his statement of economic interpretation embraced the much later Marxian conception of the "historical role of classes." His ideas were shaped by the character and the form of the economic conflict which he and the other founding fathers knew and in which he and they participated on one side or the other.

V

The proposition that government ought to rest upon the dominion of property was a cardinal tenet of faith among both the Federalists and Republicans. On this there was no disagreement between them. The great bone of contention was the kind of property on which political power should rest. The Republicans thought that it should rest on the small landed proprietors. The Federalists maintained that it should rest on mobile property, the wealth of the moneyed interests. These right- and left-wing champions of American democracy, as we have already noted, did not represent different classes but rather different fractions of the propertied class. Thus, when viewed in its true historical light, the conflict between Hamilton and Jefferson will be seen as a struggle between small and large capitalists. That this conflict took the form of the opposition of the forces of agrarianism to finance and commerce was inevitable because of the peculiar character of emerging American capitalism.

Unlike England, 18th-century America had no landless proletariat and no factory system to absorb and transform it into a modern wage-earning class. Also, unlike England, America had no landed nobility to contest the economic power and the political supremacy of rising captains of industry. English society, at the end of the Industrial Revolution, was stratified into three definitely formed and conscious classes; the landed nobility, the capitalists, and the wage-earners. In England, middle-class democracy took the form of a struggle of these industrial capitalists, supported by the wage-earners, to wrest political power from the nobility. All of this was foreign to America directly after the Revolutionary War.

In some respects the economic scene in America and, in consequence, the class arrangement, resembled that of revolutionary France in spite of the remnants of feudalism that plagued the establishment of democracy in that country. In France, as in America, the factory system had not made its appearance. Neither country had as yet become divided into industrial capitalists and proletarians. In each an emergent capitalist class was amassing wealth through financial manipulations, speculations, and mercantile transactions, but not through manufacturing industry. Over against the expanding wealth of these financiers, speculators, and merchants, stood the small property of the peasant farmer, self-employed handicraftsman, and shopkeeper. In France, the men of small wealth united with those of greater affluence to destroy the old feudal orders of church, crown, and nobility. In America, national independence was achieved by the union of identical economic forces. And, in America, as in France, after revolution had established the bourgeois republic, the great and small forces of democracy split into antagonistic factions. On the left stood the radicals proclaiming the dominion of the small proprietors, petty traders, and handicraftsmen as the only valid democracy. On the right were to be found the conservatives to whom democracy could only mean the hegemony of the financial and commercial powers. Since France and America were both predominantly agricultural, it was quite natural that in both countries left-wing or petty bourgeois democracy in espousing the rights of the common man should take an agrarian economic basis. But in France, this common-man tradition never acquired the uniqueness that it did in America. In America, it became more deeply embedded in social thought than in any other country.

In this new empire where feudalism had never been known and where virgin forests, untapped natural resources, and free land permitted every man, it seemed, to start from scratch in the race for enrichment, equalitarianism acquired an unprecedented and vital reality. Under these peculiarly American conditions the only conflict that could arise was the conflict between those who had acquired a little and those who had accumulated a great deal. This conflict envisioned by the founding fathers was devoid of class-consciousness. The participants were all common men, laborers who aspired to become capitalists, and capitalists who had been laborers.

This logic of the past dominates the thought of many present-day leaders in the party of Jefferson as well as in that of Hamilton. Thus to them a capitalist is a retired laborer. By the same token accumulated wealth represents the past labor of its owners or, at least, the stored-up labor of their forebears. But if, in retrospect, one regards these early possessors of wealth as acquisitive men, he must pronounce the same verdict on the little men-on-the-make. They were no less acquisitive than the wealthy. At heart, the little man, whether farmer or small business entrepreneur, was as much a buccaneer seeking unearned increment as any of the great financiers and speculators of his day. The problem that was of greatest moment to him was the preservation of free and equal competition for all in the exploitation of the country's natural resources and economic opportunities. This has always been the chief aspiration of petty bourgeois democracy whether led by Jefferson, Jackson, Bryan, the trust-busters of the late nineteenth and early twentieth century, or the present-day advocates of soft money, agricultural subsidies, and the protection of the small business man.

The common-man philosophy, however, while traditionally associated with Jeffersonian democracy, has found champions in the party of business and finance. Jefferson himself never expressed greater faith in it than Lincoln, the first standard bearer of the party of big business. Speaking at New Haven at the beginning of the Civil War, Lincoln said: "I take it that it is best to leave each man free to acquire property as fast as he can. Some will get wealthy. I don't believe in any law to prevent a man from getting rich; it would do more harm than good. So while we don't propose any war upon capital, we do wish to allow the humblest man an equal chance to get rich with anybody else. When one starts poor, as most do in the race of life, free society is such that he knows he can better his conditions; he knows that there is no fixed condition of labor for his whole life. . . . I want every man to have a chance. . . ."

Though shrewd in their discernment of the forces at work in early American society and, at times, prophetic in their predictions of the economic future of the country, none of the founding fathers was a systematic economic thinker. They were all of them special pleaders for different propertied interests. The divergence in their economic views was determined by the struggle between those who had and those who were getting. Their theory of society embraced no struggle between those who had and those who had not. This outlook of the founding fathers continued to dominate American social thought long after the industrial situation had changed. Though weakened, it persists to-day, and distorts the essential conflict in a fully developed capitalism.

RALPH J. BUNCHE (1904-   )

Ralph Bunche, born in Detroit and educated at the University of California at Los Angeles and Harvard, is now head of the department of political science at Howard University. He has made investigations of imperialism in Africa, as a Social Science Research Fellow, and of the Negro in American political life, as a staff member of the Carnegie-Myrdal Study of the Negro. He is the author of *A World View of Race* (1936) and of articles in scholarly magazines. "Disfranchisement of the Negro" is here used by permission of the author.

[The Disfranchisement of the Negro][1]

THE THEORY HABITUALLY OFFERED by the South for its persistent refusal to grant to black citizens their constitutional right of suffrage may be properly described as catastrophic. Symbolic of this theory are the legendary nicks in the marble steps of North Carolina's magnificent Capitol building at Raleigh. These nicks were chipped out, it is alleged, by the liquor kegs which the boisterous black legislators of Reconstruction days rolled down the steps. Garrulous old-time southern politicians can out-do Orson Welles in narrating horrendous tales of those days when the South was plagued by a pestilence of black politicians. They tell, and with rather more enjoyment than rancor, of their participation in "nigger vote buying," and in "nigger vote stealing," which frequently led to fights between rival hi-jackers; of a traffic in which the coin was sometimes liquor and sometimes women; and finally, of how, like the Pied Piper of Hamlin, they marched the Negro and his vote to the polls with music. This is the legendary picture that is conjured up by many white southerners today when they are confronted with the issue of Negro enfranchisement. They still profess to fear that Negro voters would be "bought at 50c a head" and "herded like sheep"[2] to the polls, although admitting that white vote-buying is a common practice in many parts of the South today.

Negro political status in the South remains under the shadow of the doctrine of the indispensability of white supremacy — — a doctrine which controls all relationships between the races there. The registration and election laws of the South are administered within this framework. Though there is no longer any real fear in the South of black domination *per se,* white supremacy remains a sure-fire political issue in the hands of the demagogue. In reality, the issue of political white supremacy is perpetuated less on the fear of independent black political power, than on the fear that some white group might gain political ascendancy by control and manipulation of a released Negro vote.

Perhaps the most striking feature of the southern political picture is the low-voting ratio, due almost as much to the disfranchisement

---

[1] A paper read before the American Political Science Association, Chicago, Illinois, December 27, 1940. The interview material cited in this paper is the product of extensive fieldwork, involving hundreds of interviews with southern officials, white and Negro citizens in connection with the comprehensive survey of the Negro in America sponsored by the Carnegie Corporation of New York.

[2] Interview with the secretary to the chairman of the ———— County Democratic Executive Committee, Alabama, March, 1940.

of large numbers of poor whites as to the political disqualification of
the Negro. The franchise problems of black and white citizens in
the South today are inter-related.[3] Negro non-voting is more than
a mere by-product of racial disunity. Non-voting of both black and
white citizens is essentially a broad derivative of the political and
economic structure of the South.

The one-party political system under which the southern Negro
is disfranchised is highly decentralized. Its main props are the local
political machines, the county courthouse "gangs" and "rings," and
it is in their operation that the real venality of southern politics,
especially in its relation to the Negro, is revealed. In their own domain
these local rings wield great powers. The probate judges, county
ordinaries, clerks, registrars, sheriffs, beat committeemen, members
of the election committees and the county party officers who make up
the "courthouse crowds" tend largely to invent their own rules;
amazingly wide discretionary powers are exercised by them; they
are ludicrously ill-informed on the provisions of the laws they are
sworn to uphold; while traffic in votes and offices is by no means rare.
This political system is characterized by a wide variety of loose and
undemocratic practices of which Negro disfranchisement is but one.
Among the characteristic abuses are found a widespread absence of
the secret ballot, frequent use of numbered ballots, severe misuse of
absentee voting, extensive double voting and voting under names of
the deceased, absence of watchers in polling places, frequent failure
to provide polling booths, habitual aid in marking ballots, loosely
kept voting lists, and such picturesque devices as "chain-letter"
balloting. Southern registration lists are very often shockingly inaccurate, even to the extent of having the tell-tale "col." opposite the
names of reputable white citizens; while purging the voting lists is
frequently little more than a gesture.

The discretion of the local registration and election officials is
so great that it is virtually impossible to make very many generalizations concerning the particular manifestations of the disfranchising
devices. It is never enough to analyze the state laws on the subject.
The local officials take the law into their own hands and there are
almost as many varieties of practices as there are counties. Even
within the same county there are changes in application of the law
as the personnel of registration boards changes. The uniformity is
in the motivation and objective sought rather than in the means
employed. The primary purpose of the disfranchising constitutions

[3] For a full account of the disfranchising movement cf. Lewinson, Paul, *Race, Class
and Party, passim.*

has been accomplished: Negro political power is effectively blacked-out.

With regard to registration in the South, for example, there is a strikingly loose interpretation of the laws in so far as white registrants are concerned. The poll tax constitutes a severe burden on poor white voting, but the registrar is seldom an obstacle of any consequence. Registration officials are almost universally lenient and paternalistic toward the southern white registrant. The laxness, the indifference to the law, the easy-going and often studied gullibility toward white registrants is almost everywhere transformed into a harsh, rigid, and hostile application of the letter of the law and often something more than the law, when Negro registrants appear.

Within the scope of this paper only a selected sampling of the many variations of the devices employed in the counties of one or another southern state to prohibit or discourage Negro registration and voting can be presented. No uniformity of practice as between states is found. In some states registration for Negroes is not too difficult, and Negroes may vote in local and bond elections, while disfranchisement in the only important elections results from an exclusion policy for the Democratic or "white" primaries. In other states registration is made extremely difficult, and in some counties quite out of the question, by the severe policies of registration officials and the hostility of the community. The most important devices in current usage are the following:

1) Exclusion from the Democratic primary. This is in actuality a "white" rather than a "Democratic" primary, for all whites, whether Democratic or Republican, are frequently admitted to it, while all Negroes are barred.

2) Requiring one or more (usually two) white character witnesses. Often the Negro applicant must have these appear in person.

3) Strict enforcement of the literacy tests against Negro applicants: *i.e.,* requiring "reasonable" interpretations of the Constitution, and always to the satisfaction of the officials.

4) Putting unreasonable questions to Negro applicants in constitutional understanding or interpretation tests, as, for example, "what is *non compos mentis* when it is applied to a citizen in legal jeopardy?"

5) Severe application of property qualifications and requiring Negro applicants only to show property tax receipts.

6) Basing rejection of Negro registrants on alleged minor mistakes in filling out registration blanks, as, for example, an applicant's error in computing his exact age by years, months, and *days.*

7) Evasion, by informing Negro applicants that registration cards

have "run out," that all members of the registration board are not on hand, that it is "closing time," or that the applicant "will be notified" in due course, though he seldom is.

8) Requiring Negro applicants to suffer long waits before the officials attend them.

9) Requiring Negro applicants to fill out their own blanks though those of white applicants are filled out for them by officials.

10) Deliberate insults, humiliations or threats by officials and/or hangers on.

11) Discarding only Negro applications for conviction of misdemeanors.

12) Requiring enrollment in Democratic clubs, from which Negroes are barred, for primary voting, as in South Carolina.

13) Severe application of the cumulative poll tax to Negro though not to white voters.

14) Loss of jobs or threat of loss of jobs by those Negroes who get "uppity" and insist on their right to register.

15) Warning prospective Negro voters in small towns that they will be "marked men" in the white community.

16) Intimidation through physical violence.

In the vast majority of cases, whether a particular Negro gets registered in the South depends upon the whim of the local registration officials. Fairly often local officials agree to permit a token registration of the "better class" Negroes, *i.e.,* the doctor, the undertaker and perhaps the principal of the Negro school. Most of the Negro registration that is permitted in the southern states is found in the larger cities. Negro registration and voting in the rural areas of the South is so meager as to be virtually non-existent. Efforts of Negroes toward registration are commonly described by southern registration officials as "trouble."

The application to Negroes of some of the restraining devices in the deep-South states can be graphically illustrated by specific episodes, which could be multiplied a hundred-fold as collected from field data.

The "white primary" rules are ordinarily brief and to the point. For instance, they limit participation to "qualified white electors, both male and female" (Arkansas), to "electors of the white race" (Louisiana), to "all white citizens" (Texas), And the party officials are equally explicit on the subject. As the Secretary-Treasurer of the County Democratic Committee in a Georgia county puts it:

"Niggers have been ruled out. It's our private affair and we don't invite them in, and that's that."[4]

[4] Interview, ———— County, Georgia, April, 1940.

The City Manager of a South Carolina town tells the story of a Negro Baptist preacher—a southern Negro educated in the North—who had tried to vote in the Democratic primary. He was greeted by a former mayor of the town with the question: "What do you want nigger?" When the preacher explained politely that he wanted to vote, he was warned to "get out and stay out if you know what's good for you."[5]

A member of the Board of Registrars of an Alabama County testifies that the registrars do not take just *anybody's* signature for Negro applicants, and explains that "it's generally a prominent lawyer or a business woman, or one of the registrars."[6]

When asked if another Negro voter might sign for a Negro applicant, this registrar responded:

"Lord no! We wouldn't take their word. There ain't many that gets by me, I tell you. They have to be mighty *good* niggers to get by *me*. I don't want you to go tellin' nobody that, 'cause they'll think I'm discriminatin' when I'm not. I've been in a nigger-town doing business for the past 20 years and I've learned to tell between 'em. I ain't discriminatin'. If they can show where they're good citizens, I'll sign for them myself. . . ."

In a central Alabama county, a member of the Board of Registrars explains that an entirely different process is employed for the registration of Negroes and whites. It is admitted that the reading and writing test is never employed by the registrars who make out the blanks for most applicants, as the questions are asked orally. The applicants must sign their own applications. Ordinarily only the first two sheets are filled out; the third sheet—for witnesses—is left blank except in a very few cases where the registrars have reason to doubt the veracity of the applicants. Negro applicants however are required to fill out their own blanks. "They can't take it outside to fill it out. We make them fill it out right in front of us."[7]

They must have two white people, qualified voters, to sign their blanks. A very few of the Negro applicants bring their witnesses with them. Most of them give the names of two white people who they think will sign for them. They are instructed to go out and get the white witnesses and have them come in to sign personally. The applications are held throughout that registration period and then

[5] Interview with the City Manager and Secretary of the ————— County Democratic Club, South Carolina, June, 1940.
[6] Interview with a member of the Board of Registrars, ————— County, Alabama, February, 1940.
[7] *Ibid.*

destroyed if the signers do not appear. Few of the signers appear, it is said. When they do appear, these white witnesses are questioned—unless they are prominent people—about how long they have known the Negro seeking registration, and as a resident at his present address. If the white witness has not known the applicant for most of his life, his signature is rejected.

Two prominent Negroes in Montgomery, Alabama, went to register in 1939. One of them filled out the blank and was asked to *bring* two responsible white citizens up to the registration office to endorse him. Though the president of a local bank had endorsed this Negro applicant, he did not get registered.[8]

In a northern Alabama county a Negro owner of a grocery store was told by a friendly probate judge that he and his wife would be registered if they could get the endorsement of some other responsible white people in town. The Negro grocer soon got registered without any trouble by getting the mayor's endorsement. The mayor, he explains, "is my friend. He's a wholesale grocer."[9]

The tax collector of a Georgia county explained that the reading and writing of the constitution qualification for registration in Georgia is not so simple because he requires a "reasonable definition."[10] He commented: "I can keep the President of the United States from registering . . . if I want to." As an example, he referred to the Supreme Court jurisdiction clause of the Constitution in Article III and exclaimed: "God, himself, couldn't understand that. I, myself, is the judge," and boasted: "It must be written to my satisfaction." This tax collector warned: "If we didn't have a law to stop niggers from registering, we should have to make one."

On occasion, when registrars in Alabama have desired to stop some Negro from registering, they have applied the constitutional interpretation test. One Negro applicant, it is reported, was told that he would have to recite the Constitution. The Negro went on to recite eloquently the Gettysburg Address, and the registrar exclaimed: "That's right. You can go ahead and register."[11]

The Negro recording secretary of a Negro Smelter Workers' Local registered for voting in Birmingham, Alabama, on December 6, 1939. He relates that in his examination he was asked—among others—the following questions: [12]

[8] Interview with a Negro leader, ————, Alabama, November 10, 1939.
[9] Interview with a Negro voter, ———— County, Alabama, March, 1940.
[10] Interview with the Tax Collector, ———— County, Georgia, February 3, 1939
[11] Interview with two Negro doctors, Alabama, November 17, 1939
[12] Interview, ————, Alabama, March, 1940

1. What form of government do we live under?
2. Name the three branches of government and tell the function of each.
3. Name the two houses of Congress. Tell how the members of each are elected?
4. How is the number of representatives determined?
5. What is the Bill of Rights. Name somè of its provisions.
6. From what country did our form of government originate?

He states that after he had fully answered all of these—which took some 20 minutes of oral examination—he was told to step aside. He moved away about 20 feet. The registrars conferred for a few minutes and then told him that he was "unanimously passed." As he puts it: "That meant I could vote as soon as I paid $21.00 back poll tax." And he paid that tax the next day.

The following is an extract from a letter written by a group of young Negro miners who futilely attempted to register in the small Alabama mining community where they worked. No Negroes before had even attempted to register in this community, near Birmingham. Word had spread beforehand to the whites that the men, members of a civic group, were planning to register. The registrar was seated in a car in front of the office when the men arrived. As the Negroes approached, they were asked to come up one at a time; the registrar proceeded to quizz each person, not even bothering to leave the car. Their letter tells the rest of the story:

"We went to the polls to vote November 6 (1930) but didn't pass our registration because of these questions: . . . (1) How many articles and amendments are there in the Constitution? (2) What is meant by *non compos mentis* when it is applied to a citizen in legal jeopardy? (3) Name the amendments in rotation. (4) What is meant by habeas corpus?"[13]

The probate judge of an Alabama county states:

"We had some trouble about nigger voting here a while back. Some of the men in these mine unions tried to register some of their nigger members. They knew they could control them, you know. One of the registrars came to me and asked me what they were going to do about it. I told her to ask them this one question and I bet not a one of them could answer it. If they couldn't, she had a right to refuse them. I told her to ask them what the Constitution meant when it said that the right of habeas corpus shall not be denied."[14]

[13] Interview, Birmingham, Alabama, May, 1940
[14] Interview with the Probate Judge, ————— County, Alabama, March, 1940

The judge got a big laugh out of this one and explained that only one Negro got by.

The chairman of the Board of Registrars of an Alabama county states that not more than five or six Negroes have been registered since he has been on the board, though several others had "offered." He does not believe that Negroes ought to be allowed to register unless they pay taxes on $500 worth of personal property or own a home, though this is far beyond the legal requirement. He has refused to register all who could not show receipts for this amount, stating

"If you want my personal opinion, I think there are damn few niggers that ought to vote in any election. You can't show me more than two in a thousand who're not' gonna vote for the first person who gives him two bits."[15]

In Louisiana there is no longer any poll tax payment required for registration, but the poll tax receipts must be got for the two preceding years in order to be eligible for registration: that is, the present year and the one immediately preceding. Once the poll tax receipts are obtained, the applicant must appear at the registration office, where a clerk presents him with a printed card. This form must be filled in at the registration office. The answers to the questions must be absolutely correct. Though the questions on the card appear very simple, there are many applicants who make mistakes. A registration official in referring to the experience of Negro applicants explained: "There are only a few niggers who know exactly when they were born or where they were born, or even where they were living."[16]

In New Orleans Negroes have had considerable difficulty in getting registered. One prominent New Orleans Negro, in his first effort to register there, in answering the question as to his age was told by the clerk that he had miscalculated his age as he had computed it without considering whether February had 28 or 29 days.[17] This same Negro—though he had registered on three previous occasions—was turned down at the registration office four consecutive times. On the fifth effort, a white clerk who knew him waited upon him and registered him without any difficulty.

A northern Alabama Negro who is himself registered and persistently tries to get other Negroes registered, knows the routine

[15] Interview with the Chairman of the Board of Registrars, ———— County, Alabama, February, 1940

[16] Interview with a registration official, New Orleans, Louisiana, November 13, 1939.

[17] Interview with a Negro voter, New Orleans, Louisiana, November 13, 1939.

well.[18] First, his Negro applicants are handed a blank—if the supply has not "accidentally" run out as it did on one occasion. The whites then were allowed to use blanks that had been spoiled before, but the Negro he had with him had to come back. Then they are told to fill out the blanks. For whites, the registrars fill the blanks out themselves. By the time the Negro has filled out the blank, one of the registrars has slipped out and they cannot register legally, they say, because all three of the registrars are not present. The Negro is then told to come back later. When he does, it is "after closing time." Closing time may be anywhere from 2:00 o'clock in the afternoon on. Or the officer may look over the application and claim to find mistakes in it. He cancels the blank and tells the applicant he must come back and try again. If the Negro applicant refuses to leave when the third officer steps out and decides to wait until he comes back, the registrar either temporarily closes the office, forcing him to leave, or ignores his application entirely, making him wait around until all whites are served and, incidentally, until it is "too late" again. Meanwhile remarks are often made to try to intimidate, or more often, to embarrass and ridicule the applicant and anyone who happens to be with him.

A former clerk in the registrar's office in Birmingham, Alabama, who served for three years, gave the following description of the methods of dealing with Negro applicants for registration.[19] Negroes would be given applications when they came in. After they had filled them out, they were told that the office would notify them when to come back for examination. All of these applications were checked by the clerk with the criminal dockets. If the applicant had failed to mention on his application that he had been convicted of any crime, either a felony or misdemeanor, his application was thrown out. If it was a felony and he noted it, the application would be discarded whether or not his citizenship had been restored. The clerk explained: "You know, when you check all the drunk cases and everything, there's hardly a nigger in town that isn't on the books." These Negro applicants were never notified. If they inquired, the court records would be cited and this was enough to frighten them into silence.

An elderly Negro in South Carolina, who is a faithful follower of "Tieless" Joe Tolbert, and who has attended Republican conventions, has done his best to get "something started" in his county among

---

[18] Interview with a Negro business man, chairman of a political club, ————, Alabama, February, 1940.

[19] Interview, Birmingham, Alabama, March 1, 1940.

Negro voters. The older Negro voters, he states, kept dying off and he could not recall there being more than a dozen Negro voters since he was a boy. He is now 59. By 1936, there were only two Negro voters left in the county—himself and his wife—and so then, he states: "I got busy and commenced working me up a bunch to go to register."[20]

He got ten or twelve who said they were willing, and most of them—eight—were registered in 1938, when the new registration began, but not that many voted because "they got discouraged." He then explained why the Negroes he had tried to recruit got discouraged:

"One who had worked in the Ford repair shop for a dozen years, got fired. His mother—an undertaker—was not bothered. Another, a school teacher, was warned by authorities that she had better not 'mess with such as that.' Still another, a Negro landowner out in the county, received a hike in taxes."

Two others were preachers and one of these men was "warned." One other was a janitor in the bank—one of the best known Negroes in the town and a good friend of the mayor. He was also fired.

"The mayor said he was surprised. He said he'd always liked him, but right there, he ruint hisself when he started foolin' with votin' . . . All that got people discouraged."

A Negro voter in a small southern town, such as Huntsville, Alabama, is something of a marked man. As one official informant in Huntsville puts it, "When a nigger votes, almost everybody in town knows about it. Besides, they're the most prominent ones in the County."[21]

A prominent Negro in the Baton Rouge community states:

"I don't know of anyone here who has had any trouble registering—such a relatively few have attempted to—but it is common knowledge that no Negro will be allowed to vote in Port Allen (a town in West Baton Rouge Parish). A man told me that when he went up to register, the registrar said to him: 'Now, listen, boy, if you just insist on registering, I'll register you. You got a right under the law, but I tell you, you've got to live here and you'll be pointed out as an uppity nigger. So, if I was you, I'd forget it. Besides, your one vote won't count nohow—don't you know I would lose my job if I let a whole lot of niggers register? I'd register you and maybe two or three others, but it won't get you nowhere. So, why don't you forget it, huh?"[22]

[20] Interview with a Negro Republican leader, ————, South Carolina, June, 1940.
[21] Interview with a Census taker, Huntsville, Alabama, February, 1940.

The threat of intimidation is a potent factor in blocking the Negro's path to the polls. It is more than coincidence that led three officials in Noxubee County, Mississippi, to repeat the platitude that there are no Negroes registered for voting in that county, none who try, and if any did "he wouldn't get home safe."[23]

The most recent southern state to abandon the poll tax is Florida. With the necessity for paying the annual levy as a prerequisite to voting swept away, Negro registration began to increase. When a city election came up in May, 1939, in Miami, the city had the largest number of Negroes in history on its voting lists. Resentment flared up in hostile demonstrations that had the Miami police department's nerves on edge for two or three days. On the night before the election, hooded riders in automobiles with hidden license plates patrolled the principal Negro residential sections. The robed men, identified as members of the Ku Klux Klan, put the torch to oil-drenched crosses on street corners. Nooses dangled menacingly from automobile windows and one dummy bearing a sign, "This nigger voted," was strung up as a grim warning. But the Negro could not be frightened away from the polling places.

The poll tax is, of course, an additional barrier to the exercise of the franchise by Negroes in the South. It is not the only barrier, nor is it the most significant. Yet in most southern states it imposes a discouraging burden on the exercise of the franchise in the only elections in which any appreciable number of Negroes are ever permitted to vote, i.e., the general elections. But the general elections are ordinarily mere gestures in the South, and so depriving the Negro of the right to vote in these elections is not, under present political conditions, depriving him of very much.

The alleged fear that the abolition of the poll tax will open the flood-gates of black political power is now often employed in the South to discredit the efforts of those who are striving to achieve some measure of democracy for at least the white population of that section. For instance, an editorial in the Tuscaloosa Alabama News employs the threat of Negro domination as the basis for its opposition to repeal of the poll tax and observes:

"This newspaper believes in white supremacy, and it believes that the poll tax is one of the essentials for the preservation of white supremacy. It does not believe in a Democracy with a small 'd,' because it knows this country never has had such a Democracy and never will have such

[22] Interview with a Negro leader, Baton Rouge, Louisiana, February, 1940.
[23] Interviews with three courthouse officials, Noxubee County, Mississippi, August, 1940.

a Democracy as long as white supremacy is preserved . . . If it is 'undemocratic' to argue for white supremacy—as it certainly is—then we plead guilty to the charge."[24]

By a congeries of such devices and attitudes the Negro is disfranchised. Certainly the direct implications to a democratic society of such denials of democratic rights to a large body of its citizens are shamefully clear. Long tolerated abuses of this kind cannot but have a deleterious effect upon the democratic fabric of the nation. The continuing cultivation of a large corps of public officials who have no respect for laws, who tend to become a law unto themselves, who wink and connive at habitual violation of the laws they are sworn to uphold, will inevitably reap bitter harvests for all Americans who regard the democratic way as essential to decent living. Already the efforts toward erasing the Negro as an active political factor have had their repercussions in the mass disfranchisement of white persons, now typical of a section of the country whose voting record is surely a travesty on democracy. In these days of institutionalized hooliganism elsewhere in the world Klan law is a vulnerable spot in our national democratic armor.

CHARLES H. THOMPSON (1896-   )

Charles H. Thompson, born in Jackson, Mississippi, was educated at Virginia Union University and the University of Chicago. As editor of *The Journal of Negro Education,* founded in 1931 at Howard University, where he is now professor of education and dean of the College of Liberal Arts, his influence upon Negro scholarship has been marked. He is the author of many articles in that journal and in *The American Teacher, School and Society, Annals of the Academy of Political and Social Science, Occupations,* and *The Crisis.* "The Education of the Negro in the United States" was published in *School and Society* (1935) and is here reprinted by permission of the author and of the magazine.

[24] November 3, 1939, quoted in "Suffrage in the South," Part I; by George C. Stoney, *Survey Graphic,* January, 1940, Vol. 29, No. 1, p. 41.

The Education of the Negro in the United States[1]

IT IS THE PRIMARY PURPOSE of this discussion to give a comprehensive and objective analysis of the problem which the Negro faces in his attempt to secure equitable educational opportunity in the United States of America. It is my specific purpose to define the problem, not to solve it. Accordingly, I shall attempt to suggest the answers to three specific questions: First, what is the comparative educational status of the American Negro to-day? Second, what are some of the basic factors which determine this status? And, third, what steps have been, and are being, taken to improve this status?

In attempting to define or understand the problem which the American Negro faces in his attempt to secure equitable educational opportunity, there are certain basic facts concerning the educational set-up in the United States as a whole which should be kept in mind. First, it should be emphasized that one of the basic assumptions underlying public education in the United States is the doctrine that, among other things, an equitable educational opportunity is the inalienable right of every American child, irrespective of his race, creed or socio-economic status. Second, it should also be remembered that public education in the United States is a function of local support and control. The public school "system" is not *a* system at all, but 48 or more independent school systems supported and controlled by the individual states, and their minor divisions. Third, because of the wide variations in the ability and willingness of local units to support public education, obviously this extreme decentralization creates a problem in providing equitable educational opportunity for American children in general, to say nothing of a disadvantaged minority. A child living in New York State in the industrial East, for example, has five times as much wealth behind his education as that same child would have if he were living in Mississippi in the agricultural South. Moreover, even within the same state just as great or greater disparities are found among the various county units, and just as frequently among the various district units within the same county. Thus, the chances of any American child, whether white or black, to obtain educational opportunity, equal or otherwise, are determined almost exclusively by the section of the country in which he might live, the state in that particular section, the county in that particular state and the district in that particular county.

Unfortunately, 9,000,000 of the 12,000,000 Negroes in the United

[1] Address delivered at the meeting of the World Federation of Education Associations, from August 10 to 17, 1935, at the University of Oxford, Oxford, England.

States live in the agricultural South. The agricultural South, comprising in the main the former slave states, is by far the poorest section of the country, by whatever criterion one may employ—financial, cultural or otherwise. Financially, the South is only about half as wealthy, per capita, as the rest of the nation; culturally, it is even more poverty-stricken; and educationally, it is about where the rest of the country was 15 or 20 years ago. Thus, even if the 9,000,000 Negroes who now reside in the South were white, their chance for educational opportunity would be less than half that of residents in other sections of the country.

But, the peculiar problem which the Negro faces in his attempt to secure equitable educational opportunity arises least of all out of the fact that he lives for the most part in the poorest section of the country. For he is thrice penalized: First, for belonging to the wrong class; second, for belonging to the wrong race; and third, for living in the wrong section of the country.

For historical reasons, which will be discussed presently, the South has insisted upon the establishment and maintenance of separate schools for white and Negro children. This policy has been sustained by the various state and federal courts in numerous decisions affecting the issue. They have consistently held that the individual states have a legal right to establish and maintain separate schools for the various races, *provided,* substantially equal accommodations are furnished each race. Consequently, Negroes are forced by law in 19 of the 48 states and the District of Columbia to attend schools set apart for them. Moreover, this mandatory separation makes easily possible, and there actually occurs, such gross discrimination that the Negro separate schools are almost invariably inferior to the white schools in the same school districts.

Some general idea of the nature and extent of this discrimination may be gleaned from the following facts: In 1930, in those states where separate schools are mandatory, the per capita expenditure for the average white child enrolled in school was $44.31, while the per capita expenditure for each Negro child enrolled was only $12.57. In other words, there was expended on the average Negro child enrolled in school only 28 per cent. as much as was expended on each white child. The range of disparity in expenditures extended all the way from substantial equality in the District of Columbia to only 12 per cent. as much for each Negro child in Mississippi.

As might be expected from the trend of per capita expenditures, Negro schools, in comparison with white schools on all levels, are provided with shorter school terms; with school equipment poorer in quality and less adequate in amount; and with teachers more poorly trained, more poorly paid and less adequate in number. For example, on the elementary school level, the typical Negro school is a one- or two-room structure—a ramshackle, dilapidated affair sadly in need of replacement and insufficient even to "house" the pupils enrolled—some 40 per cent. more classrooms being needed if the Negro pupils enrolled are to have anything approximating even the seating facilities provided for the white pupils in the same communities. The average Negro teacher has 40 per cent. more children; and, although she has 70 per cent. as much training, nevertheless she receives only 41 per cent. as much salary. The school term is 1½ to 2 months shorter—thus making it necessary for the average Negro pupil to spend 9 or 10 years to complete the same curriculum that the white child in the same community has an opportunity to complete in 8 years.

On the secondary school level, one third (33.5 per cent.) of the white high-school educables are enrolled in high school, while less than one tenth (9.5 per cent.) of the Negro high-school educables are so enrolled. This disparity in high-school enrolment is due mainly to three factors: First, to the poor Negro elementary school just described; second, to the fact that twice as many Negro pupils of high-school age are wage-earners; and third, and most important, to the fact that high-school facilities are not available to Negroes in the same proportion as to whites. In a recent survey, for example, it was found that in 230 counties, although there was at least one high school for whites in each of these counties, yet in not one of these counties was there a single high school for Negroes—and, this, despite the fact that approximately 160,000 (158,939) Negro pupils of high-school age resided there, and despite the fact that in no county was the Negro population less than one-eighth of the total population. And even where high-school facilities are provided, the same gross disparities in school equipment, number and training of teachers and in length of school term are found as were observed in the case of the elementary school.

On the college and university level, the same sort of situation obtains—only it is more acute because it inherits the cumulative deficiencies of the two lower schools. There are approximately 250,000 white students in colleges in the South, as compared with less than 25,000 Negro students, although the ratio of whites to Negroes in this area is only 3 or 4 to 1. On the average, the states provide for 16 white students in higher institutions supported by state funds to each Negro student provided for in similarly supported institutions—

ranging from 6 to 1 in North Carolina to 39 to 1 in Texas. The majority of all the white college students in this area (56 per cent.) are receiving their education in state-supported colleges and universities, while only two fifths of the Negro students are enrolled in similar institutions. In addition to these facts, it should be observed that there is not a single state-supported institution in this area where a Negro may pursue graduate or professional education, although in these same states, in 1930, there were approximately 11,000 (11,037) white students pursuing graduate and professional education at public expense.

These facts reveal that the separate Negro school, although it is legal only when substantially equal facilities are provided, is unmistakably the occasion and the instrument of gross discrimination in the provision of publicly supported education for whites and Negroes in these states. While Negroes have some occasion to rejoice that their schools have steadily improved for the past 30 years, nevertheless, as far as educational opportunity equal to that provided for whites is concerned, the little advance that Negro schools have made is like the progress of an ox-cart compared with that of an automobile. For example, in 1900 the discrimination in per capita expenditure for white and Negro pupils was only 60 per cent. in favor of the white pupils, but, by 1930, this disparity had increased to the almost incredible extent of 253 per cent. Moreover, this almost incredible increase in the disparity between white and Negro schools occurred, despite the fact that public school revenues in these states have increased some eight- or ten-fold, and despite the fact that the relationship between the races is alleged to have been tremendously improved. Thus, four fifths of the Negroes in the United States find themselves forced by law to attend schools set apart for them, which are almost invariably characterized by such notorious and increasing discrimination that, until this situation is remedied, they have no chance of securing educational opportunity equal in any respect to that enjoyed by whites in the same communities.

The other one fifth of the Negro population live in the northern and western sections of the country. Their problem of securing equitable educational opportunity is, in the main, only different in degree from that of the majority who reside in the southern section, just described. For the most part, they are illegally segregated for educational purposes—and in some cases legally, by permissive legislation—but they receive educational accommodations more nearly substantially equal to those of the whites than is true in the South.

From this brief summary description it is obvious that the crux of the Negro's attempt to obtain equitable educational opportunity is the separate Negro school. Not only does it permit and encourage gross discrimination, but as an instrument of social policy it connotes and enforces an inferior status, which in itself is the very antithesis of equal opportunity, educational or otherwise. However, the separate Negro school is not an isolated phenomenon. In fact, it is hardly a phenomenon at all. It is rather a symbol of the inferior social, economic and political status of the Negro in American life in general; and, as such, his inferior educational opportunities are to be explained in terms of this status.

As far as economic status is concerned, the American Negro is the mud-sill of our present economic order. According to the Federal Census for 1930, of the 5½ million Negroes gainfully occupied, 83 per cent. were farmers, workers in industry and domestic workers, as compared with only 55 per cent. of the native white population engaged in such occupations. Thus, Negroes are engaged, in considerably greater proportion, in the most poorly paid and unstable occupations in the country, and the large majority of them are thereby forced to live on or below the subsistence level, even in normal times. They are the most economically insecure group in America to-day. They are the "last hired and the first fired." When depression comes, as it did, they are the first fired not only because they are Negroes but because they are also engaged in labor that can be most easily dispensed with. Accordingly, at the present time, while 20 to 25 per cent. of the white workers are unemployed, we find roughly 40 to 50 per cent., or twice as many, Negroes without employment.

As far as political status is concerned, the American Negro is a quasi-alien in his native land. Legally, he has the right to vote, hold office and perform every other duty and enjoy every other privilege incident to American citizenship. And, while the small minority living in the northern, western and border states do actually exercise their suffrage rights—in one state electing a Negro congressman, and in several other states electing Negroes to the State legislature and to other local offices—nevertheless, in the South, where the majority of the Negroes live, they have been practically disfranchised by discrimination, intimidation and the Democratic primary. Thus, they have little or no voice in the management of the political units in which they reside. The political machinery is run by the white people and mainly for the white people in the communities in which it exists. As a consequence, they get inferior school facilities, inferior sanitation, little or no police protection; in fact, little or none of the conveniences which other taxpayers in the community expect and get.

Obviously, the Negro's inferior status is by no means an accident; it is the result of a studied and deliberate attempt on the part of the white majority to restrict the Negro minority to an inferior caste status. Quite naturally, slavery has had much to do with this development. For even before the slaves were emancipated, the seeds of enmity and hate had sprung up, growing out of the economic competition of the "poor whites" and the slaves in the South, on the one hand, and the free Negro workman and white worker in the North, on the other.

The general political effect of emancipation in the South was the decline of the political monopoly of the slave-holding aristocracy and the increasing and ultimate ascendancy of the "poor whites." By the late nineties the governmental machinery of the former slave states was almost entirely in the hands of the "poor whites"—the bitter and uncompromising enemy of the Negro during slavery. Thus, their new power was employed in the paradoxical attempt to improve their own status by degrading the status of the Negro. Their motto was: "Keep the Negro in his place"—which meant any place that would leave no doubt in any one's mind that the Negro was supposed to be an inferior caste. In addition, as pointed out by DuBois in his *Black Reconstruction*,[2] ". . . a determined psychology of caste was built up. In every possible way it was impressed and advertised that the white was superior and the Negro an inferior race. This inferiority must be publicly acknowledged and submitted to. Titles of courtesy were denied colored men and women. Certain signs of servility and usages amounting to public and personal insult were insisted upon. The most educated and deserving black man was compelled in many public places to occupy a place beneath the lowest and least deserving of the whites." And I might add that this sort of psychology continues to be emphasized, in more subtle form, in the public press, over the radio, on the cinema screen and even in the halls of learning.

Under such conditions as we have just described, it is perfectly clear why the comparative educational status of the Negro is so low. And, it is equally obvious that he will not obtain educational opportunity, equal in any respect to that of his white "neighbors," until he achieves a socio-economic-political status. that more nearly approaches theirs.

What steps have been, and are being, taken to improve the status

[2] W. E. B. DuBois, *Black Reconstruction*, New York, 1935.

of the Negro in the American social order? Quite obviously, the Negro has not stood idly by and accepted the inferior status that has been, and is being, foisted upon him. On the contrary, he has put forth, and is still putting forth, some rather strenuous efforts in opposition. While the following five general movements do not explicitly cover all the detailed activities in this sphere, yet they are sufficiently typical and general to give a fairly comprehensive understanding of the final aspect of the problem which the Negro faces in his effort to secure equitable educational opportunity.

One of the first and most obvious steps minority groups have employed to improve their status is migration. As far as the American Negro is concerned, migration has been characterized by two phases. The first phase began even before emancipation, in the form of colonization movements to other countries. The effort and subsequent failure to colonize the free Negro in Liberia and in other countries will readily be recalled.

The second and the more significant phase has been the migration of Negroes from the southern farms and rural areas to the cities of both the North and South. Since 1900, "over a million Negroes have migrated to Southern cities; while a million and a half have gone to urban areas of the North." This urbanization of the Negro has had several important effects upon his status. First, even in southern cities, the Negro's life is freer and safer; the very nature of the urban environment has made it impossible to subject him to the same restrictions and to enforce the same racial taboos which are possible in the villages and rural areas. Moreover, it is not without significance that the majority of lynchings occur in the small towns and villages. Second, urbanization has increased the stratification of the Negro population. Third, the very act of moving from the country to the city, even in the South, gives the Negro better schools. And, in the northern cities, while in many instances his children are still forced to go to separate schools, nevertheless they receive educational accommodations, substantially equal to those of the whites.

A second type of effort put forth in behalf of the Negro might be generally designated as interracial activities, and is best typified by the activities of the Commission on Interracial Cooperation and the various philanthropic agencies, such as the General Education Board, the Rosenwald Fund, the Jeanes and Slater Funds and the Phelps-Stokes Fund.[3]

[3] Other organizations whose activities should be included under this head are: the interracial departments of the Y. M. C. A. and the Y. W. C. A., interracial work of the Federal Council of Churches of Christ in America and the National Urban League.

The personnel of these organizations is generally interracial, the majority being white. Their program is frankly conservative and opportunistic, being confined almost entirely to the correction of the more flagrant instances of abuse and to attempts to get the "better" class of whites to appreciate the assets of the Negro group in their midst.

Without any intention of disparaging the efforts of such praiseworthy organizations, any objective appraisal forces the conclusion that they fall far short of making any fundamental change in the status of the American Negro. For, in the first place, their efforts do not reach the large mass of whites, who constitute the real basis of the race problem in America; and, in the second place, these organizations either do not possess the power or do not dare or care to use it, to change the status of the Negro in any fundamental sense.

As far as improving the educational level of Negroes is concerned, much has been done by the philanthropic agencies with the little money at their disposal. But, when it is considered that it would cost $200,000,000 more than is now being spent on Negro schools in the South merely to raise them to the present level of the white schools in the same areas, and an additional $50,000,000 a year to keep them there, one gains some idea of the inadequacy of the 10 or 12 million dollars now being spent each year on Negro schools and other activities by these agencies. Nor can we find comfort in the thought that the philanthropy of these agencies is stimulating a fairer spirit on the part of the white officials who disburse the public school funds. For, during the past 30 years, as already noted, the discrimination between the expenditures on white and Negro schools, instead of decreasing, has increased over fourfold.

A third effort by Negroes to improve their status grows out of the fact that, in a democratic government, the normal means of expressing approval and voicing protest reside in the citizens' right to vote and resort to the courts. Thus, from the beginning, the Negro has resorted to the political machinery of the state in an effort to improve his lot. It has already been noted that only in the northern and border states do Negroes have the opportunity to resort to the ballot, to any appreciable extent. And here, they do use their ballot fairly effectively in improving their status.

It will be recalled that, in the South, where the majority of the Negroes live, some 90 per cent. of them are disfranchised. As a consequence, they have been forced to substitute the complex and expensive process of litigation for the ballot box. What other groups have been and are able to do through exercise of their suffrage rights, these Negroes have tried and are trying to do by resort to the courts.

Since 1865, Negroes have brought some 225 cases before the state and federal higher courts. These cases have been primarily concerned with an attempt to remove such curtailments and deprivations of their civil liberties as exclusion from jury service; segregation in schools, on common carriers and in public places; residential segregation; disfranchisement; laws against intermarriage; and legal segregation accompanied by discrimination in accommodations. In 94, or approximately 42 (41.7) per cent., of these cases, the decision has been in favor of the Negro. The courts have ruled rather consistently, however, that without contravening any of the Negro's rights as a citizen, the states may legally make race distinctions but not race discriminations.

Despite the rather obvious and important limitations of court action, many Negroes, represented chiefly by the National Association for the Advancement of Colored People, feel that the advantages gained outweigh any of the disadvantages that may and do accrue. In fact, they contend that, in many instances, the Negro has no other choice. For, in the first place, it is the only alternative at his command which can challenge in any effective manner some of the more flagrant and immediate abuses which he suffers under the policy and practice of segregation. In the second place, they point out that the Negro has gained favorable decisions in 42 per cent. of the cases he has brought; and, as far as circumvention of decisions is concerned, it is not a universal practice. And, in the third place, they contend that court action is one of the most effective means Negroes have at their disposal for making and remaking public opinion, as the Scottsboro case so eloquently testifies.

A fourth effort on behalf of the Negro to improve his status is the attempt to enlist his cooperation and affiliation with various aspects of the radical labor movement in the country, such as socialism and particularly communism. The philosophy and programs of the various elements of this movement are well known. Efforts on behalf of the Negro, particularly communistic, have included a wide variety of projects, ranging all the way from the very immediate and practical activities of insisting upon the removal of the color bar and color discrimination in trade unions and other workers' organizations to the utopian proposal of a Negro socialist state in the black-belt of the South.

Without attempting to prophesy, even by implication, the future value of this movement as a means of improving the American Negro's status, it should be pointed out that the following are some of the factors which undoubtedly account, in large part, for its indifferent or little success up to the present: First, in the United States, it has not been possible to develop a radical class-consciousness even among white workers; in fact, they are hardly organization-conscious, since less than one fourth of the 25,000,000 organizable white workers are organized. Second, the assumption that "the cause of the Negro's inferior position in American life is primarily economic, and only, secondarily, if at all, racial" has not proved to be a realistic comprehension of the problem. For, despite the obvious identity of the economic interests of white and black workers, and despite the good intentions of the leaders of the movement, the majority of white workers, dominated more by race prejudice than class consciousness, have rather persistently refused to unite on any other basis than subordination of the Negro. Third, and in view of these facts, Negroes have refused to be the spearhead of the attack, for fear lest while they are fighting a class war from the front they will be subject to a race attack from the rear.

A final movement by Negroes to improve their status grows out of the fact that they are forced to live a highly segregated life throughout the country in general. The idea has been urged that Negroes should make a virtue of their necessity; that they should capitalize their segregation to improve their status, by developing economic and cultural self-sufficiency. Thus, Negroes have elected, or have been forced, to attempt to build a little Negro society, in every essential respect a replica of the dominant social organization around them. With the idea of developing an independent black economy, they have developed a number of Negro business enterprises of one sort or another. Through the necessity of cultural survival, they have developed their own institutions, such as the church, the press, and the school. And, at least one serious suggestion has been made that a similar procedure be employed to regain the franchise.[4]

Despite the fact that this movement has given opportunity for the development of Negro leadership and has given considerable opportunity for cultural attainment, yet it is clear to most intelligent Negroes that the ultimate end of such efforts is, and must be, an economic and cultural cul-de-sac. For, in the first place, with "credit, basic industry, and the state" controlled by whites, the limitations of an independent black economy are obvious. And, in the second place,

[4] Dr. Raymond Leslie Buell, of the Foreign Policy Association, in an address (in Washington, D. C.) last spring suggested that the way out for the Negro, in the South, politically, consisted in devising a scheme whereby Negroes would be allowed proportional representation in the various political units; whereby Negroes would vote only for Negroes, and whites, only for whites; and presumably whereby Negroes would vote only on those measures affecting Negroes, and whites, only on those affecting whites.

the fact that "cultures develop by constant borrowing and adaptation, rather than by isolated evolution of some unique racial quality" suggests that cultural self-sufficiency is merely the beginning of cultural decadence. Moreover, it appears fairly clear that as long as the Negro is a minority group in America, segregation will not only carry with it the stigma of inferiority, whether justified or not, but will leave an easily identifiable and relatively impotent minority exposed to any and all sorts of discriminatory and predatory practices by a dominant and ruthless majority.

Accordingly, the American Negro is confronted by the dilemma of segregation. He finds himself apparently faced by immediate economic and cultural degradation, if he does not develop his separate life and institutions; and he perceives that the more self-sufficient he makes his separate institutions, apparently the further he moves away from his ultimate goal of full participation in American life on equal terms with any other citizen, regardless of color. Because the Negro does not, in most cases, have a choice between segregation and nonsegregation, his real problem is: Given segregation as a fact, how can he use it as a means to his ultimate goal? Thus, the Negro is forced into the paradoxical position of building up his segregated life and institutions with one hand, and fighting against the necessity for them with the other. Hence, the improvement of his status in the American social order in general, as well as his advance toward more equitable educational opportunity is primarily conditioned by his success in this effort.

It is obvious from the brief survey which I have attempted to give that the problem which the American Negro faces in his attempt to secure equitable educational opportunity for his children is not an isolated phenomenon; it is an integral part of the Negro's struggle for status in American life in general. The extent to which he will secure educational opportunity equal in any respect to his white "neighbors" is dependent upon the extent to which he can achieve a status more nearly approaching theirs. The efforts by and on behalf of the Negro to improve his status have been and are many and varied. Many of them have been and are sentimental, without much regard for, or comprehension of, the reality of the problem; many of them have been and are decidedly opportunistic, without any, or due, regard for their ultimate consequences; and many of them have been and are based upon high ideals and a realistic approach to the question. But it is equally clear that none of them has solved the problem, and all of them may be necessary.

ALAIN LOCKE (1886)

Born in Philadelphia, Alain LeRoy Locke was educated at the Philadelphia School of Pedagogy, Harvard, Oxford, and the University of Berlin. From 1907 to 1910 he was a Rhodes Scholar from Pennsylvania. Since 1916, with the exception of 1925-1927, when engaged in research and literary work, and in 1927, when exchange professor at Fisk, he has been teaching at Howard University, where he is at present head of the department of philosophy. As editor of the Bronze Booklets and as author of numerous articles, including *Opportunity's* annual retrospective reviews of literature on the Negro, he is an important molder of Negro opinion. As interpretation of the Negro Renaissance, his *The New Negro* (1925) is a landmark of the movement. Locke is also the author of *Race Contacts and Race Relations* (1916), *Four Negro Poets* (1927), *Negro Art: Past and Present* (1936), *The Negro and His Music* (1936), *The Negro in Art* (1941), and, with Bernhard J. Stern, *When Peoples Meet: a Study in Race and Culture Contact* (1941). With Montgomery Gregory he has edited *Plays of Negro Life* (1927). The following is the title essay from *The New Negro* and is used by the permission of the publishers, A. & C. Boni, and of the author.

The New Negro

IN THE LAST DECADE something beyond the watch and guard of statistics has happened in the life of the American Negro and the three norns who have traditionally presided over the Negro problem have a changeling in their laps. The Sociologist, the Philanthropist, the Raceleader are not unaware of the New Negro, but they are at a loss to account for him. He simply cannot be swathed in their formulae. For the younger generation is vibrant with a new psychology; the new spirit is awake in the masses, and under the very eyes of the professional observers is transforming what has been a perennial problem into the progressive phases of contemporary Negro life.

Could such a metamorphosis have taken place as suddenly as it has appeared to? The answer is no; not because the New Negro is not here, but because the Old Negro had long become more of a myth than a man. The Old Negro, we must remember, was a creature of moral debate and historical controversy. His has been a stock figure perpetuated as an historical fiction partly in innocent sentimentalism, partly in deliberate reactionism. The Negro himself has contributed his share to this through a sort of protective social mimicry forced upon him by the adverse circumstances of dependence. So for generations in the mind of America, the Negro has been more of a formula than a human being—a something to be argued about, condemned or defended, to be "kept down," or "in his place," or "helped up," to be worried with or worried over, harrassed or patronized, a social bogey or a social burden. The thinking Negro even has been induced to share this same general attitude, to focus his attention on controversial issues, to see himself in the distorted perspective of a social problem. His shadow, so to speak, has been more real to him than his personality. Through having had to appeal from the unjust sterotypes of his oppressors and traducers to those of his liberators, friends and benefactors he has had to subscribe to the traditional positions from which his case has been viewed. Little true social or self-understanding has or could come from such a situation.

But while the minds of most of us, black and white, have thus burrowed in the trenches of the Civil War and Reconstruction, the actual march of development has simply flanked these positions, necessitating a sudden reorientation of view. We have not been watching in the right direction; set North and South on a sectional axis, we have not noticed the East till the sun has us blinking.

Recall how suddenly the Negro spirituals revealed themselves; suppressed for generations under the stereotypes of Wesleyan hymn harmony, secretive, half-ashamed, until the courage of being natural brought them out—and behold, there was folk-music. Similarly the mind of the Negro seems suddenly to have slipped from under the tyranny of social intimidation and to be shaking off the psychology of imitation and implied inferiority. By shedding the old chrysalis of the Negro problem we are achieving something like a spiritual emancipation. Until recently, lacking self-understanding, we have been almost as much of a problem to ourselves as we still are to others. But the decade that found us with a problem has left us with only a task. The multitude perhaps feels as yet only a strange relief and a new vague urge, but the thinking few know that in the reaction the vital inner grip of prejudice has been broken.

With this renewed self-respect and self-dependence, the life of the Negro community is bound to enter a new dynamic phase, the buoyancy from within compensating for whatever pressure there may be of conditions from without. The migrant masses, shifting from country-side to city, hurdle several generations of experience at a leap, but more important, the same thing happens spiritually in the life-attitudes and self-expression of the Young Negro, in his poetry, his art, his education and his new outlook, with the additional advantage, of course, of the poise and greater certainty of knowing what it is all about. From this comes the promise and warrant of a new leadership. As one of them has discerningly put it:

> We have tomorrow
> Bright before us
> Like a flame.
>
> Yesterday, a night-gone thing
> A sun-down name.
>
> And dawn today
> Broad arch above the road we came.
> We march!

This is what, even more than any "most creditable record of fifty years of freedom," requires that the Negro of today be seen through other than the dusty spectacles of past controversy. The day of "aunties," "uncles" and "mammies" is equally gone. Uncle Tom and Sambo have passed on, and even the "Colonel" and "George" play barnstorm rôles from which they escape with relief when the public spotlight is off. The popular melodrama has about played itself out, and it is time to scrap the fictions, garret the bogeys and settle down to a realistic facing of facts.

First we must observe some of the changes which since the traditional lines of opinion were drawn have rendered these quite obsolete. A main change has been, of course, that shifting of the Negro population which has made the Negro problem no longer exclusively or even predominantly Southern. Why should our minds remain sectionalized, when the problem itself no longer is? Then the trend of migration has not only been toward the North and the Central Midwest, but city-ward and to the great centers of industry—the problems of adjustment are new, practical, local and not peculiarly racial. Rather they are an integral part of the large industrial and social problems of our present-day democracy. And finally, with the Negro rapidly in process of class differentiation, if it ever was warrantable to regard and treat the Negro *en masse* it is becoming with every day less possible, more unjust and more ridiculous.

In the very process of being transplanted, the Negro is becoming transformed.

The tide of Negro migration, northward and city-ward, is not to be fully explained as a blind flood started by the demands of war industry coupled with the shutting off of foreign migration, or by the pressure of poor crops coupled with increased social terrorism in certain sections of the South and Southwest. Neither labor demand, the bollweevil nor the Ku Klux Klan is a basic factor, however contributory any or all of them may have been. The wash and rush of this human tide on the beach line of the northern city centers is to be explained primarily in terms of a new vision of opportunity, of social and economic freedom, of a spirit to seize, even in the face of an extortionate and heavy toll, a chance for the improvement of conditions. With each successive wave of it, the movement of the Negro becomes more and more a mass movement toward the larger and more democratic chance—in the Negro's case a deliberate flight not only from countryside to city, but from medieval America to modern.

Take Harlem as an instance of this. Here in Manhattan is not merely the largest Negro community in the world, but the first concentration in history of so many diverse elements of Negro life. It has attracted the African, the West Indian, the Negro American; has brought together the Negro of the North and the Negro of the South; the man from the city and the man from the town and village; the peasant, the student, the business man, the professional man, artist, poet, musician, adventurer and worker, preacher and criminal, exploiter and social outcast. Each group has come with its own separate motives and for its own special ends, but their greatest experience has been the finding of one another. Proscription and prejudice have thrown these dissimilar elements into a common area of contact and interaction. Within this area, race sympathy and unity have determined a further fusing of sentiment and experience. So what began in terms of segregation becomes more and more, as its elements mix and react, the laboratory of a great race-welding. Hitherto, it must be admitted that American Negroes have been a race more in name than in fact, or to be exact, more in sentiment than in experience. The chief bond between them has been that of a common condition rather than a common consciousness; a problem in common rather than a life in common. In Harlem, Negro life is seizing upon its first chances for group expression and self-determination. It is—or promises at least to be—a race capital. That is why our comparison is taken with those nascent centers of folk-expression and self-determination which are playing a creative part in the world today. Without pretense to their political significance, Harlem has the same rôle to play for the New Negro as Dublin has had for the New Ireland or Prague for the New Czechoslovakia.

Harlem, I grant you, isn't typical—but it is significant, it is prophetic. No sane observer, however sympathetic to the new trend, would contend that the great masses are articulate as yet, but they stir, they move, they are more than physically restless. The challenge of the new intellectuals among them is clear enough—the "race radicals" and realists who have broken with the old epoch of philanthropic guidance, sentimental appeal and protest. But are we after all only reading into the stirrings of a sleeping giant the dreams of an agitator? The answer is in the migrating peasant. It is the "man farthest down" who is most active in getting up. One of the most characteristic symptoms of this is the professional man himself migrating to recapture his constituency after a vain effort to maintain in some Southern corner what for years back seemed an established living and clientele. The clergyman following his errant flock, the physician or lawyer trailing his clients, supply the true clues. In a real sense it is the rank and file who are leading, and the leaders who are following. A transformed and transforming psychology permeates the masses.

When the racial leaders of twenty years ago spoke of developing race-pride and stimulating race-consciousness, and of the desirability of race solidarity, they could not in any accurate degree have anticipated the abrupt feeling that has surged up and now pervades the awakened centers. Some of the recognized Negro leaders and a powerful section of white opinion identified with "race work" of the older order have indeed attempted to discount this feeling as a "passing phase," an attack of "race nerves" so to speak, an "aftermath of the war," and the like. It has not abated, however, if we are to gauge by the present tone and temper of the Negro press, or by the shift in popular support from the officially recognized and orthodox spokesmen to those of the independent, popular, and often radical type who are unmistakable symptoms of a new order. It is a social disservice to blunt the fact that the Negro of the Northern centers has reached a stage where tutelage, even of the most interested and well-intentioned sort, must give place to new relationships, where positive self-direction must be reckoned with in ever increasing measure. The American mind must reckon with a fundamentally changed Negro.

The Negro, too, for his part, has idols of the tribe to smash. If on the one hand the white man has erred in making the Negro appear to be that which would excuse or extenuate his treatment of him, the Negro, in turn, has too often unnecessarily excused himself because of the way he has been treated. The intelligent Negro of today is resolved not to make discrimination an extenuation for his shortcomings in performance, individual or collective; he is trying to hold himself at par, neither inflated by sentimental allowances nor depreciated by current social discounts. For this he must know himself and be known for precisely what he is, and for that reason he welcomes the new scientific rather than the old sentimental interest. Sentimental interest in the Negro has ebbed. We used to lament this as the falling off of our friends; now we rejoice and pray to be delivered both from self-pity and condescension. The mind of each racial group has had a bitter weaning, apathy or hatred on one side matching disillusionment or resentment on the other; but they face each other today with the possibility at least of entirely new mutual attitudes.

It does not follow that if the Negro were better known, he would be better liked or better treated. But mutual understanding is basic for any subsequent cooperation and adjustment. The effort toward this will at least have the effect of remedying in large part what has been the most unsatisfactory feature of our present stage of race relationships in America, namely the fact that the more intelligent and representative elements of the two race groups have at so many points got quite out of vital touch with one another.

The fiction is that the life of the races is separate, and increasingly so. The fact is that they have touched too closely at the unfavorable and too lightly at the favorable levels.

While inter-racial councils have sprung up in the South, drawing on forward elements of both races, in the Northern cities manual laborers may brush elbows in their everyday work, but the community and business leaders have experienced no such interplay or far too little of it. These segments must achieve contact or the race situation in America becomes desperate. Fortunately this is happening. There is a growing realization that in social effort the co-operative basis must supplant long-distance philanthropy, and that the only safeguard for mass relations in the future must be provided in the carefully maintained contact of the enlightened minorities of both race groups. In the intellectual realm a renewed and keen curiosity is replacing the recent apathy; the Negro is being carefully studied, not just talked about and discussed. In art and letters, instead of being wholly caricatured, he is being seriously portrayed and painted.

To all of this the New Negro is keenly responsive as an augury of a new democracy in American culture. He is contributing his share to the new social understanding. But the desire to be understood would never in itself have been sufficient to have opened so completely the protectively closed portals of the thinking Negro's mind. There is still too much possibility of being snubbed or patronized for that. It was rather the necessity for fuller, truer self-expression, the realization of the unwisdom of allowing social discrimination to segregate him mentally, and a counter-attitude to cramp and fetter his own living—and so the "spite-wall" that the intellectuals built over the "color-line" has happily been taken down. Much of this reopening of intellectual contacts has centered in New York and has been richly fruitful not merely in the enlarging of personal experience, but in the definite enrichment of American art and letters and in the clarifying of our common vision of the social tasks ahead.

The particular significance in the re-establishment of contact between the more advanced and representative classes is that it promises to offset some of the unfavorable reactions of the past, or at least to re-surface race contacts somewhat for the future. Subtly the conditions that are molding a New Negro are molding a new American attitude.

However, this new phase of things is delicate; it will call for less charity but more justice; less help, but infinitely closer understanding. This is indeed a critical stage of race relationships because of the likelihood, if the new temper is not understood, of engendering sharp group antagonism and a second crop of more calculated prejudice. In some quarters, it has already done so. Having weaned the Negro, public opinion cannot continue to paternalize. The Negro to-day is inevitably moving forward under the control largely of his own objectives. What are these objectives? Those of his outer life are happily already well and finally formulated, for they are none other than the ideals of American institutions and democracy. Those of his inner life are yet in process of formation, for the new psychology at present is more of a consensus of feeling than of opinion, of attitude rather than of program. Still some points seem to have crystallized.

Up to the present one may adequately describe the Negro's "inner objectives" as an attempt to repair a damaged group psychology and reshape a warped social perspective. Their realization has required a new mentality for the American Negro. And as it matures we begin to see its effects; at first, negative, inconoclastic, and then positive and constructive. In this new group psychology we note the lapse of sentimental appeal, then the development of a more positive self-respect and self-reliance; the repudiation of social dependence, and then the gradual recovery from hyper-sensitiveness and "touchy" nerves, the repudiation of the double standard of judgment with its special philanthropic allowances and then the sturdier desire for objective and scientific appraisal; and finally the rise from social disillusionment to race pride, from the sense of social debt to the responsibilities of social contribution, and offsetting the necessary working and commonsense acceptance of restricted conditions, the belief in ultimate esteem and recognition. Therefore the Negro today wishes to be known for what he is, even in his faults and shortcomings, and scorns a craven and precarious survival at the price of seeming to be what he is not. He resents being spoken of as a social ward or minor, even by his own, and to being regarded a chronic patient for the sociological clinic, the sick man of American Democracy. For the same reasons, he himself is through with those social nostrums and panaceas, the so-called "solutions" of his "problem," with which he and the country have been so liberally dosed in the past. Religion, freedom, education, money—in turn, he has ardently hoped for and peculiarly trusted these things; he still believes in them, but not in blind trust that they alone will solve his life-problem.

Each generation, however, will have its creed, and that of the present is the belief in the efficacy of collective effort, in race co-operation. This deep feeling of race is at present the mainspring of Negro life. It seems to be the outcome of the reaction to proscription and prejudice; an attempt, fairly successful on the whole to convert a defensive into an offensive position, a handicap into an incentive. It is radical in tone, but not in purpose and only the most stupid forms of opposition, misunderstanding or persecution could make it otherwise. Of course, the thinking Negro has shifted a little toward the left with the world-trend, and there is an increasing group who affiliate with radical and liberal movements. But fundamentally for the present the Negro is radical on race matters, conservative on others, in other words, a "forced radical," a social protestant rather than a genuine radical. Yet under further pressure and injustice iconoclastic thought and motives will inevitably increase. Harlem's quixotic radicalisms call for their ounce of democracy today lest tomorrow they be beyond cure.

The Negro mind reaches out as yet to nothing but American wants, American ideas. But this forced attempt to build his Americanism on race values is a unique social experiment, and its ultimate success is impossible except through the fullest sharing of American culture and institutions. There should be no delusion about this. American nerves in sections unstrung with race hysteria are often fed the opiate that the trend of Negro advance is wholly separatist, and that the effect of its operation will be to encyst the Negro as a benign foreign body in the body politic. This cannot be—even if it were desirable. The racialism of the Negro is no limitation or reservation with respect to American life; it is only a constructive effort to build the obstructions in the stream of his progress into an efficient dam of social energy and power. Democracy itself is obstructed and stagnated to the extent that any of its channels are closed. Indeed they cannot be selectively closed. So the choice is not between one way for the Negro and another way for the rest, but between American institutions frustrated on the one hand and American ideals progressively fulfilled and realized on the other.

There is, of course, a warrantably comfortable feeling in being on the right side of the country's professed ideals. We realize that we cannot be undone without America's undoing. It is within the gamut of this attitude that the thinking Negro faces America, but with variations of mood that are if anything more significant than the attitude itself. Sometimes we have it taken with the defiant ironic challenge of McKay:

> Mine is the future grinding down today
> Like a great landslip moving to the sea,
> Bearing its freight of debris far away
> Where the green hungry waters restlessly
> Heave mammoth pyramids, and break and roar
> Their eerie challenge to the crumbling shore.

Sometimes, perhaps more frequently as yet, it is taken in the fervent and almost filial appeal and counsel of Weldon Johnson's:

> O Southland, dear Southland!
> Then why do you still cling
> To an idle age and a musty page,
> To a dead and useless thing?

But between defiance and appeal, midway almost between cynicism and hope, the prevailing mind stands in the mood of the same author's *To America*, an attitude of sober query and stoical challenge:

> How would you have us, as we are?
>   Or sinking 'neath the load we bear,
> Our eyes fixed forward on a star,
>   Or gazing empty at despair?
>
> Rising or falling? Men or things?
>   With dragging pace or footsteps fleet?
> Strong, willing sinews in your wings,
>   Or tightening chains about your feet?

More and more, however, an intelligent realization of the great discrepancy between the American social creed and the American social practice forces upon the Negro the taking of the moral advantage that is his. Only the steadying and sobering effect of a truly characteristic gentleness of spirit prevents the rapid rise of a definite cynicism and counter-hate and a defiant superiority feeling. Human as this reaction would be, the majority still deprecate its advent, and would gladly see it forestalled by the speedy amelioration of its causes. We wish our race pride to be a healthier, more positive achievement than a feeling based upon a realization of the shortcomings of others. But all paths toward the attainment of a sound social attitude have been difficult; only a relatively few enlightened minds have been able as the phrase puts it "to rise above" prejudice. The ordinary man has had until recently only a hard choice between the alternatives of supine and humiliating submission and stimulating but hurtful counter-prejudice. Fortunately from some inner, desperate resourcefulness has recently sprung up the simple expedient of fighting prejudice by mental passive resistance, in other words by trying to ignore it. For the few, this manna may perhaps be effective, but the masses cannot thrive upon it.

Fortunately there are constructive channels opening out into which the balked social feelings of the American Negro can flow freely. Without them there would be much more pressure and danger than there is. These compensating interests are racial but in a new and enlarged way. One is the consciousness of acting as the advance guard of the African peoples in their contact with Twentieth Century civilization; the other, the sense of a mission of rehabilitating the race in world esteem from that loss of prestige for which the fate and conditions of slavery have so largely been responsible. Harlem, as we shall see, is the center of both these movements; she is the home of the Negro's "Zionism." The pulse of the Negro world has begun to beat in Harlem. A Negro newspaper carrying news material in English, French and Spanish, gathered from all quarters of America, the West Indies and Africa has maintained itself in Harlem for over five years. Two important magazines, both edited from New York, maintain their news and circulation consistently on a cosmopolitan scale. Under American auspices and backing, three pan-African congresses have been held abroad for the discussion of common interests, colonial questions and the future co-operative development of Africa. In terms of the race question as a world problem, the Negro mind has leapt, so to speak, upon the parapets of prejudice and extended its cramped horizons. In so doing it has linked up with the growing group consciousness of the dark-peoples and is gradually learning their common interests. As one of our writers has recently put it: "It is imperative that we understand the white world in its relations to the non-white world." As with the Jew, persecution is making the Negro international.

As a world phenomenon this wider race consciousness is a different thing from the much asserted rising tide of color. Its inevitable causes are not of our making. The consequences are not necessarily damaging to the best interests of civilization. Whether it actually brings into being new Armadas of conflict or argosies of cultural exchange and enlightenment can only be decided by the attitude of the dominant races in an era of critical change. With the American Negro, his new internationalism is primarily an effort to recapture contact with the scattered peoples of African derivation. Garveyism may be a transient, if spectacular, phenomenon, but the possible rôle of the American Negro in the future development of Africa is one of the most constructive and universally helpful missions that any modern people can lay claim to.

Constructive participation in such causes cannot help giving the Negro valuable group incentives, as well as increased prestige at home and abroad. Our greatest rehabilitation may possibly come through such channels, but for the present, more immediate hope rests in the revaluation by white and black alike of the Negro in terms of his artistic endowments and cultural contributions, past and prospective. It must be increasingly recognized that the Negro has already made very substantial contributions, not only in his folk-art, music especially, which has always found appreciation, but in larger, though humbler and less acknowledged ways. For generations the Negro has been the peasant matrix of that section of America which has most undervalued him, and here he has contributed not only materially in labor and in social patience, but spiritually as well. The South has unconsciously absorbed the gift of his folk-temperament. In less than half a generation it will be easier to recognize this, but the fact remains that a leaven of humor, sentiment, imagination and tropic nonchalance has gone into the making of the South from a humble, unacknowledged source. A second crop of the Negro's gifts promises still more largely. He now becomes a conscious contributor and lays aside the status of a beneficiary and ward for that of a collaborator and participant in American civilization. The great social gain in this is the releasing of our talented group from the arid fields of controversy and debate to the productive fields of creative expression. The especially cultural recognition they win should in turn prove the key to that revaluation of the Negro which must precede or accompany any considerable further betterment of race relationships. But whatever the general effect, the present generation will have added the motives of self-expression and spiritual development to the old and still unfinished task of making material headway and progress. No one who understandingly faces the situation with its substantial accomplishment or views the new scene with its still more abundant promise can be entirely without hope. And certainly, if in our lifetime the Negro should not be able to celebrate his full initiation into American democracy, he can at least, on the warrant of these things, celebrate the attainment of a significant and satisfying new phase of group development, and with it a spiritual Coming of Age.

JAMES A. PORTER (1905-   )

James A. Porter, born in Baltimore, was educated at Howard and New York universities. He has taught at Howard, where he is now assistant professor of art. In 1933 he was the winner of the Harmon Award for portraiture. His articles on art have appeared in *Art Front, Art in America and Elsewhere, Opportunity,* and *The American Magazine of Art.* The following is used by permission of the author.

Henry Ossawa Tanner

HENRY O. TANNER, born in Pittsburgh, Pennsylvania, on June 21, 1859, was still a very young man when Edmonia Lewis and Bannister were showing their work among the collections of the Centennial Exposition. He had awakened, however, to an interest in painting at the age of thirteen years. He himself has told the circumstances surrounding that moment. One day, he and his father were walking along a path that ran through the Fairmount Park in Philadelphia, not long after the family had taken up residence in that city. Seeing a painter at work on a landscape that involved a big tree and a high knoll located nearby in the park, they paused for a while to watch him. Suddenly the boy asked his father this question: "If that man wants to paint that tree, why doesn't he go closer to it?" His father answered that the painter only wished to suggest the tree, not to copy it. The boy had no further question; but the very next day, with a terrible and inexplicable eagerness he himself began to paint, using the ordinary brushes of a house-painter upon the board backs of an old geography book, his memory of the landscape which he had seen the artist trying to organize the day before.

We are happy to be able to study the early part of his life which has, on its productive side, received little critical attention.[1] There is now reason to think of Tanner as a historical figure in American art. And now, also, there is reason to be as thorough as information permits in delineating the main lines of his youthful career.

It cannot be said that Tanner's early paintings are or should be the most interesting to Americans because many of them were produced in this country. Racial, national, or local interests are not entirely absent from them, but figure in them only in a quite subordinate way. It is true that some of this artist's first efforts were directed to portraiture both in clay and in oils; but his subjects were selected from both racial groups in America. His treatment of these subjects had no aestheticoracial bias. If we may refer to his very earliest tendencies, then it will appear that from the beginning he was attracted to themes that contained an element of abstraction. At the risk of being misunderstood, we shall say one of universality. From the outset, his work has borne the mark of a reflective, probing spirit. This value, in later years, was sought for and found by this painter in themes of a religious character.

Tanner, in his boyhood, modeled the animals in the "zoo" at Philadelphia. We have already mentioned his reaction to the sight of a man painting natural objects such as trees and grass. His spontaneous interest in nature took firm hold on him when he came under the influence of the painter of marines, Alexander Harrison, whose work had been accessible to him in an exhibition gallery in Philadelphia. His paintings made the young artist impatient to test his own reactions before the stirring element of old *Oceanus*. For this purpose he quickly repaired to the vicinity of Atlantic City. During a brief stay he completed a sufficient number of canvases to compose a sizeable exhibition, which was an opportunity obtained for him by a friend and admirer. By this time, he had already acquired an effective if laborious technic, for he had been for some time a student at the Pennsylvania Academy of Fine Arts. Indeed, one of his subjects done at the seaboard is now in the Pennsylvania Academy. It is entitled "A Windy Day on the Meadows."

The painter's father, the now deceased Bishop Benjamin Tucker Tanner, gave him all the support that his slender means permitted. Still, the young man found himself confronted with seemingly insurmountable obstructions to his career. For a while he took a teaching

---

[1] Since these paragraphs were written the world has been informed of Henry O. Tanner's death in Paris, France, May 25, 1937.

position at Clark University in Atlanta, Georgia, in order to contribute toward the expenses of his vocation. Even then he was forced to open a studio of photography in order to supplement a less than meager salary. It was during this time (the late 1880's), that Tanner resumed the painting of animal pictures. These, together with certain previously completed works, he found necessary to sell at prices ridiculously low, some of them yielding as little as fifteen dollars apiece.

The patronage and encouragement of friends was not entirely denied him. First of all, he developed a real friendship with his first instructor in painting at the Pennsylvania Academy, Thomas Eakins, whose commendation of his work had the effect of turning other friends toward him.[2] Daniel A. Payne, who had been influential among still earlier Negro aspirants for an art education, was one of Tanner's first patrons. This appreciative man appraised the gift of the artist and made a prediction concerning it that has been largely fulfilled. "From specimens of his paintings in my possession," said he, "and from other pieces which he has produced, I think that he will go down to history as one of the most successful of American artists which the present century has brought forth." Tanner made a bust of the venerable prelate. By an early writer it has been described as a very creditable effort. Three of his oil paintings are upon the walls of the library of Wilberforce University, Wilberforce, Ohio, where they were placed by Bishop Payne. These have been described as "seascapes —one, somewhat Turneresque in its dashing impressionist style of representing a storm at sea; the other two small panels, rich in coloring . . . giving a hint of future excellence."

There are several works belonging to this period that possess outstanding merit and really lead one into the heart of Tanner's artistic problem. Among them are the portraits of his father and mother now owned by Mrs. Sadie Alexander of Philadelphia, and a large landscape done at Atlantic City. The first-named works remind one of the painting of Thomas Eakins at its most humanly penetrating and richly psychological moments. Not the "pale" but the warm cast of thought hangs over them. The pigments have darkened noticeably but the strength of the artist's impression remains. And so we see in them the evidence of the artist's deep humanity and spiritual sensitiveness. In each case the image is brought out in sturdy relief against a rich lake-saturated background, reducing the surface to a schematized simplicity analogous to that of a small Cranach or Clouet portrait.

[2] A portrait of H. O. Tanner, made by Thomas Eakins and presented along with other works by the "American Master" to the Pennsylvania Museum of Art, has for some reason been left out of the permanent installation of the collections.

Another prelate who came to the aid of Tanner in the days of his earliest need was Bishop Joseph Crane Hartzell of the Methodist Episcopal Church. This man and his wife afforded the means by which he received his first opportunity to go abroad to study art. It will be remembered that during the Atlanta period the artist had resumed the painting of animals. He continued with landscape painting in the mountains of North Carolina and essayed, as well, two or three genre subjects. Of the latter class of work the most outstanding, to the writer's mind, is "The Banjo Lesson," now at Hampton Institute, Hampton, Virginia. The composition of the painting can be set down as an example of the developed style of Tanner's "first period." The placing of the two very appealing figures in a deep space warmly illuminated by the glow of an unseen hearth fire, the radical perspective of the floor and the objects on it, the poetic play of the dark masses of the figures against the luminous background, are fundamental traits of this style which reappear with greater significance in later paintings. Works like this and others made up the exhibition held by Tanner in Cincinnati in 1891. From the standpoint of sales, the exhibition was a failure; and it was just at this depressing point in the artist's career that Bishop Hartzell stepped in and showed the quality of his friendship by giving "all that he would take" for each unsold item. The total amount realized did not exceed three hundred dollars.

With this and some additional funds Tanner made his way to Paris, where, in 1891, he began his studies at the Julian Academy under Benjamin Constant. Like many other American artists he found it necessary to seek valuable instruction and impressions abroad. His reasons for so doing were not in all respects the same as those of his white American comrades whom he met in the great mecca of the art world. Already he had felt that if he was to escape the limitations imposed by American race-prejudice, he must attain to a place in the mind of a cosmopolitan public where he might work beyond its range. In working toward such a place he suffered both physically and mentally. His physical suffering meant leading the life of an impoverished art student in Paris during three or four years, living at least during the first year on an allotment of five francs a day. Mentally, his suffering consisted of the shocks that naturally attended the uprooting of projects already begun, though not broadly developed, in the *milieu* of American life and landscape. Such pictures as "The Banjo Lesson" and his portraits of Negro personages had raised some hope that "a portrayer of Negro life had arisen indeed." But the considerable versatility of interest manifested by the artist directed him away from this narrower preoccupation with illustration and race-propaganda.

Four years after Tanner's first year of study abroad, he sent to the salon "The Sabot Makers," a work that received favorable attention. Like the "Banjo Lesson" it was a work of genre interest, but it dealt with the lives of some Breton folk; and can be summed up as a rather humorous and facile comment on the leisure pursuits or the play of Breton peasants. It is a species of social study; but the artist had no idea of stating any social or aesthetic problem. Instead, he appears to be devoted to nature and to the search for expressive syntheses of rich psychological situations. The son of a minister, he does not seek here to sermonize. The incident selected is a pleasant one, and the artist has played upon it as lightly and skillfully as might a clever composer on a scherzo theme. Here, no pathetic realism clashes with the fancy of the artist's brush, only a happy, if excessively pedantic statement of rustic buffoonery entertains us.

The summers that Tanner spent in Brittany were hardly different in result from those that he had spent at consistent painting in America. The only differences were those of greater personal freedom and the enjoyment of a sense of enlarged manhood, an awareness of self-responsibility that must have fed his ambition and his energies. He had friends at Pont-Aven, some artists, who had come to see what Gauguin had discovered there, and whose common interest, in all likelihood, ably reinforced his spirit.

In the year 1892, the painter had returned to this country for a brief visit, bringing back with him a number of canvases that had been done in the course of the summer excursions to Brittany. Some of the titles were "Bois d'Amour," "Evening Near Pont-Aven," "Rocks at Concarneau," "Return of Fishing Boats" and "The Foster Mother." These, together with other works previously done in America, were exhibited at Earle's galleries in Philadelphia in 1892.

"The Banjo Lesson," previously mentioned, was among those examples. It now hangs in the library of Hampton Institute, Hampton, Virginia, where it keeps the company of a "Lion's Head," which W. S. Scarborough tells us was a preliminary study for one of the beasts depicted in the later "Daniel in the Lion's Den."

Apart from an enlarged social experience, increased knowledge of historical arts, and some solid progress to boot, the painter had added little to the stature he had attained in such paintings as the "Banjo Lesson" and the early portraits of his father and mother. He persisted in the vein of genre until the year 1895, when he suddenly determined to paint religious subjects—i. e., to reinterpret many of the pictorially suggestive episodes of the Bible. This decision made, he set to work in the methodical fashion of the academic masters under whom he had lately sat. It is difficult for an artist to divest himself of the teachings he has whole-heartedly received without first going through a period of struggle and disillusionment. In Tanner's case, the precepts had been reinforced by personal friendship for at least one teacher, Benjamin Constant. But more important than this, he had set his mind upon achieving a success in the academic salons.

The first result of this new but unintegrated phase of his work was the composition "Daniel in the Lion's Den" which brought to the painter an "honorable mention," after an appreciative gesture on the part of the painter Gérôme had caused it to be re-hung in a place of honor. This picture is not a great and original work, but it is not, on the other hand, a slavish exercise in the approved academic manner. The archaeological tendency exemplified in the art of a man like Gérôme lingers in the piece of "atmospheric setting" that suggests the tiled wall of an Assyrian palace. The compositional effect, however, is massive, and the juxtaposition of massive forms and frail prophet is in this piece an effective device. The freshness of the artist's viewpoint has imparted new life to a trite subject and vanquished the coldness of a school technic. By a sort of artistic alchemy the character of the prophet has been evoked for us, and even the dim light of his dungeon contributes to the suggestion of a bleak and powerful isolation that symbolizes his strength or the strength of his God in him. The very "souls of the beasts" have been sketched in their forms with great effect. They are like hulking shadows whose reality divides and makes more terrible the gloom of the place. A United Press dispatch of that year of the salon has been put into my hands by the artist. It reads as follows:

"Henry O. Tanner . . . is again to the front with a large canvas representing "Daniel in the Lion's Den." The prophet is in a large chamber of Assyrian brick, on whose walls are shown a frieze of coloured lions. Part of a gallery or balcony dominates the prison, from which supposedly the king occasionally witnessed the sport provided for his amusement below. Daniel is leaning against a projection which serves to give additional strength to the great walls of the construction. The moonlight enters through a window or trapdoor over his head and catches on his folded hands and richly embroidered robe. The upper part of the body is in shadow with the head turned towards the window above. In the deep shadow are the dark bodies of the lions walking restlessly up and down, their fiery eyes giving additional terror to the darkness. One lion is resting on his haunches near Daniel, part of his head and paw being in the line of the moonlight, while in the background a streak of moonlight catches the back of another lion."

In the next canvas submitted to the salon jury the original tendencies already indicated as part of the artist became identified with a weighty and plastic style of painting that has never altogether departed from later phases of his work. The canvas of which we speak is the now famous "Raising of Lazarus" which has for some time been exhibited along with other American works owned by the French government in the gallery of the *Jeu-de-Paume,* in Paris. This work created quite a sensation among the visitors to the salon of 1897. It attracted both popular and critical attention, "won for the artist his first salon triumph," and entrained a new and unfamiliar luxury of remunerative commissions. The popular success that came with this effort must have confirmed him in his decision to devote the greater part of his productivity to interpretations of scriptural themes. A medal of the third class was awarded for this work and an offer of purchase from the Ministry of Fine Arts was at once accepted.

* * * * *

Tanner's travels in the Holy Land, following his first salon triumph, were also a phase of his new inspiration, the search for atmosphere. This interest, when compared to that which later took him to Algiers and other parts of North Africa, seems rather pedantic; for it is significant that in these later visits he re-thought or revised his impressions of oriental life. His first attitude was that of the research-worker or the anthropologist visiting Palestine in order to collect the most idiosyncratic data on racial types and customs, mindful, too, of what traces of tradition there might be. His purposes had been made more urgent by the backing of the late Rodman Wanamaker who was then collecting the works of French and American artists abroad. Both the "Judas" of the Carnegie Institute in Pittsburgh and the "Nicodemus" of the Pennsylvania Academy represent a distilled, more visionary kind of orientalism. We can see that the artist is getting away from large orchestrations of figures. He is no longer persuaded by the illustrator's conscience. He selects simpler events, a more general color scheme and more rugged forms. Certainly, his last attempt in the old bombastic style, which he had inherited from Gérôme and his colleagues, was the "Wise and Foolish Virgins," a large canvas which was first exhibited in 1908. This work was also purchased by Rodman Wanamaker; but it has never figured among the really important contributions of the artist. It is a grand summation of all the defects as well as many of the qualities of Tanner's academic period.

A religious painter or a painter of religious subjects is looked upon today as more or less of an anachronism. Notwithstanding, both the spiritual and the artistic conviction of Tanner's work, especially that done after 1900, is hard to deny. Even before that date, the world might have looked to him as the first real modern exponent of religious painting. Many superficial works have been produced in both Europe and America since Tanner's career began, but if all cases be considered on their intrinsic merits, it will be seen that Tanner's commands respect because of its genuineness. The phrases used by Guy Pène DuBois in a comparative criticism of some religious compositions by George Bellows and Henry O. Tanner can be quoted in support of this contention. He illustrates by comparing Bellow's "Crucifixion" and the values shown in it to Tanner's approach to religious subjects.

". . . George Bellows might here, in perfectly good grace, have accepted the challenge of the old masters. Having recently seen the religious pictures by Henry O. Tanner at the Grand Central Gallery, I am easily convinced that if Mr. Bellows did accept the challenge, he did it, on technical and not on religious grounds. Mr. Tanner paints religious subjects because they impress him. It is possible that Mr. Bellows paints them because they will impress someone else. . . .

"It may be, however, that Mr. Bellows has suddenly become modern. In that case the subject matter which he employs is without point except as it may be an excuse, excuse by way of compromise with the public idiosyncrasy, for an arrangement of forms. Mr. Tanner, who paints religious subjects because they impress him, might (another guess) see, in this, something on the verge of sacrilege. But this, again, is not for me to say. . . . With Mr. Bellows in his 'Crucifixion,' painting is the result of an attitude, unrelated to subject matter or art."

With Tanner continual practice brought increasing clarity to pictorial exposition. The work of his middle period betrays a definite struggle to reconcile simple color and terse, incomplicated drawing. One sign of this struggle is a definite preference for the low-pitched subtle colors of moonlight. "The Disciples on the Road to Bethany" is one of the best examples from this period. It is followed by other very strong studies in nocturnal color-harmony which deserve mention here, such as the remarkable "Christ Walking on the Water" (now in Des Moines, Iowa), "The Miraculous Draft of Fishes" in which the famous "Tanner blues" and blue-greens confect a surface comparable to irridescent enamel. The absolute masterpiece of this period is the "Disciples at the Tomb" which reposes in the Art Institute of Chicago. This work brings out painter as close to the real essentials of painting as he has ever come. It is a bold, unusual conception of the theme, depending, like a cinematographic "close-up" on the ability of the human visage to convey pathetic feeling. The warm, glowing color has been put on in brusque impasto technic, without fussiness or excessive modelling. The picture stands at the very apex of Tanner's effort as a religious painter. William R. Lister might well have been looking at it when he wrote that "he [Tanner] is a practical believer in the fact of spirit. His somber, dramatic portrayals of moving scriptural scenes unite modern art with religion, as in those earlier days when immortal masters pictured on walls or canvas the earnest faith and profound soul-experiences of humanity."

In his declining years Tanner's painting lost much of its force. The old sincerity persisted; lived also the painter's ability to suggest infinite meaning with a reduced palette,—an artist's application of understatement. One very outstanding picture of his postwar days is "Christ at Emmaus." This large work in acid yellows, shining greens and resonant blues, is one of Tanner's most alluring contributions. His drift toward rugged drawing of the forms and dramatic, plastically manipulated color reaches its most expansive stage in this canvas. So rough-hewn is this painting that the light upon the face of Christ and around the fingers of his up-raised hands has the weight and the function of a second plastic outline around those parts of the figure. From this, it was but a step to the relief effects given to some of his half-tempera and half-oil paintings of which the very last was that one recently bought through subscription for the art gallery at Howard University.

Such audacious painting could scarcely be conventional; it was too individual. The sign of this man's originality was his belief in himself. He was once called the Dean of American painters in Paris. I asked a certain American painter to tell me exactly what this appellation was meant to convey. "Well," he answered, "in Tanner's case it meant the most original American painter in Paris."

JAMES WELDON JOHNSON (1871-1938)

James Weldon Johnson (see also pp. 168, 324) was well equipped to write of the early appearances of Negroes on the stage, because of his personal experiences in the show business. The following excerpt, from *Black Manhattan* (1930), is reprinted by permission of Mrs. Grace Nail Johnson and of Alfred A. Knopf, Inc., the publishers.

[Early Negro Shows]

BEGINNING QUITE EARLY, coloured singers made considerable headway on the concert stage. Contrary to what holds true at the present time, the most successful of them were women. As far back as 1851, Elizabeth Taylor Greenfield, known as the "Black Swan," attracted attention by singing for the Buffalo (New York) Musical Association. She followed this appearance with concerts before discriminating audiences in the larger cities and towns upstate in New York, and through New England and the Middle Western states. She then decided to visit Europe. Thereupon the citizens of Buffalo tendered her a benefit concert, which took place on March 7, 1853. A few weeks later she appeared in a successful concert before a very large audience in New York City; and on April 6 she sailed for England. She made an astonishing impression on the English public, and on May 4, 1854, she was "commanded to attend at Buckingham Palace" and sing before Queen Victoria. The "Black Swan" died in Philadelphia in 1876. Just about the time of her death the Hyers sisters, Anna Madah and Emma Louise, were at the top of their popularity. These two sisters, one a soprano and the other a contralto, gave concerts in which they were well received throughout all the Northern and Western states. Then came the first coloured singer with both the natural voice and the necessary training and cultivation, Mme Marie Selika. Mme Selika studied under good teachers in the United States and in Europe, becoming proficient in German and French, especially German, which she made her second language. She sang with success in this country and abroad. She is at present a teacher of singing in the Martin-Smith School of Music in Harlem. Several others gained notice also, among them Flora Batson, who possessed an almost unnatural range and was a marvellous singer of ballads.

But the most popular of all these women singers was Sissieretta Jones, known as the "Black Patti." The height of her career was so recent that her name and fame will be recalled by a great many who read these lines. She had most of the qualities essential in a great singer: the natural voice, the physical figure, the grand air, and the engaging personality. Sissieretta Jones had studied and been singing in concert for several years, but first gained wide publicity by her singing at a Jubilee Spectacle and Cake-Walk which was staged at Madison Square Garden April 26-8, 1892, for which she had been specially engaged. She sang three nights and carried off the honours of the affair. The next day the New York papers gave her space and headlines, and by one critic she was dubbed "Black Patti." Her manager was emboldened to take her to the Academy of Music, which had been dark all the week, and she sang there to large audiences for two nights immediately after the close of the Jubilee. So great was the sensation she created that there was talk of having her sing the dark roles in *Aida* and *L' Africaine* at the Metropolitan Opera House. In fact, she was signed by Abbey, Schöffel, and Grau, then managers of the Metropolitan, but the plans for grand opera were not carried out, and she was booked on the concert stage. Later she came under the management of Major Pond. In September 1892 she was invited by President Harrison to sing at a White House reception. Later in the same month she was engaged to sing for a week at the Pittsburgh Exposition as soloist with Levy's Band. That season she toured the country as soloist with the band. The following year she was engaged again to sing at the Pittsburgh Exposition, this time as soloist with Gilmore's Band. She then made a concert tour of Europe, which lasted nearly a year.

When "Black Patti" returned, she came under the management of Voelckel and Nolan of New York, who carried out their plan of taking Sissieretta Jones off the concert stage and presenting her in an all-Negro show. They engaged Bob Cole to write it; and in the same season with *Oriental America,* "Black Patti's Troubadours" was produced. "Black Patti's Troubadours," too, in a general way followed the minstrel pattern. The first part was a sketchy farce interspersed with songs and choruses and ending with a buck-dance contest. Then followed an olio. The finale was termed: "The Operatic Kaleidoscope," and in it "Black Patti" appeared in songs and operatic selections with the chorus. She took no other part in the show, but was the great drawing card. The Troubadours played season after season for a number of years. One reason for the long life of the show was "Black Patti's" great popularity in the South. The Troubadours, alone among the larger coloured shows, was able to play successfully in the South. Sissieretta Jones has retired from both the theatrical and the concert stage and lives at her home in Providence, Rhode Island.

During the first season of the Troubadours, while the company was playing at Proctor's Fifty-eighth Street Theatre in New York, Bob Cole had a serious disagreement with Messrs. Voelckel and Nolan regarding salary. Not reaching a satisfactory agreement, he gathered up the music that he had written and walked out with it. This action led to his arrest, and he was hailed into court. Before the magistrate he declared: "These men have amassed a fortune from the product of my brain, and now they call me a thief; I won't give it up!" However, as is usual, the stronger side won. But the rupture between Bob Cole and the managers of the Troubadours marked an epoch in Negro theatricals, for he began at once to plan a play of his own. In the season of 1898-9 he came out with *A Trip to Coontown,* the first Negro show to make a complete break from the minstrel pattern, the first that was not a mere potpourri, the first to be written with continuity and to have a cast of characters working out the story of a plot from beginning to end; and, therefore, the first Negro musical comedy. It was furthermore, the first coloured show to be organized, produced, and managed by Negroes. Some of the best performers then on the stage united with Cole in *A Trip to Coontown;* among them Billy Johnson, who became Cole's partner and was the Johnson of the first Cole and Johnson combination; Sam Lucas, and Jesse Shipp, who later was the directing genius in the construction of the Williams and Walker plays. *A Trip to Coontown* ran three seasons.

The summer of 1898 marked another great step forward. Will Marion Cook composed the music to a sketch entitled *Clorindy—The Origin of the Cake-Walk,* with lyrics by Paul Laurence Dunbar. The play was produced by George W. Lederer at the Casino Roof Garden and ran the entire summer season. The cast included Ernest Hogan, a veteran minstrel and a very funny, natural-black-face comedian; and Miss Belle Davis, who later made a success in Europe and stayed there. Hogan was a notable exception among black-face comedians; his comic effects did not depend upon the caricature created by the use of cork and a mouth exaggerated by paint. His mobile face was capable of laughter-provoking expressions that were irresistible, notwithstanding the fact that he was a very good-looking man. Some critics ranked him higher than Bert Williams. He had greater unction than Bert Williams and by that very token lacked Williams's subtlety and finish. *Clorindy* was the talk of New York. It was the first demonstration of the possibilities of syncopated Negro music. Cook was the first competent composer to take what was then known as rag-time and work it out in a musicianly way. His choruses and finales in *Clorindy,* complete novelties as they were, sung by a lusty chorus, were simply breath-taking. Broadway had something entirely new.

The following summer another musical playlet, *Jes Lak White Folks,* written by Cook, was produced at the New York Winter Garden. In this playlet Cook was less fortunate in his sketch material and in his cast; Hogan had gone to the Antipodes at the head of the Senegambians under the management of M. B. Curtis of "Sam'l of

Posen" fame. Curtis skipped and left the company stranded in Australia. *Jes Lak White Folks* had among its principals a girl named Abbie Mitchell, who was later to be important in Negro musical comedy and dramatics. Irving Jones was the comedian. Will Marion Cook continued to develop his distinctive style in composing the music for the later shows of Williams and Walker.

Williams and Walker came from out of the West. They came singing one of the catchiest songs of the day, "Dora Dean," which they themselves had written after the quite adequate inspiration of a sight of Miss Dora Dean, one of the famed beauties of the *Creole Show*. They reached New York in 1896. They had been together as a team for several years, undergoing all the special vicissitudes of a coloured vaudeville team of the period, when they were engaged to appear in *The Gold Bug*, produced at the Casino Theatre by Canary and Lederer. *The Gold Bug* did not quite catch Broadway's fancy, but Williams and Walker did; and after the failure of the Casino show they were engaged for the famous Koster and Bial's, where they played a record run of forty weeks. It was during this engagement that Williams and Walker made the cake-walk not only popular, but fashionable. They were assisted by two girls; one of them, Stella Wiley, was the cleverest coloured soubrette of the day. Cake-walk pictures posed for by the quartet were reproduced in colours and widely distributed as advertisements by one of the big cigarette concerns. And the execution of cake-walking became such a society fad that on Sunday morning, January 16, 1898, Williams and Walker, dressed just a point or two above the height of fashion, dared, as a publicity stunt, to call at the home of William K. Vanderbilt and leave the following letter:

To. Mr. William K. Vanderbilt
Corner of Fifty-second Street and Fifth Avenue
New York

Dear Sir:

In view of the fact that you have made a success as a cake-walker, having appeared in a semi-public exhibition and having posed as an expert in that capacity, we, the undersigned world-renowned cake-walkers, believing that the attention of the public has been distracted from us on account of the tremendous hit which you have made, hereby challenge you to compete with us in a cake-walking match, which will decide which of us shall deserve the title of champion cake-walker of the world.

As a guarantee of good faith we have this day deposited at the office of the New York *World* the sum of $50. If you purpose proving to the public that you really are an expert cake-walker we shall be pleased to have you cover that amount and name the day on which it will be convenient for you to try odds against us.

Yours very truly,

WILLIAMS AND WALKER.

Regarding the size of the stakes, Williams, who habitually left all business matters to Walker, is reported as saying: "It's a shame to take the money, so make the stakes small, George."

The two comedians next tried the London music-halls, but the English appeared not to be able to understand or appreciate their particular brand of humour; so they came back to New York and went out at the head of a mediocre show, *A Senegambian Carnival,* which promptly stranded. They followed with *4—11—44,* afterwards changed to *The Policy Players.* This was also a failure. In 1900 they brought out *The Sons of Ham,* and in this humorous-pathetic musical farce they struck their stride. In 1902 they produced *In Dahomey* and made Negro theatrical history by opening at the very centre of theatredom, at the New York Theatre in Times Square. In the spring of 1903 *In Dahomey* was taken to London. The two principals, remembering their reception in the London music-halls, were somewhat apprehensive about the venture; but the show was a success and ran for seven months at the Shaftesbury Theatre, afterwards touring the provinces. The unquestioned stamp of approval was put on it when at the end of the first month the company received a royal command for a performance at Buckingham Palace, on June 23. The performance was part of the celebration in honour of the ninth birthday of the present Prince of Wales and was given on a stage erected on the lawn. *In Dahomey* made the cake-walk a social fad in England and France. In 1906 Williams and Walker opened with *In Abyssinia* at the Majestic Theatre in Columbus Circle, New York. This was followed by *Bandana Land* in 1907.

Bandana Land was the last play in which Williams and Walker appeared together; during its run George Walker's health broke and he never again stepped on the stage. The Williams and Walker company was, all in all, the strongest Negro theatrical combination that has yet been assembled.[1] In addition to Williams and Walker there were Jesse Shipp, Alex Rogers, Will Marion Cook, and Ada Overton. Mr. Shipp had had long theatrical experience, beginning with minstrelsy, and he it was who worked out the details of the

---

[1] Written in 1930 (Editors' Note).

construction of the plays, after the idea had been discussed and adopted by the above-named heads. Mr. Rogers was the lyricist and the author of the words to many of the most popular of the Williams and Walker songs; among them: "Why Adam Sinned," "I May Be Crazy, but I Ain't No Fool," "The Jonah Man," "Bon Bon Buddy, the Chocolate Drop," and "Nobody." He also contributed much of the droll humour and many of the ludicrous situations for which these plays were noted. Mr. Cook, of whom we have already spoken, was the composer-in-chief. Ada Overton (Mrs. George Walker) was beyond comparison the brightest star among women on the Negro stage of the period; and it is a question whether or not she has since been surpassed. She was an attraction in the company and not many degrees less than the two principals. And there was also one of the best singing choruses ever heard on a musical-comedy stage. Of course the main strength of the combination centered in the two comedians; George Walker as the sleek, smiling prancing dandy, and Bert Williams as the slow-witted, good-natured, shuffling darky. Together they achieved something beyond mere fun; they often achieved the truest comedy through the ability they had to keep the tears close up under the loudest laughter.

Bert Williams went out alone in 1909 in *Mr. Lode of Kole,* which had little success and was the last Negro show in which he ever appeared. The next year he was engaged for the Ziegfeld *Follies* and remained a member of the cast for practically ten seasons. In 1920 he was the star in *Broadway Brevities,* and in 1922 the star in *The Pink Slip,* which after a tryout was rewritten and called *Under the Bamboo Tree.* He was a sick man when he went out with this last play; and after it had been on the road but a few weeks, he had to be brought back to New York. He died March 11, 1922, not yet forty-seven years old. Bert Williams goes down as one of America's great comedians. He has had few equals in the art of pantomine—a judgment with which those who saw him in his poker scene will agree. In the singing of a plaintive Negro song he was beyond approach. His singing of "Nobody" was perfection.

After three seasons with Cole and Johnson's *A Trip to Coontown* Bob Cole, in 1901, formed a partnership with another Johnson, this time J. Rosamond Johnson, the musician and singer, and the new Cole and Johnson became head-liners in big-time vaudeville. They sang their own songs and were a success in this country and in Europe. In the mean time they collaborated on the writing of white musical plays, and through this some of their songs gained world-wide popularity. In 1906 Cole and Johnson wrote and appeared in a

musical play called *The Shoofly Regiment,* which played in New
York at the Bijou Theatre on Broadway. In 1908 they came out in
another play of their own, *The Red Moon.* Each of these plays was a
true operetta with a well-constructed book and a tuneful, well-
written score. On these two points no Negro musical play has
equalled *The Red Moon.* The Cole and Johnson combination lacked
any such funmakers as were Williams and Walker, but in some
other respects they excelled their great rivals; their plays, on the
whole, were better written, and they carried a younger, sprightlier,
and prettier chorus, which, though it could not sing so powerfully,
could outdance the heavier chorus of the other company by a margin.

The break in health that ended the careers of Bob Cole and George
Walker, and the defection of Bert Williams to the white stage, all
happening within a brief period of time, put a sudden stop to what
had been a steady development and climb of the Negro in the
theatre. In this first decade of the century plays headed by Ernest
Hogan and Smart and Williams, and S. H. Dudley, and some other
performers, were produced, but all these shows, though organized
in New York, were road shows and of secondary merit. The Hogan
shows, *Rufus Rastus* and *The Oyster Man,* were the most important
of them. Hogan might have carried on, because he was a splendid
comedian and had a New York reputation; but he died a short
while before George Walker's retirement.

Then came an interval, and the efforts of the Negro in New York
in the theatre were for a while transferred to Harlem.

W. E. B. DuBOIS (1868-   )

"Of The Sorrow Songs," the first essay on the spirituals, by a Negro
and in many respects still one of the best, was written by W. E. B.
DuBois (see also p. 763) in *The Souls of Black Folk* (1903). It is one
of the best-known essays of that most influential volume. DuBois's
first real acquaintance with the spirituals occurred when he was a
student at Fisk University, famous for its Jubilee Singers. "Of The
Sorrow Songs" is reprinted by permission of the author.

Of the Sorrow Songs

I walk through the churchyard
To lay this body down;
I know moon-rise, I know star-rise;
I walk in the moonlight, I walk in the starlight;
I'll lie in the grave and stretch out my arms,
I'll go to judgment in the evening of the day,
And my soul and thy soul shall meet that day,
When I lay this body down.

THEY THAT WALKED in darkness sang songs in the olden days—Sorrow Songs—for they were weary of heart. And so before each thought that I have written in this book I have set a phrase, a haunting echo of these weird old songs in which the soul of the black slave spoke to men. Ever since I was a child these songs have stirred me strangely. They came out of the South unknown to me, one by one, and yet at once I knew them as of me and of mine. Then in after years when I came to Nashville I saw the great temple builded of these songs towering over the pale city. To me Jubilee Hall seemed ever made of the songs themselves, and its bricks were red with blood and dust of toil. Out of them rose for me morning, noon, and night, bursts of wonderful melody, full of the voices of my brothers and sisters, full of the voices of the past.

Little of the beauty has America given the world save the rude grandeur God himself stamped on her bosom; the human spirit in this new world had expressed itself in vigor and ingenuity rather than in beauty. And so by fateful chance the Negro folk-song—the rhythmic cry of the slave—stands today not simply as the sole American music, but as the most beautiful expression of human experience born this side the seas. It has been neglected, it has been, and is, half despised, and above all it has been persistently mistaken and misunderstood; but notwithstanding, it still remains as the singular spiritual heritage of the nation and the greatest gift of the Negro people.

Away back in the thirties the melody of these slave songs stirred the nation, but the songs were soon half forgotten. Some. like "Near the lake where drooped the willow," passed into current airs and their source was forgotten, others were caricatured on the "minstrel" stage and their memory died away. Then in war-time came the singular Port Royal experiment after the capture of Hilton Head, and perhaps for the first time the North met the Southern slave face to face and heart to heart with no third witness. The Sea Islands of the Carolinas,

where they met, were filled with a black folk of primitive type, touched
and moulded less by the world about them than any other outside the
Black Belt. Their appearance was uncouth, their language funny,
but their hearts were human and their singing stirred men with power.
Thomas Wentworth Higginson hastened to tell of these songs, and
Miss McKim and others urged upon the world their rare beauty. But
the world listened only half credulously until the Fisk Jubilee Singers
sang the slave songs so deeply into the world's heart that it can never
wholly forget them again.

There was once a blacksmith's son born at Cadiz, New York, who
in the changes of time taught school in Ohio and helped defend Cincinnati from Kirby Smith. Then he fought at Chancellorsville and
Gettysburg and finally served in the Freedmen's Bureau at Nashville.
Here he formed a Sunday-School class of black children in 1866, and
sang with them and taught them to sing. And then they taught him
to sing, and when once the glory of the Jubilee songs passed into the
soul of George L. White, he knew his life-work was to let those
Negroes sing to the world as they had sung to him. So in 1871
the pilgrimage of the Fisk Jubilee Singers began. North to Cincinnati
they rode,—four half-clothed black boys and five girl-women,—led by
a man with a cause and purpose. They stopped at Wilberforce, the
oldest of Negro schools, where a black bishop blessed them. Then they
went, fighting cold and starvation, shut out of hotels, and cheerfully
sneered at, ever northward; and ever the magic of their songs kept
thrilling hearts, until a burst of applause in the Congregational Council
at Oberlin revealed them to the world. They came to New York and
Henry Ward Beecher dared to welcome them, even though the metropolitan dailies sneered at his "Nigger Minstrels." So their songs conquered till they sang across the land and across the sea, before Queen
and Kaiser, in Scotland and Ireland, Holland and Switzerland. Seven
years they sang and brought back a hundred and fifty thousand dollars to found Fisk University.

Since their day they have been imitated—sometimes well, by the
singers of Hampton and Atlanta, sometimes ill, by straggling quar-
tettes. Caricature has sought again to spoil the quaint beauty of the
music, and has filled the air with many debased melodies which vulgar
ears scarce know from the real. But the true Negro folk-song still
lives in the hearts of those who have heard them truly sung and in the
hearts of the Negro people.

What are these songs, and what do they mean? I know little of
music and can say nothing in technical phrase, but I know something
of men, and knowing them, I know that these songs are the articulate

message of the slave to the world. They tell us in these eager days that life was joyous to the black slave careless and happy. I can easily believe this of some, of many. But not all the past South, though it rose from the dead, can gainsay the heart-touching witness of these songs. They are the music of an unhappy people of the children of disappointment; they tell of death and suffering and unvoiced longing toward a truer world, of misty wanderings and hidden ways.

The songs are indeed the siftings of centuries; the music is far more ancient than the words, and in it we can trace here and there signs of development. My grandfather's grandmother was seized by an evil Dutch trader two centuries ago; and coming to the valleys of the Hudson and Housatonic, black, little, and lithe, she shivered and shrank in the harsh north winds, looked longingly at the hills, and often crooned a heathen melody to the child between her knees. . . .

The child sang it to his children and they to their children's children, and so two hundred years it has traveled down to us and we sing it to our children, knowing as little as our fathers what its words may mean, but knowing well the meaning of its music.

This was primitive African music; it may be seen in larger form in the strange chant which heralds "The Coming of John":

> "You may bury me in the East,
> You may bury me in the West,
> But I'll hear the trumpet sound in that morning."

—the voice of exile.

Ten master songs, more or less, one may pluck from this forest of melody—songs of undoubted Negro origin and wide popular currency, and songs peculiarly characteristic of the slave. One of these I have mentioned. Another whose strains begin this book is "Nobody knows the trouble I've seen." When struck with a sudden poverty, the United States refused to fulfil its promise of land to the freedman, a brigadier-general went down to the Sea Island to carry the news. An old woman on the outskirts of the throng began singing this song; all the mass joined with her, swaying. And the soldier wept.

The third song is the cradle-song of death which all men know,— "Swing low, sweet chariot,"—whose bars begin the life story of "Alexander Crummel." Then there is the song of many waters, "Roll, Jordan, roll," a mighty chorus with minor cadences. There were many songs of the fugitive like that which opens "The Wings of Atlanta," and the more familiar "Been a-listening." The seventh is the song of the End and the Beginning—"My Lord, what a morning! when the stars begin to fall;" a strain of this is placed before "The

Dawn of Freedom." The song of groping—"My way's cloudy"—
begins "The Meaning of Progress"; the ninth is the song of this chapter—"Wrestlin' Jacob, the day is a-breaking,"—a paean of hopeful
strife. The last master song is the song of songs—"Steal away,"—
sprung from "The Faith of the Fathers."

There are many of the Negro folk-songs as striking and characteristic as these, as, for instance, the three strains in the third, eighth, and
ninth chapters; and others I am sure could easily make a selection on
more scientific principles. There are, too, songs that seem to me a step
removed from the more primitive types: there is the maze-like medley,
"Bright sparkles," one phrase of which heads "The Black Belt;" the
Easter carol, "Dust, dust, and ashes"; the dirge, "My Mother's took
her flight and gone home"; and that burst of melody hovering over
"The Passing of the First-Born"—"I hope my mother will be there
in that beautiful world on high."

These represent a third step in the development of the slave song, of
which "You may bury me in the East" is the first, and songs like
"Steal away" are the second. The first is African music, the second
Afro-American, while the third is a blending of Negro music with the
music in the foster land. The result is still distinctively Negro and the
method of blending original, but the elements are both Negro and
Caucasian. One might go further and find a fourth step in this
development, where the songs of the white America have been distinctively influenced by the slave songs or have incorporated whole
phrases of Negro melody, as "Swanee River" and "Old Black Joe."
Side by side, too, with the "minstrel" songs, many of the "Gospel"
hymns, and some of the contemporary "coon" songs,—a mass of music
in which the novice may easily lose himself and never find the real
Negro melodies.

In these songs, I have said, the slave spoke to the world. Such a
message is naturally veiled and half articulate. Words and music have
lost each other and new cant phrases of a dimly understood theology
have displaced the older sentiment. Once in a while we catch a strange
word of unknown tongue, as the "Mighty Myo," which figures as a
river of death; more often slight words or mere doggerel are joined to
music of singular sweetness. Purely secular songs are few in number
partly because many of them were turned into hymns by a change of
words, partly because the frolics were seldom heard by the stranger,
and the music less often caught. Of nearly all the songs, however, the
music is distinctly sorrowful. The ten master songs I have mentioned
tell in word and music of trouble and exile, of strife and hiding; they
grope toward some unseen power and sigh for rest in the End.

The words that are left to us are not without interest, and, cleared of evident dross, they conceal much of real poetry and meaning beneath conventional theology and unmeaning rhapsody. Like all primitive folk, the slave stood near to Nature's heart. Life was a "rough and rolling sea" like the brown Atlantic of the Sea Islands; the "Wilderness" was the home of God, and the "lonesome valley" led to the way of life. "Winter'll soon be over," was the picture of life and death to a tropical imagination. The sudden wild thunder-storms of the South awed and impressed the Negroes,—at times the rumbling seemed to them "mournful," at times imperious:

> "My Lord calls me,
> He calls me by the thunder,
> The trumpet sounds it in my soul."

The monotonous toil and exposure is painted in many words. One sees the ploughman in the hot, moist furrow, singing:

> "Dere's no rain to wet you,
> Dere's no sun to burn you,
> Oh, push along, believer,
> I want to go home,

The bowed and bent old man cries, with thrice-repeated wail:

> "O Lord, keep me from sinking down,"

and he rebukes the devil of doubt who can whisper:

> "Jesus is dead and God's gone away."

Yet the soul-hunger is there, the restlessness of the savage, the wail of the wanderer, and the plaint is put in one little phrase:

> "My soul wants something that's new, that's new.

Over the inner thoughts of the slaves and their relations one with another the shadow of fear ever sung, so that we get but glimpses here and there, and also with them, eloquent omissions and silences. Mother and child are sung, but seldom father; fugitive and weary wanderer call for pity and affection, but there is little of wooing and wedding; the rocks and the mountains are well known, but home is unknown. Strange blending of love and helplessness sings through the refrain:

> "Yonder's my ole mudder,
> Been waggin' at de hill so long;
> 'Bout time she cross over,
> Git home bime-by."

Elsewhere comes the cry of the "motherless" and the "Farewell, farewell, my only child."

Love-songs are scarce and fall into two categories—the frivolous and light, and the sad. Of deep successful love there is ominous silence, and in one of the oldest of these songs there is a depth of history and meaning:

> "Poor Rosy, poor gal;
> Poor Rosy, poor gal;
> Rosy break my poor heart
> Heaven shall-a-be my home."

A black woman said of the song, "It can't be sung without a full heart and a troubled sperrit." The same voice sings here that sings in the German folk-songs:

> "Jetz Geh i' an's brunele, trink' aber net."

Of death the Negro showed little fear, but talked of it familiarly and even fondly as simply a crossing of the waters, perhaps—who knows?—back to his ancient forests again. Later days transfigured his fatalism, and amid the dust and dirt the toiler sang:

> "Dust, dust and ashes, fly over my grave,
> But the Lord shall bear my spirit home."

The things evidently borrowed from the surrounding world undergo characteristic change when they enter the mouth of the slave. Especially is this true of Bible phrases. "Weep, O captive daughter of Zion," is quaintly turned into "Zion, weep-a-low," and the wheels of Ezekiel are turned every way in the mystic dreaming of the slave, till he says:

> "There 's a little wheel a-turnin' in-a-my heart."

As in olden time, the words of these hymns were improvised by some leading minstrel of the religious band. The circumstances of the gathering, however, the rhythm of the songs, and the limitations of allowable thought, confined the poetry for the most part to single or double lines, and they seldom were expanded to quatrains or longer tales, although there are some few examples of sustained efforts, chiefly paraphrases of the Bible. Three short series of verses have always attracted me,—the one that heads this chapter, of one line of which Thomas Wentworth Higginson has fittingly said, "Never, it seems to me, since man first lived and suffered, was his infinite longing for peace uttered more plaintively." The second and third are descriptions of the Last Judgment,—the one a late improvisation, with some traces of outside influence:

> "Oh, the stars in the elements are falling,
> And the moon drips away into blood,
> And the ransomed of the Lord are returning unto God,
> Blessed be the name of the Lord."

And the other earlier and homelier picture from the low coast lands:

> "Michael, haul the boat ashore,
> Then you'll hear the horn they blow,
> Then you'll hear the trumpet sound,
> Trumpet sound the world around,
> Trumpet sound for rich and poor,
> Trumpet sound the Jubilee,
> Trumpet sound for you and me."

Through all the sorrow of the Sorrow Songs there breathes a hope—a faith in the ultimate justice of things. The minor cadences of despair change often to triumph and calm confidence. Sometimes it is faith in life, sometimes a faith in death, sometimes assurance of boundless justice in some fair world beyond. But whichever it is, the meaning is always clear: that sometimes, somewhere, men will judge men by their souls and not by their skins. Is such a hope justified? Do the Sorrow Songs sing true?

The silently growing assumption of this age is that the probation of races is past, and that the backward races of today are of proven inefficiency and not worth the saving. Such an assumption is the arrogance of peoples irreverent toward Time and ignorant of the deeds of men. A thousand years ago such an assumption, easily possible, would have made it difficult for the Teuton to prove his right to life. Two thousand years ago such dogmatism, readily welcome, would have scouted the idea of blond races ever leading civilization. So woefully unorganized is sociological knowledge that the meaning of progress, the meaning of "swift" and "slow" in human doing, and the limits of human perfectability, are veiled, unanswered sphinxes on the shores of science. Why should Aeschylus have sung two thousand years before Shakespeare was born? Why has civilization flourished in

Europe, and flickered, flamed, and died in Africa? So long as the world stands meekly dumb before such questions, shall this nation proclaim its ignorance and unhallowed prejudices by denying freedom of opportunity to those who brought the Sorrow Songs to the Seats of the Mighty?

Your country? How came it yours? Before the Pilgrims landed we were here. Here have we brought our three gifts and mingled them with yours: a gift of story and song—soft, stirring melody in an ill-harmonized and unmelodious land; the gift of sweat and brawn to beat back the wilderness, conquer the soil, lay the foundations of this vast economic empire two hundred years earlier than your weak hands could have done it; the third, a gift of the Spirit. Around us the history of the land has centered for thrice a hundred years; out of the nation's hearts we have called all that was best to throttle and subdue all that was worst; fire and blood, prayer and sacrifice, have billowed over this people, and they found peace only in the altars of the God of Right. Nor has our gift of the Spirit been merely passive. Actively we have woven ourselves with the very warp and woof of this nation,—we fought their battles, shared their sorrow, mingled our blood with theirs, and generation after generation have pleaded with a headstrong, careless people to despise not Justice, Mercy and Truth, lest the nation be smitten with a curse. Our song, our toil, our cheer, and warning have been given to this nation in blood-brotherhood. Are not these gifts worth the giving? Is not this work and striving? Would America have been America without her Negro people?

Even so is the hope that sang in the songs of my fathers well sung. If somewhere in this whirl and chaos of things there dwells Eternal Good, pitiful yet masterful, then anon in His good time America shall rend the Veil and the prisoned shall go free . . . .

E. SIMMS CAMPBELL (1906-   )

E. Simms Campbell was born in St. Louis and studied at the Art Institute in Chicago. As a cartoonist he has contributed to *The New Yorker, Esquire, Opportunity,* and the old *Life.* His articles on jazz, blues, and the dance, illustrated by his own drawings, have appeared in *Esquire.* He has won prizes at the Art Institute and in the 1924 and 1925 Minneapolis exhibitions; in 1928 he won the *St. Louis Post-Dispatch* black and white contest and in 1936 the Hearst Prize. The following selection is used by permission of the author and of the editors of *Esquire* magazine.

[Early Jam]

IN THE LATE EIGHTIES and early nineties, the era of tinsel and gilt, heavy furniture and mustache cups, swing was born. Where it was born is particularly important, because this may account for its irrelevance and utter rowdyism, its very elemental nature. Memphis, St. Louis and a host of Southern towns claim credit although New Orleans seems logically to have the preference because of the great number of ragtime Negro musicians gathered there.

At this time—New Orleans was steeped in wickedness, bawdy houses running full blast, faro games on most street corners and voluptuous creole beauties soliciting trade among the welter of gamblers, steamboat men and hustlers of every nationality. New Orleans was not unique in this respect, as most American cities had their proscribed redlight district, but New Orleans was more colorful. Spaniards, Italians, Germans, French and French Negro, Swedish, and a great spattering of Portuguese—and all of them speaking creole, the handy bastard French, the patois French which even today has not changed one iota from its original form.

Here in this port of all nationalities, this western hemisphere Marseilles, came a conglomerate group of itinerant musicians—Coon shouters, honky-tonks, black butt players (Negro musicians who could not read music)—all of them seeking their pot of gold in this paradise of pleasure. Most of them had little or no training in their respective instruments but they had a rhythm and a timing that appealed to the catholic tastes of this segment of America. The sky was the limit in "hot" ballads and there was no such thing as controlled music. New York was too far away and New Orleans was the mecca of entertainment to these Southern minstrels.

True, respectable New Orleans as well as respectable America sang and played Irish ditties or saccharine sentimental tear jerkers—*Whisper Your Mother's Name*—the Curse of Saloons and the Little Nellie's Gone Astray creations. All America cried in its beer over them, but the gulf was too wide for pleasure-loving America to span, from Stephen Foster's *Old Folks at Home* to the sedate piano music (song and chorus) of the horsehair parlor days.

Barber shop chords were all right too, but New Orleans had gone on a bender—and when a man or a city goes pleasure-mad they want music with "umph"—something that's on the naughty side, that tickles the senses, that starts them bunnyhugging. Ragtime filled this bill perfectly.

Possibly the first ragtime number originated in a bagnio and I know of more than a score that were actually created in them, having traced them back to the musicians who wrote them, tracing others through musicians who had played in bands with the original composer —although I must confess that nothing is harder actually to track down than a musical score. It is stolen from so many sources—the so-called Classics are dipped in and musicians are as jealous and touchy about giving credit to their fellows as prima donnas. A few of the numbers I actually saw created, written all over the backs of envelopes and policy number slips in all-night joints in St. Louis (pardon my misspent youth) and I have heard these same numbers, fifteen years later, presented for the edification of swing enthusiasts on the concert stage. Without mentioning names, many of our greatest swing artists have played, at some time or another, in these dens of iniquity or halls of learning—according to your esthetic tastes.

One thing, you may be certain they were never created in a classroom where harmony and composition were taught. It is sometimes sad to contemplate, but few lasting contributions to popular music have ever been born in cloistered surroundings.

Ta-Ra-Ra-Boom-Dee-A was written in the house of Babe Connors, one of the more colorful Negro madams, in 1894. It was essentially ragtime—in 4-4 time, the name rag being given because the playing was ragged—one played between the beats, not on them, just as swing today is irregular but is played in a faster tempo—a stepped-up version. If you have ever seen Negroes dancing, that is dancing two-steps and one-steps and waltzes, you will notice that they do not dance exactly in time with the music. They dance to the rhythm of the number and are usually in step. It's this "feel" of the dance that's important and once one has the rhythm, there is no need to wonder or worry if you are exactly in time to the music. It was as natural for Negroes to create ragtime as it was for the rest of America to fall in step with them.

But coming back to the madams, these house-mothers of wayward America, they were continually on the lookout for added attractions to their establishments. With the rise of vaudeville, they now hoped to please their patrons with special music as well as other forms of special entertainment.

Every house with any pretentions to class had a beautiful mahogany upright piano, strewn with the usual bric-a-brac, cupid, Daphne and Apollo and ornate throws and the ever-present mandolin attachment. It added tone. A friend of mine who used to play the piano in the famous Everleigh Club of Chicago mentioned that they had a gold piano—where he composed many a piece—and where his tips were the highest he had ever received, then or since.

These madams were ever on the hunt for good musicians, but particularly good piano players, as a piano could be toned down and the less noise in the wee hours of the morning, the better. Possibly a tired Romeo could be coaxed into spending just a little more if the music fitted in with his mood.

The usual procedure would be to invite the chosen entertainer to stay at the house while he was in the city—and musicians at that time were not getting any hundred a week for their playing—and his cakes and coffee were free, with of course all the liquor he wished to hold. He could play any way he wanted to as long as he was good, and he could improvise all he wanted—just so long as he didn't stop. No matter how often he played certain numbers, the audience was continually changing. Here, when liquor, used to fight off exhaustion, had befogged the brain, many of the discordant and eerie chords were born. I have talked with many a swing musician who has admitted that he has improvised these weird minor chords in these houses and one of them used to chew calabash weed to keep him going.

Because of the tremendous amount of energy needed to play four to six shows a day, and then doubling every night to augment their meager wages, many musicians fell into this pernicious habit.

Negro musicians were paid next to nothing, the finer white dance halls barring them, and their greatest revenue came from playing "gigs" (outside jobs—special groups of three or four who were especially hired to play for wealthy white patrons at private house parties) and in playing in the finest sporting houses.

Many of them have played the Redlight Circuit from New Orleans to Seattle.

You must remember at that time that Negroes had no union of their own, were not admitted to white unions, and it was impossible for them to market their songs unless they sold them outright to white publishers—and the top price was fifteen dollars, with ten being about the average. These smart publishers would keep the scores of songs stowed away in drawers, much as a man keeps gilt-edged bonds, and at a propitious time they would revise here and there—change the title and lo!—a popular hit tune was often launched on the market in New York. It often made a song writer who never would have reached the top, unless he had the ideas of these Negroes to fall back on.

True, many a white musician shared the same fate, but he was not continually relegated to the bottom as were these early-day Negro pioneers.

This shunting aside naturally made the Negro draw into himself. With no outlet to exchange ideas on music other than with members of his own race, he became more and more essentially Negroid in musical feeling and in interpretation. Jam sessions are as old as the hills among them—it was their only medium of expressing themselves, of learning—and it was the training school for the colored boy who hoped some day to become an accomplished musician. None of them had enough money to study their instruments, learning everything they knew from these early jam sessions, improvising and going ahead purely on natural ability. All of them patterned their playing after some musical giant who was the legendary John Henry of his day, some powerful cornetist or piano-playing fool whose exploits on his chosen instrument were known throughout colored America. Camp meetings, funerals and lodge dances gave the embryo musician his first chance, and much later, about 1908 I believe, when the T. O. B. A. (Theatrical Owners Booking Agency) was formed, these musicians as well as entertainers had an opportunity to play before small theatres in the colored sections of various cities.

Before that time, minstrels and itinerant peddlers of tunes would go from town to town, but because of the precarious way in which they made a living, many towns never had opportunity to hear them. Now this was all changed. Bessie Smith, Mamie Smith, Ma Rainey, Ida Cox, Clarence Williams, Butterbeans and Susie, all great names in the "blues" constellation of Negroes throughout the United States, were swinging and playing the blues years before white America recognized them. Tom Turpin of St. Louis, Scott Joplin, Jellyroll Morton were the early great swing pianists, and by great I mean that their pieces were as intricate as Bach. They wrote trick arrangements, exciting tempos, difficult passages, and at this time the great Handy was writing, *Atlanta Blues, St. Louis Blues, New Orleans Blues, Memphis Blues, Beale Street Blues, Rampart Blues, Market Street Blues*—all these were written before 1912—just about the time Benny Goodman was six years old.

And later—the great flood of records, records that are now collector's items to the swing enthusiast. A respectable family of the nineteen twenties would not be found dead with any of these abominable discs in their homes.

The old Decca records, Columbia, Okeh, but particularly the Paramount and Black Swan or Race records as they were called. This meant especially made for the Negro race as few white people would ever buy them. I quote from old catalogues of mine and the names are authentic. *Red Hot Mamma* and *Drunk Man's Strut, Lonnie Johnson's*

Blues, Salty Dog Blues (which had particularly low-down lines), *Mr. Freddie's Blues, Barrelhouse Blues, Toad Frog Blues, Ride Jockey Ride, Death Letter Blues, Mean Man Blues, Lemon Jefferson's Blues, The Woman Ain't Born, Grave Yard Bound, Long Gone Blues, Black Hand Blues*—the list is endless. *Mecca Flat Blues*, named after a row of disorderly houses in Chicago and even *Tickler*, which is a swing standby today. . . .

All through the nineteen twenties, this endless stream of Blues records—and who bought them? Dealers did not and the chances are ten thousand to one that you haven't five of them in your collection. They were a solace to Negro domestics, who after working for hours over laundry tubs, mopping floors and shining brass, would go to the dingy comfort of a one-room flat in the Negro tenements and there put these records on their victrolas. It was a release from things white—they could hum—pat their feet—and be all colored. "Blues blues—jes' as blue as ah can be—Nogood man done lef'—and lef' po' me."

These were true expressions, expressed as illiterates would talk and they were sung husky and plaintively. Even Negroes often tire of Spirituals, no matter how good they are. They wanted something earthy and salty, something that touched their lives intimately—they wanted to hear a Negro man moan on his guitar and cut loose on a piano—they KNEW this man—he was probably just like Joe or Tom or Ed who ran off with some no good gal in Memphis and left her stranded here in this flat. True, *Japanese Sandman* and *Avalon* and the others were nice but none of them meant anything to a Negro domestic—all salvation and happiness and roses and cottages were for whites—but the blues. "Lawd, lawd—they's cullud—and cain't nobody take that away fum us."

Sporting houses were possibly the next best bets for these records and they bought them by the armful. The records sold for fifty cents with a top price of seventy-five and they were continually needing replacement as the patrons would play certain favorites over and over again until the grooves in the discs were worn down. Every joint from New Orleans all through the Delta up to St. Louis, Kansas City, Chicago, Detroit, on out to the coast had stacks of these records. Dim lights—and the blues—the low-down gutbucket blues—heady music as intoxicating as any of the wares for sale.

Perhaps Jellyroll Morton, so named for his famous blues, *The Jellyroll Blues*, was the first Negro and the first man, black or white, to play blues with an orchestra and to devote his whole life to perfecting them. He along with, though much later, Charlie Creath, Bennie Moton, Fletcher Henderson and a host of creative geniuses played St. Louis and turned out records by the score that were decidedly frowned upon by many white musicians. This was my first actual contact with these men. St. Louis being a river town, was one of the main points touched by this small band of pathfinders.

They streamed up from New Orleans and Memphis and played jazz the length and breadth of the Mississippi and many was the hot sticky summer night when I, along with many of my friends, listened breathless as these masters of weird melodies shot their golden notes out over a muddy river. Perhaps we were the first jitterbugs—but we had no white companions then—just a bunch of colored kids who loved to listen to these masters.

During the summer, on Monday nights, the Negroes of St. Louis were privileged to use the older of two paddle-wheel steamers for their boat excursions. I remember the names of both of them—*The J. S.* and the *St. Paul*—The *St. Paul* was the one we used. Lodges and fraternal orders of all sorts would get together and have a benefit—to this day I have never found out what the benefits were for—but they always meant plenty of ice cream and cake for us, and above all—music, the blues. Music that was decidedly frowned upon by respectable Negro and white families, but we kids loved it. These boat rides usually ended up in fist fights, knife fights and bottle throwing contests. Drinking St. Louis corn, packed on the boat like cattle, bunnyhugging to the tunes of Jellyroll Morton, some too ardent boy friend would cut in on another's girl—then fireworks! I can still see an excited crew, red-faced and panting among a sea of black faces, trying to restore order—and then the clear strains of Charlie Creath's trumpet drowning out the noise and the scuffling. Charlie Creath of the one lung (he had literally blown his other lung out in New Orleans proving his superiority over other trumpet players)—Charlie had cut loose on the *St. Louis Blues*.

Fights and even gun play meant nothing to these musicians who had seen it all too often—Charlie was playing a monumental solo— OH PLAY IT, MR. CHARLIE, PLAY IT—. The trumpet was in the clear now, it would not be denied—sweet and hot, the staccato notes splintered among the crowd and even the boy wielding the knife was transfixed. Someone bellowed out, "Oh play it, Mr. Charlie, play that thing!" There was laughter and the tenseness disappeared—the trumpet was laughing now—"What's a few cuts—doctor below deck'll fix 'em up and BOY—does you realize we on'y got a half-hour t'dance?"

The crowd that had formed a semicircle to watch the men fight surged forward and blended together—they were one—Charlie had won another fight.

Then and there I decided I would quit drawing and become a trumpet player or anyway a jazz pianist. Drawing was a silent art—a lonely one—but a musician, why he could work wonders before a crowd and everybody could SEE him while he worked. I remember practicing diligently by the hour on my piano lessons. True they were such exciting things as barcaroles, but in some unfathomable way I knew that sooner or later they would lead me to the *Beale Street Blues* and I would burst forth like Athena, a finished jazz pianist.

These early Negro geniuses were evolving the present-day swing. Many of the popular tunes of the day were written by whites as well as Negroes but there was this undercurrent of music—this music behind even the blues—this forbidden land as it were, that only a kid with all eyes and ears could catch. There were glimpses of it on these stolen boat rides when a lean black man would become intoxicated with the rhythm of his playing and break off into a magnificent solo—leaving the piece that the orchestra played entirely and swinging out into musical no-man's-land. He was swaying the crowd—he was "sending" them, as the jitterbugs say today, and I was an apt disciple—I was willing to be "sent."

This was a masterful exhibition on the spur of the moment of technical virtuosity fused with inspirational playing. If that wasn't swing—then there's no such animal.

The bunnyhug was accepted by conservative St. Louis, with only an occasional raising of eyebrows, but on the levee front, where I was forbidden to go—HERE was where music was really played. How well I remember a heavy black fellow they called Bootstrap—I never heard him called by any other name—who frequented the dives on the river front. He and I were buddies. He had always wanted to draw and I had always wanted to play the piano. Bootstrap and his stubby fingers, playing effortlessly on the black and yellow keys (I do not remember a single piano in any of the river joints that had white keys, all were yellow with age) had a habit of hunching his shoulders over the piano and rolling the bass. And he knew every word of every gutbucket piece that was ever played on the levee front. All the words were unprintable. "Dat's de belly rub, kid—ain't got no name, but jes' de belly rub"—and he'd float exciting chord after chord together, all of them below middle C.

People just shut their eyes and swayed when Bootstrap attacked a piano.

Coming home from one of these enthralling sessions, I had worked up to the *Double Eagle March* and used to give fair exhibitions on *Dardanella,* I inadvertently started to play Bootstrap's piece in the sanctity of our parlor. Faltering, but nonetheless, the Belly Rub. My aunt Edith, who was teaching me, rushed downstairs and asked me where I had learned such trash. Needless to say I was silent—a friend taught me. The Belly Rub was banned from the house and I was smartly rapped on my knuckles.

That surely must have been the way most of America felt toward these early Negro troubadours who had brought their musical creations forth. I do not mean the composers, both Negro and white, who wrote for Tin Pan Alley or the hundreds who were writing the popular music of the day, I mean the true jazz disciples, the gutbucket boys who were as expressive in their field as any Beethoven was in his. It was not polite music—fit only for beer joints and brothels. Finding no ready reception for their pieces, they played them where they felt they would be appreciated and the joints and brothels did appreciate them.

Swing is electrical, it electrifies people and causes mass hysteria— creating an animal enthusiasm to ears not trained to hear essentially good music. Thus your jitterbugs. They can't stand it when the minor chords and melodies break down their inhibitions—they have to give vent to their feelings in shouts and body gyrations. That's what the noted composer Will Vodery told me. Vodery is a Negro who arranged all the music for Florenz Ziegfeld's shows and discovered George Gershwin for America in 1916 and brought him to the attention of Ned Wayburn.

Will Vodery very definitely does not like swing music. "Well what do you think, Cab?" I asked the dapper Cab Calloway, who with Will Vodery is writing the new show for New York's Cotton Club and who was the first one to call swing fans jitterbugs. Cab smiled and nodded to Vodery—Vodery must have been traveling fast going down through the years, remembering all of the men I have mentioned, blending the old with the new, and his eyes lighted up as he chuckled—"Elmer, your friend Bootstrap was nearer to the truth than anybody; Swing is still the Belly Rub."

KATHERINE DUNHAM (1912-)

Born in Chicago, Katherine Dunham ˙organized dance groups and gave recitals even as a child. At the University of Chicago she com- bined her love of the dance with an interest in anthropology. In 1935 and 1936 the Rosenwald Foundation awarded her fellowships to study native dancing in Jamaica, Martinique, Trinidad, and Haiti. In 1939-1940 she gave a highly successful series of concerts illus- trating the authentic dances of the Caribbean and of the United

States. She and her group have since had important roles in *Cabin In the Sky*. She arranged the dances for the Chicago company of *Run, Lil Children* and was staff choreographer for the Labor Stage production of *Pins and Needles* in 1939-40. Miss Dunham has written articles on the native Caribbean dances in *Esquire* and she has lectured on the primitive dance at several universities. The following essay is reprinted by permission of the author.

The Negro Dance[1]

BUT THE PRESSURE of European culture upon the Negroes transplanted to the West Indies was of a different kind. . . . The political, economic, and social organization of the West Indies was no longer tribal, and the entire structure of social and art traditions which had been based upon the tribal form lost its functional validity. Accordingly, this structure began to disintegrate; and the process of disintegration was accelerated tremendously by the impact of European culture upon the now vulnerable African traditions.

My personal observation has been that the French, on the whole, were less concerned with dominating culturally their colonial peoples than the English, and consequently the integrity of African culture and the sanctity of African religious tradition persists to a greater extent in, for example, Haiti and Martinique than in Jamaica or Trinidad. Even so, in the interior of most of the Islands of the Caribbean, one can still find African forms which have survived vigorously in the almost-tribal organization of isolated communities; and these forms are replaced more and more by European influences as one nears the relatively urban communities of the port towns.

Although the survival of African dances in their intact form is most typical of inland communities in the West Indies, North America also furnishes material for observation.

[1] This essay, too long to appear in its entirety, gave first a definition of the dance as "rhythmic motion, singly or in a group for any one of several purposes" (for [1] play, [2] the stimulation or release of emotional or physical tension, [3] the expression of social relationships, and [4] the exhibition of individual or group skill). Since the dance is essentially emotional, forms of the dance have a tenacity greater than other cultural forms. The dances of the Polynesians, the Aztecs, and the American Indian show how dance patterns, though altered in function, remain fairly stable in form. The primitive African dance was largely "bound up functionally with the whole body of religious beliefs and practices," though of course there were war and social dances. In explaining her use of the word "primitive," Miss Dunham denies the connotations of either loose, or inferior, or simple, pointing out the integration and formalization of the tribal cultures of the West African empires, whence came most of the slaves for the New World.—Editors' Note.

"Early in the 19th century, soon after the Louisiana Purchase, slaves were allowed for the first time to assemble for social and recreational diversion. The most popular meeting place was a large open field at Orleans and Rampart, known as Congo Square. In earlier times the space had been a ceremonial ground of the Oumas Indians. Today, landscaped with palm trees, it forms a part of the municipal grounds called Beauregard Square. The Negroes, however, still speak of the place as Congo Square, in memory of the days when it was an open, dusty field, its grass worn bare by the stomping and shuffling of hundreds of restless bare feet. A century ago, slaves met there every Saturday night to perform the tribal and sexual dances which they had brought with them from the Congo.

"Before the Civil War the Congo Dances were one of the unusual sights of New Orleans to which tourists were always taken. At times almost as many white spectators as dancers gathered for the festive occasions. That the Negroes had not forgotten their dances, even after years of repression and exile from their native Africa, is attested by descriptive accounts of the times . . . .

". . . Though discontinued during the war, the Congo Dances were again performed after the emancipation and were not entirely abandoned even two decades later, when a correspondent of the *New York World* reported:

"'A dry-goods box and an old pork barrel formed the orchestra. These were beaten with sticks or bones, used like drumsticks so as to keep up a continuous rattle, while some old men and women chanted a song that appeared to me to be purely African in its many vowelled syllabification . . . In the dance the women did not move their feet from the ground. They only writhed their bodies and swayed in undulatory motions from ankles to waist . . . The men leaped and performed feats of gymnastic dancing . . . Small bells were attached to their ankles . . . I asked several old women to recite them (the words of the song) to me, but they only laughed and shook their heads. In their patois they told me—'No use, you would never understand it. C'est le Congo!'"

According to Herbert Asbury,[2] from whom the above description is taken, the favorite dances of the Negroes at the Congo Square were the Calinda and the Bamboula, both of which are still performed in Haiti. Both of these were, to be sure, embellished with copious borrowings from the French contre-danses, but in their fundamental pattern and movement were clearly African.

Still another instance emerges when we compare the following description by Père Labat, Jesuit missionary writing in 1742, of a

[2] H. Asbury: *The French Quarter*, Chapter VIII.

dance performed in Santo Domingo, with dances performed on some
of the islands off South Carolina.

"The dancers are placed in two lines, facing each other, men on one
side, women on the other. Those who are tired of dancing and the
spectators form a circle about the dancers and drum players. The most
skilful sings a song that he composes on the spur of the moment on
whatever subject he deems fitting the refrain of which is sung by all
the spectators and is accompanied by clapping of the hands. As for the
dancers, they hold their hands a little like those who dance while playing
castanettes . . . they jump, execute turns, approach within two or
three feet of each other, retreat in cadence until the sound of the drum
commands them to come together, beating their thighs together, that is,
the men against the women."

Persons who have visited the islands off South Carolina have
described dances in a manner as to call Père Labat's description
strikingly to mind.

However, such a direct retention of African forms in North
America is certainly the exception rather than the rule, and the West
Indies are still a more fertile field for the analysis of the survival of
the dance in its shift from tribal to folk culture. Apart from the two
extremes—the close-to-tribal organization of isolated interior communities and the cosmopolitanism of port rum-shops—the characteristic and predominant culture of the West Indies may be termed
the folk stage of acculturation. Here the conflict between the disin-
tegrating African traditions and the powerful European influences
is still very active and has resulted in many and varied attempts at
compromise and resolution.

For one thing, it was inevitable that as Negroes became more
and more inducted into the religious practices of various European
cultures; the dance and ceremonial forms which were an integral
part of African religious practices would gradually become absorbed
to some degree into the new religious life, and to a greater degree
into the new secular life. Haiti, for example, offers an interesting
instance of neatly combining Catholic and traditional African
ideologies. Every *vaudoun* ceremony begins with a Catholic litany
which, once performed, is promptly forgotten for the remainder of
the ceremony, which is almost purely African. Another example is
that of associating the portrait of St. Patrick driving the snakes out
of Ireland with Damballa, the traditional African snake-god. And
this inverted interpretation is accomplished with apparently the
greatest of ease!

In North America, however, there is less compromise and more real assimilation of African religious forms into European religious ideology. In 1938-39 I had occasion to direct a group in the Federal Writers' Project in an investigation of religious and magic cults in the city. Here, while the ideology was clearly and definitely Christian (with added flourishes), the entire pattern of religious behavior associated with it was almost as purely African. The rhythmic percussion-type hand-clapping and foot-stamping, the jumping and leaping, the "conversion" or "confession" in unknown tongues which is a form of possession or ecstasy (induced, in some cases, by a circle of "saints" or "angels" closing in upon the person in rhythmic motion of a dance), the frequent self-hypnosis by motor-activity of the shoulders—all these African forms were present. This last type of movement, for example, is called "zepaules" in Haiti, and is formally recognized there as a basic dance movement of great ritualistic importance in *vaudoun* practice. In general form, even in function, the motor activity connected with the religious expression of "store-front" churches in this country is strikingly similar to that of the Haitian peasant.

More often, however, the disintegration of African religious ideology under the impact of European influences led to the incorporation of the forms of its dance into secular dance. The West Indies, representing that stage of folk culture in which such transitions are apparent, provides, once more, some excellent examples.

In the more formalized of secular dances, in the dance-halls at carnival time, the young people of Haiti perform what they refer to as *do-ba* dances, whose characteristic feature is a wave-like motion of the spine performed in a squatting position, back forward, body bent double. The *do-ba* begins in an erect position, but gradually, by a simultaneous forward movement of shoulders and back, is lowered until the dancer is in an almost squatting position. Anyone who has seen the dance to Damballa, snake-god of the Rada-Dahomey cult, will certainly recognize the secular *do-ba* as a derivative of the ritual in imitation of the undulations of the snake-god. In the ritual, the low squatting position is the climax of the dance and usually indicates a state of supreme religious ecstasy, bordering on or participating in a state of possession by the snake-god to whom the dance is sacred. In the secular dance, the climax of intensity is also reached at the same point, although, of course, the ecstasy is not, in these cases, of the religious impetus.

Another instance of the secularization of a religious ritual is the *bonga* or *banda* of Trinidad. My experience with this dance was when it was presented to me as a part of a funeral ritual. It has a definitely sexual character, in keeping with African philosophy which closely associates procreation with death, perhaps as a compensatory effort. I have been told, however, that the same general movements and patterns are freely incorporated into carnival dances also.

So far we have spoken first of the incorporation of African religious dance patterns into Christian ideology; and we have considered, as well, examples of the degeneration of African religious dance patterns into secular dance. It remains to consider the interaction of African secular dance with European secular dance. The *beguine,* which is practically the national dance of Martinique, is a striking example of just this type of combination.

"There is not much variation. The *beguine* can be danced in two manners. One, a two-step with a very tricky little movement from side to side of the head and shoulders, while the lower body swings to each side on slightly bent knees. This is the *beguine* taken from the sixth figure of the *contre-danse* or *haute-taille,* Martinique version of the European contre-danse and quadrille. It is still the *beguine* of the salon, and now and then at the Boule Blanche a couple will separate, and with mincing steps advance toward and recede from each other before closing in the conventional *beguine.* But that is rare. The real *beguine* of the Boule Blanche, the '*beguine-beguine*', is a work of muscular art, with no particular floor pattern . . . Sometimes too, the *beguine* is more fundamental. As with the Negro Delsuc. Delsuc is black. He comes from St. Pierre. He has not long been in Fort de France, and the bright lights are a little intoxicating. But he dances the *beguine* as his grandfather danced the *Thum'bwa'*—intensely, fervently, passionately. He has a good partner . . . They dance the *beguine* as a ritual of fecundity. The consummation is in the dance itself. The conventional two-step has reduced itself to a slight elevation of first one hip then the other—a shifting of the weight. Now their hips are moving and they describe a double circle at opposite ends of a loop—a figure eight—*La Peau Fromage* —*beguine* of the old St. Pierre before the catastrophe. But Delsuc and his partner are dancing only to the tambour and the movement is no longer side to side, but under and up, hips looping on rigid torso, knees bent, heads lowered as they look into each others' eyes, moving a half inch to the right with each under and up movement, each revolution of the abdomen. Strong feet and arches keep the rhythm smooth. They find a pleasure in the artistry of the dance. . . . As the music finishes and the floor clears, without a word they turn apart, seek chairs on the opposite sides of the room, and await the next dance, eyes roving the opposite wall for another partner. The dance ends there for them. They have enjoyed it. They are satisfied in the accomplishment of an artistic feat—in matching techniques . . . Now I dance the *beguine*

. . . . and I find that it is not simply a matter of individual expression; the dance has certain standardized movements, and those who carry it to extreme or take advantages of these movements for an open sex thrill are in disfavor, even at the Boule Blanche.[3]

In interior Jamaica, as well, the "set" dances proceed step by step through 17th century French court forms of minuet only to culminate in a finale, the like of which no French court ever witnessed but which, to the Jamaicans, is part and parcel of the "set" dances. In Haiti, the *Caribinea,* or *contre-danse* is a native adaptation of the European social dance. Innumerable such examples, especially from the French colonies, could be cited. . . .

Thus we see that in the history of the Negro, the transition from tribal to folk culture expressed itself in three ways as far as the dance is concerned: 1. the use of African ritual patterns for the expression of Christian ideology; 2. the degeneration of religious ritual patterns, by virtue of the disintegration of the ideology which sustained them, into secular use; and 3. the combination of secular African patterns with the secular patterns of whatever European nation happened to dominate the territory.

By the time we come to analyze the transition from folk to urban culture, as the next stage in the acculturation of the Negro, the problem becomes more difficult; for by now the patterns are so intermixed, and so dissipated and broken, that tracing them from one complex to another is at times almost impossible. Sometimes the transition is implicit in the difference in the organization, the social procedures which are involved, in the dance as we proceed from country community to urban center.

In Haiti, for example, the common dance of the rum shops and public houses in town is the *meringue.* This might be described under the general term of ballroom dance, but, as is true of the closely related national dances of the other islands, the *meringue* has definitely undergone radical changes in character on being introduced into an urban setting. These dances in town call for no unusual knowledge or skill, and no leader. Men pay to enter an establishment and dance with the women, or buy rum for the privilege of dancing, and leave at will. Here are all young or middle-aged people—people still very active sexually, who seek stimulus and outlet for a definite localized urge.

In the country, the dances which are performed at a "bamboche"— any get-together not connected with any religious rite and not falling

[3] K. Dunham: "Boule Blanche," in *Esquire Magazine,* September, 1939.

into the category of a seasonal dance—are organized differently. The *bamboche* may have, as its primary feature, a wedding celebration, the departure of a notable in the community, part of a feast-day entertainment, or any other excuse. Here, in contrast with the organization of dances in the city, there is a *mait' la danse,* usually one of the best dancers in the neighborhood. He must have a female partner, and she too must be an outstanding dancer. Everyone usually knows each other well. Not only are both young and old equally active, but the older ones usually lead since here the premium is not upon physical attractiveness, but upon skill; and the repertoire of dances is so long and complex that only the older ones are competent to lead. In general, while there is no hierarchy of officials, there is a definite air of something more or less planned, definitely communal. Behavior and sanctions are understood. The dances are not. just accidental or the outgrowth of an urge for personal excitement or expression. They are group dances according to a set pattern, and necessitate a certain amount of skill in execution, the exhibition of which is another factor in bringing these people together.

It is not at all necessary to remain afield for examples of the movement from dance patterns of folk cultures to those of our urban centers. It just so happened that, at the very time that the Lindy Hop was first becoming popular in New York, I myself was in Jamaica, studying the dances there. When I returned to New York and saw the Lindy Hop for the first time, it was apparent to me that almost the entire pattern and certainly many of the specific movements were very similar to those urban Jamaican popular dances known as the *sha-sha,* or *mento* which I had just been recording. This similarity was due, in part, no doubt, to the influence of the Jamaicans who had emigrated to America in increasing numbers. But it was due, also, I feel, to the fact that the patterns and the movements were fundamentally familiar, as part of a deep tradition of folk-dancing, to American Negroes.

Another of our currently popular dance forms, the *"Big Apple,"* seems to me to have its derivation in the category of "circle" dances represented by the plantation "Juba" dance. In its original African form, the *Juba* or *Jumba* or *Majumba,* as it is called in the West Indies, is primarily a competitive dance of skill. One person steps forward in the circle of dancers and begins exhibiting his skill, whereupon he is joined by a member of the opposite sex who joins him in this exhibition. The people in the circle may rotate for a certain number of measures in one direction, then in another for an equal number of measures, or may remain stationary, all the while clapping rhythmically and encouraging the competitors with song and verse. While this pattern is not exclusively African, it is typical. The "Juba," as this dance in a modified form came to be known in America, was a very popular plantation folk dance and a whole tradition of Juba music was evolved in connection with it. No doubt it was influenced, to some extent, by the square dance. Certainly, however, the recently popular "Big Apple" belongs in this tradition and when danced with the particular rhythm and abandon characteristic of such Negro gathering places as the Savoy ballroom in Harlem, assumes an aspect very similar to that of the original *Jumba.*

This detailed consideration of the dances of tribal and folk cultures has been motivated by recognition of the fact that American Negro dance is a product of this particular line of development. The various European influences, the tribal origins, the disintegration of the dance of religious ritual into that of social and finally of individual expression are part of American Negro dance history. But here the dance has developed into the final urban stage under sociological pressures which do not exist to as marked a degree in the West Indies. The entire process has here been accelerated and condensed, not only by the uniquely rapid industrialization of America but also by the position of Negro culture within American society.

We have already discussed in some details those expressions of the transition from dance patterns of tribal to those of folk culture such as the *Calinda* and *Bamboula* in New Orleans, and the dances of the islands off South Carolina. The plantation dances, most of them in the tradition of the circle-and-hand-clapping dances of Africa and influenced, at the same time, by the English square dance and the French quadrille, represent that period of American Negro folk dancing which can be compared to that of the contemporary West Indies. Out of this period emerged the minstrel tradition, which was in essence a forerunner of the urbanization of Negro folk-dance patterns.

The minstrel period of Negro dance is particularly important in that, for the first time, the influence of Negro culture upon the American white culture becomes apparent. Previously it had been the Negro culture which had experienced the effects of foreign influence. The Negro had borrowed from the quadrille just as he had borrowed the finery of American white culture, although, to be sure, he had interpreted them both in his own unique manner. Now the entertainment value of Negro dance and musical expressions became recognized and whereas these forms had previously been repressed[4] or looked upon with completely alien eyes, black-face minstrel bands now began to exploit those very forms.

The rise of the black-face minstrel bands achieved the induction of Negro culture into American culture not in terms of an appreciation of Negro cultural expressions as art forms but on the basis of their entertainment value. This instrument of fusion between the two cultures resulted not only in jazz bands, a fact of American musical history which is well known, but provided the meeting ground for sand-dancing, bucking, and winging on the one hand with the Irish clog on the other. The result was the current, highly-stylized form of tap-dancing. The minstrel bands also served to make the Negro newly conscious of the value of his own expression, and when he saw it adapted by the whites, he drew on his own inventiveness in addition to his store of culture material. It is not merely the inventiveness of the Negro, but this rich background which enters into white American culture and tempers its art forms much as that of the Moors tempered those of Spain.

The Cakewalk tradition may properly be considered the urbanization of the plantation folk-dances, incorporating in the whole such separate figures as the Black Annie, the Pas Mala, the Strut, the Palmer House, and later Walkin' the Dog, Ballin' the Jack, and other individual expressions.

In moving pictures brought back from a West African sojourn Dr. Melville J. Herskovits recorded ceremonial dances, some of the steps of which bore a remarkable resemblance to that popular dance of the post-world war era, the Charleston. Again, in Haiti, I found the Charleston in the dance *La Martinique;* and in terms of the retention of choreographic forms through transition periods, I would say that such a dance must have been known during the North American folk period. I have certainly seen possessed devotees in "store-front" churches propelling themselves up and down the aisles with a practically pure Charleston step. It is not so surprising, then,

[4] The legal measures taken in New Orleans (Asbury: *The French Quarter*) to prohibit the assembly of Negroes for any reason, including dancing, are typical. In 1751 "any assembly of Negroes or Negresses, either under pretext of dancing, or for any other cause" was forbidden entirely. Later, however, "recognizing the value of recreation and a measure of social intercourse in keeping the Negro contented with his lot," the American authorities, following the Louisiana Purchase, permitted assemblies which continued far into the night. This permission was later qualified, in 1817, by an ordinance directing that "the assemblies of slaves for the purpose of dancing or other merriment, shall take place only on Sundays, and solely in such open or public places as shall be appointed by the Mayor." Congo Square was the place appointed for this purpose and such gatherings, held under strict police supervision, were rigidly terminated at sunset. Discontinued after twenty years, this custom was resumed in 1845 on the same basis.

that at one point the Charleston should have become such a popular and general expression of American culture.

Frequently, when watching the variations on the Lindy Hop in the Savoy Ballroom, I have seen individualizations which might have come directly from folk, even tribal, eras; and certainly the great sweep of Latin American dances brings with it choreographic patterns rich in African and Creole African lore.

In America, the inevitable assimilation of the Negro and his cultural traditions into American culture as such has given African tradition a place in a large cultural body which it enjoys nowhere else. While, during the cultural segregation, the African traditions were more modified here than elsewhere, those which persisted now have a sound functional relationship towards a culture which is contemporary, rather than towards one which is on the decline; and therefore such traditions as have been retained are assured of survival as long as the large, strong cultural body of which they are a part survives. With the re-establishment of a functional relationship towards society as a whole (rather than to a cult) the traditions are strengthened and re-emerge with new vigor. The current vogue of West Indian dances, bringing with it a refreshment of African traditions, adds enormously to this resurgence. The curious fact is that it will be the American Negro, in his relatively strong position as part of American culture, who, in the final analysis, will most probably guarantee the persistence of African dance traditions.

WENDELL PHILLIPS DABNEY (1865-   )

Wendell Phillips Dabney, born in Richmond, Virginia, is editor of the Cincinnati *Union,* one of the last of the journals in which the personality of the editor is stronger than the rigorous gathering of the news. He studied at Oberlin and was for many years paymaster for the city of Cincinnati. The columns of the *Union* are filled with chatty, often satiric articles and comment. Dabney has known most of the Negro celebrities in music, the theatre, literature, sports, and politics. His "historical, sociological, and biographical" *Cincinnati's Colored Citizens* appeared in 1926; his *Maggie Walker, Her Life and Deeds* was published in 1927. The selection printed below is used by permission of the author.

A Visit to Dunbar's Tomb

BRR—THE PHONE. I lifted the receiver. "Is that you, Phil?" came a soft, vibrant, masculine voice. "Yes," I answered. "How are you?" "All right." "Do you know who this is?" "Not yet." "Why, my dear boy, 'tis your old friend, M—— C——, president of the National Employment Agency, famous newspaper magnate, and representative of the Negro Press Association." "Welcome to our city. Thought 'twas your gentle voice I heard. Where are you?" "At the Sterling. Come down and take dinner with me." "Who will pay for it?" "Why I will, of course. You may consider me at present a black J. Pierpont Morgan, Jr." "Good. Coming at once."

In ten minutes I was in the Crescent Club suite, Hotel Sterling. Found Col. C—— in great shape financially and physically. The feast was sent over from "The Puritan." The menu, worthy of Lucullus. The service, superb.

It seems that my friend had in a way been emulating Sojourner Truth, Levi Coffin, and other great Underground Railway heroes of antebellum days. They helped slave Negroes to come North, while C—— had been helping free Negroes to the same destination. Said heroes were probably in heaven for their labor of love, while our friend C—— got his here in cold cash. Negro labor was in such great demand that the agents of Southern capitalists tried hard to keep it South, while agents of Northern capitalists were working desperately to get it North. Some one had to run the gauntlet and do seductive missionary work below Mason and Dixon's line, and no one was better fitted in appearance, dramatic ability, diplomacy, and intellectual equipment than M—— C——.

The incidents of this story happened several years ago. M—— had just returned from the cotton fields, doffed the habiliments of that section, and gotten, as he said, in good company by means of the phone and my love for gastronomic delicacies. The dinner over, amid the smoke of perfectos and the aroma of rare, though contraband wine, we talked of celebrities—Negro celebrities if you please—whom we had known. As a matter of fact, there is no real difference between white and black celebrities except the complexion and heights attainable. Internally and temperamentally they are very much alike. Heroes to the general public, but to their friends just good fellows who have reached by the subtle touch of destiny, greater elevation on the ladder of fame. But that's another story.

C—— finally said, "Let's go to Dayton and visit the tomb of

Paul Laurence Dunbar." "Can't get away, C———." "Oh, nonsense, I will stand all the expense," he quickly replied. "You were a good fellow when I was broke." "All right, then, we will go."

The next day, Sunday, we took the train, a parlor car, for our journey of fifty-five miles! Dinner was ordered and we strolled into the diner. Col. C——— was a picture of grandeur. Five feet six inches in height, superabundant tissue uncorsetted, complexion decidedly brunette, hair true to nature. Clad in aristocratic Southern garb, white flannel pants and coat, white silk shirt, soft collar, flowing tie, large Panama hat, sombrero style. Yes, decidedly, C——— was a most imposing personality. No "Wallingford" had a more majestic air. Every functionary with whom he came in contact, black or white, rendered homage, and they were given tips that seemed like golden drips from the Count of Monte Cristo.

We arrived in Dayton. A limousine took us to the tomb. There we sat in contemplation for an hour, though we surreptitiously took several libations in honor of Paul, alternately tossing up as to who should consume his part of the beverage. Inspiration having arrived, Col. C——— walked around the immense boulder, waving his Panama sombrero with one hand, appropriately gesticulating with the other while he quoted Dunbar's death song:

> Lay me down beneaf de willers in de grass,
> Whah de branch'll go a singing as it pass,
> An' w'en I's a-layin' low,
> I kin heah it as it go,
> Singing, 'Sleep my honey, tak your res' at las'.

Despite the charm and beauty of the poem, I kept wondering if Dunbar could see C———'s gestures and kangaroo glide around the tomb. If so, all the sanctity of heaven would not be able to keep him from laughing. Well, everything comes to an end except death and taxes. At last my host said, "Dabney, let's go and see Matilda." "All right," said I, "Is she good-looking, is she brainy, or both?" "Don't you know Matilda?" "No," I replied. "Why, she's Paul Laurence Dunbar's mother." "Oh, yes, I have met her. Do you know her well?" "No, I don't know her at all, but a pilgrimage to the son's tomb would not be complete without paying our respects to his mother." Argument could not change him, so out to the limousine. The driver, impressed by C———'s appearance, had patiently waited three hours.

A plain, two-story brick house. Well did I remember, for it was there "Bob" Troy and I talked and jested with Dunbar only a few days before he died, and it was there we found his repartee as snappy, his wit as scintillating as in the earlier days, when fortune was lavishing upon him her sweetest smiles, her choicest favors.

A touch of the bell, a head thrust from the window, footsteps. The door opened. Around were seated several white ladies, gentlemen and girls. At the end of the room was Mrs. Dunbar, Paul's mother. Her dark face, thin, attenuated, surrounded by a halo of snow-white hair, brought to mind the ancient mothers of our race, unspoiled, unsoiled by the debasing touch of serfdom. She was rendered every reverence, upon her was riveted every eye, 'til C—— came. Into the limelight, "armed and eager for the fray," he leaped. With one sweep of the arm he drew attention, then calmly announced, "Mrs. Matilda Dunbar, ladies and gentlemen, this is my friend Wendell Phillips Dabney, paymaster of Cincinnati, newspaper editor, ex-musician and a friend of Paul's. That's all. Everybody knows me. I am M—— C——, Paul's old chum and roommate. He always called me 'Nappy M——', in jovial allusion to the abnormal curling propensity of my hair, which has always run true to form. He taught me to read his poetry as he read it, and I bar no one in this wide, wide world when it comes to its rendition and interpretation." A hush fell upon the audience. Paul's mother was forgotten. A tall, blonde young lady said, "Mr. C——, I am so glad you came. I'm going to read at our college celebration one of Mr. Dunbar's poems, entitled: 'When Malindy Sings'." C—— said, "I will teach you how to read it right now." "Thank you so much, Mr. C——," she replied. "Here is my book." "No! No!" said C——. "I only get the real inspiration when I read from some book Paul has handled." So Paul's aunt went upstairs, although his mother protested vigorously against what she evidently considered a desecration. C—— read the poem. After modestly acknowledging the thunders of applause, he said, "The subject of that poem was his dear, old mother."

"The dear, old mother" angrily remarked: "Strange I never heard that before; 'tis a wonder he didn't tell me something about it. My name ain't Malindy."

C—— said, "My dear madam, that's not at all strange. He told me many things he never told you or anybody else."

That settled the matter. C—— then read another poem about slavery times. After the usual plaudits, he made this statement: "There were some very bright spots in those good old days." "Hold on there," cried Mrs. Dunbar, starting up, outstretched arms, blazing eyes. "Don't you dare tell me there was anything good about slavery. Were you ever a slave?"

"No, ma'am," quickly said C——. "I didn't say slavery was good; I said some of the days were good."

"Don't you dare tell me," she repeated, "that there was anything good about it. I was a slave, taken from my mother when only seven years old, worked in the fields, whipped and beaten like a dog. I ran away and escaped, starved in the woods for weeks, as I stole from place to place, until I got far away from those slaveholding brutes! Don't you dare tell me there's anything good about slavery."

She fell back exhausted. It was a most embarrassing moment for everybody but C———. He stepped into the silence as bravely as Napoleon ordered a charge of "the Old Guard."

"Ahem, ahem!" He cleared his throat. "Ladies and gentlemen, I am awfully glad that you are here. It makes me feel that Paul is near." He then talked about the wonderful tomb, the depth of the many poems, the fascinations permeating the short stories of Dunbar, and the hypnotic glamor engendered by their perusal.

The people finally got up to go, and as C——— ushered them out and walked on the front porch inviting them to call again, Mrs. Dunbar said to me, "I often heard Paul speak of you, and I remember you coming here, but who in the name of God is that man with you? I never saw him before," she said, "and I don't care if I never see him again. He has taken entire possession of my house. Why listen, he is inviting them to call again. Where in the world did he come from?"

C——— returned and made mention of another subject, which was taboo. More fireworks. C——— survived, as calmly cool as Stonewall Jackson amid the hail and shell of battle. We said goodbye to the few persons left behind, and again took the limousine that lingered so patiently in its dalliance upon greatness.

I was very quiet. C——— was voluble, verbose and as usual, full of pose and poise. "Oh what thinkest thou, Dabney," said he. "Of thee," said I. "You have the d——est amount of gall and nerve that in my half century and ten years of life, among every grade, class, kind, and color of man, I have ever seen. I take off my hat to the one and only, M——— C———! When God created you, C———, he broke the mold in order that there should be left no other real specimen of your kind!—Selah."

> There may be some few
> Who remind us of thee,
> But they are imitations
> As your friends can well see.

The thirty bucks demanded by the limousine were grandly paid. To each other we sadly said au revoir. " 'Twas the end of a perfect day." He went to New York and to Cincinnati returned Dabney.

WALTER WHITE (1893   )

Walter White's name, more than any other, is associated with the fight to stamp out lynching in America (see also p. 181). His *The Fire in the Flint* (1925) is still one of America's most powerful lynching novels, though the subject has since attracted numerous novelists, white and Negro. His *Rope and Faggot: A Biography of Judge Lynch* (1929), written on a Guggenheim fellowship, was the first important study of the phenomenon of lynching. "I Investigate Lynching" is a record of White's personal investigations of lynching. White has had many similar experiences since which have not been, and perhaps cannot be, collected in print. White is what many call a "voluntary" Negro, that is, a Negro who cannot be distinguished from white. "I Investigate Lynchings" is reprinted by permission of the author and the *American Mercury,* in which it first appeared.

I Investigate Lynchings

NOTHING CONTRIBUTES SO MUCH to the continued life of an investigator of lynchings and his tranquil possession of all his limbs as the obtuseness of the lynchers themselves. Like most boastful people who practice direct action when it involves no personal risk, they just can't help talk about their deeds to any person who manifests even the slightest interest in them.

Most lynchings take place in small towns and rural regions where the natives know practically nothing of what is going on outside their own immediate neighborhoods. Newspapers, books, magazines, theatres, visitors and other vehicles for the transmission of information and ideas are usually as strange among them as dry-point etchings. But those who live in so sterile an atmosphere usually esteem their own perspicacity in about the same degree as they are isolated from the world of ideas. They gabble on *ad infinitum,* apparently unable to keep from talking.

In any American village, North or South, East or West, there is no problem which cannot be solved in half an hour by the morons who lounge about the village store. World peace, or the lack of it, the tariff, sex, religion, the settlement of the war debts, short skirts, Prohibition, the carryings-on of the younger generation, the superior moral rectitude of country people over city dwellers (with a wistful eye on urban sins)—all these controversial subjects are disposed of quickly and finally by the bucolic wise men. When to their isolation is added an emotional fixation such as the rural South has on the Negro, one can sense the atmosphere from which spring the Heflins, the Ku Kluxers, the two-gun Bible-beaters, the lynchers and the anti-evolutionists. And one can see why no great amount of cleverness or courage is needed to acquire information in such a forlorn place about the latest lynching.

Professor Earle Fiske Young of the University of Southern California recently analyzed the lynching returns from fourteen Southern States for thirty years. He found that in counties of less than 10,000 people there was a lynching rate of 3.2 per 100,000 of population; that in those of from 10,000 to 20,000 the rate dropped to 2.4; that in those of from 20,000 to 30,000, it was 2.1 per cent; that in those of from 30,000 to 40,000, it was 1.7, and that thereafter it kept on going down until in counties with from 300,000 to 800,000 population it was only 0.05.

Of the forty-one lynchings and eight race riots I have investigated for the National Association for the Advancement of Colored People during the past ten years all of the lynchings and seven of the riots occurred in rural or semi-rural communities. The towns ranged in population from around one hundred to ten thousand or so. The lynchings were not difficult to inquire into because of the fact already noted that those who perpetrated them were in nearly every instance simple-minded and easily fooled individuals. On but three occasions were suspicions aroused by my too definite questions or by informers who had seen me in other places. These three times I found it rather desirable to disappear slightly in advance of reception committees imbued with the desire to make an addition to the lynching record. One other time the possession of a light skin and blue eyes (though I consider myself a colored man) almost cost me my life when (it was during the Chicago race riots in 1919) a Negro shot at me thinking me to be a white man.

II

In 1918 a Negro woman, about to give birth to a child, was lynched with almost unmentionable brutality along with ten men in Georgia. I reached the scene shortly after the butchery and while excitement yet ran high. It was a prosperous community. Forests of pine trees gave rich returns in turpentine, tar and pitch. The small towns where the farmers and turpentine hands traded were fat and rich. The main streets of the largest of these towns were well paved and lighted. The stores were well stocked. The white inhabitants belonged to the class of Georgia crackers—lanky, slow of movement and of speech, long-necked, with small eyes set close together, and skin tanned by the hot sun to a reddish-yellow hue.

As I was born in Georgia and spent twenty years of my life there, my accent is sufficiently Southern to enable me to talk with Southerners and not arouse their suspicion that I am an outsider. (In the rural South hatred of Yankees is not much less than hatred of Negroes.) On the morning of my arrival in the town I casually dropped into the store of one of the general merchants who, I had been informed, had been one of the leaders of the mob. After making a small purchase I engaged the merchant in conversation. There was, at the time, no other customer in the store. We spoke of the weather, the possibility of good crops in the Fall, the political situation, the latest news from the war in Europe. As his manner became more and more friendly I ventured to mention guardedly the recent lynchings.

Instantly he became cautious—until I hinted that I had great admiration for the manly spirit the men of the town had exhibited. I mentioned the newspaper accounts I had read and confessed that I had never been so fortunate as to see a lynching. My words or tone seemed to disarm his suspicion. He offered me a box on which to sit, drew up another one for himself, and gave me a bottle of Coca-Cola.

"You'll pardon me, Mister," he began, "for seeming suspicious but we have to be careful. In ordinary times we wouldn't have anything to worry about, but with the war there's been some talk of the Federal government looking into lynchings. It seems there's some sort of law during wartime making it treason to lower the man power of the country."

"In that case I don't blame you for being careful," I assured him. "But couldn't the Federal government do something if it wanted to when a lynching takes place, even if no war is going on at the moment?"

"Naw," he said, confidently, obviously proud of the opportunity of displaying his store of information to one whom he assumed knew nothing whatever about the subject. "There's no such law, in spite of all the agitation by a lot of fools who don't know the niggers as we do. States' rights won't permit Congress to meddle in lynching in peace time."

"But what about your State government—your Governor, your sheriff, your police officers?"

"Humph! Them? We elected them to office, didn't we? And the niggers, we've got them disfranchised, ain't we? Sheriffs and police and Governors and prosecuting attorneys have got too much sense to mix in lynching-bees. If they do they know they might as well give up all idea of running for office any more—if something worse don't happen to them——" This last with a tightening of the lips and a hard look in the eyes.

I sought to lead the conversation into less dangerous channels. "Who was the white man who was killed—whose killing caused the lynchings?" I asked.

"Oh, he was a hard one, all right. Never paid his debts to white men or niggers and wasn't liked much around here. He was a mean 'un, all right, all right."

"Why, then, did you lynch the niggers for killing such a man?"

"It's a matter of safety—we gotta show niggers that they mustn't touch a white man, no matter how low-down and ornery he is."

Little by little he revealed the whole story. When he told of the manner in which the pregnant woman had been killed he chuckled and slapped his thigh and declared it to be "the best show, Mister, I ever did see. You ought to have heard the wench howl when we strung her up."

Covering the nausea the story caused me as best I could, I slowly gained the whole story, with the names of the other participants. Among them were prosperous farmers, business men, bankers, newspaper reporters and editors, and several law enforcement officers.

My several days of discreet inquiry began to arouse suspicions in the town. On the third day of my stay I went once more into the store of the man with whom I had first talked. He asked me to wait until he had finished serving the sole customer. When she had gone he came from behind the counter and with secretive manner and lowered voice he asked, "You're a government man, ain't you?" (An agent of the Federal Department of Justice was what he meant.)

"Who said so?" I countered.

"Never mind who told me; I know one when I see him," he replied, with a shrewd harshness in his face and voice.

Ignorant of what might have taken place since last I had talked with him, I thought it wise to learn all I could and say nothing which might commit me. "Don't you tell anyone I am a government man; if I *am* one, you're the only one in town who knows it," I told him cryptically. I knew that within an hour everybody in town would share his "information."

An hour or so later I went at nightfall to the little but not uncomfortable hotel where I was staying. As I was about to enter a Negro approached me and, with an air of great mystery, told me that he had just heard a group of white men discussing me and declaring that if I remained in the town overnight "something would happen" to me.

The thought raced through my mind before I replied that it was hardly likely that, following so terrible a series of lynchings, a Negro would voluntarily approach a supposedly white man whom he did not know and deliver such a message. He had been sent, and no doubt the persons who sent him were white and for some reason did not dare tackle me themselves. Had they dared there would have been no warning in advance—simply an attack. Though I had no weapon with me, it occurred to me that there was no reason why two should not play at the game of bluffing. I looked straight into my informant's eyes and said, in as convincing a tone as I could muster: "You go back to the ones who sent you and tell them this: that I have a damned good automatic and I know how to use it. If anybody attempts to molest me tonight or any other time, somebody is going to get hurt."

That night I did not take off my clothes nor did I sleep. Ordinarily in such small Southern towns everyone is snoring by nine o'clock. That night, however, there was much passing and re-passing of the hotel. I learned afterward that the merchant had, as I expected, told generally that I was an agent of the Department of Justice, and my empty threat had served to reinforce his assertion. The Negro had been sent to me in the hope that I might be frightened enough to leave before I had secured evidence against the members of the mob. I remained in the town two more days. My every movement was watched, but I was not molested. But when, later, it became known that not only was I not an agent of the Department of Justice but a Negro, the fury of the inhabitants of the region was unlimited—particularly when it was found that evidence I gathered had been placed in the hands of the Governor of Georgia. It happened that he was a man genuinely eager to stop lynching—but restrictive laws against which he had appealed in vain effectively prevented him from acting upon the evidence. And the Federal government declared itself unable to proceed against the lynchers.

III

In 1926 I went to a Southern State for a New York newspaper to inquire into the lynching of two colored boys and a colored woman. Shortly after reaching the town I learned that a certain lawyer knew something about the lynchers. He proved to be the only specimen I have ever encountered in much travelling in the South of the

Southern gentleman so beloved by fiction writers of the older school. He had heard of the lynching before it occurred and, fruitlessly, had warned the judge and the prosecutor. He talked frankly about the affair and gave me the names of certain men who knew more about it than he did. Several of them lived in a small town nearby where the only industry was a large cotton mill. When I asked him if he would go with me to call on these people he peered out of the window at the descending sun and said, somewhat anxiously, I thought, "I will go with you if you will promise to get back to town before sundown."

I asked why there was need of such haste. "No one would harm a respectable and well-known person like yourself, would they?" I asked him.

"Those mill hands out there would harm anybody," he answered.

I promised him we would be back before sundown—a promise that was not hard to make, for if they would harm this man I could imagine what they would do to a stranger!

When we reached the little mill town we passed through it and, ascending a steep hill, our car stopped in front of a house perched perilously on the side of the hill. In the yard stood a man with iron gray hair and eyes which seemed strong enough to bore through concrete. The old lawyer introduced me and we were invited into the house. As it was a cold afternoon in late Autumn the gray-haired man called a boy to build a fire.

I told him frankly I was seeking information about the lynching. He said nothing but left the room. Perhaps two minutes later, hearing a sound at the door through which he had gone, I looked up and there stood a figure clad in the full regalia of the Ku Klux Klan. I looked at the figure and the figure looked at me. The hood was then removed and, as I suspected, it was the owner of the house."

"I show you this," he told me, "so you will know that what I tell you is true."

This man, I learned, had been the organizer and kleagle of the local Klan. He had been quite honest in his activities as a Kluxer, for corrupt officials and widespread criminal activities had caused him and other local men to believe that the only cure rested in a secret extra-legal organization. But he had not long been engaged in promoting the plan before he had the experience of other believers in Klan methods. The very people whose misdeeds the organization was designed to correct gained control of it. This man then resigned and ever since had been living in fear of his life. He took me into an adjoining room after removing his Klan robe and there showed me a considerable collection of revolvers, shot guns, rifles and ammunition.

We then sat down and I listened to as hair-raising a tale of Nordic moral endeavor as it has ever been my lot to hear. Among the choice bits were stories such as this: The sheriff of an adjoining county the year before had been a candidate for reëlection. A certain man of considerable wealth had contributed largely to his campaign fund, providing the margin by which he was reëlected. Shortly afterwards a married woman with whom the sheriff's supporter had been intimate quarreled one night with her husband. When the cuckold charged his wife with infidelity, the gentle creature waited until he was asleep, got a large butcher knife, and then artistically carved him up. Bleeding more profusely than a pig in the stock yards, the man dragged himself to the home of a neighbor several hundred yards distant and there died on the door-step. The facts were notorious, but the sheriff effectively blocked even interrogation of the widow!

I spent some days in the region and found that the three Negroes who had been lynched were about as guilty of the murder of which they were charged as I was. Convicted in a court thronged with armed Klansmen and sentenced to death, their case had been appealed to the State Supreme Court, which promptly reversed the conviction, remanded the appellants for new trials, and severely criticized the judge before whom they had been tried. At the new trial the evidence against one of the defendants so clearly showed his innocence that the judge granted a motion to dismiss, and the other two defendants were obviously as little guilty as he. But as soon as the motion to dismiss was granted the defendant was rearrested on a trivial charge and once again lodged in jail. That night the mob took the prisoners to the outskirts of the town, and told them to run, and as they set out pumped bullets into their backs. The two boys died instantly. The woman was shot in several places, but was not immediately killed. One of the lynchers afterwards laughingly told me that "we had to waste fifty bullets on the wench before one of them stopped her howling."

Evidence in affidavit form indicated rather clearly that various law enforcement officials, including the sheriff, his deputies, various jailers and policemen, three relatives of the then Governor of the State, a member of the State Legislature and sundry individuals prominent in business, political and social life of the vicinity, were members of the mob.

The revelation of these findings after I had returned to New York did not add to my popularity in the lynching region. Public sentiment in the State itself, stirred up by several courageous newspapers, began to make it uncomfortable for the lynchers. When the sheriff found things getting a bit too unpleasant he announced that he was going to ask the grand jury to indict me for "bribery and passing for white." It developed that the person I was supposed to have paid money to for execution of an affidavit was a man I had never seen in the flesh, the affidavit having been secured by the reporter of a New York newspaper.

An amusing tale is connected with the charge of passing. Many years ago a bill was introduced in the Legislature of that State defining legally as a Negro any person who had one drop or more of Negro blood. Acrimonious debate in the lower house did not prevent passage of the measure, and the same result seemed likely in the State Senate. One of the Senators, a man destined eventually to go to the United States Senate on a campaign of vilification of the Negro, rose at a strategic point to speak on the bill. As the story goes, his climax was: "If you go on with this bill you will bathe every county in blood before nightfall. And, what's more, there won't be enough white people left in the State to pass it."

When the sheriff threatened me with an indictment for passing as white, a white man in the State with whom I had talked wrote me a long letter asking me if it were true that I had Negro blood. "You did not tell me nor anyone else in my presence," he wrote, "that you were white except as to your name. I had on amber-colored glasses and did not take the trouble to scrutinize your color, but I really did take you for a white man and, according to the laws of ————, you may be." My informant urged me to sit down and figure out mathematically the exact percentage of Negro blood that I possessed and, if it proved to be less than one-eighth, to sue for libel those who had charged me with passing.

This man wrote of the frantic efforts of the whites of his State to keep themselves thought of as white. He quoted an old law to the effect that "it was not slander to call one a Negro because everybody could see that he was not; but it was slanderous to call him a mulatto."

IV

On another occasion a serious race riot occurred in Tulsa, Okla., a bustling town of 100,000 inhabitants. In the early days Tulsa had been a lifeless and unimportant village of not more than five thousand people, and its Negro residents had been forced to live in what was considered the least desirable section of the village, down near the railroad. Then oil was discovered nearby and almost overnight the village grew into a prosperous town. The Negroes prospered along with the whites, and began to erect comfortable homes, business establishments, a hotel, two cinemas and other enterprises, all of these springing up in the section to which they had been relegated. This was, as I have said, down near the railroad tracks. The swift growth of the town made this hitherto disregarded land of great value for business purposes. Efforts to purchase the land from the Negro owners at prices far below its value were unavailing. Having built up the neighborhood and knowing its value, the owners refused to be victimized.

One afternoon in 1921 a Negro messenger boy went to deliver a package in an office building on the main street of Tulsa. His errand done, he rang the bell for the elevator in order that he might descend. The operator, a young white girl, on finding that she had been summoned by a Negro, opened the door of the car ungraciously. Two versions there are of what happened then. The boy declared that she started the car on its downward plunge when he was only halfway in, and that to save himself from being killed he had to throw himself into the car, stepping on the girl's foot in doing so. The girl, on the other hand, asserted that the boy attempted to rape her in the elevator. The latter story, at best, seemed highly dubious—that an attempted criminal assault would be made by any person in an open elevator of a crowded office building on the main street of a town of 100,000 inhabitants—and in open daylight!

Whatever the truth, the local press, with scant investigation, published lurid accounts of the alleged assault. That night a mob started to the jail to lynch the Negro boy. A group of Negroes offered their services to the jailer and sheriff in protecting the prisoner. The offer was declined, and when the Negroes started to leave the sheriff's office a clash occurred between them and the mob. Instantly the mob swung into action.

The Negroes, outnumbered, were forced back to their own neighborhood. Rapidly the news spread of the clash and the numbers of mobbers grew hourly. By daybreak of the following day the mob numbered around five thousand, and was armed with machine-guns, dynamite, rifles, revolvers and shotguns, cans of gasoline and kerosene, and—such are the blessings of invention!—airplanes. Surrounding the Negro section, it attacked, led by men who had been officers in the American army in France. Outnumbered and out-equipped, the plight of the Negroes was a hopeless one from the beginning. Driven further and further back, many of them were killed or wounded, among them an aged man and his wife, who were slain as they knelt at prayer for deliverance. Forty-four blocks of property were burned after homes and stores had been pillaged.

I arrived in Tulsa while the excitement was at its peak. Within a few hours I met a commercial photographer who had worked for five years on a New York newspaper and he welcomed me with open arms when he found that I represented a New York paper. From him I learned that special deputy sheriffs were being sworn in to guard the town from a rumored counter attack by the Negroes. It occurred to me that I could get myself sworn in as one of these deputies.

It was even easier to do this than I had expected. That evening in the City Hall I had to answer only three questions—name, age, and address. I might have been a thug, a murderer, an escaped convict, a member of the mob itself which had laid waste a large area of the city—none of these mattered; my skin was apparently white, and that was enough. After we—some fifty or sixty of us—had been sworn in, solemnly declaring we would do our utmost to uphold the laws and constitutions of the United States and the State of Oklahoma, a villainous-looking man next me turned and remarked casually, even with a note of happiness in his voice: "Now you can go out and shoot any nigger you see and the law'll be behind you."

As we stood in the wide marble corridor of the not unimposing City Hall waiting to be assigned to automobiles which were to patrol the city during the night, I noticed a man, clad in the uniform of a captain of the United States Army, watching me closely. I imagined I saw in his very swarthy face (he was much darker than I, but was classed as a white man while I am deemed a Negro) mingled inquiry and hostility. I kept my eye on him without appearing to do so. Tulsa would not have been a very healthy place for me that night had my race or my previous investigations of other race riots been known there. At last the man seemed certain he knew me and started toward me.

He drew me aside into a deserted corner on the excuse that he had something he wished to ask me, and I noticed that four other men with whom he had been talking detached themselves from the crowd and followed us.

Without further introduction or apology my dark-skinned newly-made acquaintance, putting his face close to mine and looking into my eyes with a steely, unfriendly glance, demanded challengingly: "You say that your name is White?"

I answered affirmatively.

"You say you're a newspaper man?"

"Yes, I represent the New York———. Would you care to see my credentials?"

"No, but I want to tell you something. There's an organization in the South that doesn't love niggers. It has branches everywhere. You needn't ask me the name—I can't tell you. But it has come back into existence to fight this damned nigger Advancement Association. We watch every movement of the officers of this nigger society and we're out to get them for putting notions of equality into the heads of our niggers down South here."

There could be no question that he referred to the Ku Klux Klan on the one hand and the National Association for the Advancement of Colored People on the other. As coolly as I could, the circumstances being what they were, I took a cigarette from my case and lighted it, trying to keep my hand from betraying my nervousness. When he finished speaking I asked him:

"All this is very interesting, but what, if anything, has it to do with the story of the race riot here which I've come to get?"

For a full minute we looked straight into each other's eyes, his four companions meanwhile crowding close about us. At length his eyes fell. With a shrug of his shoulders and a half-apologetic smile, he replied as he turned away, "Oh, nothing except I wanted you to know what's back of the trouble here."

It is hardly necessary to add that all that night, assigned to the same car with this man and his four companions, I maintained a considerable vigilance. When the news stories I wrote about the riot (the boy accused of attempted assault was acquitted in the magistrate's court after nearly one million dollars of property and a number of lives had been destroyed) revealed my identity—that I was a Negro and an officer of the Advancement Society—more than a hundred anonymous letters threatening my life came to me. I was also threatened with a suit for criminal libel by a local paper, but nothing came of it after my willingness to defend it was indicated.

V

A narrower escape came during an investigation of an alleged plot by Negroes in Arkansas to "massacre" all the white people of the State. It later developed that the Negroes had simply organized a cooperative society to combat their economic exploitation by landlords, merchants, and bankers, many of whom openly practiced peonage. I went as a representative of a Chicago newspaper to get the facts. Going first to the capital of the State, Little Rock, I interviewed the Governor and other officials and then proceeded to the scene of the trouble, Phillips county, in the heart of the cotton-raising area close to the Mississippi.

As I stepped from the train at Elaine, the county seat, I was closely watched by a crowd of men. Within half an hour of my arrival I had been asked by two shopkeepers, a restaurant waiter, and a ticket agent why I had come to Elaine, what my business was, and what I thought of the recent riot. The tension relaxed somewhat when I implied I was in sympathy with the mob. Little by little suspicion was lessened and then, the people being eager to have a metropolitan newspaper give their side of the story, I was shown "evidence" that the story of the massacre plot was well-founded, and not very clever attempts were made to guide me away from the truth.

Suspicion was given new birth when I pressed my inquiries too insistently concerning the share-cropping and tenant-farming system, which works somewhat as follows: Negro farmers enter into agreements to till specified plots of land, they do receive usually half of the crop for their labor. Should they be too poor to buy food, seed, clothing and other supplies, they are supplied these commodities by their landlords at designated stores. When the crop is gathered the landowner takes it and sells it. By declaring that he has sold it at a figure far below the market price and by refusing to give itemized accounts of the supplies purchased during the year by the tenant, a landlord can (and in that region almost always does) so arrange it that the bill for supplies always exceeds the tenant's share of the crop. Individual Negroes who had protested against such thievery had been lynched. The new organization was simply a union to secure relief through the courts, which relief those who profited from the system meant to prevent. Thus the story of a "massacre" plot.

Suspicion of me took definite form when word was sent to Phillips county from Little Rock that it has been discovered that I was a Negro, though I knew nothing about the message at the time. I walked down West Cherry street, the main thoroughfare of Elaine, one day on my way to the jail, where I had an appointment with the sheriff, who was going to permit me to interview some of the Negro prisoners who were charged with being implicated in the alleged plot. A tall, heavy-set Negro passed me and, *sotto voce,* told me as he passed that he had something important to tell me, and that I should turn to the right at the next corner and follow him. Some inner sense bade me obey. When we had got out of sight of other persons the Negro told me not to go to the jail, that there was great hostility in the town against me and that they planned harming me. In the man's manner there was something which made me certain he was telling the truth. Making my way to the railroad station, since my interview with the prisoners, (the sheriff and jailer being present,) was unlikely to add anything to my story, I was able to board one of the two trains a day out of Elaine. When I explained to the conductor—he looked at me so inquiringly—that I had no ticket because delays in Elaine had given me no time to purchase one, he exclaimed. "Why, Mister, you're leaving just when the fun is going to start! There's a damned yaller nigger down here passing for white and the boys are going to have some fun with him."

I asked him the nature of the fun.

"Wall, when they get through with him," he explained grimly, "he won't pass for white no more."

IRA DeA. REID (1901-)

Ira DeA. Reid, born at Clifton Forge, Virginia, was educated at Morehouse, the University of Pittsburgh, and Columbia. He has taught in Texas, West Virginia, and at Atlanta University, where he is now professor of sociology. He is the author of a number of local studies, such as *The Negro in New Jersey*, and of *The Negro Immigrant* (1939), *Negro Youth, Their Social and Economic Background* (1939), *In a Minor Key* (1940), and with Arthur Raper, of *Sharecroppers All* (1941). "Mrs. Bailey Pays the Rent" is from *Ebony and Topaz* and is here reprinted by permission of the author and of the National Urban League.

Mrs. Bailey Pays the Rent

"Won't you come home Bill Bailey?
    Won't you come home,"
She mourns the whole day long.
"I'll do the cooking, I'll pay the rent,
    I know I've done you wrong.
Remember that rainy evening
    I drove you out,
With nothing but a fine tooth comb?
    Ain't that a shame,
    I know I'm to blame,
Bill Bailey, won't you please come home?"

                    —Old popular song.

FOR MANY YEARS it has been the custom of certain portions of the Negro group living in Southern cities to give some form of party when money was needed to supplement the family income. The purpose for giving such a party was never stated, but who cared whether the increment was used to pay the next installment on the "Steinway" piano, or the weekly rent? On the one hand, these parties were the life of many families of a low economic status who sought to confine their troubles with a little joy. On the other hand, they were a wild form of commercialized recreation in its primary stages. Humor was the counterpart of their irony.

No social standing was necessary to promote these affairs. Neither was one forced to have a long list of friends. All that the prospective host required to "throw" such an affair would be a good piano player and a few girls. Of course you paid an admission fee—usually ten cents—which was for the benefit of some Ladies Auxiliary—though it may have been an auxiliary to that particular house. The music invited you, and the female of the species urged that you remain. The neighborhood girls came unescorted, but seldom left without an escort. Dancing was the diversion and there is no reason to doubt that these affairs were properly named "SHIN-DIGS."

There was "Beaver Slide," that supposedly rough section of the Negro district, situated in the hollow between two typically Georgian Hills. Here lived a more naïve group of Negroes whose sociables were certain to make the passers by take notice. The motto for their affairs seemed to be "Whosoever will, let him come, and may the survived survive." Twenty to thirty couples packed into two small rooms, "slow-dragging" to the plaintive blues of the piano player, whose music had a bass accompaniment furnished by his feet. The piano was opened top and front that the strains may be more distinct, and that the artist may have the joy of seeing as well as hearing his deft touches (often played by "ear") reflected in the mechanics of the instrument. They were a free "joy-unconfined" group. Their conventions were their own. If they wished to guffaw they did—if they wished to fight they did. But they chiefly danced—not with the aloofness of a modern gigolo but with fervor. What a picture they presented! Women in ginghams or cheap finery, men in peg top trousers, silk shirts, "loud" arm bands, and the ever present tan shoes with the "bull dog" toe. Feet stamped merrily—songs sung cheerily—No blues writer can ever record accurately the tones and words of those songs—they are to be heard and not written—bodies sweating, struggling in their effort to get the most of the dance; a drink of "lightning" to accelerate the enthusiasm—floors creaking and sagging —everybody happy.

During the dance as well as the intermission, you bought your refreshments. This was a vital part of the evening's enjoyment. But what food you could get for a little money! Each place had its specialties—"Hoppinjohn," (rice and black-eyed peas) or Mulatto rice (rice and tomatoes), Okra gumbo, Sweet potato pone—sometimes Chicken —Chitterlings—Hog maws—or other strictly southern dishes. You ate your fill. Dancing was resumed and continued until all were ready to leave—or it had suddenly ended in a brawl causing the "Black Maria" to take some to the station house and the police sending the remaining folk to their respective homes.

And there were those among us who had a reverential respect for such affairs. At that time there was no great popularity attached to a study of the Negro in his social environment. These were just plain folks having a good time. On the other hand, they were capable of description, and to those of us who knew, they were known as "struggles," "break-downs," "razor-drills," "flop-wallies" and "chitterling parties." They were in fact as well as in fancy. It was a struggle to dance in those crowded little rooms, while one never knew if the cheaply constructed flooring would collapse in the midst of its sagging and creaking. What assurance did one have that the glistening steel of a razor or "switch blade" would not flash before the evening's play was done? And very often chitterlings were served—yet by the time forty sweating bodies had danced in a small parlor with one window— a summer's evening—and continued to dance—well the party still deserved that name. But Mrs. Bailey paid her rent.

NEWS ITEM: Growing out of economic stress, this form of nocturnal diversion has taken root in Harlem—that section known as the world's largest Negro centre. It's correct and more dignified name is "Parlor Social," but in the language of the street, it is caustically referred to as a "house rent party."

With the mass movement of Southern Negroes to Northern Cities, came their little custom. Harlem was astounded. Socially minded individuals claimed that the H. C. L. with the relative insufficiency of wages was entirely responsible for this ignominious situation; that the exorbitant rents paid by the Negro wage earners had given rise to the obnoxious "house rent party." The truth seemed to be that the old-party of the South had attired itself à la Harlem. Within a few years the custom developed into a business venture whereby a tenant sought to pay a rent four, five and six times as great as was paid in the South.

It developed by-products both legal and otherwise, hence it became extremely popular.

Yes sir thats my baby and I don't mean maybe
you will find her at
A SOCIAL WHIST PARTY
given by
MRS. EMILY WILLIAMS
at 124 West 135th Street, Apt. 26
on Thursday evening, November 26, 1925
Music by Prof. Campbell
Refreshments Served
bring your friends

Papa is mad about the way you do,
So meet the gang and Skoodle um Skoo at
A SOCIAL WHIST PARTY
to be given
At the residence of JAS. BENEFIELD
At 20 West 134th Street ground fl. E.
Saturday evening Sept. 3rd 1927
Good Music   Refreshments served

If you cant Charleston or do the pigeon
Wing You sure can shake that thing at a
SOCIAL PARTY
given by
STEWART & HOLTON
6 Bradhurst Ave.
Saturday Evening. Sept. 25, '26
Good Music and Refreshments

Save your tears for a rainy day,
We are giving a party where you can play
With red mammas and too bad Sheabas
Who wear their dresses above their knees
And mess around with whom they please.
At a
SOCIAL PARTY
Given by
Mrs. Helen Carter & Mrs. Mandy Wesley
Sept. 24th, 1927   at 227 West 18th St.
1 flight up   Back
GOOD MUSIC   REFRESHMENTS

Leaving me, Papa, it's hard to do,
because Mama done put that thing on
you.
A NOVELTY MATINEE DANCE
by
CHINK
116 West 144th Street.   Apt. 27
Sunday, June 27th from 4 until ?
Plenty Music   Refreshments served
—Printing Studio 79 West 131st Street

Papa, if you want to see Mama do the Black
Bottom, come to
A SOCIAL PARTY
given by
MRS. KELLY
8 WEST 134th STREET, 1 flight, west side
Saturday Evening, February 5, 1927
Good Music   Refreshments served

There has been an evolution in the éclat of the rent party since it has become "Harlemized." The people have seen a new light, and are no longer wont to have it go unnamed. They called it a "Parlor Social." That term, however, along with "Rent Party" is for the spoken word. "Social Whist Party" looks much better in print and has become the prevailing terminology. Nor is its name restricted to these. Others include "Social Party," "Too Terrible Party," "Too Bad Party," "Matinee Party," "Parlor Social," "Whist Party," and "Social Entertainment." And, along with the change in nomenclature has come a change in technique. No longer does the entrepreneur depend upon the music to welcome his stranger guests; nor does he simply invite friends of the neighborhood. The rent party ticket now turns the trick.

There straggles along the cross-town streets of North Harlem a familiar figure. A middle aged white man, bent from his labor as the Wayside Printer, is pushing a little cart which has all of the equipment necessary for setting up the rent party ticket. The familiar tinkle of his bell in the late afternoon brings the representative of some family to his side. While you wait, he sets up your invitation with the bally-hoo heading desired, and at a very reasonable price. The grammar and the English may be far from correct, but they meet all business requirements since they bring results. What work the Wayside Printer does not get goes to the nearest print shop; some of which specialize in these announcements.

A true specimen of the popular mind is expressed in these tickets.

The heading may be an expression from a popular song, a slang phrase, a theatrical quip or "poetry." A miscellaneous selection gives us the following: "Come and Get it Fixed"; "Leaving Me Papa, It's Hard To Do Because Mama Done Put That Thing On You"; "If You Can't Hold Your Man, Don't Cry After He's Gone, Just Find Another"; "Clap Your Hands Here Comes Charlie and He's Bringing Your Dinah Too"; "Old Uncle Joe, the Jelly Roll King is Back in Town and is Shaking That Thing"; "Here I am Again. Who? Daddy Jelly Roll and His Jazz Hounds"; "It's Too Bad Jim, But if You Want To Find a Sweet Georgia Brown, Come to the House of Mystery"; "You Don't Get Nothing for Being an Angel Child, So you Might as Well Get Real Busy and Real Wild."

And at various parties we find special features, among them being "Music by the Late Kidd Morgan"; "Music by Kid Professor, the Father of the Piano"; "Music by Blind Johnny"; "Music by Kid Lippy"; "Skinny At the Traps"; "Music Galore"; "Charge de Affairs Bessie and Estelle"; "Here You'll Hear that Sweet Story That's Never Been Told"; "Refreshments to Suit"; "Refreshments by 'The Cheater'." All of these present to the average rent party habituée, a very definite picture of what is to be expected, as the card is given to him on the street corner, or at the subway station.

The parties outdo their publicity. There is always more than has been announced on the public invitation. Though no mention was made of an admission fee, one usually pays from twenty-five to fifty cents for this privilege. The refreshments are not always refreshing, but are much the same as those served in parts of the South, with gin and day-Old Scotch extra. The Father of the Piano lives up to his reputation as he accompanies a noisy trap drummer, or a select trio composed of fife, guitar, and saxophone.

Apart from the admission fee and the sale of food, and drinks, the general tenor of the party is about the same as one would find in a group of "intellectual liberals" having a good time. Let us look at one. We arrived a little early—about nine-thirty o'clock. The ten persons present were dancing to the strains of the Cotton Club Orchestra via radio. The drayman was just bringing two dozen chairs from a nearby undertaker's establishment, who rents them for such affairs. The hostess introduced herself, asked our names, and politely informed us that the "admittance fee" was thirty-five cents, which we paid. We were introduced to all, the hostess not remembering a single name. Ere the formality was over, the musicians, a piano player, saxophonist, and drummer, had arrived and immediately the party took on life. We learned that the saxophone player had been in big time vaudeville; that he could make his instrument "cry"; that he had quit the stage to play for the parties because he wanted to stay in New York.

There were more men than women, so a poker game was started in the next room, with the woman who did not care to dance, dealing. The music quickened the dancers. They sang "Muddy Water, round my feet—ta-ta-ta-ta-ta-ta-ta." One girl remarked—"Now this party's getting right." The hostess informed us of the menu for the evening—, Pig feet and Chili—Sandwiches *à la carte,* and of course if you were thirsty, there was some "good stuff" available. Immediately, there was a rush to the kitchen, where the man of the house served your order.

For the first time we noticed a man who made himself conspicuous by his watchdog attitude toward all of us. He was the "Home Defense Officer," a private detective who was there to forestall any outside interference, as well as prevent any losses on the inside on account of the activity of the "Clean-up Men." There were two clean-up men there that night and the H. D. O. had to be particularly careful lest they walk away with two or three fur coats or some of the household furnishings. Sometimes these men would be getting the "lay" of the apartment for a subsequent visit.

There was nothing slow about this party. Perfect strangers at nine o'clock were boon companions at eleven. The bedroom had become the card room—a game of "skin" was in progress on the floor while dice were rolled on the bed. There was something "shady" about the dice game, for one of the players was always having his dice caught. The musicians were still exhorting to the fifteen or twenty couples that danced. Bedlam reigned. It stopped for a few minutes while one young man hit another for getting fresh with his girl while dancing. The H. D. O. soon ended the fracas.

About two o'clock, a woman from the apartment on the floor below rang the bell and vociferously demanded that this noise stop or that she would call an officer. The hostess laughed in her face and slammed the door. Some tenants are impossible! This was sufficient, however, to call the party to a halt. The spirit—or "spirits" had been dying by degrees. Everybody was tired—some had "dates"—others were sleepy —while a few wanted to make a cabaret before "curfew hour." Mrs. Bailey calmly surveyed a disarranged apartment, and counted her proceeds.

* * * * *

But the rent parties have not been so frequent of late. Harlem's new dance halls with their lavish entertainment, double orchestra, and "sixteen hours of continuous dancing," with easy chairs and refreshments available are ruining the business. They who continue in this venture of pleasure and business are working on a very close margin both socially and economically, when one adds the complexity illustrated by the following incident:

A nine year old boy gazed up from the street to his home on the "top floor, front, East Side" of a tenement on West 134th Street about eleven-thirty on a Friday night. He waited until the music stopped and cried, "Ma! Ma! I'm sleepy. Can I come in now?" To which a male voice, the owner of which had thrust his head out of the window, replied,—"Your ma says to go to the Midnight Show, and she'll come after you. Here's four bits. She says the party's just got going good."

ALLISON DAVIS (1902-   )

A native of Washington, D. C., Allison Davis was educated at Williams College, Harvard, the London School of Economics, and the University of Chicago. He has taught English at Hampton Institute, anthropology at Dillard, and has lectured on child development at the University of Chicago. Besides a number of essays in literary criticism, reviews, and poems published in magazines, Davis has contributed "The Distribution of Blood-Groups and Its Bearing on the Concept of Race" to *Political Arithmetic* (1938), edited by Lancelot Hogben; and, with W. Lloyd Warner, "A Comparative Study of American Caste," to *Race Relations and the Race Problem,* edited by Edgar T. Thompson, (1939). His books are *Children of Bondage* (1940), an American Youth Commission Study, written with John Dollard, and *Deep South* (1941), a cultural anthropological study written with Elizabeth Davis and Burleigh and Mary Gardener. The following is reprinted by permission of the author and of *Opportunity: Journal of Negro Life.*

A Glorious Company

THERE IS AN OLD Negro song in which the band of those destined for Heaven, with the prophets and King Jesus, are safely transported thither aboard a train! This journey by train to their last, long station is but an accentuated expression of the fascination and mystery which trains hold for Negroes of the south. I have often thought that the Negro farmhand would lose heart once for all, were it not for the daily encouragement he takes from the whistle of his favorite locomotives. Tied to his plow, under the red, burning sun, or aching with the loneliness of the sterile night, he can find all his desire for escape, all the courage he lacks in the face of the unknown, mingled with his inescapable hopelessness, in the deep-throated, prolonged blast of the express-train, like a challenge to untravelled lands, a terrifying cry to his petty township.

A journey by train for no more than three or five miles fills the poor Negroes of the south with confidence and elation. They are not only holiday makers; they are seekers and adventurers. With all their children and world's gear about them, they leave nothing more precious than a squalid, smoke-painted shanty, with its empty pigsty; who knows, then, if perchance they may not find a changed life in the next town or county, and never return? It is pitiable they should not yet have learned they have no fair country, and that oppression rides with them. Yet, no one who has not had his world bounded into less clean and metaphorical limits than those of a nut-shell can understand the hope which these, who journey from home, feel at the possibility of escape.

To them, the mere fact of motion suggests new independence, and incites their trammeled spirits with unbounded enthusiasm. They are rolling, in a rolling world, and at every local station exhort their friends, from the windows, to join the band.

> "Git on boa'd, little children,
> Dere's room for many a mo.'"

is the spirit, if not the letter, of their greeting.

Aboard, they are all friends, drawn by their common adventure. A gambler and bully-boy lavishes his famed courtliness on a withered, old sister, brave in her antebellum finery, and falls at length into her "revival" plans. I have often noticed a fine-looking type of old gentleman, whose rich, brown skin, and soft, curly hair lend him a gentility the Jewish patriarchs lacked. He seems destined to encounter some buxom, dark-skinned "fancy woman," who cleverly leads him into his favorite discourses on the virtues of renunciation and purity. Trained in flattery by her mode of life, she sits like a rapt student at her master's feet. And if, by unlucky goodness of heart, she offers him a pint of her own home-made "sperrits," knowing the indigence of the pure in heart, he will feel the simple testimony, and forgive.

There will be also the irreconcilables, like this white-skinned lady from the north. She feels only the indignity of the segregated train, and suffers from a kind of hyperaesthesia in this crude gathering of her own people. The odors from their full meal of fried chicken—I have seen even the delectable cabbage in lunch-boxes—arouse in her a genuine hatred of the whole clan, and she would enjoy lynching those wayworn sisters who unshoe their tortured feet. These black folk from whom she shrinks, however, are incorrigibly gentle and courteous, and seek by persistent attentions to make her comfortable,—even to talk with her like a fellow-being in a world of trouble. But her thoughts are fixed, with bitter longing, on the parlor car.

And yet, among the Florida tourists, from the observation car through the dining and lounging cars, down to this truncated segment of the baggage car, she would find no wit and smiles to put zest in the journey, like these about her. Starvation, one's own ignorance, persecution, hard luck, and the way of woman, all are turned into laughter, now reckless, and now ultimately philosophic. A jet-black woman is laughed at by her equally dark escort for spending time and effort to rouge and powder;—and she sees the ridiculous futility of her vanity, and laughs more heartily than he! A consumptive of huge frame jokingly threatens the young porter for treading on his feet, and cannot laugh without pain. And in one corner, in spite of the scowls of the conductor, a one-legged miner sings rich harmonies to his guitar, strumming with fervent sympathy, *Wonder Where's Dem Hebrew Children?* That *he* should look to Palestine two thousand years ago for homeless ones to pity!

More animated and cheerful is the story-teller, touched by just enough of the grape,—turned corn now in this makeshift world—to inspire him to a longer tale of his wanderings. He knows himself a romantic protagonist for this young college-boy who listens, and carries his adventures farther into the hero-world. There, sweet brown girls cherish him, or "evil womans" betray him, according to the powers of the grape. For the most part, he has had Herculean jobs in the mines or on the docks, and harder luck with his women than Samson; but now that he's once again "railroading, behind an eight-driving engine, with the rails ringing," his confidence returns. Tomorrow, nay tonight at the end of his fare, he may be hungry and in the park; but as he talks now, homelessness and starvation are dangers in romance, no more fatal than the wounds of the archangels, which bleed ichor, and heal forthwith!

So it is with them all, escaping the weight of hardship and persecution by some exhilaration of the moment. In an hour now, many will be left at their lonely, country station, while the great engine burns its fiery trail across the black sky, driving on into other lands with happier children. But now they are still in a band and confident. Their pride and courage are fortified by the swaggers of the porter, for he is one of their own; they feel it a strange and hopeful dispensation that he should be here to guide them safely in. So they roll on into a mystery.

In the great, city station, this sense of mystery becomes at once awful and exhilarating. They give porters tips of five cents in a beautiful trance of lavishness. The marble under their feet is turned to buoyant ether, and the great dome above draws their spirits in prayers and hallelujahs. And their exhilaration is the keener because against this brilliant spectacle, they can see in their mind's eye the alley-shack where they will come into the city's life. Now they feel only that here is a journey finished in a new and better land, full of light and splendor.

They have not gone this journey of physical hardship and spiritual cramping without the strength of hope and faith. This faith they will not lose in the newer lands to which they must eventually come, for it is revived daily by the barest victory over disease and poverty, and these will travel with them, to chasten. They go also with humility, which we will not think meanness of spirit, until we have known the daily bitterness of being forced to resign hope and manhood. And if they are humble, having faith in their journey, and courage still to face it with laughter and friendliness, perhaps they may be allowed to go in their stocking-feet, at ease over their dinner of cabbage, until they shall understand the ways of our fine lady, and some day, perchance, even of the Florida tourists.

HORACE MANN BOND (1904-   )

Horace Mann Bond, born in Nashville, Tennessee, was educated at Lincoln University and the University of Chicago. He has taught education at Lincoln, Langston, Alabama State, Fisk, and Dillard, where he was dean of the College; he is now president of Fort Valley State College. He is the author of *The Education of the Negro in the American Social Order* (1934) and *Negro Education in Alabama: a Study in Cotton and Steel* (1939). His article, "A Negro Looks at His South," appeared in *Harper's Magazine* in 1933 and is here reprinted by permission of the author and of *Harper's Magazine*.

A Negro Looks at His South

THE PROFESSIONAL SOUTHERNER is with us again, boldly proclaiming the virtues of his agrarian economy, his pride in race, his scorn of lesser breeds. The shouting and the tumult bring to the public mind the old, old picture of the quintessential Southron, the fine flower of Anglo-Saxon gentility, the Nordic par excellence in his dominance of the scene. The region is made articulate by the self-expression of these white men and women, and the Negro is merely a bit of back-stage scenery used to deepen the effect of the leading silhouette. In the South the white man is the Southerner, the Negro—well, a Negro.

Now, this classification is all very well, but I would protest that the term thus used is faulty, and that the fault is not in the Negro, but in the cavalier manner in which the accolade of Southern citizenship, of participation in the fate of the region, has been appropriated by white persons. For two or three hundred years all of my ancestors were born in the South, and the record of the last hundred years, beginning when the memory of grandparents has enabled me to pierce the chaos of slavery, convinces me that they did no unprofitable service in the development of the region. All of my kinspeople live in the South to-day, and of them the same thing may be said, in all due modesty. Most of my life has been lived in this section, and all of the hope I cherish for the future is laid there. There are probably eight or nine million Negroes who, in the same manner, are Southerners—using the phrase in the most catholic manner—people whose forbears were born in the South, whose lives have been lived there, and whose hope of future security and happiness is intimately bound up with the fortunes of the section. These people are Southerners, and I am a Southerner.

It is, therefore, of interest to the Negro in general, and to me, to inquire into the nature of the geographical portion, the psychological entity, which is called the South. It will not be doubted that we have left our impress on the region. Customs, politics, society, all of the deeper and more extensive ramifications of culture bear the imprint of those of us who, being Southerners, are also Negroes. This forest would not have been transformed into a fertile delta had it not been for us; that constitution would not have been framed had it not been for us; that speech would not have its rare flavor had it not been for the softer inflections contributed by our vocal mannerisms. Charleston would be devoid of its graces without the Negro, and

Louisiana have no tradition of good society, nor even the crown of the cosmopolitan city of New Orleans, had there been no striving, sweating, singing Negroes to make secure a foundation for culture. On the other hand, we may claim to having done less for retrogression than for progress. If competition with the Negro drove many whites to primitive mountain fastnesses, to stagnation and decay, competition with other whites has done the same in New England and the Middle States. Without us the South would certainly have had as many "po' white trash" and, without us, few if any of those "to the manor born."

As a child, I saw the South in miniature, in little microcosms that gave a touch of the larger reality. But it is not enough to pick cotton, or shell "goobers," or paddle one's bare toes lovingly in the pleasant, sticky red mud of a North Georgia hillside. Look at your South in a black-belt county in Alabama, then go a scant hundred miles to the north, to the hill country where you will find an entire county without a Negro family, and you will see an entirely different South. In the last few years I have had occasion to look at the section from the vantage point of rice farms, sugar-cane farms, cotton farms; from cotton-mill towns, port towns, steel towns, coal-mining towns, tobacco towns, and towns which had no apparent distinction aside from their common creation by the patron devil of such communities.

In such excursions into the back country the traveler is thrown among all sorts of people, white and black. I recall one man in a small town located near the Red River in Louisiana in whose house I stayed for two months. He was the janitor of the local white Baptist church. His wife was a delightful old black amazon who grumbled continually at the "Whi' folks," for making her husband work so hard, and at him for letting them abuse his hours of labor. And yet she was always ready to tell me, by the hour, with a pride that was almost pathetic, of a little white girl she had nursed, and whom she adored from afar, as that child grew into womanhood.

Another man whose hospitality I enjoyed for nearly a month was leading grocer to the Negro community, gasoline-station proprietor, and undertaker to all and sundry, white and black, in the little town nestled under the Mississippi River levee, where he lived. Still another was a Negro doctor who owned a plantation of three thousand acres on the river, below Natchez, and who complained of the laziness of his tenants quite as mournfully as any white land owner could have done. In North Carolina on one occasion I stayed for two weeks with a bootlegger who enjoyed the lavish patronage of white train-crews; but the next week found me domiciled with an old widowed woman who insisted on reading at least two chapters from the Bible before she prepared my breakfast in the morning. Two nights I spent in the meager cabin of a tenant in Louisiana who boasted of having cleared five dollars last year, a return for a year of labor which is no mean accomplishment with cotton selling at nine and ten cents the pound. By far the most entertaining of my hosts in the back-country, however, was a highly respected Negro in a small village of a certain State, who added to his income as drayman a considerable sum derived from the re-distilling, for the county sheriff, of the liquor captured by that functionary in sporadic raids over the countryside. I do not know what disposition the sheriff made of the doubly purified stuff, as my host was a teetotaler.

These Southerners—Negroes if you must—represent bits of the mosaic which when pieced together give a fairly satisfactory portrait of the section. Like them are the white people one meets in every capacity: policemen who believe that every Negro in an automobile is a bootlegger; filling-station proprietors who refuse to inspect the motor oil in a Negro's automobile, where there is no competition, but who rush to dust off the minutest speck of dirt from a windshield if there is another station on the opposite corner; a little white boy who throws a brick at my car for no particular reason other than that I am a Negro; another white boy whose father owns a thousand acres, and who toils in mud to his knees to free me from an apparently bottomless pit, and then haughtily refuses to accept anything from a "nigger" in payment for the work of an hour and the strength of two good mules; while ten miles away a surly Negro tenant refuses to budge from his cabin to help me extract my automobile from a like difficulty until I have pledged him five dollars, coin of the realm. Here is the owner of a large store who delays me for an hour while I listen patiently to his interested and intelligent discussion of the Negro and his virtues and vices; while across the way another storekeeper may hurl a bottle at my head if I do not take my hat off when I pass the threshold. Here is a white man who has killed at least three Negroes in cold blood, with no more ado about it; while he may have as his neighbor the old man I heard of in a Louisiana town who thought he had been insulted by a Negro tenant who had been his playmate as a boy. The old man hitched his horse to his buggy, told the Negro to hop in, and drove to a deserted neck of woods where he ordered the Negro to get out and fight him, fair fist and skull. The old man was no match for his tenant and was considerably battered; but he merely swore the

Negro to secrecy and drove him amicably back to town. Someone, it seemed, had seen the affray and relayed the news; but when the old man was approached to verify the scandalous rumor he only said, "Jim's my nigger, and it's none 'er yore damned business how I handle him."

The cities, too, have their own uniqueness. The comparison between the cities, and the citizens, black and white, of two such Alabama centers as Birmingham and Montgomery becomes odious. The slums of Birmingham are the wretched hovels of the creatures of Steel and Coal, and the well-to-do houses the fantastic creation of the abysmal *nouveau-riche,* while in Montgomery the slum-dwellers are still human beings, charming in their squalor, and the wealthier homes bear the relaxed countenance of accustomed luxury. Atlanta and Durham are full of "go-getters," while Natchez and Mobile still retain the charming atmosphere of men and women who arrived, and obtained, some time before the present era.

II

If Negroes are Southerners, we cannot avoid looking upon the South with as candid a view as those other Southerners who are white, nor can we avoid a touch of that sectional partisanship which gives to us the common touch. In the little Negro college where I spent four years the student body was almost equally divided between boys from the North and the South. I still remember the most popular theme for our sophomoric arguments, and these were endless. No matter how any argument began, it always drifted around to an inter-sectional debate, with boys from New Jersey and New York high schools hotly attacking the South, and with boys from Arkansas and Georgia as vigorously defending their home States. It is no mistake to assume that your true Southerner, like your man of family, brings to any internal discussion a venerable tradition, a tangle of notions derived from daily contacts with men and the means of human communication. In assessing the mental cast of the Southerner Negro it is too often forgotten that the books he studies in school, the newspapers he reads, and the radio to which he listens not infrequently, all alike are instruments seeking the end, consciously or not, of the preservation of a cultural entity. The text-books adopted by the State are carefully scanned by censors eager to eliminate any deprecatory remarks concerning the Old South, and these instruments of culture carry their propaganda as neatly into kink-thatched heads as into the consciousness of the Nordic youngster.

What the result is in sustaining a state of mind in Negroes similar to that of whites is quite apparent, though liable to more perplexing evidences of the cultural aim sought for in the former instance. I know scores of Negro lads bearing with unconscious irony the name of Robert E. Lee Jones, or Smith, or Brown; I could list a baker's dozen of Stonewall Jacksons, and I even know two colored youngsters who proudly bear the illustrious cognomen of Jefferson Davis. Indeed, I know more Negro lads named for the great Confederate general who fought to perpetuate slavery than those bearing the name of the Great Emancipator. Booker T. Washington, the sage of Tuskegee, has been perhaps the most prolific source of suggestion for fathers who sought a worthy name for their offspring; but never, in the length and breadth of my travels in the South, have I ever seen a lad christened for William Edward Burghardt DuBois, for four decades the foremost radical and intellectual of his race.

The initiation of the Negro child into the cult of the South is not alone confined to this process of furnishing subjects for hero-worship. The customs and exploits of the region likewise belong to him. What the White South reads, he reads; and what the White South debars, is barred from him. In five years of teaching I have seen but six youngsters of college grade out of a total of four or five hundred in my classes during that time who had read that immortal picture of antebellum Negro life, *Uncle Tom's Cabin*. As a matter of fact, these unhappy creatures, surrounded from youth by illiterates, deprived, for the most part, of public or private libraries, and products of public schools wretched beyond imagining, have seldom read anything but their school text-books and the Comic Supplement of the daily prints. In this, of course, they are much like the majority of their white fellow-Southerners. But at least in these school books they read of the chivalrous deeds of men and women of the Old White South, and now and then an acknowledgment of the perfection in servitude achieved by some devoted black coachman or cook. They swallow without a retch the fantastic stories of the iniquities of Reconstruction and the detailed accounts of Negro legislators portrayed as scoundrels and ignoramuses. These accounts are supplemented by inspired essays which attempt to be redolent with the charm of the Old Plantation, and the perfumed fragrance of the magnolias and cape jessamine evokes for them as readily as for white youths a sublime land of Never-Never, of chaste ladies and brave men with the graces of the perfect gentlewoman and gentleman, of mint-juleps, sugar-cured hams, and gracious manners.

The shrewder members of the race are quick to capitalize this picture of the olden time, and it has been for a long time a source of amusement to me, mixed at times with a certain amount of indignation, to see how cleverly they aid white persons in the recreation of the legend. Dignified school principals become the embodiment of the courtly black servitors of a past regime as they entertain the members of some hungry school board. I know dozens of such public functionaries whose only manifestation of educational proficiency consists in the ability to serve succulent fried chicken and hot biscuits to visiting inspectors. The larger State schools in the South for Negroes owe many of their more considerable appropriations to the fine art of culinary blandishment. Once, when I was teaching at such a school, the biennial visit of the appropriations committee of the State Legislature was announced. I looked forward to incisive questions and a searching analysis from these ferret-eyed protectors of the public funds. Vain expectations! But I was young then. On the day of the visit the entire teaching staff was marshalled by order of the president of the school to a nearby pea patch, where, enrobed in blue jeans and calico, our scholarly faculty awaited the arrival of these patrons of the arts. The eyes of the visitors sparkled with enthusiasm when they were informed by the president that what they saw was no unusual occurrence in this State college, dedicated as it was to the great ideals of honest labor and toil.

From the pea patch the legislators passed hastily around the campus, finally to rest in the spacious Home Economics Department, the best equipped in the entire school. Here they were served mountainous plates of fried chicken, together with beaten biscuits fit for an epicure (these viands had been prepared by an old Negro woman who had been imported for the occasion, although all the credit was given to the chipper domestic science staff). From this shrine they proceeded to the school auditorium, where with brimming eyes and distended stomachs they listened to Jubilee Songs—"Plantation Melodies"—sung by the student body. They departed, praising the superior work of our institution, not having been in a single classroom, not having asked a single question about the efficiency or training of the teaching staff. The school that year received the largest appropriation in its history. It can be said with much truth that fried chicken and Negro spirituals have done more for Negro education than all the philanthropic foundations and their agents have ever accomplished.

These things, of course, pertain to a High Art, the practices of a menial translated to a higher sphere, where they prosper amazingly. Negroes have a name for it; among themselves, they dub the Art, "Fooling the White Folks." A successful practitioner in this high calling becomes in the public prints "a highly respected Negro man," or "a Negro of the old order who has many white friends in this vicinity." At the death of such a one, no matter how humble (for humbleness is an added degree of virtue), one may look forward to at least a half-column of newspaper comment, and a number of "leading white citizens," always including prominent preachers and the town mayor, at one's funeral. No master of social psychology approaches the technic perfected by the Southern Negro in such matters.

If it may not be regarded as too immodest a declaration, I should like to claim for myself some progress in this art. Frequently I hear anxious queries from colored friends who know that I travel constantly in the back-country and wonder how I escape injury and insult from the natives in the dark hinterlands of Alabama and Mississippi. The technic is easy. I learned it all in one day from an elderly Negro guide who led me through a hundred miles of tangled Alabama woods in search of three rural schools tucked away in the heart of the wilderness. He had worked for white people for fifty years, and by dint of prodigious thrift had at last retired with a considerable competency. Now, when we stopped at crossroads stores for information he was quick to doff his hat and preface his every sentence with "Mister," and every interrogation with "Sir." If one has occasion to say "Yes" or "No," the monosyllables must always be followed with the respectful "Sir."

There is no denying that the system works. One day while driving through a little North Carolina village I violated every traffic law known to man, as well as others known only to the inhabitants of this drab mill village. I was promptly haled before the local bar of justice. By assiduous practice of the Art, I emerged with never a fine, not even a reprimand; indeed, a fine encomium was mine: "You act like a good darky, so I'm gointa let you go." I challenge any other motorist, white or black, to drive through that town at fifty miles an hour, as I had done, and escape unscathed. On the one occasion when I did not practice the Art I came near faring badly. In a little express station in Selma, Alabama, I attempted to insure a package of documents for five hundred dollars. The clerk was surly; I had interrupted him in a game of coon-can with several other loungers. He eyed my package suspiciously. "Whatcha got in there, money?" Forgetfully I answered:

"No."

Then he exploded. "Say, I'm a white man; say 'Sir' to me." And he flourished a long dirk before my face.

I quickly regained the situation.

"Excuse me, Mister; my mistake, Sir."

Although he eyed me suspiciously again, as if to discover some hidden irony in my answer (he was a very dirty white man), he finished expressing my parcel with no more ado.

III

This Art, of course, stripped of its intention, is no more than the common politeness in which, I believe, every Southern Negro child is instructed; it is a code laid down without application to race. I can well remember that my old grandmother insisted that I should say "Sir" to all men, and "Mam," for Madame, to all women, and always raise my hat when I wished to ask a question. It is part of my Southern training, and on numerous occasions I have been told testily, by Northern-bred Negro women, "I wish you wouldn't 'Mam' me so much; it's so Southern, and besides, it makes me feel so old!" But no matter how I guard my tongue, that inbred "Sir" or "Mam" will out in ordinary conversation.

Now this, in my opinion, is the very crux of the Southern situation. There are always two dicta that always restrain me when I essay wholesale criticism. The first is that well-known aphorism, "It is impossible to indict a people," and the other, the pithy comment of the illustrious Frenchman, "No generalization is correct, not even this one." And yet, despite the many exceptions, despite the efforts of Mr. Allen Tate and his fellow "Neo-Confederates" to extol the gentility of the former Southern scene, I am convinced that the White South of the present may be indicted on the basis of its undeveloped gentility. The Negro in the past generally had most of his dealings with men of property. It will be remembered that in antebellum times only one out of five whites in the South owned slaves, and since those halcyon days the great majority of the Negro's contacts as domestic servant and farm tenant have been with the propertied classes. As a rule, then, the Negro is accustomed to dealing with gentlemen, and all other whites are still to him the "poor white trash" whom my parents so loftily despised. Most of the hypocritical subterfuges of the present, accordingly, are mechanisms adopted by Negroes to sustain the illusion that his masters are still gentlemen, which, sadly enough, is no longer the case. By social training, by school books, by tradition, Negroes, if lackeys, are at least "gentlemen's gentlemen." In actuality, he finds that poor whites have come into the kingdom, with a taste for its distinction though devoid of its graces; and with subtle skill he feeds the taste of these Rotarian Southrons who have succeeded to the places of the long-dead mighty of another age.

It is possible, of course, that the White South of to-day reserves its nobility of soul for whites in a segregated world, as it reserves the best theater seats and railroad accommodations. But this, indeed, has in every age been the crucial test of the true gentleman: his bearing toward his inferiors. There is an anecdote of General Robert E. Lee, which is to the point. It is said that while serving as president of Washington College, after the War, he was accosted by an old Negro man who raised his hat to the General. Lee in turn doffed his hat, much to the dismay of a friend who witnessed the scene and reproached him for having tipped his hat to a nigger." Lee replied, "I cannot afford to let a Negro be more polite than I." *Noblesse oblige* has merit as a test. In general the white Southerner of to-day reacts to the Negro like a man who has but recently achieved status, and who leans over backwards to avoid any suspicion of irregularity. He is afraid to be gracious in manner to Negroes becauses his friendliness might be criticized as the eccentricities of a "nigger-lover." On numerous occasions I have heard State and local educational officials protest their desire to give Negroes a fairer proportion of the public funds, but invariably they admit an unwillingness to face the electorate behind them. Many of the older breed of Southerners were sufficiently confident of their status to be able to afford gentility in their relationship with their Negro slaves, knowing that simple humanity would not dislodge them from their positions. Even after the War there were men like Wade Hampton, of South Carolina, owner of huge plantations in that State and in Mississippi, soldiers like John B. Gordon, statesmen like Henry Grady and Benjamin Hill of Georgia, men who could advocate with sincerity decent treatment for Negroes and adequate schooling for them in public addresses. General Gordon campaigned for office in 1866, before the Negro was enfranchised, on a platform of free schools for Negroes. What modern Alabama or Georgia politician would do this? Not one; the modern breed runs to the contrary.

Witness the great men of the last two decades. Vardaman of Mississippi, Heflin of Alabama, Blease of South Carolina. These men have all, it is true, been more or less discredited with their constituencies, principally because of the very fury which they generated. But Bilbo still reigns in Mississippi. Mr. Bilbo, it will be remembered, responded to the protest telegram of a Negro Association against a lynching in the pungent words: "Go to Hell." Recently Mr. Bilbo's close friend and kinsman, Bura Hilbun, was tried on the charge of embezzling eighty-five thousand dollars of Rosenwald Fund monies, given in his care to aid in building Negro schools. A hung jury resulted in a mistrial, and Mr. Hilbun went free. But if Mr. Bilbo is finally repudiated by the Mississippi electorate, it will not be due to the scandals in his administration relating to Negro schools, but rather to his activities in connection with four State white institutions which resulted in the withdrawal of recognition from these schools by accrediting agencies. In place of Prentiss, Mississippi accepts such men as her leaders.

The luminous pen of Mr. Bowers has recently revivified the "Tragic Era" of Reconstruction. But it is largely forgotten that the men who wrested the control of politics from Negroes and Carpet-baggers were content to let the State Constitutions adopted by those legendary freebooters endure for years to come, after they had seized control. Warmoth has shown how the white Democrats of Louisiana, of which he was a reconstruction governor, were as assiduous in corralling corrupt Negro votes as the Black Republicans, and that many of the most earnest grabbers were ex-Confederate officers. Mr. Heflin has recently obtained an investigation of the election which resulted in his defeat, and his vivid accusations of ballot manipulation beggar any description ever made of the evil deeds of Negro reconstruction politicians. The recent disclosures regarding the handling of State monies in Tennessee shows a situation at least parallel to the most devious dealing of the Reconstruction "Parson" Brownlow of that State.

The election of Hayes in 1876 is generally regarded as the end of Reconstruction. Yet the first white Democrat to be elected governor in Louisiana after 1876 appointed a Negro, P. B. S. Pinchback, as well as numerous school-board members from Negroes in the various counties of the State. We have all witnessed that peculiar phenomenon, following upon stock-market crashes and bank failures, by which loud complaints of loss are heard on the part of those who have just discovered large shareholdings or deposits which hitherto had been rather successfully concealed from the knowledge of acquaintances. The like symptom of human frailty has in large part afflicted the White South. The real aristocracy, the heaviest losers in the *débâcle,* appear to have taken the issue of arms in the manner of good sportsmen, which is the manner of the gentleman. They strove mightily to regain control of the political situation, and they succeeded. Then, from the ranks of the poor whites, there arose those long-haired evangels who disputed control with the genteel, culminating in the Populism which swept the South in the nineties. By the end of that decade the old order had passed away; the new people from the hill-country were in the saddle, and the Negro found himself entirely in the hands of a ruler who had never known Uncle Mose, except as his eternal economic competitor.

IV

By far the most detestable crystallization of these uncharitable characteristics of the New Southerner is to be found in the white Northerner come South to settle and to live. One must except, of course, those noble souls who in times past braved social ostracism to come as teachers of the benighted Negroes in little mission colleges here and there. If the newly arrived white Southerner leans over backward to avoid criticism from his constituent hill-billies, the Northerner makes himself absurd by his haste in adopting the protective coloration of local prejudice. In all hotels the guests most abusive of help are more than likely to be Northerners, and I have heard numerous cooks and maids, employed seasonally by persons wintering in the South, give their infallible verdict, "They's the meanest kind of po' white trash." This sense of proportionate values in menials is not due to different standards of efficiency between Northern whites and Southerners. I have known cooks who worked for ten, twelve, fourteen hours a day without complaint for Southern whites, while cherishing a secret scorn for their Northern mistresses who gave them lighter hours and fewer tasks.

Many of the white Northerners who have come to the South are from the Middle West, and their ideal for the New South, is apparently, the re-creation in the Black Belt of Indiana civilization. The ideal has charmed the minds of the new type of Southern business man, in great part, and from Savannah to San Antonio the Rotary idea is rampant. Men from the two sections are, in fact, brothers under the skin—men fresh from the soil, educated in moribund denominational colleges or crass state institutions, with a great hunger for the Almighty Dollar. I have no desire to intimate that the great Main Street area has not its proper ratio of gently bred citizens; but it is a certainty that the product is not exported to the South. One meets these exiles everywhere in the South. Many of them bring a sturdy faith in the Grand Old Party, and promptly excise the poor Negro from the sinecures attaching to the affiliation with that Republican ghost by setting up a "lily-white" regime. The process of thus "purifying" the party has been immensely facilitated during the presidency of that great and good native-born Iowan, Mr. Herbert Hoover.

If more proof is needed of the similarity in type between the New white Southerner and the New Middle-Westerner, an inspection of records of violent race clashes will furnish confirmatory evidence. In proportion to the number of Negroes in the population, the Middle West of recent years has been as ready to mete out extra-legal justice to Negroes as the South. One of the most savage lynchings of 1930 occurred in the charming (Midwestern) city of Marion, Indiana. The butchery of almost two hundred Negroes in East St. Louis immediately after the World War was unequalled in downright atrocity even by the Elaine, Arkansas, massacre of the same period. The first lynching of 1931 occurred in Maryville, Missouri, and this town is a scant thirty miles from the Iowa border. Ten years ago I saw a sign at Rising Sun, Indiana, such as I have seen nowhere in the South: "Nigger, Don't let the Sun go down on you in This Town." I do not know whether it still stands, but as late as two years ago I was told of another sign in a nearby Indiana village that read: "Nigger, Read and Run; If You Can't Read, Run Anyway."

It may be well that the culture of the Old South has been exaggerated. Certainly the romanticists have been too egregious in their praise. Olmstead in his travels found many "big houses" that were mere cottages, and lordly masters who in fact presided over a few flea-bitten dogs and mangy mules, plus a few unkempt Negroes. To-day one may travel through a dozen counties in the Deep South, where Sherman never penetrated, and yet discover no habitations save log huts which antedate the War Between the States. Whatever damage the great destroyer may have done to the legendary great mansions of Georgia and South Carolina, his failure to march through the far reaches of Alabama and Central Mississippi should have left some such structures still erect, if they ever actually existed. But at least the Old Order was sufficiently virile to produce a tradition and to cultivate an ideal. It matters not if that tradition had no actual seat aside from certain seaboard cities and the Mississippi Delta. It is enough that it did produce here and there an expert in the art of living. Ideals, though held by a few, may affect the behavior of the many. With the wider diffusion of literacy to-day we may be permitted to ask as much of the present. Stonewall Jackson, before the War Between the States, took time to teach a Negro Sunday School class. One cannot imagine the hero of Manassas presiding at one of our modern *autos-da-fé,* or excusing it under any circumstance. General John B. Gordon of Georgia publicly advocated schools for Negroes. In 1880, six years after the Negro had been thrust from politics by this man and others, the county of Wilcox, in the Black

Belt of Alabama, expended $1.45 per capita Negro child for educational purposes. In 1928, with the New Order in full control, this same county expended 69 cents per capita Negro child. Surely the old masters would have done no less.

V

I have said but little of the Black South, and much of the White South. Sixty-five years ago a Northern agent came to a school for Freedmen in Atlanta, and in talking to the students asked them what message he should carry back to the philanthropists who had sent him. A little ragged boy arose and said, "Tell 'em we'se a-risin'." That urchin, now far advanced in age, is to-day president of a bank in Philadelphia.

I believe his hope is as true to-day as it was in those troublous times immediately after Emancipation. Yesterday I was in a school-house converted from an abandoned plantation cabin. The teacher was a girl of seventeen, hardly more literate than her advanced pupils. Fifty-six children were present, but the total enrollment was ninety-eight. That teacher received thirty dollars a month for a four months' term, and from her poor teaching I doubt if half of her pupils returned to the cotton fields one whit wiser than when they entered. In the county where this school is located fifty-five per cent of the Negro adult population is illiterate. The short school, irregular attendance, and poor teaching are undoubtedly graduating yearly hundreds from the ranks of these school children to those of adult illiterates.

What land the Negroes own in this Red River valley they bought twenty- thirty years ago. With cotton at nine cents a pound, or less, they barely live from harvest to harvest. The county is building new roads to afford unemployment relief, but while the rural whites are welcomed to those jobs, the rural Negroes in far more desperate straits are told not to apply, as they will not be hired.

In Birmingham two years ago I sat beside a Negro teacher in an educational meeting. Two hours later that inoffensive boy was shot to death by two policemen dressed in plain-clothes, who stopped him on a side street like any common highwayman and interpreted his gesture to escape as sufficient cause for opening fire upon him. They were exonerated the next day for "justifiable homicide." In that city and in others I have seen innumerable pool-rooms crowded with vicious Negroes, thieves, gamblers, the dregs of life.

On Beale Street in Memphis one evening, a month ago, I saw three viragoes dragged to a patrol wagon, shrieking curses that would put the hardiest sailor to shame. Five minutes later, in the next block, I saw two men engage in a stabbing duel and saw one flee as a crowd gathered around the gashed body of the victim. In New Orleans one may see the old Tango District running full blast, and in Montgomery I have counted seven houses of prostitution cheek by jowl with two Negro churches. Montgomery is at least tolerant in this respect, for of these places, two were staffed by white women, and two by Negro women, for white patronage, while the remainder were reserved for Negroes exclusively.

All this I have seen, and more, of human misery and degradation in this South, which I call my own. But the day after my stroll in Beale Street I came to the bridge across the Mississippi River at Vicksburg, at sunset. If you ever see that vivid color spread slowly over the swamps on the Louisiana side, as you stand on the bluffs across the river, you will realize how one may love the South and claim it as one's own. An hour later I "gave a lift" to a Negro trudging along the highway. He was a tenant farmer, but he told me proudly of a son who was a student at Tuskegee Institute. Another day, there were children in a back-county school singing a spiritual I had never heard before; and down the road a mile, a dozen ragged men dragging my automobile from a morass, emerging muddy, cold, and shivering, but refusing to accept a cent for their services when told that I was working for the Rosenwald Fund. "Cap'n Julius? Nossuh, we cain't take no money fo' that!" And these men were tenants, selling a drought-stricken cotton crop for nine cents a pound.

These white people, these black people, are Southerners, but what is more, they are intensely human. And so long as the Negro Southerner can still laugh and sing and see visions, he will get along. We are inveterate optimists, and though the White South gives us nothing better than Vardamans and Bleases and Bilbos, we still believe that "We'se a-risin'."

But if a need be enunciated, that prime necessity for all of us who are Southerners, white and black alike, in my opinion must lie in the appearance of more genuine Southern white gentlemen. Some there are, of course. Such men as Aycock of North Carolina there have been in the darkest days, and the Inter-racial movement of later years has found the type here and there in increasing numbers. These men come to their human relationships with sufficient gentility and assured status as not to be ashamed to be decent where Negroes are concerned.

One wonders if this new order of nobility will arise from the vast educational activity now so popular in the South. Perhaps; at any rate, when I see the magnificent structures being erected in every rural community for whites, with transportation bringing accredited high schools within the reach of every white child, I am not so inclined to become bitter, so long as this consoling thought remains in mind. These excellent schools, of course, are being erected and maintained at a corresponding sacrifice of adequate educational facilities for Negroes. In the county where these lines are written, the county receives from State funds $7.88 for every child, black as well as white. Of this amount, a little more than two dollars is spent on Negro children, per capita, while all the balance goes to the white schools, together with all of the local county and district taxes for school purposes. If the Negro schools are conducted for but four months, in miserable shacks, by teachers receiving an annual salary of less than $140, while the white schools enjoy every advantage, the disparity is worth while if from these white schools there comes a generation of men and women who realize that nobility carries with it certain obligations.

RAYFORD W. LOGAN (1897-   )

Rayford W. Logan was born in Washington, D. C., in 1897, and was educated in the public schools of that city, at Williams College, and at Harvard. In the First World War he served as lieutenant in the 372nd Infantry of the 93rd Division, which was brigaded with French troops. He lived abroad for several years (see below). He has taught at Virginia Union University, Atlanta University, and as professor of history at Howard University. In 1932-1933 he served as assistant to Carter G. Woodson in the Association for the Study of Negro Life and History. He has been a speaker for the Foreign Policy Association and has contributed to *The Crisis, Hispanic American Historical Review, Inter-American Quarterly, The Journal of Negro Education, The Journal of Negro History, The Nation, Opportunity, Phylon, Revista de Historia de America,* and *World Tomorrow.* He edited *The Attitude of the Southern White Press Toward Negro Suffrage, 1932-1940* (1940), and wrote *The Diplomatic Relations of the United States with Haiti, 1776-1891* (1941). The following is reprinted by permission of the author.

The Confessions of an Unwilling Nordic

NEGROES CAN ATTAIN only to a fixed level of education, acquire only a limited amount of wealth, travel only in certain degrees of latitude and longitude. If an individual is found out of these circumscribed milieux, he is not a Negro. He is an East Indian or a Brazilian, a Senegalese or a Tahitian, but not a Negro, and most certainly not an American Negro.

The following stories will strain the credulity of the readers of THE WORLD TOMORROW who, of course, have no preconceived ideas concerning Negroes. Remember, however, that an American Negro is the author, and that while he can imitate, he can not create. (See Lothrop Stoddard, Madison Grant, Imperial Wizard Evans, and other authorities.)

When I say that I am a Negro, I mean one of those who should not be able to "pass." Otherwise, there would be no point to this tale. My hair is what French people call *frisés;* my color, yellow. My features betray my African ancestry. In a southern city my brother, who can pass for a Nordic, was afraid to let me accompany him into a white restaurant. But it seems that I do not conform to some arbitrary conception of a Negro's speech, behavior, and dress. Through no fault of my own I have acquired an education superior to that of many of my lords and masters. I am a graduate of an old New England college—no, it is not Amherst—which prides itself on the number of high government officials, men of letters, and in the earlier days, soldiers of Christ that it has contributed to society. By osmosis, perhaps, I imbibed some of the learning and culture of this institution. As a result I have found myself in some very amusing, embarrassing, and edifying predicaments.

It was one of my favorite professors who first suggested what a dangerous anomaly I had become. At the close of a conversation concerning my future, he concluded:

"Upon whatever career you embark, always be colored."

"Why—," I looked at my hands and felt my hair. "Why, that should not be very difficult," I concluded with a puzzled laugh.

But it was. I had the first proof of my professor's perspicacity a few days after our conversation. While on the way to Washington to spend the Easter holidays of 1917, I left the train at North Philadelphia in order to stretch my legs. Upon returning, I found an enormous white man occupying most of the seat. With some diffidence I squeezed in beside him and pretended to sleep.

My fellow-traveler probably felt that there was no use to occupy the same seat unless you are going to talk. He interrupted my feigned slumbers by asking the name of some stream that we were passing. He appeared so totally ignorant of the geography of the section that I queried:

"Is this your first trip South?"

"No, this is my first trip North."

I eased off a little in my corner.

"My home is in Waco, Texas,"—I looked around for another seat— "I have just been up to the Quaker City on business."

"Is that so? I have a classmate from Waco, a fine chap,—."

"You don't say. I know his people well. I believe that his daddy is my wife's cousin. Say, he sure showed those folks up North how to play baseball, didn't he? . . . But it takes a lot of money to go there."

I did not deem it necessary to inform my corpulent friend that a scholarship made it possible for me to attend this ultra-exclusive school. By this time I was convinced that he had no idea that, perhaps for the first time in his life, he was riding with a colored man. I decided to sound him on the one subject about which I knew he could talk most fluently and authoritatively. Without too much abruptness I turned our conversation to lynching.

"We students of sociology are very much interested in this matter of lynching. Above all, we are trying to arrive at the reasons."

"Rape. All a 'nigger' "—I needed no further proof of his blissful ignorance—"thinks about is white women."

"But we up North are told that rape is responsible for only a comparatively small number of lynchings. I have read of one case in which the alleged cause was an argument about a mule."

"Hum . . . . ('Alleged' seemed to be giving him some difficulty.) Maybe so. But you folks don't know 'niggers' as we do. All you know is what you read about 'em. I don't approve of lynching myself as a general rule, but I tell you we have to lynch one every now and then to keep 'em in their place. If we didn't they'd get so uppity that we couldn't handle them."

"I see. They must be making some progress then."

"Progress!" he snorted. "How can a darky make any progress? The curse of Ham is upon him. A 'nigger' won't never be nothing but a 'nigger.' And the worst ones is them that's got white blood in 'em. (I was tempted to ask how they got it, but remembered in time that that was irrelevant.) The only 'niggers' that's ever amounted to anything is them that's got nothing but black blood. The only great 'darky' was Booker T. Washington, and he was coal black. *He* didn't have any high-falutin' ideas about sending a 'coon' to college."

"That hardly tallies with the opinion of our professor of American literature. He has frequently told us that one of the greatest stylists in America is Dr. DuBois, who, as you know, is almost white."

"Of course. That's due to the white blood in him."

This illuminating inconsistency inspired me to further questioning.

"What about voting? Do Negroes vote in Texas?"

"That depends. I make the 'niggers' on my farm vote for prohibition. When a 'darky' gets drunk, he don't want to work. When option is up, I line 'em up, march 'em to the polls and see that every damn one of 'em votes against liquor. But that is the only time I allow my 'niggers' to vote."

Deciding that I had learned enough and that I had listened at sufficient length to his insulting terms, I drifted off into the causes of the World War. We agreed that in the last analysis the conflict was a result of contending nationalities. This led my entertaining traveler to remark about the complexity of races in America. He himself had the blood of four or five peoples in his veins. Forseeing his question, I tried to avert it by concocting a story of an American boy whose English mother, born in India, had married in Turkey his French father, born in Martinique. This tickled him, but could not divert his thought.

"And what was the nationality of your ancestors?" For a moment I remembered my professor's admonition. But since we had not yet reached Baltimore and since there were still no other seats in the train, I quibbled.

"My case is almost as bad. My first name is German, my middle name, my mother's, is one of the oldest in England, and my last seems to be a favorite among the Irish saloon-keepers along Washington Street in Boston."

He chuckled until the window rattled. Then we chatted about less dangerous things almost into Washington. As the train was pulling into Union Station, he gave me his card, told me that he was staying at the ———— Hotel with his cousin, the Representative from some district in Texas, and invited me to call to see him. I have often wondered whether he ever found from my classmate the identity of his inquisitive companion.

My next similar experience had for its setting the American hospital at Mailly, France. Probably no other colored officer had preceded me there, because this was in the early days of July, 1918. After the regulation bath, I found myself in a private room with a white orderly attending me. From the beginning, I realized that he never suspected that I was colored. Had he done so, the initial shock would have prevailed over his obligation to serve his superior. We Negroes have learned to look for that forced laugh, spontaneous irritation, or speechless amazement which many white men can not hide when they unexpectedly find themselves in the presence of their ubiquitous pest. Without an inquiring glance, my orderly set to work arranging my clothes, asking about my needs, giving me such information as would be helpful. I avoided conversation as much as possible, for I knew the only two subjects about which he was likely to talk: women and Negroes.

But he evidently thought it a part of his duties to help me beguile the time. One afternoon when he came to get the dishes, he asked to what regiment I had belonged. I told him, adding that it was a colored regiment. Instead of staring at me quizzically as I had expected, he ejaculated:

"Damn. Weren't you afraid of 'em? They say that them 'niggers' can fight like hell, but I wouldn't want to be with 'em. Didn't they ever try to bump you off?"

"Bump me off? What for?"

"Just 'cause you're white. I've heard it said that a white officer dassn't go in front of 'em up there at the front less the 'darkees' shoot 'em down from behind."

"But what do they want to kill them for? I don't know any who have been killed in our outfit."

"You're darned lucky then. Maybe you know how to treat them, but lemme tell you, I wouldn't want to be with 'em for all the *vin rouge* in France.—I guess they can guzzle plenty of cognyac, can't they?"

"No. Our soldiers are the same as any others."

"Well, they ain't got no chance if they ever come around here. We done told these frogs not to let one light in a cafe, and if we ever ketch a woman with one of 'em, we'll run her out of town. Why, these bloody idiots believe they've got tails like monkeys."

A call from another patient prevented him from continuing his revelations.

By this time I had decided never to disillusion any one who unbosomed himself to me so confidentially. At first I had wanted to "bawl out" the soldier for the use of words that are anathema to any self-respecting Negro. But the information obtained was well worth the price of my silence.

My most bewildering situation confronted me at Camp Pontanezen near Brest. To this day I do not know how the blunder occurred. I suppose, however, that the colonel commanding the casuals merely glanced at my record, found that I had considerable court-martial experience, spoke German and French fluently, and had a record at my previous camp of "excellent." It probably never dawned upon him that I was not white. Whatever may be the explanation, I was assigned to duty with a new convoy that had just come over from America to join the Army of Occupation in Germany.

I expected the order to be rescinded as soon as I reported to duty. But the commanding officer undoubtedly concluded that since I was attached to a white outfit I must be white. The situation became truly piquant the following day when the company commander called me to give these instructions:

"Mr.—, I am leaving for Paris at once. You will have complete charge of the company during my absence."

And so I am perhaps the only colored officer who actually commanded a white company in the A. E. F. For a week white shavetails, non-coms and "bucks" obeyed my orders with an alacrity that stupefied me. At no time did any one seem to suspect that an unwritten law of the American Army was being merrily trampled under foot.

On the appointed day we prepared to entrain for Ehrenbreitstein. One white orderly was busy shining my shoes. Another was packing my bedding roll. In the midst of all this stir and confusion the captain came in from Paris and at the same time arrived orders from headquarters relieving me from duty with the regiment. The captain expressed sincere regret that I could not accompany them. I have never known whether the order was due to my being colored or a casual.

Some time afterwards I met the same captain while he was on leave in Paris. As soon as he saw me, he rushed up and kissed me on both cheeks.

"I certainly am sorry that they left you behind. That would have been a rich joke to have had a colored officer in a white outfit up in Germany. I swear I believe that I was the only one who knew the truth and I didn't care a rap."

Thus, the one person who apparently recognized the colored gentleman in the corded wood appreciated the joke too much to betray him.

After the war I decided to remain in France, where I would not, as I thought, run the risk of humiliating experiences. But I counted without the thousands of Americans who were roaming over Europe during those halcyon days when the German and Polish mark, the Austrian crown and the French franc were cascading toward zero.

One day in Vienna a woman, after eyeing me rather intently, approached and said in German:—

"You have your Key?"

When she had verified in most minute detail my Phi Beta Kappa key, she informed me that her husband had been professor of German Literature at —————— University before the war. Without giving me an opportunity to express my delight at meeting a compatriot in such a distant land, she continued:—

"Of course, I left America with my husband, who is a German. We are already planning to return—this was in 1921—since the feeling against us is rapidly declining. And we have no bitterness against you Americans. You were fooled into the war. The only thing that we can not forgive is your using 'niggers' against us. It was bad enough for the Frenchmen to use Africans, but to send 'darkies' from America, that was a crime against civilization. And for Woodrow Wilson to have committed such a folly! It was all right to use them as stevedores perhaps, but to have them kill white men! It is a wonder that they did not revolt when they returned to America.

"And ever since the war, Vienna has been flooded with them. We are hardly able to live from hand to mouth while these jazz band players strut around in fur coats and diamonds. I even saw one the other day driving an automobile. . . . It is positively disgusting the way the kids have gone crazy over them. You can see twenty or more following one every time he goes out in the street. And worst of all I have seen women dancing with them. It makes my blood run cold. We ought to form a society here to teach the 'darkies' that they have no more rights than in America. *I* am going back to America, where they know how to behave themselves."

Naturally, the richest yarn comes last. If it does not rank with Baron Muenchhausen's best, I'm a prevaricator.

The stock exchange panic of April, 1920, found me "long" on dollars. The blow was such a severe one that my physician ordered me to Dax to take a rest cure. And so I went down to that delightful town on the Adour, as renowned for the stentorian voice of the train announcer as for the celebrities who come to take the baths in order to rid themselves of their real or fancied pains. Among the persons in the first class dining room were Mme. Poincaré and M. and Mme. Fallières. As far as I could judge there were no Americans. I felt free therefore to mingle with the guests, most of whom spoke French and

German. I enjoyed the theatre, the mock bull fight, came down to dinner every evening in Tuxedo, as did the other guests, had a bank telephone me the quotations from the Bourse, played bridge and billiards.

One evening as I was knocking the balls around waiting for dinner, a woman walked in.

"Would Madame like to play?" I inquired in French.

"Why, yes. I think that we have time for a short game, say twenty-five points."

The accent was not pure, but at the time my ear was not attuned sufficiently to distinguish the nationality of the person speaking. We had a rather exciting game, interspersing our shots with jokes about our ailments. The *Maître d'hôtel* announced dinner just as the last point was scored.

I laid aside my cue and stepped back with my most perfect European bow in order to allow my charming opponent to pass. But she had to satisfy her curiosity.

"Pardon me, but is the gentleman Polish?"

"Why, no, Madame, I am an American."

"You American? Whoever saw an American who looked like you? Besides," she changed suddenly to English, "you can't fool me. You may be able to fool these Europeans, but we Americans can recognize one another anywhere. Come now, there is no use in continuing your incognito. We all know that you are a Polish prince."

When I had recovered, I blurted:—

"Since you are an American, you will certainly recognize an American Negro."

She nearly screamed with delight.

"You a 'nigger'! A 'nigger' here in Dax, staying at this hotel, speaking French better than I can, eating in the first class dining room while I eat in the second! That is the cleverest disguise I have ever heard in my life. A Polish prince passing for a 'nigger.' That is *too* funny."

Once, however, I had to establish my real identity in order to escape too tangible evidence of "conduct unbecoming an officer and a gentleman." Brest was likewise the scene of this episode. It came about in this way.

On July 4, 1919, an American officer, temporarily a victim of *eau-de-vie,* cognac and Pommery, threw a French flag from the window of a restaurant down into the *Rue de Siam.* "Old Gimlet Eye" had a harder time preventing a pitched battle between the French and

Americans than he ever had chasing Chinese or bull-dozing Haitians. The feelings of the French, of course, remained extremely bitter.

As I was returning to camp one night shortly after this unfortunate incident, I passed four French sailors on the dimly lighted road. Without a word of warning one of them initiated me into the taste of Brittany mire. Fortunately, all four tried at the same time to pommel me. They made no effort to rob me. Their one desire seemed to be to commit assault and battery with the greatest degree of efficiency and thoroughness, and to use all possible variations of *"sale Américain,"* *"sacré Américain,"* and others that I hope I misunderstood.

The effectiveness of their blows and the repetition of their oaths finally reminded me that I was not an American, but only a Negro. I told them so. I appealed to their friendship for Negroes. A punch on the nose and a jab to the ribs punctuated my statement and my appeal. Then, as one fist sought an unbruised spot on my face, I grabbed it and rubbed it over my hair.

"Tiens, he *is* colored. His hair is *frisés . . . . Mille pardons, mon ami . . .* We thought you were white."

Their apologies were profuse; their dismay touching. They escorted me back to camp singing "La Madelon."

I am opposed to segregation in any form. I am likewise opposed to class legislation of any description. But if Heflin or Blease succeeded in having passed a law requiring all anomalous Negroes to wear on their exterior garments and on the windshield of their automobile a sign, "colored," I should comply most willingly.

RICHARD WRIGHT (1909-)

"The Ethics of Living Jim Crow," which Richard Wright (see also pp. 105, 401) has drawn from his own experiences, was first published in the Federal Writers' Project's *American Stuff* (1937) and is used by permission of the author and of Harper & Brothers.

The Ethics of Living Jim Crow

MY FIRST LESSON in how to live as a Negro came when I was quite small. We were living in Arkansas. Our house stood behind the railroad tracks. Its skimpy yard was paved with black cinders. Nothing green ever grew in that yard. The only touch of green we could see was far away, beyond the tracks, over where the white folks lived.

But cinders were good enough for me, and I never missed the green growing things. And anyhow, cinders were fine weapons. You could always have a nice hot war with huge black cinders. All you had to do was crouch behind the brick pillars of a house with your hands full of gritty ammunition. And the first wooly black head you saw pop out behind another row of pillars was your target. You tried your very best to knock it off. It was great fun.

I never fully realized the appalling disadvantages of a cinder environment till one day the gang to which I belonged found itself engaged in a war with the white boys who lived beyond the tracks. As usual we laid down our cinder barrage, thinking that this would wipe the white boys out. But they replied with a steady bombardment of broken bottles. We doubled our cinder barrage, but they hid behind trees, hedges, and the sloping embankments of their lawns. Having no such fortifications, we retreated to the brick pillars of our homes. During the retreat a broken milk bottle caught me behind the ear, opening a deep gash which bled profusely. The sight of blood pouring over my face completely demoralized our ranks. My fellow-combatants left me standing paralyzed in the center of the yard, and scurried for their homes. A kind neighbor saw me and rushed me to a doctor, who took three stitches in my neck.

I sat brooding on my front steps, nursing my wound and waiting for my mother to come from work. I felt that a grave injustice had been done me. It was all right to throw cinders. The greatest harm a cinder could do was leave a bruise. But broken bottles were dangerous; they left you cut, bleeding, and helpless.

When night fell, my mother came from the white folks' kitchen. I raced down the street to meet her. I could just feel in my bones that she would understand. I knew she would tell me exactly what to do next time. I grabbed her hand and babbled out the whole story. She examined my wound, then slapped me.

"How come yuh didn't hide?" she asked me. "How come yuh aw-ways fightin'?"

I was outraged, and bawled. Between sobs I told her that I didn't have any trees or hedges to hide behind. There wasn't a thing I could have used as a trench. And you couldn't throw very far when you were hiding behind the brick pillars of a house. She grabbed a barrel stave, dragged me home, stripped me naked, and beat me till I had a fever of one hundred and two. She would smack my rump with the stave, and, while the skin was still smarting, impart to me gems of Jim Crow wisdom. I was never to throw cinders any more. I was never to fight any more wars. I was never, never, under any conditions, to fight *white* folks again. And they were absolutely right in clouting me with the broken milk bottle. Didn't I know she was working hard every day in the hot kitchens of the white folks to make money to take care of me? When was I ever going to learn to be a good boy? She couldn't be bothered with my fights. She finished by telling me that I ought to be thankful to God as long as I lived that they didn't kill me.

All that night I was delirious and could not sleep. Each time I closed my eyes I saw monstrous white faces suspended from the ceiling, leering at me.

From that time on, the charm of my cinder yard was gone. The green trees, the trimmed hedges, the cropped lawns grew very meaningful, became a symbol. Even today when I think of white folks, the hard, sharp outlines of white houses surrounded by trees, lawns, and hedges are present somewhere in the background of my mind. Through the years they grew into an overreaching symbol of fear.

It was a long time before I came in close contact with white folks again. We moved from Arkansas to Mississippi. Here we had the good fortune not to live behind the railroad tracks, or close to white neighborhoods. We lived in the very heart of the local Black Belt. There were black churches and black preachers; there were black schools and black teachers; black groceries and black clerks. In fact, everything was so solidly black that for a long time I did not even think of white folks, save in remote and vague terms. But this could not last forever. As one grows older one eats more. One's clothing costs more. When I finished grammar school I had to go to work. My mother could no longer feed and clothe me on her cooking job.

There is but one place where a black boy who knows no trade can get a job. And that's where the houses and faces are white, where the trees, lawns, and hedges are green. My first job was with an optical company in Jackson, Mississippi. The morning I applied I stood straight and neat before the boss, answering all his questions with sharp yessirs and nosirs. I was very careful to pronounce my *sirs* distinctly, in order that he might know that I was polite, that I knew where I was, and that I knew he was a *white* man. I wanted that job badly.

He looked me over as though he were examining a prize poodle. He questioned me closely about my schooling, being particularly insistent about how much mathematics I had had. He seemed very pleased when I told him I had had two years of algebra.

"Boy, how would you like to try to learn something around here?" he asked me.

"I'd like it fine, sir," I said, happy. I had visions of "working my way up." Even Negroes have those visions.

"All right," he said. "Come on."

I followed him to the small factory.

"Pease," he said to a white man of about thirty-five, "this is Richard. He's going to work for us."

Pease looked at me and nodded.

I was then taken to a white boy of about seventeen.

"Morrie, this is Richard, who's going to work for us."

"What yuh sayin' there, boy!" Morrie boomed at me.

"Fine!" I answered.

The boss instructed these two to help me, teach me, give me jobs to do, and let me learn what I could in my spare time.

My wages were five dollars a week.

I worked hard, trying to please. For the first month I got along O. K. Both Pease and Morrie seemed to like me. But one thing was missing. And I kept thinking about it. I was not learning anything, and nobody was volunteering to help me. Thinking they had forgotten that I was to learn something about the mechanics of grinding lenses, I asked Morrie one day to tell me about the work. He grew red.

"Whut yuh tryin' t' do, nigger, git smart?" he asked.

"Naw; I ain' tryin' t' git smart," I said.

"Well, don't, if yuh know whut's good for yuh!"

I was puzzled. Maybe he just doesn't want to help me, I thought. I went to Pease.

"Say, are you crazy, you black bastard?" Pease asked me, his gray eyes growing hard.

I spoke out, reminding him that the boss had said I was to be given a chance to learn something.

"Nigger, you think you're *white*, don't you?"

"Naw, sir!"

"Well, you're acting mighty like it!"

"But, Mr. Pease, the boss said . . ."

Pease shook his fist in my face.

"This is a *white* man's work around here, and you better watch yourself!"

From then on they changed toward me. They said good-morning no more. When I was just a bit slow in performing some duty, I was called a lazy black son-of-a-bitch.

Once I thought of reporting all this to the boss. But the mere idea of what would happen to me if Pease and Morrie should learn that I had "snitched" stopped me. And after all, the boss was a white man, too. What was the use?

The climax came at noon one summer day. Pease called me to his work-bench. To get to him I had to go between two narrow benches and stand with my back against a wall.

"Yes, sir," I said.

"Richard, I want to ask you something," Pease began pleasantly, not looking up from his work.

"Yes, sir," I said again.

Morrie came over, blocking the narrow passage between the benches. He folded his arms, staring at me solemnly.

I looked from one to the other, sensing that something was coming.

"Yes, sir," I said for the third time.

Pease looked up and spoke very slowly.

"Richard, *Mr.* Morrie here tells me you called me *Pease.*"

I stiffened. A void seemed to open up in me. I knew this was the show-down.

He meant that I had failed to call him *Mr.* Pease. I looked at Morrie. He was gripping a steel bar in his hands. I opened my mouth to speak, to protest, to assure Pease that I had never called him simply *Pease,* and that I had never had any intentions of doing so, when Morrie grabbed me by the collar, ramming my head against the wall.

"Now be careful, nigger!" snarled Morrie, baring his teeth. "I heard yuh call 'im *Pease!* 'N' if yuh say yuh didn't, yuh're callin' me a lie, see?" He waved the steel bar threateningly.

If I had said: "No, sir, Mr. Pease, I never called you *Pease.* I would have been automatically calling Morrie a liar. And if I had said: Yes, sir, Mr. Pease, I called you *Pease,* I would have been pleading guilty to having uttered the worst insult that a Negro can utter to a southern white man. I stood hesitating, trying to frame a neutral reply.

"Richard, I asked you a question!" said Pease. Anger was creeping into his voice.

"I don't remember calling you *Pease,* Mr. Pease," I said cautiously. "And if I did, I sure didn't mean . . ."

"You black son-of-a-bitch! You called me *Pease,* then!" he spat, slapping me till I bent sideways over a bench. Morrie was on top of me, demanding:

"Didn't yuh call 'im *Pease?* If you say yuh didn't, I'll rip yo' gut string loose with this f—kin' bar, yuh black granny dodger! Yuh can't call a white man a lie 'n' git erway with it, you black son-of-a-bitch!"

I wilted. I begged them not to bother me. I knew what they wanted. They wanted me to leave.

"I'll leave," I promised. "I'll leave right *now*."

They gave me a minute to get out of the factory. I was warned not to show up again, or tell the boss.

I went.

When I told the folks at home what had happened, they called me a fool. They told me that I must never again attempt to exceed my boundaries. When you are working for white folks, they said, you got to "stay in your place" if you want to keep working.

2

My Jim Crow education continued on my next job, which was portering in a clothing store. One morning, while polishing brass out front, the boss and his twenty-year-old son got out of their car and half dragged and half kicked a Negro woman into the store. A policeman standing at the corner looked on, twirling his nightstick. I watched out of the corner of my eye, never slackening the strokes of my chamois upon the brass. After a few minutes, I heard shrill screams coming from the rear of the store. Later the woman stumbled out, bleeding, crying, and holding her stomach. When she reached the end of the block, the policeman grabbed her and accused her of being drunk. Silently I watched him throw her into a patrol wagon.

When I went to the rear of the store, the boss and his son were washing their hands at the sink. They were chuckling. The floor was bloody, and strewn with wisps of hair and clothing. No doubt I must have appeared pretty shocked, for the boss slapped me reassuringly on the back.

"Boy, that's what we do to niggers when they don't want to pay their bills," he said, laughing.

His son looked at me and grinned.

"Here, hava cigarette," he said.

Not knowing what to do, I took it. He lit his and held the match for me. This was a gesture of kindness, indicating that even if they had beaten the poor old woman, they would not beat me if I knew enough to keep my mouth shut.

"Yes, sir," I said, and asked no questions.

After they had gone, I sat on the end of a packing box and stared at the bloody floor till the cigarette went out.

That day at noon, while eating in a hamburger joint, I told my fellow Negro porters what had happened. No one seemed surprised. One fellow, after swallowing a huge bite, turned to me and asked:

"Huh. Is tha' all they did t' her?"

"Yeah. Wasn't tha' enough?" I asked.

"Shucks! Man she's a lucky bitch!" he said, burying his lips deep into a juicy hamburger. "Hell, it's a wonder they didn't lay her when they got through."

3

I was learning fast, but not quite fast enough. One day, while I was delivering packages in the suburbs, my bicycle tire was punctured. I walked along the hot, dusty road, sweating and leading my bicycle by the handle-bars.

A car slowed at my side.

"What's the matter, boy?" a white man called.

I told him my bicycle was broken and I was walking back to town.

"That's too bad," he said. "Hop on the running board."

He stopped the car. I clutched hard at my bicycle with one hand and clung to the side of the car with the other.

"All set?"

"Yes, sir," I answered. The car started.

It was full of young white men. They were drinking. I watched the flask pass from mouth to mouth.

"Wanna drink, boy?" one asked.

I laughed, the wind whipping my face. Instinctively obeying the freshly planted precepts of my mother, I said:

"Oh, no!"

The words were hardly out of my mouth before I felt something hard and cold smash me between the eyes. It was an empty whisky bottle. I saw stars, and fell backwards from the speeding car into the dust of the road, my feet becoming entangled in the steel spokes of my bicycle. The white men piled out, and stood over me.

"Nigger, ain' yuh learned no better sense'n tha' yet?" asked the man who hit me. "Ain' yuh learned t' say *sir* t' a white man yet?"

Dazed, I pulled to my feet. My elbows and legs were bleeding. Fists doubled, the white man advanced, kicking my bicycle out of the way.

"Aw, leave the bastard alone. He's got enough," said one.

They stood looking at me. I rubbed my shins, trying to stop the flow of blood. No doubt they felt a sort of contemptuous pity, for one asked:

"Yuh wanna ride t' town now, nigger? Yuh reckon yuh know enough t' ride now?"

"I wanna walk," I said, simply.

Maybe it sounded funny. They laughed.

"Well, walk, yuh black son-of-a-bitch!"

When they left they comforted me with:

"Nigger, yuh sho better be damn glad it wuz us yuh talked t' tha' way. Yuh're a lucky bastard, 'cause if yuh'd said tha' t' somebody else, yuh might've been a dead nigger now."

4

Negroes who have lived South know the dread of being caught alone upon the streets in white neighborhoods after the sun has set. In such a simple situation as this the plight of the Negro in America is graphically symbolized. While white strangers may be in these neighborhoods trying to get home, they can pass unmolested. But the color of a Negro's skin makes him easily recognizable, makes him suspect, converts him into a defenseless target.

Late one Saturday night I made some deliveries in a white neighborhood. I was pedaling my bicycle back to the store as fast as I could, when a police car, swerving toward me, jammed me into the curbing.

"Get down and put up your hands!" the policemen ordered.

I did. They climbed out of the car, guns drawn, faces set, and advanced slowly.

"Keep still!" they ordered.

I reached my hands higher. They searched my pockets and packages. They seemed dissatisfied when they could find nothing incriminating. Finally, one of them said:

"Boy, tell your boss not to send you out in white neighborhoods this time of night."

As usual, I said:

"Yes, sir."

5

My next job was a hall-boy in a hotel. Here my Jim Crow education broadened and deepened. When the bell-boys were busy, I was often called to assist them. As many of the rooms in the hotel were occupied by prostitutes, I was constantly called to carry them liquor and cigarettes. These women were nude most of the time. They did not bother about clothing even for bell-boys. When you went into their rooms, you were supposed to take their nakedness for granted, as though it startled you no more than a blue vase or a red rug. Your presence awoke in them no sense of shame, for you were not regarded as human. If they were alone, you could steal sidelong glimpses at them. But if they were receiving men, not a flicker of your eyelids must show. I remember one incident vividly. A new woman, a huge, snowy-skinned blonde, took a room on my floor. I was sent to wait upon her. She was in bed with a thick-set man; both were nude and uncovered. She said she wanted some liquor, and slid out of bed and waddled across the floor to get her money from a dresser drawer. I watched her.

"Nigger, what in hell you looking at?" the white man asked me, raising upon his elbows.

"Nothing," I answered, looking miles deep into the blank wall of the room.

"Keep your eyes where they belong, if you want to be healthy!"

"Yes, sir," I said.

6

One of the bell-boys I knew in this hotel was keeping steady company with one of the Negro maids. Out of a clear sky the police descended upon his home and arrested him, accusing him of bastardy. The poor boy swore he had had no intimate relations with the girl. Nevertheless, they forced him to marry her. When the child arrived, it was found to be much lighter in complexion than either of the two supposedly legal parents. The white men around the hotel made a great joke of it. They spread the rumor that some white cow must have scared the poor girl while she was carrying the baby. If you were in their presence when this explanation was offered, you were supposed to laugh.

7

One of the bell-boys was caught in bed with a white prostitute. He was castrated, and run out of town. Immediately after this all the bell-boys and hall-boys were called together and warned. We were given to understand that the boy who had been castrated was a "mighty, mighty lucky bastard." We were impressed with the fact that next time the management of the hotel would not be responsible for the lives of "trouble-makin' niggers."

8

One night, just as I was about to go home, I met one of the Negro maids. She lived in my direction, and we fell in to walk part of the way home together. As we passed the white night-watchman, he slapped the maid on her buttock. I turned around, amazed. The watchman looked at me with a long, hard, fixed-under stare. Suddenly he pulled his gun, and asked:

"Nigger, don't yuh like it?"

I hesitated.

"I asked yuh don't yuh like it?" he asked again, stepping forward.

"Yes, sir," I mumbled.

"Talk like it, then!"

"Oh, yes, sir!" I said with as much heartiness as I could muster.

Outside, I walked ahead of the girl, ashamed to face her. She caught up with me and said:

"Don't be a fool; yuh couldn't help it!"

This watchman boasted of having killed two Negroes in self-defense.

Yet, in spite of all this, the life of the hotel ran with an amazing smoothness. It would have been impossible for a stranger to detect anything. The maids, the hall-boys, and the bell-boys were all smiles. They had to be.

9

I had learned my Jim Crow lessons so thoroughly that I kept the hotel job till I left Jackson for Memphis. It so happened that while in Memphis I applied for a job at a branch of the optical company. I was hired. And for some reason, as long as I worked there, they never brought my past against me.

Here my Jim Crow education assumed quite a different form. It was no longer brutally cruel, but subtly cruel. Here I learned to steal, to dissemble. I learned to play that dual role which every Negro must play if he wants to eat and live.

For example, it was almost impossible to get a book to read. It was assumed that after a Negro had imbibed what scanty schooling the state furnished he had no further need for books. I was always borrowing books from men on the job. One day I mustered enough courage to ask one of the men to let me get books from the library in his name. Surprisingly, he consented. I cannot help but think that he consented because he was a Roman Catholic and felt a vague sympathy for Negroes, being himself an object of hatred. Armed with a library card, I obtained books in the following manner: I would write a note to the librarian, saying: "Please let this nigger boy have the following books." I would then sign it with the white man's name.

When I went to the library, I would stand at the desk, hat in hand, looking as unbookish as possible. When I received the books desired I would take them home. If the books listed in the note happened to be out, I would sneak into the lobby and forge a new one. I never took any chances guessing with the white librarian about what the fictitious white man would want to read. No doubt if any of the white patrons had suspected that some of the volumes they enjoyed had been in the home of a Negro, they would not have tolerated it for an instant.

The factory force of the optical company in Memphis was much larger than that in Jackson, and more urbanized. At least they liked to talk, and would engage the Negro help in conversation whenever possible. By this means I found that many subjects were taboo from the white man's point of view. Among the topics they did not like to discuss with Negroes were the following: American white women; the Ku Klux Klan; France, and how Negro soldiers fared while there; French women; Jack Johnson; the entire northern part of the United States; the Civil War; Abraham Lincoln; U. S. Grant; General Sherman; Catholics; the Pope; Jews; the Republican Party; slavery; social equality; Communism, Socialism; the 13th and 14th Amendments to the Constitution; or any topic calling for positive knowledge or manly self-assertion on the part of the Negro. The most accepted topics were sex and religion.

There were many times when I had to exercise a great deal of ingenuity to keep out of trouble. It is a southern custom that all men must take off their hats when they enter an elevator. And especially did this apply to us blacks with rigid force. One day I stepped into an elevator with my arms full of packages. I was forced to ride with my hat on. Two white men stared at me coldly. Then one of them very kindly lifted my hat and placed it upon my armful of packages. Now the most accepted response for a Negro to make under such circumstances is to look at the white man out of the corner of his eye and grin. To have said: "Thank you!" would have made the white man *think* that you *thought* you were receiving from him a personal service. For such an act I have seen Negroes take a blow in the mouth. Finding the first alternative distasteful, and the second dangerous, I hit upon an acceptable course of action which fell safely between these two poles. I immediately—no sooner than my hat was lifted—pretended that my packages were about to spill, and appeared deeply distressed with keeping them in my arms. In this fashion I evaded having to acknowledge his service, and, in spite of adverse circumstances, salvaged a slender shred of personal pride.

How do Negroes feel about the way they have to live? How do they discuss it when alone among themselves? I think this question can be answered in a single sentence. A friend of mine who ran an elevator once told me:

"Lawd, man! Ef it wuzn't fer them polices 'n' them ol' lynch-mobs, there wouldn't be nothin' but uproar down here!"

CHRONOLOGY

1776: July 4, Declaration of Independence; Hopkins, "Dialogue Concerning the Slavery of the Africans"

1777: Vermont abolishes slavery

1780: Population of the United States: 2,781,000; Pennsylvania abolishes slavery

1780: First African Baptist Church, Richmond, founded

1783: Treaty of Paris

1784: Methodist Episcopal Church formed, adopting a rule for the freeing of members' slaves (suspended in six months)

1786: New York African free school established

1787: Northwest Ordinance, prohibiting slavery in the Northwest Territory; Jefferson, *Notes on Virginia; The Federalist* (1787-1788)

1787: Free African Society organized by Absalom Jones and Richard Allen

1789: Constitution of the United States adopted; French Revolution begins

1789: *The Interesting Narrative of the Life of Olaulah Equiano, or Gustavus Vassa, the African*

1790: Population of the United States: 3,929,214

1790: Negro Population: 757,208 (19.3%)

1791: Haitian uprising under L'Ouverture; Bill of Rights

1792: Brackenridge, *Modern Chivalry*

1793: Haitian proclamation of freedom; first Fugitive Slave Law; Eli Whitney invents the cotton gin

1794: First convention of Abolition Societies meets in Philadelphia; Act to prohibit American vessels from supplying slaves to another country; Dwight, *Greenfield Hill*

1794: Richard Allen and Absalom Jones' *A Narrative of the Black People during the Late Awful Calamity in Philadelphia;* Zoar Methodist Episcopal Church organized in Philadelphia

1796: Varick establishes colored Methodist Episcopal church in New York City

1800: Population of the United States: 5,308,483; Capital moved to Washington

1797: George Moses Horton (1797-c. 1883), Northampton County, North Carolina

1801: Haitian declaration of independence

1800: Negro Population: 1,002,037 (18.9%); Gabriel insurrection, Henrico County, Virginia

1802: Lydia Maria Child (1802-1880)

1803: Louisiana Purchase; Ralph Waldo Emerson (1803-1882), Boston

1804: Nathaniel Hawthorne (1804-1864), Salem, Massachusetts

1807: John Greenleaf Whittier (1807-1892), Haverhill, Massachusetts; Henry Wadsworth Longfellow (1807-1882), Portland, Maine

1808: Further importation of slaves prohibited

1809: Abraham Lincoln (1809-1865), Kentucky; Edgar Allan Poe (1809-1849), Boston

1810: Population of the United States: 7,239,881; Theodore Parker (1810-1860), Lexington, Massachusetts; Elihu Burritt (1810-1879), New Britain, Connecticut

1810: Negro Population: 1,377,808 (19%); Charles Remond (1810-1873), Salem, Massachusetts

1811: Harriet Beecher Stowe (1811-1896), Litchfield, Connecticut

1811: Daniel A. Payne (1811-1893), Charleston, South Carolina

1812: War of 1812

1812: Martin R. Delany (1812-1885), Charlestown, Virginia

1813: Battle of Lake Erie

1814: Hartford Convention; Treaty of Ghent

1815: Lundy organizes the Union Humane Society, St. Clairsville, Ohio; Richard Henry Dana, Jr. (1815-1881), Cambridge Massachusetts; *North American Review* founded

1816: African Methodist Episcopal Church organized in Philadelphia

1817: American Colonization Society organized; First Seminole War; Henry David Thoreau (1817-1862), Concord, Massachusetts

1817: Frederick Douglass (1817-1895), Talbot County, Maryland

1819: Florida purchased; Congress empowers President to use navy to suppress slave trade; Walt Whitman (1819-1892), Huntington, Long Island; James Russell Lowell (1819-1891), Cambridge, Massachusetts; Herman Melville (1819-1891), New York City

1820: Negro Population: 1,771,656 (18.4%); George B. Vashon (1820-1878)

1821: African Methodist Episcopal Zion church organized in New York; William Still (1821-1902), Burlington County, New Jersey

1820: Population of the United States: 9,638,453

1822: Denmark Vesey insurrection, Charleston, South Carolina

1821: Liberian colony established; Lundy begins *The Genius of Universal Emancipation,* Mt. Pleasant, Ohio

1825: Frances E. W. Harper (1825-1911), Baltimore

1826: James Russwurm graduates from Bowdoin; James Bell (1826-1902), Gallipolis, Ohio

1824: Samuel Bowles establishes the Springfield *Republican*

1827: Captain and Mrs. Basil-Hall in America

1827: *Freedom's Journal,* edited by Samuel Cornish and John Russwurm, founded

1828: Tariff of Abominations

1829: Lundy and Garrison editing the *Genius of Universal Emancipation* in Baltimore

1829: Oblate Sisters of Providence founded in Baltimore by Dominican refugee; David Walker, *Appeal;* Horton, *Hope of Liberty*

1830: Population of the United States: 12,866,020; Weld begins his antislavery campaign

1830: Negro Population: 2,328,642 (18.1%); James M. Whitfield (1830-1870), Boston, Massachusetts

1831: Garrison founds *The Liberator*; Weld converts Birney to the antislavery position

1831: First convention of people of color, Philadelphia; Southampton insurrection led by Nat Turner

1832: South Carolina's Ordinance of Nullification; Kennedy, *Swallow Barn*

1832-1835: Removal of Florida and Georgia Indians

1833: American Anti-slavery Society organized; Rev. Dr. Furman of South Carolina proclaims slaveholding established by Holy Scripture; Prudence Crandall's school closed, Canterbury, Connecticut; Captain Hamilton, *Men and Manners in America*; Mrs. Child's *Appeal in Favor of That Class of Americans Called Africans*

1833: Robert Purvis attends first Antislavery Convention

1834 Lane Seminary debates; British emancipation of slaves; *Southern Literary Messenger* founded

1835: Finney called to Oberlin College, where students, regardless of sex or color, were to be educated; Noyes Academy, New Canaan, New Hampshire, destroyed by mob violence for accepting Negro students; Taney appointed chief justice; antislavery mails seized and burned at Charleston; Seminole War, 1835-1842; Garrison mobbed; De Tocqueville, *Democracy in America*; Longstreet, *Georgia Scenes*; Simms, *The Yemassee*

1836: People of the District of Columbia present memorial to Congress asking for the abolition of slavery in their territory; Tucker, *The Partisan Leader*

1837: Elijah P. Lovejoy killed by proslavery mob in Alton, Illinois; Wendell Phillips makes his first antislavery speech in protest; Harriet Martineau, *Society in America*; Emerson,

1837: James McCune Smith returns to New York from the University of Glasgow

"The American Scholar";
Whittier, *Abolition Poems*

1838: First gag resolution, banning
antislavery petition discussion;
Whittier begins to edit *The
Pennsylvania Freeman*; Phila-
delphia mob destroys Lundy's
Pennsylvania Hall

1839: Liberty Party holds convention
at Warsaw, N. Y.; *Amistad*
case

1840: Population of the United States:
17,069,453; Liberty Party
casts 7,069 votes; *The Dial*
founded; Brisbane, *Social Destiny of Man*

1841: *Creole* case and Giddings Resolutions; Brook Farm (1841-
1846); Greeley founds the
New York *Tribune*; David Lee
Child and Mrs. Lydia Maria
Child begin editing the *National Anti-Slavery Standard*

1842: Dickens in America; Longfellow, *Poems on Slavery*; Hawthorne, *Twice-Told Tales*;
Sidney Lanier (1842-1881),
Macon, Georgia

1843: Wesleyan Methodist Connection, opposing slavery and intoxicating liquors, organized;
Whittier, "Massachusetts to
Virginia," after Latimer fugitive slave case

1844: Whittier, *Voices of Freedom*;
Georgia Washington Cable
(1844-1925), New Orleans

1845: Methodist Episcopal Church,
South, organized; Southern
Baptist Convention organized;
Texas annexed; Irish immi-
gration as result of famine in
Ireland; Mowatt, *Fashion*;
Lowell begins to write for *The
Pennsylvania Freeman*

1846: Wilmot Proviso; Mexican War
(1846-1848); Melville, *Typee*;
Hooper, *Adventures of Simon
Suggs*

1847: Free and Independent Republic
of Liberia established

1848: Lowell becomes corresponding
editor of the *National Anti-
Slavery Standard;* publishes

1838: Douglass escapes from slavery;
David Ruggles establishes the
Mirror for Liberty, first Negro
magazine; William Whipper
establishes the *National Reformer* in Philadelphia; Remond begins career as anti-
slavery lecturer

1839: Samuel Ringgold Ward becomes
minister of the Congregational
Church and agent for the
American Anti-slavery Society

1840: Negro Population: 2,873,648
(16.8%); Remond goes to
London for the World Anti-
slavery Convention

1841: Daniel Payne, "An Original
Poem Composed for the Soirée
of the Vigilant Committee of
Philadelphia"; Garrison meets
Douglass at Nantucket anti-
slavery meeting

1842: Congregation of the Sisters of
the Holy Family established
at New Orleans

1843: William Wells Brown becomes
lecturer for the Western New
York Anti-slavery Society; Delany's *Mystery* (1843-1847)
established in Pittsburgh; Garnet delivers "An Address to
the Slaves of the United States
of America" at Buffalo

1845: Douglass goes to England to
lecture; first edition of the
*Narrative of the Life of Fred-
erick Douglass*

1846: *Correspondence between the
Rev. Samuel H. Cox . . . and
Frederick Douglass, a Fugitive
Slave,* first extant Douglass
pamphlet

1847: Douglass' *North Star* begins publication; *Narrative of William
W. Brown* published by the
Massachusetts Anti-slavery Society; Still begins to work with
the Pennsylvania Anti-slavery
Society

1848: W. W. Brown, *Antislavery*

Biglow Papers; Foster, *Songs of the Sable Harmonists*; Joel Chandler Harris (1848-1908), Eatonton, Georgia

1849: California Gold Rush; German immigration as result of Revolution of 1848; Melville, *Mardi*

1850: Population of the United States: 23,191,876; Fugitive Slave Law and Compromise of 1850; slave trade prohibited in the District of Columbia after January 1, 1851; Hawthorne, *The Scarlet Letter*; Lafcadio Hearn (1850-1894), Leucadia, Greece; Charles Egbert Craddock (1850-1922), Murfreesboro, Tennessee; *Harper's* founded

1851: Christiana (Pa.) riot; Shadrach case, both involving fugitive slaves; Melville, *Moby Dick*; Hawthorne, *The House of Seven Gables*; Whittier, "Ichabod"; *Uncle Tom's Cabin* begins in *The National Era*

1852: *Uncle Tom's Cabin* produced as a play in Troy, New York; Mrs. Eastman, *Aunt Phyllis' Cabin*

1853: *A Key to Uncle Tom's Cabin;* Lieber, *On Civil Liberty*; Thomas Nelson Page (1853-1922), Hanover Co., Va.; Irwin Russell (1853-1879), Port Gibson, Mississippi

1854: Kansas-Nebraska Bill; Anthony Burns's rendition; Fitzhugh, *Sociology for the South*; Mrs. Hentz, *The Planter's Northern Bride*

Harp; Ward establishes the *Impartial Citizen,* in Syracuse

1849: W. W. Brown goes to Britain as a lecturer, delivering more than a thousand addresses in five years; *The Life of Josiah Henson . . .; Narrative of Henry Box Brown;* Harriet Tubman escapes from slavery; G. W. Williams (1849-1891), Pennsylvania; Archibald H. Grimké (1849-1930), Charleston, South Carolina

1850: Negro Population: 3,638,808 (15.7%); *Narrative of Sojourner Truth, Northern Slave;* Francis J. Grimké (1850-1938), Charleston, South Carolina

1851: Douglass breaks with Garrison, joins the Liberty Party; Delany enters Harvard Medical School; William Nell, *Services of Colored Americans in the Wars of 1776 and 1812;* Albery A. Whitman (1851-1902), Kentucky

1852: W. W. Brown's *Three Years in Europe* published in England; Delany, *The Condition, Elevation, Emigration, and Destiny of the Colored People of the United States . . .; Christian Recorder* begins publication

1853: W. W. Brown's *Clotel, or the President's Daughter,* first novel by an American Negro; Ward goes to England to lecture for the Anti-slavery Society of Canada; Crummell goes to Liberia after graduating from Queen's College, Cambridge; Whitfield, "America," *Autographs of Freedom*

1854: Colored Colonization Convention; Lincoln University founded as Ashmun Institute; Douglass delivers *Claims of the Negro Ethnologically Considered* at Western Reserve commencement; W. W. Brown manumitted

1855: Massachusetts citizens purchase Anthony Burns for $1300; Lowell appointed to Harvard; Whitman, *Leaves of Grass*; Longfellow, *The Song of Hiawatha*; Melville, *Benito Cereno*

1856: Battle of Ossawatomie; Brooks attacks Sumner; first Republican National Convention, Philadelphia; Mrs. Stowe's *Dred*

1857: Dred Scott decision; *Atlantic Monthly* founded, Lowell editing the magazine to 1861; Whittier, *Collected Poems*

1858: Lincoln-Douglas debates; crew of the *Echo*, slave ship seized by U. S. brig *Dolphin*, freed by grand jury in Columbia, S. C.

1859: John Brown at Harper's Ferry; Mrs. Child asks permission to nurse Brown; last slave ship, *The Clothilde*, lands in Mobile Bay; Boucicault, *The Octoroon*, playing in New York; Darwin, *Origin of the Species*; Helper, *The Impending Crisis*

1860: Population of the United States: 31,443,790; Lincoln elected president; South Carolina secedes; Child-Mason-Wise correspondence; Hamlin Garland (1860-1940), Wisconsin

1861: Civil War (1861-1865)

1862: Antietam; Freedmen's Relief Association; *Artemus Ward: His Book*; O. Henry (1862-1910), Greensboro, N. C.

1863: Emancipation Proclamation; West Virginia admitted to the Union, establishes public schools for Negroes; Gettysburg and Lincoln's Gettysburg Address; Vicksburg

1864: Sherman in Georgia; Locke, *Nasby Papers*

1865: Lincoln's Second Inaugural Address; Appomattox; assassination of Lincoln; Freedmen's Bureau established; Thirteenth Amendment; Phillips con-

1855: Douglass, *My Bondage and My Freedom;* Ward, *The Autobiography of a Fugitive Negro* (London); Ward goes to Jamaica; W. W. Brown, *Sketches of Places and People Abroad;* Nell, *The Colored Patriots in the American Revolution*

1856: Wilberforce founded by the Methodist Episcopal Church; Rogers, *Repeal of the Missouri Compromise Considered;* Charles Chesnutt (1856-1932), Cleveland

1858: Brown, *The Escape,* first play by a Negro author; National Colonization Convention in Cleveland; Booker T. Washington (1858-1915), Hales Ford, Virginia

1859: *Echo* slaves returned to Liberia. Delany, *Blake, or the Huts of America; The Rev. J. W. Loguen, as a Slave and as a Freeman;* Hamilton's *Anglo-African Magazine* begins publication

1860: Negro Population: 4,441,830 (14.1%)

1861: Mary Peake establishes school at Fortress Monroe, Virginia, out of which Hampton Institute grew; Joseph S. Cotter, Sr. (1861-   ), Bardstown, Kentucky

1863: W. W. Brown, *The Black Man . . .;* Kelly Miller (1863-1939), Winnsboro, South Carolina

1865: Delany commissioned a major in the Union army; Shaw, Atlanta, Wayland (Virginia Union) founded

tinues Anti-Slavery Society; E. L. Godkin founds *The Nation*; Whitman, *Drum Taps*

1866: Civil Rights Act; Tennessee re-admitted; race riots in New Orleans; Locke, *Swingin' round the Circle*

1867: Reconstruction begins; Ku Klux Klan organized; Alaska purchased; T. W. Higginson, "Negro Spirituals," *Atlantic Monthly*; W. F. Allen *et al.*, *Slave Songs of the United States*; Helper, *Nojoque*

1868: Fourteenth Amendment; Johnson impeached

1869: Union Pacific completed; Mark Twain, *Innocents Abroad*

1870: Population of the United States: 39,818,449; Fifteenth Amendment; Enforcement Act; Ku Klux Klan; organization of Standard Oil Company; American Anti-slavery Society comes to an end; *Scribner's* founded; Higginson, *Army Life in a Black Regiment*; Frank Norris (1870-1902), Chicago

1871: Whitman, *Democratic Vistas*; Howells becomes editor of the *Atlantic*; Stephen Crane (1871-1900), Newark, New Jersey; Theodore Dreiser, (1871-), Terre Haute, Indiana

1872: Horace Greeley dies; Twain, *Roughing It*; Gertrude Stein (1872-), Baltimore

1873: Warner and Twain, *The Gilded Age*

1874: Civil Rights act; W. C. T. U. founded; Vicksburg, Mississippi, race riots; Amy Lowell (1874-1925), Brookline, Massachusetts; Ellen Glasgow (1874-), Richmond, Virginia

1866: Fisk University founded

1867: Howard University chartered; Talladega, Morehouse, Johnson C. Smith founded; W. W. Brown, *The Negro in the American Rebellion;* W. E. B. DuBois (1868-), Great Barrington, Massachusetts

1868: J. W. Menard, elected to Congress from Louisiana, refused seat by the House; G. W. Williams organizes student body at Howard on a military basis; Mrs. Keckley, *Behind the Scenes*

1869: Douglass founds the *New National Era* (1869-1872), Washington; Clark, Morgan founded; Langston dean of the Howard Law School; James D. Corrothers (1869-1919), Cass County, Michigan

1870: Negro Population: 4,880,009 (12.7%); Colored Methodist Episcopal Church organized at Jackson, Tennessee; Hiram R. Revels elected to the United States Senate from Mississippi

1871: Fisk Jubilee Singers make first concert tour

1872: Douglass' Rochester house and papers destroyed by fire; *Southern Workmen* founded at Hampton; Still, *The Underground Railroad;* Elliot's Emancipation Oration; Paul Laurence Dunbar (1872-1906), Dayton, Ohio; James Weldon Johnson (1872-1930), Jacksonville, Florida

1873: Crummell returns from Liberia as rector of St. Luke's, Washington; Mrs. Harper, *Sketches of Southern Life;* Bennett College founded

1874: G. W. Williams graduates from Newton Theological Seminary; W. W. Brown, *The Rising Son*

1875: Robert Frost (1875-   ), San Francisco; J. E. Spingarn (1875-1940), New York City

1876: Harrison-Tilden election; Twain, *Tom Sawyer*; Jack London (1876-1916), San Francisco; Ole Rölvaag (1876-1931), Norway; Sherwood Anderson (1876-1941), Camden, Ohio; Willa Cather (1876-   ), Winchester, Virginia

1877: Withdrawal of federal troops from the South; Morgan, *Ancient Society*; Page, "Uncle Gabe's White Folks," *Scribner's*; Lanier, *Poems*

1878: Hearn's Creole Sketches begin to appear in New Orleans newspapers; Carl Sandburg, Galesburg, Illinois, and Upton Sinclair, Baltimore (1878-   ).

1879: Cable, *Old Creole Days*; Tourgee, *A Fool's Errand*; Cooke, *Stories of the Old Dominion*; George, *Progress and Poverty*; Vachel Lindsay (1879-1931), Springfield, Illinois

1880: Population of the United States: 50,155,783; Harris, *Uncle Remus: His Songs and Sayings*; Tourgee, *Bricks without Straw*

1881: American Federation of Labor organized; Howells leaves the *Atlantic Monthly*; Cable, *Madame Delphine*; Henry James, *Portrait of a Lady*; Carl Schurz joins *The Nation* staff

1882: John F. Slater Fund created; Twain, *Life on the Mississippi*; Howells, *A Modern Instance*; Whitman, *Specimen Days*

1883: Civil Rights Act invalidated; opening of Brooklyn Bridge; Pulitzer purchases *World*; Howe, *The Story of a Country Town*; L. F. Ward, *Dynamic Sociology*; Sumner, *What Social Classes Owe to Each Other*

1884: Slaughter-House Cases: first opinion indicating the use to

1875: Knoxville College founded; Blanche K. Bruce of Mississippi elected to the United States Senate; Carter G. Woodson (1875-   ), Buckingham County, Virginia

1877: Whitman, *Not a Man and Yet a Man*

1878: Flipper, *The Colored Cadet at West Point*; William Stanley Braithwaite, (1878-   ), Boston

1879: Negro exodus to Kansas; T. Thomas Fortune goes to New York, edits *The Rumor* (later, The New York *Globe*); *The Washington Bee* founded

1880: Negro Population: 6,580,793 (13.1%); W. W. Brown, *My Southern Home*

1881: Booker T. Washington opens Tuskegee Institute; Spelman College founded; *Life and Times of Frederick Douglass;* Scarborough, *First Lessons in Greek*

1882: Benjamin G. Brawley (1882-1939), Columbia, South Carolina

1883: G. W. Williams, *History of the Negro Race*

1884: Whitman, *The Rape of Florida*

which the Fourteenth Amendment was to be put in protecting business; Twain, *Huckleberry Finn*; Page, "Marse Chan" in *Century Magazine*; Craddock, *In the Tennessee Mountains*

1885: Howells, *The Rise of Silas Lapham*

1886: Haymarket Riot; Howells in "The Editor's Easy Chair," *Harper's*; H. James, *The Bostonians*

1887: Founding of the Catholic University of America; Page, *In Ole Virginia*

1888: Daniel Hand fund created; Cable, *The Negro Question*; Russell, *Poems*; Allen, "Two Gentlemen of Kentucky"; Bellamy, *Looking Backward*

1889: John D. Rockefeller makes his first gift to the University of Chicago

1890: Population of the United States: 62,947,714; Mississippi constitution points way to disfranchisement of Negroes; William James, *The Principles of Psychology*; Riis, *How the Other Half Lives*; Grady, *The New South*

1891: Beginnings of the Populist Party; eleven Italians lynched in New Orleans; deaths of Lowell and Melville; Smith, *Colonel Carter of Cartersville*; Allen, "King Solomon of Kentucky"; Garland, *Main Travelled Roads*

1892: Homestead, Pennsylvania, and Coeur d'Alene, Idaho, strikes; deaths of Whitman and Whittier; Howells, *An Imperative Duty*

1893: Chicago World's Fair; Grace King, *Balcony Stories*; Turner, "The Significance of the Frontier in American History"; Ward, *The Psychic Factors of Civilization*

1894: Coal strike; Coxey's Army; Pullman and railroad strikes; first motion picture; Twain, *Pud-*

1887: Chesnutt publishes "The Goophered Grapevine," is admitted to bar in Cleveland; William J. Simmons' biographical dictionary, *Men of Mark;* Fortune begins to edit *The New York Age*

1888: Bishop Payne, *Recollections of Seventy Years*

1890: Negro Population: 7,488,676 (11.9%)

1891: Schomburg comes to America; Langston takes seat in the House of Representatives; A. H. Grimké, *Life of Charles Sumner;* Penn, *The Afro-American Press*

1892: John H. Murphy founds the Baltimore *Afro-American*

1893: Dunbar, *Oak and Ivy*

1894: Langston, *From the Virginia Plantation to the National Capital*

AMERICAN SCENE	NEGRO WORLD
d'nhead Wilson; Kate Chopin, *Bayou Folk*	1895: Bob Cole, *A Trip to Coontown*, first musical produced and managed by Negroes; Alice Moore (Dunbar-Nelson), *Violets and Other Tales;* Williams and Walker arrive in New York (Tony Pastor's); Booker T. Washington delivers his Atlanta Exposition Address (September)
1895: Cuban rebellion; Crane, *Red Badge of Courage*	
1896: Plessy v. Ferguson: Louisiana jim-crow law upheld by the Supreme Court	1896: DuBois, *The Suppression of the African Slave Trade;* DuBois goes to Atlanta as professor of economics and history; Dunbar, *Lyrics of Lowly Life*
1897: Alaska gold rush; Glasgow, *The Descendant*	1897: Crummell founds the American Negro Academy in Washington; Tanner completes "The Resurrection of Lazarus"; D. W. Davis,. *Weh Down Souf';* Scarborough, "Negro Folk-Lore and Dialect"
1898: Spanish-American War; Hawaiian Islands annexed; Puerto Rico and the Philippines annexed; Wilmington, North Carolina, riots; Markham, "The Man with the Hoe"	1898: Cook and Dunbar, *Clorindy;* Cotter, *Links of Friendship;* Dunbar, *Folks from Dixie, The Uncalled*
1899: Philippine insurrection; Burton, *Old Plantation Hymns*; Norris, *McTeague*; Veblen, *The Theory of the Leisure Class*	1899: Chesnutt, *The Conjure Woman, The Wife of His Youth, Frederick Douglass;* Dunbar, *Lyrics of the Hearthside;* DuBois, *The Philadelphia Negro*
1900: Population of the United States: 75,994,575; Boxer Rebellion, China; Long and Belasco, *Madame Butterfly*; Dreiser, *Sister Carrie*	1900: Negro Population: 8,833,994 (11.6%); Chesnutt, *The House behind the Cedars;* Dunbar, *The Love of Landry, The Strength of Gideon;* Washington, *Up from Slavery,* begins in the *Outlook; The Chicago Defender* founded; first meeting of the National Negro Business League, Boston
1901: Hay-Pauncefote treaty; Norris, *The Octopus*; Carnegie, *The Gospel of Wealth*; Cable, *The Cavalier*	1901: Monroe Trotter founds the *Boston Guardian*; Whitman, "The Octoroon"; Chesnutt, *The Marrow of Tradition;* Dunbar, *The Fanatics, The Sport of the Gods* (in *Lippincott's*)
1902: John D. Rockefeller establishes the General Education Board; anthracite coal mine strike; Virginia constitution disfranchising Negroes; Riis, *The Battle with the Slum*; Dixon, *The Leopard's Spots*	1902: Dunbar, Cook, Shipp and Rogers, *In Dahomey*
1903: Panama revolts from Colombia; Wright brothers fly their plane at Kitty Hawk, North Carolina	1903: Dubois, *Souls of Black Folk;* Dunbar, *Lyrics of Love and Laughter, In Old Plantation Days*

1904: Page, *The Negro, the Southerner's Problem*; Steffens, *The Shame of the Cities*; Glasgow, *The Deliverance*

1905: Industrial Workers of the World organized; Federal Council of Churches organized; London, *The War of the Classes*; Dixon, *The Clansman*

1906: San Francisco earthquake and fire; segregation of Japanese children in San Francisco schools; Atlanta, Georgia, and Brownsville, Texas, riots; construction of Panama Canal begins; Henry Adams, *The Education of Henry Adams*; Sinclair, *The Jungle*

1907: William James, *Pragmatism*; Sumner, *Folkways*; Rauschenbusch, *Christianity and the Social Crisis*

1908: Springfield, Illinois, riots; *Social Creed of the Churches*

1909: North Pole reached by Peary and Henson; Commission to investigate Liberian affairs; Stein, *Three Lives*; Sheldon, *The Nigger*

1910: Population of the United States: 93,402,151; Carnegie Corporation chartered; Lomax, *Cowboy Songs*; Moody, *The Faith Healer*; Robinson, *The Town down the River*

1912: Roosevelt forms the Progressive Party; first Rosenwald aid to rural schools; Harriet Monroe founds *Poetry: a Magazine of Verse*

1913: Department of Labor created; Smith-Lever bill; grandfather clause, disfranchising Negroes, held unconstitutional; Max Eastman edits *The Masses* (later, *The Liberator*)

1914: Lindsay, *The Congo and Other Poems*; Amy Lowell, *Sword Blades and Poppy Seeds*; *The Little Review* founded

1915: Panama Canal opened; *Lusitania* sunk; Ford's Peace Ship; *Some Imagist Poets, 1915;* Masters,

1904: Braithwaite, *Lyrics of Life and Love;* Dunbar, *The Heart of Happy Hollow*

1906: James Weldon Johnson consul in Venezuela; Williams and Walker in *Abyssinia;* Allen, *Rhymes, Tales and Rhymed Tales;* Cotter, *Caleb, the Degenerate;* DuBois, "Litany of Atlanta"

1907: Locke graduates from Harvard, wins Rhodes scholarship for Pennsylvania; Braithwaite, *The House of Falling Leaves;* Williams and Walker in *Bandanna Land*

1908: Cole and Johnson write and play in *Red Moon*

1909: Miller, *Race Adjustment;* founding of the National Association for the Advancement of Colored People

1910: Negro Population: **9,827,763** (10.7%); DuBois made director of publicity, editor of *The Crisis* for the N. A. A. C. P.; first edition of Brawley, *The Negro in Literature and Art in the United States*

1911: National Urban League organized; Bert Williams joins *Ziegfeld Follies*; DuBois, *The Quest of the Silver Fleece*

1912: McKay comes to America to study at Tuskegee; J. W. Johnson, *The Autobiography of an Ex-Colored Man*

1913: Harriet Tubman dies, Auburn, New York; Dunbar, *Complete Poems*

1914: N. A. A. C. P. exposes and blocks anti-intermarriage, segregation laws in the District of Columbia, and bill to exclude Negroes from the army and the navy; Cromwell, *The Negro in American History;* W. C. Handy, "St. Louis Blues"; Mamie Smith makes the first blues recording

1915: Booker T. Washington dies; first Spingarn Medal for achievement presented to E. E. Just;

Spoon River Anthology; New Republic founded; D. W. Griffith's motion picture, *The Birth of a Nation*

1916: Virgin Islands purchased; Mexican border clashes; Dewey, *Democracy and Education;* Sandburg, *Chicago Poems;* Amy Lowell, *Men, Women, and Ghosts*

1917: United States enters World War I; Smith-Hughes bill; East St. Louis race riots; Julius Rosenwald Fund established; Torrence, *Three Plays for a Negro Theatre*

1918: Wilson's fourteen points; Armistice; Sandburg, *Cornhuskers;* Joyce's *Ulysses* appearing in *The Little Review*

1919: Chicago, Washington riots; Sherwood Anderson, *Winesburg, Ohio;* Frank, *Our America;* Mencken, *The American Language;* Veblen, *The Higher Learning in America*

1920: Population of the United States: 105,710,620; Nineteenth Amendment ratified; Sandburg, *Smoke and Steel;* Anderson, *Poor White;* O'Neill, *The Emperor Jones*

1921: Tulsa race riots; Dos Passos, *Three Soldiers;* Robinson, *Collected Poems*

1922: T. S. Eliot, *The Waste Land;* Sinclair Lewis, *Babbitt;* Eugene O'Neill, *The Hairy Ape;* Tate, Ransom, Davidson found *The Fugitive;* Gonzales, *The Black Border*

Association for the Study of Negro Life and History founded; J. W. Work, *Folk Songs of the American Negro*

1916: Tenth Cavalry and Twenty-fourth Infantry with Pershing's Mexican punitive force; J. W. Johnson becomes secretary of the N. A. A. C. P.; first issue of the *Journal of Negro History*, Woodson as editor; Locke, *Race Contacts and Inter-racial Relations*

1916-1919: Great migration of Southern Negroes to Northern industrial centers

1917-1918: 367,710 Negroes inducted into the military service; 1400 officers commissioned

1918: Walter White joins N. A. A. C. P. staff; Miller, *The Appeal to Conscience*

1919: Washington, Chicago race riots; Pan-African Congress, Paris; Claude McKay's "If We Must Die," in *The Liberator*; Fletcher Henderson's first Roseland Orchestra, first large Negro band to play Broadway

1920: Negro Population: 10,463,131 (9.9%); "King" Oliver organizes his Creole Jazz Band; DuBois, *Darkwater*

1921: C. S. Johnson becomes director of research and publicity for the National Urban League; Frazier in Denmark; McKay goes to Russia; Handy, *Loveless Love;* Sissle and Blake, *Shuffle Along;* Gilpin plays *The Emperor Jones*; J. W. Johnson, *The Book of American Negro Poetry;* Brawley, *A Social History of the American Negro*

1922: Garvey's Universal Negro Improvement Association reaching height of its influence; *Shuffle Along* reaches Broadway, first of a series of popular musicals; first edition of Woodson, *The Negro in Our History;* McKay, *Harlem*

1923: District of Columbia minimum wage law held unconstitutional; Frank, *Holiday;* Cather, *A Lost Lady;* O'Neill, *All God's Chillun Got Wings*

1924: *The American Mercury* founded; Green, *In Abraham's Bosom;* E. Dickinson, *Complete Poems;* Peterkin, *Green Thursday*

1925: Scopes (evolution) trial, Dayton, Tennessee; Dos Passos, *Manhattan Transfer;* Dreiser, *An American Tragedy;* Lewis, *Arrowsmith;* Glasgow, *Barren Ground;* Anderson, *Dark Laughter;* Van Vechten, *Nigger Heaven;* Heyward, *Porgy,* and *Mamba's Daughters;* Gaines, *The Southern Plantation;* Odum and Johnson, *The Negro and His Songs*

1926: Hemingway, *The Sun Also Rises;* Mumford, *The Golden Day;* Sheldon and MacArthur, *Lulu Belle;* Odum and Johnson, *Negro Workaday Songs;* Sandburg, *Abraham Lincoln, The Prairie Years*

1927: Sacco and Vanzetti executed; great Mississippi flood; Roberts, *My Heart and My Flesh;* Adams, *Congaree Sketches;* Peterkin, *Black April;* Theatre Guild's *Porgy;* Rölvaag, *Giants in the Earth;* Sandburg, *The American Songbag;* Parrington, *Main Currents in American Thought,* Vols. I and II; Beard and Beard, *The Rise of American Civilization*

1928: Benet, *John Brown's Body;* Peterkin, *Scarlet Sister Mary;* Odum, *Rainbow Round My Shoulder;* Bradford, *Ol' Man Adam an' His Chillun;* White, *American Negro Folk-Songs*

1929: Collapse of the New York stock market, followed by business depression; Botkin edits first *Folk-Say: A Regional Miscellany;* Bynner, *Indian Earth;* Wolfe, *Look Homeward,*

Shadows; G. D. Johnson, *Bronze*

1923: *Opportunity: Journal of Negro Life* begins publication, C. S. Johnson, editor; Toomer, *Cane*

1924: *Crisis* and *Opportunity* prizes for creative expression announced; Miller, *The Everlasting Stain;* Fauset, *There Is Confusion;* Miller and Lyles in *Runnin' Wild;* DuBois, *The Gift of Black Folk*

1925: Garvey imprisoned; Sweet trial (residential segregation case), Detroit; Locke edits Harlem number of the *Survey Graphic, The New Negro;* Johnson and Johnson, *The Book of American Negro Spirituals;* Cullen, *Color;* White, *Fire in the Flint;* Louis Armstrong's Hot Five recording

1926: Florence Mills in *Blackbirds;* Handy and Niles, *Blues;* Jessye, *My Spirituals;* Hughes, *The Weary Blues;* White, *Flight,* Walrond, *Tropic Death*

1927: Garvey deported; J. W. Johnson, *God's Trombones;* Hughes, *Fine Clothes to the Jew;* Charles S. Johnson (ed.), *Ebony and Topaz;* Wesley, *Negro Labor in the United States;* Louis Armstrong organizes own band, playing at the Sunset, Chicago; Duke Ellington opens at the Cotton Club, Harlem

1928: Fisher, *The Walls of Jericho;* McKay, *Home to Harlem;* DuBois, *Dark Princess;* Fauset, *Plum Bun;* Larsen, *Quicksand*

1929: Cullen, *The Black Christ;* McKay, *Banjo;* Thurman, *The Blacker the Berry*

Angel; Green, *The House of Connelly;* Rice, *Street Scene*

1930: Population of the United States: 122,775,046; *I'll Take My Stand;* Connelly, *The Green Pastures;* Gold, *Jews without Money*

1931: Faulkner, *Sanctuary;* MacLeish, *Conquistador;* O'Neill, *Mourning Becomes Electra;* Rourke, *American Humor;* Stribling, *The Forge;* Caldwell, *American Earth*

1932: Reconstruction Finance Corporation established; World War veterans' "Bonus March" on Washington; F. D. Roosevelt elected; Faulkner, *Light in August*

1933: Depression measures of the New Deal: banks closed by Presidential order, Civilian Conservation Corps, Civilian Works Authority, Farm and Unemployment Relief bills, T. V. A. bill, National Industrial Recovery Act, Home Owners' Loan bill; Stribling, *The Store;* Stein, *Autobiography of Alice B. Toklas;* Barnes, *The Antislavery Impulse*

1934: *Culture in the South;* Young, *So Red the Rose;* Mumford, *Technics and Civilization;* Josephson, *The Robber Barons;* March, *Come in at the Door;* Peters and Sklar, *Stevedore;* Wexley, *They Shall Not Die*

1935: Works Progress Administration established, including the Federal Arts Projects; National Labor Relations Board; Social Security Act; N. R. A. declared unconstitutional; First American Writers' Congress; Cohn, *God Shakes Creation;* Wolfe, *Of Time and the River;* Caldwell, *Kneel to the Rising Sun;* Odets, *Waiting for Lefty;* Gershwin, *Porgy and Bess;* J. A. and Alan Lomax, *American Ballads and Folk Songs*

1930: Negro Population: 11,891,143 (9.7%); J. W. Johnson, *Saint Peter Relates an Incident and Black Manhattan;* Hughes, *Not Without Laughter;* C. S. Johnson, *The Negro in American Civilization*

1931: Fauset, *The Chinaberry Tree;* Bontemps, *God Sends Sunday; The Journal of Negro Education* founded; Spero and Harris, *The Black Worker*

1932: Defection from the Republican party in the Hoover-Roosevelt campaign; Brown, *Southern Road;* McKay, *Gingertown;* Fisher, *The Conjure Man Dies;* first Negro detective novel

1933: First Scottsboro trials; J. W. Johnson, *Along This Way;* McKay, *Banana Bottom;* Fauset, *Comedy, American Style*

1934: Hughes, *The Ways of White Folks;* C. S. Johnson, *The Shadow of the Plantation;* J. W. Johnson, *Negro Americans, What Now?*

1935: Harlem race riots; beginning of the "swing" fad; Davis, *Black Man's Verse;* Hurston, *Mules and Men;* Henderson, *Ollie Miss;* Bontemps, *Black Thunder;* Hughes's *Mulatto* begins longest run enjoyed by play by a Negro

AMERICAN SCENE	NEGRO WORLD
1936: Agricultural Adjustment Act declared unconstitutional; C.I.O. unions suspended; Dos Passos, *The Big Money;* Eliot, *Collected Poems;* publication of *The Dictionary of American English* begins; Brooks, *The Flowering of New England;* Lomax and Lomax, *Negro Folk Songs as Sung by Lead Belly;* Shaw, *Bury the Dead;* Faulkner, *Absalom, Absalom!*	1936: Brawley, *Paul Laurence Dunbar;* Harris, *The Negro as Capitalist;* Lee, *River George*
1937: "Sit-down" strikes; Saxon, *Children of Strangers;* Steinbeck, *Of Mice and Men;* Benton, *An Artist in America;* Dollard, *Caste and Class in a Southern Town*	1937: Hurston, *Their Eyes Were Watching God;* Turpin, *These Low Grounds*
1938: Mumford, *The Culture of Cities;* Blitzstein, *The Cradle Will Rock; These Are Our Lives;* Meade, *The Back Door;* Caldwell, *Southways;* MacLeish, *Land of the Free*	1938: Gaines v. University of Missouri provides for equal educational facilities; Brawley, *Negro Builders and Heroes;* Wright, *Uncle Tom's Children*
1939: World War II; Steinbeck, *The Grapes of Wrath;* Sandburg, *Abraham Lincoln, The War Years; Mamba's Daughters* produced; Hobson, *American Jazz Music;* Sargent, *Jazz: Hot and Hybrid;* Ramsey and Smith, *Jazzmen*	1939: Turpin, *O Canaan!;* Frazier, *The Negro Family in the United States;* DuBois, *Black Folk, Then and Now*
1940: Population of the United States: 131,669,275; F. D. Roosevelt re-elected for a third term; Cather, *Sapphira and the Slave Girl;* McCullers, *The Heart Is a Lonely Hunter;* Adamic, *From Many Lands;* Faulkner, *The Hamlet;* Hemingway, *For Whom the Bell Tolls;* Caldwell, *Trouble in July*	1940: *Phylon* established with DuBois as editor; American Youth Commission volumes; *The Negro in Virginia;* Wright, *Native Son;* DuBois, *Dusk of Dawn;* Hughes, *The Big Sea;* McKay, *Harlem; Negro Metropolis*
	1941: Mitchell vs. Interstate Commerce Commission, Illinois Central Railroad, Chicago, Rock Island and Pacific Railway Company, et cetera; Locke, *The Negro in Art;* Richard Wright, *Twelve Million Black Voices;* William Attaway, *Blood on the Forge;* Davis and Gardiner, *Deep South*

INDEX

OF AUTHORS AND SELECTIONS

BLACK HISTORY

Other Books of Interest

Individual titles in Series I, II, and III of the Arno Press collection THE AMERICAN NEGRO: HIS HISTORY AND LITERATURE are listed on the following pages. These reprints are, in many instances, the actual records of those who were part of the Negro experience; they encompass the economic, political, and cultural history of the Negro from colonial time to the present. The 139 cloth-bound books in the collection are listed alphabetically by author/editor; immediately following is a list of the titles which are also available in paperback.

The books in THE AMERICAN NEGRO collection were selected by an Editorial Advisory Board made up of the following members:

William Loren Katz, General Editor, and author of **Eyewitness: The Negro in American History** and **Teacher's Guide to American Negro History**

Arthur P. Davis, Professor of English, Howard University

Jean Blackwell Hutson, Curator, The Schomburg Collection, New York Public Library

Sara D. Jackson, National Archives, Washington, D.C.

Ernest Kaiser, The Schomburg Collection, New York Public Library

Ulysses Lee (deceased), Professor of English, Morgan State College

James M. McPherson, Professor of History, Princeton University

Dorothy B. Porter, Curator, Negro Collection, Howard University

Benjamin Quarles, Professor of History, Morgan State College

Darwin T. Turner, Dean of the Graduate School, North Carolina A & T College

Doxey A. Wilkerson, Professor of Education, Yeshiva University

Individual volume prices are shown along with the International Standard Book Number (ISBN) which should be used to order. When ordering, please add 35¢ per copy to cover postage and handling costs. New York State residents please add applicable sales tax. To order, or for an annotated brochure, please write to: ARNO PRESS, 330 Madison Avenue, New York, N.Y. 10017.

The American Negro Academy Occasional Papers, Numbers 1-22.................... ISBN 0-405-01913-0 $21.50

Andrews, Sydney **The South Since the War:** As Shown by Fourteen Weeks of Travel and Observation in Georgia and the Carolinas.............ISBN 0-405-01847-9 $12.00

The Anglo-African Magazine, Volume 1, 1859...........ISBN 0-405-01803-7 $12.50

Anti-Negro Riots in the North, 1863....................ISBN 0-405-01848-7 $ 3.50

Atlanta University **Atlanta University Publications, Numbers 1, 2, 4, 8, 9, 11, 13, 14, 15, 16, 17, 18**......................................ISBN 0-405-01804-5 $30.00

Atlanta University **Atlanta University Publications, Numbers 3, 5, 6, 7, 10, 12, 19, 20** ISBN 0-405-01914-9 $33.00

Bell, Howard H. (editor) **Minutes of the Proceedings of the National Negro Conventions, 1830-1864** ....ISBN 0-405-01916-5 $17.00

Bell, Howard H. **A Survey of the Negro Convention Movement, 1830-1861**............ ISBN 0-405-01915-7 $12.00

Bonner, T. D. **The Life and Adventures of James P. Beckworth, Mountaineer, Scout, and Pioneer, and Chief of the Crow Nation of Indians**......ISBN 0-405-01850-9 $16.00

Botume, Elizabeth Hyde **First Days Amongst the Contrabands**...................... ISBN 0-405-01805-3 $10.50

Brown, Sterling **The Negro in American Fiction** and **Negro Poetry and Drama**.......... ISBN 0-405-01851-7 $10.50

Brown, Sterling; Davis, Arthur P. and Lee, Ulysses (editors) **The Negro Caravan**....... ISBN 0-405-01852-5 $35.00

Brown, William Wells **Clotel, or, the President's Daughter**..ISBN 0-405-01853-3 $ 8.00

Carleton, George W. (editor) **The Suppressed Book About Slavery!**.................... ISBN 0-405-01806-1 $13.50

Cashin, Herschel V., et al. **Under Fire With the Tenth U.S. Cavalry**.................. ISBN 0-405-01854-1 $12.00

Chestnutt, Charles W. **The Marrow of Tradition**..........ISBN 0-405-01855-X $10.00

The Chicago Commission on Race Relations **The Negro in Chicago:** A Study of Race Relations and a Race Riot.........................ISBN 0-405-01807-X $15.00

Child, Lydia Maria **An Appeal in Favor of That Class of Americans Called Africans**...... ISBN 0-405-01808-8 $ 7.00

Child, Lydia Maria **The Freedmen's Book**...............ISBN 0-405-01809-6 $ 8.50

Clark, Peter **The Black Brigade of Cincinnati:** Being a Report of Its Labors and a Muster-roll of Its Members; Together With Various Orders, Speeches, etc. Relating to It.... ISBN 0-405-01917-3 $ 4.50

Coffin, Levi **Reminiscences of Levi Coffin, the Reputed President of the Underground Railroad:** Being a Brief History of the Labors of a Lifetime in Behalf of the Slave, With the Stories of Numerous Fugitives, Who Gained Their Freedom Through His Instrumentality, and Many Other Incidents...................ISBN 0-405-01810-X $16.50

Commissioner of Education in the District of Columbia **History of Schools for the Colored Population:** Part I: In the District of Columbia; Part II: In the United States........ ISBN 0-405-01918-1 $ 7.50

Craft, William and Ellen **Running a Thousand Miles for Freedom:** Or, the Escape of William and Ellen Craft From Slavery...............ISBN 0-405-01923-8 $ 5.00

Cullen, Countee **Color** ....ISBN 0-405-01919-X $ 4.50

Culp, D. W. (editor) **Twentieth Century Negro Literature:** Or, a Cyclopedia of Thought on the Vital Topics Relating to the American Negro by One Hundred of America's Greatest Negroes.........................ISBN 0-405-01856-8 $20.00

Cummings, John **Negro Population in the United States, 1790-1915**................ ISBN 0-405-01811-8 $23.50

Hurston, Zora Neale **Dust Tracks On A Road:** An Autobiography................................
.... ISBN 0-405-01927-0 $12.00

Jacques-Garvey, Amy (editor) **Philosophy and Opinions of Marcus Garvey, Volume I**....
.... ISBN 0-405-01821-5 $ 3.50

Jacques-Garvey, Amy (editor) **Philosophy and Opinions of Marcus Garvey, Volume II**....
.... ISBN 0-405-01873-8 $10.00

Jay, William, and Clarke, James Freeman **The Free People of Color:** On the Condition of
the Free People of Color in the United States; Present Condition of the Free Colored
People of the United States....................ISBN 0-405-01928-9 $ 4.50

Johnson, James Weldon **Black Manhattan**..............ISBN 0-405-01822-3 $13.00

Jones, Thomas Jesse (editor) **Negro Education:** A Study of the Private and Higher Schools
for Colored People in the United States..............ISBN 0-405-01874-6 $35.00

Katz, Bernard (editor) **The Social Implications of Early Negro Music in the United
States** ....ISBN 0-405-01875-4 $ 7.50

Katz, William Loren (editor) **Five Slave Narratives:** A Compendium................
.... ISBN 0-405-01823-1 $15.00

Keckley, Elizabeth H. **Behind the Scenes:** Or, Thirty Years a Slave, and Four Years in the
White House .... ISBN 0-405-01824-X $ 9.00

Kerlin, Robert T. **The Voice of the Negro 1919**...........ISBN 0-405-01825-8 $ 7.50

Kester, Howard **Revolt Among the Sharecroppers**.........ISBN 0-405-01876-2 $ 3.50

King, Edward **The Great South:** A Record of Journeys in Louisiana, Texas, the Indian
Territory, Missouri, Arkansas, Mississippi, Alabama, Georgia, Florida, South Carolina,
North Carolina, Kentucky, Tennessee, Virginia, West Virginia, and Maryland........
.... ISBN 0-405-01929-7 $28.50

Langston, John Mercer **From the Virginia Plantation to the National Capitol:** Or, the First
and Only Negro Representative in Congress From the Old Dominion...............
.... ISBN 0-405-01877-0 $18.00

Larsen, Nella **Passing** ....ISBN 0-405-01930-0 $ 8.00

Livermore, George **An Historical Research Respecting the Opinions of the Founders of
the Republic on Negroes as Slaves, as Citizens, and as Soldiers**..................
.... ISBN 0-405-01878-9 $ 6.50

Locke, Alain **The Negro and His Music** and **Negro Art, Past and Present**..............
.... ISBN 0-405-01879-7 $ 8.00

Locke, Alain (editor) **The New Negro:** An Interpretation...ISBN 0-405-01826-6 $ 9.00

Lockwood, Lewis C. J., and Forten, Charlotte **Two Black Teachers During the Civil War:**
Mary S. Peake, the Colored Teacher at Fortress Monroe; Life on the Sea Islands....
.... ISBN 0-405-01931-9 $ 5.00

Love, Nat **The Life and Adventures of Nat Love, Better Known in the Cattle Country as
"Deadwood Dick"** .... ISBN 0-405-01827-4 $ 6.00

Lynch, John R. **The Facts of Reconstruction**.............ISBN 0-405-01828-2 $10.00

McKay, Claude **A Long Way From Home**..................ISBN 0-405-01880-0 $12.00

May, Samuel J. **Some Recollections of Our Anti-Slavery Conflict**.................
.... ISBN 0-405-01829-0 $10.50

Mayer, Brantz **Captain Canot, or Twenty Years of An African Slaver:** Being an Account of
His Career and Adventures On the Coast, In the Interior, On Shipboard, and In the
West Indies ....ISBN 0-405-01830-4 $14.50

Miller, Kelly **An Appeal To Conscience:** America's Code of Caste, a Disgrace to Democracy
.... ISBN 0-405-01881-9 $ 3.50

Miller, Kelly **Out of the House of Bondage**..............ISBN 0-405-01882-7 $ 7.50

Miller, Kelly **Race Adjustment:** Essays on the Negro in America, and The Everlasting Stain
.... ISBN 0-405-01831-2 $20.50

National Association for the Advancement of Colored People **Thirty Years of Lynching
in the United States, 1889-1918** ....ISBN 0-405-01932-7 $ 4.50

National Negro Conference **Proceedings of the National Negro Conference, 1909**......
.... ISBN 0-405-01890-8 $ 7.00

Nell, William C. **The Colored Patriots of the American Revolution, With Sketches of Several Distinguished Colored Persons:** To Which Is Added a Brief Survey of the Condition and Prospects of Colored Americans........ISBN 0-405-01832-0 $12.00

Nesbit, William, and Williams, Samuel **Two Black Views of Liberia:** Four Months In Liberia, or African Colonization Exposed; Four Years In Liberia, a Sketch of the Life of Rev. Samuel Williams ....ISBN 0-405-01936-X $ 5.50

Nichols, J. L., and Crogman, William H. **Progress of a Race:** Or, the Remarkable Advancement of the American Negro From the Bondage of Slavery, Ignorance, and Poverty To the Freedom of Citizenship, Intelligence, Affluence, Honor, and Trust............
.... ISBN 0-405-01883-5 $16.50

O'Connor, Ellen M., and Miner, Myrtilla **Myrtilla Miner: A Memoir** and **The School for Colored Girls in Washington, D.C.**....................ISBN 0-405-01933-5 $ 5.50

Ottley, Roi **New World A-Coming:** Inside Black America....ISBN 0-405-01833-9 $11.50

Ovington, Mary White **The Walls Came Tumbling Down**....ISBN 0-405-01884-3 $ 9.50

Payne, Daniel A. **History of the African Methodist Episcopal Church**.................
.... ISBN 0-405-01885-1 $15.00

Payne, Daniel A. **Recollections of Seventy Years**.........ISBN 0-405-01834-7 $10.00

Pearson, Elizabeth Ware (editor) **Letters From Port Royal, Written at the Time of the Civil War** ....ISBN 0-405-01886-X $10.50

Penn, I. Garland **The Afro-American Press and Its Editors**..ISBN 0-405-01887-8 $18.00

Porter, Dorothy (editor) **Negro Protest Pamphlets:** A Compendium..................
.... ISBN 0-405-01888-6 $ 7.00

Porter, James A. **Modern Negro Art**....................ISBN 0-405-01889-4 $10.00

Rollin, Frank A. **Life and Public Services of Martin R. Delany:** Sub-Assistant Commissioner, Bureau Relief of Refugees, Freedmen, and of Abandoned Lands, and Late Major 104th U.S. Colored Troops....................ISBN 0-405-01934-3 $13.00

Schurz, Carl **Report on the Condition of the South**........ISBN 0-405-01938-6 $ 5.00

Scott, Emmett J. **Negro Migration During the War**........ISBN 0-405-01891-6 $ 6.00

Scott, Emmett J. **Scott's Official History of the American Negro in the World War**......
.... ISBN 0-405-01892-4 $18.00

Siebert, Wilbur H. **The Underground Railroad from Slavery to Freedom**............
.... ISBN 0-405-01835-5 $14.50

Silvera, John D. **The Negro in World War II**.............ISBN 0-405-01893-2 $14.00

Simmons, William J. **Men of Mark:** Eminent, Progressive, and Rising..............
.... ISBN 0-405-01836-3 $39.50

Sinclair, William A. **The Aftermath of Slavery:** A Study of the Condition and Environment of the American Negro ....ISBN 0-405-01894-0 $11.00

Smedley, R. C. **History of the Underground Railroad:** In Chester and the Neighboring Counties of Pennsylvania ....ISBN 0-405-01895-9 $14.00

South Carolina Constitutional Convention **Proceedings of the Constitutional Convention of South Carolina:** Held at Charleston, S. C., Beginning January 14th and Ending March 17th, 1868 ....ISBN 0-405-01837-1 $28.00

Spiller, G. (editor) **Papers on Inter-Racial Problems:** Communicated to the First Universal Race Congress Held at the University of London, July 26-29, 1911..............
.... ISBN 0-405-01935-1 $17.50

Steward, T. G. **The Colored Regulars in the United States Army:** With a Sketch of the History of the Colored American and an Account of His Services in the Wars of the Country, From the Period of the Revolutionary War to 1899....................
.... ISBN 0-405-01896-7 $10.50

Still, William **The Underground Railroad:** A Record of Facts, Authentic Narratives, Letters, etc., Narrating the Hardships, Hair-Breadth Escapes and Death Struggles of the Slaves in Their Efforts for Freedom, as Related by Themselves and Others, or Witnessed by the Author . . . . ISBN 0-405-01838-X $25.00

Stowe, Harriet Beecher **The Key to Uncle Tom's Cabin:** Presenting the Original Facts and Documents Upon Which the Story is Founded Together With Corroborative Statements Verifying the Truth of the Work . . . . ISBN 0-405-01839-8 $15.50

Taylor, Susie King **Reminiscences of My Life in Camp With the 33rd United States Colored Troops Late 1st S. C. Volunteers** . . . . ISBN 0-405-01840-1 $ 4.00

Thorne, Jack (David Bryant Fulton) **Hanover, Or the Persecution of the Lowly, A Story of the Wilmington Massacre** . . . . ISBN 0-405-01937-8 $ 5.50

Thurman, Wallace **The Blacker the Berry** . . . . ISBN 0-405-01897-5 $ 8.00

Torrence, Ridgely **The Story of John Hope** . . . . ISBN 0-405-01939-4 $16.50

Trowbridge, J. T. **The South:** A Tour of Its Battle-Fields and Ruined Cities, A Journey Through the Desolated States, and Talks With the People. ISBN 0-405-01898-3 $18.00

Truth, Sojourner **Narrative of Sojourner Truth:** A Bondswoman of Olden Time, Emancipated by the New York Legislature in the Early Part of the Present Century, With a History of Her Labors and Correspondence Drawn From Her "Book of Life" . . . . ISBN 0-405-01841-X $11.50

Turner, Edward Raymond **The Negro in Pennsylvania:** Slavery — Servitude — Freedom, 1639-1861 . . . . ISBN 0-405-01899-1 $10.00

Turner, Lorenzo Dow **Africanisms in the Gullah Dialect** . . . . ISBN 0-405-01900-9 $12.50

Walker, David and Garnet, Henry Highland **Walker's Appeal in Four Articles** and **An Address to the Slaves of the United States of America** . . ISBN 0-405-01901-7 $ 4.50

Walker, Margaret **For My People** . . . . ISBN 0-405-01902-5 $ 5.00

Ward, Samuel Ringgold **Autobiography of a Fugitive Negro:** His Anti-Slavery Labours in the United States, Canada and England . . . . ISBN 0-405-01842-8 $12.50

Warner, Robert Austin **New Haven Negroes, A Social History**. ISBN 0-405-01940-8 $14.00

Washington, Booker T. **Working with the Hands:** Being a Sequel to "Up from Slavery" Covering the Authors Experiences in Industrial Training at Tuskegee . . . . ISBN 0-405-01941-6 $11.00

Washington, Booker T; DuBois, W. E. B; Dunbar, Paul Laurence, et al. **The Negro Problem:** A Series of Articles by Representative American Negroes of Today . . . . ISBN 0-405-01903-3 $ 7.00

Washington, Booker T; Wood, N. B., and Williams, Fannie Barrier **A New Negro for a New Century** . . . . ISBN 0-405-01904-1 $13.50

Webb, Frank J. **The Garies and Their Friends** . . . . ISBN 0-405-01905-X $12.00

Weld, Theodore Dwight **American Slavery As It Is:** Testimony of a Thousand Witnesses . . . . ISBN 0-405-01843-6 $ 7.00

Wells-Barnett, Ida **On Lynchings** . . . . ISBN 0-405-01849-5 $ 7.50

West, Dorothy **The Living Is Easy** . . . . ISBN 0-405-01942-4 $14.00

White, Walter **A Man Called White** . . . . ISBN 0-405-01906-8 $12.00

White, Walter **Rope and Faggot:** A Biography of Judge Lynch . . . . ISBN 0-405-01907-6 $ 9.00

Williams, George W. **History of the Negro Race in America from 1619 to 1880:** Negroes as Slaves, as Soldiers, and as Citizens; Together With a Preliminary Consideration of the Unity of the Human Family, an Historical Sketch of Africa, and an Account of the Negro Governments of Sierra Leone and Liberia . . . . . . ISBN 0-405-01844-4 $34.50

Wilson, Joseph T. **The Black Phalanx:** A History of the Negro Soldiers of the United States in the Wars of 1775-1812, 1861-65 . . . . ISBN 0-405-01845-2 $15.50

Woodson, Carter G. **The Education of the Negro Prior to 1861:** A History of the Education of the Colored People of the United States From the Beginning of Slavery to the Civil War . . . . ISBN 0-405-01846-0 $14.00

W. P. A. Writer's Project **The Negro in Virginia**.........ISBN 0-405-01910-6 $12.00

W. P. A. Writer's Project **These Are Our Lives**...........ISBN 0-405-01911-4 $13.50

Wright, Richard R., Jr. **The Negro in Pennsylvania:** A Study in Economic History......
.... ISBN 0-405-01908-4 $ 7.00

Wright, Richard **Twelve Million Black Voices:** A Folk History of the Negro in the United States .... ISBN 0-405-01909-2 $10.00

Paperbacks

Baker, Henry E. **The Colored Inventor:** A Record of Fifty Years...................
.... ISBN 0-405-01943-2 $ 1.00

Brown, William Wells **Clotel, or, the President's Daughter**..ISBN 0-405-01951-3 $ 2.45

Delany, Martin Robinson **The Condition, Elevation, Emigration, and Destiny of the Colored People of the United States:** Politically Considered..ISBN 0-405-01952-1 $ 2.45

Douglass, Frederick **My Bondage And My Freedom**........ISBN 0-405-01967-X $ 3.95

Dunbar, Paul Laurence **The Strength of Gideon and Other Stories**..................
.... ISBN 0-405-01953-X $ 3.45

Fisher, Rudolph **The Walls of Jericho**...................ISBN 0-405-01954-8 $ 3.25

Fortune, Timothy Thomas **Black and White:** Land, Labor, and Politics in the South....
.... ISBN 0-405-01955-6 $ 3.25

Garrison, William Lloyd **Thoughts on African Colonization:** Or an Impartial Exhibition of the Doctrines, Principles, and Purposes of the American Colonization Society Together With the Resolutions, Addresses, and Remonstrances of the Free People of Color....
.... ISBN 0-405-01956-4 $ 3.25

Griggs, Sutton E. **Imperium in Imperio**.................ISBN 0-405-01957-2 $ 2.45

Herndon, Angelo **Let Me Live**.........................ISBN 0-405-01958-0 $ 3.75

Higginson, Thomas Wentworth **Black Rebellion**........ ISBN 0-405-01959-9 $ 2.45

Jacques-Garvey, Amy (editor) **Philosophy and Opinions of Marcus Garvey** 2 volumes in 1
.... ISBN 0-405-01960-2 $ 4.50

Katz, Bernard (editor) **The Social Implications of Early Negro Music in the United States**
.... ISBN 0-405-01961-0 $ 2.45

Katz, William Loren (editor) **Five Slave Narratives:** A Compendium.................
.... ISBN 0-405-01962-9 $ 3.75